PSYCHOLOGY
IN YOUR LIFE

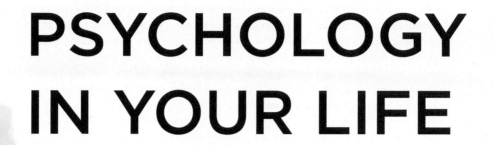

PSYCHOLOGY IN YOUR LIFE

SARAH GRISON
Parkland College

TODD F. HEATHERTON
Dartmouth College

MICHAEL S. GAZZANIGA
University of California, Santa Barbara

W. W. NORTON & COMPANY
NEW YORK • LONDON

W. W. Norton & Company has been independent since its founding in 1923, when William Warder Norton and Mary D. Herter Norton first published lectures delivered at the People's Institute, the adult education division of New York City's Cooper Union. The firm soon expanded their program beyond the Institute, publishing books by celebrated academics from America and abroad. By mid-century, the two major pillars of Norton's publishing program—trade books and college texts—were firmly established. In the 1950s, the Norton family transferred control of the company to its employees, and today—with a staff of four hundred and a comparable number of trade, college, and professional titles published each year—W. W. Norton & Company stands as the largest and oldest publishing house owned wholly by its employees.

Editor: Sheri L. Snavely
Electronic Media Editor: Patrick Shriner
Developmental Editor: Susan Weisberg
Project Editor: Kurt Wildermuth
Managing Editor, College: Marian Johnson
Manuscript Editor: Christianne Thillen
Assistant Editor: Shira Averbuch
Media Assistant: George Phipps
Marketing Manager, Psychology: Lauren Winkler
Production Manager: Sean Mintus
Photo Manager: Patricia Marx
Photo Editor: Michael Fodera
Photo Researcher: Julie Tesser
Permissions Manager: Megan Jackson
Permissions Clearing: Bethany Salminen
Design Director: Rubina Yeh
Text Design: Faceout Studio

Composition: cMPreparé
Manufacturing: Transcontinental

Library of Congress Cataloging-in-Publication Data
Grison, Sarah.
    Psychology in your life/Sarah Grison, Parkland College, Todd F. Heatherton, Dartmouth College, Michael S. Gazzaniga, University of California, Santa Barbara. – First edition.
pages cm
    Includes bibliographical references and indexes.
    ISBN 978-0-393-92139-7 (pbk. : alk. paper) 1. Developmental psychology—Textbooks. 2. Psychology—Textbooks. I. Heatherton, Todd F. II. Gazzaniga, Michael S. III. Title.
    BF713.G75 2015
    150—dc23   2013043523

W. W. Norton & Company, Inc., 500 Fifth Avenue, New York, NY 10110-0017
www.wwnorton.com

W. W. Norton & Company, Ltd., Castle House, 75/76 Wells Street, London WIT 3QT

234567890

For all teachers who inspire
others, especially
Ken Kotovsky and Steve Tipper

With gratitude,

Sarah Heatherton and James Heatherton

Lilli, Emmy, Garth, Dante,
and Rebecca

ABOUT THE AUTHORS

SARAH GRISON is an Associate Professor of Psychology at Parkland College. She brings 18 years of psychology teaching experience to *Psychology in Your Life*. Sarah's research examines how psychological research can be applied to teaching and learning. She teaches introductory psychology regularly and puts her laboratory and classroom research into practice to improve student learning and actively engage students in large lectures. She has created and taught courses to support novice teachers in developing their skills. Sarah is a certified Teacher-Scholar who previously was recognized each year on the University of Illinois List of Excellent Teachers. She has won the University of Illinois Provost's Initiative for Teaching Advancement Award and the Association for Psychological Science Award for Teaching and Public Understanding of Psychological Science. She is a member of the Association for Psychological Science; the American Educational Research Association; the International Mind, Brain, and Education Society; and the American Psychological Association (Division 2, Society for Teaching of Psychology).

TODD F. HEATHERTON is the Lincoln Filene Professor in Human Relations in the Department of Psychological and Brain Sciences at Dartmouth College. He teaches introductory psychology every year. His recent research takes a social brain sciences approach, which combines theories and methods of evolutionary psychology, social cognition, and cognitive neuroscience to examine the neural underpinnings of social behavior. He was elected president of the Society of Personality and Social Psychology in 2011 and has served on the executive committees of the Association of Researchers in Personality and the International Society of Self and Identity. He received the Petra Shattuck Award for Teaching Excellence from the Harvard Extension School in 1994, the McLane Fellowship from Dartmouth College in 1997, and the Friedman Family Fellowship from Dartmouth College in 2001. He is a fellow of the American Psychological Association, the Association for Psychological Science, the Society of Experimental Social Psychology, the Society for Personality and Social Psychology, and the American Association for the Advancement of Science.

MICHAEL S. GAZZANIGA is Distinguished Professor and Director of the Sage Center for the Study of the Mind at the University of California, Santa Barbara. In his career, he has introduced thousands of students to psychology and cognitive neuroscience. He founded and presides over the Cognitive Neuroscience Institute and is founding editor-in-chief of the *Journal of Cognitive Neuroscience*. He is past president of the American Psychological Society and a member of the American Academy of Arts and Sciences, the Institute of Medicine, and the National Academy of Sciences. He has held positions at the University of California, Santa Barbara; New York University; the State University of New York, Stony Brook; Cornell University Medical College; and the University of California, Davis. He has written many notable books, including, most recently, *Who's in Charge?: Free Will and the Science of the Brain*.

CONTENTS IN BRIEF

PREFACE

Everyone who has taught introductory psychology remembers that first time. Most instructors have a humorous story about being handed the textbook just a few days before class began and being pointed in the direction of the classroom. We, the authors of *Psychology in Your Life*, certainly remember our first experiences. One of us was in a hot and windowless attic teaching discussion sections at Carnegie Mellon. Another one of us was trying to overcome the imposter syndrome, teaching at Harvard in a building named after William James. And yet another one of us was trying to hold the attention of 800 students at the University of California, Santa Barbara, right before the 1967 Summer of Love. Whether we were teaching as graduate students or doctoral students or as faculty, all of us were hooked on the experience. We are passionate for the field. As teachers, we strive to communicate the excitement of psychology as a science to students and help them understand how relevant psychology is to their lives. We hope this book achieves both of these goals. At the same time, we designed this book to facilitate student learning and support instructors everywhere who yearn for more teaching resources than merely a textbook and the location of their classroom.

Providing support to both teachers and students is more important now than ever before because both teachers and students are experiencing a "perfect storm" of challenges. Teachers must teach more students in a wider variety of course formats, support learning in many different students, and also figure out how to assess student learning. Often, we must achieve these goals with fewer resources, less support, and little training. Students also face many obstacles to their learning. They may be less prepared to be successful in college-level courses, encounter significant difficulties in reading complex information, and need to use a variety of ways to learn material, including learning-by-doing. At the same time, today's students may have significant constraints on time and money and have many responsibilities with family and jobs. Even the most motivated students can be overwhelmed by so many challenges. We are aware of all of these challenges because we are psychology teachers and researchers too. For many years, we have taught introductory psychology in both small sections and large lecture halls, to tens of thousands of college students. Some of these students were in honors programs. Others were at risk of academic underachievement. Over the years, we have learned many lessons from these experiences, including the simple fact that *one size does not fit all*.

Psychology in Your Life was created to meet the needs of a wide variety of students and the teachers who work with them on a daily basis. The book is based on the experiences of students in introductory psychology classes who yearn to be successful in learning the material but who don't always know how to do so. And it is guided by psychological research that reveals which teaching practices best engage students, get them to actively work with the material, and enhance their learning. In short, *Psychology in Your Life* is designed to support success both in instructors' teaching psychology and in students' learning how to apply psychological concepts to daily life.

How does *Psychology in Your Life* support the needs of teachers and students at the same time? Quite simply, by acknowledging the fact that *great teaching and great learning go together.* After all, great teaching can help students learn, but students play an important active role in their own learning. Students can learn in the absence of great teaching. But when teachers get the support they need, they can have an incredibly important impact in facilitating the learning processes. We created *Psychology in Your Life* to reflect the three interconnected activities that must occur in excellent educational environments: teaching, learning, and investigating improvements. These three activities are reflected in the interconnected framework of all aspects of *Psychology in Your Life*, which is: I Teach, I Learn, I Improve.™

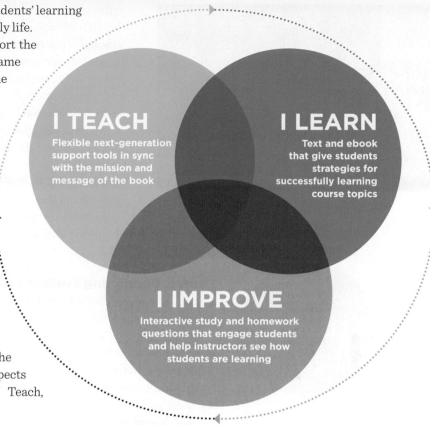

I TEACH
Flexible next-generation support tools in sync with the mission and message of the book

I LEARN
Text and ebook that give students strategies for successfully learning course topics

I IMPROVE
Interactive study and homework questions that engage students and help instructors see how students are learning

I Teach: Supporting Teachers' Success The first aspect of the I Teach, I Learn, I Improve™ approach honors the fact that as teachers we aim to support student learning of both course information and certain skills that will help them in their academic, professional, and personal lives. However, at the same time, teachers need support in achieving these results. Accordingly, we have two main goals in supporting teachers, both of which are achieved through the Interactive Instructor's Guide (IIG) for *Psychology in Your Life*. The IIG is an online repository of resources on both course content and pedagogical tools.

First, we aim to support teachers in preparing the best classes by providing easy access to course materials that support students in achieving the Learning Goals. The reality is that teachers differ in their goals for student learning. Teachers focus on particular content goals and deemphasize others. Teachers may also focus on developing students' skills, such as in application, critical thinking, or scientific thinking. When teacher's use the IIG, they can choose resources that focus on the **Learning Goals** and skills that are most relevant to their courses. With mere hours to prepare for class, all teachers need to do is open the IIG and click on the resources they can use for class, including PowerPoint lecture slides, in-class activities, clicker questions, original Demonstration Videos, and video clip suggestions. Resources are tagged in the IIG by chapter, section, and Learning Goal, so teachers can easily see how resources support learning the specific content and skills. Sorting and searching functions enable teachers to use the IIG flexibly, to find resources based on specific criteria.

A second goal is to support the continuous professional development of teaching skills. We remember the dread we felt when we began to teach with few or no support materials. And even today, with our combined experience of nearly 75 years of teaching, we still find ourselves hunting at times for new in-class

I TEACH

activities to demonstrate concepts. So, to support teachers' skills, the IIG includes two types of original videos. **Demonstration Videos** for instructors provide step-by-step instructions for doing in-class demonstrations of 30 important concepts found in the textbook. These instructions come from teachers experienced in engaging their students in demonstrations and class activities. Accompanying each video are printed summaries, which include both lists of materials needed to re-create the demonstrations and handouts where needed. In addition, **Teaching Videos** offer brief observations to less experienced teachers about which concepts students tend to find challenging. In presenting strategies for overcoming these challenges, the videos refer to specific pedagogical support in the textbook as well as to resources in the instructor support materials. Other Teaching Videos focus on the importance of certain pedagogical practices.

I Learn: Supporting Student Learning The second aspect of the I Teach, I Learn, I Improve™ framework is dedicated to putting into practice the techniques that psychological research indicates will support best student learning. Accordingly, the textbook and enhanced e-book for *Psychology in Your Life* are both designed based on the fact that students are best able to learn content and skills when they actively work with the material.

One goal is to support students' ability to read the text material and learn by providing them with clear **Learning Goals** *and* **Reading Activities** *for each major concept (or* **Big Question***) in a chapter.* The Learning Goals focus both on specific content and on developing more-complex thinking skills (from remembering the material to understanding, applying, analyzing, and evaluating it). The Reading Activities give students questions to answer that target the content and thinking skills described in the associated Learning Goals. Of course, some of the material in introductory psychology can be difficult for students to learn. All teachers know how hard it is for students to understand the process of classical conditioning! So **Learning Tips** are provided in each chapter, to anticipate confusion and support students in successfully answering the Reading Activities and achieving the Learning Goals.

6.1 What Are the Three Ways We Learn?

📖 LEARNING GOALS	✏️ READING ACTIVITIES	LEARN
a. Remember the key terms about learning.	List all of the boldface words and write down their definitions.	
b. Understand the three main types of learning.	Describe these types of learning using your own words.	
c. Apply learning to your life.	Provide examples from your own experience of the two types of non-associative learning.	
d. Understand how the brain changes during learning.	Summarize in your own words how long-term potentiation explains learning in the brain.	

Because relating new information to what we already know improves learning, another goal is to help students apply psychological concepts to their academic, professional, and personal lives. To achieve this goal, the textbook and enhanced e-book include several application features. **Has It Happened to You?** features describe interesting and engaging examples of concepts that students may have encountered in their daily lives. **Try It Yourself** features explain how students can try out psychological concepts, such as how to use operant conditioning to change someone's behavior. And **Using Psychology in Your Life** features explain how students can apply the principles to improve their lives, such as by using behavior modification to improve exercise habits.

Lastly, many teachers believe it is important for students to develop critical thinking and scientific thinking skills that will support them in their academic and professional pursuits. To that end, the textbook and enhanced e-book include features that improve these core skills. **Being a Critical Consumer** features provide case studies where students critically evaluate statements and questions they encounter in the media about psychological research, such as *does playing violent video games cause aggressive behavior?* **Scientific Thinking** features reinforce the fact that psychology is an empirical science and help students understand the steps in the scientific method: hypothesis, research methods, results, and conclusion. Ultimately, this feature can help develop students' scientific thinking skills, including analysis and evaluation, when they apply the steps of the scientific method to specific research studies mentioned in the chapter.

I Improve: Supporting Excellence in Teaching and Learning The final aspect of the I Teach, I Learn, I Improve™ approach provides information on the quality of educational experiences by revealing student performance and learning. Through the textbook, the enhanced e-book, and the **Norton Smartwork** online learning environment, we achieve this goal in two main ways.

Research shows that students learn material best when they are repeatedly tested on it. Students always need fast and simple ways to quiz themselves on their learning immediately after reading material in the textbook. Because of these facts, the textbook provides an appendix of chapter-specific **Quizzes.** Students can take each self-quiz and check their answers. The enhanced e-book provides two forms of self-quizzing. In addition to an interactive version of the self-quiz at the end of each chapter, the e-book includes **Study Questions** at the end of each section. In both the textbook and the e-book, because each question is associated with a specific Learning Goal in the chapter, students can easily see which goals they have and have not mastered, and return to the appropriate sections of the text to review material.

Repeated testing with engaging, interactive tools that also provide rich feedback to students supports learning. The Norton Smartwork online learning environment offers interactive homework assignments that enable students to test their performance. Multiple-choice **Pre-Lecture/Post-Study Quizzes** can be assigned to assess learning. **Intervention Study Assignments,** in various question types, provide students with answer-specific feedback. This feedback, on both correct answers and incorrect answers, helps students improve their thinking about the questions and the concepts.

***Psychology in Your Life*: Helping Teachers and Students Weather the Storm of Educational Challenges** We return now to where we began: Both teachers and students are currently experiencing a "perfect storm" of challenges. Instructors are teaching more students who differ greatly in preparation for college-level work, but the instructors have less training and support than ever. These unique challenges require a different approach to teaching and learning. In response, I Teach, I Learn, I Improve™ provides the first integrated package of textbook, e-book, teaching support, and assessment tools that are centered on core content and skill goals and are designed based on psychological research on teaching and learning. We believe that *Psychology in Your Life* provides a unique educational system that supports student learning and teaching skills while providing evidence about positive educational outcomes. We have spent several years working hard to make this vision into a reality. Now we give *Psychology in Your Life* to you, so that these tools might help teachers support learning in their students, and so that students can learn from their teachers.

ACKNOWLEDGMENTS

Like teaching and learning, writing a textbook and developing unique and integrated educational tools for teachers and students are joint efforts. Our work to support teachers and students in *Psychology in Your Life* has depended so much on the support that we received in the years we have been engrossed in this project.

First, we wish to thank our families for their unwavering support. Our spouses and significant others have been incredibly understanding and generous when we worked through family vacations. Repeatedly. And our children and grandchildren have patiently waited for us to finish working on the days when they wanted to spend time with us. We are very grateful to each of you.

It has been our good fortune to have been joined by so many talented individuals during the process of developing *Psychology in Your Life*. We are extremely grateful to our colleagues who lent their expertise in psychology to writing material for the textbook. Carrie V. Smith, at the University of Mississippi, wrote the Being a Critical Consumer features. She's an excellent teacher, and her efforts will help train students to be educated consumers of information. Debra Mashek, at Harvey Mudd College, wrote the Using Psychology in Your Life features. Her engaging and insightful voice will help students use psychology to improve their own lives. We thank Beth Morling, at the University of Delaware, for her expert advice on our research methods coverage. We are very grateful to Ines Segert, at the University of Missouri, for offering advice about each chapter of the book and checking the accuracy of the text, figures, and captions.

We are also very grateful to the faculty, graduate students, and undergraduates at the University of Illinois, Urbana-Champaign. Many of the teaching and learning principles we used in *Psychology in Your Life* were inspired by the teaching of Dr. Sandra Goss Lucas, who has spent many years training graduate students in pedagogical best practices. In addition, many of the teaching practices used in this book have been empirically tested with the undergraduate students in introductory psychology, who helped us learn more about what helped them learn. And what did not. Most importantly, we wish to thank the graduate student teachers and researchers from the University of Illinois, Urbana-Champaign, for sharing with us their knowledge of psychological concepts and of evidence-based teaching and learning pedagogies. It is only with their expertise that we have been able to develop the materials to support teachers' skills in the Interactive Instructor's Guide and student learning in Norton Smartwork and in the Test Bank. So Crystal Carlson, Genevieve Henricks-Lepp, Jennifer Wiedenbenner, Angela Isaacs, and Lauren Bohn, we thank you. Your dedication to this project, boundless energy, and drive for excellence are truly inspirational. Daniel Kolen, you are a fast learner about psychology, and your keen eye and production talent have perfected our video materials to support both the students and teachers. You are a true gem in your profession, and we are grateful to call you one of us—a member of "The Team."

Focus Group Participants We were guided and advised by fun, insightful, and committed introductory psychology teachers who attended several focus groups held in Chicago; Houston; Washington, D.C.; St. Pete Beach; and Reno. They all read chapters, gave advice about level and detail, and helped to hone the look, feel, and content of the book and support program. We extend a special thank you to Laura Hebert, at Angelina College, for consulting her class several times to help us choose the best possible title for the textbook. We also thank Gregg Gold, at Humboldt State, for his excellent accuracy checking of an early version of the learning chapter. And we extend a special thank you to the Washington, D.C., focus group members/Mike Gazzaniga lunch club for the lively discussion on teaching, split-brain research, and life in general.

Carol Anderson, *Bellevue College*

Sherry Ash, *San Jacinto College*

Tom Brothen, *University of Minnesota*

Danice Brown, *Southern Illinois University*

Adam Butler, *University of Northern Iowa*

Tom Capo, *University of Maryland University College*

Eric Currence, *Ohio State University*

Ramezan Dowlati, *NVCC Loudoun*

Mike Dudley, *Southern Illinois University*

Kimberley Duff, *Cerritos College*

Bryan Fantie, *American University*

David Foster, *Western Oregon University*

Ilija Gallego, *Houston Community College*

Gregg Gold, *Humboldt State*

Christine Grela, *McHenry County College*

Laura Hebert, *Angelina College*

Tony Hermann, *Bradley University*

George Hernandez, *Rock Valley College*

Dominique Hubbard, *NVCC Alexandria*

Lynnel Kiely, *Harold Washington College*

Rosalyn King, *NVCC Loudoun*

Mary Johannesen-Schmidt, *Oakton Community College*

Sheryl Leytham, *Grand View University*

Ayanna Lynch, *Bowie State University*

Stefanie Mitchell, *San Jacinto College*

Fernando Ortiz, *Santa Ana College*

Kathy Peterson, *Grand View University*

Marylou Robins, *San Jacinto College*

Armida Rosiles, *South Plains College*

John Scarbrough, *Lincoln Land Community College*

Mary Ann Schmitt, *NVCC Manassas*

Dale Smith, *Olivet Nazarene*

John Stachula, *Saint Ambrose University*

Margot Underwood, *Joliet Junior College*

Christopher Warren, *California State Long Beach*

Mary Waterstreet, *Saint Ambrose University*

Linda Weldon, *CCBC Essex*

Cara Williams, *Moraine Valley Community College*

Glenda Williams, *Lone Star College*

Andrea Zabel, *Midland College*

Clare Zaboroski, *San Jacinto College*

Reviewers The chapters were thoroughly reviewed as they moved through the editorial and production process. Reviewers included star teachers who checked for issues such as level, detail, pacing, and readability, which supports student comprehension. Reviewers also included experts who checked for scientific accuracy and helped us find the right balance of correctness, clarity, and concision. Our reviewers showed extraordinary attention to detail and understanding of the student experience. We are grateful to all the reviewers listed here. Their efforts reflect a deep commitment to excellence in psychology and in teaching students about the importance and applicability of our field.

Carol Anderson, *Bellevue College*

Nicole Arduini-Van Hoose, *Hudson Valley Community College*

Holly Beard, *Midlands Technical College*

Richard Bernstein, *Broward College*

Bernardo Carducci, *Indiana University Southeast*

Pamela Case, *Richmond Community College*

Scott Cohn, *Western State Colorado University*

Barbara Corbisier, *Blinn College*

Dale Doty, *Monroe Community College*

Gina Dow, *Denison University*

Michael Dudley, *Southern Illinois University Edwardsville*

Laura Flewelling, *Johnston Community College*

Shannon Gadbois, *Brandon University*

Gregg Gold, *Humboldt State University*

Jeffrey Green, *Virginia Commonwealth University*

Laura Hebert, *Angelina College*

Tasha Howe, *Humboldt State University*

Karin Hu, *City College of San Francisco*

Mary Johannesen-Schmidt, *Oakton Community College*

Jennifer Johnson, *Bloomsburg University of Pennsylvania*

Patricia Kemerer, *Ivy Tech Community College Northeast*

Yuthika Kim, *Oklahoma City Community College*

Karen Kwan, *Salt Lake Community College*

Sheryl Leytham, *Grand View University*

Debbie Ma, *California State University, Northridge*

Pam Marek, *Kennesaw State University*

Daniel McConnell, *University of Central Florida*

Matthias Mehl, *University of Arizona*

Arthur Olguin, *Santa Barbara City College*

David Payne, *Wallace Community College*

Nambrath Rajkumari Wesley, *Brookdale Community College*

Randi Shedlosky, *York College of Pennsylvania*

Aya Shigeto, *Nova Southeastern University*

Nancy Simpson, *Trident Technical College*

Martha Weaver, *Eastfield College*

The Norton Team To realize a vision, you must take a first step. For *Psychology in Your Life,* the first step was a leap of faith, when W. W. Norton & Co. saw the possibilities of what this project could bring to teachers and students. As the oldest and largest independent publishing company, Norton has created some of the best-respected and iconic books in modern times. The excellence of these works makes Norton stand out as a beacon among publishers. Because the company is wholly owned by its employees, the employees are the heart and soul of this excellence. *Psychology in Your Life* exists because of the extraordinary contributions of so many people at Norton.

At the top of the list is Sheri Snavely, the editor of *Psychology in Your Life.* When Sarah and Sheri first discussed this project, many publishing companies were interested in taking a new approach to developing evidence-based educational products. While representatives from many companies wanted to hear about this project, Sheri wanted to learn about it through experience. She asked to sit in on Sarah's introductory psychology class. No one from another company had asked to do that, but Sheri needed to see if Sarah was a teacher who actually "walked the walk" of supporting student learning in class. That hands-on approach enabled Sheri to see the value in the vision. Together with her fellow Norton editor Peter Lesser, Sheri brought *Psychology in Your Life*—and the ideas behind it—to Norton. Sheri's leadership and guidance have provided a constant star to keep us oriented in the right direction. She has our utter gratitude, respect, and admiration. We are also deeply thankful for the receptive audience we found in Roby Harrington, the director of Norton's College Division; Julia Reidhead, the editorial director of the College Division; and Karl Bakeman, the editorial director for Digital Media.

One of our key goals for this textbook was providing appropriate, sufficient, and accurate information about psychology while supporting students' abilities to understand the material. The book's developmental editor, Susan Weisberg, drew on her vast experience to help us make the text accessible while maintaining the integrity of the content. The book's copyeditor, Christianne Thillen, further refined the prose while keeping a close eye on content. The project editor, Kurt Wildermuth, then performed the herculean task of carrying the chapters through the many stages from manuscript editing to publication. Kurt expertly mentored us through these many processes, and he should be knighted for his sage advice, expertise, and patience. The production manager, Sean Mintus, helped us work with Dragonfly Media Group to create clear and accurate explanatory graphics. Sean also kept us meeting our deadlines with the compositor and printer, carefully and considerately granting us extra time when necessary.

Most textbooks have media components. The media component for *Psychology in Your Life* is different in that the media supports both teachers and students. This focus required a shift in the approach to media and the development of many new tools. The new vision for the electronic media in *Psychology in Your Life* is the brainchild of Patrick Shriner, electronic media editor extraordinaire. Patrick's expertise and creativity helped guide us in crafting many new tools to support teachers' skills, including the development of the Interactive Instructor's Guide (IIG) and the creation of original Demonstration Videos and Teaching Videos. Patrick and the amazing associate media editor, Callinda Taylor, worked tirelessly with us and the team of teacher-researchers at the University of Illinois to design all aspects of the e-book, IIG, Norton Smartwork, and the Test Bank around the core Learning Goals in the textbook. We spent so much time together developing these tools that we began to feel like a group of siblings. The end result of these long hours of joint work is something remarkable: media that is part of an integrated package, connected to all aspects of *Psychology in Your Life*.

Another of our goals, for the textbook and the e-book, was to use design and graphics to enhance learning. The material needed to be both relevant to students and visually compelling. Norton's hugely talented College design director, Rubina Yeh, worked with Faceout Studio to create this book's beautiful design, from the gorgeous chapter openers to the elegant interior. Norton's corporate art director, Debra Morton Hoyt, guided Faceout in the creation of the intriguing cover. We are also grateful for the keen eyes of Julie Tesser, photo researcher, and Mike Fodera, photo editor, who helped us select the best photographs to correctly demonstrate psychological principles. If patience is a virtue, then Julie and Mike represent consummate virtuousness.

Behind the scenes, Shira Averbuch, assistant editor, and George Phipps, media assistant, ensured that many processes have gone smoothly. Their intelligence and organizational abilities helped guide us through invigorating and informative focus groups with talented teachers, rigorous reviewing and accuracy checking, and assembling the IIG, Norton Smartwork, and the Test Bank. In the constant juggling act of developing a textbook and educational tools, Shira and George have shown themselves to be master jugglers.

One of the greatest joys in developing *Psychology in Your Life* has been working with Lauren Winkler, our energetic and creative marketing manager. Lauren helped us convert an abstract vision to an easily communicated reality. She has a natural instinct for explaining complex ideas in simple terms, and her attention to detail in pursuing this goal is unwavering. We are deeply grateful to Lauren for helping realize our vision of an integrated teaching and learning platform: I Teach, I Learn, I Improve.™

Norton's sales managers and sales representatives are truly invested in supporting teachers and students. Their expertise, insight, and mission focus make them extraordinary advocates for excellence in education. We extend particular gratitude to the dedicated science specialists—Peter Ruscitti, Heidi Shadix, and Rebecca Andragna—who travel tirelessly on the book's behalf.

Finally, we thank the teachers we have met at conferences and meetings, where we have exchanged ideas about challenges in teaching and how to address those challenges. By contributing to the ideas behind *Psychology in Your Life*, those teachers have become part of the extended Norton team.

CONTENTS

4 Development Across the Life Span

8 Thinking and Intelligence 266

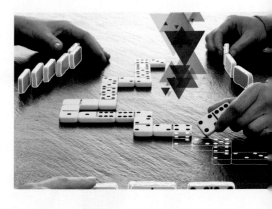

9 Motivation and Emotion 306

10 Health and Well-Being 346

11 Social Psychology 380

12 Self and Personality

PSYCHOLOGY IN YOUR LIFE

Introducing the World of Psychology

1

YOU'RE DRIVING DOWN THE STREET, talking on your cell phone as you negotiate the traffic, stop signs, and pedestrians. Then the driver in front of you stops suddenly. You frantically drop the phone and swerve, barely avoiding a collision. Your heart is pounding as you realize what could have happened.

BIG QUESTIONS

FIGURE 1.1

Psychology in Daily Life: The Dangers of Using a Cell Phone While Driving
Kelsey Raffaele took this photo of herself (photo courtesy of her mother, Bonnie Raffaele). Bonnie Raffaele helped get a new law passed in their state that prevents novice drivers from using cell phones while driving. For more information on the dangers of using a cell phone while driving, please visit thekdrchallenge.com/Kelsey_s_Story.html.

Kelsey Raffaele, a 17-year-old high school senior in Michigan, wasn't so lucky (**Figure 1.1**). In January 2010, Kelsey was driving through town after school and decided to pass a slower vehicle in front of her. When she saw an oncoming vehicle in the passing lane, she misjudged the distance and crashed. Kelsey spoke her last words on her cell phone as she talked with her best friend, Stacey Hough: "Oh [no], I'm going to crash."

If you are like 70 percent of the people in the United States, you talk on a cell phone every day when you are driving. This habit is so common that most of us never think twice about it. That's exactly what Stacey Hough reported. She was driving behind Kelsey at the time of the accident. "[We] used our phones all the time behind the wheel. We never thought anything would come of it," said Stacey. "Until it happen[s], you don't think it could happen."

Statistics contradict people's intuition that they can drive safely when talking on the phone. The National Highway Traffic Safety Administration estimates that about 1.4 million car crashes each year, a little less than one-third of all car crashes, involve drivers who are using cell phones. Cell phone use is reported in about 18 percent of distracted driving fatalities. The common wisdom is that these accidents happen because the driver has only one hand on the wheel while holding the phone with the other. Because of this habit, several states have enacted laws that require the use of hands-free phones while driving. But even when they have two hands on the steering wheel, can people really drive safely while talking on the phone?

Unfortunately, we cannot use intuition to answer questions like this one. Intuition fails here because what seems to be obvious is rarely the whole story. Behind the "obvious" are mental processes that cause us to think and act in certain ways. In fact, according to the latest research findings, a driver's performance is similar whether he is holding a phone or using a hands-free device. This finding implies that the absence of one hand on the steering wheel is not the problem. The distraction of the conversation is the main reason drivers miss the important visual and audio cues that ordinarily would help them avoid a crash.

Having all the data can help us make informed decisions about what actions to take. In the case of cell phones and driving, the research suggests that current legislation is not likely to reduce risk. Instead, we must limit cell phone use while driving. But how can public policies succeed in getting people not to use cell phones when driving, if these drivers believe they are not at risk? Could manufacturers create cell phones and other in-car products that are less distracting when drivers use them? And how might we understand which drivers are most at risk and provide intervention for them?

When you decided to take a psychology course, you probably did not think it would deal with issues such as cell phone use. But questions like these are at the forefront of psychological research. This text introduces you to current topics and looks at how you can use psychology to think critically and guide your daily life. Just imagine what this knowledge might have done for Kelsey Raffaele—and for the thousands of other people like her who perish in distracted driving accidents every year.

1.1 Why Is Psychology Important to You?

📖 LEARNING GOALS	✏️ READING ACTIVITIES	**LEARN**
a. Remember the key terms about psychology.	List all of the boldface words and write down their definitions.	
b. Apply critical thinking to your life.	Use the three critical thinking questions to come to an appropriate conclusion about an issue in your life.	
c. Apply psychology to your life.	Give three examples of how the material and/or skills you learn in this course can help you improve your life.	

Understanding and applying the principles of psychology can affect us in critical ways. For example, psychology can help us understand why we should not talk on our cell phones while driving. It can also help us understand other people. Do you remember when Lady Gaga wore a meat dress to the MTV music awards? Why did she do it (**Figure 1.2**)? Or think about the last time a friend or family member did something that really surprised you. You may have wanted to understand that person's motives, thoughts, desires, intentions, moods, actions, and so on.

All of us want to know whether other people are friends or enemies, leaders or followers, likely to reject us or fall in love with us. We also want to understand ourselves—why we like or don't like *Jersey Shore* or *Here Comes Honey Boo Boo*, why we love the people we do, why we get so angry when someone laughs at us, or why we made that "stupid mistake." Psychology can help us understand other people and ourselves. In turn, this understanding can help us improve our friendships, work more effectively in groups, be better parents, and have more success in our academic work and at our jobs. In short, psychology can help us improve our lives.

Psychology Explains Our Mental Activity and Behavior

We saw in this chapter's opening story that people believe they can talk on a cell phone and still drive safely. This story is important because it shows that we cannot use our intuition to truly understand people or to predict behavior. By contrast, **psychology** is the systematic, objective study of our mental activity and our behavior.

Mental activity lets us perceive the world. That is, we use our senses—sight, smell, taste, hearing, and touch—to take in information from outside ourselves. Through mental activity, we interpret that information—each of us in our own unique ways. These processes of the mind, of receiving and interpreting information, are responsible for all of our memories, thoughts, and feelings. By contrast, the term *behavior* refers to all of our actions that result from sensing and interpreting information. It is important to remember that both our mental activity and our behavior are produced by our brains. In recent years, technology such as brain imaging has provided great

FIGURE 1.2

Understanding People
Psychology can help us understand ourselves. It also provides insight into why other people think and behave as they do, such as why Lady Gaga wore a meat dress to the 2010 MTV Video Music Awards.

psychology
The study of mental activity and behavior, which are based on brain processes.

Which picture(s) show aspects of psychology? See the answer below.

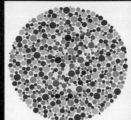

This woman is experiencing depression.

These people are friends.

This couple enjoys the thrill of roller coaster rides.

This is a color blindness test (see the 5?).

The design of this door is confusing—push or pull?

Answer: All of these pictures reflect psychology because they suggest the presence of mental processes and behavior that depend on brain activity.

insight into how our brains process information to let us think about and respond to information in the world around us.

So psychology focuses on mental activity, behavior, and brain processes. The areas of investigation range from the simple to the complex. What are some of the topics of interest in psychology? Using the Try It Yourself feature, see if you can figure out the answer.

Are you getting the impression that every aspect of what we think and do relates to psychology? Then you are right. You might be surprised to know that as you sit reading this textbook, you are experiencing psychology. Your eyes move across the page so you can see the words and understand their meaning. You are thinking about what is written, but maybe you are also feeling hungry. Perhaps you are thinking about someone you just met. You want to do well in this class, so you take notes on what you are reading in order to remember it. Psychology is a part of every moment of your life because everything you are thinking and doing relates to psychology.

Psychology Teaches Us to Think Critically

Do you believe in extrasensory perception (ESP)? ESP refers to the supposed ability to receive information directly through the mind, not through the physical senses such as vision or hearing. However, there is no compelling scientific support for ESP or mental telepathy. Yet according to a 2005 survey (Musella, 2005), 41 percent of Americans believe in ESP. What's more, about 37 percent of people believe in mental telepathy—the idea that one person can read another person's mind. Before taking a psychology course, many students believe things they've heard about the brain, mental activity, and behavior without stopping to think about why they believe what they do. But a main goal of this course is to teach you to stop and investigate before you believe. In other words, in this course, you will learn to think critically.

STEPS IN CRITICAL THINKING In **critical thinking,** we systematically evaluate information to reach reasonable conclusions based on the evidence. Three steps are involved in becoming a skilled critical thinker.

The first step in critical thinking is to ask "What am I being asked to believe or accept?" Here we use friendly skepticism: Keeping an open mind about a new idea or claim, but being cautious instead of accepting the information at face value. This combination of openness and caution is easy to achieve when a claim does not fit with our personal views. But we especially need to practice friendly skepticism when we think that we already "know" something.

The second step in critical thinking is to ask "What evidence is provided to support the claim?" Here, we use logic and reasoning to determine whether there are holes in the evidence or whether the information might be biased. For example, does the person presenting the information have a personal or political agenda?

The last step of critical thinking is to ask "What are the most reasonable conclusions?" Here, we consider whether there might be alternative explanations for the claim. We also make our final decisions about whether we believe the claim or not.

The Learning Tip explains how this book will help you develop strong critical thinking skills. Essentially, you will practice using these three steps to evaluate claims you see in the popular media. The media love a good story, and they often jump on findings from psychological research. Unfortunately, as you will see, media reports can be distorted or even totally wrong.

EVALUATING PSYCHOLOGY IN THE NEWS One example of new psychology research that was turned into an overblown news report concerns the so-called Mozart effect. According to the original research, research participants showed significant but temporary gains in performing one type of task after listening to a Mozart sonata for 10 minutes, compared with listening to relaxation instructions or silence (Rauscher & Shaw, 1993).

News outlets quickly reported these results, but they misunderstood or misrepresented the findings with headlines that suggested that listening to Mozart was a way to increase intelligence (**Figure 1.3**). Even people surrounded by professional advisors can fall prey to such media reports. In this case, the governor of Georgia, Zell Miller, set aside $105,000 of the state budget to provide classical music to each of the approximately 100,000 children born in the state each year. Though the babies and their parents may have enjoyed the music, there is no evidence that listening improved the infants' intelligence.

LEARNING TIP: Developing Critical Thinking Skills

Throughout this textbook, Being a Critical Consumer features will help you develop critical thinking skills. These features present recent news articles from the popular press that make claims about psychological research. Each time you read a Being a Critical Consumer feature, try to answer the three key questions about the claim being made:

1. What am I being asked to believe or accept?
2. What evidence is provided to support the claim?
3. What are the most reasonable conclusions?

critical thinking
Systematically evaluating information to reach reasonable conclusions best supported by evidence.

Breaking News: Listening to Mozart Makes People Smarter

October 14, 1993

Recent research in psychology reveals that listening to Mozart increases intelligence. After reading about the power of the "Mozart effect," the governor of Georgia, Zell Miller, set aside a chunk of the state budget to provide classical music to every child born in the state each year.

According to Miller, the "Mozart effect"

FIGURE 1.3

Thinking Critically About Psychology in the News
Media reports seek to grab attention. The claims can be based on psychological research, but they can also be hype. Consider what happened when research revealed small gains in one type of performance task after participants listened to a Mozart sonata for 10 minutes. The media dubbed these gains the Mozart effect and falsely reported that listening to Mozart could make people smarter.

Thinking critically about claims in psychology will help you in your daily life. This ability will also help you study successfully in this and other classes. Indeed, one study found that students who use critical thinking skills complete an introductory psychology course with a more accurate understanding of the subject than do students who complete the same course without using critical thinking skills (Kowalski & Taylor, 2004).

Psychology Helps Us Succeed in School and at Work

Apart from a good grade, what do you hope to get out of this class? You'll find this class valuable whether it ends up being the only psychology course you ever take, you become a psychology major, or you plan to pursue a graduate degree and become a psychologist. Studying psychology can pave the way for success both in your schoolwork and in your professional life.

ACADEMIC SUCCESS Learning about psychology's major issues, theories, and controversies will help you succeed in your academic work. For example, in Chapter 7 you will learn how attention and memory work. This material will help you read and remember information better. In Chapter 9, you will learn about the connections between motivation and emotion. This information will help you motivate yourself to succeed.

Furthermore, as you learn about these psychological concepts, you will be developing important abilities: analyzing information by breaking it into pieces, evaluating ideas by drawing conclusions about them, and communicating about psychological concepts. In short, when you follow the simple rules in Using Psychology in Your Life, you will be well on your way to using psychological principles to help you achieve success in your schoolwork.

PROFESSIONAL SUCCESS Studying psychology will also prepare you for success in your professional life (**Figure 1.4**). Teachers and education professionals need to understand how people's thinking, social abilities, and behaviors develop over time (Chapter 4). Health care workers need to know how to relate to their patients, how patients' behaviors are linked to health, and what motivates or discourages patients from seeking medical care or following treatment plans (Chapter 10). People in business, marketing, advertising, and sales need

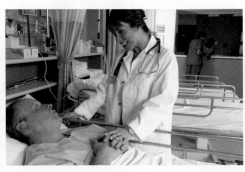

(a)

(b)

(c)

FIGURE 1.4

Studying Psychology Develops Career Skills

Studying psychology helps people develop skills they can use in a wide range of careers. **(a)** Teachers need to understand how people learn. **(b)** People in medical professions need to know how to gauge people's moods and their motivations to recover. **(c)** To convince people to buy products, salespeople need to understand the relationship between motivation and emotion.

USING PSYCHOLOGY IN YOUR LIFE:

How Can Psychology Help Me Study?

Knowing about psychology can be useful to you in many ways, even if you do not pursue a career in the field. The following learning strategies are all based on psychological research, and they will help you learn more efficiently and work more productively. Try practicing these techniques during this course and beyond, and you will see the benefits both in school and in your career.

1. **THE RIGHT GOALS LEAD TO SUCCESS**—Throughout your life, you will set countless short-term and long-term goals for yourself, from getting that enormous pile of laundry done to succeeding in your job. In your coursework, it is important to choose goals that are challenging yet attainable. Then divide each goal into specific, achievable steps, or subgoals, and reward yourself when you reach a milestone. Even a small achievement is worth celebrating!

2. **A LITTLE STRESS MANAGEMENT GOES A LONG WAY**—Stress is a fact of life. A moderate amount of stress can improve your performance by keeping you alert, challenged, and focused. However, too much stress has the opposite effect and can diminish your productivity, interfere with your sleep, and even take a toll on your health. When the pressure is on in school, seek healthy ways to manage your stress, such as exercising, writing in a journal, spending time with friends, practicing yoga, or meditating.

3. **CRAMMING IS A CRUMMY WAY TO LEARN**—You have a busy life, and it is always tempting to postpone studying until the night before an exam. But there is too much to learn to do that. You might be able to remember enough information to pass the exam the next day, but research shows that your learning won't last. To make learning stick, you need to space out your study sessions over the semester and build in plenty of time for active reviews.

4. **LEARNING IS AN ACTIVE ENDEAVOR**—The more effort you put into studying actively over many days, the more benefit you will receive. Every time you learn something, you create "memory traces" in your brain. And by working with the information, you strengthen the memory traces, so you will be more likely to recall the memory in the future. As a result, merely rereading a chapter is not as effective as actively working with the information. Be sure to write down information as you read, answer questions about the topics, and so on.

5. **EXPLAINING ENHANCES UNDERSTANDING**—Memorizing information—for example, by writing definitions—is likely to result in shallow learning that is easily forgotten. By contrast, a deeper level of learning results when we connect information with what we already know. As you study for this course, be sure to describe concepts in your own words and apply the concepts to your life.

6. **THERE ARE MANY WAYS TO LEARN**—People process information in two channels: visual and verbal. So another strategy for creating durable learning is to use both visual and verbal information. Supplement the notes you take with visuals such as concept maps, graphs, flowcharts, and other types of diagrams. Doing so makes you more likely to remember the information. And by emphasizing the connections among important ideas, you are also more likely to see the big picture.

to know how attitudes are formed or changed and how well people's attitudes predict their behavior (Chapter 11). Basically, as humans dealing with other humans, we all need to know psychology. Prospective employers in most fields—including business, education, law enforcement, medicine, social services, child care, and retail sales—know how important it is to understand people. Smart employers look for applicants who have knowledge and skills that come from training in psychology.

Some students become so fascinated by psychology that they devote their lives to studying the brain, mental activity, and behavior. And if you are thinking about a career in psychology or a related field, there is good news. According to the U.S. Department of Labor (U.S. Bureau of Labor Statistics, 2009), opportunities for people with graduate degrees in psychology are expected to grow by about 12 percent by 2018. The outlook is equally positive in many other countries around the world. Developing countries, for example, are increasingly addressing the psychological well-being of their citizens. These efforts are providing hands-on opportunities for people trained in psychology to use their knowledge and skills. As they discover, psychology is an exciting field. Researchers around the globe are reporting new insights into issues that great scholars of the past tried to understand. These insights are helping to explain the very nature of what it means to be human.

LEARN

✓ **1.1 CHECKPOINT: Why Is Psychology Important to You?**

- We experience psychological issues every minute of our lives, but we cannot understand them based on common sense alone.

- Psychology is the scientific study of mental activity, behavior, and the brain.

- Studying psychology helps improve critical thinking skills and study skills. It also helps develop skills that make people successful in their jobs.

1.2 What Do Psychologists Investigate?

LEARNING GOALS	READING ACTIVITIES **LEARN**
a. Remember the key terms about what psychologists investigate.	List all of the boldface words and write down their definitions.
b. Apply the nature/nurture debate to your own life.	Give examples of how your thoughts and behavior are influenced by nature and by nurture.
c. Understand the three psychology schools of thought that investigated the conscious mind and the unconscious mind.	Describe in your own words each school of thought that investigated the conscious mind and the unconscious mind.
d. Evaluate the four psychology schools of thought that investigate behavior and mental activity.	Assess why psychology schools of thought shifted to investigating behavior and mental activity.

For as long as people have been able to think, we have been trying to understand ourselves and others. The goal of understanding human thought and behavior actually originated in philosophy. Indeed, some of the most important questions that psychologists now examine intrigued ancient scholars thousands of years ago. However, since scientists began to systematically investigate psychological processes over a century ago, we have made incredible progress in understanding how people think and behave.

Psychology Originated in Philosophical Questions

In ancient Greece, early philosophers, such as Aristotle and Plato, debated psychological issues. Was how a person thought and acted inborn—in other words, did thinking and behavior result from a person's biological nature? Or were thinking and behavior acquired through education, experience, and culture—for example, did they result from how a person was nurtured? Psychologists have carried on this *nature/nurture debate* for as long as psychology has been a field of study. Psychologists now widely recognize that both nature and nurture influence our psychological development. Throughout this book, you will see many examples of how nature and nurture influence each other so much that they are hard to separate.

Another classic question in psychology is the *mind/body problem.* Are the mind and the body separate and distinct? Or is the mind simply our own personal experience of the physical brain's activity? The ancient Greeks and Romans knew that the brain was essential for normal mental functioning. Their understanding came largely from their observations of people who suffered blows to the head, then lost consciousness or experienced changes in certain mental abilities, or both. By contrast, at other points in history, scholars believed that the mind was separate from and in control of the body. This claim was partly based on the strong religious belief that humans have a divine and immortal soul. In this view, the soul is separate from the physical body and departs from the body upon death.

In the 1600s, the French philosopher René Descartes suggested the idea of *dualism,* that the mind and the body are separate yet intertwined (**Figure 1.5**). The body, Descartes argued, was nothing more than an organic machine governed by "reflex." In keeping with the prevailing religious beliefs, he concluded that the rational mind was divine and separate from the physical body. Today, psychologists reject dualism. The current view among psychologists is that the mind emerges from activity—information processing—in the brain.

Psychologists Investigate the Conscious and Unconscious Mind

Historically, philosophers used thinking and intuition to answer the big questions about who we are. However, in the mid-1800s in Europe, psychology arose as a scientific field of study and then spread throughout the world. During this time, different ways of thinking about psychology emerged. After a school of thought emerged, it would dominate for a while. When the flaws of that approach became apparent, a new school of thought would emerge. Let's look at how several schools of thought have laid the foundation for the modern science of psychology (**Table 1.1**).

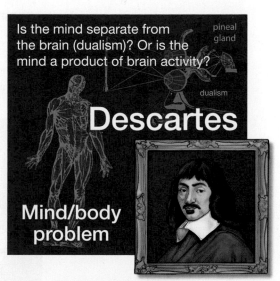

Is the mind separate from the brain (dualism)? Or is the mind a product of brain activity?

pineal gland

dualism

Descartes

Mind/body problem

FIGURE 1.5

Descartes and the Mind/Body Problem: Dualism
According to the philosopher René Descartes, the mind and the body are separate yet intertwined. As discussed throughout this book, psychologists now reject this idea, called dualism. Instead, they view the mind as a product of brain processes.

TABLE 1.1

SCHOOL OF THOUGHT AND INFLUENTIAL SCIENTISTS	GOAL
Structuralism • Wilhelm Wundt • Edward Titchener	Identify the basic parts, or structures, of the conscious mind
Functionalism • William James • Charles Darwin	Describe how the conscious mind aids adaptation to an environment
Psychoanalytic theory • Sigmund Freud	Understand how unconscious thoughts cause psychological disorders
Gestalt psychology • Max Wertheimer • Wolfgang Köhler	Study subjective perceptions as a unified whole
Behaviorism • John B. Watson • B. F. Skinner	Describe behavior in response to environmental stimuli
Cognitive psychology • George Miller • Ulric Neisser	Explore internal mental processes that influence behavior
Social psychology • Kurt Lewin	Investigate how the presence of others affects people's thoughts and actions

EXPERIMENTAL PSYCHOLOGY BEGINS Experimental psychology began in 1879, when Wilhelm Wundt established the first psychology laboratory (**Figure 1.6**). Wundt based his investigations on a realization: Psychological processes are the products of brain activity, so they must take time to occur. The time it takes to complete a psychological task is called *reaction time*. Wundt inferred that

FIGURE 1.6
Wundt's Experimental Psychology Laboratory
Wilhelm Wundt **(third from left)** established the first psychology laboratory in Germany in 1879. This event marked the beginning of modern experimental psychology.

more-complex psychological tasks would require more brain activity and so would take longer than simple tasks. To this day, researchers use reaction time to study psychological processes, although their equipment is far more modern.

Wundt was not satisfied with studying mental reaction times. He developed a new method to measure people's conscious experiences. This method was called *introspection*. In using introspection, research participants had to reflect and report on their thoughts about their personal experiences of objects. For example, participants would experience a series of objects and say which one they found the most pleasant. Wundt's work investigating conscious experiences was critical to the development of psychology. He trained many of the great early psychologists who went on to establish psychological laboratories throughout Europe, Canada, and the United States.

STRUCTURALISM: COMPONENTS OF THE CONSCIOUS MIND One of Wundt's students was Edward Titchener (**Figure 1.7**). Titchener pioneered a school of thought that became known as **structuralism.** This school is based on the idea that conscious experience can be broken down into underlying parts. Titchener believed that if psychologists could understand the basic elements of conscious experience, they would have a scientific basis for understanding the mind.

Suppose a research participant was played a musical tone or shown an object, such as an apple. Through introspection, the participant would analyze the subjective experience. In this way, the researcher would understand the component parts of the participant's experience, such as the quality and intensity of the stimulus (**Figure 1.8**). Although Wundt ultimately rejected the use of introspection, Titchener relied on the method throughout his career.

The general problem with introspection is that it is personal and unique to each person who is having the experience. In other words, each of us brings to introspection a unique way of perceiving things. Researchers cannot determine whether participants in a study are using introspection in a similar way. Over time, psychologists largely abandoned introspection because it was not a reliable method for understanding psychological processes across different people. Even so, Wundt, Titchener, and other structuralists were important because they helped develop a pure science of psychology with its own vocabulary and set of rules.

FUNCTIONALISM: PURPOSE OF THE CONSCIOUS MIND One critic of structuralism was William James (**Figure 1.9**). James suggested that structuralism failed to capture the most important aspects of mental experience. He argued that the mind was much more complex than its elements and could not be broken down. Psychologists who used the structural approach, he said, were like people

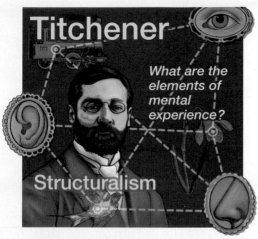

FIGURE 1.7

Edward Titchener
Edward Titchener founded structuralism. This school used introspection to investigate the basic parts of the conscious mind.

"It's red. It's bright."

FIGURE 1.8

Structuralism and Introspection
In structuralism, a person would perform introspection about an object. For example, the person might report on the quality ("red") and intensity ("bright") of an apple. The person's verbal reports were thought to reveal the basic parts of the conscious mind.

FIGURE 1.9

William James
William James, the founder of functionalism, investigated the function of the conscious mind. He wanted to understand how the operations of the mind help people adapt to environmental demands.

structuralism
An early school of psychology that explored the structures of the mind through introspection.

FIGURE 1.10

Darwin and Natural Selection
Charles Darwin observed that species change over time. Such change enables species to adapt and survive. The mechanism of change—the engine of evolution—is called natural selection. These ideas led to the development of evolutionary theory.

functionalism
An early school of psychology concerned with the adaptive purpose, or function, of mind and behavior.

natural selection
In evolutionary theory, the idea that those who inherit characteristics that help them adapt to their particular environments have a selective advantage over those who do not.

FIGURE 1.11

Sigmund Freud
Sigmund Freud founded psychoanalytic theory. Freud used psychoanalysis to treat unconscious mental forces that conflicted with acceptable behavior and produced psychological disorders.

trying to understand a house by studying each of its bricks individually. More important to James was that the bricks together formed a house and that a house has a particular function. In short, the mind's elements mattered less than the mind's usefulness to people. This approach came to be known as **functionalism.**

According to functionalism, the mind came into existence over the course of human evolution. The mind works as it does to help preserve human life over time. In other words, the mind helps humans adapt to environmental demands. Thanks to the mind, humans survive and pass along their genes to future generations.

EVOLUTIONARY THEORY: NATURAL SELECTION AIDS SURVIVAL

One of the major influences on functionalism was the work of the naturalist Charles Darwin. In 1859, Darwin published his revolutionary book *On the Origin of Species.* This work introduced the world to *evolutionary theory.* Darwin had studied the variations in species and in individual members of species. He reasoned that species change over time. Earlier philosophers and naturalists had discussed the possibility that species might evolve. But Charles Darwin was the first to present the mechanism of evolution, which he called **natural selection** (**Figure 1.10**).

The basic units of natural selection are genes. These genes contain hereditary information, which is passed from parents to offspring. But in the inheritance of genes, random mutations occur. These mutations produce variations in individuals. Some of these changes—specific physical characteristics, skills, and abilities—make an individual better adapted to its environment. Individuals with such adaptations will be more likely to survive and reproduce than individuals without the adaptations. And because the individuals survive and reproduce, their genes are passed on to offspring. This idea has come to be known as "survival of the fittest." But survival of the fittest doesn't happen only once. Presumably, the offspring of the fittest will in turn survive and reproduce. The offspring of their offspring will survive and reproduce. And so on. As the adaptive genes are passed on to more and more offspring of succeeding generations, a species will change. This kind of change is called evolution.

Darwin's ideas have deeply influenced science, philosophy, and society. Rather than being a specific area of scientific inquiry, evolutionary theory is a way of thinking that can be used to understand many aspects of mind and behavior (Buss, 1999).

PSYCHOANALYTIC THEORY: UNCONSCIOUS CONFLICTS

Twentieth-century psychology was profoundly influenced by one of its most famous thinkers, Sigmund Freud (**Figure 1.11**). Freud was trained in medicine. At the beginning of his career, he worked with people who had nervous system disorders, such as the paralysis of various body parts. He found that many of his patients had few medical reasons for their paralysis. Soon he came to believe that psychological factors were causing their conditions. To try to understand the connections between psychology and physical problems, Freud developed *psychoanalytic theory.*

Freud concluded that much of human behavior is determined by mental processes operating below the level of conscious awareness. He believed that these unconscious mental forces included both troubling childhood experiences blocked from memory and sexual urges that conflicted with acceptable behavior. By creating psychological blockages within the individual, these forces produced psychological discomfort and even mental disorders.

From his theories, Freud developed the practice of *psychoanalysis*. In this therapeutic approach, the therapist and the patient work together to bring the contents of the patient's unconscious into the patient's conscious awareness (**Figure 1.12**). Once the patient's unconscious conflicts are revealed, the therapist helps the patient deal with them constructively. Freud was influential in shaping the public view of psychology. Many of his ideas are difficult to test using scientific methods, but psychologists widely accept the idea of unconscious mental processes.

Psychologists Explore Behavior and Mental Activity

In the early twentieth century, psychological researchers shifted away from studying the conscious and unconscious experiences of the mind. Some researchers, such as the Gestalt psychologists, believed that mental experience cannot be broken down into common underlying parts. Other researchers, such as the behaviorists, believed that the conscious mind and the unconscious mind were not appropriate topics for psychological investigation. The ideas of Gestalt psychology, behaviorism, and subsequent schools are the basis for modern psychological research on mental activity. Modern research, in turn, leads to new treatments for psychological disorders.

GESTALT PSYCHOLOGY: EXPERIENCING THE "WHOLE" Gestalt psychology developed in opposition to structuralism. This new school of thought sought to understand how people perceive information. The most prominent Gestalt psychologists included Max Wertheimer (**Figure 1.13**) and Wolfgang Köhler.

In 1912, the Gestalt psychologists began to explore how people experience sensory input. For example, why can two people view an object in very different ways? How can one person look at an object more than once and see it differently each time? You can experience such a shift in the Try It Yourself feature. Research into such questions led to the development of

FIGURE 1.12
Psychoanalysis in Our Lives
Psychoanalysis has had a large impact on the treatment of psychological disorders. But today most clinical psychologists use different techniques to treat psychological disorders.

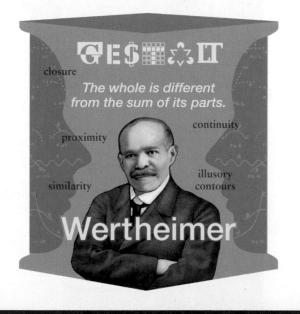

The whole is different from the sum of its parts.

closure
continuity
proximity
similarity
illusory contours

FIGURE 1.13
Max Wertheimer
Max Wertheimer was a founder of Gestalt psychology. According to this school of thought, people's experiences cannot be broken down into parts. Instead, perception is unique for each person and is affected by context.

TRY IT YOURSELF: Gestalt Theory and the Whole Versus the Parts

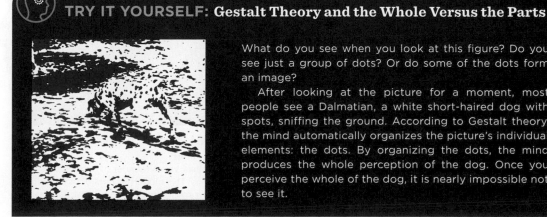

What do you see when you look at this figure? Do you see just a group of dots? Or do some of the dots form an image?

After looking at the picture for a moment, most people see a Dalmatian, a white short-haired dog with spots, sniffing the ground. According to Gestalt theory, the mind automatically organizes the picture's individual elements: the dots. By organizing the dots, the mind produces the whole perception of the dog. Once you perceive the whole of the dog, it is nearly impossible not to see it.

Gestalt theory. According to this set of ideas, the perception of objects is a personal experience. In other words—in direct contrast with structuralism—what a person experiences is different from all of the constituent elements of an object. The Gestalt perspective has influenced many areas of psychology, including the study of vision and our understanding of human personality.

BEHAVIORISM: STIMULI AND RESPONSES In 1913, the psychologist John B. Watson (**Figure 1.14**) challenged the focus on conscious and unconscious mental processes as being unscientific. He felt that if psychology was going to be a science, it had to stop trying to study mental events that could not be observed directly. Instead, Watson believed that animals—including humans—learned all behaviors through environmental factors. Specifically, Watson believed that psychologists needed to study the environmental stimuli, the behavioral triggers, in particular situations. By understanding the stimuli, people could predict the animals' behavioral responses in those situations. Watson developed the school of **behaviorism,** which investigates the observable environmental effects on behavior. Watson's views have been furthered by thousands of psychologists, including B. F. Skinner.

Behaviorism dominated psychological research well into the early 1960s. Behaviorists established many basic principles that are still viewed as critical to understanding behavior (**Figure 1.15**). At the same time, enough evidence has accumulated to show that thought processes really do influence behavior. Few psychologists today describe themselves as strict behaviorists.

COGNITIVE PSYCHOLOGY: MENTAL ACTIVITY In the second half of the twentieth century, evidence slowly emerged that learning was not as simple as the behaviorists believed. For example, learning theorists such as Edward Tolman showed that animals could learn just by observation even if they were not triggered to learn by a reward in the environment. Other findings were also difficult for behaviorism to explain and suggested that mental functions were important for understanding behavior.

In 1957, George A. Miller (**Figure 1.16**) and his colleagues, including Ulric Neisser, launched the cognitive revolution in psychology. Today, **cognitive psychology**

FIGURE 1.14

John B. Watson
John Watson founded behaviorism, the scientific study of how observable environmental factors affect behavior.

FIGURE 1.15

Behaviorism in Our Lives
Many people use the principles of behaviorism to train animals. To increase a desired behavior, the trainer provides an environmental stimulus that is rewarding. Here, a woman gives a treat reward to a dog that sits up on command. The same principles of behaviorism can be used to teach a child how to behave in a desirable way.

FIGURE 1.16

George Miller
George Miller was a founder of cognitive psychology. This modern school of psychology uses experimental methods to investigate how people think, remember, pay attention, make decisions, and solve problems.

is concerned with investigating mental functions such as intelligence, thinking, language, attention, learning, memory, problem solving, and decision making (**Figure 1.17**). While some early cognitive psychologists focused exclusively on mental processes, others recognized that the brain was important to cognition. In the early 1980s, cognitive psychologists joined forces with computer scientists, philosophers, and researchers who studied the brain. The goal of this collaboration was to develop an integrated view of mind and brain. During the next decade, cognitive neuroscience emerged. This field studies the brain mechanisms that underlie thought, learning, and memory.

SOCIAL PSYCHOLOGY: SITUATIONS SHAPE BEHAVIOR During the mid-twentieth century, many psychologists came to understand that people's behaviors were affected by the presence of others. This realization occurred partly because people sought to understand the atrocities committed in Europe before and during World War II. Why had apparently normal Germans, Poles, and Austrians willingly participated in the murders of innocent men, women, and children? And why did some people in these countries put their own lives at risk to save others?

A key lesson from this research was that most people are strongly influenced by social situations. With this idea in mind, researchers emphasized a scientific, experimental approach to understanding how people are influenced by others. Pioneers in this area included the Gestalt-trained psychologist Kurt Lewin (**Figure 1.18**). The field that emerged from this work is **social psychology.** This school focuses on the power of situations and on the way people are shaped by their interactions with others (**Figure 1.19**).

PSYCHOLOGY INFORMS THERAPY These movements in psychology have greatly influenced the development of methods to treat psychological disorders. For instance, the rise of behaviorism led to therapies designed to modify behavior rather than deal with underlying mental conflicts. Behavior modification methods continue to work very well in a range of situations. For example, behavior modification can be used to train people with intellectual impairments or to treat clients who are especially anxious and fearful. The cognitive revolution led therapists to recognize the important role of thought processes in psychological disorders.

FIGURE 1.17
Cognitive Psychology in Our Lives
Cognitive psychology reveals how we pay attention, remember, solve problems, and make decisions. This information can be used to improve our learning and our daily lives. Indeed, many of the features in this textbook are based on the principles of cognitive psychology, so using this book will help you learn.

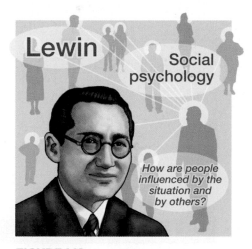

FIGURE 1.18
Kurt Lewin
Kurt Lewin founded modern social psychology. He pioneered the use of experimental research to investigate how people influence each other.

FIGURE 1.19
Social Psychology in Our Lives
The rise of social psychology means that we have a stronger understanding of how people are influenced by others and by social situations. In some cases, this influence may be negative, when a person is isolated from his peers. But in other cases the presence of others can have very positive effects.

social psychology
The study of how people are influenced by their interactions with others.

As a result, therapies were developed to correct faulty ways of thinking (such as "I am a complete failure" and "If I fail this test, my parents will kill me").

In addition, today's more sophisticated understanding of the nature/nurture debate affects the treatment of psychological disorders. Psychologists now believe that many psychological disorders result as much from the brain's "wiring" (nature) as from the way people are reared and treated (nurture). For many conditions, behavioral and cognitive therapies are effective (see Chapter 14). For other conditions, the most effective treatments are drugs that alter brain chemistry. In some situations, the best treatment is a combination of therapy and drugs. According to the research, no universal treatment or approach fits all psychological disorders (Kazdin, 2008).

✓ **1.2 CHECKPOINT: What Do Psychologists Investigate?**

- The classic questions in psychology, such as the nature/nurture debate and the mind/body problem, originated in philosophy.
- Early psychological schools of thought explored the conscious mind and the unconscious mind. Later schools of thought explored mental activity and behavior.
- Behaviorism is based on the idea that objective, observable behavior should be the focus of psychological inquiry.
- Cognitive psychology investigates unseen mental processes and how they affect our thinking.
- Social psychology explores how the presence of other people affects our thinking and behavior.

1.3 Who Are Psychologists Today?

📖 LEARNING GOALS	✏️ READING ACTIVITIES
a. Remember the key terms about who psychologists are today.	List all of the boldface words and write down their definitions.
b. Analyze how psychologists do research at four different levels of analysis.	Differentiate between the four levels of analysis for the research question "What motivates a person to overeat at a holiday meal?"
c. Apply the eight subfields of psychology to your own life.	Give four examples of how research from different subfields could have a positive impact on your life.
d. Understand the five ethical issues in psychological research.	Summarize in your own words the five ethical guidelines that psychologists must address in their research.

Do you enjoy listening to music? Why do you like some kinds of music and not others? Do you prefer some types of music when you are in a good mood and other types when you are feeling down? If you listen to music while you study, does it affect how you learn? Let's look at how psychologists today investigate interesting questions such as these.

Psychologists Work Across Levels of Analysis

You just learned that psychological researchers study mental activity and behavior. But today these researchers would take different approaches to studying a topic such as the effects of music on thought and actions. They might examine, for instance, how musical preferences vary among individuals and across cultures, how music affects emotional states and thought processes, and even how the brain perceives sound as music rather than noise. Let's see how psychologists today might research this one topic in diverse ways across four levels of psychological analysis.

DIFFERENT LEVELS OF PSYCHOLOGICAL ANALYSIS **Table 1.2** outlines the four broadly defined levels of analysis that reflect current approaches to investigating topics in psychology: biological, individual, social, and cultural.

The *biological level of analysis* deals with how the physical body influences our thoughts and behavior. The last three decades have seen tremendous growth in understanding the biological bases of mental activities. We now know that genes affect thoughts, actions, feelings, and disorders and that certain psychological processes are associated with activity in specific parts of the brain. Psychologists today who work at this level of analysis have shown that musical training changes brain structures associated with learning and memory (Herdener et al., 2010).

TABLE 1.2

Four Levels of Psychological Analysis

	LEVEL OF ANALYSIS	FOCUS	WHAT IS STUDIED?
	Biological	Brain systems	Neuroanatomy, animal research, brain imaging
		Neurochemistry	Neurotransmitters and hormones, animal studies, drug studies
		Genetics	Gene mechanisms, heritability, twin and adoption studies
	Individual	Individual differences	Personality, gender, developmental age groups, self-concept
		Perception and cognition	Thinking, decision making, language, attention, memory, vision
		Behavior	Observable actions, responses, physical movements
	Social	Interpersonal behavior	Groups, relationships, persuasion, influence, workplace interactions
		Social cognition	Attitudes, stereotypes, perceptions
	Cultural	Thoughts, actions, behaviors in different societies and cultural groups	Norms, beliefs, values, symbols, ethnicity

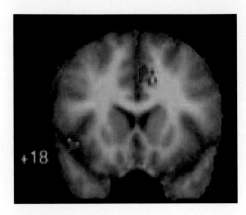

FIGURE 1.20

Your Brain on Music

Certain regions of the brain are associated more with organized sounds than with scrambled sounds. The highlighted region on the left becomes more active when you hear spoken language or music. Noise does not activate that region.

Listening to pleasant music increases activation of brain regions associated with positive experiences (Koelsch, Offermanns, & Franzke, 2010). And music appears to be treated by the brain as a special category of auditory information (**Figure 1.20**). One 35-year-old woman whose brain was damaged lost the ability to recognize even the most familiar tunes, although other aspects of her memory system and language system were intact (Peretz, 1996).

The *individual level of analysis* focuses on individual differences in personality and mental processes that affect perception and understanding. In the case of music, researchers who work at this level of analysis look for individual differences in music's effects on mood, memory, and decision making (Levitin, 2006). Have you ever had a bad romantic breakup and spent a lot of time listening to sad songs? Studies have shown that listening to certain types of music changes people's moods and makes their feelings more intense (Baumgartner, Lutz, Schmidt, & Jäncke, 2006). Indeed, young children listening to sad music tend to interpret a story negatively, and those listening to happy music tend to interpret a story more positively (Ziv & Goshen, 2006). And when participants listen to music from childhood, they recall specific memories from that period (Janata, 2009).

Was there ever a time when you were sad and a friend dragged you to a party? In that situation or a similar one, what happened to your mood? The *social level of analysis* involves investigating how groups affect people's interactions and people's influence on each other. In studying the effects of music, researchers look at the types of music people prefer when in groups versus when they are alone. They also investigate whether certain types of music promote negative behaviors. For instance, certain types of rap music have been associated with violence and drug use (Miranda & Claes, 2004). Similarly, people who prefer heavy metal, punk, reggae, and techno music are more likely to use alcohol, drugs, and tobacco than are people who prefer pop or classical music (Mulder et al., 2009). However, listening to music with prosocial lyrics led participants to be more empathic and increased their helping behavior (Greitemeyer, 2009). Such associations do not mean that listening to music always *causes* these behaviors. Perhaps people who already behaved that way also developed those musical preferences.

The *cultural level of analysis* explores how people's thoughts, feelings, and actions are similar or different across cultures. **Culture** is made up of beliefs, values, rules, norms, and customs that people learn from one another when they share a common language or environment. If you have friends from other cultures, or if you listen to world music, you're aware that different cultures prefer different types of music (**Figure 1.21**). Part of the explanation may lie in the music itself. For instance, African music has rhythmic structures different from those in Western music (Agawu, 1995), which may be due to the important role of dancing and drumming in these cultures. Further, attitudes about people who are different from us can affect our perceptions of their musical styles. For example, societal attitudes toward rap and hip-hop music in the United States and United Kingdom revealed subtle prejudicial attitudes against blacks and a greater willingness to discriminate against them (Reyna, Brandt, & Viki, 2009).

As these examples show, when the research question calls for it, psychologists today investigate a question across different levels of analysis in an interconnected way. And conducting innovative research at several levels of analysis creates a broader understanding of both mental processes and behavior. Throughout this book, you will see how this multilevel approach has led to breakthroughs in psychological understanding. The Gestalt psychologists were right: The whole is different from the sum of its parts.

culture

The beliefs, values, rules, and customs that exist within a group of people who share a common language and environment and that are transmitted through learning from one generation to the next.

FIGURE 1.21
Cultural Differences in Music
Differences across cultures can include musical traditions and preferences. **(a)** Traditional African music involves complex rhythms, organic instrumentation, and an emphasis on drumming. **(b)** By contrast, modern pop music in Korea, K-pop, involves glossy production, electronic elements, and the visual dazzle of girl bands or boy bands.

Psychologists Investigate Many Different Topics

A psychologist's career involves predicting behavior or understanding mental activity. Psychologists today achieve this aim by working in many different settings depending on whether their primary focus is on research, teaching, clinical practice with patients, or applying scientific findings to improving the quality of daily living.

Researchers who study the brain, the mind, and behavior may work in schools, businesses, universities, or clinics (**Figure 1.22a**). Some psychological practitioners apply the findings of psychological research to helping people in need of psychological treatment, designing safe and pleasant work environments, counseling people on career paths, or helping teachers design better educational experiences. The distinction between psychological research and clinical psychology can be fuzzy. Many researchers are also clinical practitioners, and many clinical psychologists study psychological disorders as well as treat them.

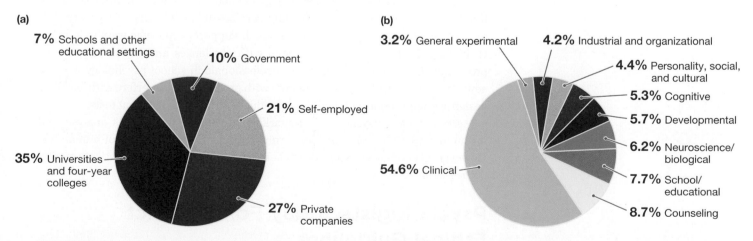

(a)
- **7%** Schools and other educational settings
- **10%** Government
- **21%** Self-employed
- **27%** Private companies
- **35%** Universities and four-year colleges

(b)
- **3.2%** General experimental
- **4.2%** Industrial and organizational
- **4.4%** Personality, social, and cultural
- **5.3%** Cognitive
- **5.7%** Developmental
- **6.2%** Neuroscience/ biological
- **7.7%** School/ educational
- **8.7%** Counseling
- **54.6%** Clinical

FIGURE 1.22

Where Psychologists Work and What They Do
(a) This pie chart shows the types of settings in which psychologists work, based on data from 2007.
(b) This pie chart shows psychology doctoral degrees awarded for the 2007–2008 academic year.

TABLE 1.3

Research-Related Subfields in Psychology

SUBFIELD	RESEARCH INTERESTS	SAMPLE RESEARCH QUESTIONS
Biological psychology	Study how biological systems give rise to mental activity.	• How do brain chemicals influence sexual behavior? • How do brain cells change during learning?
Cognitive psychology/ Neuroscience	Study attention, perception, memory, problem solving, and language, often based on brain processes.	• What makes some problems harder to solve than others? • How do cell phones distract people when they drive?
Developmental psychology	Study how people change from infancy through old age.	• How do children learn to speak? • How can older adults maintain mental abilities as they age?
Personality psychology	Study enduring characteristics that people display over time and across circumstances.	• Why are some people shy? • How do genes, circumstances, and culture shape personality?
Social psychology	Study how people are affected by the presence of others and how they form impressions.	• When are people influenced by others to behave in certain ways? • How do people form or dissolve intimate relationships?
Cultural psychology	Study how people are influenced by the societal rules that dictate behavior in their cultures.	• How do societal rules influence interpersonal behavior? • Do societal rules create differences in perception?
Clinical psychology	Study the factors that cause psychological disorders and the best methods to treat them.	• What factors lead people to feel depressed? • How does the brain change as a result of therapy for depression?
Industrial/organizational psychology	Study issues pertaining to industry and the workplace.	• How can building morale help motivate workers? • How can equipment be designed so workers can easily perform duties and avoid accidents?

The diverse nature of modern psychology is outlined in **Table 1.3,** which shows the wide range of interests psychologists have across the eight main subfields in the discipline. **Figure 1.22b** gives the percentages of psychologists who recently received doctoral degrees in those subfields.

In many of these subfields, psychologists conduct research. In other subfields, psychologists focus more on providing services to individuals and groups. For example, counseling psychology professionals support people who want to improve their daily lives by helping them cope with challenges and crises in personal, professional, and academic domains. Professionals in school psychology work in educational settings. They help students with problems that interfere with learning, design age-appropriate curricula, and conduct aptitude achievement tests.

As you can see, psychology is remarkably diverse in its levels of analysis and its subfields. Psychologists are concerned with nearly every aspect of human life. However, all psychologists follow strict ethical guidelines as they investigate mental processes and behavior.

Psychologists Today Follow Strict Ethical Guidelines

When psychologists conduct research, they must fully consider the ethical issues involved. Are they asking the participants to do something unreasonable? Are the participants risking physical or emotional harm from the study? To ensure the participants' well-being, all colleges, universities, and research institutes have strict guidelines in place regarding research. All researchers must follow those guidelines (**Figure 1.23**).

The guardians of the ethical guidelines at schools and other institutions where research is conducted are **institutional review boards (IRBs).** These boards consist of administrators, legal advisers, trained scholars, and members of the community. The members review all proposed research to ensure that it meets scientific standards. For research to be ethical, five main issues must be addressed.

1. Privacy: Researchers must respect participants' privacy. For example, it is ethical to observe people without their knowledge in public, such as at an airport. It is not ethical to observe private behaviors without people's knowledge.

2. Confidentiality: Participants' information must be kept secret. It can be made available only to the few people who need to know it. This confidentiality prevents other people from linking the study's findings to the actual participants.

3. Informed consent: *Informed consent* means that people must be told about the research, and they can choose to participate or not. Usually, the participant gives consent in writing before the study begins.

4. Deception: Sometimes, knowing a study's specific goals could alter the participants' behavior. That alteration could make the results meaningless. In such a case, the researchers may use deception to mislead participants about the study. If deception is used, once the study is completed the researchers must inform the participants of the study's goals and explain why deception was necessary.

5. Risks: Researchers cannot ask participants to endure unreasonable pain or discomfort. However, potential gains from research sometimes require asking participants to expose themselves to some risk to obtain important findings. The *risk/benefit ratio* is an analysis of whether the research is important enough to be worth placing participants at some risk.

In fact, you can experience psychological research yourself if you volunteer to participate in studies at your school. By participating in this research, you can learn more about the field. You will also contribute to the scientific understanding of how humans think and behave. And you will be protected by rigorous ethical guidelines.

institutional review boards (IRBs)
Groups of people responsible for reviewing proposed research to ensure that it meets the accepted standards of science and provides for the physical and emotional well-being of research participants.

FIGURE 1.23
Student Participants
When you volunteer to participate in psychological research, you will be protected by ethical guidelines as you learn about psychology and contribute to the field.

 1.3 CHECKPOINT: Who Are Psychologists Today?

- Psychologists today investigate diverse questions across one or more of four levels of analysis: biological, individual, social, and cultural.

- Psychologists now work in many settings.

- Across a wide variety of subfields, psychological researchers investigate different aspects of mental activity and behavior.

- Psychologists must adhere to all ethical guidelines when conducting scientific research.

1.4 How Do Psychologists Conduct Research?

![] LEARNING GOALS	![] READING ACTIVITIES	LEARN
a. Remember the key terms about the scientific method.	List all of the boldface words and write down their definitions.	
b. Analyze the cycle of the scientific method.	Change Figure 1.24 to show how you could scientifically investigate distracted driving when people use their cell phones.	
c. Understand the three psychological research methods.	Describe each method and its pros and cons in your own words.	
d. Apply correlations to your life.	Give two examples of correlations in your life.	

You've decided to buy a new a smartphone, but you aren't sure which one is best. You've seen ads for many different brands and models, all with different specifications, but can you believe what they say? You might ask your friends what smartphone they like. Or you might go to an expert authority, such as an electronics retailer, to compare specifications and features. Maybe you go online to look at product reviews and consumer comments. We answer questions in our daily lives by using these sorts of techniques all the time. But psychologists can't answer questions based on beliefs, hearsay, rumor, or even expert opinions.

Psychologists Use the Scientific Method

Psychology is a science. Because they are scientists, psychologists gain accurate knowledge about behavior and mental processes only by observing the world and measuring various aspects of it. This approach is called *empiricism*. To be confident about the conclusions drawn from their observations, psychologists conduct empirical research using the **scientific method.**

There are three key aspects of the scientific method. First, the scientific method requires that psychologists follow several carefully planned, systematic steps. Second, the processes that psychologists use in the scientific method must be objective—that is, free from bias. Third, the procedures must be reproducible. This statement means that if other psychologists repeat the same procedures with similar people, they would expect to obtain the same results. Only when the scientific method is followed can we be confident that our empirical results provide a true understanding of mental activity and behavior.

FIVE STEPS IN THE SCIENTIFIC METHOD The process of the scientific method includes the five steps shown in **Figure 1.24.** Let's look at each step in turn.

Psychologists study research questions they find interesting. Psychologists are often people-watchers, and when they see a person behaving in a puzzling way, they want to understand that behavior. The process of understanding follows the scientific method. The scientific method usually begins with a **theory** (see Figure 1.24, Step 1). Typically, a psychologist develops a theory to explain some interesting or puzzling phenomenon—an observable thing—the psychologist has noticed. A theory is an explanation or model of how the phenomenon works. The theory consists of interconnected ideas or concepts that are used to explain prior research findings and to make predictions about future events.

scientific method
A systematic procedure of observing and measuring phenomena (observable things) to answer questions about *what* happens, *when* it happens, *what causes* it, and *why*. This process involves a dynamic interaction between theories, hypotheses, and research methods.

theory
A model of interconnected ideas or concepts that explains what is observed and makes predictions about future events.

hypothesis
A specific prediction of what should be observed if a theory is correct.

descriptive methods
A research method that provides a systematic and objective description of what is occurring.

A clearly stated theory is important because it is the basis for the next step of the scientific method: developing a **hypothesis** (see Figure 1.24, Step 2). A hypothesis is a specific, testable prediction about the theory. Any one theory is usually tested by several separate hypotheses, all testing various aspects of the theory.

Now you move to the third step in the scientific method: testing the hypothesis (see Figure 1.24, Step 3). There are three main types of research methods you can use to test your research question: descriptive, correlational, and experimental (**Figure 1.25**). Which method you use depends on the goal of your research, as described in the next section.

In Step 4 of the scientific method, you analyze the data to see whether your hypothesis is supported (see Figure 1.24, Step 4). First, you summarize the raw data using *descriptive statistics*. Then you use *inferential statistics* to determine whether differences really exist between sets of numbers in descriptive statistics. Both of these forms of analysis are described in Appendix A: Analyzing Data in Psychological Research, at the back of the book.

After the completion of this step, you must determine what issues need additional investigation (see Figure 1.24, Step 5). Remember, no single study gives us a definitive answer about any psychological topic. A study tells us only what happened in a particular set of circumstances. As a result, scientists never say they have proved a theory. However, we generally can feel more confident about scientific findings when the particular study and its outcomes are repeated by the same researcher or others. When the results from two or more studies are the same, or at least support the same conclusion, the findings are more likely to be trustworthy. For psychology studies, the findings add to our understanding of mental activity, behavior, or both.

Descriptive Methods Describe What Is Happening

Now that you have learned the five steps of the scientific method, let's look in more detail at Step 3: testing with a certain research method. Your choice of one of three research methods (see Figure 1.25) depends on the goal of your research. If the goal of your research is describing behavior, then you would use one of the **descriptive methods** to collect data to test your hypothesis.

A descriptive method provides a snapshot of what is occurring at a specific point in time. As a result, this technique is especially valuable in the early stages of research. During the early stages, researchers are trying to see whether a particular phenomenon exists. Let's look at three descriptive methods you might use: observational studies, self-reports, and case studies.

FIGURE 1.24
Cycle of the Scientific Method

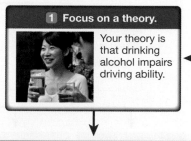

1 Focus on a theory.

Your theory is that drinking alcohol impairs driving ability.

2 State a hypothesis.

Your hypothesis is that people who consume more alcohol will tend to display poorer motor control in driving than will people who consume less alcohol.

3 Test with a research method.

You test your hypothesis by selecting the most appropriate research method. You then collect data to evaluate your hypothesis. For example, in an experiment you might have some participants in your study drink alcohol and others drink tonic water.

4 Analyze the data.

You analyze the data using appropriate statistical techniques and draw conclusions. If the data do not support your hypothesis, you either discard the theory or revise it (and make plans to test the revision). See, at the back of the book, Appendix A: Analyzing Data in Psychological Research.

5 Report results and embark on further inquiry.

You submit results to research journals and present them at conferences to share them with the scientific community. Then you continue the process by refining your theory, making further predictions, and testing hypotheses.

FIGURE 1.25
Types of Research Methods

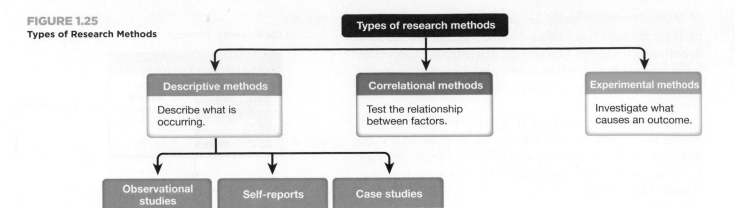

OBSERVATIONAL STUDIES *Observational studies* are a specific type of descriptive method. They involve systematically assessing and coding observable behavior (**Figure 1.26**). By coding, we mean determining which previously defined category the behavior fits into. For example, researchers might note the types of gestures people make when meeting at an airport. They might group the behaviors of nonhuman animals that have been injected with drugs that affect brain function.

Observational studies can be used either in the laboratory or in natural environments. Some researchers observe behavior at regular time intervals. These intervals may be as short as seconds or minutes, or they may be as long as years, entire lifetimes, and even across generations. By using intervals, the researchers can keep track of what research participants do at specific points in time.

It is often hard to observe a situation without seeing what we expect or want to see. In conducting observational studies, researchers must guard against *observer bias*. Bias refers to errors in observation that occur because of the observer's expectations. Observer bias can especially be a problem if cultural norms favor behaving in certain ways. For instance, in many societies women are freer to express

Observational studies are a descriptive research method. They involve observing and classifying behavior, either with intervention by the observer or without intervention by the observer.

Advantages	Especially valuable in the early stages of research, when trying to determine whether a phenomenon exists. Can take place in a laboratory or a real-world setting.
Disadvantages	Errors in observation can occur because of an observer's expectations (*observer bias*). Observer's presence can change the behavior being witnessed (*reactivity*).

FIGURE 1.26

Observational Studies

(left) The evolutionary psychologist Lawrence Sugiyama, here hunting with a bow and arrow, has conducted fieldwork in Ecuadorian Amazonia among the Shiwiar, Achuar, Shuar, and Zaparo peoples.
(right) The primatologist Jane Goodall observes a family of chimpanzees.

With intervention

Without intervention

Hypothesis: Being observed can lead participants to change their behavior.

Research Method:

1 During studies of the effects of workplace conditions at the Hawthorne Plant, a Western Electric manufacturing plant, the researchers manipulated several independent variables. These variables included the levels of lighting, pay incentives, and break schedules.

2 The researchers then measured the dependent variable: the speed at which workers did their jobs.

Result: The workers' productivity increased when they were being observed, regardless of how the independent variable was changed.

Conclusion: Being observed can lead participants to change their behavior, because people often act in particular ways to make positive impressions.

sadness than men are. As a result, in coding men's and women's facial expressions, an observer may be more likely to rate female expressions as indicating sadness. The observer may tend to rate men's expressions of sadness as annoyance or some other emotion.

Another problem with observational studies is that they can produce artificial behavior. Such behavior will not reflect how people naturally behave. For example, the presence of an observer might alter the behavior being observed. Suppose people want to make a positive impression on an observer. They may act differently when they believe they are being observed. Such an alteration is called *reactivity*. A classic study on a form of reactivity, the Hawthorne effect, is described in the Scientific Thinking feature.

SELF-REPORTS For some kinds of research, observational studies are not appropriate. A different descriptive method consists of obtaining *self-reports* from research participants (**Figure 1.27**).

Questionnaires or surveys can be used to gather data from a large number of people in a short time. These research tools are easy to administer as well as cost-efficient. With groups that cannot be studied through questionnaires or surveys (for example, young children), interviews can be used. Interviews are also helpful in getting more details about the respondents' opinions, experiences, and attitudes. That is, the answers during the interview may lead the researchers to ask questions they had not planned.

A problem common to all self-report methods is that people's answers can involve personal biases called *self-report bias*. Sometimes people may not reveal personal information that casts them in a negative light. If you are in your

Self-reports are a descriptive research method that involves asking questions of research participants. The participants then respond in any way they feel is appropriate or select from among a fixed number of options.

Advantages	Self-reports such as surveys and questionnaires can be used to gather data from a large number of people. They are easy to administer, cost-efficient, and a relatively fast way to collect data. Interviewing people face-to-face gives the researcher the opportunity to explore new lines of questioning.
Disadvantages	People can introduce biases into their answers (*self-report bias*). They may not recall information accurately.

Surveys and questionnaires

Interviews

twenties, imagine having an interviewer around your parents' age ask you to describe intimate aspects of your sex life. If you are an older student, imagine a twenty-something interviewer asking the same question. How truthful would you be? Researchers have to consider whether their questions might lead a person to respond in a way that is most socially acceptable. Any distortion of the truth—whether it is meant to please or displease—will present a biased view. Psychologists therefore design self-reports so that people feel comfortable providing information. For example, the researchers make clear to the participant that all responses will be confidential.

CASE STUDIES *Case studies* involve intensive examination of a few unique people or organizations (**Figure 1.28**). For example, case studies of people with brain injuries have provided a wealth of evidence about which parts of the brain are involved in various psychological processes. In one case, a man who was

Case studies are a descriptive research method that involves intensive examination of one person or organization or a few individuals or organizations.

Advantages	Can provide a lot of data.
Disadvantages	Can be very subjective. If a researcher has a preexisting theory (for example, people who are socially awkward are dangerous), this theory can bias what is observed, investigated, and recorded. The results cannot be generalized from a single case study to the population.

FIGURE 1.28
Case Studies
(left) In December 2012, a 20-year-old gunman went on a shooting spree at Sandy Hook Elementary School, in Newtown, Connecticut. The gunman killed twenty-six teachers and young students before killing himself. (right) The gunman's name was Adam Lanza. This photo shows Lanza as a seemingly happy and healthy young boy. The Sandy Hook shooting provides a case study of how an individual can become disturbed enough to commit a terrible act.

accidentally stabbed through the middle part of the brain with a fencing foil lost the ability to store new memories (Squire & Moore, 1979). This study was important for indicating which parts of the brain are involved in memory.

Case studies of people with psychological disorders are used frequently in psychology. The major problem with these clinical case studies is that it is difficult to know whether the researcher's theory about the cause of the psychological disorder is correct. The researcher has no control over the person's life and is forced to make assumptions about the effects of various life events.

Correlational Methods Test Associations

Descriptive methods are limited because the observations, surveys, and case studies are done only on people who are already engaging in the behaviors being studied. So descriptive methods can only help us see what's occurring. When we want to examine the relationship between two factors, we have to use **correlational methods.** Correlational studies let us look at two factors at the same time. This comparison enables us to examine how one factor is related to another factor. How so? In correlational methods, the investigators do not alter the factors being studied or claim that one factor causes the other (**Figure 1.29**). They simply measure the two factors and then determine the degree of association between the two variables.

As an example, say you form the hypothesis "There is a relationship between drinking alcohol and showing impaired motor skills." You could use a correlational method to test this hypothesis. To do so, you might measure people's self-reported alcohol use and also their self-reported car accident history. These data would enable you to compare how drinking alcohol and driving performance are related. The data do not, however, show causation—they do not establish that drinking alcohol actually *caused* the performance. Why not? A few potential problems prevent researchers from drawing causal conclusions from correlational studies.

CORRELATION IS NOT CAUSALITY One problem with correlational studies is in knowing the direction of the relationship between variables. That is, can we determine what causes what? This sort of ambiguity is known as the *directionality problem.*

correlational methods
A research method that examines how variables are naturally related in the real world. The researcher makes no attempt to alter the variables or assign causation between them.

Correlational research methods examine how variables are related, without intervention by the observer.

Advantages — Rely on naturally occurring relationships. May take place in a real-world setting.

Disadvantages — Cannot demonstrate causal relationships (that one thing happened because of the other). Cannot show the direction of the cause/effect relationship between variables (*directionality problem*). An unidentified variable may be involved (*third variable problem*).

FIGURE 1.29
Correlational Methods
Correlational methods help us understand whether two factors are associated. A correlation may exist between how overweight parents are and how overweight their children are. A correlational study cannot demonstrate the cause of this relationship, which may include biological tendencies to gain weight, lack of exercise, and high-fat diets.

Eating Pizza Cuts Cancer Risk

Diet of Fish Can Prevent Teen Violence

Does Your Neighborhood Cause Schizophrenia?

Housework Cuts Breast Cancer Risk

FIGURE 1.30

Correlations in the News

When the media present results from correlational studies, the reports often suggest that one factor causes the other. In such cases, we need to think critically and remember that just because two events are associated with each other, we cannot say whether one causes the other.

For example, suppose you survey a large group of people about their sleeping habits and their levels of stress. Those who report sleeping badly also report having a higher level of stress. Does lack of sleep increase stress levels, or does increased stress lead to shorter and worse sleep? The cause/effect relationship in this example could go in either direction. As shown in the Learning Tip, both lack of sleep and more stress could be causes. But both of them also could be effects. In short, because of the directionality problem, correlational methods cannot tell us what causes a certain outcome.

Another drawback of all correlational studies is the *third variable problem*. Suppose a researcher assumes that variable A causes variable B. Or suppose the researcher assumes B causes A. What if a third variable, C, causes both A and B? Consider the relationship between drinking and driving. People who are very stressed in their daily lives may be more likely to drink before driving. Stress also may make them distracted while driving. Thus, the cause of both drinking and bad driving may be the third variable, stress. The Learning Tip also explains why the third variable problem prevents us from understanding what causes an outcome in a study using correlational methods. In fact, sometimes the third variable is not even identifiable (**Figure 1.30**).

These examples may make it seem that we should simply disregard the results of correlational studies. On the contrary, correlational studies still provide important information about the natural relationships between variables, enabling researchers to make valuable predictions. For example, correlational research has identified a strong relationship between depression and suicide. For this reason, clinical psychologists often assess symptoms of depression to determine suicide risk. In addition, researchers who conduct correlational studies use statistical procedures to rule out potential third variables and directionality problems. Once they have shown that a relationship between two variables holds even when potential third variables are taken into account, researchers can be more confident that the relationship is meaningful. In any case, to truly understand psychological findings, it is important to understand the difference between correlation and causation, as shown in the Being a Critical Consumer feature.

LEARNING TIP: Problems Determining Causality in Correlational Methods

The directionality problem and the third variable problem are the two main reasons that correlational methods prevent us from being able to state that changes in one variable actually cause changes in another. Here is a way to visualize these problems in correlational methods.

The Directionality Problem

Lack of sleep (A) is correlated with greater stress (B).

- Does less sleep cause more stress? (A → B)

    or

- Does more stress cause less sleep? (B → A)

The Third Variable Problem

Drinking before driving (A) is correlated with being distracted while driving (B).

- Stress (C) causes some people to drink before driving. (C → A)

    and

- Stress (C) causes some people to be distracted while driving. (C → B)

Kim finished reading Chapter 1 of her psychology text and put the book down. As a first-semester student, she was a bit nervous about taking introductory psychology because she hadn't studied psychology in high school and wasn't really sure what it was about. However, her advisor felt that the course might be helpful for Kim as a marketing major. Her friends told her that the class and the professor were really good.

Kim was surprised at how much she enjoyed reading the first chapter of the book. She had not realized how varied the study of psychology is. She especially liked reading about how psychologists conduct research. As she turned on her computer, she thought, *I wonder how much of the information I read about every day involves psychological research.*

On her startup page, she saw a list of news headlines. One, from the news service Reuters, caught her attention: "Spanking Kids Can Cause Long Term Harm." *What did that mean? Can spanking* cause *harm to kids over a long term? Was that statement based on psychological research?* The headline was making a causal claim, and Kim wanted to know how the writer could make that claim. Flipping through the chapter she had just read, she found the statement that only experimental methods can establish causation. In addition, she read, random assignment to groups is necessary in an experiment to avoid confounds and ensure that one factor caused a particular outcome. *If there was a research study, how was it done? Was one set of parents told to spank their children and one set of parents not allowed to spank theirs? Was that an ethical way to conduct a study?* Kim also reread the review of ethical guidelines in the chapter. Research, it said, should try to avoid exposing people to unreasonable pain or discomfort. *Would making parents spank their children be ethical?*

Kim was now very curious about this study. Her professor, Dr. Parretti, had told Kim's class that people should be critical consumers of the research they read about in the popular press. Sometimes headlines are meant to grab attention but do not accurately or completely describe the research that was done. *Could this be one of those cases where the research said one thing but the press said another?*

Determined to get to the bottom of the question, Kim thought, *It's likely that correlational methods were used to study this topic, probably with self-reports. Researchers could have measured whether spanking occurred in the home and then measured psychological outcomes, such as aggressive behavior and mental health problems. But would this experiment have warranted the news headlines she had read?* With a quick search, she found other headlines about the study. From *U.S. News and World Report:* "Spanking Produces Troubled Kids, Study Contends." From *Huffington Post:* "Children Who Get Physical Punishment Tend Toward Aggression." From *Globe and Mail:* "Study Links Spanking to Later Mental Disorders." Even the headlines seemed to focus on slightly different aspects of the study!

When Kim found the original study, she saw that the headlines didn't completely match what was written by the journalists or the actual scientists. The published study had collected 20 years of data on the topic, but it proposed only a correlation between spanking and harm to children, not a causal relationship. Even without a causal relationship, Kim was convinced that the correlations they did find were important and that there is a link between spanking one's children and negative outcomes for that child. Kim thought, *Maybe this psychology class is going to be pretty useful! It's teaching me ways to criticize what I read on the Internet!*

Experimental Methods Test Causation

So we now know that if a psychologist is using a correlational method, the research will uncover whether a relationship exists between factors. The researcher will not control the situation and so cannot determine whether one factor causes the other. Therefore, if the goal of the research is to determine causation, the psychologist must use a different type of research method. To determine whether one factor causes the other, **experimental methods** must be used to test the hypothesis (**Figure 1.31**).

VARIABLES AND OPERATIONAL DEFINITIONS To begin understanding experimental methods, let's return to the research example concerning alcohol consumption and motor skills. In this case, the hypothesis might be "Consuming more alcohol will cause poorer driving skills."

experimental methods
A research method that tests causal hypotheses by manipulating independent variables and measuring the effects on dependent variables.

FIGURE 1.31

Experimental Methods
Experimental research methods
provide information about the causes
of particular mental activities or
behaviors.

Experimental research methods examine how one variable that is manipulated by researchers affects another variable.

Advantages	Provide control over independent variables, so can demonstrate that one thing causes another. Avoid the *directionality problem*.
Disadvantages	Varying something other than the independent variable (a *confound*) can affect the dependent variable and lead to inaccurate conclusions. Often take place in an artificial setting.

1	2	3	4	5
Researcher manipulates...	Researcher randomly assigns subjects to...	Researcher measures...	Researcher analyzes results.	Conclusion
independent variable	control group or experimental group	dependent variable	Are the data in the control group different from the data in the experimental group?	The explanation either supports or does not support the hypothesis. Are there confounds, which would lead to alternative explanations?

FIGURE 1.32

Participants in an Experiment With Simulated Driving
An experiment investigating how alcohol consumption affects driving skills can be performed safely by having participants use a driving simulator or play a driving game. Information about the participants' driving skills would be recorded electronically.

independent variable
In an experiment, the variable that the experimenter manipulates to examine its impact on the dependent variable.

dependent variable
In an experiment, the variable that is affected by the manipulation of the independent variable.

To perform an experiment that will test a hypothesis, the researcher manipulates one variable. This variable is called the **independent variable.** In an example experiment, on drinking alcohol and driving skills, the independent variable would be alcohol consumption. However, to ensure that the research is objective and systematic, you have to define the alcohol consumption more specifically. In other words, you must create an *operational definition* of the variable. To operationally define the independent variable of alcohol consumption, you can bring the amount of alcohol in each person's blood to a predetermined level. That level is described by blood alcohol content (BAC). In this experiment, let's say you manipulate BAC to range from 0.0 (no alcohol) to 0.01–0.05 (relaxed feeling; sense of well-being; impaired thought, judgment, and coordination) to 0.06–0.10 (loss of inhibitions; extraversion; impaired reflexes, depth perception, peripheral vision, and reasoning). Note that the legal limit for driving is 0.08.

After manipulating the independent variable, you measure the effect of that factor on a second factor. The second factor is called the **dependent variable.** In your experiment, the dependent variable is driving skills. Instead of letting your participants drive, you would measure their skills safely as they use a driving simulator or play a driving game on a computer (**Figure 1.32**).

Just as you need to operationally define the independent variable, you need to operationally define the dependent variable. Again, these procedures ensure that the research is systematic and objective. One option for the dependent variable might be to measure the amount of time it takes participants playing the driving computer game to stop the car when an obstacle appears in the road. In this case, the operational definition of driving skills is in milliseconds of stopping time. Another operational definition of driving skills would be how many times the person playing the driving game crashes the virtual car. Often, a single dependent variable can have many operational definitions.

GROUPS Your experiment tests the hypothesis that the dependent variable (driving skills, as measured by either the number of virtual crashes or how long it takes the driver to stop the car) is affected by the independent variable (the amount of alcohol consumed, as shown by BAC). But how do you know if the change in the dependent variable is really caused by your manipulation of the independent variable?

To clarify the relationship between your variables, you assign some participants in the study to a **control group.** In this case, participants assigned to the control group drink something nonalcoholic, such as tonic water, instead of alcohol. To make sure that both groups expect to be drinking alcohol, you might disguise the tonic water by using lemon or even some alcohol rubbed along the rim of the glass. However, the participants in the **experimental group** experience the manipulation you are interested in. In this case, they consume enough alcohol to reach a certain BAC level. Because you disguise the tonic water, all the study participants think they are drinking alcohol. You then compare the effects of drinking tonic water in the control group with the effects of drinking alcohol in the experimental group (or more than one experimental group, if you include several levels of BAC in the study).

The benefit of using an experimental method is that the researcher can study the causal relationship between the two variables. Suppose the independent variable (BAC in our example) consistently influences the dependent variable (driving skills). The independent variable is then assumed to cause the change in the dependent variable. The experiment makes it possible to rule out alternative explanations, such as third variables. In addition, because the experimenter determines when the independent variable (here, the BAC level) is administered, the experimenter can be sure that this variable comes first in time. In this way, the experimenter also solves the directionality problem.

CONTROL IS NECESSARY TO DETERMINE CAUSALITY A properly performed experiment depends on rigorous control. Here, control means the steps taken by the researcher to minimize the possibility that anything other than the independent variable will affect the experiment's outcome. When conducting an experiment, a researcher needs to ensure that the only thing that varies is the independent variable. That way, the researcher knows that the independent variable—nothing else—has affected the dependent variable. Anything that affects a dependent variable and that may unintentionally vary between the study's different experimental conditions is known as a *confound*.

Consider a confound in your hypothetical study of alcohol consumption and driving skills. Suppose the computer game used to assess driving when participants are sober has an automatic transmission. Now suppose the game used with intoxicated participants has a manual transmission (stick shift). If you're not

control group
In an experiment, a comparison group of participants that receives no intervention or receives an intervention that is unrelated to the independent variable being investigated.

experimental group
In an experiment, one or more treatment groups of participants that receive the intervention of the independent variable being investigated.

💡 **LEARNING TIP: Dependent and Independent Variables**

WHEN YOU SEE	PLEASE THINK	MEANING
<u>In</u>dependent variable	<u>In</u> control of the experimenter	The experimenter manipulates what the participant does, sees, experiences, is exposed to, and so on.
<u>Depend</u>ent variable	<u>Depend</u>s on what the participant does	The experimenter measures only what the participant does.

familiar with both types of transmissions, you might think they're equal. However, driving a car with a manual transmission takes more skill than driving one with an automatic transmission. As a result, a change in driving performance might actually be caused by the type of car driven in the computer game. In this example, the drivers' skills might be confounded with the type of transmission. The presence of a confound would make it impossible to determine the true effect of BAC on driving performance.

The more confounds and thus alternative explanations that can be eliminated, the more confident a researcher can be that the change in the independent variable is causing the change (or effect) in the dependent variable. Control represents the foundation of the experimental approach, because it allows the researcher to rule out alternative explanations for the observed data. As consumers of research, we all need to think about confounds that could be causing particular results that are reported in the news.

RANDOM ASSIGNMENT REMOVES CONFOUNDS One possible confound in a study is preexisting differences between groups that are assigned to different conditions. Consider your study of drinking and driving. What happens to the results if the people assigned to have many drinks just happen to be heavy drinkers? Some heavy drinkers develop such a tolerance to alcohol that they show few outward signs of intoxication even when their blood alcohol levels are high enough to knock out a typical person (Chesher & Greeley, 1992). By contrast, some participants might become intoxicated on very small amounts of alcohol. Either group might distort the results. The distorted results would indicate that the effects of alcohol on driving are lesser or greater than they would be in the general population.

Of course, individual differences are bound to exist among participants. For example, any of your groups might include some people with low tolerance for alcohol and some people with high tolerance, some people with excellent coordination and some people with poor coordination. How do you keep these differences from being a problem? You use **random assignment** (**Figure 1.33a**). This method gives each potential research participant an equal chance of being assigned to any level of the independent variable (BAC level, for example). Differences between participants will tend to average out when participants are assigned randomly to either the control group or one or more of the experimental groups. Random assignment balances out known and unknown factors.

SAMPLING Now that you know about random assignment, what types of participants would you choose for your hypothetical study? Selecting participants is as important as choosing a research method. Psychologists typically want to know that their findings generalize. In other words, the results should apply to people beyond the individuals in the study. When studying the effects of drinking alcohol on driving skills, you want to know more than how the specific participants behaved. Ultimately, you want to discover general laws about human behavior. Such laws will enable you, other psychologists, and people in general to predict how drinking alcohol affects driving performance.

The general group you want to know about is your *population*. For instance, you might want your results to generalize to college students, to students who belong to

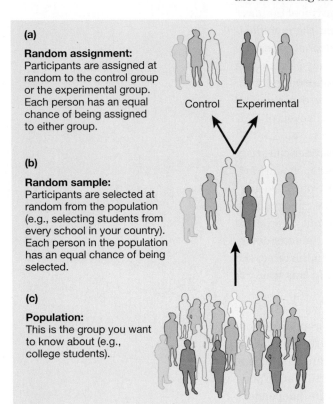

(a)

Random assignment:
Participants are assigned at random to the control group or the experimental group. Each person has an equal chance of being assigned to either group.

Control   Experimental

(b)

Random sample:
Participants are selected at random from the population (e.g., selecting students from every school in your country). Each person in the population has an equal chance of being selected.

(c)

Population:
This is the group you want to know about (e.g., college students).

FIGURE 1.33
Random Assignment and Random Sampling
For the results of an experiment to be considered useful, researchers must use random assignment and random sampling.

random assignment
Placing research participants into the conditions of an experiment in such a way that each participant has an equal chance of being assigned to any level of the independent variable.

sororities and fraternities, to women, to men over the age of 45, and so on. To learn about the population, you study a subset, or a small number, from it. That subset, the people you actually study, is the *sample*. Sampling is the process you use to select people from the population to be in the study.

One way to represent the whole population is to take a **random sample** (**Figure 1.33b–c**). This method gives each member of the population an equal chance of being chosen to participate. Most of the time, however, researchers will use a sample consisting of people who are conveniently available for the study. Even if you wanted your results to generalize to all students in your country or in the world, you would probably use a sample from your own college or university. Even though a sample from your own college might not look like all students in the country, it seems reasonable to expect that the effect of alcohol on human motor skills would be about the same, no matter where you sampled them from. It is important for researchers to recognize that their results might not generalize to other samples that are quite different, such as people from other cultures (Henrich, Heine, & Norenzayan, 2010).

In reading this chapter, you have learned what psychologists have investigated in the past, what they research today, and how they use the scientific method to understand thought and behavior. It's time to learn about psychology in your life.

random sample
A sample that fairly represents the population because each member of the population had an equal chance of being included.

1.4 CHECKPOINT: How Do Psychologists Conduct Research?

- Psychologists use empiricism to investigate psychological topics by following the five steps of the scientific method.

- Descriptive methods allow description of what is occurring.

- Correlational methods investigate the relationship between factors.

- Only experimental methods make it possible to determine a cause and effect relationship between variables.

BIG PICTURE

BIG QUESTION

LEARNING GOALS

1.1 Why Is Psychology Important to You?

a. Remember the key terms about psychology.

b. Apply critical thinking to your life.

c. Apply psychology to your life.

1.2 What Do Psychologists Investigate?

a. Remember the key terms about what psychologists investigate.

b. Apply the nature/nurture debate to your own life.

c. Understand the three psychology schools of thought that investigated the conscious mind and the unconscious mind.

d. Evaluate the four psychology schools of thought that investigate behavior and mental activity.

1.3 Who Are Psychologists Today?

a. Remember the key terms about who psychologists are today.

b. Analyze how psychologists do research at four different levels of analysis.

c. Apply the eight subfields of psychology to your own life.

d. Understand the five ethical issues in psychological research.

1.4 How Do Psychologists Conduct Research?

a. Remember the key terms about the scientific method.

b. Analyze the cycle of the scientific method.

c. Understand the three psychological research methods.

d. Apply correlations to your life.

KEY TERMS

CHECKPOINT

psychology
critical thinking

- We experience psychological issues every minute of our lives, but we cannot understand them based on common sense alone.
- Psychology is the scientific study of mental activity, behavior, and the brain.

- Studying psychology helps improve critical thinking skills and study skills. It also helps develop skills that make people successful in their jobs.

structuralism
functionalism
natural selection
Gestalt theory
behaviorism
cognitive psychology
social psychology

- The classic questions in psychology, such as the nature/nurture debate and the mind/body problem, originated in philosophy.
- Early psychological schools of thought explored the conscious mind and the unconscious mind. Later schools of thought explored mental activity and behavior.

- Behaviorism is based on the idea that objective, observable behavior should be the focus of psychological inquiry.
- Cognitive psychology investigates unseen mental processes and how they affect our thinking.
- Social psychology explores how the presence of other people affects our thinking and behavior.

culture
institutional review boards
    (IRBs)

- Psychologists today investigate diverse questions across one or more of four levels of analysis: biological, individual, social, and cultural.
- Psychologists now work in many settings.
- Across a wide variety of subfields, psychological researchers investigate different aspects of mental activity and behavior.

- Psychologists must adhere to all ethical guidelines when conducting scientific research.

scientific method
theory
hypothesis
descriptive methods
correlational methods
experimental methods
independent variable
dependent variable
control group
experimental group
random assignment
random sample

- Psychologists use empiricism to investigate psychological topics by following the five steps of the scientific method.
- Descriptive methods allow description of what is occurring.
- Correlational methods investigate the relationship between factors.

- Only experimental methods make it possible to determine a cause and effect relationship between variables.

For a self-quiz on this chapter, go to the back of the book and find Appendix B: Quizzes.

The Role of 2 Biology in Psychology

IN 2012, JACK OSBOURNE (**Figure 2.1**), the 26-year-old son of Ozzy and Sharon Osbourne, celebrated the arrival of his daughter Pearl. Just two weeks later, he noticed a disturbing problem with his vision. He told *People* magazine (July 9, 2012) about an experience he had at a gas station: "I was talking to the attendant, and all of a sudden a black dot appeared in my vision. . . . I was like, 'That's weird.' The next day I woke up and the dot had turned into a cigar shape." Jack's vision kept getting worse, until he could barely see out of his right eye. After a series of tests, doctors determined that Jack was in the early stages of multiple sclerosis.

BIG QUESTIONS

2.1 **How Do Our Nervous Systems Affect Thinking and Behavior?**

2.2 **How Do the Parts of Our Brains Function?**

2.3 **How Do Our Brains Communicate With Our Bodies?**

2.4 **How Do Nature and Nurture Affect Our Brains?**

FIGURE 2.1

Around the Globe, 2.5 Million People Have Multiple Sclerosis

Jack Osbourne is one of millions of people with multiple sclerosis. This disease damages nerve cells in the brain.

Multiple sclerosis (MS) is a disorder of the nervous system that is typically diagnosed in people between ages 20 and 40. MS affects the brain and the spinal cord, so that movements become jerky and people lose the ability to coordinate their actions. Gradually, the ability to move, see, and think all become severely impaired. MS affects about 2.5 million people throughout the world. It is incurable, but in some forms of the disease the symptoms are now manageable.

The symptoms of MS make clear that our nervous system is critical for thinking normally and behaving normally. The nervous system consists partly of nerve cells, also known as neurons. MS limits the ability of neurons to send signals to each other and to receive each other's signals. To picture how a neuron operates, imagine the plastic around a wire, such as the cord from a lamp or an appliance. The plastic insulates the wire, allowing electrical current to run to the lamp so it can turn on. Without that insulating layer, electricity will never reach the lamp. One part of the neuron, like the lamp cord, is covered by a fatty layer that enables the neuron to transmit signals to other neurons and other parts of the body. In MS, the fatty layer deteriorates, and normal communication between neurons is short-circuited.

To learn about psychology, you need to understand how neural communication enables us to think and behave. You also need to see how both nature and nurture affect these processes. We cannot understand thought and behavior without understanding our underlying biological processes.

2.1 How Do Our Nervous Systems Affect Thinking and Behavior?

nervous system

A network of billions of cells in the brain and the body, responsible for all aspects of what we feel, think, and do.

The **nervous system** is a network of billions of cells in the brain and the body. This system is responsible for all aspects of what we feel, think, and do. The nervous system has three basic functions: (1) receive sensory input from the world through vision, hearing, touch, taste, and smell; (2) process the information in the brain by paying attention to it, perceiving it, and remembering it; and (3) respond to the information by acting on it. To experience these functions, see Try It Yourself.

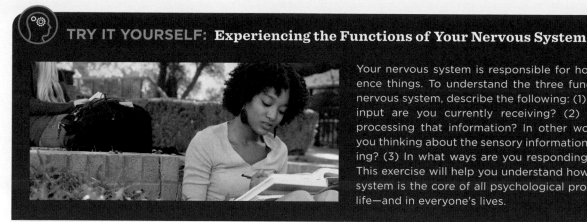
These three functions are a result of processing in two divisions of the nervous system. The **central nervous system** consists of the brain and the spinal cord, which both contain massive numbers of nerve cells. The **peripheral nervous system** consists of the nerve cells in the soft organs in the rest of the body (**Figure 2.2**). These two units are separate, but they interact constantly. For example, when you touch a sharp tack, the peripheral nervous system registers that sensory signal and transmits the information to the central nervous system. The central nervous system organizes and evaluates that information, then directs the peripheral nervous system to perform specific behaviors, such as moving your hand away from the tack. These two systems work together every moment of our lives, enabling us to think and act.

central nervous system
The part of the nervous system that consists of the brain and the spinal cord.

peripheral nervous system
The part of the nervous system that enables nerves to connect the central nervous system with the muscles, organs, and glands.

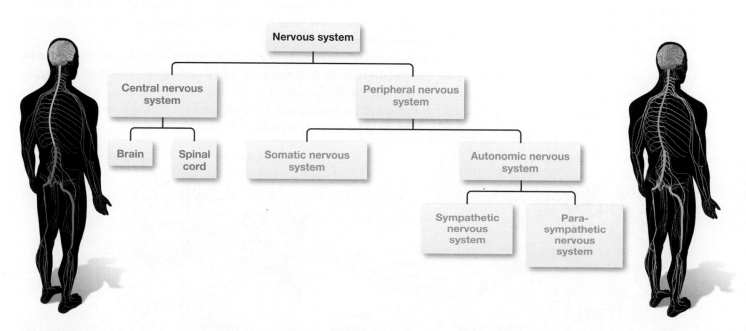

FIGURE 2.2

The Nervous System
The main divisions of the nervous system are the central nervous system and the peripheral nervous system. Together with their subdivisions, these systems (1) receive sensory input, (2) process it further, and (3) respond to it.

Neurons Are the Basic Units of Our Nervous Systems

Both divisions of the nervous system are made up of smaller units. These units are the nerve cells, or **neurons** (**Figure 2.3**). Individual neurons receive, integrate, and transmit information in the nervous system. Each neuron communicates with tens of thousands of other neurons. But the neurons do not communicate randomly or by chance. Instead, they communicate selectively with other neurons. Through this selective communication, neurons form networks. The networks of billions of neurons sending and receiving signals make possible all the complex aspects of human thought and behavior. Through maturation and experience, the networks develop and strengthen. In other words, permanent alliances form among groups of neurons. Those alliances enable the neurons to process information strongly and efficiently.

We are able to think and act because neurons are able to communicate with each other. And neural communication is possible because of the neuron's structure, in addition to the neuron's electrical and chemical properties.

STRUCTURE OF NEURONS Let's examine the four parts of a neuron that enable it to communicate with other neurons. These parts are the dendrites, the cell body, the axons, and the terminal buttons (**Figure 2.4**).

The **dendrites** are short, branchlike extensions. They detect signals from neighboring neurons. In the **cell body,** the information received from thousands of other neurons is collected and integrated (joined together). Once the incoming information has been integrated in the cell body, electrical impulses are transmitted along the **axon.** Axons vary tremendously in length. In fact, the longest axons stretch all the way from the spinal cord to each of the big toes. In everyday language, we commonly refer to neurons as nerves, as in the phrase "pinched nerve." In this context, a nerve is a bundle of axons that carry information between the brain and other specific locations in the body. At the end of the axon are knoblike structures called *terminal buttons*.

The site where communication occurs between neurons is called the **synapse.** In the synapse, the neurons do not actually touch each other. Instead, they communicate by sending chemicals into a tiny gap between the terminal buttons of the sending neuron and the dendrites of the receiving neurons. The chemicals leave one neuron, cross the synapse, and pass signals along to the dendrites of other neurons.

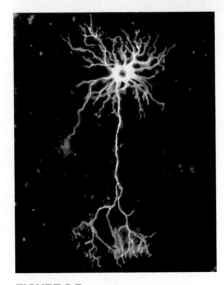

FIGURE 2.3
Human Nerve Cell
This is a nerve cell, also known as a neuron. Neurons are the basic units of the human nervous system.

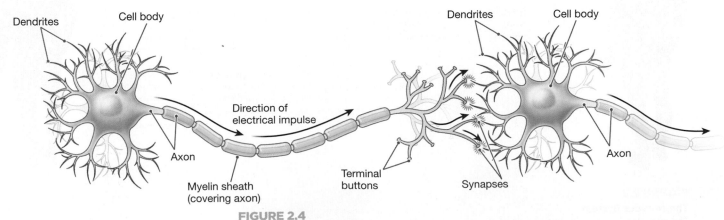

Dendrites Cell body

Direction of electrical impulse

Axon

Myelin sheath (covering axon)

Terminal buttons

Synapses

Dendrites Cell body

Axon

FIGURE 2.4
Neuron Structure
Messages are received by the dendrites, processed in the cell body, transmitted along the axon, and sent to other neurons via chemical substances released from the terminal buttons to the dendrites of the receiving neuron. The details of these processes are shown in Figures 2.5 and 2.6.

ELECTRICAL PROPERTIES OF NEURONS Parts of the neuron are covered with a *membrane,* a thin covering. This barrier separates the inside of the neuron from the outside environment. The membrane is semipermeable. In other words, some substances move through the membrane. These substances may move from outside the neuron to the inside or from inside the neuron to the outside.

The membrane contributes to neural communication by regulating the neuron's electrical activity. It is important to know that the inside and the outside of a neuron have different electrical charges. Think of the positive and negative ends of a battery. The neuron begins in a *resting state*. During this state, the electrical charge inside the neuron is slightly more negative than the electrical charge outside.

Now imagine the neuron is stimulated enough that it is going to send a message to another neuron. This stimulation causes molecules such as sodium and potassium to move through the membrane. When this change occurs, the electrical charge across the membrane changes. The inside of the neuron becomes more positive than the outside. If the neuron is stimulated enough, it fires an **action potential** down the axon to the terminal buttons, where chemicals are released into the synapse. The neuron then returns to the resting state. In this way, one neuron is able to send a message to another neuron. Let's examine the action potential and the process of neural communication in more detail.

Action Potentials Allow Neurons to Communicate With Each Other

Neurons communicate with other neurons in three phases (**Figure 2.5**). During the transmission phase (Step 1), neurons pass signals to receiving neurons. During the reception phase (Step 2), neurons receive signals from neighboring

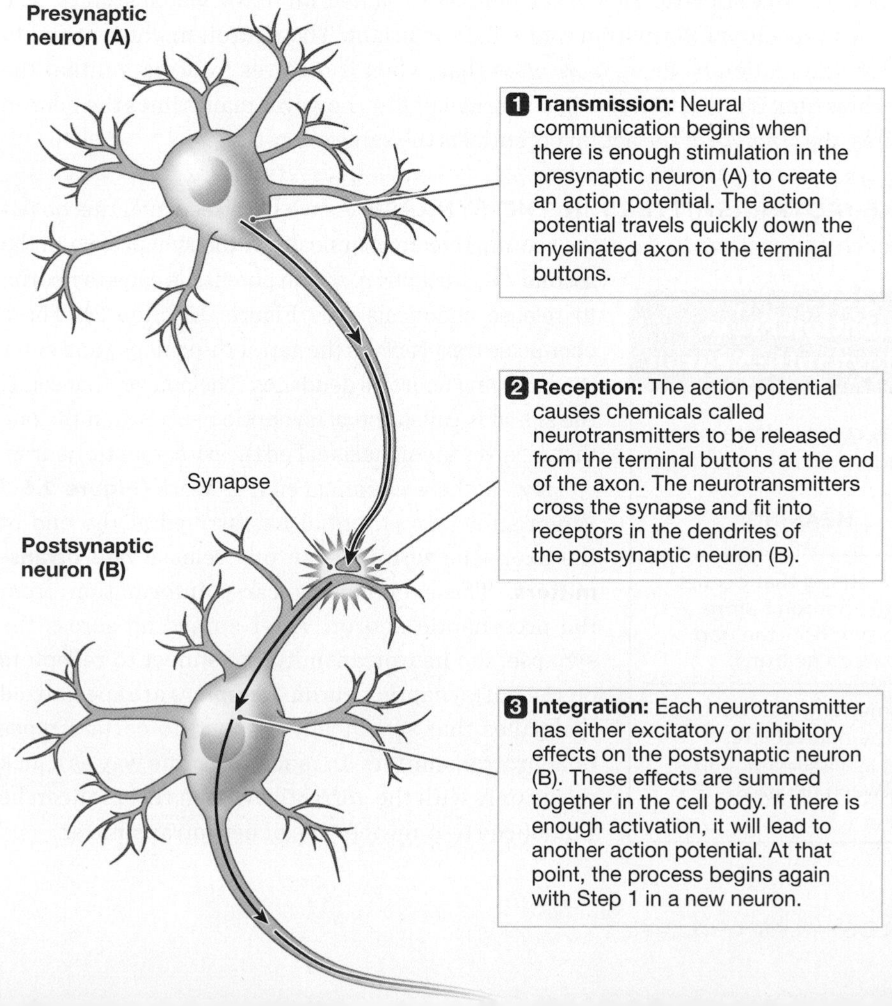

dendrites
Branchlike extensions of the neuron with receptors that detect information from other neurons.

cell body
Part of the neuron where information from thousands of other neurons is collected and integrated.

axon
A long, narrow outgrowth of a neuron that enables the neuron to transmit information to other neurons.

synapse
The site where communication occurs between neurons through neurotransmitters.

action potential
The neural impulse that travels along the axon and then causes the release of neurotransmitters into the synapse.

Presynaptic neuron (A)

1 Transmission: Neural communication begins when there is enough stimulation in the presynaptic neuron (A) to create an action potential. The action potential travels quickly down the myelinated axon to the terminal buttons.

Synapse

Postsynaptic neuron (B)

2 Reception: The action potential causes chemicals called neurotransmitters to be released from the terminal buttons at the end of the axon. The neurotransmitters cross the synapse and fit into receptors in the dendrites of the postsynaptic neuron (B).

3 Integration: Each neurotransmitter has either excitatory or inhibitory effects on the postsynaptic neuron (B). These effects are summed together in the cell body. If there is enough activation, it will lead to another action potential. At that point, the process begins again with Step 1 in a new neuron.

FIGURE 2.5

Three Steps of Neural Communication
This graphic shows the three steps of neural communication: (1) transmission, (2) reception, and (3) integration.

neurons. During integration (Step 3), neurons assess the incoming signals. Then this neural communication process can be repeated, with signals transmitted to yet more neurons. Now let's look at each of these steps in turn.

ACTION POTENTIALS In the first step, a neuron is stimulated by signals from other neurons. The stimulated neuron may transmit this information to other neurons (see Figure 2.5, Step 1). What determines whether the neuron will transmit the information it has received? When a neuron is stimulated, the electrical charge inside the neuron becomes more positive than the charge outside the neuron. If the electrical charge changes enough, the action potential begins. Traveling along the axon like a wave, the action potential moves away from the cell body. It moves down the axon and toward the terminal buttons.

The action potential travels quickly along the axon. This fast movement is made possible by the fatty layer that insulates the axon. The fatty casing is called the *myelin sheath*. Because the myelin sheath makes neural communication so quick, you are able to move your hand away from a sharp tack fast enough to keep from getting hurt. However, recall from the chapter opener that Jack Osbourne's vision was affected because multiple sclerosis destroys the myelin sheath. Axons that have no insulation cannot effectively continue the action potential. In short, when neurons lose the myelin sheath, they lose the ability to communicate.

To communicate, a neuron fires an action potential. A neuron cannot fire just a little bit: It either fires or it does not. How often a neuron fires an action potential can change, though, depending on how much stimulation the neuron receives. To understand this idea, suppose you are playing a video game in which you fire missiles by pressing a button. Every time you press the button, a missile is launched at the same speed as the previous one. It makes no difference how hard you press the button. However, if you press faster, missiles will fire more rapidly one after another. Now suppose the missile launcher is a neuron in the visual system. The neuron receives information that a light is bright. The neuron might respond to that stimulation by firing *more often* than when it receives information that the light is dim. But whether the light is bright or dim, however many times the neuron fires, the *strength* of the action potential is the same every time.

NEUROTRANSMITTERS IN THE SYNAPSE As we have seen, neurons do not touch one another. Instead, they communicate chemically at the synapse. So in the second step, reception, action potentials cause a neuron to release chemicals (see Figure 2.5, Step 2). These chemicals travel across the gap at the synapse and enter the receiving neuron's dendrites. The neuron that sends the signal is called the *pre*synaptic neuron, and the one that receives the signal is called the *post*synaptic neuron.

How do these chemical signals work (**Figure 2.6**)? When an action potential has arrived at the end of the axon, the terminal buttons release **neurotransmitters.** These chemicals carry information from the presynaptic neuron. After spreading across the synapse, the neurotransmitters connect to receptors on the postsynaptic neuron. *Receptors* are specialized molecules that specifically respond to certain types of neurotransmitters. In much the same way as a lock opens only with the correct key, each receptor can be influenced by only one type of neurotransmitter.

LEARNING TIP: Communication From Presynaptic Neuron to Postsynaptic Neuron

It will be easy to understand how neurons communicate with each other if you remember the following.

WHEN YOU SEE	PLEASE THINK	MEANING
Presynaptic	Before the synapse	Something that occurs in the neuron before the synapse (the gap between neurons)
Postsynaptic	After the synapse	Something that occurs in the neuron after the synapse (the gap between neurons)

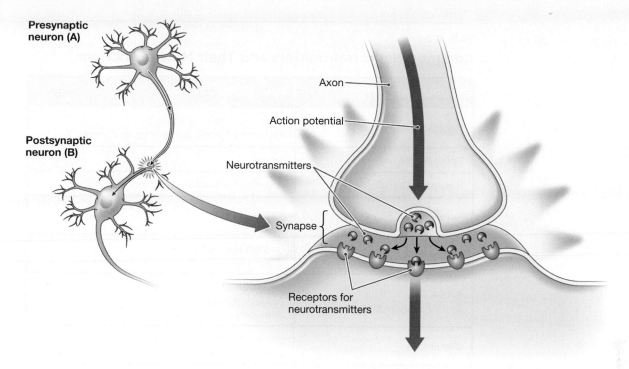

Presynaptic
neuron (A)

Postsynaptic
neuron (B)

Axon

Action potential

Neurotransmitters

Synapse

Receptors for
neurotransmitters

FIGURE 2.6
Neurotransmitters Move Across the Synapse
The action potential in the presynaptic neuron results in the release of neurotransmitters from terminal buttons. These neurotransmitters cross the synapse and bind to specific receptors on the dendrites of the postsynaptic neuron.

Once neurotransmitters are released into the synapse, they stimulate specific receptors. This stimulation continues until the presynaptic neuron stops releasing the neurotransmitters, it reabsorbs them, or they are destroyed in the synapse.

EXCITATORY AND INHIBITORY SIGNALS In the third step, integration, the postsynaptic neuron processes incoming signals (see Figure 2.5, Step 3). The binding of neurotransmitters with their receptors on the postsynaptic neuron can produce signals of two types: excitatory or inhibitory. As the name indicates, excitatory signals excite the neuron—they increase the likelihood that it will fire. Inhibitory signals inhibit the neuron—they decrease the likelihood that it will fire. Any individual signal received by the neuron has little influence on whether the neuron fires. Instead, thousands of excitatory and inhibitory signals are added together within the cell body of the neuron. If the total amount of excitatory input goes past a certain threshold, the postsynaptic neuron fires an action potential. After firing, the neuron returns to its slightly negative resting state. The process repeats hundreds of times per second.

Neurotransmitters Influence Our Mental Activity and Behavior

Much of our knowledge about neurotransmitters has come from research on how drugs and toxic substances affect emotion, thought, and behavior. Drugs that enhance the actions of neurotransmitters are known as *agonists*. Drugs that inhibit the actions of neurotransmitters are known as *antagonists*. Addictive drugs, such as heroin and cocaine, have their effects because they are chemically similar to naturally occurring neurotransmitters. The receptors cannot sense the difference between the ingested drug and the real neurotransmitter released from a presynaptic neuron. Remember, a neurotransmitter fits a receptor the way a key fits a lock. However, the receptor-lock cannot tell a real neurotransmitter-key from a forgery. The receptor can be affected by either a neurotransmitter or a drug that resembles the neurotransmitter.

TABLE 2.1

Common Neurotransmitters and Their Major Functions

NEUROTRANSMITTER	FUNCTIONS
Acetylcholine	Motor control over muscles Attention, memory, learning, and sleeping
Epinephrine	Energy
Norepinephrine	Arousal and alertness
Serotonin	Emotional states and impulse control Dreaming
Dopamine	Reward and motivation Motor control over voluntary movement
GABA (gamma-aminobutyric acid)	Inhibition of action potentials Anxiety reduction Intoxication (through alcohol)
Glutamate	Enhancement of action potentials Learning and memory
Endorphins	Pain reduction Reward

To assess how neurotransmitters affect behavior, researchers often inject agonists or antagonists into animals' brains. For instance, scientists may want to test the hypothesis that a certain neurotransmitter in a specific brain region leads to increased eating. Injecting an agonist into that brain region should increase an animal's eating. Injecting an antagonist should decrease its eating. Such studies help in the development of drug treatments for many psychological and medical disorders.

There are many kinds of neurotransmitters. Some neurotransmitters are particularly important in understanding how we think, feel, and behave (**Table 2.1**).

ACETYLCHOLINE Maybe you have seen ads for Botox or known someone who received Botox injections to remove wrinkles. Botox treatments depend on the action of *acetylcholine*, the neurotransmitter responsible for motor control. After moving across the synapses, acetylcholine binds with receptors on muscle cells. This chemical binding makes the muscles contract.

Where does Botox come in? Botulism, a form of food poisoning, inhibits the release of acetylcholine. The resulting paralysis of muscles leads to difficulty in chewing, difficulty in breathing, and often death. In small, much less toxic doses, the botulism bacteria (popularly known as Botox) paralyze muscles that produce wrinkles in certain areas. The affected areas include the forehead (**Figure 2.7**). Because the effects of Botox wear off over time, a new dose of botulism needs to be injected every 2 to 4 months. But Botox also paralyzes the facial muscles we use to express emotions, as in smiling and frowning. If too much Botox is injected, the result can be an expressionless face.

In addition to regulating motor control, acetylcholine is also involved in some complex mental processes. For example, acetylcholine influences attention, memory, learning, and sleeping. Because acetylcholine plays a role in

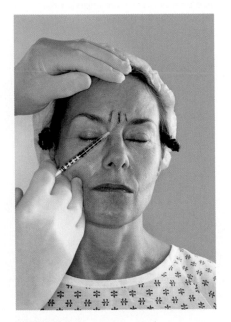

FIGURE 2.7

Acetylcholine and Botox

The neurotransmitter acetylcholine is responsible for motor control between nerves and muscles. Botox inhibits the release of acetylcholine, paralyzing muscles. Here, a woman gets a Botox injection to remove wrinkles in her forehead.

attention and memory, drugs that are acetylcholine antagonists can cause temporary amnesia. In a similar way, diminished acetylcholine functioning is associated with Alzheimer's disease, a condition characterized primarily by severe memory deficits (Geula & Mesulam, 1994). Drugs that are acetylcholine agonists may enhance memory and decrease symptoms of Alzheimer's. So far, though, drug treatments for the disease have had only limited success.

EPINEPHRINE You've certainly experienced an adrenaline rush. This effect is the sudden burst of energy that seems to take over your whole body. The adrenaline rush results from a release of the neurotransmitter *epinephrine,* formerly called adrenaline. Epinephrine binds to receptors throughout the body. The resulting rush is part of a system called the fight-or-flight response. This system prepares the body for dealing with threats from the environment (**Figure 2.8**).

The neurotransmitter related to epinephrine, *norepinephrine,* is involved in states of arousal and alertness. Norepinephrine is especially important for noticing what is going on around you.

SEROTONIN The neurotransmitter *serotonin* is involved in a wide range of psychological activities. It is especially important for emotional states, impulse control, and dreaming. A lack of serotonin is thought to contribute to sad and anxious moods, food cravings, and aggressive behavior. Some drugs, such as Prozac, that are used to treat a wide array of mental and behavioral disorders—including depression, obsessive-compulsive disorders, eating disorders, and obesity—leave more serotonin in the synapse to bind with the postsynaptic neurons (Tollefson, 1995).

DOPAMINE *Dopamine* has many important brain functions. Its most important functions are motivation and reward. Consider that people eat when they're hungry, drink when they're thirsty, and have sex when they're aroused. What physiological system motivates these activities? Behaviors such as these activate dopamine receptors, and the increased dopamine produces a desire to perform the behavior.

By contrast, a lack of dopamine may be involved in problems with movement. Severe loss of dopamine is connected to Parkinson's disease. First identified by the physician James Parkinson in 1917, Parkinson's is a degenerative and fatal neurological disorder. It affects about 1 in every 200 older adults and occurs in all known cultures. Most people with Parkinson's do not experience symptoms until after age 50, but the disease can occur earlier in life. For example, the actor Michael J. Fox was diagnosed with Parkinson's at age 30.

With Parkinson's disease, the dopamine-producing neurons in the midbrain slowly die off. The resulting lack of dopamine causes disturbances in motor function: rigid muscles, tremors, and difficulty initiating voluntary action. You can see these symptoms in the shuffling walk of a person with the disease. In the later stages of the disorder, people experience severe cognitive and mood disturbances. Injections of one of the chief chemical building blocks of dopamine, L-DOPA, help the surviving neurons produce more dopamine. When L-DOPA is used to treat Parkinson's disease, patients often have a remarkable, though temporary, recovery.

GABA AND GLUTAMATE The main inhibitory neurotransmitter is *GABA* (gamma-aminobutyric acid). It is more widely distributed throughout the brain

FIGURE 2.8

Epinephrine and Adrenaline Rush
Certain activities, such as bungee jumping, release the neurotransmitter epinephrine. You feel the effect of epinephrine as a sudden burst of energy, sometimes called an adrenaline rush.

than most other neurotransmitters. Without the inhibitory effect of GABA, the excitation of neurons might get out of control and spread through the brain chaotically. In fact, epileptic seizures may be caused by low levels of GABA (Upton, 1994).

Drugs that are GABA agonists (e.g., Valium) are widely used to treat anxiety disorders. The increased inhibitory effect provided by these drugs helps calm anxious people. Alcohol has similar effects on GABA receptors. As a result, people typically experience alcohol as relaxing. GABA reception may also be the primary mechanism that causes alcohol to interfere with motor coordination.

In contrast, *glutamate* is the main excitatory neurotransmitter. It is involved in fast-acting neural transmission throughout the brain. Glutamate receptors aid learning and memory by strengthening synaptic connections.

ENDORPHINS You've no doubt heard about, or perhaps experienced, "runner's high." This psychological state results from a release of *endorphins*. Endorphins are a class of neurotransmitters involved in reward, such as runner's high, as well as in natural pain reduction. Pain is useful because it signals that we are hurt or in danger. That signal should then prompt us to try to escape or withdraw. If you didn't experience pain when you touched a hot stove, you wouldn't know that you should pull your hand away before being badly injured.

Pain can interfere with adaptive functioning, however. If pain prevents us from eating, competing, or mating, then people will fail to pass along their genes. Endorphins' painkilling, or analgesic, effects help us perform these behaviors even when we are in pain. In humans, drugs that bind with endorphin receptors (e.g., morphine) reduce the subjective experience of pain. Apparently, morphine does not block the nerves that transmit pain signals. Instead, it alters the way pain is experienced. In other words, people still feel pain, but they report a sense of detachment such that they do not care about the pain (Foley, 1993).

 2.1 CHECKPOINT: How Do Our Nervous Systems Affect Thinking and Behavior?

- The central nervous system processes information in the brain and the spinal cord. The peripheral nervous system processes information in the soft organs.

- The nervous system has three primary tasks: It receives information, it integrates that information, and it passes signals to other neurons to allow thought and action.

- Neurons are the basic units of the nervous system.

- Changes in a neuron's electrical charge elicit an action potential. The action potential causes the release of neurotransmitters that are received by other neurons.

- Neurons communicate with each other through neurotransmitters. Each particular neurotransmitter has specific effects on thought and behavior.

2.2 How Do the Parts of Our Brains Function?

As we saw at the beginning of this chapter, the nervous system has two main divisions: the peripheral nervous system and the central nervous system (see Figure 2.2). The central nervous system consists of the brain and the spinal cord. Our basic biological processes, such as our heartbeat, breathing, and reflexes, all depend on the spinal cord. But everything we are and do depends on the brain. To truly understand how we see, hear, remember, interact with others, and sometimes experience psychological disorders, we need to understand the main structures of the brain.

Understanding of Our Brains Has Developed Over Time

In the first animals, nervous systems were little more than a few specialized cells with the capacity for electrical activity. Today, an adult human brain weighs about 3 pounds (1.4 kilograms) and is quite complex. We can think of the brain as a collection of interacting neural circuits that have accumulated and developed throughout human evolution. In adapting to the environments where humans have lived, the brain has evolved. As a result of evolution, specialized mechanisms in the brain regulate our breathing, food intake, sexual behavior, and body fluids. Likewise, sensory systems in the brain aid our navigation and help us recognize friends and foes.

EARLY STUDIES OF THE BRAIN By the beginning of the nineteenth century, early psychologists agreed that mental processes were a result of brain function. What's more, anatomists understood the brain's basic structure reasonably well. But debates raged over how the brain produced mental activity. Did different parts of the brain do different things? Or were all areas of the brain equally important in mental activities such as problem solving and memory?

In the early nineteenth century, the neuroscientist Franz Gall and his assistant, the physician Johann Spurzheim, proposed their theory of phrenology. Gall and Spurzheim based their theory on the idea that different areas of the brain perform different functions. Phrenology was the practice of assessing personality traits and mental abilities by measuring bumps on the human skull. Phrenology was popular until as late as the 1930s. At that time, an enterprising company manufactured 33 psychographs—devices used to analyze personality based on the locations and

FIGURE 2.9

Phrenology and the Psychograph
(a) In phrenological maps, each region of the skull is associated with a different feature of personality to reflect processes occurring in the brain under the skull.
(b) Psychographs were sold to the public and were claimed to "do the work of a psychoanalyst" by showing "your talents, abilities, strong and weak traits, without prejudice or flattery."

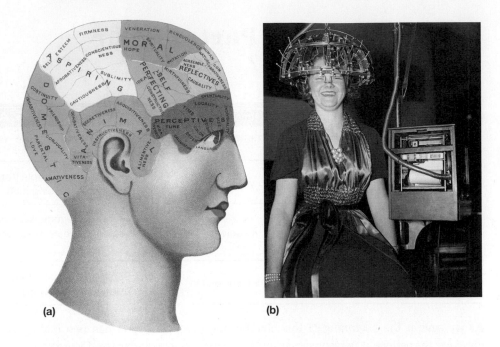

(a)　　　　(b)

sizes of skull bumps. Because these machines were featured at state fairs and amusement parks, it is unlikely that many people, if any, took the personality readings seriously (**Figure 2.9**). But phrenology was influential. People paid attention to this theory because it was based on the seemingly scientific principle that brain functions had specific locations in the brain. Although bumps on the skull did not turn out to be related to personality, the idea of localization of brain function was an important insight. At the time, the technology was not available to test the theory scientifically.

The first strong evidence that brain regions perform specialized functions came from the work of the physician and anatomist Paul Broca (Finger, 1994). In 1861, Broca performed an autopsy on a patient. The patient had been able to understand language, but had lost the ability to say anything other than one word. When Broca examined the patient's brain, he found a large section of damaged tissue in the front left side (**Figure 2.10a**). Broca concluded that this particular region in the left hemisphere of the brain was important for speech. Broca's theory has survived the test of time. This left frontal region, now confirmed to be crucial for producing speech, became known as **Broca's area** (**Figure 2.10b**).

CONTEMPORARY BRAIN RESEARCH For most of human history, theorists and researchers did not have methods for studying mental activity as it occurred in the working brain. Over the last century, scientists have developed various methods to study the brain in action.

The first method developed was a way to record the electrical activity of neurons firing in the brain. A researcher fits electrodes onto the participant's scalp. The electrodes act like small microphones, but they pick up the brain's electrical activity instead of sounds. The device that records this activity is called an *electroencephalograph* (EEG; **Figure 2.11a**). This measurement is useful because different behavioral states produce different and predictable EEG patterns. An EEG can reveal, for example, when someone is falling asleep. It has also shown that the brain is very active even when the body is at rest, especially during dreams.

The brain's electrical activity is associated with changes in the flow of blood carrying oxygen and nutrients to the active brain regions. These changes can be measured with several different brain imaging methods.

Broca's area
A small portion of the left frontal region of the brain; this area is crucial for producing speech.

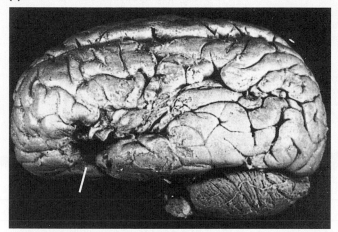

(a)

(b)

Broca's area

FIGURE 2.10

Broca's Area

(a) Paul Broca studied a patient's brain and identified the lesioned area in the left frontal lobe as crucial for producing speech. **(b)** This illustration shows the location of Broca's area.

The main brain imaging method used today in psychological research is *functional magnetic resonance imaging* (fMRI; **Figure 2.11b**). This technique measures changes in the blood's oxygen level. These changes enable the researchers to assess the brain's blood flow. Using this method, they are then able to map the working brain. For example, the participant performs a mental task (thinks about something), such as deciding whether a face looks happy or sad. During the task, the researchers scan the participant's brain. The participant then does a task that differs from the first in only one way. The researchers then compare brain images to examine differences in activity associated with the task.

How do researchers determine whether a brain region is important for a task? Ideally, they want to compare performances when that area is working effectively and when it is not. The method used for this purpose is *transcranial magnetic stimulation* (TMS; **Figure 2.11c**). This technique uses a very fast and powerful magnetic field to momentarily disrupt activity in a specific brain region. For example, placing the TMS coil over areas of the brain involved in language will disrupt a person's ability to speak. This technique has its limitations. In particular, it can be used only for short durations to examine brain areas close to the scalp. When used along with imaging, however, it is a powerful method for examining which brain regions are necessary for specific psychological functions.

FIGURE 2.11

Measures of Brain Activity

There are several ways to measure how the brain responds to tasks or events. These methods give us insight into how thinking and action depend on our biological processes.

(a)

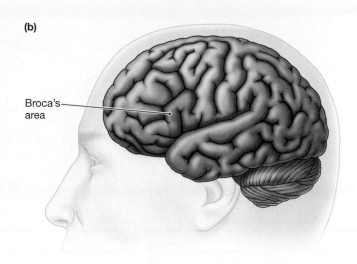

An electroencephalograph (EEG) measures the brain's electrical activity.

(b)

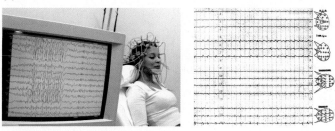

Functional magnetic resonance imaging (fMRI) maps mental activity during a mental task by assessing the blood's oxygen level in the brain.

(c)

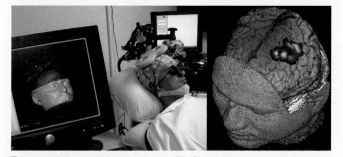

Transcranial magnetic stimulation (TMS) momentarily disrupts brain activity in a specific brain region.

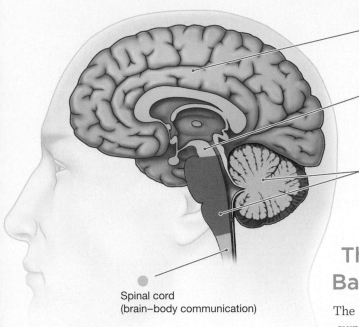

Forebrain
(motivation, emotion,
complex thought)

Midbrain
(movement)

Hindbrain
(survival
functions)

Spinal cord
(brain–body communication)

FIGURE 2.12

Three Main Brain Divisions
Shown here are the hindbrain, the
midbrain, and the forebrain, plus the
spinal cord.

Contemporary brain research using these methods has greatly advanced our understanding of the brain. Just how important is measuring brain activity? For researchers who want to understand the inner workings of the brain, imaging is equivalent to the telescope for astronomers. In the following sections, we'll learn how brain research reveals the three main divisions of the brain: the *hindbrain,* the *midbrain,* and the *forebrain.* Each of these divisions is associated with particular mental processes and particular behaviors (**Figure 2.12;** also see the Learning Tip).

The Hindbrain and Midbrain House Basic Programs for Our Survival

The lower part of the brain contains structures that are essential for survival. These structures control breathing, heartbeat, swallowing, and moving. These areas of the brain are connected to the rest of the body

LEARNING TIP: Processing in the Brain

HINDBRAIN	**BRAINSTEM:** breathing, heart rate, other survival mechanisms
	CEREBELLUM: motor learning, coordination, balance
MIDBRAIN	**SUBSTANTIA NIGRA:** initiation of voluntary motor activity
FOREBRAIN (SUBCORTICAL STRUCTURES)	**THALAMUS:** sensory information (except smell)
	HYPOTHALAMUS: regulation of body functions (e.g., temperature) and motivation (e.g., hunger, thirst)
	HIPPOCAMPUS: formation of new memories
	AMYGDALA: association of emotions with experiences
	BASAL GANGLIA: motor planning and movement, reward
FOREBRAIN (CORTICAL STRUCTURES)	**OCCIPITAL LOBES:** vision
	PARIETAL LOBES: touch, spatial information
	TEMPORAL LOBES: hearing, memory
	FRONTAL LOBES: planning, movement, complex thought

through the spinal cord. The cord is a rope of nerves running inside the spine, from just above the pelvis to the base of the skull (see Figure 2.12).

The spinal cord's most important job is communication between the brain and the rest of the body. The spinal cord carries sensory information up to the brain and carries motor signals from the brain to the body parts to initiate action. For example, the spinal cord coordinates reflexes—such as the way your leg moves when a doctor taps your knee or how your arm moves when you jerk your hand away from a flame.

The cord is composed of two distinct tissue types. One type is gray matter, which is dominated by the cell bodies of neurons. The other type is white matter, which consists mostly of axons and the myelin sheaths that surround them. People sometimes mistakenly call the brain our gray matter. However, both gray matter and white matter are located throughout the brain and the spine.

HINDBRAIN At the base of the skull, the spinal cord thickens and becomes more complex. Here, the cord changes into the first structure of the hindbrain, the *brain stem* (**Figure 2.13**). The brain stem houses the nerves that control the most basic functions of survival, including heart rate, breathing, swallowing, vomiting, urination, and orgasm. Thus a significant blow to this region can cause death. Gagging is one of the many reflexes that emerge from the brain stem.

The **cerebellum** is a large extension in the hindbrain. It is connected to the back of the brain stem (see Figure 2.13). Its size and convoluted surface make it look like an extra brain. In fact, the name *cerebellum* comes from the Latin word for "little brain."

The cerebellum is essential for proper motor function. Damage to the different parts of the cerebellum produces very different effects. Damage to the very bottom causes problems with head tilt and balance. Damage to the ridge that runs up the back of the cerebellum affects walking. Damage to the lobes on either side causes a loss of coordination in the limbs. For example, the person could not reach out smoothly to pick up a pen.

The cerebellum's most obvious role is in motor learning and motor memory. For example, the cerebellum makes it possible for you to ride a bicycle effortlessly—and to do so while planning your next meal. In fact, the cerebellum may be involved in

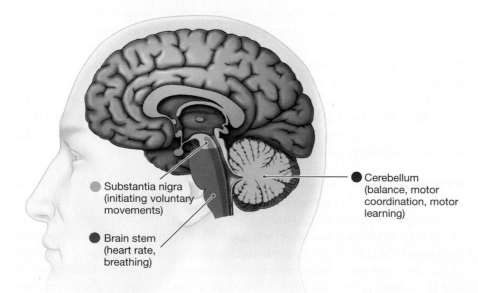

Substantia nigra (initiating voluntary movements)

Brain stem (heart rate, breathing)

Cerebellum (balance, motor coordination, motor learning)

FIGURE 2.13

The Hindbrain and the Midbrain
This drawing shows where the hindbrain (brain stem and cerebellum) and the midbrain (substantia nigra) are located. The view shows the brain as though you could see inside to its middle.

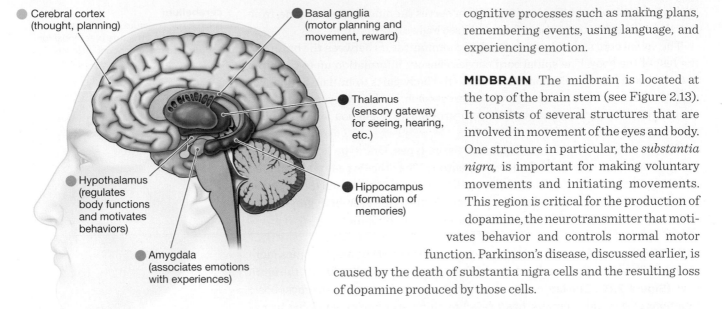

Cerebral cortex
(thought, planning)

Basal ganglia
(motor planning and
movement, reward)

Thalamus
(sensory gateway
for seeing, hearing,
etc.)

Hypothalamus
(regulates
body functions
and motivates
behaviors)

Hippocampus
(formation of
memories)

Amygdala
(associates emotions
with experiences)

FIGURE 2.14

The Forebrain
This drawing shows where the forebrain regions (the cerebral cortex and the five subcortical structures) are located. The view shows the brain as though you could see inside to its middle.

cognitive processes such as making plans, remembering events, using language, and experiencing emotion.

MIDBRAIN The midbrain is located at the top of the brain stem (see Figure 2.13). It consists of several structures that are involved in movement of the eyes and body. One structure in particular, the *substantia nigra,* is important for making voluntary movements and initiating movements. This region is critical for the production of dopamine, the neurotransmitter that motivates behavior and controls normal motor function. Parkinson's disease, discussed earlier, is caused by the death of substantia nigra cells and the resulting loss of dopamine produced by those cells.

Forebrain Subcortical Structures Control Our Motivations and Emotions

Above the midbrain is the forebrain. The forebrain includes two main areas: the cerebral cortex and the five subcortical structures (**Figure 2.14**). The intricate surface that makes up the outermost part of the forebrain is called the cerebral cortex. We will discuss the functions of the cerebral cortex shortly. Below this structure are the forebrain subcortical regions. This name simply means that these regions are under the cortex.

Some subcortical structures are important for psychological functions. These structures include the thalamus, the hypothalamus, the hippocampus, the amygdala, and the basal ganglia. Some of these structures belong to the limbic system. *Limbic* is from the Latin word for "border." The limbic system serves as the border between the parts of the brain that evolved earliest (the hindbrain and the midbrain) and the part that evolved more recently (the cerebral cortex). The brain structures in the limbic system are especially important for controlling motivated behaviors, such as eating and drinking. These structures are also important for controlling emotions.

THALAMUS The **thalamus** is the gateway to the cortex (see Figure 2.14). In other words, this structure receives almost all incoming sensory information, organizes it, and relays it to the cortex. The only exception to this rule is the sense of smell. Smell is the oldest and most fundamental sense. From the nerves in the nose, smell has a direct route to the cortex. During sleep, the thalamus partially shuts out incoming sensations to help the person stay asleep.

thalamus
A subcortical forebrain structure; the gateway to the brain for almost all incoming sensory information before that information reaches the cortex.

hypothalamus
A subcortical forebrain structure involved in regulating bodily functions. The hypothalamus also influences our basic motivated behaviors.

HYPOTHALAMUS The **hypothalamus** is the brain's master regulatory structure (see Figure 2.14). It is indispensable to the body's survival. "Hypo" means below, so the hypothalamus is located below the thalamus. It receives input from almost everywhere in the body and brain, and it sends its influence to almost everywhere in the body and brain. It affects the functions of many internal organs. It also regulates body temperature, body rhythms such as sleeping and waking, blood pressure, and blood glucose (also known as blood sugar). It is also involved in the motivations for many behaviors, including drinking, eating, aggression, and sex.

HIPPOCAMPUS The **hippocampus** plays an important role in the formation of new memories (see Figure 2.14). Its name comes from the Greek word for "sea horse," because of this structure's sea horse–like shape. The hippocampus seems to form new memories by creating new neural connections within the cerebral cortex for each new experience.

The hippocampus may be involved in how we remember the arrangements of both places and objects in space. For example, it may help us recall how streets are laid out in a city or how furniture is positioned in a room. An interesting study to support this theory focused on London taxi drivers. Maguire and colleagues (2003) found that one region of the hippocampus was much larger in London taxi drivers' brains than in the brains of most other London drivers. London taxi drivers are well known for their expertise. To acquire a commercial license, these taxi drivers must take a rigorous exam testing their knowledge of the city's streets. Is a person with a large hippocampus more likely to drive a taxi? Or does the hippocampus grow because of navigational experience?

In the Maguire study, the volume of gray matter in the hippocampal region was highly correlated with the number of years of experience as a taxi driver. In other words, it is possible the hippocampus changes with experience. But recall from Chapter 1 that correlation does not prove causation. The Maguire study did not *conclude* that the hippocampus changes with experience. However, research does show that the hippocampus is important for navigating in our environments (Nadel et al., 2013).

AMYGDALA If you are like most people, you would probably jump if you encountered a large snake. This response shows your **amygdala** in action (see Figure 2.14). The name comes from the Latin word for "almond," because of the structure's almond-like shape. The amygdala is located immediately in front of the hippocampus. It serves a vital role in learning to associate things in the world (such as a snake) with emotional responses (such as fear). The amygdala also intensifies memory during times of emotional arousal. For example, a frightening experience can be seared into your memory for life (although your memory of the event may not be completely accurate).

The amygdala plays a special role in responses to stimuli that elicit fear. This adaptive function helps protect animals from danger. The amygdala is also involved in evaluating the emotional significance of a facial expression (Adolphs et al., 2005). Imaging studies have found that the amygdala is activated especially strongly in response to a fearful face (Whalen et al., 2001). But the amygdala also functions in the processing of more-positive emotions, including sexual arousal. Hamann and colleagues (2004) have found that activity within the amygdala increases when people view sexually arousing stimuli, such as nude photos or videos of sexual activity. The same study also found that amygdala activation is markedly higher in men. This finding suggests that the amygdala may be involved when men respond more strongly to visual sexual stimuli than women do.

BASAL GANGLIA Before crossing a street, do you automatically look for cars? If so, you most likely learned this habit when you were a child. In drawing on this knowledge and performing this action, you're relying on your *basal ganglia* (see Figure 2.14). The basal ganglia are subcortical structures that are crucial for planning and producing movement. There is evidence that damage to the basal ganglia can impair the learning of habits, such as automatically looking for cars.

hippocampus
A subcortical forebrain structure that is associated with the formation of memories.

amygdala
A subcortical forebrain structure that serves a vital role in our learning to associate things with emotional responses and in processing emotional information.

One structure in the basal ganglia is the nucleus accumbens. This structure is important for experiencing reward and motivating behavior. Think about eating food you like or looking at someone you find attractive. Your thoughts might lead you to want to eat that food or spend time with that person. What makes this happen? Nearly every pleasurable experience activates dopamine neurons in the nucleus accumbens. In other words, the dopamine boost makes you want to eat the food or spend time with the person. One brain imaging study found that viewing expensive sports cars led to greater activation of the nucleus accumbens in men than did viewing less expensive economy cars (Erk, Spitzer, Wunderlich, Galley, & Walter, 2002). The more desirable objects are, the more they activate basic reward circuitry in our brains.

The Cerebral Cortex of the Forebrain Processes Our Complex Mental Activity

The outer layer of the forebrain is called the *cerebral cortex*. This layer gives the brain its distinctive wrinkled appearance (see Figure 2.14). (*Cortex* is the Latin word for "bark." In reality, the cortex feels more like a hard-boiled egg than tree bark.) In humans, the cerebral cortex is relatively large. If you could flatten it out, the cortex would be about the size of a large sheet of newspaper. However, because it is folded in against itself so many times, the cortex fits within the skull. It is the site of all thoughts, detailed perceptions, and complex behaviors. It enables us to comprehend ourselves, other people, and the outside world.

The cortex is divided into two halves. These halves are called the left hemisphere and the right hemisphere. Each cerebral hemisphere has four areas, which are called lobes: the occipital, parietal, temporal, and frontal lobes. Each lobe has specialized functions (**Figure 2.15a**). In addition, areas within each lobe process

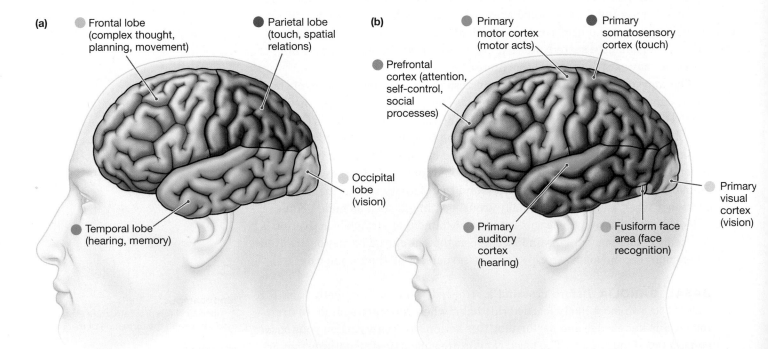

FIGURE 2.15

Lobes and Processing Centers of the Cerebral Cortex
(a) This diagram identifies the four lobes of the cerebral cortex. **(b)** The colored areas in this diagram mark important regions within the lobes. Each region processes specific information.

specific information (**Figure 2.15b**). The hemispheres are connected by a structure called the *corpus callosum*. This massive bridge consists of millions of axons. It allows information to flow between the hemispheres (**Figure 2.16**).

LOBES OF THE CEREBRAL CORTEX The **occipital lobes** are at the back portion of the head (see Figure 2.15a). These lobes are devoted almost exclusively to vision, and they include many distinct visual areas. By far the largest of these areas is the primary visual cortex (see Figure 2.15b). The primary visual cortex is the major destination and processor of visual information. Recall from the chapter's opening story that Jack Osbourne has multiple sclerosis. One of the first symptoms Osbourne experienced was a visual disturbance. This effect was most likely due to neurons becoming demyelinated (losing myelin) in his primary visual cortex.

The primary visual cortex is surrounded by a patchwork of secondary visual areas. These areas process various qualities of the visual input, such as its colors, forms, and motions.

The **parietal lobes** are devoted partially to touch (see Figure 2.15a). Their labor is divided between the left and right cerebral hemispheres. The information received by the hemispheres is actually reversed: The left hemisphere receives touch information from the right side of the body, and the right hemisphere receives touch information from the left side of the body. In each parietal lobe, this sensory information is directed to the primary somatosensory cortex (see Figure 2.15b). The name of this structure might be long and intimidating, but it simply refers to a strip of brain matter in the front part of the lobe, running from the top of the brain down the sides.

In the primary somatosensory cortex, touch information from one body part registers in the cortex near regions where touch information is registered from nearby body parts (**Figure 2.17,** right side). For example, sensations on the fingers register in the cortex near where sensations on the hand are registered. More cortical area is devoted to the body's more sensitive areas, such as the face and the fingers. As a result, the classic representation of the primary somatosensory area is like a distorted version of the entire body.

occipital lobes
Regions of the cerebral cortex at the back of the brain; these regions are important for vision.

parietal lobes
Regions of the cerebral cortex in front of the occipital lobes and behind the frontal lobes; these regions are important for the sense of touch and for picturing the layout of spaces in an environment.

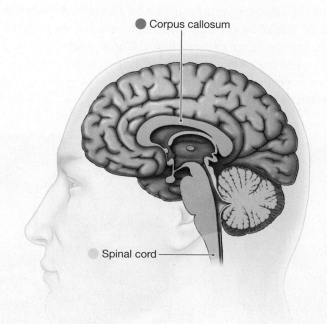

Corpus callosum

Spinal cord

FIGURE 2.16
The Corpus Callosum
This fibrous structure connects the two hemispheres of the cerebral cortex.

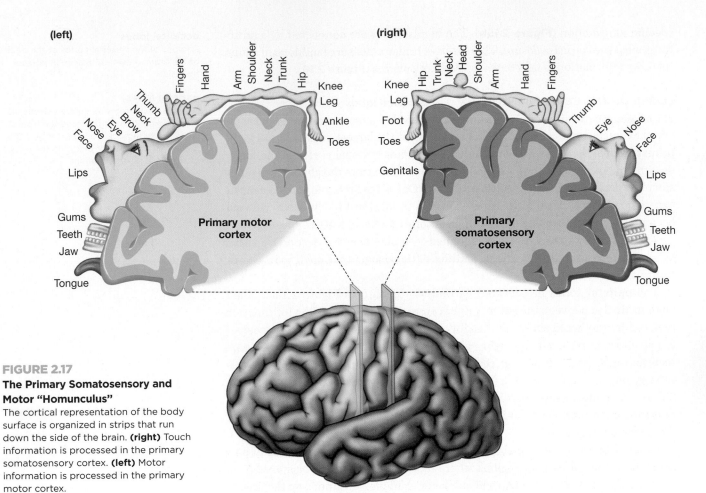

(left)

Fingers Hand Arm Shoulder Neck Trunk Hip Knee Leg Ankle Toes

Thumb Neck Brow Eye Nose Face Lips Gums Teeth Jaw Tongue

Primary motor cortex

(right)

Knee Leg Foot Toes Genitals

Hip Trunk Neck Head Shoulder Arm Hand Fingers Thumb Eye Nose Face Lips Gums Teeth Jaw Tongue

Primary somatosensory cortex

FIGURE 2.17

The Primary Somatosensory and Motor "Homunculus"
The cortical representation of the body surface is organized in strips that run down the side of the brain. **(right)** Touch information is processed in the primary somatosensory cortex. **(left)** Motor information is processed in the primary motor cortex.

This representation of the somatosensory area is known as the somatosensory homunculus. (*Homunculus* comes from the Greek word for "little man.") The representation is based on mappings by the pioneering neurological researcher Wilder Penfield. Penfield created these mappings as he examined patients who were to undergo surgery for epilepsy (**Figure 2.18a**). Penfield's aim was to perform the surgery without damaging brain areas vital for functions such as speech. With the patient awake, Penfield applied a local anesthetic to the scalp. He then electrically stimulated regions of the patient's brain (**Figure 2.18b**). During the stimulation, Penfield asked the patient to report what he was experiencing. Penfield's studies provided important evidence about the amount of brain tissue devoted to each sensory experience.

(a)

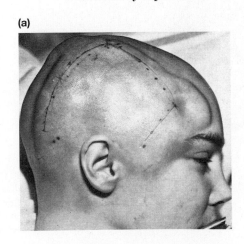

(b)

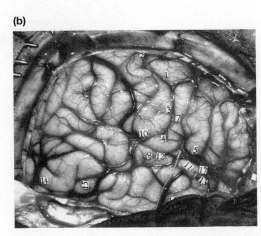

FIGURE 2.18

Mapping the Somatosensory Homunculus
(a) This photograph shows one of Wilder Penfield's patients immediately before direct stimulation of the brain. **(b)** Here you can see the exposed surface of the patient's cortex. The numbered tags mark locations that were electrically stimulated.

A stroke or other damage to the right parietal region can result in the neurological disorder called hemineglect. Patients with this syndrome fail to notice anything on their left sides. While looking in a mirror, they will shave or put makeup on only the right side of the face. If two objects are held up before them, they will see only the one on the right. When asked to draw a simple object, they will draw only its right half (**Figure 2.19**).

The **temporal lobes** (see Figure 2.15a) hold the primary auditory cortex (see Figure 2.15b). This brain region is responsible for hearing. In addition, the temporal lobes include visual areas specialized for recognizing detailed objects, such as faces. Also within the temporal lobes are the hippocampus and the amygdala (both critical for memory, as discussed earlier).

At the intersection of the temporal and occipital lobes is the fusiform face area (see Figure 2.15b). This region is much more active when you look at faces than when you look at other things. Other regions of the temporal lobe are more activated by objects, such as houses or cars, than by faces. If your fusiform face area were damaged, you would have trouble recognizing people but not objects.

The **frontal lobes** are essential for planning and movement (see Figure 2.15a). The rear portion of the frontal lobes is the primary motor cortex (see Figure 2.15b). This structure includes neurons that send messages directly to the spinal cord to move the body's muscles. The functions of the primary motor cortex are divided down the middle of the body, like those of the primary somatosensory cortex: The left hemisphere controls the right arm, for example, whereas the right hemisphere controls the left arm. In addition, motor information for a body part is processed in cortical areas that are near regions that process motor acts for nearby body parts (see Figure 2.17, left side). In people with multiple sclerosis, neurons in a specific area of the motor cortex become demyelinated (lose myelin). As a result, the person has trouble moving that specific body part.

PREFRONTAL CORTEX The rest of the frontal lobes consists of the *prefrontal cortex* (see Figure 2.15b). In humans, this structure occupies about 30 percent of the brain. Scientists have long thought that our extraordinarily large prefrontal cortex makes humans unique in the animal kingdom. There is recent evidence, however, that what separates humans from other animals is not how much of the brain the prefrontal cortex occupies. Instead, the difference between the human brain and the brains of other animals is in the complexity and organization of these neural circuits (Bush & Allman, 2004; Schoenemann, Sheehan, & Glotzer, 2005).

The entire prefrontal cortex is critical for rational thought. It is also especially important for many aspects of human social life. It provides both our sense of self and our capacity to empathize with others or feel guilty about harming them. Particular parts of the prefrontal cortex are responsible for directing and maintaining attention, keeping ideas in mind while distractions bombard us from the outside world, and developing and acting on plans.

Psychologists have learned a great deal of what they know about how brain regions work by carefully studying people whose brains have been damaged by disease or injury. Perhaps the most famous historical example of brain damage is the case of Phineas Gage (**Figure 2.20a**). The first modern theories of the prefrontal cortex's role in both personality and self-control were based on Gage's case.

In 1848, Gage was a 25-year-old foreman on the construction of Vermont's Rutland and Burlington Railroad. One day, he dropped a tool called a tamping iron, which was over a yard long and an inch in diameter. The iron rod hit a rock, igniting some blasting powder. The resulting explosion drove the rod into his cheek,

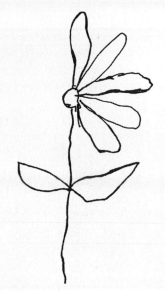

FIGURE 2.19
Hemineglect
This drawing was made by a patient with hemineglect who has damage to the parietal lobe in the right hemisphere. The patient did not draw much of the flower's left side.

temporal lobes
Regions of the cerebral cortex below the parietal lobes and in front of the occipital lobes; these regions are important for processing auditory information and for perceiving objects and faces.

frontal lobes
Regions of the cerebral cortex at the front of the brain; these regions are important for movement and complex processes (rational thought, attention, social processes, etc.).

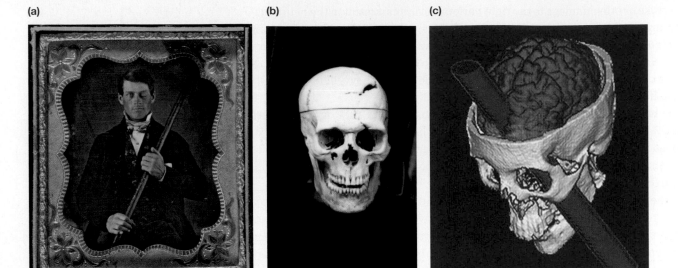

(a)   **(b)**   **(c)**

FIGURE 2.20

Phineas Gage

(a) This recently discovered photo shows Gage holding the rod that passed through his skull. **(b)** Here you can see the hole in the top of Gage's skull. **(c)** This computer-generated image reconstructs the likely path of the rod through the skull.

through his frontal lobes, and out through the top of his head (**Figure 2.20b**). Gage was still conscious as he was hurried back to town on a cart. Able to walk, with assistance, upstairs to his hotel bed, he wryly remarked to the awaiting physician, "Doctor, here is business enough for you." He said he expected to return to work in a few days. In fact, Gage lapsed into unconsciousness and remained unconscious for two weeks.

Physically, Gage recovered remarkably well. Unfortunately, the accident led to major personality changes. Whereas the old Gage had been regarded by his employers as "the most efficient and capable" of workers, the new Gage was not. As one of his doctors later wrote,

> The equilibrium or balance, so to speak, between his intellectual faculties and animal propensities seems to have been destroyed. He is fitful, irreverent, indulging at times in the grossest profanity . . . impatient of restraint or advice when it conflicts with his desires. . . . A child in his intellectual capacity and manifestations, he has the animal passions of a strong man.

In sum, Gage was "no longer Gage." He could not get his foreman's job back. Instead, Gage exhibited himself in various New England towns and at the New York Museum (owned by the circus showman P. T. Barnum). He worked at the stables of the Hanover Inn at Dartmouth College. After a decade, Gage's health began to decline, and in 1860 he started having epileptic seizures and died within a few months. At first, the medical community used Gage's recovery to argue that the entire brain works uniformly and that the healthy parts of Gage's brain had taken over the work of the damaged parts. However, Gage's severe psychological impairments eventually led the group to recognize that some areas of the brain have specific functions.

Reconstruction of Gage's injury clearly shows that the prefrontal cortex was the area most damaged by the tamping rod (Damasio, Grabowski, Frank, Galaburda, & Damasio, 1994; **Figure 2.20c**). Recent studies of patients with similar injuries reveal that this brain region is particularly concerned with social processes. For example, it is responsible for following social norms, understanding what other people are thinking, and feeling emotionally connected to others. People with damage to this region do not typically have problems with memory or general knowledge. They often have serious disturbances in their ability to get along with others.

In the late 1930s, mental health professionals developed a new treatment for many patients with psychological disorders—especially patients who could not control their emotions. The procedure was called a lobotomy, and it was a deliberate damaging of the prefrontal cortex (**Figure 2.21**). This form of brain surgery generally left patients lethargic and emotionally flat. As a result, the patients were much easier to manage in mental hospitals. But it also left them disconnected from their social surroundings, as Gage was. Most lobotomies were performed in the late 1940s and early 1950s. With the arrival of drugs to treat psychological disorders, the lobotomy was phased out.

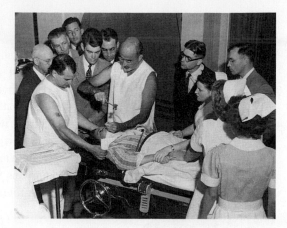

FIGURE 2.21
Lobotomy
This photo shows Dr. Walter Freeman performing a lobotomy in 1949.

 2.2 CHECKPOINT: How Do the Parts of Our Brains Function?

- The hindbrain includes the brain stem, which regulates basic survival functions, and the cerebellum, which is essential for movement and control of balance.

- The midbrain includes the substantia nigra, which is responsible for initiating voluntary motor activity.

- Together, the five subcortical structures of the forebrain control memory formation, emotions, and motivated behaviors.

- The four lobes of the forebrain and associated cortical areas are responsible for the most complex processing.

2.3 How Do Our Brains Communicate With Our Bodies?

📖 LEARNING GOALS	✏️ READING ACTIVITIES
a. Remember the key terms about the peripheral nervous system and the endocrine system.	List all of the boldface words and write down their definitions.
b. Analyze how the somatic nervous system processes information.	Identify how your somatic nervous system functions when you touch a hot pan.
c. Apply the autonomic nervous system to your life.	Provide examples of two experiences you have had, one processed by the sympathetic system and one by the parasympathetic system.
d. Understand the endocrine system.	Summarize in your own words how the testes and ovaries secrete certain hormones that influence sexual development and behavior.

When you decide to move your arm, most of the time your arm moves. When you watch a sad movie, your eyes may produce tears. How do the parts of your body get the information from your brain that makes them respond the way they do?

Have you ever had your knee-jerk reflex tested at the doctor's office? If so, you probably sat on a table. When the doctor used a tool to tap a spot just below your knee, your leg involuntarily jerked up. This procedure illustrates how your somatic nervous system allows reflexes to occur: Nerves process information about the tap, and signals are processed through the spinal cord. This processing causes your leg to move. The communication happens in an instant because the signals never have to reach your brain. Instead, the reflex signals are processed only in the spinal cord.

somatic nervous system
A part of the peripheral nervous system; this part transmits sensory signals and motor signals between the central nervous system and the skin, muscles, and joints.

autonomic nervous system
A part of the peripheral nervous system; this part transmits sensory signals and motor signals between the central nervous system and the body's glands and internal organs.

Recall that the nervous system consists of the central nervous system (the brain and the spinal cord) and the peripheral nervous system (all the nerves in the rest of the body; see Figure 2.2). The peripheral nervous system transmits a variety of information to the central nervous system. It also responds to messages from the central nervous system to perform specific behaviors or make bodily adjustments. The peripheral nervous system has two primary components: the somatic nervous system and the autonomic nervous system. In producing psychological activity, the nervous system also interacts with the hormones of the endocrine system. Let's examine how these various interactions affect thought and behavior.

Our Somatic Nervous System Detects Sensory Input and Responds

The **somatic nervous system** transmits signals to and from the central nervous system through nerves. Specialized receptors in the skin, muscles, and joints send sensory information to the spinal cord, which relays it to the brain. In addition, the central nervous system sends signals through the somatic nervous system to muscles, joints, and skin to initiate or inhibit movement.

To get a sense of how fast this process can work, think of the last time you touched something hot or accidentally touched a sharp object, such as a tack. Those signals triggered your body's nearly instantaneous sensory experience of the impact. In the case of the sharp tack, these signals would immediately trigger movement of your finger off the painful object.

This process controls movement. For instance, suppose you are using a pen to take notes. You are contracting and relaxing your hand muscles and finger muscles to adjust your fingers' pressure on the pen. When you want to use the pen, your brain sends messages to your finger muscles so they move in specific ways. Receptors in both your skin and your muscles send back messages to help determine how much pressure is needed to hold the pen. This simple act of using a pen is a remarkable symphony of neural communication. Yet most of us employ motor control so easily that we rarely think about it. Some movement does, in fact, occur without information ever being processed in the brain. These movements are reflexes, such as the knee-jerk reflex discussed in Has It Happened to You? For each reflex action, a handful of neurons simply convert sensation into action based on processing only within the spinal cord.

Our Autonomic Nervous System Regulates the Body Automatically

The second major component of the peripheral nervous system is the **autonomic nervous system** (see Figure 2.2). As its name suggests, the autonomic nervous system automatically regulates the body's internal environment (see the Learning Tip). It accomplishes this regulation by stimulating glands (such as sweat glands) and by maintaining internal organs (such as the heart). Nerves in the autonomic nervous system also carry signals from the glands and internal organs to the central nervous system. These signals provide information about, for example, the fullness of your stomach or how anxious you feel.

The autonomic nervous system has two divisions: the *sympathetic* nervous system and the *parasympathetic* nervous system (see Figure 2.2). Both divisions

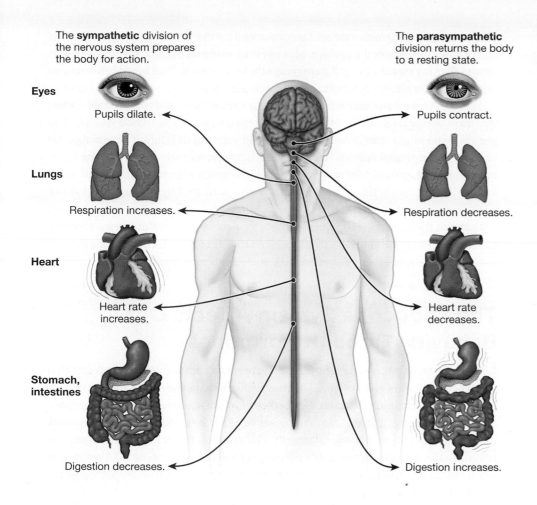

The **sympathetic** division of the nervous system prepares the body for action.

The **parasympathetic** division returns the body to a resting state.

Eyes

Pupils dilate.

Pupils contract.

Lungs

Respiration increases.

Respiration decreases.

Heart

Heart rate increases.

Heart rate decreases.

Stomach, intestines

Digestion decreases.

Digestion increases.

control the activity of organs and glands. They do so by providing signals that travel from the central nervous system to the organs and glands and back again (**Figure 2.22**).

To understand these signals, imagine that you hear a fire alarm. In the second after you hear the alarm, signals go out to parts of your body that automatically prepare them for action. As a result, blood flows to the muscles that move your skeleton. Epinephrine is released, increasing your heart rate and blood sugar. Your lungs take in more oxygen. Your pupils dilate to maximize visual sensitivity. You perspire to keep from overheating. These preparatory actions are prompted by the autonomic nervous system's sympathetic division. If a fire exists, you are physically prepared to flee. If the alarm turns out to be false, your heart will return to its normal steady beat, your breathing will slow, and you will stop perspiring.

LEARNING TIP: Remembering the Autonomic Nervous System

WHEN YOU SEE	PLEASE THINK	MEANING
Autonomic nervous system	Automatic processes	Processes that are out of a person's control, such as blood pressure, heart rate, and respiration.

This return to a normal state will be prompted by the parasympathetic division of the autonomic nervous system. Most of your internal organs are controlled by inputs from sympathetic and parasympathetic systems. The more aroused you are, the greater the sympathetic system's dominance.

It doesn't take a fire alarm to activate your sympathetic nervous system. When you meet someone you find attractive, for example, your heart beats quickly, you perspire, you might start breathing heavily, and your pupils dilate. These responses occur because sexual arousal has activated the sympathetic division of the autonomic nervous system. The responses provide nonverbal cues during social interaction. The sympathetic nervous system is also activated by psychological states such as anxiety or unhappiness. If people worry a great deal or do not cope well with stress, their bodies are in a constant state of arousal. Important research in the 1930s and 1940s by Hans Selye demonstrated that chronic activation of the sympathetic nervous system is associated with such medical problems as heart disease and asthma.

The Endocrine System Affects Our Behavior Through Hormones

Like the nervous system, the **endocrine system** is a communication network that influences thoughts and actions. The main difference between the two systems is in their forms of communication: The nervous system uses electrochemical signals, and the endocrine system uses chemicals called hormones. Both systems work together to regulate psychological activity. For instance, the brain receives information from the nervous system about potential physical or psychological threats. The brain communicates with the endocrine system to release hormones that prepare the organism to deal with those threats.

Hormones are chemical substances released into the bloodstream by endocrine glands. The endocrine glands include the pineal gland (see Chapter 3), the adrenal glands (see Chapter 10), the pituitary gland, the thyroid, and the testes or ovaries (**Figure 2.23**). Once released, hormones travel through the bloodstream until they reach their target tissues. Because they travel through the bloodstream, hormones can take from seconds to hours to have an effect. Once hormones are in the bloodstream, their effects can last for a long time and affect multiple body regions. Many different kinds of hormone action take place. Let's consider two types.

HORMONES, SEXUAL DEVELOPMENT, AND BEHAVIOR One example of hormonal influence is our sexual development and sexual behavior. The main endocrine glands influencing sexual behavior are the gonads: the testes, in males, and the ovaries, in females. Although people often talk about "male" and "female" hormones, both males and females produce both hormones. What differs is the quantity: *Androgens,* such as testosterone, are more prevalent in males. *Estrogens,* such as estradiol, are more prevalent in females. Gonadal hormones influence the development of secondary sex characteristics (e.g., breast development in females, growth of facial hair in males). Gonadal hormones also influence adult sexual behavior.

For males, being able to perform sexually depends on having at least a minimum amount of testosterone. Surgical removal of the testes, or castration, before puberty diminishes the capacity for developing an erection and lowers sexual interest. A man who is castrated after puberty will be able to perform sexually if he receives an injection of testosterone. Testosterone injections do not increase sexual behavior in healthy men, however. This finding suggests that a healthy man needs only the minimum amount of testosterone to perform sexually (Sherwin, 1988).

endocrine system
A communication system that uses hormones to influence thoughts and actions.

hormones
Chemical substances, released from endocrine glands, that travel through the bloodstream to targeted tissues; the tissues are later influenced by the hormones.

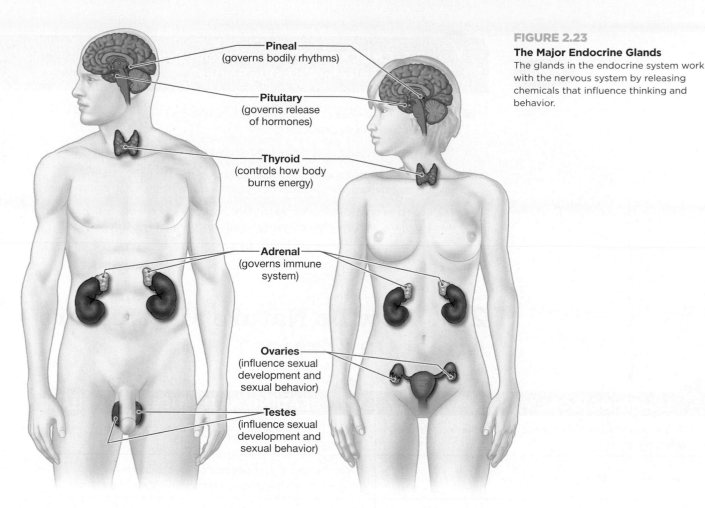

Pineal
(governs bodily rhythms)

Pituitary
(governs release
of hormones)

Thyroid
(controls how body
burns energy)

Adrenal
(governs immune
system)

Ovaries
(influence sexual
development and
sexual behavior)

Testes
(influence sexual
development and
sexual behavior)

In females, the influence of gonadal hormones is much more complex. Many nonhuman female animals experience a defined period, called estrus, when the female is sexually receptive and fertile. During estrus, the female displays behaviors designed to attract the male. Surgical removal of the ovaries terminates estrus. The female is no longer receptive, and her sexual behavior ends. Injections of estrogen will reinstate estrus.

Human female sexual behavior may have more to do with androgens than estrogens (Morris, Udry, Khan-Dawood, & Dawood, 1987). According to pioneering work by Barbara Sherwin (1994, 2008), women with higher levels of testosterone report greater interest in sex, and testosterone injections increase women's sexual interest after surgical removal of the uterus.

HORMONES AND PHYSICAL GROWTH Growth hormone (GH) prompts bone, cartilage, and muscle tissue to grow or helps them regenerate after injury. Since the 1930s, some people have used GH to increase body size and strength. Many athletes have sought a competitive advantage by using GH. For example, in early 2013 the legendary cyclist Lance Armstrong admitted to using GH and other hormones, including testosterone, to gain a competitive advantage. In an interview with Oprah Winfrey, Armstrong claimed it was impossible for any cyclist to win a major championship without doping (**Figure 2.24**).

FIGURE 2.24

Growth Hormone and Cycling
In January 2013, Lance Armstrong appeared on *The Oprah Winfrey Show* to admit using doping techniques to enhance his cycling performance.

- The peripheral nervous system includes the somatic nervous system and the autonomic nervous system.

- The somatic nervous system allows movement of the muscles and joints.

- The autonomic nervous system automatically regulates the body's internal environment through the sympathetic division and the parasympathetic division.

- The endocrine system includes glands that produce and release hormones that travel through the bloodstream and influence a variety of processes.

2.4 How Do Nature and Nurture Affect Our Brains?

📖 LEARNING GOALS	✏️ READING ACTIVITIES
a. Remember the key terms about how nature and nurture affect the brain.	List all of the boldface words and write down their definitions.
b. Apply the effects of genetics to your life.	Describe one of your physical or psychological characteristics that was primarily influenced by genetics.
c. Understand how behavioral genetics studies the interaction of genes and environment.	Summarize the results of twin studies in your own words.
d. Apply the effects of environment to your life.	Describe one of your characteristics that was primarily influenced by the environment in which you were raised.

As you know from the chapter's opening story, Jack Osbourne is experiencing the symptoms of multiple sclerosis (MS). Did he inherit this condition from his parents? Could environmental influences, such as childhood nutrition, be involved? We don't know exactly what causes MS. Some researchers believe that unknown environmental triggers produce the condition and that people inherit a predisposition to respond to those triggers. Whatever the cause, how Osbourne copes with MS will depend at least in part on his psychological makeup.

So far, we have looked at the basic biological processes underlying psychological functions. Now we return to the question of nature or nurture. Recall from Chapter 1 that nature and nurture always work together to make us who we are. At the moment of conception, we inherit the **genes** we will possess for the rest of our lives. But how much of who we are depends on our genetic makeup? And how much of who we are depends on environmental influences, such as the household and the culture we are raised in? To begin answering these questions, see Try It Yourself.

Until fairly recently, genetic research focused almost entirely on whether people possessed certain types of genes. For example, did they have the genes for particular psychological disorders? It is important to discover the effects of individual genes. However, this approach misses the critical role of environmental factors in how genes work. Geneticists still study the inheritance of particular

genes
The units of heredity, which partially determine an organism's characteristics.

characteristics, but they also study gene expression. They examine the processes that turn genes "on" and "off." Their research reveals that our environment affects how our genes are expressed and therefore how they influence our thoughts, feelings, and behavior.

Genes Affect Our Thoughts and Behavior

Lenore Wexler had so little control over her movements that she stumbled across the street. A policeman watched her and then asked her why she was drinking so early in the day. Wexler was not drinking, however. She was showing the first symptoms of Huntington's disease, a disorder that affects the nervous system and damages specific parts of the brain (**Figure 2.25**). The damage results in abnormal body movements such as a jerky walk; loss of ability to walk, write, or speak; emotional and personality changes, such as extreme anxiety and depression; dementia; and eventually death.

Lenore Wexler was the mother of Nancy Wexler, who is a neuropsychologist and geneticist. After her mother's death from Huntington's in 1978, Wexler dedicated herself to finding the gene for the disorder that had killed her mother. Though knowing which genes are involved in Huntington's has not yet led to a cure, it can help people decide whether they want to take the risk of having children and possibly passing along the gene. If a parent has Huntington's, that parent's biological child has a 50/50 chance of developing the disorder. Because symptoms often do not appear before the affected person is around 40, many of those with Huntington's often have children before they realize they have the genetic disorder. Thanks to the work of Nancy Wexler and her colleagues, people who have relatives with Huntington's can now take a genetic test to find out if they carry the gene for the disease and then decide whether they want to risk having children.

We all know that genes control many physical characteristics, such as sex and eye color. The inheritance of Huntington's helps us understand that genes also influence our predispositions to particular diseases, including cancer and alcoholism. What about other factors, such as personality, intelligence, and athletic talent? There, too, genes have their influence. So can genes influence individual choices, such as whether we will get divorced or what careers we have?

Increasingly, research indicates that genes lay the groundwork for many human traits. From this perspective, people are born essentially like undeveloped photographs: The image is already captured, but the way it eventually appears can vary based on the development process. Your genetic makeup is called your *genotype*. The genotype is set at the moment of conception and never changes. Your observable physical and psychological characteristics are called your *phenotype*. These factors are influenced in part by the genotype. They are also affected by environmental factors. In other words, they can change. Your current height—your phenotype—is influenced by your genotype. It was also influenced by your environment, such as childhood diet.

Suppose a person inherits a predisposition to alcoholism (nature). If she is raised in a nondrinking environment and spends time with only moderate social drinkers (nurture), that predisposition may never be expressed. Psychologists

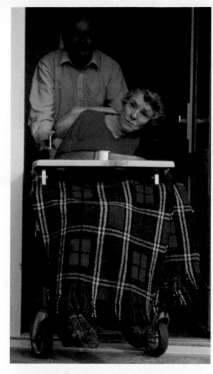

FIGURE 2.25

Huntington's Disease Affects the Brain, Thoughts, and Behavior Huntington's disease is an extreme example of how we are affected by our genes.

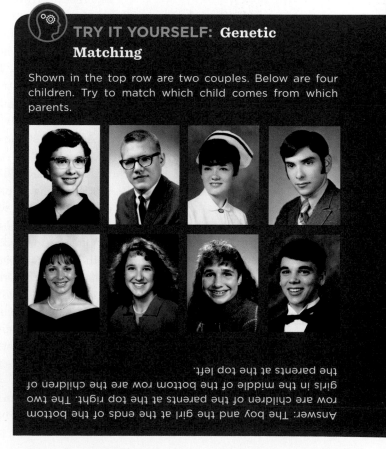

TRY IT YOURSELF: Genetic Matching

Shown in the top row are two couples. Below are four children. Try to match which child comes from which parents.

Answer: The boy and the girl at the ends of the bottom row are children of the parents at the top right. The two girls in the middle of the bottom row are the children of the parents at the top left.

study the ways that nature, nurture, and their combination affect psychological characteristics. In other words, they study the ways that genes are expressed in distinct environments.

Genes Interact With Environment to Influence Us

"I'm so different from the rest of this family! I must be adopted!" Did you ever think that when you were a child? Most of us, at one time or another, have marveled at how different siblings can be. Even siblings raised around the same time and in the same household have their individual appearances, individual personalities, and so on. The differences are to be expected, however.

Siblings always share some genes and often share much of their environment. But most siblings do not have identical genes or identical life experiences. Within the household and outside it, environments differ subtly and not so subtly. Siblings have different birth orders. Their mother may have consumed different foods and other substances during the different pregnancies. The siblings may have different friends and teachers. Their parents may treat them differently. The study of how genes and environment interact to influence psychological factors is known as *behavioral genetics*. Scientists in this field use two methods to assess the degree to which traits are inherited: twin studies and adoption studies.

Twin studies compare similarities between different types of twins to determine the genetic basis of specific traits. **Monozygotic twins** are identical. They result from one zygote (fertilized egg) dividing in two (**Figure 2.26a**). Because they come from the same fertilized egg, both twins have the same genetic makeup. **Dizygotic twins** are sometimes called fraternal or non-identical twins. They result when two separately fertilized eggs develop in the mother's womb simultaneously (**Figure 2.26b**). Because they come from two separately fertilized eggs, these twins are no more similar genetically than any other pair of siblings.

How do researchers use this information to judge genetic influence? They focus on a specific trait. They compare how similar monozygotic twins are in phenotypes (observable traits and characteristics) with how similar dizygotic twins are. The increased similarity in that trait is considered most likely due to genotypes (genetic influences).

Adoption studies compare the similarities between biological relatives and adoptive relatives. Adopted nonbiological siblings may share similar home environments, but they will have different genes. Therefore, researchers assume that similarities among adopted siblings who are not biologically related have more to do with environment than with genes. However, growing up in the same home turns out to have relatively little influence on many traits, such as personality.

One way to conduct a study is to compare twins who have been raised together with twins who were raised apart. In a classic study, Thomas Bouchard and his colleagues at the University of Minnesota identified more than 100 pairs of identical and fraternal twins, some raised together and some raised apart (Bouchard et al., 1990). The researchers examined a variety of these twins' characteristics, including intelligence, personality, well-being, achievement, alienation, and aggression. The general finding from the Minnesota Twin Project was that identical twins, whether raised together or not, were likely to be similar.

The "Jim twins" were among the most famous case studies to emerge from this project. These twin brothers were separated at birth and raised by different families. Both families named their new son James. What's more, each James went on to marry a woman named Linda, divorce Linda and marry a woman named Betty,

monozygotic twins
Identical twins; these siblings result from one zygote splitting in two, so they share the same genes.

dizygotic twins
Fraternal twins; these siblings result from two separately fertilized eggs, so they are no more similar genetically than non-twin siblings are.

(a) Monozygotic (identical) twins

One sperm fertilizes
one egg ...

... and the zygote
splits in two.

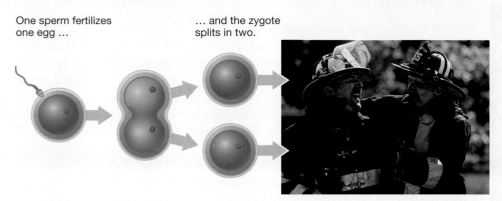

(b) Dizygotic (fraternal) twins

Two sperm fertilize
two eggs ...

... which become
two zygotes.

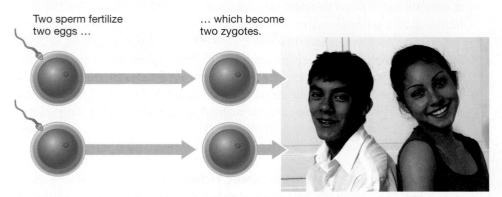

FIGURE 2.26
Twins
(a) Identical twins result when one fertilized egg splits in two. Gerald Levey and Mark Newman are identical twins who were separated at birth. When reunited at age 31, they discovered they were both firefighters and had similar personality traits.
(b) Fraternal twins, such as this pair pictured during their 13th birthday party, result when two separate eggs are fertilized at the same time.

name a son James Alan (or James Allen), and name a dog Toy. On top of that, both twins were part-time law enforcement officers who drove Chevrolets and vacationed in Florida. They were the same height and weight, chain-smoked the same brand of cigarettes, and drank the same brand of beer. No one would seriously suggest there are genes for naming dogs Toy or for marrying and divorcing women named Linda. However, the many similarities in the Jim twins' lives point to the strong genetic influences in shaping personality and behavior.

Some critics have argued that most of the adopted twins in the Minnesota study were raised in relatively similar environments. This similarity came about, in part, because adoption agencies try to match the child to the adoptive home. But this argument does not explain the case of the identical twins Oskar Stohr and Jack Yufe (Bouchard et al., 1990). Oskar and Jack were born in Trinidad in 1933. Oskar was raised a Catholic in Germany and eventually joined the Nazi Party. Jack was raised in the Jewish faith in Trinidad and lived for a while in Israel. Few twins have such different backgrounds. Yet when they met at an interview for the study, Oskar and Jack were wearing similar clothes, exhibited similar mannerisms, and shared odd habits, such as flushing the toilet before using it, dipping toast in coffee, storing rubber bands on their wrists, and enjoying startling people by sneezing loudly in elevators.

Critics feel that nothing more than coincidence is at work in these case studies. They argue that any two people of the same age would exhibit many surprising similarities just by coincidence, even though their lives differed in most other ways. Studies also fail to examine the many ways these twins differ on key traits. But twins and other relatives share similarities beyond coincidental attributes and behavior quirks. For instance, intelligence and personality traits such as shyness tend to run in families, indicating a strong genetic component.

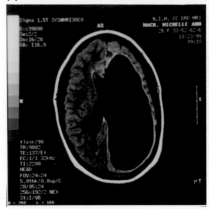

(a)

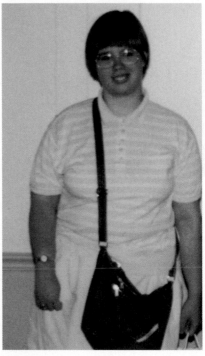

(b)

FIGURE 2.27

Michelle Mack and a Case of Extreme Plasticity

(a) While in her mother's womb, Michelle suffered a stroke that obliterated her left hemisphere (shown here as the black area on the right). Over time, Michelle's right hemisphere took over the duties of the left hemisphere—language production and moving the right side of the body—to a surprising extent. Michelle's case shows the plasticity of the brain.

plasticity
A property of the brain that causes it to change through experience, drugs, or injury.

Environment Changes Our Brains

When Michelle Mack was a youngster, her parents realized that she was different from other children. They couldn't explain these differences. When Michelle was 27 years old, they learned that she was missing the left hemisphere of her brain (**Figure 2.27**). Doctors suspected that Michelle's condition was the result of a stroke she experienced in the womb.

Without a left hemisphere, Michelle should have shown severe deficits in skills processed in that half of the brain. For example, the left hemisphere controls language, and it controls motor actions for the right side of the body. Losing a hemisphere as an adult would result in devastating loss of function. But Michelle's speech is only minimally affected. And she can move the right side of her body, although with some difficulty. Michelle is able to lead a surprisingly independent life. She graduated from high school, has a job, pays her bills, and does chores. Where did her capabilities come from? Her right hemisphere developed language processing capabilities as well as functions that ordinarily occur across both hemispheres.

Michelle Mack's case shows that nurture can influence nature. Over time, Michelle interacted with the world. Her experiences enabled her brain to reorganize itself. Her right hemisphere took over processing for the missing left hemisphere. In fact, despite the great precision and the specificity of its connections, the brain is extremely adaptable. Over the course of development, throughout our constant stream of experience, and after injury, the brain continually changes. This property is known as **plasticity.** It reflects the interactive nature of biological and environmental influences.

STRENGTHENING EXISTING CONNECTIONS Brain plasticity is what allows us to learn. Throughout life, we learn new things that we remember. All our memories are reflected in the brain's physical changes. Psychologists now believe that the changes are mainly in the strength of existing connections. One possibility is that when two neurons fire simultaneously, the connection between them strengthens. The strengthened connection then makes these neurons more likely to fire together in the future. By contrast, the connection between two neurons tends to get weaker if the neurons do not keep firing simultaneously. This theory can be summarized by the catchphrase *neurons that fire together, wire together*.

BRAIN REORGANIZATION Sometimes, the brain undergoes some reorganization, which is another example of brain plasticity. That is, entirely new connections develop between neurons. This new growth is a major factor in recovery from brain injury. Following an injury in the cortex, the surrounding gray matter assumes the function of the damaged area. Think of the healthy gray matter as a local business scrambling to pick up the customers of a newly closed competitor. The remapping seems to begin immediately, and it continues for years. Such plasticity involves all levels of the central nervous system, from the cortex down to the spinal cord.

Brain reorganization is much more common in children than in adults. As an extreme example, consider young children who have epilepsy so severe that it paralyzes one or more of their limbs. To control the epilepsy, surgeons may remove an entire cerebral hemisphere. Just as in the case of Michelle Mack, the remaining hemisphere eventually takes on most of the lost hemisphere's functions. The children regain almost complete use of their limbs. If this procedure were performed on adults, however, the lack of a cerebral hemisphere would result in severe motor deficits. With less chance of brain reorganization, the adults would lose all the functions of the missing hemisphere.

How Can I Overcome a Learning Disability and Succeed?

Have you been diagnosed with a learning disability? Do you suspect you might have one, such as dyslexia, that might give you trouble with reading, spelling, or writing? According to the National Center for Learning Disabilities (2009), a learning disability is a "neurological disorder that affects the brain's ability to receive, process, store, and respond to information." The new academic and organizational challenges of college might make the disability more apparent. But a learning disability isn't a recipe for failure. Many people with learning disabilities—such as the celebrity chef Jamie Oliver, who has dyslexia—become very successful.

If you have a learning disability or suspect you have one, the first thing to do is get in touch with your campus's disability support services staff or a member of the student affairs staff (e.g., the dean of students, a director of residence life, or a mental health counselor on your campus). Don't delay out of fear of embarrassment or shyness. These people will help you get access to resources that you can use if and when you need them (such as when the workload becomes very intense).

If your learning disability is verified, disability support staff will work with you to determine what is needed to level the playing field for you. What does "level the playing field" mean? Imagine if one football team had to play blindfolded while the opposing team could see perfectly. The game would be unfair for the blindfolded team. Thankfully, students with learning disabilities do not have to go through college wearing their own versions of blindfolds. Schools must provide equal opportunity to the benefits of education for individuals with learning disabilities.

Given your particular situation, some types of accommodations will be helpful and others will not. Disability support office staff will let your professors know whether you are entitled to a specific type of accommodation. For example, you might need extra time to complete an exam. Importantly, they will not tell your professors about the specific nature of your learning disability. They will simply note that you have one. If you wish, you can also speak directly with individual professors about your learning disability and the kinds of resources likely to help you. Linda Tessler, a psychologist who works with people with learning disabilities, writes:

> It must be clear that you are not asking for standards to be lowered. You are using tools to help you perform. To pass, you must perform the task that your classmates perform. You may, however, need to get there in a different way. (Tessler, 1997)

Will a learning disability prevent you from succeeding? Not if you can help it, and you can help it by advocating for yourself. Line up the resources you need to ensure that you are able to succeed.

FEMALE AND MALE BRAINS In most ways, the brains of females and males are similar. The few differences come from the interplay of biological and environmental effects on the brain. Everything we experience alters the brain. Because females and males differ in both their hormonal makeup and their life experiences, it makes sense that their brains would develop somewhat differently.

Males generally have larger brains than females. Jay Giedd and his colleagues (1997) at the U.S. National Institutes of Health reported that boys' brains are approximately 9 percent larger than girls' brains, and there are some differences in the rate of maturation for different parts of the brain for girls and boys. For both sexes, the sizes of brain structures are highly variable. In brains and brain structures, larger is not necessarily better.

As we saw earlier, one hemisphere can be more generally dominant for a certain cognitive function (such as language production; see Figure 2.10). For males, the left hemisphere generally governs language abilities (**Figure 2.28a**). For females,

Carlos was excited to be back in school. He had been an average student in high school, but after graduation he was just not ready for college. He spent one very unproductive semester at state college. Then he spent eight years in the army, including two tours of duty overseas. Now Carlos knew he was ready for higher education. Classes and readings did not seem like obligations. They were chances to learn new things.

While reading Chapter 2 of his psychology textbook, Carlos became interested in brain laterality. *How cool is it that the left side of my brain controls the right side of my body and vice versa?* Carlos was left-handed. From childhood, he had been able to list famous "southpaws" (Julius Caesar, Napoleon Bonaparte, Marilyn Monroe, and Barack Obama, to name a few). Now he wondered if being in this minority (estimated between 5 percent and 30 percent of people) made him think any differently from people in the majority. He laughed. *Please tell me there is some benefit to never having scissors that suit my hand!*

At the *Huffington Post,* Carlos found a news article: "11 Little Known Facts About Left-Handers." He had read these sorts of stories for years. Would his newly acquired psychology background help him separate the facts from the fiction in this article? One of the claims was that "Lefties make better artists." *Is this possible? Does being left-handed really make me a better artist?*

Reading the article more closely, he decided this claim was overstated. According to one scientific study, left-handed people engage in more-divergent thinking. In other words, they think outside the box. According to another study, lefties appear to be more drawn to careers in the arts, sports, and information technology. *Is that the evidence? These are associations, so being left-handed is linked with creativity.*

But these results don't mean that being left-handed makes *me more creative.* Carlos thought some more. *Maybe it's OK to just have correlational data here. After all, it would be hard to do an experiment on this topic.*

Carlos now began looking for research that would show a relationship between handedness and actual brain behavior. *I remember the finding that women use both sides of the brain when they listen, whereas men use just one side of the brain. Maybe researchers have shown that left-handed people use the sides of the brain differently than right-handed people do.*

Indeed, the same article claimed that "Left-handers get angrier." That research on left-handedness suggested that lefties might be more prone to negative emotions. And lefties' brains can show more imbalance between the right and left hemispheres when processing negative emotions. *Those findings are still associational, but they show a convincing and interesting link between handedness and brain activity. Of course, I can't tell if lefties are born this way or if years of frustration with right-handed scissors and right-handed desks have influenced my anger levels and brain activity!*

however, language processes are somewhat distributed more across the hemispheres (**Figure 2.28b**). One source of data that supports this distinction is people's experiences following strokes. Even when patients are matched on the brain location and severity of the damage caused by a stroke, women are less impaired in

FIGURE 2.28

How Males and Females Process Language

Researchers used fMRI to study men and women while they listened to someone reading aloud. As these fMRI images show, **(a)** the men listened with one side of their brains, and **(b)** the women listened with both sides of their brains. Note that in both sets of images, the left side of the brain is shown on the right side.

(a) **Males**

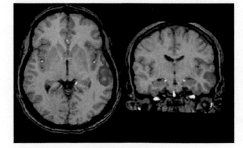

(b) **Females**

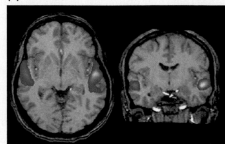

language use than men are (Jiang, Sheikh, & Bullock, 2006). A possible reason for women's better outcomes is that, because language is represented in both halves of women's brains, damage to half of a woman's brain will have less effect on her language abilities.

A related hypothesis is that compared with hemispheres of a man's brain, the hemispheres of a woman's brain are connected by more neural fibers. Remember that a thick band of neurons, the corpus callosum, connects the brain's two halves (see Figure 2.16). Some researchers have found that a portion of this connective tissue is larger in women (Gur & Gur, 2004).

Before we can be confident about sex-related differences in the brain, more research must be done. Meanwhile, keep in mind that female and male brains are similar in many—perhaps most—ways.

 2.4 CHECKPOINT: How Do Nature and Nurture Affect Our Brains?

- Both genes and environment affect who we are and what we do.

- The genes we inherit from our parents affect our physical attributes and the ways we think and behave.

- Behavioral genetics uses twin studies to examine how genes and environment interact to influence mental activity and behavior.

- Environment affects brain function and psychological characteristics through plasticity, strengthening neural connections, brain reorganization, and the effects of gender.

BIG QUESTION

LEARNING GOALS

2.1
How Do Our Nervous Systems Affect Thinking and Behavior?

a. Remember the key terms about the divisions of the nervous system and neurons.

b. Apply the three functions of the nervous system to your own life.

c. Analyze the four steps in neural communication.

d. Apply neurotransmitters to your life.

2.2
How Do the Parts of Our Brains Function?

a. Remember the key terms about brain regions and processes.

b. Apply the three main brain divisions to your own life.

c. Remember the five forebrain subcortical regions.

d. Understand the four lobes of the cerebral cortex.

2.3
How Do Our Brains Communicate With Our Bodies?

a. Remember the key terms about the peripheral nervous system and the endocrine system.

b. Analyze how the somatic nervous system processes information.

c. Apply the autonomic nervous system to your life.

d. Understand the endocrine system.

2.4
How Do Nature and Nurture Affect Our Brains?

a. Remember the key terms about how nature and nurture affect the brain.

b. Apply the effects of genetics to your life.

c. Understand how behavioral genetics studies the interaction of genes and environment.

d. Apply the effects of environment to your life.

KEY TERMS

nervous system
central nervous system
peripheral nervous
system
neurons
dendrites
cell body
axon
synapse
action potential
neurotransmitters

CHECKPOINT

- The central nervous system processes information in the brain and the spinal cord. The peripheral nervous system processes information in the soft organs.

- The nervous system has three primary tasks: It receives information, it integrates that information, and it passes signals to other neurons to allow thought and action.

- Neurons are the basic units of the nervous system.

- Changes in a neuron's electrical charge elicit an action potential. The action potential causes the release of neurotransmitters that are received by other neurons.

- Neurons communicate with each other through neurotransmitters. Each particular neurotransmitter has specific effects on thought and behavior.

Broca's area
cerebellum
thalamus
hypothalamus
hippocampus
amygdala
occipital lobes
parietal lobes
temporal lobes
frontal lobes

- The hindbrain includes the brain stem, which regulates basic survival functions, and the cerebellum, which is essential for movement and control of balance.

- The midbrain includes the substantia nigra, which is responsible for initiating voluntary motor activity.

- Together, the five subcortical structures of the forebrain control memory formation, emotions, and motivated behaviors.

- The four lobes of the forebrain and associated cortical areas are responsible for the most complex processing.

somatic nervous system
autonomic nervous system
endocrine system
hormones

- The peripheral nervous system includes the somatic nervous system and the autonomic nervous system.

- The somatic nervous system allows movement of the muscles and joints.

- The autonomic nervous system automatically regulates the body's internal environment through the sympathetic division and the parasympathetic division.

- The endocrine system includes glands that produce and release hormones that travel through the bloodstream and influence a variety of processes.

genes
monozygotic twins
dizygotic twins
plasticity

- Both genes and environment affect who we are and what we do.

- The genes we inherit from our parents affect our physical attributes and the ways we think and behave.

- Behavioral genetics uses twin studies to examine how genes and environment interact to influence mental activity and behavior.

- Environment affects brain function and psychological characteristics through plasticity, strengthening neural connections, brain reorganization, and the effects of gender.

For a self-quiz on this chapter, go to the back of the book and find Appendix B: Quizzes.

3 Consciousness

THE SNOWBOARD CHAMPION KEVIN PEARCE, the Arizona congresswoman Gabrielle Giffords, and many military personnel who have served in Iraq and Afghanistan—what do these people have in common? All have suffered traumatic brain injury, or TBI, a condition in which a person's brain is damaged by an external force, such as a violent blow or penetration by an object, such as a bullet. The consequences of TBI vary, but victims are often in a coma for varying lengths of time. TBI is not the only situation in which people may be in a coma; a comatose state may also result from particular diseases and medical events, such as a stroke. What does it mean to be in a coma? Is the person conscious at all? Is he aware of his surroundings? Can she think and feel? There are no simple answers to these questions.

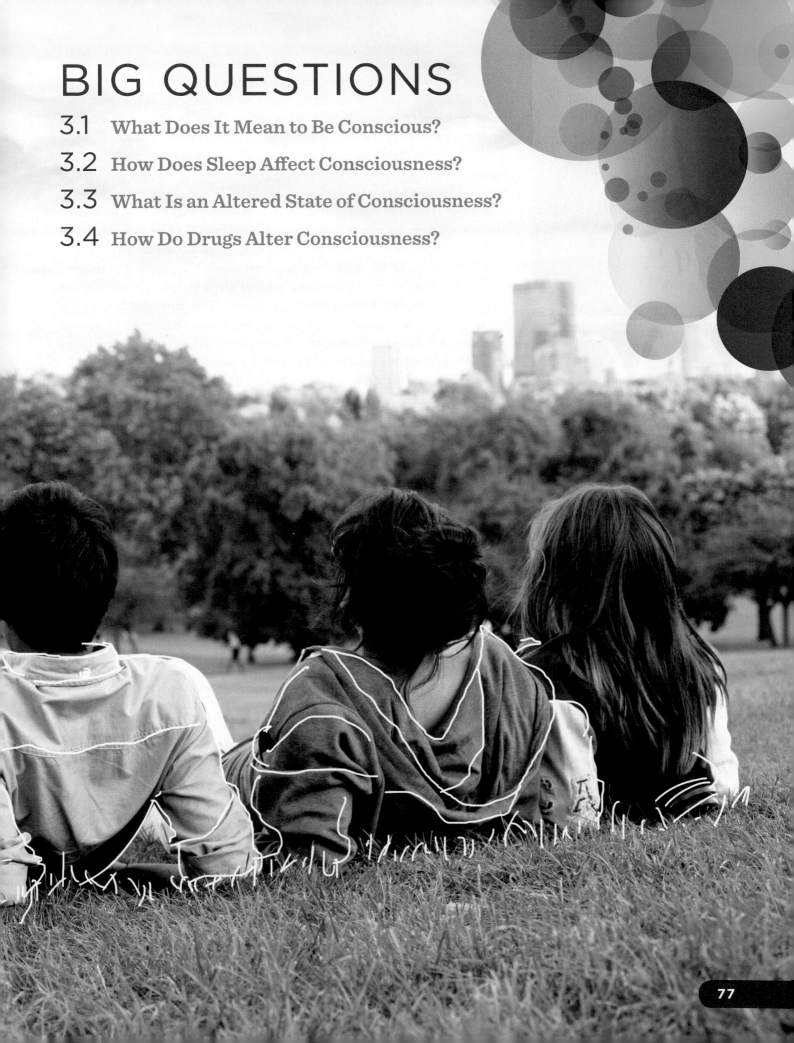

BIG QUESTIONS

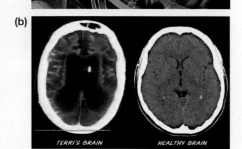

(a)

(b)

FIGURE 3.1

Minimally Conscious State Versus Persistent Vegetative State
(a) Jan Grzebski was in a minimally conscious state for 19 years before he awoke and reported that he had been aware of events around him. **(b)** Terri Schiavo spent more than 15 years in a persistent vegetative state before she was taken off life support. Her parents and their supporters believed she showed some awareness. But the dark areas of the brain scan on the left indicate that her cortex had deteriorated beyond recovery. There could not have been activity in these areas.

Consider the case of the Polish railroad worker Jan Grzebski, who, after being hit by a train in 1988, fell into a coma. Nineteen years later, at age 67, he woke up. Grzebski reported that during his coma, he remembered events that were going on around him, including his children's marriages. He tried to speak a few times, but he was not understood (Scislowska, 2007). From Grzebski's report, it is clear that even during his coma, he had some awareness of what was happening around him. He is described as being in a minimally conscious state during his coma (**Figure 3.1a**).

In other cases, it is hard to tell whether people in comas are conscious. Terri Schiavo, a young woman in Florida, spent more than 15 years in a coma. She went into the coma after her heart temporarily stopped, resulting in a lack of oxygen to her brain for several minutes. Terri seemed to respond to external stimuli and even laughed sometimes, making some people believe she was conscious. But brain scans revealed that the parts of her brain that would allow her to consciously produce these responses were either destroyed or showed no activity. Because of these results, some physicians argued that Terri could not choose to perform the behaviors. They said she wasn't conscious.

Terri's husband wanted to terminate her life support, but her parents wanted to continue it. Both sides waged a widely reported legal battle that lasted for years. A court finally ruled in 2005 that Schiavo's life support could be terminated. After her death, an autopsy confirmed substantial and irreversible damage throughout her brain, especially in cortical regions that are important for consciousness. Many experts now take this report as conclusive evidence that Terri had no awareness during her coma and was in a persistent vegetative state (**Figure 3.1b**).

The chances of recovery for people in a minimally conscious state, such as Jan, are much better than for those in a persistent vegetative state, such as Terri. So the question of consciousness clearly is more than an academic issue: It can be a battleground for life-and-death decisions. Trying to answer the question of "What is consciousness?" is one of the most fundamental issues in psychology. In this chapter, we explore what it means to be conscious and explain how consciousness depends on brain activity.

3.1 What Does It Mean to Be Conscious?

📖 **LEARNING GOALS**	✏️ **READING ACTIVITIES**	**LEARN**
a. Remember the key terms about consciousness.	List all of the boldface words and write down their definitions.	
b. Apply the two levels of consciousness.	Provide an example of each level of consciousness from your life.	
c. Analyze the impact of unconscious processing.	Identify when subliminal messages *do* versus *do not* affect thinking and behavior.	
d. Apply the global workspace model to your life.	Provide examples of how the five regions of your brain process your awareness of specific information.	
e. Understand consciousness in a person with a split brain.	Describe how a person with a split brain experiences visual information presented to each hemisphere and whether the person can or cannot verbally report that information.	

How can someone who is in a coma be conscious? The very possibility seems to contradict our traditional understanding of the term. The cases discussed in the chapter opener, however, highlight two points that are at the core of this chapter: First, people can be conscious of their surroundings even when they do not appear to be. Second, conscious experiences are associated with brain activity. Because of the very nature of consciousness, conscious experiences differ from person to person. So to understand the relationship between the brain and consciousness, we need to consider how conscious experiences differ.

consciousness
The combination of a person's subjective experience of the external world and the person's mental activity; this combination results from brain activity.

Consciousness Is a Subjective Experience

Consciousness refers to our moment-by-moment subjective experiences. And subjective experiences are personal and unique to whoever is experiencing them, as described in the Learning Tip. Listening to music on your iPod is one example of a subjective experience. Reflecting on the songs you hear and what they mean to you is another. You know you are conscious because you are experiencing the outside world through your senses and because you are aware of what you are thinking. But what gives rise to your consciousness?

Philosophers have long debated the nature of consciousness. As we saw in Chapter 1, in the seventeenth century René Descartes stated that the mind is distinct from the brain. This view is called dualism. Most psychologists reject dualism for *materialism,* the idea that the brain and the mind are inseparable, and that the processing of the brain is what allows the experiences of the mind. According to materialism, the activity of neurons in the brain produces consciousness: the sight of a face, the smell of a rose. More specifically, for each experience—each sight, each smell—there is an associated pattern of brain activity. The activation of this particular group of neurons in the brain gives rise to that particular conscious experience.

Given that processing in the brain underlies consciousness, each of us will experience consciousness personally—that is, subjectively—based on how our own brains process the external world and our internal mental activity. So, we cannot know if any two people experience the world in exactly the same way. For example, you think an apple tastes sweet, but your friend might find it sour. If you and your friends are looking at the same car, does the color look the same to all of you?

So even though conscious experiences exist, their subjective nature makes them difficult to study empirically. However, psychology has provided some

---

💡 LEARNING TIP: Understanding Subjectivity

The concepts of *subjective* and *objective* are important in psychology. It's easy to understand the difference between them if you remember the information shown in this chart.

WHEN YOU SEE	PLEASE THINK	MEANING
Subjective	Information is <u>subject</u> to your own personal view.	Other people will not experience that information in the same way, because it would be <u>subject</u> to their own view.
Objective	Information is an <u>object</u> that all people view the same way.	Other people will experience that information in the same way, because it is an <u>object</u> seen in the same way by all.

HAS IT HAPPENED TO YOU?

Experiencing the Shift in Levels of Consciousness

Before reading further, try to remember what you ate for lunch yesterday. If you were able to do this, you just experienced the shift between the two levels of consciousness.

Before reading this, you most likely were not thinking about what you had for lunch yesterday. If that's true, you were unconscious of this bit of information—that is, you were not aware of it. When you were asked to recall the information, you might have thought for a minute, and then the answer probably popped into your mind. At that point, you were fully conscious of what you ate for lunch. You might even have recalled many details of the experience. This shift is a seemingly simple feat. But behind this shift are all of the intricacies of how the brain helps you direct attention to the information you want or need to be aware of and experience.

means to understand conscious experiences. This approach helps all people to view mental processing and behavior in the same way, free from their own personal perspectives.

There Are Different Levels of Consciousness

Remember when you first learned how to drive? You probably paid very close attention to everything you needed to do and where all the stop signs and other cars were. But, once you have been driving for several years, it might seem as if you are on autopilot sometimes. You might go down a familiar road, paying no attention to how you drive and what's around you. Across these two experiences, your quantity, or amount, of consciousness is very different. Describing the levels of consciousness helps us to understand our experiences based on how much attention we pay to external stimuli and internal mental processes at a specific moment. Our levels of consciousness also reveal how aware we are of these experiences.

Our level of consciousness varies continuously throughout the day. When we are fully *conscious,* we are very alert. We pay attention to information and are acutely aware of our experiences. We notice that we are fully conscious when we are performing difficult or unfamiliar tasks, such as learning to drive. In situations of this kind, we use slow and effortful controlled processes that we need for the task, and we are completely aware while doing so (**Figure 3.2**).

Now consider a different situation. As you read this chapter, do you always focus intently on the material? Or do you find that sometimes you begin daydreaming and then realize you have no idea what you just read? In other words, you were going through the motions of reading, but you were mostly *unconscious* of what you read. In general, all of us can execute routine and well-learned tasks, such as reading, by using automatic processes. These processes are fast and effortless. However, because we are not fully conscious of engaging in such tasks, we won't remember some of the details of the experiences. Our lack of awareness will prevent the actions from leaving lasting impressions on us. Suppose, for instance, you drive to a familiar destination on autopilot. You probably won't remember the vehicles you pass or how many traffic lights you stop at.

There is a limit to how many things the mind can be consciously aware of at the same time, however. Even though multitasking is now a way of life, we almost never successfully complete even automatic tasks, such as reading or driving, while doing other things, such as talking on a cell phone or texting. This is a simple psychological fact: We have only so much attention available to consciously experience and respond to information. This is why it is so dangerous to talk on a cell phone or text while driving, as discussed in Chapter 1.

Unconscious Processing Sometimes Affects Behavior

Have you ever had a slip of the tongue, when you were thinking one thing and said another? Most people have, at some point, made this classic mistake. It is called a Freudian slip—where we express an unconscious thought at an inappropriate time or in an inappropriate social context. As we try to overcome our blunder, we wonder why it happened.

Considerable evidence indicates that people are affected by thoughts, stimuli, and events they are not aware of (Gladwell, 2005). **Subliminal perception** refers to times when our sensory systems are processing stimuli but, because the stimuli last only a short time or are subtle, we are generally not aware of them. Over the last several decades, many researchers have explored different ways that unconscious processing during subliminal perception can influence thinking and behavior. For example, in a classic experiment by Nisbett and Wilson (1977), participants were asked to examine pairs of obviously associated words, such as *ocean* and *moon*. Then they were asked to view single words, such as *detergent*, and merely state what other words came to mind. Nisbett and Wilson wanted to find out if viewing the word pairs would influence which words came to mind when participants viewed single words. And if so, would the participants be conscious of this influence?

Indeed, the researchers found that when given the word pair *ocean–moon*, followed by the word *detergent*, participants typically said the word *tide*. Because the moon affects the ocean and the tides, it is not surprising that participants chose the word *tide* with the word pair. What is surprising is that when the participants were asked why they said "tide," they usually gave reasons pertaining to the detergent's brand name, such as "My mom used Tide when I was a kid." This response shows that participants were not aware that the word pair had influenced their thoughts and behavior.

A variety of evidence indicates that much of our everyday behavior occurs without our awareness or intention (Bargh & Morsella, 2008; Dijksterhuis & Aarts, 2010). This automatic activity seems to happen because we can be influenced by cues from the environment even if we are not aware of them. For example, in one study people were shown pictures of various objects while they were in an fMRI scanner (see Chapter 2). Some of these objects were appetizing pictures of food, although participants did not realize that food cues were relevant. The more activity there was in brain reward regions specifically for the food pictures, the more weight people gained over the next 6 months (Demos, Heatherton, & Kelley, 2012). This brain activity indicates that some people seem to be especially susceptible to processing cues about food, even if they don't consciously notice it. In turn, this unconscious processing of food cues may be related to their weight gain.

Though material presented subliminally can influence how people process information, it has little or no effect on complex thinking and actions. For example, advertisers have long been accused of using subliminal cues to get people to buy their products (see Try It Yourself). However, buying a product is a result of many cognitive processes, and the evidence suggests that subliminal messages have quite small effects on purchasing behavior (Greenwald, 1992).

Brain Activity Gives Rise to Consciousness

Despite what you might see in some movies, scientists cannot—yet—read your intimate thoughts by looking at your brain activity. However, psychology is beginning to reveal how brain activity may give rise to specific subjective experiences. For instance, psychologists can identify objects you are seeing by looking at your brain activity (Kay, Naselaris, Prenger, & Gallant, 2008). In one study, researchers used fMRI to determine, based on the pattern of brain activity at that moment, which picture the participants were seeing: a house, a shoe, a bottle, or a face (O'Toole, Jiang, Abdi, & Haxby, 2005).

Psychologists now examine, even measure, consciousness and other mental states that once were considered too subjective to be studied. For example, Frank

subliminal perception
The processing of information by sensory systems without a person's conscious awareness.

TRY IT YOURSELF:
Subliminal Perception

Try to pick out the subliminal message in this advertisement.

Break out the frosty bottle

and keep your tonics dry!

GILBEYS GIN

Answer: The ice cubes spell out S-E-X.

Hypothesis: Specific patterns of brain activity can predict what a person is seeing.

Research Method:

1 Participants were shown images with houses superimposed on faces.

2 Participants were asked to report whether they saw a house or a face.

3 Researchers used fMRI to measure neural responses in participants' brains when the participants reported seeing the house or the face.

Results: When participants reported seeing a face, there was greater activity in one temporal lobe region, the fusiform face area. However, when participants reported seeing a house, there was greater activity in different temporal lobe regions, ones associated with object recognition. (For discussions of what information is processed in the brain regions, see Chapter 2.)

Conclusion: Awareness of certain information is associated with activity in the brain region that processes that particular sensory information.

Tong and colleagues (Tong, Nakayama, Vaughan, & Kanwisher, 1998) studied the relationship between consciousness and neural responses in the brain. Participants were shown images of houses that were superimposed on faces. When participants reported seeing a face, neural activity increased within the temporal lobe regions associated with face recognition—the fusiform face area. When participants reported seeing a house, neural activity increased within different temporal lobe regions, ones associated with object recognition. This finding suggests that different types of sensory information are processed by different areas in the brain. Importantly, these specific neural processes are associated with awareness of particular information. You can read more about this study in the Scientific Thinking feature.

THE GLOBAL WORKSPACE MODEL The **global workspace model** is a psychological theory that is based on this brain activity research. The global workspace model proposes that consciousness arises as a function of which brain circuits are active (Baars, 1988; Dehaene, Changeux, Naccache, Sachur, & Sergent, 2006). To put it another way: You experience your brain regions' activity as conscious awareness of specific information. For instance, when you listen to music, your conscious experience results from activation in particular brain regions. Those regions are processing the sound of the music, the meaning of the lyrics, perhaps your memories of hearing the song in the past, and the emotional states those memories produce. Your total experience results from the simultaneous activity of all the different brain regions supporting these psychological processes.

The key idea of the global workspace model is that no one area of the brain is responsible for general "awareness." Instead, specific areas of the brain process certain types of information. The processing in these brain areas produces

global workspace model
Consciousness is a product of activity in specific brain regions.

conscious experience of the particular information (**Figure 3.3**). From this perspective, consciousness is the mechanism that makes us actively aware of information so that we can prioritize what information we need or want to deal with at any moment.

THE SPLIT BRAIN One way researchers have gained a better understanding of the conscious mind is by studying people who have had brain surgery. For example, in a few rare cases, epilepsy does not respond to modern medications. Surgeons then may remove the part of the patient's brain where epileptic seizures begin. Another strategy, pioneered in the 1940s and still sometimes practiced when other interventions have failed, is to cut connections within the brain to isolate the site where the seizures begin. After the procedure, a seizure that begins at that site is less likely to spread throughout the cortex.

As you know from Chapter 2, the brain has a right hemisphere and a left hemisphere. The major connection between the hemispheres is the corpus callosum, a massive bundle of neural fibers (**Figure 3.4a;** see also Figure 2.16). The corpus callosum can be severed without damaging the gray matter (**Figure 3.4b**), so that the two halves of the brain are almost completely isolated from each other. The resulting condition, called **split brain,** has provided many important insights into the basic organization and specialized functions of each brain hemisphere.

What is it like to have your brain split in half? Perhaps the most striking thing about people whose brains have been divided surgically is that, unlike those who have had other types of brain surgery, they have no immediately apparent problems. In fact, some early investigations suggested the surgery had not affected the patients in any apparent way. They could walk and talk normally, think clearly, and interact socially. There was one important difference, however. In a series of tests on the first people with split brains, Michael Gazzaniga and Roger Sperry (1967) came up with a stunning result: Just as the brain had been split in two, so had the conscious mind! To understand what this finding means, consider how the two halves of the brain usually process information.

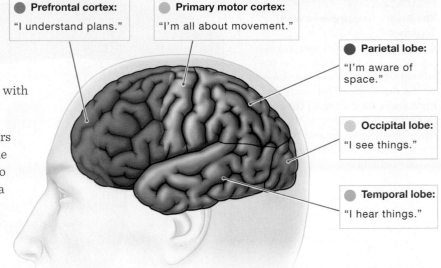

● **Prefrontal cortex:** "I understand plans."

● **Primary motor cortex:** "I'm all about movement."

● **Parietal lobe:** "I'm aware of space."

● **Occipital lobe:** "I see things."

● **Temporal lobe:** "I hear things."

FIGURE 3.3

Areas of the Brain That Process Awareness of Information

A central theme in cognitive neuroscience is that awareness of different aspects of the world is associated with processing in different parts of the brain. This simplified diagram indicates major areas where processing leads to awareness.

split brain

A condition in which the corpus callosum is surgically cut, and the two hemispheres of the brain do not receive information directly from each other.

(a)

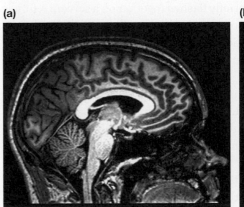

(b)

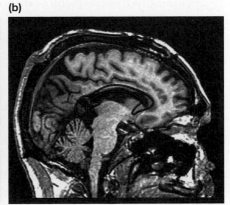

FIGURE 3.4

Split Brain

(a) This image shows the brain of a person whose corpus callosum is intact. **(b)** This image shows the brain of a patient whose corpus callosum has been removed (as indicated by the red outline). With the corpus callosum removed, the two hemispheres of the brain are almost completely separated.

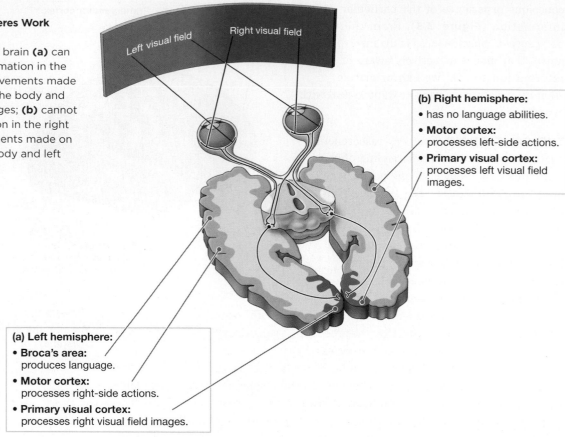

FIGURE 3.5

The Brain's Hemispheres Work Together

A person with a split brain **(a)** can talk *only* about information in the left hemisphere—movements made on the right side of the body and right visual field images; **(b)** cannot talk about information in the right hemisphere—movements made on the left side of the body and left visual field images.

Left visual field

Right visual field

(b) Right hemisphere:
- has no language abilities.
- **Motor cortex:** processes left-side actions.
- **Primary visual cortex:** processes left visual field images.

(a) Left hemisphere:
- **Broca's area:** produces language.
- **Motor cortex:** processes right-side actions.
- **Primary visual cortex:** processes right visual field images.

When you look ahead, everything you see that is located to the left of your nose (the left visual field) is processed by the right side of your occipital lobe. What you see that is located to the right of your nose (the right visual field) is processed by the left side of your occipital lobe. Similarly, movements of your left hand are controlled by the right motor cortex while movements of your right hand are controlled by the left motor cortex. And in most people, the left hemisphere is dominant for processing language. Normally, the right hemisphere has little ability to produce language. In all people, each half of the brain processes different information. So people with a split brain can give us insight into how a single hemisphere processes sensory, motor, and language information (**Figure 3.5**).

Let's imagine that two pictures are briefly flashed together on a screen: A fork is shown in the right visual field, and a spoon is shown in the left visual field. A person with a split brain can verbally report seeing the fork shown in the right visual field, but he cannot report seeing the spoon in the left visual field. Why does this limitation occur?

The left hemisphere (or "left brain") receives only information about the picture in the right visual field. Because the left hemisphere controls speech, the picture on the right (fork) is the only picture a person with a split brain can talk about (**Figure 3.6a**). By contrast, the right hemisphere (or "right brain") has processed the picture of the spoon on the left. The right hemisphere normally can't produce a verbal report to name the picture, because that side of the brain has no language abilities. And since the person's corpus callosum is severed,

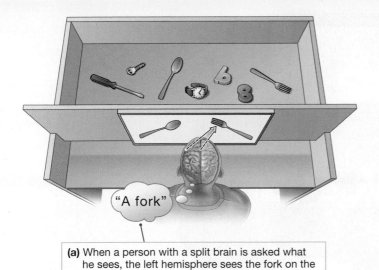

(a) When a person with a split brain is asked what he sees, the left hemisphere sees the fork on the right side of the screen and can verbalize that.

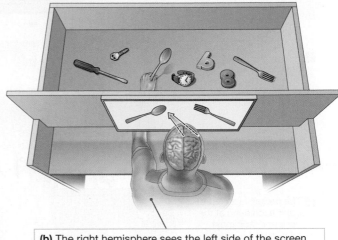

(b) The right hemisphere sees the left side of the screen, but cannot verbalize what is seen. However, the person can pick up the correct object using the left hand.

FIGURE 3.6

Investigating the Hemispheres in the Split Brain
This illustration explains the effects of a split brain on the hemispheres and on the person's responses. **(a)** Someone with a split brain can name an object only if it is shown in the right visual field and processed in the left hemisphere, where language is produced. **(b)** The same person can use his left hand to reach for an object that is shown in the left visual field and processed in the right hemisphere.

the visual information cannot pass from the right hemisphere to the left hemisphere to be verbalized.

However, the right brain can act on visual information it has processed about the spoon in the left visual field. Remember, the right hemisphere controls the opposite hand. Accordingly, the left hand can pick up a spoon from a selection of objects (**Figure 3.6b**). Thus, the limitations and abilities of the person with a split brain show us that splitting the brain produces two "half brains." Each half of the brain processes information independently from the other.

Normally, the abilities of each hemisphere complement those of the other. For instance, the right brain is generally good at spatial relationships, whereas the left brain is hopeless at them. In one experiment, a participant with a split brain is given a pile of blocks and a drawing of a simple arrangement in which to put them, such as a square. When using the left hand, controlled by the right brain, the participant arranges the blocks effortlessly. But when using the right hand, controlled by the left brain, the participant has a difficult time creating the square. During this dismal performance, the right brain makes the left hand try to slip in and help!

THE INTERPRETER This phenomenon reveals an important dimension to the relationship between the brain's hemispheres: They work together to reconstruct our conscious experiences. Again, this collaboration can be demonstrated in people with split brains. In one experiment, a participant with a split brain—known as J.W.—saw different images flash simultaneously on the left and right sides of a screen (**Figure 3.7**). Below those images was a stationary row of other images. J.W. was asked to point with each hand to the bottom image most related to the image flashed on that side of the screen above.

For example, in one trial, a picture of a chicken claw was flashed to J.W.'s left hemisphere, and a snow scene was flashed to his right hemisphere. In response to the image of the claw, J.W.'s right hand (controlled by the left brain) pointed to a picture of a chicken. In response to the snow scene, his left hand (controlled by the right brain) pointed to a picture of a snow shovel. It's important to remember that in people with a split brain, such as J.W., the left hemisphere can verbalize

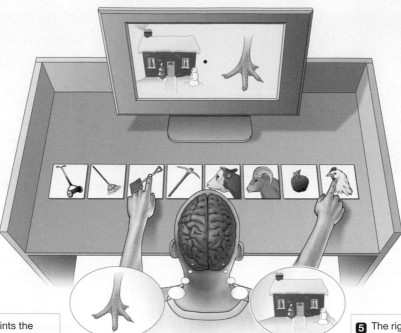

1 A person with a split brain watches as different images flash simultaneously on the left and right.

2 Below the screen is a row of other images.

3 The person is asked to point each hand at the bottom image most related to the image flashed on that side of the screen.

4 The left hemisphere points the right hand at a picture of a chicken head. The left hemisphere says that the chicken claw goes with the chicken head.

5 The right hemisphere points the left hand at a picture of a snow shovel. The left hemisphere decides that the shovel is used to clean up after chickens. (It does not see the snow scene.)

FIGURE 3.7

The Left Hemisphere Interpreter
On the basis of limited information, the left hemisphere interprets behavior that is processed in the right hemisphere.

information processed on that side of the brain (e.g., the chicken claw), but it has no access to visual information processed in the right hemisphere (e.g., the snow scene). So, when J.W. was asked why he pointed to those pictures, he used his left brain to reply, "Oh, that's simple. The chicken claw goes with the chicken, and you need a shovel to clean out the chicken shed." The left brain could not verbalize the relationship between the shovel and the snow scene, which was processed in the right hemisphere. Instead, it interpreted the left hand's pointing to the shovel in a way that was consistent with the only knowledge available to the left brain: the chicken claw.

In short, the left hemisphere tends to construct a world that makes sense. The sense-constructing activity in the left hemisphere is called the *interpreter*. This term means that the left hemisphere is interpreting what the right hemisphere has done (Gazzaniga, 2000). In the last example, the left hand was controlled by the disconnected right hemisphere. The left hemisphere interpreter created a ready way to explain the left hand's action. The left hemisphere's explanation, however, was unrelated to the right hemisphere's real reason for commanding that action. Yet to J.W., the movement seemed perfectly logical once the action had been interpreted.

Experiencing consciousness with a split brain is extremely rare, of course. Nearly all people have two hemispheres that communicate and cooperate on the tasks of daily living and awareness of experiences. The popular media have sometimes exaggerated the findings of this research. They have suggested that certain people are "left brain" logical types and others are "right brain" artistic types. It is true that the hemispheres are specialized for certain functions, such as language or spatial navigation. Still, conscious awareness and most cognitive processes involve the coordinated efforts of both hemispheres.

3.1 CHECKPOINT: What Does It Mean to Be Conscious?

- Consciousness is how the brain allows us to be aware of and experience the external world and our internal mental activity.

- There are two levels of consciousness, which vary in the amount of attention to and awareness of our experiences.

- Information that is processed subliminally—that is, without conscious awareness—can influence basic thinking and behavior for only short periods of time.

- Conscious experiences are a result of activity in five specific regions of the brain that cause us to be aware of specific types of information.

- People with split brains have a unique experience of consciousness: They are aware of only information presented to the one hemisphere that processes that information. And they can verbalize only information processed in the left hemisphere.

3.2 How Does Sleep Affect Consciousness?

📖 LEARNING GOALS	✏️ READING ACTIVITIES
a. Remember the key terms about sleep.	List all of the boldface words and write down their definitions.
b. Analyze how brain activity reveals four stages of sleep.	Compare brain activity during the four stages of sleep versus alert wakefulness.
c. Apply the three reasons people need to sleep.	Provide, in relation to your own life, three examples of why you need to sleep.
d. Understand the five common sleep disorders.	Describe each sleep disorder using your own words.

It's midnight, and you've finally gotten into bed. But you're so nervous about a job interview in the morning that you're sure you'll be up all night worrying. The next thing you know, the alarm is going off at 7:00 AM. Once again, your brain did that mysterious thing, and you fell asleep. What was your brain doing during those seven hours? Why do we sleep?

People commonly think that the brain shuts itself down during sleep. In fact, many brain regions are more active when we are asleep than when we are awake. And evidence indicates that some complex thinking, such as working on difficult problems, occurs in the brain even when we are sleeping (Walker & Stickgold, 2006). Given that brain activity is the basis for consciousness, what are our conscious experiences during sleep? Before we answer that question, let's consider how sleep fits into life.

Sleep Is Part of the Normal Rhythm of Life

Brain activity and other physiological processes are regulated into daily patterns known as **circadian rhythms** (*circadian* roughly translates to "about a day"). Sleep/wake cycles operate according to circadian rhythms, as do body temperature and hormone levels. Circadian rhythms are influenced by the cycles of light and dark. Even when removed from light cues, however, we (and nonhuman animals as well) continue to show these rhythms.

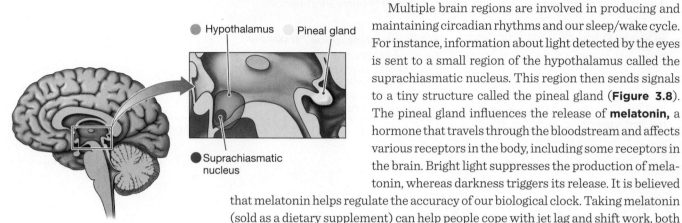

Multiple brain regions are involved in producing and maintaining circadian rhythms and our sleep/wake cycle. For instance, information about light detected by the eyes is sent to a small region of the hypothalamus called the suprachiasmatic nucleus. This region then sends signals to a tiny structure called the pineal gland (**Figure 3.8**). The pineal gland influences the release of **melatonin,** a hormone that travels through the bloodstream and affects various receptors in the body, including some receptors in the brain. Bright light suppresses the production of melatonin, whereas darkness triggers its release. It is believed that melatonin helps regulate the accuracy of our biological clock. Taking melatonin (sold as a dietary supplement) can help people cope with jet lag and shift work, both of which interfere with circadian rhythms. Taking melatonin also appears to help people fall asleep, although it is unclear why this happens.

Individuals differ tremendously in how much they sleep. Infants sleep much of the day. As adults, we spend about one-third of our time sleeping, an average of around 8 hours per night. Some adults report needing 9 or 10 hours of sleep a night to feel rested, whereas others report needing only a few hours. People tend to sleep less as they age. However, researchers were skeptical when a 70-year-old retired nurse, Miss M., reported sleeping only about an hour a night—that is, until she agreed to participate in a study. On her first two nights in a research laboratory, Miss M. was unable to sleep, apparently because of the excitement. But on her third night, she slept for only 99 minutes, then awoke refreshed, cheerful, and full of energy (Meddis, 1977). You might like the idea of sleeping so little and having all those extra hours of spare time. But bear in mind that most of us do not function well on so little sleep.

FIGURE 3.8

Pineal Gland and Sleep/Wake Cycles
Changes in light register in the suprachiasmatic nucleus of the hypothalamus. The hypothalamus then signals the pineal gland. The pineal gland influences the production of melatonin, which signals the body that it is time to sleep or wake up.

Consciousness Changes During Sleep

How is being awake different from being asleep? The difference has as much to do with conscious experience as with biological processes. When you sleep, your conscious experience of the outside world is largely turned off. To some extent, however, you remain aware of your surroundings and your brain still processes certain information. Your mind analyzes potential dangers, controls body movements, and shifts body parts to maximize comfort. This is why people who sleep next to children or pets tend not to roll over onto them and why, after infancy, most people do not fall out of bed while sleeping.

Before the development of objective methods to assess brain activity, most people believed the brain went to sleep along with the rest of the body. As we discussed in Chapter 2, invention of the electroencephalograph, or EEG, in the 1920s enabled researchers to measure the brain's electrical activity. When you are awake and fully conscious, you experience many different sources of sensory

circadian rhythms
The regulation of biological cycles into regular, daily patterns.

melatonin
A hormone, released in the brain, that aids regulation of circadian rhythms because bright light reduces production and darkness increases production.

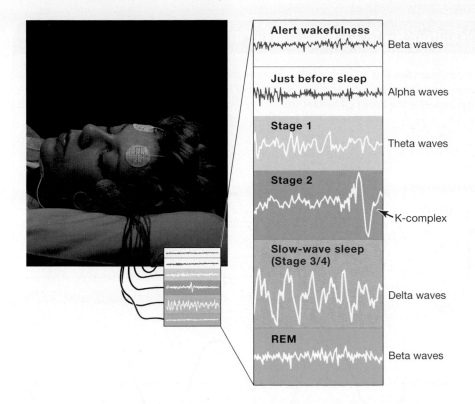

FIGURE 3.9
Brain Activity During Sleep
These EEG patterns are examples of electrical brain activity during different stages of normal sleep.

activity. As a result, the neurons in your brain are extremely active. An EEG shows this brain activity as short, frequent, irregular electrical signals called beta waves (shown in **Figure 3.9**). When you really focus your attention on something, or when you close your eyes and relax, brain activity slows and becomes more regular, producing the electrical pattern known as alpha waves.

FOUR STAGES OF SLEEP As EEG readings indicate, sleep occurs in stages that are marked by changes in consciousness (see Figure 3.9; also see the Learning Tip on p. 90). When you drift off to sleep, you enter stage 1, shown on the EEG as theta waves. You can easily be aroused from stage 1, and if awakened, you will probably deny that you were sleeping. In this light sleep, you might see fantastical images or geometric shapes. Or you might have the sensation of falling or that your limbs are jerking.

As you progress to stage 2, your breathing becomes more regular, and you become less sensitive to external stimulation. When the EEG shows bursts of brain activity called *K-complexes,* you are really asleep. Some researchers believe that these bursts are signals from brain mechanisms involved with shutting out the external world and keeping people asleep (Steriade, 1992).

The progression to deep sleep occurs through stages 3 and 4, which are seen as one stage because the brain activity is nearly identical (Silber et al., 2007). This period is marked by large, regular delta waves, and it is often referred to as **slow-wave sleep.** People in slow-wave sleep are very hard to wake and are often disoriented when they do wake up. People still process some information in slow-wave sleep, however, because the mind continues to evaluate the environment for potential danger. For example, parents in slow-wave sleep can be aroused by their children's cries. Yet they can blissfully sleep through the sounds of sirens or traffic noise, which are louder than the crying children but are not necessarily relevant.

After about 90 minutes of sleep, the sleep cycle reverses, returning to stage 1. At this point, the EEG suddenly shows a flurry of beta wave activity that usually represents an awake, alert mind. The eyes dart back and forth rapidly beneath

HAS IT HAPPENED TO YOU?
The Hypnic Jerk

Have you ever been falling asleep when suddenly a part of your body twitched? Or maybe you were dozing off in class and your whole body jerked? Either way, you were most likely aware of your movement, which is called a hypnic jerk. Experts don't know exactly what causes hypnic jerks, but many agree that they come from the muscles' responding to brain activity that occurs at the start of stage 1 sleep. Because these jerks shift us briefly out of stage 1 sleep, we become aware that we just moved. This conscious awareness usually does not last long, though. It fades when we slip back into sleep for the night, or at least for the class period.

slow-wave sleep
Stages 3 and 4 of deep sleep, when EEGs reveal large, regular delta waves and sleepers are hard to awaken.

An EEG of the brain's electrical activity can seem like just a bunch of chicken scratches. But to understand how these waveforms reveal the stages of sleep and consciousness, you need to focus on only two things: the height of the waveforms (amplitude) and the distance between the peaks (wavelength).

(a) EEG waveforms that are shorter in height (lower amplitude) and have a smaller distance between the peaks (shorter wavelength) indicate brain activity that is associated with awareness of information. That information can be in the external world, as in alert wakefulness. Or it can be in our own minds when we are dreaming, as occurs during REM sleep.

(b) By contrast, EEG waveforms that are relatively taller in height (higher amplitude) and have a longer distance between the peaks (longer wavelength) indicate brain activity that is associated with deep sleep.

Notice that as we move through the stages of sleep, EEG waveforms always increase in height and in the distance between the peaks. This combined pattern indicates that we are falling more deeply asleep.

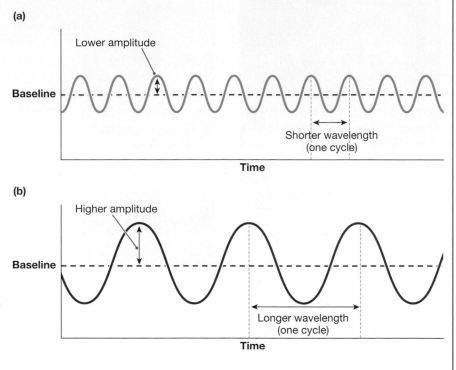

REM sleep

The stage of sleep when EEGs show beta wave activity associated with an awake, alert mind, and sleepers experience rapid eye movements, dreaming, and paralysis of motor systems.

FIGURE 3.10

Stages of Sleep

This chart shows how the four stages of sleep progress over the course of the night.

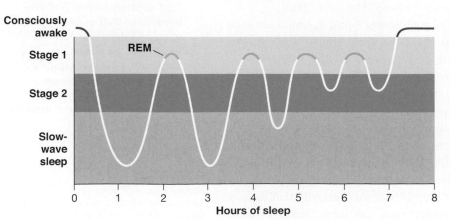

closed eyelids. Because of these rapid eye movements, this stage is called **REM sleep.** It is sometimes called paradoxical sleep because of the paradox of a sleeping body with an active brain. Indeed, some regions of the brain are more active during REM sleep than during wakefulness. But although the brain is active during REM episodes, most of the body's muscles are paralyzed. At the same time, the body shows signs of genital arousal: Most males of all ages develop erections, and most females of all ages experience clitoral engorgement.

REM sleep is psychologically significant because of its relation to dreaming. When people are awakened during REM sleep, about 80 percent of the time they report dreaming. By contrast, they report dreaming during non-REM sleep less than half the time (Solms, 2000). What's more, as we will see later in the chapter, dreams differ in these two types of sleep.

THE REPEATING SLEEP CYCLE Over the course of a typical night, we cycle through the stages of sleep about five times. As shown in **Figure 3.10,** we progress from stage 1 sleep to slow-wave sleep, then to REM sleep. As morning approaches, the sleep cycle becomes shorter, and we spend relatively more time in REM sleep. You may say you slept like a log all night long, but it's probably not quite true. People briefly awaken many times during the night, although they do not remember these awakenings in the morning. As people age, they sometimes have more difficulty going back to sleep after awakening.

People Dream While Sleeping

Dreams are one of life's great mysteries. Why do our minds conjure up images, fantasies, stories that make little sense, and scenes that ignore physical laws and rules of both time and space? Why does the mind confuse these conjurings with reality? Although they sometimes incorporate external sounds or other sensory experiences that happen while we sleep, **dreams** are the products of our consciousness. Some people claim they do not dream, or never remember their dreams, but everyone dreams unless a brain injury or medication interferes. In fact, the average person spends 6 years of his or her life dreaming. Yet no one knows if dreaming serves any biological function.

REM DREAMS AND NON-REM DREAMS We dream during both REM and non-REM sleep. But in the two types of sleep, the content of our dreams differs. REM dreams are more likely to be bizarre. They may involve intense emotions, visual and auditory hallucinations (but rarely taste, smell, or pain), and an uncritical acceptance of illogical events. You fly, are chased by monsters, or tunnel through the center of the earth. Non-REM dreams feel normal, like every-day life. They may concern ordinary activities such as deciding what clothes to wear or taking notes in class.

The activity of different brain regions during REM and non-REM sleep may be responsible for the different types of dreams and our experiences of them. During non-REM sleep, many brain regions are generally deactivated. In contrast, during REM sleep, some areas of the brain show increased activity, whereas others show decreased activity (Hobson, 2009; **Figure 3.11**). The content of REM dreams results from the activation of brain structures associated with motivation, emotion, and reward (e.g., the amygdala). The visual association areas are

dreams
Products of consciousness during sleep in which a person confuses images and fantasies with reality.

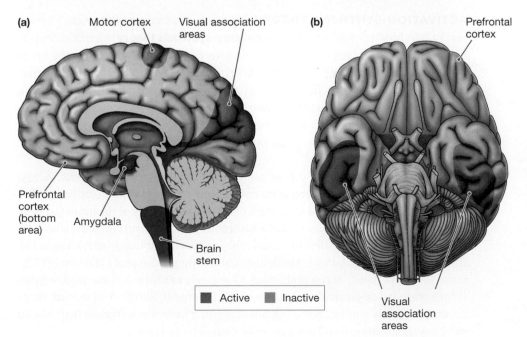

(a)
Motor cortex
Visual association areas
Prefrontal cortex (bottom area)
Amygdala
Brain stem

■ Active ■ Inactive

(b)
Prefrontal cortex
Visual association areas

FIGURE 3.11
Brain Activity During REM Sleep
These two views of the brain show the regions that are active (red) and inactive (blue) during REM sleep. **(a)** As seen here from the side, the motor cortex, the brain stem, and visual association areas are active. So is the amygdala, which is involved in emotion. The prefrontal cortex is inactive. **(b)** This view from beneath the brain shows other visual association areas that are active. This view also reveals the bottom of the prefrontal cortex, which is inactive.

also activated. At the same time, the prefrontal cortex becomes less activated (Schwartz & Maquet, 2002). As we saw in Chapter 2, the prefrontal cortex is necessary for processing self-awareness, reflective thought, and conscious input from the external world. Because this brain region is less active during REM dreams, the brain's emotion centers and visual association areas interact without rational thought. The disconnect between feelings and logic contributes to the wilder images in REM dreams.

WHAT DO DREAMS MEAN? Perhaps we should ask, do dreams mean anything? Sigmund Freud presented one of the first major theories of dreams. According to Freud, dreams contain hidden content that represents unconscious conflicts in the mind of the dreamer. The *manifest content* is the way visual information is seen (manifested) in the dream and remembered by the dreamer. For example, you might see images in your dream that have you flying through the air, away from dark storm clouds. The *latent content* is the meaning behind what is being visually manifested. In this example, the meaning behind the visual images in the dream might be that you are trying to get away from a problem with your parents. Some theorists believe that the manifest content disguises the latent content to protect the dreamer from directly confronting a conflict.

Virtually no support exists for Freud's ideas that dreams represent hidden conflicts and that objects in dreams have special symbolic meanings. Daily life experiences do, however, influence the content of dreams. For example, you may be especially likely to have dreams with anxiety-producing content while studying for exams.

Some dreams have thematic structures, unfolding as events or stories rather than as jumbles of disconnected images. Still, such structures apparently hold no secret meanings. Although your dreams may seem uniquely your own, many common themes occur in dreams. Have you ever dreamed about showing up for an exam and being unprepared or finding that you are taking the wrong test? Many people in college have dreams like these. Even after you finish school and no longer take exams routinely, you probably will have similar dreams about being unprepared. Retired professors sometimes dream about being unprepared to teach classes.

ACTIVATION-SYNTHESIS THEORY The sleep researchers John Alan Hobson and Robert McCarley proposed the **activation-synthesis theory** to explain dreaming (Hobson & McCarley, 1977). According to this theory, neurons in the brain fire randomly during sleep. This random firing can activate parts of the brain that normally process sensory input, such as sights, sounds, and smells. The sleeping mind tries to make sense of the resulting sensory activity by combining it with stored memories, and the result is our experience of having a dream. From this perspective, dreams are simply the side effects of mental processes produced by random neural firing.

In 2000, Hobson and his colleagues revised the activation-synthesis theory. They wanted to take into account recent findings in cognitive neuroscience. For instance, they suggested that activation of the limbic regions of the brain (such as the amygdala), which are associated with emotion and motivation, is the source of the emotional content of dreams. They also proposed that the deactivation of the frontal cortices contributes to the delusional and illogical aspects of dreams. Critics of Hobson's theory argue that dreams are rarely as chaotic as we might expect if they were based on random brain activity (Domhoff, 2003). And indeed, most dreams are fairly similar to waking life—they just have some strange features. In sum, psychologists are still not sure what causes us to dream.

activation-synthesis theory
Dreams are the result of the brain's attempts to make sense of random brain activity by synthesizing the activity with stored memories.

Sleep Is an Adaptive Behavior

In Chapter 1, we discussed how certain traits are adaptive for a species. That is, each species has traits that help it to survive and reproduce in a changing environment. At first glance, sleep hardly seems adaptive. Tuning out the external world for periods of time can be a threat to survival if a predator pounces or you drive your car into a tree. But we cannot avoid the need to sleep. Eventually our bodies shut down, and we sleep whether we want to or not.

But why do we sleep? Most animals sleep, even if they have peculiar sleeping styles. For instance, in some dolphin species the cerebral hemispheres take turns sleeping. So sleep must serve an important biological purpose. In other words, it must help us adapt and respond in our environment. Researchers have proposed three reasons that sleeping is adaptive and beneficial to us: restoration, preservation, and facilitation of learning.

THREE BENEFITS OF SLEEP Think about the last time you engaged in demanding physical activity—maybe spending the day helping a friend move or running a long race. Most likely you slept longer than usual afterward. According to the *restorative theory,* sleep allows the body, including the brain, to rest and repair itself. Growth hormone, released during deep sleep, helps bring about the repair of damaged tissue. Sleep apparently enables the brain to replenish energy stores and also strengthens the immune system (Hobson, 1999).

According to the *circadian rhythm theory,* sleep has evolved to preserve animals, including humans, from harm. Sleep keeps creatures quiet and inactive when the danger of attack is greatest—usually when it is dark. Each day, animals need only a limited amount of time to accomplish the necessities of survival, such as obtaining food. As a result, it is adaptive for animals to spend the rest of the time inactive, preferably hidden. So an animal's typical amount of sleep depends on how much time that animal needs to obtain food, how easily it can hide, and how vulnerable it is to attack. Small animals tend to sleep a lot. Large animals that are vulnerable to attack, such as cows and deer, sleep little. Large predatory animals, which are generally not vulnerable, sleep a lot (**Figure 3.12**). We humans depend greatly on vision for survival. We are adapted to sleeping at night because our early ancestors were more at risk in the dark.

Scientists have also proposed that sleep is important because it is involved in strengthening neural connections that serve as the basis of learning. The general idea of this *consolidation theory* is that circuits wired together during the waking period are consolidated, or strengthened, during sleep (Wilson & McNaughton, 1994). When research participants in one study slept after learning word lists, their recall was better than in control conditions where participants remained awake after learning the lists (Drosopoulos, Schulze, Fischer, & Born, 2007).

Both slow-wave sleep and REM sleep appear to be important for learning to take place, but people may be especially likely to perform better if they dream about the task while sleeping. In one study, participants learned how to run a complex maze. Those who then slept for 90 minutes went on to perform better on the maze than participants who hadn't slept. Those who dreamed about the maze performed the best of all (Wamsley, Tucker, Payne, Benavides, & Stickgold, 2010).

Indeed, there is some evidence that students experience more REM sleep during exam periods, when they might be consolidating a great deal of information (Smith & Lapp, 1991). Changes in sleep patterns over the life cycle also support the argument that sleep, especially REM sleep, promotes the development of brain circuits for learning. Infants and the very young, who learn an enormous amount in a few years, sleep the most and also spend the most time in REM sleep.

FIGURE 3.12
Sleeping Predator
After a fresh kill, a lion may sleep for days.

FIGURE 3.13

Sleep Deprivation
Students may try to avoid sleep. But sleep will catch up with them!

✗ SLEEP DEPRIVATION CAN IMPAIR FUNCTION We've all gone through periods when we didn't get enough sleep. Does the occasional lack of sleep harm us? Many laboratory studies have examined the effects of temporary sleep deprivation on physical and cognitive performance. Surprisingly, most studies find that two or three days of sleep deprivation have little effect on strength, athletic ability, or the performance of complex tasks. If you find yourself nodding off over your textbook after a night without sleep, however, you're not alone (**Figure 3.13**). When deprived of sleep, people find it difficult to perform quiet tasks, such as reading, and nearly impossible to perform boring or mundane tasks.

By contrast, a long period of sleep deprivation does decrease cognitive performance. People who suffer from chronic sleep deprivation may experience attention lapses and reduced short-term memory. Studies with rats have found that extended sleep deprivation compromises the immune system and leads to death. Sleep deprivation is also dangerous and potentially disastrous because it makes people prone to microsleeps, in which they fall asleep during the day for a few seconds or even a minute (Coren, 1996).

If your main style of studying is the all-nighter, then findings that link sleep to learning should make you think twice. In one recent study, students who were sleep deprived for just one night showed reduced activity the next day in the hippocampus, a brain area essential for memory (Yoo, Hu, Gujar, Jolesz, & Walker, 2007). These sleep-deprived students also showed poorer memory at later testing. The researchers found substantial evidence that sleep does more than consolidate memories. Sleep also seems to prepare the brain for its memory needs for the next day.

Sleep deprivation also interferes with the body's hunger signals, contributing to overeating and weight gain (late-night pizza run, anyone?). It impairs motor abilities, contributing to accidents and injuries. Sleep deprivation also increases anxiety, depression, and distress. And—to add insult to injury—others perceive us as less attractive when we are sleep deprived, compared with when we are well rested (Axelsson et al., 2010).

When you finally do sleep after a long period of deprivation, you will enter the REM stage more quickly and will have more REM dreams than usual. This REM rebound after deprivation implies that REM sleep is a particularly important part of the sleep process (Suchecki, Tiba, & Machado, 2012).

Sleep Disorders Are Relatively Common Throughout Life

Nearly everyone occasionally has trouble falling asleep or going back to sleep after waking up during the night. When the continual inability to sleep causes significant problems in daily life, the problem has reached the point of being a sleep disorder.

INSOMNIA It's 3:00 AM, and you're turning over in bed for what seems like the 500th time. You're exhausted, but your brain refuses to turn off, and you're beginning to feel desperate. Now and then, each of us has a hard time sleeping. If you experience this problem chronically, you might have a sleep disorder. **Insomnia** is a sleep disorder in which a person's mental health and ability to function are reduced by the chronic inability to sleep. Indeed, insomnia is associated with diminished psychological well-being, including feelings of depression (Bootzin & Epstein, 2011; Hamilton et al., 2007).

Researchers estimate that between 12 percent and 20 percent of adults have insomnia; it is more common in women than in men and in older adults than in

insomnia
A disorder characterized by an inability to sleep.

younger adults (Espie, 2002; Ram, Seirawan, Kumar, & Clark, 2010). It is hard to estimate how many people truly have insomnia, however. One reason is that many people who believe they are poor sleepers overestimate how long it takes them to fall asleep and often underestimate how much sleep they get in a typical night. Some people even experience pseudoinsomnia, in which they basically dream they are not sleeping. Their EEGs would show they were sleeping. But if you woke them, they would claim they had been awake.

Ironically, a major cause of insomnia is worrying about sleep. When you experience this kind of insomnia, you may be tired enough to sleep. As you try to fall asleep, however, you worry about whether you will get to sleep and may even panic about how a lack of sleep will affect you. This anxiety leads to heightened arousal, which interferes with normal sleep patterns. It's a vicious cycle.

If you look at the many TV ads and the pharmacy shelves filled with both prescription pills and over-the-counter sleep aids, it would seem that medication is a simple way to deal with insomnia. Sleeping pills may work in the short run, but they can cause significant problems down the road. People may come to depend on the pills to help them sleep. Then if they try to stop taking the pills, they may lie awake wondering whether they can get to sleep on their own.

As a better alternative, you might try preventing or even curing insomnia by changing your habits. You can read about some techniques in this chapter's Using Psychology in Your Life feature, on p. 96. For more serious insomnia, the most successful treatment combines drug therapy with cognitive-behavioral therapy (CBT). CBT helps people overcome their worries about sleep and relieves the need for the drugs, which should be discontinued before the end of therapy (Morin et al., 2009). CBT is discussed at length in Chapter 14.

SLEEP APNEA Another fairly common sleep disorder is **sleep apnea.** While asleep, a person with this disorder stops breathing for short periods because his throat closes. In struggling to breathe, the person briefly awakens and gasps for air.

Sleep apnea is most common among middle-aged men and is often associated with obesity, although it is unclear if obesity causes sleep apnea or sleep apnea contributes to obesity (Pack & Pien, 2011; Spurr, Graven, & Gilbert, 2008). Sleep apnea causes people to sleep poorly, feel tired in the daytime, and even have problems such as an inability to concentrate while driving. What's more, sleep apnea is associated with cardiovascular problems and stroke.

Because they do not remember awakening frequently during the night, people with sleep apnea are typically unaware of their condition. The main symptom that may bring it to their attention is loud snoring that disturbs a partner. For serious cases, physicians often prescribe a device that blows air into the nose or mouth while the person sleeps (**Figure 3.14**).

NARCOLEPSY A student who falls asleep during a lecture is likely sleep deprived, but a professor who falls asleep while lecturing is probably experiencing an episode of **narcolepsy.** In this rare disorder, extreme sleepiness occurs during normal waking hours. During an episode of narcolepsy, a person may experience the muscle paralysis that accompanies REM sleep, perhaps causing her to go limp and collapse. Obviously, people with narcolepsy have to be very careful about the activities they engage in. Unexpectedly falling asleep can be dangerous or fatal, depending on the situation. Evidence suggests that narcolepsy is a genetic condition that affects transmission of a specific neurotransmitter in the hypothalamus (Chabas, Taheri, Renier, & Mignot, 2003; Nishino, 2007). The most widely used treatments for this condition are drugs that act as stimulants.

sleep apnea
A disorder in which a person, while asleep, stops breathing because the throat closes; the condition results in frequent awakenings during the night.

narcolepsy
A sleep disorder in which a person experiences excessive sleepiness during normal waking hours, sometimes going limp and collapsing.

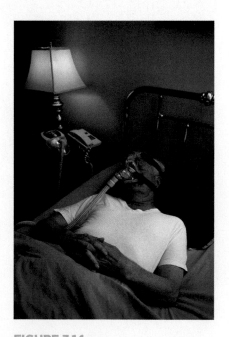

FIGURE 3.14
Sleep Apnea
This man has sleep apnea. While he sleeps, a continuous positive airway pressure device blows air into his nose or mouth to keep his throat open.

USING PSYCHOLOGY IN YOUR LIFE:

How Can I Develop Better Sleep Habits?

If you don't get enough sleep, you are setting yourself up for poor mental health, poor physical health, and academic difficulties. You probably know this from personal experience as well as from what you've read. But even though you may have the best intentions, sleep may sometimes play hard to get. Anxiety, excitement, getting too tired, or having bad sleep habits may leave you lying in bed, dog-tired but wide awake. Here are some strategies that can help you develop better sleep:

1. **Establish a routine to help set your biological clock.** Every day, go to bed at the same time and wake up at the same time. Changing the time you go to bed or wake up each day alters your regular nightly sleep cycle and can disrupt other physiological systems.

2. **Avoid alcohol and caffeine in the evening.** Alcohol might help you get to sleep more quickly, but it will interfere with your sleep cycle and most likely make you wake up early the next day. Caffeine is a stimulant, so it will prevent you from falling asleep.

3. **Exercise regularly.** Regular exercise will help maintain your sleep cycle. However, exercising creates arousal that interferes with sleep, so do not exercise right before going to bed. Instead, do a little stretching before bedtime to help your mind and body relax.

4. **Remember, your bed is for sleeping.** Most of us do not sleep in our kitchens, nor should we eat in our beds. Or watch TV. Or study. Your mind needs to associate your bed with sleeping. The best way to make that association is to use your bed only for sleeping. And maybe a little cuddling.

5. **Relax.** Do not worry about the future (easier said than done, right?). Write down things to do or worries on a notepad and then put them aside until the next day. Have a warm bath or listen to soothing music. Download a couple of meditation and relaxation podcasts, and use the techniques to help you deal with stress and guide you to restfulness.

6. **Get up.** When you cannot fall asleep, get up and do something else. Do not lie there trying to force sleep (we all know how well that works, or rather does not work). If you start feeling sleepy a bit later, go back to bed and give sleep another chance.

7. **Let bygones be bygones.** When you have trouble falling asleep on a particular night, do not try to make up for the lost sleep by sleeping late the next morning or napping during the day. Those zzzz's are gone. You want to be sleepy when you go to bed the next night. Sleeping late, napping, or both will make the next night's sleep more difficult.

The sleep attitudes and habits you establish during college will be with you for the rest of your life. Set yourself up for academic success, and for physical and mental health, by making good sleep a priority and taking charge of your sleep.

For additional resources, visit the National Sleep Foundation's Web site at www.sleepfoundation.org.

An Example of What Not to Do

An Example of What to Do

BEING A CRITICAL CONSUMER:
Is the Sleeping Brain Ever Really Asleep?

It's only a month into the first semester, and I already feel behind, James thought. He was excited about starting college, but he hadn't been quite prepared for the amount of studying that was required. He liked all his classes (well, maybe except his algebra course), but he loved his psychology class. In high school, a psychologist had helped his best friend, Lorenzo, deal with the death of Lorenzo's mother. At that point, James had decided to major in psychology. Now, after finishing Chapter 3 of his psychology textbook, he was already hooked.

James had been especially interested when reading the section about sleep deprivation. Since starting college, he wasn't sure he had gotten more than six hours of sleep in any night. He also was really surprised to learn that the brain is still so active even during sleep, especially during REM sleep. *No wonder I'm always so tired—my brain never shuts down!*

James decided to look online for additional information about sleep. At the *Huffington Post,* his attention was drawn to an interesting headline: "Sounds of Arguing Affect Babies' Brains, Even While They're Asleep." James read the article and found out that, as part of a 2013 research study, 20 babies aged 6–12 months slept in an fMRI machine. As James knew from reading Chapter 2, fMRI measures blood flow in various areas of the brain. Blood flow indicates how active a particular region is. While the babies slept, half of them heard a male voice saying nonsense sentences in an angry tone of voice. The other half heard the same nonsense syllables said by the man in a neutral tone of voice. Some of the babies had parents who verbally fought a lot, whereas some of the babies had parents who seldom argued. By using fMRI, the researchers found that in the parts of the brain responsible for regulating stress and emotion, babies from high-conflict homes showed greater brain activity in response to the angry voice than to the neutral voice. *That's sort of sad,* James thought, *but also kind of cool—more evidence that the brain processes the environment even during sleep.*

Intrigued, James looked for other stories covering this research. At *FoxNews.com,* he found the same article with a slightly different title: "Sounds of Arguing Affect Sleeping Babies' Brains." *That seems like a fair headline, too—it just presents the basic facts of the study.* But at *Telegraph .co.uk,* he found a much more shocking headline: "Arguing Parents Could Damage Their Baby for Life, Study Claims." *Is that really what they found? Did the other articles I read fail to mention that these infants were followed later in life?* James read the *Telegrap*h article more closely. He noticed that although the details of the study were not different, the journalist seemed to go a step further and speculate on what the findings of the study might mean even though the study's main author was not saying such things.

James felt frustrated because some interesting, possibly important ideas were being presented in a way that might mislead readers. He decided to post a comment on *Telegraph.co.uk* reminding the *Telegraph*'s readers that the study had not, in fact, followed the babies later in life. Submitting his own two cents made James think, *Some furthur research could be done here.* He noticed that the study used only male voices. In addition, it focused only on verbal conflict. *Would babies have responded the same to an angry female voice? Do homes with physical conflict have the same effect?* James yawned loudly. More investigation could be done tomorrow. It was time for Mr. Psychology to get some sleep!

REM BEHAVIOR DISORDER AND SLEEPWALKING *REM behavior disorder* is roughly the opposite of narcolepsy. In this condition, the normal paralysis that accompanies REM sleep is disabled. People who experience REM behavior disorder act out their dreams while sleeping. Often, in acting out dreams, they strike their sleeping partners. No treatment exists for this rare sleep disorder. The condition is caused by a neurological deficit and is most often seen in elderly males.

By contrast, sleepwalking is most common among young children. Technically called *somnambulism*, this relatively common behavior occurs during slow-wave sleep, typically within the first hour or two after falling asleep. During an episode, the person is glassy-eyed and seems disconnected from other people and/or the surroundings. Contrary to popular belief, no harm is done if the sleepwalker is awakened during the episode. Being gently walked back to bed is safer for the sleepwalker than being left to wander around and potentially get hurt.

✓ **3.2 CHECKPOINT: How Does Sleep Affect Consciousness?**

- We experience changes in consciousness when we sleep as we become less aware of the external world, yet we are still able to respond when necessary.

- Sleep has four stages. Each stage is characterized by brain activity that is the basis for how we experience that stage of sleep.

- We dream differently during REM sleep than during non-REM sleep.

- Three theories have been proposed to explain why sleeping is beneficial.

- Five disorders affect the experience of sleeping.

3.3 What Is an Altered State of Consciousness?

📖 LEARNING GOALS	✏️ READING ACTIVITIES
a. Remember the key terms about altered states of consciousness.	List all of the boldface words and write down their definitions.
b. Apply altered states of consciousness to your life.	Provide two examples of variations in the quality, or clarity, of your conscious experiences.
c. Understand how hypnosis affects consciousness.	Summarize the two theories of how hypnosis may, or may not, alter awareness.
d. Understand how meditation and flow may alter consciousness.	Describe in your own words the ways that meditation and flow affect awareness.

We can describe consciousness by noting the level, or amount, of consciousness that we have at any one moment. But we can also describe a state of consciousness. This state is not determined by the level of consciousness—by whether a person is conscious or unconscious. It is determined by the *quality* of consciousness. In other words, how clearly do we experience the external world? How clearly do we experience the internal world, and how organized are our thoughts? An altered state of consciousness occurs when the external world seems much more or less clear to us than usual, and when our thoughts are much more or less organized than usual.

There Are Different Altered States of Consciousness

When you hear the phrase *altered consciousness*, your first thought might be of intense meditation, drug-induced hallucinations, or something out of zombie movies. And it is true that a person's state of consciousness, or quality of awareness, can be altered in extreme ways. Indeed, the opener for this chapter describes two people who were in comas. Jan Grzebski was in a minimally conscious state. Terri Schiavo was in a persistent vegetative state.

Because overt actions by a person in a minimally conscious state and a person in a persistent vegetative state may look similar, behavior cannot reveal what altered state a person is experiencing. However, brain imaging may be useful for identifying the extent of a patient's brain injury and likelihood of recovery, and it may provide insight into their consciousness during the coma. For example, one 23-year-old woman who was in a coma could not give any outward signs of awareness. But researchers wondered whether she was able to understand language and respond to the experimenters' requests. When she was asked to imagine playing tennis or walking through her house (Owen et al., 2006), the woman's pattern of brain activity became quite similar to the patterns of control participants who also imagined playing tennis or walking through a house (**Figure 3.15**).

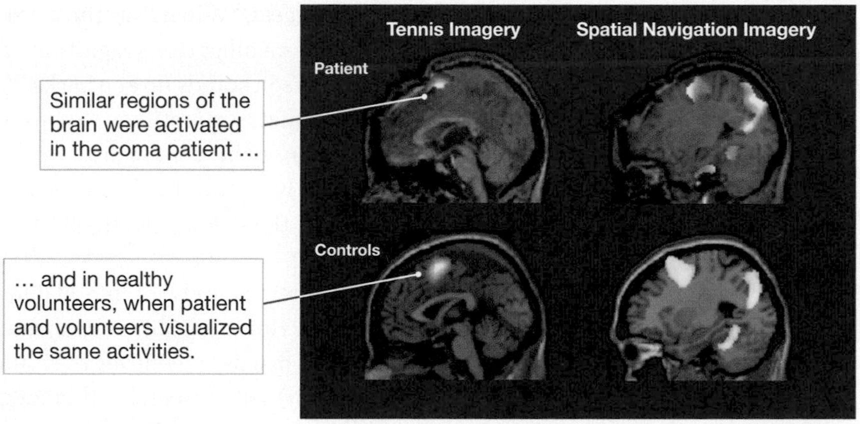

We have just been looking at cases of extremely altered states. Less dramatic changes occur in consciousness naturally over the course of the day. These natural changes are often caused by what is happening in the environment or what we are doing. For instance, learning to play a piece on the piano might produce intense concentration. By contrast, watching television might lead to "zoning out," with little awareness beyond what is on the screen. In this section, we consider three ways a person can purposely reach an altered state of consciousness: hypnosis, meditation, and immersion in an action.

FIGURE 3.15

In a Coma but Conscious
The brain images on the top are from the patient, a young woman in a coma who showed no visible signs of conscious awareness. The images on the bottom are a composite from the control group, which consisted of healthy volunteers. Both the patient and the control group were told to visualize playing tennis and walking around. Right after the directions were given, the neural activity in the patient's brain appeared similar to the neural activity in the control group's brains.

Hypnosis Can Produce Changes in Perception, Memory, and Action

In June 2012, Maxime Nadeau, a young hypnotist-in-training, hypnotized a group of 13- and 14-year-old girls during a performance at a school in Quebec, Canada. But things didn't go exactly as planned: Nadeau was unable to bring several of the girls out of hypnosis. He had to call on his mentor, Richard Whitbread, to break the spell. Whitbread did so and later told the Canadian Broadcasting Company: "There were a couple of students who had their heads lying on the table, and there were [others] who, you could tell, were in trance. . . . The eyes were open and there was nobody home." What does it mean that "nobody was home"? Were the girls really in a trance? Can a hypnotist produce a real change in mental state, or is hypnosis just good theater? What exactly is hypnosis?

FIGURE 3.16
Hypnotized?
Are hypnotized people in an altered state of consciousness, or are they just playing a part suggested to them by the hypnotist?

POSTHYPNOTIC SUGGESTION In **hypnosis,** a person, responding to suggestions, experiences changes in memory, perception, and/or voluntary action (Kihlstrom, 1985; Kihlstrom & Eich, 1994). Psychologists generally agree that hypnosis affects some people, but they do not agree on whether hypnotists can produce a genuinely altered state of consciousness (Jamieson, 2007).

A hypnotist may work with one or more people at a time. To begin the hypnosis, the hypnotist makes a series of suggestions such as, "You are becoming sleepy.... Your eyelids are drooping.... Your arms and legs feel very heavy." As the listener falls more deeply into the hypnotic state, the hypnotist makes more suggestions. "You cannot move your right arm," "You feel warm," and so on. If everything goes according to plan, the listener follows all the suggestions as though they are true (**Figure 3.16**).

Sometimes the hypnotist suggests that, after the hypnosis session, the listener will experience some change. Such a posthypnotic suggestion is usually accompanied by the instruction to not remember the suggestion. For example, a hypnotist might suggest, "When I say the word *dog*, you will stand up and bark like a dog. You will not remember this suggestion." And, much to the delight of the audience, later on the person stands up and barks like a dog.

Therapists sometimes hypnotize patients and give them *posthypnotic suggestions* to help them lose weight or quit smoking. But evidence suggests that hypnosis has quite modest effects on these behaviors. There is clear evidence, however, that some posthypnotic suggestions can at least subtly influence behaviors.

Consider a study of moral judgment conducted by Thalia Wheatley and Jonathan Haidt (2005). Participants received a posthypnotic suggestion to feel a pang of disgust whenever they read a neutral, or non-offensive, word (e.g., the word *often*). After receiving this suggestion, participants made more-severe moral judgments when reading stories that included the word *often*, even when the stories were not immoral. Like people in split-brain studies, the participants were surprised by their reactions and sometimes made up justifications for their harsh ratings, such as saying that the lead character seemed "up to something." This result suggests that the left hemisphere interpreter might be involved in people's understanding their own behavior when that behavior results from posthypnotic suggestion or other unconscious influences.

To the extent that hypnosis works, it relies more on the person being hypnotized than on the skill of the hypnotist. Indeed, tests for hypnotic suggestibility show that hypnosis works primarily for people who are highly suggestible (Kallio & Revonsuo, 2003). Researchers cannot precisely identify the personality characteristics of people who can or cannot be hypnotized, but suggestibility is related to getting absorbed in activities easily, not being distracted easily, and having a rich imagination (Balthazard & Woody, 1992; Crawford, Corby, & Kopell, 1996; Silva & Kirsch, 1992). Furthermore, a person who dislikes the idea of being hypnotized or finds it frightening would probably not be hypnotized easily. To be hypnotized, a person must go along with the hypnotist's suggestions willingly. There is no reliable evidence that people will do things under hypnosis that they would normally object to.

TWO THEORIES OF HYPNOSIS Some psychologists believe that a person under hypnosis essentially plays the role of a hypnotized person. The person is not faking, but acts the part as if in a play, willing to perform actions called for by the "director," the hypnotist. According to this **sociocognitive theory of hypnosis,** hypnotized people behave as they expect hypnotized people to behave, even if those expectations are faulty (Kirsch & Lynn, 1995; Spanos & Coe, 1992).

hypnosis
A social interaction during which a person, responding to suggestions, experiences changes in memory, perception, and/or voluntary action.

sociocognitive theory of hypnosis
Hypnotized people are not in an altered state, but they behave in a way that is expected in that situation.

An alternative theory, the **dissociation theory of hypnosis,** acknowledges the importance of social context, but views hypnosis as a truly altered state. According to this theory, hypnosis is a trancelike state in which conscious awareness is separated, or dissociated, from other aspects of consciousness (Gruzelier, 2000). In support of this theory, many brain imaging studies have found alterations in the brain activity of a hypnotized person (Rainville, Hofbauer, Bushnell, Duncan, & Price, 2002). In one of the earliest such studies, Stephen Kosslyn and colleagues (2000) demonstrated that when hypnotized participants were asked to imagine black-and-white objects as having color, they showed activity in visual cortex regions involved in color perception. Hypnotized participants asked to drain color from colored images showed diminished activity in those same brain regions. This activity pattern did not occur when participants were not hypnotized. These results indicate that hypnotic suggestion may indeed change brain function. And if brain function is changed during hypnosis, then maybe hypnosis really does alter consciousness. After all, it seems unlikely that a person could alter his brain activity to please a hypnotist, even if that hypnotist is a psychological researcher.

HYPNOSIS FOR PAIN One of the best supported uses of hypnosis is *hypnotic analgesia,* a form of pain reduction. Laboratory research has demonstrated that this technique works reliably (Hilgard & Hilgard, 1975; Nash & Barnier, 2008). For instance, a woman who plunges her arm into extremely cold water will feel great pain, and the pain will intensify over time. On average, a person can keep the arm in the water for only about 30 seconds, but a person experiencing hypnotic analgesia can hold out longer. As you might expect, people high in suggestibility who experience hypnotic analgesia can tolerate the cold water the longest (Montgomery, DuHamel, & Redd, 2000).

There is considerable evidence from clinical settings that hypnosis is effective in dealing with acute pain (e.g., during surgery and dental work) and chronic pain (e.g., from arthritis, cancer, or diabetes; Patterson & Jensen, 2003). A patient can also be taught self-hypnosis to improve recovery from surgery.

Hypnotic analgesia may work by changing the patient's interpretation of pain rather than by diminishing pain. That is, the patient feels the sensations associated with pain, but feels detached from those sensations (Price, Harkins, & Baker, 1987). An imaging study confirmed this pattern by showing that although hypnosis does not affect the sensory processing of pain, it reduces brain activity in regions that process the emotional aspects of pain (Rainville, Duncan, Price, Carrier, & Bushnell, 1997).

Findings such as these provide considerable support for the dissociation theory of hypnosis. It seems unlikely that either expectations about hypnosis or social pressure to not feel pain could explain how people experiencing hypnotic analgesia are able to undergo painful surgery and not feel it. Nor is it likely that expectations or social pressure could result in the altered brain activity seen during hypnotic analgesia.

Meditation Affects Cognitive Processing and Brain Function

With a growing awareness of different cultural and religious practices and alternative approaches to medicine, people in the West have become more interested in examining Eastern techniques of altering consciousness, including **meditation (Figure 3.17)**. Different forms of meditation are central to many Eastern religions, including Hinduism, Buddhism, and Sikhism. But the common

dissociation theory of hypnosis
Hypnotized people are in an altered state where their awareness is separated from other aspects of consciousness.

meditation
A practice in which intense contemplation leads to a deep sense of calmness that has been described as an altered state of consciousness.

FIGURE 3.17
Meditation
When meditating, people try to reach an altered state of consciousness by relaxing deeply.

thread among all of these religions is that through intense contemplation, the meditator develops a deep sense of tranquility that has been described as an altered state of consciousness.

There are three basic forms of meditation. In *concentrative meditation,* you focus your attention on one thing, such as your breathing pattern, a mental image, or a specific phrase (sometimes called a mantra). In *mindfulness meditation,* you let your thoughts flow freely, paying attention to them but not examining their meaning or reacting to them in any way.

Religious forms of meditation are meant to bring spiritual enlightenment. Most forms of meditation popular in the West are not necessarily religious. They are meant primarily to expand the mind, bring about feelings of inner peace, and help people deal with the tensions and stresses in their lives.

The meditation practice perhaps best known in the West is *transcendental meditation (TM).* This form involves meditating with great concentration for 20 minutes twice a day. In a 2006 study, a large number of heart patients were randomly assigned to TM or an educational program. After 16 weeks, the patients practicing TM improved more than the control group on a number of health measures, such as blood pressure, blood lipids, and insulin resistance (Paul-Labrador et al., 2006). Unfortunately, this study does not show which aspects of TM produced the health benefits. Was it simply relaxing, or was it an altered state of consciousness?

Psychologists also study how meditation affects cognitive processing and brain function (Cahn & Polich, 2006). One such study found that subjects who completed meditation training showed greater stress reduction and more significant improvement in attention than a group that received simple relaxation training (Tang et al., 2007).

Some researchers argue that long-term meditation brings about structural changes in the brain that help maintain brain function over the life span. For instance, although the volume of gray matter typically diminishes with age, one study found that this volume did not diminish in older adults who practiced Zen meditation (Pagnoni & Cekic, 2007). This finding suggests that Zen meditation might help preserve cognitive functioning as people age. However, remember from Chapter 1 that correlation does not prove causation. People who meditate may differ substantially from people who do not, especially regarding lifestyle choices such as diet and taking care of their health. Careful empirical research should contribute significantly to our understanding of meditation's effects.

Flow Activities Can Lead to Altered Consciousness

Hypnosis and meditation are activities specifically intended to alter a person's state of consciousness. But participation in an intense sport or an intense religious ceremony can also lead to altered consciousness.

Here's a situation you've likely heard about or even experienced yourself: A marathon runner goes from feeling pain and fatigue to being euphoric and feeling a glorious release of energy. Commonly known as runner's high, this state is partially mediated by physiological processes (especially endorphin release; see Chapter 2). It also occurs due to a shift in the state of consciousness. Religious ceremonies can create similar alterations of consciousness. Indeed, such rituals often involve chanting, dancing, or other behaviors as a way for people to lose themselves in religious ecstasy. Like meditation, religious ecstasy directs attention away from the self and allows the practitioners to focus on their spiritual awareness (**Figure 3.18**).

FIGURE 3.18

Religious Ecstasy

This woman appears to be overcome with religious ecstasy during a ceremony in an African-Christian church in Nigeria. In such cases, people experience altered consciousness when their attention is directed away from themselves and onto spiritual awareness.

One psychological theory about such peak experiences is based on the concept of **flow,** "a particular kind of experience that is so engrossing and enjoyable [that it is] worth doing for its own sake even though it may have no consequence outside itself" (Csikszentmihalyi, 1999, p. 824). Flow is a state of altered consciousness in that you lose track of time, forget about your problems, and fail to notice other things going on (Csikszentmihalyi, 1990). Flow experiences have been reported during many activities, including playing music (O'Neil, 1999) or a moderately challenging version of the computer game *Tetris* (Keller & Bless, 2008), participating in sports (Jackson, Thomas, Marsh, & Smethurst, 2001), and simply doing satisfying jobs (Demerouti, 2006). In the view of the psychologist Mihaly Csikszentmihalyi (1999), flow experiences bring personal fulfillment and make life worth living.

ESCAPING THE SELF Our conscious thoughts can be dominated by worries, frustrations, and feelings of personal failure. Sometimes people get tired of dealing with life's problems and try to make themselves feel better through escapist pursuits. Potential flow activities such as sports or work may help people escape thinking about their problems, but people engage in such activities mainly to feel fulfilled. The difference is between escaping and engaging. Sometimes people choose to escape the self rather than engage with life: To forget their troubles, they drink alcohol, take drugs, play video games, watch television, surf the Web, text, and so on. The selective appeal of escapist entertainment is that it distracts people from reflecting on their problems or their failures, thereby helping them avoid feeling bad about themselves.

Some escapist activities—such as running or reading—tend to have positive effects, some tend to be relatively harmless distractions, and some tend to come at great personal expense. For example, people obsessively playing online games such as *World of Warcraft* have lost their jobs and even their marriages (**Figure 3.19**). They have even taken the lives of their offspring: In South Korea in 2010, Kim Jae-beom and his common-law wife, Kim Yun-jeong, neglected their 3-month-old daughter to the point that she died of starvation. The couple reportedly spent every night raising a virtual daughter as part of a role-playing game they engaged in at an Internet café. Some ways of escaping the self can also be associated with self-destructive behaviors, such as binge eating, unsafe sex, and, at the extreme, suicide. According to the social psychologist Roy Baumeister (1991), people engage in such behaviors because they want to escape their problems by reducing self-awareness. The state of being in lowered self-awareness may reduce long-term planning, reduce meaningful thinking, and help bring about uninhibited actions. The next section of this chapter looks at a common way people try to escape their problems—namely, using drugs or alcohol to physiologically alter consciousness.

flow
A highly focused, altered state of consciousness, when awareness of self and time diminishes due to being completely engrossed in an enjoyable activity.

FIGURE 3.19
Escapist Entertainment
Simple entertainment can shift toward obsession when a person continually tries to escape from his problems.

 3.3 CHECKPOINT: What Is an Altered State of Consciousness?

- Normally, our state of consciousness allows us to experience the external world and our thoughts clearly. Altered consciousness makes the outer world more or less vivid and our thoughts more or less organized.

- Patterns of brain activity suggest that people who have been hypnotized experience a shift in consciousness and are not simply faking it.

- Altered states of consciousness may be achieved through three forms of meditation.

- In cases of extreme physical exertion or profound religious experiences, people can experience a type of altered consciousness called a flow state.

3.4 How Do Drugs Alter Consciousness?

Throughout history and across all cultures, people have discovered that ingesting certain substances can alter their mental states. Some of those altered states can be similar to the flow experience we described earlier. Others can be very pleasant for a brief period. However, some of those mental states, especially over the long term, can have negative consequences, including injury or death. According to the United Nations Office on Drugs and Crime (2009), upward of 250 million people around the globe use illicit drugs each year. Here we look at the effects of drug use from the perspective of psychology.

People Use—and Abuse—Many Psychoactive Drugs

Drugs are a mixed blessing. If they are the right ones, taken under the right circumstances, they can provide relief from severe pain or a moderate headache. They can help people suffering from depression lead more satisfying lives. They can help children who have attention-deficit/hyperactivity disorder settle down and learn better. But many of these same drugs can be used for "recreational" purposes: to alter physical sensations, consciousness, thoughts, moods, and behaviors in ways that users believe are desirable. This recreational use can sometimes have negative consequences.

Psychoactive drugs are mind-altering substances that change the brain's neurochemistry by activating neurotransmitter systems. The effects of a particular drug depend on which neurotransmitter systems it activates. Drugs also differ in the effects they have on the user. **Stimulants** are drugs that increase behavior and mental activity. By contrast, **depressants** decrease behavior and mental activity. **Hallucinogenics** are drugs that change the subjective experiences of perception, thought, and emotion. In this section, we consider a few common psychoactive drugs. Some of these drugs have legitimate medical uses, but all of them are commonly abused outside of treatment.

STIMULANTS Cocaine and amphetamines are drugs that act as stimulants. So are caffeine and nicotine. Stimulants activate the sympathetic nervous system, increasing heart rate and blood pressure. They improve mood, but they also make people become restless, and they disrupt sleep. Stimulants generally cause these effects by allowing the neurotransmitter dopamine (see Chapter 2) to remain in the synapse between neurons longer, which prolongs the impact of dopamine. However, sometimes stimulants also increase the release of dopamine by neurons (Fibiger,

stimulants
Psychoactive drugs that increase both mental processes and physical activity.

depressants
Psychoactive drugs that decrease both mental processes and physical activity.

hallucinogenics
Psychoactive drugs that affect perceptual experiences and evoke sensory images even without sensory input.

1993). Dopamine seems to be involved in drug use in two ways. First, the increased dopamine is associated with greater reward, or increased liking (Volkow, Wang, & Baler, 2011). Second, the increased dopamine leads to a greater desire to take a drug, even if that drug does not produce pleasure. Thus sometimes an addict *wants* a drug even if she does not *like* the effects of the drug (Kringelbach & Berridge, 2009). Available evidence suggests that dopamine is particularly important for the wanting aspect of addiction.

Cocaine is an example of a stimulant. It is derived from the leaves of the coca bush, which grows primarily in South America. Cocaine has a long history of legal use in America. John Pemberton, a pharmacist from Georgia, was impressed with cocaine's effects. In 1886, he added the drug to soda water for easy ingestion, creating Coca-Cola (**Figure 3.20**). In 1906, the U.S. government outlawed cocaine, so it was removed from the drink. To this day, coca leaves are still used in the making of Coke, but the active ingredient has been removed. Illegal use of cocaine occurs when the drug is inhaled (snorted) as a powder or smoked in the form of crack cocaine. Users experience a wave of confidence and feel good, alert, energetic, sociable, and wide awake. Cocaine produces its stimulating effects by increasing the concentration of dopamine in the neural synapse. These short-term effects are especially intense for crack cocaine users. But habitual use of cocaine in large quantities can lead to paranoia, psychotic behavior, and violence (Ottieger, Tressel, Inciardi, & Rosales, 1992).

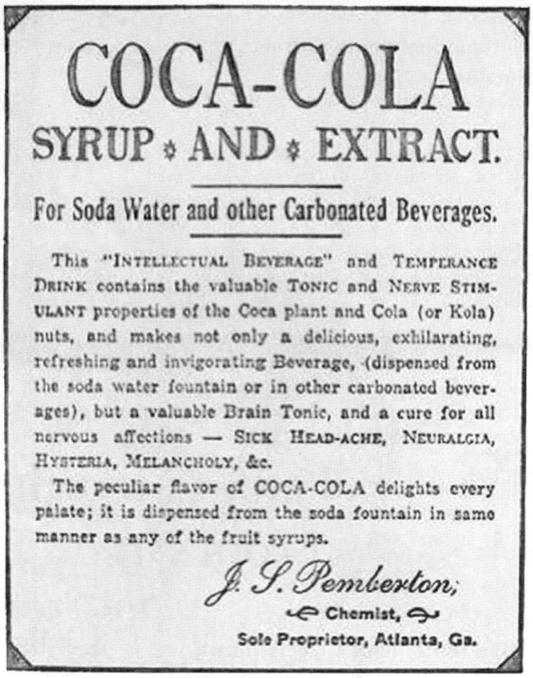

Methamphetamine (meth) is also a stimulant. Meth is the world's second most commonly used illicit drug, after marijuana (Barr et al., 2006). However, the use of meth may be declining (Gonzales, Mooney, & Rawson, 2010). This drug was first developed in the early twentieth century as a nasal decongestant, but its recreational use became popular in the 1980s. The National Institute of Drug Abuse (2006) estimates that around 4 percent of the U.S. population has tried methamphetamine. One factor that has encouraged use of this drug and may explain its popularity is how easy it is to make using common over-the-counter drugs and simple lab methods. By blocking the reuptake of dopamine and increasing its release, methamphetamine yields much higher levels of dopamine in the synapse. Methamphetamine stays in the body and brain much longer than, say, cocaine, so its effects are prolonged. Over time, methamphetamine damages various brain structures, including the frontal lobes (**Figure 3.21**). The drug's effects on the temporal lobes and the limbic system may explain the harm done to memory and emotion in long-term users (Kim et al., 2006; Thompson et al., 2004). Methamphetamine also causes considerable damage to the rest of the body (**Figure 3.22**).

DRUGS WITH HALLUCINOGENIC EFFECTS Several drugs have hallucinogenic effects that alter sensation and perception. These drugs include *MDMA* and marijuana. MDMA (ecstasy) has become popular since the 1990s. It produces an energizing effect similar to that of stimulants, but it also causes slight hallucinations, so it has properties of both classes of drugs. The drug first became popular among young adults in nightclubs and at all-night parties known as raves. According to the National Institute of Drug Abuse (2010), MDMA use by high school students increased from 3.7 percent to 4.7 percent between 2009 and 2010. MDMA is associated with less dopamine release and more serotonin release than methamphetamines. The serotonin release may explain ecstasy's hallucinogenic properties. Although many users believe it to be relatively safe, researchers have documented a number of impairments from

FIGURE 3.20

Early Coke Ad

This advertisement's claim that Coca-Cola is "a valuable Brain Tonic" may have been made because the company included cocaine in the drink before 1906.

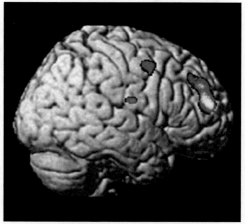

FIGURE 3.21

Methamphetamine's Effects on the Brain

This image is a combination of the brain scans from 29 methamphetamine addicts. The red and yellow areas represent the brain damage that typically occurs in the frontal cortex because of methamphetamine abuse (Kim et al., 2006). Such damage may explain the cognitive problems that occur with methamphetamine use.

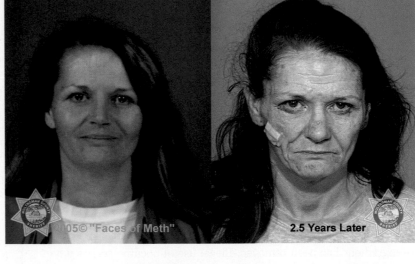

2005© "Faces of Meth" 2.5 Years Later

(a)

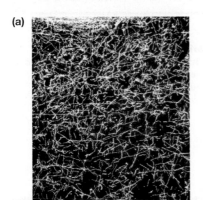

(b)

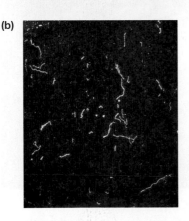

FIGURE 3.23

MDMA's Effects on the Brain
(a) This image shows serotonin nerve fibers in the cortex of a normal monkey.
(b) This image shows the same brain area of a monkey that received multiple doses of MDMA (ecstasy). Eighteen months after the monkey received the MDMA, the monkey's serotonin nerve fibers (white) remain drastically reduced.

long-term ecstasy use, especially memory problems and a diminished ability to perform complex tasks (Kalechstein, De La Garza, Mahoney, Fantegrossi, & Newton, 2007). Because ecstasy also depletes serotonin, users often feel depressed when the drug's rewarding properties wear off (Fischer, Hatzidimitriou, Wlos, Katz, & Ricaurte, 1995; **Figure 3.23**).

Marijuana consists of the dried leaves and flower buds of one type of cannabis plant. This is the most widely used illicit drug in the world. Many drugs can easily be categorized as a stimulant, a depressant, or a hallucinogen, but marijuana has the effects of all three classes of drugs. The psychoactive ingredient in marijuana is THC, or tetrahydrocannabinol. This chemical produces a relaxed mental state, an uplifted or contented mood, and some perceptual and cognitive distortions. Marijuana users report that THC makes perceptions more vivid, and some say it especially affects taste. However, most first-time marijuana users do not experience the "high" obtained by more experienced users. Novice smokers might use inefficient techniques, they might have trouble inhaling, or both. Users apparently must learn how to appreciate the drug's effects (Kuhn, Swartzwelder, & Wilson, 2003). In this way, marijuana differs from most other drugs. Generally, the first time someone uses a drug other than marijuana, the effects are very strong, and subsequent uses lead to tolerance, in which a person has to use more of the drug to get the same effect.

Marijuana is also used for its medicinal properties. For instance, cancer patients undergoing chemotherapy report that marijuana is effective for overcoming nausea. Nearly 1 in 4 AIDS patients reports using marijuana to relieve nausea and pain (Prentiss, Power, Balmas, Tzuang, & Israelski, 2004). The medical use of marijuana is legal in many countries and American states. Nevertheless, this practice is controversial due to the possibility that chronic use can cause health problems or lead to abuse of the drug.

DEPRESSANTS The most commonly used depressant drug is alcohol. *Opiates* are another type of depressant, and these include heroin, morphine, and codeine. These drugs provide enormous reward value, producing feelings of relaxation, insensitivity to pain, and euphoria. Heroin provides a rush of intense pleasure that most addicts describe as similar to orgasm. The rush evolves into a pleasant, relaxed stupor. Heroin and morphine are highly addictive, perhaps because they have dual physical effects: They increase pleasure by binding with opiate receptors and increase wanting of the drug by activating dopamine receptors (Kuhn et al., 2003).

Opiates have been used to relieve pain for hundreds of years. Indeed, before the twentieth century, heroin was widely available without a prescription and was marketed by Bayer, the aspirin company (**Figure 3.24**). The benefits of short-term opiate use to relieve severe pain seem clear. But long-term opiate use to relieve chronic pain is much more likely to lead to abuse or addiction than is short-term use (Ballantyne & LaForge, 2007). Moreover, long-term use of opiates is associated with a number of neurological and cognitive deficits, such as attention and memory problems (Gruber, Silveri, & Yurgelun-Todd, 2007). Thus clinicians need to be cautious in prescribing opiates, such as Vicodin, especially when the drugs will be used for long periods.

Alcohol Is the Most Widely Abused Drug

Perhaps you know someone who drank a lot of alcohol, experienced a blackout, and can't remember the details. Alcohol is a depressant that, like other addictive drugs, may offer its rewards by activating dopamine receptors. But it also interferes with the neurochemical processes involved in memory, and memory loss can follow excessive alcohol intake. Heavy long-term alcohol intake can cause extensive brain damage. Korsakoff's syndrome, a disorder sometimes caused by alcoholism, is characterized by both severe memory loss and intellectual deterioration.

Many societies have a love/hate relationship with alcohol. On the one hand, moderate drinking is an accepted part of social interaction and may even be good for health. On the other hand, alcohol is a major contributor to many societal problems, such as spousal abuse and other forms of violence. Although the percentage of traffic fatalities due to alcohol is dropping, alcohol is a factor in more than one-third of fatal accidents (Mayhew, Brown, & Simpson, 2002). One study found that approximately one-third of college students reported having had sex during a drinking binge, and the heaviest drinkers were likely to have had sex with a new or casual partner (Leigh & Schafer, 1993), thus increasing their risk for exposure to sexually transmitted diseases. The overall cost of problem drinking in the United States—including lost productivity due to employee absence, health care expenses, and so on—is estimated to be more than $100 billion each year.

GENDER DIFFERENCES IN ALCOHOL CONSUMPTION ACROSS CULTURES
The World Health Organization conducts a massive, ongoing international study of gender-related and culture-related differences in alcohol consumption (Obot & Room, 2005). The study's main premise is that to understand alcohol consumption worldwide, we need to study the ways alcohol is used, by men and by women, across cultural and social contexts. The authors call the gap between men and women in alcohol consumption "one of the few universal gender differences in human social behavior" (Wilsnack, Wilsnack, & Obot, 2005, p. 1).

As you might suspect, in every region of the world, men drink a lot more than women across a wide variety of measures (e.g., drinking versus abstinence, heavy drinking versus occasional drinking, alcohol-related disorders). Men are twice as likely to report binge drinking (having five or more drinks in one evening), chronic drinking, and recent alcohol intoxication. Gender gaps in binge drinking may be smaller among university students, however.

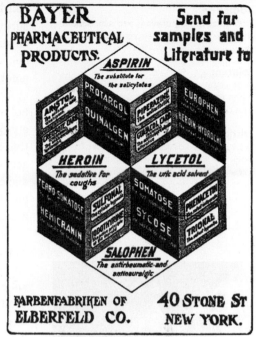

FIGURE 3.24
Early Heroin Ad
Before 1904, Bayer advertised heroin as "the sedative for coughs."

addiction
Compulsive drug craving and use, despite the negative consequences of using the drug.

tolerance
A physical effect of addiction that occurs when a person needs to take larger doses of a drug to experience its effect.

withdrawal
A physical and psychological effect of addiction that occurs when a person experiences anxiety, tension, and cravings after discontinuing use of an addictive drug.

(a)

(b)

FIGURE 3.25

Physical Dependence Versus Psychological Dependence
In addiction, both types of dependence can force people to go to extremes. **(a)** In physical dependence, a person develops a tolerance to the effects of a drug. As a result, the person must consume more of the drug to prevent the adverse physical side effects of withdrawal. Someone addicted to alcohol might even abuse products that contain alcohol, such as cough syrup. **(b)** Casinos encourage a psychological dependence on gambling. People suffering from this dependence spend increasing amounts of time and money gambling, to the point where their lives are seriously disrupted.

EXPECTATIONS ABOUT ALCOHOL Alan Marlatt is a leading researcher on substance abuse. Marlatt (1999) has noted that in many cultures, people view alcohol as the "magic elixir," capable of increasing social skills, sexual pleasure, confidence, and power. They anticipate that alcohol will have positive effects on their emotions and behavior. For example, people tend to think that alcohol reduces anxiety, so both light and heavy drinkers turn to alcohol after a difficult day. Alcohol *can* interfere with the way the brain processes suggestions of threats, so anxiety-provoking events may be less troubling when people are intoxicated. However, this effect occurs only if people drink *before* the anxiety-provoking events. In fact, according to the research, drinking after a hard day can increase people's focus on and obsession with their problems (Sayette, 1993). What's more, although moderate doses of alcohol are associated with more-positive moods, larger doses are associated with more-negative moods.

Expectations about alcohol's effects are learned very early in life, through observation. Children may see that people who drink seem to have a lot of fun and that drinking is an important part of many celebrations. Teenagers may view drinkers as sociable and grown up, two things they desperately want to be. Studies have shown that children who have very positive expectations about alcohol are more likely to start drinking and become heavy drinkers than children who do not share those expectations (Leigh & Stacy, 2004).

Addiction Has Physical and Psychological Aspects

Addiction is behavior that remains compulsive despite its negative consequences. Addiction to drugs and alcohol has both physical and psychological factors. In physical dependence, a user develops **tolerance** to the substance, needing to consume more to achieve the same subjective effect (**Figure 3.25a**). If the user fails to ingest the substance, he will experience symptoms of **withdrawal,** a physical and psychological state characterized by feelings of anxiety, tension, and cravings for the addictive substance.

The physical symptoms of withdrawal vary widely from drug to drug and from individual to individual. The symptoms commonly include nausea, chills, body aches, and tremors. A person can be psychologically dependent, however, without showing tolerance or withdrawal. Though we focus here on addiction to substances that alter consciousness, people can also become psychologically dependent on behaviors, such as shopping or gambling (**Figure 3.25b**).

How do people become addicted? One central factor appears to be dopamine activity in the limbic system, which underlies the rewarding properties of taking drugs (Baler & Volkow, 2006). As a powerful reinforcer, any behavior that leads to increased dopamine activity is likely to be repeated. Activating dopamine receptors leads to both pleasure and the desire to take more of the drug. It is possible that genes predispose some people to be more responsive to the reinforcing properties of drugs, making them more vulnerable to addiction.

Only about 5 percent to 10 percent of people who use drugs become addicted. Indeed, more than 90 million Americans have experimented with illicit drugs, yet most of them use drugs only occasionally or try them for a while and then stop. Further, Jonathan Shedler and Jack Block (1990) found that people who had experimented with drugs as adolescents were better adjusted in adulthood than both people who had never tried them and people who were heavy users. This finding does not suggest, however, that everyone should try drugs or that parents should encourage drug experimentation. We cannot know in advance how an individual will react to a drug.

Though we can't predict who will become addicted, we can identify some adolescents who are especially likely to experiment with illegal drugs and to abuse alcohol. Children who are attracted to novelty and risk taking and have poor relationships with their parents are more likely to associate with trouble-making peers and to use alcohol, tobacco, and drugs (Wills, DuHamel, & Vaccaro, 1995). It is also possible that an inherited predisposition to sensation seeking may predict behaviors, such as affiliating with drug users, that increase the possibility of substance abuse.

Indeed, there is some evidence for genetic components of addiction, especially alcoholism. There is little direct evidence, however, for a single "alcoholism" or "addiction" gene. Instead, people inherit a cluster of characteristics. Inherited factors such as risk-taking and impulsivity, a reduced concern about personal harm, or a predisposition to finding chemical substances pleasurable may make some people more likely to explore drugs and enjoy them.

Does the family or social environment determine alcohol and drug use? Social learning theorists have emphasized the roles of parents, the mass media, and peers, including self-identification with high-risk groups (e.g., "stoners" or "druggies"). Teenagers want to fit in somewhere, even with groups that society perceives as deviant. Children imitate the behavior of role models, especially those they admire or identify with. Consider children who, during their preschool and elementary school years, have seen their parents drinking alcohol routinely. These children tend to have positive attitudes about alcohol and to begin drinking early (Sher, Grekin, & Williams, 2005).

3.4 CHECKPOINT: How Do Drugs Alter Consciousness?

- People can physically alter their consciousness by using drugs that change the way they think, feel, and act.

- Commonly used psychoactive drugs—such as cocaine, amphetamines, MDMA, opiates, and alcohol—produce psychological and behavioral effects by affecting neurotransmitter systems.

- Alcohol is the most widely abused drug. There are pronounced gender differences in alcohol use across all societies.

- Excessive drug use can lead to addiction. Addiction is characterized by physical dependence, with tolerance and withdrawal, and by psychological dependence.

- Addiction is influenced by personality factors, such as sensation seeking. The environment, or the context in which drug use occurs, also influences addiction.

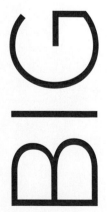

3.1
What Does It Mean to Be Conscious?

a. Remember the key terms about consciousness.

b. Apply the two levels of consciousness.

c. Analyze the impact of unconscious processing.

d. Apply the global workspace model to your life.

e. Understand consciousness in a person with a split brain.

3.2
How Does Sleep Affect Consciousness?

a. Remember the key terms about sleep.

b. Analyze how brain activity reveals four stages of sleep.

c. Apply the three reasons people need to sleep.

d. Understand the five common sleep disorders.

3.3
What Is an Altered State of Consciousness?

a. Remember the key terms about altered states of consciousness.

b. Apply altered states of consciousness to your life.

c. Understand how hypnosis affects consciousness.

d. Understand how meditation and flow may alter consciousness.

3.4
How Do Drugs Alter Consciousness?

a. Remember the key terms about drugs.

b. Apply the effects of the three classes of psychoactive drugs.

c. Understand how each drug within the three classes alters peoples' state of consciousness.

d. Analyze the two aspects of addiction: tolerance and withdrawal.

KEY TERMS

CHECKPOINT

consciousness
subliminal perception
global workspace model
split brain

- Consciousness is how the brain allows us to be aware of and experience the external world and our internal mental activity.

- There are two levels of consciousness, which vary in the amount of attention to and awareness of our experiences.

- Information that is processed subliminally—that is, without conscious awareness—can influence basic thinking and behavior for only short periods of time.

- Conscious experiences are a result of activity in five specific regions of the brain that cause us to be aware of specific types of information.

- People with split brains have a unique experience of consciousness: They are aware of only information presented to the one hemisphere that processes that information. And they can verbalize only information processed in the left hemisphere.

circadian rhythms
melatonin
slow-wave sleep
REM sleep
dreams
activation-synthesis theory
insomnia
sleep apnea
narcolepsy

- We experience changes in consciousness when we sleep as we become less aware of the external world, yet we are still able to respond when necessary.

- Sleep has four stages. Each stage is characterized by brain activity that is the basis for how we experience that stage of sleep.

- We dream differently during REM sleep than during non-REM sleep.

- Three theories have been proposed to explain why sleeping is beneficial.

- Disorders affect the experience of sleeping.

hypnosis
sociocognitive theory of
    hypnosis
dissociation theory of hypnosis
meditation
flow

- Normally, our state of consciousness allows us to experience the external world and our thoughts clearly. Altered consciousness makes the outer world more or less vivid and our thoughts more or less organized.

- Patterns of brain activity suggest that people who have been hypnotized experience a shift in consciousness and are not simply faking it.

- Altered states of consciousness may be achieved through three forms of meditation.

- In cases of extreme physical exertion or profound religious experiences, people can experience a type of altered consciousness called a flow state.

stimulants
depressants
hallucinogenics
addiction
tolerance
withdrawal

- People can physically alter their consciousness by using drugs that change the way they think, feel, and act.

- Commonly used psychoactive drugs—such as cocaine, amphetamines, MDMA, opiates, and alcohol—produce psychological and behavioral effects by affecting neurotransmitter systems.

- Alcohol is the most widely abused drug. There are pronounced gender differences in use across all societies.

- Excessive drug use can lead to addiction. Addiction is characterized by physical dependence, with tolerance and withdrawal, and by psychological dependence.

- Addiction is influenced by personality factors, such as sensation seeking. The environment, or the context in which drug use occurs, also influences addiction.

For a self-quiz on this chapter, go to the back of the book and find Appendix B: Quizzes.

4 Development Across the Life Span

WHO ARE YOU RIGHT NOW? Are you the same person you were at 13, and 8, and 3? Almost certainly the answer is no. As virtually all people do, you have changed in many ways over the years.

Now look at **Figure 4.1**. How old do you think the infant was? Her name was Brooke Greenberg, and in this photo she was 19 years old. She was being held by her younger sister, 16-year-old Carly. In 1993, Brooke was born prematurely. At first, she seemed to develop normally. But at about the age of 19 months, after various medical problems, Brooke stopped growing. Her brain also seemed to stop changing developmentally. In lots of ways, until her death in 2013, Brooke seemed to be "frozen" as a toddler.

BIG QUESTIONS

FIGURE 4.1

Brooke Greenberg: The Infant Who Didn't Change
Brooke Greenberg was 19 years old here and was being held by her younger sister. In most ways, Brooke looked and acted like a toddler. The fact that Brooke did not grow or change may provide insight into "normal" human development.

Brooke was happy and laughed a lot. She enjoyed music and shopping trips to the mall, but she refused to engage in activities she didn't like. At such times, Brooke's family thought of her as a typically rebellious teenager. However, she couldn't speak, so she expressed herself with sounds like those an infant would make. She couldn't walk, so she traveled in a stroller. She had the bone development of a 10-year-old, but she still had all of her baby teeth. She wore diapers. Her family took care of Brooke her entire life.

Brooke's stalled development in many, but not all, areas baffled doctors over the years. They named the unknown cause of Brooke's disjointed development *Syndrome X.* Her condition was extremely rare, but by working to understand why Brooke did not develop and age, scientists may have begun to better understand the changes that occur throughout all of our lives.

4.1 How Do We Develop in the Womb?

📖 **LEARNING GOALS**	✏️ **READING ACTIVITIES**	**LEARN**
a. Remember the key terms related to prenatal development.	List all of the boldface words and write down their definitions.	
b. Understand the three prenatal periods.	Summarize in your own words the physical changes that occur in each period.	
c. Apply information about teratogens and their effects during prenatal development.	Describe three hypothetical cases showing the effects of teratogens during prenatal development.	
d. Analyze how biology and environment affect prenatal development.	Organize a table showing how nature and nurture each affect prenatal development.	

developmental psychology
The scientific study of how humans change over the life span, from conception until death.

It may surprise you to learn that who you are right now has been partly determined by how you developed during the *prenatal period,* from the time of conception until birth. But it's true: Before each of us is born, we are influenced by nature (genetics and biology) and nurture (environment). **Developmental psychology** explores the changes that occur as we grow, starting in the prenatal period and continuing through the other stages of our lives. Developmental changes can be grouped in three domains: physical, socio-emotional, and cognitive (**Figure 4.2**). Let's look at these domains in more detail.

FIGURE 4.2

Interactions Between Three Developmental Domains and the Environmental Context
Humans develop physically, socially, emotionally, and cognitively. Change in each area affects, and is affected by, change in other areas.

Physical: growth of the body and changes in the brain, sensory and motor skills, and hormones

Cognitive: how our mental processes and abilities to think and communicate change over time

Socio-emotional: changes in how we understand ourselves, interact with others, and experience and regulate emotions

Prenatal Development Occurs in Three Phases

Think about starting with just two cells, and 9 months later ending up with a human being. It's a truly amazing process. From conception until birth, prenatal development occurs in three major periods. The **germinal period** begins when the sperm from the male unites with the egg from the female (**Figure 4.3a**). This union creates the zygote, the first cell of a new life. The zygote begins to divide rapidly

germinal period

The period in prenatal development from conception to two weeks after fertilization of the egg, when the zygote divides rapidly and implants in the uterine wall.

(a) (b) (c)

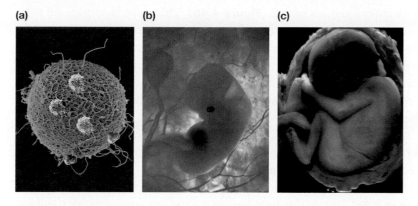

FIGURE 4.3

Development in the Womb

(a) In the germinal period, the union of egg and sperm forms a zygote that implants in the uterine wall within 2 weeks. **(b)** The embryonic period, from 2 weeks to 2 months, is when the organs develop in the embryo. **(c)** The fetal period, from 2 months until birth, is a time of tremendous physical growth and brain development that prepares the baby to survive outside the womb.

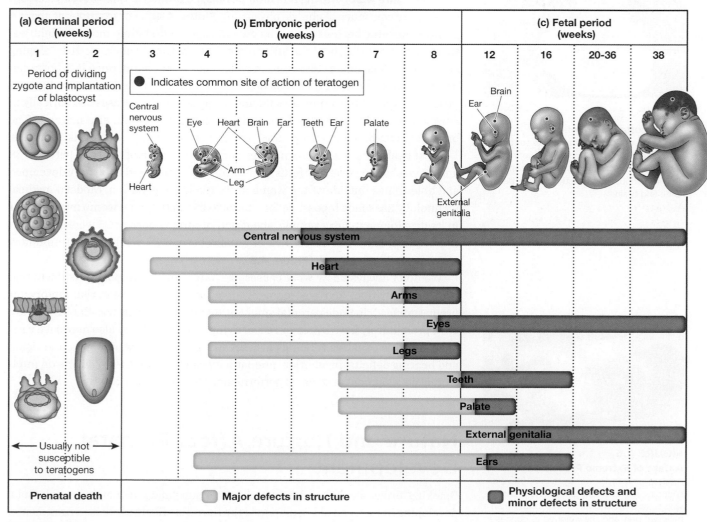

FIGURE 4.4

Bodily Changes in the Three Developmental Periods

embryonic period
The period in prenatal development from 2 to 8 weeks after conception, when the brain, spine, major organs, and bodily structures begin to form in the embryo.

fetal period
The period in prenatal development from 8 weeks after conception until birth, when the brain continues developing, bodily structures are refined, and the fetus grows in length and weight and accumulates fat in preparation for birth.

FIGURE 4.5

The Importance of Folic Acid
Nutritional deficiencies can cause serious birth defects. Early in pregnancy, eating dark leafy greens, such as spinach, can prevent serious malformations of the baby's spine and brain.

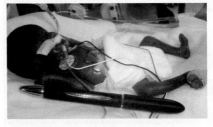

FIGURE 4.6

A Case of Extreme Prematurity
Amillia Sonja Taylor was born in 2006, after spending just 21 weeks and 6 days in the womb. At birth, she was a little longer than a ballpoint pen, and she weighed 10 ounces—less than the weight of a can of soda.

into 2 cells, then 4 cells, then 8 cells, and so on, becoming a ball of cells called a blastocyst (**Figure 4.4a**). A placenta begins to form to nourish and protect it. Just 7 or 8 days after fertilization, the blastocyst is implanted in the uterine wall and the next stage of development begins. If any abnormalities occur during this earliest stage of development, the result is usually a miscarriage before the woman even knows she is pregnant.

From about 2 weeks to 2 months, the developing human is known as an embryo (**Figure 4.3b**). The **embryonic period** is the most important time for physical development of the spinal cord, brain, and all internal organs, including the heart, lungs, liver, kidneys, and sex organs (**Figure 4.4b**). This stage is considered to be the critical time for organ formation. If development goes wrong, the organ(s) will develop improperly, and miscarriage or birth defects may result. For example, if the mother has not consumed enough of the nutrient folic acid during the first month of prenatal development, the embryo's spinal cord and brain may not develop properly. If the embryo then survives, the baby may be born with serious birth defects, such as spina bifida. For this reason, women who want to become pregnant are encouraged to eat foods such as spinach, broccoli, citrus fruits, beans, and avocado, which all contain good amounts of folic acid, or take prenatal vitamins containing folic acid (**Figure 4.5**).

From 2 months of prenatal development until birth, the growing human is called a fetus (**Figure 4.3c**). During this **fetal period,** no new structures develop, but the whole body continues to change physically (**Figure 4.4c**). For example, at about 4 months the fetus begins to move its own muscles; a first-time mother might feel these movements by about the fifth month. The eyes and eyelids finish developing at 6 months. The organs also finish developing, so the infant, once it is born, can breathe on its own and digest food taken by mouth. In the last 3 months of prenatal growth, the fetus accumulates fat under the skin and increases dramatically in length and weight. While the fetus is growing larger, its brain also matures. The brain begins to process sensory input and motor output, and basic thinking begins.

Most healthy full-term pregnancies end with the birth of the baby between 38 and 42 weeks. However, the fetus is traditionally considered to be fully developed and able to live outside of the womb at 28 weeks of gestation. Modern medical technology has made it possible for a fetus to live outside the womb much earlier in its development. For example, about half of infants born at 25 weeks of gestation survive, and up to 10 percent of fetuses born at 22 weeks of gestation now survive outside the womb (**Figure 4.6**).

We don't always know what causes premature birth, although it is likely that genetics, nutrition, and environment all play roles. The clear risk factors for premature birth include parental smoking, drinking, and drug use. Babies who are born prematurely have a greater risk of dying as infants. They also may have various disabilities, such as cerebral palsy, breathing and feeding problems, and vision and hearing deficits. In addition, prematurity can have long-term effects on intellectual development and school performance (Nomura et al., 2009).

Nature and Nurture Affect Prenatal Development

Smoking, drugs, alcohol, pollutants, and other substances can make us sick. But a developing human can also experience the harmful effects of such environmental factors. The same placenta that provides oxygen and nutrients to the baby helps protect it from harmful substances. Even so, certain environmental agents can pass through the placenta and sometimes have terrible consequences.

teratogens
Environmental agents that can harm prenatal development.

TERATOGENS Teratogens (from the Greek *tera,* which means "monster") are substances that cause birth defects. As shown in the Learning Tip on p. 118, there are several classes of teratogens, and the impact of any one depends on when exposure occurs during prenatal development and how long that exposure lasts. The physical effects of exposure to certain teratogens can be obvious at birth. However, some teratogens have effects that are not apparent until the child is much older, including disorders involving language, reasoning, attention, social behavior, and/or emotions. There are no standards about how much exposure to any teratogen is safe for normal physical, socio-emotional, and cognitive development. Even small exposure to teratogens can sometimes have terrible effects.

DRUGS AND ALCOHOL The use of recreational drugs—such as opiates, cocaine, or marijuana—during pregnancy can affect not only the mother, but also the developing human and its long-term development during childhood and beyond. Premature birth and other complications have been associated with the use of all these drugs during pregnancy (Gillogley, Evans, Hansen, Samuels, & Batra, 1990; Sherwood, Keating, Kavvadia, Greenough, & Peters, 1999). For instance, babies of women taking opiates, particularly methadone, have two to three times greater risk for unexplained sudden death in infancy (Davidson Ward et al., 1990). Cocaine use has also been linked to sudden infant death (Hulse, Milne, English, & Holman, 1998; Kandall & Gaines, 1991). Among infants exposed to opiates during prenatal development, 55 percent to 94 percent show symptoms of withdrawal as newborns, including irritability, high-pitched crying, tremors, vomiting, diarrhea, and rapid breathing (American Academy of Pediatrics, 1998).

We've been talking about how a woman's behavior before or during pregnancy might affect her baby, but mothers are only half the story when it comes to creating new humans. So potential fathers, as well as mothers, must be cautious about their diets, exposure to toxins, and use of substances. Though less research has been done on the effects of men's health and lifestyles on prenatal development, there is now evidence that fathers' behaviors affect sperm, which in turn influences prenatal development. For example, paternal smoking may be related to infant hydrocephalus (a dangerous excess of fluid in the brain), and paternal alcohol use is related to infant heart defects (Savitz, Schwingle, & Keels, 1991).

Both women and men can impair prenatal development with the most commonly used teratogen: alcohol. Women who drink alcohol when pregnant are gambling with their baby's development, because alcohol can lead to a variety of defects. The most severe disorder is *fetal alcohol syndrome (FAS),* which results in abnormalities such as a small head, malformations of the face and limbs, heart defects, and abnormal brain development (Abel, 2006; **Figure 4.7**). Besides these physical impairments, FAS babies often have a low birth weight, slight mental retardation, and behavioral and cognitive problems (Guerri, 2002). In the United States, FAS is estimated to occur in between 0.2 and 2.0 cases per 1,000 live births, though the actual numbers could be higher (Centers for Disease Control and Prevention, 2004). For this reason, many health workers recommend that women completely avoid drinking any alcohol when they are pregnant or trying to become pregnant (Mukherjee, Hollins, Abou-Saleh, & Turk, 2005). We now know that men might want to follow the same advice.

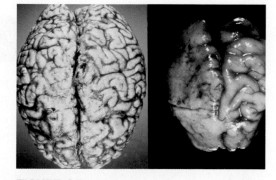

FIGURE 4.7
Fetal Alcohol Syndrome
Compare **(a)** the brain of a normal 6-week-old baby with **(b)** the seriously deformed brain of a baby of the same age with fetal alcohol syndrome (FAS).

This table will help you understand the various classes of teratogens and their effects.

LEGAL DRUGS	**ALCOHOL:** fetal alcohol syndrome, facial malformations, mental retardation, learning difficulties
	NICOTINE: miscarriage, still birth, low birth weight, mental retardation, learning difficulties
	CAFFEINE: miscarriage, low birth weight
RECREATIONAL DRUGS	**COCAINE:** low birth weight, breathing problems, seizures, learning difficulties, irritability
	MARIJUANA: irritability, nervousness, tremors
INFECTIONS	**GERMAN MEASLES (RUBELLA):** blindness, deafness, heart defects, brain damage
	SYPHILIS: mental retardation, deafness, meningitis
ENVIRONMENTAL FACTORS	**RADIATION (X-RAYS):** higher incidence of cancer, physical deformities
	MERCURY: mental retardation, blindness

4.1 CHECKPOINT: How Do We Develop in the Womb?

- Human development occurs in three interacting domains: biological, socio-emotional, and cognitive.

- In the prenatal period, both nature (inborn genetics and biological traits) and nurture (environment) affect human development.

- Prenatal development occurs in three periods: germinal, embryonic, and fetal.

- Teratogens are environmental agents with adverse physical effects during prenatal development and potentially long-term cognitive and behavioral effects.

4.2 How Do Infants and Children Develop Over Time?

📖 **LEARNING GOALS**	✏️ **READING ACTIVITIES**
a. Remember the key terms about how infants and children develop.	List all of the boldface words and write down their definitions.
b. Understand motor and sensory development in an infant.	Summarize these physical changes in a table using your own words.
c. Apply socio-emotional aspects of child development to real life.	Describe the attachment style and temperament of an infant or child you know.
d. Understand the four stages of cognitive development in children.	Summarize the main aspects of development in each of the stages using your own words.
e. Analyze the three stages of language development in childhood.	Organize the three stages of development in a table that includes the typical age of the child and an example of what they might say.

Have you ever interacted with a newborn baby? Do you have the sense that newborns are helpless? In fact, babies arrive in the world with basic abilities that ensure their survival. In *infancy,* beginning at birth and lasting between 18 and 24 months, babies can suck for nourishment and see the face of a caregiver who feeds them. They can cry when hungry, which makes parents want to feed them. Infants can also smile and bond with caregivers to develop attachments that ensure their survival. And they can remember and learn. These abilities aid infants' survival until *childhood,* which ends between ages 11 and 14. Both infancy and childhood are times of great change across all three developmental domains (shown in Figure 4.2).

Infants and Children Change Physically

As infants and children develop, the brain changes in two critical ways. First, myelinated axons form synapses with other neurons. Recall from Chapter 2 that myelin ensures efficient communication between neurons by functioning like the plastic that insulates electrical wires. Through the synaptic connections between neurons, regions of the brain can communicate and process information. Far more of these connections initially develop than the infant brain will ever use, but this growth gives every brain the potential to adapt well to any environment. Second, over time and with experience, the synaptic connections are refined to preserve the most important and helpful connections. This refinement is a case of "use it or lose it." Connections that are not used will decay and disappear. But the effect is a brain that can process information more efficiently.

Unfortunately, sometimes infants and young children are raised in environments that do not stimulate their brains (**Figure 4.8a**). In these cases, very few synaptic connections are made. As a result, these under-stimulated brains will be less able to process complex information, solve problems, or allow the children to develop advanced language skills (Perry, 2002; **Figure 4.8b**). But the reverse is also true: When infants and young children are able to explore the external world, and

(a)

(b)

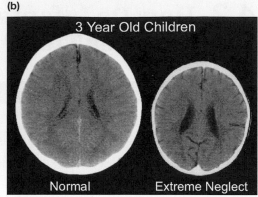

3 Year Old Children

Normal   Extreme Neglect

(c)

FIGURE 4.8

Environmental Stimulation and Brain Development
(a) Some infants and children are raised in environments that provide little stimulation or comfort. **(b)** These images illustrate the impact of neglect on the developing brain. The brain scan on the left is from a healthy 3-year-old child with an average head size. The brain scan on the right is from a 3-year-old child with minimal exposure to language, touch, and social interaction, who has a significantly smaller head. **(c)** The best brain development takes place in environments with rich stimulation and comforting contact with caregivers.

when they have ample opportunities to move, talk, and read, their brains are stimulated. In short, when the brain is stimulated, the brain is encouraged to develop (**Figure 4.8c**). And when the brain develops, it can support the individual's rich physical, socio-emotional, and cognitive development.

INBORN REFLEXES Babies come into the world hardwired with basic motor reflexes that aid survival. For example, infants must eat in order to grow, and they are born with innate, unlearned reflexes that help them find food. When an infant is stroked at the corner of her mouth, she will show the *rooting reflex*. That is, she turns and opens her mouth in anticipation of food (**Figure 4.9a**). If she finds a nipple where she has turned, the infant will show the *sucking reflex*. Automatically closing her mouth on the nipple, she will begin to suck to eat (**Figure 4.9b**).

Another inborn reflex that aids survival is the *grasping reflex* (**Figure 4.9c**). If you stroke an infant's palm, he automatically curls his fingers around the stroked area (see the Try It Yourself feature on p. 122). Some scholars believe that this survival mechanism persists from our prehistoric ancestors. Young primates need to be carried from place to place, so grasping their mothers is an adaptive reflex. Though such inborn reflexes help infants survive in the first months of life, being able to move on purpose is another matter entirely. Babies have to learn these *motor skills*.

MOTOR SKILLS Have you ever watched an infant trying to lift her head to look around? At first, the infant's head wobbles on neck muscles that are underdeveloped. (This is why it is so important to cradle a baby's head in your hand, so you can help control the head until the baby learns to do so herself.) It takes a lot of practice before the infant learns to move her head to look at a caregiver and turn toward a voice she recognizes.

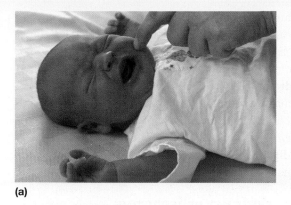
(a)

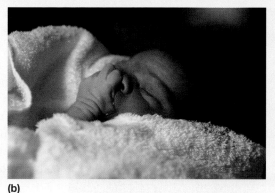
(b)

(c)

FIGURE 4.9

Infant Reflexes

Infants are born with innate abilities that help them survive, including the **(a)** rooting reflex, **(b)** sucking reflex, and **(c)** grasping reflex.

In the first years of life, children progress from moving their heads to sitting up, standing, and walking. The process of developing these motor skills can be seen as a sequence of steps that usually occur within a predictable range of ages. The process is called **maturation (Figure 4.10)**. Maturation was originally thought to be determined only by nature, not by nurture. For an example of nature's effects on development, consider that Brooke Greenberg could not walk primarily because of her biological deficits. But then, even in cases of normal brain development, occasionally a child reverses a couple of maturation steps or even skips one. The fact that not all babies crawl is an example of how nurture also affects maturation.

When infants sleep on their backs, they often skip the crawling phase. Perhaps infants who sleep on their backs do not develop the stomach muscles needed to

maturation

Physical development of the brain and body that prepares an infant for voluntary movement, such as rolling over, sitting, and walking.

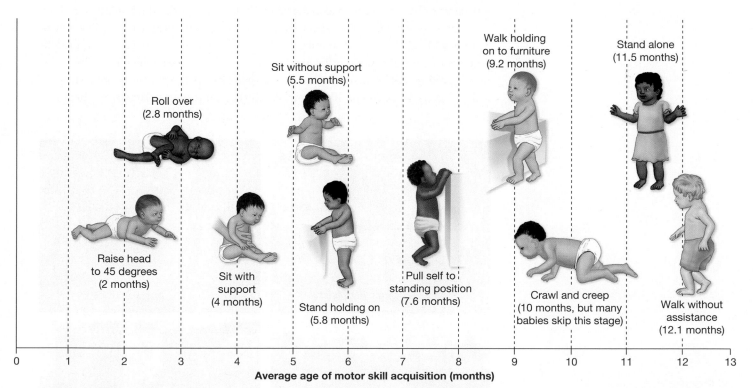

Average age of motor skill acquisition (months)

Roll over (2.8 months)

Sit without support (5.5 months)

Walk holding on to furniture (9.2 months)

Stand alone (11.5 months)

Raise head to 45 degrees (2 months)

Sit with support (4 months)

Stand holding on (5.8 months)

Pull self to standing position (7.6 months)

Crawl and creep (10 months, but many babies skip this stage)

Walk without assistance (12.1 months)

FIGURE 4.10

Physical Maturation and Learning to Walk

Usually, a human baby learns to walk without formal teaching, in a sequence that is typical of all humans. However, the age when a child develops a certain skill varies a lot, so the average age of acquisition is shown here. A child might deviate from this sequence—for example, by skipping the crawling phase—yet still develop normal walking abilities.

TRY IT YOURSELF: Survival Reflexes

If you know a newborn or a young infant, you can observe the innate survival reflexes. The baby can be anywhere from a day old to several months old, though babies show these reflexes less as they develop. Be sure to try this exercise when the baby is fully awake and alert and is in a comfortable and safe position—for example, nestled in a caretaker's arms. But don't freak out if the baby doesn't display the expected results. Some deviation is perfectly acceptable. Anyone concerned about the development of a particular infant should seek the advice of a pediatrician.

Rooting reflex: Gently caress the baby's cheek down to the corner of his mouth. The baby should turn his head toward the cheek that was stroked and might even open his mouth a bit.

Sucking reflex: If you have engaged the rooting reflex and the infant has opened his mouth, place the rubber tip of a pacifier or a baby bottle in the baby's mouth. He may start to suck.

Grasping reflex: Place a finger in the palm of the baby's hand, or gently stroke his palm, and the baby will close his fingers over his palm, perhaps around your finger.

crawl. In any case, pediatricians strongly recommend that infants sleep on their backs. Why? Since the mid-1980s, research has shown that placing infants on their backs for sleeping reduces greatly the incidence of sudden infant death syndrome (SIDS). Preventing SIDS is far more important than making sure that babies crawl before walking. And skipping the crawling phase does not affect long-term motor development! So some differences in maturation, caused by how an individual is nurtured, can be perfectly natural. You have to consider the circumstances.

DYNAMIC SYSTEMS PERSPECTIVE Development in any domain (physical, socio-emotional, or cognitive) takes place through complex interactions. The factors involved are the person's biology, the person's active exploration of an environment, and the constant feedback provided within the person's cultural context (Smith & Thelan, 2003). The dynamic systems theory of development can be seen in the way that children often achieve developmental milestones at different paces, depending on the culture in which they are raised (**Figure 4.11**).

As an example of the dynamic systems theory of development, one study (Super, 1976) focused on the motor development of Kipsigi infants in western Kenya. Kipsigi parents in the Kohwet village placed their babies in shallow holes in the ground so the babies could practice sitting upright. The parents also marched their babies around while placing their own arms under the babies' arms, so the children could practice walking. These infants walked about 1 to 2 months earlier than American and European infants who spent a lot of time in cribs and playpens. Middle-class Kipsigi families who had moved to Westernized homes in a larger city let their infants both sleep in cribs and lie in playpens like their Western counterparts. However, they still

FIGURE 4.11
Dynamic Systems Theory
Throughout life, every new form of behavior emerges through consistent interactions between a person's biological aspects and that person's cultural and environmental contexts.

deliberately taught their infants motor skills using traditional Kipsigi methods. These urban Kipsigi infants walked 2 weeks later than the rural infants in Kohwet but 1 week earlier than infants in Boston, Massachusetts.

SENSORY DEVELOPMENT To learn, infants need information. They get information from the world by hearing, seeing, smelling, tasting, and perceiving touch. Some of these sensory abilities are more fully developed at birth than others. The earliest fully developed sensory abilities are directly connected with the infant's survival. For instance, 2-hour-old infants prefer sweet tastes to all other tastes (Rosenstein & Oster, 1988). This preference makes sense because breast milk is sweet, so infants are born with a built-in mechanism that makes them want to drink this nutritious milk. Infants also have a good sense of smell, especially for scents associated with feeding.

When infants are born, they can also hear quite well. They startle at loud sounds and turn their heads in the direction of everyday sounds. Infants even hear well enough to prefer specific sounds. For instance, a newborn can change her sucking pattern in order to hear her mother's voice (DeCasper & Fifer, 1980). The newborn's ability to recognize and discriminate her mother's voice makes sense because a fetus starts hearing that voice inside the womb at 4½ months. Infants' abilities to recognize and locate sounds improve as they gain experience with objects and people and as the auditory cortex develops further. By the age of 6 months, babies have a nearly adult level of hearing (DeCasper & Spence, 1986).

By contrast, newborns have quite poor vision. Initially they can see only about 8–12 inches from their heads and cannot make out the differences between colors. They can see high-contrast patterns better than they see patches of gray (Fantz, 1966; **Figure 4.12**). These visual abilities are adaptive in that they let the infant focus on what is most important: the mother's breast, which provides nutrition, and her face, which provides important social information.

By about 2 months, infants can see differences among blue, green, and red, and their visual acuity for distant objects increases rapidly over the first 6 months (**Figure 4.13;** Teller, Morse, Borton, & Regal, 1974). As long as babies have access to rich visual experiences and the brain and parts of the eye develop normally, they can see in a way that is similar to adults when they are about a year old. Once again, development has proceeded thanks to complex interactions of dynamic systems.

FIGURE 4.12

Babies Are Born Able to See High Contrast
The innate ability to see large blocks of black and white helps a baby survive. It lets the baby locate her mother's nipple, which contrasts in color with the surrounding tissue, in order to eat.

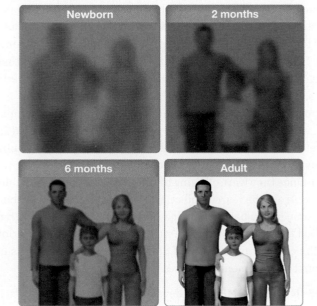

FIGURE 4.13

Infants' Visual Abilities Improve With Experience
Newborns have poor visual acuity and poor ability to see colors. These capacities improve rapidly over the first 6 months of life. At about a year of age, the infants' visual abilities are similar to those of adults.

Infants and Children Change Socially and Emotionally

Humans are social animals. We spend a good part of our lives getting along with other people, or trying to, and it's not always easy. How do we learn how to do it? Infants and children develop socially and emotionally by interacting with others. Our early experiences with our primary caregivers—such as a mother, a father, a grandparent, a day care teacher—are critical for developing the bonds that are essential for socio-emotional development. During this stage, we first learn how to communicate with others, how to behave appropriately in various situations, and how to establish and maintain relationships. During later stages, this development enables us to live successfully in the world with others.

EARLY ATTACHMENT All infants—including those with brain damage and disabilities, such as Brooke Greenberg—have a fundamental need to form strong connections with caretakers. These connections with caretakers help ensure the infants' survival and development, and they should persist over time and across situations. In order to help develop these connections, all infants display an inborn set of behaviors that motivate adults to care for them (Bowlby, 1982).

For example, an infant can cry immediately after birth. The crying provokes psychological, physiological, and behavioral reactions in caregivers, who typically offer the newborn comfort, food, or both. In virtually every culture studied, men, women, and children raise the pitch of their voices when talking to babies. They know intuitively that babies can hear and will pay attention to high-pitched voices. In response, the babies maintain eye contact with the people speaking (Fernald, 1989; Vallabha, McClelland, Pons, Werker, & Amano, 2007). Between 4 and 6 weeks of age, most infants display a first social smile, which typically creates powerful feelings of love in caregivers (**Figure 4.14**). When these inborn abilities create the necessary connections, what sort of "caring" do caregivers provide?

During the late 1950s, psychologists generally believed the care an infant needed was based primarily on getting food from his mother. However, the psychologist Harry Harlow wondered if care was really about providing food, or about something else entirely (Harlow & Harlow, 1966). To investigate this question, as you can see in the Scientific Thinking feature, Harlow placed infant rhesus monkeys in a cage with two surrogate "mothers." One mother was made of wire and provided milk through a bottle. The second mother was made of soft terrycloth, but did not give milk. Harlow found that the monkeys approached the wire mother only when they were hungry. The rest of the day, they clung to the cloth mother. To these monkeys, caring was really about having comforting contact, so they became attached to the cloth mothers, because of their softness.

As an important part of his experiment, Harlow tested the monkeys' attachment to the two mothers in various ways. For example, he placed in the cage a menacing metal robot with flashing eyes and large teeth. Upon seeing the robot, the infants always ran to the mother that provided comfort, never to the mother that fed them. Once they were clinging to the cloth mother, they would calm down and actually confront the feared object. Harlow repeatedly found that the infants were calmer, braver, and better adjusted overall when near the cloth mother. The mother-as-food theory of attachment was shown to be wrong. Harlow's findings established the critical importance of comforting touch and reassurance in the socio-emotional development of infants.

VARIATIONS IN ATTACHMENT To develop socio-emotional bonds, infants need physical closeness with and comfort from caregivers. At about 8 to 12 months,

FIGURE 4.14
Infant Attachment Behaviors
Newborns behave in ways, such as smiling, that make their caretakers want to nurture them.

Hypothesis: Infant monkeys will form an attachment to a surrogate mother that provides comfort.

Research Method: Infant rhesus monkeys were put in a cage with two different "mothers":

1 One mother was made of cloth, but could not give milk.

2 The other was made of wire, but could give milk.

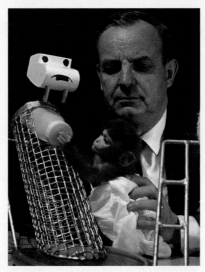

Results: The monkeys clung to the cloth mother and went to it for comfort in times of threat. The monkeys approached the wire mother only when they were hungry.

Conclusion: Infant monkeys will prefer and form an attachment to a surrogate mother that provides comfort over a wire surrogate mother that provides milk.

Note: Photographs are not available from the original experiments. These images are from the CBS television show *Carousel,* which filmed Harlow simulating versions of his experiments in 1962.

however, the infants begin to crawl or toddle and start to move away from caregivers. When they cannot see their attachment figures or are left with babysitters or strangers they don't know, they often show signs of distress (Waters, Matas, & Sroufe, 1975; **Figure 4.15**). This phenomenon, *separation anxiety,* occurs in all

(a)

(b)

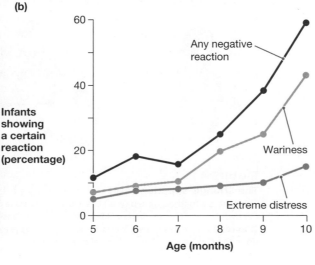

Infants showing a certain reaction (percentage)

Any negative reaction

Wariness

Extreme distress

Age (months)

FIGURE 4.15

Separation Anxiety

(a) Beginning at about 8 months of age, infants show distress when separated from caregivers. **(b)** This separation anxiety increases dramatically as the infants approach their first year of life.

Have you ever been in a room with a baby when the parent left for a minute? Or have you seen an infant left with a babysitter he didn't know? How did the infant react in these situations? If he was 8–12 months old, he probably started to cry or even scream. The infant may have been experiencing separation anxiety, a condition of great distress when the caregiver is out of sight. It is a completely normal reaction for infants at this age. The infant you saw was most likely fine as soon as a loved one comforted him. In fact, you were probably left more shaken by the experience than the infant was!

human cultures. You've probably seen babies displaying separation anxiety. You can read about two typical situations in Has It Happened to You?

To study variations in infant attachment, the developmental psychologist Mary D. Salter Ainsworth created the *strange-situation test* (**Figure 4.16**). In a playroom, a child, a caregiver, and a friendly but unfamiliar adult participate in a series of eight semi-structured separations and reunions between the child and each adult. Over the course of the eight episodes, the child experiences increasing

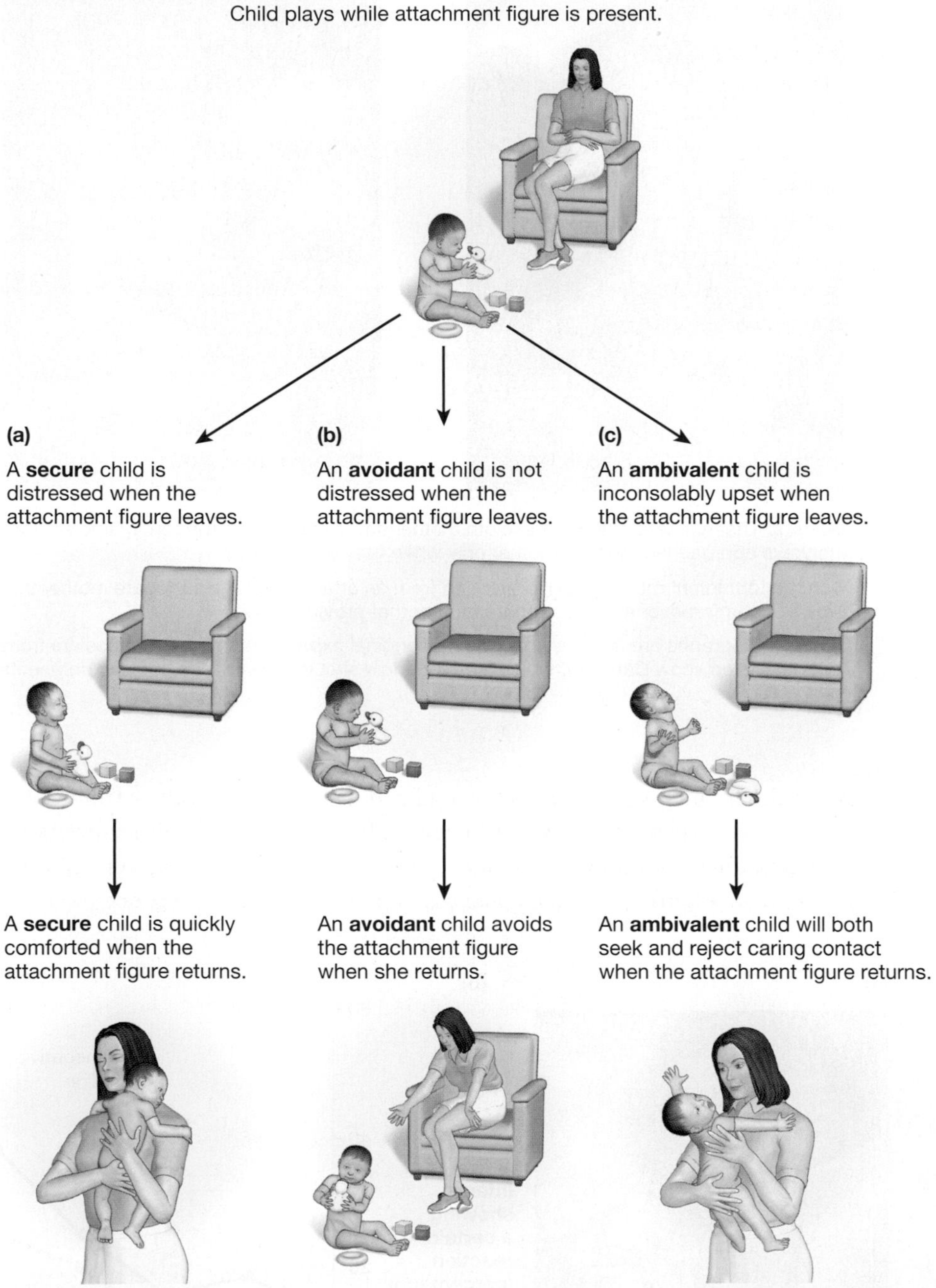

Child plays while attachment figure is present.

(a) A **secure** child is distressed when the attachment figure leaves.

(b) An **avoidant** child is not distressed when the attachment figure leaves.

(c) An **ambivalent** child is inconsolably upset when the attachment figure leaves.

A **secure** child is quickly comforted when the attachment figure returns.

An **avoidant** child avoids the attachment figure when she returns.

An **ambivalent** child will both seek and reject caring contact when the attachment figure returns.

FIGURE 4.16
The Strange-Situation Test
This test is a method of exploring the attachment style of an infant or child: **(a)** secure, **(b)** avoidant, or **(c)** ambivalent. Attachment style is based on two factors, shown here. **(top row)** How does the child respond when the caretaker leaves the room? **(bottom row)** How does the child respond when the caretaker returns?

distress and a greater need for the caregiver to be close by. How well the child copes with distress, and the strategies he uses to do so, show the kind of attachment the child has to the caregiver. The researchers observe the test through a one-way mirror in the laboratory and record the child's activity level and actions such as crying, playing, and paying attention to the mother and the stranger. Using the strange-situation test, Ainsworth has identified the following three attachment styles (Ainsworth, Blehar, Waters, & Wall, 1978).

In **secure attachment,** the child is happy to play alone and is friendly to the stranger as long as the attachment figure is present. When the attachment figure leaves the playroom, the child is distressed, whines or cries, and shows signs of looking for the attachment figure. When the attachment figure returns, the child usually reaches out her arms to be picked up and then is happy and quickly comforted by the caregiver. The child then feels secure enough to return to playing (see Figure 4.16a). As in Harlow's findings, the caregiver is a source of security in times of distress. After a distressing separation, a securely attached infant will be soothed immediately when the caregiver picks her up. When parents have a secure attachment style, approximately 60 percent to 65 percent of their children show secure attachment (Van IJzendoorn, 1995; **Figure 4.17**).

The remaining 35 percent to 40 percent of children display one of the types of insecure attachment (see Figure 4.17). Those with **avoidant attachment** do not get upset or cry at all when the caregiver leaves, and they may prefer to play with the stranger rather than the parent during their time in the playroom. They may also avoid the caregiver upon the caregiver's return (see Figure 4.16b). Those with **ambivalent attachment** may cry a great deal when the caregiver leaves the room, yet both seek and reject caring contact when the caregiver returns and tries to calm them down (see Figure 4.16c). Insecurely attached infants have learned that their caregiver is not available, or only inconsistently available, to soothe them when they are distressed. These children may be emotionally neglected or actively rejected by their attachment figures.

Decades of research show that secure attachments are related to better socio-emotional functioning in childhood, better peer relations, and successful adjustment at school (e.g., Bohlin, Hagekull, & Rydell, 2000; Granot & Mayseless, 2001). In contrast, insecure attachments have been linked to poor outcomes later in life, such as depression and behavioral problems (e.g., Munson, McMahon, & Spieker, 2001). In cases of insecure attachment, interventions may help the caregivers acquire the skills to increase the likelihood of secure attachments forming.

Infants and Children Change Cognitively

Two-year-old Rowen is in her car seat looking at a book. She asks her father, who is driving the car, "What's this?" Her father replies, "Sorry, I am looking at the road. I can't see what you see there in the backseat." But Rowen doesn't understand, so she keeps asking the same question. Young children cannot put themselves in another person's shoes to understand what that person senses, thinks, or feels. However, through exchanges such as this one, children begin to learn about the world around them. Rowen, like most children, will eventually realize that other people's perspectives are different from her own. Social interactions can also reveal how children think about the world.

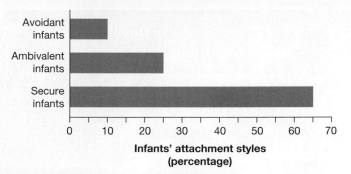

Infants' attachment styles (percentage)

FIGURE 4.17

Variations in Attachment Style
This chart breaks down what percentage of children (of parents who have a secure attachment style) show a secure, an avoidant, or an ambivalent attachment style.

secure attachment
The attachment style for most infants, who are confident enough to play in an unfamiliar environment as long as the caregiver is present and are readily comforted by the caregiver during times of distress.

avoidant attachment
The attachment style for infants who are somewhat willing to explore an unfamiliar environment, but do not look at the caregiver when the caregiver leaves or returns, as though they have little interest in the caregiver.

ambivalent attachment
The attachment style for infants who are unwilling to explore an unfamiliar environment but seem to have mixed feelings about the caregiver—they cry when the caregiver leaves the room, but they cannot be consoled by the caregiver upon the caregiver's return.

DEVELOPING THEORY OF MIND Infants take a big step in cognitive development when they begin to understand who they are and how they think about the world. To determine whether an infant can recognize who she is, researchers will stick a small red dot on her forehead or nose, then place her in front of a mirror. If the infant stares at the dot, touches it, or tries to rub it away, she clearly knows the dot is unusual. She is aware enough of who she is and what she looks like that she can separate herself from the red dot. If there is an infant in your life, you can follow the steps in Try It Yourself to see if he has developed this cognitive ability.

Once an infant becomes self-aware enough to recognize herself in a mirror, she can learn that her thoughts are different from those of other people (Gergely & Csibra, 2003; Sommerville & Woodward, 2005). The capacity to understand that other people have minds and intentions is called *theory of mind* (Baldwin & Baird, 2001). In one study demonstrating theory of mind in infants, an adult begins handing a toy to an infant, but then stops. On some trials, the adult acts unwilling to hand over the toy, teasing the infant with the toy or playing with it herself. On other trials, the adult becomes unable to hand it over, "accidentally" dropping it or being distracted by a ringing telephone. Infants older than 9 months showed greater signs of impatience—for example, reaching for the toy—when the adult was unwilling than when the adult was unable (Behne, Carpenter, Call, & Tomasello, 2005).

This and other studies (e.g., Onishi & Baillargeon, 2005) that use age-appropriate methods provide strong evidence that children begin to read intentions in the first year of life. By the end of the second year, perhaps even by 13 to 15 months of age, children become very good at reading intentions (Baillargeon, Li, Ng, & Yuan, 2009). In other words, even though preschool-age children tend to view the world based only on their own perspectives, they have the cognitive ability to understand others' perspectives. And as infants and children acquire theory of mind, they develop the ability to think in increasingly sophisticated ways.

PIAGET'S THEORY OF COGNITIVE DEVELOPMENT
How do we account for the differences between the way children think and the way adults think? Are children merely inexperienced? Do they simply not have the skills and knowledge that adults normally learn over time? The developmental psychologist Jean Piaget investigated how children's thinking changes as they develop (**Figure 4.18**). By exploring the mental abilities of his own three children and many others, Piaget discovered that children's minds work in a different way than those of adults.

Specifically, Piaget proposed that we change how we think as we form new *schemas,* or ways of thinking about how the world works. Piaget described

FIGURE 4.18

Jean Piaget
Piaget's work with young children was the basis for his idea that thinking becomes more sophisticated as we progress through a series of stages of cognitive development.

two ways that we develop a schema. During **assimilation,** we place a new experience into an existing schema, or mental representation about that information. During **accommodation,** we create a new schema or dramatically alter an existing one to include new information that otherwise would not fit into the schema. For example, a 2-year-old might see a cow for the first time and shout, "Doggie!" After all, a cow has four legs and fur and is certainly not a human. Thus, based on a schema about dogs that the child has developed, the label "doggie" can be considered logical. But the toddler's parent says, "No, honey, that's a cow! See, it doesn't say 'arf'! It says 'moo'! And it is much bigger than a dog." Because the child cannot easily assimilate this new information into the existing schema about dogs, he must now create a new schema about cows, through the process of accommodation. The constant repeating experience of assimilation and accommodation allow a child to develop increasingly sophisticated schemas over time. Piaget's research became the basis for his influential theory that children go through four progressively complex stages of cognitive development. These stages are described next and summarized in **Figure 4.19.**

assimilation
The process we use to incorporate new information into existing frameworks for knowledge.

accommodation
The process we use to create new frameworks for knowledge or drastically alter existing ones to incorporate new information that otherwise would not fit.

Stage	Characterization
1 Sensorimotor (birth–2 years)	• Starts to mentally represent information acquired through the senses and motor exploration. • Begins to act intentionally—for example, pulls a string to set a mobile in motion or shakes a rattle to make a noise. • Achieves object permanence by realizing that things continue to exist even when no longer present to the senses. 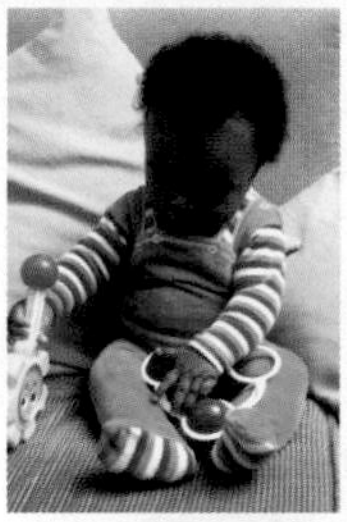
2 Preoperational (2–7 years)	• Learns to use language and to represent objects by images and words. • Thinking is egocentric, where the child has difficulty taking the viewpoint of others. • Can think intuitively, not logically. • Classifies objects by a single feature—for example, groups red blocks regardless of shape. 
3 Concrete operational (7–12 years)	• Can think logically about concrete objects and events. • Achieves conservation of number, volume, mass, and weight. • Classifies objects by several features and can order them in a series along a single dimension, such as size. 
4 Formal operational (12 years and up)	• Can think logically about abstract propositions and test hypotheses systematically. • Becomes concerned with hypothetical issues, the future, and ideological problems. 

FIGURE 4.19
Piaget's Stages of Cognitive Development
Piaget described how children's thinking abilities are characterized across four stages of cognitive development.

Use this graphic to help you understand the difference between the two ways that thinking develops as described by Jean Piaget.

Assimilation is when a child first absorbs new information into a schema, even if he does so incorrectly (see part [a] of the figure). In this case a child might initially try to assimilate "butterfly" into the schema "birds." After all, this creature does have wings and fly.

During **accommodation,** two things can happen. One thing is to modify the existing schema (see part [b] of the figure). For example, the child modifies the existing schema, "birds," to clarify what information is part of that schema. For example, birds have beaks, so a butterfly is not a bird. Alternatively, another thing that can happen is to create a new schema (see part [c]). In our example, the child creates a new, perhaps even broader schema of "flying animals." This new, broader schema might be appropriate for birds, but also allow things that are not birds but do fly, such as a butterfly.

By continually repeating the processes of assimilation and accommodation, infants and children gradually change how they think about the world around them.

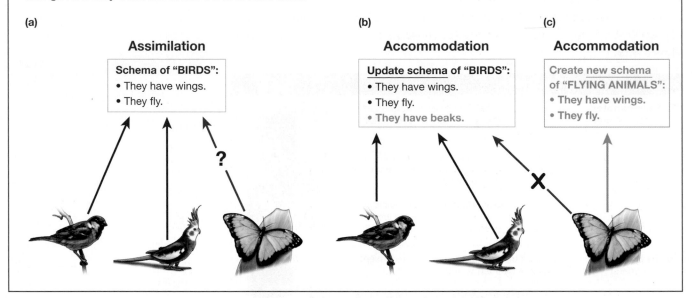

SENSORIMOTOR STAGE: BIRTH TO 2 YEARS According to Piaget, children from birth until about age 2 are in the **sensorimotor stage** of cognitive development. During this period, they acquire information primarily through their senses and motor exploration. Thus very young infants' understanding of objects occurs when they react reflexively to the sensory input from those objects. For example, they learn by sucking on a nipple, grasping a finger, or seeing a face. They progress from being reflexive to being reflective—that is, capable of mentally representing the external world and their experiences with increasingly complex schemas.

As infants begin to control their motor movements, they develop their first schemas. These conceptual models consist of mental representations of the actions that can be performed on certain kinds of objects. For instance, the sucking reflex begins as a reaction to the sensory input from the nipple. Soon the infant realizes she can suck other things, such as a bottle, a finger, a toy, or a blanket. Piaget described sucking other objects as an example of assimilation to the schema of sucking. But sucking a toy or a blanket does not result in the same experience as the reflexive sucking of a nipple. The difference between these experiences leads the child to alter the sucking schema to include new experiences and information. For example, while sucking a blanket, she may create a new schema that includes using less force than sucking on a bottle. She uses the process of accommodation to create this new schema.

sensorimotor stage
The first stage in Piaget's theory of cognitive development; during this stage, infants acquire information about the world through their senses and motor skills.

preoperational stage
The second stage in Piaget's theory of cognitive development; during this stage, children think symbolically about objects, but they reason based on intuition and superficial appearances rather than logic.

According to Piaget, one important cognitive concept developed in this stage is *object permanence*—the understanding that an object continues to exist even when it is hidden from view. Piaget noted that until 9 months of age, most infants will not search for objects they have seen being hidden under a blanket. At around 9 months, they will look for the hidden object by picking up the blanket. Still, their search skills have limits. For instance, after watching his parent hide a toy under a blanket several times, an 8-month-old child finds the toy. If the parent then hides the toy under a different blanket, in full view of the child, the child will still look for the toy in the first hiding place. Even in this more difficult task, a child's full comprehension of object permanence was, for Piaget, one key accomplishment of the sensorimotor period.

PREOPERATIONAL STAGE: 2 TO 7 YEARS According to Piaget, children from about 2 to 7 years of age can begin to think about objects not in their immediate view. They have developed conceptual models of how the world works. During this **preoperational stage,** children begin to think symbolically. For example, they can pretend that a stick is a sword or a wand. However, Piaget believed that children at this stage cannot think operationally—in other words, they cannot imagine the logical outcomes of performing certain actions on certain objects. Instead, they use intuitive reasoning based on superficial appearances.

For instance, children at this stage have no understanding of the *law of conservation*. This law states that even if the appearance of a substance changes in one dimension, the properties of that substance remain unchanged. For example, if you pour a short, wide glass of water into a tall, narrow glass, the amount of water does not change. But if you ask children in the preoperational stage which glass contains more, they will pick the tall, narrow glass because the water is at a higher level. The children will make this error even when they have seen someone pour the same amount of water into each glass or when they pour the liquid themselves. They cannot understand that the narrower diameter of the taller glass makes the water level higher (**Figure 4.20**).

The lack of conservation skills is thought to be due to a key cognitive limitation of the preoperational period: *centration*. This limitation occurs when a child cannot think about more than one detail of a problem solving task at a time. The child "centers" on only one detail or aspect of the problem, so his ability to think logically is limited.

Another cognitive characteristic of the preoperational period is *egocentrism*. Preoperational thinkers generally view the world through their own experiences. They can understand how others feel, and they are able to care about others, but their thought processes tend to revolve around their own perspectives. For example, a 2-year-old may play hide-and-seek by placing a box over her head, believing that if she cannot see other people, other people cannot see her (**Figure 4.21**).

1 A young child understands that two identical short glasses contain the same amount of water.

2 Here, the child observes the water from one of the short glasses poured into the tall glass.

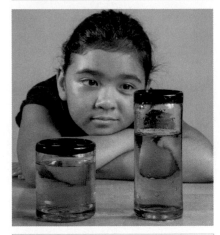
3 When asked which one contains more water, the child will point to the taller glass, even though the amount of water poured in is the same as the amount of water in the short glass.

FIGURE 4.20
Conservation Task Based on Volume
In the preoperational stage, according to Piaget, children reason intuitively, not logically. As a result, these children cannot yet understand the concept of conservation, which is shown here in a task focusing on the volume of a liquid.

FIGURE 4.21
Egocentrism
This toddler is playing hide and seek with her mother. Because the toddler's head is in the box and she cannot see the mother, she believes that the mother also cannot see her.

concrete operational stage
The third stage in Piaget's theory of cognitive development; during this stage, children begin to think about and understand logical operations, and they are no longer fooled by appearances.

formal operational stage
The final stage in Piaget's theory of cognitive development; during this stage, people can think abstractly, and they can formulate and test hypotheses through logic.

Instead of viewing this egocentric thinking as a limitation, modern scholars agree with Piaget that such "immature" skills prepare children to take special note of their immediate surroundings and learn as much as they can about how their own minds and bodies interact with the world. A clear egocentric focus prevents them from trying to expand their schemas too much before they understand how they think about and understand their own experiences (Bjorklund, 2007).

CONCRETE OPERATIONAL STAGE: 7 TO 12 YEARS At about 7 years of age, according to Piaget, children enter the **concrete operational stage.** They remain in this stage until adolescence. Piaget believed that humans do not develop logic until they begin to think about and understand operations. A classic operation is an action that can be undone: A light can be turned on and off, a stick can be moved across the table and then moved back, and so on. According to Piaget, when children are able to understand that an action is reversible, they can begin to understand concepts such as conservation. Children in this stage are not fooled by superficial transformations, such as how the volume of liquid can look different in glasses of varying size. Instead, they can reason logically about problems.

Although using operations is the beginning of logical thinking, Piaget believed that children at this stage reason only about concrete things. That is, they reason about objects they can act on in the world. They are not yet able to reason abstractly, or hypothetically, about what might be possible. For this reason, children in first, second, and third grades often use objects to do math. They use their fingers to add and subtract, and they group objects, such as tokens, to multiply and divide. They cannot do these operations in their heads. By using concrete information, children in this stage can think in much more logical and less egocentric ways than children in the preoperational stage. However, according to Piaget, they cannot truly engage in sophisticated scientific and abstract thinking until they reach adolescence.

FORMAL OPERATIONAL STAGE: 12 YEARS TO ADULTHOOD Piaget's final stage of cognitive development is the **formal operational stage.** Here, people can reason in sophisticated, abstract ways. Formal operations involve critical thinking, characterized by the ability to form a hypothesis about something and test the hypothesis through logic. Critical thinking also involves using information to systematically find answers to problems. To study this ability, Piaget gave teenagers and younger children four flasks of colorless liquid and one flask of colored liquid. He then explained that the colored liquid could be obtained by combining two of the colorless liquids. Adolescents, he found, systematically try different combinations to obtain the correct result, whereas younger children just randomly combine liquids. Adolescents are also able to consider abstract notions and think about many viewpoints at once. Lastly, this kind of thinking is characterized by an ability to envision the future and predict the consequences of certain actions.

NEW WAYS OF THINKING ABOUT PIAGET'S THEORY Piaget's theory revolutionized the understanding of cognitive development. And he was right about many things. For example, infants do learn about the world through sensorimotor exploration. Also, people do move from intuitive, illogical thinking to a more logical understanding of the world. However, modern research has revealed that we have to consider Piaget's theory more flexibly.

For example, we now know that Piaget underestimated the ages at which certain skills develop. Contemporary researchers using age-appropriate methods

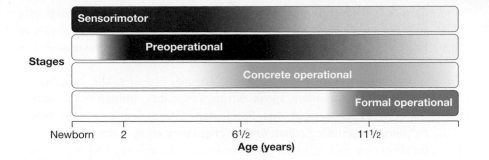

have found that object permanence develops in the first few months of life, rather than at 8 or 9 months of age, as Piaget thought (Baillargeon, 1987). In his various testing protocols, Piaget may have confused infants' cognitive abilities with their physical capabilities. Because of this, he may have underestimated the age at which some thinking skills develop. For example, infants may not be able to grasp a hidden object, but they may understand that it still exists.

In addition, psychologists now think of cognitive development in terms of trends rather than strict stages. People gradually shift from one or more ways of thinking to other ways of thinking, so they may exhibit skills from different stages simultaneously (**Figure 4.22**). For example, while a certain child might not understand the conservation of volume (see Figure 4.20), she may be able to perform a conservation task based on number (**Figure 4.23**). This view of cognitive development is consistent with our understanding of brain development. Cognitive development may not necessarily follow strict and uniform stages, because different areas of the brain are responsible for different skills (Bidell & Fischer, 1995; Case, 1992; Fischer, 1980).

1 A 4-year-old is shown two rows of marbles. Each row has the same number of marbles, but one row is spread out. When asked which row has more marbles, the 4-year-old says the longer row.

2 However, when asked to count the marbles in each row, the 4-year-old counts correctly and states that the two rows have the same number of marbles.

FIGURE 4.23
Conservation Task Based on Number
When a task is performed in an age-appropriate manner, children are able to show conservation of number much earlier than they can show conservation of volume (see Figure 4.20).

Language Develops in an Orderly Way

Recall that 19-year-old Brooke Greenberg, whose physical and mental development essentially stopped when she was a toddler, could communicate only by making infant-like sounds. The ability to speak in sentences develops as the brain changes and as cognitive abilities become more sophisticated. It is important to recognize that as children develop social skills, they also improve their language abilities. Thanks to language, we can live in complex societies where our ability to communicate helps us learn the history, rules, and values of our culture or cultures. Language also enables us to communicate across cultures and to learn much more than other animals can. How does this remarkable ability, communication through language, develop?

FROM ZERO TO 60,000 Language is a system of using sounds and symbols according to grammatical rules. It can be viewed as a hierarchical structure: Sentences can be broken down into smaller units, called phrases, and phrases can be broken down into words (**Figure 4.24a**). Each word consists of one or more *morphemes* (the smallest units that have meaning, including suffixes and prefixes). Each morpheme consists of one or more *phonemes* (basic sounds; **Figure 4.24b**). For example, the word *asked* has two morphemes ("ask" and "ed") and four phonemes (the sounds you make when you say the word: /a/s/k/t/).

(a)

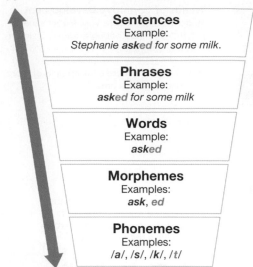

Sentences
Example:
*Stephanie **asked** for some milk.*

Phrases
Example:
***ask**ed for some milk*

Words
Example:
***ask**ed*

Morphemes
Examples:
ask**, **ed

Phonemes
Examples:
/a/, /s/, /k/, /t/

(b)

FIGURE 4.24

Organization of Language
(a) Language is organized hierarchically. Sentences and phrases are created from words, words are created from morphemes, and morphemes are created from phonemes. **(b)** In learning to read, these children are combining phonemes into morphemes.

babbling
Intentional vocalization, often by an infant, that does not have a specific meaning.

telegraphic speech
The tendency for toddlers to speak using rudimentary sentences that are missing words and grammatical markings but follow a logical syntax and convey a wealth of meaning.

overregularization
The tendency for young children to incorrectly use a regular syntax rule where they should use an exception to the rule.

Syntax is the system of rules about how words are combined into phrases and how phrases are combined to make sentences. For example, English syntax dictates that we say *Stephanie asked for some milk,* not *Stephanie some milk for asked.*

Infants are born ready to learn language. In fact, the language or languages that mothers speak during pregnancy influence the listening preferences of newborns. For instance, Canadian newborns whose mothers spoke only English during pregnancy show a strong preference for sentences in English as compared with sentences in Tagalog, a major language of the Philippines. Newborns of mothers who spoke both Tagalog and English during pregnancy pay attention to both languages (Byers-Heinlein, Burns, & Werker, 2010). Further, up to 6 months of age, a baby can discriminate all the speech sounds that occur in all languages, even if the sounds do not occur in the language spoken in the baby's home (Kuhl, 2006; Kuhl et al., 2006; Kuhl, Tsao, & Liu, 2003).

From hearing sounds immediately after birth and then learning the sounds of their own languages, babies develop the ability to speak. Without working very hard at it, humans appear to go from babbling as babies to employing a full vocabulary of about 60,000 words as adults. Learning to speak follows a distinct path. During the first months of life, newborns' actions—crying, fussing, eating, and breathing—generate all their sounds. In other words, babies' first verbal sounds are cries, gurgles, grunts, and breaths. From 3 to 5 months, they begin to coo and laugh. From 5 to 7 months, they begin **babbling,** using consonants and vowels. From 7 to 8 months, they babble in syllables (*ba-ba-ba, dee-dee-dee*).

By the end of their first year, infants around the world are usually saying their first words. These first words typically combine phonemes into morphemes to label items in their environment (*kitty, milk*), simple action words (*go, up, sit*), quantifiers (*all gone! more!*), qualities or adjectives (*hot*), socially interactive words (*bye, hello, yes, no*), and even internal states (*boo-boo* after being hurt; Pinker, 1984). Thus even very young children use words to perform a wide range of communicative functions. They name, comment, and request.

By about 18 to 24 months, children's vocabularies start to grow rapidly. They put words together and form basic sentences of roughly two words. Though these mini-sentences are missing some words, they have what is known as syntax. Typically, the word order indicates what has happened or should happen: For example, "Throw ball—all gone" translates as *I threw the ball, and now it's gone.* The psychologist Roger Brown called these utterances **telegraphic speech** because the children speak as if they are sending a telegram. They put together bare-bones words according to conventional rules (Brown, 1973).

As children use language in increasingly sophisticated ways, they sometimes overapply new grammatical rules. This tendency is called **overregularization.** For example, when children learn that adding *-ed* makes a verb past tense, they add *-ed* to every verb, even verbs that do not follow that rule. Thus they may say "runned" or "holded" even though they may have said "ran" or "held" at a younger age. This trend usually lasts through the early elementary school years, when children begin to master irregular forms of words. Such overregularizations reflect an important aspect of language acquisition: Children are not simply repeating what they have heard others say. After all, they most likely have not heard anyone say "runned." Instead, these errors occur because children recognize patterns in spoken grammar and then apply the patterns to new sentences they never heard before (Marcus, 1996; Marcus et al., 1992).

Salma smiled as she walked the aisles at Target. *It is so weird,* she thought. *Every psychology chapter I read seems to have some connection to my life!* Although she loved the readings for her major (criminal justice), reading for psychology was just so different. She had put off taking psychology until her junior year, and now she was wishing she had taken it much earlier. When reading Chapter 2, she had become fascinated by endorphins. She had just started jogging, and although she had experienced a runner's high, she had not known there was a name and an explanation for it. After learning more about dreams in Chapter 3, she and her friend James had joked with each other about some odd dreams they started having. Today, right after she had finished reading Chapter 4, Salma received an Evite to her cousin's baby shower. On her way to Target, she thought: *I wonder if I can use my newfound knowledge of developmental psychology to pick a really good gift?*

As she walked down the aisles of the store, Salma became annoyed about her limited choices. All the clothes and toys for infant girls seemed to be pink. All the clothes and toys for infant boys seemed to be blue. *Do little boys really prefer blue things and little girls really prefer pink things? Or is it just that adults think boys should like blue and girls should like pink?*

Recalling Chapter 4, Salma knew that infants had very poor color detection at birth. *So at what age might children develop color preferences?* Putting on her detective hat, she left the store and went to the library in search of a psychological study that might solve the Case of the Pink and Blue Toy Aisles. When she looked up "color preferences" and "gender," the first article she found was perfect. The title was "Pretty in Pink: The Early Development of Gender-Stereotyped Colour Preferences." The study participants were six groups of children: those less than a year old, 1-year-olds, 2-year-olds, 3-year-olds, 4-year-olds, and 5-year-olds. The researchers showed each child pairs of different objects, such as a Koosh ball and a measuring cup. One of the objects was pink. They measured what proportion of time the child reached for the pink object.

Salma was intrigued. The answer of whether or not there was a pink preference depended on the child's age. In children 2 years old or younger, girls showed no significantly greater preference for pink than boys did. However, from age 3 onward, girls showed a statistically significant preference for pink objects as compared to boys. What's more, starting at age 3, boys demonstrated an avoidance of pink. *Mystery solved: Female children 3 years of age and older really do pick pink when given a choice!*

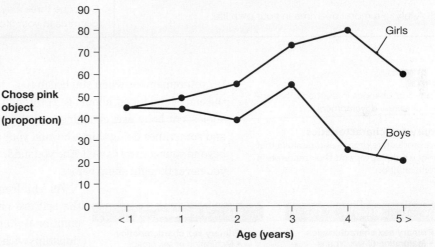

Still, Salma began to wonder whether children had developed their own color preferences or whether toy makers had created this preference in children. The article she read demonstrated the preference, but the purpose of this study was only to note if the preference existed. The study didn't and couldn't say more about the source of the preference. *Did girls learn that pink toys were for them and thus developed the preference? Or was preferring pink a part of female development and toy makers just knew that? Would little girls start to like green if their favorite toys came out in that color? Sounds like another study needs to be done!*

4.2 CHECKPOINT: How Do Infants and Children Develop Over Time?

- We are born with innate reflexes, but through experiences we learn to move and process sensory information.
- Forming strong attachments with caregivers early on supports appropriate social interactions and emotion regulation.
- Infants' and children's cognitive abilities become more advanced with time and experience as they move through four stages of cognitive development.
- Children develop language skills starting with the production of phonemes and eventually moving to speaking full sentences.

4.3 How Do Adolescents Develop?

LEARNING GOALS	READING ACTIVITIES
a. Remember the key terms related to adolescent development.	List all of the boldface words and write down their definitions.
b. Understand the physical changes in puberty.	Summarize the changes in primary and secondary sex characteristics and when they occur in boys and girls, using your own words.
c. Apply socio-emotional aspects of development to your own adolescence.	Provide a description of the development of your sense of identity, including gender and ethnic identity.
d. Analyze a moral dilemma in your own life.	Describe three ways you could reason morally about a dilemma in your life based on Kohlberg's theory.

LEARN

puberty
The physical changes in the body that are a part of sexual development.

primary sex characteristics
The reproductive organs and genitals that distinguish the sexes and their maturation for reproduction.

Do you remember when you began to go through *adolescence*? This period starts at the end of childhood, about age 11 through 14, and lasts until about age 18 or 21. Your adolescent body was changing in major ways, parts of it growing into new shapes and sometimes doing things beyond your control. Your emotions may have seemed beyond your control as well. And you suddenly may have felt wildly attracted to people you never thought about before.

As children approach adolescence, all aspects of the self are changing. Physical changes occur, socio-emotional changes emerge as part of renegotiating relationships with parents and peers, and cognitive changes arise as part of the potential emergence of critical and analytical thinking. Taken together, changes in these three domains (see Figure 4.2) lay the foundation for the development of a sense of personal identity.

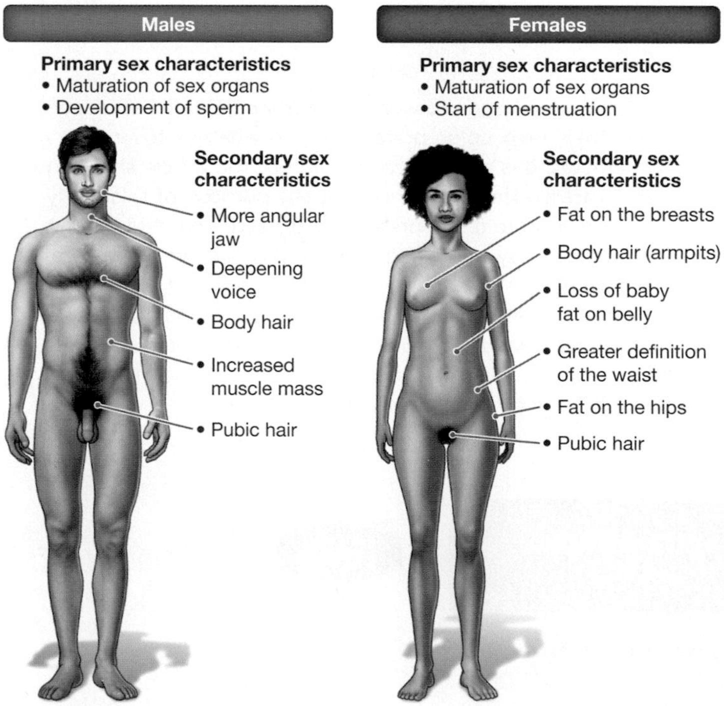

FIGURE 4.25
Physical Development During Adolescence
As boys and girls enter puberty, they develop primary and secondary sex characteristics.

Adolescents Develop Physically

Physically, adolescence is characterized by the onset of sexual maturity and the ability to reproduce. **Puberty,** a roughly two-year developmental period, marks the beginning of adolescence. Puberty typically begins between 8 and 14 years for females and between 10 and 14 years for males. Most girls complete pubertal development by the age of 16, and boys finish by the age of 18 (Lee, 1980).

ONSET OF PUBERTY When you were around 10 or 12 years old, did you seem to grow overnight? This adolescent growth spurt, a rapid, hormonally driven increase in height and weight, is a clear dividing line between childhood and the start of puberty. During puberty, hormone levels increase throughout the body, stimulating many physical changes. Puberty brings the development of the **primary sex characteristics** (**Figure 4.25**). That is, the male and female sex organs mature, menstruation begins in girls, and sperm develop in boys. Also developing at this time are the **secondary sex characteristics** (see Figure 4.25). That is, boys and girls experience greater growth of body hair, often first as darker and thicker hair on the legs, then pubic hair, then in other places. Boys' muscle mass increases, their voices deepen, and their jaws become more angular. Girls lose baby fat on their bellies as their waists become more defined, and they also develop fat deposits on the hips and breasts (Lee, 1980).

Puberty may seem to be purely physical, but it is affected by environment. For example, a girl who lives in a stressful environment or has insecure attachments to caregivers is likely to begin menstruating earlier than a girl in a peaceful, secure environment (Wierson, Long, & Forehand, 1993). This finding suggests that a girl's body responds to stress as a threat. Because the body feels threatened, it speeds up the need to reproduce in order to continue the girl's gene pool. Thus environmental forces trigger hormonal changes, which send the girl into puberty (Belsky, Houts, & Fearon, 2010). Because boys do not have an easily identifiable pubertal event like menstruation in girls, we know less about the effects of environment on puberty in boys. Boys and girls experience similar changes in brain development during adolescence, however, so researchers are able to identify a few key characteristics of the teenage brain.

BRAIN CHANGES DURING ADOLESCENCE While teenagers are experiencing pubertal changes, their brains also are in an important phase of reorganization. Synaptic connections are being refined, and gray matter is increasing. However, the frontal cortex of the brain is not fully developed until the early 20s. An adolescent's limbic system—the motivational and emotional center of the brain—tends to be more active than the frontal cortex. As a result, although teenagers are *able* to think critically, they often have a difficult time doing so. Instead, they are more likely to act irrationally and engage in risky behaviors than adults are (Blakemore & Choudhury, 2006; Casey, Jones, & Somerville, 2011). Because teenagers have the ability to understand the consequences of their actions, it is important to educate them about behavioral consequences. If parents, teachers, community members, and other adults are supportive and provide the proper guidance and discipline, adolescents will know that people who care about them will help them avoid making poor decisions (Steinberg & Sheffield, 2001).

Adolescents Develop Socially and Emotionally

"Who am I?" This question, which opened the chapter, may be foremost in an adolescent's thoughts. As we progress through adolescence, each of us begins to develop a sense of identity, of who we are. How we define ourselves is influenced by many factors, including the culture in which we are raised, our gender, and our beliefs about personal characteristics such as race, sex, and age. The quest for identity is an important challenge during development, especially in Western cultures, where individuality is valued. As adolescents seek to understand how they fit into the world and to imagine what kind of person they will become later in life, they build on the preceding developmental stages.

STAGES OF PSYCHOSOCIAL DEVELOPMENT The psychologist Erik Erikson proposed a theory of human development that emphasized age-related psychosocial challenges and their effects on social functioning across the life span. Erikson

secondary sex characteristics
Sex-differentiating characteristics that are not directly related to reproduction but that develop during the hormonal changes of puberty.

identity versus role confusion
Fifth stage of Erikson's theory of psychosocial development, where adolescents face the challenge of figuring out who they are.

thought of identity development as being composed of eight stages, ranging from an infant's first year of life to old age (**Table 4.1**). Because it recognizes the importance of the entire life span, Erikson's theory has been extremely influential in developmental psychology. However, a theory is only as good as the evidence that supports it, and few researchers have tested Erikson's theory directly.

Erikson conceptualized each life stage as having a major developmental "crisis"—a challenge to be confronted. All of these crises are present throughout life, but each takes on special importance at a particular stage. Although each crisis provides an opportunity for psychological development, a lack of progress may impair further psychosocial development (Erikson, 1980). However, if the crisis is successfully resolved, the challenge provides skills and attitudes that the individual will need to face the next challenge successfully. Successful resolution of the early challenges depends on the supportive nature of the child's environment as well as the child's active search for information about his competence. According to Erikson's theory, adolescents face perhaps the most fundamental challenge: how to develop an adult identity. This crisis of **identity versus role confusion** includes addressing questions about our own femininity and masculinity as well as our ethnic and cultural identity.

TABLE 4.1

Erikson's Eight Stages of Psychosocial Development

STAGE	AGE	MAJOR PSYCHOSOCIAL CRISIS	SUCCESSFUL RESOLUTION OF CRISIS
1. Infancy	0–2	Trust versus mistrust	Children learn that the world is safe and that people are loving and reliable.
2. Toddler	2–3	Autonomy versus shame and doubt	Encouraged to explore the environment, children gain feelings of independence and positive self-esteem.
3. Preschool	4–6	Initiative versus guilt	Children develop a sense of purpose by taking on responsibilities, but they also develop the capacity to feel guilty for misdeeds.
4. Childhood	7–12	Industry versus inferiority	By working successfully with others and assessing how others view them, children learn to feel competent.
5. Adolescence	13–19	Identity versus role confusion	By exploring different social roles, adolescents develop a sense of identity.
6. Young adulthood	20s	Intimacy versus isolation	Young adults gain the ability to commit to long-term relationships.
7. Middle adulthood	30s to 50s	Generativity versus stagnation	Adults gain a sense that they are leaving behind a positive legacy and caring for future generations.
8. Old age	60s and beyond	Integrity versus despair	Older adults feel a sense of satisfaction that they have lived a good life and developed wisdom.

SOURCE: Erikson (1959).

GENDER IDENTITY Children as young as 2 years old often ask other children, "Are you a boy or girl?" And even at this age, they can correctly identify themselves as boys or girls. Whether children think they are male or female is part of their **gender identity.** At 2, children base this information on biological differences. Psychologists refer to these biological differences as *sex*. But as children develop into adolescents, their gender identity also is based on differences between males and females that result from socialization. Psychologists refer to these differences as *gender*. The distinction between sex and gender is not always easy to make, because the biological and psychosocial aspects of being female or male are usually so entwined that we cannot separate them (Hyde, 2005).

Your gender identity shapes how you behave. Every culture has rules about what behaviors are appropriate for males and what are appropriate for females. **Gender roles** are behaviors that differ between males and females because of cultural influences, expectancies, or learning. Children develop their expectations about the genders by observing their parents, peers, teachers, and the media. By watching movies and television shows, for example, many children over the past few generations have come to believe that being a firefighter is a male job, being a nurse is a female job, and so on. Such portrayals help to develop and reinforce gender stereotypes, which are commonly held beliefs about men and women. The separation of boys and girls into different play groups is a powerful socializing force as well, and we can also find many examples of stereotyping in children's toys (**Figure 4.26a**). However, these days many toy companies are designing and marketing their products to make them attractive to children of both genders (**Figure 4.26b**).

Males and females are biologically similar in many respects, but the brains of men and women differ in some ways. For example, men generally show greater responsiveness to pictures of sexual imagery. Is this difference caused by some inherent property of the male brain, by the ways that boys are treated during development, or both? We don't know the answer to that question, but we know that nature and nurture play prominent roles in the development of gender identity. The case of Bruce Reimer is an extraordinary example of the interplay of sex and gender in the development of gender identity.

BRUCE REIMER: A UNIQUE CASE OF GENDER IDENTITY In 1966, seven-month-old Bruce Reimer and his twin brother, Brian, underwent routine circumcisions. Although the procedure is common and usually has no complications, Bruce's penis was badly damaged. As recounted in John Colapinto's book, *As Nature Made Him: The Boy Who Was Raised as a Girl* (2000), experts counseled Bruce's parents that sexual reassignment was the best course of action for Bruce's psychological well-being. Bruce was castrated (his testes were removed) when he was 22 months old. He was renamed Brenda and raised as a girl alongside her twin brother (**Figure 4.27**).

Brenda was socialized as a girl; she had long hair, her parents dressed her in feminine clothes, and they encouraged her to play with other girls. But Brenda was teased for being rough and aggressive, and she was not comfortable or happy as a child. At age 11, Brenda was given hormones to initiate the development of female secondary sexual characteristics. But the hormones made Brenda feel even more uncomfortable, and developing breasts caused her intense embarrassment and horror. Ultimately, Brenda's parents were forced to acknowledge that she was not—nor would she ever truly be—a girl. Brenda recalled that when they told her the truth, that she was born a boy, "Suddenly it all made sense why I felt the way I did. I wasn't some sort of weirdo. I wasn't crazy."

(a)

(b)

FIGURE 4.26
Development of Gender Roles
(a) Historically, many children's toys have promoted gender stereotyping.
(b) Currently, toy companies are trying to make these types of toys in versions that appeal to girls.

gender identity
Each person's beliefs about being male or female.

gender roles
The characteristics associated with being male or being female, because of cultural influence or learning.

FIGURE 4.27
Brian and Brenda (Bruce) Reimer
This photo shows Brian and Brenda (Bruce) Reimer as children. Only his short haircut distinguishes Brian as the boy. Because they were identical twins, the situation was ideal for studying the effects of culture on gender identity.

FIGURE 4.28
David (Bruce) Reimer
This photo shows David (Bruce) living as a man.

Brenda immediately decided to return to being male. She changed her name to David and underwent surgery to create a functional artificial penis for sexual intercourse. David met and married a woman with three children, and for many years he lived an apparently happy family life (**Figure 4.28**). Unfortunately, David's marriage failed, and he suffered a series of financial setbacks. After the death of his twin brother, he became despondent. David killed himself in May 2004 at age 38. Most psychologists believe the stress of being a boy raised as a girl contributed to identity problems that troubled him throughout his life.

David's life suggests that gender identity begins very early in prenatal development. It results from a complex cascade of hormones, changes in brain structure and function, and environmental forces in the womb (Swaab, 2004). Even though David did not have testicles to generate hormones, hormones still circulated in his infant brain and contributed to his sense of being masculine. In the 1960s, people generally favored environmental explanations for most differences between males and females. In hindsight, it seems clear that changing the appearance of a child's genitals, injecting the child with hormones, or treating the child as belonging to a certain gender will not turn that person from a boy into a girl, or vice versa.

ETHNIC IDENTITY Along with a gender identity, each adolescent must establish an ethnic identity. Culture shapes much of who we are as we develop a full sense of identity during adolescence. Culture also determines whether each person's identity will be accepted or maligned. In a multiracial country such as the United States, questions of racial or ethnic identity can be complicated. Forming an ethnic identity can be a particular challenge for adolescents of color.

Children entering middle childhood have some awareness of their ethnic identities. That is, they know the labels and attributes that the dominant culture applies to their ethnic group. During middle childhood and adolescence, children in ethnic minority groups often engage in additional processes aimed at ethnic identity formation (Phinney, 1990). The factors that influence these processes vary widely among individuals and groups.

For instance, a child of Mexican immigrants may struggle to live successfully in both a traditional Mexican household and a Westernized American neighborhood and school. The child may have to serve as a "cultural broker" for his family, perhaps translating materials sent home from school, calling government agencies or insurance companies, and handling more adultlike responsibilities than other children the same age. In helping the family adjust to the stress of life as immigrants in a foreign country, the child may feel additional pressures, but he may also develop important skills in communication, negotiation, and caregiving (Cooper, Denner, & Lopez, 1999). And by successfully negotiating these tasks, a child can develop a bicultural identity. That is, the child strongly identifies with two cultures and seamlessly combines a sense of identity with both groups (Vargas-Reighley, 2005). A child in this situation who develops a bicultural identity is likely to be happier, better adjusted, and have fewer problems in adult social and economic roles.

PARENTS AND PEERS If you were asked for one adjective that best describes "teenager," what would you say? The odds are high that it would be *rebellious*. Recall from the opening story that even 19-year-old Brooke Greenberg, who was frozen in the body of a 19-month-old toddler, displayed this rebellious nature by refusing to do things she did not like. Throughout the world, it seems that as adolescents develop their own identities, they come into more conflict with their parents.

For most families, this conflict leads only to minor annoyances. It can actually help adolescents develop important skills, including negotiation, critical thinking, communication, and empathy (Holmbeck, 1996). According to Erikson's theory, negotiating a pathway to a stable identity requires breaking away from childhood beliefs by questioning and challenging parental and societal ideas (Erikson, 1968). But even though adolescents and their parents may disagree and sometimes argue, across cultures parents have a great deal of direct influence on their children's individual behaviors, values, and sense of autonomy (Feldman & Rosenthal, 1991). Parents also indirectly affect social development by influencing children's choices about friends (Brown, Mounts, Lamborn, & Steinberg, 1993; Cairns & Cairns, 1994).

Peers play a crucial role in identity development. Peer groups are created when teenagers form friendships with others who have similar values and worldviews (**Figure 4.29a**). Observers outside the peer groups tend to place teenagers who dress or act a certain way into groupings, called *cliques* (**Figure 4.29b**). The observers often see members of cliques as virtually interchangeable, and community members may respond to all youths from that group in similar ways (Urberg, Degirmencioglue, Tolson, & Halliday-Scher, 1995). The teenagers, however, often see themselves as unique and individual, or as connected to a small subset of close friends, not just as members of a certain clique. The friendships created in these peer groups provide an important sense of belonging, social support, and acceptance.

Adolescents Develop Cognitively

Think back to the story of Bruce Reimer, the boy who was raised as a girl. Did his parents make the right choice when they decided on sexual reassignment for him? That decision was especially difficult because it wasn't just a matter of physical health. It also involved morality. Moral choices, large ones and small ones alike, affect other people. Ideally, the ability to consider questions about morality develops during childhood and continues into adulthood.

MORAL REASONING AND MORAL EMOTIONS Moral development is the way people learn to decide between behaviors with competing social outcomes. In other words, when is it acceptable to take an action that may harm others or that may break implicit or explicit social contracts? Theorists typically divide morality into moral reasoning, which depends on cognitive processes, and moral emotions. Moral emotions, such as embarrassment and shame, are considered self-conscious emotions. They are called self-conscious because they involve how people think about themselves. For example, the emotional experience of sadness might become the self-conscious emotional experience of shame when it is yourself you feel sad about. It is important to note, however, that moral reasoning is affected by moral emotions (Moll & de Oliveira-Souza, 2007). The development of moral emotions is vital to acting morally.

Psychologists who study the cognitive processes of moral behavior have focused largely on Lawrence Kohlberg's stage theory. Kohlberg (1984) tested moral-reasoning skills by asking people to respond to hypothetical situations in which someone was faced with a moral dilemma. For example, should a person steal a drug to save his dying wife because he could not afford the drug? Kohlberg

(a)

(b)

FIGURE 4.29
Peers and Cliques
(a) Adolescents develop strong friendships with peers who share similar interests and values. **(b)** Outside observers might tend to place the young men in this peer group into a single clique, "punks," and would tend to react to all of them in similar ways. Each adolescent, however, might view himself as an individual.

Bullying

Have you ever been the victim of bullying? Have you seen children or adolescents being bullied? Have you ever bullied someone? Bullying is when someone repeatedly uses physical power or control over another person, behaving aggressively in a way that is unwanted (Espelage and Holt, 2012). There are many types of bullying:

- Physical: physical contact that hurts a person—for example, hitting, kicking, punching, taking away an item and destroying it—and physical intimidation, such as threatening someone and frightening him enough to make him do what the bully wants.

- Verbal: name-calling, making offensive remarks, or joking about a person's appearance, religion, gender, ethnicity, sexual orientation; and verbal intimidation.

- Social: spreading rumors or stories about someone, excluding someone from a group on purpose, or making fun of someone by pointing out her differences.

- Cyber: sending aggressive, threatening, and/or intimidating messages, pictures, or information using social media, computers (e-mail and instant messages), or cell phones (text messaging and voicemail).

Bullying is a complex behavior with many contributing factors. However, experts tend to agree that bullies might not strongly feel the moral emotions of guilt and shame (Hymel, Rocke-Henderson, & Bonanno, 2005). Bullies also often show increased moral disengagement, such as indifference or pride, when explaining their behavior and more-positive attitudes about using bullying to respond to difficult social situations. Because bullying tends to get people what they want and society traditionally turns a blind eye to it, bullying goes on. However, both kids who are bullied and those who bully others can have serious, lasting problems.

So what can you do? Here are three steps adults should take when they see an act of bullying occurring among children and adolescents:

1. **Stop the bullying on the spot:** Intervene in a calm and respectful manner, separate the children, make sure they are safe, and get any needed medical help.

2. **Find out what happened:** Once you have separated the kids, get all of their views on what happened. Seek evidence from other people who witnessed the act. Do not jump to conclusions or place blame.

3. **Support the kids involved:** Listen to the person being bullied, assure him that it's not his fault, and work to resolve the bullying situation. Also work with the person doing the bullying to help him realize his behavior is wrong, understand why he bullies, and take steps to reduce the behavior.

By modeling good moral reasoning and good moral behavior, and reducing the rewards associated with bullying, you can help children and adolescents develop appropriate moral values. Even other kids can learn to be more than bystanders and help reduce bullying. For more information on how to respond to bullying and prevent it, visit www.stopbullying.gov.

was most concerned with the reasons people provided for their answers, rather than the answers themselves. He devised a theory of moral judgment that involved three main levels of moral reasoning.

At the **preconventional level,** people solve the moral dilemma in terms of self-interest or pleasurable outcomes. For example, a person at this level might say, "He should steal the drug because he could get away with it." At the **conventional level,** people's responses conform to rules of law and order or focus on others' approval or disapproval. For example, a person at this level might say, "He should take the drug because everyone will think he is a bad person if he lets his wife die." At the **postconventional level,** the highest level of moral reasoning, people's responses center on complex reasoning. This reasoning concerns abstract principles that transcend laws and social expectations. For example, a person at this level might say, "Sometimes people have to break the law if the law is unjust." Thus Kohlberg believed advanced moral reasoning to include considering the greater good for all people and giving less thought to personal wishes or fear of punishment.

Not all psychologists agree with moral-reasoning theories such as Kohlberg's. Critics fault these theories for emphasizing only the cognitive aspects of morality and neglecting emotional issues that influence moral judgments, such as shame, pride, or embarrassment. They believe that moral actions, such as helping others in need, are influenced more by emotions than by cognitive processes.

Finally, not everyone progresses through the stages of moral development at the same rate or in the same order. How can a parent, guardian, or other authority figure help guide a younger person's moral development? According to the research, there is great value in showing the general consequence of a specific behavior. Saying, "You made Chris cry. It's not nice to hit, because it hurts people" is more effective than saying simply, "Don't hit people." Such explanation promotes children's sympathetic attitudes, appropriate feelings of guilt, and awareness of other people's feelings. The resulting attitudes, feelings, and awareness then influence the children's moral reasoning and behavioral choices, which also help instill moral values that guide behavior throughout life. This cycle of moral development can be readily seen in cases of bullying, as described in Using Psychology in Your Life.

preconventional level
Earliest level of moral development; at this level, self-interest and event outcomes determine what is moral.

conventional level
Middle level of moral development; at this level, strict adherence to societal laws and the approval of others determine what is moral.

postconventional level
Highest level of moral development; at this level, decisions about morality depend on abstract principles and the value of all life.

 4.3 CHECKPOINT: How Do Adolescents Develop?

- During puberty, both males and females undergo physical changes, including development of primary and secondary sex characteristics and changes in the brain.

- Adolescence is the time when teens confront the psychosocial conflict of identity versus role confusion.

- The establishment of gender identity reflects the interaction of nature (biological factors of sex and hormones) and nurture (gender socialization).

- During adolescence, cognitive development leads to more-sophisticated moral reasoning.

4.4 How Do We Develop in Adulthood?

Sometimes we see adults doing things that make us think, "They're acting like kids," and not in a good way. What does it mean to be an adult? For many years, developmental psychologists focused on childhood and adolescence, as if most important aspects of development occurred by age 20 and then people did not change anymore. In recent decades, researchers working in a wide range of fields have demonstrated that throughout adulthood, important changes occur physically, socio-emotionally, and cognitively (see Figure 4.2). Therefore, many contemporary psychologists consider development from the perspective of the entire life span. Their goal is to understand how mental activity and social relations change over the entire course of life. *Adulthood,* then, becomes an important topic for study. Beginning at the end of adolescence, lasting through old age and concluding with death, adulthood makes up most of life. The developmental changes during adulthood vary from stage to stage.

Our Bodies Change in Adulthood

Our bodies are ready to reproduce when we reach our teens. We peak in fitness during our 20s. So, evolutionarily speaking, a 40-year-old is quite old. In fact, for most of their history, humans lived only a few decades. As recently as the beginning of the twentieth century, the average life expectancy in the United States was only 47 years. However, since 1900, through modern medicine and improvements in hygiene and in food availability, we have increased the average human life expectancy by about 30 years.

EARLY TO MIDDLE ADULTHOOD It's the prime of life! Really? Between the ages of 20 and 40, we actually experience a steady decline in muscle mass, bone density, eyesight, and hearing (Shephard, 1997). As we approach middle age, we start to notice that we can no longer drink as much alcohol, eat as much junk food, or get by on as little sleep as we could in our 20s. That "middle-age spread," the accumulating fat around the belly, becomes harder and harder to work off. Thus nutrition, exercise, and a healthy lifestyle are important in early adulthood. First, it is much harder to get in shape after middle age. Second, the better physical and psychological shape we are in during early adulthood, the fewer significant declines we will see as we age.

TRANSITION TO OLD AGE In Western societies, people are living much longer, and the number of people over age 85 is growing dramatically. Indeed, it is becoming commonplace for people to live beyond 100. By 2030, more than 1 in 5 Americans will be over age 65, and these older people will be ethnically diverse, well educated, and physically fit (National Research Council, 2006). With this "graying" of the population in Western societies, much greater research attention has been paid to the lives of people over age 60.

Our view of the elderly is changing a great deal as the baby boom generation ages. Many older adults work productively well past their 70s. For instance, nearly 40 percent of U.S. federal judges are over 65 (Markon, 2001). Popular-music stars such as Madonna, Bruce Springsteen, and the Rolling Stones are still performing well into their 50s, 60s, and beyond, certainly defying common stereotypes of older people (**Figure 4.30**).

Nevertheless, the body and mind start deteriorating more rapidly at about age 50. The cosmetics and plastic surgery industries are booming as we try to cover up superficial physical changes such as the graying of hair and the wrinkling of skin. But some of the most serious changes affect the brain, whose frontal lobes shrink proportionally more than other brain regions (Cowell et al., 1994). Scientists once believed that cognitive problems such as confusion and memory loss were a normal, inevitable part of aging. They now recognize that most older adults remain alert; they just do everything a bit more slowly.

FIGURE 4.30
Changing Views of the Elderly
The Rolling Stones, now in their 60s and early 70s, are still making music after nearly 50 years.

Adults Develop Lifelong Social and Emotional Bonds

Despite its sometimes rocky road, adolescence can be an exciting and gratifying time. Ideally, during this period we meet new friends, learn new ideas, and consolidate our emerging sense of identity. Successfully meeting the challenges of adolescence prepares us to face the challenges of adulthood. This new set of challenges reflects the need to find meaning in our lives.

PSYCHOSOCIAL CHALLENGES Think back to Erikson's theory that we develop psychosocially through eight life stages (see Table 4.1). According to Erikson, successful adult development includes having intimate relationships with friends and partners, giving back to society, and viewing life in a generally positive light, even through the many ups and downs or tragedies.

Young adulthood is the time of Erikson's sixth stage. The psychosocial challenge during this stage, **intimacy versus isolation,** involves forming and maintaining committed friendships and romantic relationships. Essentially, as young adults we are finding people to share life with in intimate ways. We are moving outward from ourselves rather than being socially isolated. Erikson emphasized the Western value of merging with others while not losing our own sense of identity. For Erikson, building a strong sense of identity in adolescence is crucial for being able to form truly intimate relationships with others in adulthood. He argued that if a person has no sense of self, it is more difficult to engage in honest, open, emotionally close relationships with others (Erikson, 1980).

Erikson's seventh-stage challenge, **generativity versus stagnation,** takes place during middle age. This stage involves contributing to future generations. Caring for children, being productive in a career, having regard for others, and

intimacy versus isolation
Sixth stage of Erikson's theory of psychosocial development, where young adults face the challenge of forming committed long-term friendships and romances.

generativity versus stagnation
Seventh stage of Erikson's theory of psychosocial development, where middle-aged adults face the challenge of leaving behind a positive legacy and caring for future generations.

(a)

(b)

(c)

FIGURE 4.31

Marriage
Across cultures, marriage remains a building block of society. If the statistics hold true, **(a)** this Sami couple in Norway, **(b)** this Amhara couple in Ethiopia, and **(c)** this Hani couple in China will report being happy in their marriages.

being concerned about the future are positive psychosocial actions of this stage. If our children turned out well, our career was satisfying, and we contributed to our community, we are more likely to leave middle age with a sense of generativity, or leaving a positive legacy. The opposite of generativity, stagnation, includes a feeling that life is going nowhere or that we are very materialistic and self-centered. Contemporary research indicates that people who are high in generativity have a more positive outlook on life (McAdams & Olson, 2010).

In old age, we reach Erikson's last challenge, **integrity versus despair.** Integrity refers to a sense of honesty about ourselves and a feeling that our lives have been well lived, so that facing death is neither scary nor depressing. For Erikson, the psychosocial challenge of late adulthood involves how we view our life, not whether that life was easy or trauma free. The crisis at this stage can be triggered by events that highlight the mortal nature of human life, such as the death of a spouse or close friend. The crisis also can be triggered by changing social and occupational roles, such as retirement. Resolving the final challenge allows us to come to terms with the reality of death. If we have many regrets, lack close relationships, or are angry about getting older, we may resolve the psychosocial conflict with a sense of despair instead of integrity. Although Erikson's theory paints a rather mixed view of old age, a great deal of evidence suggests that older adults are much more satisfied with their lives than was traditionally believed. One recent study of older adults between ages 65 and 92 found that life satisfaction generally increased over an 8-year period (Gana, Bailly, Saada, Joulain, & Alaphilippe, 2013).

MARRIAGE In adulthood, people devote a great deal of effort to achieving and maintaining satisfying relationships. Around the world, the vast majority of people marry at some point in their lives or form some type of permanent bond with a relationship partner (**Figure 4.31**). However, the percentage of people who marry is declining slowly in most industrialized countries, and people today marry later in life than did those in the past (Grossman, 2005).

Research shows that marriage benefits the individuals involved. For example, married people generally live longer than people who were never married, were divorced, or were widowed (Waite, 1995). When people's income rises (as by combining two salaries through marriage), they are able to live in safer neighborhoods, have better health care, eat better, and so on. Compared with those who are unmarried, married people typically experience greater happiness and joy and are at less risk for psychological disorders such as depression (Robles & Kiecolt-Glaser, 2003).

The benefits of marriage are more significant for men than for women, however. Studies suggest that men may benefit from marriage because their wives make sure they smoke less, eat more healthily, and go to the doctor. Women serve as the primary social support for their husbands. Married men report higher sexual and relationship satisfaction than do cohabiting and single men; but across these same groups, women report no difference. Married women report more emotional satisfaction, however, than cohabiting or single women do.

Still, marriage is not a cure-all. Unhappily married people are at greater risk for poor health and even mortality than happily married people. In general, people who are in unhappy marriages, are separated, or are divorced have many physical and psychological struggles, ranging from depression to physical illness to violent behavior (Carrère, Buehlman, Gottman, Coan, & Ruckstuhl, 2000). Note, though, that these studies are largely correlational. It could be that happy, well-adjusted people are more likely to get married and not that marriage causes good outcomes for people. Or perhaps unhappy, negative people have both health problems and strained marriages.

The good news is that according to national surveys, at any given time the vast majority of married people report satisfaction with their marriages. Those reporting the most satisfaction tend to have sufficient economic resources, share decision making, and together hold the view that marriage should be a lifelong commitment (Amato, Johnson, Booth, & Rogers, 2003). Having a successful marriage contributes to a sense of generativity in middle adulthood, as does having children.

HAVING CHILDREN The birth of a first child is a profound event for most couples. In fact, this arrival changes their lives in almost every respect. Seeing a baby's first social smile, watching the first few tentative steps, and hearing a child say "Mommy" or "Daddy" are powerful rewards for parents. Being a parent is central to the identity of many adults. They often become immersed in their children's lives, making sure their children have playmates, exposing them to new experiences, and seeking ways to make them happy and healthy.

Research shows that children can strain a marriage, however, especially when time and money are tight. Consistently, couples with children, especially those with adolescent children, report less marital satisfaction than those who are childless (Belsky, 1990; Cowan & Cowan, 1988). Most couples feel their love will be enough to make the birth of a baby a blissful time. These couples often receive a rude awakening when they are sleep deprived, agitated, and less than skilled at caring for their new bundle of joy, especially during the first months (Cowan & Cowan, 1988).

Contemporary researchers are trying to find ways to prepare parents for parenthood so the transition does not put such a strain on the relationship. For example, Philip and Carolyn Cowan, a married couple who are also marriage researchers, have found that many couples do not discuss roles and responsibilities before they have a child. This failure to communicate leads to misunderstandings and feelings of resentment after the child's birth. The Cowans recommend that couples have serious and detailed conversations about all aspects of their lives and how they will approach each task after the baby is born.

Partners who report their early married life as chaotic or negative are more likely to find that having a baby does not bring them closer together or solve their problems. Instead, raising the child increases the existing strain. Teaching newlyweds or young partners how to communicate and understand each other's needs may prevent divorce, and it may also allow the couple to enjoy parenting when their children are young as well as when they grow older and the children leave home (Shapiro, Gottman, & Carrère, 2000).

FINDING MEANING IN LATER LIFE People of all ages want to find meaning in life. But meaning often becomes a preoccupation for the elderly. As people grow older, they perceive time to be limited, so they adjust their priorities to emphasize emotionally meaningful events, experiences, and goals (Carstensen, 1995; Fung & Carstensen, 2004). For instance, they may choose to spend more time with a smaller group of close friends and avoid new people. They may spend an increasing amount of time reflecting on their lives and sharing memories with family members and friends. As they look back on their lives, older adults report more positive emotions than negative ones (Pasupathi & Carstensen, 2003).

The message here is that older adults want to savor their final years by putting their time and effort into meaningful and rewarding experiences. To the extent that they consider their time well spent, older adults are satisfied and can live their final years gracefully. This result is especially likely if throughout their lives they have worked hard to maintain their physical health, their social ties, and their cognitive capacities.

The Mental Abilities of Adults Begin to Decline

Yes, the baby boom generation is filling a large percentage of judgeships and providing us with some still-favorite entertainers. That generation has also given rise to the common phrase *a senior moment*—the inability to remember something we knew a moment before. In that moment, we know we're just not as sharp as we once were.

Although we may not notice until later adulthood, our cognitive abilities begin declining much earlier. It's difficult to pinpoint exactly what causes the decline. The frontal lobes, which play an important role in certain types of memory and many other cognitive skills, typically shrink as people grow older. One of the most consistent and identifiable cognitive changes is a slowing of mental processing speed. As early as the mid-20s, it takes us longer to process a sensory input and react with a motor response, and the response time becomes greater as we age (Era, Jokela, & Heikkinen, 1986).

Some of the observed decline may result from sensory-perceptual changes that occur with age. For instance, our sensitivity to visual contrast decreases, so activities such as climbing stairs or driving at night may become more difficult and more dangerous. Sensitivity to sound also decreases with age, especially the ability to tune out background noise. This change may make older people seem confused or forgetful when they simply are not able to hear well enough. And unfortunately, aging also affects memory and intelligence.

INTELLIGENCE AND MEMORY For 7 years, the Seattle Longitudinal Study tracked participants between the ages of 25 and 81 to address questions of intelligence during aging (Schaie, 1990). By testing cognitive abilities such as verbal and mathematical skills, the researchers found that intellectual decline does not occur until people are in their 60s or 70s. Further, they found that people who were healthy and stayed mentally active demonstrated less decline. Older adults take longer to learn new information. Still, once they learn it, they use that information as efficiently as young adults do. Moreover, older adults have accumulated a great deal of knowledge over their lives and therefore tend to know more than younger adults. Perhaps for this reason, we often view older adults as wise.

Older people tend to have difficulty with memory tasks that require juggling multiple pieces of information at the same time. Tasks that call for them to do several things at once, such as driving while listening to the radio, also prove difficult. Although memory and the speed of processing may decline, the continued ability to learn new information may offset those losses in terms of daily functioning.

Older adults who experience a dramatic loss in mental ability may be experiencing **dementia.** This brain condition causes gradual decline in thinking, memory, and behavior. Dementia has many causes, including excessive alcohol intake and HIV. But for older adults, the major causes are Alzheimer's disease and small strokes that affect the brain's blood supply. After age 70, the risk of dementia increases with each year of life. Approximately 3 percent to 5 percent of people will develop Alzheimer's disease by age 70 to 75, and 6.5 percent will develop the disease after age 85 (Kawas, Gray, Brookmeyer, Fozard, & Zonderman, 2000).

dementia
Severe impairment in intellectual capacity and personality, often due to damage to the brain.

The initial symptoms of Alzheimer's are typically minor memory impairments, but the disease eventually progresses to more serious difficulties, such as forgetting daily routines (**Figure 4.32**). It takes about 4 years for people to progress from mild cognitive impairment to a diagnosis of Alzheimer's (Kawas et al., 2000). Eventually, the person loses all mental capacities, including memory and language. Many people with Alzheimer's also experience profound personality changes. While we do not know the exact cause of Alzheimer's, some people seem to have a genetic predisposition to its development.

Besides a genetic predisposition to Alzheimer's (Corder et al., 1993), there may be genetic predispositions to other kinds of dementia. That picture may seem grim, but a predisposition is not a hopeless case, because environment also has an impact. Decades of research show that challenging one's brain by learning new tasks, working puzzles, reading, remaining socially active, and maintaining physical exercise at least 3 days per week is associated with a significantly lower risk of dementia (Fratiglioni, Paillard-Borg, & Winblad, 2004; Larson et al., 2006). As you age, playing an active role in your own development may help make adulthood transitions nonthreatening, even deeply rewarding experiences (**Figure 4.33**).

Despite the physical, social, and emotional challenges of aging, most older adults are healthy and happy. Except for dementia, older adults have fewer mental health problems, including depression, than younger adults (Jorm, 2000). Indeed, some individuals thrive in old age, especially those with adequate financial resources and good health (Crosnoe & Elder, 2002). Most older adults report being just as satisfied with life, if not more so, as younger adults are (Mroczek & Kolarz, 1998). As noted earlier, one study found that life satisfaction increased for older adults over an 8-year period.

Thus this chapter ends where it began, with a reminder that all aspects of human development result from a complex interplay of influences. These influences include genes, hormones, family, social ties, culture, and each individual's motivations and actions. We all play active roles in our own development. We are not passively absorbing our environments, nor are we solely ruled by our genes. How we experience each phase of the life span depends on our own perceptions, the social support we receive, and the choreographed dance between nature and nurture.

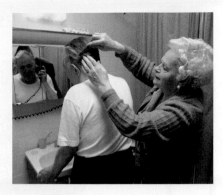

FIGURE 4.32
Impairments from Alzheimer's Disease
A woman helps her husband, who has Alzheimer's disease. This brain condition, which is the major cause of dementia, occurs in the elderly.

FIGURE 4.33
Maintaining Health and Happiness
Most older adults report being very happy. Engaging in activities that stimulate the brain (doing crossword puzzles) and the body (swimming and walking) is associated with staying healthy and happy for as long as possible.

 4.4 CHECKPOINT: How Do We Develop in Adulthood?

- Physical changes are inevitable, especially after the age of 50. Keeping in shape during early adulthood means we will see less significant decline as we grow old.

- In adulthood, we experience several psychosocial conflicts, which we resolve by developing long-term relationships, having children and satisfying careers, and feeling satisfied.

- Cognitive abilities decline as we grow old, but only some older adults experience dementia.

- Despite the declines of older adulthood, many elderly people thrive, reporting this period as the happiest time of life.

BIG PICTURE

4.1

How Do We Develop in the Womb?

a. Remember the key terms related to prenatal development.

b. Understand the three prenatal periods.

c. Apply information about teratogens and their effects during prenatal development.

d. Analyze how biology and environment affect prenatal development.

4.2

How Do Infants and Children Develop Over Time?

a. Remember the key terms about how infants and children develop.

b. Understand motor and sensory development in an infant.

c. Apply socio-emotional aspects of child development to real life.

d. Understand the four stages of cognitive development in children.

e. Analyze the three stages of language development in childhood.

4.3

How Do Adolescents Develop?

a. Remember the key terms related to adolescent development.

b. Understand the physical changes in puberty.

c. Apply socio-emotional aspects of development to your own adolescence.

d. Analyze a moral dilemma in your own life.

4.4

How Do We Develop in Adulthood?

a. Remember the key terms about adult development.

b. Understand physical development as we age.

c. Evaluate socio-emotional changes in adulthood.

d. Apply the cognitive aspects of development in adulthood.

KEY TERMS

CHECKPOINT

developmental psychology
germinal period
embryonic period
fetal period
teratogens

- Human development occurs in three interacting domains: biological, socio-emotional, and cognitive.

- In the prenatal period, both nature (inborn genetics and biological traits) and nurture (environment) affect human development.

- Prenatal development occurs in three periods: germinal, embryonic, and fetal.

- Teratogens are environmental agents with adverse physical effects during prenatal development and potentially long-term cognitive and behavioral effects.

maturation
secure attachment
avoidant attachment
ambivalent attachment
assimilation
accommodation
sensorimotor stage
preoperational stage
concrete operational stage
formal operational stage
babbling
telegraphic speech
overregularization

- We are born with innate reflexes, but through experiences we learn to move and process sensory information.

- Forming strong attachments with caregivers early on supports appropriate social interactions and emotion regulation.

- Infants' and children's cognitive abilities become more advanced with time and experience as they move through four stages of cognitive development.

- Children develop language skills starting with the production of phonemes and eventually moving to speaking full sentences.

puberty
primary sex characteristics
secondary sex characteristics
identity versus role confusion
gender identity
gender roles
preconventional level
conventional level
postconventional level

- During puberty, both males and females undergo physical changes, including development of primary and secondary sex characteristics and changes in the brain.

- Adolescence is the time when teens confront the psychosocial conflict of identity versus role confusion.

- The establishment of gender identity reflects the interaction of nature (biological factors of sex and hormones) and nurture (gender socialization).

- During adolescence, cognitive development leads to more-sophisticated moral reasoning.

intimacy versus isolation
generativity versus stagnation
integrity versus despair
dementia

- Physical changes are inevitable, especially after the age of 50. Keeping in shape during early adulthood means we will see less significant decline as we grow old.

- In adulthood, we experience several psychosocial conflicts, which we resolve by developing long-term relationships, having children and satisfying careers, and feeling satisfied.

- Cognitive abilities decline as we grow old, but only some older adults experience dementia.

- Despite the declines of older adulthood, many elderly people thrive, reporting this period as the happiest time of life.

For a self-quiz on this chapter, go to the back of the book and find Appendix B: Quizzes.

5 Sensation and Perception

WHAT DO YOU EXPERIENCE when you see the color red or eat chocolate? If you are like most people, you experience red as a visual phenomenon. You may associate this color with stoplights or stop signs. You experience eating chocolate as a sweet taste. You may associate this taste with pleasure. But not everyone would agree with these descriptions.

William hates driving because, to him, the sight of road signs tastes like a gross mixture of pistachio ice cream and earwax (McNeil, 2006). For Michael, any personal name has a specific taste—for example, the name "John" tastes like corn bread (Simner et al., 2006). Another person experiences each day of the week, or month of the year, as a particular color—Monday is red, Tuesday is indigo, December is yellow, and so on (Ramachandran & Hubbard, 2003). Other people experience colors as smells, sights as sounds, or sounds as colors and shapes.

BIG QUESTIONS

This condition, where people receive sensory input in one form and experience it in another form, is called synesthesia. If you have never experienced synesthesia, it is almost impossible to imagine. However, the condition is not that rare. Estimates of the percentage of the population that report these cross-sensory experiences range from 1 in 2,000 to 1 in 200. And reports of people with synesthesia date as far back as ancient Greece (Ferry, 2002). But modern psychological research is revealing how people have these unique perceptual experiences.

The explanation is in the brain. For example, during brain scans taken of people with color-number synesthesia who looked at black numbers on a white background, researchers found neural activity in the brain area responsible for color vision. Control participants without synesthesia did not show activity in this brain area when they looked at the same numbers (Ramachandran, 2003). Each person who has synesthesia experiences it in a very consistent way. For example, a certain number always appears to be one particular color (**Figure 5.1**). Color-number synesthesia may occur because the brain area involved in seeing colors is near the brain area involved in understanding numbers. Specifically, these two brain areas may somehow be connected, or one area of the brain might have adopted another area's role.

Research into synesthesia can give us insight into how people process sensory input as well as how our brains help us perceive sensory information in our own unique ways. The perceptual system is stunningly intelligent in its ability to guide us around. For example, right this minute your brain is making millions of calculations to produce a coherent experience of your environment. Neurons inside your brain do not directly experience the outside world. Instead, they communicate with other neurons inside your brain. Your conscious experience of the world emerges from this communication. And this all happens in milliseconds.

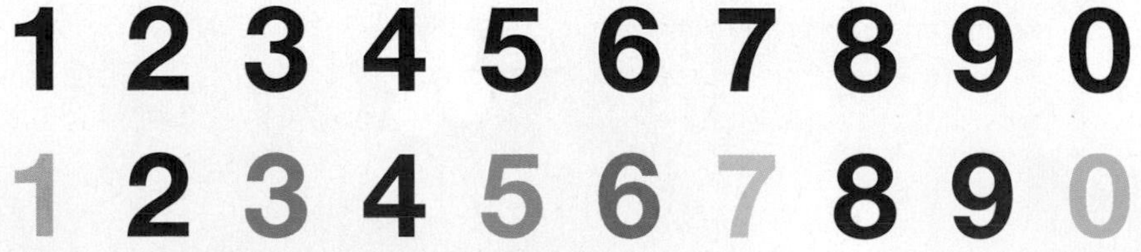

FIGURE 5.1

Synesthesia Shows Unusual Relationships Between Sensation and Perception
In synesthesia, sensory input in one form is experienced in another form. In color-number synesthesia, each number is seen as a particular color.

5.1 How Do Sensation and Perception Affect Us?

LEARNING GOALS	READING ACTIVITIES
a. Remember the key terms about sensation and perception.	List all of the boldface words and write down their definitions.
b. Apply the four steps from sensation to perception to your life.	Using a sensory input you have experienced, describe the four steps from sensation to perception.
c. Understand absolute threshold and difference threshold.	Use your own words to compare absolute threshold and difference threshold.
d. Apply signal detection theory to real life.	Use signal detection theory to explain the four ways new parents could respond to their baby's crying.

Imagine you take half a grapefruit out of the refrigerator and dig into it with a spoon. Some juice splashes out of the fruit and hits your nose and mouth. What do your senses tell you? You smell some strong fragrance. You feel something cold on your skin. You taste something sharp on your tongue. So far, your experience consists of raw sensation. Your sensory systems have detected features of the juice.

Sensation is the detection of physical stimuli from the world around us and the sending of that information to the brain. Physical stimuli can be light waves, sound waves, food molecules, odor molecules, temperature changes, or pressure changes on the skin. In sensing the splash of the grapefruit juice, you are sensing food molecules, odor molecules, slight temperature changes, and slight pressure changes.

Perception is the brain's further processing of sensory information. This processing results in our conscious experience of the world. The essence of perception is interpreting sensation. That is, our perceptual systems (as opposed to our sensory systems) translate sensation into information that is meaningful and useful. In the above example, perception is interpretation of the sensory stimuli of cold droplets, a strong smell, and a sharp taste as qualities of grapefruit.

But even when people experience the exact same sensory input (sensation), they experience that input differently (perception). If you like grapefruit, you might experience this splash as at least partly pleasant. If you dislike grapefruit—suppose your father has insisted that you eat it—you might experience the splash as totally unpleasant. The Try It Yourself exercise on p. 156 will help you begin to understand the differences between sensation and perception.

Our Senses Detect Physical Stimuli, and Our Brains Process Perception

Suppose you are driving, and the traffic signal changes from red to green. Believe it or not, there is actually no red or green color in the signal or in the light you see. Instead, your eyes and brain enable you to see the redness or greenness of the light. Objects in the physical world don't actually have color. Each object reflects light waves of particular lengths. Our visual systems interpret those waves as different colors.

sensation
The sense organs' detection of external physical stimulus and the transmission of information about this stimulus to the brain.

perception
The processing, organization, and interpretation of sensory signals in the brain; these processes result in an internal neural representation of the physical stimulus.

If you and your friends look at the same car, will you all agree on the color? Check it out with this example:

1. Look only at the picture of the car. Decide what color the car is. Then look at the color bar and decide which color sample is most similar to how you see the color of the car. Write down both of your answers.
2. Now ask a few other people to do the things in step 1.
3. Most likely, some people have labeled the car color the same way you did. Some people have chosen different labels. However, the label a person chooses for the color doesn't tell us what that person has actually perceived.
4. But even people who labeled the car the same way you did might have chosen a different color sample from the one that you chose. This result suggests you had different perceptions of the same color.

What does this demonstration show? The sensory input, the sensation, is the same for people. Yet each person has a unique perception of that input. Taken together, sensation and perception make up all of our individual experiences with the world.

sensory receptors
Sensory organs that detect physical stimulation from the external world and change that stimulation into information that can be processed by the brain.

transduction
A process by which sensory receptors change physical stimuli into signals that are eventually sent to the brain.

So how do light waves get changed into information that the brain can process? Special cells in our eyes respond to these different wavelengths and change that physical signal into information that the brain can interpret. If you are driving and your brain receives information about a green traffic light, your brain most likely will interpret that light as meaning "Go."

FROM SENSATION TO PERCEPTION To understand more clearly both sensation and perception, imagine that you drive up to a traffic signal as it turns green. The green light is actually the physical stimulus in the form of light waves (**Figure 5.2,** Step 1). That stimulus is detected by specialized cells called **sensory receptors.** The receptors' detection of the stimulus is sensation (see Figure 5.2, Step 2).

In a process called **transduction,** the sensory receptors change the stimulus input to signals that the brain can understand (see Figure 5.2, Step 3). In some cases, such as taste, transduction directly results in neurons' firing action

1 Physical stimulus: A traffic light turns green. The green light is a physical stimulus.

2 Sensation: The light waves are detected by sensory receptors in the driver's eyes.

3 Transduction: The sensory receptors translate the physical stimulus into signals. Those signals will become neural signals.

4 Perception: The neural signals travel along nerve fibers to the thalamus. Then cortical areas in the brain process the signals and construct a representation of a green light. The brain interprets the light as indicating "Start driving!"

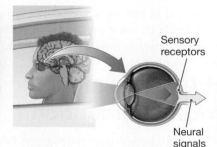
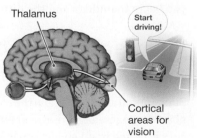

FIGURE 5.2
From Sensation to Perception
Here is a summary of the four steps in the process of changing sensory input into a personal experience. The example is for sensation and perception of vision, but the steps in general also apply to hearing, taste, smell, and touch. However, information about smell is not processed through the thalamus.

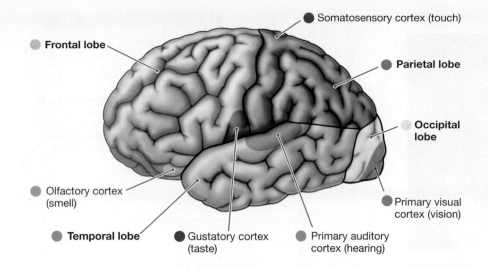

Somatosensory cortex (touch)

Frontal lobe

Parietal lobe

Occipital lobe

Olfactory cortex (smell)

Primary visual cortex (vision)

Temporal lobe

Gustatory cortex (taste)

Primary auditory cortex (hearing)

FIGURE 5.3

The Brain's Primary Sensory Areas
Except for smell, all sensory input is first processed through the thalamus. Then inputs are sent to cortical regions that process information about vision, hearing, taste, smell, and touch.

potentials (to review the firing of action potentials, see Chapter 2). For vision, more processing must happen before the information is coded as action potentials. When the brain does process the action potentials, you will interpret them as green light. You will also register the meaning of that traffic signal as "Go." This further processing of the information following transduction is perception (see Figure 5.2, Step 4).

This example demonstrates the general processes of sensation and perception. However, the details are slightly different for each sense. In this chapter, you will learn about the four steps of sensation and perception for each major sensory system. In each case, a physical stimulus is detected, specialized sensory receptors transduce the stimulus information, and neurons fire action potentials. These action potentials are the sensory information that is sent to specific regions of the brain for interpretation (**Figure 5.3**).

The sum of this activity, across all of your senses, is your huge range of perceptions. And your perceptions add up to your experience of the world. If you get splashed with grapefruit juice or see the color of a traffic light, your sensations and perceptions enable you to interpret the information and respond appropriately. For example, you decide the juice is delicious or you accelerate the car.

There Must Be a Certain Amount of a Stimulus for Us to Detect It

Stop reading for a moment and listen. What do you hear? Perhaps voices in the next room or music down the hall. But can you hear the buzzing of the fly that you see on the window across the room? How much physical stimulus is required for our sense organs to detect sensory information? How much change in the physical stimulus is required before we notice that change in the sensory information?

THRESHOLD TO DETECT SENSORY INFORMATION An enormous amount of physical stimulation from the world around you reaches your sensory receptors. Even so, you do not notice much of it. Physical stimulation has to go beyond some level before you experience a sensation. The **absolute threshold** is the

absolute threshold
The smallest amount of physical stimulation required to detect a sensory input half of the time it is present.

(a)

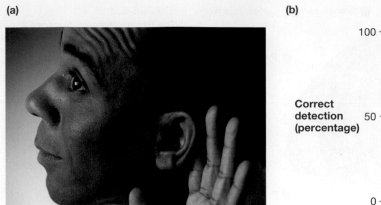

(b)

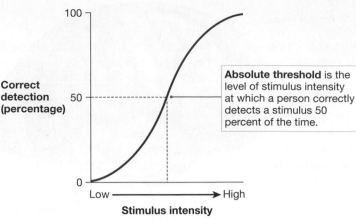

Absolute threshold is the level of stimulus intensity at which a person correctly detects a stimulus 50 percent of the time.

Correct detection (percentage)

100

50

0

Low ———————→ High

Stimulus intensity

FIGURE 5.4

Absolute Threshold

(a) Can this man detect a soft sound, such as a whisper? **(b)** This graph shows the relationship between the intensity of stimulus input and a person's ability to correctly detect the input. The absolute threshold is the point of stimulus intensity that a person can correctly detect half the time.

minimum amount of physical stimuli required before you detect the sensory input (**Figure 5.4**). You can also think of the absolute threshold as the smallest amount of a stimulus a person can detect half of the time the stimulus is present. For instance, how loudly must someone in the next room whisper for you to hear it? In this case, the absolute threshold is the quietest whisper you could hear half the time. **Table 5.1** lists some approximate minimum levels of physical stimuli that are required to detect sensory input for each sense.

A **difference threshold** is the smallest difference that you can notice between two pieces of sensory input. In other words, it is the minimum amount of change in the physical stimulus required to detect a difference between one sensory experience and another. Suppose your friend is watching a television show. You are reading and not paying attention to what's on the screen. If a commercial comes on that is louder than the show, you might look up, noticing that something has changed. In this case, the difference threshold is the minimum change in volume required for you to detect a difference.

TABLE 5.1

Absolute Threshold to Detect Input for Each Sense

SENSE	MINIMUM SENSORY INPUT REQUIRED FOR DETECTION
Taste	1 teaspoon of sugar in 2 gallons of water
Smell	1 drop of perfume diffused into the entire volume of six rooms
Touch	A fly's wing falling on your cheek from a distance of 0.04 inch
Hearing	The tick of a clock at 20 feet under quiet conditions
Vision	A candle flame 30 miles away on a dark, clear night

SOURCE: Galanter (1962).

difference threshold
The minimum difference in physical stimulation required to detect a difference between sensory inputs.

The difference threshold increases as the stimulus becomes more intense. Say you pick up a 1-ounce jar of spice and a 2-ounce jar of spice. You will easily detect the difference of 1 ounce. Now pick up a 5-pound package of flour and a package that weighs 5 pounds and 1 ounce. The same difference of 1 ounce between these two will be harder to detect, maybe even impossible to detect.

The principle at work here is called *Weber's law*. This law is based on the work of the nineteenth-century psychologist Ernst Weber. The law states that the *just-noticeable difference* between two sensory inputs is based on a proportion of the original sensory input rather than on a fixed amount of difference. What does that mean? Assume the overall stimulus input is less intense (as in the case of the 1-ounce container). A specific change in input (say 1 ounce) can easily be detected by a person. But now assume the original stimulus is more intense (as in the case of the 5-pound package). That same change in input (1 ounce) is much harder to detect. Weber's law may sound complex. But as shown in Has It Happened to You?, we experience difference thresholds all the time.

SIGNAL DETECTION THEORY The concept of an absolute threshold means that either you saw something or you did not. Your detection depended on whether the intensity of the sensory input was above or below the threshold. But can your judgment also affect your ability to detect sensory input? **Signal detection theory** accounts for human judgment in sensation. This theory states that detecting a sensory input, called the *signal*, requires making a judgment, called the *response*, about the presence or absence of the signal, based on uncertain information (Green & Swets, 1966).

To understand this theory, think about the many jobs where people have to decide if items are imperfect. In restaurants, servers check the food before it goes out to the customers. In retail stores, employees check products before they go on display. Signal detection theory explains how situations like these can have one of four outcomes (**Figure 5.5**). If a signal is present—such as a flaw in a food order—and the person responds to it, the outcome is called a *hit*. If the person does not respond to the signal, the outcome is a *miss*. By contrast, if there is no signal but the person responds anyway, the outcome is a *false alarm*. If there is no signal and the person does not respond, the outcome is a *correct rejection*.

The person's sensitivity to the signal is usually computed by comparing the hit rate with the false alarm rate. This comparison corrects for any bias the participant might bring to the situation. Signal detection theory also explains

signal detection theory
Detection of a faint stimulus requires a judgment—it is not an all-or-none process.

(a)

(b)

Response given?
(For example:
Detect the flaw?)

Signal present? (For example: Is there a flaw?)		Yes	No
	Yes	Hit (correct)	Miss (mistake)
	No	False alarm (mistake)	Correct rejection (correct)

FIGURE 5.5

Signal Detection Theory
(a) Have you ever had a job where you had to look for flaws in food orders or products? **(b)** According to signal detection theory, there are four possible outcomes when a person is asked to detect the presence of a sensory input, such as a flaw. These outcomes depend on whether an input is present. They also depend on the person's ability to judge the presence of an input. This theory accounts for people's biases in making judgments about whether a stimulus is present.

sensory adaptation
A decrease in sensitivity to a constant level of stimulation.

how a worker can be biased in situations like these. Imagine that a server gets paid extra money every time he notices that an order has a flaw, such as the wrong vegetable, and asks the cook to correct that flaw before the order goes to the table. Or imagine that a retail worker receives a bonus every time she detects damaged goods and removes them from the shelves. This financial incentive will result in workers being biased toward responding when they see flaws. This bias will result in more hits but also more false alarms. By contrast, imagine the worker has to pay a financial penalty every time he wrongly delays a food order or she wrongly removes a retail product. The worker will have the opposite bias: toward not responding to a flaw. This bias will result in more misses but also more correct rejections.

Signal detection theory helps us understand how a person can be biased toward responding, or not responding, even given the same amount of sensory input. As you can imagine, all sorts of factors influence the decision to respond to a particular sensory input. Consider, for example, the person's experience, motivation, attention, training, and knowledge of the consequences of whatever response is made.

SENSORY ADAPTATION Our sensory systems are tuned to notice changes in our surroundings. It is important for us to be able to notice such changes because they might require responses. It is less important to keep responding to unchanging stimuli. **Sensory adaptation** is a decrease in sensitivity to a constant level of stimulation.

For example, imagine that you are studying and work begins at a nearby construction site. When the equipment starts up, the sound seems particularly loud and annoying. After a few minutes, the noise seems to have faded into the background. If a stimulus is presented continuously, the responses of the sensory systems that detect it tend to diminish over time. Similarly, when a continuous stimulus stops, the sensory systems usually respond strongly as well. If the construction noise suddenly halted, you would likely notice the silence.

5.1 CHECKPOINT: How Do Sensation and Perception Affect Us?

- Sensation is the detection of light, sound, touch, taste, and smell. Perception is how the brain interprets this information.

- Sensory receptors transduce sensory input into signals. Except for smell, this information is sent to the thalamus and relevant parts of the cortex for further processing.

- Absolute threshold and difference threshold describe how much physical stimulus must be present for detection to happen.

- Signal detection theory explains how our judgments affect our ability to detect input.

- Our senses adapt to constant stimulation and detect changes in our environment.

5.2 How Do We See?

LEARN

📖 LEARNING GOALS	✏️ READING ACTIVITIES
a. Remember the key terms about visual sensation and perception.	List all of the boldface words and write down their definitions.
b. Understand the four steps in visual sensation and perception.	Summarize in your own words the pathway from visual sensory input to processing in cortical areas.
c. Analyze the two theories of color perception.	Differentiate between trichromatic theory and opponent process theory.
d. Understand the three categories of object perception.	Organize a table that names the three categories of object perception mechanisms and summarizes each category in your own words.
e. Apply depth perception and motion perception to your own life.	Explain cues that have helped you perceive depth and motion, providing one example of each type of perception from your life.

Does a place look safe or dangerous? Does a person look friendly or hostile? Given that we acquire information through our senses, vision is an extremely important source of knowledge. Yet sight seems so effortless, so automatic, that most of us take it for granted. But every time you open your eyes, nearly half your brain springs into action. Your brain is racing to make sense of the light waves arriving in your eyes. Of course, the brain can do this only based on sensory signals from the eyes.

Sensory Receptors in Our Eyes Detect Light

People sometimes describe the human eye as working like a crude camera. This analogy means that the eye focuses light to form an image. But the comparison does not do justice to the processes that enable you to see information. Intricate processes in your eyes are required for you to see as familiar an image as the face of a friend.

FOCUSING LIGHT IN THE EYE What is the first step in seeing something, such as a chair or the face of a friend? Believe it or not, light bounces off that object. That light enters your eyes in the form of light waves (**Figure 5.6**). The waves pass through the *cornea* of your eye. The cornea is the eye's thick, transparent outer layer (see Figure 5.6, Step 1).

The light then passes through the *pupil*. This feature is the small opening that looks like a dark circle at the center of the eye. The *iris,* a circular muscle, gives eyes their color and controls the pupil's size to determine how much light enters the eye. In dim lighting, the iris allows the opening of the pupil to become larger to let more light into the eye. The iris also increases the size of the pupil when you see something you like, such as a beautiful painting or a cute baby (Tombs & Silverman, 2004).

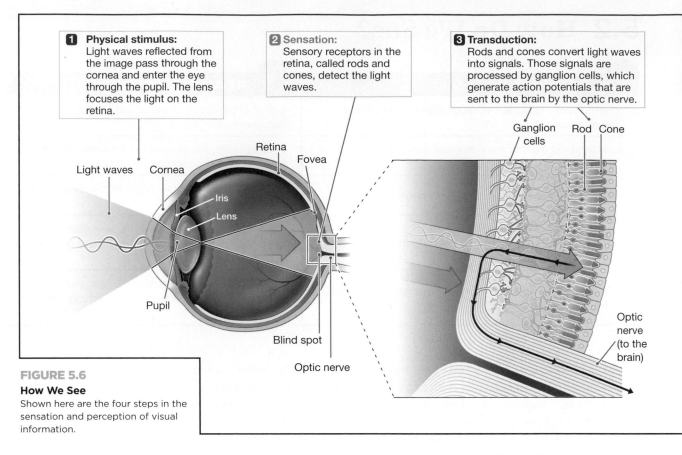

1 **Physical stimulus:**
Light waves reflected from the image pass through the cornea and enter the eye through the pupil. The lens focuses the light on the retina.

2 **Sensation:**
Sensory receptors in the retina, called rods and cones, detect the light waves.

3 **Transduction:**
Rods and cones convert light waves into signals. Those signals are processed by ganglion cells, which generate action potentials that are sent to the brain by the optic nerve.

Ganglion cells

Rod Cone

Light waves
Cornea
Retina
Fovea
Iris
Lens
Pupil
Blind spot
Optic nerve

Optic nerve (to the brain)

FIGURE 5.6
How We See
Shown here are the four steps in the sensation and perception of visual information.

lens
The adjustable, transparent structure behind the pupil; this structure focuses light on the retina, resulting in a crisp visual image.

retina
The thin inner surface of the back of the eyeball; this surface contains the sensory receptors.

rods
Sensory receptors in the retina that detect light waves and transduce them into signals that are processed in the brain as vision. Rods respond best to low levels of illumination, and therefore do not support color vision or seeing fine detail.

cones
Sensory receptors in the retina that detect light waves and transduce them into signals that are processed in the brain as vision. Cones respond best to higher levels of illumination, and therefore they are responsible for seeing color and fine detail.

Behind the iris, muscles change the shape of the **lens.** If you look at something far from you, your lenses will flatten. This flattening enables you to focus on something in the distance. If you look at something close to you, your lenses will thicken so you can focus. If you look at something too close to you, your eyes will feel uncomfortable. They are straining because the muscles cannot make the lenses any fatter. At that point, you have to back away a bit to see the object.

Together, the cornea and lens focus light so you see objects accurately. Light is actually focused more by the cornea than by the lens. Because the lens is adjustable, it fine-tunes how the light is bent. Glasses and contact lenses provide clear, focused vision by helping the lens bend the light. As we get older, the muscles of the lens lose their ability to change the shape of the lens. As a result, it becomes hard to focus on near objects. After about age 50, most of us have to hold our menus far away from us to be able to read them, or we need to get reading glasses to bend the light more than our lenses can.

RODS AND CONES The cornea and the lens work to focus light on the **retina,** the thin inner surface of the back of the eye (see Figure 5.6, Step 2). The retina contains the **rods** and **cones,** which allow sensation of the light waves. The rods and cones are the sensory receptors in the eye that transduce light waves into signals (see Figure 5.6, Step 3). The name of each type of visual sensory receptor cell comes from its distinctive shape.

Each retina holds approximately 120 million rods and 6 million cones. Near the center of the retina is a small region called the *fovea*. Here, cones are densely packed. Cones are spread throughout the rest of the retina (except in the blind spot, as you will see shortly). However, they become increasingly scarce near the outside edge. Cones are responsible primarily for vision under bright conditions and for seeing both color and detail. When you look at the faces in Figure 5.6, do you see

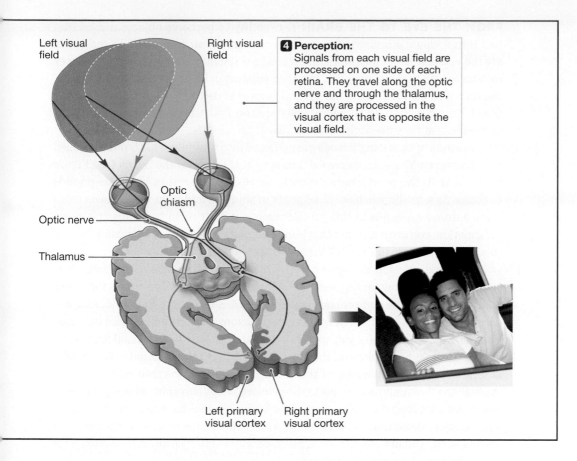

Left visual field

Right visual field

4 Perception:
Signals from each visual field are processed on one side of each retina. They travel along the optic nerve and through the thalamus, and they are processed in the visual cortex that is opposite the visual field.

Optic chiasm

Optic nerve

Thalamus

Left primary visual cortex   Right primary visual cortex

them clearly? If so, it is your cones that are processing the small features of each face and the colors of the clothes.

Unlike cones, the rods are concentrated at the retina's edges. None are in the fovea. Also unlike cones, rods respond well at extremely low levels of light. Rods are responsible primarily for night vision. They do not support color vision, and they are poor at providing information about fine details. For these reasons, on a moonless night, objects appear in shades of gray. If you look directly at a very dim star on a moonless night, the star will appear to vanish because its light will fall on the fovea, where there are no rods. If you look just to the side of the star, the star will be visible, because its light will fall just outside the fovea, where there are rods.

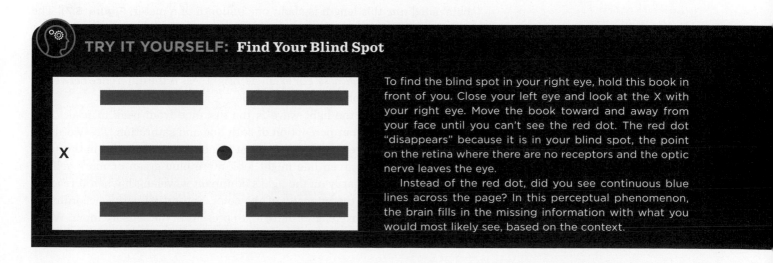

TRY IT YOURSELF: Find Your Blind Spot

X

To find the blind spot in your right eye, hold this book in front of you. Close your left eye and look at the X with your right eye. Move the book toward and away from your face until you can't see the red dot. The red dot "disappears" because it is in your blind spot, the point on the retina where there are no receptors and the optic nerve leaves the eye.

Instead of the red dot, did you see continuous blue lines across the page? In this perceptual phenomenon, the brain fills in the missing information with what you would most likely see, based on the context.

FROM THE EYE TO THE BRAIN Our ability to perceive objects means that this initial visual stimulation must be processed in our brains. Rods and cones are the visual sensory receptors that transduce the information from light waves into messages that are modified by other support cells in the retina. But finally, the information about what the eye has sensed is delivered to the *ganglion cells* (see Figure 5.6, Step 3). Ganglion cells are the first true neurons in the visual system in that they fire action potentials.

The axons of each ganglion cell are gathered into a bundle. This bundle is called the *optic nerve.* The optic nerve exits the eye at the back of the retina (see Figure 5.6, Step 4). At the point where the optic nerve exits the retina, there are no rods or cones. As a result, you have blind spots in your left and right visual fields. Your brain automatically fills in this gap. Because you don't seem to be missing visual information, you are not aware that blind spots exist in your field of vision. To find these blind spots, do the Try It Yourself activity on p. 163.

Half of the axons in the optic nerves cross to the other side of the brain. The rest of the axons stay on the same side of the brain. The point where the axons cross is known as the optic chiasm (see Figure 5.6, Step 4). Say you are looking at a point in the distance. The arrangement of the axons causes all the visual information to the left of the point you are staring at (the left side of the visual field) to be sent to the right hemisphere of the brain. Everything to the right side of that point is sent to the left hemisphere of the brain. In each case, the information passes through the thalamus and travels to the *primary visual cortex* in the occipital lobes (see Figure 5.6, Step 4). This region of the brain provides basic information about what is seen. Basic information includes the orientation, size, and movement of objects in the visual field. However, more-complex information is processed later on in other specialized brain regions.

We Perceive Color Based on Physical Aspects of Light

When you look at Figure 5.6, how do you know what colors the clothes are? An object appears to be a particular color because of two factors: the wavelengths of light that the object reflects and how the receptors in the eye process the light. Because of these two factors, we can identify millions of different shades of color.

PHYSICAL EXPERIENCE OF COLOR For humans, visible light consists of electromagnetic waves ranging in length from about 400 to 700 nanometers (abbreviated *nm;* this length is about one billionth of a meter; **Figure 5.7**). The physical qualities of this light correspond to the perception of color in different ways (**Figure 5.8**). One physical quality of light is the *amplitude.* The amplitude is the height of the light wave from base to peak. Psychologically, people experience this quality as *brightness.* For example, brightness is the difference between a bright blue and a dark blue of the same shade.

The *wavelength* of the light wave is the distance from peak to peak. This distance determines your perception of both hue and saturation. The word *hue* refers to the distinctive characteristics that place a particular color in the spectrum. For example, a green hue might look more blue-green or more yellow-green, depending primarily on the light's dominant wavelength when it reaches the eye. *Saturation* is the intensity of the color. Saturation varies according to how many different wavelengths of light are present in the sensory input. When

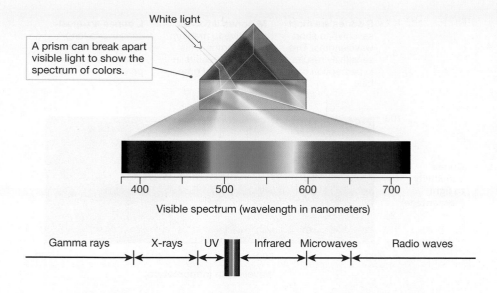

A prism can break apart visible light to show the spectrum of colors.

White light

400   500   600   700

Visible spectrum (wavelength in nanometers)

Gamma rays | X-rays | UV | Infrared | Microwaves | Radio waves

FIGURE 5.7

Visible Light
When white light shines through a prism, the spectrum of color that is visible to humans is revealed. As shown here, the visible color spectrum is only a small part of the electromagnetic spectrum: It consists of electromagnetic wavelengths from just under 400 nm (perceived as the color violet) to just over 700 nm (perceived as the color red).

only one wavelength of light is present, this wavelength primarily stimulates one type of cone receptor. That simple stimulation will yield a perception of a "pure" basic color, such as a vibrant blue, yellow, or red. In other words, we see the color as highly saturated. By contrast, when there are many wavelengths of light present, these wavelengths will stimulate many types of cone receptors. This complex stimulation will yield a perception of a less saturated color, such as a pale pastel pink.

TRICHROMATIC THEORY Most of us would have no problem saying that a certain flower is yellow rather than blue. But how do we know that? How do the physical aspects of light become the colors we perceive? Here our cone receptors come into play.

The **trichromatic theory** relates color perception to cone receptors. *Trichromatic* means "three-color." According to this theory, color perception results from activity across three different types of cone receptors. Each type of receptor is

trichromatic theory
There are three types of cone receptor cells in the retina that are responsible for color perception. Each type responds optimally to different, but overlapping, ranges of wavelengths.

Short wavelength: The distance between peaks is short, so we perceive blue. Because only one wavelength is present, this blue is highly saturated, or "pure."

Long wavelength: The distance between peaks is long, so we perceive red. Because only one wavelength is present, this red is highly saturated, or "pure."

High amplitude: The height between baseline and peak is high, so we perceive the color as being bright.

Low amplitude: The height between baseline and peak is low, so we perceive the color as being dark.

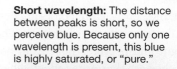
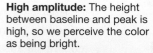
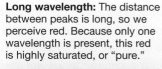
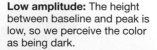

Baseline

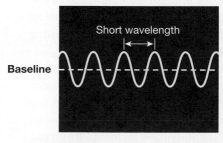
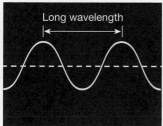
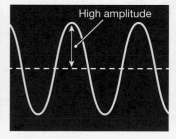
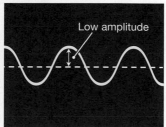

Short wavelength

Long wavelength

High amplitude

Low amplitude

FIGURE 5.8

Physical Aspects of Light Relate to Color Perception
The amplitude and wavelength, physical aspects of visible light, are processed into the perceptual experiences of brightness, hue, and saturation.

FIGURE 5.9

Trichromatic Theory Explains Color Perception

Our perception of hue is determined by the wavelength of the visible light that reaches the eye. This graph shows how each type of cone best absorbs light of different wavelengths.

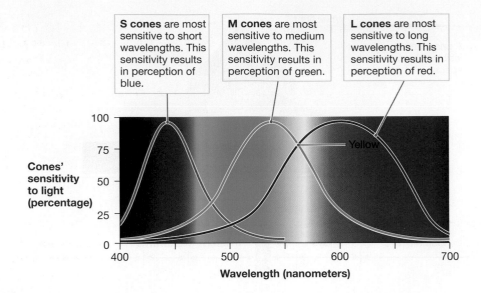

S cones are most sensitive to short wavelengths. This sensitivity results in perception of blue.

M cones are most sensitive to medium wavelengths. This sensitivity results in perception of green.

L cones are most sensitive to long wavelengths. This sensitivity results in perception of red.

(a) Additive color mixing

(b) Subtractive color mixing

FIGURE 5.10

Additive and Subtractive Color Mixing
(a) Additive color mixing is the combining of wavelengths of light. The varying proportions of wavelength mixtures determine the particular colors of light we perceive. **(b)** By contrast, subtractive color mixing is the combining of pigments. The varying proportions of pigment mixtures determine the particular colors of paint we perceive.

sensitive to different wavelengths of light (**Figure 5.9**). Specifically, S cones are most sensitive to short wavelengths. This sensitivity leads to our ability to see blue. M cones are most sensitive to medium wavelengths. This sensitivity enables us to see green. L cones are most sensitive to long wavelengths. Thanks to this sensitivity, we can see red. So, because wavelengths of light at about 570 nm stimulate the M and L cones equally, we perceive yellow.

Trichromatic theory also explains how we see a color based on the mixing of different wavelengths. What you see is determined by many wavelengths. When they are added together, the wavelengths have a combined influence on the eye's receptors. For this reason, the combining of wavelengths is called *additive color mixing*. Such mixing is used by lighting designers in the theater (**Figure 5.10a**). For example, lighting designers can create yellow light by presenting a light of 570 nm. Alternatively, they can combine medium wavelengths that stimulate M cones (seen as green) and long wavelengths that stimulate L cones (seen as red). As far as the brain can tell, yellow light is the same as a combination of green light and red light. Either way, everyone in the theater sees the light as yellow. When red, green, and blue light are mixed, the combination looks white. This white light results because all of the visible wavelengths are present.

How we see colors in paint works somewhat differently. Paint colors are determined by pigments. Pigments are chemicals on the surfaces of objects. These chemicals absorb different wavelengths of light and prevent them from being reflected. Whichever wavelengths are *not* absorbed are therefore reflected by the pigment and enter the eye. In other words, the color of a pigment is determined by the wavelengths that the pigment *does not absorb*. For this reason, the combining of pigments is called *subtractive color mixing* (**Figure 5.10b**).

Blue paint looks blue because the pigment does not absorb short wavelengths (about 440 nm). Yellow paint looks yellow because the pigment does not absorb medium and long wavelengths (about 570 nm). When these pigments are mixed, the combination absorbs a greater range of wavelengths. The color we see is due to the reflected wavelengths that are "left over." When blue and yellow pigments are mixed, the leftover wavelengths—the ones not absorbed by the combination—are about 530 nm. As a result, the combination looks green. Similarly, when red, yellow, and blue pigments are mixed, the combination looks black. The black pigment results because nearly all the wavelengths of light of the visible spectrum are absorbed.

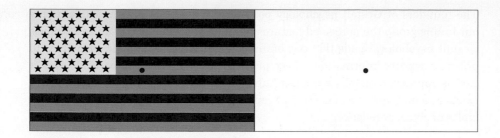

FIGURE 5.11
Afterimages Reveal Color Opposites
Focus on the dot in the middle of the flag and stare at the flag for at least 30 seconds. Then look at the dot to the right, on the white background. What do you see? You should see a red, white, and blue American flag. This result occurs due to processing in the ganglion cells.

OPPONENT PROCESS THEORY Some aspects of color vision cannot be explained by the responses of our cone receptors. For example, we have trouble visualizing certain color mixtures. It is easier to imagine reddish yellow or bluish green, say, than reddish green or bluish yellow. Moreover, the trichromatic theory does not explain certain perceptual experiences. For instance, some colors appear to be opposites (**Figure 5.11**). When we stare at a red image for some time, we see a green afterimage when we look away. When we stare at a green image, we see a red afterimage when we look away. Likewise, when we stare at a blue image for some time, we see a yellow afterimage when we look away. When we stare at a yellow image, we see a blue afterimage. These perceptual afterimage effects are better explained by **opponent-process theory.**

opponent-process theory
The proposal that ganglion cells in the retina receive excitatory input from one type of cone and inhibitory input from another type of cone, creating the perception that some colors are opposites.

To understand color opposites, we move to the next stage in visual processing. Remember that cones are receptors that detect wavelengths of light. The cones process that sensory input, and that processing ultimately leads to our perception of colors. Cones send the information to ganglion cells. The ganglion cells fire action potentials to send visual information to the brain. Some types of ganglion cells make it seem that red and green are opposites, whereas other types make it seem that yellow and blue are opposites. The ways that these different ganglion cells respond to cone input explains why we see colors as opposites.

Ultimately, how the brain converts light waves to the experience of color is quite complex. On the one hand, it can be understood by considering the response of cones to different wavelengths. On the other hand, processing by the ganglion cells leads to seeing colors as opposites. But what about people with color-number synesthesia (described at the start of this chapter)? These people perceive colors in written numbers even when the wavelengths the numbers are presented in will cause most people to perceive only black and white. This phenomenon reveals how each person's perception of color, and other aspects of visual perception, are based on how that person's own, unique brain processes information. Most synesthetes never know—until they test their perceptions—that their perceptions are different from other people's.

We Perceive Objects by Organizing Visual Information

Look at **Figure 5.12.** What do you see? In this reversible figure, some people see a younger woman. Some people see an older woman. As the psychologist James Enns (2005) notes, very little of what we call "seeing" takes place in the eyes. What we see results from processing in the brain. In this case, then, how does information about the object's features get organized into our individual visual experiences?

One explanation is based on the theory of Gestalt psychologists that perception is more than simply gathering sensory input (see Chapter 1). The German word *Gestalt* means "shape" or "form." In psychology, *Gestalt* means "organized whole."

FIGURE 5.12
Reversible Figure
What do you see when you look at this figure? Some see the face of a younger woman (her ear, her jawline, and a black necklace). Other people see the face of an older woman (an eye, a nose, and a black, open mouth).

The founders of Gestalt psychology postulated a series of laws to explain how our brains group the perceived features of a visual scene into organized wholes. Gestalt psychology holds that our brains use a number of built-in principles to organize sensory information. These principles explain why we perceive, say, "a car" as opposed to metal, tires, glass, hubcaps, fenders, and so on. For us, an object exists as a unit, not as a collection of separate features. Let's consider these principles of object perception.

FIGURE AND GROUND One of the visual perception system's most basic principles is organizing visual features into an object. In discussions of Gestalt principles, an object is a figure that is distinct from the background. The background is referred to as the ground. In identifying any figure, the brain assigns the rest of the scene to the ground. A classic illustration of this principle is the reversible figure (again, see Figure 5.12). Here, you can go back and forth in perceiving two possible figures—the younger woman or the older woman—but you cannot perceive them both at the same time. The "correct" assignment of figure and ground is ambiguous. Sometimes you perceive the relationship one way, and sometimes you perceive it the other way. This illusion demonstrates how visual perception of figure and ground is dynamic and ongoing.

GROUPING Whether the object is a reversible figure or an "ordinary" object in the world, your visual system seeks to form a coherent image of what you are seeing. To form that image, the system must determine what parts "go together." This process is called **grouping.** The Gestalt psychologists identified several principles that explain how visual grouping works (**Figure 5.13**).

Have you ever seen many geese together in one area? We tend to visually put the individual geese into one large group, a flock, because they look alike and they stay close together. This example shows how we group visual information based on the *proximity* of parts and by the *similarity* of parts. By clustering visual elements based on proximity and similarity, we are able to consider the scene as a whole rather than as the individual parts.

Now think about a common experience: You see a person, but the person is partially obscured by a table. Why didn't you perceive the person and the table as

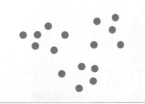

ⓐ Proximity:
Close figures are grouped as an object. So we see these 16 dots as three groups of objects.

ⓑ Similarity:
Similar figures are grouped in an object. So we see this rectangle as having two locked pieces.

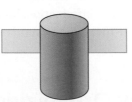

ⓒ Continuity:
Intersecting lines are interpreted as continuous. So we see the green bar as one piece that continues behind the purple cylinder.

ⓓ Closure:
Figures with gaps are interpreted as complete. So we see the figure as one whole triangle.

ⓔ Illusory contours:
Contours are perceived even when they do not exist. So we see the contours of a square here.

FIGURE 5.13

Gestalt Principles of Grouping
Gestalt psychology describes several principles of grouping that explain how we perceive features of the visual field as a unified, whole object.

FIGURE 5.14
Ross Ice Shelf and Mount Erebus
(a) The pilots on Air New Zealand Flight 901 expected to see the flat terrain of the Ross Ice Shelf in Antarctica. **(b)** This expectation led to tragic consequences when the pilots failed to see Mount Erebus, a 12,000-foot-high volcano, directly in their flight path.

parts of the same object? Clearly, we can determine what parts of visual input go together to make coherent forms. We can make out the person and the table, not the person-table. Three additional Gestalt principles are at work here: the *continuity* of a line, *closure* of gaps, and the creation of *illusory contours*.

BOTTOM-UP AND TOP-DOWN PROCESSING How do we assemble information about parts into a perception of a whole object? According to most models, perceptual organization is hierarchical. Specifically, perception of objects and patterns occurs through **bottom-up processing.** This term means that processing begins with the external world and the sensory input, which is detected by sensory receptors. Then the information is processed from these basic, lower levels to higher, more conceptual levels within the brain.

Perception also includes **top-down processing.** This term means that information at higher levels of conceptual processing can influence object perception at lower, more basic levels in the processing hierarchy. Information at higher levels includes our prior experiences and our expectations. Unfortunately, faulty expectations can lead to faulty perceptions. On November 28, 1979, Air New Zealand Flight 901 crashed into the slopes of Mount Erebus, on Ross Island in Antarctica. The crash killed 237 passengers and 20 crew members. The pilots believed they were flying over the Ross Ice Shelf, where there are no mountains, so they reduced altitude to give the passengers a better view of the spectacular Antarctic landscape (**Figure 5.14a**). However, the plane was actually far off course. Given the whiteout conditions and the pilots' expectations, the flight crew failed to notice the 12,000-foot volcano looming in front of them (**Figure 5.14b**). In this case, top-down expectations influenced bottom-up processing of the visual information the pilots were seeing, and the consequences were tragic.

bottom-up processing
The perception of objects is due to analysis of environmental stimulus input by sensory receptors; this analysis then influences the more complex, conceptual processing of that information in the brain.

top-down processing
The perception of objects is due to the complex analysis of prior experiences and expectations within the brain; this analysis influences how sensory receptors process stimulus input from the environment.

LEARNING TIP: Bottom-Up and Top-Down Processing

To remember what it means to process information from the bottom up or the top down, just remember this tip.

WHEN YOU SEE	PLEASE THINK	MEANING
<u>Bottom</u>-up	Processing based on information about the <u>basic</u> stimulus properties	The processing of information that is based on the properties of the stimulus in the world
<u>Top</u>-down	Processing based on information in your brain, at the <u>top</u> of your body	The processing of information that is based on your knowledge, personal experiences, and expectations

When We Perceive Depth, We Can Locate Objects in Space

Look up from this book and reach for something in front of you, perhaps a pen or a coffee cup. To accomplish this simple task, you need to perceive the object coherently. You also have to know where the object is in space. Without this spatial ability, it would be very difficult to navigate in the world and interact with things and people. In fact, our brains use two types of cues to help us perceive depth. **Binocular depth cues** are based on input from both eyes together. **Monocular depth cues** are based on input from one eye alone.

BINOCULAR DEPTH PERCEPTION Look at the objects around you. You see them as three-dimensional. Indeed, they are three-dimensional. Yet inside your eyes, once the light reflected from the images hits your retinas, all of the depth information is lost. The information is represented on the retinas in two dimensions only, just as it would be in a photograph. How can we perceive depth in the world if it is processed on the flat retinas in two dimensions?

To understand the process, look at something very close up. Hold your hand or your book up to your face. Repeatedly blink your left eye and then your right eye. When you do this, does whatever you are looking at quickly change positions from the left to the right and back again? This perception of "jumping" occurs because the retina of each eye has a slightly different view. Together, the different views on the retina are called *binocular disparity*. This phenomenon is one of the ways we perceive depth.

Because each eye has a slightly different view, the brain has access to two different, though overlapping, retinal images. The brain uses the disparity between these two retinal images to compute distances to nearby objects. By computing distances, the brain enables us to perceive depth (**Figure 5.15**). But binocular disparity is an important cue for depth perception only when the objects are relatively close to us. And it requires using both eyes. So another set of cues also helps us perceive depth.

MONOCULAR DEPTH PERCEPTION Photographs, movies, videos, and television images are flat. Flat images have no depth, yet we perceive depth in them. What's more, we perceive this three-dimensionality in two-dimensional images just by using one eye. For this reason, another set of visual cues are called monocular depth cues. Artists routinely use these cues to create a sense of depth, so monocular depth cues are also called *pictorial depth cues*. For example, when you look at **Figure 5.16,** you can see depth in the picture in several ways. The Renaissance painter, sculptor, architect, and engineer Leonardo da Vinci first identified many of these cues, which include *occlusion, height in field, relative size, familiar size, linear perspective,* and *texture gradient.*

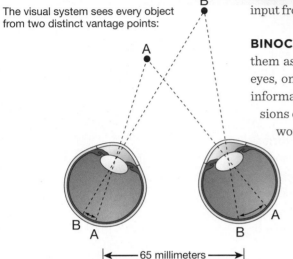

The visual system sees every object from two distinct vantage points:

B

A

The distance between retinal images of objects A and B is different in the left eye…

from the distance between A and B in the right eye. This is an important cue for depth.

B A

A B

|← 65 millimeters →|

FIGURE 5.15

Binocular Disparity

We use both eyes to perceive depth through binocular disparity, where each retina has a slightly different view of the world.

Cues in Our Brains and in the World Allow Us to Perceive Motion

You see something move. A person walks by, or a car whizzes past. You are aware of all this motion because you are sensing changes in illumination on your retinas. Changes in illumination, together with object recognition processes, enable

binocular depth cues
Cues of depth perception that arise because people have two eyes.

monocular depth cues
Cues of depth perception that are available to each eye alone.

FIGURE 5.16
Pictorial Depth Cues
We can perceive depth with just one eye. In this image, six monocular depth cues create the illusion of distance. Monocular depth cues are also called pictorial depth cues.

a **Occlusion:** A near object (woman's head) blocks an object that is farther away (the building).

b **Height in field:** Objects that are lower in the visual field (woman) are seen as nearer than objects that are higher in the visual field (man on the sidewalk at [c]).

c **Relative size:** Objects that are farther away (man on the sidewalk) project a smaller retinal image than close objects of a similar size (man on the street next to [b]).

d **Familiar size:** We know how large familiar objects are (car), so we can estimate how far away they are by the size of their retinal images.

e **Linear perspective:** Seemingly parallel lines (sidewalk) appear to converge in the distance.

f **Texture gradient:** As a uniformly textured surface recedes, its texture continuously becomes denser (pattern on the pavement).

you to perceive that an object is in motion, changing locations. Two phenomena offer insights into how the visual system perceives motion: motion aftereffects and stroboscopic motion.

MOTION AFTEREFFECTS *Motion aftereffects* may occur when you gaze at a moving image for a long time and then look at a stationary scene. You experience a momentary impression that the new scene is moving in the opposite direction from the moving image. This illusion is also called the waterfall effect, because if you stare at a waterfall and then turn away, the scenery you are now looking at will seem to move upward for a moment.

Motion aftereffects are strong evidence that motion-sensitive neurons exist in the brain. According to the theory that explains this illusion, the visual cortex has neurons that respond to movement in a given direction. When you stare at a moving sensory input long enough, these direction-specific neurons start adapting to the motion. That is, they become fatigued and so are less sensitive. If the sensory input is suddenly removed, the motion detectors that respond to all the other directions are more active than the fatigued motion detectors. Thus you see the new scene moving in the other direction.

STROBOSCOPIC MOTION Motion pictures are called movies because they seem to be moving. Actually, though, movies are made up of still images. Each image is slightly different from the one before it. When the series is presented fast enough, we perceive the illusion of motion pictures. This perceptual illusion is called *stroboscopic motion* (**Figure 5.17**).

FIGURE 5.17
How Moving Pictures Work
This static series would appear transformed if you spun the wheel. With the slightly different images presented in rapid succession, the stroboscopic movement would tell your brain that you are watching a moving horse.

In 1912, the Gestalt psychologist Max Wertheimer conducted experiments on stroboscopic motion. Wertheimer flashed, at different intervals, two vertical lines placed close together. When the interval was less than 30 milliseconds, observers thought the two lines were flashing simultaneously. When the interval was greater than 200 milliseconds, they saw two lines being flashed at different times. Between those times, movement illusions occurred: When the interval was about 60 milliseconds, the line appeared to jump from one place to another. At slightly longer intervals, the line appeared to move continuously. This phenomenon has brought us to productions such as *Inception* and *The Amazing Spider-Man*. In other words, all the special effects, fancy camera work, and fast editing you see in today's movies are ways of manipulating a very simple perceptual trick.

✓ 5.2 CHECKPOINT: How Do We See?

- In visual sensation, rods and cones transduce light waves into visual information. This information is sent to the thalamus and primary visual cortex for perceptual processing.

- Trichromatic theory and opponent-process theory explain two ways that we perceive color.

- We perceive objects by determining figure and ground, by using grouping principles, and through bottom-up and top-down processing.

- We perceive depth based on how the brain processes binocular cues and monocular cues.

- We perceive motion by processing motion aftereffects and stroboscopic motion.

5.3 How Do We Hear?

📖 LEARNING GOALS	✏️ READING ACTIVITIES
a. Remember the key terms about auditory sensation and perception.	List all of the boldface words and write down their definitions.
b. Understand the four steps in auditory sensation and perception.	Summarize in your own words the pathway from auditory sensory input to processing in cortical areas.
c. Apply pitch perception to your own life.	Describe how temporal coding and place coding allow you to perceive a low-pitched sound and a high-pitched sound.
d. Understand how sound intensity allows perception of a sound's location.	Summarize in your own words how you localize sound based on the intensity of what you hear.

Like seeing, hearing is an important source of information about the world. Suppose you are driving along a crowded, curving street. You can't see all the vehicles behind you. Suddenly you hear a siren coming toward you from back there. The siren lets you know that you should pull over to let an emergency vehicle pass.

Hearing is also called *audition*. This sensory mechanism enables us to determine what is happening in our environments. It provides a medium for spoken language. It brings pleasure to our lives, such as through music. In this section, let's begin by discussing how sound waves are transduced in the auditory system. Then we'll look at how we perceive the richness of sound information.

Auditory Receptors in Our Ears Detect Sound Waves

The world is full of sound. A song plays, a person speaks, the TV drones, an overhead light hums. But everything you hear is merely changes in air pressure produced within your hearing distance. Just as objects in the world have no essential color, these changes in air pressure have no sound. Instead, your ability to hear is based on the intricate interactions of various regions of the ear and on processing in the brain.

An age-old question asks, "If a tree falls in the woods and no one is there to hear it, does it make a sound?" The answer is no. The falling of the tree makes vibrations in the air. It is only the way our ears and brains process the vibrations in the air that creates the perception of sound.

FROM THE EAR TO THE BRAIN Suppose you hear music, such as the sound of a saxophone. The sound waves from the music are the sensory input (**Figure 5.18**). The process of hearing begins when sound waves arrive at the shell-shaped structure of your *outer ear* (see Figure 5.18, Step 1). The odd shape of the outer ear actually is functional: The shell shape increases the ear's ability to capture sound waves and then funnel the waves down the auditory canal. When you have trouble hearing something, it helps to cup or bend your outer ear because you funnel even more sound waves into the auditory canal.

Next, the sound waves from the music travel down the auditory canal to the **eardrum.** The eardrum is a membrane stretched tightly across the canal. This membrane marks the beginning of the *middle ear.* When the sound waves hit the eardrum, they make it vibrate. The vibrations of the eardrum are transferred to three tiny bones, which together are called the *ossicles.* The ossicles amplify the vibrations even more. If you have ever experienced an ear infection, you know how important the eardrum is to hearing. When fluid builds up behind the eardrum, the membrane cannot vibrate properly, so it seems as if you have cotton in your ears. You can't really hear much of anything.

At the start of the *inner ear,* the amplified vibrations reach the *oval window.* Though its name makes it seem like an opening, the oval window is actually another membrane. That membrane vibrates in turn. The oval window is located within the **cochlea,** a fluid-filled tube that curls into a snail-like shape. Running through the center of the cochlea is the thin *basilar membrane.* The oval window's vibrations create pressure waves in the cochlear fluid that make the basilar membrane move in a wave. Movement of the basilar membrane stimulates the bending of **hair cells.** These cells are the sensory receptors for detecting auditory input (see Figure 5.18, Step 2).

The bending of the hair cells then causes them to transduce the auditory information into signals (see Figure 5.18, Step 3). This transduction initiates the creation of action potentials in the *auditory nerve.* The auditory nerve sends the information to the sensory processing center of the thalamus and finally to the *primary auditory cortex* in the brain (see Figure 5.18, Step 4). This region of the cortex processes the information. As a result, you perceive the music as coming from a saxophone.

eardrum
A thin membrane that marks the beginning of the middle ear; sound waves cause the eardrum to vibrate.

cochlea
A coiled, bony, fluid-filled tube in the inner ear that houses the sensory receptors.

hair cells
Sensory receptors located in the cochlea that detect sound waves and transduce them into signals that ultimately are processed in the brain as sound.

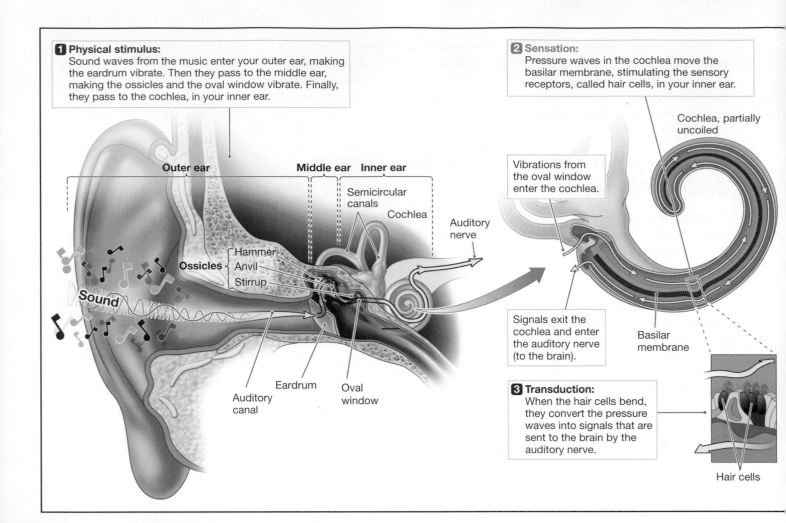

1 Physical stimulus:
Sound waves from the music enter your outer ear, making the eardrum vibrate. Then they pass to the middle ear, making the ossicles and the oval window vibrate. Finally, they pass to the cochlea, in your inner ear.

2 Sensation:
Pressure waves in the cochlea move the basilar membrane, stimulating the sensory receptors, called hair cells, in your inner ear.

Cochlea, partially uncoiled

Vibrations from the oval window enter the cochlea.

Signals exit the cochlea and enter the auditory nerve (to the brain).

Basilar membrane

3 Transduction:
When the hair cells bend, they convert the pressure waves into signals that are sent to the brain by the auditory nerve.

Hair cells

Outer ear   Middle ear   Inner ear

Semicircular canals

Cochlea

Auditory nerve

Ossicles { Hammer, Anvil, Stirrup

Sound

Eardrum   Oval window

Auditory canal

USING PSYCHOLOGY IN YOUR LIFE:

Hearing Deficiencies From Listening to Loud Music With Ear Buds

You see it all the time: young adults, teenagers, and increasingly even young children using ear buds to listen to music on portable devices. The music is often so loud that people around them can hear it too. It may surprise you to learn that this common activity has been linked with noise-induced hearing loss (NIHL) in nearly 13 percent of American children between the ages of 6 and 19—affecting more than 5 million young people (Centers for Disease Control, 2013). Furthermore, research suggests that some people in their 20s have hearing loss to a degree that has traditionally been seen in 50-year-olds. But the good news is that you don't have to give up your iPod. If you know a little bit about how your body processes sound waves to hear music, then you can prevent hearing loss in these situations.

Any loud noise can damage hearing. People who work in noisy environments, such as factories, often experience hearing loss, especially if they don't wear ear protection. This hearing loss occurs because loud sounds produce sound waves with greater amplitudes. These waves stimulate hair receptors in the basilar membrane much more than do soft sounds, which produce sound waves with smaller amplitudes. When hair cells in the basilar membrane of the cochlea are repeatedly overstimulated, they lose the ability to transduce sound waves.

One cause of damage to the hair cells is the volume, or loudness, of the sound, which is measured in decibels (dB). The measured volume of some sounds may surprise you—in the following table, for example, you can see that a portable music player at maximum volume can be louder than a rock concert! But volume is not the only source of damage. The length of exposure to the noise is also important. For example, hearing an 85-dB noise for 8 hours causes the same amount of damage as 90 dB for 2 hours or 100 dB for 15 minutes. Listening to the music player at top volume for 2 minutes can

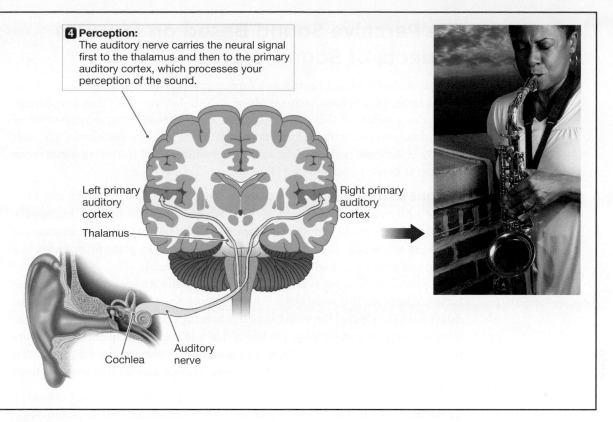

4 Perception:
The auditory nerve carries the neural signal first to the thalamus and then to the primary auditory cortex, which processes your perception of the sound.

Left primary auditory cortex

Right primary auditory cortex

Thalamus

Cochlea

Auditory nerve

FIGURE 5.18

How We Hear

Shown here are the four steps in the sensation and perception of auditory information.

produce hearing loss. But listening with ear buds adds 6–9 dB of volume because the sound waves are produced inside the auditory canal, close to the eardrum. In this situation, just 15 seconds of exposure can cause hearing loss. The result is similar to the effect of listening to the noise from jet engines.

So how can you enjoy your music and avoid hearing loss? Just follow these simple rules.

1. **Use the 60/60 rule.** Listen to your portable music device for 60 minutes at 60 percent of the maximum volume. If you can't tell what 60 percent of maximum volume is, just use a volume where you can still understand someone speaking to you in a normal voice from an arm's length away. After 60 minutes, give your ears a break for a while. This recovery time significantly reduces the chance of damaging your hearing.

2. **Don't use ear buds.** Instead, use headphones that go over your ears. Noise dampening or canceling headphones are even better. These headphones reduce the noise that you hear around you, so you don't feel the need to increase the volume on your music player.

3. **Ringing ears are sending a warning.** If your ears are ringing, buzzing, or roaring, or sounds seem muffled or distorted 24 hours after you've been exposed to loud noise, have your hearing checked by a doctor. Hearing loss can be temporary and decrease over time, and your doctor can help you avoid further, more permanent damage.

NOISE IN THE ENVIRONMENT	LOUDNESS IN DECIBELS (APPROXIMATE)	LISTENING TIME UNTIL DAMAGE TO HAIR CELLS (APPROXIMATE)
Whisper Normal conversation Vacuum cleaner	20 40–60 70	Safe for any length of time
Vehicle traffic	85	8 hours
Gas lawnmower	90	2 hours
Average rock concert	100	15 minutes
Portable music player at maximum volume	110	2 minutes
When using ear buds	*116–119*	*15 seconds*
Jet engine Gunshot Rocket launch	140 165 180	Immediate damage occurs

We Perceive Sound Based on Physical Aspects of Sound Waves

The psychologist Daniel Levitin is a former professional musician. In his best-selling book, *This Is Your Brain on Music* (2006), Levitin notes that music illustrates the wonders of the auditory system. Each person's unique perception of music depends on how that information is processed in the person's brain. Through activity in different regions of the brain, the features of all the instruments come together to create the experience of music.

LOUDNESS AND PITCH OF SOUNDS Recall that what you eventually hear begins with changes in air pressure. The pattern of changes in air pressure over a period of time is a sound wave (**Figure 5.19**). The height of the sound waves is called the amplitude. The amplitude determines our perception of loudness: We hear sound waves with higher amplitudes as louder sounds.

The distance between peaks of sound waves is the wavelength. And the time between the peaks in wavelength is called the *frequency*. The frequency of the waves determines the pitch of the sound, which is how high or low the sound is. You hear a higher frequency as a higher-pitched sound and a lower frequency as a lower-pitched sound. The frequency of a sound is measured in vibrations per second, called *hertz* (abbreviated Hz). Most humans can detect sound waves with frequencies from about 20 Hz to about 20,000 Hz.

TEMPORAL AND PLACE CODING Most of the sounds we hear, from conversations to concerts, are made up of many frequencies. Those frequencies activate a broad range of hair cells. How does the firing of hair cells signal different frequencies of sound, such as high notes and low notes in a song? In other words, how is pitch coded by the auditory system? There are two mechanisms for encoding the frequency of a sound wave. Both of these mechanisms operate at the same time in the basilar membrane.

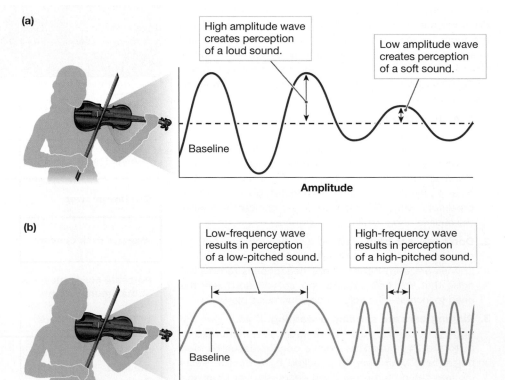

(a)

High amplitude wave creates perception of a loud sound.

Low amplitude wave creates perception of a soft sound.

Baseline

Amplitude

(b)

Low-frequency wave results in perception of a low-pitched sound.

High-frequency wave results in perception of a high-pitched sound.

Baseline

Frequency

FIGURE 5.19

Physical Aspects of Sound Waves Relate to Perception of Loudness and Pitch

The amplitude and frequency of sound waves are processed into the perceptual experiences of loudness and pitch.

Temporal coding is the process of encoding relatively low frequencies. For example, when you hear a tuba, temporal coding is involved. For this type of coding, cochlear hair cells fire at a rate that matches the frequency of the sound wave. For instance, a 1,000-Hz tone causes hair cells to fire 1,000 times per second. This strict matching between the frequency of auditory stimulation and the firing rate of the hair cells occurs up to about 4,000 Hz. At higher frequencies, temporal coding can be maintained only if hair cells fire in volleys. That is, different groups of cells take turns firing, so that the overall temporal pattern matches the sound frequency.

The second mechanism for encoding frequency is **place coding.** Different frequencies are encoded by receptors at different locations on the basilar membrane. This membrane responds to sound waves like a clarinet reed, vibrating in resonance with the sound. Higher frequencies, such as the frequency of a train whistle, vibrate better at the membrane's base by the oval window. Lower frequencies, such as the frequency of a foghorn, vibrate more toward the membrane's tip. The frequency of a sound wave, therefore, is encoded by the hair cell receptors on the area of the basilar membrane that vibrates the most.

After the hair cells have fired based on the frequency of a sound wave, processing in the brain enables us to perceive that pitch. The processing of pitch takes place in the primary auditory cortex. Auditory neurons in the thalamus extend their axons to the primary auditory cortex. There, other neurons code the frequency of the auditory stimuli. The neurons toward the rear of the auditory cortex respond best to sounds at higher frequencies. The neurons toward the front of the auditory cortex respond best to sounds at lower frequencies.

LOCALIZATION Suppose you hear a siren while driving, but you can't tell which direction the sound is coming from. Locating the origin of a sound is called localization. This ability is an important part of auditory perception. However, the hair cells cannot code where events occur. Instead, the brain integrates the different sensory information coming from each of our two ears.

Much of our understanding of auditory localization has come from research with barn owls. These nocturnal birds have finely tuned hearing, which helps them locate their prey. In fact, in a dark laboratory, a barn owl can locate a mouse through hearing alone.

The owl uses two cues to locate a sound (**Figure 5.20**). The first cue is the time when the sound arrives in each ear. The second cue is the amplitude, or intensity, of the sound wave in each ear. Unless the sound comes from exactly in front or in back of the owl, the sound will reach one ear first. Whichever side it comes from, it

temporal coding
The perception of lower-pitched sounds is a result of the rate at which hair cells are stimulated by sound waves of lower frequencies.

place coding
The perception of higher-pitched sounds is a result of the location on the basilar membrane where hair cells are stimulated by sound waves of varying higher frequencies.

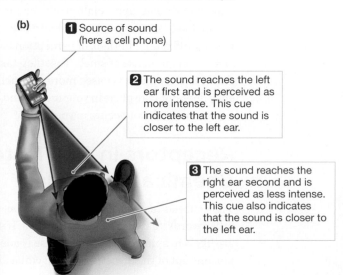

(a)

(b)

1 Source of sound (here a cell phone)

2 The sound reaches the left ear first and is perceived as more intense. This cue indicates that the sound is closer to the left ear.

3 The sound reaches the right ear second and is perceived as less intense. This cue also indicates that the sound is closer to the left ear.

FIGURE 5.20

Perceiving Location and Loudness of Sound
(a) Both barn owls and **(b)** humans draw on the intensity and timing of sounds to locate where sounds are coming from.

will sound softer on the other side because the owl's head acts as a barrier. These differences in timing and intensity are minute, but they are not too small for the owl's brain to detect and act on. Although a human's ears are not as finely tuned to the locations of sounds as an owl's ears are, the human brain uses information from the two ears in a similar way to localize sounds.

✓ **5.3 CHECKPOINT: How Do We Hear?**

- In auditory sensation, hair cells transduce sound waves into auditory information. The auditory nerve sends this information to the thalamus and the primary auditory cortex for perceptual processing.

- We perceive pitch based on temporal coding and place coding.

- Our pitch perception results from processing in neurons in the auditory cortex that respond best to certain frequencies.

- We perceive the location of a sound when the brain compares the time and the intensity of a sound as it arrives at each ear.

5.4 How Can We Taste and Smell?

📖 **LEARNING GOALS**	✏️ **READING ACTIVITIES** LEARN
a. Remember the key terms about sensation and perception of taste and smell.	List all of the boldface words and write down their definitions.
b. Apply the four steps in sensing and perceiving taste and smell to your own life.	Using the four steps in the pathway from sensory input to processing in cortical areas, describe your perception of the flavor of your favorite food.
c. Understand the reasons humans have evolved the senses of taste and smell.	Describe in your own words how the senses of taste and smell are important to the survival of humans.

When you think about your favorite foods, you can almost taste them. But regardless of whether you swoon over a grilled steak, chow mein with mustard greens, or a spicy salsa, your appreciation of a certain food depends on more than taste alone. As you likely know from having had a cold, food seems tasteless when your nose is really stuffed up. This lack of perception happens because our sense of taste relies heavily on our sense of smell. Together, taste and smell produce the experience of *flavor*. In fact, flavor is based more on smell than on taste. This perceptual experience does not take place in your mouth and nose, however. Like seeing and hearing, experiencing flavor occurs in your brain.

Receptors in Our Taste Buds Detect Chemical Molecules

The sense of taste is also called *gustation*. Gustation has an adaptive function. In other words, taste is related to survival. If something you eat tastes really bad, you are likely to spit it out. This response is adaptive, because the job of taste is to keep poisons out of the digestive system while allowing good food in.

FROM THE MOUTH TO THE BRAIN Suppose you taste a lemon (**Figure 5.21**). The physical stimulus that causes you to taste this food consists of chemical molecules that dissolve in saliva (see Figure 5.21, Step 1). The *taste receptors* are the sensory receptors that detect the chemical molecules. They are located in the **taste buds** (see Figure 5.21, Step 2). On the tongue, the taste buds reside in tiny, mushroom-shaped structures called **papillae.** But the taste buds are also spread throughout the mouth and throat. Most individuals have approximately 8,000 to 10,000 taste buds.

Food, fluid, or any other substance (e.g., dirt) will stimulate the taste buds. At that point, the taste receptors transduce the sensory input into action potentials (see Figure 5.21, Step 3). The taste information is sent to other brain regions through a set of nerves, primarily the *facial nerve* (see Figure 5.21, Step 4). After processing by the thalamus, the information is further processed in the *gustatory cortex*.

FIVE MAIN TASTES Like the other senses, taste involves a nearly infinite variety of perceptions. These perceptions arise from the activation of unique combinations of receptors. Scientists once believed that different regions of the tongue are more sensitive to certain tastes, but we now know that the different taste buds are spread relatively uniformly throughout the tongue and mouth (Lindemann, 2001). Every taste experience is composed of a mixture of five basic qualities: sweet, sour, salty, bitter, and umami (Japanese for "savory" or "yummy"; pronounced "oo-MOM-ee"). Umami is the most recently recognized taste sensation (Krulwich, 2007). If you have eaten foods such as meat, cheese, or mushrooms, you may have noticed how they seem to be bursting with flavor. If so, you have experienced umami. Researchers are still investigating how the cells in the taste buds lead to perception of all five of these taste qualities.

Some people experience taste sensations intensely. This trait is determined largely by genetics. These individuals, known as supertasters, are highly aware of flavors and textures and are more likely than others to feel pain when eating very spicy foods (Bartoshuk, 2000). Supertasters have nearly six times as many taste buds as normal tasters. The more taste buds you have, the more intense your taste experiences will be.

Although it might sound enjoyable to experience intense tastes, many super-tasters are especially picky eaters because particular tastes can overwhelm them. When it comes to sensation, more is not necessarily better. Being a supertaster may also affect health. Supertasters tend to avoid bitter-tasting foods, which they find extremely distasteful. This avoidance may put the supertasters at risk for some cancers that bitter foods may protect against (Basson et al., 2005). The upside is that supertasters also dislike the taste of fatty, sugary foods, so they tend to be thin and may have a lower risk of cardiovascular disease. You can take the test in Try It Yourself, on p. 180, to see if you are a supertaster.

TASTE PREFERENCE Do you love or hate anchovies? Each of us has individual taste preferences. These preferences come partly from our different numbers of taste receptors. The same food can actually taste different to different people, because the sensation associated with that food differs in their mouths. The texture of food also affects taste preferences: Whether a food is soft or crunchy, creamy or granular, tender or tough affects perception of the sensory experience. Another factor is whether the food causes discomfort, as can happen with spicy chilies. But cultural factors influence taste preferences as well.

Cultural influences on food preferences begin in the womb. One study of infant food preferences found that, through their own eating behaviors before

taste buds
Structures, located in papillae on the tongue, that contain the sensory receptors called taste receptors.

papillae
Structures on the tongue that contain groupings of taste buds.

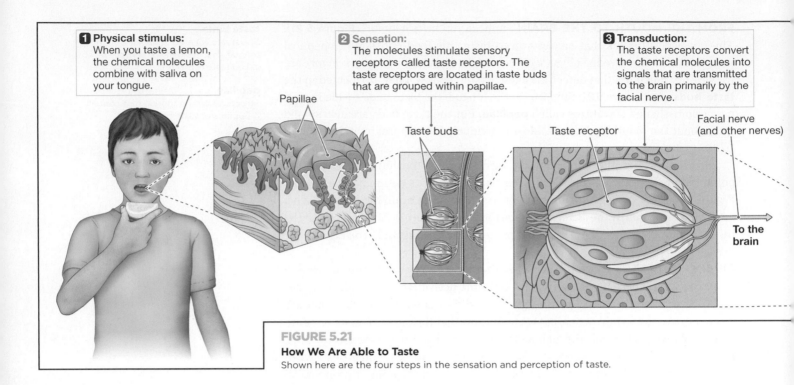

1 Physical stimulus:
When you taste a lemon, the chemical molecules combine with saliva on your tongue.

2 Sensation:
The molecules stimulate sensory receptors called taste receptors. The taste receptors are located in taste buds that are grouped within papillae.

3 Transduction:
The taste receptors convert the chemical molecules into signals that are transmitted to the brain primarily by the facial nerve.

Papillae

Taste buds

Taste receptor

Facial nerve (and other nerves)

To the brain

FIGURE 5.21

How We Are Able to Taste

Shown here are the four steps in the sensation and perception of taste.

and immediately following birth, mothers apparently pass their eating preferences on to their offspring (Mennella, Jagnow, & Beauchamp, 2001). The details of this study are summarized in the Scientific Thinking feature on p. 181. Once again, as noted throughout this book, the effects of nature and nurture are impossible to separate.

TRY IT YOURSELF: Are You a Supertaster?

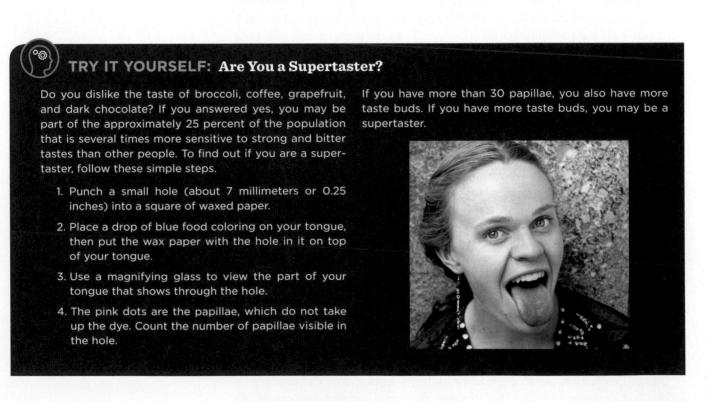

Do you dislike the taste of broccoli, coffee, grapefruit, and dark chocolate? If you answered yes, you may be part of the approximately 25 percent of the population that is several times more sensitive to strong and bitter tastes than other people. To find out if you are a super-taster, follow these simple steps.

1. Punch a small hole (about 7 millimeters or 0.25 inches) into a square of waxed paper.

2. Place a drop of blue food coloring on your tongue, then put the wax paper with the hole in it on top of your tongue.

3. Use a magnifying glass to view the part of your tongue that shows through the hole.

4. The pink dots are the papillae, which do not take up the dye. Count the number of papillae visible in the hole.

If you have more than 30 papillae, you also have more taste buds. If you have more taste buds, you may be a supertaster.

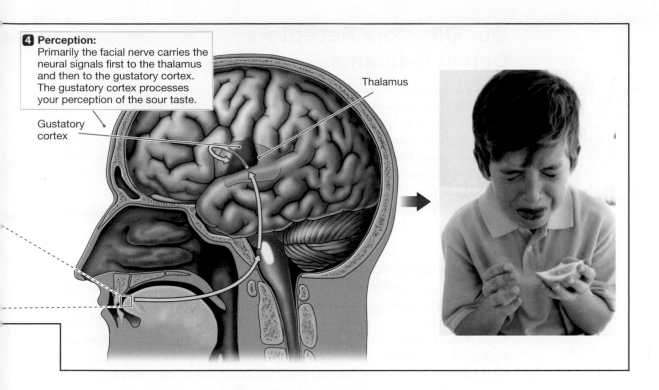

4 Perception:
Primarily the facial nerve carries the neural signals first to the thalamus and then to the gustatory cortex. The gustatory cortex processes your perception of the sour taste.

Gustatory cortex

Thalamus

 SCIENTIFIC THINKING:
Infant Taste Preferences Affected by Mother's Diet

Hypothesis: Taste preferences in newborns are influenced by their mothers' food preferences during the months immediately before and after birth.

Research Method: Pregnant women were assigned at random to one of four groups. They were instructed to drink a certain beverage every day for two months before the baby's birth and two months after the baby's birth:

	Before birth	After birth
Group 1:	carrot juice	water
Group 2:	carrot juice	carrot juice
Group 3:	water	carrot juice
Group 4:	water	water

Results: Babies whose mothers were in Groups 1, 2, or 3 preferred the taste of carrot juice more than did babies whose mothers were in Group 4 and did not drink carrot juice.

Conclusion: Babies become familiar with the taste of foods their mothers consume around the time of their birth, and they prefer familiar tastes.

Our Olfactory Receptors Detect Odorants

olfactory epithelium
A thin layer of tissue, deep within the nasal cavity, containing the olfactory receptors; these sensory receptors produce information that is processed in the brain as smell.

When a dog is out for a walk, why does it sniff virtually every object and creature it encounters? The sense of smell, which is also called *olfaction,* is the dog's main way of perceiving the world. Our sense of smell is much weaker than that of dogs, and in fact of many animals. For example, dogs have 40 times more olfactory receptors than humans do and are 100,000 to 1 million times more sensitive to odors. Our less developed sense of smell comes from our ancestors' reliance on vision. Yet the importance of smell to us in our daily lives is made clear, at least in Western cultures, by the vast sums of money we spend on fragrances, deodorants, and mouthwash.

FROM THE NOSE TO THE BRAIN Of all the senses, olfaction has the most direct route to the brain. But it may be the sense we understand the least. Like taste, smell begins when you sense chemical molecules that come from outside your body. The chemical molecules are called *odorants.* Say you smell a fresh loaf of bread (**Figure 5.22**). The odorants pass into your nose and through the upper and back portions of the nasal cavity (see Figure 5.22, Step 1). In the nose and the nasal cavity, a warm, moist environment helps the sensory receptors, called *olfactory receptors,* detect the odorant molecules. The olfactory receptors are embedded within the **olfactory epithelium.** This layer of tissue, as thin as a dime, is located deep in the nasal cavity (see Figure 5.22, Step 2).

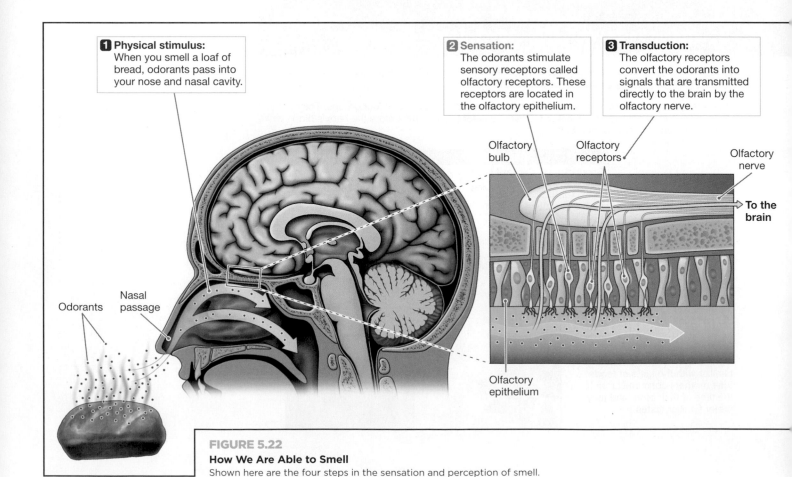

1 Physical stimulus: When you smell a loaf of bread, odorants pass into your nose and nasal cavity.

2 Sensation: The odorants stimulate sensory receptors called olfactory receptors. These receptors are located in the olfactory epithelium.

3 Transduction: The olfactory receptors convert the odorants into signals that are transmitted directly to the brain by the olfactory nerve.

Olfactory bulb

Olfactory receptors

Olfactory nerve

To the brain

Odorants

Nasal passage

Olfactory epithelium

FIGURE 5.22
How We Are Able to Smell
Shown here are the four steps in the sensation and perception of smell.

The olfactory receptors transduce the odorants into signals that the brain will ultimately process (see Figure 5.22, Step 3). These signals are processed in the **olfactory bulb,** the brain center for smell. From the olfactory bulb, which is just below the frontal lobes, the *olfactory nerve* transmits smell information to various brain regions, including the *olfactory cortex* (see Figure 5.22, Step 4). Unlike all other forms of other sensory information, smell signals bypass the thalamus, the early relay station in the brain.

TEN THOUSAND SMELLS There are thousands of olfactory receptors in the olfactory epithelium. Each receptor responds to different odorants. Humans can detect about 10,000 smells, but researchers are still exploring how the receptors transduce odorants into the perception of these distinct smells. One possibility is that each type of receptor is uniquely associated with a specific odor. For example, one type of receptor would encode only the scent of roses. This explanation is unlikely, however, given the huge number of scents we can detect. A more likely possibility is that each odor stimulates several receptors and that the activation pattern across several types of receptors determines the final olfactory perception (Lledo, Gheusi, & Vincent, 2005). Remember that in all sensory systems, sensation and perception result from both the specificity of receptors and the larger pattern of receptor responses.

SMELL PERCEPTION Information about whether a smell is pleasant or unpleasant is processed in the brain's prefrontal cortex. The smell's intensity is processed in the amygdala, a brain area involved in emotion and memory

olfactory bulb
A brain structure above the olfactory epithelium in the nasal cavity; from this structure, the olfactory nerve carries information about smell to the brain.

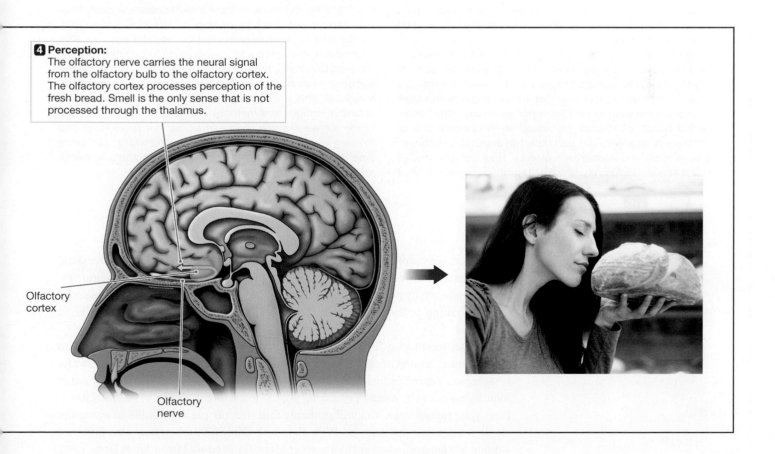

4 Perception:
The olfactory nerve carries the neural signal from the olfactory bulb to the olfactory cortex. The olfactory cortex processes perception of the fresh bread. Smell is the only sense that is not processed through the thalamus.

Olfactory cortex

Olfactory nerve

Kim was pretty pleased with herself. She had finished the reading for her Marketing 101 class and was about to start on psychology. She was looking forward to it, actually, because reading about psychology did not feel like work. Even her friends were interested in what she was learning in class. However, sometimes they asked her things that seemed like "pop psychology" rather than the real psychology she was learning. For example, when Kim was reading the consciousness chapter, one of her friends asked about "homicidal somnambulism." This term refers to when people kill other people, and the killers claim to have been sleepwalking. These cases are incredibly rare. Kim smiled and wondered, *What will my friends latch on to in this chapter?*

To relax before settling down with her textbook, Kim logged on to her Facebook account and started chatting with her friend Anton. The conversation turned to her reading, and Kim mentioned some of Chapter 5's subject headings, such as "How Can We Taste and Smell?" Anton asked if she knew why people remember things better based on smell. When he gave the example of how smelling a particular perfume always reminded him of his grandmother, Kim became curious about the phenomenon. *Is there any scientific evidence for this? Maybe Anton just misses his grandmother so much he thinks he smells her perfume everywhere.* Anton even mentioned that, according to a doctor on TV, loss of smell is an early diagnostic sign of Alzheimer's disease (a condition associated with memory loss).

On the Web, Kim found references to a lot of research on memory and the sense of smell. For example, according to one study, people exposed to the smell of rosemary had a greater ability to remember to do things (prospective memory) than people who were not exposed to that smell. And a bunch of studies, discussed at the Department of Veterans Affairs Web site, had found an association between loss of smell and Alzheimer's disease. However, the studies didn't show conclusively whether the brain degeneration of

Alzheimer's causes the loss of smell, or if the loss of smell makes Alzheimer's more likely. *Maybe the truth,* Kim thought, *is that aging is related to both Alzheimer's and changes in smell. Still, I guess some of those Internet claims actually have been the subject of real psychological research.*

The articles were interesting, but they did not help Kim understand why smell and memory would be linked. When she read Chapter 5, the picture became much clearer. As the textbook explained, the olfactory system runs through the amygdala. This brain region is associated with the process of both emotions and memory. *This connection makes total sense! As we are perceiving smell, we are processing and thinking about the things that are happening at the same time. The sensory processing and the thinking help us create memories.*

(Anderson, Christoff, et al., 2003). Because of the amygdala's role in processing smell, it is not surprising that olfactory stimuli can evoke feelings and memories. For example, many people find that the aromas of certain holiday foods, the smell of bread baking, or the fragrances of particular perfumes generate fond childhood memories.

We can readily say whether an odor is pleasant or offensive to us. We can discriminate among thousands of different odors. However, according to the researchers Yaara Yeshurun and Noam Sobel (2010), most people are pretty bad at identifying odors by name. Try asking people to name the smells of odorous items from your refrigerator. You will probably find that people are unable to name the smell at least half the time (de Wijk, Schab, & Cain, 1995). You may also find that women are generally better than men at identifying odors (Bromley & Doty, 1995; Lehrner, 1993; Schab, 1991).

- In taste sensation, taste receptors transduce chemical molecules into taste information. The facial nerve sends this information to the thalamus and gustatory cortex for perceptual processing.

- We detect five basic taste sensations: sweet, sour, salty, bitter, and umami (savory).

- In the sensation of smell, olfactory receptors transduce odorants and send smell information to the olfactory bulb. The olfactory nerve then transmits the signals to the olfactory cortex for perceptual processing.

- We can perceive and discriminate about 10,000 smells. But we are generally poor at naming odors.

5.5 How Do We Feel Touch and Pain?

LEARNING GOALS	READING ACTIVITIES
a. Remember the key terms about touch and pain sensation and perception.	List all of the boldface words and write down their definitions.
b. Understand the four steps in touch sensation and perception.	Summarize in your own words the pathway from tactile sensory input to processing in cortical areas.
c. Apply pain sensation and perception to your life.	Describe how you would sense and perceive banging your knee on the corner of a table.
d. Understand ways to control perception of pain.	Describe in your own words how you can reduce your perception of pain.

When you see, hear, taste, or smell something, receptors in just one small part of your body have been stimulated. But for the sense of touch, receptors exist all over your body. In fact, the skin is the largest organ for sensory reception.

Receptors in Our Skin Detect Temperature and Pressure

Suppose you are splashed with cold water. Water or anything else that makes contact with your skin provides tactile stimulation (**Figure 5.23,** Step 1). Tactile stimulation produces the experience of touch. Touch conveys sensations of temperature, of pressure, and of pain. It also delivers a sense of where our limbs are in space.

FROM THE SKIN TO THE BRAIN Specialized receptors detect temperature and pressure (see Figure 5.23, Step 2). These sensory receptors are embedded within the skin. For sensing temperature, there are **warm receptors** and **cold receptors.** Intense hot or cold stimuli can trigger both warm and cold receptors, however. Such simultaneous activation can produce strange sensory experiences, such as

warm receptors
Sensory receptors in the skin that detect the temperature of stimuli and transduce it into information processed in the brain as warmth.

cold receptors
Sensory receptors in the skin that detect the temperature of stimuli and transduce it into information processed in the brain as cold.

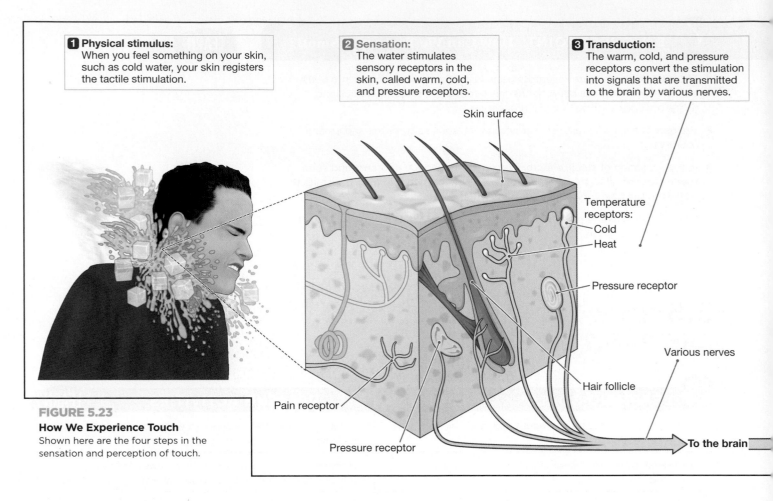

1 Physical stimulus: When you feel something on your skin, such as cold water, your skin registers the tactile stimulation.

2 Sensation: The water stimulates sensory receptors in the skin, called warm, cold, and pressure receptors.

3 Transduction: The warm, cold, and pressure receptors convert the stimulation into signals that are transmitted to the brain by various nerves.

Skin surface

Temperature receptors:
Cold
Heat

Pressure receptor

Various nerves

Hair follicle

Pain receptor

Pressure receptor

To the brain

FIGURE 5.23

How We Experience Touch
Shown here are the four steps in the sensation and perception of touch.

pressure receptors
Sensory receptors in the skin that detect tactile stimulation and transduce it into information processed in the brain as different types of pressure on the skin.

fast fibers
Sensory receptors in skin, muscles, organs, and membranes around both bones and joints; these myelinated fibers quickly convey intense sensory input to the brain, where it is perceived as sharp, immediate pain.

slow fibers
Sensory receptors in skin, muscles, organs, and membranes around both bones and joints; these unmyelinated fibers slowly convey intense sensory input to the brain, where it is perceived as chronic, dull, steady pain.

a false feeling of wetness. In addition, there are five types of **pressure receptors.** Some of these receptors are nerve fibers at the base of hair follicles. These receptors respond to movement of the hair. Four other types of pressure receptors are capsules in the skin. These receptors respond to continued vibration; to light, fast pressure; to light, slow pressure; or to stretching and steady pressure.

With tactile stimulation, such as being splashed with cold water, these receptors transduce the information into signals that will be sent to the brain (see Figure 5.23, Step 3). When skin is touched above the neck, the information is sent directly into the brain through *cranial nerves* (those that connect directly to the brain; see Figure 5.23, Step 4). When the touch is below the neck, the information is sent to the spinal cord and then *spinal nerves* transmit that information to the brain. In both cases, touch information travels first through the thalamus and then to the *somatosensory cortex*. In the somatosensory cortex, the information is processed.

PERCEPTION OF TOUCH How do you know where on your body you're being touched? In the 1940s, the neurosurgeon Wilder Penfield studied patients undergoing brain surgery. Penfield discovered that electrical stimulation of the primary somatosensory cortex could evoke the perception of touch in different regions of the body (Penfield & Jasper, 1954). Parts of the body that are located near each other, such as the hand and arm, are processed in adjacent brain areas in the somatosensory cortex. In this way, the body is effectively mapped out according to physical proximity. We saw this mapping in the homunculus of Figure 2.17 (right side).

For the most sensitive regions of the body, such as lips and fingers, a great deal of cortex is dedicated to processing touch. For less sensitive areas, such as the

4 Perception:
For touches above the neck, cranial nerves send neural signals to the brain. But for touches below the neck, neural signals are sent to the spinal cord, and spinal nerves transmit them to the brain. Signals travel to the thalamus and then to the area of the somatosensory cortex that processes the body part that was touched. This processing makes you perceive the cold water on your neck.

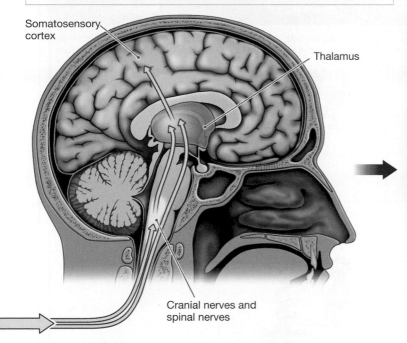

Somatosensory cortex

Thalamus

Cranial nerves and spinal nerves

back and the calves, very little cortex is dedicated to processing touch. Caressing certain parts of the body feels so good because more of your brain processes that information.

We Detect Pain in Our Skin and Throughout the Body

Ouch! You reach for a pan on the stove, not knowing that the handle is really hot. You pull your hand away quickly before you get badly burned. Just as taste can prevent you from eating something harmful, pain is part of a warning system that stops you from continuing activities that may harm you. Children born with a rare genetic disorder that leaves them insensitive to pain usually die young, no matter how carefully they are supervised. They simply do not know how to avoid activities that harm them or to report when they are ill (Melzack & Wall, 1982).

TWO TYPES OF PAIN RECEPTORS Most experiences of pain result when damage to the skin triggers pain receptors. The nerves that carry pain information are thinner than those for temperature and for pressure. These thinner nerves are found in all body tissues that sense pain: skin, muscles, membranes around both bones and joints, organs, and so on.

Two kinds of nerve fibers carry pain information to the brain. **Fast fibers** have myelinated axons. As described in Chapter 2, these axons are like heavily insulated electrical wires. They carry information very quickly. Fast fibers carry information that is perceived as sharp, immediate pains. By contrast, **slow fibers** have

It's easy to remember what type of pain we perceive based on information carried by fast fibers and by slow fibers.

When you see:	Please think:	Meaning:
Fast fibers	About being hit with the pointy edge of the letter F (for <u>Fast</u>).	Fast fibers carry information that we perceive as sharp, immediate pain.
Slow fibers	About being hit with the curved edge of the letter S (for <u>Slow</u>).	Slow fibers carry information that we perceive as dull, steady pain.

nonmyelinated axons. Without the insulation around these "wires," some of the signal "leaks" out. Slow fibers carry information about chronic, dull, steady pains.

Suppose you had burned yourself on a hot pan handle (**Figure 5.24**). The moment your skin touched the pan, you would have felt a sharp, fast, localized pain. Then you would have felt a slow, dull, more diffuse pain. In this case, the fast fibers were activated by strong physical pressure and temperature extremes. The slow fibers were activated by changes in the damaged skin tissue. Both fast pain and slow pain are adaptive. Fast pain leads us to recoil from harmful objects and therefore is protective. Slow pain keeps us from using the affected body parts and therefore helps them recover from injury. Like all other sensory experiences, the actual perception of pain is created by the brain.

CONTROLLING PAIN When you are in pain, does the pain feel worse when you're wide awake and active or when you're trying to sleep? Distraction can reduce your perception of pain. When

FIGURE 5.24
Types of Pain
A painful touch, such as a burn, creates two types of pain. Activation of fast fibers leads to perception of intense pain. Activation of slow fibers leads to the perception of duller, throbbing pain.

ready for sleep, you generally try to remove distractions. As a result, the pain probably feels more intense. Without distractions, you might focus on or worry about the pain, thus increasing your pain perception. So, as you prepare for a painful procedure or suffer after one, try to distract yourself. Don't focus on or worry about the pain. Watching an entertaining movie can help reduce pain perception, especially if it is funny enough to elevate your mood. And Swedish researchers found that listening to music was an extremely effective means of reducing post-operative pain, perhaps because it helps patients relax (Engwall & Duppils, 2009).

Keep in mind, however, that severe pain is a warning that something in the body is seriously wrong. If you experience severe pain, you should be treated by a medical professional.

(a)

(b)

Internal Sensory Systems Help Us Function in Space

Humans, like other animals, have several internal sensory systems in addition to the five primary senses. These systems help us find and maintain our position in space. One such system is the *kinesthetic sense*. Some researchers group the kinesthetic sense with the touch senses. Kinesthetic sensations come from receptors in muscles, in tendons, and in joints. This information enables us to coordinate voluntary movement and is invaluable in avoiding injury.

You experience your kinesthetic sense every day. For example, you can pinpoint your position in space. You register the movements of your body and your limbs. Without these abilities, you would be unable to perform activities such as yoga (**Figure 5.25a**).

The *vestibular sense* uses information from receptors in structures of the inner ear called the semicircular canals (see Figure 5.18). These canals contain a liquid that moves when the head moves, bending hair cells in the canals. The bending generates signals that inform us of the head's rotation. In this way, it is responsible for a sense of balance. Balance enables us to perform activities such as riding a bike or walking on a balance beam (**Figure 5.25b**).

If an inner-ear infection or standing up quickly has made you dizzy, you have experienced a disturbance in your vestibular sense. And the experience of being seasick or carsick results in part from conflicting signals arriving from the visual system and the vestibular system.

FIGURE 5.25

Kinesthetic and Vestibular Senses
(a) Our kinesthetic sense tells us how our body and limbs are positioned in space.
(b) Our vestibular sense allows us to maintain balance.

 5.5 CHECKPOINT: How Do We Feel Touch and Pain?

- In touch, sensory receptors transduce information about pressure and temperature. Nerves then send this information to the thalamus and somatosensory cortex for perception.

- For pain, fast fibers transduce information about immediate, sharp pain. Slow fibers transduce information about chronic, dull pain.

- Our kinesthetic sense lets us judge where our body and limbs are in space. The vestibular sense aids balance by judging direction and intensity of head movements.

BIG PICTURE

5.1
How Do Sensation and Perception Affect Us?

a. Remember the key terms about sensation and perception.
b. Apply the four steps from sensation to perception to your life.
c. Understand absolute threshold and difference threshold.
d. Apply signal detection theory to real life.

5.2
How Do We See?

a. Remember the key terms about visual sensation and perception.
b. Understand the four steps in visual sensation and perception.
c. Analyze the two theories of color perception.
d. Understand the three categories of object perception.
e. Apply depth perception and motion perception to your own life.

5.3
How Do We Hear?

a. Remember the key terms about auditory sensation and perception.
b. Understand the four steps in auditory sensation and perception.
c. Apply pitch perception to your own life.
d. Understand how sound intensity allows perception of a sound's location.

5.4
How Can We Taste and Smell?

a. Remember the key terms about sensation and perception of taste and smell.
b. Apply the four steps in sensing and perceiving taste and smell to your own life.
c. Understand the reasons humans have evolved the senses of taste and smell.

5.5
How Do We Feel Touch and Pain?

a. Remember the key terms about touch and pain sensation and perception.
b. Understand the four steps in touch sensation and perception.
c. Apply pain sensation and perception to your life.
d. Understand ways to control perception of pain.

KEY TERMS

sensation
perception
sensory receptors
transduction
absolute threshold
difference threshold
signal detection theory
sensory adaptation

lens
retina
rods
cones
trichromatic theory
opponent-process theory
grouping
bottom-up processing
top-down processing
binocular depth cues
monocular depth cues

eardrum
cochlea
hair cells
temporal coding
place coding

taste buds
papillae
olfactory epithelium
olfactory bulb

warm receptors
cold receptors
pressure receptors
fast fibers
slow fibers

CHECKPOINT

- Sensation is the detection of light, sound, touch, taste, and smell. Perception is how the brain interprets this information.

- Sensory receptors transduce sensory input into signals. Except for smell, this information is sent to the thalamus and relevant parts of the cortex for further processing.

- Absolute threshold and difference threshold describe how much physical stimulus must be present for detection to happen.

- Signal detection theory explains how our judgments affect our ability to detect input.

- Our senses adapt to constant stimulation and detect changes in our environment.

- In visual sensation, rods and cones transduce light waves into visual information. This information is sent to the thalamus and primary visual cortex for perceptual processing.

- Trichromatic theory and opponent-process theory explain two ways that we perceive color.

- We perceive objects by determining figure and ground, by using grouping principles, and through bottom-up and top-down processing.

- We perceive depth based on how the brain processes binocular cues and monocular cues.

- We perceive motion by processing motion aftereffects and stroboscopic motion.

- In auditory sensation, hair cells transduce sound waves into auditory information. The auditory nerve sends this information to the thalamus and the primary auditory cortex for perceptual processing.

- We perceive pitch based on temporal coding and place coding.

- Our pitch perception results from processing in neurons in the auditory cortex that respond best to certain frequencies.

- We perceive the location of a sound when the brain compares the time and the intensity of a sound as it arrives at each ear.

- In taste sensation, taste receptors transduce chemical molecules into taste information. The facial nerve sends this information to the thalamus and gustatory cortex for perceptual processing.

- We detect five basic taste sensations: sweet, sour, salty, bitter, and umami (savory).

- In the sensation of smell, olfactory receptors transduce odorants and send smell information to the olfactory bulb. The olfactory nerve then transmits the signals to the olfactory cortex for perceptual processing.

- We can perceive and discriminate about 10,000 smells. But we are generally poor at naming odors.

- In touch, sensory receptors transduce information about pressure and temperature. Nerves then send this information to the thalamus and somatosensory cortex for perception.

- For pain, fast fibers transduce information about immediate, sharp pain. Slow fibers transduce information about chronic, dull pain.

- Our kinesthetic sense lets us judge where our body and limbs are in space. The vestibular sense aids balance by judging direction and intensity of head movements.

For a self-quiz on this chapter, go to the back of the book and find Appendix B: Quizzes.

Learning

THE PARTY WAS GREAT, the DJ was cool, and the food was terrific. Especially the shrimp—and you ate a lot of them. But almost immediately something didn't feel right, and you ended up having a night that you would like to forget. Even now, a year later, the sight, the smell, and the thought of shrimp makes you feel ill. You never eat them anymore.

Sound familiar? Maybe it wasn't shrimp, but if you've ever had a similar response to a misadventure with food, you have experienced *conditioned taste aversion*, a particular form of learning. Conditioned taste aversion is not limited to humans. You can see a striking example of it in the way wolves have learned not to prey on domestic livestock.

BIG QUESTIONS

6.1 **What Are the Three Ways We Learn?**

6.2 **How Do We Learn by Classical Conditioning?**

6.3 **How Do We Learn by Operant Conditioning?**

6.4 **How Do We Learn by Watching Others?**

FIGURE 6.1

Wolves Experiencing Conditioned Taste Aversion

Conditioned taste aversion helps train wolves not to eat domestic livestock when wolves are reintroduced to areas in the United States.

Gray wolves of the Northern Rocky Mountain region were native to Yellowstone National Park when the park was created in 1872. By the 1970s, however, all the wolves in the park had been killed as part of a predator control plan. Some gray wolves remained in the lower 48 states, but in 1974 the species was listed as endangered. In 1987, the U.S. Fish and Wildlife Service announced a recovery plan to reintroduce wolves to Yellowstone Park. At the same time, some conservation groups were proposing to reintroduce other subspecies of wolves, such as the Mexican wolf, to other parts of the United States. In all of these regions, the local farmers and ranchers were afraid the wolves would prey on their sheep and cattle. An important part of all the reintroduction plans, therefore, was gaining the support of the farmers and ranchers by finding creative ways to limit predation by wolves. Here is where the psychology behind conditioned taste aversion came into play.

Sheep carcasses treated with nonlethal doses of poison were placed where wolves would find them (**Figure 6.1**). After eating the meat, the wolves immediately vomited. Just as you now avoid food that made you sick in the past, the wolves soon learned to associate eating sheep with becoming ill. So they avoided preying on sheep. As a result, many ranchers stopped opposing reintroduction of wolves. Thus conditioned taste aversion for the flavor of sheep's meat has allowed the wolves to flourish in regions where agriculturists would normally exterminate them. Today, in several regions of the United States, wolves have been taken off the endangered species list.

Using conditioned taste aversion to help wolves learn not to eat sheep is an example of how psychology can be put to work in "the real world." The principles behind the wolves' learning are also the basis for some of the ways that humans learn. In this chapter, we examine how learning takes place. This material represents some of psychology's major contributions to our understanding of behavior. Learning theories have been used to improve quality of life and to train humans as well as nonhuman animals to learn new tasks. To understand all behavior, we need to know what learning is.

6.1 What Are the Three Ways We Learn?

📖 **LEARNING GOALS**	✏️ **READING ACTIVITIES** **LEARN**
a. Remember the key terms about learning.	List all of the boldface words and write down their definitions.
b. Understand the three main types of learning.	Describe these types of learning using your own words.
c. Apply learning to your life.	Provide examples from your own experience of the two types of non-associative learning.
d. Understand how the brain changes during learning.	Summarize in your own words how long-term potentiation explains learning in the brain.

Learning is a change in behavior that results from experience. Learning is central to almost all areas of human existence. It makes possible our basic abilities (such as walking and speaking) and our complex ones (such as flying airplanes, performing surgery, or maintaining intimate relationships). What music you like, how you choose to dress, social rules about how close you stand to someone else, cultural values about whether you exploit or preserve the environment—learning helps shape all these and many other aspects of daily life. One of the basic questions we must ask, then, is: How do we learn?

learning
A change in behavior, resulting from experience.

habituation
A decrease in behavioral response after lengthy or repeated exposure to a stimulus.

We Learn From Experience

The processes that allow us to learn have been debated for centuries, though more formal learning theory arose in the early twentieth century. Formal learning theory was developed partly because some psychologists were not satisfied with the Freudian ideas then at the heart of psychological theorizing. Recall from Chapter 1 that Freud and his followers used verbal report techniques, such as dream analysis and free association. They aimed to assess the unconscious mental processes that they believed were the primary determinants of behavior. But other psychologists argued that Freudian theory was unscientific and ultimately meaningless, and they developed theories of behavior and learning that were based on events others could observe.

John Watson, in particular, rejected any psychological approach that did *not* focus on what could be observed directly (Watson, 1924). According to Watson, observable behavior was the only valid indicator of psychological activity. Recall that this idea was the basis for the approach that came to be known as behaviorism. In formulating his ideas on behaviorism, Watson was influenced by the seventeenth-century philosopher John Locke. An infant, Locke argued, is a *tabula rasa* (Latin for "blank slate"). Born knowing nothing, the infant develops over time by acquiring all of its knowledge through sensory experiences. Building on this foundation, Watson stated that environment and its associated effects on animals were the only determinants of learning.

Behaviorism was also the basis for B. F. Skinner's groundbreaking studies of animals, often using pigeons or rats. Skinner designed these experiments to discover the basic rules of learning. He found that by giving an animal food for doing particular actions, he could radically change that animal's behavior.

Modern psychologists agree that learning results from an individual's experience. Learning occurs when an animal or human benefits from experience so that its behavior is better adapted to the environment. Indeed, the ability to learn is crucial for all creatures. To survive, animals and humans need to learn things such as which sounds indicate potential dangers, what foods are dangerous, and when it is safe to sleep. Psychologists have divided learning into three main types: non-associative learning, associative learning, and learning by watching others. All of these types of learning are described in this chapter.

(a)

(b)

FIGURE 6.2

Two Forms of Non-Associative Learning

(a) Habituation: Suppose you live or work in a noisy environment. You learn to ignore the constant noise, because you do not need to respond to it. **(b)** Sensitization: Suppose you're in the backseat with your brother. He keeps annoying you, until finally you threaten to strike him.

We Learn in Three Ways

In *non-associative learning*, a person learns about one stimulus, which is information in the external world. A stimulus could be a sight, smell, or sound, for example. One important form of non-associative learning is **habituation,** where an individual is exposed to a stimulus for a long time, or repeatedly. Eventually, the individual's behavioral response to that stimulus decreases (**Figure 6.2a**).

TRY IT YOURSELF: Habituation

Right now, you can experience learning about a stimulus through habituation. Sit back and listen to the background sounds wherever you are. Perhaps you can hear the hum of a light, a computer fan whirring, or music playing nearby. But did you notice this noise before it was pointed out to you? No, because you habituated to it. And in a few minutes, because of habituation, you will probably stop noticing the noise again.

sensitization
An increase in behavioral response after lengthy or repeated exposure to a stimulus.

Habituation happens particularly if the stimulus is neither harmful nor rewarding. For example, if an animal experiences a new stimulus, such as hearing a sound, it will pay attention for a while, because the sound might indicate a potential danger. If the sound does not result in a threat, the animal soon learns to ignore it. In our everyday lives, we also constantly habituate to meaningless events around us (see Try It Yourself).

Sensitization is a second form of non-associative learning. It takes place when an individual is exposed to a stimulus for a long time, or many times, and then has an increased behavioral response. In general, sensitization leads to heightened preparation to respond in an important situation where there is some potential harm or reward (**Figure 6.2b**). For instance, suppose that while you are studying, you smell something burning. You probably will not habituate to this smell, because it is an important stimulus. You might focus even greater attention on the smell to determine whether it is just a candle, another student burning her dinner, or something potentially dangerous.

Unlike non-associative learning, *associative learning* requires understanding how two or more pieces of information are related to each other. Associations develop through two types of conditioning. The first type, classical conditioning, occurs when you learn that two stimuli go together. For example, if you always hear a certain kind of music during scary scenes in a movie, you learn to feel anxious whenever you hear that music. The second type, operant conditioning, occurs when you learn that a behavior leads to a particular outcome. For example, you

LEARNING TIP: Types of Learning

This graphic will help you understand the relationship between the three main types of learning and all of the subtypes.

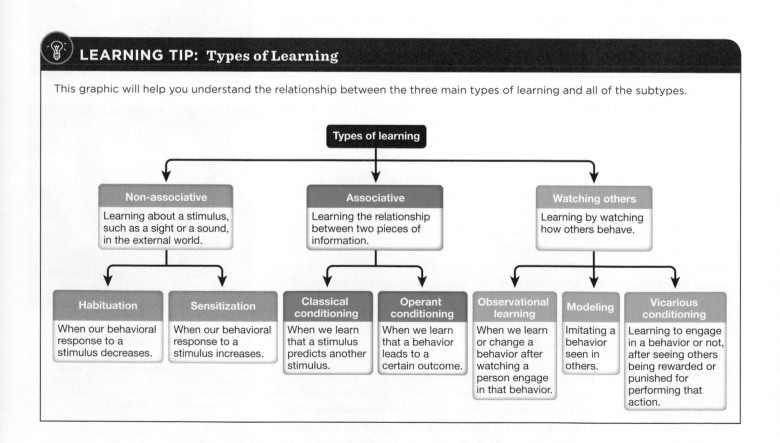

learn that studying leads to better grades. The third type of learning—*learning by watching others*—is just what it sounds like. Both humans and animals can learn by watching others, such as through observational learning, modeling, and vicarious conditioning. For example, you might have learned the latest popular dance by watching a YouTube video.

These main ways that we learn are summarized in the Learning Tip on p. 196. In later sections of the chapter, we consider each type of learning in more detail. First, let's look briefly at what happens in the brain when we learn.

The Brain Changes During Learning

All the types of learning we've just described result from experience. But what happens in the brain during learning? Exposure to environmental events actually causes changes in the brain that allow learning to occur. As discussed in Chapter 2, the psychologist Donald Hebb proposed that learning results from alterations in the connections between synapses. Recall that, according to Hebb, when one neuron excites another, some change takes place that strengthens the connection between the two neurons ("cells that fire together, wire together"). After that original event, the firing of one neuron becomes increasingly likely to cause the firing of the other neuron.

To understand how learning occurs in the brain, researchers have investigated the enhanced activity that results from the strengthening of synaptic connections between neurons. This phenomenon is known as *long-term potentiation (LTP)*. This term is easy to remember if you know that the word *potent* suggests something is "strong." So potentiation indicates strengthening of synaptic connections that allow us to learn. A lot of evidence supports the idea that long-term potentiation is involved in learning and memory (Beggs et al., 1999; Cooke & Bliss, 2006). For instance, LTP effects are most easily observed in brain sites known to be active in learning and memory, such as the hippocampus. What's more, the same drugs that improve learning also lead to increased LTP, and those that block learning also block LTP.

 6.1 CHECKPOINT: What Are the Three Ways We Learn?

- Learning is a change in behavior that results from experience. There are three main types of learning.

- Non-associative learning about a stimulus happens through habituation and sensitization.

- Associative learning about relationships between events occurs through classical conditioning and operant conditioning.

- Learning also occurs when we watch what others do.

- Learning occurs when synaptic connections in the brain become stronger over time through long-term potentiation (LTP).

6.2 How Do We Learn by Classical Conditioning?

HAS IT HAPPENED TO YOU?

Experiencing Classical Conditioning

Does the smell of french fries make your mouth water? If so, then simply seeing the sign for a restaurant with fries you like may have made your mouth water. If this happened, you were classically conditioned!

classical conditioning
A type of learned response in which a neutral object comes to elicit a response when it is associated with a stimulus that already produces a response.

It's only a movie, but when the music starts to play, we feel tense as we watch the woman descend into the dark basement. The music helps make the situation scary. We just know that something bad is about to happen to her. But how do we know this? We know it because we have learned the association between the presence of certain music and bad things happening to the characters in the movie. This kind of learning is so familiar because it has happened to all of us (see Has It Happened to You?). We even describe it with a familiar phrase: acting like Pavlov's dog. But what was Pavlov's dog, and what does it have to do with learning?

Through Classical Conditioning, We Learn That Stimuli Are Related

Ivan Pavlov was a Russian physiologist who won a Nobel Prize in 1904 for his research on the digestive system (**Figure 6.3a**). Pavlov was interested in the salivary reflex, which is an automatic and unlearned response that occurs when food is presented to a hungry animal, including a human. To investigate the digestive system, Pavlov created an apparatus that measured how various types of food placed into a dog's mouth resulted in different amounts of saliva (**Figure 6.3b**).

Like so many major scientific advances, Pavlov's contribution to psychology started with a simple observation. One day, he realized that the dogs he was studying were salivating before they actually tasted their food. In fact, the dogs began to salivate the moment they saw the bowls that contained the food or whenever the lab technician who usually delivered the food walked into the room. Pavlov's genius was in recognizing that this behavioral response was a window into the working mind. Unlike innate reflexes, such as salivating when actually tasting the food, salivating at the sight of a bowl or of a person is not automatic. Therefore, that response must have been acquired through experience by associating two stimuli with each other. In other words, the dogs showed learning by **classical conditioning.** This insight led Pavlov to devote the rest of his life to studying the basic principles of learning.

1 The dog was presented with a bowl that contained meat.

2 A tube carried the dog's saliva to a container.

3 The container was connected to a device that measured the amount of saliva.

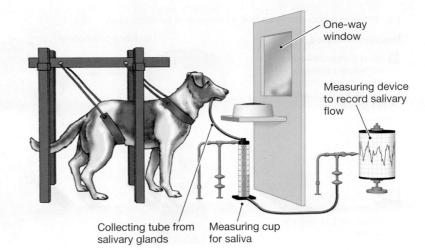

One-way window

Measuring device to record salivary flow

Collecting tube from salivary glands

Measuring cup for saliva

FIGURE 6.3

Pavlov's Apparatus and Classical Conditioning
(a) Ivan Pavlov, pictured here with his colleagues and one of his canine subjects, conducted groundbreaking work on classical conditioning.
(b) Pavlov's apparatus collected and measured a dog's saliva.

PAVLOV'S EXPERIMENTS REVEAL THE FOUR STEPS IN CLASSICAL CONDITIONING The Scientific Thinking feature on p. 200 describes classical conditioning as revealed by Pavlov's research. In addition, the Learning Tip on p. 201 will help you learn the four main terms associated with classical conditioning.

Classical conditioning always begins with a stimulus that naturally elicits a response. In other words, the stimulus produces the response, much like a reflex. In the case of Pavlov's research, the presentation of food causes the salivary reflex and no learning is required to produce the salivation. As shown in Step 1 of the Scientific Thinking feature, Pavlov called the food the **unconditioned stimulus (US),** because nothing is learned about the stimulus. Pavlov called the salivation elicited by food the **unconditioned response (UR).** The response is "unconditioned" because it is an unlearned behavior, like any simple reflex.

In Step 2, a *neutral stimulus* is presented. The neutral stimulus can be anything that the dog can see or hear, but it must not be associated with the UR. Pavlov used a metronome as the neutral stimulus. The metronome is a device that helps musicians keep time to music by making rhythmic clicking sounds, but it does not cause salivation.

Step 3 of the process is the conditioning trials. Now the neutral stimulus is presented along with the unconditioned stimulus that reliably produces the unconditioned response. Recall that the unconditioned stimulus here was the food, and the neutral stimulus was the clicking of a metronome. This is when the dog begins to associate the two stimuli, food and the clicking metronome, and we say the animal is learning.

In Step 4, the critical trials, we see evidence that the dog has learned the association between the food and the metronome. This is because presenting the clicking metronome alone, without the presence of the food, now makes the dog salivate. We now say that the animal has been classically conditioned. At this point, the metronome is called the **conditioned stimulus (CS),** because its clicking sound causes the dog to salivate only after the dog has gone through the process of conditioning. In our example, the dog has learned the relationship between the metronome and the food. Similarly, the salivation elicited by the metronome is now called the **conditioned response (CR),** because it is a behavior that occurs only after conditioning. In this case, both the unconditioned and the conditioned

unconditioned stimulus (US)
A stimulus that elicits a response that is innate and does not require any prior learning.

unconditioned response (UR)
A response that does not have to be learned, such as a reflex.

conditioned stimulus (CS)
A stimulus that elicits a response only after learning has taken place.

conditioned response (CR)
A response to a conditioned stimulus; a response that has been learned.

Hypothesis: A dog can learn that a metronome predicts food.

Research Method:

1. Food (**unconditioned stimulus**) causes a reflexive response, salivation (**unconditioned response**).

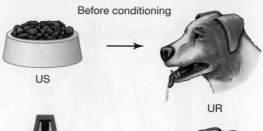

Before conditioning

US

UR

2. The clicking metronome (*neutral stimulus*) does not cause the dog to salivate.

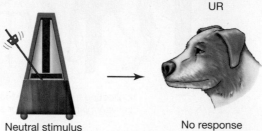

Neutral stimulus

No response

3. During conditioning trials, the clicking metronome is presented to the dog along with food so that the dog begins to learn the two stimuli are associated.

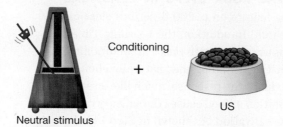

Conditioning

+

Neutral stimulus

US

4. During critical trials, the clicking metronome (**conditioned stimulus**) is presented without the food, and the dog salivates (**conditioned response**).

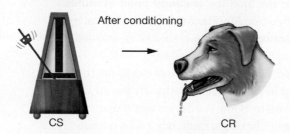

After conditioning

CS

CR

Result: The conditioned response shows that the dog learned that the metronome predicted the arrival of food.

Conclusion: The dog was classically conditioned to associate the metronome with food. In other words, the dog salivated when hearing the sound of the metronome because it learned that the metronome predicted the arrival of food.

responses are salivation, but they are not identical. The conditioned response usually is weaker than the unconditioned response. Thus the metronome sound alone produces less saliva than the food does.

Now let's go back to the scenario at the beginning of this section. As you watch the movie and see the woman descending into the basement in the middle of the night, you have a natural feeling of fear about this scary situation. In this case, the stimulus and your response to it are unconditioned. Now imagine a kind of music begins to play in the movie. You first heard that music earlier in the movie, but you did not notice it very much. But now you realize that it seems

In classical conditioning, the word *conditioned* simply means "learned," as shown below.

WHEN YOU SEE	PLEASE THINK	MEANING
<u>Unconditioned</u> stimulus	Stimulus that is <u>not learned</u>	Something that instinctively (innately) prompts a reaction
<u>Unconditioned</u> response	Response that is <u>not learned</u>	Reaction that is elicited instinctively (innately)
<u>Conditioned</u> stimulus	Stimulus that is <u>learned</u>	Something that prompts a reaction only after learning has occurred
<u>Conditioned</u> response	Response that is <u>learned</u>	Reaction that is elicited only after learning has occurred

to come on just before something bad happens to a character in the movie. You will probably start to feel tense as soon as you hear the music. You have learned that the music, the conditioned stimulus, predicts scenes where terrible things happen to the characters. This learning makes you feel tense as you watch the movie, because that feeling is the conditioned response (**Figure 6.4**).

Just as Pavlov's studies revealed, the conditioned stimulus (music) produces a somewhat weaker, or slightly different, response than does the unconditioned stimulus (the scary scene). Because this association is learned, the conditioned response may be more a feeling of tension or anxiety than one of fear. But suppose you later hear this music in a different setting, such as on the radio. Again you will feel tense, even though you are not watching the movie. You have been classically conditioned to feel anxious when you hear the music.

FIGURE 6.4

Classical Conditioning in Thrillers
In many suspenseful or scary movies, the soundtrack music becomes intense just before something exciting or terrible happens. The classic 1975 movie *Jaws* uses this classical conditioning technique to make us feel afraid, as the "duh-duh, duh-duh" theme music always plays just before the shark attacks.

Learning Varies in Classical Conditioning

Like many other scientists of his time and in the decades since, Pavlov believed that conditioning is how animals adapt to their environments. By learning to predict what objects bring pleasure or pain—for instance, learning that the clicking of a metronome predicts the appearance of food—animals acquire new adaptive behaviors.

ACQUISITION The gradual formation of a learned association between a conditioned stimulus (here, a metronome) and an unconditioned stimulus (here, food) to produce the conditioned response (here, salivation) is known as **acquisition** (**Figure 6.5a**).

From his research, Pavlov concluded that for an animal to acquire a learned association, the two stimuli must occur at the same time. But later research has shown that the strongest conditioning occurs when the conditioned stimulus is presented slightly before the unconditioned stimulus. Thus, in the case of Pavlov's dogs, if the metronome (CS) comes just *before* the food (US), this will produce a stronger acquisition of a salivation response (CR) than if the metronome comes at the same time as, or after, the food. The metronome's role in predicting the food is an important part of classical conditioning because it alerts the dog that food is

acquisition
The gradual formation of an association between conditioned and unconditioned stimuli.

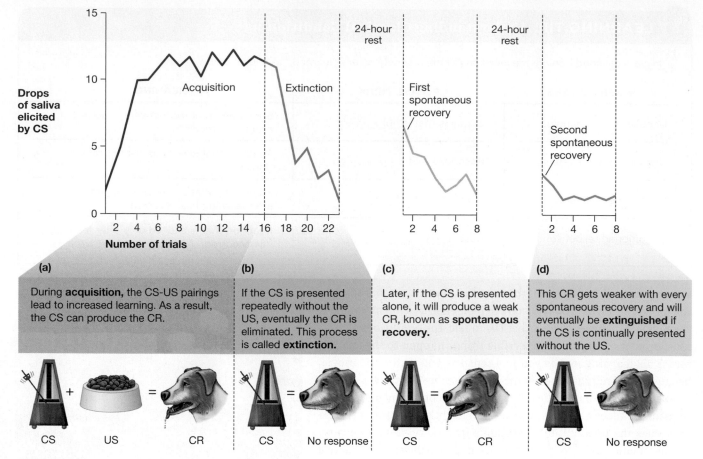

FIGURE 6.5

Acquisition, Extinction, and Spontaneous Recovery
Classical conditioning varies in strength and persistence, as shown by these three conditioning processes.

In figure (panels):

(a) During **acquisition,** the CS-US pairings lead to increased learning. As a result, the CS can produce the CR.

(b) If the CS is presented repeatedly without the US, eventually the CR is eliminated. This process is called **extinction.**

(c) Later, if the CS is presented alone, it will produce a weak CR, known as **spontaneous recovery.**

(d) This CR gets weaker with every spontaneous recovery and will eventually be **extinguished** if the CS is continually presented without the US.

coming. This process is even easier to understand in our movie example, where the music is setting you up to feel anxious just before you watch the woman go into the basement. The next time you watch a thriller, pay attention to the way the music gets louder just before a scary part begins, and notice how it makes you feel.

EXTINCTION But what happens in this example if the food is never again presented with the metronome? In other words, once the salivation behavior (CR) is acquired, how long does it continue even without presentation of the food (US)? Animals sometimes have to learn when associations are no longer adaptive. Normally, after standard classical conditioning, the metronome (CS) leads to salivation (CR) because the animal learns to associate the metronome with the food (US). If the metronome is presented many times and food does not arrive, the animal learns that the metronome is no longer a good predictor of food. Because of this new learning, the animal's conditioned salivary response to the metronome gradually disappears. This process is known as **extinction.** The conditioned response is extinguished when the conditioned stimulus is no longer paired with the arrival of the unconditioned stimulus (**Figure 6.5b**). Extinction is actually a form of learning that takes the place of the previous association. Through extinction, the animal learns that the original association no longer holds true (Bouton, 1994; Bouton, Westbrook, Corcoran, & Maren, 2006). Although extinction reduces the strength of the associative bond, it does not completely eliminate that bond.

SPONTANEOUS RECOVERY Imagine that a long time after extinction, the sound of the metronome is again presented. In this case, the most adaptive response by the dog is to see if the metronome will once again predict the arrival of food. When this

extinction
A process in which the conditioned response is weakened when the conditioned stimulus is repeated without the unconditioned stimulus.

occurs, the extinguished conditioned response of salivation is reactivated in a process called **spontaneous recovery** (**Figure 6.5c**). This recovery will fade quickly and lead to extinction once again, however, unless the CS is paired with the US again. Even a single presentation of the CS with the US will reestablish the CR, but the response will get weaker again if CS-US pairings do not continue (**Figure 6.5d**).

GENERALIZATION, DISCRIMINATION, AND SECOND-ORDER CONDITIONING

In any learning situation, hundreds of possible stimuli can be associated with the unconditioned stimulus to produce the conditioned response. How does the brain determine which stimulus is worth responding to? For instance, suppose we classically condition a dog so that it salivates (CR) when it hears a 1,000-hertz (Hz) tone (CS) that is paired with food (US). After the CR is established, the dog will also salivate when it hears tones close to 1,000 Hz. The farther the tones are from 1,000 Hz, the less the dog will salivate. **Stimulus generalization** occurs when stimuli that are similar, but not identical, to the CS produce the CR. Generalization is adaptive, because in nature animals seldom repeatedly experience the CS in an identical way. Slight differences in background noise, temperature, lighting, and so on lead to slightly different perceptions of the CS. Thanks to these different perceptions, animals learn to respond to variations in the CS (**Figure 6.6a–b**).

Of course, generalization has limits. Sometimes it is important for animals to distinguish among similar stimuli. For instance, two plant species might look similar, but one of them might be poisonous. In **stimulus discrimination,** an animal learns to differentiate between two similar stimuli if one is consistently associated with the US and the other is not (**Figure 6.6c**). Pavlov and his students demonstrated that dogs could learn to make very fine distinctions between similar stimuli. You may have used stimulus discrimination to learn which ringtone or phone music belongs to which of your friends.

spontaneous recovery
A process in which a previously extinguished response reemerges after the conditioned stimulus is presented again.

stimulus generalization
Learning that occurs when stimuli that are similar but not identical to the conditioned stimulus produce the conditioned response.

stimulus discrimination
A differentiation between two similar stimuli when only one of them is consistently associated with the unconditioned stimulus.

(a)

(b)

(c)

FIGURE 6.6

Stimulus Generalization and Stimulus Discrimination
Stimulus generalization and stimulus discrimination are important components of learning. These processes may take place even when a learned response has not been classically conditioned. **(a)** When people touch poison ivy and get an itchy rash, they learn to fear this three-leafed plant, and so they avoid it. **(b)** People may then experience stimulus generalization if they fear and avoid similar three-leafed plants—even nonpoisonous ones, such as fragrant sumac. By teaching people to avoid three-leafed plants, stimulus generalization therefore helps keep people safe. **(c)** People may also experience stimulus discrimination related to poison ivy. They do not fear and avoid dissimilar plants—such as Virginia creeper, which has five leaves and is nonpoisonous. If stimulus discrimination did not occur, fear of poison ivy would cause us to avoid activities near wooded areas, such as hiking and gardening.

Now consider what might happen if another stimulus is added to the situation. You know that in one of Pavlov's early studies, a dog learned to associate a tone (CS) and food (US) so that the tone (CS) led to salivation (CR). In a second training session, a black square was repeatedly presented at the same time as the tone (CS). The dog salivated (CR) even though no food (US) was presented. After a few trials, the black square was presented alone, and again the dog salivated (CR). In such cases, the first conditioned stimulus (the tone) became associated with another stimulus (the black square), which was then indirectly associated with the US (food). Effectively, the black square became the second conditioned stimulus (CS-2), which elicited the conditioned response of salivation even when presented alone, without the US or the original CS. This phenomenon is known as *second-order conditioning*.

Second-order conditioning helps account for the complexity of learned associations, especially in people. For instance, suppose a child has been conditioned to associate money with desirable objects, such as candy and toys. Now suppose that whenever the child's uncle visits, the uncle gives the child some money. Through second-order conditioning, the child will learn to associate the uncle with money. If the child feels affection for the uncle, some of that affection will come from the association with money (Domjan, 2003).

We Learn Fear Responses Through Classical Conditioning

Many people are afraid of certain things, but some people's fears can get in the way of their daily functioning. For example, do you know anyone who is so afraid of spiders that he feels panicky when he even looks at a picture of one? Such extreme fear reactions, or phobias, may be the result of classical conditioning. A *phobia* is an acquired fear that is very strong in comparison to the real threat of an object or of a situation. Common phobias include the fear of heights, enclosed places, insects, snakes, or the dark. According to classical-conditioning theory, phobias develop through generalization of a fear experience, as when a person stung by a wasp develops a fear of all flying insects. (Phobias are discussed further in Chapter 13.)

THE CASE OF LITTLE ALBERT John Watson is known as the father of behaviorism. He was one of the first researchers to demonstrate the role of classical conditioning in the learning of phobias. In 1919, Watson asked a wet nurse at the Johns Hopkins clinic to let him use her son in what became a classic study. The study began when the boy, who became known as "Little Albert," was 9 months old. Watson and his lab assistant presented Little Albert with various neutral objects, including a white rat, a rabbit, a dog, a monkey, costume masks, and a ball of white wool. Albert showed a natural curiosity about these items, but he displayed no apparent emotional responses.

When Albert was 11 months old, the conditioning trials began. This time, as they presented the white rat and Albert reached for it, Watson smashed a hammer into an iron bar, producing a loud clanging sound (**Figure 6.7**). The sound scared the child, who immediately withdrew and hid his face. Watson did this a few more times, at intervals of five days, until Albert would whimper and cringe when the rat was presented alone. Thus the US (loud sound) led to a UR (fear). Eventually, the pairing of the CS (rat) with the US (loud sound) led to the rat alone producing a CR (fear). The fear response generalized to other stimuli that Watson had presented along with the rat at the initial meeting. Over time, Albert became frightened of them all, including the rabbit and the ball of wool. Even a Santa Claus with a white

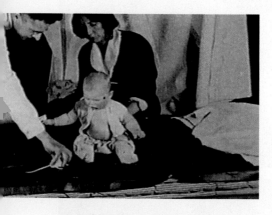

FIGURE 6.7

Case Study of "Little Albert" Reveals Phobias Are Learned Through Classical Conditioning

Little Albert learned to associate a white rat with a loud sound that made Albert feel afraid. Eventually Albert showed the conditioned fear response when he saw the white rat. This case study revealed that phobias could be learned through classical conditioning.

beard produced a fear response. Thus Watson demonstrated that phobias could be brought about by classical conditioning.

Though Albert was emotionally stable when the study began, and Watson believed the study would cause him little harm, Watson's conditioning of Albert has long been criticized as unethical. Today an ethics committee probably would not approve such a study. Watson had planned a series of trials where he would continually present the feared items to Albert paired with more pleasant things, but Albert's mother removed the child from the study before Watson could conduct the trials. We don't know how his later life might have been affected by the study. Tragically, Albert died at the age of 6, likely of meningitis, a brain infection (Beck, Levinson, & Irons, 2009).

COUNTERCONDITIONING A colleague of Watson's—the behavioral pioneer Mary Cover Jones—did use this method successfully to reduce phobias. Jones eliminated the fear of rabbits in a 3-year-old by bringing a rabbit closer as she provided the child with a favorite food (Jones, 1924). Such classical-conditioning techniques have since proved valuable in developing very effective behavioral therapies to treat phobias. In the example above, where a person might have a phobia of spiders, a clinician might expose the client to spiders while having him engage in an enjoyable task. This technique, called *counterconditioning,* may help the client overcome the phobia.

The behavioral therapist Joseph Wolpe has developed a formal treatment based on counterconditioning (Wolpe, 1997). If you were undergoing Wolpe's treatment, called *systematic desensitization,* first you would be taught how to relax your muscles. Then you would be asked to imagine the feared object or situation while you continued to use the relaxation exercises. Eventually, you would be exposed to the feared stimulus while relaxing. The general idea is that the $CS \rightarrow CR_1$ (fear) connection can be broken by developing a $CS \rightarrow CR_2$ (relaxation) connection. Psychologists now believe that in breaking such a fear connection, repeated exposure to the feared stimulus is more important than relaxation.

Adaptation and Cognition Influence Classical Conditioning

Pavlov's original explanation for classical conditioning was that any two events presented together would produce a learned association. In other words, any object or phenomenon could be converted to a conditioned stimulus when associated with any unconditioned stimulus. Pavlov and his followers believed that the strength of the association was determined by factors such as the intensity of the conditioned and unconditioned stimuli. For example, a louder metronome or a larger piece of meat would produce stronger associations than a quieter metronome or a smaller piece of meat. In the mid-1960s, a number of challenges to Pavlov's theory suggested that some conditioned stimuli were more likely to produce learning than others.

EVOLUTIONARY INFLUENCES Let's return for a moment to the situation we used to open this chapter: your response to shrimp after your bad experience with it at the party. Such conditioned taste aversion is the result of classical conditioning. We also saw conditioned taste aversion in the gray wolves of the Northern Rocky Mountain region that stopped preying on sheep after becoming ill from eating poisoned sheep meat. In the case of the wolves, when the sheep carcass (CS)

FIGURE 6.8
Fearing Dangerous Things Is a Helpful Adaptive Response
This cat is showing a fear response to the dog. The tendency for animals and humans to fear dangerous things, such as predators and poisonous plants, makes sense. After all, being biologically prepared to fear potentially dangerous situations makes survival more likely.

was paired with the poison (US), the wolves that ate the meat vomited. They associated feeling sick with the sheep (CR), so it was adaptive for them to stop preying on the sheep (CR). However, research conducted by the psychologist John Garcia and colleagues showed that certain pairings of stimuli are more likely to become associated than others (Garcia & Koelling, 1966).

Conditioned taste aversions like these are easy to produce with smell or taste, but they are very difficult to produce with light or sound. This difference makes sense, because smell and taste are the main cues that guide an animal's eating behavior. From an evolutionary viewpoint, animals that quickly associate a certain flavor with illness, and therefore avoid that flavor, will be better adapted. That is, they will be more likely to survive and pass along their genes.

However, auditory and visual stimuli may have survival value for particular animals in particular environments. Thus animals may learn adaptive responses that are related to the potential dangers associated with the stimuli. For example, monkeys can more easily be conditioned to fear snakes than to fear objects such as flowers or rabbits (Cook & Mineka, 1989). The psychologist Martin Seligman (1970) has argued that animals are genetically programmed, or biologically prepared, to fear specific objects. Preparedness helps explain why animals tend to fear potentially dangerous things (e.g., snakes, fire, heights) rather than objects that pose little threat (e.g., flowers, shoes, babies; **Figure 6.8**).

COGNITIVE INFLUENCES Until the 1970s, most learning theorists were behaviorists. They were concerned only with observable stimuli and observable responses. Since then, there has been more emphasis on trying to understand the mental processes that are the basis of conditioning. An important principle has emerged from this work: Classical conditioning is a way that animals come to *predict* the occurrence of events.

The psychologist Robert Rescorla (1966) conducted one of the first studies that highlighted the role of cognition in learning. He argued that for learning to take place, the conditioned stimulus must accurately predict the unconditioned stimulus. For instance, a stimulus that occurs *before* the US is more easily conditioned than one that comes *after* it. Even though both are close to the US in time, the stimulus that comes before the US is more easily learned because it predicts the US. We saw this effect in the example of creepy music before scary scences in movies.

The cognitive model of classical learning states that an animal learns to expect that some predictors (potential CSs) are better than others. According to this model, the strength of the CS-US association is determined by how unexpected or surprising the US is. When an animal encounters a new stimulus, it pays attention to it. The more surprising the US, the harder an animal tries to understand how it happened. Figuring out the US helps the animal predict when it will happen again. The result of this effort is greater classical conditioning of the new event (CS) that predicted the US.

Suppose you always use an electric can opener to open a can of dog food. Your dog associates the sound of the can opener (CS) with the appearance of food (US). The dog has the conditioned response (CR) of wagging its tail when it hears that sound. Now say the electric can opener breaks, and you replace it with a manual one. According to the cognitive model of learning, the unexpected appearance of the food (US) without the electric can opener sound (CS) will cause your dog to pay attention to events in the environment that might have produced the food. Soon the dog will learn to associate being fed with use of the new can opener (new CS; **Figure 6.9**).

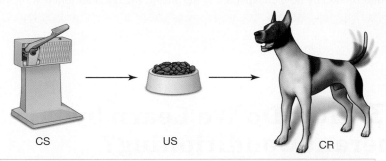

CS   US   CR

1 A dog learns to associate an electric can opener (**conditioned stimulus**) with the arrival of food (**unconditioned stimulus**). This association causes the dog's tail to wag (**conditioned response**).

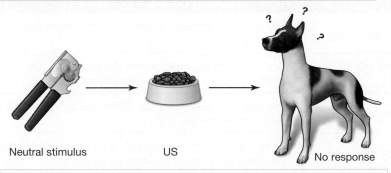

Neutral stimulus   US   No response

2 The dog is surprised when a manual can opener (*neutral stimulus*) replaces the electric one. Because it is surprised, the dog does not show the conditioned response.

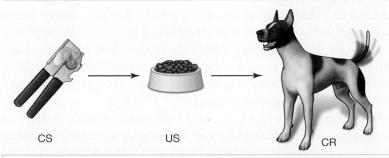

CS   US   CR

3 The dog now pays attention to the environment and so comes to associate the new can opener (**conditioned stimulus**) with the arrival of food (**unconditioned stimulus**). Now the manual can opener (new conditioned stimulus) becomes the better predictor of the expected event: food. As a result, the manual can opener elicits the **conditioned response**.

FIGURE 6.9
The Role of Cognition in Learning
The cognitive model of learning emphasizes the role of prediction and expectation in learning.

6.2 CHECKPOINT:
How Do We Learn by Classical Conditioning?

- In Pavlov's classical conditioning, a conditioned stimulus that is predictably associated with an unconditioned stimulus produces a learned, conditioned response.

- Six factors affect the strength and persistence of learning from classical conditioning.

- Phobias may develop when classical conditioning leads to generalization of a fear experience. Techniques based on classical conditioning, such as counterconditioning, can be used to treat phobias.

- Classical conditioning helps animals learn responses that aid survival. The cognitive model states that the amount of conditioning that occurs is determined by how unexpected or surprising the unconditioned stimulus is.

6.3 How Do We Learn by Operant Conditioning?

📖 LEARNING GOALS	✏️ READING ACTIVITIES
a. Remember the key terms about operant conditioning.	List all of the boldface words and write down their definitions.
b. Understand the four types of reinforcement and punishment in operant conditioning.	Summarize in your own words the four ways that reinforcement and punishment affect behavior.
c. Apply the four schedules of reinforcement.	Provide an example of each of the four schedules of reinforcement in your life.
d. Apply the three cognitive aspects of conditioning.	Describe an example from your own life of learning via a cognitive map, latent learning, and insight.

You know that if you study, you're likely to get a better grade on an exam. That seems like an obvious connection, but how did you learn this association? Not through classical conditioning. That form of conditioning is a relatively passive process. For example, an animal learns predictive connections between stimuli, no matter what the animal does. So when we look at an example of classical conditioning, we cannot conclude that learning to behave in a certain way has occurred because of the consequences of the animal's action.

However, our behaviors often represent the way to reach a desired outcome. These behaviors are instrumental—they are done for a purpose. We study to get good grades, we eat our favorite dessert because it tastes delicious, and so on. We learn that behaving in certain ways leads to positive outcomes and behaving in other ways results in negative outcomes, and this knowledge affects how we act in the future. This type of associative learning, where we learn the relationship between a behavior and its consequences, and the relationship affects our future actions, is called **operant conditioning.**

operant conditioning
A learning process in which the consequences of an action determine the likelihood that the action will be performed in the future.

Animals Learn Through the Outcomes of Their Actions

Research on how animals learn the effects of an action began in the late nineteenth century, in Cambridge, Massachusetts, at the home of the psychologist William James. A young graduate student named Edward Thorndike was working with James. Thorndike performed the first reported carefully controlled experiments in comparative animal psychology. Specifically, he studied whether nonhuman animals showed signs of intelligence.

THORNDIKE'S EXPERIMENTS REVEAL THE EFFECTS OF ACTION To conduct his research, Thorndike built a puzzle box—a small cage with a trapdoor (**Figure 6.10a**). The trapdoor would open if the animal inside performed a specific action, such as pulling a string. Thorndike placed food-deprived animals, at first chickens but later cats, inside the puzzle box to see if they could figure out how to escape.

To motivate the cats, Thorndike placed food just outside the box (**Figure 6.10b,** Step 1). When first placed in the box, the cat usually made several unsuccessful attempts to escape. After 5 to 10 minutes of struggling, the cat would accidentally step on the lever that pulled the string, and the door would open (see **Figure 6.10b,** Step 2). Thorndike would then return the cat to the box and repeat the trial. During each of the following trials, the cat more and more quickly pushed the lever. Soon it learned to escape from the puzzle box within seconds (see **Figure 6.10b,** Step 3). Thorndike's research led him to develop a general theory of learning. According to this *law of effect,* any behavior that leads to a "satisfying state of affairs" is likely to occur again. Any behavior that leads to an "annoying state of affairs" is less likely to occur again.

(a)

(b)

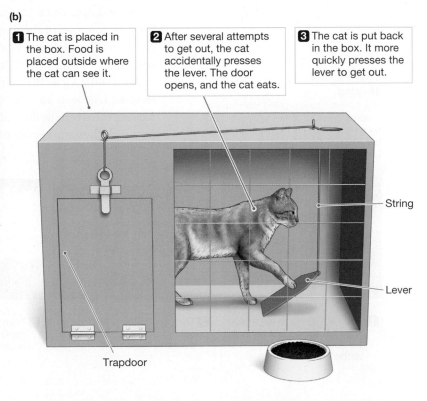

1 The cat is placed in the box. Food is placed outside where the cat can see it.

2 After several attempts to get out, the cat accidentally presses the lever. The door opens, and the cat eats.

3 The cat is put back in the box. It more quickly presses the lever to get out.

String

Lever

Trapdoor

FIGURE 6.10

Thorndike's Puzzle Box

(a) Thorndike's experiments used puzzle boxes, like the one shown here. **(b)** The box was designed to assess learning in animals, and Thorndike used it in developing the law of effect. Because stepping on the lever to pull the string led to the satisfying state where the cat could escape from the box, the cat stepped on the lever more quickly the next time it was in the box.

Learning Varies in Operant Conditioning

B. F. Skinner developed a more formal learning theory based on the law of effect. Skinner, the psychologist most closely associated with operant conditioning, chose the term *operant* to express the idea that animals *operate* on their environments to produce effects. Operant conditioning is the learning process in which an action's consequences determine how likely that action is to be performed in the future. Skinner also coined the term *reinforcer* to describe a stimulus that occurs after a response and increases the likelihood that the response will be repeated. Skinner believed that behavior—studying, eating, driving on the proper side of the road, and so on—occurs because it has been reinforced.

To test his theory, Skinner developed a simple device that is now known as a Skinner box. Inside the box, a lever that can be pressed (operant) is connected to a food supply (reinforcer). An animal, usually a rat or pigeon, is placed in the Skinner box. Through operant conditioning, the animal learns that pressing the lever results in food (**Figure 6.11**).

Lever

Food tray

FIGURE 6.11

Skinner Box

In B. F. Skinner's research, an animal received a reinforcer, such as food, after pressing a lever (operant). Getting the food made the animal more likely to repeat that action. Learning a response in this way is called operant conditioning.

SHAPING In operant conditioning, providing the reinforcer before the animal displays the appropriate behavior usually does not lead to learning. Inside a Skinner box, an animal has so little to do that it usually makes the right correct response: It presses the lever or key fairly quickly. Outside a Skinner box, however, the same animal might be distracted and take longer to perform the action you are looking for. Rather than wait for the animal to spontaneously perform the action, you can use an operant-conditioning technique to teach the animal to do so. This powerful process, called *shaping*, consists of reinforcing behaviors that are increasingly similar to the desired behavior.

For example, suppose you are trying to teach your dog to roll over. At first, you reward the dog for any behavior that even slightly resembles rolling over, such as lying down. Once this behavior is established, you selectively reinforce it. That is, you reward the dog each time it gets closer to performing the behavior you want. For instance, you might reward the dog for rolling onto one side. Next you might reward it for lying on its back. This system eventually produces the desired behavior as the animal learns what behavior is being reinforced. Indeed, shaping has been used to condition animals to perform amazing feats: pigeons playing table tennis, dogs playing the piano, pigs doing housework such as picking up clothes and vacuuming, and so on (**Figure 6.12**).

FIGURE 6.12

Shaping

The operant conditioning technique of shaping consists of reinforcing behaviors that are increasingly similar to the desired behavior. Shaping can be used to train animals to perform unusual behaviors.

1 If you are trying to teach your dog to surf, you first reward the dog for approaching the surfboard.

2 Then you reward the dog for getting on the surfboard and standing there.

3 Then you reward the dog for continuing to stand on the board as the waves move it.

4 As the dog learns what behavior is being reinforced, it eventually learns to produce the desired behavior: surfing!

Shaping has also been used to teach people. People with psychological disorders can learn appropriate social skills, children with autism spectrum disorder can learn language, and individuals with differences in developmental abilities can learn life skills. More generally, parents and educators often use shaping to encourage appropriate behavior in children. For example, they praise children for their first, often unreadable, attempts at handwriting.

REINFORCERS CAN BE CONDITIONED The most obvious reinforcers are those necessary for survival, such as food or water. Because they satisfy biological needs, they are called *primary reinforcers*. From an evolutionary standpoint, the learning value of primary reinforcers makes a great deal of sense: Animals that repeatedly perform behaviors that are reinforced by food or water are more likely to survive and pass along their genes.

Many apparent reinforcers do not directly satisfy biological needs, however. Receiving a grade of A on your term paper, a compliment on your art project, or a raise at work can all be reinforcing. Events or objects that serve as reinforcers but do not satisfy biological needs are called *secondary reinforcers*. These reinforcers are established through classical conditioning. We learn to associate a neutral stimulus, such as money, with a primary reinforcer such as food (US). Money is really only pieces of metal or slips of paper, but these and other neutral objects become meaningful conditioned stimuli (CS) thanks to their associations with unconditioned stimuli.

REINFORCER POTENCY Some reinforcers are more powerful than others. The psychologist David Premack (1959; Holstein & Premack, 1965) theorized about how a reinforcer's value could be determined. The key is the amount of time an animal, when free to do anything, engages in a specific behavior associated with the reinforcer. For instance, given freedom of choice, children more often eat ice cream than spinach. Ice cream is therefore more reinforcing for children than spinach is. One great advantage of Premack's theory is that it can account for differences in individual peoples' values. For people who eat ice cream more often than spinach, ice cream serves as a stronger reinforcer.

A logical application of Premack's theory, called the *Premack principle,* is that a more valued activity can be used to reinforce the performance of a less valued activity. When parents tell their children, "Eat your spinach and then you'll get dessert," they're using the Premack principle. You've probably used it on yourself a few times: "After I finish reading this chapter, I'll watch that video" (**Figure 6.13**).

FIGURE 6.13

The Premack Principle in Our Daily Lives
When you were younger, did you have to eat your dinner before you got your dessert? If so, then you experienced the Premack principle firsthand. In this case, you had to accept the less desired food in order to receive the food you really wanted.

Reinforcement and Punishment Influence Operant Conditioning

positive reinforcement
The addition of a stimulus to increase the probability that a behavior will be repeated.

negative reinforcement
The removal of a stimulus to increase the probability that a behavior will be repeated.

positive punishment
The addition of a stimulus to decrease the probability that a behavior will recur.

negative punishment
The removal of a stimulus to decrease the probability that a behavior will recur.

Reinforcement and punishment have opposite effects on behavior. Reinforcement makes a behavior more likely to be repeated, and punishment makes that behavior less likely to occur again. Furthermore, in both positive reinforcement and positive punishment, a stimulus is added. But in negative reinforcement or negative punishment, a stimulus is removed. The operant conditioning terminology can be confusing, so let's look at each of these concepts next. **Figure 6.14** also gives an overview of all these situations, and the Learning Tip will help you remember the terms correctly.

POSITIVE AND NEGATIVE REINFORCEMENT Both positive and negative reinforcement *increase* the likelihood of a certain behavior. **Positive reinforcement** is the *addition* of a stimulus that increases the probability that a behavior will be repeated. Positive reinforcement is often called *reward,* and when behaviors are rewarded, the actions increase in frequency. For example, feeding a rat after it presses a lever will increase the probability that the rat will press the lever again (see Figure 6.14a). Similarly, when you receive praise from your boss or an increase in pay, your response is to work harder. In contrast, **negative reinforcement** increases behavior by *removing* a stimulus. Negative reinforcement occurs when a rat presses a lever to turn off a painful electric shock. The rat will be more likely to press the lever again in the future (see Figure 6.14b).

Negative reinforcement is common in everyday life. You take a pill to get rid of a headache. You close your door to shut out noise. You change the channel to avoid watching an awful show. You pick up a crying baby. In each case, you are trying to stop a stimulus. If the action you take successfully reduces the stimulus, then the next time you have a headache, hear noise in your room, see an awful program, or are with a crying baby, the more likely you are to repeat the behavior that reduced the stimulus. Your behavior has been negatively reinforced. However, be aware that negative reinforcement is not the same as punishment.

POSITIVE AND NEGATIVE PUNISHMENT By contrast, both positive and negative punishment *reduce* the likelihood that a behavior will be repeated. **Positive**

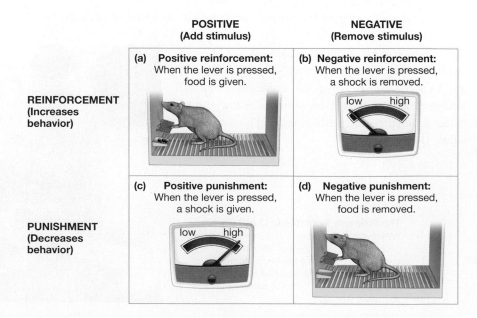

	POSITIVE (Add stimulus)	**NEGATIVE** (Remove stimulus)
REINFORCEMENT (Increases behavior)	**(a) Positive reinforcement:** When the lever is pressed, food is given.	**(b) Negative reinforcement:** When the lever is pressed, a shock is removed.
PUNISHMENT (Decreases behavior)	**(c) Positive punishment:** When the lever is pressed, a shock is given.	**(d) Negative punishment:** When the lever is pressed, food is removed.

FIGURE 6.14

Reinforcement and Punishment
This graphic will help you understand the four types of reinforcement and punishment.

punishment is when the *addition* of a stimulus decreases the probability of a behavior being repeated. This happens when a rat receives an electric shock for pressing a lever, which makes it less likely to press the lever again (see Figure 6.14c). If a teenager gets a speeding ticket, then she has experienced positive punishment, which should make her less likely to speed in the future. However, by *removing* a stimulus, **negative punishment** decreases the likelihood a behavior will be repeated. For example, when a rat presses a lever and food is removed, the rat is not likely to press the lever again (see Figure 6.14d). And when a teenager loses driving privileges for speeding, he has received negative punishment that should prevent speeding in the future. As these examples show, negative and positive forms of punishment should produce the same result: The teen will be less likely to speed the next time he or she gets behind the wheel.

SCHEDULES OF PARTIAL REINFORCEMENT How often should a reinforcer be given? To produce fast learning, behavior might be reinforced each time it occurs. This process is known as *continuous reinforcement.* In the real world, behavior is seldom reinforced continuously. Animals do not find food each time they look for it, and people do not receive praise each time they behave acceptably. Instead, occasional reinforcement of behavior is more common. This is called *partial reinforcement.*

The effect of partial reinforcement on conditioning depends on the reinforcement schedule. Partial reinforcement can be given on a predictable basis, which is called a fixed schedule, or on an unpredictable basis, called a variable schedule. Partial reinforcement can also be given based on either the passage of time, called an interval schedule, or the number of behavioral responses, called a ratio schedule. Crossing how reinforcement is given with how consistently it is given provides the four most common schedules of reinforcement, as shown in **Figure 6.15** and in the Learning Tip on p. 214.

LEARNING TIP: Four Types of Reinforcement and Punishment

It's easy to remember the difference between the four types of reinforcement and punishment: positive reinforcement, negative reinforcement, positive punishment, and negative punishment. Ask these two questions to get it right:

1. Is a stimulus added or taken away?
   - If a stimulus is *added,* then this is "positive."
   - If a stimulus is *taken away,* then this is "negative."
2. After adding or taking away a stimulus, does the behavior increase or decrease?
   - If the behavior *increases,* then this is "reinforcement."
   - If the behavior *decreases,* then this is "punishment."

If you put together the two words from your answers to questions 1 and 2, you will know which of the four types of reinforcement and punishment is being used.

FIGURE 6.15

Effect of Reinforcement Schedules on Behavior

The curves show cumulative responses under different schedules of reinforcement over time. The steeper the line, the greater the response rate.

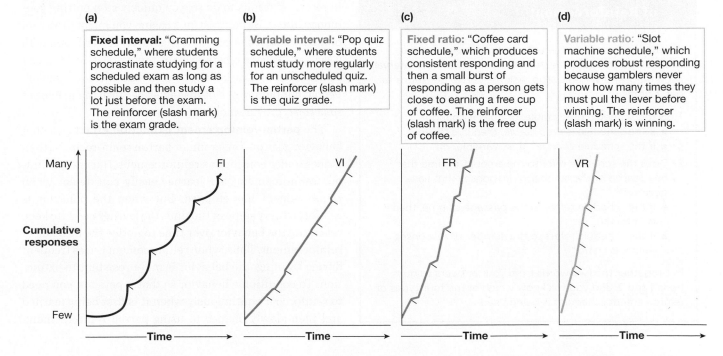

(a)

Fixed interval: "Cramming schedule," where students procrastinate studying for a scheduled exam as long as possible and then study a lot just before the exam. The reinforcer (slash mark) is the exam grade.

(b)

Variable interval: "Pop quiz schedule," where students must study more regularly for an unscheduled quiz. The reinforcer (slash mark) is the quiz grade.

(c)

Fixed ratio: "Coffee card schedule," which produces consistent responding and then a small burst of responding as a person gets close to earning a free cup of coffee. The reinforcer (slash mark) is the free cup of coffee.

(d)

Variable ratio: "Slot machine schedule," which produces robust responding because gamblers never know how many times they must pull the lever before winning. The reinforcer (slash mark) is winning.

fixed interval schedule (FI)
Reinforcing the occurrence of a particular behavior after a predetermined amount of time since the last reward.

variable interval schedule (VI)
Reinforcing the occurrence of a particular behavior after an unpredictable and varying amount of time since the last reward.

fixed ratio schedule (FR)
Reinforcing a particular behavior after that behavior has occurred a predetermined number of times.

variable ratio schedule (VR)
Reinforcing a particular behavior after the behavior has occurred an unpredictable and varying number of times.

partial-reinforcement extinction effect
The greater persistence of behavior under partial reinforcement than under continuous reinforcement.

Many jobs pay employees on a **fixed interval schedule (FI),** where reinforcement is given after a fixed amount of time has passed. For example, say people earn $10 for each hour they work. One feature of fixed interval schedules is a scalloping pattern. "Scalloping" refers to a series of circle segments that look like the edge of a scallop shell. The rises in this pattern mean that behavior continually increases just before the opportunity for reinforcement, and then behavior drops off after reinforcement (see Figure 6.15a). You're probably familiar with this pattern in your courses that have regularly scheduled examinations. Students often slack off a bit after an exam and then "cram" their studying into the time just before the next exam.

Variable interval schedules (VI) provide reinforcement after an unpredictable amount of time has passed. A good example of a VR schedule is the pop quiz schedule, in which students know that they could face a quiz at any time (see Figure 6.15b). As you might guess, VR schedules lead to more consistent response rates than FI schedules. In a class with pop quizzes, you cannot slack off in studying, because you need to be ready for a quiz at any time.

By contrast, in a **fixed ratio schedule (FR),** reinforcement is given after a fixed number of responses—for instance, a system that pays a factory worker by the piece or a coffee card rewards program that gets you a free cup of coffee after you buy 10 cups (see Figure 6.15c). Fixed ratio schedules often elicit more robust responding than FI schedules. For example, factory workers paid by the piece are usually more productive than those paid by the hour, especially if the workers receive incentives for higher productivity.

Variable ratio schedules (VR) provide reinforcement after an unpredictable number of responses. An example is slot machines: They may pay out a consistent amount over the long term, but you never know which pull of the handle will result in winning money (see Figure 6.15d).

Besides affecting the number of responses, the schedule of reinforcement also affects how long a behavior persists. Continuous reinforcement is highly effective for teaching a behavior. If the reinforcement is stopped, however, the behavior is quickly extinguished. For instance, normally when you put money in a vending machine, it gives you a product in return. If it fails to do so, you quickly stop putting your money into it. By contrast, at a casino you might drop a lot of money into a slot machine that rarely rewards you with a jackpot. Psychologists explain this persistent behavior as the effect of a variable ratio schedule of reinforcement: People put money in slot machines because the machines *sometimes* provide monetary rewards.

The **partial-reinforcement extinction effect** says that behavior goes on longer under partial reinforcement than it does under continuous reinforcement. During continuous reinforcement, the learner easily can detect when reinforcement has stopped. But when the behavior is reinforced only some of the time, the learner needs to keep repeating the behavior over time to notice the absence of reinforcement. Thus, when reinforcement is less frequent during training, the behavior is more resistant to extinction. To condition a behavior so that it persists, you need to reinforce it continuously when it is first being learned and then slowly change to using partial reinforcement.

LEARNING TIP: Four Schedules of Reinforcement

It's easy to remember the difference between the four schedules of reinforcement: fixed interval, variable interval, fixed ratio, and variable ratio. Ask these two questions to get it right:

1. Is the schedule predictable, or does it change?
   - If the schedule is *predictable,* then it is "fixed."
   - If the schedule *changes,* it is "variable."

2. Does the schedule refer to the amount of time that has passed or the number of responses that have occurred?
   - If the schedule refers to the *passage of time,* then it is "interval."
   - If the schedule refers to the *number of responses,* then it is "ratio."

Put together the two words from your answers to questions 1 and 2, and you will know which of the four types of reinforcement schedules is being used.

Parents naturally follow this strategy in teaching their children behaviors such as toilet training.

The persistence of partially reinforced behaviors also provides an important lesson for trying to extinguish unwanted behaviors. For instance, suppose your cat meows when demanding to be fed. You try to ignore it, because you don't want to reinforce the behavior. But once in a while, you break down and feed the cat. You've just made it even harder to extinguish the behavior. The longer you take to break down, the more persistent the cat will be. To extinguish the behavior, you have to consistently withhold reinforcement. The same is true for a child who demands a candy bar at the grocery store. To stop the child from making demands, you refuse to buy the candy bar. Then, any other time the child demands that you buy an item, you refuse again and again.

Operant Conditioning Affects Our Lives

Now imagine that a child demands a candy bar at a grocery store, the parent says no, and the child throws a temper tantrum. The exasperated parent yells, "If you don't stop screaming, you're going to get a smacked bottom!" Will this approach produce the desired behavior?

PARENTAL PUNISHMENT IS INEFFECTIVE To make their children behave, parents sometimes use punishment as a means of discipline. Many contemporary psychologists believe that punishment is often applied ineffectively, and that it may have unintended and unwanted consequences. Research has shown that for punishment to be effective, it must be reasonable, unpleasant, and applied immediately so that the relationship between the unwanted behavior and the punishment is clear (Goodall, 1984; O'Leary, 1995). Obviously, this means there is considerable potential for confusion.

Sometimes punishment is wrongly applied after a behavior that is actually desirable. For example, if a student is punished after admitting to cheating on an exam, he may then associate the punishment with being honest rather than with the original offense. As a result, the student learns not to tell the truth. As Skinner once pointed out, one thing people learn from punishment is how to avoid it. Rather than learning how to behave appropriately, they may learn not to get caught.

Punishment can also lead to negative emotions, such as fear and anxiety. Through classical conditioning, these emotions may become associated with the person who administers the punishment. If a child learns to fear a parent or teacher, the long-term relationship between child and adult may be damaged (Gershoff, 2002).

In addition, punishment often fails to offset the reinforcing aspects of the undesired behavior. In real life, any behavior can be reinforced in multiple ways. For instance, thumb sucking may be reinforced because it makes a child feel good, because it provides relief from negative emotions, and because it eases hunger. Punishment may not be enough to offset such rewards, and it may reinforce the child's secrecy about thumb sucking.

For these and other reasons, most psychologists agree with Skinner's recommendation that reinforcement is a better way than punishment to teach desirable behavior (**Figure 6.16**). A child complimented for being a good student is likely to perform better academically than one punished for doing poorly. After all, reinforcing good behavior tells the child what to do. Punishing the child for bad behavior does not tell the child how to improve.

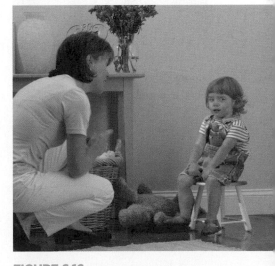

FIGURE 6.16

Parents Should Avoid the Use of Punishment

In general, using reinforcement to improve children's behavior is more effective than using punishment. In reinforcing children's behavior, it is especially important to say what they *should* be doing instead of what they *should not* be doing.

One form of punishment that most psychologists believe is especially ineffective is physical punishment, such as spanking (see the Being a Critical Consumer feature in Chapter 1). Even so, spanking is very common. Nearly three-quarters of American parents spank their children and apparently believe it is effective (Gallup, 1995). As noted by Alan Kazdin and Corina Benjet (2003), beliefs about the appropriateness of spanking are related to religious beliefs, cultural views, and legal issues. Many countries (e.g., Austria, Denmark, Israel, Sweden, and Italy) have banned physical punishment in homes or schools. Even the United Nations has passed resolutions discouraging it.

Researchers have provided evidence of many negative outcomes associated with spanking, especially severe spanking (Bender et al., 2007). These problems include poor parent/child relations, weaker moral values, mental health problems, increased delinquency, and future child abuse. One concern is that physical punishment teaches the child that violence is an appropriate behavior for adults. We discuss such imitative behavior later in this chapter.

How often do mild forms of spanking cause problems? That question is open to debate (Baumrind, Larzelere, & Cowan, 2002), but the evidence indicates that other forms of punishment, such as taking away cell phone or Internet access, are more effective for decreasing unwanted behaviors (Kazdin & Benjet, 2003). Many psychologists believe that any form of punishment is less effective than using positive reinforcement to increase the likelihood of engaging in "better" behaviors. By rewarding the behaviors they wish to see, parents are able to increase those behaviors while building more positive bonds with their children.

BEHAVIOR MODIFICATION *Behavior modification* is the use of operant-conditioning techniques to eliminate unwanted behaviors and replace them with desirable ones. The general reasoning behind behavior modification is that most unwanted behaviors can be unlearned. Conditioning strategies are widely used, for example, to teach people to be more productive at work, to save energy, and to drive more safely. Children with severe learning disabilities can be trained to communicate and to interact. As we discuss in Chapter 14, operant conditioning techniques are also effective for treating many psychological conditions.

One widespread behavior modification method draws on the principle of secondary reinforcement. Chimpanzees can be trained to perform tasks in exchange for tokens, which they can later trade for food. The tokens thus reinforce behavior, and the chimps work as hard to obtain the tokens as they work to obtain food. Prisons, mental hospitals, schools, and classrooms often use *token economies,* in which people earn tokens for completing tasks and lose tokens for behaving badly. The people can later trade their tokens for objects or privileges (**Figure 6.17**). Here, the rewards not only reinforce good behavior but also give participants a sense of control over their environment.

FIGURE 6.17
Token Economies Change Behavior
Many teachers give tokens (or stickers or pencils) for obeying class rules, turning in homework on time, and helping others. At some future point, the tokens can be exchanged for rewards, such as fun activities or extra recess time.

Biology and Cognition Influence Operant Conditioning

Behaviorists such as B. F. Skinner believed that all behavior could be explained by straightforward conditioning principles. In reality, as described in this section, reinforcement explains only certain human behaviors. On the one hand, biological factors can either increase the effects of reinforcers or limit their effects on learning. On the other hand, reinforcement does not always have to be present for learning to take place.

Can Behavior Modification Help You Exercise Regularly?

The Centers for Disease Control and Prevention report that less than half of adults meet the goal of exercising 30 minutes a day, 5 days per week (U.S. DHHS, 2008). Maybe you intend to exercise daily, but then struggle to find the time to get to the gym. Or maybe you make working out a priority for a few weeks and then stop. How can psychology help you stick with your exercise program?

Just as psychologists use operant conditioning to change the behaviors of animals, including humans, you can condition yourself to perform healthful behaviors. Consider these steps:

1. **Identify a behavior you wish to change.** First, you need to decide what behavior you wish to modify. In this case, you want to increase your level of physical activity.

2. **Set goals.** Set goals that are realistic, specific, and measurable. If your current exercise program consists of a daily race to beat the closing elevator door, setting a goal to run 10 miles per day every day this month is not realistic. A goal of "exercise more" is too vague. Instead, set a goal that you can accomplish in a relatively short time, and one you can measure objectively. For example: Walk up the three flights of stairs at work at least four days this week; or attend three yoga sessions this week; or walk at least 10,000 steps each day this week. Setting goals you can meet quickly allows for more opportunities for reinforcement. If your ultimate goal is to have 30 minutes of moderate exercise 5 days per week, you need to set small, incremental subgoals that you can reinforce along the way.

3. **Monitor your behavior.** Monitor your behavior for a week before you begin your new physical activity regimen. This will likely move you toward your goal, since you will be more conscious of your behavior. It will also give you a baseline against which you can measure your progress. Record your observations. If you have a smartphone, you might download an app for recording physical activity. Or you can register at an exercise-tracking Web site. Or just use a paper notebook.

4. **Select a reinforcer and decide on a reinforcement schedule.** When you choose a reinforcer, pick something attainable that you genuinely find enjoyable. For example, perhaps for every yoga class you attend, you will earn one song from iTunes. Or you could give yourself a penny for every hundred steps you take each day. Later, when the money adds up, you can use it to buy something you do not normally spend money on.

5. **Reinforce the desired behavior.** To bring about the behavior change you want to see, you need to reinforce the desired behavior whenever it occurs. Be consistent. Suppose that if you work out at the gym three times this week, you treat yourself to a movie. This is important: If you do not work out at the gym three times this week, do not go to the movie. You may be tempted to go anyway, but if you want the behavior modification to work, you have to resist. If you do not behave appropriately, you do not receive the reinforcer. Allow yourself no exceptions.

6. **Modify your goals, reinforcements, or reinforcement schedules, as needed.** Once you begin consistently hitting your stated goals, make the goals more challenging. Add more days of exercise per week, more minutes, or more reps per workout. If you find yourself getting bored with a reinforcer, mix it up a bit. Just be sure to select reinforcers that are genuinely appealing. And change the reinforcement schedule so you have to work harder to get the reward—for example, delay the reinforcement until you've completed two workouts rather than one.

Of course, you can use these principles to address other behaviors, such as procrastinating on your studies, neglecting to call your family, spending too much time on Facebook, and so on. For now, just pick one behavior you want to modify and try following the steps described. Once you get the hang of it, see if you can translate these steps to other areas of your life. You might amaze yourself with the power of behavior modification.

DOPAMINE ACTIVITY AFFECTS REINFORCEMENT Recall that Skinner and other traditional behaviorists defined reinforcement strictly in terms of whether it increased behavior. They were uninterested in *why* it increased behavior—whether any personal feelings might be involved, for instance. After all, they believed that mental states were impossible to study empirically.

Studies of learning have made it clear, however, that positive reinforcement works in two ways: It provides the subjective experience of pleasure, and it increases the desire for the object or event that produced the pleasure. If you behave in a way that produces a favorable outcome—for instance, studying for an exam and then getting an A—the experience creates responses in the brain that support studying for exams again.

Both the liking and wanting involved in positive reinforcement are a result of biological factors, particularly the neurotransmitter dopamine (Schultz, 2010; Wise & Rompre, 1989; Volkow, Wang, & Baler, 2011). When hungry rats are given food, they experience increased dopamine release in the regions of the brain that process reward information: the greater the hunger, the greater the dopamine release (Rolls, Burton, & Mora, 1980). Food tastes better when you are hungry, and water is more rewarding when you are thirsty, because more dopamine is released when you have been deprived.

In operant conditioning, dopamine has a biological influence on how reinforcing something is. Drugs that block dopamine's effects disrupt operant conditioning. On the other hand, drugs that enhance dopamine activation, such as cocaine and amphetamines, increase the reinforcing value of stimuli. This effect helps explain why dopamine is involved in addictive behavior, especially in terms of increased desire for the addictive substance. We will discuss dopamine and addiction further in Chapter 9.

BIOLOGY CONSTRAINS REINFORCEMENT Though behavior can be shaped through reinforcement, we now know that animals have a hard time learning behaviors that run counter to their evolutionary adaptation. A good example of such biological constraints comes from the experience of Marian and Keller Breland. These psychologists used operant-conditioning techniques to train animals for commercials (Breland & Breland, 1961). Many of their animals refused to perform certain tasks they had been taught. For instance, a raccoon learned to place coins in a piggy bank, but eventually it refused to perform this task. Instead, the raccoon stood over the piggy bank and briskly rubbed the coins in its paws. This rubbing behavior was not reinforced; in fact, it delayed reinforcement. One explanation for the raccoon's behavior is that the task it was supposed to perform was incompatible with its innate, biologically determined, adaptive behaviors. The raccoon associated the coin with food and treated it the same way: Rubbing food between the paws is hardwired for raccoons (**Figure 6.18**).

Conditioning is most effective when the association between the response and the reinforcement is consistent with the animal's built-in biological predispositions. For instance, the psychologist Robert Bolles has argued that animals have built-in defense reactions to threatening stimuli (Bolles, 1970). Pigeons can be trained to peck at keys to obtain food or secondary reinforcers, but it is difficult to train them to peck at keys to avoid electric shock. They can learn to avoid shock by flapping their wings, however, because wing flapping is their natural means of escape.

LEARNING WITHOUT REINFORCEMENT Another challenge to the idea that reinforcement is responsible for all behavior is the fact that learning can take place

FIGURE 6.18

Biology Constrains Learning Through Operant Conditioning

Animals have a hard time learning behaviors that go against their biological predispositions. For example, raccoons are hardwired to rub food between their paws, as this raccoon is doing. They have trouble learning *not* to rub objects.

without reinforcement. Edward Tolman, an early cognitive theorist, argued that reinforcement has more impact on *performance* than on *acquisition* of knowledge through learning. This difference is easy to understand if you think of your school-work. For example, if you earn a grade of C on an exam, this suggests that your performance on that day is about average. However, does that performance give any information about whether you truly learned the material?

Tolman's research investigated the answer to this question. In his experiments, rats had to learn to run through complex mazes to obtain food. Tolman believed that each rat developed a **cognitive map.** That is, during an experiment, each rat held in its brain a representation of the particular maze. That representation was based on the things and spaces the rat had seen inside the maze. The rat used this knowledge of the environment to help it find the food quickly.

To test his theory, Tolman and his students studied three groups of rats (**Figure 6.19**). The rats in Group 1 traveled through the maze, but received no reinforcement: They reached the "goal box," but found no food in the box. On later trials, rats continued to wander through the maze slowly, making many "wrong turns" on the way to the goal box. The rats in Group 2 received reinforcement on every trial because there was food in the goal box. On each of the following trials, these rats found the box faster and with fewer errors. The rats in Group 3 started receiving reinforcement only after the first 10 trials. For the first 10 days, they performed as slowly and incorrectly as the unrewarded rats in Group 1. But the rats in Group 3 showed something amazing when they received their first reward on day 11. Suddenly, these rats very quickly and accurately navigated the maze to get to the goal box. In fact, they performed even better than rats in Group 2 that had been rewarded regularly (Tolman & Honzik, 1930).

Tolman's results suggest that the third group of rats had learned a cognitive map of the maze all along. However, based on their performance once the reinforcement began, the Group 3 rats did not use that map to reveal their learning until they started being rewarded. In other words, they were learning even without reinforcement, a situation Tolman termed **latent learning.** The reinforcement led to demonstration of this learning over time through improved performance.

Tolman's results help us understand that your grade of C on an exam shows average performance, but the grade does not indicate whether you learned the material. Learning happens over time, and performance is just a snapshot of what happens at one moment along that longer timeline. If the teacher gave a similar exam again but with a reward for success, you might perform much better. And in comparison with your first attempt, this better performance on the second try

cognitive map
A visuospatial mental representation of an environment.

latent learning
Learning that takes place in the absence of reinforcement.

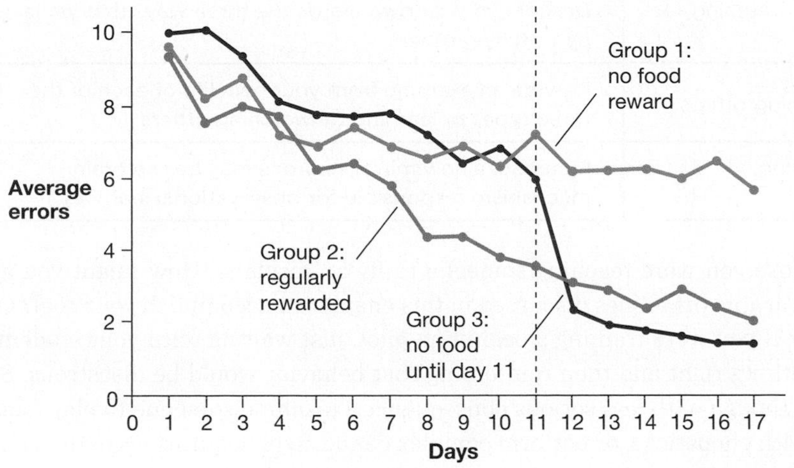

FIGURE 6.19

Tolman's Study of Latent Learning
Rats that were regularly reinforced for correctly running through a maze (Group 2) showed improved performance over time compared with rats that did not receive reinforcement (Group 1). Rats that were not reinforced for the first 10 trials but were reinforced thereafter showed an immediate change in performance (Group 3). Note that between days 11 and 12 Group 3's average number of errors decreased dramatically.

insight learning
A sudden understanding of how to solve a problem after a period of either inaction or thinking about the problem.

would reveal learning. In sum, reinforcement affects performance, and changes in performance over time reveal learning.

Another form of learning that takes place without reinforcement is **insight learning.** In this form of problem solving, a solution suddenly emerges after a delay—a period of either inaction or thinking through the problem. You probably have had this sort of experience. After mulling over a problem for a while and seeming to get nowhere, suddenly you know the answer. The presence of reinforcement does not fully explain insight learning, but it helps determine whether the behavior will be repeated.

6.3 CHECKPOINT: How Do We Learn by Operant Conditioning?

- Operant conditioning involves learning the association between a behavior and its consequences. This learning changes future behavior.

- Reinforcement increases the likelihood that a behavior will be repeated. By contrast, punishment reduces the likelihood that a behavior will be repeated.

- Positive reinforcement and positive punishment change behavior by adding a stimulus. Negative reinforcement and negative punishment change behavior by removing a stimulus.

- There are four schedules of reinforcement, and each schedule has a different effect on behavior.

- Biological conditions, such as the release of dopamine or innate constraints, influence learning. Cognitive processes, such as cognitive maps, latent learning, and insight, also influence learning.

6.4 How Do We Learn by Watching Others?

📖 **LEARNING GOALS**	✏️ **READING ACTIVITIES**
a. Remember the key terms related to learning by watching others.	List all of the boldface words and write down their definitions.
b. Understand the three types of learning by watching others.	Describe in your own words the three ways that we learn by watching others.
c. Apply the three types of learning by watching others.	Provide an example from your own life of each of the three types of learning by watching others.
d. Understand what happens in the brain during observational learning.	Summarize how mirror neurons may be the brain mechanism responsible for observational learning.

Suppose you were teaching someone to fly an airplane. How might you apply the learning principles discussed in this chapter to accomplish your goal? Obviously, if you were training a beginning pilot, just waiting until your student did something right and then reinforcing that behavior would be disastrous. Similarly, though with less serious consequences, teaching someone to play football, eat with chopsticks, or perform complex dance steps requires more than simple reinforcement. We learn many behaviors not by doing them, but by watching others do them. This is true not only for mechanical skills, because we learn social etiquette by watching others. We sometimes learn to be anxious in particular situations by seeing that other people are anxious. We often get our attitudes about politics and religion from parents, peers, teachers, and the media. In general, we learn by watching others in these three ways: observational learning, modeling, and vicarious conditioning.

Three Ways We Learn Through Watching

Observational learning occurs when an individual either acquires or changes a behavior after viewing at least one performance of that behavior. This kind of learning is a powerful adaptive tool for both humans and other animals. Offspring can learn basic skills by watching adults perform those skills. They can learn which things are safe to eat by watching what adults eat, and they can learn to fear dangerous objects and situations by watching adults avoid them. Young children are sponges, absorbing everything that goes on around them (**Figure 6.20**). This behavior can be a bad thing too. When a young child starts to curse, you know the child learned that behavior from an adult, a sibling, or a peer.

observational learning
The acquisition or modification of a behavior after exposure to at least one performance of that behavior.

FIGURE 6.20
Observational Learning
This boy is not just watching his grandfather woodworking. Through observational learning, he is acquiring the skills to do woodworking himself.

 SCIENTIFIC THINKING:
Bandura's Bobo Doll Studies Reveal Observational Learning

Hypothesis: Children can acquire behaviors through observation.

Research Method:

1 Two groups of preschool children were shown a film of an adult playing with a large inflatable doll called Bobo.

2 One group saw the adult play quietly with the doll (activity not shown below).

3 The other group saw the adult attack the doll (activity shown in top row below).

Result: When children were allowed to play with the doll later, those who had seen the aggressive display were more than twice as likely to act aggressively toward the doll.

Conclusion: Exposing children to violence may encourage them to act aggressively.

modeling
The imitation of behavior through observational learning.

BANDURA'S RESEARCH REVEALS LEARNING THROUGH OBSERVATION

The psychologist Albert Bandura conducted the most thorough work on observational learning in the 1960s. In a now-classic series of studies, Bandura divided preschool children into two groups. One group watched a film of an adult playing quietly with a large inflatable doll called Bobo. The other group watched a film of the adult attacking Bobo furiously: whacking the doll with a mallet, punching it in the nose, and kicking it around the room. As shown in the Scientific Thinking box, when the children were later allowed to play with a number of toys, including the Bobo doll, those who had seen the more aggressive display were more than twice as likely to act aggressively toward the doll (Bandura, Ross, & Ross, 1961).

Bandura's results suggest not only that people learn through observation, but that exposing children to violence is associated with acting aggressively. But is that correct? This question comes up frequently in relation to the violent TV shows, movies, and video games that are common in our culture. If you had children, would you let them watch violent TV shows or play violent video games? The discussion in Being a Critical Consumer (p. 224) might help you answer that question.

LEARNING THROUGH MODELING Can you remember learning to tie your shoes? It probably happened as you watched your parents using slow and exaggerated motions, repeated many times. After your parents demonstrated how to tie shoes, you would have tried it yourself, making an effort to imitate them. Because humans can learn through observation, they readily imitate the actions of others and learn new things. The imitation of observed behavior is commonly called **modeling.**

Within a few days (or even hours) of birth, human newborns will model actions seen in others, such as sticking out the tongue and making facial expressions. And infants will continue to model gestures and other actions as they develop (**Figure 6.21**). Nonhuman animals may also be imitators. Indeed, one study found that infant macaque monkeys imitate facial expressions when they are 3 days old (Ferrari et al., 2006). However, research is unclear on whether nonhuman animals engage in imitation in the same way that humans do.

Modeling in humans is influenced by many factors. Generally, we are more likely to imitate the actions of models who are attractive, have high status, and are somewhat similar to ourselves. In addition, modeling is effective only if the observer is physically capable of imitating the behavior. Simply watching Michael Phelps blast through the water in the 100-meter butterfly does not mean we could do that if we jumped in the pool. And the influence that models have on behavior often occurs implicitly—we are not aware that our behaviors are being altered. People might not even be aware that they have changed their ways of speaking or dressing to resemble those of celebrities. Overwhelming evidence says, however, that we imitate what we see in others. And we especially model the behaviors of people we admire.

Adolescent smoking is a particularly striking example of modeling behavior. For example, adolescents whose favorite actors smoke in movies are much more likely to smoke (Tickle, Sargent, Dalton, Beach, & Heatherton, 2001). In addition, the more smoking that adolescents observe in movies, the more positive their attitudes about smoking become, and the more likely they are to begin smoking (Sargent et al., 2005; **Figure 6.22**). Surprisingly, these effects are strongest among children whose parents do not smoke. Why would this be so? Movies tend to glamorize the habit, often presenting images of smokers as mature, cool, sexy—things adolescents want to be, and different from how they see their parents. Adolescents do not generally decide to smoke after watching one movie

FIGURE 6.21
Early Modeling
Babies frequently show learning by watching and then imitating behaviors and expressions.

FIGURE 6.22
Modeling and Smoking
Eye-catching movie images such as this one, from the 2012 James Bond movie *Skyfall*, contribute to viewers' sense that smoking is a mature, cool, sexy behavior. Because people learn to model what they see, they readily imitate the actions of people they admire, including movie stars who smoke.

that makes smoking seem glamorous. But repeated demonstrations shape their attitudes about smoking and subsequently lead to imitation. As adolescent viewers learn to associate smoking with people they admire, even fictional movie characters, they incorporate the general message that smoking is desirable.

LEARNING THROUGH VICARIOUS CONDITIONING Another factor that determines whether a person imitates a model is whether he or she observes the model being rewarded for performing the behavior. In the study mentioned earlier, Bandura and colleagues showed children a film of an adult aggressively playing with a Bobo doll, but this time the film ended in one of three different ways (Bandura et al., 1963). In the first version, the control condition, the adult experienced no consequences for the aggressive behavior. In the second version, the adult was rewarded for the aggressive behavior with candy and praise. In the third version, the adult was punished for the behavior by being both spanked and verbally reprimanded.

When the children were subsequently allowed to play with the Bobo doll, those who observed the model being rewarded for aggressive behavior were much more likely to be aggressive toward the doll than were the children who watched the control condition of the film. In contrast, those who saw the model being punished were less likely to be aggressive than were those in the control group. Through **vicarious conditioning,** people learn about the consequences of an action by watching others being rewarded or punished for performing the action. This in turn affects people's own likelihood to engage in that behavior at a later time (**Figure 6.23**).

These findings do not mean that the children who did not show aggression did not learn the behavior. Later, the children were offered small gifts to perform the model's actions, and all—even those who had watched the model being punished—performed the aggressive actions reliably. As we noted earlier, a key distinction in learning is between the *acquisition* of a behavior and its *performance*. In this case, all the children acquired the behavior. In other words, they learned it. But only those who saw the model being rewarded performed the behavior. That is, not until the children themselves were actually rewarded for acting in that way did they all perform the behavior. Direct rewards prompted the children in the control group to reveal the behavior they had acquired.

Watching Others Results in Cultural Transmission

All humans belong to the same species and share the vast majority of genes. Around the world, however, there is enormous cultural diversity in what people think and how they behave. Would you be the same person if you had been raised in a small village in China, or in the jungles of South America, or in the mountains of Afghanistan? Probably not, since your religious beliefs, your values, even your musical tastes are shaped by the culture in your part of the world. Each piece of knowledge about a culture that can be shared, such as knowing it is a bad idea to text while driving, is a *meme*. Memes can be learned in many ways, such as conditioning through association or reinforcement. However, many memes are learned by watching the behavior of other people.

Evolutionary psychologists view memes as similar to genes. Like genes, memes are selectively passed on from one generation to the next. But unlike the

FIGURE 6.23

Learning Through Vicarious Conditioning

When a person observes someone else being rewarded or punished for a particular behavior, the observer may learn to do, or not do, the same thing. This type of learning happens all the time with siblings. Because this boy is watching his sister get a "talking to" after behaving badly, he will probably learn to not make the same mistake that she made.

vicarious conditioning
Learning the consequences of an action by watching others being rewarded or punished for performing the action.

Carlos's twin sons had finally gone to bed. They were particularly wound up tonight since they had just celebrated their 12th birthday and wouldn't stop playing the new video game they had received. Carlos was looking forward to some peace and quiet so he could read Chapter 6.

As he read, Carlos became intrigued about the research on observational learning. *I wonder if my sons are learning to be like the characters they see in the video games they play?* This question had crossed his mind after the Newtown, Connecticut, school massacre in 2012. Many of the news reports suggested that violent video games could have been a cause of the shooter's behavior. Carlos wondered: *Do people learn to be violent by playing video games?* Throughout the semester, Dr. Parretti had encouraged the students to be on the lookout for psychological research that could have real-life implications. *Was there psychological research on this topic? What kind of study would convince me that children learn aggression from video games?*

Carlos thought about correlational studies and what those would look like in this case. *I guess a study could ask a group of kids how much they play video games and then measure how aggressive they are.* Those sorts of studies seemed pretty easy to conduct, but they left too many questions unanswered. If researchers found a correlation between frequency of video game playing and aggression, then maybe one did lead to the other, but in which direction? *Maybe aggressive kids just like video games more, so they play them more often.* Or maybe some other factor could be driving them both. *Maybe it could have something to do with the children's feelings of social isolation at school—kids who have fewer friends may be both more aggressive and more likely to entertain themselves with video games.*

What would it take for Carlos to be completely convinced that children learn to be violent from video games? He would want to see an experimental study. In this study, researchers would have one group of people play a violent video game while another group played a nonviolent video game. *That arrangement would tell us whether children learn to be violent by playing any video game or violent games in particular.*

The next day, with his professor's help, Carlos found an interesting study done by Barlett and Rodeheffer (2009). This study looked at different types of video games and different outcomes. Study participants were randomly assigned to play either a realistic, violent video game (people shooting, as in "Conflict Desert Storm") or a nonviolent video game ("Hard Hitter Tennis"). While participants played the game, their physical arousal—for instance, their heart rate—was measured. Every 15 minutes, the researchers used a word completion task to measure the participants' aggressive thoughts. They also used a questionnaire, the State Hostility Scale, to measure participants' aggressive feelings. After playing for 45 minutes, people who played realistic, violent video games had more aggressive feelings, more aggressive thoughts, and a higher heart rate than those who played nonviolent video games.

Carlos was impressed with how convincing the results were. Playing the violent video games clearly caused people to think aggressive thoughts *and* feel more aggressive. Carlos thought, *This study does not say that violent video games cause school shootings. But if these games make my sons think aggressive thoughts and feel more aggressive, that's a good enough reason to be more careful about the ones they play.*

transmission of genes through natural selection, which typically occurs slowly over thousands of years, memes can spread quickly. For example, people's adoption of the Internet is a meme that occurred worldwide. But some memes, such as fads, die out quickly.

Even nonhuman animals show this kind of passing along of knowledge. One good example of the cultural transmission of knowledge is the case of Imo, a macaque monkey. In the 1950s, researchers who were studying monkeys in Japan threw some sweet potatoes onto a sandy beach for the macaques there to eat. Imo developed the habit of washing her sweet potatoes in the ocean to remove the sand. Within a short time, other monkeys copied Imo, and soon many monkeys were washing their potatoes before eating them. Through this type of learning, this meme has continued to be passed along from one generation to the next, and monkeys at this beach still wash their potatoes (Dugatkin, 2004; **Figure 6.24**).

Biology Influences Observational Learning

Suppose you're watching somebody handle a piece of paper and that person gets a paper cut. You might find yourself flinching as if you received the cut.

What happens in the brain during observational learning? When you watch someone performing an action, *mirror neurons* in your brain become activated (Iacoboni, 2009). Mirror neurons are especially likely to become activated when you observe someone making a movement that has some goal, such as reaching for a glass of water. Your mirror neurons are not activated when you see just the water glass or when you see a person just sitting. But these same mirror neurons become activated when *you* reach for a glass of water. Every time you watch another person engaging in an action, similar neural circuits are firing in your brain and in the other person's brain.

Scientists are debating the function of mirror neurons. This system may support observational learning. However, the firing of mirror neurons in the observer's brain does not always lead that person to actually imitate the behavior being observed. Therefore, some theorists think that mirror neurons may help us explain and predict others' behavior. In other words, mirror neurons may allow us to step into the shoes of people we observe so we can better understand those people's actions. One theory is that mirror neurons are the neural basis for empathy. Empathy is the emotional response of feeling what other people are experiencing, such as our flinching when someone else receives a paper cut.

FIGURE 6.24

Memes

In the 1950s, a Japanese macaque named Imo developed the meme of washing sweet potatoes in the ocean. Imo's fellow monkeys observed this behavior and copied it. As shown here, the descendants of these macaques continue the behavior of washing sweet potatoes in the ocean.

 6.4 CHECKPOINT: How Do We Learn by Watching Others?

- Humans learn basic and complex skills, beliefs, attitudes, habits, and emotional responses by watching others. Three types of learning by watching are observational learning, modeling, and vicarious learning.

- Watching others also allows transmission of cultural information.

- Mirror neurons become active when we observe a goal-directed behavior. This response may be a neural basis of observational learning.

BIG QUESTION	LEARNING GOALS

BIG PICTURE

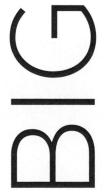

6.1
What Are the Three Ways We Learn?

a. Remember the key terms about learning.

b. Understand the three main types of learning.

c. Apply learning to your life.

d. Understand how the brain changes during learning.

6.2
How Do We Learn by Classical Conditioning?

a. Remember the key terms about classical conditioning.

b. Apply the four steps of classical conditioning.

c. Apply the concepts of acquisition, extinction, spontaneous recovery, generalization, and discrimination.

d. Analyze the acquisition of a phobia and counterconditioning to reduce a phobia.

6.3
How Do We Learn by Operant Conditioning?

a. Remember the key terms about operant conditioning.

b. Understand the four types of reinforcement and punishment in operant conditioning.

c. Apply the four schedules of reinforcement.

d. Apply the three cognitive aspects of conditioning.

6.4
How Do We Learn by Watching Others?

a. Remember the key terms related to learning by watching others.

b. Understand the three types of learning by watching others.

c. Apply the three types of learning by watching others.

d. Understand what happens in the brain during observational learning.

KEY TERMS

CHECKPOINT

learning
habituation
sensitization

- Learning is a change in behavior that results from experience. There are three main types of learning.

- Non-associative learning about a stimulus happens through habituation and sensitization.

- Associative learning about relationships between events occurs through classical conditioning and operant conditioning.

- Learning also occurs when we watch what others do.

- Learning occurs when synaptic connections in the brain become stronger over time through long-term potentiation (LTP).

classical conditioning
unconditioned stimulus (US)
unconditioned response (UR)
conditioned stimulus (CS)
conditioned response (CR)
acquisition
extinction
spontaneous recovery
stimulus generalization
stimulus discrimination

- In Pavlov's classical conditioning, a conditioned stimulus that is predictably associated with an unconditioned stimulus produces a learned, conditioned response.

- Six factors affect the strength and persistence of learning from classical conditioning.

- Phobias may develop when classical conditioning leads to generalization of a fear experience. Techniques based on classical conditioning, such as counterconditioning, can be used to treat phobias.

- Classical conditioning helps animals learn responses that aid survival. The cognitive model states that the amount of conditioning that occurs is determined by how unexpected or surprising the unconditioned stimulus is.

operant conditioning
positive reinforcement
negative reinforcement
positive punishment
negative punishment
fixed interval schedule (FI)
variable interval schedule (VI)
fixed ratio schedule (FR)
variable ratio schedule (VR)
partial-reinforcement
    extinction effect
cognitive map
latent learning
insight learning

- Operant conditioning involves learning the association between a behavior and its consequences. This learning changes future behavior.

- Reinforcement increases the likelihood that a behavior will be repeated. By contrast, punishment reduces the likelihood that a behavior will be repeated.

- Positive reinforcement and positive punishment change behavior by adding a stimulus. Negative reinforcement and negative punishment change behavior by removing a stimulus.

- There are four schedules of reinforcement, and each schedule has a different effect on behavior.

- Biological conditions, such as the release of dopamine or innate constraints, influence learning. Cognitive processes, such as cognitive maps, latent learning, and insight, also influence learning.

observational learning
modeling
vicarious conditioning

- Humans learn basic and complex skills, beliefs, attitudes, habits, and emotional responses by watching others. Three types of learning by watching are observational learning, modeling, and vicarious learning.

- Watching others also allows transmission of cultural information.

- Mirror neurons become active when we observe a goal-directed behavior. This response may be a neural basis of observational learning.

For a self-quiz on this chapter, go to the back of the book and find Appendix B: Quizzes.

7 Memory

SCOTT HAGWOOD IS AN ORDINARY MAN. He was a mediocre student in high school and college, then became a businessman and consultant. He is somewhat reserved and is uncomfortable being in the spotlight. But he is in the spotlight a lot: He is a four-time winner of the USA Memory Championship and one of only 122 Grand Masters of memory. Scott Hagwood's memory abilities may be among the best developed in the world. To become a Grand Master of memory, he had to compete at official competitions. He also had to show that he could memorize 1,000 digits in less than an hour, the order of 10 shuffled decks of playing cards in under an hour, and the order of one shuffled deck of cards in less than two minutes (**Figure 7.1**).

BIG QUESTIONS

7.1 **How Do We Acquire Memories?**

7.2 **How Do We Maintain Memories Over Time?**

7.3 **What Are Our Different Long-Term Storage Systems?**

7.4 **How Do We Access Our Memories?**

FIGURE 7.1
Memory Competition
At the USA Memory Championship, a member of the competitive memory team from the University of Pennsylvania is using a strategy to make information more meaningful and easy to remember. In this chapter, you will learn such tools, and they can help you improve your memory skills.

What makes Hagwood amazing is that he was not born with extraordinary memory skills. As an adult, he learned that he had thyroid cancer. A common complication of the disease is deficits in memory. Hagwood became concerned because "I didn't have a great memory to begin with. I thought there might be something I could do to help facilitate my memory." So he set out to improve his memory before it was impaired by his medical condition.

Hagwood taught himself how to use memory tools to be successful at the USA Memory Championship. These memory tools are based on the idea that the more meaningful something is, the easier it is to remember. For example, to memorize playing cards, competitors mentally link each playing card with a person, an action, or an object. Every group of three or more cards makes a sentence. Edward Cooke, a 23-year-old competitor and Grand Master from England, explains that when he sees a three of clubs, a nine of hearts, and a nine of spades, this group of three cards triggers a visual image of "Brazilian lingerie model Adriana Lima in a Biggles biplane shooting at his old public-school headmaster in a suit of armor." While the technique may sound silly, it creates a meaningful and vivid image that is easy to remember.

But this example covers only three cards. Contestants must memorize the order of 10 decks of cards—that's 520 cards—in less than an hour. To keep all the images in order, contestants take a "mental walk" through a familiar location. There, the visual images are "placed" in predetermined locations along the walk. Cooke's mental walk begins at his favorite pub in Oxford, England. It ends at a nearby hotel. When he must recall the cards, he takes this mental walk and sees all the images in the places where he put them. Then he can recall them in the correct order.

Feats such as these seem superhuman. But Scott Hagwood's case provides a simple message: We all can improve our memory just by learning and using simple techniques. Thinking back to his school days, Scott now realizes that he was able to understand the material. He simply didn't know how to study properly. Now Scott tours the country, teaching "regular people" how to improve their memory. In this chapter, you will learn the same tips that Scott teaches, as we discuss what memory is and how it works.

7.1 How Do We Acquire Memories?

📖 **LEARNING GOALS**	✏️ **READING ACTIVITIES** **LEARN**
a. Remember the key terms about memory and encoding.	List all of the boldface words and write down their definitions.
b. Analyze the three phases of information processing in acquisition of a memory.	Identify how you encoded, stored, and can retrieve a specific memory that you have.
c. Understand how attention affects memory.	Summarize in your own words how the presence or absence of attention influences the encoding of a memory.
d. Apply filter theory to your ability to selectively attend to important information.	Use filter theory to explain how you can attend to relevant information during a lecture and ignore irrelevant information.

Memory is the nervous system's capacity to acquire and retain information and skills. This capacity allows us to take information from experiences and store it for retrieval later. The skills shown by the contestants at the USA Memory Championship make it seem that we remember information in the same way a video camera captures and faithfully retrieves events. But that's not the case at all. Unlike in video recording, not all experiences are equally likely to be remembered. Some life events leave no lasting memory. Other life events are remembered but later forgotten. Still others remain for a lifetime. We have multiple memory systems, and each memory system has its own "rules." For example, the processes that underlie memory for information we will need to retrieve in 10 seconds are different from the processes that underlie memory for information we will need to retrieve in 10 years.

In addition, unlike video recordings, our memories are often incomplete, biased, and distorted. Two people's memories of the same event can differ greatly, because each person stores and retrieves memories of the event differently. We tend to remember personally relevant information and filter our memories through our own perceptions and knowledge of related events. In other words, memories are not "truth," but our perception of what occurred. And this perception is altered during the processes of acquiring, maintaining, and re-accessing the memories.

We Acquire Memories by Processing Information

To understand the three processing phases of memory, consider that right now you are reading the information in this textbook. Presumably, you are trying to remember the information. In the **encoding** phase, your brain changes information—for example, what you see on the page when you are reading this text—into a meaningful neural code that it can use (**Figure 7.2,** Step 1). The **storage** phase is how you maintain the coded representation in a network of neurons in the brain. Storage can last a fraction of a second or as long as a lifetime. Think of this phase as maintaining the text material from when you read it until you take the test, or even longer (see Figure 7.2, Step 2). As we will see later in the chapter, there are

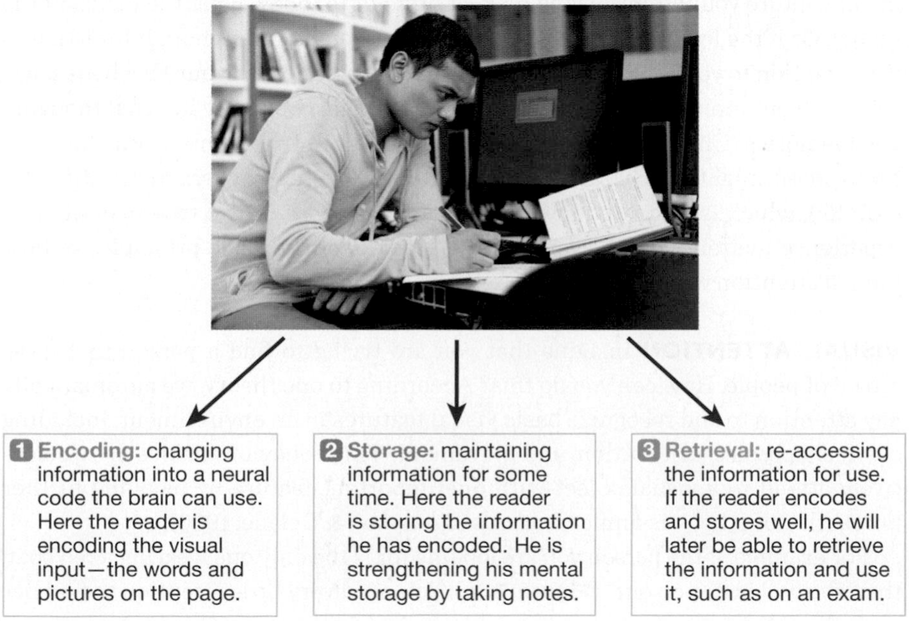

memory
The nervous system's capacity to acquire and retain skills and knowledge for later retrieval.

encoding
The processing of information so that it can be stored.

storage
The retention of encoded representations over time.

1 Encoding: changing information into a neural code the brain can use. Here the reader is encoding the visual input—the words and pictures on the page.

2 Storage: maintaining information for some time. Here the reader is storing the information he has encoded. He is strengthening his mental storage by taking notes.

3 Retrieval: re-accessing the information for use. If the reader encodes and stores well, he will later be able to retrieve the information and use it, such as on an exam.

FIGURE 7.2
Three Phases of Information Processing in Memory

retrieval
The act of recalling or remembering stored information when it is needed.

attention
Focusing mental resources on information; allows further processing for perception, memory, and response.

at least three storage systems, which differ in how long they store information. In **retrieval,** the third phase of memory, you re-access the information. Think of this phase as bringing to your mind a previously encoded and stored memory when it is needed, such as when you need to answer a question on your psychology exam (see Figure 7.2, Step 3). Unfortunately, we all know that sometimes we experience memory failure. If memory were like a video recorder, we would never get an exam question wrong. But we do get things wrong, and this is in part due to how we pay attention to the information.

Attention Allows Us to Encode a Memory

Many students say they have memory problems. Specifically, they have trouble remembering the material covered in class and in their textbooks. But their problems often have nothing to do with the way their brains work. Rather, they do not pay attention when they are supposed to be learning. If you overload your system by studying while checking e-mail, texting, and watching television, you will do worse at all these tasks than if you focused on one task at a time (Manhart, 2004).

Starting when you were very young, you've probably heard your parents and teachers telling you to "pay attention." To get information into memory, we need to pay attention to it. That is, we need to be alert and focus on the information. Think about the difference between the words *look* and *see,* and between *listen* and *hear. Look* and *listen* refer to directing certain mental processes, called **attention,** to some information. We do so at the cost of paying less attention to other information, however. In fact, the word *pay* implies that costs are associated with attending to some information but not to others. That is, attention is limited. When it is divided among too many tasks or the tasks are difficult, our performance on each task suffers. In short, if we do not pay attention to *look* or *listen,* then we cannot even process sensory input to *see* or *hear.* In this case, we will not have a memory of that information.

Having limited attention helps us to function in the world. Imagine what your life would be like if you could not block out the irrelevant information that comes at you all the time. A task as simple as listening to your instructor during class requires focused attention. If a classmate recently colored her hair purple, that might capture your attention and make it difficult to follow what the instructor is saying. Or if the lecture is somewhat boring, you might find it more interesting to pay attention to your own thoughts, another conversation, or your Facebook page. In short, your attention can be distracted by external cues or by internal thoughts and memories (Chun, Golomb, & Turk-Browne, 2011). In extreme cases, this inattentiveness might be characterized as attention-deficit/hyperactivity disorder (ADHD), which is discussed in Chapter 13. However, it is also true that all of us experience inattentiveness every day. Let's consider the basic principles of how human attention works.

(a)

(b)

FIGURE 7.3

Visual Attention to the Feature of Color

(a) It requires less attention to process a single feature of an object, such as when you need to find a person in a red coat. **(b)** It requires greater attention to process two features, such as a woman in a red coat. This example shows that attention is limited and that we need to direct attentional resources to what is important.

VISUAL ATTENTION Imagine that you are trying to find a person in a large crowd of people. How can you do this? According to one theory, we automatically pay attention to and recognize basic visual features in an environment, including color, shape, size, orientation, and movement. This behavior enables us to selectively attend to a visual object with one important feature by blocking further processing of other, dissimilar features (Treisman & Gelade, 1980).

For example, if the person you are looking for is the only one wearing a red coat, then she will just "pop out" (**Figure 7.3a**). You need very little attention to find her in the crowd, and finding her will take less time. By contrast, searching for a visual object with two features is slower and more difficult and requires more attention. If you are searching for a woman wearing a red coat when some men in the crowd are wearing red coats, finding the woman will be harder and take longer (**Figure 7.3b**). This task—searching for an object with two features—reveals how attention is a limited process. It is hard to perform two attentionally demanding tasks at the same time. You can feel the effort required in a similar task if you do the Try It Yourself activity.

AUDITORY ATTENTION Auditory attention is also limited. Imagine that you are at a party, talking with a friend. Suddenly you hear someone behind you mention your name, or a particularly juicy piece of gossip captures your attention. Your attention now focuses on that conversation, so you will lose the thread of your original conversation. This example again shows that it is hard to perform two attention-demanding tasks at the same time.

Selective-listening studies examine what we do with auditory information that is not attended to. In studies by Cherry (1953), participants wore headphones that delivered one message to one ear and a different message to the other ear. Each person was asked to attend to one message and "shadow" it by repeating the message aloud (**Figure 7.4**). Later on, the participants often had no knowledge about the content of the unattended message. However, when a participant's own name was presented as part of the unattended message, participants reported hearing their name, though they knew nothing about the rest of the message. This finding shows that some important information is attended to. To be important, information has to be personally relevant, such as your name or the name of someone close to you, or it has to be particularly loud or different in some obvious physical way.

Selective Attention Allows Us to Filter Unwanted Information

According to this research, attention selectively allows us to focus on what is important in a situation. It generally also allows us to ignore what is irrelevant. Let's apply this principle to your experience in class: If you focus attention on listening to the instructor, you are likely to encode the information so it can be stored in memory. By contrast, if you pay attention to your classmate's purple hair or your Facebook page, you may never encode the lecture information. Later on, you probably won't consciously remember the material from class. This example shows how some stimuli demand all of our attention and nearly prevent the ability to attend to anything else.

FILTER THEORY In 1958, the psychologist Donald Broadbent developed *filter theory* to explain how we selectively attend to the most important information. In this model, attention is like a filter. Important information is allowed through the filter, but irrelevant information is prevented from getting through the filter. However, what is important enough to get through the filter? And what happens to information that is filtered out, or ignored? Is it not processed at all?

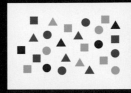

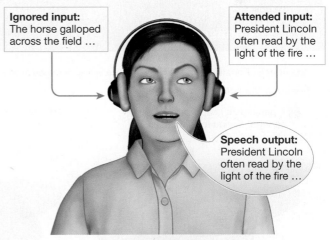

Ignored input: The horse galloped across the field …

Attended input: President Lincoln often read by the light of the fire …

Speech output: President Lincoln often read by the light of the fire …

FIGURE 7.4

Auditory Attention to "Shadow" Message in One Ear

In this task, the participant receives a different auditory message in each ear and must repeat, or "shadow," just one of the messages. Typically, the person has no memory of the other message. This result shows that attention is limited and that we remember only what we pay attention to.

change blindness
An individual's failure to notice large visual changes in the environment.

Some stimuli, such as those that evoke emotions, can readily capture our attention because they provide important information about potential threats in our environment (Phelps, Ling, & Carrasco, 2006). Faces are a good example of stimuli that are allowed through the attentional filter because they provide important social information. For example, a face indicates whether someone is a potential mate (i.e., has an attractive face) or may intend to cause physical harm (i.e., has an angry face). Indeed, a series of studies found that the attentional system prioritizes faces, especially when they appear threatening, over less meaningful stimuli (West, Anderson, & Pratt, 2009).

Studies such as these indicate that decisions about what to attend to are made early in the perceptual process. In certain situations, however, unattended information can "leak" through the filter to be processed at least to some extent. We saw such a situation with the selective listening participants who heard their name mentioned in the unattended message. On the other hand, because we cannot attend to everything in the vast array of visual information available, often we are "blind" to even large changes in our environment. This phenomenon is known as **change blindness.**

CHANGE BLINDNESS If the person you were talking to suddenly changed into another person, would you notice? The answer seems obvious: Of course you would. However, when this question was explored experimentally, the results were surprising (Simons & Levin, 1998). In this research, shown in the Scientific Thinking feature, participants were approached by a stranger who asked for directions. Then the stranger was momentarily blocked from the participants' view by a large object and replaced with another person of the same sex and race. Surprisingly, half of the people giving directions never noticed that they were talking to a different person.

When giving directions to a stranger, we normally do not attend to the distinctive features of the stranger's face or clothing. If we are unable to recall those features

---

SCIENTIFIC THINKING:
Change Blindness

Hypothesis: People can be "blind" to large visual changes around them.

Research Method:

1 A participant is approached by a stranger asking for directions.

2 The stranger is momentarily blocked by a larger object.

3 While being blocked, the original stranger is replaced by another person.

Results: Half the participants giving directions never noticed they were talking to a different person (as long as the replacement was of the same race and sex as the original stranger).

Conclusion: Change blindness results from inattention to certain visual information.

later, it is not because we forgot them. More likely, it is because we processed those features very little in the first place. Because we didn't process the features, they were never encoded into memory. After all, how often do we need to recall such information?

As change blindness illustrates, we can attend to only a limited amount of information. Large discrepancies exist between what most of us believe we can pay attention to and what we do actually attend to. As a result, our perceptions of the world are often inaccurate. However, we have little awareness of our perceptual failures. We simply do not know how much information we miss in the world around us. Every time we miss a piece of information, we don't encode the information for storage in memory. In other words, every time we fail to pay attention, we most likely will not create a memory of the information.

7.1 CHECKPOINT: How Do We Acquire Memories?

- Memories are created by encoding information from sensory input. Encoded information is maintained in storage. Retrieval allows accessing of previously encoded and stored information.

- Visual attention can be focused on encoding one feature of an object more quickly and effortlessly than two or more features.

- It is difficult to focus auditory attention on encoding more than one message at a time, and most unattended auditory information is not processed.

- Selective attention filters out irrelevant information and causes people *not* to notice large changes in the environment.

7.2 How Do We Maintain Memories Over Time?

📖 LEARNING GOALS	✏️ READING ACTIVITIES
a. Remember the key terms about storage of memories.	List all of the boldface words and write down their definitions.
b. Understand sensory storage.	Explain in your own words how visual sensory storage and auditory sensory storage provide perceptual continuity.
c. Understand the relationship between short-term storage and working memory.	Summarize how using working memory to chunk information increases the capacity and duration of short-term storage.
d. Apply encoding processes in long-term storage to your life.	Provide a description of how you have used maintenance rehearsal and elaborative rehearsal to encode and maintain two memories in long-term storage.
e. Understand how information is organized in long-term storage based on semantic meaning.	Describe how association networks explain why hearing "fire engine" is more likely to make a person remember "ambulance" than "red."

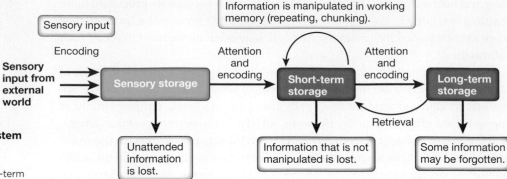

FIGURE 7.5

Three-Part Memory Storage System
This model proposes three different memory stores: (1) sensory storage, (2) short-term storage, and (3) long-term storage. Each memory store retains different encoded input, and each store has its own duration and capacity.

Have you been paying attention to what you are reading in this chapter? If you have, then you should be able to answer this question: What is the first phase of processing involved in creating a memory? Did you remember that the first step is when information is processed for memory by encoding it in the brain (see Figure 7.2)? Now we will explore the second key phase, in which memories are stored so that the information can be used at a later time.

So how is information maintained over time through storage? In 1968, the psychologists Richard Atkinson and Richard Shiffrin proposed that we have three different types of memory stores: sensory storage, short-term storage, and long-term storage (**Figure 7.5**). Each of these memory stores retains different encoded input, and each has the capacity to maintain a certain amount of information for a certain length of time. For a summary of these memory stores, see **Table 7.1.** Next we look at the three memory stores in more detail.

TABLE 7.1

The Three Memory Stores

	SENSORY STORAGE	**SHORT-TERM STORAGE**	**LONG-TERM STORAGE**
Function of storage	• Creates perceptual continuity for the world around us	• Maintains information for immediate use	• Stores information for re-access and use at a later time
Encoding for storage	• In the sense it is experienced: visual, auditory, taste, smell, and touch	• Primarily auditory • Also visual and semantic	• Primarily semantic • Also visual and auditory • Dual coding provides richest encoding
Duration of storage	• Up to a few seconds, depending on the sense	• About 20 seconds • Indefinite with working memory manipulation of items	• Probably unlimited
Capacity of storage	• Vast due to huge amount of sensory input	• About 7 items, plus or minus 2 • Using working memory aids capacity	• Probably unlimited

Sensory Storage Allows Us to Maintain Information Very Briefly

"You're not paying attention to me." Most of us are likely to have heard that complaint at some point. In that situation, even if you were thinking about something else, you may have been surprised, and relieved, to find that you could repeat the last few words the other person spoke. Sensory storage is the reason you can do this.

FIVE TYPES OF SENSORY STORES Recall from Chapter 5 that we obtain all our information about the world through our senses: vision, hearing, taste, smell, and touch. This sensory information is the basis for all of our memories. When you see someone twirling a sparkler, for instance, the visual input to your eyes is transduced into a neural signal that is processed in your brain. One way this sensory input is processed is through encoding into sensory storage. Here, the sensory input—the sparkler—leaves a visual trace in the nervous system for just a fraction of a second. In this way, **sensory storage** is a very brief maintenance system for sensory information. In this case, the system lets you see the trail of light left by the sparkler just long enough to see the message written in the sparkler's light (**Figure 7.6**).

In the same way that one type of sensory storage very briefly maintains visual input, four other types of sensory stores maintain all the other sensory input: auditory, smell, taste, and touch. These kinds of input are not what we usually think of as memory, because each sensory store is so brief that we are unaware it is operating. However, sensory storage of all this vast amount of input is important because it allows us to have a coherent experience of the world around us.

DURATION AND CAPACITY OF SENSORY STORAGE How long can information be maintained in sensory storage? And how much information can be maintained? In a classic 1960 study, the cognitive psychologist George Sperling provided the initial answers to these questions for visual sensory storage.

Three rows of four letters were flashed on a screen for one-twentieth of a second (**Figure 7.7a**). Then participants were asked to recall all 12 of the letters (i.e., provide a whole report). Most people could name only three or four letters (**Figure 7.7b,** blue line). But they stated that they believed they had seen all the letters. Perhaps participants actually had a very brief memory for all 12 of the items. But in the time it took them to name the first 3 or 4 letters, they forgot the other 8 or 9 letters.

To test this interpretation, Sperling repeated the study, but he asked participants to report just one of the three rows of letters (i.e., partial report). They knew which row they had to report based only on hearing a high-, medium-, or low-pitched sound (see Figure 7.7a). When the sound occurred immediately after the letters disappeared, the participants correctly remembered almost all the letters in the signaled row. But when there was a longer delay between the disappearance of the letters and the sound, participants recalled fewer letters in the signaled row. Based on this result, Sperling concluded that participants maintained many of the 12 items in sensory storage for about one-third of a second (see Figure 7.7b, green line). After that very brief period, the trace of the memory in sensory storage faded progressively until it was no longer accessible.

By maintaining a large amount of information for a fraction of a second, sensory storage enables us to experience the world as a continuous stream of information rather than as discrete sensations (see Table 7.1). You can see this for yourself in

FIGURE 7.6

Sensory Storage
When you stand in front of a sparkler, you can see the word *LOVE* spelled by the sparkler because the visual input is maintained briefly in sensory storage.

sensory storage
A memory storage system that very briefly holds a vast amount of information from the five senses in close to their original sensory formats.

(a)

Rows of letters	Tone signaling which row to report
GTFB	High tone
QZCR	Medium tone
KPSN	Low tone

(b)

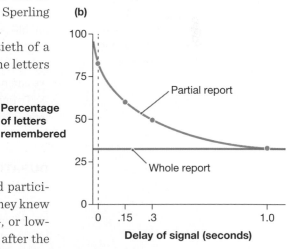

Percentage of letters remembered

FIGURE 7.7

Duration and Capacity of Sensory Storage
A clever experiment investigated visual sensory storage. **(a)** Twelve letters were flashed. In the whole report condition, participants had to name all 12 letters. In the partial report condition, they heard a tone that signaled which row of 4 letters to report. **(b)** According to the results of the partial report condition, many of the 12 letters are maintained in sensory storage for about one-third of a second.

short-term storage
A memory storage system that briefly holds a limited amount of information in awareness.

working memory
An active processing system that allows manipulation of different types of information to keep it available for current use.

the Has It Happened to You? feature. Also thanks to visual sensory storage, you can enjoy a movie. A movie is actually a series of still pictures that follow each other very closely in time. But your sensory storage retains information just long enough for you to connect one image with the next in a smooth way so that the images look like continuous action. Indeed, sensory memory is what explains the phenomenon of stroboscopic motion discussed in Chapter 5. Although sensory storage provides continuity, we can't remember all the vast amount of information that comes in through our senses because we do not pay attention to most of it. It is only when we focus our attention that information is processed into short-term storage.

Working Memory Allows Us to Actively Maintain Information in Short-Term Storage

What do you do when you need to remember a phone number, such as 463-5456, for a few seconds? If you are like most people, you probably repeat the numbers silently in your head until you can write them down or call them. Some people may remember the number temporarily by visualizing the numbers. Your ability to maintain the numbers by repeating or visualizing them for a time shows the important role of short-term storage in maintaining information.

Researchers initially saw **short-term storage** as simply a buffer, or holding place. A small amount of information could be encoded, primarily based on auditory information but also based on visual information, and maintained for only a short time. According to this view, we could remember a phone number for a few seconds, but there was no mechanism to actively manipulate information in short-term storage. Newer research has revealed that short-term storage includes the important process of **working memory.** As the name implies, working memory enables us to work on the information we have in short-term storage (Baddeley, 2002; Baddeley & Hitch, 1974). So working memory allows us to actively process sounds, images, and ideas. This mechanism lets us repeat a phone number so that we can maintain it longer in short-term storage.

To understand the relationship between short-term storage and working memory, let's examine the duration and capacity of short-term storage (see Table 7.1). We'll see how working memory can increase these qualities.

DURATION OF SHORT-TERM STORAGE To investigate how long information is maintained in short-term storage, researchers gave participants a string of three meaningless letters to remember, such as *X C J* (Peterson & Peterson, 1959). Then participants had to count backward by threes from 100 for a period of time before being asked to recall the letters. As shown in **Figure 7.8,** if the participants did no backward counting, then they recalled about eight letter strings. However, after only six seconds of backward counting, participants recalled fewer than four letter strings. By 18 seconds of counting, most people could not recall any of the letter strings. So, in the best case, people can remember about eight items in short-term storage. In addition, short-term storage lasts up to 20 seconds when people don't use working memory processes to actively maintain the information they want to remember.

By contrast, if people are allowed to use working memory to manipulate the letters by repeating them over and over, then the information can be maintained for at least as long as the person continues to pay attention to repeating the letters.

This research indicates that although short-term storage may be a "location" for maintaining memories, working memory allows manipulation of sounds, images, and ideas for longer maintenance in short-term storage (Baddeley, 2002; Baddeley & Hitch, 1974).

CAPACITY OF SHORT-TERM STORAGE Completing the backward-counting task in the example just described makes it impossible to repeat the letters using working memory. This effect shows that without working memory, we can hold only a limited amount of information in short-term storage at a time. The cognitive psychologist George Miller noted that the capacity limit of short-term storage is generally seven items (plus or minus two), which is referred to as the *memory span* (Miller, 1956). Notice that this memory span is consistent with the research findings in Figure 7.8, where participants remembered eight letter strings. Even so, Miller's estimate may be too high, as some research suggests that short-term storage may be limited to as few as four items (Conway et al., 2005). Some individuals have a smaller or larger memory span. Capacity of short-term storage increases as children develop (Garon, Bryson, & Smith, 2008) and decreases with advanced aging (McCabe et al., 2010). Do the activity in Try It Yourself to check your own memory span.

Because short-term storage is limited in capacity, you might expect people to have great difficulty remembering a string of letters such as NHTSACAFBIMSCIAILDEA. These 20 letters would tax even the largest memory span. But what if we organized the information into smaller, meaningful units? For instance, NH TSA CA FBI MS CIA IL DEA. Here the letters are shown grouped together to produce abbreviations for states and acronyms for U.S. federal government agencies. This process of using working memory to organize information into meaningful groups or units is known as **chunking.** The more efficiently you chunk information, the more you can remember.

Chunking makes information much easier to recall for two reasons. First, by using working memory, we can reduce the 20 items to be recalled into 7 chunks, and 7 items are within the capacity of our memory span. Second, as you saw when we described the use of memory tools in the USA Memory Championship, meaningful units are easier to remember than nonsense units. Meaningful units are easier to remember because they draw on information that we already know. In short, chunking shows how working memory can increase the capacity of short-term storage, just as repetition can extend the duration of short-term storage.

Master chess players use this memory tool when they glance at a scenario on a chessboard, even for a few seconds, and later reproduce the exact arrangement of pieces (Chase & Simon, 1973). They instantly chunk the board into a number of meaningful units based on their prior experience with the game. If the pieces are arranged on the board in ways that make no sense in terms of chess, however, experts are no better than novices at reproducing the board. In general, the greater your expertise with the material, the more efficiently you can chunk information. As a result, you will be able to transfer more information into long-term storage, and you will be able to access and use that information later when you need it.

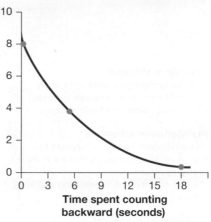

Number of letter strings correctly recalled

Time spent counting backward (seconds)

FIGURE 7.8

Duration and Capacity of Short-Term Storage

In an experiment that explored short-term storage, it was found that about 8 items can be maintained for about 20 seconds when a person is prevented from using working memory processes.

chunking
Using working memory to organize information into meaningful units to make it easier to remember.

TRY IT YOURSELF: Digit Span Task

1. Have a friend read the first row of numbers to you at the rate of one per second.

2. When they are done reading, write down the numbers in the order you heard them.

3. Repeat the process with each row until you reach a row where you fail to recall the numbers in the correct order.

4. Whichever row your memory failed on, go to the row above it and count the number of digits that you were correctly able to recall in that row. This number is your short-term storage digit span. For example, if you made a mistake on the row 19223530, but recalled all the numbers in row 0401473, then your memory span is 7 items.

925
8642
37654
627418
0401473
19223530
486854332
2531971768
85129619450
918546942937

Long-Term Storage Allows Us to Maintain Memories Relatively Permanently

long-term storage
A memory storage system that allows relatively permanent storage, probably of an unlimited amount of information.

maintenance rehearsal
Using working memory processes to repeat information based on how it sounds (auditory information); provides only shallow encoding of information and less successful long-term storage.

elaborative rehearsal
Using working memory processes to think about how new information relates to ourselves or our prior knowledge (semantic information); provides deeper encoding of information for more successful long-term storage.

Do you remember the phone number that was given at the beginning of the section on short-term storage? Unless you really paid attention and repeated the number, it's unlikely that you remember it. You might have maintained the information in short-term storage for a few seconds, but it was probably not processed into long-term storage.

When people talk about memory, they usually are referring to this relatively permanent type of memory. To envision **long-term storage,** try to imagine everything you know and everything you are likely to know in your lifetime. It is hard to imagine how much information that might be, because you can always learn more. Unlike the other two memory stores, long-term storage has nearly limitless capacity and duration (see Table 7.1). This type of storage enables you to remember nursery rhymes from childhood, the meanings and spellings of words you rarely use (such as *aardvark*), what you had for lunch yesterday, and so on. Given the billions of sensory experiences and thoughts we have each day, some type of filtering system must limit what goes into long-term storage. So what gets prioritized for encoding into long-term storage?

Generally, information that helps us adapt to our environment is likely to be transformed into a memory held in long-term storage. Evolutionary theory helps explain how we decide in advance what information will be useful. Memory allows both human and nonhuman animals to use information in ways that assist in reproduction and survival. For instance, recognizing a predator and remembering an escape route will help an animal avoid being eaten and thus give it an advantage over animals that fail to learn from their experiences. For humans, remembering which objects are edible, which people are friends and which ones are enemies, and how to get home are all critical for survival. The key is that this information must be deeply encoded into long-term storage for us to remember it.

ENCODING FOR LONG-TERM STORAGE We have seen that paying attention to information allows it to be encoded into short-term storage. To store information more permanently, we also need to use attentional processing to encode that information into long-term storage.

According to the *levels of processing model,* the more deeply an item is processed during encoding, the more meaning it has and the better it is remembered (Craik & Lockhart, 1972). Encoding can be achieved through two types of rehearsal. **Maintenance rehearsal,** simply repeating the item over and over, provides shallow encoding of information. This rehearsal is based on how the item sounds (auditory information). **Elaborative rehearsal** encodes the information more deeply. This rehearsal is based on meaning (semantic information). For example, we think about the item conceptually or decide whether it refers to ourselves. In other words, in this type of rehearsal, we encode information more deeply when it is meaningful to us and we can link it to knowledge already in our long-term storage. Contestants in the USA Memory Championship use elaborative encoding to remember playing cards by linking each card with a person, action, or object that the competitor knows.

How does encoding work according to the levels of processing model? Suppose you show research participants a list of words and then ask them to do one of three things. You might ask them to make simple perceptual judgments, such as whether each word is printed in capital or lowercase letters. This task requires the

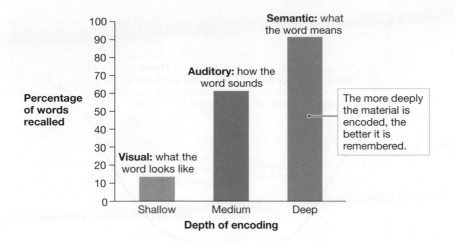

FIGURE 7.9

Deeper Encoding Aids Long-Term Storage
If participants are asked to remember a list of words based on how the words look, how they sound, or what they mean, they usually have better recall after processing the meaning of the information. This result suggests that deeper encoding aids long-term storage.

processing of visual information. Or you might ask the participants to judge the sound of each word, such as whether the word rhymes with *boat*. This task calls for the processing of auditory information. Or you might ask them about each word's meaning, as in "Does this word fit in the sentence *They had to cross the _____ to reach the castle?*" This task requires semantic processing. Once participants have completed the task, you might ask them to remember as many words as possible. You would find that words processed based on semantics, or meaning, are remembered the best (**Figure 7.9**). Brain imaging studies have shown that deep encoding based on semantics activates more brain regions than shallow encoding and that this greater brain activity is associated with better memory (Kapur et al., 1994). Together, these findings suggest that deeper encoding improves the likelihood of long-term storage, which then improves the likelihood of remembering.

You can see for yourself how encoding works according to levels of processing. Think back to that phone number mentioned earlier. Even if you used maintenance rehearsal to repeat the phone number to yourself, you probably did not remember it. This failure to store the phone number in long-term storage shows how attention and memory function hand in hand: We attend just enough to complete the current task and lose information that seems irrelevant to us or insignificant.

Now suppose you are reminded of the number, 463-5456. You also learn that this is the phone number of a potter, who chose the last four digits, 5456, because they correspond to the letters *KILN*, which is an oven used in pottery making. Are you more likely to remember the number? If so, your ability to remember is increased because you are using elaborative rehearsal to encode the information more richly. You are encoding not just on visual or auditory information about the number but on semantic information about the word *KILN*. In fact, you might have used a combination of both visual and semantic encoding, called *dual coding,* which is a very successful method of transferring the information into long-term storage.

LONG-TERM STORAGE VERSUS SHORT-TERM STORAGE By now it should be clear that long-term storage differs from short-term storage in several ways. Long-term storage lasts longer and has a far greater capacity, and it depends on deep encoding of information. But is long-term storage truly a different type of memory than short-term storage?

Some evidence that short-term storage and long-term storage are separate systems comes from research that required people to recall a long list of words. The ability to recall items from the list depended on the order of presentation. That

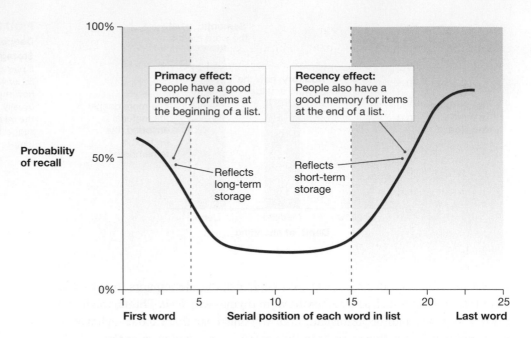

is, people remembered items presented early or late in the list better than items in the middle of the list. The *primacy effect* refers to the better memory people have for items presented at the beginning of the list. The *recency effect* refers to the better memory people have for the most recent items, the ones at the end of the list (**Figure 7.10**).

One explanation for the primacy and recency effects relies on a distinction between short-term storage and long-term storage. When research participants study a long list of words, they rehearse the earliest items the most. As a result, that information is transferred into long-term storage. By contrast, the last few items are still in short-term storage when the participants have to recall the words immediately after reading them. This research suggests that primacy effects are due to retrieving information from long-term storage, whereas recency effects are due to retrieving information from short-term storage.

Our Long-Term Storage Is Organized Based on Meaning

Imagine if a library put each of its books wherever there was empty space on a shelf. To find a particular book, a librarian would have to look through the entire inventory book by book. This type of random storage would not work well for books, and it would not work well for memories. When an event or some information is important enough, you want to be able to retrieve it later. How is information organized for long-term storage so it is easy to retrieve later on?

As we discussed in Chapter 5, our sensory experiences are transformed by our brains into our perceptions of those experiences. For instance, when your visual system senses a shaggy, four-legged animal and your auditory system senses barking, you perceive a dog. But you do not have a tiny picture of a dog stored in your head. Instead, the concept of "dog" is a mental representation for a category of animals that share certain features, such as having fur and barking. The mental representation for "dog" differs from that for "cat," even though the two are similar in many ways. You also have mental representations for complex and abstract ideas, including beliefs and feelings. What all of the representations have in common is that they include semantic information about the concepts and what those concepts mean to you. Long-term storage is based on the meaning of these semantic mental representations.

SCHEMAS If we maintain memories in long-term storage according to their meaning, how do we determine the meanings of particular memories? Chunking is a good way to encode groups of items for long-term storage. The more meaningful the chunks, the better we will store them and remember them. Decisions about how to chunk information depend on *schemas,* ways of structuring memories in long-term storage that help us perceive, organize, process, and use information. As we sort out incoming information, schemas guide our attention to the relevant features. Thanks to schemas, we can construct new memories by filling in holes within existing memories, overlooking inconsistent information and interpreting meaning based on our experiences.

Although schemas help us make sense of the world, they can lead to biased encoding. In a classic demonstration conducted in the early 1930s, the psychologist Frederic Bartlett (1932) asked British participants to listen to a Native American folktale. The story involved supernatural experiences, and it was difficult to understand for non–Native Americans unfamiliar with such tales. Fifteen minutes later, Bartlett asked the participants to repeat the story exactly as they had heard it. The participants altered the story greatly. They also altered it consistently, so that it made sense from their own cultural standpoint, or schema. Sometimes they simply forgot the supernatural parts they could not understand. In other words, pieces of information that do not fit into our preexisting schemas can be hard to encode into long-term storage.

In addition, schemas also affect your ability to retrieve information from long-term storage. Read the following paragraph carefully:

> The procedure is actually quite simple. First arrange things into different bundles depending on makeup. Don't do too much at once. In the short run this may not seem important, however, complications easily arise. A mistake can be costly. Next, find facilities. Some people must go elsewhere for them. Manipulation of appropriate mechanisms should be self-explanatory. Remember to include all other necessary supplies. Initially the routine will overwhelm you, but soon it will become just another facet of life. Finally, rearrange everything into their initial groups. Return these to their usual places. Eventually they will be used again. Then the whole cycle will have to be repeated. (Bransford & Johnson, 1972, p. 722)

Now, can you say what this paragraph was specifically about? You probably cannot say exactly. If you can't say what it was about, do you think you will remember it well or be able to answer questions about it? What if we tell you that the paragraph is describing washing clothes. Go back and reread the paragraph. Notice how your schema for doing laundry can help you understand and remember how the words and sentences are connected to one another. In a research setting, college students who read this paragraph knowing that it was about washing clothes found it easy to understand and relatively straightforward to recall. In short, having a schema about information can help you remember it later on.

ASSOCIATION NETWORKS Another way that the meaning of information is organized in long-term storage is based on *networks of associations*. In a network model proposed by the psychologists Allan Collins and Elizabeth Loftus (1975), an item's distinctive features are linked in a way that identifies the item. Each unit of information in the network is a node. Each node is connected to many other nodes. The resulting network is like the linked neurons in your brain, but the nodes are simply bits of information, not physical objects (**Figure 7.11**). For example, when you look at a fire engine, all the nodes that represent a fire engine's features, such as "red," are activated. The resulting activation pattern across nodes gives rise to the knowledge that the object is a fire engine rather than, say, a car, a vacuum cleaner, or a cat.

An important feature of network models is that activating one node increases the likelihood that closely associated nodes in the same category will also be activated. As shown in Figure 7.11, the closer the nodes, the stronger the association between them and therefore the more likely it is that activating one node will activate the other. Seeing a fire engine activates linked nodes, so you will quickly recognize other vehicles, such as "ambulance." In fact, you will recognize vehicles more quickly than you will recognize items in other categories, such as an apple, which is a fruit.

The main idea here is that activating one node increases the likelihood that closely linked nodes will become active. This idea is central to *spreading activation models* of memory. According to these models, information that is heard or seen activates specific nodes for memories in long-term storage. This activation increases the ease of access of stored information to linked material. Easier access of stored information means easier retrieval.

Think about the huge amount of material in your memory. It is amazing how quickly you can search through that long-term storage and obtain the memories you need. Each time you hear a sentence, you have to remember what all the words mean. You also have to recall all the relevant information that helps you understand the sentence's overall meaning. For this process to occur, the information needs to be organized logically. Imagine trying to find a specific file on a full 600-gigabyte hard disk by opening one file at a time. Searching that way would be hopelessly slow. Instead, most computer disks are organized into folders, within each folder are more-specialized folders, and so on. Associative networks in the brain work similarly. The network is organized by category. Because the categories are structured in a hierarchy, they provide a clear and explicit blueprint for where to find needed information quickly.

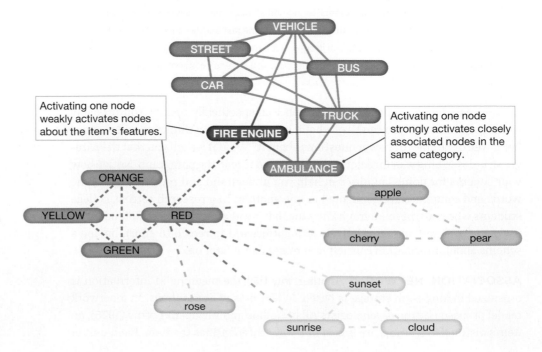

FIGURE 7.11

A Network of Associations
Memories are organized in long-term storage based on the meaning of information. Concepts are connected through their associations. The closer the concepts are to each other, the stronger the association between them. Activation of a concept (fire engine) spreads to close associates and activates them (dark whole lines). But far associates become only weakly activated (lighter dashed lines).

Activating one node weakly activates nodes about the item's features.

Activating one node strongly activates closely associated nodes in the same category.

7.2 CHECKPOINT: How Do We Maintain Memories Over Time?

- A huge amount of visual, auditory, taste, smell, and touch information is maintained in sensory storage for up to a few seconds to ensure continuous sensory experiences.

- Short-term storage keeps about 8 items available for current use for up to 20 seconds. Active processing in working memory increases both this capacity and this duration.

- Long-term storage of memories is relatively permanent and virtually limitless for deeply encoded information.

- Information in long-term storage is organized based on meaning through schemas and association networks.

7.3 What Are Our Different Long-Term Storage Systems?

📖 **LEARNING GOALS**	✏️ **READING ACTIVITIES** LEARN
a. Remember the key terms about long-term storage systems and brain processes.	List all of the boldface words and write down their definitions.
b. Apply the two forms of explicit memory to your life and explain whether they are affected by retrograde amnesia.	Provide an example of an episodic memory and a semantic memory you have, and explain whether you would recall them if you developed retrograde amnesia today.
c. Understand implicit memory and whether anterograde amnesia affects it.	Explain whether a person with anterograde amnesia could or could not learn a new motor task, such as riding a bicycle.
d. Understand how the brain processes memories.	Summarize in your own words the brain areas that contribute to explicit memory and implicit memory.

Henry Molaison, one of the most famous people in memory research, was born in 1926 and died in 2008 (**Figure 7.12**). In vital ways, though, his world stopped in 1953, when he was 27 years old. As a young man, Molaison suffered from severe epilepsy, which caused seizures that made it impossible for him to lead a normal life. Molaison's seizures originated in the temporal lobes of his brain and spread from there to other parts of the brain. Because the anticonvulsive drugs available at that time could not control his seizures, surgery was the only choice for treatment. The reasoning behind this surgery was that if the seizure-causing portion of his brain was removed, he would stop having seizures. So in September 1953, Molaison's doctors removed parts of his medial temporal lobes, the

FIGURE 7.12
Henry Molaison (H.M.)
Known to the world only by his initials, Molaison became one of the most famous people in memory research by participating in countless experiments. He died at a nursing home on December 2, 2008.

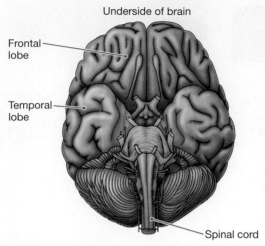

Underside of brain

Frontal lobe

Temporal lobe

Spinal cord

FIGURE 7.13

Surgery on H.M.'s Brain
The portions of the medial temporal lobe that were removed from H.M.'s brain are indicated by the blue regions.

area in the middle of the temporal lobes, including the hippocampus (**Figure 7.13**).

The surgery quieted Molaison's seizures, but it had an unexpected and very unfortunate side effect: He lost the ability to store most types of new information in long-term storage. This condition, called amnesia, includes two basic types. In **retrograde amnesia,** people lose memories for past events, facts, people, and even personal information (**Figure 7.14a**). By contrast, in **anterograde amnesia,** people lose the ability to form new memories (**Figure 7.14b**). After his surgery, Molaison experienced antero-grade amnesia. Until his death, the larger world did not know Molaison's real name or what he looked like. His privacy was guarded by the researchers who studied how anterograde amnesia affected his memory abilities. But the knowledge provided by this research with Molaison (known as H.M.) is the basis for what we know about the types of memories in long-term storage.

An older view of memory was that all memories were basically the same type. In the late 1970s and early 1980s, cognitive psychologists began to challenge this view. They argued that memory is not just one thing. Rather, they saw it as a process that involves several interacting systems (Schacter & Tulving, 1994). The systems have a common function: to retain and use information. However, they encode and store different types of information in different ways. Research on H.M.'s memory abilities in the past few decades has been critical in helping us understand that long-term storage is actually made up of several memory systems. Specifically, H.M. showed us that brain damage can affect memories that we intentionally retrieve and describe: These are called explicit memories. However, brain damage may not affect memories that we display

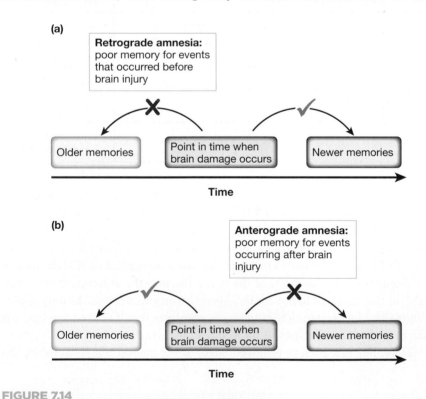

(a)

Retrograde amnesia: poor memory for events that occurred before brain injury

Older memories — Point in time when brain damage occurs — Newer memories

Time

(b)

Anterograde amnesia: poor memory for events occurring after brain injury

Older memories — Point in time when brain damage occurs — Newer memories

Time

FIGURE 7.14

Retrograde and Anterograde Amnesia
Amnesia involves two forms of memory loss. **(a)** Retrograde amnesia is an inability to access memories that were created before the brain damage (see red X). **(b)** Anterograde amnesia is an inability to create new memories after the brain damage (see red X).

retrograde amnesia
A condition in which people lose the ability to access memories they had before a brain injury.

anterograde amnesia
A condition in which people lose the ability to form new memories after experiencing a brain injury.

This graphic will help you remember the relationship between the two main types of memory in long-term storage and the subtypes.

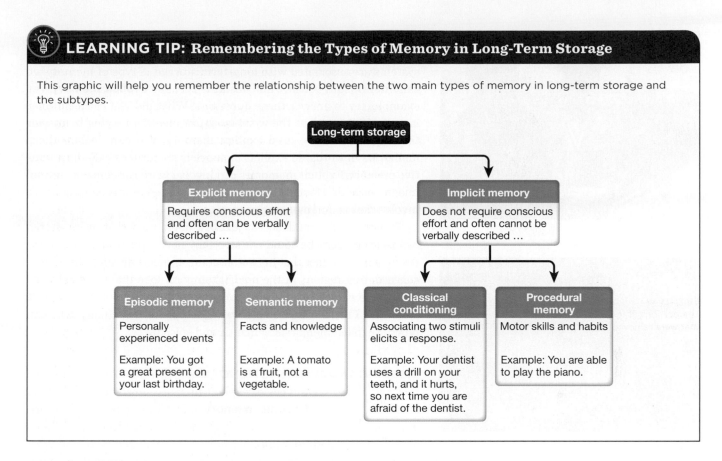

by our behavior, such as how to ride a bike. These are called implicit memories. These two types of memories, along with their subtypes, are shown in the Learning Tip.

Our Explicit Memories Involve Conscious Effort

According to the psychologists who tested H.M., his IQ was slightly above average. His thinking abilities remained intact after his surgery. He could hold a normal conversation as long as he was not distracted, though he forgot the conversation in a minute or less. H.M.'s ability to hold a conversation showed that he was still able to remember things for short periods. After all, to grasp the meaning of spoken language, a person needs to remember the words recently spoken, such as the beginning and end of a sentence. So his short-term storage was intact.

In addition, after the surgery, H.M. could still talk about things he knew at the time of the surgery. He could describe members of his family and memories from his childhood, explain the rules of baseball, and so on. So H.M. could clearly access information that was already in long-term storage at the time of the surgery. After the surgery, however, H.M. could not encode new memories in long-term storage. He never remembered what day of the week it was, what year it was, or his own age. People who worked with H.M.—such as the psychologist Brenda Milner, who followed his case for over 40 years—had to introduce themselves to him every time they met. Because of his profound memory loss, he remembered nothing from minute to minute. As H.M. put it, "Every day is alone in itself."

(a)

(b)

FIGURE 7.15

Two Types of Explicit Memory
(a) One type of explicit memory is episodic memory. Episodic memory enables people to recall and describe their prior experiences, as these veterans are doing. **(b)** Another type of explicit memory is semantic memory, a person's knowledge of facts. Game shows such as *Jeopardy!* test semantic memory. In 2004, Ken Jennings (pictured here) became the longest defending champion on *Jeopardy!* when he won 75 games in a row.

explicit memory
The system for long-term storage of conscious memories that can be verbally described.

episodic memory
A type of explicit memory that includes a person's personal experiences.

semantic memory
A type of explicit memory that includes a person's knowledge about the world.

AMNESIA AND EXPLICIT MEMORY The study of H.M.'s anterograde amnesia helped researchers discover that different memory systems are associated with long-term storage. A type of memory we can intentionally retrieve and describe is called **explicit memory.** For example, try to answer these questions: What did you eat for dinner last night? What does the word *aardvark* mean? In trying to answer these questions, you used explicit memory. You can declare these memories in words, so explicit memory is sometimes called declarative memory. Explicit memories can involve words or concepts, visual images, or both. Most of the examples presented in this chapter so far involve the explicit memory system.

Though H.M. could access explicit memories that were stored before his surgery, he could not store any new explicit memories after the surgery. The fact that his anterograde amnesia affected this ability suggests that regions in the medial temporal lobe that were removed during the surgery are critical for long-term storage of new explicit memories. Further research has shown that there are actually two main types of explicit memories: semantic and episodic.

EPISODIC AND SEMANTIC MEMORY In 1972, Endel Tulving observed that people have two types of explicit memory: episodic memory and semantic memory. **Episodic memory** refers to our personal experiences and includes information about the time and place each experience occurred (**Figure 7.15a**). Memories of where you were and what you did on your sixteenth birthday, for example, are part of your episodic memory. **Semantic memory** is our knowledge of facts independent of personal experience. We might not remember where or when we learned a fact, but we know it (**Figure 7.15b**). For instance, most people know what Jell-O is. They know the capitals of places they have never visited. Even people who have never played baseball know that three strikes mean the batter is out.

Scientists have learned a great deal about memory by studying people like H.M. and others who have impaired memory. Evidence that episodic and semantic systems of explicit memory are separate can be found in cases of brain injury in which a person's semantic memory is intact even though episodic memory is impaired. Researchers found this pattern in three British people who had experienced brain damage as children (Vargha-Khadem et al., 1997). Each of the three developed poor memory for episodic information. As children, they had trouble reporting what they had for lunch, what they had watched on television 5 minutes earlier, or what they did during summer vacation. Their parents reported that the children had to be constantly monitored to make sure they remembered things as basic as going to school. Remarkably, these three children attended mainstream schools and did reasonably well. Moreover, when tested as young adults, their IQs fell within the normal range. They learned to speak and read, and they could remember many facts. For instance, one of the three, at age 19, was asked, "Who is Martin Luther King Jr.?" The person answered, "An American; fought for Black rights, Black rights leader in the 1970s; got assassinated." In other words, despite their brain damage, these people were able to encode and retrieve semantic memories from long-term storage. But they could not remember their own personal experiences.

Our Implicit Memories Function Without Conscious Effort

We have seen that after his surgery H.M. could not form new explicit memories. Let's explore H.M.'s memory abilities a bit more to see how they reveal the existence of a second form of memory: implicit memory.

H.M. was able to learn some new things after his surgery, such as motor tasks. But he could not state that he had learned these things. In one series of tests, he was asked to trace the outline of a star while watching his hand in a mirror (**Figure 7.16**). Most people do poorly the first few times they try this difficult task. On each of three consecutive days, H.M. was asked to trace the star 10 times. His performance improved over the three days. This finding indicated that he had retained some information about the task. Given his deficits in explicit memory, H.M. could not recall ever having performed the task previously. Nevertheless, his ability to learn new motor skills enabled him to get a job at a factory. There, he mounted cigarette lighters on cardboard cases.

IMPLICIT MEMORY AND AMNESIA H.M.'s retained memory abilities after the surgery reveal a second memory system for long-term storage. This system contrasts with H.M.'s deficits in explicit memory. **Implicit memory** refers to memories that we are not conscious of. Because you cannot declare implicit memories in words, this system is sometimes called non-declarative memory. Implicit memory influences our lives in subtle ways. For example, advertisers rely on implicit memory to influence our purchasing decisions. Constant exposure to brand names makes us more likely to think of them when we buy products. If you find yourself wanting a particular brand, you might be unconsciously remembering advertisements for that brand, even if you cannot recall the specifics.

Because H.M. could form new implicit memories after the surgery, his behavior suggests that parts of the medial temporal lobe that were removed are not necessary for storing these types of memories. This idea further suggests that implicit memory is a second unique long-term storage system. Furthermore, there are two main types of implicit memories: classical conditioning and procedural memories.

CLASSICAL CONDITIONING AND PROCEDURAL MEMORY

Implicit memories do not require conscious attention. They happen automatically, without deliberate effort. There are two main types of implicit memory. Classical conditioning, which we discussed in Chapter 6, employs implicit memory (**Figure 7.17a**). For example, if you always experience fear at the sight of a person in a white lab coat, you might have past associations between a person in a white lab coat and pain. This memory is implicit.

Suppose you are driving. Suddenly, you realize you have been daydreaming and have no episodic memory of the past few minutes. During that time, you employed implicit memories of how to drive and where you were going. Because you drew on that information, you did not crash the car or go in the wrong direction.

implicit memory
The system for long-term storage of unconscious memories that cannot be verbally described.

FIGURE 7.16

H.M.'s Performance in Mirror Drawing
When H.M. got better at mirror drawing over time, he showed that he could form new implicit memories (procedural) after his surgery. When he could not remember doing the mirror drawing task, H.M. showed that he could not form new explicit memories (episodic) after his surgery. These findings are evidence for the existence of multiple memory systems in long-term storage.

(a)

(b)

FIGURE 7.17

Two Types of Implicit Memory
(a) One type of implicit memory includes classical conditioning. For example, a person may learn to associate a stimulus, such as a spider, with a certain response, such as fear. **(b)** A second type of implicit memory is procedural memory, or motor memory. This type includes knowing how to ride a bicycle or play the piano.

This type of implicit memory is called **procedural memory** (**Figure 7.17b**). It involves motor skills, habits, and other behaviors employed to achieve goals, such as coordinating muscle movements to ride a bicycle or following the rules of the road while driving.

Procedural memories are generally so unconscious that most people find that consciously thinking about automatic behaviors interferes with the smooth production of those behaviors. The next time you are riding a bicycle, try to think about each step involved in the process. How does that conscious effort affect the action?

Procedural memories tend to last a long time. Once you learn to ride a bike, you most likely will always be able to ride one. It would take brain damage for you to lose that skill.

Prospective Memory Lets Us Remember to Do Something

"When you see Juan, tell him to call me, okay? And don't forget to bring the DVD tonight so we can watch the movie." Unlike the other types of memory we have discussed so far, **prospective memory** is future oriented. It means that we will remember to do something at some future time (Graf & Uttl, 2001).

Prospective memory comes with a cost. Recall that the cognitive effort involved in paying attention to certain information makes us unable to attend closely to other information. In the same way, remembering to do something takes up valuable cognitive resources. This type of memory reduces either the number of items we can deal with in short-term storage or the number of things we can attend to and process in working memory (Einstein & McDaniel, 2005).

In a study of prospective memory, participants had to learn a list of words (Cook, Marsh, Clark-Foos, & Meeks, 2007). In one condition, the participants also had to remember to do something. For example, they had to press a key when they saw a certain word. That group—the participants who had to remember to do something—took longer to learn the list than the control group that learned the same list of words but did not have to remember to do something.

Cues can help prospective memory. For example, seeing Juan might automatically trigger your memory. You would then effortlessly remember to give Juan the message. But particular environments do not always have obvious cues for certain prospective memories. So you might not encounter a cue for remembering to bring the DVD. Prospective memory for events without cues is the reason sticky notes are so popular (**Figure 7.18a**). In this case, you might stick a note that says "Bring

FIGURE 7.18

Prospective Memory
People use several tools to assist prospective memories. **(a)** Some of us use sticky notes to remind us to do things. **(b)** Some of us use a device, such as a smartphone, to remember appointments and deadlines.

(a)

(b)

DVD" on the steering wheel of your car. By jogging your memory, the note saves you the effort of remembering. For an even more urgent reminder, you might set your cell phone alarm or use an electronic calendar (**Figure 7.18b**).

Memory Is Processed by Several Regions of Our Brains

Over the past twenty years, memory researchers have made tremendous progress in understanding what happens in the brain when we acquire, store, and retrieve memories. The research on people with memory disorders clearly reveals that there are separate long-term storage systems. Moreover, distinct brain regions are involved in processing information pertaining to different long-term stores.

MEMORY'S PHYSICAL LOCATIONS Not all brain areas are equally involved in memory. A great deal of specialization occurs. In fact, different brain regions are responsible for storing different aspects of information (**Figure 7.19**).

Recall that H.M.'s anterograde amnesia left him unable to learn new explicit memories. However, he remained able to learn new implicit memories. H.M.'s surgery removed regions within the temporal lobes, such as the hippocampus. Clearly, this area is important for the ability to store new explicit memories. However, the temporal lobes are less important for implicit memories such as procedural memories and classical conditioning.

By contrast, the cerebellum plays a role in implicit memory systems. It is especially involved in procedural memory for learning motor actions. The amygdala is especially important for another type of implicit memory. Recall that in classical conditioning, an animal may unconsciously learn to be afraid of something. But an animal without an amygdala cannot learn to fear objects that signal danger.

The take-home message here is that memory does not "live" in one part of the brain. Memory is distributed among different brain regions. So if you lose one particular brain cell, you will not lose a memory.

CONSOLIDATION OF MEMORIES Your brain is different than it was before you began reading this chapter. Reading the chapter is making some of your neural connections stronger. At the same time, new neural connections should be developing—especially in your hippocampus. Neural connections that support memory have become stronger, and new synapses have been constructed (Miller, 2005). This process is known as **consolidation.** Through consolidation, your experiences become your lasting memories.

The medial temporal lobes are responsible for coordinating and strengthening the connections among neurons when we learn something. This region, including the hippocampus, is particularly important for the formation of new memories. The actual storage of memories, however, occurs in the particular brain regions engaged during the perception, processing, and analysis of the material being learned. For instance, visual information is stored in the cortical areas involved in visual perception. Sound is stored in the areas involved in auditory perception. Now think about memories of those sensory experiences. Remembering something we have seen or heard involves reactivating the same cortical circuits that

procedural memory
A type of implicit memory that involves motor skills and behavioral habits.

prospective memory
Remembering to do something at some future time.

consolidation
A process by which immediate memories become lasting through long-term storage.

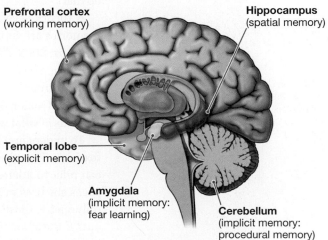

Prefrontal cortex
(working memory)

Hippocampus
(spatial memory)

Temporal lobe
(explicit memory)

Amygdala
(implicit memory: fear learning)

Cerebellum
(implicit memory: procedural memory)

FIGURE 7.19

Brain Regions Associated With Memory
We all have several different memory systems for long-term storage. Specific brain regions are responsible for processing information for each of the long-term stores.

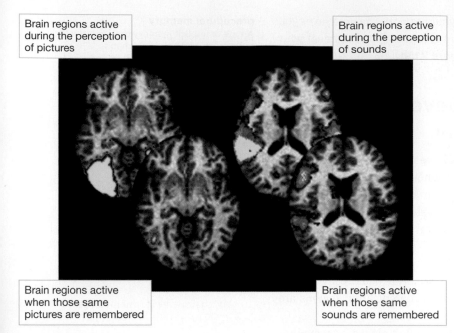

Brain regions active during the perception of pictures

Brain regions active during the perception of sounds

Brain regions active when those same pictures are remembered

Brain regions active when those same sounds are remembered

FIGURE 7.20

Brain Activation During Perception and Remembering

These four horizontally sliced brain images were acquired using magnetic resonance imaging. In each pair, the top image shows the brain activity for sensory-specific perception. The bottom image shows the regions of the sensory cortex that are activated when that sensory-specific information is remembered. Notice that the perceptions and the memories both activate similar cortical areas.

were involved when we first saw or heard the information (**Figure 7.20**). It is almost as if the brain is reexperiencing what we saw or heard. This reexperience occurs even though the original stimulus is no longer in front of us.

The medial temporal lobes are important for coordinating the storage of information between the different cortical sites and also are involved in strengthening the connections between these sites (Squire, Stark, & Clark, 2004). Think about what Google does for the Internet. Google doesn't store all the information on the Internet, but it provides links to where that information is stored. That's what the medial temporal lobes do for memories. Once the connections between different brain sites are strengthened sufficiently, the medial temporal lobes become less important for memory. H.M.'s surgery removed parts of his medial temporal lobes. Without those parts, he could not make new memories (at least ones he could talk about). He still was able to retrieve old memories.

To understand the basic consolidation process, consider this example. While reading this chapter, you have come to understand that *medial* means "in the middle." Now that you have acquired this information, you need to think about it over time so that it will be consolidated in your memory. A good night's sleep might also help this process. There is compelling evidence that sleep helps with the consolidation of memories and that disturbing sleep interferes with learning.

RECONSOLIDATION OF MEMORIES All of us have probably wished we could forget some things that are particularly embarrassing or painful. Could we actually do that?

A theory developed by Karim Nader and Joseph LeDoux proposes that once memories are activated, they need to be consolidated again for long-term storage (LeDoux, 2002; Nader & Einarsson, 2010). This process is known as *reconsolidation*. When memories for past events are retrieved, those memories can be affected by new circumstances, so reconsolidated memories may differ from their original versions (Nader, Schafe, & LeDoux, 2000). In other words, our memories begin as versions of what we have experienced, but they might change when we use them.

To understand how reconsolidation works, think of a student working with her textbook. Then the student returns the book to its place on her bookshelf so that she can refer to it later. While working, the student might turn down the edges of the pages she uses most frequently. When she retrieves the book later, it might naturally open to those pages. What if some pages become damaged to the point of falling out? If the student looks for those pages later, she won't be able to find them. The idea here is that the book placed back on the shelf is now different from the one the student started with. The dog-eared pages make some information easier to access, and the damaged pages make other information impossible to access. Reconsolidation actually changes our memories every time we access them.

According to this theory, reconsolidation occurs each time a memory is activated and placed back in storage. This process may explain why our memories for events can change over time. Think about another intriguing possibility: Could

Halfway into his first semester at college, James was feeling confident. He had learned a lot and received good grades on his midterm exams. When he checked Facebook to see how his friends were, he was especially happy to find out that his friend Lorenzo was doing well at his university. James and Lorenzo had been friends since they were little boys, when they met at Little League. They had joined the same Boy Scout troop and moved up the ranks to Eagle Scout together. But their senior year had been difficult: Lorenzo's mother was killed in a car crash. She had been driving, and Lorenzo was in the passenger seat. Lorenzo had been haunted by powerfully negative memories of that day, and he went through a period where he just wasn't himself. With some help from a psychologist, Lorenzo had improved. Although James had hoped they would go to the same university, he was simply glad that his friend was functioning well enough to attend college and even enjoy it.

James took a break from his computer and started reading Chapter 7 of his psychology textbook. Thinking about memory made him wonder, *Will Lorenzo ever forget the details of that crash? Is there a technique for erasing memories? So many conditions can be treated with medication now. Will we ever be able to just pop a pill and forget something we don't want to remember?* Curious but expecting to find nothing, James did an Internet search for "pill for losing a memory." At the online version of *Wired* magazine, he found an article that actually described how such a pill would work. *Can an article on the Internet really be trusted?* This one seemed quite informative. The writer had even interviewed the researchers, rather than just relying on a journalistic point of view. This piece was reporting, not an editorial.

The article covered a lot of the same material that James had just read about how memories are formed. As James knew from his textbook reading, memories are not set in stone. Every time we access them, they are altered ever so slightly. According to the *Wired* article, this kind of change helps explain the success of talk therapy. *Right! Talking about his memories helped Lorenzo.* In talk therapy, a patient can discuss painful memories in a controlled, safe space with the help of a therapist. When the painful memories are

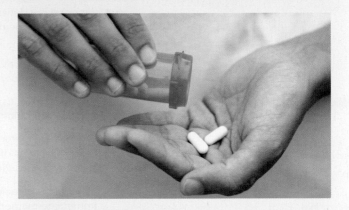

recalled in a less threatening way, the memories themselves can become less threatening. That is, they are associated with less negative emotions. *Lorenzo hasn't forgotten the car crash, but it doesn't seem to bother him the way it used to. But what if he could just get rid of that memory?*

The article described a molecule, PKMzeta, that exists in synapses. When this molecule was not present, some memories apparently disappeared. Researchers had found drugs that blocked the activity of PKMzeta. Through testing, the researchers were able to inhibit this molecule so that specific memories were deleted but other attached memories were not. The research had been done only on rats, and other research contradicts these findings. But in the future, with more testing, researchers may develop pills that let us choose to erase some specific memories that we want to stop recalling.

The article also considered the ethical issues regarding such a pill. What if it falls into the wrong hands? Should we delete painful memories, even though pain is part of being human? In fact, pain can be educational, teaching us not to do particular things. *Would Lorenzo ever want to take such a pill? Is there some benefit to remembering that day?* Ultimately, James gained a better understanding of the basic process of memory. *Memory is complicated but fascinating. Knowledge about that process has huge potential for helping people!*

bad memories be erased by activating them and then interfering with reconsolidation of them (**Figure 7.21**)? Recently, researchers have shown that using the classical conditioning technique of extinction during the period when memories are susceptible to reconsolidation can be an effective method of altering bad memories (Schiller et al., 2010; for a discussion of extinction, see Chapter 6).

FIGURE 7.21

Altering Memories
In the 2004 movie *Eternal Sunshine of the Spotless Mind*, Joel Barish (played by Jim Carrey) undergoes a procedure that eliminates memories of his former girlfriend. The movie is fiction, but real-life researchers are investigating how using behavioral techniques or drugs can alter memories.

7.3 CHECKPOINT: What Are Our Different Long-Term Storage Systems?

- Amnesia is a deficit in long-term storage. Retrograde amnesia is the inability to recall past memories. Anterograde amnesia is the inability to form new memories.

- Explicit memories that we consciously remember include personal events (episodic memory) and general, factual knowledge (semantic memory).

- Implicit memories are processed without conscious effort and include classical conditioning and procedural memories of motor skills.

- Prospective memory is remembering to do something in the future, and it has "costs" in terms of reducing attentional resources and impairing short-term storage and working memory processing.

- Multiple brain regions process memory information. Through consolidation, immediate memories become lasting memories. Memories may be altered through reconsolidation.

7.4 How Do We Access Our Memories?

📖 **LEARNING GOALS**	✏️ **READING ACTIVITIES**
a. Remember the key terms about how we access memories from long-term storage.	List all of the boldface words and write down their definitions.
b. Understand how retrieval cues improve access to memories in long-term storage.	Explain, in your own words, three ways that retrieval cues can be used to retrieve memories in long-term storage.
c. Apply forgetting to your own long-term storage of memories.	Demonstrate the three ways to forget memories in long-term storage with one example of each from your own life.
d. Understand how memories in long-term storage can become distorted.	Compare, in your own words, the four ways that memories in long-term storage can become distorted.

Scott Hagwood and the other USA Memory Championship contestants are able to store large amounts of information in their brains by using various processing techniques. But when it comes time to compete, how do they actually "remember" the information? How do they get the information out of storage?

Up to this point, we have focused on two phases of memory. In the first phase, we acquire memories through encoding. In the second phase, we maintain information through storage in one of three memory storage systems. The third phase of processing information is to re-access the stored memories at a later date to use that information in some way. Four processes affect our ability to access stored memories, as shown in the Learning Tip.

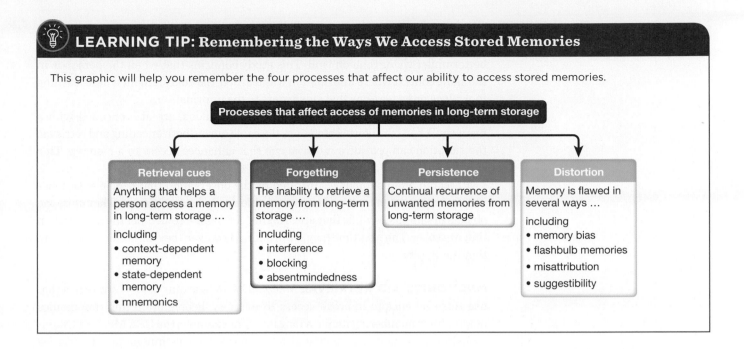

LEARNING TIP: Remembering the Ways We Access Stored Memories

This graphic will help you remember the four processes that affect our ability to access stored memories.

Processes that affect access of memories in long-term storage

Retrieval cues	Forgetting	Persistence	Distortion
Anything that helps a person access a memory in long-term storage ... including • context-dependent memory • state-dependent memory • mnemonics	The inability to retrieve a memory from long-term storage ... including • interference • blocking • absentmindedness	Continual recurrence of unwanted memories from long-term storage	Memory is flawed in several ways ... including • memory bias • flashbulb memories • misattribution • suggestibility

Retrieval Cues Help Us Access Our Memories

Encountering stimuli can automatically trigger memories. So a **retrieval cue** can be anything that helps us access a memory. Think about the smell of turkey, a favorite song from years past, a familiar building, and so on. The properties of any experience are encoded with a memory and can later aid retrieval of that memory.

CONTEXT AND STATE AID RETRIEVAL The context of an event includes details such as the physical location, odors, and background music. That context is encoded along with the memory. As a result, the context produces a sense of familiarity that helps us retrieve the memory (Hockley, 2008).

In a dramatic research demonstration of this *context-dependent memory* effect, two groups of scuba divers learned lists of words. Some divers learned the words on land. Other divers learned the words under water (Godden & Baddeley, 1975; **Figure 7.22a**). Later on, both groups recalled the words better when they were in the same environment where they had learned them (**Figure 7.22b**). That is, when

retrieval cue
Anything that helps a person access information in long-term storage.

(a)

(b)

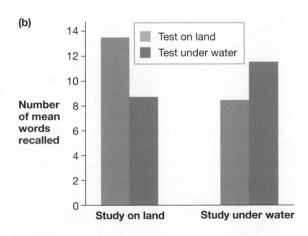

- Test on land
- Test under water

Number of mean words recalled

Study on land Study under water

FIGURE 7.22
Context–Dependent Memory
A unique study showed that the context of a memory can help retrieve that memory. **(a)** People learned lists of words either on land or under water. **(b)** Later on, they remembered more words if they were tested in the same environment where they had learned the words.

forgetting
The inability to access a memory from long-term storage.

divers learned information on land, they recalled that information better on land than under water. When divers learned the words under water, they recalled them better under water than on land. This study confirms that when the person is in the same context where information was learned, the environment where learning took place provides a cue that aids access to the information.

Like physical context, internal cues, such as mood, are also encoded with a memory. When our internal states are the same during both encoding and retrieval, the situation can provide a retrieval cue that enhances access to a memory. This effect is known as *state-dependent memory.*

Research on this topic was inspired by the observation that people experiencing alcoholism often can't find important objects, such as paychecks. They store the objects in safe places while they are drinking, but cannot remember the places when they are sober. The next time they are drinking, however, they may remember where they put the objects.

MNEMONICS AID RETRIEVAL *Mnemonics* are learning aids or strategies that use retrieval cues to improve access to memory. People often find mnemonics helpful for remembering items in long lists. For example, the USA Memory Championship contestants use mnemonics for their feats. One mnemonic, the *method of loci,* consists of associating items you want to remember with physical locations. The contestants use the method of loci to remember the order of playing cards by visualizing cards in certain locations on a mental walk through a familiar place.

You can practice techniques of this kind. You may not become a memory contest champion, but you can improve your ability to access memories in long-term storage. Suppose you want to remember a grocery list of items to buy from the store. First, you might visualize parts of the physical layout of some familiar location, such as your bedroom. Then you would associate the list of items to buy with certain places in the room. You might picture your open dresser drawer filled to the top with apples, a loaf of bread snuggled in your bed under a comforter, and a waterfall of milk flowing down your curtains. When you later need to remember the items, you would visualize your room and retrieve the information associated with each location.

We Forget Some of Our Memories

Ten minutes after you see a movie, you probably remember plenty of the details. The next week, you might remember mostly the plot and the main characters. Years later, you might remember only the gist of the story. You might not remember having seen the movie at all. We forget far more than we remember. **Forgetting** is the inability to access memory from long-term storage. This inability is a normal, everyday experience.

The study of forgetting has a long history in psychology. In the late nineteenth century, the psychologist Hermann Ebbinghaus examined how long it took him to relearn lists of unfamiliar nonsense syllables (e.g., vut, bik, kuh). Ebbinghaus found that when he repeatedly practiced with the syllables, it took him less time to relearn them the next day. In other words, the more time he spent learning material, the less he forgot. His results are shown in a forgetting curve (**Figure 7.23**). Luckily, most of

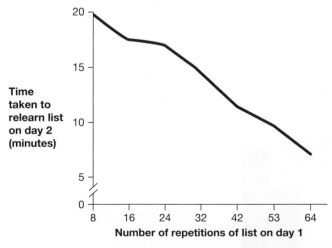

Time taken to relearn list on day 2 (minutes)

Number of repetitions of list on day 1

FIGURE 7.23

Forgetting Curve
Research shows that when a person repeatedly practices with nonsense syllables, it takes her less time to relearn them later on.

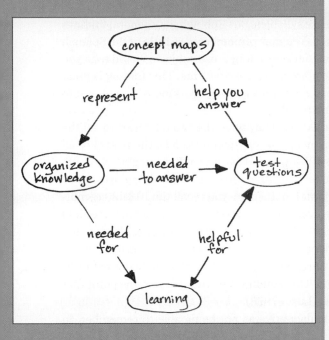

How Can I Remember Information for Exams?

What part of the college experience do most students particularly dislike? There's a good chance you said "exams." Psychology can't make exams go away, but it can help make them easier to deal with. Here are some tools that can help you study more effectively and remember information more easily.

1. **Distribute learning.** Though pulling an all-nighter is a college classic, cramming does not work. Six sessions of 1 hour each, spread over days or weeks, are much better for learning than one 6-hour marathon because you will store information better (Cepeda, Pashler, Vul, Wixted, & Rohrer, 2006).

2. **Process deeply.** When you are learning something new, do not just read or repeat the material. Shallow processing won't help your memory. Instead, think about the meaning of the material and how the concepts are related to each other and to your life. Using deeper processing, such as by making material personally relevant, is an especially good way to remember it easily.

3. **Practice.** To make your memories more durable, you need to practice retrieving the information you are trying to learn. In fact, repeated testing is a more effective memory-building strategy than spending the same amount of time rereading or reviewing information you have already read (Roediger & Karpicke, 2006). Answering practice questions will help you remember the information during exams.

4. **Overlearn.** With material in front of us, we are often overly confident that we "know" the information and believe we will remember it later. But recognition is easier than recall. As a result, information in a book might not be as accessible when the book is closed and you have to answer questions about what you read. If you want to be able to recall information, you need to put in extra effort when encoding the material. Even after you *think* you have learned it, test yourself by trying to recall the material a few hours and a few days after studying. Keep rehearsing until you can recall the material easily.

5. **Picture images.** Creating a mental image is an especially good way to remember something. Visual imagery strategies include making a sketch to help you link ideas to images, creating a flowchart to show how some process unfolds over time, or drawing a concept map that shows the relationships between ideas.

6. **Make mnemonics.** Whatever their goals for remembering, people employ many types of mnemonics. For example, how many days are there in September? In the Western world, at least, most people can readily answer this question thanks to the old jingle that begins "Thirty days has September." Another common type of mnemonic is the acronym, such as HOMES to remember the great lakes (Huron, Ontario, Michigan, Erie, and Superior). To use all of the strategies we've described, you need to remember them. As a first step toward improving your study skills, try to create an acronym to remember these six strategies, using the first letter of each strategy: DPPOPM.

us do not need to memorize nonsense syllables. But Ebbinghaus's general findings apply to meaningful material as well. You may remember very little of the Spanish or calculus you took in high school, but relearning these subjects would take you less time and effort than it took to learn them the first time. This finding is great news for students: When you spend more time actively working with material to learn it, you will forget less of the material.

Most people feel bad about forgetting. They wish they could better recall the material they study for exams, the names of childhood friends, the names of all seven dwarfs who lived with Snow White, what have you. But imagine what life would be like if you could not forget. Imagine, for example, walking up to your locker. You want to recall its combination. Instead, you recall the 10 or 20 combinations for all the locks you have ever used. A Russian newspaper reporter had nearly perfect memory. If someone read him a tremendously long list of items and he visualized the items for a few moments, he could recite the list, even many years later. But his memory was so cluttered with information that he had great difficulty functioning in normal society. This condition tortured him to the point that he eventually was institutionalized (Luria, 1968).

Not being able to forget is as maladaptive as not being able to remember. In this way, forgetting is a desirable and useful aspect of human memory. Forgetting may even be necessary for survival. Normal forgetting helps us remember and use important information. There are three main ways that we forget: interference, blocking, and absentmindedness.

INTERFERENCE When Ebbinghaus studied nonsense syllables, he observed forgetting over time. Many early theorists argued that such forgetting results from the decay of the particular memory trace in a person's brain. Some evidence does indicate that unused memories are forgotten. However, research over the last few decades has established that most forgetting occurs because of interference from other information. There are two types of interference.

In **retroactive interference,** access to older memories is impaired by newer memories. Say you're about to take a psychology test. You study the psychology material, and then you study some history material. Your performance on the psychology test might suffer because the psychology material you studied first is harder to access due to interference from the history material you studied second (**Figure 7.24a**). By contrast, in **proactive interference,** access to newer memories is impaired by older memories. In this case, when you take your psychology test, your performance on that test might suffer because you recall the older information that you studied first, the history material, not the newer information you studied second, the psychology material (**Figure 7.24b**).

(a)

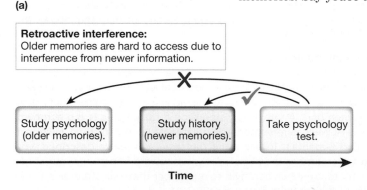

Retroactive interference:
Older memories are hard to access due to interference from newer information.

Study psychology (older memories). | Study history (newer memories). | Take psychology test.

Time

(b)

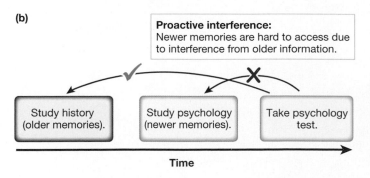

Proactive interference:
Newer memories are hard to access due to interference from older information.

Study history (older memories). | Study psychology (newer memories). | Take psychology test.

Time

FIGURE 7.24

Retroactive and Proactive Interference

(a) Retroactive interference occurs when retrieving old memories (here, psychology material) is hard due to interference from new memories (here, history material). **(b)** Proactive interference occurs when retrieving new memories (psychology material) is hard due to interference from old memories (history material).

BLOCKING You can't recall the name of a favorite song. You forget the name of someone you are introducing. You "blank" on some lines when acting in a play. This type of forgetting is called *blocking*. Blocking occurs when we are temporarily unable to remember something. It is frustrating but common.

Roger Brown and David McNeill (1966) described another good example of blocking: the *tip-of-the-tongue phenomenon*. Here, people experience great frustration as they try to recall specific words. For instance, when asked to provide a word that means "patronage bestowed on a relative, in business or politics" or "an astronomical instrument for finding position," people often struggle (Brown, 1991). Sometimes they know which letter the word begins with, how many syllables it has, and even what it sounds like. Even with these partial retrieval cues, they cannot pull the precise word into working memory. (Did you know the words were *nepotism* and *sextant*?)

Blocking often occurs because of interference from words that are similar in some way, such as in sound or meaning, and that are repeatedly experienced. For example, you might repeatedly call an acquaintance Margaret although her name is Melanie. The tip-of-the-tongue phenomenon increases with age, perhaps because older people have more memories that might interfere.

ABSENTMINDEDNESS *Absentmindedness* is the inattentive or shallow encoding of events. The major cause of absentmindedness is failing to pay attention (**Figure 7.25**). For instance, you absentmindedly forget where you left your keys because, when you put them down, you were also reaching to answer your phone. You forget the name of a person you are talking with because, when you met him 5 minutes earlier, you were wondering where your keys went. You forget whether you took your vitamins this morning because you were deciding whether to study for your psychology test or your history test.

Recall that when prospective memory fails, you fail to remember to do something that you were planning to do. This form of absentmindedness often occurs because you are caught up in another activity. This lack of attention can have serious consequences. In the United States over the past decade, more than 300 children have died because they were left unattended in hot cars (49 died in 2010 alone). In many cases, the parent forgot to drop off the child at day care on the way to work. It is easy to imagine forgetting your lunch in the car, but your child? Fortunately, such incidents are rare, but they seem to be especially likely when the parent's typical routine does not include day care drop-off duty. While the parent is driving, his or her brain shifts to "autopilot" and automatically goes through the process of driving to the workplace instead of stopping at day care first.

Our Unwanted Memories May Persist

Sometimes you want to forget something but have difficulty doing so. **Persistence** occurs when unwanted memories recur despite our desire not to have them. Some unwanted memories are so traumatic that they destroy the life of the individual who suffers from them.

One prominent example of persistence occurs in posttraumatic stress disorder (PTSD), in which people experience extremely stressful episodes after having had a traumatic experience. During a PTSD episode, they relive the traumatic experience. PTSD is a serious mental health problem, affecting 7.8 percent of people in the United States alone (Kessler, Sonnega, Bromet, Hughes, & Nelson, 1995). The most common causes of PTSD include events that threaten people or those close to them. For example, the unexpected death of a loved one, a physical or sexual assault,

FIGURE 7.25
Absentmindedness
The celebrated musician Yo-Yo Ma is pictured here with his $2.5 million eighteenth-century cello. This instrument was returned to Yo-Yo Ma after he absentmindedly left it in a cab.

persistence
The continual recurrence of unwanted memories from long-term storage.

Have you ever experienced absentmindedness? Maybe you left one room to get something from another, but completely forgot what you wanted once you were there. This type of forgetting happens to all of us at one time or another.

The easiest way to overcome absentmindedness in a situation like this is to go back to the room where you were thinking about getting that object. In fact, if returning to the room jogs your memory, then you have experienced the effect of context dependence as well.

distortion
Human memory is not a perfectly accurate representation of the past, but is flawed.

military combat, a car accident, a natural disaster, or seeing someone badly injured or killed can all lead to PTSD.

Considerable research is under way to produce drugs that will erase unwanted memories. One drug, propranolol, blocks norepinephrine receptors. If it is given right around the time of a traumatic experience, the memories and fear response for that event are reduced, and the effect lasts for months (Cahill, Prins, Weber, & McGaugh, 1994; Pitman et al., 2002). Drugs such as propranolol might have side effects, however. Alternatively, as we discussed earlier, extinction can be used during reconsolidation to yield similar results, potentially without side effects (Schiller et al., 2010).

Erasing memories leads to many ethical questions. If we can erase traumatic memories, should we remove only the memories of traumas that were beyond the sufferer's control? Or should a person be treated for suffering a guilty conscience after an intentional malicious act? Will reducing memories to take the emotional sting out of life make us less human?

Our Memories Can Be Distorted

You may think that you remember everything about your senior prom just as it happened. But research has shown clearly that human memory provides less-than-accurate portrayals of past events. In fact, human memory is really quite flawed. In general, **distortion** occurs in memory in four ways: memory bias, flashbulb memories, misattribution, and suggestibility.

MEMORY BIAS *Memory bias* is the changing of memories over time so that they become consistent with our current beliefs or attitudes. As one of psychology's greatest thinkers, Leon Festinger (1987), put it: "I prefer to rely on my memory. I have lived with that memory a long time, I am used to it, and if I have rearranged or distorted anything, surely that was done for my own benefit."

We tend to recall our past beliefs and past attitudes as being consistent with our current ones. Often, we revise our memories when they contradict our attitudes and beliefs. We also tend to remember events as casting us in prominent roles or favorable lights. We exaggerate our contributions to group efforts. We take credit for successes and blame failures on others. And we remember our successes more than our failures.

FLASHBULB MEMORIES Do you remember where you were when you first heard about the Boston Marathon bombings (**Figure 7.26a**)? Some events lead to what Roger Brown and James Kulik (1977) termed *flashbulb memories*. These vivid memories seem like a flash photo, capturing the circumstances in which we first learned of a surprising and consequential or emotionally arousing event. In 1977, Brown and Kulik interviewed research participants about their memories of the assassination of U.S. president John F. Kennedy. The participants described these 14-year-old memories in highly vivid terms. The details included who they were with, what they were doing or thinking, who told them or how they found out, and what their emotional reactions were to the event. Flashbulb memories are an example of episodic memory. They are not like the problem of persistence, however. They are not recurring unwanted memories.

An obvious problem affects research into the accuracy of flashbulb memories. Researchers have to conduct a study immediately after an event occurs so they can compare the memories of people at different times. The explosion of the U.S. space shuttle *Challenger*, on January 28, 1986, provided a unique opportunity for

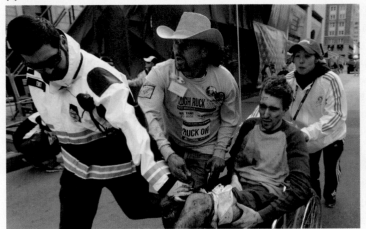

FIGURE 7.26
Flashbulb Memories
Surprising and consequential or emotionally arousing events can produce flashbulb memories. For example, **(a)** the Boston Marathon bombings, in 2013; and **(b)** the attacks on the World Trade Center in 2001.

research on this topic. Ulric Neisser and Nicole Harsch (1993) had 44 psychology students fill out a questionnaire the day the shuttle exploded. When they tested the students' memories three years later, only three students had perfect recall. The rest were incorrect about multiple aspects of the situation. We are all likely to experience inaccurate flashbulb memories, even for traumatic events that we think we remember well, such as the attacks on the World Trade Center in 2001 (**Figure 7.26b**).

Other researchers have documented better memory for flashbulb experiences. For example, for three years after the airline hijackings and attacks on the World Trade Center and Pentagon on September 11, 2001, a study was conducted of more than 3,000 people across the United States (Hirst et al., 2009). Memories related to 9/11—such as where the person first heard about the attacks and her knowledge about the events—declined somewhat during the first year. Memory remained stable thereafter. As might be expected, people who were living in New York City on 9/11 had, over time, the most accurate memories of the World Trade Center attacks.

People are more confident about their flashbulb memories than they are about their ordinary memories (Talarico & Rubin, 2003). Although flashbulb memories are not perfectly accurate, they are at least as accurate as memory for ordinary events. Any event that produces a strong emotional response is likely to produce a vivid, although not necessarily accurate, memory (Christianson, 1992). Or a distinctive event might simply be recalled more easily than a trivial event, however inaccurate the result. It is also possible that greater media attention to major events leads to greater exposure to the details of those events, thus encouraging better memory (Hirst et al., 2009).

MISATTRIBUTION *Misattribution* occurs when we misremember the time, place, person, or circumstances involved with a memory. Source amnesia is a form of misattribution that occurs when we have a memory for an event but cannot remember where we encountered the information. Consider your earliest childhood memory. How vivid is it? Are you actually recalling the event? How do you know you are not remembering either something you saw in a photograph or a story related to you by

FIGURE 7.27

Cryptomnesia

The 2006 novel *How Opal Mehta Got Kissed, Got Wild, and Got a Life* turned into a possible case of cryptomnesia. The author was a student at Harvard University named Kaavya Viswanathan. Viswanathan admitted that several passages in the work were taken from books that she read in high school. As a result, *How Opal Mehta Got Kissed* had to be recalled from bookstores. Perhaps Viswanathan, thinking she had come up with new material, had retrieved other people's writing from memory.

family members? Most people cannot remember specific memories from before age 3. The absence of early memories may be due to the early lack of language as well as to frontal lobes that are not fully developed.

An intriguing example of source misattribution is *cryptomnesia*. Here, we think we have come up with a new idea, but really we have retrieved an old idea from memory and failed to attribute the idea to its proper source (Macrae, Bodenhausen, & Calvini, 1999; **Figure 7.27**). Consider students who take verbatim notes while conducting library research. Sometimes these students experience the illusion that they have composed the sentences themselves. This mistake can later lead to an accusation of plagiarism. (Be especially vigilant about recording the source of verbatim notes while you are taking them.)

George Harrison, the late Beatle, was sued because his 1970 song "My Sweet Lord" is strikingly similar to the song "He's So Fine," recorded in 1962 by the Chiffons. Harrison acknowledged having known "He's So Fine," but vigorously denied having plagiarized it. He argued that with a limited number of musical notes available to all musicians, and an even smaller number of chord sequences appropriate for rock and roll, some compositional overlap is inevitable. In a controversial verdict, the judge ruled against Harrison.

SUGGESTIBILITY During the early 1970s, a series of important studies conducted by Elizabeth Loftus and colleagues demonstrated that when people are given misleading information, this information affects their memory for an event. In one experiment, Loftus and John Palmer (1974) showed participants a videotape of a car accident. When participants heard the word *smashed* applied to the tape, they estimated the cars to be traveling faster than when they heard *contacted, hit, bumped,* or *collided.* One week later, they were asked if they had seen broken glass on the ground in the video. No glass broke in the video, but nearly one-third of those who heard *smashed* falsely recalled having seen broken glass. Very few of those who heard *hit* recalled broken glass. The way that the question was asked apparently influenced their memory for the information. This research reveals the *suggestibility* of memories in long-term storage.

The suggestibility of memories in long-term storage creates problems for one of the most powerful forms of evidence in our justice system: the eyewitness account. Research has demonstrated that very few jurors are willing to convict an accused individual on the basis of circumstantial evidence alone. But if just one person says, "That's the one!" then conviction becomes much more likely. This effect occurs even if it is shown that the witness had poor eyesight or some other condition that raises questions about the testimony's accuracy. The power of eyewitness testimony is troubling because witnesses are so often in error. Gary Wells and his colleagues (1998) studied 40 cases in which DNA evidence indicated that a person had been falsely convicted of a crime. They found that in 36 of these cases, the person had been misidentified by at least one eyewitness (**Figure 7.28**). Why is eyewitness testimony so prone to error?

First, recall the phenomenon of change blindness. Research on this error showed that a person fails to notice that the person she was talking with has been

FIGURE 7.28

Eyewitness Accounts Can Be Unreliable

William Jackson **(top)** served five years in prison because he was wrongly convicted of a crime based on the testimony of two eyewitnesses. Note the similarities and differences between Jackson and the real perpetrator **(bottom)**.

replaced with a new person (see Scientific Thinking, p. 234). Eyewitness testimony depends critically on paying sufficient attention to an incident when it happens, rather than after it happens. If we are not attending to the information, it won't be encoded and stored in a way that is accurate. Ultimately, then, the testimony is prone to error because often the eyewitness is not paying attention to the right details when the event happens.

Further, the memories of eyewitnesses become distorted over time. Taryn Simon is a photographer. For the *New York Times,* Simon created *The Innocents,* a photo essay of people who were wrongfully convicted of crimes they did not commit. Mostly, these people were convicted because of faulty eyewitness testimony (**Figure 7.29**). As Simon explained, "Police officers and prosecutors influence memory—both unintentionally and intentionally—through the ways in which they conduct the identification process. They can shape, and even generate, what comes to be known as eyewitness testimony" (Simon, 2003). Simon described many compelling examples of memory's flexibility. One victim, Jennifer Thompson, misidentified her attacker after being shown multiple images of possible assailants. According to Thompson, "All the images became enmeshed to one image that became Ron, and Ron became my attacker" (quoted in Simon, 2003, para. 3).

Lastly, how good are observers, such as jurors, at judging eyewitnesses' accuracy? The general finding from a number of studies is that jurors cannot tell the difference between accurate eyewitnesses and inaccurate ones (Clark & Wells, 2008; Wells, 2008). The problem is that eyewitnesses who are wrong are just as confident as eyewitnesses who are right. They may even be *more* confident. Eyewitnesses who vividly report trivial details of a scene are probably less credible than those with poor memories for trivial details. After all, eyewitnesses to real crimes tend to be focused on the weapons or on the action and fail to pay attention to minor details. Thus strong confidence for minor details may be a cue that the memory is likely to be inaccurate or even false. Nevertheless, some people are particularly confident, and jurors find them convincing.

FIGURE 7.29
Fallibility of Memory
On July 3, 2008, Patrick Waller **(left)** was exonerated of a crime for which he had been wrongly convicted and sent to prison for 15 years. DNA evidence convinced the jury to reverse Waller's conviction.

 7.4 CHECKPOINT: How Do We Access Our Memories?

- Retrieval cues help us access information in long-term storage by providing information about the context in which the information was encoded.

- Forgetting, due to interference, blocking, or absentmindedness, makes us unable to access information from long-term storage.

- Persistence is the recurrence of unwanted memories. It is common among individuals with posttraumatic stress disorder.

- Memories can become distorted through memory bias, flashbulb memories, misattribution, and suggestibility.

7.1
How Do We Acquire Memories?

a. Remember the key terms about memory and encoding.

b. Analyze the three phases of information processing in acquisition of a memory.

c. Understand how attention affects memory.

d. Apply filter theory to your ability to selectively attend to important information.

7.2
How Do We Maintain Memories Over Time?

a. Remember the key terms about storage of memories.

b. Understand sensory storage.

c. Understand the relationship between short-term storage and working memory.

d. Apply encoding processes in long-term storage to your life.

e. Understand how information is organized in long-term storage based on semantic meaning.

7.3
What Are Our Different Long-Term Storage Systems?

a. Remember the key terms about long-term storage systems and brain processes.

b. Apply the two forms of explicit memory to your life and explain whether they are affected by retrograde amnesia.

c. Understand implicit memory and whether anterograde amnesia affects it.

d. Understand how the brain processes memories.

7.4
How Do We Access Our Memories?

a. Remember the key terms about how we access memories from long-term storage.

b. Understand how retrieval cues improve access to memories in long-term storage.

c. Apply forgetting to your own long-term storage of memories.

d. Understand how memories in long-term storage can become distorted.

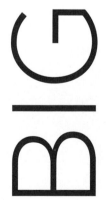

KEY TERMS

CHECKPOINT

memory
encoding
storage
retrieval
attention
change blindness

- Memories are created by encoding information from sensory input. Encoded information is maintained in storage. Retrieval allows accessing of previously encoded and stored information.

- Visual attention can be focused on encoding one feature of an object more quickly and effortlessly than two or more features.

- It is difficult to focus auditory attention on encoding more than one message at a time, and most unattended auditory information is not processed.

- Selective attention filters out irrelevant information and causes people *not* to notice large changes in the environment.

sensory storage
short-term storage
working memory
chunking
long-term storage
maintenance rehearsal
elaborative rehearsal

- A huge amout of visual, auditory, taste, smell, and touch information is maintained in sensory storage for up to a few seconds to ensure continuous sensory experiences.

- Short-term storage keeps about 8 items available for current use for up to 20 seconds. Active processing in working memory increases both this capacity and this duration.

- Long-term storage of memories is relatively permanent and virtually limitless for deeply encoded information.

- Information in long-term storage is organized based on meaning through schemas and association networks.

retrograde amnesia
anterograde amnesia
explicit memory
episodic memory
semantic memory
implicit memory
procedural memory
prospective memory
consolidation

- Amnesia is a deficit in long-term storage. Retrograde amnesia is the inability to recall past memories. Anterograde amnesia is the inability to form new memories.

- Explicit memories that we consciously remember include personal events (episodic memory) and general, factual knowledge (semantic memory).

- Implicit memories are processed without conscious effort and include classical conditioning and procedural memories of motor skills.

- Prospective memory is remembering to do something in the future, and it has "costs" in terms of reducing attentional resources and impairing short-term storage and working memory processing.

- Multiple brain regions process memory information. Through consolidation, immediate memories become lasting memories. Memories may be altered through reconsolidation.

retrieval cue
forgetting
retroactive interference
proactive interference
persistence
distortion

- Retrieval cues help us access information in long-term storage by providing information about the context in which the information was encoded.

- Forgetting, due to interference, blocking, or absentmindedness, makes us unable to access information from long-term storage.

- Persistence is the recurrence of unwanted memories. It is common among individuals with posttraumatic stress disorder.

- Memories can become distorted through memory bias, flashbulb memories, misattribution, and suggestibility.

For a self-quiz on this chapter, go to the back of the book and find Appendix B: Quizzes.

8 Thinking and Intelligence

IN 2012, AN ENGLISH 4-YEAR-OLD named Heidi Hankins did something unusual—she joined Mensa, the international society for people with extremely high intelligence (**Figure 8.1a**). Psychological testing indicated that Heidi has an intelligence quotient, or IQ, of 159, just a point or two below Albert Einstein and Stephen Hawking. (The average IQ is 100, and people are considered gifted when they score above 130.) Heidi's parents chose to have her tested because she seemed quite remarkable from an early age. She could speak in full sentences before age 1 and taught herself to read by using a computer at 18 months. At age 2, she was reading at a level typical of children many years older. In all other respects, Heidi is a normal young child. She even likes to play with Lego building blocks and Barbie dolls.

BIG QUESTIONS

8.1 **What Is Thinking?**

8.2 **How Do We Make Decisions and Solve Problems?**

8.3 **What Is Intelligence?**

8.4 **How Do We Measure Intelligence?**

(a)

(b)

FIGURE 8.1

Extraordinary Intelligence and Thinking

(a) At age 4, Heidi Hankins displayed an intelligence quotient of 159. This IQ qualified her to join Mensa, the international society for people with extremely high intelligence. **(b)** At age 15, Phiona Mutesi used her excellent thinking skills in reasoning, solving problems, and decision making to become the youngest African chess champion ever.

Now consider Phiona Mutesi, a young girl who grew up in very different circumstances (**Figure 8.1b**). Phiona was raised in an extremely poor neighborhood in Kampala, the capital of Uganda. In 2005, unable to read or write, sleeping on the streets, and desperate for food, the 9-year-old Phiona traveled with her brother to meet a missionary who promised a bowl of porridge to any child who would try chess. Phiona developed a love for the game. She also discovered that she was very good at it. Indeed, at age 15 Phiona became her country's chess champion, and the youngest African chess champion ever (Crothers, 2012). Chess requires reasoning about possible moves, solving tactical problems, and making good decisions. How was Phiona, a child with no education, able to think so skillfully and become a master at this difficult game?

Because Heidi is thought to be highly intelligent, and Phiona shows excellent thinking skills, you might get the idea that intelligence and thinking are two different things. But actually they are connected, because a person's ability to show intelligence is linked to having excellent thinking skills. The important point is that we can all improve our thinking. Thinking helps us act intelligently. And by acting intelligently, we can improve our personal lives, our academic work, and our professional careers. In this chapter, we explore aspects of thinking, such as decision making and problem solving. We also explore how thinking relates to intelligence.

8.1 What Is Thinking?

LEARNING GOALS	✏️ **READING ACTIVITIES** LEARN
a. Remember the key terms about representations used in thinking.	List all of the boldface words and write down their definitions.
b. Apply analogical and symbolic representations to your life.	Provide one example each of analogical and symbolic representations that you have used.
c. Understand how concepts are organized according to the three models of thinking.	Summarize in your own words how each of the three models of thinking would organize the concept "bird."
d. Apply schemas and stereotypes to your life.	Use the idea of schemas to explain a positive or negative stereotype that you have.

The chapter opener described Phiona Mutesi's extraordinary thinking skills in playing chess. But thinking does not have to be extraordinary—we are thinking throughout our daily lives. In fact, you are thinking right now. Are you thinking about Phiona's skills, the game of chess, or how she has risen above the circumstance she was born in? This chapter considers the nature of thought: how we represent ideas in our minds, and how we use these ideas to solve problems and make decisions.

Thinking Is the Manipulation of Mental Representations

Representations of the external world are all around us. For example, a road map represents streets. A menu represents food options. A photograph represents a particular part of the world.

As we saw in Chapter 5, representations are created when sensory input is changed into signals the brain can process. When we look at a chair, for instance, our eyes transduce the light into signals, and the brain processes the signals into an image that we call "chair." In other words, patterns of brain activity provide meaningful information about objects we encounter in our environments. **Thinking** is the mental manipulation of these representations.

Cognitive psychologists study thought and the understanding that results from thinking. For these scientists, the challenge is to understand the nature of our internal, mental representations of information around us. For example, when are the internal representations in our minds like maps or pictures? And when are they more abstract, like language?

ANALOGICAL AND SYMBOLIC REPRESENTATIONS When we think about information, we use two basic types of internal representations: analogical and symbolic.

Analogical representations usually correspond to images. They have some characteristics of actual objects. Therefore, they are *analogous* to actual objects. For example, maps correspond to geographical layouts. Family trees depict branching relationships between relatives. A clock corresponds directly to the passage of time. **Figure 8.2a** is a drawing of a violin from a particular perspective. This drawing is an analogical representation.

In our mind's eye, we often form images without trying. For example, think about a lemon. Did your "lemon" thought take the form of an image that resembled an actual lemon? Did you see the lemon's yellow, waxy, dimpled skin? Did your mouth water (a different sort of mental image)?

Studies have shown that when you retrieve information from memory, as when you recall a picture you recently saw, the representation of that picture in your mind's eye parallels the representation in your brain the first time you saw the picture (Kosslyn, Thompson, Kim, & Alpert, 1995; Stokes, Thompson, Cusack, & Duncan, 2009). In one study, participants were either shown four objects—food, tools, faces, and buildings—or asked to recall those objects (Reddy, Tsuchiya, & Serre, 2010). The brain activity was surprisingly similar for the initial sight of a specific object and the later remembering of that object. In other words, neural activity occurs when we look at objects. That neural activity can be reactivated when we think about the objects.

Of course, no "picture" exists inside your head. As we saw in Chapters 2 and 5, neural activity consists of electrical impulses that cause groups of neurons to fire. The experience simply seems like viewing a picture inside your head. And the mental image is not perfectly accurate. Instead, it generally matches the physical object it represents. By using mental images, you can answer questions about objects that are not in your presence. For example, what color is a lemon? Manipulating mental images also allows you to think about your environment in novel and creative ways. Novel and creative thinking can help you solve problems.

By contrast, **symbolic representations** are abstract. These representations usually consist of words or ideas. They do not have relationships to physical

thinking
The mental manipulation of representations of information we encounter in our environments.

analogical representations
Mental representations that have some of the physical characteristics of objects.

symbolic representations
Abstract mental representations that consist of words or ideas.

(a)   (b)

Violin

FIGURE 8.2

Analogical Versus Symbolic Representations
(a) Analogical representations, such as this picture of a violin, have some characteristics of the objects they represent. **(b)** Symbolic representations, such as the word *violin*, are abstract and do not have relationships to the physical qualities of objects.

qualities of objects in the world. The word *hamburger* is a symbolic representation that usually represents a cooked patty of beef served on a bun. The word *violin* stands for a musical instrument (**Figure 8.2b**). There are no correspondences between what a violin looks like, what it sounds like, and the letters or sounds that make up the word *violin*. The individual characters that make up the word stand for what a violin is, but the letters are arbitrary. You cannot "see" any part of a violin in the shape of the letters *v-i-o-l-i-n*.

Together, both analogical and symbolic representations form the basis of human thought, intelligence, and the ability to solve the complex problems of everyday life or of special challenges. For instance, recall Phiona from the chapter opener. Like most expert chess players, Phiona probably has rich images in her mind of where the pieces will be on the chessboard many moves in the future (analogical representations). What's more, she likely uses information about specific chess strategies that she has read about (symbolic representations). Taken together, Phiona's rich and accurate mental representations and her ability to manipulate them skillfully are a large part of her success in chess.

MENTAL MAPS Most of us can pull up a visual image of Africa's contours even if we have never seen the actual contours with our own eyes. Such *mental maps* include a combination of analogical and symbolic representations. But how accurate are our mental maps?

Consider this question: Which is farther east, San Diego, California, or Reno, Nevada? If you are like most Americans, you answered that Reno is farther east than San Diego. But, as you can see from the map in **Figure 8.3,** the reverse is true. Even if you formed an analogical representation of a map of the western United States, your symbolic knowledge probably told you that a city on the Pacific Coast is farther west than a city in a state that does not border the Pacific Ocean. In this case, a symbolic representation yielded a wrong answer.

Mental maps can sometimes lead to errors because we can represent only a limited range of knowledge. Although our general knowledge is correct, it does not take into account the way Nevada extends to the west and the Pacific Coast near Mexico slants to the east. Regularizing irregular shapes is a shortcut we use unconsciously for organizing and representing information in memory. Such shortcuts are generally useful, but they can lead to errors.

Thinking Depends on Categorization of Concepts

Much of our thinking, such as the idea of where San Diego and Reno are, reflects visual and verbal representations of objects in the world. It also reflects what you know about the world. Say that you are shown a drawing of a small yellow object and asked to identify it. Your brain forms a mental image (analogical representation) of a lemon and provides you with the word *lemon* (symbolic representation). So far, so good.

But picturing a lemon and knowing its name do not tell you what you can do with a lemon. You also know that certain parts of a lemon are edible and that lemon juice usually tastes strong and sour. This additional information helps you know that you can make lemonade by diluting the juice with water and adding sugar. In short, what you know about a lemon and how you think about it influences what

FIGURE 8.3

Mental Maps Can Be Inaccurate
In our mental maps, we cannot represent all analogical and symbolic information with perfect accuracy. As a result, our mental maps sometimes lead us to incorrect thinking. For example, San Diego is actually farther east than Reno.

you do with a lemon. How do we organize representations of objects so that we can think about them—and interact with them—effectively and efficiently?

SCHEMAS AND THE CATEGORIZATION OF CONCEPTS Recall from Chapter 7 that our long-term memories are organized based on schemas. Schemas are our prior knowledge and experience with information. Schemas are also related to the organization of analogical and symbolic representations in our minds. To understand the relationship between schemas and representations, consider two musical situations: a country music dance (**Figure 8.4a**) and a symphony orchestra performance (**Figure 8.4b**).

First, schemas are useful because many of the most commonly encountered situations have consistent attributes. For example, you might expect to see guitars and fiddles at a country music dance, but you probably don't expect to see them in an orchestral concert. There, you would expect to see violins and trumpets instead. Second, schemas are useful because people have specific roles within the context of a situation. Your country music schema would include people dancing, but your orchestral schema would not include dancing. Finally, schemas are useful because they allow us to think efficiently about objects by categorizing them.

When we use a schema to group things based on shared properties, we create a *category* about the information. For example, based on the schema for Types of Music, we can create these two categories: Country Music Instruments and Orchestral Music Instruments (**Figure 8.5a**). Some instruments might exist in just one category or the other (the guitar is used in country bands, and the trumpet is used in orchestras). However, other instruments belong in both categories. For example, the violin, which is used in orchestras, is the same thing as a fiddle, which is used in country music.

Besides creating a category with several things together, we also create a **concept** to store unique knowledge about each specific member of a category (**Figure 8.5b**). For example, our concept of a guitar includes the knowledge that it "usually has six strings and is played by plucking." Our concept of a trumpet is based on knowing that "it is made of brass tubing and it is played by blowing into it." A concept can include knowledge about a relation between items (such as "violins are smaller than guitars" or "watermelons are heavier than lemons"). Or it can consist of information about certain dimensions of each item (such as pitch or sweetness).

(a)

(b)

FIGURE 8.4

Schemas About Types of Music Events
Our experiences with music create memories that are organized into schemas.
(a) Because of our schemas about country music concerts, we expect to see guitars and fiddles and people dancing.
(b) Because of our schemas about orchestral music concerts, we expect to see violins and trumpets and people sitting still while listening.

concept
A mental representation of objects, events, or relations around common themes.

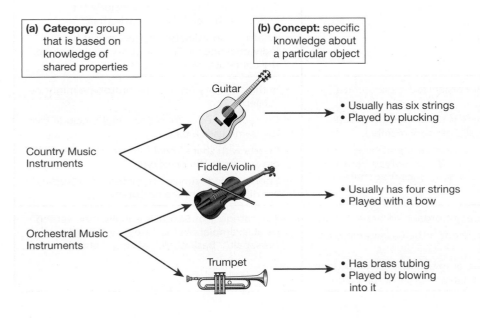

(a) Category: group that is based on knowledge of shared properties

(b) Concept: specific knowledge about a particular object

Guitar
- Usually has six strings
- Played by plucking

Country Music Instruments

Fiddle/violin
- Usually has four strings
- Played with a bow

Orchestral Music Instruments

Trumpet
- Has brass tubing
- Played by blowing into it

FIGURE 8.5

Schema for Types of Music Includes Categories and Concepts
(a) Schemas allow us to group objects into categories based on shared properties. In our example, we might have two categories for instruments. **(b)** In turn, categories are made up of concepts, which are stored information about each unique object. The category of Country Music Instruments might include the concept "guitar." The category of Orchestral Music Instruments might include the concept "trumpet."

One concept can be stored in more than one category. For example, "fiddle/violin" is used in both country music and orchestral music.

defining attribute model
A way of thinking about concepts: A category is characterized by a list of features that determine if an object is a member of the category.

In sum, then, we use a common theme to group information by categorizing concepts together based on their similarities and differences. The common theme is a schema. This grouping method is a very efficient way to organize information in our minds, because it ensures that we do not have to store every instance of an object, relationship, or dimension individually. Instead, we store concepts based on the properties shared by certain items, or particular ideas.

There is evidence that specific regions of the brain are dedicated to processing certain concepts. Recall from Chapter 2 that the fusiform face area is a cortical area at the intersection of the brain's temporal and occipital lobes. The fusiform face area is especially responsible for processing faces. Recent fMRI research has also revealed that different areas in the occipital and temporal lobes of the brain are specialized for processing concepts about animals and tools (Martin & Chao, 2001). As described in **Table 8.1,** three models explain how concepts are organized into categories to allow us to think about objects.

DEFINING ATTRIBUTE MODEL According to the **defining attribute model** of concepts, each concept is characterized by a number of attributes that are necessary for an object to be a member of a category. For the category of Musical Instruments, the defining attributes would include "is a device that produces sound" and "is used to make music" (**Figure 8.6**). We can then organize musical instruments into a hierarchy of subordinate categories based on the type of instrument, such as Wind Instruments or String Instruments. So "guitar" is a concept. This concept is part of the subordinate category of String Instruments. The concept belongs in that category because of the attributes of guitar, which includes "has six strings," "strings can be plucked or strummed," and so on.

TABLE 8.1

Models of Organizing Concepts

MODEL	WAY OF CATEGORIZING CONCEPTS	EXAMPLE FOR THE CATEGORY "SPORTS"
Defining attribute model	• Concepts are organized in hierarchical categories. • Concepts are characterized by attributes (features) necessary for an object to be a member of a category. • No one concept in the category is a better fit than any other.	• The category of Sports refers to "an athletic activity, often competitive, requiring physical skill." • One subordinate category could be Team Sports. This category could include the concepts "baseball" and "basketball." • Another subordinate category might be Individual Sports. This category could include the concepts "skiing" and "surfing."
Prototype model	• Concepts are organized in hierarchical categories. • The prototype is the concept that is the "most typical" category member. • Other concepts are categorized as similar or different from the prototype based on how many characteristics they share with the prototype.	• In the category Sports, the prototype might be "baseball." • Characteristics of "baseball" might include that the game uses a ball. • Sports with shared characteristics ("basketball") are similar to the prototype. • Sports with dissimilar characteristics ("surfing") are different from the prototype.
Exemplar model	• Concepts are not organized hierarchically. • No single concept is the best member of a category. • All examples, or exemplars, of concepts in a category equally represent the category.	• The category of Sports is equally represented by all exemplars in the category (including "baseball," "basketball," "surfing," etc.).

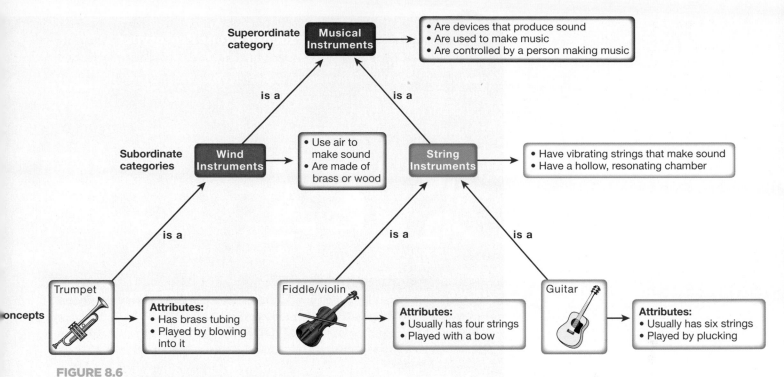

FIGURE 8.6

The Defining Attribute Model of Concepts

In the defining attribute model, each concept is associated with certain attributes that are necessary for that object to be a member of a category. The concept "guitar" is characterized by having strings that are plucked to produce music. Because of these attributes, the concept "guitar" belongs to the subordinate category of String Instruments.

The defining attribute model is appealing, but it doesn't reflect the reality of how we organize representations in our minds. Consider the instruments used in the musical *Stomp*. The performers make music with many unconventional objects, such as trash cans and brooms (**Figure 8.7**). According to the defining attribute model, there are three reasons that we should never consider these objects to be instruments. First, the model suggests that a concept, such as a trash can, either belongs in a category or, in this case, does not. But *Stomp* shows us that the real answer is more like "it depends on how you use the object." Second, this model suggests that each attribute is equally important in defining a category. But our trash can example shows how in reality we may perceive that "is used to make music" is the most important attribute for membership to the category of Musical Instruments. Lastly, the model says that all members fit into the category equally well. But if we decide that a trash can is a part of the category Musical Instruments, you probably still think a guitar is a better example of that category.

PROTOTYPE MODEL An alternative to the defining attribute model of concept organization is the **prototype model.** According to this model, concepts are organized based on the "most typical member," or prototype, of a category. The most typical member has certain characteristics. We decide whether an item belongs in the category by comparing its characteristics to those of the prototype (see Try It Yourself on p. 274).

For example, many people consider an orange to be the prototypical concept for the category of Fruit. Oranges have seeds, are edible, and taste sweet, so items that

FIGURE 8.7

The Unusual Musical Instruments in *Stomp*

The musical *Stomp* demonstrates that we can use unusual objects, such as trash cans and broomsticks, to make music. The defining attribute model does not explain how we can do this.

prototype model
A way of thinking about concepts: Within each category, there is a best example—a prototype—for that category.

TRY IT YOURSELF: Identify Your Prototypes

Please answer the following two questions. Then check the answers printed upside down. Lastly, read the explanations to understand your thought processes.

Questions:

1. Think of "a bird." What comes to your mind?

2. Now think of "a hero." What comes to mind? (Based on Decyk, 1994.)

Typical Answers:

Black Mask (China)   Superman (U.S.)   Kiwi (New Zealand)   Robin (U.S.)

Explanations of Thought Processes:

What we think is a prototypical concept varies, and it depends on our life experiences. However, within a culture, people will be fairly consistent in choosing what they consider is the best representation of a category.

1. So, if you live in the United States, you probably thought of a bird such as a robin or a sparrow. For you, these examples are most likely prototypical birds because they are among the best members of the category of Birds. However, if you live in New Zealand, you might have thought of a different bird—for example, a kiwi.

2. For a hero, most people in the United States think of a superhero, such as Superman or Spider-Man. Some people think of a "real" hero, such as a police officer or a firefighter. Few people think of a woman, a child, or an animal, all of whom can be heroes. People from China tend to think of Black Mask, a superhero popular in that country.

share most or all of these characteristics are also considered Fruit (**Figure 8.8**). Concepts that don't share many of these traits are not thought of as members of that category. Thus most people do not think of tomatoes and olives as fruits, even though they are. The same idea applies to Musical Instruments. A trash can has few traits in common with what might be thought of as a prototypical Musical Instrument, such as a guitar. Nevertheless, *Stomp* once again shows us that a trash can might be considered a musical instrument, because it does produce musical sounds. It is just a non-prototypical instrument.

One positive feature of the prototype model is that it is very flexible in allowing concepts to be members of a category even when they may not be a great representation of the category. So, an olive is a fruit even though it doesn't have many of the characteristics of an orange (see Figure 8.8). A drawback of this flexibility is that

FIGURE 8.8

The Prototype Model of Concepts
According to the prototype model, some concepts in a category are prototypes. That is, they are more representative of that category than are other concepts in the category. For this reason, an orange seems to be the prototype of the category Fruit. By contrast, olives do not seem to be very representative of the category.

		Oranges	Grapes	Tomatoes	Olives
Characteristics	Seeds	✓	✓	✓	
	Edible	✓	✓	✓	✓
	Sweet	✓	✓		

a specific person may choose a prototype as the best representation of a category for many different reasons. For example, an orange may be considered as the prototype of fruit because it is the most common member of that category. Or it may be because it represents a combination of the typical attributes in the category. Unfortunately, the prototype model cannot distinguish between these possibilities.

EXEMPLAR MODEL The **exemplar model** addresses this flexibility concern in the prototype model by suggesting that a category has no single concept as its best representation. Instead, people form a fuzzy representation based on their experiences. That is, all the concepts in a category form the basis for the category. The concepts are called *exemplars*. And the exemplar model accounts for the observation that some category members are more prototypical than others: The prototypes are simply concepts that we have encountered more often.

For instance, your representation of cats is made up of all the cats you have encountered in your life. If you see an animal in a house, you compare this animal with your memories of other animals you have encountered. If it more closely resembles the cats you have encountered (as opposed to the dogs, squirrels, rats, and other animals), you conclude it is a cat—even if it is an odd-looking cat (**Figure 8.9**). Similarly, according to this model, all types of instruments, including trash cans, are equally good exemplars of the category Musical Instruments.

STEREOTYPES The defining attribute, prototype, and exemplar models all explain how we use schemas to categorize concepts and how we represent these concepts in our minds. But in our daily lives, our knowledge and thinking about concepts extends well beyond a simple list of facts about objects. To demonstrate this capacity, let's return to the example of the country music dance and the orchestral concert.

When you first looked at each of the pictures in Figure 8.4, did any particular thoughts enter your mind about one or the other? For example, maybe you thought that only wealthy people listen to orchestral music. Or maybe you thought about how country music is uplifting and easy to dance to. Thus, although our schemas enable us to think efficiently about related concepts, they can lead to generalizations about events, objects, and people. These generalizations are called **stereotypes.** As shown in the Scientific Thinking feature, schemas cause us to begin developing stereotyped thinking at a very young age.

One common stereotype, described in Chapter 4, pertains to gender roles. Gender roles are the socially prescribed behaviors for females and males (**Figure 8.10a**). They represent a type of schema that operates at the unconscious

FIGURE 8.9
The Exemplar Model of Concepts
The exemplar model holds that all members of a category are exemplars. For example, even this strange-looking feline—a brown tortie, white, and tabby sphinx—is an exemplar of the category of Cats.

exemplar model
A way of thinking about concepts: All concepts in a category are examples (exemplars); together, they form the category.

stereotypes
Cognitive schemas that allow for easy, fast processing of information about people, events, or groups, based on their membership in certain groups.

(a)   (b)

FIGURE 8.10
Schemas and Stereotypes
(a) Many people have this schema about gender roles: Men work to provide for the family, and women stay at home and raise the children. However, this schema leads to stereotyping about what roles men and women play in a family. **(b)** Increasingly, however, men are staying home with the children while women work outside the home.

Hypothesis: Preschoolers' behaviors will reveal stereotyped thinking based on schemas about how adults use alcohol and tobacco.

Research Method: Children used props and dolls to act out a social evening for adults. As part of the role play, each child selected items from a miniature grocery store stocked with 73 different products. The items on the shelves included beer, wine, and cigarettes.

Results: Out of 120 children, 34 (28 percent) "bought" cigarettes, and 74 (62 percent) "bought" alcohol. Children were more likely to buy cigarettes if their parents smoked. They were more likely to buy beer or wine if their parents drank alcohol at least monthly or if they viewed PG-13 or R-rated movies in which adults were pictured drinking.

Conclusion: Children's play behavior suggests they are highly attentive to the use and enjoyment of alcohol and tobacco and have well-established expectations about how cigarettes and alcohol fit into social situations. Observation of adult behavior, especially parental behavior, may influence preschool children to develop these stereotypes to view smoking and drinking as normal in social situations. These stereotypes may then relate to behaviors adopted later in life.

level. In other words, we follow gender roles without consciously knowing we are doing so. For example, when children and teens are asked to draw a scientist, very few draw women, because they unconsciously associate being a scientist with being male (Chambers, 1983).

One reason we need to become aware of how schemas direct our thinking about concepts is that they may unconsciously cause us to act on our stereotypes. For example, until fairly recently, orchestra conductors invariably chose men for principal positions because the conductors believed that women did not play as well as men. The schema of women as inferior musicians interfered with the conductors' ability to rate women objectively at auditions. However, experience has the power to change schemas and overcome stereotypes. After recognizing this bias, the top North American orchestras began holding auditions with the musicians hidden behind screens and their names withheld from the conductors. Since these methods were instituted, the number of women in orchestras has increased considerably (Gladwell, 2005). When we are all aware of how our schemas influence our thinking, we can do our best to overcome this unconscious tendency to stereotype (**Figure 8.10b**).

- Thinking is manipulating mental representations of objects we encounter in our environment.

- In thinking, we use analogical representations, which usually correspond to images, and symbolic representations, which usually correspond to words or ideas.

- Concepts are symbolic representations of items that are categorized on the basis of defining attributes, prototypes, or exemplars.

- Schemas, mental representations that are organized based on experience and knowledge, allow for efficient thinking but can lead to stereotypes.

8.2 How Do We Make Decisions and Solve Problems?

📖 LEARNING GOALS	✏️ READING ACTIVITIES LEARN
a. Remember the key terms about reasoning, decision making, and problem solving.	List all of the boldface words and write down their definitions.
b. Understand the three main biases in decision making.	Explain in your own words how heuristics, framing, and the paradox of choice can lead to faulty decision making.
c. Apply problem solving strategies to your life.	Provide two examples of problem solving in your life and describe what strategy you used to solve each of them.
d. Understand the three strategies for overcoming obstacles in problem solving.	Summarize in your own words the three ways that changing representations helps overcome obstacles in problem solving.

What to eat for breakfast, what to wear, what time to leave for work or class—these choices may not be life changing, but they are examples of the many decisions you make throughout every day. You also solve problems, such as figuring out how to organize the paper you're writing or how to break bad news to someone. In the previous section, we looked at how we represent and organize our knowledge about the world. How do we use that knowledge to guide our daily actions? Thinking enables us to make decisions and solve problems.

Sometimes the terms *reasoning, decision making,* and *problem solving* are used interchangeably, but they are not really the same thing. In **reasoning,** you determine if a conclusion is valid. To do so, you use information that you believe is true. For example, your friend has concluded that the boy band One Direction is the greatest singing group of all time. What information would you consider in judging whether that conclusion is valid? In this case you probably use *informal reasoning*—for example, based on people's opinions, hearsay, or how often you hear the band's songs on the radio. By contrast, psychologists engage in *formal reasoning* by using the standardized and objective procedures of the scientific method to collect empirical evidence and test hypotheses to see if they are valid (see Chapter 1). In this case, the opinions of others and hearsay are not relevant.

reasoning
Using information to determine if a conclusion is valid or reasonable.

FIGURE 8.11

Decision Making and Problem Solving
Two forms of thinking that are experienced in our daily lives: **(a)** decision making and **(b)** problem solving.

(a)

You use **decision making** to select between options. In 2008, a 9-month-old girl's uncle had to decide whether to carry her through a burning apartment building or drop her several stories into the arms of a police officer waiting below. The uncle said, "I looked into his eyes and saw that he would catch her. Then I let her go."

(b)

You use **problem solving** to overcome obstacles. For example, how did this man solve the problem of getting out of the corner he painted himself into?

We see this contrast between informal and formal reasoning quite often in our daily lives. You might choose a spot for a holiday based on the opinions of your friends (informal reasoning) or based on research that you do to find out the temperature, cost, and available activities (formal reasoning). Similarly, physicians often lament that their patients reject weight-loss regimens and other medical therapies that are supported by science, but they readily accept ones supported by personal testimonials of friends and family (Diotallevi, 2008).

Decision making is another form of thinking. In this case, you select among alternatives (**Figure 8.11a**). Usually, you identify important criteria and determine how well each alternative satisfies these criteria. For example, say you need to choose between taking a course in psychology or a course in another topic. What criteria would you use in making this decision?

Problem solving is yet another form of thinking. In general, you have a problem when a barrier or a gap exists between where you are and where you want to be. To solve the problem, you overcome obstacles to move from your present state to your desired goal state (**Figure 8.11b**). For example, if you decide to enroll in the psychology class, but it conflicts with another course in your schedule, you have a problem that you must solve, perhaps by dropping the conflicting class.

How We Think Biases Decision Making

In the 1970s, Amos Tversky and Daniel Kahneman spearheaded research to identify the ways that people make everyday decisions. In particular, they investigated why many of our decisions are not based on perfect logic. Instead, our decisions are based on processes that enable us to make decisions quickly—that is, without taking time to consider all the possible pros and cons. In recognition of this important research, Kahneman received the 2002 Nobel Prize in Economic Sciences. (Tversky was deceased when the prize was awarded.)

Now let's look at a typical everyday decision. Imagine that you have a round pool and you want a cover for it. How can you decide what size of pool cover to buy?

decision making
Attempting to select the best alternative among several options.

problem solving
Finding a way around an obstacle to reach a goal.

One rational way to answer this question is by thinking about the area of the circle that is the pool's opening. For example, you could multiply pi (3.1416) by the radius of the pool squared. This formula, which you may remember from algebra, is an *algorithm* for calculating the area of a circle. An algorithm is a set of procedures to follow when thinking and making a decision. When followed correctly, the algorithm will always yield the correct result. In this case, the area of the circle you're looking to find is the opening of the pool. But would you actually use this algorithm to decide on the pool cover size?

Instead, you might note whether the pool is small, medium, or large. You would then choose a cover by matching what is available at the store to what you think the size of your pool is. This approach is not completely rational, nor is it guaranteed to produce the correct result. But as Kahneman and Tversky revealed, this type of thinking leads us to make "rule of thumb" decisions that are generally fine—good enough in our daily lives.

HEURISTICS When we use a rule of thumb as an informal way to make a decision, we are using what is known as a **heuristic.** We may not even be aware of taking these mental shortcuts, because heuristic thinking often occurs unconsciously. But heuristics are useful because they require minimal cognitive resources. They allow us to focus our attention on other things. Heuristic thinking is also adaptive, because it allows us to make decisions quickly rather than weighing all the evidence each time we have to decide. Tversky and Kahneman identified several heuristics that we commonly use to make decisions in our daily lives. Let's consider two of them.

The *availability heuristic* is the tendency to make a decision based on information that comes most easily to mind. In other words, we tend to rely on information that is easy to retrieve (**Figure 8.12**). Consider this question: In most industrialized countries, are there more farmers or more librarians? If you live in an agricultural area, you probably said farmers. If you live in an urban area, you probably said librarians. Most people who answer this question think of the librarians they know about and the farmers they know about. If they can retrieve many more instances in one category, they assume it is the larger category. In fact, most industrialized countries have many more farmers than librarians. Because people who live in cities and suburbs tend not to meet many farmers, they are likely to believe there are more librarians. Another way to think about availability is as the prototype that comes to mind (i.e., it is readily available in memory) when we think about a specific concept. This kind of thinking implies that we tend to rely on prototypes in making decisions.

The *representativeness heuristic* also reveals that we make decisions based on prototypes. This heuristic is the tendency to place people or objects in a category if they are similar to the concept that is the prototype. We use this heuristic when we base a decision on how closely each option matches what we already believe. For example, say that Helena is intelligent, ambitious, and scientifically minded. She enjoys working on mathematical puzzles, talking with other people, reading, and gardening. Would you guess that she is a cognitive psychologist or a postal worker? Most people, employing the representativeness heuristic, would guess that Helena is a cognitive psychologist because her characteristics better match their prototype of psychologists.

The representativeness heuristic can lead to faulty reasoning if we fail to take other information into account. One very important bit of information is the *base rate,* which is how frequently an event occurs. For example, there are many more postal workers than cognitive psychologists, so the base rate for postal workers

FIGURE 8.12
The Availability Heuristic
In 2012, Hurricane Sandy damaged parts of New Jersey. Most people remembered the news footage of devastation, so tourists decided to vacation elsewhere. Atlantic City had to launch an advertising campaign to combat this availability heuristic and show that the boardwalk was repaired and the casinos were open for business. Only then did tourists start returning to the city.

heuristic
A shortcut (rule of thumb or informal guideline) used to reduce the amount of thinking that is needed to make decisions.

FIGURE 8.13

The Impact of Framing on Decision Making

The framing of the gas prices makes it seem very attractive to pay in cash in order to get the discount. What if the sign at a competing gas station stated that if you used a credit card to pay for the gas, there would be an additional charge of five cents per gallon? Which gas station would you buy gas from?

framing
How information is presented affects how that information is perceived and influences decisions.

(a)

(b)

is higher than that for cognitive psychologists. Therefore, any given person, including Helena, is much more likely to be a postal worker. People generally do not pay much attention to base rates in reasoning, focusing instead on whether the information is more representative of one prototype or another. Although Helena's traits may be more representative of cognitive psychologists overall, they also likely apply to a large number of postal workers.

As Tversky and Kahneman demonstrated, heuristics result in biases, and biases may lead to errors. Consider the commonly believed heuristic that a high price equals high quality. Although laboratory studies show that one type of soap is basically as good as any other, many consumers believe that "fancy" soaps are superior. Unfortunately, we cannot be aware of every heuristic we rely on. But we can be aware of frequently used ones, such as the availability and representativeness heuristics. Once we know that such shortcuts can lead us to make faulty judgments, we can use heuristics more carefully as we seek to make rational decisions.

FRAMING If we are completely rational in how we make decisions, then we should consider the possible alternatives and choose the one with the most value. For example, would you be more likely to buy a package of ground beef if it were described as "75 percent lean" or if it were described as "25 percent fat"? If you are like most people, you find the first description much more appealing, and so you would be likely to purchase that meat (Sanford, Fay, Stewart, & Moxey, 2002). But in reality, the information on each label is the same—it is just presented in a different way. (In other words, "75 percent lean" means "25 percent fat.") So people should choose each alternative equally. But we don't, which shows that we do not always make decisions rationally. Instead, the way information is presented can alter how we perceive and make decisions about it. This effect is known as **framing.** Framing can significantly influence decision making in a variety of situations (**Figure 8.13**).

THE PARADOX OF CHOICE Five hundred cable channels! Fifty choices at a restaurant buffet! Thirty different styles of running shoes to choose from! What more could we ask for? In Western cultures, not being able to choose violates our sense of freedom. But when too many options are available, especially when all of them are attractive, we experience conflict and indecision.

Although some choice is better than none, too much choice can be frustrating and unsatisfying, and ultimately it can impair our thinking (Schwartz, 2004). This effect was demonstrated in a study where shoppers at a grocery store were presented with a display of either 24 or 6 varieties of jam to sample (Iyengar & Lepper, 2000). The shoppers also received a discount coupon for any variety of jam. The greater variety attracted more shoppers, but it failed to produce more sales. Only 3 percent of shoppers at the display with many choices bought jam (**Figure 8.14a**). By contrast, 30 percent of the shoppers at the display with

FIGURE 8.14

Too Much Choice

As part of Iyengar and Lepper's study, **(a)** one display presented 24 jams, and **(b)** the other display presented 6 jams. Bar-code labels on the jars indicated whether people bought more from one group of jams or the other. The results indicated that having many possibilities can make it difficult to choose one item.

We tend to believe that the more options we have, the better. But it can be frustrating to select a cereal when the supermarket has a hundred choices. Having too much choice can also be harmful in our personal lives.

Historically, people were set in their careers, married, and having children before age 25. In modern industrialized nations, young adults now delay these life decisions for years as they explore options in careers and possible mates (Grossman, 2005). With so many choices, young adults may spend years trying to find the right job and the perfect life partner.

But according to psychologist Barry Schwartz, having nearly unlimited choice may be related to an increase in clinical depression in modern countries: "If virtually every choice you make fails to live up to expectations and aspirations [you will come to] the conclusion that you can't do anything right" (2004, p. 215). So what can we do to avoid this problem?

Schwartz divides people into *satisficers* and *maximizers*. Satisficers live according to a philosophy of "good enough," choosing an option that most closely matches what they want. They do not go through every apple to find the very best one, nor do they date every available person to choose a life partner. Satisficers tend to be happy with their choices, perhaps because they did not strive to make the perfect decision.

By contrast, maximizers devote a lot of time and effort to making the best decisions. They feel paralyzed when they have to select between equally attractive choices and they question the choice they finally make. As a result, they generally are more disappointed with their decisions and are more likely to experience regret.

Schwartz believes that to be more satisfied with life, we should make choices that meet our needs even if those choices are not the best. And we should focus on the positive aspects of our decisions. In fact, making daily decisions based on satisficing saves time and mental energy and helps us avoid feeling disappointed. In our personal lives, satisficing can help us to feel happy enough with the choices we made so we don't dwell on bad decisions and suffer adverse mental health effects.

USING PSYCHOLOGY IN YOUR LIFE:

How to Make Decisions When There Are Too Many Choices

limited choices bought jam (**Figure 8.14b**). In a later study, the same investigators found that people choosing among a small number of chocolates were more satisfied with the products they selected than were people who chose from a wider variety.

We Solve Problems to Achieve Goals

How do you get into your car when you have locked the keys inside? How can you make enough money to spend your spring break somewhere nice? What do you have to do to get a grade of A in this course? Our thoughts are often focused on our goals and how to achieve them. Even so, there aren't always simple and direct means of attaining a particular goal. We must use knowledge to determine how to move from our current state to the goal state, and we must use good strategies to overcome obstacles. How we think about the problem can help or hinder our ability to find effective solutions.

SUBGOALS Once we have identified a goal, how do we get to it? How do we proceed from one step to the next to the next, what errors do we typically make in negotiating tricky or difficult steps, and how do we decide on more efficient (or, in some cases, less efficient) solutions? In many cases, solving the problem requires breaking the task into *subgoals*. Reaching each subgoal will result in achieving the

FIGURE 8.15

The Tower of Hanoi Problem
(a) Try to solve the Tower of Hanoi problem. You can use a quarter, a nickel, and a penny, and a sheet with three dots on it to represent the three pegs.
(b) The way to solve this problem, and many others, is by creating and meeting several subgoals.

(a)

The goal: Move the disks to the peg on the other end. You can move only one disc at a time. You cannot place a larger disc on top of a smaller disc.

(b)

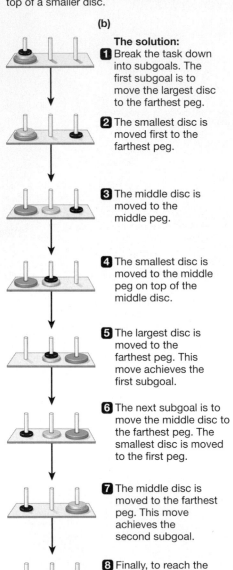

The solution:
1 Break the task down into subgoals. The first subgoal is to move the largest disc to the farthest peg.

2 The smallest disc is moved first to the farthest peg.

3 The middle disc is moved to the middle peg.

4 The smallest disc is moved to the middle peg on top of the middle disc.

5 The largest disc is moved to the farthest peg. This move achieves the first subgoal.

6 The next subgoal is to move the middle disc to the farthest peg. The smallest disc is moved to the first peg.

7 The middle disc is moved to the farthest peg. This move achieves the second subgoal.

8 Finally, to reach the main goal, the smallest disc is moved to the farthest peg.

main goal of solving the problem. You can see a classic example of this method in **Figure 8.15.**

Using subgoals is important for many problems. Suppose a high school senior has decided she would like to become a doctor. To achieve this goal, she needs first to attain the more immediate subgoal of being admitted to college. To get into college, she needs to meet another subgoal: earning good grades in high school. This subgoal would require developing good study skills and paying attention in class. Breaking down a problem into subgoals is an important component of problem solving. When you are facing a complex problem and the next step is not obvious, identifying the appropriate steps or subgoals and their order can be challenging. Let's consider some approaches you can follow.

WORKING BACKWARD When the appropriate steps for solving a problem are not clear, proceeding from the goal state to the initial state can help yield a solution. This process is called *working backward*. Consider the water lily problem (Fixx, 1978, p. 50):

Water lilies double in area every 24 hours. On the first day of summer there is only one water lily on the lake. It takes 60 days for the lake to be completely covered in water lilies. How many days does it take for half of the lake to be covered in water lilies?

One way to solve this problem is to work from the initial state to the goal state: You figure that on day 1 there is one water lily, on day 2 there are two water lilies, on day 3 there are four water lilies, and so on, until you discover how many water lilies there are on day 60 and you see which day had half that many. It will take you quite a while to solve the problem this way. But consider what happens if you work backward, from the goal state to the initial state. If on day 60 the lake is covered in water lilies and water lilies double every 24 hours, then half the lake must have been covered in water lilies on day 59. In this case, working backward helps you solve the problem more quickly and easily.

ANALOGY Imagine that a surgeon needs to use a laser at high intensity to destroy a patient's tumor. The surgeon must aim the laser very precisely to avoid destroying healthy surrounding tissue. This example poses a very difficult problem. The problem cannot be solved by using subgoals or working backward (**Figure 8.16a**).

The surgeon remembers reading a story about a general who wanted to capture a fortress. The general needed to move a large number of soldiers up to the fortress, but all the roads to the fortress were planted with mines. A large group of soldiers would have set off the mines, but small groups could travel safely. So the general divided the soldiers into small groups and had each group take a different road to the fortress, where the groups converged and attacked together.

Because the surgeon's problem has constraints analogous to the general's problem, she gets the idea to aim several lasers at the tumor from different angles. By itself, each laser will be weak enough to avoid destroying the living tissue in its path. But the combined intensity of all the converging lasers will be enough to destroy the tumor (**Figure 8.16b**).

Finding an appropriate *analogy* for a problem can help us achieve our goals, the way it did for the surgeon (Reeves & Weisberg, 1994). Analogous solutions work, however, only if we recognize the similarities between the problem we face now and those we have solved before (Keane, 1987; Reeves & Weisberg, 1994).

SUDDEN INSIGHT Often, we do not recognize that something is a problem until it seems unsolvable and we feel stuck. For example, it is only when you spot the

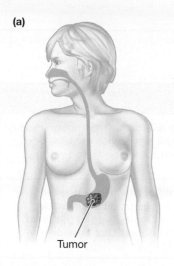
(a)

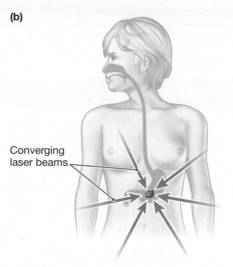
(b)

Converging
laser beams

Tumor

The goal: A surgeon must use a laser at high intensity to destroy a tumor deep inside a patient's body without destroying healthy surrounding tissue.

The solution: The surgeon recalls a story of a general with a similar problem. She uses the story as an analogy to solve her problem. Based on this analogy, she uses several laser beams at a lower intensity but aims them all to converge on one area.

FIGURE 8.16
Using Analogies
(a) Try to solve this tumor problem. It may help you to return to p. 282 and read the next paragraph of the text, which discusses a similar problem—the "fortress problem." **(b)** The solution to the fortress problem is an analogy that can be applied to solving the tumor problem.

keys in the ignition of your locked car that you know you have a problem. As you stand there pondering the problem for a period of time, a solution may pop into your head. *Insight* is the metaphorical lightbulb that goes on in your head when you suddenly realize the solution to a problem.

In 1925, the Gestalt psychologist Wolfgang Köhler conducted one of psychology's most famous studies on insight. Convinced that some nonhuman animals could behave intelligently, Köhler studied whether chimpanzees could solve problems. He placed bananas beyond a chimp's reach and provided objects that the chimp could use to reach the bananas. Could the chimp figure it out (**Figure 8.17**)?

First the chimp just jumped at the bananas. That didn't work. Then the chimp began a period of repeatedly looking at the bananas and walking around to the objects in the enclosure. Finally, the chimp began to use the objects to get at the food. Eventually, the chimp was able to stack up several boxes and stand on them to reach the bananas. Köhler argued that these actions were examples of insight. Having solved the problem, the chimps transferred the solution to new, similar problems and solved them quickly. These additional solutions confirmed that the chimp's behavior had resulted from insight learning (see Chapter 6).

Table 8.2 summarizes how we can use subgoals, working backward, analogies, and insight to help us solve many problems. But some problems are harder to solve than others. Sayings such as "think outside the box" have become clichés (at least in Western cultures) for how we might go about solving difficult problems. Let's look next at what this approach actually involves.

We Overcome Obstacles to Solve Problems

"Have you heard about the new restaurant that opened on the moon? It has great food but no atmosphere!" The premise of this joke is that *atmosphere* means one thing in the restaurant schema but something else in the context of the moon. Humor often violates an expectation, such as the meaning of *atmosphere*. To "get" the joke, we have to rethink some common representation. We can think of getting a joke as a kind of problem solving. In problem solving, we often need to revise a mental representation to overcome an obstacle to thinking successfully.

FIGURE 8.17
Insight in Chimpanzees
Chimpanzees try to solve problems, such as reaching bananas that are too high.

The goal: The chimpanzees want to reach the bananas, which are out of reach.

The solution: As shown here, the chimp in Köhler's study seemed to suddenly realize a solution. It stacked several boxes on top of each other and stood on them to reach the bananas. This behavior suggested that the chimp solved the problem through insight.

TABLE 8.2

Problem Solving Techniques

TECHNIQUE	CHARACTERISTICS	SAMPLE PROBLEM	SOLUTION
Subgoals	Identify the goal state and several subgoals to be achieved.	Talia wants to repair the car muffler, but she doesn't have enough money to pay for repairs.	To reach the goal of having enough money for repairs, she researches the best price, cuts spending for a month, and works more.
Working backward	Begin from the goal state and work backward to the current state.	Bradley wants to graduate in 2 years, but he isn't sure what courses he needs to take.	First he identifies the credits needed to graduate, then the credits needed per term, then the credits needed this term, and finally the classes that provide the needed credits for this term.
Analogy	Identify a previously solved problem that is similar to the current problem.	Roberto cooks beef with broccoli, but the broccoli ends up soggy.	He thinks about how, when he mows the lawn with his shirt on, his shirt gets damp with sweat. In the same way, moisture from the beef ruins the broccoli. Next time, he cooks the beef and broccoli separately, then combines them.
Insight	Take a break from actively thinking about the problem.	Amelia has a hard time solving a difficult calculus problem.	She puts the problem away for a while. When she returns later on, the answer pops into her mind.

restructuring

Thinking about a problem in a new way in order to solve it.

RESTRUCTURING One strategy that problem solvers commonly use to overcome obstacles is **restructuring** the problem. This technique consists of representing the problem in a novel way. Ideally, the new mental view reveals a solution that was not visible under the old problem structure. The revelation leads to the sudden "Aha!" moment that is characteristic of insight.

In one now-famous study, Scheerer (1963) gave each participant a sheet of paper that had a square of nine dots on it (**Figure 8.18a**). The task was to connect all nine dots, using at most four straight lines, without lifting the pencil off the page. As shown in **Figure 8.18b,** one solution is to literally think outside the box: to realize that keeping the lines within the box is not a requirement. People don't usually realize this. Instead, they tend to think that the lines must stay within the box, even

(a) **The goal:** Connect the dots by using at most four straight lines. Most participants consider only solutions that fit within the square formed by the dots.

(b) **The solution:** Restructure the mental representation to include solutions in which the lines can extend beyond the boundary formed by the dots.

FIGURE 8.18

The Nine-Dot Problem

(a) Cover part (b) of this figure and then try solving this difficult problem. **(b)** By restructuring the problem in a new way, you can solve it more easily.

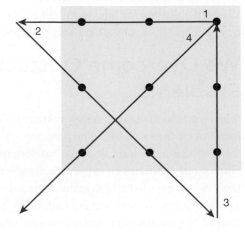

though that restriction is never explicitly stated. Solving the problem requires restructuring the representation by eliminating assumed constraints.

OVERCOMING MENTAL SETS In trying to solve a problem, we commonly think back to how we have solved similar problems. We tend to persist with previous strategies. These established ways of thinking are known as **mental sets.** Mental sets are often useful because they may save us the time and effort of searching for new types of solutions. But sometimes they make it difficult to find the best solution. Consider this question: What happens once in June, once in July, and twice in August? If you are like most people, you are probably trying to think of various summertime activities or events that happen more in August than in June or July. But the correct answer is "the letter *u*." Thinking about things that happen during summer months leads you to expect the question to be about events, not the letters that make up the words. If this happened to you, then you have just experienced the effects of a mental set.

OVERCOMING FUNCTIONAL FIXEDNESS In a 1954 study, Karl Duncker gave participants a candle, a pack of matches, a box of tacks, and the following challenge: *Using only these objects, attach the candle to the wall in such a way that the candle can be lit and burn properly* (**Figure 8.19a**). Can you think of how this might be done?

Most people have difficulty in coming up with an adequate solution. They struggle because they have mental representations about the typical functions of particular objects. This kind of obstacle is called **functional fixedness.** To overcome functional fixedness, we need to reinterpret the objects' potential functions (**Figure 8.19b**). If the participants in Duncker's study reinterpret the function of the tack box, a solution emerges: The side of the box can be tacked to the wall so that it creates a stand. The candle is then placed on the box and lit. In general, participants have difficulty viewing the box as a possible stand when it is being used as a container for the tacks. When participants are shown representations of this problem with an empty box and the tacks on the table next to the box, they solve the problem somewhat more easily.

In general, people who have excellent thinking skills can demonstrate the abilities to create, change, and manipulate internal representations to make decisions and solve problems. These abilities are just one reason that Phiona Mutesi, discussed in the chapter opener, excels at playing chess. However, do Phiona's thinking skills mean that she is intelligent? So far in this chapter, we have considered how we use knowledge when we think. Now it's time to consider what it means to think intelligently.

✓ 8.2 CHECKPOINT: How Do We Make Decisions and Solve Problems?

- Reasoning is evaluating information, arguments, and beliefs to draw a conclusion. Reasoning can be informal or formal.

- Decision making is often faulty because it is based on using heuristics or framing. The paradox of choice contributes to the difficulty of decision making.

- In problem solving, we overcome obstacles to reach a goal by using subgoals, analogy, and/or insight, or by working backward.

- We can solve difficult problems by restructuring the representation and overcoming mental sets and functional fixedness.

FIGURE 8.19
Overcoming Functional Fixedness
(a) Try to solve the candle problem.
(b) To solve this difficult problem, people must overcome functional fixedness.

(a)

The goal: Attach the candle to the wall using only a pack of matches and a box of tacks.

(b)

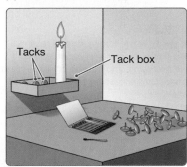

The solution: The box for the tacks can be used as a stand for the candle, and the candle can be lit with the matches.

LEARN

mental sets
A tendency to approach a problem in the same way that has worked in the past, which may make it harder to solve a problem.

functional fixedness
A tendency to think of things based on their usual functions, which may make it harder to solve a problem.

8.3 What Is Intelligence?

LEARNING GOALS	✏️ READING ACTIVITIES LEARN
a. Remember the key terms about intelligence.	List all of the boldface words and write down their definitions.
b. Understand general intelligence.	Explain in your own words how general intelligence is based on the single-factor model as revealed by IQ scores.
c. Apply the four theories of multiple intelligences to your life.	Provide four examples of intelligence in people you know, basing each example on a different theory of multiple intelligences.
d. Analyze the contributions of nature and nurture to the development of your own intelligence.	Identify one way that your intelligence has been influenced by nature and another way that it has been influenced by nurture.

intelligence
The ability to use knowledge to reason, make decisions, make sense of events, solve problems, understand complex ideas, learn quickly, and adapt to environmental challenges.

Look at the people in **Figure 8.20.** Which of these people do you believe are intelligent? You may believe that only some of the people are intelligent, or that they are all intelligent but in different ways. How did you make your decision about who is intelligent?

Sometimes our thinking leads to great ideas and creative discoveries. At other times our thinking leads to bad decisions and regret. Some people seem to be better at thinking about and using knowledge than others, and we often say those people are intelligent. Thus **intelligence** is the ability to use knowledge to reason, make

(a)

Albert Einstein developed the general theory of relativity. He is considered by many to be the "father of modern physics." His intelligence quotient (IQ) is thought to have been 160.

(b)

The contestants at the 2012 Scripps National Spelling Bee demonstrated their spelling skills. They drew on their knowledge of word meanings, word origins, and the rules and irregularities of English.

(c)

The rapper, songwriter, producer, and actor Eminem is one of the best-selling musicians in the world. In July 2012, Eminem became the first person to reach 60 million "friends" on Facebook.

(d)

In 2012, the Austrian skydiver Felix Baumgartner successfully free fell from Earth's stratosphere, from a height of 28,000 feet.

(e)

The talk-show host, media mogul, and philanthropist Oprah Winfrey is arguably one of the most influential women in the world. She was the first African American billionaire.

FIGURE 8.20

Who Is Intelligent?
Which of these people are intelligent? Why do you think so?

decisions, make sense of events, solve problems, understand complex ideas, learn quickly, and adapt to environmental challenges. In other words, intelligence is complex and multifaceted.

One General Factor May Underlie Intelligence

We all know people who are especially talented in some areas but weak in others. For example, someone may write brilliant poems but cannot solve difficult calculus problems. Is it correct to say he is intelligent? The question is whether intelligence reflects one overall talent or many individual ones.

IQ SCORES REVEAL INTELLIGENCE If you have ever taken an intelligence test, you no doubt noticed that it included many different types of questions concerning math, English, and other knowledge and skills. As a result of your performance on the test, you were given one overall score, called an **intelligence quotient,** or **IQ.** Modern intelligence tests, which we discuss later in the chapter, are all variants of the first assessment of intelligence, developed by the psychologist Alfred Binet and his collaborator Theodore Simon, in the early 1900s (**Figure 8.21**).

The French government encouraged Binet to identify children in the French school system who needed extra attention and special instruction. Binet proposed that intelligence is best understood as a collection of high-level mental processes. Accordingly, Binet and Simon developed a test for measuring each child's vocabulary, memory, skill with numbers, and other mental abilities. The result was the Binet-Simon Intelligence Scale.

One assumption underlying the test was that each child might do better on some components by chance, but how the child performed on average across the different components would indicate his or her overall level of intelligence. Indeed, Binet found that scores on his tests were consistent with teachers' beliefs about the children's abilities. They were also consistent with the children's grades.

The result was an intelligence test with many different types of questions that yielded a single IQ score. This type of test reflects the theoretical idea that one general factor underlies intelligence. Indeed, recall from the chapter opener that Heidi Hankins has an extremely high IQ score. As a result of that score, Heidi was admitted to Mensa, the international society for people with extremely high intelligence. Look back at Figure 8.20 to see which of the people is considered intelligent based partly on his IQ score.

GENERAL INTELLIGENCE Charles Spearman (1904) used statistical methods to investigate scores on the various types of questions in intelligence tests. Spearman found that people who scored high on one type of item also tended to score high on other types of items. In general, people who are very good at a specific ability, such as math, are also good at other abilities, such as writing, problem solving, and other mental challenges. Spearman viewed **general intelligence** as the single, common factor that contributes to performance on any intellectual task (**Figure 8.22**). In his view, general intelligence tends to yield higher IQ scores on intelligence tests.

Intelligence is due to one general factor.

Binet
Intelligence quotient

FIGURE 8.21

Alfred Binet
Binet, depicted here with a child research participant, launched the approach of assessing intelligence by using the intelligence quotient.

intelligence quotient (IQ)
An index of intelligence originally computed by dividing a child's estimated mental age by the child's chronological age, then multiplying this number by 100.

general intelligence
The idea that one general factor underlies intelligence.

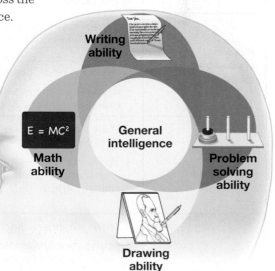

FIGURE 8.22

General Intelligence: A Single Factor of Intelligence
As depicted in this cluster of overlapping ovals and circle, Spearman viewed general intelligence as the single factor of intelligence. This underlying factor influences an individual's specific abilities related to intelligence, such as writing and math.

fluid intelligence
Intelligence that reflects the ability to process information, particularly in novel or complex circumstances.

crystallized intelligence
Intelligence that reflects both the knowledge a person acquires through experience and the ability to use that knowledge.

multiple intelligences
The idea that people have many different types of intelligence that are independent of one another.

Moreover, research has shown that general intelligence influences important life outcomes. For example, things that are affected by general intelligence, such as performance in school and at work, can influence everything from socioeconomic status to health. Indeed, general intelligence may directly affect our health. As medical knowledge rapidly advances and becomes more complex, trying to keep up with and process all this new information is a challenge. People who are higher in general intelligence have an advantage in meeting that challenge. Those with higher scores on intelligence tests may be more literate about health issues, accumulate greater health knowledge, follow medical advice, and understand the link between behavior and health (Gottfredson, 2004a). This provocative idea warrants further investigation because it could have important implications for the medical system and the way doctors communicate medical advice.

There May Be Multiple Aspects of Intelligence

Most psychologists agree that some form of general intelligence exists. But researchers also recognize that intelligence can be characterized in alternative ways. Let's look at some of the theories of intelligence and how they compare with the model of general intelligence, as summarized in **Table 8.3.**

TABLE 8.3
Theories of Intelligence

MODEL	KEY CHARACTERISTICS	EXAMPLE
General intelligence	• There is a single factor underlying intelligence. • This factor tends to yield higher IQ scores.	• Marisol's high IQ score reveals that she has high general intelligence.
Fluid and crystallized intelligence	• General intelligence is made up of fluid and crystallized intelligence. • Fluid intelligence: thinking quickly and flexibly in novel, complex situations. • Crystallized intelligence: knowledge from experience that is used to solve problems.	• Michael shows fluid intelligence when he quickly and calmly thinks of another way to present his data after his laptop dies. • Elena's strong crystallized intelligence helps her know the answers to crossword puzzles.
Multiple intelligences	• Many intelligences are not measurable by IQ tests. • These intelligences include musical, bodily-kinesthetic, linguistic, mathematical/logical, spatial, intrapersonal, and interpersonal.	• Brian can play any tune on his guitar after hearing it once. He is probably high in musical intelligence. • Shanice shows high intrapersonal intelligence when she creates a study plan based on knowledge of her own study habits.
Triarchic theory	• There are three aspects of intelligence. • Analytical intelligence: skill in solving problems and puzzles. • Creative intelligence: ability to think in new and interesting ways. • Practical intelligence: skill in dealing with everyday tasks.	• Viktor shows strong analytical intelligence because he is a highly strategic chess player. • John shows creative intelligence because he can survive anywhere with just a few dollars in his pocket. • Zahara may be low in practical intelligence because she constantly loses her car keys.
Emotional intelligence	• Emotional intelligence: skills in managing emotions and recognizing them in other people.	• When Glynnis feels herself getting angry with her boss, she takes a walk so she can calm down. She likely has high emotional intelligence.

FLUID AND CRYSTALLIZED INTELLIGENCE Raymond Cattell (1971) proposed that general intelligence actually consists of two specific types of intelligence (**Figure 8.23**). **Fluid intelligence** involves information processing, especially in novel or complex circumstances, such as reasoning, drawing analogies, and thinking quickly and flexibly. In contrast, **crystallized intelligence** involves knowledge we acquire through experience, such as vocabulary and spelling (look back at Figure 8.20b) and cultural information, and the ability to use this knowledge to solve problems (Horn, 1968; Horn & McArdle, 2007). Fluid intelligence is somewhat analogous to working memory, whereas crystallized intelligence is somewhat analogous to long-term memory. Because both fluid and crystallized intelligence are components of general intelligence, people who score high on one factor also tend to score high on the other. This finding suggests that strong crystallized intelligence is likely aided by strong fluid intelligence.

MULTIPLE INTELLIGENCES Whereas Cattell argued that fluid and crystallized intelligence both contribute to general intelligence, Howard Gardner (1983) proposed a theory of **multiple intelligences.** Gardner identified several different types of intellectual talents that are independent of one another (**Figure 8.24**). For example, he proposed that *musical intelligence* enables some people to discriminate subtle variations in pitch or in timbre and therefore to have above average musical abilities (see Figure 8.20c). Among the other intelligences Gardner proposed are *bodily-kinesthetic* (the ability of athletes and dancers to control their motions with exquisite skill, as shown in Figure 8.20d), *linguistic* (excellent verbal skills), *mathematical/logical* (the ability to calculate and think sequentially), *spatial* (thinking in terms of images and pictures), *intrapersonal* (self-understanding), and *interpersonal* (social understanding).

Gardner's theory is important partly because it recognizes that people can be average or even deficient in some aspects of intelligence and outstanding in others. According to Gardner, each person has a unique pattern of intelligences. No one should be viewed as "smarter" than others, just differently talented. Some psychologists find this is a feel-good philosophy with little basis in fact. These critics have questioned whether being able to control body movements or compose music is truly a form of intelligence or should instead be considered a specialized talent. Does clumsiness or tone deafness indicate a lack of intelligence?

There are still no standardized ways to assess many of Gardner's intelligences. In fact, Gardner believes that standard testing methods cannot capture the true essence of different types of intelligence. Thus, to support his theory, Gardner

Fluid intelligence   **Crystallized intelligence**

FIGURE 8.23

Multiple Intelligences: Fluid and Crystallized Intelligence
Cattell saw general intelligence as made up of two types of intelligence. Fluid intelligence represents working memory processes and information processing that allow us to think quickly and flexibly. Crystallized intelligence pertains to information in long-term storage, such as knowledge we acquire through experience, including vocabulary and spelling.

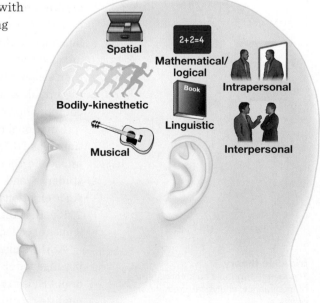

FIGURE 8.24

Multiple Intelligences: Gardner's Theory of Multiple Intelligences
Howard Gardner has theorized that people have many types of intelligence that are independent of each other.

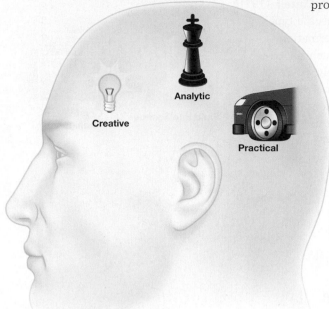

FIGURE 8.25
Multiple Intelligences: Sternberg's Triarchic Theory
Robert Sternberg has theorized that intelligence can take three forms: analytical, practical, and creative.

triarchic theory
The idea that people have three types of intelligence: analytical, creative, and practical.

provides examples of people who have exhibited particular talents, such as the artist Pablo Picasso, the dancer Martha Graham, the physicist Albert Einstein, and the poet T. S. Eliot. Each of these figures was especially talented in his or her field. What contradicts Gardner is that these people were also talented in many respects, and all were high in general intelligence (Gottfredson, 2004b). By contrast, many of us can think of someone we know who is very skilled in one particular way, for example in playing a certain sport, but who may not have shown high general intelligence in academic endeavors or on intelligence tests.

Another psychologist who proposed there are different types of intelligence is Robert Sternberg. Sternberg theorized (1999) that people have three types of intelligence, which he described in his **triarchic theory** (**Figure 8.25**). *Analytical intelligence* is similar to that measured by standard intelligence tests—being good at problem solving, completing analogies, figuring out puzzles, and similar challenges. *Creative intelligence* involves the ability to gain insight and solve novel problems—to think in new and interesting ways. *Practical intelligence* refers to dealing with everyday tasks, such as knowing whether a parking space is large enough for your vehicle, being a good judge of people, being an effective leader, and so on.

Evidence for the existence of multiple intelligences is that many phenomenally successful public figures did not excel academically. For example, Oprah Winfrey was born in poverty, became a teen mother, and has no college degree. Nevertheless, she has become one of the most influential women in the world as a media proprietor, talk-show host, actress, producer, and philanthropist. Arguably, her vast accomplishments are a result of intelligence in several domains, including analytical, creative, and practical intelligence (see Figure 8.20e).

EMOTIONAL INTELLIGENCE *Emotional intelligence (EI)* was conceived by the psychologists Peter Salovey and John Mayer and subsequently popularized by the science writer Daniel Goleman. This form of intelligence consists of four abilities: managing our own emotions, using our emotions to guide our thoughts and actions, recognizing other people's emotions, and understanding emotional language (Salovey & Grewel, 2005; Salovey & Mayer, 1990). People high in EI are good at understanding emotional experiences in themselves and others, then responding to those emotions productively. Regulating our moods, resisting impulses and temptations, and controlling our behaviors are all important components of EI.

Emotional intelligence is correlated with the quality of people's personal relationships (Reis et al., 2007). The idea of emotional intelligence has had a large impact in schools and industry, and programs have been designed to increase students' and workers' emotional intelligence. These efforts may be valuable, since emotional intelligence is a good predictor of high school grades (Hogan et al., 2010). In addition, people high in emotional intelligence cope best with the challenges of college exams (Austin, Saklofske, & Mastoras, 2010).

At the same time, some critics have questioned whether EI really is a type of intelligence or whether it stretches the definition of intelligence too far. Whether or not EI is a type of intelligence, the concept highlights the idea that many human qualities are important and advantageous for those who have them.

Salma had a particular interest in reading about criminals. She looked for online collections of such stories, such as *Slate's* feature "Dumb Criminal of the Week." After reading one story, she wondered, *How could someone rob a house but leave his own cell phone behind? How is criminality related to intelligence? Committing any crime is not smart. But if I were going to commit a crime, I think I'd be more clever about it.*

In considering these issues, Salma applied some of the knowledge she'd learned in her psychology class. *How would a researcher find a link between IQ and criminal behavior?* On the Web, she found many articles about such a link. According to research studies covered in the articles, there was a negative correlation between IQ and criminal behavior. There was also a negative correlation between IQ and violent/aggressive behavior. In other words, as intelligence went up, criminal behavior and violent/aggressive behavior went down. *But these are correlations. Could the link be causal? And if the link is causal, which way does the causality work? Does having a low IQ cause people to commit crimes, or does committing crimes cause people's IQs to decrease?*

The problem was that these variables could not be tested directly. In other words, neither criminal behavior nor IQ could be manipulated. *And let's not even begin to think about outside variables, such as life stress and neighborhood characteristics. But experimentation isn't possible without manipulation, and causal explanations can't be determined without an experiment. What if we looked at IQ and criminal behavior over time, as in a longitudinal study?* Although an experiment can best help determine if outside variables are at work, Salma thought a longitudinal study could at least nail down which factor came first in time.

At *Motherjones.com,* she found a 2013 article by Kevin Drum. This piece discussed lead as an outside variable. Lead didn't cause both IQ and crime. But it appeared to cause lower IQ, and lower IQ then might have resulted in more criminal behavior. Drum discussed research that linked childhood lead exposure, even at low levels, to deficits in IQ. These links seemed related to two different trends over the last few decades: the decline in the use of leaded gas (and in car emissions with lead) and the fall of crime rates. Since the 1970s, the use of leaded gas had declined. Since the 1990s, crime rates had decreased substantially. *So let's think about this link. When kids were growing up in the '70s, they were exposed to more lead. This exposure may have negatively*

affected their IQs. When these same kids grew up, their deficits in IQ may have been associated with committing crimes. If these links are true, that's one possible reason why crime rates have fallen in the past few decades. My generation was not exposed to as much lead as my parents' and grandparents' generations were!

According to Drum, lead exposure and criminal behavior might not have been linked just through decreases in IQ. Lead exposure resulted in a loss of white matter in the brain—*and white matter speeds the brain's communication with itself, so it's part of intelligence.* But lead exposure also resulted in a loss of gray matter. Gray matter might be lost especially in the prefrontal cortex, which is responsible for reasoning and impulse control—*and impulse control helps prevent us from committing crimes. What do these findings add up to? IQ may be part of the reason for criminal behavior, but other brain functioning may matter too.*

Salma also liked this word of caution from Drum: "Needless to say, not every child exposed to lead is destined for a life of crime. Everyone over the age of 40 was probably exposed to too much lead during childhood, and most of us suffered nothing more than a few points of IQ loss." But how could we really judge the effects of all the substances we ingested? And how could we calculate the effects of all the IQ points lost across populations? Salma found herself pondering further research possibilities on pollutants, psychology, and society.

Intelligence Is a Result of Genes and Environment

Think back to Heidi Hankins, discussed in the chapter opener. Does showing exceptional intelligence very early in her life mean that Heidi was born with a certain amount of intelligence? Is everyone born with particular intelligence, or is intelligence a product of how we are raised and the environment we are in?

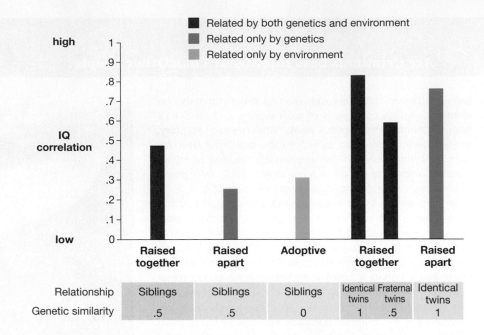

FIGURE 8.26

Genes and Intelligence
This graph represents average IQ correlations obtained from family, adoption, and twin study designs. Siblings raised together show more similarity than siblings raised apart or siblings who are adopted and raised together. However, as shown by the red and blue bars on the right, the highest correlations are found among identical twins, whether they are raised in the same household or not. Overall, the greater the degree of genetic relation, the greater the correlation in intelligence.

To understand intelligence, we must once again return to questions of nature and nurture and examine the effects of genes and the environment on influencing intelligence.

Consider one example: Humans have a genetic capacity for having a large vocabulary, but every word in a person's vocabulary is learned in a particular environment (Neisser et al., 1996). Moreover, the specific words we learn are affected by the culture where we are raised, the amount of schooling we receive, and our general social context. Thus even if intelligence has a genetic component, the way we express intelligence is affected by our circumstances. Instead of seeking to demonstrate whether nature or nurture is the more important factor, psychologists try to identify how each crucial factor contributes to intelligence.

BEHAVIORAL GENETICS As we saw in Chapter 2, behavioral geneticists study the genetic basis of behaviors and traits such as intelligence. Many twin and adoption studies have made it clear that genes help determine intelligence, but it is hard to measure the extent of genetic effects (**Figure 8.26**). For example, studies show that twins raised apart are highly similar in intelligence. Though this finding seems to support the importance of genetics in the development of intelligence, it fails to consider the ways people interact with and alter their environments. Even when raised apart, twins might have similar experiences (Flynn, 2007). Suppose the twins have inherited a higher than average verbal ability. Adults who notice this ability might read to the twins more often and give them more books. The "intelligence gene" has eluded researchers, probably because thousands of genes contribute to intelligence and each one of them has only a small effect (Plomin & Spinath, 2004).

ENVIRONMENTAL FACTORS Recall from Chapter 4 that a variety of factors influence our development before we are born as well as when we are infants and children. These factors also affect the development of intelligence. For example, we know that poor nutrition can affect brain development and result in lower

(a)   (b)

FIGURE 8.27

Optimal Environments Help Develop Intelligence

There are many ways that parents can provide an enriched environment that will support the development of intelligence in their children. Good practices include **(a)** reading books to children and **(b)** providing children with intellectual opportunities from a young age.

intelligence. Other environmental influences that can lead to lower intelligence include prenatal factors (e.g., the parents' intake of drugs and alcohol) and post-natal factors (e.g., family, social class, education, cultural beliefs, and our own drug and alcohol use). On the positive side, an enriched environment can aid in the development of intelligence in many ways (**Figure 8.27**).

For instance, breast-feeding during infancy has been shown to enhance cognitive development. Two large studies—following more than 3,000 people from birth to age 18 or 27—found that breast-feeding for more than 6 months produced a 5- to 7-point difference in IQ (Mortensen, Michaelsen, Sanders, & Reinisch, 2002). There is also an apparent relation between birth weight and intelligence later in life (Shenkin, Starr, & Deary, 2004; **Figure 8.28**).

Not surprisingly, the intellectual opportunities a child receives affect intelligence. For instance, schooling encourages the development of children's brains and cognitive capacities. As Stephen Ceci (1999) notes, the more years that children remain in school, the higher their IQs will be. And students who start school at a younger age because of where their birth dates fall on the calendar have higher test scores than their same-age peers who start school a year later. Schooling not only builds knowledge. Schooling also teaches critical thinking skills, such as being able to think abstractly and learn strategies for solving problems (Neisser et al., 1996). Overall, the evidence is considerable that environmental factors contribute to intelligence.

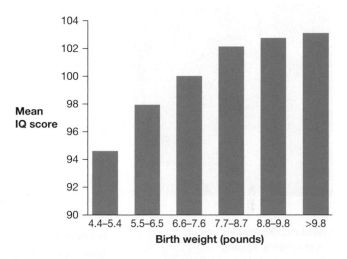

Mean IQ score (y-axis: 90, 92, 94, 96, 98, 100, 102, 104)

Birth weight (pounds) (x-axis: 4.4–5.4, 5.5–6.5, 6.6–7.6, 7.7–8.7, 8.8–9.8, >9.8)

FIGURE 8.28

Birth Weight and Intelligence

For children whose birth weight is within the normal range, IQ scores increase along with birth weight.

 8.3 CHECKPOINT: What Is Intelligence?

- General intelligence is the idea that a single unifying factor underlies intelligence.

- Alternative theories state that people have many intelligences, such as fluid and crystallized intelligence, multiple intelligences, the three intelligences included in triarchic theory, and emotional intelligence.

- Behavioral genetics has demonstrated that genes influence intelligence. However, environmental factors also influence intelligence.

8.4 How Do We Measure Intelligence?

📖 **LEARNING GOALS**	✏️ **READING ACTIVITIES**	**LEARN**
a. Remember the key terms about how intelligence is measured.	List all of the boldface words and write down their definitions.	
b. Analyze the three common types of psychometric tests of intelligence.	Distinguish how the three common types of psychometric tests are similar and different.	
c. Understand the relationship between cognitive performance and intelligence.	Describe in your own words three ways in which cognitive performance reveals intelligence.	
d. Apply the concept of stereotype threat to the real world.	Provide an example of how you have experienced stereotype threat in your life or seen it in others.	

FIGURE 8.29

Standardized Procedures in Psychometric Testing

All psychometric tests, including achievement tests, aptitude tests, and intelligence tests, are standardized tests. They are administered in a consistent way and have procedures to allow for objective scoring. These students are taking the SAT for their applications to college.

reliability
How consistently a psychometric test produces similar results each time it is used.

validity
How well a psychometric test measures what it is intended to measure.

achievement test
A psychometric test that is designed to test what knowledge and skills a person has learned.

aptitude test
A psychometric test that is designed to test a person's ability to learn—that is, the person's future performance.

We have considered a number of theories of what intelligence is. But as we saw in Chapter 1, to determine whether a theory is valid, we have to test it scientifically. Ever since Alfred Binet began to investigate intelligence in France in the early 1900s, Binet's work has formed the basis for the development of psychometric tests that accurately measure intelligence.

Intelligence Is Assessed With Psychometric Tests

All *psychometric tests* have some features in common. They are standardized tests, designed to be given in a consistent way, with uniform procedures for scoring in an objective way (**Figure 8.29**). In other words, psychometric tests must have **reliability:** People's results should be similar each time they take the test. In addition, psychometric tests must have **validity:** They should measure what they claim to measure—a specific aspect of intelligence.

However, psychometric tests differ based on the specific aspect of intelligence they are supposed to measure. Psychometric tests fall into three main categories that measure slightly different, but overlapping, aspects of intelligence: achievement tests, aptitude tests, and intelligence tests.

ACHIEVEMENT AND APTITUDE TESTS To be admitted to college, you may have taken a test such as the ACT or the SAT. These two different types of psychometric tests measure different aspects of intelligence. A standardized **achievement test** assesses current skills and knowledge. The ACT is an achievement test that measures the knowledge you acquired in high school. Another achievement test is the exam taken by U.S. schoolchildren every three years, as mandated by the federal No Child Left Behind Act (2001).

By contrast, the SAT is a standardized **aptitude test** that measures your ability to learn in the future. Various aptitude tests are also used to predict what tasks people will perform with skill. Employers sometimes use aptitude tests to determine whether a prospective employee will be successful in a certain position. For both achievement and aptitude tests, the stakes can be high because people's performances can greatly affect their lives.

TRY IT YOURSELF: IQ Test Items

You can experience questions from an IQ test yourself by answering the example items below (similar to those used in the WAIS III).

1. The verbal portion of IQ tests contains questions about knowledge and language.
   a. General Knowledge: What day of the year is Independence Day in the United States?
   b. Vocabulary: What does *corrupt* mean?
   c. Comprehension: Why do people buy home insurance?
2. The performance portion of IQ tests includes nonverbal tasks.
   a. Picture Arrangement: The pictures below tell a story. Put them in the right order to tell the story.

   b. Object Assembly: If these pieces are put together correctly, they make something. Put them together as fast as you can.

   c. Digit-Symbol Substitution: Using the code below, fill in the missing information in the test picture.

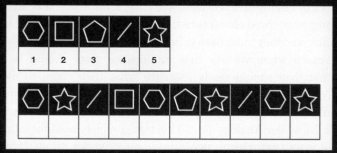

INTELLIGENCE TESTS Ever since Binet designed his original method of measuring intelligence in 1904, several modern intelligence tests have been developed. In 1919, the psychologist Lewis Terman, at Stanford University, modified the Binet-Simon test and established normative scores (average scores for each age) for American children. This test—commonly known as the Stanford-Binet test—remains among the most widely used intelligence tests for children in the United States. In 2003, the test was revised for the fifth time.

In 1939, the psychologist David Wechsler developed an intelligence test for use with adults. The Wechsler Adult Intelligence Scale (WAIS)—the most current version is the WAIS-IV, released in 2008—has two parts, as illustrated in Try It

mental age
An assessment of a child's intellectual standing compared with that of same-age peers; determined by comparing the child's test score with the average score for children of each chronological age.

Yourself. Each part consists of several tasks. The *verbal* part measures aspects such as comprehension, vocabulary, and general knowledge. The *performance* part involves nonverbal tasks, such as arranging pictures in proper order, assembling parts to make a whole object, and identifying a picture's missing features.

INTELLIGENCE QUOTIENT An intelligence score is based on how correctly people answer questions on intelligence tests. Binet's original test assessed a child compared with same-age peers. Binet introduced the important concept of **mental age.** This measure is determined by comparing a child's test score with the average score for children of each chronological age.

Say an 8-year-old gets right most of the test questions that other 8-year-olds get right, but does not correctly answer questions that a 9-year-old gets right. Binet would characterize that child as having a mental age of 8. If the 8-year-old can correctly answer most of the questions an average 10-year-old would get right, he would have a mental age of 10. When the child's chronological age equals his mental age, this result indicates that the child's intelligence is typical of children in his age group.

The psychologist Wilhelm Stern refined Binet's scoring system by developing the intelligence quotient. A child's IQ is computed by dividing the child's mental age by the child's chronological age and multiplying the result by 100. To calculate the IQ of the 8-year-old with a mental age of 10, for instance, we calculate $(10/8) \times 100$. The result is 125, a very high IQ.

The formula breaks down when used with adults, however. Therefore, the IQs of adults are measured in comparison with the average adult and not with adults at different ages. Today, the average IQ is set at 100. Across large groups of people, the distribution of IQ scores forms a bell curve. The bell curve is also known as a *normal distribution*. Most people are close to the average. Fewer and fewer people score at the tails of the distribution (**Figure 8.30**).

VALIDITY AND RELIABILITY How do we know that intelligence tests are actually good indicators of intelligence? As we noted earlier, for psychometric tests to be useful, they must have three characteristics: They must be standardized, they must have reliability, and they must have validity.

What do we mean when we say that intelligence tests should be valid? We are saying that they should really measure what they claim to measure (**Figure 8.31a**). To explore the validity of intelligence tests, researchers analyzed data from 127 different studies. As part of these 127 studies, more than 20,000 participants took the Miller Analogy Test. This test is widely used for admission to graduate school as well as for hiring decisions in many work settings. It requires test takers to complete analogies such as "Fingers are to hands as toes are to ____."

FIGURE 8.30

The Distribution of IQ Scores
IQ is a score on a normed test of intelligence. That is, each person's score is relative to the scores of the large number of people who already took the test. The average, or mean, score on intelligence tests is 100. As shown in this bell curve, approximately 68 percent of people have an IQ score between 85 and 115.

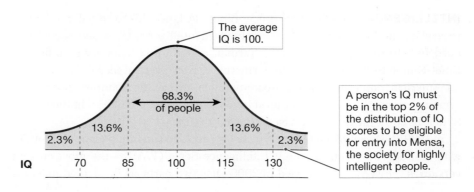

The average IQ is 100.

68.3% of people

13.6%   13.6%
2.3%   2.3%

IQ   70   85   100   115   130

A person's IQ must be in the top 2% of the distribution of IQ scores to be eligible for entry into Mensa, the society for highly intelligent people.

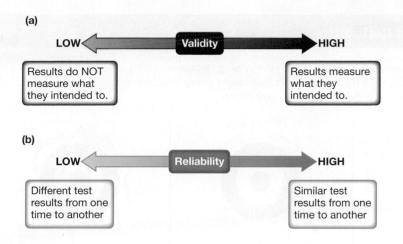

(a)

LOW ◄———— Validity ————► HIGH

Results do NOT measure what they intended to.

Results measure what they intended to.

(b)

LOW ◄———— Reliability ————► HIGH

Different test results from one time to another

Similar test results from one time to another

FIGURE 8.31
Validity and Reliability
An intelligence test that is a good indicator of intelligence has two key aspects.
(a) Good intelligence tests must have validity. That is, they should measure what they intend to: intelligence. **(b)** Good intelligence tests must also have reliability. In other words, people should score similarly each time they take the test.

The researchers found that scores on the Miller Analogy Test predicted not only graduate students' academic performances but also individuals' productivity, creativity, and job performance in the workplace (Kuncel, Hezlett, & Ones, 2004). The data suggest modest correlations between IQ and work performance, IQ and income, and IQ and jobs requiring complex skills.

By contrast, if an intelligence test has reliability, the results for a person will be stable and consistent over time. That is, someone who takes the same intelligence test multiple times should have a similar score each time (**Figure 8.31b**). Reliability is tied to validity. If a test is valid, then it will also be reliable. But even when a test is reliable, it is not necessarily valid. You can get the same score on a test over many trials, whether or not the test actually measures what it is supposed to measure. The relationship between reliability and validity is summarized in the Learning Tip on p. 298.

Even when an IQ test is a valid, reliable measurement of general intelligence, it is not always an accurate predictor of success in school or work. In fact, additional factors contribute to life success (Neisser et al., 1996). For example, people from privileged backgrounds tend to have higher IQs. However, they also tend to have other advantages, such as family contacts, access to internships, and acceptance to schools that can cater to their needs. Even if two people have more or less equal IQ and social background, the person working twice as many hours per week may have a better chance of accomplishing his goals (Lubinski, 2004). Another study found that children's self-control was much better than IQ in predicting final grades (Duckworth & Seligman, 2005). In other words, IQ may be important, but it is only one of the factors contributing to success in the classroom, the workplace, and life generally.

CULTURAL BIAS One important criticism of intelligence tests is that they may penalize people who belong or don't belong to particular cultures or groups. That is, doing well on intelligence tests often requires knowing the language and culture of the mainstream.

For instance, consider this analogy:

STRING is to GUITAR as REED is to

a. TRUMPET

b. OBOE

c. VIOLIN

d. TROMBONE

This graphic provides an analogy that will help you understand the relationship between validity and reliability in intelligence tests. Just as the goal in archery is to hit the red bull's-eye target every time, the goal of an intelligence test is to measure intelligence as it was designed to do every time.

ARCHERY ANALOGY	**Valid:** The shots <u>did hit</u> the intended target. **Reliable:** Repeated shots <u>did result</u> in very similar outcomes.	**Not valid:** The shots <u>did not hit</u> the intended target. **Reliable:** Repeated shots <u>did result</u> in very similar outcomes.	**Not valid:** The shots <u>did not hit</u> the intended target. **Not reliable:** Repeated shots <u>did not result</u> in very similar outcomes.
TRANSFER TO INTELLIGENCE TESTS	**Valid:** The test <u>did measure</u> intelligence as it was designed to do. **Reliable:** Repeated testing <u>did result</u> in very similar IQ scores.	**Not valid:** The test <u>did not measure</u> intelligence as it was designed to do. **Reliable:** Repeated testing <u>did result</u> in very similar IQ scores.	**Not valid:** The test <u>did not measure</u> intelligence as it was designed to do. **Not reliable:** Repeated testing <u>did not result</u> in very similar IQ scores.

Are you familiar with all these instruments? Do you know what a reed is? To solve this analogy, you need to know that an oboe uses a reed to make music, just as a guitar uses strings to make music. If you were not exposed to this information, you could not answer the question.

In addition, some words mean different things to different groups. How we answer a test item is determined by the meaning of that item in our culture. When Randy Jackson described someone's performance on *American Idol* as "da bomb," he did not mean she "bombed," or did badly. He meant it was "cool"—which did not mean it was cold. And so on. A person's exposure to mainstream language and mainstream culture affects which meaning of a word comes most quickly to mind, or even if she knows the meaning at all.

What it means to be intelligent also varies across cultures. Most measures of IQ reflect values of what is considered important in modern Western culture, such as being quick-witted or speaking well. But what is adaptive in one society is not necessarily adaptive in others. One approach to dealing with cultural bias is to use items that do not depend on language. The nonverbal performance measures on the WAIS, for example, may be a more neutral way to test intelligence. Other culture-neutral tests show a series of patterns and ask the test taker to identify the missing pattern (**Figure 8.32**).

The task is to identify the missing shape in this sequence.

Choose from the eight shapes below to complete the sequence above:

The solution is the first triangle in the bottom row.

FIGURE 8.32

Removing Bias From Tests

According to the creators of this test, the task should not yield differences in intelligence based on a person's culture. However, you should be a bit skeptical of this claim, because it is not easy to remove all cultural biases from tests.

In general, it is difficult to detect and quantify the bias in intelligence assessments. It is also difficult to remove all forms of bias from testing. For example, doing well on tests, among them IQ tests, simply matters more to some people in some cultures than it does to others. This situation tends to yield more favorable test results for those people who wish to do well.

Intelligence Is Associated With Cognitive Performance

Psychometric tests provide a good way to measure IQ based on the premise that intelligence is a single factor. But as we've seen, other models propose that intelligence has multiple aspects. In the late 1800s, the scientist Sir Francis Galton believed that intelligence was related to the speed of neural responses and the sensitivity of sensory/perceptual systems. The smartest people, Galton believed, had the quickest responses, keenest perceptions, and most efficient brains. Other psychologists believe that intelligence is supported by cognitive processes such as mental processing, working memory, and attention. How can such aspects of intelligence be measured?

SPEED OF MENTAL PROCESSING People who do not seem very intelligent are sometimes described as "a bit slow." Though that description may sometimes be hurtful, it actually might be accurate. People who score lower on intelligence tests consistently respond more slowly on tests of reaction time than those who score higher on intelligence tests (Deary, 2000). Psychologists test reaction time in two ways.

A test of *simple reaction time* might require you to press a computer key as quickly as possible whenever a stimulus appears on the screen. For example, "Press the X key every time you see an X." A more difficult test might require you to choose, again as quickly as possible, the correct response for the stimulus presented. For example, "Press the X key every time you see an X, or press the A key every time you see an A." Scores on intelligence tests are related even more strongly to this *choice reaction time* (Jensen, 1998).

WORKING MEMORY AND ATTENTION General intelligence scores are also closely related to working memory (Conway, Kane, & Engle, 2003). Many studies of the relationship between working memory and intelligence differentiate between simple tests of memory and memory tests that require some form of secondary processing. On a simple test of memory, you would be asked to listen to a list of words and then repeat the list in the same order (**Figure 8.33a**). Performance on these tests is related only weakly to general intelligence (Engle, Tuholski, Laughlin, & Conway, 1999). In contrast, memory tests that have two components show a strong relation between working memory and general intelligence (**Figure 8.33b**; Gray & Thompson, 2004; Kane, Hambrick, & Conway, 2005; Oberauer, Schulze, Wilhelm, & Süß, 2005).

The link between working memory and general intelligence may be attention. Paying attention, especially while being bombarded with competing information or other distractions, enables you to stick to a task until you complete it successfully (Engle & Kane, 2004). The

FIGURE 8.33
Memory Tasks
(a) In a simple test of memory, a participant listens to a short list of words and then repeats the words in order. **(b)** Memory tests that have two components show a stronger association between working memory and general intelligence. In this case, a participant has to solve math operations as words are presented. Once again, the person has to repeat the words in the order they are presented (adapted from Conway et al., 2003).

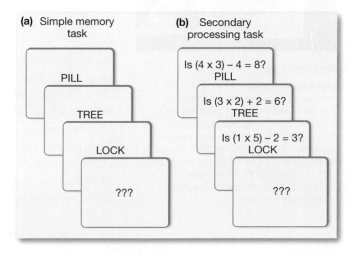

FIGURE 8.34

Einstein's Extraordinary Brain
Sandra Witelson with Einstein's brain in her lab at McMaster University.

FIGURE 8.35

Stephen Wiltshire
Despite his autism, Stephen Wiltshire had published a book of his remarkably accurate, expressive, memory-based drawings by the time he was a young teenager. Here, in October 2010, he holds his drawing of an architectural site in London, England. Wiltshire observed the site briefly, then completed the picture largely from memory.

importance of staying focused makes sense in light of the relationship between general intelligence and the accomplishment of novel, complex tasks. The question, then, is whether brain regions that support working memory are involved in general intelligence.

INTELLIGENCE AND THE BRAIN Intelligent people are sometimes called "brainy," but how are the brain and intelligence related? Does a bigger brain make you smarter?

Many studies have documented a relationship between brain size and intelligence (McDaniel, 2005). However, these findings are only correlations, so we cannot say for certain that brain size determines differences in intelligence.

Sandra Witelson, a Canadian neuroscientist at McMaster University, has her own personal collection of brains—125 of them, all from Canadians. She also has an enviable specimen from outside Canada: She is the official keeper of Albert Einstein's brain (**Figure 8.34**). Einstein's brain is rather unremarkable in overall size and weight. But the parietal lobe—the portion of the brain used in visual thinking and spatial reasoning—is 15 percent larger than average. This relationship is interesting, but we don't know whether Einstein's genius was due to the size of this brain region or whether he spent so much time thinking about particular phenomena that the result was an increase in the size of his parietal lobe. Together, these possibilities provide a great example of the directionality problem (see Chapter 1).

SAVANTS How would you like to be able to read a page of this textbook in 8 to 10 seconds? Perhaps less useful but even more impressive would be the ability to recite all the zip codes and area codes in the United States by their assigned regions, or to name hundreds of classical music pieces by hearing only a few notes of each work. These amazing abilities are just a few of the extraordinary memory feats demonstrated by Kim Peek (Treffert & Christensen, 2006).

Peek, who died in 2008, was the inspiration for the character played by Dustin Hoffman in the 1988 movie *Rain Man*. He memorized the contents of over 9,000 books, but he could not button his own clothes or manage any of the usual chores of daily living, such as making change. Peek was born, in 1951, with an enlarged head and many brain anomalies, including a missing corpus callosum, the thick band of nerves that connects the brain's two halves. He also had abnormalities in several other parts of his brain, especially the left hemisphere. He scored 87 on an intelligence test, but clearly this number did not adequately describe his intelligence.

Peek and people like him are known as *savants*. They have minimal intellectual capacities in most domains, but at a very early age each savant shows an exceptional ability in some "intelligent" process. For example, a savant's exceptional ability may be related to math, music, or art. The neurologist and author Oliver Sacks (1995) recounts the story of Stephen Wiltshire, an artistic savant. Wiltshire has autism spectrum disorder. In childhood, it took him the utmost effort to acquire enough language to accomplish simple verbal communication. Even so, years after taking a single glance at a place, Wiltshire can draw a highly accurate picture of it (**Figure 8.35**). We know very little about savants. The combination of prodigious memory and the inability to learn seemingly basic tasks is a great mystery.

Many Factors Determine Group Differences in Intelligence

When you hear that Nobel Prize winners, Supreme Court justices, or members of Mensa have high IQs, you probably are not surprised or bothered. The idea that some people may be smarter than the average person is not very controversial. A more controversial claim is that there are differences in intelligence between people of different races.

The most controversial aspect of intelligence testing over the last century has been the idea that genetics can explain overall differences in intelligence scores between racial groups. In a 1969 paper, Arthur Jensen created a firestorm of controversy by asserting that African Americans are, on average, less intelligent than white Americans. Given the importance of intelligence to educational and career attainment, claims that some groups are superior to others require close scrutiny, and it is important to discuss controversial and sensitive topics with an eye to being as fair to all sides as possible.

The debate continues about differences in African Americans' and white Americans' scores on measures of intelligence. Multiple studies over the past 30 years have found that—although *many* African Americans have higher intelligence scores than most white Americans—on average whites score about 10 to 15 points higher than African Americans on most measures of intelligence. What might be the cause of this group difference?

BIOLOGICAL DIFFERENCES The first issue to consider is whether "race" is a biologically meaningful concept. Many psychologists and anthropologists believe it is not. The vast majority of genes—perhaps as many as 99.9 percent—are identical among all humans. Further, the increase in interracial relationships in many countries means that a growing proportion of the population is racially mixed (**Figure 8.36a**). People increasingly identify themselves as biracial and multiracial to reflect their full racial and ethnic heritages (**Figure 8.36b**). Some genetically based biological differences do exist between people who identify themselves as black and those who identify themselves as white. But it is unlikely that differences in skin color and hair type relate to the mental capacities that underlie intelligence.

ENVIRONMENTAL DIFFERENCES Even if there are differences in IQ score between races, we cannot conclude that race *causes* the differences if there are any environmental differences between the groups. On average, African Americans have very different life circumstances than white Americans. On average, African Americans make less money, are more likely to live in poverty, have fewer years of education and lower-quality health care, and are more likely to face prejudice and discrimination.

Around the world, minority groups that are the targets of discrimination—such as the Maori in New Zealand, the burakumin in Japan, and the Dalits in India—have lower intelligence scores on average. John Ogbu (1994) argues that poor treatment of minority-group members can make them pessimistic about their chances of success within their cultures. This may make them less likely to believe that hard work will pay off for them, in turn lowering their motivational level and therefore their performance. This explanation is plausible, but it is not

(a)

(b)

FIGURE 8.36

Multiracial Americans
Most methods of classifying race depend on self-report, in which people group themselves into categories. This method is increasingly difficult to use as people become more multiracial. **(a)** This woman represents a "racial composite" of Americans in the twenty-first century, similar to the composite presented by *Time* magazine. **(b)** In the United States, families are increasingly multiracial. Here, Maya Soetoro-Ng, the sister of President Barack Obama, is shown with her husband, Konrad Ng, and their children.

FIGURE 8.37
Stereotype Threat
Stereotype threat may lead black students
to perform poorly on some standardized
tests.

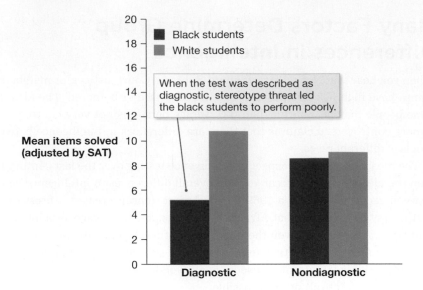

stereotype threat
Apprehension about confirming negative
stereotypes related to a person's own
group.

a clear-cut basis for understanding the differences in test scores between African Americans and white Americans (Neisser et al., 1996). Let's consider one other explanation.

STEREOTYPE THREAT Research over the past decade has provided an important reason that some racial groups may score lower on standardized tests of intelligence. **Stereotype threat** is the apprehension or fear that some people might experience if they believe that their performances on tests might confirm negative beliefs about their racial group (Steele & Aronson, 1995; **Figure 8.37**). As noted by the psychologist Toni Schmader (2010), stereotype threat causes distraction and anxiety, interfering with performance by reducing the capacity of short-term memory and undermining confidence and motivation.

Steven Spencer and his colleague Gregory Walton researched many stereotype threat studies involving a number of different groups from several countries and reached two general conclusions. First, they found that stereotyped groups perform worse than non-stereotyped groups when they are being evaluated. This effect is reversed when the threat is reduced, such as when an exam is presented as non-evaluative (Walton & Spencer, 2009). Second, they found that interventions to reduce the effects of stereotype threat are often successful. For instance, even simply informing people about the negative consequences of stereotype threat can prevent them from showing the effects (Johns, Schmader, & Martens, 2005).

In another study, encouraging African American students to write about important personal values appeared to protect them from stereotype threat, perhaps because it led them to focus on positive aspects of their lives rather than on stereotypes about their group (Cohen, Garcia, Apfel, & Master, 2006). Other studies have found that strengthening peer relations and social connections can help prevent stereotype threat. Indeed, Canadian aboriginal children performed better academically in school environments that provided opportunities to develop social skills and create friendships (Baydala et al., 2009).

Stereotype threat applies to any group that is subject to a negative stereotype. For instance, women tend to do more poorly than men when taking an exam on which they believe men typically outscore women, but they often perform as well as men on the same test if they do not hold such a belief (Schmader, Johns, & Forbes, 2008; Spencer, Steele, & Quinn, 1999). One study used fMRI to examine the neural mechanisms underlying stereotype threat (Krendl, Richeson, Kelley, & Heatherton, 2008). The researchers found that women who had been reminded about the negative stereotypes concerning women's math ability solved fewer math problems correctly and responded more slowly. Most important, they had more activation in the brain regions involved in social and emotional processing, suggesting that they were anxious about their performance. By contrast, the women in the control group who had not been told the negative stereotypes showed greater activation in neural networks associated with mathematical learning. These results support the idea that anxiety about confirming stereotypes interferes with performance.

The idea that there are differences in intelligence between the sexes or different races is based on the way we think: by making generalizations about people. We described how these stereotypes led orchestra conductors to choose men for principal positions because the conductors believed that women were not as good musicians. But recall that the conductors have been able to overcome this stereotype by ensuring that both men and women received equal and fair tryouts. We can all learn from this example. By being aware of our tendency to stereotype one group as more intelligent than the other, we can work to overcome stereotypes so that our thinking can more closely reflect reality.

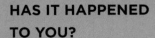

 8.4 CHECKPOINT: How Do We Measure Intelligence?

- Intelligence is assessed with three different types of psychometric tests: achievement, aptitude, and intelligence tests.

- Intelligence is related to cognitive performance in terms of the speed of mental processing, working memory, and attention.

- Race differences in intelligence are hard to assess because of environmental differences.

- Stereotype threat influences test scores when people believe that their performance might confirm negative stereotypes about their sex or race.

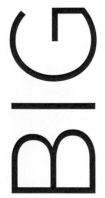

BIG PICTURE

8.1
What Is Thinking?

a. Remember the key terms about representations used in thinking.

b. Apply analogical and symbolic representations to your life.

c. Understand how concepts are organized according to the three models of thinking.

d. Apply schemas and stereotypes to your life.

8.2
How Do We Make Decisions and Solve Problems?

a. Remember the key terms about reasoning, decision making, and problem solving.

b. Understand the three main biases in decision making.

c. Apply problem solving strategies to your life.

d. Understand the three strategies for overcoming obstacles in problem solving.

8.3
What Is Intelligence?

a. Remember the key terms about intelligence.

b. Understand general intelligence.

c. Apply the four theories of multiple intelligences to your life.

d. Analyze the contributions of nature and nurture to the development of your own intelligence.

8.4
How Do We Measure Intelligence?

a. Remember the key terms about how intelligence is measured.

b. Analyze the three common types of psychometric tests of intelligence.

c. Understand the relationship between cognitive performance and intelligence.

d. Apply the concept of stereotype threat to the real world.

KEY TERMS

CHECKPOINT

thinking
analogical representations
symbolic representations
concept
defining attribute model
prototype model
exemplar model
stereotypes

- Thinking is manipulating mental representations of objects we encounter in our environment.

- In thinking, we use analogical representations, which usually correspond to images, and symbolic representations, which usually correspond to words or ideas.

- Concepts are symbolic representations of items that are categorized on the basis of defining attributes, prototypes, or exemplars.

- Schemas, mental representations that are organized based on experience and knowledge, allow for efficient thinking but can lead to stereotypes.

reasoning
decision making
problem solving
heuristic
framing
restructuring
mental sets
functional fixedness

- Reasoning is evaluating information, arguments, and beliefs to draw a conclusion. Reasoning can be informal or formal.

- Decision making is often faulty because it is based on using heuristics or framing. The paradox of choice contributes to the difficulty of decision making.

- In problem solving, we overcome obstacles to reach a goal by using subgoals, analogy, and/or insight, or by working backward.

- We can solve difficult problems by restructuring the representation and overcoming mental sets and functional fixedness.

intelligence
intelligence quotient (IQ)
general intelligence
fluid intelligence
crystallized intelligence
multiple intelligences
triarchic theory

- General intelligence is the idea that a single unifying factor underlies intelligence.

- Alternative theories state that people have many intelligences, such as fluid and crystallized intelligence, multiple intelligences, the three intelligences included in triarchic theory, and emotional intelligence.

- Behavioral genetics has demonstrated that genes influence intelligence. However, environmental factors also influence intelligence.

reliability
validity
achievement test
aptitude test
mental age
stereotype threat

- Intelligence is assessed with three different types of psychometric tests: achievement, aptitude, and intelligence tests.

- Intelligence is related to cognitive performance in terms of the speed of mental processing, working memory, and attention.

- Race differences in intelligence are hard to assess because of environmental differences.

- Stereotype threat influences test scores when people believe that their performance might confirm negative stereotypes about their sex or race.

For a self-quiz on this chapter, go to the back of the book and find Appendix B: Quizzes.

9 Motivation and Emotion

FOR THE FIRST YEAR OF HER LIFE, GABRIELLE WAS HOMELESS, living with her family in the back of a van. When her father left, her mother supported four young children by herself. Even though the family was poor, Gabrielle's mother enrolled her in gymnastics when she was 6 years old. Gabrielle, an African American, was bullied by teammates who told her to get a nose job and called her "their slave." Yet Gabrielle completely dedicated herself to gymnastics (**Figure 9.1a**). When she was 8 years old, she became a Virginia State Gymnastics champion.

BIG QUESTIONS

(a)

(b)

FIGURE 9.1

Gabby Douglas's Motivation to Succeed

(a) Gabby came from a humble background, but she was motivated to inspire others. She worked hard to become the best gymnast in the world. (b) In 2012, Gabby became the Olympic gold medalist in the gymnastics team and individual all-around competitions. Gabby's story shows the relationship between our emotions and our motivations to behave in certain ways.

When she was 14, Gabrielle moved to Iowa and lived with a host family in order to train with a famous gymnastics coach. She was terribly homesick. She almost quit. But she kept on, and at 16 she won the national championship that sent her to the 2012 Olympics. Gabrielle told the *New York Times,* "I'm going to inspire so many people. Everybody will be talking about, how did she come up so fast? But I'm ready to shine." (Macur, 2012). And shine she did, taking the gold and inspiring a nation of admirers.

In 2012, Gabrielle Douglas, better known as Gabby, became the Olympic gold medalist in both the gymnastics team and individual all-around competitions (**Figure 9.1b**). Her achievements are historic. Gabby is the first woman of color, and the first African American gymnast, to earn the title of Individual All-Around Champion in gymnastics. In addition, Gabby is the first American to win gold in both the individual all-around and team gymnastics competitions at the same Olympics. When Gabby was asked how she overcame so many obstacles to soar so high, she said, "I've had a lot of hardships in my life and in my career, but I never let that hurt what I do in the gym. I've always put my heart into gymnastics and pushed myself every single day, no matter what else was going on."

Experts say that the keys to success are motivation and persistent drive. Those qualities are crucial whether a person is trying to succeed at the Olympics, in school, or at a job. This chapter examines the factors that motivate our behavior. For example, how do we set goals? What makes us work hard and consistently to achieve those goals? This chapter also examines how our motivation and emotions are tied together. We are motivated to act and succeed because of how we feel. And reaching our goals after dedicated hard work leads to a deep sense of satisfaction and happiness. Gabby Douglas's story shows that each of us can have rewarding experiences as long as we are motivated to succeed.

9.1 What Motivates Our Behavior?

📖 **LEARNING GOALS**	✏️ **READING ACTIVITIES**	LEARN
a. Remember the key terms about motivation.	List all of the boldface words and write down their definitions.	
b. Understand the five main factors that motivate us to behave in a certain way.	Summarize in a table how motivation is affected by needs, drives, incentives, arousal, and pleasure.	
c. Apply intrinsic and extrinsic motivation to your life.	Provide one example of each to explain how you can use intrinsic motivation to reach a goal and extrinsic motivation to meet a different goal.	
d. Apply achievement motivation to your life.	Describe three changes you can make to demonstrate high need achievement in your schoolwork or job.	

What inspires you to get up in the morning? Why do you choose to eat certain foods? Does being in a sexual relationship interest you? Questions such as these are real-world instances of more general questions about why we do what we do. As Gabby Douglas's story shows, our motivation to do—or not do—certain things, and our emotions about those activities, strongly influence our behavior every day. In fact, the words *emotion* and *motivation* come from the same Latin word: *movere*, "to move."

Many Factors Influence Motivation

Most of the general theories of motivation emphasize four basic qualities. First, motivation is *activating*—it stimulates us to do something. For instance, the desire to be fit might motivate you to get up and go for a run on a cold morning. Second, motivation is *directive*—it guides our behaviors toward meeting specific goals or needs. Hunger motivates you to eat, thirst motivates you to drink, and pride (or fear or many other feelings) motivates you to study for exams. Third, motivation helps us *sustain* our behavior until we achieve our goals or satisfy our needs. Hunger gnaws at you until you find something to eat, whereas a desire to win drives you to practice foul shots until you succeed. Fourth, motives *differ in strength,* depending on the person and on the situation. Thus **motivation** refers to factors of varying strength that energize, direct, or sustain behavior (**Figure 9.2**). A wide range of factors motivate our behaviors, as described in **Table 9.1**.

SATISFACTION OF NEEDS What do we really need to do to stay alive? Of course, we need air, food, and water to survive. But satisfying our basic biological needs is not enough to live a fully satisfying life. We also have social needs, including the need for achievement and the need to be with others. A **need,** then, is a state of deficiency that can be either biological (e.g., water) or social (e.g., being with other people). Either way, needs lead to goal-directed behaviors. Failure to satisfy a need leads to psychological or physical problems.

In the 1940s, the psychologist Abraham Maslow proposed a "need theory" of motivation that became very influential. Maslow believed that people are driven by many needs, which can be described in a **need hierarchy** (**Figure 9.3**). Survival

(a)　　(b)

(c)　　(d)

FIGURE 9.2

What Motivates Us?
When we look at people, in life or in photos, we see their behaviors. For example, they may be **(a)** dressing warmly, **(b)** studying, **(c)** eating with friends and family, or **(d)** embracing and kissing. And while we may think we know why people act as they do, we actually can't see their internal motivations. Throughout this chapter, we will refer back to the examples in this figure as we consider people's motivations and behaviors.

motivation
Factors of differing strength that energize, direct, and sustain behavior.

need
A state of biological or social deficiency.

need hierarchy
An arrangement of needs, in which basic survival needs must be met before people can satisfy higher needs.

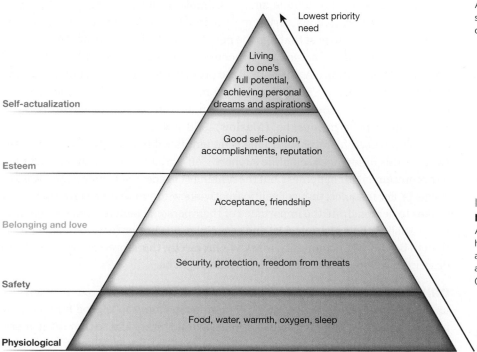

Lowest priority need

Self-actualization — Living to one's full potential, achieving personal dreams and aspirations

Esteem — Good self-opinion, accomplishments, reputation

Belonging and love — Acceptance, friendship

Safety — Security, protection, freedom from threats

Physiological — Food, water, warmth, oxygen, sleep

Highest priority need

FIGURE 9.3

Need Hierarchy
According to Maslow's hierarchy of needs, humans must satisfy basic needs (such as for food and water) before they can address higher needs for personal growth (such as for self-actualization).

TABLE 9.1

Factors That Motivate Our Behaviors

FACTOR	DESCRIPTION	EXAMPLE
Satisfaction of needs	In a need hierarchy, a need is a state of being deficient in biological or social factors. The deficiency motivates the person to engage in behaviors that make up for it (i.e., help satisfy the need).	Mike's job didn't pay enough money to guarantee that he could pay for housing and food for his family. He took a second job to help pay the bills.
Drive reduction	A drive is an internal psychological state that motivates behaviors that will satisfy a certain need. When the need is satisfied, the drive is reduced.	Teddy felt very cold in his apartment. This feeling created a drive that motivated Teddy to put on a sweater to satisfy his need for warmth. Once he felt warmed, the drive was reduced.
Incentives	Incentives are external factors that motivate behaviors.	Knowing she could win the tennis championship was a good incentive that motivated Aya to practice hard.
Optimal level of arousal	Each person has his own optimal level of arousal, somewhere from low to high. We are motivated to engage in behaviors that fit with our preferred level of arousal.	Rhonda and Jake are an odd couple. She prefers calmness, so she stays in and watches movies in the evening. He prefers excitement, so he goes out to clubs at night.
Pleasure principle	The pleasure principle says that people are motivated to engage in behaviors that make them feel good and to avoid behaviors that cause pain.	Sarah was completely full after dinner. She ordered the flourless chocolate cake anyway because she knew it would taste so good.

needs (such as food and water) can be placed at the bottom of the hierarchy, based on the idea that they must be satisfied first. Needs such as personal growth can be placed at the top of the hierarchy. To experience personal growth, Maslow believed, people must not only meet their biological needs. They must also meet the needs to feel safe and secure, to feel loved, and to have a good opinion of themselves.

Maslow's theory is an example of *humanistic psychology*. The humanistic school views people as striving toward personal fulfillment. From this perspective, human beings are unique among animals because we continually try to improve ourselves. In considering motivation, humanists focus on the person. For example, they suggest that it is the person who desires food, not the person's stomach. A state of *self-actualization* occurs when people achieve their personal dreams and aspirations. A self-actualized person is living up to her potential and therefore is truly happy. Maslow writes, "A musician must make music, an artist must paint, a poet must write, if he is ultimately to be at peace with himself. What a man *can* be, he *must* be" (Maslow, 1968, p. 46).

Maslow's need hierarchy has long been embraced in education and business. Even so, this order lacks scientific support. Self-actualization might or might not be a requirement for happiness, but the ranking of needs is not as simple as Maslow suggests. For instance, think of political activists who starve themselves in hunger strikes to demonstrate the importance of their personal beliefs. Some people who have satisfied their physiological and security needs prefer to be left alone rather than to be part of a community. Maslow's hierarchy, therefore, is more useful as a description of how important various needs might be.

DRIVE REDUCTION AND INCENTIVES Many bars set out free snacks, usually nuts or potato chips, for their customers. Doing so is good for business, because the saltiness of the snacks makes people thirsty and so they drink more. By providing salty treats, bars are creating a need for fluids. What motivates us

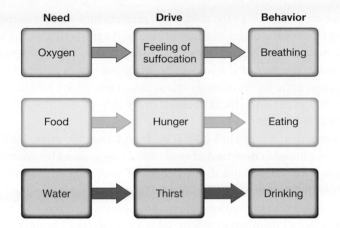

Need	Drive	Behavior
Oxygen	Feeling of suffocation	Breathing
Food	Hunger	Eating
Water	Thirst	Drinking

FIGURE 9.4

Needs, Drives, and Behaviors According to Drive Reduction
According to drive reduction, a need is a deficiency in some area that creates a drive—an internal psychological state. The drive motivates a person to behave in ways to satisfy that need.

to satisfy our needs? A **drive** is a psychological state that motivates a person to satisfy a need. A particular drive encourages behaviors that will satisfy a particular need (**Figure 9.4**). In our example, the salty snacks create the drive of thirst to satisfy the need for fluids. The drive of thirst then encourages the purchase of a beverage to drink.

Basic biological drives, such as thirst or hunger, help animals maintain a stable condition. A stable condition is also called equilibrium. In the 1920s, the physiologist Walter Cannon coined the term *homeostasis* to describe the tendency for bodily functions to remain in equilibrium. A good analogy is a home heating and cooling system controlled by a thermostat. You set the thermostat to some desired temperature. The temperature is a *set point*. This set point indicates homeostasis for the system. If the actual temperature is different from the set point, the furnace or air conditioner gets feedback that makes it adjust the temperature. Similarly, the human body regulates temperature to a set point (**Figure 9.5**).

drive
A psychological state that, by creating arousal, motivates an organism to engage in a behavior to satisfy a need.

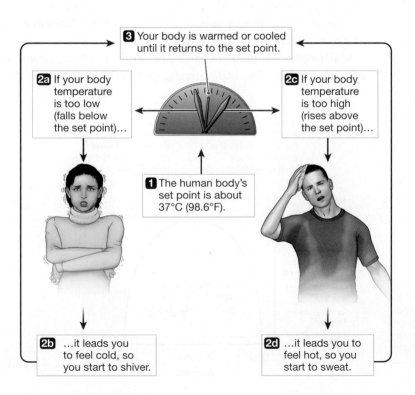

3 Your body is warmed or cooled until it returns to the set point.

2a If your body temperature is too low (falls below the set point)...

2c If your body temperature is too high (rises above the set point)...

1 The human body's set point is about 37°C (98.6°F).

2b ...it leads you to feel cold, so you start to shiver.

2d ...it leads you to feel hot, so you start to sweat.

FIGURE 9.5

A Model of Homeostasis
A thermostat is an external example that shows how homeostasis works inside the body. **(1)** An individual's internal thermostat is set at a comfortable temperature. **(2a)** If the person's body temperature falls below the set point, **(2b)** then the person feels cold and shivers. **(3)** The person gets warmer to reach the set point. **(2c)** By contrast, if the person's body temperature moves above the set point, **(2d)** then the person feels hot and sweats. **(3)** The person gets cooler to reach the set point.

HAS IT HAPPENED TO YOU?

Needs and Drives

Have you ever felt thirsty and drunk a soda or bottle of water, only to feel thirsty again soon afterward? If that beverage truly satisfied the drive—thirst—then you should have stopped needing a drink for a while. Beverage companies know how our needs and drives work, and they use that knowledge to increase their business. In short, companies produce beverages that will not quench your thirst. The next time you choose a beverage—any beverage—look at the label. If you see "salt," "sodium," "sodium chloride," or "minerals" on the label, then you will probably feel thirsty soon after drinking that beverage. You need more fluid and will have the drive to buy another beverage.

arousal
Physiological activation (such as increased brain activity) or increased autonomic responses (such as increased heart rate, sweating, or muscle tension).

incentives
External objects or external goals, rather than internal drives, that motivate behaviors.

FIGURE 9.6

Graph of the Yerkes-Dodson Law
According to this law, performance increases with arousal until an optimal point. Here, the optimal point is the top of the curve. Below that point of moderate arousal and above it, arousal interferes with performance.

When we are too warm or too cold, brain mechanisms initiate responses such as sweating (to cool the body) or shivering (to warm the body). At the same time, we become motivated to perform behaviors such as taking off or putting on clothes (as suggested in the case of the woman dressing warmly in Figure 9.2a). Models such as this are useful for describing various basic biological drives, such as hunger and thirst. You experience them yourself every day, as described in the Has It Happened to You? feature.

The psychologist Clark Hull (1943) built on Cannon's work. Hull proposed that when an animal is deprived of some need (such as water, sleep, or sex), a drive increases in proportion to the degree of deprivation. The hungrier you are, the more driven you are to find food. The drive creates **arousal.** Arousal is a sense of tension that encourages you to do something to reduce the drive. For example, you eat a late-night snack to reduce your drive of hunger.

If a behavior consistently reduces a drive over time, it becomes a *habit.* The likelihood that a behavior will occur is due to both drive and habit. For instance, suppose you feel the need to forget your troubles. To satisfy that need, you feel driven to distract yourself, so you go to YouTube and watch videos of cute animals. Watching those videos makes you forget your troubles, and that outcome reinforces further video viewing. Over time, you might develop the habit of watching cute animal videos, especially when you are stressed.

Drives push us to reduce a sense of tension when we have an unmet need. We are also pulled toward certain things in our environments. **Incentives** are external things, rather than internal drives, that motivate behaviors. For example, getting a good grade on an exam is an incentive for studying hard.

AROUSAL AND PERFORMANCE Because drives motivate behavior by creating arousal, you might think that more arousal will lead to more motivation and thus to better performance. But that's not necessarily the case. The *Yerkes-Dodson law* describes the relationship between arousal, motivation, and performance. This law was named after the two researchers who formulated it, in 1908. This law states that performance increases with arousal up to an optimal point. After that point, more arousal will result in decreasing performance. A graph of this relationship is shaped like an upside-down *U* (**Figure 9.6**).

As the Yerkes-Dodson law predicts, students perform best on exams when they feel moderate anxiety. Too little anxiety can make them inattentive or

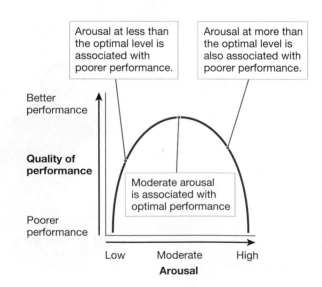

Arousal at less than the optimal level is associated with poorer performance.

Arousal at more than the optimal level is also associated with poorer performance.

Better performance

Quality of performance

Poorer performance

Moderate arousal is associated with optimal performance

Low   Moderate   High

Arousal

(a)

(b)

FIGURE 9.7

People Differ in Their Optimal Level of Arousal

Each of us has a different level of optimal arousal that motivates us to behave in certain ways. **(a)** Some people have a lower level of optimal arousal. These people tend to prefer calmer activities, such as reading, which keep arousal at an optimal lower level. **(b)** Other people have a higher level of optimal arousal. They tend to prefer exciting activities, such as skydiving, which raise arousal to an optimal higher level.

unmotivated, and too much anxiety can interfere with their thinking ability. Likewise, athletes have to pump themselves up for their events, but they can fall apart under too much stress.

All of us function better with some arousal. Activities that arouse us and capture our attention can be stimulating, exciting, or even frightening. We each prefer a certain level of arousal, which can be low (**Figure 9.7a**) or high (**Figure 9.7b**). In other words, everyone is motivated to engage in behaviors based on their own *optimal level of arousal.* Too much arousal overwhelms us. Too little arousal leaves us bored. Answer the questions in the Try It Yourself feature to determine what your optimal level of arousal is.

PLEASURE Sigmund Freud proposed that needs are satisfied based on the *pleasure principle.* According to Freud, the pleasure principle motivates people to seek pleasure and avoid pain. This idea is central to many theories of motivation. We do things that feel good. If something feels good, we do it again. Sexual activity is a perfect example. People generally engage in various sexual behaviors because of the pleasure those behaviors provide. They may engage in those behaviors despite not wanting to reproduce.

The idea that pleasure motivates behavior helps us understand why we behave in ways that do not necessarily satisfy our biological needs. For example, we eat dessert even when we are not hungry. But the pleasure principle also makes sense from an

---

TRY IT YOURSELF: Are You a Sensation Seeker?

Do you prefer more rather than less arousal? Use this chart to determine whether you are a sensation seeker. Choose the number that reflects how you feel about each statement.

Strongly disagree	Somewhat disagree	Neither disagree nor agree	Somewhat agree	Strongly agree
1	2	3	4	5

(a) I would like to explore strange places. _____
(b) I like to do frightening things. _____
(c) I like new and exciting experiences, even if I have to break the rules. _____
(d) I prefer friends who are exciting and unpredictable. _____

Scoring:
Add your four answers and divide by four. Your score reveals whether you tend to avoid or seek out new sensations.

1.0 to 1.99: You may strongly avoid sensation seeking; you may prefer a very low level of internal arousal.

2.0 to 2.99: You may mildly avoid sensation seeking; you may prefer a somewhat low level of internal arousal.

3.0 to 3.99: You may mildly tend toward sensation seeking; you may prefer a somewhat high level of internal arousal.

4.0 and above: You may strongly tend toward sensation seeking; you may prefer a very high level of internal arousal.

Your score is a rough indication of whether you are motivated toward activities that raise or lower your level of arousal. It also suggests your optimal level of arousal. This level is the point at which you will perform the best in most circumstances.

SOURCE: Stephenson, Hoyle, Palmgreen, & Slater (2003).

(a)

(b)

FIGURE 9.8

Extrinsic and Intrinsic Motivation
(a) Extrinsic motivation is an external factor that causes us to behave in a certain way. That factor is a reward. A major example is money. **(b)** Intrinsic motivation causes us to behave in a certain way simply because the activity, or the result of the activity, is enjoyable.

extrinsic motivation
A desire to perform an activity because of the external goals that activity is directed toward.

intrinsic motivation
A desire to perform an activity because of the value or pleasure associated with that activity, rather than for an apparent external goal or purpose.

evolutionary perspective. Both positive and negative motivations are adaptive. For instance, food, sex, and companionship are typically associated with pleasure, so we are motivated to seek them out. Big, fierce animals are associated with pain, so we are motivated to avoid them (Watson, Wiese, Vaidya, & Tellegen, 1999). A good example of this principle is the finding that animals prefer to eat sweet foods (Steiner, 1977). Sweetness usually indicates that food is safe to eat. By contrast, most poisons and toxins taste bitter, so it is not surprising that animals avoid bitter tastes.

Some Behaviors Are Motivated for Their Own Sake

Although 14-year-old Gabby Douglas felt homesick, she kept on with her gymnastics training. Gabby was directed toward **extrinsic motivation.** Extrinsic motivation is the desire to achieve an external goal. For example, when you work to earn a good grade or a paycheck, you are extrinsically motivated (**Figure 9.8a**). Not all of our behavior is extrinsically motivated.

INTRINSIC MOTIVATION Consider the activities people find most satisfying, such as reading a good novel, taking a walk, or listening to music. Many of these activities seem to fulfill no obvious purpose other than enjoyment. Such activities are directed toward **intrinsic motivation.** Intrinsic motivation is the desire to get the value or pleasure from the activity with no apparent external goal (**Figure 9.8b**). We can assume—or hope—that in performing gymnastics, Gabby Douglas also experiences intrinsic motivation.

Some intrinsically motivated activities may satisfy our natural curiosity and creativity. After playing with a new toy for a long time, children start to lose interest and will seek out something new. Playful exploration is characteristic of all mammals and especially primates. For example, monkeys will work hard, without an external reward, to solve relatively complex puzzles (Harlow, Harlow, & Meyer, 1950). One function of play is that it helps us learn about the objects in an environment. This activity clearly has survival value. That is, knowing how things work enables us to use those objects for more serious tasks.

Similarly, many of us are driven toward creative pursuits. Maybe we produce artwork. Maybe we modify recipes with new ingredients. We may do these things simply because we enjoy activities that allow us to express our creativity. *Creativity* is the tendency to generate ideas or alternatives that may be useful in solving problems, communicating, and entertaining ourselves and others (Franken, 1988).

SELF-DETERMINATION AND SELF-PERCEPTION In Chapter 6, we looked at a basic principle of learning theory: When a behavior is rewarded, the person will increase that behavior. This idea seems logical. The surprising thing is that extrinsic rewards may undermine intrinsic motivation.

In a classic study, children were invited to draw with colored marking pens (Lepper, Greene, & Nisbett, 1973). Most children find this activity intrinsically motivating. One group of children was extrinsically motivated to draw by being led to expect a "good player award." Another group of children was rewarded unexpectedly following the task. A third group was neither rewarded nor led to expect a reward. Later, there was a free-play period. Children who were expecting an extrinsic reward spent much less time playing with the pens than did the children who were never rewarded or the children who received an unexpected reward. The first group of children responded as though it was their job to draw with the colored pens. In other words, why would they play with the pens for free when they were used to being paid? There are two explanations for this behavior.

According to *self-determination theory,* extrinsic rewards may reduce the intrinsic value of an activity because such rewards undermine our feeling that we are choosing to do something for ourselves. In contrast, feeling free to choose makes us feel good about ourselves and inspires us to do our most creative work (Deci & Ryan, 1987).

According to *self-perception theory,* we are seldom aware of our specific motives. Instead, we make inferences about our motives according to what seems to make the most sense (Bem, 1967). Suppose someone gives you a big glass of water. After drinking the whole thing, you exclaim, "Wow, I must have been thirsty!" You believe you were thirsty because you drank the whole glass. You make this assumption even though you were not aware of being thirsty. When we cannot come up with obvious explanations for our behaviors—that we expected a reward, for instance—we conclude that we simply like the behaviors. Being rewarded for engaging in an activity, however, gives us an alternative explanation for engaging in it. The alternative explanation is that we didn't perform the behavior just for fun. Instead, we performed the behavior because of the reward. So without the reward, we have no reason to engage in the behavior. The reward has replaced the goal of pure pleasure.

We Set Long-Term Goals

What would you like to be doing 10 years from now? What things about yourself would you change? So far, we have focused on motivation to fulfill short-term goals, such as satisfying our hunger or spending a pleasurable afternoon. But we have long-term aspirations as well. Our aspirations might not be as newsworthy as Gabby Douglas's Olympic dreams, but they matter greatly to us. What motivates us to fulfill those goals?

In the 1930s, the personality psychologist Henry Murray (1938) proposed a number of basic *psychosocial needs,* including the needs for power, autonomy, achievement, and play. The study of psychosocial needs has yielded important insights into what motivates human behavior. A key insight is that people are especially motivated to achieve personal goals.

Good goals motivate us to work hard, but what is a good goal? Challenging—but not overly difficult—and specific goals are best (Locke & Latham, 1990). Challenging goals encourage effort, persistence, and concentration. In contrast, goals that are too easy or too hard can undermine motivation and lead to failure. Dividing specific goals into concrete steps also leads to success, just as setting subgoals is helpful in solving problems (see Chapter 8). If you are interested in running the Boston Marathon, for instance, your first goal might be gaining the stamina to run 1 mile. When you can run a mile, you can set another goal and eventually build up to running the 26-mile marathon. Focusing on concrete, short-term goals helps in achieving long-term goals.

SELF-EFFICACY AND ACHIEVEMENT MOTIVATION Personal expectations for success play an important role in motivation. For instance, if you believe studying hard will lead to a good grade on an exam, you will be motivated to study.

achievement motivation
The need, or desire, to attain a certain standard of excellence.

Self-efficacy is the expectation that your efforts will lead to success (Bandura, 1977a). This expectation helps get you going. If you have low self-efficacy—if you do not believe your efforts will pay off—you may be too discouraged even to study for the exam. People with high self-efficacy often set challenging goals that lead to success. However, those with inflated self-views may set goals they cannot possibly achieve. Again, goals that are challenging but not overwhelming usually are most likely to lead to success.

People differ in how much they pursue challenging goals. **Achievement motivation** is the need, or desire, to do well relative to standards of excellence (achievement may be the motivation for the student studying hard in Figure 9.2b). Compared with those low in achievement motivation, students high in achievement motivation sit closer to the front of classrooms, score higher on exams, and obtain better grades in courses relevant to their career goals (McClelland, 1987). Students with high achievement motivation also are more realistic in their career aspirations. Those high in achievement motivation set challenging but attainable personal goals. Those low in achievement motivation set extremely easy or impossibly high goals.

DELAYED GRATIFICATION Suppose that you are applying to graduate school and the entrance exam is coming up soon. You know you should stay in and study, but all your friends are going out to the basketball game and are begging you to come with them. Which would you do?

One common challenge in meeting our long-term goals is postponing immediate gratification. In a series of now-classic studies, children were given the choice of waiting to receive a preferred toy or food item or having a less preferred toy or food item right away (Mischel, Shoda, & Rodriguez, 1989). Some children were better at delaying gratification than other children were.

How did some of the children in these studies manage to delay gratification (**Figure 9.9**)? Given the choice between eating one marshmallow right away or eating two after several minutes, some 4-year-olds used strategies to help them not eat the marshmallow while they waited. One strategy was simply ignoring the tempting item rather than looking at it. For example, some of them covered their eyes or looked away. Alternatively, some children were able to ignore the item by the related strategy of self-distraction: They sang, played games, or pretended to sleep. On average, older children were better at delaying gratification. Very young children tended to look directly at the item they were trying to resist, making the delay especially difficult.

The ability to delay gratification is an indicator of success in life. Children able to delay gratification at age 4 were rated 10 years later as being more socially competent and better able to handle frustration. The ability to delay gratification in childhood has also been found to predict higher SAT scores and better school grades (Mischel et al., 1989).

We Have a Need to Belong

We often hear that "humans are social animals." This statement is not just a way of saying that people like parties. Over the course of human evolution, our ancestors who lived with others were more likely to survive, reproduce, and pass along their genes. Children who stayed with adults were more likely to survive until their reproductive years, because the adults would protect and take care of them. Similarly, adults who developed long-term, committed relationships were more likely to reproduce and to have children who survived to reproduce. Successful groups

1 Ignore tempting items by looking away.

2 Ignore tempting items through self-distraction.

FIGURE 9.9

Delaying Gratification

It is often hard to meet long-term goals because there is no immediate reward, or gratification, for our hard work. Luckily, several techniques can help us cope with delaying gratification. Some of those techniques are shown here.

How Can You Satisfy a Need to Belong?

People have a strong need to form stable and satisfying relationships with friends, family, romantic partners, colleagues, and the community. But we are also often told to "look out for number one," suggesting that our self-interest should be a primary motivator. Jennifer Crocker is a research psychologist interested in the ways that motivations influence our sense of well-being. Crocker has examined two motivational perspectives. These perspectives are based on *egosystem goals* and *ecosystem goals*. Both perspectives have important implications for our ability to satisfy the need to belong.

*Ego*system goals motivate us to build and maintain other people's impressions of us. People motivated by egosystem goals focus on proving themselves, showing their good qualities, and validating their worth. Such people prioritize their own perceived needs over those of others (Crocker, Olivier, & Nuer, 2009). When we are so focused on building and maintaining others' perceptions of us, we see relationships with others in terms of winning and losing: If I win, you lose. If you win, I lose. Crocker's research shows that students who hold these goals became more depressed and anxious during their first semester in college. These goals are also associated with problematic alcohol use (Moeller & Crocker, 2009).

In contrast, people with *eco*system goals perceive themselves as part of a system where their own circumstances are linked to those of others. They prioritize the needs of others because they understand these social connections and care about the well-being of others (Crocker et al., 2009). These individuals are likely to think that both people can benefit from a situation, and that they are responsible for working together to make that happen. Students who hold ecosystem goals tend to be less depressed and anxious during their first semester in college. They are more engaged in their courses and more eager to learn from failure. In a nutshell, people with ecosystem goals seem to enjoy a host of positive benefits.

How might you cultivate your ecosystem goals and satisfy your need to belong? Three strategies will help you see yourself as more interconnected in relationships with others.

1. **Think and write about your personal values and priorities.** The ability to think beyond the self is at the heart of ecosystem goals. Interestingly, you can do this by clarifying your own values. Write down the values that are important to you, and explain why they are important. A study by Crocker and her colleagues found that people who did that felt more loving, joyful, giving, empathic, connected, sympathetic, grateful, and so on (Crocker, Niiya, & Mischkowski, 2008).

2. **Think about goals you have that would help other people.** Ask yourself how the tasks in your everyday life support your other-oriented goals. For example, if you are interested in studying medicine, you might say, "I want to help relieve other people's physical pain." You might then see your organic chemistry class as an opportunity to learn something that will help in future work with patients rather than as a difficult barrier that could show the world you are not cut out to be a doctor.

3. **Be grateful.** Other people touch our lives in many ways that we can be thankful for. One way to identify and appreciate moments of humanity and moments of connection is to keep a gratitude journal. Each evening before you go to bed, think of an instance or two where you were affected in a good way by another person. The event might be something small, such as when a kind driver made room for you to merge into traffic. It might be something larger, such as when a friend sat with you for hours as you grieved the loss of a loved one.

need to belong theory
The need for interpersonal attachments is a fundamental motive that has evolved for adaptive purposes.

FIGURE 9.10
Making Friends
We generally have a need to belong. This need motivates us to form friendships and join social groups.

shared food, provided mates, and helped care for children, including orphans. Some survival tasks (such as hunting large mammals or looking out for predatory enemies) were best accomplished by group cooperation. It therefore makes great sense that, over the millennia, humans have lived in groups.

The **need to belong theory** states that the need for social relations is a fundamental motive that has evolved for adaptive reasons (Baumeister & Leary, 1995). This theory explains why most people make friends easily (**Figure 9.10**). All societies have some form of group membership, though the types of groups may differ (Brewer & Caporael, 1990). Not belonging to a group increases risk for various negative consequences, such as illness and premature death (Cacioppo, Hughes, Waite, Hawkley, & Thisted, 2006). Such ill effects suggest that the need to belong is a basic motive that drives behavior. The need to belong motivates people the same way that hunger drives people to seek food and avoid dying from starvation.

If humans have a fundamental need to belong, then it is reasonable to expect that we have ways of detecting whether we are included in particular groups (MacDonald & Leary, 2005). In other words, given the importance of being a group member, people need to be sensitive to signs that the group might reject them. Indeed, evidence indicates that people feel anxious when facing exclusion from their social groups. Further, people who are shy and lonely tend to worry most about social evaluation and pay much more attention to social information (Gardner, Pickett, Jefferis, & Knowles, 2005). The take-home message is that just as a lack of food causes hunger, a lack of social contact causes emptiness and despair.

In the movie *Cast Away,* Tom Hanks's character becomes stranded on a deserted island. The man has such a strong need for companionship that he begins carrying on a friendship with a volleyball he calls Wilson (named for the manufacturer, whose name is on the ball). As the film reviewer Susan Stark (2000) notes, this film convinces us that "human company, as much as shelter, water, food and fire, is essential to life as most of us understand it."

  9.1 CHECKPOINT: What Motivates Our Behavior?

- Motivations include factors of differing strengths that activate, direct, and sustain behaviors that satisfy a need.

- Needs, drives, incentives, arousal, and pleasure all affect motivation.

- Extrinsically motivated acts are directed toward the achievement of an external goal. Intrinsically motivated acts are performed simply because they are pleasurable.

- We are motivated to achieve our long-term goals. People with high self-efficacy and high need achievement are more likely to set challenging but attainable goals.

- We have a fundamental need to belong. This need motivates us to make friends and avoid social exclusion. But it creates feelings of emptiness and despair in the absence of other people.

9.2 What Motivates Eating and Sexual Behavior?

LEARN LEARNING GOALS	READING ACTIVITIES
a. Remember the key terms about the motivations to eat and to have sexual relations.	List all of the boldface words and write down their definitions.
b. Analyze how four biological systems influence our motivation to eat.	Describe the ways that the stomach, bloodstream, hormones, and brain influence our motivation to eat.
c. Apply the idea that learning affects your motivation to eat.	Provide examples of how conditioning, familiarity, and culture influence your motivation to eat.
d. Understand two ways that biology affects the motivation for sexual behavior.	Summarize how the sexual response cycle and hormones affect our motivation to engage in sexual behavior.
e. Apply cultural rules to motivation for sexual behavior.	Provide an example of how your motivation for sexual behavior (or the avoidance of sexual behavior) is affected by cultural rules.

Eating and having sexual relations are sensitive topics. Yet these behaviors are very highly motivated. After all, they are fundamental for our individual survival and the survival of our species. Here you will learn the factors that motivate people to eat (or not) and engage in sexual behavior (or not).

Many Biological Systems Motivate Eating

For a long time, scientists believed that eating was a classic homeostatic system. That is, people would normally eat when they felt hungry and stop eating when they were full. Some sort of "detector" would notice deviations from the set point and would signal that a person should start or stop eating. But where did the hunger signals come from? The search for the hunger detector has led scientists from the stomach and the bloodstream to hormones and the brain.

STOMACH AND BLOODSTREAM Your stomach rumbles in the middle of class or while you are at work. You immediately know what that means: You are hungry. But is this really true? Internal contractions and expansions of the stomach can indeed make your stomach growl. However, over the past century, research has established that these movements are not major causes of hunger and eating. Indeed, people who have had their stomachs surgically removed due to illness continue to report feeling hungry even though they no longer have a stomach that growls.

Other research has pointed to the existence of receptors in the bloodstream that monitor levels of vital nutrients. One theory proposes that the bloodstream is monitored for its glucose levels. Glucose is the primary fuel for metabolism and is especially crucial for neuronal activity. It therefore makes sense for animals to become hungry when they are deficient in glucose. Another theory proposes a set point for the amount of body fat a person has. In this scenario, when a person loses body fat, hunger signals motivate eating and a return to the set point. Having multiple systems that motivate eating ensures the consumption of adequate nutrition.

HORMONES With obesity on the rise around the world, considerable research is under way to find out whether manipulating hormones can help prevent or treat the condition. Two main hormones are involved in our experience of hunger and eating behaviors.

Leptin is the hormone involved in fat regulation. As we eat and store the food energy as fat, leptin is released from our fat cells. The released leptin travels to the hypothalamus, the brain region that controls many homeostatic systems. There it acts to stop eating behavior, perhaps by making food less appetizing (Farooqi et al., 2007). Because leptin acts slowly, however, it takes considerable time after eating before leptin levels change in the body. Therefore, leptin may be more important for long-term body fat regulation than for short-term eating control.

The hormone **ghrelin** originates in the stomach. It surges before meals and decreases after we eat, so it may play an important role in triggering hunger (Abizaid, 2009; Higgins, Gueorguiev, & Korbonits, 2007). When people lose weight, an increase in ghrelin motivates additional eating, in part by making food more rewarding (Zorrilla et al., 2006).

THE BRAIN The hypothalamus is the brain structure that most influences eating. Early research revealed that damage to the hypothalamus could dramatically change eating behavior and body weight. One of the first observations occurred in 1939, when researchers discovered that patients with tumors of the hypothalamus became obese. Brain structures other than the hypothalamus are also involved in eating behavior. For instance, a region of the frontal cortex called the gustatory cortex processes taste cues such as sweetness and saltiness (Rolls, 2007). Seeing tasty food makes a person crave it, and this response is associated with activity in the limbic system, the main brain region involved in wanting and liking (Volkow, 2007).

Of course, sometimes we eat when we are not hungry. At other times, we avoid eating even though we are not full. How much any one biological mechanism contributes to eating behavior, including the eating disorders described in Chapter 10—obesity, anorexia nervosa, and bulimia nervosa—is unclear. Many factors influence how we eat. They include learning and culture, which we will look at next.

Eating Is Influenced by Learning

Everyone needs to eat to survive. But eating is also one of life's greatest pleasures, and we do a lot of it. Most people in industrialized countries consume between 80,000 and 90,000 meals during their lives—that's more than 40 tons of food! Around the globe, special occasions often involve elaborate feasts, and much of the social world revolves around eating. This aspect of eating is greatly affected by learning. The eating behaviors shown in Figure 9.2c are most likely motivated by learning what foods to eat, what time to eat, and how to eat from common plates of food.

CONDITIONED TO EAT What time did you eat lunch yesterday? Most people, all around the world, eat lunch at about the same time of day—somewhere between noon and 2 PM. On a physiological level, this practice makes little sense. After all, people differ greatly in metabolic rate, the amount they eat for breakfast, and the amount of fat they have stored for long-term energy needs. But we don't eat lunch at noon because we have deficient energy stores. We do it because we have been classically conditioned to associate eating with regular mealtimes.

(a)

(b)

FIGURE 9.11
Familiarity Influences Food Preferences
People tend to prefer eating the foods they
are familiar with. **(a)** If as a child you ate
wheat or multigrain bread, you are likely to
do so as an adult. **(b)** By contrast, if you ate
white bread as a child, then as an adult you
are more likely to still eat white bread.

The internal clock that indicates mealtime is much like Pavlov's metronome, which we described in Chapter 6. The internal clock leads to various anticipatory responses that motivate eating behavior and prepare the body for digestion. The sight and smell of tasty foods activates physiological systems that increase hunger. Just thinking about treats—freshly baked bread, pizza, a decadent dessert—may initiate similar reactions that make you hungry.

FAMILIARITY AND EATING PREFERENCES As a child, were you raised in a household that ate whole grain bread or white bread (**Figure 9.11**)? Or maybe rice or tortillas? Now as an adult, which do you prefer? If you are like most people, you probably eat the same type of food that you ate as a child. Familiarity generally shapes food preferences. The more experience we have with a food, the more we will continue to eat it.

People's avoidance of unfamiliar foods makes evolutionary sense because unfamiliar foods may be dangerous or poisonous, so avoiding them is adaptive (Galef & Whiskin, 2000). Getting children to like new foods often involves exposing them to small amounts at a time until they grow accustomed to the taste. Infants and toddlers also learn to try foods by observing their parents and siblings. Children are much more likely to eat a new food offered by their mother than the same food offered by a friendly stranger. This behavior, too, makes sense from an evolutionary standpoint. After all, if Mom eats something, it must be safe to eat.

Of course, what we prefer to eat is also determined by the ethnic, cultural, and religious values of our own upbringing and experiences. For example, Kosher Jews eat beef but not pork. Hindus eat pork but not beef. Ethnic differences in food preference often continue when a family moves to a new country, so culturally transmitted food preferences powerfully affect our eating habits.

CULTURAL INFLUENCES Would you eat a bat? In the Seychelles islands, bat is a delicacy. (It tastes something like chicken.) What we will eat has little to do with logic and everything to do with what we learn is "food" (see Has It Happened to You?). Some of the most nutritious foods are not eaten in North America, because they are viewed as disgusting. For instance, fried termites, a favorite in Zaire, have

HAS IT HAPPENED TO YOU?

Food and Traditions

Do you eat turkey and cranberries in July? Many Americans eat these foods at Thanksgiving but not at other times of the year. Every family has its own traditions for what and how they eat. The particular choices may be due to ethnicity, religion, or other reasons. Family food traditions are especially strong around particular holidays. Does the culture of your family sometimes set up a motivation for you to eat (or not eat) certain things? If so, you have learned the motivation to eat based on cultural experiences.

Our Culture Influences What We View as Tasty
Crickets are a popular snack among Cambodians. This vendor in Phnom Penh is offering what is considered to be a tasty treat in that culture: fried crickets.

more protein than beef. Insects are nutritious, and in many countries they are eaten as tasty treats (**Figure 9.12**). At the same time, people from other cultures might be nauseated by some North American favorites, such as Jell-O or peanut butter. Even when people are starving to death, they may refuse to eat perfectly nutritious substances because they are culturally unfamiliar. In Naples in 1770, people died because they were suspicious of the potatoes sent to relieve their famine. In Ireland during the potato famine (1845–1852), many people died because they refused to eat corn sent from America.

We Have a Drive for Sexual Relations

In movies, television shows, video games, and advertising, sex is all around us. Sexual desire has long been recognized as one of humanity's most durable and powerful motivators. Most human beings have a significant desire for sex, but sex drive varies considerably among individuals and across circumstances. Variation in the frequency of sex can be explained both by individual differences and by society's dominating influence over how and when individuals engage in sexual activity.

For much of the history of psychology, the study of sex was taboo. The idea that women were motivated to have sex was almost unthinkable. In fact, many theorists believed women were incapable of enjoying sex. In the 1940s, the pioneering work of Alfred Kinsey and his colleagues provided shocking—for the times—evidence that women's sexual attitudes and behaviors were in many ways similar to those of men. In Kinsey's surveys of thousands of Americans, he found that more than half of both men and women reported premarital sexual behavior, that masturbation was common in both sexes, that women enjoyed orgasms, and that homosexuality was much more common than most people believed.

Kinsey's surveys were controversial, but he showed a deep respect for collecting data as a way of answering a research question. More than 50 years after he began his work, we know a great deal more about sexual behavior. Still, the topic makes many people uncomfortable. In this section, we examine what psychology has learned about the motivation for sex.

SEXUAL BEHAVIOR Kinsey's research during the 1940s demonstrated how little most people knew about human sexual behavior. Despite his eye-opening contributions, ignorance about the physiology of sex persisted into the 1960s, when William Masters and Virginia Johnson began laboratory studies of sexual behavior. Their sample was somewhat biased, because all the research participants were people willing to be filmed while having intercourse or masturbating. Nonetheless, Masters and Johnson gained considerable insight into human sexual behavior.

The most enduring contribution of their research was the identification of the **sexual response cycle.** This predictable pattern of physical and psychological responses consists of four phases. The phases differ between men and women (**Figure 9.13**).

The *excitement phase* (see Figure 9.13a–b) occurs when people contemplate sexual activity or when they begin kissing and touching in a sensual manner. During this stage, blood flows to the genitals. People report feelings of sexual arousal. For men, the penis begins to become erect. For women, the clitoris becomes swollen, the vagina expands and secretes fluids, and the nipples enlarge.

sexual response cycle
A four-stage pattern of physiological and psychological responses during sexual activity.

(a)

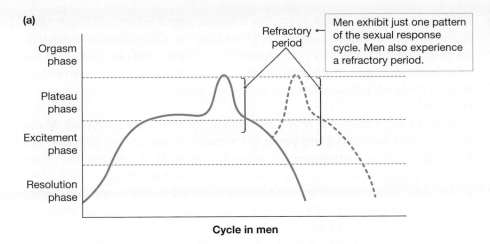

Refractory period ← Men exhibit just one pattern of the sexual response cycle. Men also experience a refractory period.

Orgasm phase
Plateau phase
Excitement phase
Resolution phase

Cycle in men

(b)

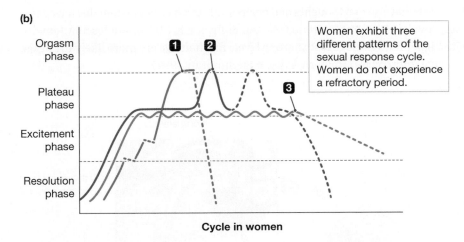

Women exhibit three different patterns of the sexual response cycle. Women do not experience a refractory period.

Orgasm phase
Plateau phase
Excitement phase
Resolution phase

Cycle in women

FIGURE 9.13

The Sexual Response Cycles of Men and Women

There are four phases in the sexual response cycle: excitement, plateau, orgasm, and resolution. However, as shown here, **(a)** men and **(b)** women experience the sexual response cycle differently.

Excitement continues into the *plateau phase* (see Figure 9.13a–b). Pulse rate, breathing, and blood pressure increase, as do the various other signs of arousal. For many people, this stage is the frenzied phase of sexual activity. Inhibitions are lifted, and passion takes control.

The plateau phase culminates in the *orgasm phase* (see Figure 9.13a–b). This stage consists of involuntary muscle contractions throughout the body, dramatic increases in breathing and heart rate, rhythmic contractions of the vagina for women, and ejaculation of semen for men. For healthy males, orgasm nearly always occurs. For females, orgasm is more variable (see Figure 9.13b, lines 1, 2, and 3). When orgasm occurs, however, women and men report nearly identical pleasurable sensations.

Following orgasm, there is a dramatic release of sexual tension and a slow return to a normal state of arousal. In this stage, the *resolution phase*, the male enters a *refractory period* (see Figure 9.13a). During this period, the man is temporarily unable to maintain an erection or have an orgasm. The female does not have such a refractory period and may experience multiple orgasms with no refractory period between each one. Again, the female response is more variable than the male response, as shown by their three separate patterns of sexual response (see Figure 9.13b). These different response cycles show that a woman may have one orgasm (line 1 in the graph), multiple orgasms (line 2), or plateau repeatedly without reaching orgasm (line 3).

HORMONES As we saw in Chapters 2 and 4, hormones affect human sexual behavior in two ways. First, they influence physical development of the brain and

androgens
A class of hormones that are associated with sexual behavior and are more prevalent in males; testosterone is one example.

estrogens
A class of hormones that are associated with sexual behavior and are more prevalent in females; estradiol is one example.

body during puberty. Second, hormones influence sexual behavior through motivation. That is, they are involved in producing and terminating sexual behaviors. Given the important role of the hypothalamus (**Figure 9.14**) in controlling the release of sex hormones into the bloodstream, it is no surprise that the hypothalamus is the brain region considered to be most important for stimulating sexual behavior.

Females and males each have some amount of all the sex hormones. Males have a greater quantity of **androgens** (for example, testosterone). Females have a greater quantity of **estrogens** (for example, estradiol). Androgens are apparently much more important for reproductive behavior than estrogens are, at least for humans. Testosterone is involved in both male and female sexual functioning (Sherwin, 2008). Males need a certain amount of testosterone to be able to engage in sex, but they do not perform better if they have more testosterone. The situation is somewhat different for women: The more testosterone they have, the more likely they are to have sexual thoughts and desires, although typically females have relatively low levels of testosterone (Meston & Frohlich, 2000). Adolescent females with higher than average testosterone levels for their age are more likely to engage in sexual intercourse (Halpern, Udry, & Suchindran, 1997).

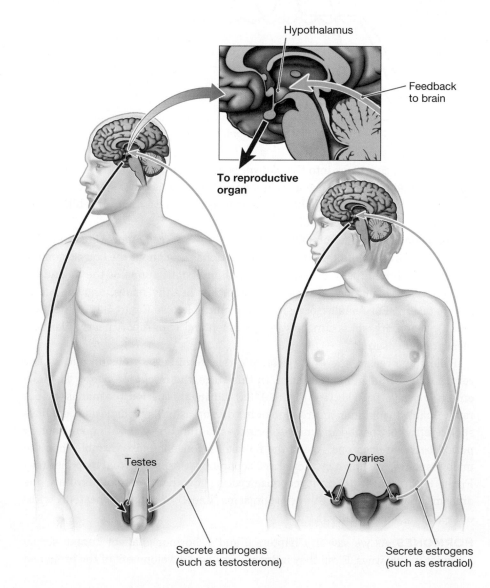

FIGURE 9.14

Brain Regions and Hormones Involved in Sexual Behaviors

The hypothalamus regulates sexual behaviors by influencing production of the sex hormones, estrogens and androgens, in the reproductive organs.

Cultural Rules Shape Sexual Interactions

Think of a romantic comedy. One attractive person meets another by chance. They spend some exciting time together, an attraction develops, and sexual behavior follows—often within a day or two, or even sooner.

In real life, the course of action is often quite different. For one thing, most people rely on their friends or social groups to meet their sex partners. And people generally do not fall into bed together as fast as they do in the movies. Most people know someone a long time before having sex. But the sexual behavior displayed by actors in movies and other media shapes our beliefs and expectations about what sexual behaviors are appropriate, and when.

Sexual customs and norms vary across cultures. Even so, all known cultures have some form of sexual morality. This consistency indicates the importance to society of regulating sexual behavior. Cultures may seek to restrain and control sex for a variety of reasons, including maintaining control over the birth rate, helping to establish paternity, and reducing conflicts.

GENDER DIFFERENCES IN SEXUAL BEHAVIOR The sexual revolution of the late twentieth century significantly changed sexual behavior in many societies. Still, the infamous *double standard* has not died. This unwritten law stipulates that premarital or casual sex is morally and socially acceptable for men but not for women. The double standard may influence male behavior. A noticeable and consistent finding in nearly all measures of sexual desire is that men, on average, have a higher level of sexual motivation than women do. In general, men masturbate more frequently than women, want sex earlier in the relationship, think and fantasize about sex more often, spend more time and money (and other resources) in the effort to obtain sex, desire more different sexual activities, initiate sex more and refuse sex less, and rate their own sex drives as stronger than women's (Baumeister, Catanese, & Vohs, 2001).

Women are generally much less willing than men to have sex with someone they do not know. In one study of 96 university students, a moderately attractive stranger approached a person of the opposite sex and said, "I have been noticing you around campus. I find you attractive. Would you go to bed with me tonight?" Not one woman said yes to the stranger's request, but three-quarters of the men agreed to the request (**Figure 9.15**). In fact, the men were less likely to agree to go on a date with the stranger than they were to agree to have sex with her (Clark & Hatfield, 1989).

To account for findings such as these, the evolutionary psychologist David Buss has proposed the **sexual strategies theory** (Buss & Schmitt, 1993). The theory suggests that throughout human history, males and females have faced different adaptive problems. As a result, the sexes use different strategies for passing along their genes to future generations.

Women's basic strategy is intensive care of a relatively small number of infants. Their commitment is to take care of children rather than simply to have many of

sexual strategies theory
Women and men have evolved distinct mating strategies because they have faced different adaptive problems over the course of human history. The strategies used by each sex maximize the probability of passing along their genes to future generations.

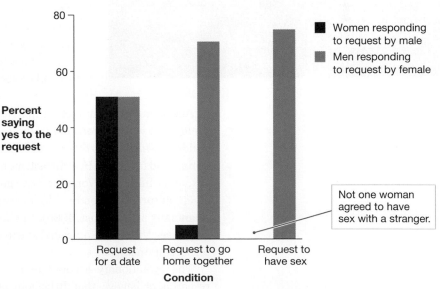

FIGURE 9.15

Sexual Behaviors and Responses
Men and women were propositioned by a stranger of the opposite sex. Both sexes were equally likely to accept a date. Men were much more willing than women to agree to go home with or have sex with the stranger.

Which of these two people do you think is more physically attractive?

(a)   **(b)**

What about these two?

(c)   **(d)**

People from Western cultures who are attracted to Caucasians often find specific features to be more attractive. The woman labeled **(b)** is typically seen as having a "sexy" face, partly due to being tanner, having higher and more prominent cheekbones, and being thinner. Similarly, the man labeled **(d)** is also seen as "sexy," because of his square jaw and prominent cheekbones. However, because what is physically attractive varies greatly across cultures and experience, it is entirely possible that you don't find any of these people attractive.

them. Once a woman is pregnant, additional matings are of no reproductive use. Once she has a small child, an additional pregnancy can put her current child at risk. In fact, biological mechanisms ensure spacing between children. For example, nursing typically makes ovulation less likely to occur.

For men, all matings may have a reproductive payoff, so men's reproductive strategies would involve having as much sex as possible. Further, they bear few of the personal costs of pregnancy, and their fertility is unaffected by getting a woman pregnant, so having children is a much less intensive commitment than it is for women. Thus the sexual strategies theory would explain why men are likely to be less cautious in their sexual behavior than women.

MATE PREFERENCES What do men and women want in their mates? Judging from all the self-help books on the subject, the question isn't easily answered. It may be easier to say what people do not want. In seeking mates, both sexes avoid certain characteristics, such as insensitivity, bad manners, loudness or shrillness, and the tendency to brag about sexual conquests (Cunningham, Barbee, & Druen, 1996).

It might seem that both men and women are likely to seek physically attractive partners (a motivation that might explain the couple's behavior in Figure 9.2d). Youth and beauty imply potential fertility. You can explore the nature of attraction in the Try It Yourself activity. But according to the sexual strategies theory, because women are limited in the number of offspring they can produce, they should be choosier in selecting mates. They should seek men who can provide resources that will help them successfully nurture their children. In other words, men should judge potential mates mainly on looks, because looks imply fertility. For their part, women should also watch for indications that their mates will be good fathers. Is there any scientific support for these ideas?

According to a study of 92 married couples in 37 cultures, women generally prefer men who are considerate, honest, dependable, kind, understanding, fond of children, well liked by others, good earners, ambitious, career oriented, from a good family, and fairly tall. By contrast, men tend to value good looks, cooking skills, and sexual faithfulness. Women value a good financial prospect more than men do. In all 37 cultures, women tend to marry older men, who often are more settled and financially stable (Buss, 1989). In short, males and females differ in the relative emphases they place on social status and physical appearance, at least for long-term relationships.

The evolutionary account of human mate selection is controversial. Some researchers believe that behaviors shaped by evolution have little impact on contemporary relationships. After all, instinctive behaviors are affected by cultural context, and cultural context is very different now than it was in early human societies. Modern human sexual behavior is influenced by contemporary norms. For example, from a biological view, it might seem an advantage for humans to reproduce as soon as they are able. But many contemporary cultures discourage sexual behavior until people are older and better able to care for their offspring. The critical point is that human behavior emerges to solve adaptive problems. To some degree, the modern world presents new adaptive challenges based on societal standards of conduct. These standards shape the context in which men and women view sexual behavior as desirable and appropriate.

We Differ in Our Sexual Orientations

Recently John Mace, a resident of New York City, got married. At the time of his wedding, Mr. Mace was 91 years old. Even more remarkably, he had waited 62 years to marry his soul mate, 84-year-old Richard Dorr (**Figure 9.16**). The two men met in 1948 at the Juilliard School of Music. They became a couple in 1950. When Mr. Mace and Mr. Dorr met, homosexuality was illegal in every state in the United States. And in most Western cultures, homosexuality was regarded as deviant and abnormal. In fact, until 1973, psychiatrists officially viewed homosexuality as a mental illness. But in reality, homosexual behavior has been noted in various forms throughout recorded history, and attitudes toward it have varied over time and place. Right now, public opinion is shifting on this topic in the United States. Indeed, in 2011, Mr. Dorr and Mr. Mace helped encourage the New York State Senate to pass the same-sex marriage bill. New York became the fifth state, and the most populous, to legalize same-sex marriage. Mr. Dorr has said that he and Mr. Mace are thrilled to marry. Mr. Mace adds that after so many years, it is "a completion" of sorts to stop feeling as though they are second-class citizens.

Classic psychoanalytic theories of sexual orientation suggested that families with a domineering mother and a submissive father might cause a child to identify with the opposite-sex parent (e.g., a boy with his mother). Such identification would translate into a sexual attraction to the same-sex parent. However, there is little or no evidence that the way parents treat their children has anything to do with sexual orientation. Likewise, no other environmental factor has been found to account for homosexuality. So does biology determine sexual orientation?

BIOLOGICAL FACTORS One approach to examining the extent to which biological factors contribute to sexual orientation explores the effect of hormones. The best available evidence suggests that prenatal exposure to hormones might play some role in sexual orientation (Mustanski, Chivers, & Bailey, 2002). For example, because of a mother's medical condition, some female fetuses are exposed to higher than normal levels of androgens during prenatal development. These females often have masculine characteristics, at birth and throughout life. Later in life, they are more likely to report being lesbians. Scientists have also studied the role of genetics in homosexuality, but so far it is unclear whether or how human sexual orientation might be encoded in our genes.

Some research suggests the hypothalamus may be related to sexual orientation. In postmortem examinations, researchers found that an area of the hypothalamus that typically differs between men and women was only half as large in gay men as in straight men (LeVay, 1991). In fact, the size of this area in gay men was comparable to its size in straight women. Although intriguing, this study can be criticized on the grounds that correlation does not mean causation. That is, a size difference in any one part of the brain cannot establish whether this area determines sexual orientation, whether being heterosexual or homosexual results in changes to brain structure or function, or whether some other factor is responsible for all these effects. For instance, some researchers believe that the size of the hypothalamus is determined by prenatal exposure to androgens.

FIGURE 9.16

Changing Perspectives on Homosexuality
When John Mace and Richard Dorr became a couple in 1950, homosexuality was illegal in every state in the United States. In 2011, the New York Senate passed the Same-Sex Marriage Act. A year later, 62 years after the start of their relationship, Mr. Mace, 91, and Mr. Dorr, 84, were finally married.

Although these findings are thought-provoking, there is currently not enough evidence to establish a causal connection between brain regions and sexual orientation. The evidence is consistent, however, that biology plays some role in sexual orientation. The question is how and when biology contributes, and to what degree.

STABILITY OF SEXUAL ORIENTATION In 2012, California passed a law that would have prevented mental health providers from attempting to change sexual orientation through psychological means. Later that year, however, a U.S. federal appeals court temporarily blocked implementation of the law. Such "conversion therapy" has been the subject of debate for decades, and opinions are often divided along political and religious lines.

There is no good evidence that sexual orientation can be changed through therapy. Few psychologists or physicians believe that sexual orientation—as opposed to specific sexual activity—is a choice or that it can be changed. In some cultures and subcultures, people may engage in same-sex behaviors for a period and then return to heterosexual behaviors. Men and women in jail, for example, often engage in temporary same-sex relationships. Moreover, some people are bisexual. Bisexual people are sexually attracted to people of both sexes and sometimes have sexual relationships with people of both sexes.

As the marriage of John Mace and Richard Dorr shows, many modern societies are increasingly acknowledging homosexuals' rights to express their sexuality. Canada, Spain, Norway, Sweden, South Africa, Portugal, and an increasing number of states in the United States allow gays and lesbians to marry. In 2013, the U. S. Supreme Court ruled that married same-sex couples were entitled to federal benefits, and it declined to consider a challenge to gay marriage in California. Around the world, other places recognize same-sex relationships in varying ways. In some ways, the contemporary world is catching up with human history. Homosexuality has always existed, whether or not homosexuals were free to be themselves.

9.2 CHECKPOINT: What Motivates Eating and Sexual Behavior?

- Our motivation to eat is influenced primarily by signals from the bloodstream, hormones, and specific regions of the brain. This motivation is not strongly influenced by signals from the stomach.

- Learning influences eating behaviors through classical conditioning, familiarity, and culture.

- Biology influences the motivation for sexual behavior based on the sexual response cycle and hormones.

- Sexual strategies theory may explain how cultural rules influence different sexual behavior between the sexes as well as variations in mate selection.

- Contemporary researchers maintain that biological factors influence sexual orientation.

9.3 How Do We Experience Emotions?

LEARN

📖 LEARNING GOALS	✏️ READING ACTIVITIES
a. Remember the key terms about how we experience emotions.	List all of the boldface words and write down their definitions.
b. Analyze the three theories of emotion.	Differentiate how each theory explains how you would feel excited happiness when you see your romantic partner.
c. Understand how the body and brain influence emotion.	Summarize in a table how the body, amygdala, and prefrontal cortex contribute to emotions.
d. Apply the regulation of emotional states to your life.	Provide examples of how you can use reappraisal, humor, and distraction to effectively regulate your negative emotions.

What makes you decide to do something? We do many things because we have to. However, emotion provides a lot of motivation for our actions. Remember Gabby Douglas's emotional statement that she was going to inspire a lot of people? Wanting to succeed and inspire people was Gabby's motivation for training so hard.

After she won the gold medals, Gabby was filled with joy. We aren't all Olympic gymnasts, but each of us seeks out events, activities, and objects that make us feel good. We avoid events, activities, and objects that make us feel bad. But what does it mean to feel something?

People have an intuitive sense of what emotion is. But from the perspective of psychology, an **emotion** is an immediate, specific response to environmental events. It is how you might feel when you receive a gift, or when you get cut off in traffic. Like motives, emotions also produce changes in thought and behavior. They are usually described as being positive or negative (**Figure 9.17**). In addition, we experience positive and negative emotions subjectively. That is, we feel the emotions in ways that are unique to each of us. You may feel the excitement of going on a roller coaster as a positive emotion. Another person might feel that excitement very negatively. Even so, we use common labels for emotions. Many theorists distinguish between primary and secondary emotions.

emotion
Feelings that involve subjective evaluation, physiological processes, and cognitive beliefs.

(a)

(b)

FIGURE 9.17
Negative and Positive Emotions Make Us Cry
Emotions can be positive or negative and are experienced subjectively. So we can show the same response, such as crying, to either negative or positive emotions. **(a)** The tears shed by the family and friends of a fallen police officer reflect their sadness. **(b)** This bride is crying because of the happiness she feels during her wedding.

primary emotions
Evolutionarily adaptive emotions that are shared across cultures and associated with specific physical states; they include anger, fear, sadness, disgust, happiness, and possibly surprise and contempt.

secondary emotions
Blends of primary emotions; they include remorse, guilt, shame, submission, and anticipation.

Basic or **primary emotions** are evolutionarily adaptive, shared across cultures, and associated with specific physical states. They include anger, fear, sadness, happiness, disgust, and possibly surprise and contempt. **Secondary emotions** are blends of primary emotions. They include remorse, guilt, submission, shame, and anticipation.

To see the difference between the two types of emotion, imagine that your boyfriend or girlfriend reports feeling neglected by you. Your first emotional response might be a primary one: anger at being accused, because you did not mean to neglect your companion. Your second emotional response might also be primary: sadness, because you inadvertently hurt your companion. Your anger and sadness might then combine into a secondary emotion: guilt, because through neglect you brought pain to someone you care about.

There Are Three Major Theories of Emotion

We feel happy, we feel sad, we feel angry, we feel impatient—but what causes us to feel these and other emotions? Three theories explain how we experience emotion, as described in the Learning Tip. The James-Lange theory explains emotions based on our bodily (physiological) responses. The Cannon-Bard theory focuses on how the brain processes information. The Schachter-Singer two-factor theory focuses on our thought processes.

JAMES-LANGE THEORY Common sense suggests that emotions lead to physical changes. Maybe your stomach is in knots because you're so worried about how you will do on an exam. Or someone makes you very angry, and you respond by gritting your teeth and clenching your fists. When we feel angry or sad or embarrassed, our bodies respond. But in 1884, William James argued that it was just the opposite.

James asserted that the physical changes we experience because of a situation lead us to feel an emotion. As he put it, "We feel sorry because we cry, angry because we strike, afraid because we tremble, [it is] not that we cry, strike, or

LEARNING TIP: Three Theories of Emotion

You can use the following table to remember the three theories of emotion.

THEORIES	DESCRIPTIONS	EXAMPLES
James-Lange theory	Bodily responses are the basis for feeling emotions.	Miguel had to give a presentation in front of his class of 50 students. His palms were sweating, and he was breathing heavily. He felt very scared. (See Figure 9.18.)
Cannon-Bard theory	Processing in the brain is the cause of emotions and bodily responses at the same time.	When Kumiko's son graduated from college, her brain processed the information. She felt overwhelming joy at the same time as her heart beat rapidly. (See Figure 9.20.)
Schacter-Singer two-factor theory	How a person thinks about and labels bodily responses is the basis for emotions.	When Leeza had a terrible car accident, her heart was racing incredibly fast. She attributed her heart beating so quickly to fear caused by the scary event. (See Figure 9.21.)

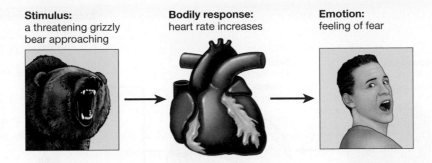

Stimulus: a threatening grizzly bear approaching

Bodily response: heart rate increases

Emotion: feeling of fear

FIGURE 9.18
James-Lange Theory of Emotion
According to this theory, when a person experiences a stimulus, he has a bodily response. Then he feels the emotion.

tremble because we are sorry, angry, or fearful" (1884, p. 190). James believed that physical changes in the body occur in distinct patterns that translate directly into specific emotions.

Around the same time, the physician and psychologist Carl Lange independently proposed a similar theory. Psychologists now refer to the **James-Lange theory** of emotion. According to this theory, we experience specific patterns of bodily responses. When we perceive those responses, we feel emotions. In the example shown in **Figure 9.18,** the man sees the bear. As a result, his heart rate increases. This response is the basis for the man's emotional response of fear.

One implication of the James-Lange theory is that if you mold your facial muscles to mimic an emotional state, it is thought that you will activate the associated emotion. In other words, facial expressions trigger the experience of emotions, not the other way around. In 1963, Silvan Tomkins proposed this idea as the *facial feedback hypothesis*. Eleven years later, James Laird (1974) tested the idea by having people hold a pencil between their teeth or with their mouths in a way that produced a smile (**Figure 9.19a**) or a frown (**Figure 9.19b**). When participants then rated cartoons, those who were made to smile found the cartoons the funniest.

CANNON-BARD THEORY In 1927, the physiologist Walter B. Cannon noted that the human mind and the human body do not experience emotions at the same speed. The mind—in other words, the brain—is quick to experience emotions. The body is much slower, taking at least a second or two to respond. Cannon also noted that many emotions produce similar bodily responses. For instance, anger, excitement, and sexual interest all produce similar changes in heart rate and blood pressure. The similarities make it too difficult for people to determine quickly which emotion they are experiencing. Therefore, Cannon, along with Philip Bard, proposed that the mind and body experience emotions independently.

According to the **Cannon-Bard theory** of emotion, the information from an emotion-producing stimulus is processed in the brain. As a result of this processing, we experience two separate things at roughly the same time: an emotion and a physical reaction. In the example in **Figure 9.20,** the man sees the bear. The

James-Lange theory
Emotions result from the experience of physiological reactions in the body.

Cannon-Bard theory
Emotions and bodily responses both occur simultaneously due to how parts of the brain process information.

(a)

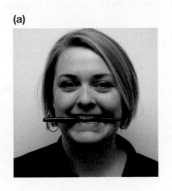

(b)

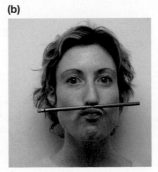

FIGURE 9.19
Facial Feedback Hypothesis
According to this hypothesis, facial expression triggers a person's experience of emotion. **(a)** When a person holds a pencil this way, the cheek muscles draw up into a smile. **(b)** But when a person holds a pencil this way, the cheek muscles draw down into a frown. In each case, the resulting expression affects the person's emotions.

FIGURE 9.20
Cannon-Bard Theory of Emotion
According to this theory, when a person experiences a stimulus, the information is processed in his brain. Then, simultaneously, he feels the emotion and the bodily reaction.

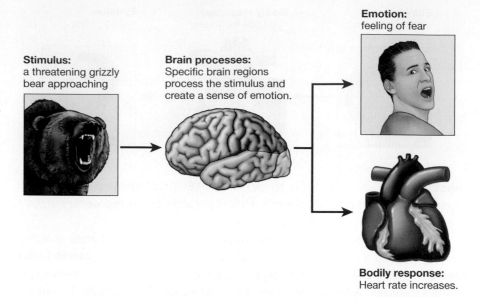

Stimulus:
a threatening grizzly bear approaching

Brain processes:
Specific brain regions process the stimulus and create a sense of emotion.

Emotion:
feeling of fear

Bodily response:
Heart rate increases.

two-factor theory
How we experience an emotion is influenced by the cognitive label we apply to explain the physiological changes we have experienced.

man's brain processes the information about the bear. The processing in the brain produces, at the same time, both the emotion of fear and bodily changes, such as an increase in heart rate.

SCHACHTER-SINGER TWO-FACTOR THEORY The social psychologists Stanley Schachter and Jerome Singer (1962) proposed a **two-factor theory** of emotion. According to this theory, a situation evokes both a physiological response, such as arousal, and a cognitive interpretation. The cognitive interpretation is called an *emotion label*. In other words, when we experience arousal, we search for its source so we can explain it cognitively. **Figure 9.21** shows a man seeing a bear. The man feels a bodily response, such as an increase in heart rate. The man then interprets that his heart rate increased because the bear is scary and threatening. Thus the interpretation of the bodily response leads to the feeling of fear.

Often the search for a cognitive explanation is quick and straightforward. That is, we generally recognize the event that led to our emotional state. But what happens when the situation is not so clear? The two-factor theory proposes that whatever we believe caused the emotion will determine how we label the emotion.

One interesting implication of the two-factor theory is that physical states caused by a situation can be attributed to the wrong emotion. Such mistaken identification of the source of our arousal is called *misattribution of arousal*.

In one exploration of this phenomenon, researchers tried to see whether people could feel romantic attraction through misattribution (Dutton & Aron, 1974). Each participant, a straight male, chose to cross either of two bridges over the Capilano River, in British Columbia. One was a narrow suspension bridge with a low rail that swayed 230 feet above raging, rocky rapids (**Figure 9.22**).

FIGURE 9.21

Schachter-Singer Two-Factor Theory
According to this theory, when a person experiences a stimulus, he has a bodily response. Then he applies an emotion label to explain the changes. Finally, he feels the emotion brought on by the situation.

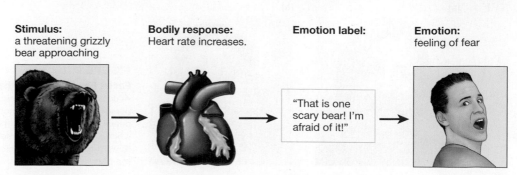

Stimulus:
a threatening grizzly bear approaching

Bodily response:
Heart rate increases.

Emotion label:
"That is one scary bear! I'm afraid of it!"

Emotion:
feeling of fear

The other was a sturdy modern bridge just above the river. At the middle of each bridge, an attractive female research assistant approached the man and interviewed him. She gave him her phone number and offered to explain the results of the study at a later date if he was interested.

According to the two-factor theory of emotion, the less stable bridge would produce bodily arousal (sweaty palms, increased heart rate). This arousal could be misattributed as attraction to the interviewer. Indeed, men interviewed on the less stable bridge were more likely to call the interviewer and ask her for a date.

Many possible confounds could affect this study (recall from Chapter 1 that confounds are hidden variables). For instance, men who were more likely to take risks might be more likely to choose a scary bridge *and* to call for a date. Nevertheless, the general idea—that people can misattribute arousal for attraction—has been supported in other studies.

Excitation transfer is a similar form of misattribution. Here, leftover physiological arousal caused by one event is transferred to a new stimulus. For example, in the period after exercise, the body returns to its baseline state slowly. The body is adjusting to persisting arousal symptoms, including an elevated heart rate. After a few minutes, most people will have caught their breath and may not realize their bodies are still aroused. So during this interim period, they are likely to transfer the residual excitation from the exercise to any event that occurs.

FIGURE 9.22
Misattribution of Arousal
Some men walked across this scary bridge. These men displayed more attraction to the female experimenter on the bridge than did the men who crossed on a safer bridge. This result suggests that the men on this bridge misattributed their physiological responses. They assumed their fast heartbeats and increased sweating were related to being attracted to the female, not to being scared by crossing the high bridge.

Both Body and Brain Are Important for Emotion

You just learned that different theories of emotion focus on the idea that we feel something based primarily on how our bodies or our brains respond to a situation. You feel fear because you see a bear and your heart starts beating fast, or because your brain processes information about the bear. Let's look more closely now at exactly what parts of our bodies and brains influence our experience of emotions.

EMOTIONS FROM BODILY RESPONSES Think about all the movies or TV shows you've seen where a law enforcement agent is trying to find out if a suspect is telling the truth. The suspect is hooked up to a polygraph—popularly known as a lie detector. The assumption behind using these devices is that people who are lying are more likely to be emotional. Because of their emotions, they will have physical reactions that show up on the polygraph.

In fact, certain emotional states do influence the body in predictable ways. When people are frightened, their muscles become tense and their hearts beat faster. Giving a talk in front of people causes many of us to perspire. Other bodily systems that are associated with certain emotional states include blood pressure, blood temperature, breathing rate, and pupil size.

THE AMYGDALA One brain region that is important for understanding emotion is the amygdala (**Figure 9.23a**). The amygdala processes the emotional significance of stimuli, and it generates immediate emotional and behavioral reactions (Phelps, 2006). According to Joseph LeDoux (2007), the processing of emotion in the amygdala is a circuit that has developed over the course of evolution to protect animals from danger. LeDoux (1996, 2007) has established the amygdala as the brain structure most important for emotional learning. For an example of emotional learning, remember how fear responses can be classically conditioned (see Chapter 6). People with damage to the amygdala might know certain objects are dangerous, but they do not seem afraid of those objects. These same people do

After reading Chapter 9 of her psychology textbook, Kim decided to watch some television. Flipping through the channels, she landed on an episode of the crime drama *Lie to Me*. She'd never seen the show before. She became interested when she discovered that the main character, Dr. Cal Lightman, was a psychologist. At one point, Lightman explained that he could detect whether a suspect was lying by watching the person's facial expressions. *Could this really happen?* Kim wondered. She was pretty certain that she should not trust a TV show to present psychological findings accurately.

After her next psychology class, Kim asked Dr. Parretti about the show. "I'm actually a fan," Dr. Parretti told her, "because the science is so good." *So at least one show has scientific validity!* Dr. Parretti explained that *Lie to Me* was inspired by the work of the psychologist Paul Ekman (who is mentioned on p. 338). In fact, Ekman was a scientific consultant for the show. In his research, Ekman has found that emotions are universal and innate. Drawing on these findings, Ekman has helped train TSA agents, FBI agents, and Secret Service agents to detect deception. People can hide their emotions to some extent, so Ekman trains people to look for what he calls "micro-emotions"—very brief, involuntary facial expressions of emotions that people aren't so good at hiding. These expressions last less than one-fifth of a second. *That is amazing! I can't believe that anyone can detect something that happens so quickly.*

Dr. Parretti later e-mailed Kim an article from the *Popular Mechanics* Web site with even more information. According to the article, 1 percent of the population is so good at detecting deception that Ekman calls them "wizards of deception detection." Even without training, these people can detect micro-emotions and lies. Kim remembered her recent phone call home, when her mother claimed to know that Kim's brother, Ken, was lying about where he'd been the night before. "How do you know?" Kim asked.

"A mother knows when her son is lying," her mother claimed. "That is how I know!"

When her mother claimed maternal intuition, it was impossible to argue with her, so Kim let the subject drop. Now she thought, *Is it possible that my mother is one of these wizards? That's unlikely, given how few of them are.* Kim wondered if what her mother called maternal intuition was in fact an ability her mother had acquired. Maybe her mother had learned how to detect micro-emotions in Ken's face, so she really could tell when he was lying.

not develop conditioned fear responses to objects associated with negative events, such as being shocked each time the object is presented.

Consider the case of S.P. This patient had a portion of her amygdala removed to reduce the frequency of epileptic seizures (Anderson & Phelps, 2000). The surgery

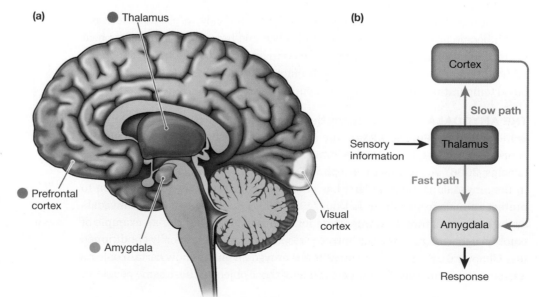

FIGURE 9.23

The Emotional Brain
(a) The two most important brain structures for processing emotion are the amygdala and the prefrontal cortex. **(b)** When sensory information reaches the thalamus, the information can take two paths. The fast path and the slow path enable us to assess and respond to emotion-producing stimuli in different ways.

was reasonably successful, and S.P. retained most of her intellectual faculties. She has a normal IQ, has taken college courses, and performs well on standardized tests of visual attention. She does not show fear conditioning, however. When she sees a picture of a blue square that has previously been accompanied by an electric shock, S.P. can tell you that the blue square is associated with shock, but her body shows no physiological evidence of having acquired the fear response.

Information reaches the amygdala along two separate pathways. The first path is a "quick and dirty" system that processes sensory information nearly instantaneously. Recall from Chapter 5 that, except for smell, all sensory information travels to the thalamus before going on to other brain structures and the related portions of the cortex. Along the fast path, sensory information travels quickly through the thalamus to the amygdala for priority processing (**Figure 9.23b**). Suppose you are walking along a hiking trail and come across an object that looks like a snake. The fast path prepares you to take evasive action.

The second path is somewhat slower, but it leads to more deliberate and more thorough evaluations. Along this slow path, sensory material travels from the thalamus to the cortex (i.e., the visual cortex or the auditory cortex). In the cortex, the information is scrutinized in greater depth before it is passed along to the amygdala. This slower processing has determined that what you saw was just a stick shaped like a snake, and you can step right over it. Theorists believe that the fast system prepares animals to respond to a threat in case the slower pathway confirms the threat (LeDoux, 2000).

As we saw in Chapter 7, emotional events are especially likely to be stored in memory. The amygdala plays a role in this process. Brain imaging studies have shown that emotional events are likely to increase activity in the amygdala and that increased activity is likely to improve long-term memory for the event (Cahill et al., 2001; Hamann, Ely, Grafton, & Kilts, 1999). In short, thanks to the amygdala, emotions such as fear strengthen memories. This adaptive mechanism enables us to remember harmful situations so we can potentially avoid them.

The amygdala also plays another role in the processing of emotions: It is involved in the perception of social stimuli. For instance, when we "read" someone's facial expressions, the amygdala helps us interpret them. Brain imaging studies demonstrate that this perception is particularly useful in the case of fearful faces (Whalen et al., 1998). People with damage to the amygdala often have difficulty evaluating the intensity of fearful faces. One study suggests that people with damage to the amygdala have difficulty using photographs to assess people's trustworthiness—a task most people can do easily (Adolphs, Sears, & Piven, 2001; **Figure 9.24**). This difficulty leads them to be unusually friendly with people they do not know. Their extra friendliness might result from a lack of the normal mechanisms for being cautious around strangers and for feeling that some people should be avoided.

THE PREFRONTAL CORTEX Another brain region that is important for understanding emotion is the prefrontal cortex (see Figure 9.23a). There is some evidence that the left and right frontal lobes are affected by different emotions. In a series of studies, Richard Davidson (2000) found that greater activation of the right prefrontal cortex is associated with negative emotion, whereas greater activation of the left hemisphere is associated with positive emotion.

Injury to the frontal lobes often impairs emotional experience. Consider the case of Elliott. Elliot was a happily married man and a successful professional who began having headaches in his early 30s. It turned out that a tumor the size of a small orange was growing behind Elliot's eyes and into his frontal lobes. Surgeons removed the tumor along with some frontal lobe tissue, and Elliott recovered

(a)

(b)

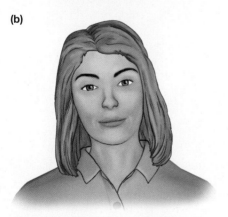

FIGURE 9.24

Evaluating Trustworthiness From Facial Expressions

People with damage to the amygdala cannot determine whether the facial expression in **(a)** or **(b)** shows trustworthiness. People with damage to the amygdala tend to be unusually friendly and not cautious with strangers.

quickly. He continued to be a reasonable, intelligent, and charming man with a superb memory. However, he no longer experienced emotion.

The neurologist Antonio Damasio (1994) showed Elliot a series of disturbing pictures, such as images of severely injured bodies. Elliot knew the pictures were disturbing. He believed that before the surgery he would have responded to them emotionally. But now he felt nothing.

Without emotions, and the link they provide to motivation, Elliot became detached from his problems and reacted to the events in his life as if they were happening to someone he was not very connected to. Elliot's brain surgery left his intellect intact. However, the surgery ultimately robbed him of his ability to function as a member of society.

We Regulate Our Emotional States

Emotions can be disruptive and troublesome. In our daily lives, circumstances often require us to harness our emotional responses. Doing so is not easy, of course. How do you mask your expression of disgust when you are obligated by politeness to eat something you dislike? How do you force yourself to be nice about losing a competition that really matters to you?

James Gross (1999) outlined several strategies people use to regulate their emotions. In *reappraisal*, we directly alter our emotional reactions to events by thinking about those events in more neutral terms. So if you get scared while watching a movie, you can remind yourself that the movie is fictional and no one is actually being hurt. Recent studies have found that engaging in reappraisal changes the activity of brain regions involved in the experience of emotion (Ochsner, Bunge, Gross, & Gabrieli, 2002).

Next we look at some other strategies for regulating emotional states. Not all of these strategies are equally successful. *Humor* is a simple, effective method of regulating negative emotions. *Thought suppression* and *rumination* are two common mistakes people make when trying to regulate mood. *Distraction* is, overall, the best way to avoid the problems that come with those mistakes.

HUMOR "Laughter is the best medicine" is a common saying. In fact, humor has many mental and physical health benefits. Most obviously, humor increases positive emotion. When we find something humorous, we smile, laugh, and enter a state of pleasurable, relaxed excitation. Research shows that laughter improves the immune system and stimulates the release of hormones, dopamine, serotonin, and endorphins. When we laugh, we experience rises in circulation, blood pressure, skin temperature, and heart rate, along with a decrease in pain perception. All of these responses are similar to those resulting from physical exercise. They are considered beneficial to short-term and long-term health.

Sometimes we laugh in situations that do not seem very humorous. For example, telling funny stories about someone at her funeral may seem odd. According to one theory, laughing in such situations helps people distance themselves from their negative emotions and strengthens their connections to others. In one study on the topic, Dacher Keltner and George Bonanno (1997) interviewed 40 people who had recently lost a spouse. The researchers found that genuine laughter during the interview was associated with positive mental health and fewer negative feelings, such as grief. Laughing was a way of coping with a difficult situation.

THOUGHT SUPPRESSION AND RUMINATION When we suppress negative thoughts, we are trying not to feel or respond to the emotion at all. Daniel Wegner and colleagues (1990) have demonstrated that suppressing negative thoughts is extremely difficult. In fact, doing so often leads to a *rebound effect*. As a result of the rebound, we actually think more about something after suppression than before. Sometimes people who are dieting try not to think about the foods they can't eat. These people often end up thinking about those foods more than if they had engaged in a distracting activity.

Rumination involves thinking about, elaborating, and focusing on undesired thoughts or feelings. This response prolongs the mood. It also hampers successful mood regulation strategies, such as distracting yourself or focusing on solutions for the problem (Lyubomirsky & Nolen-Hoeksema, 1995).

DISTRACTION You're going to the dentist tomorrow morning. Just thinking about the root canal work you're going to have is making your evening unpleasant. So you distract yourself by going out with friends. Distraction involves doing or thinking about something other than the troubling activity or thought. By focusing attention elsewhere, distraction temporarily helps us stop focusing on our difficulties.

Some distractions backfire, however. We may end up thinking about other problems. Or we may engage in maladaptive behaviors, such as overeating or binge drinking. A healthier strategy might involve watching a movie that captures your attention. Choose a movie that will not remind you of your troubled situation. Otherwise, you might simply find yourself wallowing in mental anguish.

9.3 CHECKPOINT: How Do We Experience Emotions?

- Emotions are a personal experience. Primary emotions are universal across cultures. Secondary emotions are blends of the primary emotions.

- Emotions are associated with bodily reactions. Emotions are a product of processing in certain parts of the brain, particularly the amygdala and the prefrontal cortex.

- The James-Lange theory, Cannon-Bard theory, and two-factor theory explain how we feel emotions, based primarily on physiological or cognitive components.

- We can successfully regulate our negative emotional states by using strategies such as reappraisal, humor, and distraction.

9.4 How Do Emotions Help Us Adapt?

📖 **LEARNING GOALS**	✏️ **READING ACTIVITIES**
a. Remember the key terms related to how emotions help us adapt.	List all of the boldface words and write down their definitions.
b. Understand how facial expressions communicate emotion and how display rules vary.	Compare when the display rules of your culture do or do not permit showing two of the universal emotions.
c. Understand the cognitive functions of emotions.	Summarize in your own words how emotions affect decision making and judgments.
d. Apply the interpersonal functions of guilt and embarrassment to your life.	Provide an example of how guilt and embarrassment have strengthened interpersonal relations in your life.

Over the course of human evolution, we have drawn on our emotions to help us respond to environmental challenges. Negative and positive experiences have guided our species to successful behaviors, such as running away when we are about to be attacked by a dangerous animal. In other words, emotions are adaptive because they prepare and guide behaviors that increase the probability of surviving and reproducing. Emotions provide information about the importance of stimuli to personal goals, and then they prepare us for actions aimed at achieving those goals (Frijda, 1994).

Facial Expressions Communicate Emotion

If someone scowls at you intensely, you are likely to feel afraid, or at least wary, of him. We interpret facial expressions of emotion to predict other people's behavior. Facial expressions provide many clues about whether our behavior is pleasing to others or whether it is likely to make them reject, attack, or cheat us. In his 1872 book, *Expression of Emotion in Man and Animals*, Charles Darwin argued that expressive aspects of emotion are adaptive because they communicate how we are feeling. Thus facial expressions, like emotions themselves, provide adaptive information.

(a)

(b)

FIGURE 9.25

Contextual Effects on Categorizing Emotional Expression

Research participants were shown images such as these and asked to categorize them as showing anger, fear, pride, sadness, disgust, surprise, or happiness. **(a)** This photo pairs a sad face with a sad posture. When the face appeared in this context, most participants categorized the expression as sad. **(b)** This photo pairs the same sad face with a fearful posture. When the face appeared in this context, most participants categorized the expression incorrectly, as fearful.

EYES AND MOUTH We convey emotional information by means of our eyes and mouth. Much of the research on facial expression is conducted by showing people isolated faces. In the real world, however, we see faces in contexts that give us cues about what emotion a person is experiencing. In one study, researchers showed identical facial expressions in different contexts and found that the context profoundly affected how people interpreted the emotion (Aviezer et al., 2008; **Figure 9.25**). Look at the photos in Try It Yourself to see if you can tell when a smile is sincere.

FACIAL EXPRESSIONS ACROSS CULTURES Does a smile mean the same thing in Bolivia or Vietnam that it means in the United States? According to Darwin, the face innately communicates emotions to others. He argued that these communications are understandable by all people, regardless of culture. Paul Ekman and colleagues (1969) tested this hypothesis in Argentina, Brazil, Chile, Japan, and the United States. In each country, participants viewed photographs of posed emotional expressions and then were asked to identify the emotional responses. In all five countries, the participants recognized the expressions as anger, fear, disgust, happiness, sadness, and surprise.

Because people in these countries had extensive exposure to each other's cultures, however, learning and not biology could have been responsible for the cross-cultural agreement. To control for that potential confounding factor, the researchers traveled to a remote area in New Guinea. The native inhabitants there had little exposure to outside cultures and received only minimal formal education. Nonetheless, they were able to identify the emotions seen in the photos fairly well. Agreement was not quite as high as in other cultures. As shown in Scientific Thinking, the researchers also asked participants in New Guinea to display certain facial expressions. They found that evaluators from other countries identified the expressions at a level better than chance (Ekman & Friesen, 1971).

Subsequent research has found general support for cross-cultural identification of some facial expressions. Support is strongest for happiness and weakest

TRY IT YOURSELF: Genuine Versus Fake Smiles

When people smile, they don't always mean it. Try to determine whether the man below is showing a genuine smile (really feeling happy) or a "fake" smile (being sociable but not actually feeling happy). The answer is below.

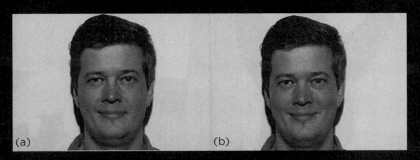

(a)   (b)

There are real differences between a genuine smile and a fake one. These differences are processed by different regions of the brain. Focusing on the mouth does not provide information about whether the smile is genuine. Instead, the eyes tell it all: When a person is genuinely happy, you will see a small crinkle at the corners of the eyes.

Answers: (a) fake, (b) genuine.

SCIENTIFIC THINKING:
Facial Expressions Across Cultures

Hypothesis: The face innately communicates emotions to others. These communications are understandable by all people, regardless of culture.

Research Method:

1 Participants in New Guinea were photographed while displaying certain facial expressions. For example, they were asked to look as if they had come across a rotting pig or as if one of their children had died.

2 Participants from other countries were asked to identify the emotions being expressed by the New Guineans.

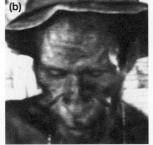

Results: People across cultures largely agreed on the meaning of different facial expressions. The examples here are **(a)** happiness, **(b)** sadness, **(c)** anger, and **(d)** disgust.

Conclusion: Recognition of facial expressions may be universal and therefore biologically based.

FIGURE 9.26
Expressions of Pride May Be Biologically Determined
In response to victory in separate judo matches, **(a)** a sighted athlete and **(b)** an athlete who was born blind both expressed their pride through similar behaviors. Because such similarities occur across cultures, the physical expression of pride appears to be biologically based.

for fear and disgust (Elfenbein & Ambady, 2002). The evidence showing that many facial expressions are universal suggests they probably have a biological basis.

FACIAL EXPRESSIONS OF PRIDE Would you expect the physical expression of pride to be biologically based or culturally specific? The psychologist Jessica Tracy has found that young children can recognize when a person feels pride. Moreover, she found that isolated populations with minimal Western contact also accurately identify the physical signs. These signs include a smiling face, raised arms, an expanded chest, and a pushed-out torso (Tracy & Robins, 2008).

Tracy and David Matsumoto (2008) examined pride responses among people competing in judo matches in the 2004 Olympic and Paralympic Games. Sighted and blind athletes from 37 nations competed. After victory, the behaviors displayed by sighted and blind athletes were very similar. This finding suggests that pride responses are innate rather than learned by observing them in others (**Figure 9.26**).

Display Rules Differ Across Cultures and Between the Sexes

Americans are loud and obnoxious. The British are cold and bland. Italians are warm and emotional. We're all familiar with such cultural stereotypes, which appear in everything from movies to advertising. These images arise in part because of **display rules.** Display rules govern how and when people exhibit emotions. Basic emotions seem to be expressed similarly across cultures. But display rules, which are learned through socialization, dictate which emotions are suitable in given situations. Display rules also may explain why the identification of facial expressions is much better within cultures than between cultures (Elfenbein & Ambady, 2002).

From culture to culture, display rules tend to be different for women and men. In particular, the rules for smiling and crying differ between the sexes. At least in North America, it is generally believed that women display emotions more readily, frequently, easily, and intensely (Plant, Hyde, Keltner, & Devine, 2000). There is evidence that this belief is true—except perhaps for emotions related to dominance, such as anger (LaFrance & Banaji, 1992). Men and women may vary in their emotional expressiveness for evolutionary reasons: The emotions most closely associated with women are related to caregiving, nurturance, and

display rules
Rules that are learned through socialization and that dictate what emotions are suitable in certain situations.

interpersonal relationships. The emotions associated with men are related to dominance, defensiveness, and competitiveness.

Women may be more likely to display many emotions. They do not necessarily experience those emotions more intensely. Even when women report more-intense emotions, their reports might reflect societal norms about how women are supposed to feel (Grossman & Wood, 1993). Perhaps because of differences in upbringing in modern Western society, women tend to be better than men at describing their emotions (Feldman Barrett, Lane, Sechrest, & Schwartz, 2000).

Ultimately, do sex differences in emotional expression reflect learned patterns of behaviors? Or do they reflect biologically based differences? Nature and nurture work together here. It is difficult—often impossible—to distinguish the effects of nature versus nurture.

Emotions Serve Cognitive Functions

For a long time, psychologists considered thinking and feeling as separate. Researchers studied decision making, memory, and other mental processes as if people were evaluating the information from a purely rational perspective. Yet our immediate emotional responses arise quickly and automatically, coloring our perceptions at the very instant we notice an object. As Robert Zajonc put it, "We do not just see 'a house': We see a *handsome* house, an *ugly* house, or a *pretentious* house" (1980, p. 154). These instantaneous evaluations subsequently guide our decision making, memory, and behavior. Therefore, psychologists now generally acknowledge that it is unrealistic to try to separate emotion from cognition (Phelps, 2006).

As Chapter 8 emphasizes, everyday cognition is far from rational. Our decisions and judgments are affected by our feelings. For example, when we are in a good mood, we tend to be persistent and to find creative, elaborate responses to challenging problems (Isen, 1993). When we are pursuing goals, positive feelings signal that we are making satisfactory progress and thereby encourage us to keep trying. According to the **affect-as-information theory** (Schwarz & Clore, 1983), we use our current moods to make decisions, judgments, and appraisals. We draw on our moods even if we do not know their sources.

DECISION MAKING Would you rather go rock climbing in the Alps or attend a performance by a small dance troupe in Paris? In considering this question, did you think rationally about all the implications of either choice? Or did you flash on how you would feel in either situation? Emotions influence our decision making in different ways. For example, anticipating how different choices might make us feel can serve as a guide in decision making. In this way, we are able to make decisions more quickly and more efficiently. And in the face of complex, multi-faceted situations, emotions serve as heuristic guides (see Chapter 8). That is, emotions provide feedback for making quick decisions (Slovic, Finucane, Peters, & MacGregor, 2002).

EMOTION AFFECTS JUDGMENTS As noted above, we use our moods to make judgments. For example, Schwarz and Clore (1983) asked people to rate their overall life satisfaction. To answer this question, people potentially must consider many factors, including living situations, expectations, personal goals, and accomplishments. In arriving at their answers, however, the research participants did not carefully consider all these factors. Instead, the participants seemed to rely on their current moods. People in good moods rated their lives as satisfactory, whereas people in bad moods gave lower overall ratings.

affect-as-information theory
People use their current moods to make decisions, judgments, and appraisals, even if they do not know the sources of the moods.

Emotions Strengthen Interpersonal Relations

FIGURE 9.27

Emotions Influence Social Bonds
Emotions can help strengthen social relationships between people. Here, the clear expressions of joy will help cement the decision of this couple to get married.

Because humans are social animals, many of our emotions involve interpersonal factors. We feel hurt when teased, angry when insulted, happy when loved, and proud when complimented. In interacting with others, we use emotional expressions as powerful tools for social communication (**Figure 9.27**).

Nevertheless, for most of the twentieth century, psychologists paid little attention to interpersonal emotions. Guilt, embarrassment, and similar phenomena were associated with Freudian thinking and therefore not studied in mainstream psychological science. Theorists have since reconsidered interpersonal emotions in view of humans' evolutionary need to belong to social groups. Thus social emotions may be important for maintaining social bonds.

GUILT STRENGTHENS SOCIAL BONDS When we believe we did something that directly or indirectly harmed another person, we experience feelings of anxiety, tension, and remorse. We label such feelings as **guilt.** The typical guilt experience occurs when we feel responsible for another person's negative emotional state. Occasionally, however, guilt can arise even when we know we are not responsible. A familiar example is survivor guilt. That is, people feel guilty for having survived accidents or catastrophes in which others have died.

Excessive feelings of guilt may have negative consequences. Guilt itself is not entirely negative. According to one theory, guilt protects and strengthens interpersonal relationships in three ways (Baumeister et al., 1994). First, feelings of guilt discourage us from doing things that would harm our relationships and encourage behaviors that strengthen relationships. For example, guilt keeps us from cheating on our partners and leads us to phone our parents regularly. Second, displays of guilt demonstrate that people care about their relationship partners, thereby affirming social bonds. Third, guilt can be used to manipulate others. This aspect of guilt is especially effective when people hold power over us and it is difficult to get them to do what we want. For instance, you might try to make your boss feel guilty so you do not have to work overtime. Children may use guilt to get adults to buy them presents or grant them privileges.

There is evidence that socialization is more important than biology in determining specifically how children experience guilt. One study involving identical and fraternal twins (Zahn-Waxler & Robinson, 1995) found that all the negative emotions showed considerable genetic influence, but guilt was unique in being highly influenced by social environment. Perhaps surprisingly, parental warmth is associated with greater guilt in children. This finding suggests that feelings of guilt arise in healthy and happy relationships. As children become citizens in a social world, they develop the capacity to empathize. As a result, they experience feelings of guilt when they transgress against others.

EMBARRASSMENT AND BLUSHING We have all experienced embarrassment, probably many times. We tend to feel embarrassed after violating a cultural

guilt
A negative emotional state associated with anxiety, tension, and agitation.

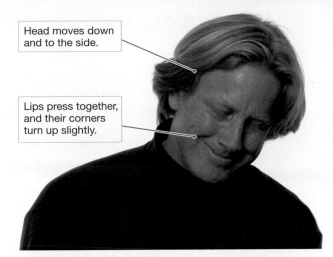

Head moves down and to the side.

Lips press together, and their corners turn up slightly.

FIGURE 9.28
Embarrassment
Embarrassment is another emotion that can increase social bonds. In this photo, the psychologist Dacher Keltner is demonstrating the classic facial signals of embarrassment.

norm, doing something clumsy, being teased, or experiencing a threat to our self-image (Miller, 1996). Some theories suggest that embarrassment remedies interpersonal awkwardness and restores social bonds. Embarrassment represents recognition of the unintentional social error. Like guilt, embarrassment may reaffirm close relationships after wrongdoing (**Figure 9.28**).

Embarrassment is often accompanied by blushing. The writer Mark Twain once said, "Man is the only animal that blushes. Or needs to." Darwin, in his 1872 book, called blushing the "most peculiar and the most human of all expressions," thereby separating it from emotional responses he deemed necessary for survival. According to recent theory and research, blushing occurs most often when people believe others might view them negatively, and blushing communicates an understanding that some type of social awkwardness occurred. This nonverbal apology is an appeasement that brings out forgiveness in others, thereby repairing and maintaining relationships (Keltner & Anderson, 2000).

 9.4 CHECKPOINT: **How Do Emotions Help Us Adapt?**

- Facial expressions communicate emotion. Some expressions of emotion are universally recognized.

- Display rules learned through socialization dictate how and when people express emotions. These rules differ between the sexes and across cultures.

- Emotions serve cognitive functions when we interpret our body's responses and use that information to make decisions and evaluate information.

- Guilt and embarrassment strengthen interpersonal relations by helping to maintain and repair social bonds.

BIG PICTURE

9.1
What Motivates Our Behavior?

a. Remember the key terms about motivation.
b. Understand the five main factors that motivate us to behave in a certain way.
c. Apply intrinsic and extrinsic motivation to your life.
d. Apply achievement motivation to your life.

9.2
What Motivates Eating and Sexual Behavior?

a. Remember the key terms about the motivations to eat and to have sexual relations.
b. Analyze how four biological systems influence our motivation to eat.
c. Apply the idea that learning affects your motivation to eat.
d. Understand two ways that biology affects the motivation for sexual behavior.
e. Apply cultural rules to motivation for sexual behavior.

9.3
How Do We Experience Emotions?

a. Remember the key terms about how we experience emotions.
b. Analyze the three theories of emotion.
c. Understand how the body and brain influence emotion.
d. Apply the regulation of emotional states to your life.

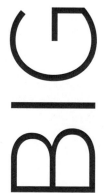

9.4
How Do Emotions Help Us Adapt?

a. Remember the key terms related to how emotions help us adapt.
b. Understand how facial expressions communicate emotion and how display rules vary.
c. Understand the cognitive functions of emotions.
d. Apply the interpersonal functions of guilt and embarrassment to your life.

KEY TERMS

motivation
need
need hierarchy
drive
arousal
incentives
extrinsic motivation
intrinsic motivation
achievement motivation
need to belong theory

CHECKPOINT

- Motivations include factors of differing strengths that activate, direct, and sustain behaviors that satisfy a need.

- Needs, drives, incentives, arousal, and pleasure all affect motivation.

- Extrinsically motivated acts are directed toward the achievement of an external goal. Intrinsically motivated acts are performed simply because they are pleasurable.

- We are motivated to achieve our long-term goals. People with high self-efficacy and high need achievement are more likely to set challenging but attainable goals.

- We have a fundamental need to belong. This need motivates us to make friends and avoid social exclusion. But it creates feelings of emptiness and despair in the absence of other people.

leptin
ghrelin
sexual response cycle
androgens
estrogens
sexual strategies theory

- Our motivation to eat is influenced primarily by signals from the bloodstream, hormones, and specific regions of the brain. This motivation is not strongly influenced by signals from the stomach.

- Learning influences eating behaviors through classical conditioning, familiarity, and culture.

- Biology influences the motivation for sexual behavior based on the sexual response cycle and hormones.

- Sexual strategies theory may explain how cultural rules influence different sexual behavior between the sexes as well as variations in mate selection.

- Contemporary researchers maintain that biological factors influence sexual orientation.

emotion
primary emotions
secondary emotions
James-Lange theory
Cannon-Bard theory
two-factor theory

- Emotions are a personal experience. Primary emotions are universal across cultures. Secondary emotions are blends of the primary emotions.

- Emotions are associated with bodily reactions. Emotions are a product of processing in certain parts of the brain, particularly the amygdala and the prefrontal cortex.

- The James-Lange theory, Cannon-Bard theory, and two-factor theory explain how we feel emotions, based primarily on physiological or cognitive components.

- We can successfully regulate our negative emotional states by using strategies such as reappraisal, humor, and distraction.

display rules
affect-as-information theory
guilt

- Facial expressions communicate emotion. Some expressions of emotion are universally recognized.

- Display rules learned through socialization dictate how and when people express emotions. These rules differ between the sexes and across cultures.

- Emotions serve cognitive functions when we interpret our body's responses and use that information to make decisions and evaluate information.

- Guilt and embarrassment strengthen interpersonal relations by helping to maintain and repair social bonds.

For a self-quiz on this chapter, go to the back of the book and find Appendix B: Quizzes.

10 Health and Well-Being

CAN SOMEONE BE TOO OBESE TO BE A GOOD PARENT? Gary Stocklaufer was a happily married man, the adoptive father of a great son, and certified by the state to be a foster parent. When his cousin was unable to raise his own baby son, Max, Stocklaufer and his wife stepped in as the child's foster parents. After three months, they filed the paperwork to adopt their cherished foster son. But the same Missouri judge who had presided over Stocklaufer's earlier adoption this time said no. The judge cited Stocklaufer's weight—at the time, between 500 and 600 pounds—as the reason for

BIG QUESTIONS

FIGURE 10.1

Gary Stocklaufer

Gary Stocklaufer is shown here weighing over 500 pounds. Stocklaufer fought against a judge's ruling that he was too obese to adopt a child. Shortly after this photograph was taken, Stocklaufer underwent surgery to help him lose weight, and the court reversed the ruling.

the denial. Apart from his weight, Stocklaufer was healthy. The judge reasoned that Stocklaufer was likely to develop a serious disease and die at a young age because he was obese (**Figure 10.1**).

When asked about the case, the judge responded that he was required to consider the welfare and best interests of the child. The National Association to Advance Fat Acceptance (NAAFA) asked publicly whether "fat = poor parenting," and it established a legal defense fund for Stocklaufer. The case was appealed. Ultimately, the judge reversed his earlier ruling because Stocklaufer had lost over 200 pounds following gastric bypass surgery.

Stocklaufer's case is only one of many similar stories in which fat people have been denied the right to adopt. Is it reasonable to consider someone's weight when deciding something as important as adoption? Given that body weight has a substantial genetic component, should potential parents be held accountable for their weight? Would it make a difference if the potential parent were following an exercise program? Could the standard of acting in a child's best interests be applied to prospective adoptive parents who smoke? What about people with diabetes or other conditions associated with a reduced life span? These questions are related to the idea that we can control our health behaviors. By doing so, we can play an active role in being healthier and living longer.

10.1 What Affects Our Health?

📖 **LEARNING GOALS**	✏️ **READING ACTIVITIES** **LEARN**
a. Remember the key terms about health and well-being.	List all of the boldface words and write down their definitions.
b. Apply the biopsychosocial model of health to your life.	Provide a description of one health issue that could be explained by this model.
c. Analyze how overeating, anorexia, bulimia, and binge eating affect health.	Differentiate between these three types of disordered eating and the causes and health effects of each.
d. Evaluate how exercising more can improve health.	Assess the physical, emotional, and cognitive benefits of exercise.

health psychology

A field that integrates research on health and on psychology; it involves the application of psychological principles to promoting health and well-being.

well-being

A positive state that includes striving for optimal health and life satisfaction.

biopsychosocial model

A model of health that integrates the effects of biological, behavioral, and social factors on health and illness.

If you ask yourself, "What affects my health?" you may think first about germs, viruses, and disease. Indeed, most people think about their health in only biological and medical terms. So you may be surprised to learn that your attitudes and behavior affect your health.

Biology, Psychology, and Social Factors Influence Health

The traditional Western medical model sees health essentially as the absence of disease. According to this model, people are patients—passive recipients of disease. The focus is on medical treatments, including drugs, designed to return patients to health. The assumption is that health professionals know best and thus should maintain control over what happens to the patients.

Psychologists and most health-care professionals take a more integrated approach to health and well-being. They believe our attitudes and behaviors are critical in staying healthy, regaining health following illness, and achieving well-being throughout our lives. In this approach, the individual plays a more active role.

Health psychology integrates research on health and on psychology. This field was launched nearly three decades ago. At that time, psychologists, physicians, and other health professionals came to appreciate the importance of lifestyle factors to physical health (**Figure 10.2**). Health psychologists do not think of health as merely the absence of disease. Instead, they apply their knowledge of psychological principles to promote health and well-being.

Well-being is a positive state in which we feel our best. To achieve this state, we need to strive for optimal health and life satisfaction. To achieve optimal health, we need to actively participate in health-enhancing behaviors.

Health and well-being is a growing area of psychology. Psychologists who study health and well-being want to understand the complex relationships between thoughts (health-related cognitions), actions, and physical and mental health. To understand those relationships, psychologists rely on the research methods of psychology. They study how our behavior and social systems affect our health. They study how ethnic and sex differences influence health outcomes. And they study how health-related behaviors and health outcomes affect our actions, thoughts, and emotions.

BIOPSYCHOSOCIAL MODEL How can your personality, thoughts, or behavior affect your health? To answer this question, you need to understand the **biopsychosocial model** (**Figure 10.3**). This model is central to understanding the difference between the traditional medical model and the approach taken by health psychologists. Here, health and illness result from a combination of factors, including biological characteristics (e.g., genetic predisposition), psychological factors (e.g., behaviors, lifestyle, stress, health beliefs), and social conditions (e.g., cultural influences, family relationships, social support).

As Figure 10.3 illustrates, our thoughts and actions affect the environments we find ourselves in. Those environments affect the biological underpinnings of our thoughts and actions. The result is a kind of continuous loop.

Suppose you are an anxious person. You have particular ways of dealing with high-anxiety situations, such as before an exam, or when you are having relationship difficulties, or if you have financial worries. For example, in such situations, eating comfort foods such as mashed potatoes, macaroni and cheese, and ice cream calms you down. If you consume these foods in excess, you will probably gain weight and eventually become overweight. Extra weight can make even moderate exercise difficult, so you may decrease your physical activity. That decrease will slow down your metabolism. A slowed metabolism will cause you to gain more weight. Being overweight may make you even more anxious. And so the circle would continue.

Throughout this chapter, we will explore how obesity, eating disorders, smoking, and stress affect health. These effects always involve the interplay between biological, social, and psychological factors.

FIGURE 10.2
The Longest-Living People
The Japanese tend to live very long lives. Their longevity is no doubt due to a combination of genetics and behavior. Pictured here are 99-year-old Matsu and 91-year-old Taido, both of Ogimi Village.

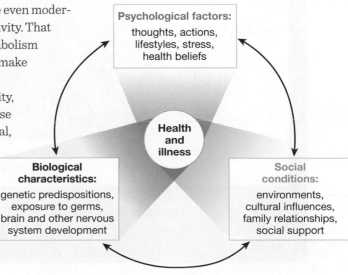

Psychological factors:
thoughts, actions, lifestyles, stress, health beliefs

Health and illness

Biological characteristics:
genetic predispositions, exposure to germs, brain and other nervous system development

Social conditions:
environments, cultural influences, family relationships, social support

FIGURE 10.3
The Biopsychosocial Model
This model illustrates how health and illness result from a combination of biological, psychological, and social factors.

Obesity Has Many Health Consequences

Obesity may not be a valid reason to prevent someone such as Gary Stocklaufer from adopting a child. Yet obesity is a major health problem with physical and psychological consequences. The most common measure of obesity is **body mass index (BMI).** BMI is the ratio of body weight to height. You can use the chart in Try It Yourself to calculate your own BMI and interpret the value obtained.

Understanding obesity requires a complex approach. You have to examine behavior, underlying biology, cognition (how we think about food and obesity), and the societal context that makes cheap and tasty food readily available. In fact, obesity is an ideal example of the biopsychosocial model of health. As you read about obesity, keep in mind the linkages between genetic predisposition, thoughts, feelings, and behaviors. Also keep in mind that these variables cycle through a continuous loop.

In Western nations, obesity has increased dramatically in recent years. For example, obesity rates have increased significantly in the United States. Fewer than 15 percent of the U.S. population met the criteria for obesity in 1980, but more than 35 percent met the criteria in 2010 (Ogden, Carroll, Kit, & Flegal, 2012). The numbers are even higher for racial and ethnic minorities. Nearly half of African American women and Mexican American women are classified as obese. Likewise, the percentage of obese children has quadrupled since the 1960s.

Extreme obesity is having a BMI over 40. This condition was almost unheard of in 1960, but it now characterizes more than 1 in 20 Americans (Ogden & Carroll, 2010; **Figure 10.4**). The increase in extreme obesity is a concern because the health

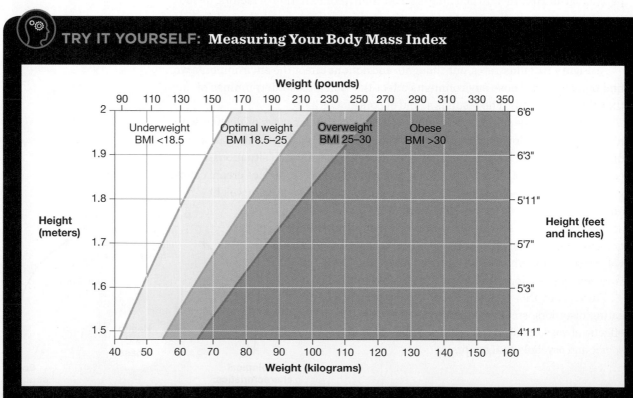

TRY IT YOURSELF: Measuring Your Body Mass Index

To determine your own body mass index (BMI), find the point at which your weight and height meet on the graph. If your BMI is above or below the optimal range (shown in yellow), then you are at greater risk for health problems.

consequences of being overweight are most apparent when people have BMIs over 35 (Flegal, Kit, Orpana, & Graubard, 2013).

Obesity is not a problem just in the United States. According to the World Health Organization, obesity has doubled around the globe since 1980 (WHO, 2011). Given the many health consequences associated with obesity, there has been great interest in understanding why people are gaining weight and what might be done to reverse this trend.

OVEREATING It may seem obvious that one factor contributing to obesity is overeating. But scientists do not know why some people can control how much they eat and others struggle with eating behaviors. A common belief is that those who overeat are lazy or unmotivated. The reality is that obese people typically try multiple diets and other "cures" to lose weight, but dieting seldom leads to permanent weight loss (Aronne, Wadden, Isoldi, & Woodworth, 2009). Most individuals who lose weight through dieting eventually regain the weight. Often, these individuals gain back more than they lost.

Think of a buffet table at a party, or perhaps at a hotel you've visited. You see platter after platter of different foods. You don't eat many of these foods at home, and you want to try them all (**Figure 10.5a**). But trying them all might mean eating more than your usual meal size. The availability of different types of food is one factor in gaining weight. Scientists have seen this behavior in studies with rats: Rats that normally maintain a steady body weight when eating one type of food eat huge amounts and become obese when they are presented with a variety of high-calorie foods, such as chocolate bars, crackers, and potato chips (Sclafani & Springer, 1976; **Figure 10.5b**). The same is true of humans. We eat much more when a variety of good-tasting foods are available than when only one or two

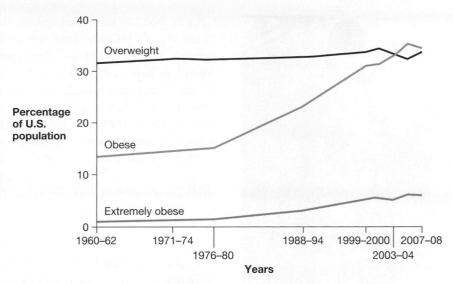

FIGURE 10.4

Changing Trends in Body Mass
This graph shows the trends in people characterized as overweight, obese, and extremely obese among adults aged 20–74 in the United States, 1960–2008.

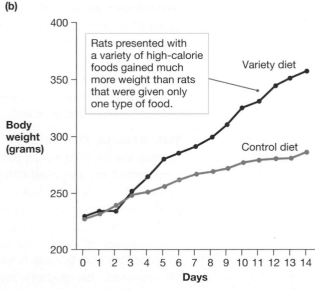

FIGURE 10.5

The Impact of Variety on Eating Behavior
(a) If you were presented with this table full of delicious foods, would you be tempted to try them all? **(b)** As shown in this graph, rats gain more weight when given variety in their diet.

FIGURE 10.6
Body Weight Is Socially Contagious
Friends tend to influence one another's sense of what body weight is appropriate. Thus friends often have similar body types.

types of food are available (Epstein, Robinson, Roemmich, Marusewski, & Roba, 2010). We also eat more when portions are larger (Rolls, Roe, & Meengs, 2007). In addition, overweight people show more activity in reward regions of the brain when they look at good-tasting foods than do individuals who are at an optimal weight (Rothemund et al., 2007). Together, these findings suggest that, in industrialized nations, the increase in obesity over the past few decades is partly explained by three factors: the availability of a variety of high-calorie foods, the large portions served in many restaurants, and individual differences in response to food cues.

Moreover, body weight is socially contagious. One study found that close friends of the same sex tend to be similar in body weight (Christakis & Fowler, 2007). This study also found that even when close friends live far apart from each other, if one friend is obese, the other one is likely to be obese as well. Studies of the social transmission of obesity suggest that the critical factor is not eating the same meals or cooking together. Instead, what matters is the implicit agreement on acceptable body weight (**Figure 10.6**). If many of your close friends are obese, implicitly you learn that obesity is normal. Thus subtle communications can affect how we think and act when we eat.

GENETIC INFLUENCE A trip to the local mall, a tourist attraction, or anyplace that families gather reveals one obvious fact about body weight: Obesity tends to run in families. Various family and adoption studies indicate that approximately half the variability in body weight can be considered to be the result of genetics (Klump & Culbert, 2007). One of the best and largest studies, carried out in Denmark during the 1980s, found that the BMI of adopted children was strongly related to the BMI of their biological parents and not at all to the BMI of their adoptive parents (Sorensen, Holst, Stunkard, & Skovgaard, 1992). Studies of twins provide even stronger evidence of the genetic control of body weight. Identical twins tend to have similar body weights whether they are raised together or raised apart (Bouchard & Pérusse, 1993; Wardle, Carnell, Haworth, & Plomin, 2008).

If genes primarily determine body weight, why has the percentage of Americans who are obese doubled over the past few decades? Genetics determines whether a person *can* become obese, but environment determines whether that person *will* become obese (Stunkard, 1996). In an important study, identical twins were overfed by approximately 1,000 calories a day for 100 days (Bouchard, Tremblay et al., 1990). Most of the twins gained some weight, but there was great variability among pairs in how much they gained (ranging from 4.3 kilograms to 13.3 kilograms, or 9.5 pounds to 29.3 pounds). Further, within each pair, there was striking similarity in how much weight the two twins gained and in which parts of the body they stored the fat. Thus genes predispose some people to obesity in environments that promote overfeeding, such as contemporary industrialized societies.

THE STIGMA OF OBESITY Think back to Gary Stocklaufer, who was once deemed too fat to be a good parent. This story illustrates the extreme stigma, or social negativity, associated with being overweight. In most Western cultures, obese individuals are viewed as less attractive, less socially adept, less intelligent, and less productive than their normal-weight peers (Dejong & Kleck, 1986).

Not surprisingly, obesity can give rise to various psychological problems. Perceiving oneself as overweight is linked to depression, anxiety, and low self-esteem (Stice, 2002). Bear in mind, however, that human obesity research is correlational. We cannot say that one factor causes the other. Maybe people with low self-esteem are more likely to put on weight.

Not all cultures stigmatize obesity. In some developing countries, being obese is a sign of being a member of the upper class. Obesity may be desirable in developing countries because it helps prevent some infectious diseases, reduces the likelihood of starvation, and is associated with having more successful births. It may also serve as a status symbol, indicating that a person can afford to eat luxuriously. In Pacific Island countries such as Tonga and Fiji, being obese is a source of personal pride, and dieting is uncommon (**Figure 10.7a**).

In most industrialized cultures, food is generally abundant. Because citizens of those countries are thus able to take food for granted, being overweight is not associated with upper-class status. Instead, it is associated with lower socioeconomic status. Indeed, in the United States fresh and nutritious food is often more expensive than high-calorie fast food. The relative affordability of fast food may contribute to people becoming overweight if they have limited finances.

The upper classes in Western cultures have a clear preference for very thin body types, as exemplified in the fashion industry (**Figure 10.7b**). The typical female fashion model is 5 feet 11 inches tall and weighs approximately 110 pounds. In other words, the standard represented by models is 7 inches taller and 55 pounds lighter than the average woman in the United States. Such extreme thinness represents a body weight that is nearly impossible for most people to achieve. Nevertheless, women report holding body weight ideals that are not only lower than average weight but also lower than what men find attractive (Fallon & Rozin, 1985).

RESTRICTIVE DIETING In contemporary Western societies, we are constantly bombarded with advertising for the latest weight-loss systems, miracle diets, and food plans that "guarantee" the shedding of pounds. But as we noted earlier, dieting is not a very effective way to lose weight permanently.

Most diets fail primarily because of the body's natural defense against weight loss (Kaplan, 2007). Body weight is regulated around a set point determined mainly by genetic influence. Consider two examples. In 1966, several inmates at a Vermont prison were challenged to increase their body weight by 25 percent (Sims et al., 1968). For six months, these inmates consumed more than 7,000 calories a day, nearly double their usual intake. If each inmate was eating about 3,500 extra calories a day (the equivalent of seven large cheeseburgers), simple math suggests that he should have gained approximately 170 pounds over the six months. In reality, few inmates gained more than 40 pounds. Most lost the weight when they went back to normal eating. Those who did not lose the weight had family histories of obesity.

At the other end of the spectrum, researchers investigated the short-term and long-term effects of semistarvation (Keys, Brozek, Henschel, Mickelsen, & Taylor, 1950). During World War II, more than 100 men volunteered to take part in this study as an alternative to military service. Over six months of being forced to reduce their food intake, the participants lost an average of 25 percent of their body weight. Most found this weight reduction very hard to accomplish. Some had great difficulty losing more than 10 pounds. The men underwent dramatic changes in emotions, motivation, and attitudes toward food. They became anxious, depressed, and listless. They lost interest in sex and other activities. They became obsessed with eating. Many of these outcomes are similar to those experienced by people with eating disorders.

Although it is possible to alter body weight, the body responds to weight loss by slowing down metabolism and using less energy. Therefore, after the body has been deprived of food, it needs less food to maintain a given body weight. Likewise, weight gain occurs much faster after weight loss (Brownell, Greenwood, Stellar, & Shrager, 1986). This pattern might explain why "yo-yo dieters" tend to become heavier over time.

DISORDERED EATING When dieters fail to lose weight, they often blame their lack of willpower. They may vow to redouble their efforts on the next diet. Repeatedly

(a)

(b)

FIGURE 10.7

Variations in Body Image

(a) In some places, people find larger body shapes more desirable. Consider these welcoming women on the island of Fatu Hiva, in French Polynesia. **(b)** By contrast, consider the thinness embodied by these models in the United States.

failing may have harmful and permanent physiological and psychological consequences. In physiological terms, weight-loss and weight-gain cycles alter the dieter's metabolism and may make future weight loss more difficult. Psychologically, repeated failures diminish satisfaction with body image and damage self-esteem. Over time, chronic dieters tend to feel helpless and depressed. Some eventually engage in more extreme behaviors to lose weight, such as taking drugs, fasting, exercising excessively, or purging.

For a vulnerable individual, chronic dieting may promote the development of a clinical eating disorder. The three most common eating disorders are anorexia nervosa, bulimia nervosa, and binge-eating disorder (Wiseman, Harris, & Halmi, 1998). Although eating disorders affect both sexes, they are more common for women.

Individuals with **anorexia nervosa** have an excessive fear of becoming fat. As a result, they restrict how much they eat. This reduction in energy intake leads to body weight that is much lower than is optimal. Anorexia most often begins in early adolescence. It was once believed that this disorder mainly affected upper-middle-class and upper-class Caucasian girls. Now race and class may no longer be defining characteristics of eating disorders (Polivy & Herman, 2002). This change might have come about because media images of a thin ideal have permeated all corners of society in the United States.

Although many young adults strive to be thin, fewer than 1 in 100 meet the clinical criteria of anorexia nervosa as described by the most recent *Diagnostic and Statistical Manual of Mental Disorders* (DSM-5), which was released in 2013 (**Table 10.1**). These criteria include both objective measures of thinness and psychological characteristics that indicate an abnormal obsession with food and body weight. Those who have anorexia view themselves as fat even though they are at a significantly low weight, often with BMIs under 17. Issues of food and weight dominate their lives, controlling how they view themselves and how they view the world. Initially, the results of self-imposed starvation may draw favorable comments, such as "You look so thin, you could be a fashion model!" These positive remarks may particularly come from friends who are also influenced by the message that skinny is beautiful. But as an anorexic person loses more and more weight, family and friends usually become concerned. The person with anorexia not only starves herself, but often engages in activities such as vomiting, abuse of laxatives, or excessive exercise to further reduce the impact of food energy that is consumed. In many cases, medical attention is required.

Anorexia is difficult to treat. Patients cling to the belief that they are overweight or not as thin as they would like to be, even when they are severely emaciated. This dangerous disorder causes a number of serious health problems, in particular a loss of bone density and heart disease. About 15 percent to 20 percent of those with anorexia eventually die from the disorder—they literally starve themselves to death (American Psychiatric Association, 2000b).

Individuals with **bulimia nervosa** alternate between dieting and binge eating. Bulimia often develops during late adolescence. Approximately 1 to 2 percent of women in high school and college meet the criteria for bulimia nervosa (see Table 10.1). These women tend to be of average weight or slightly overweight. They regularly binge eat, feel their eating is out of control, worry excessively about body weight issues, and engage in one or more compensatory behaviors, such as self-induced vomiting, excessive exercise, or the abuse of laxatives. In men, bulimia is more common than anorexia nervosa. However, most people with bulimia are women.

anorexia nervosa
An eating disorder characterized by excessive fear of becoming fat and therefore restricting energy intake to obtain a significantly low body weight.

bulimia nervosa
An eating disorder characterized by dieting, binge eating, and purging.

TABLE 10.1
DSM-5 Diagnostic Criteria for Eating Disorders

CRITERIA FOR ANOREXIA NERVOSA	CRITERIA FOR BULIMIA NERVOSA	CRITERIA FOR BINGE-EATING DISORDER
A. Restriction of energy intake relative to requirements, leading to significantly low body weight in the context of age, sex, developmental trajectory, and physical health. *Significantly low weight* is defined as a weight that is less than minimally normal or, for children and adolescents, less than what is minimally expected. B. Intense fear of gaining weight or of becoming fat, or persistent behavior that interferes with weight gain, even though a person is at a significantly lower weight. C. Disturbances in the way in which one's body weight or shape is experienced, undue influence of body weight or shape on self-evaluation, or persistent lack of recognition of the seriousness of the current low body weight.	A. Recurrent episodes of binge eating. An episode of binge eating is characterized by both of the following: 1. Eating, in a discrete period of time (e.g., within any 2-hour period), an amount of food that is definitely larger than what most individuals would eat in a similar period of time under similar circumstances. 2. A sense of lack of control over eating during the episode (e.g., a feeling that one cannot stop eating or control what or how much one is eating). B. Recurrent inappropriate compensatory behaviors in order to prevent weight gain, such as self-induced vomiting, misuse of laxatives, diuretics, or other medications; fasting; or excessive exercise. C. The binge eating and inappropriate compensatory behaviors both occur, on average, at least once a week for 3 months. D. Self-evaluation is unduly influenced by body shape and weight. E. The disturbance does not occur exclusively during episodes of anorexia nervosa.	A. Recurrent episodes of binge eating. An episode of binge eating is characterized by both of the following: 1. Eating, in a discrete period of time (e.g., within any 2-hour period), an amount of food that is definitely larger than what most individuals would eat in a similar period of time under similar circumstances. 2. A sense of lack of control over eating during the episode (e.g., a feeling that one cannot stop eating or control what or how much one is eating). B. The binge-eating episodes are associated with three (or more) of the following: 1. Eating much more rapidly than normal. 2. Eating until feeling uncomfortably full. 3. Eating large amounts of food when not feeling physically hungry. 4. Eating alone because of feeling embarrassed by how much one is eating. 5. Feeling disgusted with oneself, depressed, or very guilty afterward. C. Marked distress regarding binge eating is present. D. The binge eating occurs, on average, at least once a week for 3 months. E. The binge eating is not associated with bulimia nervosa or anorexia nervosa.

SOURCE: American Psychiatric Association (2013).

Whereas those with anorexia nervosa cannot easily hide their self-starvation, binge eating tends to occur secretly. When ordering large quantities of food, those with bulimia nervosa pretend they are ordering for a group. They often hide the massive quantities of food they buy for binges. They try to vomit quietly or seek out little-used bathrooms to avoid being heard while they vomit. Although bulimia is associated with serious health problems, such as dental and cardiac disorders, it is seldom fatal (Keel & Mitchell, 1997).

A disorder similar to bulimia is **binge-eating disorder.** The American Psychiatric Association officially recognized binge eating as a disorder in 2013. People with this disorder engage in binge eating at least once a week, but they do not purge. These individuals often eat very quickly, even when they are not hungry. Those with binge-eating disorder often experience feelings of guilt and embarrassment, and they may binge eat alone to hide the behavior. Many people with

binge-eating disorder
An eating disorder characterized by binge eating that causes significant distress.

Smoking Is a Global Phenomenon
(a) These men are smoking in Tiananmen Square, in Beijing, China. **(b)** These smokers belong to the Mentawi people, a seminomadic hunter-gatherer tribe in the coastal and rain forest regions of Indonesia.

(a)

(b)

binge-eating disorder are obese. Compared to bulimia, binge-eating disorder is more common among males and ethnic minorities (Wilfley, Bishop, Wilson, & Agras, 2007).

Smoking Is a Leading Cause of Death

Like obesity and eating disorders, smoking has a large impact on our health. Despite overwhelming evidence that smoking cigarettes leads to premature death, millions around the globe continue to light up (Carmody, 1993). Increasing numbers of people in low-income countries are smoking (**Figure 10.8**). Thirty percent of all smokers worldwide are in China. Ten percent are in India. Twenty-five percent come from Indonesia, Russia, the United States, Japan, Brazil, Bangladesh, Germany, and Turkey combined. The Centers for Disease Control and Prevention reported that in 2009, about 1 in 5 American adults was a current smoker. According to the World Health Organization (2008), tobacco causes 5.4 million deaths worldwide every year. Smoking is blamed for more than 440,000 deaths per year in the United States, and it decreases the typical smoker's life by more than 12 years (Centers for Disease Control and Prevention, 2010a).

Smoking causes numerous health problems. Examples include heart disease, respiratory ailments, and various cancers. Cigarette smoke also causes health problems for nonsmoking bystanders. As a result, smoking has been banned in many public and private places. Smokers also endure scoldings from physicians and loved ones concerned for their health and welfare. Besides spending money on cigarettes, smokers pay significantly more for life insurance and health insurance. Why do they continue to smoke? Why does anyone start?

Most smokers begin in childhood or early adolescence. In the 1990s, every day, nearly 5,000 Americans aged 11 to 17 smoked their first cigarette (Gilpin, Choi, Berry, & Pierce, 1999). About half of these young smokers will likely continue smoking into adulthood, and one-third of those will die from smoking (United States Department of Health and Human Services, 2001). Fortunately, after an increase in the 1990s, adolescent smoking decreased significantly over the last decade (Johnston, O'Malley, Bachman, & Schulenberg, 2011; **Figure 10.9**). Regular smoking dropped from approximately 13 percent to 7 percent of adolescents, and the number of adolescents who even try smoking dropped by 33 percent (Centers for Disease Control and Prevention, 2010c).

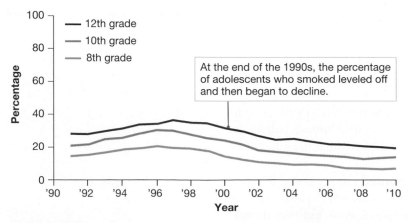

At the end of the 1990s, the percentage of adolescents who smoked leveled off and then began to decline.

FIGURE 10.9

Adolescents and Smoking
This graph shows the percentages of adolescents who smoked in the given years.

It is hard to imagine any good reason to start smoking. First attempts at smoking often involve a great deal of coughing, watering eyes, a terrible taste in the mouth, and feelings of nausea. So why do kids persist? Most researchers point to powerful social influences as the leading cause of adolescent smoking (Chassin, Presson, & Sherman, 1990). Research has demonstrated that adolescents are more likely to smoke if their parents or friends smoke (Hansen et al., 1987; **Figure 10.10**). They often smoke their first cigarettes in the company of other smokers, or at least with the encouragement of their peers. Though many adolescent smokers overestimate the number of adolescent and adult smokers (Sherman, Presson, Chassin, Corty, & Olshavsky, 1983), they may take it up to fit in with the crowd.

Other studies have pointed out that "being a smoker" can have a powerful influence on young people. Adolescents might also be affected by media images of smokers. Television shows and movies often portray smokers in glamorous ways that appeal to adolescents (see Figure 6.22). Researchers in Germany found that among German children aged 10 to 16, the more they watched popular North American movies that depicted smoking, the more likely they were to try smoking (Hanewinkel & Sargent, 2008). Children take up smoking partially to look "tough, cool, and independent of authority" (Leventhal & Cleary, 1980, p. 384). Thus smoking may be one way for adolescents to enhance their self-image as well as their image with peers (Chassin et al., 1990).

By the 12th grade, 50 percent to 70 percent of adolescents in the United States have had some experience with tobacco products (Centers for Disease Control and Prevention, 2010c; Mowery, Brick, & Farrelly, 2000). Of course, it is hard to look tough while gasping and retching. So even though most adolescents try one or two cigarettes, most of them do not become regular smokers. Still, many of the adolescents who experiment with smoking do go on to smoke on a regular basis (Baker, Brandon, & Chassin, 2004).

Over time, casual smokers become addicted. Nicotine is the active drug in tobacco, and this drug is widely acknowledged as the primary factor in motivating and maintaining smoking behavior (Fagerström & Schneider, 1989; United States Department of Health and Human Services, 2004). Once the smoker becomes hooked on nicotine, going without cigarettes will lead to unpleasant withdrawal symptoms, including distress and heightened anxiety (Russell, 1990). Some people appear especially susceptible to nicotine addiction, perhaps because of genetics (Sabol et al., 1999). Nicotine leads to increased activation of dopamine neurons. This activation has a reinforcing effect and encourages further use.

Changing Habits Can Improve Health

Many people struggle to improve their health by curbing their bad habits. But how likely are we to really control our health-related behaviors, such as eating too much, smoking, and not exercising enough? Consider weight loss. For weight-loss programs to be successful, people need to make permanent lifestyle changes (**Figure 10.11**). These changes include altering eating habits, increasing exercise, dealing with temptations to eat, and enlisting family members to help. People who are not obese but want to shed extra pounds can join support groups to help them exercise more and eat better.

POSITIVE EFFECTS OF EXERCISE Physical exercise helps control appetite, increase metabolism, and burn calories. For these reasons, exercise is an essential element of any weight control program. In general, the more we exercise, the better our physical and mental health. One type of exercise, aerobics, temporarily increases breathing and heart rate. Aerobic exercise is especially good for cardiovascular

FIGURE 10.10
Social Influence on Smoking
Adolescents are strongly affected by social situations. They are more likely to smoke if their friends or parents smoke.

(a)

(b)

FIGURE 10.11
Creating Healthy Habits
People who are overweight can improve their health through a combination of lifestyle changes, such as **(a)** eating healthy foods and **(b)** exercising.

health; it lowers blood pressure and strengthens the heart and lungs (Lesniak & Dubbert, 2001). Scientists do not know exactly how exercise generates all of its positive effects. It makes us feel good because we know it is good for us. It helps us build self-confidence and cope with stress. It affects neurotransmitter systems involved in reward, motivation, and emotion. It also enhances both the growth of new neurons and neural connections and the production of synaptic connections.

Research clearly shows the benefits of exercise in almost every aspect of our lives, including enhanced memory and improved cognition (Harburger, Nzerem, & Frick, 2007). As little as 10 minutes of exercise can promote feelings of vigor and enhance mood, although at least 30 minutes of daily exercise is associated with the most positive mental state (Hansen, Stevens, & Coast, 2001). In fact, there is compelling evidence that exercise can contribute to positive outcomes for the treatment of depression (Craft & Perna, 2004). Exercise may also help in the treatment of addiction and alcoholism (Read & Brown, 2003).

Still, unlike societies throughout most of human history, modern Western society allows people to exert little physical energy. People drive to work; take elevators; spend hours watching remote-controlled television; spend even more hours online; use various labor-saving devices, such as dishwashers; and then complain about not having time to exercise. Once people are out of shape, it is difficult for them to start exercising regularly.

Fortunately, it is never too late to start exercising and receiving its positive benefits. Sedentary adults between the ages of 60 and 79 participated in a study on the benefits of exercise (Colcombe et al., 2006). These participants were randomly assigned to either six months of aerobic training (such as running or fast dancing) or six months of a control group. Those who received aerobic training significantly increased their brain volume, including both white (myelinated) matter and gray matter. The control group experienced no comparable changes. Another study focused on older adults with moderate memory problems (Lautenschlager et al., 2008). These participants were randomly assigned to an exercise group (3 hours a week for two weeks) or to a control group. The exercise group improved in their overall cognition, including memory. The control group showed no changes. The researchers concluded that exercise reduces cognitive decline in older adults with moderate memory problems.

QUITTING SMOKING Just as people can improve their health by exercising, they can also improve their health by kicking a smoking habit. But how can people quit smoking cigarettes? Their best chances involve several actions at once. To assist with the withdrawal symptoms, they can use nicotine replacement, such as patches or gum. They can avoid places where other people smoke. They can substitute behaviors that are healthier than smoking. Unfortunately, like other addicts, smokers may need to "hit rock bottom" before realizing they have to change their behavior. The psychologist David Premack discusses a case study of a man who quit smoking because of something that happened as he was picking up his children at the city library:

> A thunderstorm greeted him as he arrived there; and at the same time a search of his pockets disclosed a familiar problem: he was out of cigarettes. Glancing back at the library, he caught a glimpse of his children stepping out in the rain, but he continued around the corner, certain that he could find a parking space, rush in, buy the cigarettes and be back before the children got seriously wet. (Premack, 1970)

For the smoker, it was a shocking vision of himself "as a father who would actually leave the kids in the rain while he ran after cigarettes." According to Premack, the man quit smoking on the spot. Not everyone can quit smoking by going "cold turkey." However, people will most likely experience improved health if they stop smoking.

- Health is not just the absence of disease. Health is a positive state of well-being.

- The biopsychosocial model explains health and illness based on biological characteristics, psychological factors, and social conditions.

- Obesity is influenced by genetics, overeating, and how we think about food and our environment.

- Extreme efforts to control weight and body shape may result in the onset of anorexia nervosa, bulimia nervosa, or binge-eating disorder.

- Smoking contributes to heart disease, cancer, and many other deadly diseases.

- Adopting healthy habits can improve health. Exercise has physical, emotional, and cognitive benefits.

10.2 How Does Stress Affect Our Health?

📖 **LEARNING GOALS**	✏️ **READING ACTIVITIES**
a. Remember the key terms about stress.	List all of the boldface words and write down their definitions.
b. Apply the idea of stressors to your life.	Provide examples of each of the stressors from your life.
c. Understand the three phases of the general adaptation syndrome (GAS).	Describe the three phases of the GAS stress response in your own words.
d. Apply stress responses to real life.	Provide an example of a stress you have experienced.

What is causing you stress right now? You might be experiencing stress because of schoolwork, family, your job, or a romantic relationship. Maybe several factors are involved.

We sometimes think of stress as something objective, outside ourselves. But the biological effects of stress result directly from the ways we think about events in our lives and the way social factors influence us. For example, some students find final exams so stressful that they get sick at exam time. Other students may see exams simply as inconveniences or even challenges to be overcome. For these students, exams do not have negative health consequences. In short, stress is another perfect example of how the biopsychosocial model explains our health. When psychologists talk about stress, then, what are they referring to?

Stressors Have a Negative Impact on Health

Stress is the set of behavioral, mental, and physical processes that occur as we attempt to deal with an environmental event or stimulus that we perceive as

stress
A group of behavioral, mental, and physical processes occurring when events match or exceed the organism's ability to respond in a healthy way.

LEARNING TIP: Stressors, Responses, and Mediating Factors

We can't see "stress." It is not a physical object. Instead, it is a set of processes within our bodies. We can understand these processes in terms of the three components of stress.

We can see stressors—events in our lives that force us to make adjustments and lead to the process of stress. We also experience responses to stressors. Finally, the effects of stressors in eliciting responses can be increased or decreased by mediating factors, such as personality and coping strategies.

Stressors	Mediating factors	Stress responses
Major life stressors	Personality	Physical
Daily hassles	Coping strategies	Psychological
		Behavioral

threatening. As the Learning Tip summarizes, stress has three components. The threatening event is called a **stressor.** The stressor elicits one or more **stress responses.** However, *mediating factors* can increase or decrease the likelihood that a stressor will elicit a stress response. Mediating factors may include personality and coping strategies.

You have experienced the connections between these three factors many times. Maybe you were in a situation where a loved one became ill. You started to feel anxious about his health, but the support of your family helped get everyone through the tough time. Or the situation could have been as simple as losing your keys. Looking for your keys made you late for work, and you became angry.

stressor
An environmental event or stimulus that threatens an organism.

stress responses
Physical, behavioral, and/or psychological responses to stressors.

major life stressors
Large disruptions, especially unpredictable and uncontrollable catastrophic events, that affect central areas of people's lives.

daily hassles
Everyday irritations that cause small disruptions, the effects of which can add up to a large impact on health.

TYPES OF STRESSORS Psychologists typically think of stressors as falling into two categories: **major life stressors** and **daily hassles.** Major life stressors are changes or disruptions that strain central areas of people's lives. Unpredictable and uncontrollable catastrophic events are especially stressful. In the fall of 2012, Hurricane Sandy, nicknamed Superstorm Sandy, was a major stressor in the lives of tens of thousands of people (**Figure 10.12a**).

Major life stressors can be choices you make as well as things out of your control. For instance, you might decide to move somewhere new. Experiencing this major event is stressful even though you made the choice. We tend to think of major life stressors as negative events, but positive experiences may also be stressors. Consider the birth of a baby. Many parents call this event as one of the most exhausting—but rewarding—experiences of their lives. Other positive stressors can include starting a new job, starting school, or getting married.

By contrast, daily hassles are stressors that are small, day-to-day irritations and annoyances. Examples include driving in heavy traffic, dealing with difficult people, or waiting in a long line (**Figure 10.12b**). The combined effects of constant daily hassles can be comparable to the effects of major life changes. By slowly wearing down personal resources, these hassles pose a threat to our coping abilities. People may get used to some hassles but not to others. For example, conflicts with other people or living in a crowded, noisy, or polluted place appear to add up to have negative effects on health and well-being. For

FIGURE 10.12

Types of Stressors

(a) Hurricane Sandy, in 2012, was a major life stressor for thousands of people. Here a man exhibits a stress response as he surveys the damage to his home on the New Jersey coastline. **(b)** By contrast, waiting on a long line at the supermarket is an example of a daily hassle. If the impacts of daily hassles add up, these stressors can have as much effect on health as major life stressors.

(a)

(b)

TRY IT YOURSELF: Student Stress Scale

To determine the amount of stress in your life, select the events that have happened to you in the past 12 months.

Event	Life Change Units	Event	Life Change Units	Event	Life Change Units
Death of close family member	100	Change in financial status	39	Change in social activities	29
Death of close friend	73	Change in major	39	Change in eating habits	28
Divorce between parents	65	Trouble with parents	39	Chronic car trouble	26
Jail term	63	New girlfriend or boyfriend	38	Change in number of family get-togethers	26
Major personal injury or illness	63	Increased workload at school	37	Too many missed classes	25
Marriage	58	Outstanding personal achievement	36	Change of college	24
Being fired from job	50	First term in college	35	Dropping more than one class	23
Failing important course	47	Change in living conditions	31	Minor traffic violations	20
Change in health of family member	45	Serious argument with instructor	30		
Pregnancy	45	Lower grades than expected	29		
Sex problems	44	Change in sleeping habits	29		
Serious argument with close friend	40				

Scoring

Next to each event is a score that indicates how much a person has to adjust as a result of the change. Both positive events (outstanding personal achievement) and negative events (major personal injury or illness) can be stressful because they require us to make adjustments. Add together the life change unit scores to determine how likely you are to experience illness or mental health problems as a result of the stress of these events.

300 life change units or more: A person has a high risk for a serious health change.
150–299 life change units: About 1 of every 2 people is likely to have a serious health change.
149 life change units or less: About 1 of every 3 people is likely to have a serious health change.

SOURCE: Adapted from Holmes & Rahe (1967).

some research studies, participants keep diaries of their daily activities. The researchers find consistently that the more intense and frequent the hassles, the poorer the physical and mental health of the participant.

To understand what stressors may be affecting you in your life, add up your stress events using the scale in Try It Yourself. In doing the activity, you will notice that some stressors cause more stress than others. These results are indicated by higher life-change unit scores for the more-stressful events. These events are more likely to elicit stress responses and require some sort of coping mechanisms. Notice also that some of the stressors are positive life events, such as getting married.

The next two sections will build on your new understanding of stressors. You will learn how you are responding to stressors. You will also learn what coping tools you are, or should be, using.

immune system
The body's mechanism for dealing with invading microorganisms, such as allergens, bacteria, and viruses.

general adaptation syndrome (GAS)
A consistent pattern of physical responses to stress that consists of three stages: alarm, resistance, and exhaustion.

We Have Several Responses to Stress

When you experience stressors, how do you react to them? Does your heart beat faster? Do you get upset? Perhaps you turn to friends for help? Or maybe you eat too much ice cream or drink too much alcohol? There is a wide range of ways in which each of us responds to stressful events in our lives.

GENERAL ADAPTATION SYNDROME In the early 1930s, the endocrinologist Hans Selye (1936) found that different types of stress produced roughly the same pattern of physiological changes. These changes include enlarged adrenal glands. They also include damage to part of the **immune system,** resulting in decreased levels of white blood cells in the blood. Selye concluded that the enlarged adrenal glands and immune system damage reduce the organism's potential ability to resist additional stressors. These effects represent a nonspecific physical stress response, which Selye called the **general adaptation syndrome (GAS).** The general adaptation syndrome consists of three stages: alarm, resistance, and exhaustion (**Figure 10.13**).

Think about a time when you were frightened. Suppose you heard a strange noise while walking alone late at night. Your heart probably started to beat faster. Maybe your palms became sweaty. This physical response is what happens in the *alarm stage* of the general adaptation syndrome. As an emergency reaction, these effects prepare the body to respond physically. That is, immediate bodily responses are aimed at boosting our physical abilities to fight or run away. At this point, our resistance decreases, making us less able to cope with additional stressors. At the same time, the body starts action in the immune system that will protect us in case we are injured while fighting or running away.

By contrast, some stressors last much longer than a temporary frightening experience. For example, students and people with difficult jobs both experience a lot of stress in an effort to do well. These people might be described as experiencing the *resistance stage* of the general adaptation syndrome. Here, the body physically prepares for a longer, more sustained attack against a stressor. The immunity to infection and disease increases somewhat as the body maximizes its defenses. Unfortunately, the body's physical fight against stress is not sustainable.

After being exposed to a stressor for a long time, the body reaches the *exhaustion stage.* The body's ability to respond to stress begins to decline. Various physiological systems, such as the immune system, begin to fail. Most of us have experienced

FIGURE 10.13

The General Adaptation Syndrome
Selye described three stages of physical response to stress. As shown here, the body may progress from alarm to resistance to exhaustion. At each stage, the ability of the body to resist more stressors is influenced. Ultimately, in the exhaustion stage, the person will be more likely to experience adverse health effects.

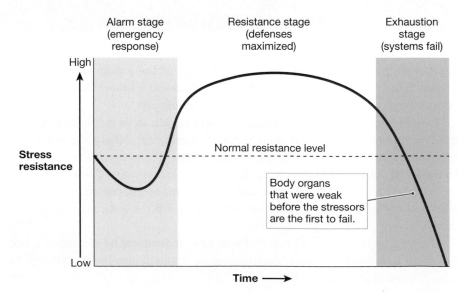

this stage in a small way: We get sick immediately after a longer period of stress, such as when studying for exams or preparing important work at our jobs. But the effects of the exhaustion stage can also have a much more severe impact. Bodily systems that were already weak before the stress become more likely to fail. This effect is one reason that people with high levels of chronic stress in their lives are more susceptible to some serious diseases.

IMMUNE RESPONSE One of Selye's central points was that stress alters the functions of the immune system. Normally, when foreign substances such as viruses, bacteria, or allergens enter the body, the immune system launches into action to destroy the invaders. Stress interferes with this natural process. More than 300 studies have demonstrated that short-term stress boosts the immune system—such as occurs during the end of the fight-or-flight response—whereas chronic stress weakens it, leaving the body less able to deal with infection (Segerstrom & Miller, 2004).

The effects of long-term stress make the body less capable of warding off foreign substances. In a clear demonstration that stress affects the immune system, shown in Scientific Thinking, Sheldon Cohen and colleagues (1991) paid healthy volunteers to have cold viruses swabbed into their noses. Those who reported the highest levels of stress before being exposed to the viruses developed worse cold symptoms and higher viral counts than those who reported being less stressed.

Apparently, when we experience high stress levels for a long time, the function of the immune system is impaired, and the probability and severity of poor health increase (Herbert & Cohen, 1993; McEwen, 2008). People who have very stressful jobs—such as air traffic controllers, combat soldiers, and firefighters—tend to have

SCIENTIFIC THINKING:
Stress and the Immune System

Hypothesis: Stress affects the immune system.

Research Method: Researchers swabbed the noses of healthy volunteers with cold viruses.

Results: Participants who reported a higher level of stress before being exposed to the cold virus developed worse cold symptoms.

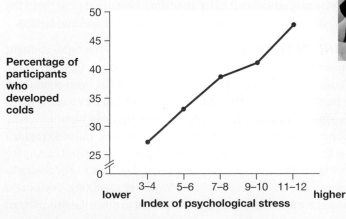

Percentage of participants who developed colds

Index of psychological stress

lower / higher

Conclusion: The functioning of the immune system can be impaired by high levels of stress.

fight-or-flight response
The physiological preparedness of animals to deal with danger.

tend-and-befriend response
Females' tendency to respond to stressors by protecting and caring for their offspring and forming social alliances.

Fight-or-Flight Response
Fight-or-flight is a physical response to stressors. This response occurs during the alarm phase of the general adaptation syndrome. It prepares a person's body to fight or run away.

HAS IT HAPPENED TO YOU?

Stress Eating

Have you ever found yourself eating a box of cookies, a bag of potato chips, or a pint of ice cream after something bad happened to you? If that's the case, then you have experienced *stress eating*. Stress eating is just what it sounds like: a response to stressors by eating, usually overeating junk foods.

Most people have experienced stress eating at one time or another. But eating as a consistent response to stress can lead to obesity and have other adverse effects on health. Instead of stress eating, try to find other ways to distract you from your stress. Consider taking a walk, reading a good book, or watching an engaging movie (Heatherton & Baumeister, 1991).

many health problems that presumably are due partly to the effects of high levels of chronic stress. Indeed, as you will see later in the chapter, stress is associated with health problems that include increased blood pressure, cardiac disease, diabetes, and declining sexual interest.

FIGHT-OR-FLIGHT RESPONSE However, short-term stress can actually boost the immune response. During the alarm phase of the general adaptation syndrome, a person or animal physically prepares to deal with the stress of an attack. This preparation is called a **fight-or-flight response** (**Figure 10.14**).

Within seconds or minutes, the fight-or-flight response enables the organism to direct its energy to dealing with the threat. It has no more physical reserves to deal with additional stressors. In this stage, the body is also most likely to be exposed to infection and disease. For example, the body might be injured in an attack. So the immune system kicks in, and the body begins fighting back. In other words, immediate physiological responses are aimed at boosting physical abilities while reducing activities that make the organism vulnerable. Recall from Chapter 2 that the physical reaction by the sympathetic nervous system includes increased heart rate, redistribution of the blood supply from skin and digestive organs to muscles and brain, deepening of respiration, and dilation of the pupils. At the same time, the body postpones less critical processes—such as food digestion—that can occur after the stressor is removed.

Selye understood that, from an evolutionary perspective, the ability to respond immediately and effectively to stressors is important to survival and reproduction. Thus this stress response was adaptive for our ancestors because it gave them the energy they needed to either outrun a predator or stand their ground and fight it.

TEND-AND-BEFRIEND RESPONSE The generalizability of the fight-or-flight response has been questioned by Shelley Taylor and colleagues (Taylor, 2006; Taylor et al., 2002). They note that in the past, stress research has been conducted primarily with male participants; less than 1 in 5 of the participants were female. The result is a sex inequality in laboratory stress studies that can blind us to the fact that men and women often respond differently to stressors. Indeed, Taylor's research has revealed that females generally respond by protecting and caring for their offspring as well as by forming alliances with social groups to reduce risks to individuals, including themselves (Taylor, 2006; Taylor et al., 2002). Taylor and colleagues coined the phrase **tend-and-befriend response** to describe this pattern (**Figure 10.15**).

Tend-and-befriend responses make sense from an evolutionary perspective. After all, females typically bear a greater responsibility for the care of offspring.

Responses that protect their offspring as well as themselves would be maximally adaptive. When a threat appears, hiding or quieting the offspring may be a more effective means of avoiding harm than trying to flee while pregnant or with a clinging infant. Furthermore, affiliating with others might provide additional protection and support.

FIGURE 10.15
Tend-and-Befriend Response
Tend-and-befriend occurs when, in response to stressors, females form social groups and care for offspring.

NEGATIVE STRESS RESPONSES Some people who feel stress head to the gym for a workout. Unfortunately, many of us have less positive responses to stress. Indeed, many problem drinkers explain that they abuse alcohol as a response to stress in their lives. When people are stressed, they also eat junk food, smoke cigarettes, use drugs, and so on (Baumeister, Heatherton, & Tice, 1994). In addition, some people are especially likely to respond to stress by overeating (Heatherton & Baumeister, 1991; see Has It Happened to You?). One study of more than 12,000 people from Minnesota found that high stress was associated with greater intake of fat, less-frequent exercise, and heavier smoking (Ng & Jeffrey, 2003). In developed nations, such habits contribute to nearly every major cause of death, including obesity (Smith, Orleans, & Jenkins, 2004).

 10.2 CHECKPOINT: How Does Stress Affect Our Health?

LEARN

- The three components of stress are stressors, stress responses, and mediating factors.

- Stress affects health when stressors, either major life events or daily hassles, require a person to make adjustments.

- The general adaptation syndrome is a response to stress. This response consists of an initial alarm phase (including the fight-or-flight response), resistance, and, if the stressor continues, exhaustion.

- Women often respond to stress with the tend-and-befriend response. Some women and men have negative responses to stress, such as overeating and smoking.

10.3 What Changes the Impact of Stressors?

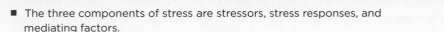 LEARNING GOALS	READING ACTIVITIES LEARN
a. Remember the key terms about stress mediators.	List all of the boldface words and write down their definitions.
b. Understand how personality traits influence the effects of stressors.	Summarize in your own words how stressors can have greater or lesser effects, depending on personality.
c. Apply strategies for coping with stress to your life.	Give an example of how you use emotion-focused coping in one stressful situation and problem-focused coping in another.

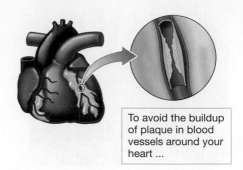

To avoid the buildup of plaque in blood vessels around your heart ...

... don't smoke

... eat healthfully

... exercise.

FIGURE 10.16

Heart Disease

To decrease your risk of heart disease, follow these simple steps to reduce the impact of stressors.

Is contemporary life making us sick? Jobs, school, family, relationships, money, time, pressure to succeed, pressure to conform, and pressure to be different are mediating factors in how we deal with stress. Mediating factors can increase or decrease the chances that we will become ill because of stress.

Before the twentieth century, most people died from infections and from diseases transmitted from person to person. But the last century saw a dramatic shift in the leading causes of mortality. According to a 2011 Census Bureau report, people in the United States are now most likely to die from heart disease, cancer, stroke, lung disease, and accidents. And there is overwhelming evidence that chronic stress is associated with the initiation and progression of a wide variety of these diseases (Cohen, Janicki-Deverts, & Miller, 2007; McEwen & Gianaros, 2011; Thoits, 2010).

Let's consider heart disease. In this illness, blood vessels around the heart become narrow or are blocked by fatty plaque. When pieces of plaque break off from the wall of a blood vessel, blood clots form around the plaque and interrupt blood flow. If a clot blocks a blood vessel that feeds the heart, the blockage causes a heart attack. If a clot blocks a vessel that feeds the brain, the blockage causes a stroke. This stress-related condition is the leading cause of death for adults in the industrialized world. According to a World Health Organization report in 2011, each year more than 7 million people die from heart attacks (**Figure 10.16**). The rate of heart disease is lower in women than in men, but heart disease is the number one killer of women.

Genetics is one of the many factors that influence heart disease. However, another critical factor is how we respond to stressors. Do we respond with negative behaviors such as overeating and smoking, which are major risk factors for heart disease? Or do we respond by directing our energy into healthy behaviors? Our responses depend partly on personality. In addition, who we are as individuals also influences how we use coping mechanisms when we are stressed.

Personality Influences How Stress Affects Us

Stress and negative emotions increase the risk of heart disease in two ways (Albus, 2010; Sirois & Burg, 2003). First, as we have discussed, people often cope with these states through behaviors that are bad for health, such as overeating, drinking excessively, or smoking. Second, over time, stress causes wear and tear on the heart, making the heart more likely to fail. Chronic stress leads to overstimulation of the sympathetic nervous system. That overstimulation causes higher blood pressure, constriction of blood vessels, changes in blood chemistry, and greater buildup of plaque on arteries. In turn, each of these conditions contributes to heart disease. For these reasons, people who tend to be stressed out are more likely to have heart disease than are people who tend to be laid back.

TYPE A AND B BEHAVIOR PATTERNS The Western Collaborative Group conducted one of the earliest tests of the hypothesis that personality affects heart disease (Rosenman et al., 1964). In 1960, this group of physicians began an 8½-year study. The participants were 3,500 men from northern California who were free of heart disease at the start of the study. The men were screened annually for established risk factors such as high blood pressure, accelerated heart rate, and high cholesterol. Their overall health practices were assessed. Personal details—such as education level, medical and family history, income, and personality traits—also were assessed.

The results indicated that a particular set of personality traits predicted heart disease. This set of traits is now known as the **Type A behavior pattern.** Type A describes people who are competitive, achievement oriented, aggressive, impatient, and time-pressed (feeling hurried, restless, unable to relax; **Figure 10.17a**). Men who exhibited these traits were much more likely to develop heart disease than were those who exhibited the **Type B behavior pattern.** Type B describes noncompetitive, relaxed, easygoing, accommodating people (**Figure 10.17b**). In fact, this study found that having a Type A personality was as strong a predictor of heart disease as having high blood pressure, high cholesterol, or smoking (Rosenman et al., 1975). Although the initial work on heart disease was done only with men, recent research shows that personality matters for women as well (Knox, Weidner, Adelman, Stoney, & Ellison, 2004; Krantz & McCeney, 2002).

HOSTILE PERSONALITIES AND DEPRESSION Research done over the 50 years since the original study has found that the original list of traits was too broad. Today we know that only certain components of the Type A behavior pattern are related to heart disease for women and men. For example, researchers have found that the most toxic factor on the list is *hostility* (Williams, 1987). Hot-tempered people who are frequently angry, cynical, and combative are much more likely to die at an early age from heart disease (Eaker, Sullivan, Kelly-Hayes, D'Agostino, & Benjamin, 2004). Indeed, having a high level of hostility while in college predicts greater risk for heart disease later in life (Siegler et al., 2003). At the same time, there is considerable evidence that negative emotional states not viewed as part of a Type A or B personality—especially depression—also predict heart disease (Miller, Freedland, Carney, Stetler, & Banks, 2003).

Of course, having a heart condition might *make* someone angry and depressed. Still, having a hostile personality and being depressed also predict the worsening of heart disease. Causes and effects might be connected in a vicious cycle. In contrast, optimistic people tend to be at lower risk for heart disease (Maruta, Colligan, Malinchoc, & Offord, 2002). How might a negative personality increase the risk of heart disease?

Think about a time when you were very angry. How did it feel? Your body likely responded by increasing your heart rate, shutting down digestion, moving more blood to your muscles—in short, preparing for fight or flight. Some people even turn red with anger or start to shake. People with hostile personalities frequently experience such physiological responses (**Figure 10.17c**). These responses take a toll on the heart. Chronic hostility can lead to the same physical symptoms as chronic stress, causing wear and tear on the heart and making it more likely to fail.

Many studies have identified the biological pathways that lead from being angry and hostile to developing heart disease. As you might expect, the repeated action of bodily responses in hostile and angry individuals affects more than just the health of their hearts. Other bodily organs suffer as well. Researchers investigated whether an association existed between hostility and chronic pulmonary disease (Jackson, Kubzansky, Cohen, Jacobs, & Wright, 2007). Chronic pulmonary disease is a progressive condition in which airflow to the lungs is reduced. This condition is a serious health risk in itself. It also contributes to coronary heart disease. Even among the young, healthy participants in this study, higher levels of hostility were related to several measures of reduced pulmonary functioning.

The evidence is clear: Hostile, angry people are at greater risk for serious diseases and earlier death than are those with more optimistic and happier personalities. This conclusion appears to be universal. A cross-cultural comparative study conducted with Japanese and non-Japanese college students replicated

(a)

(b)

(c)

FIGURE 10.17

Personality Traits Predict Heart Disease
(a) People with Type A behavior pattern are ambitious, aggressive, and impatient. They tend to respond more to stressors and are more likely to develop heart disease. **(b)** People with Type B behavior pattern are noncompetitive, easygoing, and relaxed. They are less adversely affected by stressors and so are less likely to develop heart disease. **(c)** People with hostile personalities are hot-tempered, angry, and combative. They have strong physical responses to stressors and are more likely to experience heart disease.

Type A behavior pattern
Personality traits characterized by competitiveness, achievement orientation, aggressiveness, hostility, restlessness, impatience with others, and an inability to relax.

Type B behavior pattern
Personality traits characterized by being noncompetitive, relaxed, easygoing, and accommodating.

(a)

(b)

FIGURE 10.18

Emotion-Focused Coping and Problem-Focused Coping
(a) In emotion-focused coping, we avoid the stressor, minimize it, distance ourselves, or try to escape by eating or drinking.
(b) In problem-focused coping, we try to address the stressor by solving problems. For example, we might consult a technical manual about how to fix a car problem.

primary appraisals
Part of coping that involves making decisions about whether a stimulus is stressful or not.

secondary appraisals
Part of coping where people decide how to manage and respond to a stressful stimulus.

emotion-focused coping
A type of coping in which people try to prevent having an emotional response to a stressor.

problem-focused coping
A type of coping in which people take direct steps to confront or minimize a stressor.

the association of anger and impatience with a wide range of health symptoms for students from all ethnic and cultural groups (Nakano & Kitamura, 2001). How might negative personality traits increase the likelihood that a person experiences coronary heart disease? Learning to manage both stress and anger improves outcomes for those who have heart disease (Sirois & Burg, 2003).

Coping Mediates the Effects of Stressors

Maybe it's an exam in a course you have to pass. Maybe you're starting a new job. Maybe the hurricane left you in the cold and dark for a week. We all experience stressful events. To deal effectively with the stressors in our lives, we use ways of thinking that enable us to manage the stressors more objectively. Richard Lazarus (1993) described a two-part appraisal process: We use **primary appraisals** to decide whether stimuli are stressful, benign, or irrelevant. When we decide that stimuli are stressful, we use **secondary appraisals** to consider how to cope with the stressor. Such thoughts also affect our perceptions of potential stressors and our reactions to stressors in the future. In other words, making cognitive appraisals can help us cope with stressful events. They can also help us prepare for stressful events.

TYPES OF COPING Susan Folkman and Richard Lazarus (1988) have grouped coping strategies into two general categories. In **emotion-focused coping,** we try to prevent an emotional response to the stressor. That is, we adopt strategies to numb the pain. Such strategies include avoidance, minimizing the problem, trying to distance ourselves from the outcomes of the problem, or engaging in behaviors such as eating or drinking (**Figure 10.18a**). For example, if you are having difficulty at school, you might avoid the problem by skipping class, minimize the problem by telling yourself school is not all that important, distance yourself from the outcome by saying you can always get a job if college does not work out, or overeat and drink alcohol to dull the pain of the problem. These strategies do not solve the problem or prevent it from happening again in the future.

Problem-focused coping involves taking direct steps to solve the problem: generating alternative solutions, weighing their costs and benefits, and choosing between them (**Figure 10.18b**). In this case, if you are having academic trouble, you might arrange for a tutor, minimize the distractions in your life, or ask for an extension on a paper you're struggling with. Given these alternatives, you could consider how likely a tutor is to be helpful, discuss the problem with your professors, and so on. People adopt problem-focused behaviors when they perceive stressors as controllable and are experiencing only moderate levels of stress. Conversely, emotion-focused behaviors may enable people to continue functioning in the face of uncontrollable stressors or high levels of stress.

The best way to cope with stress depends on personal resources and on the situation. Most people report using both emotion-focused coping and problem-focused coping. Emotion-based strategies are usually effective only in the short run. For example, if your partner is in a bad mood and is giving you a hard time, just ignoring her until the mood passes can be the best option. In contrast, ignoring your partner's drinking problem will not make it go away, and eventually you will need a better coping strategy. Problem-focused coping strategies do not work, however, unless the person with the problem can do something about the situation.

Besides problem-focused coping, two other strategies can help people use positive thoughts to deal with stress (Folkman & Moskowitz, 2000). When using this cognitive process, you would focus on possible good things—the proverbial silver

Reducing Exam Anxiety

Almost everyone has felt nervous about an upcoming exam. But sometimes exam jitters can seem to get out of hand. You walk into the exam room and suddenly your heart is beating rapidly, your breathing rate increases, and your palms get sweaty. When you begin the exam, all the information you knew seems to fly from your brain and be totally inaccessible. Later on, after the exam, you may have wondered, "How could I have gotten so many questions wrong? I knew those answers!" This extremely common experience of stress is called exam anxiety.

Recalling the three components of stress can help you understand and cope with this experience. The stressor is the actual exam itself. The stress response is in part physical: Your sympathetic nervous system prepares you to "fight or flee" from the test, which causes the increase in heart rate, respiration, and perspiration. There are also emotional responses, including fear and anxiety, and cognitive responses, which prevent you from accessing information that you had stored in your brain. Fortunately, there are four coping strategies you can use to reduce the impact of the stressor and these responses.

1. **Change how you think about the exam.** Thinking repeatedly about the worst-case scenario—I'll flunk the course; I'll never get a job; everyone will think I'm stupid—will increase the impact of the stressor. Instead, use a technique called positive reappraisal. Instead of viewing the exam as scary, view it as a challenge that you can meet successfully.

2. **Get plenty of sleep the night before the exam.** Avoid unhealthy behaviors, such as drinking alcohol. Many of the behaviors that stressed-out college students may engage in—skipping sleep, drinking alcohol, smoking cigarettes—further exacerbate the problem of stress (Glaser & Kiecolt-Glaser, 2005).

3. **Arrive at the exam several minutes early.** Relax and take some deep breaths. Your body can keep up the sympathetic nervous system response for only a short time. So if you can get there early and give your body time to overcome the response, your heart rate and breathing will return to normal. Taking a few minutes to write down what is making you anxious about the exam may also help you reduce stress and get a higher exam grade (Ramirez & Beilock, 2011).

4. **Finally, use good test-taking skills as you work through the exam.** Underline important parts of questions. Cross off answers you know are wrong. Take time to check every answer and come back to ones you are unsure of. Reconsider them after you have worked through all the questions, because you continue to learn as you take the exam.

If you follow these steps, you are likely to experience less exam anxiety and also get better exam grades. This result creates a positive cycle. As you get better grades on your exams, you will find it easier to eliminate exam anxiety.

lining—in the current situation. One strategy is to compare yourself to those who are worse off. This *downward comparison* has been shown to help people cope with serious illnesses. For example, if you were diagnosed with diabetes, you could recognize that diabetes is not as serious as cancer. That is, your situation is not as bad as for those who have cancer (downward comparison). Another strategy is to give positive meaning to ordinary events. For example, you could take time to enjoy the positive moments in your life, such as eating a delicious meal, watching a good movie, or enjoying a sunset. Finding the positive in events can help distract us from feeling stressed. Using Psychology in Your Life, on p. 369, describes how the various coping mechanisms can help you reduce the effects of stress in an area that almost all students experience: exam anxiety.

INDIVIDUAL DIFFERENCES IN COPING A family-oriented holiday such as Christmas may have you feeling anxious. Perhaps you're dreading all the food preparation or having to see your cranky uncle. Meanwhile, your friend may be looking forward to it as a chance to spend relaxing time with his relatives. People differ widely in their perceptions of how stressful life events are.

Some people seem stress resistant because they are so capable of adapting to life changes by viewing events constructively (**Figure 10.19a**). This trait is called *hardiness* (Kobasa, 1979). Hardiness has three components: commitment, challenge, and control. People high in hardiness are committed to their daily activities, view threats as challenges or as opportunities for growth, and see themselves as being in control of their lives. People low in hardiness typically feel alienated, fear or resist change, and view events as beyond their control (e.g., being under someone else's control).

A related idea is *resilience*. Generally, some people are more resilient than others, better able to cope in the face of adversity (Block & Kremen, 1996). When faced with hardships or difficult circumstances, resilient individuals "bend without breaking." As a result, they are able to bounce back quickly when bad things happen (**Figure 10.19b**). Those who are highest in resilience are able to use their emotional resources flexibly to meet the demands of stressful situations (Bonanno, 2004).

Can resilience be taught? Some researchers believe that people can become more resilient by following particular steps (Algoe & Fredrickson, 2011). The steps in this process include coming to understand when particular emotions are adaptive, learning specific techniques for regulating both positive and negative emotions, and working to build healthy social and emotional relations with others.

INVOLVING THE FAMILY One of the most stressful events in life is dealing with illness or pain. At some point in life, many of us will experience a serious medical condition, or our loved ones may suffer from illness or chronic pain. Can family members help each other cope with such situations?

Including family members in a treatment plan for a chronically ill person might seem important. According to the research, however, such inclusion often is not effective (Martire & Schulz, 2007). A major problem is that the ill person may feel as though family members are controlling her life rather than providing assistance. And as we have seen, being in control of essential decisions in your life is a central component of hardiness.

Family interventions can be beneficial when family members promote the person's feeling of being in control. Some behaviors that seem to help when a family member has a chronic illness include motivating the patient to make his own health and life choices and to carry out the activities of everyday living, modeling healthy behaviors, providing rewards, and pointing out the positive consequences of caring for the person who is ill (Martire & Schulz, 2007). For example, family

(a)

(b)

FIGURE 10.19

Hardiness and Resilience
Some people are better at coping with stressors than others are. **(a)** People with hardiness seem less affected by stressors because they view them as an opportunity to do something constructive. Former Congresswoman Gabrielle Giffords has displayed hardiness, as she has begun to campaign for gun control and background checks in the wake of being shot. **(b)** People who show resilience in the face of stressors tend to respond flexibly and bounce back quickly. This woman shows resilience after the 2011 floods in Taiwan by using a bike to transport supplies.

BEING A CRITICAL CONSUMER: Can Pets Help Reduce Stress?

On a Friday night, Carlos took his sons, Diego and David, to the farmer's market. Carlos's wife was at an out-of-town conference. He and the boys needed some fresh vegetables to go with the burgers and fries they'd be having for dinner. Down one of the aisles, they saw a sign: "Free Puppies to a Good Home!" Before Carlos could redirect his boys' attention, Diego and David had raced to the crate of adorable little mutts.

"Daddy!" Diego shouted. "We want a puppy!"

"Can we please have one?" David added.

"What would you do with a puppy?" Carlos asked. He knew this fight would be tough.

A dog would guard the house, the boys explained. It would give them someone else to play with. It would help clean the house.

"Help clean the house?" Carlos asked.

"When we drop food at the dinner table," Diego explained, "the dog could lick it up!" Carlos was unconvinced.

Then David offered, "Dad, the puppy would be great for you too. It would help you with your stress!"

Carlos was surprised at his son's attempt at persuasion. *How do these kids even know about stress?* he thought. *Have I seemed stressed out? Are dogs good for stress?* Knowing that he couldn't just show up at home with a puppy, Carlos confirmed that the man giving away the puppies planned to be at the market the next day.

That night, Carlos wondered about how to bring up this issue with his wife. He thought about David's statement that puppies were good for stress. *When the Student*

Association ran that Stress-Less Midterm Week program, they included Pet-a-Puppy Day. Some of the guys I was deployed with, who had a difficult time readjusting, were assigned dogs. Is there any research to support this link between pets and stress relief?

At the *USA Today* Web site, Carlos found an article about various ways that dogs were used to decrease stress. As he knew, dogs had been used to help veterans. They had also been used to help reduce stress in witnesses during court cases and in children during exams. Scientific research wasn't the focus of the article, however. Carlos did a bit more Web searching. At www.promises.com, a treatment center presented information about the effects of pets on stress. Research had found a correlation between pet ownership and lower baseline heart rates. In addition, when experimenters placed their study participants in stressful situations, people with their pets did not seem to become as physically stressed as people without their pets. Even more amazingly, researchers found that people experienced less stress with a pet than they did when they were with a close friend or spouse!

The past few weeks had been pretty stressful for Carlos. After reading Chapter 10, he knew that his work, socializing, and daily activities included both positive and negative stressors. He could use some stress relief. Now he picked up the phone to call his wife and discuss the idea of getting a puppy. Was he crazy—too stressed out to think clearly? Not at all. *It's not every day that my boys want something that would be healthy for the whole family.*

members might prepare food for the person or help her practice relaxation techniques. By providing motivation, encouragement, and emotional support, families can also assist the patient in adjusting to life with the illness.

✓ 10.3 CHECKPOINT: What Changes the Impact of Stressors?

- Chronic stress is associated with adverse health effects, including heart disease, cancer, stroke, and lung disease.

- Personality differences—including Type A and B behavior patterns, hostility, and depression—can explain differential effects of stress on people and disparities in health.

- How we think about stressors, in deciding if they are harmful (primary appraisals) and how to cope with them (secondary appraisals), affects how stressors influence us.

- Emotion-focused coping and problem-focused coping can mediate stress and the effects on health.

10.4 Can a Positive Attitude Keep Us Healthy?

LEARNING GOALS	READING ACTIVITIES LEARN
a. Remember the key terms about positivity.	List all of the boldface words and write down their definitions.
b. Understand happiness and psychological well-being.	Summarize the characteristics of happiness and well-being.
c. Apply the effects of positivity to your own health.	Provide three examples of how a positive attitude can have beneficial effects on your health.
d. Understand how social support and spirituality benefit health and well-being.	Explain in your own words how to improve health and well-being through social support and spirituality.

As we have seen throughout this chapter, stress and negative emotions, especially hostility, can affect our health in negative ways. What about the opposite? Can positive experiences and a positive attitude keep us healthy? Can they even make us healthier?

Positive Psychology Emphasizes Well-Being

In the 1990s, some psychologists began studying what is positive in the human experience. The **positive psychology** movement encouraged the scientific study of qualities such as faith, values, creativity, courage, and hope (Seligman & Csikszentmihalyi, 2000). The earliest emphasis in positive psychology was on understanding what makes people truly happy. According to positive psychologists, happiness has three components: (a) positive emotion and pleasure, (b) engagement in life, and (c) a meaningful life (Seligman, Steen, Park, & Peterson, 2005).

For example, college students high in authentic happiness might experience pleasure when interacting with other students (component a), might be actively engaged in class discussions and course readings (component b), and might find meaning in how the material influences their lives (component c). More recently, the positive psychology movement has placed a greater emphasis on overall well-being. In his book *Flourish* (2011), Seligman argues that a truly successful life is not just about happiness (i.e., pleasure, engagement, and meaning). It is also about good relationships and a history of accomplishment.

A SENSE OF WELL-BEING The new positive psychology emphasizes the strengths and virtues that help people thrive. Its primary aim is an understanding of psychological well-being (Diener, 2000). Recall that to achieve well-being, a positive state where we feel our best, we need to strive for optimal health and life satisfaction by actively participating in health-enhancing behaviors.

Enhancing well-being has become an important issue for governments. In 2010, the Prime Minister of the United Kingdom, David Cameron, announced a new well-being scale that would be used to understand the state of the nation. And in the United States, a new biannual survey called the Well-Being Index investigates people's sense of well-being across six areas. These areas include life evaluation,

positive psychology
The study of the strengths and virtues that allow people and communities to thrive.

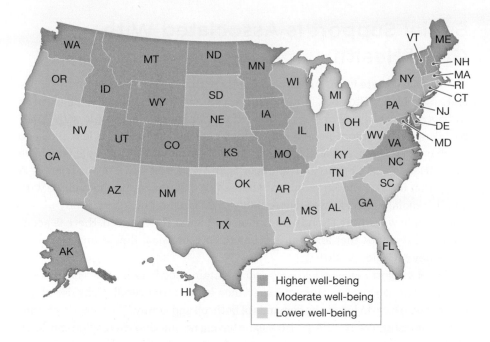

FIGURE 10.20
Well-Being in the USA
These 2009 data are from Gallup's Well-Being Index. Each day, 500 people in the United States were surveyed about their lives, emotional health, work environment, physical health, healthy behaviors, and access to food and shelter. The data reveal a general pattern of people's satisfaction with their lives.

Higher well-being
Moderate well-being
Lower well-being

emotional health, work environment, physical health, healthy behavior, and basic access (to housing, food, water, etc.; **Figure 10.20**). These new tools should help governments understand individual and collective issues about well-being. The new understanding, in turn, should enable leaders to develop strategies and policies to enhance people's well-being.

Well-being tends to vary across cultures. The wealthiest countries often have the highest levels of satisfaction. These findings fit well with the proposal, described in Chapter 9, that people need to satisfy basic needs such as food, shelter, and safety before they can address self-esteem needs. People who are resilient—that is, who can bounce back from negative events—experience positive emotions even when under stress (Tugade & Fredrickson, 2004). According to the broaden-and-build theory, positive emotions prompt people to consider novel solutions to their problems. Thus resilient people tend to draw on their positive emotions in dealing with setbacks or negative life experiences (Fredrickson, 2001).

HEALTH BENEFITS OF POSITIVITY AND WELL-BEING Can positive emotions and well-being be linked with good health (**Figure 10.21**)? To address this question, one team of researchers asked more than 1,000 patients in a large medical practice to fill out questionnaires about their emotional traits (Richman et al., 2005). The questionnaires measured positive emotions (hope and curiosity) and negative emotions (anxiety and anger). Two years after receiving the questionnaires, the researchers used the patients' medical files to see if there was a relationship between these emotions and three broad types of diseases: hypertension, diabetes, and respiratory tract infections. Higher levels of hope were associated with reduced risk of these diseases. Higher levels of curiosity were associated with reduced risk of hypertension and diabetes.

Other research reveals that being generally positive has multiple beneficial effects on the immune system (Marsland, Pressman, & Cohen, 2007). People with a positive attitude show enhanced immune system functioning and live longer than their less positive peers (Dockray & Steptoe, 2010; Xu & Roberts, 2010). They have fewer illnesses after exposure to cold germs and flu viruses (Cohen, Alper, Doyle, Treanor, & Turner, 2006). In other words, across multiple studies and types of measures, positive emotions are related to considerable health benefits.

FIGURE 10.21
Health Effects of Laughter
Laughing clubs, such as this one in India, believe in laughter as therapy and as a way to keep in shape.

Social Support Is Associated With Good Health

We often associate isolation and loneliness with depression and other psychological problems. But social interaction appears to be beneficial for physical as well as mental health. For example, one study has shown that people with larger social networks (more people they interact with regularly) are less likely to catch colds (Cohen, Doyle, Skoner, Rabin, & Gwaltney, 1997). People who have more friends also appear to live longer than those who have fewer friends. A study that used a random sample of almost 7,000 adults found that people with smaller social networks were more likely to die during the 9-year study period than people with more friends (Berkman & Syme, 1979). Indeed, there is accumulating evidence that loneliness predicts both physical illness and mortality (Hawkley & Cacioppo, 2010).

Social support helps people cope and maintain good health in two basic ways. First, people with social support experience less stress overall. Consider single parents who have to juggle the demands of both job and family. The lack of a partner means more tasks to handle. It also means having no one who shares the emotional challenges. Social support can take tangible forms, such as providing material help or assisting with daily chores. Second, social support enables us to better cope with stressful events. To be most effective, social support needs to imply that people care. When family, friends, or organized support groups offer expressions of caring and willingness to listen to problems, it can lessen the negative effects of stress.

MARRIAGE CAN BE GOOD FOR YOUR HEALTH The research on social support clearly shows that positive relationships are good for health. Marriage is generally our most intimate and long-lasting supportive relationship, and it has many health advantages (**Figure 10.22**). Most studies of marriage and well-being focus on the ways that marital partners can support each other by helping each other deal with stress, assisting in meeting life's demands, and encouraging each other's healthful behavior. In fact, an international study that involved more than 59,000 people from 42 countries found that the effect of marriage on well-being was fairly similar in all the countries studied, despite their diversity (Diener, Gohm, Suh, & Oishi, 2000). There were cross-cultural similarities in regard to marriage. In addition, men and women derived approximately equal benefits from marriage. For instance, being single leads to greater mortality for both women and men.

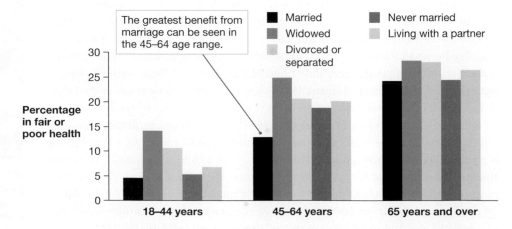

FIGURE 10.22

Relationship Between Marriage and Health

Positive social relationships, including marriage, are good for our health. This finding is shown in data from the National Health Interview Surveys in the United States from 1999 to 2002.

Comparable data are not available for gays or lesbians who are married or in long-term, marriage-like relationships. It is reasonable to expect, however, that homosexuals would receive the same benefits from this kind of social support as heterosexuals. Indeed, in one recent study, gay and lesbian couples in long-term, committed relationships were indistinguishable from straight couples in terms of the quality of the relationship and various physiological indicators of health (Roisman, Clausell, Holland, Fortuna, & Elieff, 2008).

Marriage is not a guaranteed path to good health. Troubled marriages are associated with increased stress, and unmarried people can be happier than people in bad marriages. For instance, research shows that people with troubled marriages and people going through a divorce or bereavement all had compromised immune systems (Kiecolt-Glaser & Glaser, 1988).

SPIRITUALITY CONTRIBUTES TO WELL-BEING For many of us, religion or spirituality provides a sense of meaning or purpose in life. And as we have seen, those factors contribute to happiness and well-being. In many studies, people who are religious report greater feelings of well-being than do people who are not religious. This feeling can be derived from a number of things. Religious people are better at coping with crises in their lives, because their religious beliefs serve as a buffer against hard knocks (Myers, 2000). On a daily basis, religious beliefs can help people achieve and maintain well-being through the social support provided by faith communities. The support can also be physical: Many religions promote healthy behaviors, such as avoiding alcohol and tobacco or eating a vegetarian diet.

The positive effects are not associated with any single religion, however. Rather, the benefits come from a sense of spirituality that occurs across religions (**Figure 10.23**). As Rabbi Harold Kushner notes, people need to feel they are "something more than just a momentary blip in the universe" (quoted in Myers, p. 64).

FIGURE 10.23
Spirituality and Well-Being
A sense of spirituality can have positive effects on well-being. That sense does not have to be connected with a particular religion.

Several Strategies Can Help Us Stay Healthy

Over the last three decades, psychologists have learned much about the complex relations between stress and health. We now know that, to be healthy, we need to cope with stress, regulate our emotions, and control our daily habits. Adopting the following strategies will help you take control of your life and enhance your health and well-being.

- **Eat natural foods.** Food fads come and go, but the basic rules never change: Eat a varied diet that emphasizes natural foods. Whole grains, fruits, and vegetables should be the major parts of that diet. But various animal products, such as poultry or other lean meats, can also be part of it. Avoid processed foods and fast foods. Avoid foods containing trans fat and other artificial types of fat that prolong store shelf life. Reading the label will tell you whether a product contains these fats.

- **Watch portion size.** Eat a varied diet in moderation, and eat only when you are hungry. Eating small, healthy snacks between meals may prevent you from becoming too hungry and overeating at your next meal. Remember that many prepared foods are sold in large portions, and large portions encourage overeating. Over time, the extra calories from large portions may contribute to obesity.

- **Drink alcohol in moderation, if at all.** According to some research, one glass of wine per day, or a similar quantity of other alcohol-containing drinks, may have cardiovascular benefits (Klatsky, 2009). But excessive alcohol consumption can cause serious health problems, including alcoholism, liver problems, some cancers, heart disease, and immune system deficiencies.

- **Keep active.** Exercise is an excellent daily strategy for keeping stress in check. Four times a week or more, engage in at least a half hour of moderate physical activity. Ignore the saying *no pain, no gain*, because pain may actually deter you from exercising over the long run. Start with moderate exercise that will not leave you breathless, and gradually increase the intensity. Look for other ways to be active, such as taking the stairs or walking to work or school.

- **Do not smoke.** Many college students and other adults begin smoking each year. Smoking eventually produces undesirable physical effects for all smokers. These problems include a hacking cough, unpleasant odor, bad breath, some cancers and other lung disease, and death at a younger age.

- **Practice safe sex.** Sexually transmitted diseases (STDs) affect millions of people worldwide—including college students. Many new HIV cases are occurring among those under age 25, who are infected through heterosexual or homosexual activity. Despite the devastating consequences of some STDs, many young adults engage in risky sexual practices, such as not using condoms. They are especially likely to engage in risky practices when using alcohol or other drugs. Ways to avoid STDs include condom use or abstinence.

- **Learn to relax.** Stress can cause many health problems. For example, conditions such as insomnia can interfere with your ability to function. By contrast, relaxation exercises can help soothe the body and mind. You might also try a relaxing activity, such as yoga (**Figure 10.24**). You can also seek help from trained counselors. One method that counselors may teach is using biofeedback to measure your physiological activity so you can learn to control your bodily responses to stress.

- **Learn to cope.** Negative events are a part of life. Learn to assess them realistically. See what might be positive about the events even as you accept the

FIGURE 10.24
Relaxing
We can improve our health and work toward a positive sense of well-being in many ways. One good method is to relax—for example, by practicing yoga.

difficulties they pose. You can learn strategies for dealing with stressors: seeking advice or assistance, attempting new solutions, distracting yourself with more pleasant thoughts or activities, reinterpreting situations humorously, and so on. Find out which strategies work best for you. The important thing is to prevent stress from consuming your life.

- **Build a strong support network.** Friends and family can help you deal with much of life's stress, from daily frustrations to serious catastrophes. Avoid people who encourage you to act in unhealthy ways or who are threatened by your efforts to be healthy. Instead, find people who share your values, who understand what you want from life, and who can listen and provide advice, assistance, or simply encouragement. Trusting others is a necessary part of social support, and it is associated with positive health outcomes.

- **Consider your spiritual life.** If you have spiritual beliefs, try incorporating them into your daily living. Benefits can come from living a meaningful life and from experiencing the support provided by faith communities.

- **Try some happiness exercises.** Many low-risk activities can quickly increase a person's happiness (Lyubomirsky, King, & Diener, 2005). For example, you can write and deliver a letter of gratitude to someone you want to thank. Once a week, write down three things that went well and describe why they went well. Act like a happy person. Sometimes just going through the motions of being happy will create happiness. By focusing on positive events and more-positive explanations of troubling ones, you may become a happier—and healthier—person.

 10.4 CHECKPOINT: Can a Positive Attitude Keep Us Healthy?

- Positive psychology has investigated happiness and emphasizes the strengths and virtues associated with psychological well-being.

- A positive, optimistic outlook provides many health benefits.

- Social support is critical to good health. People in good marriages have higher well-being and reduced mortality rates.

- Spirituality and social and physical support from faith communities all contribute to a sense of well-being.

BIG PICTURE

BIG QUESTION

LEARNING GOALS

10.1
What Affects
Our Health?

a. Remember the key terms about health and well-being.

b. Apply the biopsychosocial model of health to your life.

c. Analyze how overeating, anorexia, bulimia, and binge eating affect health.

d. Evaluate how exercising more can improve health.

10.2
How Does
Stress Affect
Our Health?

a. Remember the key terms about stress.

b. Apply the idea of stressors to your life.

c. Understand the three phases of the general adaptation syndrome (GAS).

d. Apply stress responses to real life.

10.3
What Changes
the Impact
of Stressors?

a. Remember the key terms about stress mediators.

b. Understand how personality traits influence the effects of stressors.

c. Apply strategies for coping with stress to your life.

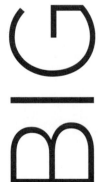

10.4
Can a Positive
Attitude Keep
Us Healthy?

a. Remember the key terms about positivity.

b. Understand happiness and psychological well-being.

c. Apply the effects of positivity to your own health.

d. Understand how social support and spirituality benefit health and well-being.

KEY TERMS

health psychology
well-being
biopsychosocial model
body mass index (BMI)
anorexia nervosa
bulimia nervosa
binge-eating disorder

stress
stressor
stress responses
major life stressors
daily hassles
immune system
general adaptation syndrome
    (GAS)
fight-or-flight response
tend-and-befriend response

Type A behavior pattern
Type B behavior pattern
primary appraisals
secondary appraisals
emotion-focused coping
problem-focused coping

positive psychology

CHECKPOINT

- Health is not just the absence of disease. Health is a positive state of well-being.

- The biopsychosocial model explains health and illness based on biological characteristics, psychological factors, and social conditions,

- Obesity is influenced by genetics, overeating, and how we think about food and our environment.

- Extreme efforts to control weight and body shape may result in the onset of anorexia nervosa, bulimia nervosa, or binge-eating disorder.

- Smoking contributes to heart disease, cancer, and many other deadly diseases.

- Adopting healthy habits can improve health. Exercise has physical, emotional, and cognitive benefits.

- The three components of stress are stressors, stress responses, and mediating factors.

- Stress affects health when stressors, either major life events or daily hassles, require a person to make adjustments.

- The general adaptation syndrome is a response to stress. This response consists of an initial alarm phase (including the fight-or-flight response), resistance, and, if the stressor continues, exhaustion.

- Women often respond to stress with the tend-and-befriend response. Some women and men have negative responses to stress, such as overeating and smoking.

- Chronic stress is associated with adverse health effects, including heart disease, cancer, stroke, and lung disease.

- Personality differences—including Type A and B behavior patterns, hostility, and depression—can explain differential effects of stress on people and disparities in health.

- How we think about stressors, in deciding if they are harmful (primary appraisals) and how to cope with them (secondary appraisals), affects how stressors influence us.

- Emotion-focused coping and problem-focused coping can mediate stress and the effects on health.

- Positive psychology has investigated happiness and emphasizes the strengths and virtues associated with psychological well-being.

- A positive, optimistic outlook provides many health benefits.

- Social support is critical to good health. People in good marriages have higher well-being and reduced mortality rates.

- Spirituality and social and physical support from faith communities all contribute to a sense of well-being.

For a self-quiz on this chapter, go to the back of the book and find Appendix B: Quizzes.

11 Social Psychology

CORY BOOKER, mayor of Newark, New Jersey, and now a United States senator, gives new meaning to the phrase *public servant*. In 2012, after returning home from a television interview, Booker noticed that his neighbor's house was in flames. He then heard someone screaming that a woman was trapped inside. Booker's security guards initially tried to hold him back. Later, one of the guards explained what happened. "He basically told me, 'This woman is going to die if we don't help her,' and what can I say to that? I let him go and without thinking twice, he just ran into the flames and rescued this young lady."

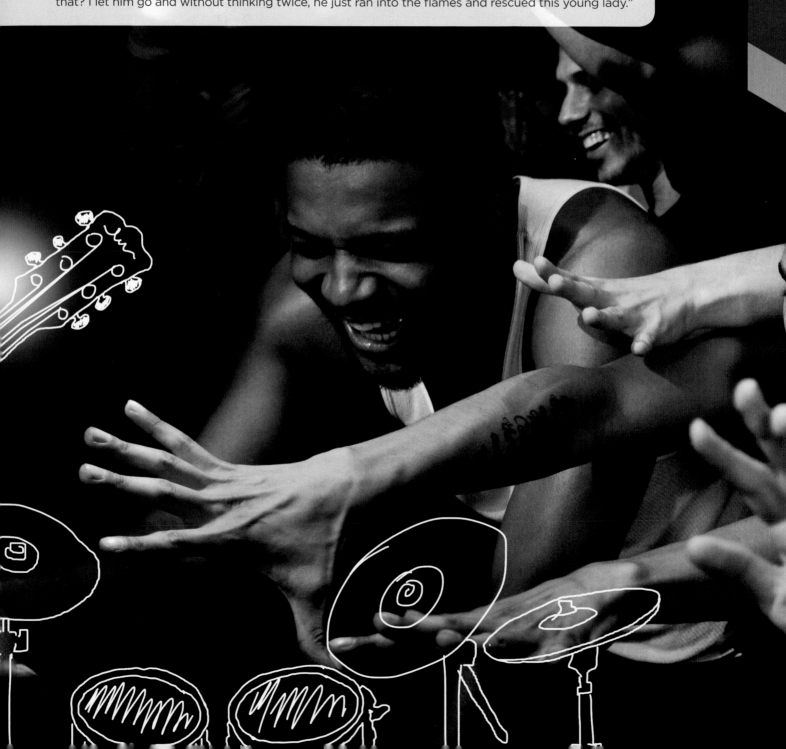

BIG QUESTIONS

FIGURE 11.1

Cory Booker's Helping Behavior
During his tenure as mayor of Newark, New Jersey, Cory Booker demonstrated many ways that people can help each other and develop strong relationships with others. Here, Booker helps dig out the snowbound car of a Newark resident. "It was very nice," said the car's owner. "I didn't expect it, so it was shocking."

Booker rushed to the second floor of the home. He felt flames behind him and saw nothing but smoky blackness in front of him. He found the woman and carried her back through the house, which by then was engulfed in flames. Although they managed to escape, Booker sustained second-degree burns and was treated for smoke inhalation.

This story shows how people sometimes risk their lives for other people. The incident is particularly striking because it was not Cory Booker's only act of heroism. In 2010, a resident of the city asked the mayor to send someone to shovel her elderly father's driveway. She feared he would have a heart attack doing it himself. Booker showed up 20 minutes later and cleared the snow himself (**Figure 11.1**). Following Hurricane Sandy in October 2012, Booker invited residents without power to eat and sleep in his house. He set up beds, made his DVD collection of sci-fi and kids' movies available, and housed and fed around 30 people a day. And on a bitterly cold day in January 2013, a reporter tweeted to the mayor that someone had left a dog outside in the freezing cold. Booker showed up on the scene and carried the shaking dog to safety. "This is brutal weather," Booker said. "You just can't leave your dogs out here on a day like this and expect them to be okay."

Every day we read about how people can be cruel to each other. We hear about bullying that leads to teen suicide, wars that victimize the innocent, gang shootouts—the list of horrors seems endless. Yet people such as Cory Booker perform acts of compassion on a large and a small scale every day. Their stories not only impress us. They also can inspire us to help others.

This chapter considers how and why we help or hurt each other, how situations and people influence the way we think and act, and how we develop strong relationships with the people in our lives. These concerns are the realm of *social psychology*. Because almost every human activity has a social dimension, research in social psychology covers a lot of territory. We'll begin by looking at how people think about other people.

11.1 How Do We Think About Other People?

📖 **LEARNING GOALS**	✏️ **READING ACTIVITIES**	**LEARN**
a. Remember the key terms pertaining to how we think about other people.	List all of the boldface words and write down their definitions.	
b. Apply the principles of snap judgments to your life.	Provide an example of how you have experienced snap judgments based on thin slices of behavior and/or facial expressions.	
c. Analyze how we make attributions based on the actor/observer bias.	Distinguish between the attributions you would make if you were fired from a job versus if a coworker were fired.	
d. Understand the difference between prejudice and discrimination and how they are affected by competition and cooperation.	Summarize in your own words the difference between prejudice and discrimination and how they are increased by competition and reduced by cooperation.	

Humans are social animals who live in a highly complex world. At any moment, hundreds of millions of people are talking with friends, forming impressions of strangers, arguing with family members, falling in love, and helping other people, as Cory Booker has done. Our regular interactions with others—even imagined others, even online "avatars"—shape who we are and how we understand the world.

We Make Snap Judgments About People

Think about what goes through your mind when you first meet someone, or even when you see someone in passing. Most likely, you very quickly make several judgments. You might think: This is someone attractive, or someone to be wary of, or someone about as intelligent as you are, or someone you'd like to know better. Many factors affect your initial impressions of someone and the way you react to him. These factors include how others describe him and how you feel about his nonverbal behavior, or body language—his movements, gestures, and facial expressions (**Figure 11.2**).

THIN SLICES OF BEHAVIOR How much can we learn from body language? The psychologists Nalini Ambady and Robert Rosenthal have found that people can make accurate judgments based on only a few seconds of observation. Ambady and Rosenthal refer to such quick views as *thin slices of behavior*. Thin slices of behavior are powerful cues for forming impressions of others.

In one research study, research participants viewed soundless 30-second film clips of college teachers lecturing (Ambady & Rosenthal, 1993). The participants were asked to rate the lecturers' teaching ability. Based solely on thin slices of behavior, the participants' ratings agreed strongly with the ratings given by the instructors' actual students. Here's another example: Videotapes of judges giving instructions to juries reveal that a judge's nonverbal actions can predict whether a jury will find the defendant guilty or not guilty (Rosenthal, 2003). Perhaps unconsciously, judges may indicate their beliefs about guilt or innocence through facial expressions, tone of voice, and gestures (**Figure 11.3**).

FACIAL EXPRESSIONS One of the first things we usually notice about another person is the face. In fact, when human babies are less than an hour old, they prefer to look at a picture of a human face rather than a blank outline of a head (Morton & Johnson, 1991). The face communicates information such as emotional state, interest, and trustworthiness. This ability to communicate is particularly true for the eyes.

We use our eyes to indicate anger, to flirt, or to catch the attention of a passing waiter. Eye contact is important in social situations, though how we perceive it depends on our culture. People from Western cultures tend to seek eye contact when they speak to someone. If the other person does not meet their eyes, they might assume, perhaps incorrectly, that she is embarrassed, ashamed, or lying. Westerners tend to view a person who looks them in the eyes as truthful and friendly. For this reason, people wearing sunglasses are often described as cold and aloof, and police officers sometimes wear sunglasses partly to seem intimidating. In other groups, such as certain Native American tribes, making direct eye contact, especially with the elderly, is considered disrespectful.

FIGURE 11.2
Reading Body Language
People's body language affects our impressions of them and their situations. How do the facial expressions and gestures of the men in this photo influence your judgment of the situation?

FIGURE 11.3
Thin Slices of Behavior
Even having a few seconds to read body language can provide sufficient cues for us to form general impressions about people. The judge shown here had summoned this defendant to court because the defendant was overdue in paying a court fine. We can tell that the judge is clearly indicating his disapproval.

We Make Attributions About Other People

When other people act kindly and heroically, we assume they are kind and heroic people. We neglect to consider the situation in which they have acted. For instance, Cory Booker said that he just did what most neighbors would do if they realized someone was trapped in a burning building. He noted also that firefighters and police officers perform those kinds of actions every day. An important lesson from social psychology is that we are usually more affected by situations than we realize. We need to keep this lesson in mind when we explain why certain events happened or why people behaved as they did. *Attributions* are our explanations for events or actions, including other people's behavior.

TYPES OF ATTRIBUTIONS In any situation, there are dozens of likely explanations for how things turn out. For example, you might have done well on a test because you studied hard, the test itself was easy, or a combination of these factors.

Fritz Heider originated attribution theory. Heider described two main types of attributions. **Personal attributions** are ways that we explain outcomes based on internal factors, such as someone's ability, mood, or effort. **Situational attributions** are explanations based on external factors, such as luck, accidents, or the actions of other people. Bernard Weiner (1974) noted that attributions can also vary on other dimensions. For example, attributions can be stable over time (permanent) or unstable (temporary). They can be controllable or uncontrollable. The weather, for instance, is situational, unstable, and uncontrollable. How would you classify good study habits?

Humans generally like order and predictability. We prefer to think that things happen for reasons, because explanations enable us to anticipate future events. But the world can be dangerous—many unexpected things happen. Suppose that a violent act, such as a rape or murder, appears to be senseless. We may make attributions about the victim, such as "She deserved it because she was wearing sexy clothes," or "He provoked it by starting the fight." Attributions of this kind are part of the *just world hypothesis*. From this perspective, victims must have done something to justify what happened to them. Such attributions make the violent act seem more understandable and more justified. They make the world seem safer and saner.

BIAS IN ATTRIBUTIONS When explaining other people's behavior, we tend to overemphasize the importance of personal factors and underestimate the importance of the situation. This tendency is so pervasive that it has been called the **fundamental attribution error.** By contrast, when we make attributions about ourselves, we tend to focus on situations rather than on our personal traits. This tendency is called the **actor/observer bias.**

The actor/observer bias refers to two tendencies. When we are the *actor* in a particular situation, our interpretation of a behavior or outcome is based on the situation. For example, we might say, "I failed the exam because it was unfair." When we are the *observer,* we interpret the same behavior, or the same outcome, based on others' personal attributes. For example, we might say, "She failed the exam because she did not study." One reason for this difference in attributions between ourselves and others is simply that we know more about the situations that we are involved in. Because we know less about the situations of other people, we tend to think that what happened was based on their personal traits. Some researchers have found that people in Eastern cultures,

personal attributions
People's explanations for why events or actions occur that refer to people's internal characteristics, such as abilities, traits, moods, or efforts.

situational attributions
People's explanations for why events or actions occur that refer to external events, such as the weather, luck, accidents, or other people's actions.

fundamental attribution error
In explaining other people's behavior, the tendency to overemphasize personality traits and underestimate situational factors.

actor/observer bias
When interpreting our own behavior, we tend to focus on situations. When interpreting other people's behavior, we tend to focus on personal attributes.

LEARNING TIP: Attributions and the Actor/Observer Bias

Here's an easy way to remember the actor/observer bias based on a situation that we are all familiar with: fender benders.

WHEN YOU SEE	PLEASE THINK	FENDER BENDER EXAMPLE
Actor	When you are the <u>actor</u>, you attribute the outcome to the <u>situation</u>.	I had a fender bender because: • The road was slippery. • The other driver went through the red light.
Observer	When you are the <u>observer</u>, you attribute the outcome to another person's <u>personal attributes</u>.	That person had a fender bender because: • She's a careless driver. • His eyesight is really bad.

(a)

such as those in Asia, are more likely than Westerners to believe that human behavior is the outcome of both personal and situational factors (Choi, Dalal, Kim-Prieto, & Park, 2003; Miyamoto & Kitayama, 2002). The Learning Tip will help you remember actor/observer bias.

We Tend to Stereotype Other People

Do all Italians have fiery tempers? Do all Canadians like hockey? Can white women rap? As we saw in Chapter 8, stereotypes are mental shortcuts that allow for easy, fast processing of social information (**Figure 11.4**). Stereotyping occurs automatically and, in most cases, outside of our awareness. In and of themselves, stereotypes are neutral. They simply reflect efficient cognitive processes. Indeed, some stereotypes are based in truth: Men tend to be more violent than women, and women tend to be more nurturing than men. However, these statements are true on average. Not all men are violent, nor are all women nurturing.

MAINTAINING STEREOTYPES Once we form stereotypes, we tend to maintain them. For instance, we might perceive a behavior in a way that is consistent with a stereotype we hold. A lawyer described as aggressive and a construction worker described as aggressive bring to mind very different images. Thus we might attribute a white man's success to hard work and determination and a black man's success to outside factors, such as luck or affirmative action.

When we encounter someone who does not fit a stereotype, we may put that person in a special category rather than change the stereotype. This practice is called *subtyping*. Thus a racist who believes African Americans are lazy may categorize the superstar Beyoncé or the politicians Cory Booker or Barack Obama as exceptions to the rule rather than as evidence that the stereotype is wrong. Forming a subtype of successful African Americans allows the racist to maintain the stereotype that most African Americans are unsuccessful.

SELF-FULFILLING PROPHECY How does being treated as a member of a stereotyped group affect a person? Stereotypes that start out being untrue can later

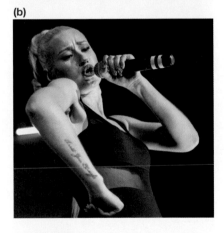

(b)

FIGURE 11.4

Stereotypes
We tend to create mental stereotypes because they are a fast, easy way to think about social information. Unfortunately, mental stereotypes are not always correct. **(a)** Does this photo, of fans at a 2010 Olympic Gold Medal hockey game between Canada and the United States, lead you to think that all Canadians like hockey? **(b)** When you think of a rapper, do you picture a Caucasian woman? Probably not. But Iggy Azalea is one of the white female rappers looking to establish themselves in this traditionally male-dominated field.

Have you ever had the feeling
that someone doesn't like you
very much? If so, this feeling
probably affected how you
treated that person—and not
for the better. Perhaps the other
person saw that you didn't treat
her very well. In turn, she treated
you poorly. Her behavior then
seemed to confirm your belief
that she didn't like you.

   This negative cycle of the self-
fulfilling prophecy can be broken
if you simply treat the other
person well. The new positive
way of interacting can become a
self-fulfilling prophecy of its own.

become true. The **self-fulfilling prophecy** is the tendency to behave in ways that
confirm our own or others' expectations.

   In the 1960s, the psychologist Robert Rosenthal and a school principal,
Lenore Jacobsen, conducted impressive research on this process. In one of
their studies, they had elementary school students take a test that supposedly
identified those who were especially likely to show large increases in IQ during
the school year. These students were labeled bloomers. Teachers were given a
list of the bloomers in their classes. At the end of the year, standardized testing
revealed that the bloomers showed large increases in IQ. However, as you might
have guessed, students on the bloomer lists had actually been chosen at random.
These students had not necessarily scored higher on the earlier test. Therefore,
their increases in IQ likely resulted from the extra attention and encouragement provided by the teachers. The teachers' expectations turned into reality—
a self-fulfilling prophecy.

   Of course, negative stereotypes can become self-fulfilling as well. When teachers expect certain students to fail, they might subtly, however unconsciously,
undermine those students' self-confidence or motivation (McKown & Weinstein,
2008). For instance, offering unwanted help, even with the best intentions, can
send the message that the teacher does not believe the student has what it takes
to succeed on his own. Have you ever experienced a self-fulfilling prophecy, either
positive or negative?

Stereotypes Can Make Us Feel and Act Certain Ways

Stereotypes may be positive, neutral, or negative. When they are negative, stereotypes can lead to prejudice and discrimination. **Prejudice** involves negative feelings,
opinions, and beliefs associated with a stereotype. **Discrimination** is the inappropriate and unjustified treatment of people as a result of prejudice. Prejudice and
discrimination are responsible for much of the conflict and warfare around the
world. Within nearly all cultures, some groups of people are discriminated against
because of prejudice. Over the last half century, social psychologists have studied
the causes and consequences of prejudice. They have looked for ways to reduce the
destructive effects of prejudice.

   Why do stereotypes so often lead to prejudice and discrimination? Psychologists have developed various theories. According to one theory, only certain types
of people are prejudiced. According to a second theory, people treat others as
scapegoats to relieve the tensions of daily living. According to a third theory, people
discriminate against others to protect their own self-esteem. One explanation,
consistent with evolutionary theory, is that it is adaptive to favor our own groups
over other groups. As a result, we tend to discriminate against people who pose
threats to our groups.

INGROUP/OUTGROUP BIAS It's the big game. You are wearing the team colors,
cheering yourself hoarse, and maybe even doing silly dances—all in the name of team
spirit. We are powerfully connected to the groups we belong to. We not only cheer them
on, we fight for them, and sometimes we are even willing to die for them. Those groups
that we belong to are *ingroups*. Those that we do not belong to are *outgroups* (**Figure 11.5**).

   Our group memberships are an important part of our social identities. Membership contributes to each group member's overall sense of self-esteem. Believing
that the groups we belong to are good groups makes us feel better about ourselves.

self-fulfilling prophecy
People's tendency to behave in ways that
confirm their own expectations or other
people's expectations.

prejudice
Negative feelings, opinions, and beliefs
associated with a stereotype.

discrimination
The inappropriate and unjustified
treatment of people as a result of
prejudice.

The separation of people into ingroup and outgroup members appears to occur early in development. Researchers have found that Caucasian 6-year-olds show as much preference for their ingroups as Caucasian adults do (Baron & Banaji, 2006).

Once we categorize others as ingroup or outgroup members, we treat them differently. For instance, we tend to view outgroup members as less varied than ingroup members. UCLA students may think Berkeley students are all alike. When they think about UCLA students, they cannot help noticing the wide diversity of student types. Of course, Berkeley students have the same view in reverse: Their student body is diverse, but one UCLA student is not much different from any other.

One consequence of categorizing people as ingroup or outgroup members is *ingroup favoritism*. For example, we are more willing to do favors for ingroup members or to forgive their mistakes or errors. Why do people value members of their own groups more highly than they value other people? We can speculate that over the course of human evolution, personal survival has depended on group survival. Those who work together to keep resources within their group and deny resources to outgroup members have a selective advantage over those who are willing to share with the outgroup. This advantage becomes especially important when groups are competing for scarce resources.

STEREOTYPES AND PERCEPTION We have seen how stereotypes can influence our beliefs and behavior. But social psychological research has shown that stereotypes can influence our basic perceptual processes. Because people are often not conscious of their stereotypes, they are also unaware of the influence of stereotypes on their perceptions.

In an experiment that demonstrated this influence, white participants were briefly shown a picture of a white face or a black face (**Figure 11.6a;** Payne, 2001). The picture appeared so briefly that participants were not aware of seeing it. After each face, a picture of either a tool or a gun appeared (**Figure 11.6b**). Participants were asked to classify the object as a "tool" or "gun" as quickly as possible. Participants who were shown a black face identified the gun more quickly and also more often mistook the tool for a gun.

COMPETITION AND COOPERATION Can the findings of social psychology be used to reduce prejudice? Can they be used to encourage peace? Since the 1950s, social psychologists have worked with politicians, activists, and others in many attempts to lessen the hostility and violence between factions.

Social psychology may be able to offer strategies for promoting intergroup harmony and producing greater tolerance for outgroups. The first study to suggest this possibility was conducted in the 1950s by Muzafer Sherif and colleagues (1961). Sherif arranged for 22 well-adjusted and intelligent white fifth-grade boys from Oklahoma City to attend a summer camp at a lake. The boys did not know each other. Before arriving at camp, they were randomly divided into two groups, the Eagles and the Rattlers. The next week, over a four-day period, the groups were pitted against each other in competition.

Group pride was extremely strong, and animosity between the groups quickly escalated. The Eagles burned the Rattlers' flag. The Rattlers retaliated by trashing

FIGURE 11.5
Ingroup/Outgroup Bias
People tend to identify strongly with the groups they are a part of. Here, during the semifinal match of the 2011 Men's World Hockey Championships, players from the Swedish team (in the yellow and blue uniforms) fight with players from the Czech team.

(a)

(b)

FIGURE 11.6
Stereotypes and Perception
(a) In one study, participants were shown a picture of a white face or a picture of a black face. **(b)** Then participants were immediately shown a picture of an object and asked to classify it as a gun or a tool. Participants primed by seeing black faces identified guns more quickly and mistook tools for guns. The study revealed that stereotypes can influence basic perceptual processes.

(a)

(b)

FIGURE 11.7

Competition and Cooperation
(a) Competition can increase hostility. For example, when the tennis greats Serena **(top, about to return the ball)** and Venus Williams play against each other in singles matches, each sister seeks to defeat the other. **(b)** By contrast, cooperation can increase tolerance and friendship. As a team in doubles matches, the Williams sisters unite to defeat their opponents.

the Eagles' cabin. Eventually, confrontations and physical fights had to be broken up by the experimenters. Phase 1 of the study was complete. Sherif had shown how easy it was to make people hate each other: Simply divide them into groups, have the groups compete against each other, and prejudice and mistreatment will result. If you've ever watched *Survivor,* you've seen this happen.

Phase 2 of the study then explored whether the hostility could be undone. Sherif reasoned that if competition led to hostility, then cooperation should reduce hostility. The experimenters created situations in which members of both groups had to cooperate to achieve necessary goals. For instance, the experimenters rigged a truck to break down. Getting the truck moving required all the boys to pull together. In an ironic twist, the boys had to use the same rope they had used earlier in a tug-of-war. After a series of tasks that required cooperation, the walls between the two sides broke down. The boys became friends across the groups. Among strangers, competition and isolation created enemies. Among enemies, cooperation created friends (**Figure 11.7**).

COOPERATION IN THE CLASSROOM The programs that most successfully bring groups together involve person-to-person interaction. A good example is the jigsaw classroom. The social psychologist Eliot Aronson developed this program with his students in the 1970s.

In the jigsaw classroom, students work together in mixed-race or mixed-sex groups. Each group member is an expert on one aspect of the assignment. For instance, when studying Mexico, one group member might focus on the country's geography, another on its history, and so on. The various geography experts from each group get together and master the material. They then return to their own groups and teach the material to their team members. In other words, each group member cooperates both within and outside of the group.

More than 800 studies of the jigsaw classroom have demonstrated that this program leads to more-positive treatment of other ethnicities. According to Aronson, children in jigsaw classrooms grow to like each other more and develop higher self-esteem than do children in traditional classrooms. The lesson is clear: Communal work toward goals can reduce prejudice and benefit all the workers.

 LEARN

11.1 CHECKPOINT: How Do We Think About Other People?

- We tend to form first impressions quickly, based on body language and facial expressions.

- The actor/observer bias is the tendency to make situational attributions to explain our behavior and personal attributions to explain other people's behavior.

- Stereotypes allow for fast, easy processing of social information. Self-fulfilling prophecies occur when we behave in ways that confirm stereotyped expectations.

- Stereotypes can lead to prejudice and discrimination, especially for those in outgroups. Engaging in activities that require cooperation reduces stereotypes and prejudice.

11.2 How Do Our Attitudes Affect Us?

Do you believe in UFOs? Do you prefer one political party, or are you an independent? Do you have strong feelings about a movie you saw recently, or about particular products or companies? We all have feelings and beliefs, also known as **attitudes.** We have attitudes about serious things, such as religion or politics. We also have them about more trivial things, such as movies and hair products.

Our attitudes are shaped by our social context. As a result, they play important roles in how we evaluate and interact with other people. For example, how you were raised influences your religious and political beliefs. Your beliefs in turn affect whether you attend a religious institution as well as which religious institution you might attend, and whether you engage in political campaigning and for which party. Moreover, your engagement in these behaviors further influences and refines your attitudes (**Figure 11.8**). For all these reasons, understanding attitudes and how they affect daily life is an important issue in social psychology.

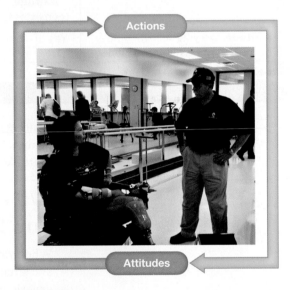

FIGURE 11.8

Interrelationship Between Attitudes and Behavior
Our attitudes affect our behavior, and our behavior affects our attitudes. Here, in 2005, the Vietnam veteran Don Sioss, a member of the Disabled Vietnam Veterans, talks with Major Ladda Tammy Duckworth about her treatment for injuries she suffered while serving as a helicopter pilot in Iraq. When veterans visit wounded soldiers, this behavior is likely to make the veterans' attitudes even stronger, so they will continue the behavior over time.

Simple and Complex Attitudes Affect Our Behavior

Let's explore some attitudes and their relationship with behavior. On the one hand, sometimes we hold attitudes and then we act in accordance with them. For example, if you believe smoking is bad for you and you do not smoke, then your behavior is consistent with your attitude. That is, you have a *simple attitude* toward smoking. On the other hand, if you believe smoking is bad for you and you do smoke, then your behavior is not consistent with your attitude. In this case, you have a *complex attitude*. You probably have some attitude toward exercising, either simple or complex, as described in the Try It Yourself feature on p. 390.

In general, the stronger and more personally relevant an attitude is, the more likely it is to predict behavior. Such attitudes also lead us to act the same way across situations related to that attitude. Consider someone who grew up in a strongly Democratic household. Suppose the person frequently heard negative comments

attitudes
People's evaluations of objects, of events, or of ideas.

TRY IT YOURSELF: **Simple or Complex Attitude Toward Exercising**

Is your attitude toward exercising simple or complex? To figure out your attitude, answer the questions in the table below. If you answer both questions the same way—both yes or both no—then you have a simple attitude toward exercising. That is, your behavior is consistent with your attitude. If you answer one question differently, then you have a complex attitude toward exercising. That is, like many people, your behavior is inconsistent with your attitude.

	Simple attitude (consistent)		Complex attitude (inconsistent)	
Attitude: Do you believe exercising makes you healthier?	Yes	No	Yes	No
Behavior: Do you exercise?	Yes	No	No	Yes

about Republicans. That person is more likely to register as a Democrat and vote Democratic than someone who grew up in a more politically neutral environment.

The more specific the attitude, the more predictive it is. For instance, your attitude toward recycling is more predictive of whether you take your soda cans to a recycling bin than are your general environmental beliefs. Attitudes formed through direct experience also tend to be better predictors of behavior. For example, think about parenthood. If you aren't a parent but plan to have children, what kind of parent do you think you will be? Your expectations aren't yet informed by direct experience of parenting. But if you have seen one child through toddlerhood, you will have formed very strong attitudes about child-rearing techniques. These attitudes will predict how you approach the early months and years of parenting your second child.

The ease or difficulty we have in retrieving an attitude from memory is called our **attitude accessibility.** The accessibility of an attitude predicts how consistent with the attitude our behavior is likely to be. Russell Fazio (1995) has shown that easily activated attitudes are more stable, predictive of behavior, and resistant to change. Thus the more quickly you recall that recycling is important to you, the more likely you are to discard a soda can into a recycling bin rather than a trash can.

We Form Attitudes Through Experience and Socialization

When you started college, you probably encountered many new people, objects, and situations. Throughout life, when we hear about things, read about them, or experience them directly, we learn about them, and we may even explore them. The information we gain through learning and exploring shapes our attitudes. Generally, we develop negative attitudes about new things more quickly than we develop positive attitudes about them (Fazio, Eisner, & Shook, 2004). Positive attitudes develop more slowly over time.

MERE EXPOSURE Think about a food you like that you could not stand when you first tried it—coffee or sushi, for instance. How did you come to like it? Typically, the more we are exposed to something, the more we tend to like it. We acquire a taste for it—sometimes literally. In a classic set of studies, Robert Zajonc (1968, 2001) exposed people to unfamiliar items either a few times or many times. Greater exposure to the item, and therefore greater familiarity with it, caused people to have more-positive attitudes about the item. This process is called the **mere exposure effect.**

The mere exposure effect is also seen in our preferences for faces. For example, when people look at normal photographs of themselves and compare them to photos with the same images reversed, they tend to prefer the reversed versions. Why would this be the case? The reversed images correspond to what we usually see when we look in the mirror, or how we are used to seeing

attitude accessibility
Ease of retrieving an attitude from memory.

mere exposure effect
The increase in liking due to repeated exposure.

ourselves (**Figure 11.9**). Our friends and family members prefer the true photographs, which correspond to how they are used to seeing us.

CONDITIONING Because our associations between things and their meanings can change, our attitudes can be conditioned. (For a full discussion of conditioning, see Chapter 6.) Advertisers often use classical conditioning to create positive attitudes about a product. When we see a celebrity that we are attracted to (say, Brad Pitt) paired with a product that we have neutral feelings about (for example, a certain perfume), we tend to develop more-positive attitudes about the product (**Figure 11.10**). After this conditioning, the formerly neutral stimulus (the perfume) alone triggers the same positive attitude response as the positively viewed object (Brad Pitt). Operant conditioning also shapes attitudes: If you are rewarded with good grades each time you study, you will develop a more positive attitude toward studying.

SOCIAL EXPOSURE Attitudes also are shaped through socialization. Caregivers, peers, teachers, religious leaders, politicians, and media figures guide our attitudes about many things. As mentioned in Chapter 6, teenagers' attitudes about clothing styles and music, about behaviors such as smoking and drinking alcohol, and about the latest celebrities are heavily influenced by their peers' beliefs. Society instills many of our basic attitudes.

FIGURE 11.9

The Mere Exposure Effect
If she is like most people, the Academy Award–winning actress Meryl Streep will prefer **(left)** her mirror image to **(right)** her photographic image. Streep is more familiar with her mirror image, which (like most of us) she no doubt sees many times every day.

Both Explicit and Implicit Attitudes Affect Us

Most white Americans say that they view African Americans positively and that they are not racist. Yet earlier in life, they may have learned societal stereotypes of African Americans that are at odds with their expressed beliefs. How do you know what your real attitude is about something?

Recall from Chapter 3 that access to our mental processes is limited and that unconscious processes can influence behavior. Our conscious awareness of our attitudes can be limited by what we want to believe, but our actions may reveal our less positive attitudes (Nosek, Hawkins, & Frazier, 2011). These unconscious attitudes can reveal themselves through subtle responses. Suppose, for example, that a nonracist white person feels more uneasy when a black person walks behind him at night than when a white person does.

Attitudes can be explicit or implicit. These different attitudes have different effects on behavior. An **explicit attitude** is one you know about and can report to other people. If you say you like bowling, you are stating your explicit attitude toward it. But maybe you always say no when friends invite you to go bowling. This behavior suggests an unconscious outlook that is different. An unconscious attitude is also known as an **implicit attitude.** Our many implicit attitudes influence our feelings and behaviors at an unconscious level (Greenwald & Banaji, 1995).

We access implicit attitudes from memory quickly, with little conscious effort or control. In this way, implicit attitudes function like implicit memories. As we saw in Chapter 7, implicit memories make it possible for us to perform actions, such as riding a bicycle, without thinking through all the required steps. Similarly, you might purchase a product endorsed by a celebrity even though you have no conscious memory of having seen the celebrity use the product. The product might simply look familiar to you. Some evidence suggests that implicit attitudes involve brain regions associated with implicit rather than explicit memory (Lieberman, 2000).

FIGURE 11.10

Classical Conditioning in Advertising to Change Attitudes
Advertisers depend on the idea that positive feelings about a celebrity can often condition a person to have a positive response to a product that is paired with that celebrity. This effect usually translates into greater sales for the product.

explicit attitude
An attitude that a person is consciously aware of and can report.

implicit attitude
An attitude that influences a person's feelings and behavior at an unconscious level.

cognitive dissonance
An uncomfortable mental state due to a contradiction between two attitudes or between an attitude and a behavior.

To assess implicit attitudes, researchers use indirect means. One method researchers use to assess implicit attitudes is a reaction time test called the Implicit Association Test (IAT; Greenwald, McGhee, & Schwartz, 1998). The IAT measures how quickly a person associates concepts or objects with positive or negative words.

Another way to assess implicit attitudes is to observe behavior. Consider the 2008 presidential election, when many observers wondered how attitudes about African Americans would affect people's willingness to vote for Barack Obama. People higher in self-reported (explicit) prejudice were indeed less likely to vote for Obama. In addition, though, people who reported low levels of prejudice but whose scores on the IAT indicated negative attitudes about blacks also were less likely to vote for Obama (Payne et al., 2010). For this second group of people, their implicit attitudes were better predictors of behavior than their explicit attitudes. You can check out your own implicit attitudes by going to the Web site for Project Implicit© at implicit.harvard.edu/implicit/. Just select a test, answer the questions, and complete the online activity.

Discrepancies Between Attitudes and Behavior Lead to Dissonance

Generally, we expect attitudes to guide behavior. We expect people to vote for candidates they like and avoid eating foods they do not like. What happens when people hold conflicting attitudes? In 1957, the social psychologist Leon Festinger answered that question by proposing the theory of **cognitive dissonance.**

 LEARNING TIP: Cognitive Dissonance

What happens when you have a complex attitude? Suppose your attitude is that it is healthy to exercise (Cognition A). On the other hand, you do not actually exercise (Behavior B). This inconsistency creates some internal conflict, or cognitive dissonance, which feels uncomfortable.

You can reduce the discomfort of cognitive dissonance in two ways. You can bring your attitude in line with your behavior—for example, by saying, "Exercising won't affect my health that much" (change Cognition A). Or you might bring your behavior in line with your attitude by beginning to exercise more (change Behavior B). Either way, the dissonance is reduced and the consistency between your attitude and your behavior will make you feel better.

COGNITIVE DISSONANCE THEORY Dissonance is a lack of agreement. According to Festinger's theory, cognitive dissonance occurs when there is a contradiction between two attitudes or between an attitude and a behavior. For example, people experience cognitive dissonance when they smoke even though they know that smoking might kill them.

A basic assumption of cognitive dissonance theory is that dissonance causes anxiety and tension. Anxiety and tension cause displeasure. Displeasure motivates people to reduce dissonance. People may reduce dissonance by changing their attitudes or behaviors. Smokers may reduce dissonance by quitting smoking or by deciding that smoking isn't so bad. They sometimes rationalize or trivialize the discrepancies, as the Learning Tip illustrates.

POSTDECISIONAL DISSONANCE Cognitive dissonance also arises when we have positive attitudes about different options, but we have to choose one option. For example, you might have trouble deciding which apartment to rent. You narrow the choice to two or three alternatives, and then you have to choose one. Once you've made your choice, *postdecisional dissonance* motivates you to focus on the chosen apartment's positive aspects and the other apartments' negative aspects. This effect occurs automatically, with little cognitive processing, and apparently without awareness (Lieberman, Ochsner, Gilbert, & Schacter, 2001).

INSUFFICIENT JUSTIFICATION In one of the original dissonance studies, each participant was asked to perform an extremely boring task for an hour (Festinger & Carlsmith, 1959). People did not like the task, but the experimenter offered the participants either $1 or $20 to lie and tell the next participant that the task was really interesting, educational, and worthwhile. Almost all the participants went along with this setup and lied to the next participant.

Later, in an apparently unrelated study, the same participants were asked how worthwhile and enjoyable the task in the earlier study actually had been. You might think that those paid $20 remembered the task as more enjoyable, but just the opposite happened. Participants who were paid $1 rated the task much more favorably than those who were paid $20 (**Figure 11.11**).

According to the researchers, this insufficient justification effect occurred because those paid $1 did not have a strong enough reason to lie. Therefore, to justify why they went along with the lie, they changed their attitudes about performing the dull task. Those paid $20 had plenty of justification for lying, because $20 was a large amount of money in 1959 (roughly equivalent to $150 today). Therefore, these participants did not experience dissonance and did not have to change their attitudes about the task.

JUSTIFICATION OF EFFORT In 2011, band members at Florida A&M University were hazing the drum major Robert Champion on a school bus. They ended up beating Champion to death. Hazing and initiation rites are major problems on college campuses. Administrators impose rules and penalties to discourage hazing, yet some groups, such as fraternities and sororities, continue to do it. The groups require new recruits to undergo embarrassing or difficult rites of passage because these endurance tests make membership in the group seem much more valuable. The tests also make the group more cohesive.

As research has shown (Aronson & Mills, 1959), when people put themselves through pain, embarrassment, or discomfort to join a group, they experience a great deal of dissonance. After all, these people typically would not choose to be in pain, embarrassed, or uncomfortable. Yet they made such a choice. They resolve the dissonance by exaggerating the importance of the group and their commitment to it. This justification of effort helps explain why people are willing to subject themselves to humiliating experiences such as hazing (**Figure 11.12**). More tragically, justification of effort may help explain why people who give up connections to family and friends to join cults or to follow charismatic leaders are willing to die rather than leave the groups. If they have sacrificed so much to join a group, they believe, the group must be extraordinarily important.

Our Attitudes Can Be Changed Through Persuasion

We are constantly bombarded by advertisements; lectures from parents, teachers, and physicians; pressure from peers; public service announcements; politicians appealing for our votes; and on and on. These signals attempt to persuade us to think or do something. **Persuasion** is the active and conscious effort to change an attitude by sending a message. In the earliest scientific work on persuasion, Carl Hovland and colleagues (1953) emphasized that persuasion is most likely to occur when people pay attention to a message, understand it, and find it convincing. They also have to remember it.

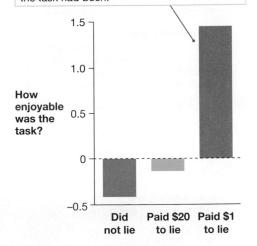

Participants who were paid only $1 to mislead a fellow participant experienced the effect of insufficient justification, a form of cognitive dissonance. This dissonance led them to increase their attitudes about how pleasurable the task had been.

How enjoyable was the task?

FIGURE 11.11
Effect of Insufficient Justification
Participants in one study performed an extremely boring task and then reported to other participants how enjoyable it was. Some participants were paid $20 to lie, and some were paid $1.

FIGURE 11.12
Justifying Effort
In early 2008, the University of Maryland removed the Delta Sigma chapter of the Delta Tau Delta fraternity from the College Park campus. Photos such as this one revealed that the fraternity's hazing included abusive alcohol consumption and mental, emotional, and physical duress.

persuasion
The active and conscious effort to change an attitude through the transmission of a message.

central route
A method of persuasion that uses high elaboration—where people pay attention to the arguments and consider all the information in the message. This method usually results in development of stronger attitudes.

peripheral route
A method of persuasion that uses low elaboration—where people minimally process the message. This method usually results in development of weaker attitudes.

Various factors affect the persuasiveness of a message (Petty & Wegener, 1998). Such factors include the source (who delivers the message), the content (what the message says), and the receiver (who processes the message). Sources that are both attractive and credible are the most persuasive. Thus television ads for medicines and medical services often feature attractive people playing the roles of physicians. Even better, of course, is when a drug company ad uses a spokesperson who is both attractive and an actual doctor. A message also may be more credible and persuasive when we perceive the source as similar to ourselves.

Of course, the arguments in the message are important for persuasion (Greenwald, 1968). Strong arguments that appeal to our emotions are the most persuasive. Advertisers also use the mere exposure effect: They repeat the message over and over in the hope that multiple exposures will make it more persuasive. For this reason, politicians often make the same statements seemingly endlessly during campaigns.

Those who want to persuade (including, of course, politicians) also have to decide whether to deliver one-sided arguments or to consider both sides of a particular issue. One-sided arguments work best when the audience is more likely to be on the speaker's side or is gullible. With a more skeptical crowd, speakers who acknowledge both sides but argue that one is superior tend to be more persuasive than those who completely ignore the opposing view.

According to Richard Petty and John Cacioppo's *elaboration likelihood model* (1986), sometimes people think carefully, or elaborate information, and sometimes they do not think too deeply. When we are motivated to process information and are able to process that information, persuasion takes the **central route** (**Figure 11.13**). That is, we elaborate the information. We pay attention to the arguments, consider all the information, and use rational cognitive processes. This route leads to strong attitudes that last over time and that we actively defend.

When we are either not motivated or unable to process information, persuasion takes the **peripheral route.** In this route, we don't think too deeply. That is, we minimally elaborate the message. When people don't think carefully, cues such as the attractiveness or status of the person making the argument influence what attitude is adopted. This route leads to more-impulsive action, as when we decide to purchase a product because a celebrity has endorsed it or because of how an advertisement makes us feel. Attitudes developed through the peripheral route are weaker and more likely to change over time.

FIGURE 11.13

The Elaboration Likelihood Model
(a) When people are motivated and able to consider information, they process it via the central route. As a result, their attitude changes reflect high elaboration. **(b)** When people are either not motivated or not able to consider information, they process it via the peripheral route. As a result, their attitude changes reflect low elaboration.

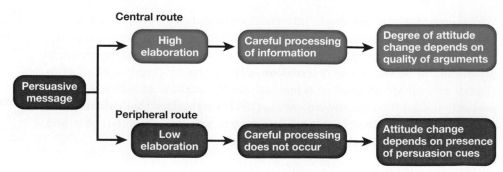

- Attitudes are evaluations of objects, events, or ideas. Attitudes can be simple or complex and can affect behavior.

- Attitudes are created by the mere exposure effect, conditioning, and socialization.

- Implicit attitudes operate at an unconscious level and affect behavior without our awareness. We are consciously aware of explicit attitudes and can state how they affect our behavior.

- Cognitive dissonance is an uncomfortable state produced by conflict between attitudes or between an attitude and a behavior.

- According to the elaboration likelihood model, attitudes are changed by persuasion through the central route or the peripheral route.

11.3 How Do Other People Influence Us?

📖 **LEARNING GOALS**	✏️ **READING ACTIVITIES**
a. Remember the key terms about the social influence of other people.	List all of the boldface words and write down their definitions.
b. Understand the four main ways that groups affect people.	Summarize group influence through social facilitation, social loafing, deindividuation, and group decision making.
c. Apply conformity, compliance, and obedience to your life.	Provide one example each of how someone influenced you to conform, comply, and obey.
d. Analyze the factors that influence us to act aggressively or prosocially.	By organizing them in a table, differentiate between the factors that tend to make us aggressive and the factors that tend to make us act prosocially.

"As soon as I'm around my parents, I act as if I'm seven years old again!" It's a common lament, and you may have said it yourself. Do you behave the same way when you are with your parents, a teacher or employer, or a romantic interest? And do you act the same way when you are alone as when you're in a group? Of course not. So far, we have considered how social factors affect our attitudes and behavior. But other people also affect us as well.

Groups Affect Individual Behavior

Although we may not go so far as to submit to hazing, we are all powerfully motivated to fit in with whatever group we are part of. As we've seen, being part of a group may be an adaptive behavior that helped our ancestors survive and reproduce. One way we try to fit in is by presenting ourselves positively. We display our best behavior and try not to offend others. We also conform to group norms, obey commands from authorities, and are influenced by others in our social groups. In fact, the desire to fit in with the group and avoid being ostracized is so great that under some

FIGURE 11.14

Influence of Groups on Behavior
(a) In social facilitation, the presence of others improves performance. For example, we run faster in a group than alone. **(b)** In social loafing, the presence of others impairs performance. For example, when other people are around to do the work, some people tend to slack off.

(a)   (b)

social facilitation
When the mere presence of others enhances performance.

social loafing
The tendency for people to work less hard in a group than when working alone.

circumstances, we willingly engage in behaviors that we otherwise would condemn. Perhaps the single most important lesson from social psychology is that the power of the social situation is much greater than most people believe.

SOCIAL FACILITATION AND SOCIAL LOAFING In the first social psychology experiment, conducted in 1897, Norman Triplett showed that bicyclists pedal faster when they ride with other people than when they ride alone. They do so because of **social facilitation** (**Figure 11.14a**). That is, the presence of others enhances performance.

In some cases, however, people work less hard in a group than when working alone. This effect is called **social loafing** (**Figure 11.14b**). Social loafing occurs when efforts are pooled, so individuals do not feel personally responsible for the group's output.

In a classic study, six blindfolded people wearing headphones were told to shout as loudly as they could. Some were told they were shouting alone. Others were told they were shouting with other people. Participants did not shout as loudly when they believed that others were also shouting (Latané, Williams, & Harkins, 1979). When people know that their individual efforts can be monitored, however, they do not engage in social loafing. Thus if a group is working on a project, each person must feel personally responsible for some component of the project for everyone to exert maximum effort (Williams, Harkins, & Latané, 1981).

(a)

(b)

FIGURE 11.15

Effect of Groups in the Stanford Prison Study and at Abu Ghraib
(a) In the Stanford prison study, student-guards took on their roles with such vigor that the study was ended early because of concerns for the well-being of the "guards" and the "prisoners." **(b)** Were soldier-guards at Abu Ghraib who harassed, threatened, and tortured prisoners just a few "bad apples," or were they normal people reacting to an extreme situation?

DEINDIVIDUATION In a classic study, the psychologists Philip Zimbardo and Chris Haney had male undergraduates at Stanford University play the roles of prisoners and guards in a mock prison (Haney, Banks, & Zimbardo, 1973). The students had all been screened and found to be psychologically stable. They were randomly assigned to their roles. What happened was unexpected and shocking. Within days, the "guards" became brutal and sadistic. They constantly harassed the "prisoners," forcing them to engage in meaningless and tedious tasks and exercises. The prisoners became helpless to resist. Although the study was scheduled to last two weeks, the researchers stopped it after only six days. The Stanford prison study demonstrated how quickly apparently "normal" students could be transformed into the social roles they were playing (**Figure 11.15a**).

In a real-life situation that has been likened to the Stanford experiment, the Abu Ghraib prison in Iraq, now named the Baghdad Central Prison, will always be remembered as the site of horrible abuses of power. During 2003, the first year of the Iraq War, American soldiers brutalized Iraqi detainees at Abu Ghraib. The soldiers raped prisoners, threatened them with dogs, beat them, placed them in humiliating positions, and forced them to perform or simulate oral sex and masturbation (**Figure 11.15b**).

When the news media began to reveal the abuse at Abu Ghraib, U.S. military and government officials were quick to claim that these were isolated incidents carried out by a small group of wayward soldiers. They emphasized that even amid the horrors of war, soldiers are expected to behave in a civilized and professional manner. The idea that only a few troubled individuals were responsible for the abuses is strangely comforting, but is it true?

The soldiers at Abu Ghraib, like the students in the Stanford study, were probably normal people who were caught up in overwhelming situations where being part of the group influenced their actions in extreme ways. Essentially, they lost their individuality, and their self-awareness, when they became part of the group. **Deindividuation** occurs when people are not self-aware and therefore are not paying attention to their personal standards.

Being self-aware typically causes people to act in ways that are consistent with their values and beliefs. When self-awareness disappears, so do inhibitions. Deindividuated people often do things they would not do if they were alone or self-aware. For example, most of us like to think we would try to help a person who was threatening suicide. But people in crowds often fail to intercede in such situations. Disturbingly, they may even egg the person on, yelling "Jump! Jump!" to someone teetering on a ledge.

People are especially likely to become deindividuated when they are aroused and anonymous and when responsibility is not clear. Rioting by fans, looting following disasters, and other mob behaviors are the products of deindividuation. Not all deindividuated behavior is so serious, of course. Fans dressing alike at a sports event and people dancing the funky chicken while inebriated at a wedding are most likely in deindividuated states and acting in ways they would avoid if they were self-aware (**Figure 11.16**).

GROUP DECISION MAKING Think back to when you were a child and all your friends were going to do something risky. Maybe they were going to dive off a high cliff or steal something from a convenience store. Did you join in?

In the 1960s, James Stoner found that groups often make riskier decisions than individuals do. Stoner called this phenomenon the *risky-shift effect*. The risky-shift effect accounts for why children in a group may try something dangerous that none of them would have tried alone. People in groups tend to make decisions that are more extreme than those made by people on their own.

Sometimes, however, groups become more cautious. Whether the group accepts more risk or becomes more cautious depends on the initial attitudes of the group members. If most of the group members are somewhat cautious, then the group becomes even more cautious. This process is known as *group polarization* (Myers & Lamm, 1976). For example, a jury that is initially skeptical is likely to become even more so after its members discuss the case. Through mutual persuasion, the decision making individuals come to agreement.

Sometimes group members are particularly concerned with maintaining a good atmosphere within the group. Therefore, for the sake of cordiality, the group may end up making a bad decision. In 1972, the social psychologist Irving Janis coined the term *groupthink* to describe this extreme form of group polarization.

Many examples of groupthink have occurred throughout history. Remember the second Bush administration's decision to go to war with Iraq over weapons of mass destruction that did not exist (as later investigations showed). Even though some members of the administration had doubts, they kept those doubts to themselves to avoid rocking the boat. Groupthink typically occurs when a group is under intense pressure, is facing external threats, or is biased in a particular direction. The group does not carefully process all the information available to it. Dissension is discouraged. Group members assure each other that they are doing the right thing.

To prevent groupthink, leaders must refrain from expressing their opinions too strongly at the beginning of discussions. The group should be encouraged to

deindividuation
A state of reduced individuality, reduced self-awareness, and reduced attention to personal standards; this phenomenon may occur when people are part of a group.

(a)

(b)

FIGURE 11.16
Deindividuation
(a) When people are excited and anonymous, like the fans at this basketball game, they tend to become less self-aware and to pay less attention to their personal standards. **(b)** When this process of deindividuation happens, people tend to act in ways that they would not normally behave.

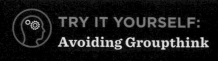

conformity
The altering of your own behaviors and opinions to match those of other people or to match other people's expectations.

consider alternative ideas. Either a group member can play devil's advocate or the group can carefully examine outside opinions. Of course, a group can make a bad decision even without falling victim to groupthink. Other factors, such as political values, can bias a group's decision making. But carefully going through the alternatives and weighing their pros and cons can help people avoid groupthink. The next time you work in a group, you can test some of the suggestions in Try It Yourself.

We Conform to the Expectations of Others

When you enter an elevator, do you face the doors or the other people? Most likely you face the doors. If you can't, you look at the floor. Looking directly at strangers in an elevator makes us, and them, uncomfortable. As a result, we conform to the expected behavior. **Conformity** is altering our behaviors or opinions to match those of others or to match what is expected of us. And conformity is a powerful form of social influence. What makes us conform?

NORMATIVE AND INFORMATIONAL INFLUENCE Social psychologists have identified two primary reasons that we conform. *Normative influence* occurs when—to be liked, to be accepted, or to avoid looking foolish—we go along with what the group does. This effect leads us to face the door in the elevator (**Figure 11.17a**). *Informational influence* occurs when we assume that the behavior of a group provides information about the right way to act. Suppose you are in a public place and see a mass of people running for the exit. In such a situation, you might assume that their behavior is giving you information about a potential emergency. If you suspect they are exiting for a good reason, informational influence would lead you to conform by running in the same direction (**Figure 11.17b**).

We have all seen examples of conformity to a group. Solomon Asch (1955) provided remarkable evidence of this behavior. Asch assembled male participants for a study of visual acuity. The participants looked at a reference line and three comparison lines. They decided which of the three comparison lines matched the reference line and said their answers aloud (**Figure 11.18**).

Normally, people are able to perform this easy task with a high level of accuracy. In these studies, Asch included just one naive (real) participant with a group of five confederates. The confederates pretended to be participants, but they actually

(a)   (b)

FIGURE 11.17
Normative and Informational Influence
People behave in the ways that others do for two main reasons. **(a)** They do this to be liked or to avoid looking foolish due to normative influence. An example of this behavior is the way that people generally stand facing the door in an elevator. **(b)** They also behave like others do when they think the group provides information about what should be done. This effect of informational influence is seen in crowds, when people start running in a particular direction—presumably away from a particular danger.

were working for the experimenter. The real participant always gave his answer last, after the five confederates gave theirs.

On 12 of the 18 trials, the confederates deliberately gave the same wrong answer. After hearing five wrong answers, the participant then had to state his answer. About one third of the time, the participant went along with the confederates: He knowingly gave an answer he knew was false. When the trials were repeated, three out of four real participants conformed to the incorrect response at least once. Why would they do this? It was not because they knew others were providing the right answer. In other words, it was not due to informational influence. Instead, people conformed because they did not want to look foolish by going against the group. That is, they conformed due to normative influence.

SOCIAL NORMS We may complain about all the rules we have to follow, but society needs rules in order to function. Imagine what would happen if you woke up one morning and decided that you would start driving on the wrong side of the road. Normative influence relies on the societal need for rules. Expected standards of conduct are called **social norms.** Social norms influence behavior in many ways. For example, they indicate which behavior is appropriate in a given situation and also how people will respond to those who violate norms. Standing in line is a social norm, and people who violate that norm by cutting in line are often sternly told to move to the back of the line. Normative influence works because we feel embarrassed when we break social norms. The next time you enter an elevator, try standing with your back to the elevator door and facing people. You may find it quite difficult to defy even this simple social norm.

People conform due to normative influence in daily life: Adolescents conform to peer pressure to smoke, jury members go along with the group rather than state their own opinions, and people stand in line to buy tickets. Sometimes, of course, we reject social norms. In a series of follow-up studies, Asch (1956) found that small group size and lack of unanimity among the group both diminish our tendency to conform.

Groups tend to enforce social norms. Research (for example, Schachter, 1951) has shown that dissenters are typically not treated well by groups. Groups enforce conformity, and those who fail to go along are rejected. The need to belong, including the anxiety associated with the fear of social exclusion, gives a group powerful influence over its members.

We Comply With the Requests of Others

We may follow social norms because we are afraid not to. We also behave in certain ways simply because others ask us to. Say your friends ask you to do a favor for them. If you do what they request, you are exhibiting **compliance.**

A number of factors increase compliance. Joseph Forgas (1998) has demonstrated that a person in a good mood is especially likely to comply. This tendency may be the basis for "buttering up" others when we want things from them. We may also comply with requests because we fail to pay attention (Cialdini, 2008). Wanting to avoid conflict, we follow a standard mental shortcut—responding without fully considering our options. If we are given a reason for a request, we are much more likely to comply, even if the reason makes little sense.

As shown in **Table 11.1,** some powerful strategies can be used to influence others to comply. Consider the *foot-in-the-door strategy:* Once people agree to a small request, they are more likely to comply with a large and undesirable request. Jonathan Freedman and Scott Fraser (1966) asked homeowners to place a large, unattractive "DRIVE CAREFULLY" sign on their front lawns. As you might imagine,

1   2   3

Comparison lines   Reference line

FIGURE 11.18
Asch's Research on Conformity
In Asch's study, participants in a group had to decide which of the three comparison lines matched the reference line and to say their answers aloud. He found that people tended to conform to social norms by giving the wrong answer, even when those norms were obviously wrong.

social norms
Expected standards of conduct, which influence behavior.

compliance
The tendency to agree to do things requested by others.

James was at a meeting of the science fiction/fantasy club. The treasurer was talking about the upcoming raffle. The club was raising money to help send some members to Comic-Con International, a large convention where actors, writers, and directors come to talk about their new science fiction/fantasy projects. James really liked the club, from its *World of Warcraft* online sessions to its campus-wide Humans versus Zombies event. He was eager to participate in the fund-raising. He had just read Chapter 11 of his psychology book and wondered, *Can I use my new knowledge of social psychology to help the club? How can we get people to comply with our request to buy raffle tickets?*

James opened his laptop and Googled *social psychology purchase request compliance*. He discovered that, according to some research, using people's names affected their willingness to make purchases. The phenomenon was called the name remembrance effect. In their first study (1995), Howard, Gengler, and Jain had student participants come to a professor's office. Previously, the participants had all said their names in class with the professor. As each student arrived at the office, the professor either greeted the student by name, claimed to remember the student's name but then seemed unable to recall it, or didn't mention the student's name at all. After their conversation, the professor asked if the participant would like to buy some cookies that his wife was selling for their church (25¢ each). The researchers measured whether participants bought cookies or not and how much they spent if they did. The participants were much more likely to buy cookies if the professor remembered their names (see graph [a]). In addition, the participants spent more money on cookies

if the professor remembered their names (see graph [b]). People even bought more or spent more if the professor forgot their names than if the professor didn't mention their names at all.

In a second study (1997), Howard, Gengler, and Jain tested the circumstances of the sale. This time, the professor again remembered, forgot, or didn't mention each participant's name, but half of the participants were asked to buy cookies in the professor's office while the other half were asked to buy them in an adjacent room. In addition, the "seller" of the cookies was no longer the professor's wife but a department secretary. *By changing the location of the cookie sales and the person selling the cookies, the researchers had removed perceived pressure from the professor to obey the request.* Regardless of whether the participants made the decision in the professor's office or the other room, and even when the seller wasn't the professor's wife, using the participants' names led to people being more likely to purchase cookies and to spend more money. *In other words, even when the circumstances of the request weren't so personal on the professor's part, the participants still bought cookies just because the professor remembered their names. This technique should work for us!*

James raised his hand. When the treasurer called on him, James explained the psychology research he'd just read about. "When people are trying to sell tickets, they should first introduce themselves and ask for people's names. Then, later in the conversation, they should be sure to call the people by their names. According to the research, our sales could double last year's." *I can't wait to see how much we make!*

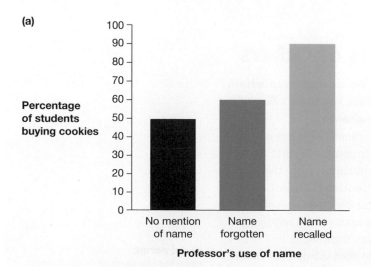

(a) Percentage of students buying cookies / Professor's use of name: No mention of name, Name forgotten, Name recalled

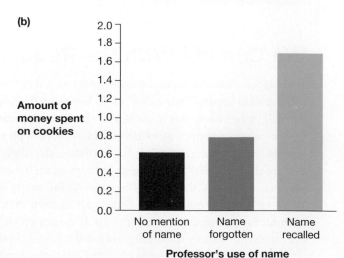

(b) Amount of money spent on cookies / Professor's use of name: No mention of name, Name forgotten, Name recalled

TABLE 11.1

The Three Ways of Inducing Compliance

STRATEGY	TECHNIQUE	EXAMPLE
Foot in the door	If you agree to a small request, you are more likely to comply with a large request.	You agree to help a friend move a couch. Now you are more likely to comply when she asks you to help her move all of her belongings to her new apartment.
Door in the face	If you refuse a large request, you are more likely to comply with a smaller request.	A marketer calls, and you refuse to answer a product questionnaire that takes 20 minutes. Now you are likely to agree to answer 5 questions about a product.
Lowballing	When you agree to buy a product for a certain price, you are likely to comply with a request to pay more for the product.	You agree to buy a used car for $4,750. When the salesman says he forgot to add some charges, you agree to buy the car for $5,275.

few people agreed to do so. However, when homeowners were first asked to sign a petition supporting legislation to reduce traffic accidents, many later agreed to put up the lawn signs. Once people commit to a course of action, they behave in ways consistent with that course.

The opposite strategy is the *door in the face:* People are more likely to agree to a small request after they have refused a large request. The second request seems modest in comparison, and people want to seem reasonable. Salespeople often use this technique when they try to sell you a moderately priced item after you've rejected an expensive one.

Another favorite sales tactic is the *lowballing* strategy. Here, a salesperson offers a product—for example, a car—for a very low price. Once the customer agrees, the salesperson may claim that the manager did not approve the price or that there will be additional charges. Whatever the reason, someone who has already agreed to buy a product will often agree to pay the increased cost.

We Obey People Who Have Authority

In the early 1960s, Stanley Milgram conducted what turned out to be one of the most famous and most disturbing psychology experiments ever done. Milgram wanted to understand why apparently normal German citizens willingly obeyed orders to injure or kill innocent people during World War II. Milgram was interested in the determinants of **obedience.** That is, he wanted to find out what factors influence people to follow orders given by an authority.

Milgram's experiment is summarized in Scientific Thinking. One participant was assigned to serve as a "teacher." The experimenter sat next to the teacher. Another participant, located in the next room, was the "learner." The learner was asked questions. Each time he gave a wrong answer, the teacher gave him what the teacher was told was an electric shock. As the test proceeded, the teacher was supposed to gradually increase the strength of the shocks.

obedience
Factors that influence people to follow the orders given by an authority.

Hypothesis: People will obey authority figures.

Research Method:

1. The participant ("teacher") was told that he must administer a shock to the "learner," located in another room, whenever he answered a question incorrectly. The learner was secretly in league with the experimenter.

2. The teacher helped the experimenter strap the learner into the machine that supposedly delivered the shocks. During the experiment, when the teacher believed he was shocking the learner, he heard a recording of the learner screaming in pain and begging the teacher to stop.

3. The teacher initially wanted to stop the study, but the experimenter insisted that he give the learner increasingly severe shocks. The real purpose of the experiment was to determine whether the teacher would obey the authority of the experimenter.

4. After the experiment, each participant teacher was introduced to the confederate learner and could see that the learner had not been harmed.

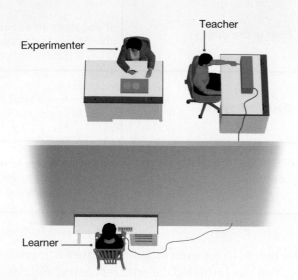

Results: Almost all of the participants tried to quit. However, nearly two-thirds of them obeyed the experimenter's directives to continue delivering shocks.

Conclusion: Most people will obey even hideous orders given by insistent authority figures. This willingness may be reduced depending on personality and making people more personally responsible for what is occurring.

In fact, the learner was a confederate of the experimenter, and the "shocks" were not real. A recording made it sound as though the learner was getting extremely painful shocks. The learner also complained of a heart condition and begged for the shocks to stop. Almost all the teachers tried to quit, especially when the learner screamed in pain. Each time, however, the experimenter ordered the teacher to continue. The experimenter stated: "The experiment requires that you continue," "It is essential that you go on," "There is no other choice; you must go on!"

Milgram was quite surprised by the results of his study. Some teachers resisted authority by saying no to the experimenter's orders. However, nearly two thirds obeyed all the experimenter's directives (**Figure 11.19**). Indeed, most of the teachers

FIGURE 11.19

Predicted and Actual Results

Psychiatrists, college sophomores, middle-class adults, and both graduate students and professors in the behavioral sciences offered predictions about the results of Milgram's experiments. Their predictions were incorrect. Most people continued shocking participants.

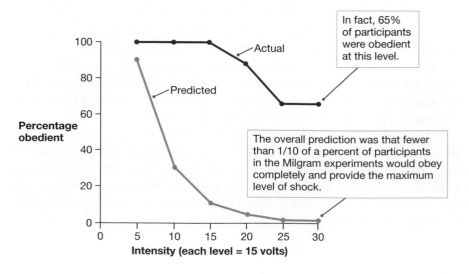

were willing to administer an apparently dangerous amount of electricity to the learner with a heart condition. These findings have been replicated by Milgram and others around the world. The conclusion of all the studies is that ordinary people can be coerced into obedience by insistent authorities. This effect occurs even when the coerced behavior goes against the way people usually would behave.

Milgram's results do not mean that people are always obedient. Indeed, some types of people, such as those who are concerned about how others view them, are more likely to be obedient (Blass, 1991). Milgram also found that some situations produced less obedience. For instance, if the teacher could see or had to touch the learner, obedience decreased. When the experimenter gave the orders over the telephone and thus was more removed from the situation, obedience dropped dramatically. So both personality and situational factors affected obedience.

Throughout his studies, Milgram was highly concerned with the participants' mental states. In systematic debriefings, he carefully revealed the true nature of the experiments to the participants. He made sure that the teachers met the confederate learners and that the teachers could see that the learners were not hurt in any way. Milgram (1974) also followed his participants over time. They reported experiencing no long-term negative effects. Actually, many people were glad they had participated. They felt they had learned something about themselves and about human nature. Most of us assume that only bullies would willingly inflict injury on others when ordered to do so. Milgram's research, and studies that followed up on it, demonstrated that ordinary people may do horrible things when ordered to do so by an authority. Although some people have speculated that these results would not be true today, a recent replication of the study found that 70 percent of the participants were obedient up to the maximum voltage in the experiment (Burger, 2009).

We Sometimes Hurt Each Other

Bullying, bar brawls, workplace intimidation—sometimes we hurt each other even when we are not being ordered to. **Aggression** involves the intention to harm someone else. Physical aggression is common among young children but relatively rare in adults. Adults' aggressive acts more often involve words, or other symbols, meant to threaten, intimidate, or emotionally harm others.

BIOLOGICAL FACTORS The biology of aggression has been studied primarily in nonhuman animals. Among nonhuman animals, aggression often occurs in the context of fighting over a mate or defending territory from intruders. Research with nonhuman animals has shown that stimulating certain brain regions or altering brain chemistry can lead to substantial changes in the level of aggression displayed. Several lines of evidence suggest that serotonin is especially important in the control of aggressive behavior (Caramaschi, de Boer, & Koolhaus, 2007). In humans, low levels of serotonin have been associated with aggression in adults and with hostility and disruptive behavior in children (Kruesi et al., 1992; Moffitt et al., 1998).

SITUATIONAL FACTORS The following situation is probably all too familiar: You are driving to an important meeting. Traffic is barely moving. As the minutes go by, you start imagining the consequences of being late. Then another driver cuts in front of you. It's a perfect setup for road rage, a common form of aggression.

In the 1930s, John Dollard and colleagues proposed the **frustration-aggression hypothesis.** This hypothesis suggests that the more frustrated we feel, the more likely we are to be aggressive. The more our goals are blocked, the greater our frustration, and therefore the greater our aggression (**Figure 11.20**).

aggression
Any behavior that involves the intention to harm someone else.

frustration-aggression hypothesis
The more frustrated we feel, the more likely we are to act aggressively.

FIGURE 11.20
Frustration Predicts Aggression
Frustration generally leads to aggression. For example, when traffic is heavy and drivers feel frustrated, they are more likely to behave aggressively. That aggressive behavior may include yelling and displaying road rage.

Frustration may lead to aggression by eliciting negative emotions. Similarly, any situation that induces negative emotions—such as being insulted, afraid, overly hot, or in pain—can trigger physical aggression even if it does not induce frustration. Negative emotions may lead to aggression because negative events activate thoughts related to fighting or escaping, and those thoughts prepare us to act aggressively. Whether we actually behave aggressively depends on the situation. If we have recently been exposed to cues of violence—for example, if we have recently watched a violent movie or been in the presence of weapons—we are more likely to act aggressively.

SOCIAL AND CULTURAL FACTORS An evolutionary approach to aggression would call for similar patterns of aggressive behavior to exist in all human societies. After all, if aggression provided a selective advantage for human ancestors, it should have done so for all humans. But the data show that violence varies dramatically across cultures and even within cultures at different times. For example, over the course of 300 years, Sweden went from being one of the most violent nations on Earth to being one of the most peaceable. Moreover, murder rates are far higher in some countries than in others (**Figure 11.21**). And analysis of crime statistics in the United States reveals that physical violence is much more prevalent in the South than in the North. Aggression may be part of human nature, but society and culture influence people's tendencies to commit acts of physical violence.

Some cultures may be violent because they subscribe to a culture of honor. In this belief system, men are primed to protect their reputations through physical aggression. For example, men in the southern United States traditionally were (and perhaps still are) raised to be ready to fight for their honor and to respond aggressively to personal threats. In a 1996 study (Cohen, Nisbett, Bowdle, & Schwarz, 1996), researchers found that participants raised in the South became more upset and were more likely to feel personally challenged when they were insulted than were participants raised in the North. They became more physiologically aroused after the insult, as measured by cortisol and testosterone

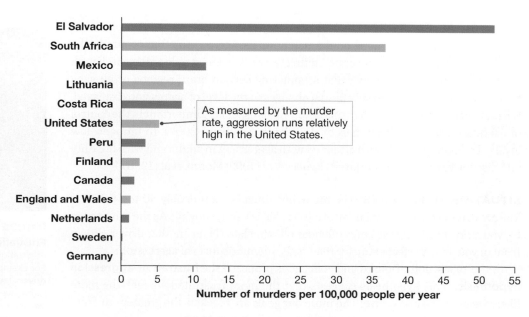

FIGURE 11.21

Aggression Varies Across Cultures

The numbers in this chart are the most recent available, from 2008. They come from the United Nations Office on Drugs and Crime (n.d.).

As measured by the murder rate, aggression runs relatively high in the United States.

Number of murders per 100,000 people per year

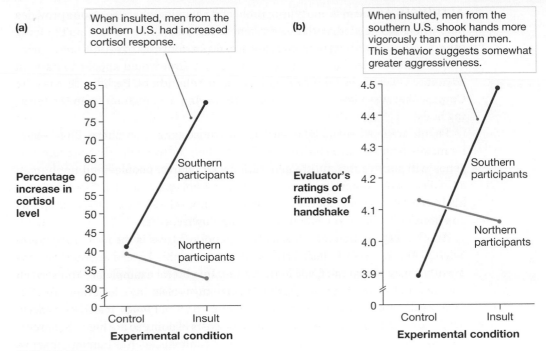

(a)

When insulted, men from the southern U.S. had increased cortisol response.

Percentage increase in cortisol level

85
80
75
70
65
60
55
50
45
40
35
30
0

Southern participants

Northern participants

Control   Insult

Experimental condition

(b)

When insulted, men from the southern U.S. shook hands more vigorously than northern men. This behavior suggests somewhat greater aggressiveness.

Evaluator's ratings of firmness of handshake

4.5
4.4
4.3
4.2
4.1
4.0
3.9
0

Southern participants

Northern participants

Control   Insult

Experimental condition

FIGURE 11.22

Aggressive Responses to Insults

According to results from studies at the University of Michigan, men in the southern United States tend to respond more aggressively to personal insults than do men in the North. This effect may partly be due to the Southerners having been raised in a culture of honor.

increases (**Figure 11.22a**). They also became more likely to act in an aggressive and dominant way for the rest of the experiment. For instance, participants raised in the South shook a new confederate's hand much more vigorously after they had been insulted than did participants raised in the North (**Figure 11.22b**).

prosocial
Acting in ways that tend to benefit others.

We Help Each Other . . . Sometimes

Think of the images of Superstorm Sandy that filled the TV news, print publications, and social media in 2012. Besides showing the devastation brought by the storm, many of the images captured the outpouring of compassion and assistance—ranging from financial contributions to hands-on home rebuilding—that occurred after the storm (**Figure 11.23**). Though we have been focusing on many negative aspects of social influence, people also behave in **prosocial** ways. That is, sometimes we act for the benefit of others.

Prosocial behaviors include offering assistance, doing favors, paying compliments, resisting the temptation to insult or throttle another person, or simply being pleasant and cooperative. By benefiting others, prosocial behaviors lead to positive interpersonal relationships. Group living, which requires people to engage in prosocial behaviors such as sharing and cooperating, may be a central human survival strategy. After all, a group that works well together is a strong group, and belonging to a strong group benefits the individual members.

FIGURE 11.23

Prosocial Behavior and "Superstorm" Hurricane Sandy

During and after Hurricane Sandy, many people acted in prosocial ways by helping others. Here, volunteers shovel sand away from a car trapped due to Hurricane Sandy in the Rockaway Beach neighborhood of Queens, New York.

altruism
The act of providing help when it is needed, with no apparent reward for doing so.

bystander apathy
The failure to offer help to people in need.

ALTRUISM Altruism is one type of prosocial behavior where someone provides help when it is needed, with no apparent reward for doing so. But isn't helping others, and even risking personal safety to do so, contrary to evolutionary principles? After all, those who protect themselves first would appear to have an advantage over those who risk their lives to help others. Perhaps this is why Cory Booker was viewed as so heroic after saving his neighbor from the burning house.

People are most altruistic toward those whose genes they share. This behavior makes evolutionary sense, because we are helping to ensure that our common genes will survive into future generations. Of course, people—and nonhuman animals as well—sometimes help nonrelatives. For example, Cory Booker risked his life to save his neighbor, someone he was not related to. Likewise, dolphins and lions will look after orphans within their own species.

Another explanation for altruism toward nonrelatives is the idea of *reciprocal helping*. According to Robert Trivers (1971), one animal helps another because the other may return the favor in the future. In a literal example of "You scratch my back, and I'll scratch yours," primates take turns cleaning each other's fur. For reciprocal helping to be adaptive, the benefits must outweigh the costs. Indeed, people are less likely to help others when the costs of doing so are high. Reciprocal helping is also much more likely to occur among animals, such as humans, that live in social groups because their species survival depends on cooperation.

BYSTANDER APATHY In 1964, a young woman named Kitty Genovese was walking home from work in a relatively safe area of New York City. An assailant savagely attacked her for half an hour, eventually killing her. At the time, a newspaper reported that 38 people had witnessed the crime, and none of them tried to help or called the police (**Figure 11.24**). Later evidence has shown that the story was wrong. In fact, there were only a few witnesses and none of them could see what was happening to Genovese (Manning, Levine, & Collins, 2007).

As you might imagine, the idea that 38 people could stand by and watch a brutal murder provoked outrage at the time. The public response prompted social psychologists to undertake research on how people react in emergencies. Shortly after the Genovese murder, Bibb Latané and John Darley examined situations that produce what they called **bystander apathy.** This term refers to the failure to offer help by those who observe someone in need. Common sense might suggest that when more people are available to help, a victim is more likely to be helped. Latané and Darley claimed, however, that each person is less likely to offer help if other bystanders are around.

To test their theory, Latané and Darley placed people in situations that indicated they should seek help. In one of the first situations, male college students were in a room, filling out questionnaires (Latané & Darley, 1968). Pungent smoke started puffing in through the heating vents. Some participants were alone. Some were with two other naive participants. Some were with two confederates, who noticed the smoke, shrugged, and continued filling out their questionnaires. When participants were on their own, most went for help. When three naive participants were together, however, few initially went for help. With the two calm confederates, only 10 percent of participants went for

38 Who Saw Murder Didn't Call the Police

A young woman name Kitty Genovese was walking home from work in a relatively safe area of New York City. The assailant savagely attacked her for half an hour, eventually killing her. At the time, a newspaper reported that 38 people had witnessed the crime, and none of them trie' to help or called the police.

FIGURE 11.24

Kitty Genovese: A True Case of Bystander Apathy?
The idea that 38 people watched Kitty Genovese's murder provoked research on bystander apathy. Although the reporting of the case was incorrect, bystander apathy does occur.

help in the first 6 minutes (**Figure 11.25**). The other 90 percent "coughed, rubbed their eyes, and opened the window—but they did not report the smoke" (p. 218).

In later studies, the researchers confronted the participants with mock crimes, apparent heart attack victims in subway cars, and people passed out in public places. The experimenters got similar results each time. Bystander apathy has been shown to occur in a wide variety of contexts. Even divinity students, while rushing to a lecture on the Good Samaritan, failed to help a person in apparent need of medical attention (Darley & Batson, 1973).

Years of research have indicated four major reasons for bystander apathy. First, bystanders expect other bystanders to help. Thus the greater the number of people who witness someone in need of help, the less likely any of them are to step forward. Second, we fear making social blunders in ambiguous situations. In the Genovese murder, the few witnesses found the situation unclear and therefore might have been reluctant to call the police. There is evidence that people feel freer to seek help as the need for help becomes clearer. Third, we are less likely to help when we are anonymous and can remain so. Therefore, if you need help, it is often wise to point to a specific person and say something like, "You, in the red shirt, call an ambulance!"

A fourth factor in deciding whether to help involves weighing two factors: How much personal harm do we risk by helping someone? And what benefits might we have to forgo if we help? Imagine you are walking to a potentially dull class on a beautiful day. Right in front of you, someone falls down, twists an ankle, and needs transportation to the nearest clinic. You probably would be willing to help. Now imagine you are running to a final exam that counts for 90 percent of your grade. In this case, you probably would be much less likely to offer assistance.

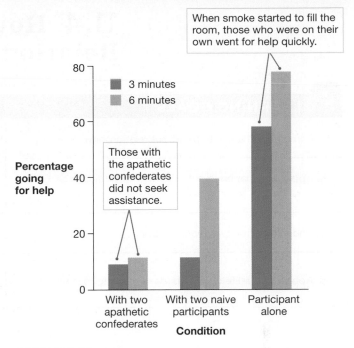

FIGURE 11.25
The Bystander Apathy Effect
In Latané and Darley's experiments, participants were asked to wait with two apathetic confederates, with two other naive participants, or alone. This chart records the participants' reactions to smoke filling the room.

 11.3 CHECKPOINT: How Do Other People Influence Us?

- Groups influence individual behavior through social facilitation, social loafing, and deindividuation, and by affecting group decision making.

- We conform to match the behaviors, opinions, or expectations of others. We also comply with requests and are obedient to authorities.

- We sometimes intend to hurt others through aggression. Aggression is influenced by biological, situational, and sociocultural factors.

- We help others through prosocial behaviors, including altruism, that maintain social relations. But sometimes we fail to help due to bystander apathy.

11.4 How Do We Develop Strong Relationships?

When you think about the social relationships that have been the most important to you, most likely you think about a romantic partner or your closest friends. These people have powerful effects on us. Whom do we choose to be our friends or lovers, how do these core social bonds develop, and why do some succeed and others fail?

Some people think that love and friendship are mysterious states to be considered only by poets. But relationships can be explored scientifically. Recently, researchers have begun to make considerable progress in identifying the factors that lead us to form relationships (Berscheid & Regan, 2005). Many of these findings support the idea that developing strong, lasting relationships with others is important to our survival as a species.

Situations and Personalities Affect Our Relationships

How did you become close with your best friend? If you are like most people, your best friend is someone that you grew up with or have lived near for a long time. He or she is probably also similar to you in a number of ways, including your core values and beliefs. In addition, your best friend probably has a lot of characteristics that you find positive. Psychologists have discovered that all these factors promote the development of friendships.

PROXIMITY In 1950, Leon Festinger, Stanley Schachter, and Kurt Back examined the effects of proximity on friends in a college dorm. *Proximity* here simply means how often people come into contact. The researchers found that the more often students come into contact, the more likely they are to become friends. Indeed, friendships often form among people who belong to the same groups, clubs, and so on. Proximity might have its effects because of familiarity: People like familiar things more than unfamiliar ones. And, as we saw earlier, when we are repeatedly exposed to something, we tend to like the thing more over time. The mere exposure effect may apply to people as well as objects.

BIRDS OF A FEATHER Birds of a feather really do flock together, and so do people who are like each other (**Figure 11.26**). People with similar attitudes, values, interests, backgrounds, personalities, and levels of attractiveness tend to like each other more than people who are dissimilar. In high school, people tend to be friends with those of the same sex, race or ethnicity, age, and year in school. College roommates who are most similar at the beginning of the school year are most likely to become good friends (Neimeyer & Mitchell, 1988). In addition, the most successful romantic couples also tend to be the most physically similar (Bentler & Newcomb, 1978; Caspi & Herbener, 1990). Of course, people can and do become friends or romantic partners with people of other races, people who are much older or younger, and so on. Such friendships and relationships tend to be based on other important similarities, such as values, education, and socioeconomic status.

PERSONAL CHARACTERISTICS We tend to especially like people who have admirable personality characteristics. This tendency holds true whether we are choosing friends or lovers. In a now-classic study, Norman Anderson (1968) asked college students to rate how much they would like others who possessed 555 different traits. As you might suspect, people most like those who have personal characteristics valuable to the group, such as kindness, dependability, and trustworthiness (**Table 11.2**). They dislike others with characteristics such as dishonesty, insincerity, and lack of personal warmth, which tend to drain group resources. People who seem overly competent or too perfect, however, make others feel uncomfortable or inadequate, and small mistakes can make a person seem more human and therefore more likable (Helmreich, Aronson, & LeFan, 1970).

FIGURE 11.26
Similarity in Attitudes and in Attractiveness
Friends and romantic partners tend to be similar in personal characteristics, attitudes, beliefs, and attractiveness. A good example of this matching is Beyoncé and Jay Z, both of whom are very attractive and successful musicians and entrepreneurs.

TABLE 11.2
The Ten Most Positive and Most Negative Personal Characteristics

MOST POSITIVE	MOST NEGATIVE
1. Sincere	1. Unkind
2. Honest	2. Untrustworthy
3. Understanding	3. Malicious
4. Loyal	4. Obnoxious
5. Truthful	5. Untruthful
6. Trustworthy	6. Dishonest
7. Intelligent	7. Cruel
8. Dependable	8. Mean
9. Open-minded	9. Phony
10. Thoughtful	10. Liar

SOURCE: Anderson (1968).

PHYSICAL ATTRACTIVENESS People also value physical attractiveness in forming relationships. But what determines physical attractiveness? Some standards of beauty, such as preferences for particular body types, appear to change over time and across cultures. Nevertheless, how people rate attractiveness is generally similar across all cultures (Cunningham, Roberts, Barbee, Druen, & Wu, 1995). For example, across all cultures, people who look after themselves, such as by having good hygiene, are viewed as more attractive.

Most people find symmetrical faces more attractive than asymmetrical ones. This preference may be adaptive, because a lack of symmetry could indicate poor health or a genetic defect. A cleverly designed study of what people find attractive (Langlois & Roggman, 1990) used a computer program to combine (or average) various faces without regard to individual attractiveness. They found that the more faces that were combined, the more the "averaged" faces were rated as attractive (**Figure 11.27**). People may view averaged faces as attractive because of the mere exposure effect. In other words, average faces may be more familiar than unusual faces. Other researchers contend that although averaged faces might be attractive, averaged faces that are initially rated as more attractive are rated more favorably than averaged faces initially rated as less attractive (Perrett, May, & Yoshikawa, 1994). Look at the photos in Try It Yourself to see if you agree.

Attractiveness can bring many important social benefits. Most people are drawn to those they find physically attractive (Langlois et al., 2000). Attractive people are less likely to be perceived as criminals, and they are given lighter sentences when convicted of crimes. They are typically rated as happier, more intelligent, more sociable, more capable, more gifted, more successful, and less socially deviant. They are paid more for doing the same work, and they have greater career opportunities. These findings point to what Karen Dion and colleagues (1972) dubbed the *"what is beautiful is good" stereotype.*

The preference for attractiveness begins early. Children as young as 6 months prefer to look at attractive faces, and young children prefer attractive over unattractive playmates (Rubenstein, Kalakanis, & Langlois, 1999). Even mothers treat their attractive children more positively than their less attractive children (Langlois, Ritter, Casey, & Sawin, 1995).

Although attractive people typically receive preferential treatment, do they actually have characteristics consistent with the stereotype that what is beautiful is good? The evidence on this issue is mixed. Attractive people tend to be more popular, more socially skilled, and healthier, but they are not necessarily smarter or happier (Feingold, 1992). Among studies of college students, for instance, the correlation

---

 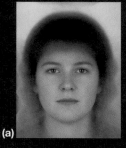

TRY IT YOURSELF: Which Face Is More Attractive?

Which face do you find more attractive? Image **(a)** represents the averaging of the faces of 60 women. Image **(b)** is the composite of the 15 faces that were initially rated as the most attractive out of that 60. Given the choice between **(a)** and **(b)**, most people prefer **(b)**. Female faces tend to be rated as most attractive when they are very symmetrical between the left and right sides and when they have stereotypically feminine features, such as larger eyes, a smaller nose, plumper lips, and a smaller chin.

(a)   **(b)**

FIGURE 11.27

"Average" Is Attractive
The more faces that are averaged together, the more attractive people find the outcome. The face on the right, a combination of 32 faces, typically is rated most attractive.

2   4   8   16   32

⟵————— Number of faces averaged together —————⟶

between objective ratings of attractiveness and other characteristics, such as grades or number of personal relationships, appears small. So why does having all the benefits of attractiveness not lead to greater happiness? Possibly, attractive people learn to distrust attention from others, especially romantic attention (Reis et al., 1982). If they believe that good things happen to them primarily because they are good-looking, they may come to feel insecure. After all, looks can change or fade with age.

Love Is a Key Part of Romantic Relationships

"Who Wrote the Book of Love?" was a hit song in 1958. But long before then, people were questioning what love is. We still do today. However, psychologists have long neglected the scientific study of love. Thanks to the pioneering work of Elaine Hatfield and Ellen Berscheid, researchers now can use scientific methods to examine this important interpersonal bond.

(a)

(b)

FIGURE 11.28
Passionate Versus Companionate Love
(a) Some romantic relationships focus on passionate love. **(b)** Other romances show the development of companionate love.

PASSIONATE AND COMPANIONATE LOVE Hatfield and Berscheid have drawn an important distinction between **passionate love** and **companionate love.** Passionate love is a state of intense longing and sexual desire, the stereotype of love we see in movies and on television. In passionate love, people fall head over heels for each other. They feel an overwhelming urge to be together. When they are together, they are continually aroused sexually (**Figure 11.28a**). Brain imaging studies show that passionate love is associated with activity in dopamine reward systems, the same systems involved in drug addiction (Fisher, Aron, & Brown, 2006; Ortigue, Bianchi-Demicheli, Hamilton, & Grafton, 2007).

People experience passionate love early in relationships. In most enduring relationships, passionate love evolves into companionate love (Sternberg, 1986). Companionate love is a strong commitment to care for and support a partner. This kind of love develops slowly over time because it is based on friendship, trust, respect, and intimacy (**Figure 11.28b**).

CHANGES IN LOVE OVER TIME Romantic relationships change over time, as the long-term pattern of sexual activity rises and then declines. Typically, for a period of months or even years, the two people experience frequent, intense desire for one another. They have sex as often as they can arrange it. Past that peak, however, their interest in having sex with each other decreases. For example, from the first year of marriage to the second, frequency of sex declines by about half. After that, the frequency continues to decline, though more gradually. In addition, people typically experience less passion for their partners over time. Unless people develop other forms of satisfaction in their romantic relationships—such as friendship, social support, and intimacy—the loss of passion leads to dissatisfaction and often to the eventual dissolution of the relationship (Berscheid & Regan, 2005).

Perhaps unsurprisingly, then, relatively few marriages meet the blissful ideals that newlyweds expect. Many contemporary Western marriages fail. In North America, approximately half of all marriages end in divorce or separation, often within the first few years. Moreover, many couples that do not get divorced live together unhappily. Some "partners" exist in a constant state of tension or as strangers sharing a home. The social psychologist Rowland Miller notes that "married people are meaner to each other than they are to total strangers" (1997, p. 12). Given that relationships inevitably change, we have to make staying in love something we are willing to work at.

passionate love
A type of romantic relationship that includes intense longing and sexual desire.

companionate love
A type of romantic relationship that includes strong commitment to supporting and caring for a partner.

WORKING TO STAY IN LOVE Even in the best relationships, some conflict is inevitable. Couples continually need to resolve such problems. Managing conflict is clearly an important aspect of any relationship, because it often determines whether the relationship will last.

John Gottman (1994) describes four interpersonal styles that typically lead couples to discord and dissolution. These maladaptive strategies are being overly critical, holding the partner in contempt (i.e., having disdain, lacking respect), being defensive, and mentally withdrawing from the relationship. For example, when one partner voices a complaint, the other partner responds with his or her own complaint. The responder may raise the stakes by recalling all of the other person's failings. People use sarcasm and sometimes insult or demean their partners. Inevitably, any disagreement, no matter how small, escalates into a major fight over the core problems. Often, the core problems center on a lack of money, a lack of sex, or both.

When a couple is more satisfied with their relationship, the partners tend to express concern for each other even while they are disagreeing (**Figure 11.29**). They manage to stay relatively calm and try to see each other's point of view. They may also deliver criticism lightheartedly and playfully (Keltner, Young, Heerey, Oemig, & Monarch, 1998).

Happy couples also differ from unhappy couples in attributional style. This term refers to how one partner explains the other's behavior (Bradbury & Fincham, 1990). Happy couples overlook bad behavior or respond constructively, a process called *accommodation* (Rusbult & Van Lange, 1996). Unhappy couples tend to view each other in the most negative ways possible. Essentially, happy couples attribute good outcomes to each other, and they attribute bad outcomes to situations. Unhappy couples attribute good outcomes to situations, and they attribute bad outcomes to each other. For example, if a couple is happy and one partner brings home flowers as a gift, the other partner reflects on the gift giver's generosity and sweetness. If a couple is unhappy and one of the partners brings home flowers as gift, the other partner wonders what bad deed the first partner is making up for. Above all, then, viewing your partner in a positive light—even to the point of idealization—may be the key to maintaining a loving relationship.

FIGURE 11.29

Working to Stay in Love

Positive interactions, such as expressing concern or making a thoughtful gesture, are ways to show your partner you care.

Overlooking Flaws to Have a Great Romantic Life

Some couples seem loving and supportive. We look at them and think, "That's the kind of relationship I'd like to have!" With other couples we may think, "That relationship seems so toxic! Why are they even together?" What different factors help create healthy and unhealthy relationships? How can their successes and failures help you create a healthy relationship that will thrive?

Sandra Murray, John Holmes, and Dale Griffin reasoned that people who fall in love and maintain that love tend to be biased toward positive views of their partners. This bias enables the lovers to reconcile two conflicting thoughts: "I love my partner" and "My partner sometimes does things that drive me crazy!" After all, people in love relationships often have to make accommodations for one another's failings.

To investigate this hypothesis, Murray and colleagues (1996) investigated partners' perceptions of each other. Their study included couples who were dating as well as married couples. The results were consistent with their predictions. Those people who loved their partners the most also idealized their partners the most. That is, they viewed their partners in unrealistically positive terms compared with how they viewed other people *and* compared with how their partners viewed themselves. Those people with the most positively biased views of their partners were more likely to be in a relationship with the same partner several months later than were those people with more realistic views of their partners.

How can you benefit from this research? Suppose your romantic partner has annoying habits, such as frequently coming home late from work or always leaving dirty dishes around the house. According to Murray and colleagues, paying attention to your partner's flaws or placing too much importance on occasional failures may make it very difficult to remain in love. If, however, you can put a positive spin on your partner's behavior, you should encounter fewer conflicting thoughts. For example, you might think of your partner's lateness as reflecting that "he's trying his best to provide for the family by working hard." In other words, if you try to idealize your partner a bit, this view may protect your relationship. This technique is one way that you can use psychology to improve your romantic life.

 11.4 CHECKPOINT: How Do We Develop Strong Relationships?

- Situational and personal factors affect the development of strong friendships and romantic relationships.
- Passionate love and companionate love are both important aspects of romantic relationships.
- We can work to stay in love, and increase satisfaction with our romantic relationships, by learning how to manage conflict and seeing our partner in a positive way.

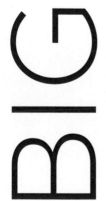

BIG PICTURE

11.1
How Do We Think About Other People?

a. Remember the key terms pertaining to how we think about other people.

b. Apply the principles of snap judgments to your life.

c. Analyze how we make attributions based on the actor/observer bias.

d. Understand the difference between prejudice and discrimination and how they are affected by competition and cooperation.

11.2
How Do Our Attitudes Affect Us?

a. Remember the key terms about simple and complex attitudes.

b. Understand the three main ways we develop attitudes.

c. Apply the idea of cognitive dissonance to your life.

d. Analyze advertisements to determine how persuasion is being used based on the elaboration likelihood model.

11.3
How Do Other People Influence Us?

a. Remember the key terms about the social influence of other people.

b. Understand the four main ways that groups affect people.

c. Apply conformity, compliance, and obedience to your life.

d. Analyze the factors that influence us to act aggressively or prosocially.

11.4
How Do We Develop Strong Relationships?

a. Remember the key terms about relationships.

b. Apply information about the effect of situations and personalities to your own relationships.

c. Understand the two types of love.

d. Apply to your life two methods of working to stay in love.

KEY TERMS

personal attributions
situational attributions
fundamental attribution error
actor/observer bias
self-fulfilling prophecy
prejudice
discrimination

attitudes
attitude accessibility
mere exposure effect
explicit attitude
implicit attitude
cognitive dissonance
persuasion
central route
peripheral route

social facilitation
social loafing
deindividuation
conformity
social norms
compliance
obedience
aggression
frustration-aggression
    hypothesis
prosocial
altruism
bystander apathy

passionate love
companionate love

CHECKPOINT

- We tend to form first impressions quickly, based on body language and facial expressions.

- The actor/observer bias is the tendency to make situational attributions to explain our behavior and personal attributions to explain other people's behavior.

- Stereotypes allow for fast, easy processing of social information. Self-fulfilling prophecies occur when we behave in ways that confirm stereotyped expectations.

- Stereotypes can lead to prejudice and discrimination, especially for those in outgroups. Engaging in activities that require cooperation reduces stereotypes and prejudice.

- Attitudes are evaluations of objects, events, or ideas. Attitudes can be simple or complex and can affect behavior.

- Attitudes are created by the mere exposure effect, conditioning, and socialization.

- Implicit attitudes operate at an unconscious level and affect behavior without our awareness. We are consciously aware of explicit attitudes

and can state how they affect our behavior.

- Cognitive dissonance is an uncomfortable state produced by conflict between attitudes or between an attitude and a behavior.

- According to the elaboration likelihood model, attitudes are changed by persuasion through the central route or the peripheral route.

- Groups influence individual behavior through social facilitation, social loafing, and deindividuation, and by affecting group decision making.

- We conform to match the behaviors, opinions, or expectations of others. We also comply with requests and are obedient to authorities.

- We sometimes intend to hurt others through aggression. Aggression is influenced by biological, situational, and sociocultural factors.

- We help others through prosocial behaviors, including altruism, that maintain social relations. But sometimes we fail to help due to bystander apathy.

- Situational and personal factors affect the development of strong friendships and romantic relationships.

- Passionate love and companionate love are both important aspects of romantic relationships.

- We can work to stay in love, and increase satisfaction with our romantic relationships, by learning how to manage conflict and seeing our partner in a positive way.

For a self-quiz on this chapter, go to the back of the book and find Appendix B: Quizzes.

12 Self and Personality

WHEN MARC BROKE UP WITH THE WOMAN he had been dating for almost a decade, Internet dating was a growing phenomenon. Marc had heard many success stories about couples who had met online, and friends encouraged him to give it a shot. But Marc wanted to find someone by being himself and doing the things that he loved in the city, such as going to museums, parks, concerts, or other cultural events. There, he hoped, he would meet a like-minded woman who enjoyed city life as much as he did. Things didn't go according to plan, however, so after a few months of being on his own, Marc decided to try Internet dating.

BIG QUESTIONS

FIGURE 12.1

Made for Each Other?
(a) This boy, determined to be himself even in the presence of a professional photographer, grew up to be "Marc." **(b)** This girl, playing her own version of Wonder Woman with earrings, grew up to be "Christine."

personality
The characteristic thoughts, emotional responses, and behaviors that are relatively stable in an individual over time and across circumstances.

When Marc joined an online dating site, he had to complete a long survey with questions about who he was, such as "Are you usually optimistic?" Marc knew himself well and could answer those questions easily. But he also had to answer questions about the characteristics he wanted in a partner. He was less sure about what qualities he was looking for in a girlfriend. Mainly, he wanted someone who *was not* his ex-girlfriend.

Over the next few months, Marc met several women he knew only from their answers to the survey questions. Invariably, on the first date, one or the other of them would decide that they did not click—they were not a match. Then, when Marc was just about fed up, he visited the site and saw a photo of a stylish-looking woman named Christine. In her profile, she described qualities he found appealing; she was adventurous, she "couldn't live without" cool sneakers and possibility. She sounded fun and positive and open. And she had a clear sense of the characteristics she was looking for in a partner: a self-sufficient, trustworthy man with his own ideas. When they finally met on a rainy Sunday, he liked the way she removed her hood before stepping inside the bar. She liked his smile. This time, it was a match.

Early childhood photos show Marc and Christine expressing many of the same characteristics—his stubbornness, her dramatic flair—that each exhibits today (**Figure 12.1**). They both alternate between preferring solitude and being outgoing. Each prefers to work alone, but each can become the catalyst for conversation at a party, a meeting, or some other gathering. During their six years together, Marc and Christine have brought out each other's best qualities. Marc thrives emotionally because he has someone to devote himself to. Because Christine's boyfriend is also her best friend, she feels confident enough to present her best self to the world.

Since the emergence of Internet dating in the 1990s, more and more people have turned to it to find romantic partners. According to a 2009 study, about 1 in 5 heterosexual couples reported meeting on the Internet, which made it second to meeting through friends as the most common method of meeting future partners (Rosenfeld, 2010). Online dating sites are based on the idea that questionnaires provide information that helps people decide whether they have compatible personalities and would be good matches for each other. This assumption seems to have worked for Marc and Christine. But does it work for everyone? To answer this, we have to explore how well people know themselves and how they understand other people.

This chapter is concerned with **personality.** Personality consists of the typical thoughts, emotional responses, and behaviors that are relatively stable in people over time and across circumstances. Everyone has a sense of their own personality. This chapter begins by talking about how we come to know ourselves. It then turns to how we come to understand other people.

We constantly try to figure out other people—to understand why they behave in certain ways and to predict their behavior. In fact, many students take psychology courses partly because they want to know what makes other people tick. In this chapter, you will learn how psychologists study personality, what personality is and where it comes from, and what knowing someone's personality can tell us about predicting that person's thoughts and behaviors.

12.1 How Do We Know Ourselves?

The story of Marc and Christine reveals how Marc had to know himself so he could find a good companion. It also shows that he had to realize what he wanted in a companion to decide whether they would be a good match. This section focuses on how we know ourselves—how we process information about ourselves, and how that processing shapes our personalities. In other words, we will look at one of the most enduring questions in psychology: "Who am I?"

Our Sense of Self Is Who We Believe We Are

When you talk about your "self," what are you actually referring to? Each of us has a notion of something we call the self, but the self is difficult to define. Your sense of self involves your mental representations of your personal experiences, such as memories and perceptions of what is going on at any particular moment. Your sense of self also includes your physical body and your conscious awareness of being separate from others and unique. In short, your sense of self is who you believe you are. This sense is sometimes called the self-concept.

For college students, the sense of self typically includes gender, age, student status, interpersonal style (e.g., shy, friendly), personal characteristics (e.g., moody, optimistic), and body image (e.g., positive, negative). Stop and think for a moment about 10 ways that you can answer the question "Who am I?" Your answers reveal your sense of self (**Figure 12.2**).

Your sense of self influences you in several ways. It affects how you think, by guiding your attention to information relevant to you. It also influences the way you behave. And it has an impact on how you feel. Because of all these connections, your self affects you every day. For example, think back to your 10 ideas about who you are. Now think about concrete ways that those ideas have influenced your thoughts, behaviors, and feelings. If you think of yourself as shy, maybe you once avoided a wild party but feel bad about not going. If you believe yourself to be optimistic, maybe you easily bounced back from a poor grade in organic chemistry and feel confident that you can improve.

FIGURE 12.2
Your Sense of Self
Each of us has a sense of who we are. Our sense of self includes memories, experiences, personal characteristics, and physical appearance.

SELF-SCHEMA Picture yourself at a loud, crowded party. You can barely hear yourself speak. But when someone across the room mentions your name, your ears perk up. As we saw in Chapter 7, psychologists explain that this effect occurs because we process information about ourselves deeply, thoroughly, and automatically. The information becomes part of our **self-schema.**

Our self-schema consists of an integrated set of memories, beliefs, and generalizations about ourselves (Markus, 1977) that is organized as a network of interconnected knowledge about the self (**Figure 12.3**). The self-schema helps each of us perceive, organize, interpret, and use information about our self. It also helps us filter information so that we are likely to notice things that are relevant to us, such as our own name. Examples of our behavior and aspects of our personality that are important to us become prominent in our self-schemas. For instance, being a good athlete or a good student may be a major component of your self-schema, but having few cavities probably is not. Thus, if you are asked whether you are ambitious, you can answer without sorting through occasions when you did or did not act ambitiously. Your self-schema summarizes the relevant past information.

Your self-schema may increase your memory for information that is relevant to you. Tim Rogers and colleagues (1977) showed that we are likely to remember adjectives better when they are used to describe our own traits than when they are used only generally. For instance, suppose you are asked, "What does the word *honest* mean?" If you are later asked to recall the word you were asked about, you might or might not recall *honest*. Suppose, however, the initial question is, "Does the word *honest* describe you?" When asked later to recall the word, you will be more likely to remember it.

What brain activity is involved in this effect? Researchers typically find that when people process information about themselves, there is activity in the middle of the frontal lobes of the brain (Gillihan & Farah, 2005; Kelley et al., 2002). Damage to the frontal lobes tends to reduce or eliminate self-awareness. Activation of the frontal lobes seems to be important for processing information about the self (Heatherton, 2011).

WORKING SELF-CONCEPT Psychologists refer to the immediate experience of the self in the here and now as the **working self-concept.** This experience is limited to the amount of personal information that is being processed at one moment in time. Because the working self-concept includes only part of the vast array of self-knowledge, the sense of self varies from moment to moment. Your self-descriptions depend on which memories you retrieve, which situation you are in, which people you are with, and your role in that situation. And they affect how you act in different situations. For instance, suppose your sense of self includes the traits *fun-loving* and *intelligent.* At a party, you might think of yourself more as fun-loving rather than intelligent. This working self-concept will influence your behavior at the party. In other words, you become more likely to act in ways that show you are fun. By contrast, when you are in class, you might think of yourself as intelligent. In that situation, your working self-concept will lead you to participate actively in the discussion.

When we consider who we are or think about different features of our personality, we often emphasize characteristics that make us distinct from others. Think back to your 10 responses to the question "Who am I?" Which answers stressed your similarity to other people or membership in a group? Which stressed your differences from other people, or at least from the people immediately around you?

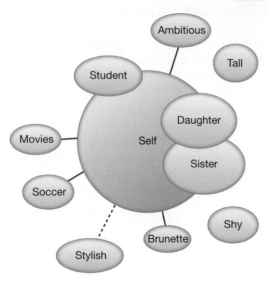

FIGURE 12.3

Self-Schema

Our self-schema consists of interrelated knowledge about ourselves. Here the concepts that are most strongly related to one person's sense of self (student, daughter, and sister) are shown overlapping with the self. Concepts that are not quite as strongly related (ambitious, movies, soccer, and brunette) are connected to the self with a solid line. Weakly related concepts (stylish) are connected to self with a dotted line. Concepts that do not relate to the self have no connecting lines.

self-schema
An integrated set of memories, beliefs, and generalizations about the self.

working self-concept
Reflects how a person thinks of herself at a certain moment.

In studies using this question, respondents are especially likely to mention features such as ethnicity, gender, or age if they differ in these respects from other people around them at the moment (**Figure 12.4**). For example, Canadians are more likely to note their nationality if they are in Boston than if they are in Toronto. Because the working self-concept guides behavior, this tendency implies that Canadians are also more likely to feel and act like "Canadians" when in Boston than when in Toronto. Most people do not want to be too distinctive, however, because generally they want to avoid standing out too much from the crowd.

SELF-ESTEEM **Self-esteem** is the affective aspect of our sense of self. Here, we evaluate how we feel about our personal characteristics. When we answer questions such as "Am I good or bad?" and "Am I worthy or unworthy?" we are making an affective evaluation about ourselves. Although self-esteem is related to our sense of self, we can objectively believe positive things about ourselves and still have low self-esteem—that is, not like ourselves very much. Conversely, we can like ourselves very much, and therefore have high self-esteem, even when objective indicators do not support such positive self-views.

Many theories propose that self-esteem is based on how we believe others perceive us. This view is known as *reflected appraisal*. When we internalize the values and beliefs expressed by people who are important in our life, we adopt those attitudes (and related behaviors) as our own. Consequently, we come to respond to ourselves in ways that are consistent with how others respond to us. From this perspective, when an important person rejects, ignores, or devalues us, we are likely to experience low self-esteem.

SOCIOMETER THEORY One theory argues that self-esteem is a mechanism for monitoring the likelihood of social exclusion (Leary et al., 1995). As we have discussed, humans have a fundamental, adaptive need to belong. When we behave in ways that make us more likely to be rejected from a social group, our self-esteem decreases. Thus self-esteem is a *sociometer,* an internal monitor of social acceptance or rejection.

When our sociometer indicates a high possibility of rejection, we experience low self-esteem (**Figure 12.5a**). In this case, we are highly motivated to improve our public image. When our sociometer indicates a low probability of rejection, we

(a) Who am I? / I am male.

(b) Who am I? / I am black.

FIGURE 12.4

Working Self-Concept

Our immediate experience of ourselves, our working self-concept, varies depending on which aspect of the self is most relevant at that moment. **(a)** Suppose a black man is working with a group of women. In that situation, his working self-concept might focus on awareness that he is a man. **(b)** Now suppose the same man is working with a group of white people. In that situation, his working self-concept might focus on awareness that he is black.

self-esteem
The affective aspect of the self.

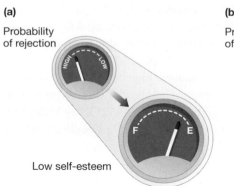

(a)
Probability of rejection

Low self-esteem

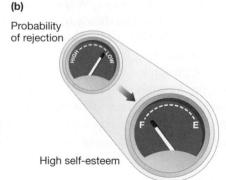

(b)
Probability of rejection

High self-esteem

FIGURE 12.5

Sociometers

(a) If the probability of rejection seems high, the person's self-esteem will tend to be low.
(b) If the probability of rejection seems low, the person's self-esteem will tend to be high.

tend to experience high self-esteem (**Figure 12.5b**). In this case, we will probably not worry about how others perceive us. Abundant evidence supports the sociometer theory, including the consistent finding that low self-esteem is highly correlated with social anxiety (Leary, 2004; Leary & MacDonald, 2003).

SELF-ESTEEM AND LIFE OUTCOMES With so much emphasis placed on self-esteem in Western culture, you might expect that having high self-esteem is the key to life success. But the evidence from psychology indicates that self-esteem may be less important than is commonly believed. A review of several hundred studies found that although people with high self-esteem report being much happier, self-esteem is weakly related to objective life outcomes (Baumeister, Campbell, Krueger, & Vohs, 2003, 2005). For instance, people with high self-esteem who consider themselves smarter, more attractive, and better liked do not necessarily have higher IQs and are not necessarily thought of more highly by others. Many people with high self-esteem are successful in their careers, but so are many people with low self-esteem. Although self-esteem has a slight relationship to some outcomes, such as academic success, the success might be what causes the high self-esteem. That is, people might have higher self-esteem because they have done well in school.

In fact, having a high opinion of yourself could even have some downsides. Violent criminals commonly have very high self-esteem. Some people become violent when they think others are not treating them with an appropriate level of respect (Baumeister, Smart, & Boden, 1996). School bullies also often have high self-esteem (Baumeister et al., 2003). Ultimately, having high self-esteem seems to make people happier, but it does not necessarily lead to successful social relationships or life success.

One characteristic associated with inflated self-esteem is *narcissism*. The term comes from a Greek myth, in which a young man named Narcissus rejected the love of others and fell in love with his own reflection in a pond. In the psychological sense, people who are narcissistic are self-centered, view themselves in grandiose terms, feel entitled to special treatment, and are manipulative. Because narcissists' greatest love is for the self, they tend to have poor relations with others (Campbell, Bush, Brunell, & Shelton, 2005), they become angry when challenged (Rhodewalt & Morf, 1998), and they tend to be unfaithful (Campbell, Foster, & Finkel, 2002).

An analysis of many studies found increasing narcissism among American college students between 1979 and 2006 (Twenge, Konrath, Foster, Campbell, & Bushman, 2008). The researchers point to a few possible contributing factors: programs aimed at increasing self-esteem among young schoolchildren (such as having them sing songs about how they are special), grade inflation that makes students feel more capable than they really might be, and a rise in the use of self-promotion Web sites such as Facebook and MySpace. However, other research has not found the same increase in narcissism, so debate continues about whether it is appropriate to say that young adults are members of "Generation Me" (Trzesniewski, Donnellan, & Roberts, 2008).

Even though we might encourage children to have high self-esteem, there is a tendency for self-esteem to fall during adolescence and be at its lowest for people, especially young women, aged 18 to 22 years (Robins et al., 2002; **Figure 12.6**). Self-esteem then typically increases across adulthood, peaking when people are in their sixties and falling off toward the end of life.

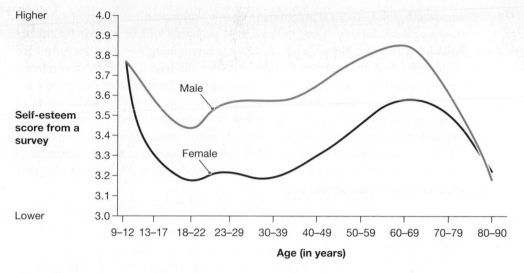

FIGURE 12.6

Self-Esteem Across the Life Span

Our self-esteem varies over our lives. Low points in self-esteem are seen in the late teens and early twenties, especially for females. Low self-esteem is also experienced toward the end of our lives. Self-esteem typically peaks when people are in their sixties.

We Try to Maintain a Positive Sense of Self

When Marc and Christine filled out their Internet dating questionnaires, they probably described themselves in positive ways. After all, why would someone be drawn to a partner who didn't like himself or herself? But it's not only on dating sites that we see ourselves positively. Most people show favoritism to anything associated with themselves. They even prefer the letters of their own names, especially their initials, to other letters (Koole, Dijksterhuis, & van Knippenberg, 2001; **Figure 12.7**).

Perhaps you have listened to the radio storyteller Garrison Keillor describe the fictional town of Lake Wobegon, where "all the children are above average." Statistically, it is impossible for *everyone* to be above average, but things are different when it comes to self-esteem. For instance, 90 percent of adults claim they are better-than-average drivers, even if they once were the driver in a car accident that landed them in the hospital (Guerin, 1994; Svenson, 1981). Similarly, when the College Entrance Examination Board surveyed more than 800,000 college-bound seniors, not a single senior rated herself or himself as below average, and a whopping 25 percent rated themselves in the top 1 percent (Gilovich, 1991). Most people describe themselves as above average in nearly every way. Psychologists refer to this phenomenon as the *better-than-average effect* (Alicke, Klotz, Breitenbecher, Yurak, & Vredenburg, 1995). People with high self-esteem are especially likely to exhibit this effect.

According to research, most people have *positive illusions*—overly favorable and unrealistic beliefs—in at least three areas (Taylor & Brown, 1988). First, most people continually experience the better-than-average effect. Second, they have unrealistic beliefs about how much they can control what happens. For example, some fans believe they help their favorite sports teams win if they attend games or

FIGURE 12.7

Favoritism

People rate letters in their own name, especially their initials, as being more beautiful than letters not in their name.

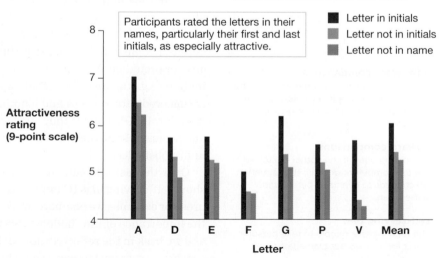

Participants rated the letters in their names, particularly their first and last initials, as especially attractive.

Legend:
- Letter in initials
- Letter not in initials
- Letter not in name

wear their lucky jerseys. Third, most people are unrealistically optimistic about their personal futures. They believe they probably will be successful, marry happily, and live long lives. Positive illusions can be adaptive when they promote optimism in meeting life's challenges, but they can lead to trouble when people overestimate their skills and underestimate their vulnerabilities.

Though life is filled with failure, rejection, and disappointment, most of us feel pretty good about ourselves. How do we maintain such positive views? Psychologists have cataloged several unconscious strategies that help us maintain a positive sense of self. Some of the most common are social comparisons and self-serving biases. As you read the following descriptions, bear in mind that psychologists do not necessarily endorse these strategies.

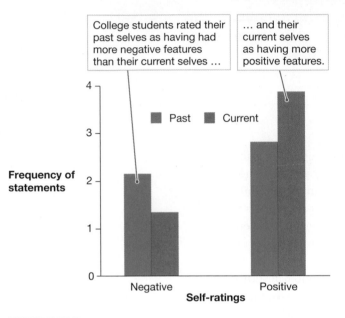

FIGURE 12.8

Temporal Comparisons of the Self
People tend to make temporal comparisons that indicate more positive perceptions of themselves now than in the past. This form of downward comparison has the effect of protecting a person's positive sense of self.

SOCIAL COMPARISONS Social comparison occurs when we evaluate our own actions, abilities, and beliefs by contrasting them with those of other people. That is, we compare ourselves with others to see where we stand. We are especially likely to make such comparisons when there is no objective standard. For instance, we might think we are doing better financially than someone else, even though a number of factors, from income to savings to lifestyle, affect financial success. Social comparisons are an important means of understanding our actions and emotions.

In general, people with high self-esteem make **downward comparisons.** That is, they contrast themselves with people inferior to themselves in the characteristic they are evaluating. People with low self-esteem tend to make **upward comparisons.** They contrast themselves with people superior to them. *Temporal comparison* is another form of downward comparison where people view their current selves as better than their former selves (Wilson & Ross, 2001; Figure 12.8). Thinking of ourselves as better than others, or as better than we used to be, tends to make us feel good about ourselves. But if we constantly compare ourselves with others who do better, we may only confirm our negative self-feelings. Has this happened to you?

SELF-SERVING BIASES People with high self-esteem tend to take credit for success but blame failure on outside factors. Psychologists refer to this tendency as the **self-serving bias.** For instance, students who do extremely well on exams often explain their performance by referring to their skills or hard work. Those who do poorly might describe the test as an arbitrary examination of trivial details. People with high self-esteem also assume that criticism is motivated by envy or prejudice. According to one theory, members of groups prone to discrimination (e.g., the disabled, ethnic minorities) maintain positive self-esteem by taking credit for success and blaming negative feedback on prejudice (Crocker & Major, 1989). Thus if they succeed, the success is due to personal strengths and occurs despite the odds. If they fail, the failure is due to external factors and unfair obstacles.

Over the last 40 years, psychologists have documented many ways that we show self-serving bias (Campbell & Sedikides, 1999). In thinking about our failures, for example, we compare ourselves with others who did worse, we diminish the importance of the challenge, we think about the things we are really good at, and we bask in the reflected glory of both family and friends. The overall picture suggests we are extremely well equipped to protect our positive beliefs about

downward comparisons
Comparing oneself to another person who is less competent or in a worse situation, which tends to protect a person's high self-esteem.

upward comparisons
Comparing oneself to another person who is more competent or in a better situation, which tends to confirm a person's low self-esteem.

self-serving bias
The tendency for people to take personal credit for success but blame failure on external factors.

ourselves. Some researchers have argued that self-serving biases reflect healthy psychological functioning (Mezulis, Abramson, Hyde, & Hankin, 2004; Taylor & Brown, 1988). Still, the earlier discussion of narcissism should make us wary of that perspective.

Our Sense of Self Is Influenced by Cultural Factors

Do you like to stand out in a crowd? If so, then maybe you have body art, color your hair brightly, wear unusual clothes, or do something that makes you seem unique. In Western cultures, particularly the United States, people often take pride in expressing themselves in ways that make them stand out from the crowd. But this is not the case for all people. In some cultures, people prefer to blend into the group. An important difference in the self is whether people view themselves as fundamentally separate from or connected to other people.

Harry Triandis (1989) has noted that some cultures emphasize the collective self more than the personal self. Such *collectivist cultures* include those in Japan, Greece, Pakistan, China, and some regions of Africa. Collectivist cultures emphasize connections to family, social groups, and ethnic groups; conformity to societal norms; and group cohesiveness. In Japan, people tend to dress similarly and respect situational norms (**Figure 12.9a**). When a family goes to a restaurant in China, all the people at the table share multiple dishes.

In contrast, *individualist cultures* emphasize rights and freedoms, self-expression, and diversity. Individuality cultures include those in northern and western Europe, Australia, Canada, New Zealand, and the United States. In the United States, people dress differently from one another, cultivate personal interests, and often enjoy standing out from the crowd (**Figure 12.9b**). When an American family goes to a restaurant, each person usually orders what he or she prefers.

In collectivist cultures, one's sense of self is determined largely by people's social roles and personal relationships (Markus & Kitayama, 1991; **Figure 12.10a**). Children in collectivist cultures are raised to follow group norms and to obey parents, teachers, and other people in authority. They are expected to find their proper place in society and not to challenge or complain about their status. By contrast, in individualist cultures, parents and teachers encourage children to be self-reliant and to pursue personal success, even at the expense of interpersonal

FIGURE 12.9
Collectivist and Individualist Cultures
(a) Eastern cultures tend to value those who fall in line with the masses. **(b)** Western cultures tend to highlight individualism.

You have probably engaged in social comparisons at some point. To find out, ask yourself these questions.

1. Have you ever compared yourself to someone who was worse off than you in some way? This downward comparison probably made you feel good and increased your self-esteem.

2. Have you compared yourself to someone who was better off than you in some way? This upward comparison probably made you feel bad and decreased your self-esteem.

3. Have you ever compared some version of yourself to a version from some point in the past? Usually we view our present selves as better than our past selves. This temporal comparison also likely increased your self-esteem.

(a)

(b)

"You're from a different culture," Mary Christine said to Salma. "So of course you think of yourself differently than how I think of myself."

Mary Christine and Salma were taking the same psychology class. They had been friends since freshman year, when they had randomly been assigned to be roommates in the dorms. Since then, they had pledged the same sorority and had continued to live together, sharing an apartment off campus. On paper, they were very different. Mary Christine came from what she called "old money" and could trace her ancestry back to the *Mayflower*. Salma's maternal grandparents had immigrated from New Delhi, India, when her mom was just 4 years old. Her father had immigrated when he was 21, coming to the United States to work on his Ph.D. in philosophy.

Mary Christine and Salma had been discussing Chapter 12 of their textbook. They were now focused on the idea of self-esteem. *Is Mary Christine right?* Salma wondered. *Does the fact that I am from a different culture mean that my self-esteem differs from hers?* In the chapter, the authors noted that some cultures are more collectivistic than others. *India is more collectivistic than the U.S. But I am Indian and American, so how do those two cultures affect how I value myself?*

"I'm not sure you're right," she told Mary Christine. "I was raised here. If I'd been raised in New Delhi, would I see myself differently?"

"Well, since we can't manipulate those variables, we can't experiment on you," Mary Christine joked. "So I don't think we can say for sure that being in America caused a change in your self-esteem."

"Right," Salma responded. "But maybe there's another way to get at the answer. How can we determine whether exposure to Western culture changes self-esteem?"

"Well, would you guess that your self-esteem is different from that of your parents? Or your grandparents?"

"I would say so. Maybe that's it! I wonder if any studies have been done looking at whether groups of people with differing levels of Western exposure have different levels of self-esteem?"

Working with the campus librarian, Mary Christine and Salma found research that examined self-esteem in people of Japanese descent (Heine & Lehman, 2004). The participants varied in their levels of Western exposure. They ranged from Japanese people who had never left Japan to third-generation Japanese-Canadians (meaning their grandparents had lived in Japan). All the groups completed the same measure of self-esteem. *This method didn't directly test whether culture "causes" changes in self-esteem,* Salma thought, *but it measured whether the groups are different and just how different.*

Salma and Mary Christine were impressed with the pattern of results found in the study (see the graph). As the exposure to Western culture increased, so did people's self-esteem. The more exposure, the higher their reported self-esteem.

Mary Christine joked, "If these results generalize, then you're becoming more like me every day."

"You bet," Salma joked back. "If we finally end up with the same self-esteem, maybe we'll be the same person!"

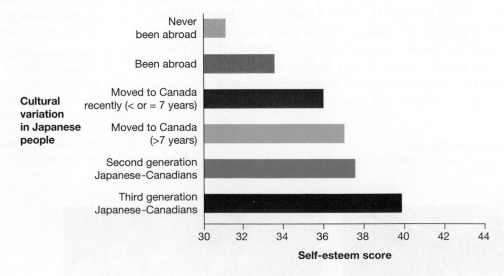

relationships. Thus children's senses of self are based on their feelings of being distinct from others (**Figure 12.10b**). Note, however, that within these broad patterns there is variability. Some people in individualist cultures have interdependent senses of self. Some people in collectivist cultures have independent senses of self.

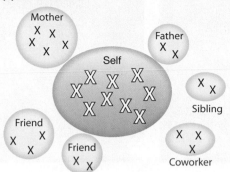

(a) Collectivist

Mother
Father
Self
Friend
Sibling
Friend
Coworker

(b) Individualist

Mother
Father
Self
Sibling
Friend
Friend
Coworker

FIGURE 12.10

Cultural Differences in Self
People's senses of self differ across cultures, and some aspects are more important to the self (as shown by the larger *X*s). **(a)** In collectivist cultures, the most important elements of a person's self tend to reside in areas where the person's sense of self is connected with others. **(b)** In individualistic cultures, the most important elements of a person's sense of self tend to reside within the person.

 12.1 CHECKPOINT: How Do We Know Ourselves?

- Our sense of self is based on three aspects: self-schema, working self-concept, and self-esteem.

- The sociometer model suggests that self-esteem is based on the likelihood that we will be accepted or rejected socially.

- We employ many strategies to maintain positive views of ourselves. These strategies include positive illusions, social comparisons, and self-serving biases.

- People from collectivist cultures tend to have interdependent senses of self. People from individualist cultures tend to have independent senses of self.

12.2 How Can We Understand Personality?

📖 LEARNING GOALS	✏️ READING ACTIVITIES
a. Remember the key terms about personality.	List all of the boldface words and write down their definitions.
b. Apply Rogers's person-centered approach to your life.	Provide an example of how conditions of worth or unconditional positive regard influenced your personality.
c. Apply the five-factor theory to people you know.	Use the five-factor theory to explain the personalities of two people you know.
d. Analyze the four approaches to understanding personality.	Describe your personality in terms of psychodynamic theory, the humanistic approach, the cognitive approach, and the trait approach.

Recall from the story that opened this chapter that Marc wasn't sure what characteristics he wanted in a girlfriend. But Christine was sure. She wanted a man who had his own ideas, was self-sufficient, and was trustworthy. Once Christine met Marc, how was she able to determine whether he had the personality she wanted? We now turn to the second issue in personality: How can we understand other

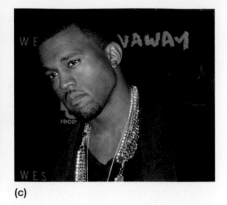

(a)   (b)   (c)

FIGURE 12.11

People's Personalities

We all have opinions about other people's personalities. How would you describe the characteristics of these people? **(a)** Simon Cowell judged the talent of singers on *American Idol* and then on *The X Factor*. He tends to give harsh critiques. **(b)** Margaret Cho is a comedian and actor who is best known for the sharp wit of her stand-up comedy routines. **(c)** Kanye West is a recording artist, record producer, and fashion designer with a flamboyant style.

people, including our friends, parents, siblings, romantic partners, and people who are in the public eye (**Figure 12.11**)?

Because humans are so complex, the discussion of personality brings together a host of topics from across psychology: How is personality influenced by nature and nurture? How much does our behavior reveal about our personality? How much does personality vary across situations? In the past century, psychologists have studied personality based on several different approaches (**Table 12.1**).

TABLE 12.1

Approaches to Personality

Approach	Description	Example
Psycho-dynamic theory	Personality is based on our unconscious wishes that create conflict between the id, ego, and superego.	Freud's psychodynamic theory: Janice will do anything to get what she wants. Janice's personality may be dominated by her id.
Humanistic approaches	Personality is based on our tendency to fulfill our potential through personal growth.	Rogers's person-centered approach: Dante always tells his children that he loves them no matter what. He is helping them reach their full potential for growth by expressing unconditional positive regard.
Cognitive approaches	Personality is based on how we think.	Rotter's expectancy theory: Maria knows that if she works hard in college, she will get high grades and this will help her get a good job. Maria seems to have an internal locus of control. See also Bandura's reciprocal determinism.
Trait approaches	Personality can be described by our characteristics.	Five-factor theory: Vivian is described by friends as very dependable but not very outgoing. According to the five-factor theory, Vivian is highly conscientious and very introverted. See also Eysenck's biological trait theory.

Psychodynamic Theory Emphasizes Unconscious Conflicts

Recall from Chapter 1 that Sigmund Freud was a physician who developed many ideas about personality by observing his patients. Freud came to believe that many of their problems were caused by psychological rather than physical factors. From his clinical work, Freud developed his **psychodynamic theory** of personality. The central idea of this theory is that unconscious forces—such as wishes, desires, and hidden memories—determine behavior. Many of Freud's ideas are controversial and not well supported by scientific research, but his theories had an enormous influence over psychological thinking for much of its early history.

UNCONSCIOUS CONFLICTS For Freud, the powerful forces that drive our behavior often conflict with each other. He also emphasized that we are typically unaware of those forces or their conflicts. For instance, you might unknowingly want to steal an object you desire. That impulse would conflict with your implicit knowledge that you could get in trouble for the theft or that society considers theft a crime. Freud believed that our conscious awareness is only a small fraction of our mental activity. That is, conscious awareness represents the proverbial tip of the iceberg, and most mental processes are going on under the surface (**Figure 12.12**).

According to this model, the *conscious* level of our mental activity consists of the thoughts that we are aware of. The *preconscious* level consists of content that is not currently in our awareness but that could be brought to awareness. This level is roughly analogous to long-term memory. The *unconscious* level contains material that the mind cannot easily retrieve. These hidden memories, wishes, desires, and motives are often in conflict. The conflicts between them produce anxiety or other psychological discomfort. To protect us from this distress, these forces and their conflicts are kept hidden from awareness. Sometimes, however, this information leaks into consciousness in "Freudian slips." For example, we may accidentally reveal a hidden motive by saying, when we meet an attractive person, "I don't think we've been seduced," instead of "introduced." Freud said these slips were not accidents. Instead, they offered a glimpse into unconscious conflicts that determine behavior.

THREE STRUCTURES OF PERSONALITY
Freud also proposed a model of how personality is organized. In this model, personality consists of three interacting structures, and these structures vary in their access to consciousness (see Figure 12.12). The first structure, the **id,** exists at the most basic level: completely submerged in the unconscious. The id operates according to the *pleasure principle,* which pushes us to seek pleasure and avoid pain. Freud called the force that drives the pleasure principle the *libido.* Although today the term *libido* has a specifically sexual connotation, Freud

psychodynamic theory
Freudian theory that unconscious forces determine behavior.

id
In psychodynamic theory, the component of personality that is completely submerged in the unconscious and operates according to the pleasure principle.

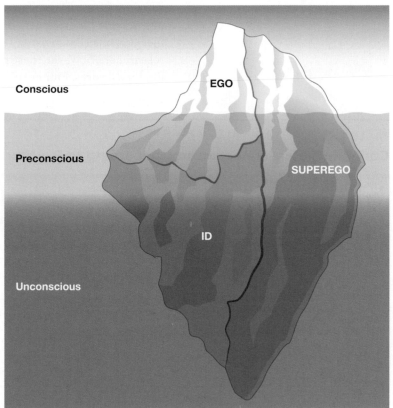

FIGURE 12.12

Freud's Psychodynamic Theory of Personality
Sigmund Freud theorized that unconscious mental activity can result in conflict between the three personality structures: the id, the ego, and the superego.

used it to refer more generally to the energy that promotes pleasure seeking. In other words, the libido acts on impulses and desires. The id is like an infant, crying to be fed whenever hungry, held whenever anxious.

The second structure, the **superego,** acts as a brake on the id. Largely in the unconscious, the superego develops in childhood and is the internalization of parental and societal standards of behavior. It is a rigid structure of morality, or conscience.

The third structure, the **ego,** mediates between the id and the superego. That is, the ego tries to satisfy the wishes of the id while being responsive to the rules of the superego. The ego operates according to the *reality principle,* which involves rational thought and problem solving. According to psychodynamic theory, unique interactions of the id, superego, and ego produce individual differences in personality.

Conflicts between the id and the superego lead to anxiety. The ego then copes with anxiety through various **defense mechanisms.** Defense mechanisms are unconscious mental strategies that the mind uses to protect itself from distress (**Table 12.2**). For instance, we often rationalize our behavior by blaming our situation. Maybe we tell our parents that we didn't call them because we were too busy studying for an exam. Finding good excuses keeps us from feeling bad and can also prevent others from feeling angry toward us.

Much of the theoretical work on defense mechanisms can be credited to Freud's daughter, Anna Freud (1936). Over the past 40 years, psychological research has provided a great deal of support for the existence of many of the defense mechanisms (Baumeister, Dale, & Sommers, 1998). According to contemporary researchers, however, these mechanisms do not relieve unconscious conflict over libidinal desires. Rather, defense mechanisms protect self-esteem.

TABLE 12.2

Common Defense Mechanisms According to Psychodynamic Theory

MECHANISM	DEFINITION	EXAMPLE
Denial	Refusing to acknowledge source of anxiety	Tanya has been diagnosed with cancer but refuses to get treatment, saying her symptoms are caused by something other than cancer.
Repression	Excluding source of anxiety from awareness	Louis cannot remember the night that he was mugged at gunpoint.
Projection	Attributing unacceptable qualities of the self to someone else	Emily is very competitive, but accuses others of being super-competitive.
Reaction formation	Warding off an uncomfortable thought by overemphasizing its opposite	Simon is a teen who is attracted to Aaron, but Simon bullies Aaron for being gay.
Rationalization	Creating a seemingly logical reason or excuse for behavior that might otherwise be shameful	Pamela drives after drinking alcohol because "everyone does it."
Displacement	Shifting the attention of emotion from one object to another, easier target	Franklin has a terrible day at work with his boss and then comes home and yells at his children.
Sublimation	Channeling socially unacceptable impulses into constructive, even admirable, behavior	Lakisha has an eating disorder and becomes a nutritionist who works with people trying to lose weight.

LEARNING TIP: Id, Ego, and Superego

Here is an easy way for you to remember the three aspects of personality described by Freud's psychodynamic theory.

The **id** is the desire for pleasure and avoidance of pain.

The **ego** resolves the conflict between the id and the superego.

The **superego** is the conscience for what is socially acceptable and moral.

PSYCHOSEXUAL DEVELOPMENT An important component of Freudian thinking is the idea that early childhood experiences have a major impact on the development of personality. Freud believed that children unconsciously aim to satisfy libidinal urges to experience pleasure. In their pursuit of these satisfactions, children go through developmental stages that correspond to the different urges. These developmental stages are called *psychosexual stages*.

In each psychosexual stage, libido is focused on one of the body's erogenous zones. *Erogenous* means "sexually arousing," and these zones are the mouth, the anus, and the genitals.

The *oral stage* lasts from birth to approximately 18 months. During this time, infants seek pleasure through the mouth. Because hungry infants experience relief when they breast-feed, they come to associate pleasure with sucking. When children are 2 to 3 years old, they enter the *anal stage*. During this time, toilet training—learning to control the bowels—leads them to focus on the anus. From age 3 to 5, children are in the *phallic stage*. That is, they direct their libidinal energies toward the genitals. Children often discover the pleasure of rubbing their genitals during this time, although they have no real sexual intent. The phallic stage is followed by a brief *latency stage*. During this time, children suppress libidinal urges or channel them into doing schoolwork or building friendships. Finally, in the *genital stage*, adolescents and adults attain mature attitudes about sexuality and adulthood. They center their libidinal urges on the capacities to reproduce and to contribute to society.

FIGURE 12.13

Freud's Theory of the Oedipus Complex During Psychosexual Development

Freud proposed that during one of the stages of psychosexual development, young boys form an attachment to their mothers and compete with their fathers for her affection. Because this unconscious desire causes conflict, Freud suggested that it is repressed, resulting in young boys' identifying more strongly with their fathers.

One of the most controversial Freudian theories applies to children in the phallic stage. According to Freud, children desire an exclusive relationship with the opposite-sex parent. For this reason, children consider the same-sex parent a rival. As a result, they develop hostility toward that parent. In boys, this phenomenon is known as the *Oedipus complex* (**Figure 12.13**). The complex is named after the ancient Greek character Oedipus, who unknowingly killed his father and married his mother. Freud believed that children develop unconscious wishes to kill their same-sex parent so they can claim the other parent. He suggested that children resolve this conflict by repressing their desires for the opposite-sex parent and identifying with the same-sex parent. That is, they take on many of that parent's values and beliefs. This theory applied mostly to boys. Freud's theory for girls was more complex and even less convincing. There is little research support for either theory.

According to Freud, progression through these psychosexual stages profoundly affects personality. For example, some people become *fixated*, or stuck, at a stage during which they receive excessive parental restriction or indulgence. Those fixated at the oral stage develop *oral personalities*. They continue to seek pleasure through the mouth, such as by smoking. They also are excessively needy. Those fixated at the anal phase may have *anal-retentive personalities*. They are stubborn and highly regulating. Anal fixation may arise from overly strict toilet training or excessively rule-based child rearing.

PSYCHODYNAMIC THEORY TODAY Sigmund Freud is the thinker most closely identified with psychodynamic theory. A number of influential scholars have modified Freud's ideas. While rejecting aspects of Freudian thinking, these scholars have embraced the notion of unconscious conflict. Contemporary *neo-Freudians* focus on social interactions, especially children's emotional attachments to their parents or primary caregivers. This focus is embodied in *object relations theory*. According to this theory, our mind and sense of self develop in relation to others ("objects") in our environment, and how we relate to these others shapes our personality. The concept of object relations is important to many professionals who conduct counseling to help people improve their relations with others.

Today, Freud's work has to be understood in the context of his time and the methods available to him. Freud was a keen observer of behavior and a creative theorist. Even so, he had no way to use objective methods to explore mental processes, such as using brain imaging to examine emotional reactions to things that might produce the conflicts predicted by psychodynamic theory. Because Freud's central premises cannot be examined through accepted scientific methods, psychologists have largely abandoned psychodynamic theories. Still, Freud's observations and ideas continue to affect personality psychology and have framed much of the research in personality over the last century (Hines, 2003; Westen, 1998).

Humanistic Approaches Emphasize Goodness in People

humanistic approaches
Ways of studying personality that emphasize self-actualization, where people seek to fulfill their potential through greater self-understanding.

Until the early 1950s, most theories of personality painted a rather bleak view of people. For example, Freud's theories emphasized a dark side filled with anxiety and conflict. Against this backdrop, a new and more positive view of personality began to emerge. **Humanistic approaches** emphasize how the unique goodness in a person, his or her own growth, and self-understanding all influence personality.

These approaches propose that we seek to fulfill our potential for personal growth through greater self-understanding. This process is called self-actualization. Abraham Maslow's theory of motivation is an example. As discussed in Chapter 9, Maslow believed that the desire to become self-actualized is the ultimate human motive (see Figure 9.3).

The most prominent humanistic psychologist, Carl Rogers, introduced a *person-centered approach* to understanding personality and human relationships. Rogers emphasized two issues as crucial in the development of personality: The first issue is our personal understanding of our lives—that is, our sense of self. The second issue is how others see us and evaluate us. In the therapeutic technique Rogers developed, the therapist would create a supportive and accepting environment. The therapist and the client would deal with the client's problems and concerns as the client understood them.

Rogers's theory highlights the importance of the way parents show affection for their children and how parents can affect personality development. Rogers believed that most parents provide love and support that is conditional. That is, the parents love their children on the condition that the children do what the parents want them to do and live up to the parents' standards.

This condition creates a discrepancy between a child's self and how her parents evaluate her. In turn, this discrepancy leads to development of a personality based on *conditions of worth* (**Figure 12.14a**). Parents who do not approve of their children's behavior may withhold their love. As a result, children quickly abandon their true feelings, dreams, and desires. They accept only those parts of themselves that elicit parental love and support. Thus people lose touch with their true selves in their pursuit of getting approval from others.

To prevent conditions of worth, Rogers encouraged parents to accept and prize their children no matter how the children behave or how close they come to meeting parents' expectations. This approach allows for consistency between a child's self and how his parents evaluate him. Such consistency leads to development of a personality based on *unconditional positive regard* (**Figure 12.14b**).

a If parents' affection for a child is conditional on the child acting in an acceptable way, the child's personality develops based solely on the aspects that get approval from others. That is, the child's personality is based on *conditions of worth*.

or

b When parents' affection for a child is unconditional, and expressed regardless of how the child acts, the child's personality can develop freely. That is, the child's personality will be based on *unconditional positive regard*.

FIGURE 12.14

Rogers's Person-Centered Approach to Personality
According to Rogers's theory, personality is influenced by how we understand ourselves and how others evaluate us, which leads to conditions of worth or unconditional positive regard.

cognitive approaches
Ways of studying personality that recognize the influence of how people think.

locus of control
The idea that personality is based on a person's perception of whether she controls the rewards and punishments that she experiences (internal locus of control) or does not control them (external locus of control).

In other words, parents might express disapproval of a child's bad behavior, but at the same time they should express their love for the child herself. According to Rogers, a child raised with unconditional positive regard would develop a healthy sense of self-esteem and would become a fully functioning person.

Cognitive Approaches Focus on How Thoughts Shape Personality

As we saw in Chapter 6, learning theory dominated most areas of psychology for the first half of the twentieth century. From this perspective, personality resulted from learned responses to patterns of reinforcement. By the 1950s, however, there was growing agreement that cognition—how we think—is important in understanding many aspects of human behavior, including personality. This emphasis has produced **cognitive approaches** to personality.

EXPECTANCY THEORY Julian Rotter (1954) developed one of the first theories of personality that included cognition. According to Rotter's *expectancy theory,* our behaviors are a part of our personality. They result from how we think about two things: our *expectancies* for reinforcement and the *values* we ascribe to particular reinforcers. For instance, suppose you are deciding whether to study for an exam or go to a party. You will probably consider whether studying will lead to a good grade and how much that grade matters to you. Then you will weigh those two considerations against two others: the likelihood that the party will be fun, and how much you value having fun.

Expectancy theory led Rotter to propose that people's personalities are based on their **locus of control.** Locus of control means whether people control the rewards and punishments that they experience. People with an internal locus of control believe that they themselves influence outcomes (**Figure 12.15a**).

a People who expect that their own actions influence events and outcomes have a personality based on an **internal locus of control.**

or

b People who expect that forces outside of their control influence events and outcomes have developed a personality based on an **external locus of control.**

FIGURE 12.15

Rotter's Expectancy Theory of Personality
According to Rotter, personality is influenced by expectations, which can lead to having an internal locus of control or an external locus of control.

TRY IT YOURSELF: What Is Your Locus of Control?

Do you believe that your efforts will lead to positive outcomes? To determine your locus of control, decide which statement best represents your position in each of these four situations.

1. A. People's misfortunes result from the mistakes they make.
    B. Many of the unhappy things in people's lives are partly due to bad luck.
2. A. In the case of the well-prepared student there is rarely, if ever, such a thing as an unfair test.
    B. Many times exam questions tend to be so unrelated to course work that studying is really useless.
3. A. Becoming a success is a matter of hard work. Luck has little or nothing to do with it.
    B. Getting a good job depends mainly on being in the right place at the right time.
4. A. What happens to me is my own doing.
    B. Sometimes I feel that I don't have enough control over the direction my life is taking.

Scoring:
- If you chose A more often, you may tend to have an internal locus of control. That is, you expect that you can control the outcome of events.
- If you chose B more often, you may tend to have an external locus of control. In other words, you expect that the outcome of events is outside your control.

SOURCE: Rotter (1966).

For example, a person with an internal locus of control might believe that she got a promotion because she worked hard. Those with an *external locus of control* believe that outcomes—and therefore their personal fates—result from forces beyond their control (**Figure 12.15b**). A person with an external locus of control could view the same promotion as being due to luck, not because of her hard work. These generalized beliefs reflect personality. What is your locus of control?

RECIPROCAL DETERMINISM In another influential theory of personality, Albert Bandura (1977) argued that three factors influence how a person acts: The first factor is the person's environment. The second factor is multiple *person factors,* which include the person's characteristics, self-confidence, and expectations. The third factor is the behavior itself. This approach to personality explains how each of these three factors affect the others to determine behavior. Because personality is explained by the interaction of all three factors, the model is called *reciprocal determinism.*

Let's look at how these factors affect personality. Imagine that a woman goes to a party. According to Bandura's model, the party is the environment. The specific features of the environment affect the person's behavior. To judge the effects, we need to know the specifics. Therefore, let's specify that most of the people at the party are men that the woman doesn't know (**Figure 12.16a**). In addition, the woman will have particular person factors. Let's say she is outgoing and sociable (**Figure 12.16b**). These characteristics have probably been rewarded by her environment in the past. For example, people, especially men, may have responded positively to her friendliness. Lastly, the woman's behavior in this situation will reflect both the environment and her person factors (**Figure 12.16c**). Specifically, at this party with many men, the woman most likely will be friendly and talkative with the men.

But if any of the factors change, then the woman's behavior will also change. For example, if men leave and as a result there are fewer men than women in the situation, the woman's behavior will change.

FIGURE 12.16

Bandura's Reciprocal Determinism Theory of Personality
Bandura proposed that three factors interact with each other to influence personality: the environment, person factors, and behavior.

a **Environment:** the situation at any given moment

b **Person factors:** characteristics, self-confidence, and expectations of success

c **Behavior:** actions in a situation

Trait Approaches Describe Characteristics

trait approaches
Ways of studying personality that are based on people's characteristics, their tendencies to act in a certain way over time and across circumstances.

According to the theories we have discussed so far, the same underlying processes occur in everyone. Individuals differ because they experience different conflicts, think differently, and so on. Other approaches to personality focus more on description than explanation. Most contemporary personality psychologists focus on **trait approaches** to personality. These approaches describe the behavioral tendencies that are generally consistent over time and across most situations.

Traits exist on a continuum. Most people fall somewhere in the middle, and relatively few are at the extremes. For instance, some of the people you know may be very shy and some just the opposite. But most are probably in the middle—they are shy in some situations but not in others. Let's look at how two trait approaches to personality focus on the ways individuals differ in basic personality characteristics.

THE BIG FIVE In the last 30 years or so, many personality psychologists have embraced the *five-factor theory*. This theory identifies five basic personality traits: *openness to experience, conscientiousness, extraversion, agreeableness, and neuroticism* (McCrae & Costa, 1999; **Figure 12.17**). For example, agreeableness reflects the extent to which a person is trusting and helpful. A person high in openness to experience is imaginative and independent. A person low in this basic trait is down-to-earth and conformist. For each factor, personality may be anywhere on a continuum from low to high.

Considerable evidence supports the five-factor theory (John, 1990). The Big Five emerge across cultures, among adults and children, even when vastly

Openness to experience	**C**onscientiousness	**E**xtraversion	**A**greeableness	**N**euroticism
Imaginative vs. down-to-earth	Organized vs. disorganized	Social vs. retiring	Softhearted vs. ruthless	Worried vs. calm
Likes variety vs. likes routine	Careful vs. careless	Fun-loving vs. sober	Trusting vs. suspicious	Insecure vs. secure
Independent vs. conforming	Self-disciplined vs. weak-willed	Affectionate vs. reserved	Helpful vs. uncooperative	Self-pitying vs. self-satisfied

FIGURE 12.17
The Five-Factor Theory of Personality
According to the five-factor theory, there are five personality traits: Openness, Conscientiousness, Extraversion, Agreeableness, and Neuroticism. Each person ranges from low to high on each personality trait.

different questionnaires assess the factors. The same five factors appear whether people rate themselves or are rated by others. Furthermore, people's "scores" on the five-factor theory traits have been shown to predict a wide variety of behaviors (Paunonen & Ashton, 2001). Their scores also have been shown to predict satisfaction with job, marriage, and life generally (Heller, Watson, & Ilies, 2004). Today, the five-factor theory dominates much of the way that psychologists study personality in humans. Some researchers have even begun to apply the ideas of personality traits to animals, as shown in the Scientific Thinking feature on p. 438.

LEARNING TIP: Remembering the Big Five

Figure 12.17 gives you an easy way to remember the personality dimensions of the five-factor theory. Taken together, the first letters of the five dimensions spell the word OCEAN. So when you need to remember the five-factor theory, just think of the OCEAN.

BIOLOGICAL TRAIT THEORY In the 1960s, the psychologist Hans Eysenck developed the *biological trait theory*. Eysenck initially proposed that personality traits had two major dimensions: how outgoing people were and whether their emotions tended to be stable or unstable (**Figure 12.18**). According to Eysenck, people vary in how outgoing they are. *Introversion* refers to how shy, reserved, and quiet a person is. *Extraversion* refers to how sociable, outgoing, and bold a person is. This dimension is similar to the extraversion trait in the Big Five theory. As we will see later in this chapter, Eysenck believed that this dimension reflects differences in biological processes.

Eysenck's second dimension refers to variability in a person's moods and emotions. People who are *stable* in emotionality tend to show consistency in moods and emotions. A person who has *unstable* emotions experiences frequent and dramatic mood swings, especially toward negative emotions, compared with a person who is more stable. Eysenck referred to these people as being *neurotic,* and indeed this dimension is similar to the five-factor theory trait of neuroticism. A neurotic person often feels anxious, moody, and depressed and generally holds a very low opinion of himself.

Eysenck also proposed a third dimension of personality traits (see Figure 12.18). Psychoticism reflects a mix of aggression, poor impulse control, self-centeredness, or a lack of empathy. The term *psychoticism* implies a level of psychological disorder that Eysenck did not intend. As a result, more-recent conceptions of this trait call it *constraint*. According to this view of the trait, people range from generally controlling their impulses to generally not controlling them (Watson & Clark, 1997). This dimension is most similar to the five-factor theory trait of conscientiousness, or how careful and organized someone is.

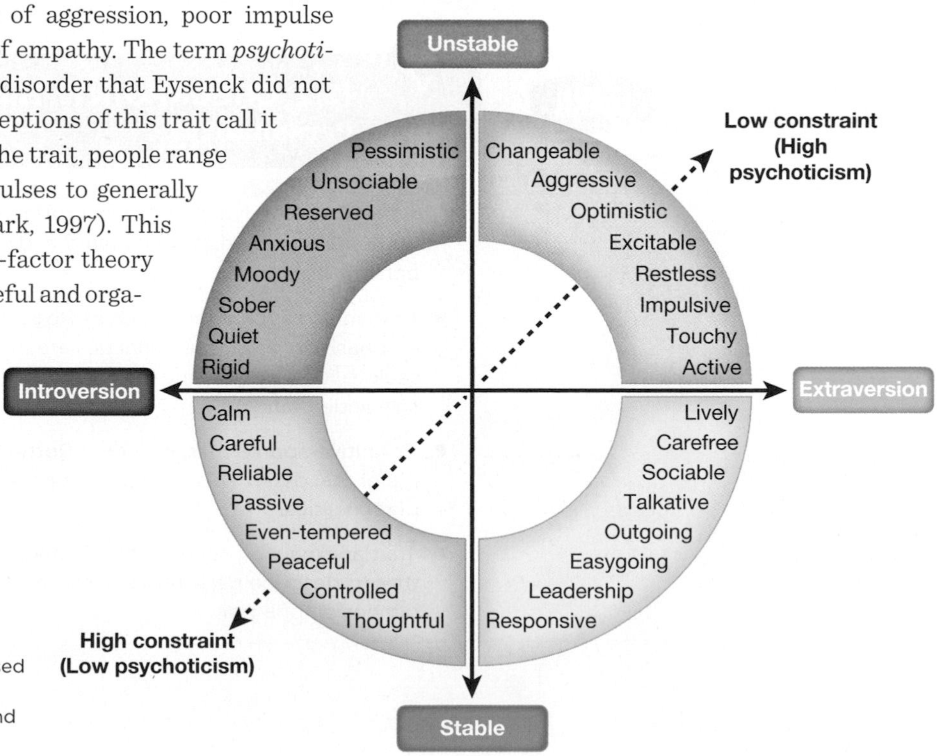

Unstable

Low constraint (High psychoticism)

Pessimistic · Changeable
Unsociable · Aggressive
Reserved · Optimistic
Anxious · Excitable
Moody · Restless
Sober · Impulsive
Quiet · Touchy
Rigid · Active

Introversion ← → **Extraversion**

Calm · Lively
Careful · Carefree
Reliable · Sociable
Passive · Talkative
Even-tempered · Outgoing
Peaceful · Easygoing
Controlled · Leadership
Thoughtful · Responsive

High constraint (Low psychoticism)

Stable

FIGURE 12.18

Eysenck's Biological Trait Theory of Personality

According to Eysenck, personality is composed of traits that occur in three dimensions: extraversion/introversion, unstable/stable, and high constraint/low constraint.

Hypothesis: Just like humans, animals can be described in terms of basic personality traits.

1 The researchers defined 44 traits and asked four observers to rate 34 spotted hyenas on each trait.

2 Using a mathematical analysis, the 44 traits were grouped into five dimensions:

ASSERTIVENESS   CURIOSITY

EXCITABILITY   HUMAN-DIRECTED
                         AGREEABLENESS

SOCIABILITY

Results: The four judges' ratings showed as much agreement as in most personality studies of humans. The five personality dimensions could not be accounted for by other factors, such as the sex or age of the hyenas.

Conclusion: The finding that hyenas can reliably be described in terms of personality traits lends support to the idea that animals, like humans, have distinct personalities.

 LEARN

✓ **12.2 CHECKPOINT: How Can We Understand Personality?**

- Freud's psychodynamic theory proposes that unconscious forces determine our behavior. Conflicts between the id, superego, and ego are the basis of our personalities.

- Humanistic approaches, such as Rogers's person-centered approach, emphasize that our personalities are influenced by inherent goodness. We seek to fulfill our potential for personal growth through greater self-understanding.

- Cognitive approaches, including Rotter's expectancy theory and Bandura's reciprocal determinism theory, propose that how we think influences our personalities.

- Trait approaches, such as the five-factor theory and Eysenck's biological trait theory, describe personality based on whether we are low or high on a certain dimension of a trait.

12.3 How Does Biology Affect Personality?

📖 LEARNING GOALS	✏️ READING ACTIVITIES	LEARN
a. Remember the key terms about the biological basis of personality.	List all of the boldface words and write down their definitions.	
b. Understand the research showing that genetics influences personality.	Explain in your own words how twin studies and adoption studies indicate that genetics influences personality.	
c. Apply temperament styles to children.	Provide an example of each of the three temperament styles in children you know.	
d. Understand how extraversion/introversion may be the result of brain processes.	Summarize how processing of arousal in the reticular activating system (RAS) may be responsible for extraversion and introversion.	

From their online profiles, Marc and Christine believed that they were compatible. And, indeed, their personalities were a good match, and their romance has blossomed. Did this happen because they were born with personality traits that were hardwired and that were a good fit for a relationship? Or did it happen because over the years, their experiences made them into who they are? As we have seen throughout this book, nature and nurture work together to produce individuals. This theme is particularly true for personality. Over the past few decades, evidence has emerged that biological factors—such as genes, brain structures, and neurochemistry—play an important role in determining personality.

Personality Is Affected by Genes and the Environment

Recall the Chapter 9 Try It Yourself exercise that let you see whether you are a sensation seeker. Maybe you don't want to do something as extreme as bungee jumping off a bridge or ice climbing. Even so, if you enjoy new experiences, there is an "adventure-seeking" aspect of your personality. And your genes are likely at least somewhat responsible.

Research has shown that certain genes can be linked with some personality traits. In fact, a gene that regulates one particular dopamine receptor has been associated with novelty seeking (Cloninger, Adolfsson, & Svrakic, 1996; Ekelund, Lichtermann, Jaervelin, & Peltonen, 1999). People with one form of this gene may be deficient in dopamine. These people tend to seek out novel experiences to increase the release of dopamine. In other words, they may be considered adventure seekers. This gene and perhaps thousands of others contribute to specific traits that are part of a person's overall personality (Weiss, Bates, & Luciano, 2008). But even if you have a genetic tendency toward being an adventure seeker, you will become this type of person only if you are raised in an environment where this trait is encouraged and supported.

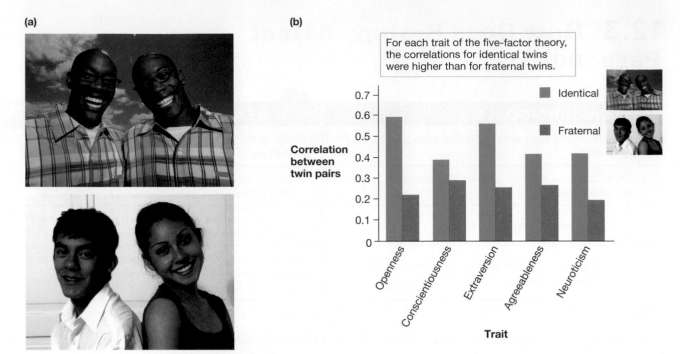

FIGURE 12.19

Identical Twins Have Similar Personalities

(a) Recall that identical twins have the same genes, are the same sex, and look the same. Fraternal twins have no more genes in common than do any two siblings. **(b)** Researchers examined the similarity between personality traits for 123 pairs of identical twins and 128 pairs of fraternal twins. Their findings show that identical twins are more similar in personality traits than are fraternal twins.

Research with identical twins provides insight into the role of genetics in personality. Recall that identical twins share nearly the same genes, whereas fraternal twins do not (**Figure 12.19a**). Numerous studies have shown that identical twins are more similar than non-identical twins in personality traits described by the five-factor theory (e.g., Jang, Livesley, & Vemon, 1996; **Figure 12.19b**). As we saw in Chapter 8, studies on twins raised apart have found that they are often as similar as, or even more similar than, twins raised together (Bouchard et al., 1990). One possible explanation for this finding is that parenting style may foster differences rather than similarities. If this explanation is correct, we might expect stronger correlations between personality traits for older twins than for younger twins, since the effects of parenting would diminish over time and the effects of genes would become stronger. And indeed, identical twins become more alike as they grow older. Siblings and fraternal twins do not become more alike.

Further evidence for the genetic basis of personality comes from adoption studies. Two children who are not biologically related but raised as siblings in the same household tend to be no more alike in personality than any two strangers randomly plucked off the street (Plomin & Caspi, 1999). Why might this be the case? One explanation is that these siblings do not share genes. Another explanation is that, even though the siblings are raised in the same home, their environments differ. After all, their ages may be different, they may have younger or older sisters or brothers, and their parents no doubt respond to each child differently. Further, the lives of siblings become less similar as they establish friendships outside the home. Their personalities slowly become increasingly individualized as their initial differences become magnified through their interactions with the world.

Moreover, the personalities of adopted children bear no significant relationship to those of their adoptive parents.

These findings and other current evidence suggest that parenting style has much less impact than has long been assumed. In other words, the similarities in personality between biological siblings and between children and their biological parents seem to have some genetic component.

The small correlations in personality among siblings might imply that parenting style has little effect. Still, parents are important. David Lykken is a leading researcher in behavioral genetics. Lykken (2000) has argued that children raised with inadequate parenting are not socialized properly. Improperly socialized children, according to Lykken, are much more likely to become delinquent or to display antisocial behavior. Thus children need adequate parenting, which most parents provide, but the particular style of parenting may not have a major impact on personality.

Our Temperaments Are Innate

If you have ever spent time around babies, you know that some babies are calm or fussy, and others are more or less active. It's easy to make judgments about babies' characteristics. We do it all the time when we say things such as "She's a happy baby," "She smiles at everyone," or "He really loves to run around!" These statements help describe the child's **temperament.** Temperament is the general tendency to feel or act in certain ways. This sense of a person is broader than personality traits. Life experiences may alter personality traits, but temperaments represent the innate biological structures of personality.

THREE ASPECTS OF TEMPERAMENT Arnold Buss and Robert Plomin (1984) have argued that three personality characteristics can be considered temperaments. *Activity level* is the overall amount of energy and behavior we exhibit (**Figure 12.20a**). For example, some children race around the house. Other children are less vigorous. Still others are slow paced. *Emotionality* describes the intensity of emotional reactions (**Figure 12.20b**). For example, some children cry often or become frightened easily. Some children anger quickly. Finally, *sociability* refers to the general tendency to affiliate with others (**Figure 12.20c**). Children high in sociability prefer to be with others rather than to be alone. According to Buss and Plomin, these three temperamental styles are the main personality factors influenced by genes. There is evidence from twin studies, adoption studies, and family studies that heredity has a powerful effect on these core temperaments. And these core temperaments, which are evident when we are children, endure throughout life.

LONG-TERM IMPLICATIONS OF TEMPERAMENT You are clearly different as an adult than you were as a child. Yet early childhood temperament appears to influence behavior and personality significantly throughout a person's development (Caspi, 2000).

One study focused on the health, development, and personalities of more than 1,000 people born during a one-year period (Caspi et al., 2002). These individuals were examined approximately every two years, and 97 percent remained in the study through their 21st birthdays. When they were 3 years old, they were classified into temperamental types. The classification at age 3 turned out to be a good predictor of personality and behaviors that appeared in early adulthood. Children whose temperaments were classified as well adjusted were less likely at the age of 21 to abuse alcohol or show antisocial disorders than were children whose

temperament
Biologically based tendency to feel or act in certain ways.

(a)

(b)

(c)

FIGURE 12.20
Three Types of Temperament
Temperaments are aspects of the personality that are more determined by biology. There are three temperaments, which are based on the degree of a child's **(a)** activity level, **(b)** emotionality, and **(c)** sociability.

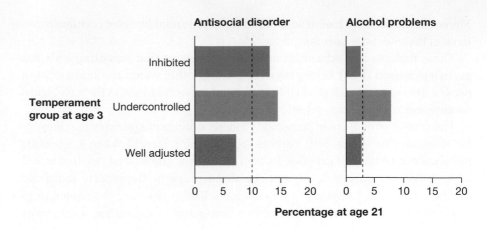

Antisocial disorder | Alcohol problems

FIGURE 12.21

Predicting Adolescent Behavior Based on Temperament at Age 3

Researchers investigated the personality development of more than 1,000 people. As shown in these graphs, the individuals who were judged as undercontrolled at age 3 were later more likely to be antisocial or to have alcohol problems. In the graphs, the dotted line indicates the average for the entire sample.

temperaments had been classified as undercontrolled at age 3 (**Figure 12.21**). In addition, inhibited children were much more likely, as adults, to be anxious, to become depressed, to be unemployed, to have less social support, and to attempt suicide. In other words, early childhood temperament may be a good predictor of later behaviors.

Research also has shown that children as young as 6 weeks show behaviors and reactions, such as being easily startled, that identify them as likely to be shy (Kagan & Snidman, 1991). This finding suggests that shyness has a strong biological influence. However, shyness has a social component as well. To reduce shyness in their children, parents can create supportive and calm environments in which children can deal with stress and novelty at their own pace. Approximately one quarter of young children identified as potentially shy are not shy later in childhood (Kagan, 2011). Once again, nature and nurture work together to influence who we are.

Personality Is Influenced by Physiology

Some theories propose that our personality is based on the biological processes that produce our thoughts, emotions, and behaviors (Canli, 2006). Most research on the neurobiological underpinnings of personality has explored the dimension of extraversion/introversion.

Recall that Hans Eysenck developed the biological trait theory (see Figure 12.18). Eysenck believed that differences in arousal produce the behavioral differences between extraverts and introverts. Our degree of arousal is based on processing in a part of the brain called the *reticular activating system (RAS)*. The RAS affects alertness. It is also involved in inducing and terminating the different stages of sleep. Eysenck proposed that the system of reticular activation differs between extraverts and introverts.

As we discussed in Chapter 9, each person prefers some level of arousal that is optimal for them. And each person also functions best at that level of arousal (see Figure 9.6). Eysenck proposed that extraverts typically are below their optimal level of arousal. In other words, extraverts are chronically under-aroused relative to their optimal level of arousal. So they often engage in activities that will increase their arousal. They seek out new situations and new emotional experiences, such as going to parties or meeting new people. And extraverts tend to perform better in stimulating situations such as these (**Figure 12.22a**). By contrast, introverts typically are above their optimal levels of arousal. These people are often over-aroused in relation to their optimal level of

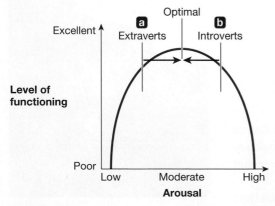

FIGURE 12.22

Optimal Arousal Influences Personality

(a) People who are extraverted have lower levels of arousal. To function optimally, they seek out exciting activities. **(b)** By contrast, people who are introverted have higher levels of arousal. To function optimally, they seek out calming activities.

arousal. Because they do not want any additional arousal, they seek out quiet solitude with few stimuli, and they perform better in these situations (**Figure 12.22b**). In short, if you are an introvert, a noisy environment will distract you. If you are an extravert, quiet places will bore you. Either way, you won't be able to complete tasks to the best of your ability.

Personality Stability Is Influenced by Biology and Situation

Genetic makeup may predispose people to have certain personality traits or characteristics. Whether these genes are expressed depends on the unique circumstances that each child faces during development. This idea is expressed in the maxim "Give me a child until he is seven, and I will show you the man." The movie director Michael Apted explores this maxim in his *Up* series of documentary films. Through the series, Apted follows the development of 14 British people. Most of the participants have been interviewed every seven years from age 7 until age 56. A striking aspect of the films is the apparent stability of personality over time. For example, the boy who was interested in the stars and science becomes a physics professor. The reserved, well-mannered, upper-class 7-year-old girl grows into the reserved, well-mannered woman in her pastoral retreat at age 35.

Are all people's personalities really so stable? Childhood temperament may predict behavioral outcomes in early adulthood, but what about change during adulthood? Clinical psychology is based on the belief that people can and do change important aspects of their lives. In fact, they exert considerable energy trying to change, attending self-help groups, reading self-help books, paying for therapy sessions, and struggling to make their lives different. But how much can people really change their personalities?

Whether personality is fixed or changeable depends largely on how we define the essential features of personality. Continuity over time and across situations is inherent in the definition of *trait*. Most research finds personality traits to be remarkably stable over the adult life span (McCrae & Costa, 1990). An analysis of 150 studies—in which nearly 50,000 participants were followed for at least one year—found strong evidence for stability in personality (Roberts & Friend-DelVecchio, 2000). People's rankings (low or high) on any personality trait were quite stable over long periods across all age ranges. Stability was lowest for young children and highest for those over age 50 (**Figure 12.23**). This finding

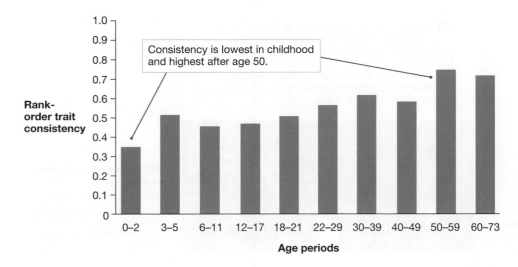

FIGURE 12.23
The Stability of Personality
After childhood, people's personality traits tend to be quite stable over time.

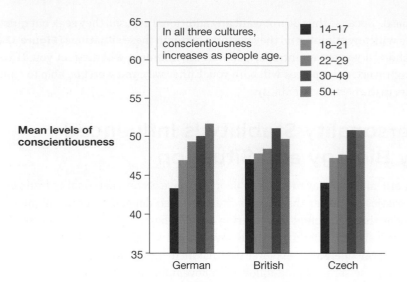

FIGURE 12.24
Conscientiousness at Different Ages in Three Cultures
The tendency for people's personalities to stabilize as they age also occurs across cultures, as shown here for the trait of conscientiousness.

In all three cultures, conscientiousness increases as people age.

14–17
18–21
22–29
30–49
50+

Mean levels of conscientiousness

German   British   Czech

HAS IT HAPPENED TO YOU?

Characteristic Adaptations

Think of a few of your basic tendencies, the traits (see Figure 12.17) that have been the basis of your personality for as long as you can remember. Have you ever had to change how you expressed those traits depending on the situation? For example, a highly agreeable person who has a job as a project supervisor might sometimes need to be less agreeable with the employees he supervises. This does not mean he is a less agreeable person; he just needs to adapt his behavior somewhat at work. If something similar has happened to you, you have experienced making characteristic adaptations to your basic tendencies.

suggests that personality changes somewhat in childhood but becomes more stable by middle age. Moreover, this pattern holds in different cultures (McCrae et al., 2000; **Figure 12.24**). These cross-cultural findings suggest that age-related changes in personality occur independently of environmental influences and therefore that personality change itself may be based in human biology. But other evidence suggests that some aspects of personality change due to life events. In one large study, the death of a spouse led to increases in neuroticism (Mroczek & Spiro, 2003).

Robert McCrae and Paul Costa (1999) emphasize an important distinction. They separate basic tendencies of personality from characteristic adaptations. **Basic tendencies** are traits determined largely by biological processes. As such, they are very stable (**Figure 12.25a**). **Characteristic adaptations** are adjustments to situational demands (**Figure 12.25b**). Such adaptations tend to be somewhat consistent because they are based on skills, habits, roles, and so on. But changes in

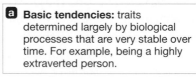

a **Basic tendencies:** traits determined largely by biological processes that are very stable over time. For example, being a highly extraverted person.

b **Characteristic adaptation:** behavior changes caused by adjustments to the situation, which tend to be consistent. For example, a highly extraverted young man will still be very extraverted as an older man, but will show that extraversion in different ways, based on what he can do at that age.

basic tendencies
Personality traits that are largely determined by biology and are stable over time.

characteristic adaptations
Changes in behavioral expression of basic tendencies based on the demands of specific situations.

FIGURE 12.25
McCrae and Costa's Model of Personality
According to this model, our personalities are made up of two tendencies: basic tendencies and characteristic adaptations.

behavior produced by characteristic adaptations do not indicate changes in basic tendencies. Consider a highly extraverted man. In his youth, he may go to parties frequently, be a thrill seeker, and have multiple sexual partners. When he is older, he will be less likely to do these things, but he may have many friends and enjoy traveling. Although the exact behaviors differ, they reflect the basic tendency of extraversion.

Overall, personality appears to be relatively stable, especially among adults. Because personality is determined partly by biological mechanisms, some personality changes are tied to changes in biological makeup. Indeed, damage to certain brain regions is associated with dramatic changes in personality, as we saw with the railroad worker Phineas Gage in Chapter 2 and Elliot in Chapter 9. The brain develops well into early adulthood, and the pace of brain development may explain the greater evidence of personality change before age 30. At the same time, people's environments tend to be relatively stable, especially after early adulthood. We tend to have one job after another with the same status level. We tend to marry people whose attitudes and personalities are similar to our own. The stability of situations likely contributes to the stability of personality.

 12.3 CHECKPOINT: How Does Biology Affect Personality?

- The results of twin studies and adoption studies suggest that personality is rooted in genetics.

- Temperament is the biologically based personality tendency that is evident in early childhood and has long-term implications for adult behavior.

- Personality traits such as extraversion/introversion are linked to biological processes, where the reticular activating system (RAS) influences level of arousal.

- Personality traits, the basic tendencies, are stable over time. This stability also suggests a biological basis for personality. However, characteristic tendencies are traits that are expressed differently, depending on the situation. These differences indicate the impact of environment on personality.

12.4 How Do We Assess Personality?

LEARNING GOALS	READING ACTIVITIES
a. Remember the key terms about how personality is measured.	List all of the boldface words and write down their definitions.
b. Understand the three ways that personality is assessed.	Summarize in a table how projective and objective measures and observational techniques are used to assess personality.
c. Apply the person/situation debate in strong and weak situations to your life.	Provide one example each of how your behavior is influenced more by personality traits in weak situations and more by the situation in strong situations.

(a)

(b)

FIGURE 12.26

Projective Measures of Personality
Projective measures provide insight into our personality by allowing a person to project unconscious thoughts onto ambiguous images, as shown here in **(a)** a Rorschach inkblot test and **(b)** a Thematic Apperception Test (TAT).

projective measures
Personality tests that examine unconscious processes by having people interpret ambiguous stimuli.

objective measures
Relatively direct assessments of personality, usually based on information gathered through self-report questionnaires or observer ratings.

If personality is all about understanding ourselves and other people, how can we be sure that our intuition about personalities is accurate? Psychology is a science. To understand personality from an objective psychological perspective, we have to be able to assess what we're talking about. Assessment was involved when Marc and Christine filled out their online dating questionnaires. Presumably, the questions were designed by psychologists and had been shown to elicit valid information about people's personalities. Questionnaires are just one way of assessing personality. Let's consider several different methods.

Several Methods Are Used to Assess Personality

Researchers do not agree on the best method for assessing the three aspects of personality: thoughts, feelings, and behaviors. The way they choose to measure personality depends largely on their theoretical orientation. For instance, trait researchers use personality descriptions. Humanistic psychologists use approaches that consider the whole person at once. Psychodynamic theorists try to assess unconscious forces. At the broadest level, assessment procedures can be grouped into projective measures, objective measures, and observational measures.

PROJECTIVE MEASURES As we have seen, psychodynamic theory considers unconscious conflicts an influence on personality. **Projective measures** explore the unconscious by having people describe or tell stories about stimulus items that are ambiguous. The general idea is that people will project their mental contents onto the ambiguous items. This process reveals hidden aspects of personality, such as motives, wishes, and unconscious conflicts. Many of these procedures have been criticized for being too subjective and insufficiently validated.

One of the best-known projective measures is the *Rorschach inkblot test* (**Figure 12.26a**). In this procedure, someone looks at an apparently abstract inkblot and describes what it appears to be. How the person describes the inkblot is supposed to reveal unconscious conflicts and other problems. The Rorschach has been criticized because it finds many normal adults and children to be psychologically disordered (Wood, Garb, Lilienfeld, & Nezworski, 2002).

Another classic projective measure is the *Thematic Apperception Test (TAT)*. In the 1930s, Henry Murray and Christiana Morgan developed the TAT to study motives related to personality, such as achievement. In this test, someone is shown an ambiguous picture and asked to tell a story about it (**Figure 12.26b**). The story is scored based on the motivational schemes that emerge. The schemes are assumed to reflect the storyteller's personal motives. Indeed, the TAT has been useful for measuring motivational traits—especially those related to achievement, power, and affiliation—and it continues to be used in contemporary research (McClelland, Koestner, & Weinberger, 1989). The TAT also reliably predicts how interpersonally dependent people are (Bornstein, 1999). For example, this test predicts how likely people are to seek approval and support from others.

OBJECTIVE MEASURES **Objective measures** of personality are straightforward assessments that do not assume unconscious influences. They usually involve self-report questionnaires or observer ratings (**Figure 12.27**). Measuring only what the raters believe or observe, these measures make no pretense of uncovering hidden conflicts or secret information. Personality researchers use these objective measures to assess how much the answers predict behavior. A questionnaire might target a specific trait, such as how much excitement someone seeks in life. More often, an objective measure will include a large inventory of traits. For example, the *NEO Personality Inventory* consists of 240 items that are designed to assess the five-factor theory personality traits.

But how objective are so-called objective personality tests? After all, they require people to make subjective judgments about themselves. And self-reports can be affected by the desire to avoid looking bad and even by the desire to view oneself in a good light. In addition, it can be difficult for researchers to compare self-reported objective measures directly, because people do not have objective standards to rate themselves against.

Suppose you are asked to rate yourself for shyness on a scale from 1 to 7. What does a 5 mean to you? Two individuals reporting a 5 on a 7-point shyness scale may not be equally shy, because the term can mean different things to different people.

PERSONALITY IN EVERYDAY LIFE Researchers have developed a number of objective measures to assess how personality emerges in daily life. One example is the electronically activated record, or EAR (Mehl, Pennebaker, Crow, Dabbs, & Price, 2001). People wear a device that unobtrusively tracks their real-world moment-to-moment interactions, picking up snippets of conversation and other auditory information. Through studies using the device, researchers have discovered various aspects of personality. One study found that the stereotype that women talk more than men is false (Mehl, Vazire, Ramirez-Esparza, Slatcher, & Pennebaker, 2007). The EAR also has been used to show that self-reports on the five-factor theory traits predict real-world behavior (Mehl, Gosling, & Pennebaker, 2006). For instance, extraverts talk more and spend less time alone. Agreeable people swear less often. Conscientious people attend class more often. And people open to experience spend more time in restaurants, bars, and coffee shops.

Do you keep your bedroom tidy or messy, warm or cold? Such aspects of your environment may predict your personality. In his 2008 book *Snoop,* Sam Gosling notes that each person's personality leaks out in many situations, such as through a Facebook profile, a personal Web page, or the condition of her bedroom or office. In a number of unrelated studies, participants who viewed public information about other people were able to form reasonably accurate impressions of how those people rated themselves on the five-factor theory personality traits.

OBSERVATIONAL METHODS Someone might be able to judge your personality by looking at your bedroom and your Facebook profile. Still, how well does that person really know you? Suppose you feel shy in new situations, as many people do. Would others know that shyness is part of your personality? Some shy people force themselves to be outgoing to mask their feelings, so their friends might have no idea that they feel shy. Other people react to their fear of social situations by remaining quiet, so observers might believe them to be cold, arrogant, and unfriendly. Ultimately, how well do observers' personality judgments predict others' behavior?

One study found a surprising degree of accuracy for trait judgments (Funder, 1995). For instance, our close acquaintances may predict our behavior more accurately than we do ourselves. This effect may occur because our friends actually observe how we behave in situations. By contrast, we may be preoccupied with evaluating other people and fail to notice

FIGURE 12.27
Objective Measures of Personality
Objective measures provide insight into personality based on people's responses in interviews or on surveys and questionnaires.

TRY IT YOURSELF: Projective Personality Test

Look at Figure 12.26a–b. What do you see in each picture? A psychologist trained in interpreting projective tests would tell you that your answers reveal something about your personality. Of course, these interpretations are very subjective.

For example, in (a) someone might see an angry fox, the body parts of a person, or a butterfly. Each answer is thought to suggest the presence of different unconscious feelings and desires, some of which are more negative than others.

With (b), a person's verbal remarks (e.g., that the test makes her feel stressed), her body language (blushing, stammering, fidgeting, etc.), and what she says the picture shows are thought to provide information about her feelings, inner conflicts, and optimism or pessimism.

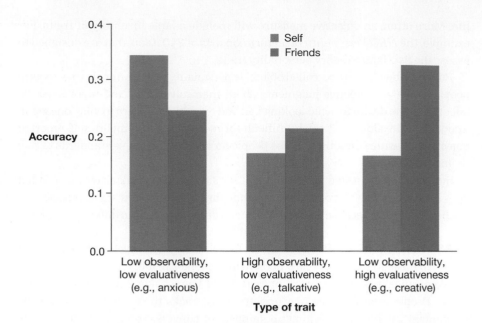

FIGURE 12.28

Self-Ratings Versus Friends' Ratings for Different Traits

This chart shows the average accuracy scores for ratings of three types of traits. As shown in the pair of bars at left, self-ratings tend to be more accurate than friends' ratings for traits that are low in both observability and evaluativeness. As shown in the middle, friends' ratings tend to be more accurate than self-ratings for traits that are high in observability and low in evaluativeness. As shown on the right, friends' ratings tend to be especially accurate for traits that are low in observability and high in evaluativeness.

our own behavior. Not surprisingly, there is evidence that we come to know others better over time, as we witness their behavior across different circumstances. Thus we are more accurate in predicting a close friend's behavior than in predicting the behavior of a mere acquaintance (Biesanz, West, & Millevoi, 2007).

How accurate are people's self-judgments in comparison to the way their friends describe them? Research suggests that we have blind spots about aspects of our personality, because we want to feel good about ourselves (Vazire & Carlson, 2011). This tendency is particularly true for highly evaluative traits—those that we care strongly about. Thus we might be accurate in knowing whether we are anxious or optimistic, because those traits are associated with feelings that can be ambiguous to observers. By contrast, our friends might be more accurate in knowing whether we are talkative or charming, because the behaviors associated with those traits are easy to observe. A key insight of this research is that a trait that is easy to observe but also highly meaningful to people, such as creativity, is more likely to be judged accurately by friends than by the person with the trait (**Figure 12.28**).

Behavior Is Influenced by Personality and Situations

Suppose you are looking for a parking space on a busy street. You see one, but you'd have to make an illegal U-turn to get it. You probably wouldn't do it if a police officer was nearby. But would you do it if there was no officer to see you? There is considerable evidence that personality traits predict behavior over time and across situations. Nevertheless, people are also highly sensitive to social context. Social norms influence behavior regardless of personality.

PERSON/SITUATION DEBATE In 1968, Walter Mischel dropped a bombshell on the field of personality. Mischel proposed that behaviors are determined more by situations than by personality traits. This idea has come to be called **situationism.** For evidence, Mischel referred to studies in which people who were dishonest in one situation were completely honest in another. Suppose a student is not totally honest with a professor in explaining why her paper is late. According to Mischel, that student may be no more likely to steal or to cheat on her taxes than another student who admits that he went to a party and didn't have time to finish his paper.

situationism
The theory that behavior is determined more by situations than by personality traits.

Do Personalities Matter in Roommate Relationships?

If you are like most college students, you share your living space with at least one roommate. Positive roommate relationships can be a highlight of your college experience and can provide a foundation for lifelong friendships. Negative roommate relationships can make your life miserable and add significant stress to your college experience. How can you use a psychological understanding of personality to help ensure a positive roommate relationship? There are no guarantees in the realm of interpersonal relationships, but the research on this topic points to some useful advice.

Carli and colleagues (1991) examined the association between personality similarity and relationship satisfaction among 30 college roommate pairs. The roommates had been randomly assigned to live together during the fall of their freshman year. After living together for six months, they completed self-report inventories. The researchers found that personality similarity between roommates was positively correlated with both relationship satisfaction and intent to live together the following year. Simply put, students liked their roommates when they were similar to them.

What do the results of this study mean for you? When it comes time to select a roommate, look for someone who is similar to you, especially in the personality traits that are most important to you. But how do you do this? You have at least three options for figuring out how a potential roommate compares with you. You can ask the potential roommate, you can ask her previous roommates, or you can rely on your own observations.

Preference for—and comfort with—a tidy versus a messy living space is not a personality trait in the same way that openness or agreeableness is a personality trait. However, this preference is certainly an individual difference worth paying attention to. Ogletree and colleagues (2005) found that a third of the college-age people they studied reported experiencing roommate conflict related to the cleanliness of their living space. So it would be a good idea to ask potential roommates questions such as those in Table 12.3.

Many colleges and universities ask students to complete personality questionnaires before matching roommates in dorms. You might already have responded to questions like those in Table 12.3 as part of your application for residence. If you and your roommate are a good fit, the system has worked.

TABLE 12.3

Level of Cleanliness Scale

Answer each item on a scale of 1 to 5, where 1 represents "very strongly disagree" and 5 represents "very strongly agree." If your answers are quite similar to those of your potential roommate, you've got at least one good indication of a satisfying arrangement.
1. I don't mind having a messy apartment.
2. It is important to me that my house or apartment is nice and neat.
3. If my house is cluttered when guests drop by, I apologize for the mess.
4. Leaving a stack of dirty dishes in the sink overnight is disgusting.
5. An overflowing trash can does not bother me.
6. It is important that anyone I live with share my cleanliness standards.
7. Leaving clothes that have been worn on a chair is an acceptable way of dealing with dirty clothes until doing laundry.

SOURCE: Ogletree et al. (2005).

(a)

(b)

FIGURE 12.29

Strong and Weak Situations
(a) A strong situation, such as a funeral, tends to discourage displays of personality. **(b)** A weak situation, such as hanging out with friends, tends to let people behave more freely.

interactionists
Theorists who believe that behavior is determined jointly by situations and underlying traits.

Mischel's critique of personality traits caused considerable rifts between social psychologists and personality psychologists. After all, social psychologists emphasize situational forces. Personality psychologists focus on individual traits. And the most basic definition of personality holds that personality is relatively stable across situations and circumstances. If Mischel was correct and there is relatively little stability, the whole concept of personality seems empty. As you might expect, there was a vigorous response to Mischel's critique. The discussion has come to be called the *person/situation debate*. Personality psychologists now agree that both the person and the situation are important.

INTERACTION OF PERSONALITY AND SITUATION How much our behavior expresses our personality varies from situation to situation (Kenrick & Funder, 1991). Suppose you are highly extraverted, aggressive, and boisterous. Your friend is shy, thoughtful, and restrained. At a party, the two of you would probably act quite differently. At a funeral, you might display similar or even nearly identical behavior. Personality psychologists differentiate between *strong situations* and *weak situations*. Strong situations (e.g., elevators, religious services, job interviews) tend to mask differences in personality, thanks to the power of the social environment (**Figure 12.29a**). Weak situations (e.g., parks, bars, one's house) tend to reveal differences in personality (**Figure 12.29b**). Most trait theorists are **interactionists.** They believe that behavior is determined jointly by situations and underlying disposition.

We also affect our social environments, however. First, we choose many of our situations. Introverts tend to avoid parties or other situations where they might feel anxious. Extraverts seek out social opportunities. Once we are in situations, our behavior affects those around us. Some extraverts may draw people out and encourage them to have fun. Other extraverts might act aggressively and turn people off. As Bandura noted, reciprocal interaction occurs between the person and the social environment so that they simultaneously influence each other.

There Are Cultural and Sex Differences in Personality

How similar are people around the world? As we have seen, there are stereotypes about people from different countries as well as about men and women. Is there any truth to these stereotypes? Does scientific evidence document differences in personality between cultures or between women and men?

One research team conducted a careful investigation of personality differences across 56 nations (Schmitt, Allik, McCrae, & Benet-Martinez, 2007). They found the five-factor theory personality traits in all 56 countries, but there were modest differences across the countries. For example, people from East Asia (Japan, China, Korea) rated themselves comparatively lower than other respondents on extraversion, agreeableness, and conscientiousness, and comparatively higher on neuroticism (**Figure 12.30**). By contrast, respondents from countries in Africa rated themselves as more agreeable, more conscientious, and less neurotic than people from most other countries rated themselves. Keep in mind, however, that the ratings might have reflected differences in cultural norms for saying good and bad things about oneself. People from East Asian countries might simply be the most modest.

What about sex? Are the stereotypes about men's and women's personalities accurate? Women and men are much more similar than different in terms

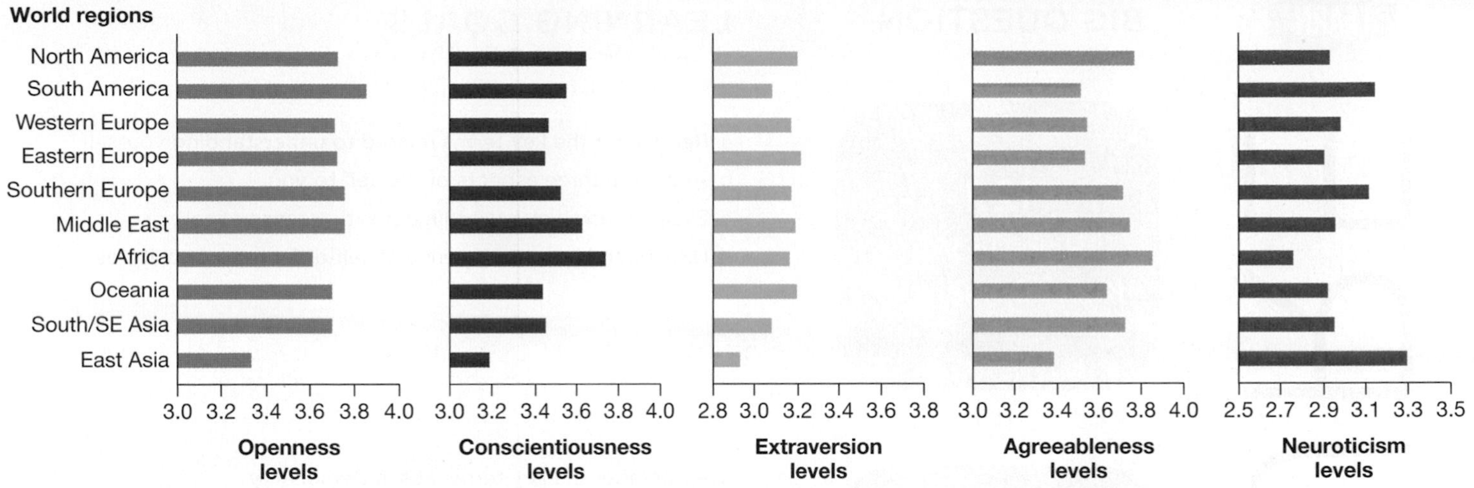

World regions
North America
South America
Western Europe
Eastern Europe
Southern Europe
Middle East
Africa
Oceania
South/SE Asia
East Asia
3.0 3.2 3.4 3.6 3.8 4.0
Openness levels
3.0 3.2 3.4 3.6 3.8 4.0
Conscientiousness levels
2.8 3.0 3.2 3.4 3.6 3.8
Extraversion levels
3.0 3.2 3.4 3.6 3.8 4.0
Agreeableness levels
2.5 2.7 2.9 3.1 3.3 3.5
Neuroticism levels

FIGURE 12.30
Cross-Cultural Research on Personality Traits
A team of more than 120 scientists investigated the five-factor theory personality traits around the world, from Argentina to Zimbabwe. This chart presents some of their findings.

of personality, but the differences between them largely support the stereotypes. That is, across various studies, women typically report and are rated as being more empathic and agreeable than men, but also as being somewhat more neurotic and concerned about feelings. By contrast, men tend to report, and are rated as, being more assertive (Costa, Terracciano, & McCrae, 2001; Feingold, 1994; Maccoby & Jacklin, 1974).

✓ 12.4 CHECKPOINT: How Do We Assess Personality?

LEARN

- Researchers use projective, objective, and observational methods to assess personality.
- Behavior is influenced by the interaction of personality traits and situations. Behavior in strong situations depends more on the situation, whereas behavior in weak situations depends more on personality traits.
- The five-factor theory personality traits are universal across cultures, but there are modest differences between cultures for each of the factors. Sex differences in personality are consistent with common sex stereotypes.

BIG PICTURE

BIG QUESTION	LEARNING GOALS
12.1 How Do We Know Ourselves?	a. Remember the key terms related to understanding yourself. b. Apply the three aspects of the self to you. c. Evaluate how you maintain a positive sense of self. d. Understand how one's sense of self differs across cultures.
12.2 How Can We Understand Personality?	a. Remember the key terms about personality. b. Apply Rogers's person-centered approach to your life. c. Apply the five-factor theory to people you know. d. Analyze the four approaches to understanding personality.
12.3 How Does Biology Affect Personality?	a. Remember the key terms about the biological basis of personality. b. Understand the research showing that genetics influences personality. c. Apply temperament styles to children. d. Understand how extraversion/introversion may be the result of brain processes.
12.4 How Do We Assess Personality?	a. Remember the key terms about how personality is measured. b. Understand the three ways that personality is assessed. c. Apply the person/situation debate in strong and weak situations to your life.

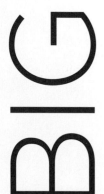

KEY TERMS

personality
self-schema
working self-concept
self-esteem
downward comparisons
upward comparisons
self-serving bias

psychodynamic theory
id
superego
ego
defense mechanisms
humanistic approaches
cognitive approaches
locus of control
trait approaches

temperament
basic tendencies
characteristic adaptations

projective measures
objective measures
situationism
interactionists

CHECKPOINT

- Our sense of self is based on three aspects: self-schema, working self-concept, and self-esteem.

- The sociometer model suggests that self-esteem is based on the likelihood that we will be accepted or rejected socially.

- We employ many strategies to maintain positive views of ourselves. These strategies include positive illusions, social comparisons, and self-serving biases.

- People from collectivist cultures tend to have interdependent senses of self. People from individualist cultures tend to have independent senses of self.

- Freud's psychodynamic theory proposes that unconscious forces determine our behavior. Conflicts between the id, superego, and ego are the basis of our personalities.

- Humanistic approaches, such as Rogers's person-centered approach, emphasize that our personalities are influenced by inherent goodness. We seek to fulfill our potential for personal growth through greater self-understanding.

- Cognitive approaches, including Rotter's expectancy theory and Bandura's reciprocal determinism theory, propose that how we think influences our personalities.

- Trait approaches, such as the five-factor theory and Eysenck's biological trait theory, describe personality based on whether we are low or high on a certain dimension of a trait.

- The results of twin studies and adoption studies suggest that personality is rooted in genetics.

- Temperament is the biologically based personality tendency that is evident in early childhood and has long-term implications for adult behavior.

- Personality traits such as extraversion/introversion are linked to biological processes, where the reticular activating system (RAS) influences level of arousal.

- Personality traits, the basic tendencies, are stable over time. This stability also suggests a biological basis for personality. However, characteristic tendencies are traits that are expressed differently, depending on the situation. These differences indicate the impact of environment on personality.

- Researchers use projective, objective, and observational methods to assess personality.

- Behavior is influenced by the interaction of personality traits and situations. Behavior in strong situations depends more on the situation, whereas behavior in weak situations depends more on personality traits.

- The five-factor theory personality traits are universal across cultures, but there are modest differences between cultures for each of the factors. Sex differences in personality are consistent with common sex stereotypes.

For a self-quiz on this chapter, go to the back of the book and find Appendix B: Quizzes.

13 Psychological Disorders

IN SEPTEMBER 2012, 15-YEAR-OLD Amanda Todd posted a soundless YouTube video displaying a series of handwritten messages that described her years of being bullied (**Figure 13.1**). It had begun in the 7th grade, when Amanda used video chat to meet people over the Internet. One man convinced her to pose topless and then threatened to blackmail Amanda unless she posted even more explicit sexual images of herself. Police informed Amanda's parents that her pictures had been widely circulated over the Internet. Students at her school started to tease her and call her names. Amanda went into a tailspin, experiencing feelings of anxiety and depression.

BIG QUESTIONS

FIGURE 13.1

The Case of Amanda Todd
Amanda Todd is shown here in a school portrait (photo courtesy of her mother, Carol Todd). Amanda experienced repeated cyberbullying so extreme that she suffered from anxiety and depression. Despite attempts to treat Amanda's problems, she ultimately decided to end her life. This case highlights how debilitating psychological disorders can be and how important it is to address the factors that cause disorders. To learn about how to prevent bullying and what to do when it happens, please visit http://www.stopbullying.gov/.
For more information about Amanda Todd, see the family's tribute site at http://amandatoddlegacy.org.

Amanda moved to a new school, but she didn't get the fresh start she had hoped for. Her tormenter followed her online, sending the damaging pictures to students and teachers at her new school. As students from both her old and new schools continued to bully Amanda, her psychological state worsened and she began to harm herself by cutting. Finally Amanda attempted suicide. Frantic to help Amanda, her parents arranged for counseling. Amanda attended another new school. She was diagnosed with anxiety and depression and given drugs to treat her symptoms. Despite these efforts, Amanda attempted suicide again a month after posting her YouTube video. This time she was successful.

Unfortunately, Amanda's case is not isolated. As we saw in Chapter 4, many adolescents and young adults are bullied, in person and over the Internet. It's natural for someone who is the victim of bullying to feel anxious or sad. Such feelings may pass with time, but if the feelings become so overwhelming that they begin to interfere with daily living, the person may be experiencing a psychological disorder. There is a strong relationship between bullying and psychological disorders. A recent study of over 1,400 participants found that being bullied during childhood is associated with psychological disorders such as anxiety and depression (Copeland, Wolke, Angold, & Costello, 2013).

The tragic case of Amanda Todd has some important messages. First, bullying can cause deep psychological harm, so we each need to do our part to prevent it, avoid taking part in it, and support people involved. Second, we need to be aware of the signs of psychological disorders so that we can seek help for ourselves, our families, and our friends. For instance, the desire to commit suicide is a symptom of the psychological disorder called major depressive disorder. This chapter will help you understand the most common psychological disorders, including their symptoms and causes. In the next chapter, you will learn about some ways professionals can treat these disorders to help people recover so that they can improve their lives.

13.1 What Is a Psychological Disorder?

📖 **LEARNING GOALS**	✏️ **READING ACTIVITIES** LEARN
a. Remember the key terms related to psychological disorders.	List all of the boldface words and write down their definitions.
b. Apply the idea of disordered thoughts, emotions, and behavior to real life.	Use the criterion "interferes with life" to consider whether the thoughts, emotions, or behavior of a person (in a movie or TV show) might be disordered.
c. Apply the diathesis-stress model to the onset of psychological disorders.	Describe how Amanda Todd's depression might be explained by the diathesis-stress model.
d. Understand the classification systems for psychological disorders.	Summarize in your own words how the *DSM-5* classification system is similar to and different from the dimensional approach to psychological disorders.

Psychological disorders, sometimes called mental disorders, are common around the globe, in all countries and all societies. These disorders reflect **psychopathology,** sickness or disorder of the mind. Psychological disorders account for the greatest amount of disability in developed countries, surpassing even cancer and heart disease (Centers for Disease Control and Prevention, 2011). Indeed, in any given year about 1 in 4 Americans over age 18 has a psychological disorder (Kessler, Chiu, Demler, & Walters, 2005). Nearly 1 in 2 Americans will have some form of psychological disorder at some point in life, most commonly depression, attention-deficit/hyperactivity disorder (ADHD), an anxiety disorder, or a substance abuse disorder (Kessler & Wang, 2008). There are enormous differences in psychopathology across the sexes: Some disorders, such as depression, are much more common in women. Others, such as antisocial personality disorder and childhood ADHD, are much more common in men (**Figure 13.2**).

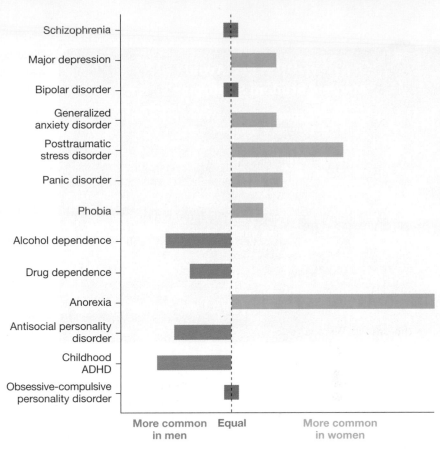

FIGURE 13.2

Sex Differences in Mental Disorders

The bars in this graph represent how common particular mental disorders are for men and for women. Note that these are relative rates, and they do not reflect the frequency of disorders for the entire population. For example, anorexia is much more likely in women than in men, but it is relatively uncommon in the population.

psychopathology
Sickness or disorder of the mind.

Disorders Interfere With Our Lives

Most of us have felt really sad on occasion or anxious when facing some difficult challenge. How can we tell if those feelings are a reasonable response to the situation or an indication of something more serious? Drawing the line between "normal" emotions, thoughts, and behaviors and a psychological disorder can be difficult. After all, different people respond to events differently, and the level of personal suffering is hard to measure objectively. However, as a rule of thumb, when a psychological problem disrupts a person's life and causes significant distress over a long period, the problem is considered a disorder rather than merely a low point of everyday life.

How do you know if someone has a psychological disorder? Behavior, especially unusual behavior, must always be considered in context. A woman running through the streets screaming, sobbing, and grabbing and hugging people might have some form of mental disorder—or she might be celebrating because she just won the lottery. Many thoughts, emotions, and behaviors that are considered acceptable in one setting may be considered deviant in other settings (**Figure 13.3**). For example, some Native American and East Asian cultures consider it a great honor to hear the voices of spirits. In urban America, this would be seen as evidence of auditory hallucinations.

So if our intuition is not enough to determine whether someone is experiencing a psychological disorder, how can we tell? In deciding whether something is psychopathology, it is important to consider four criteria: (1) Does it deviate from cultural norms for what is acceptable? In other words, does it vary from how a person is expected to think, feel, or act in a given situation? (2) Is it maladaptive?

FIGURE 13.3

Psychological Disorder or Not?

In some places, seeing a homeless man behaving in this way might not be considered to be unusual. That's not true on the streets in Notting Hill, a fashionable area of London.

TRY IT YOURSELF: Avoid "Medical Student Syndrome"

As you read this chapter, you may realize that someone you are close to—a friend, a family member—or even you may be experiencing impaired thoughts, emotions, or behavior. However, even if particular symptoms seem to describe a person you know perfectly, resist the urge to make a diagnosis. Just like medical students who worry they have every disease they learn about, you need to guard against overanalyzing yourself and others. Indeed, we are not clinicians, so we cannot correctly assess and actually diagnose another person's mental health status. At the same time, what you learn in this chapter and the next (on treating disorders) may help you understand mental health problems you or others might experience, and to support the person in getting the proper diagnosis and treatment.

etiology
Factors that contribute to the development of a disorder.

That is, does the thought, feeling, or behavior interfere with the person's ability to respond appropriately? (3) Is it self-destructive, does it cause the individual personal distress, or does it threaten other people in the community? (4) Does it cause discomfort and concern to others?

As described in the Learning Tip, these criteria are important, but there are some problems with each one. Therefore, psychopathology is increasingly defined as occurring when thoughts, emotions, and/or behaviors impair good daily functioning. For example, someone concerned about germs may wash his hands more than average, and that behavior deviates from the norm. On the one hand, such behavior may be beneficial—after all, it is the best way of avoiding contagious disease. The same behavior, however, can prevent someone from living a normal life if he cannot stop until he has washed his hands raw. Indeed, the diagnostic criteria for all the major disorder categories require that the symptoms of the disorder must interfere with at least one aspect of the person's life, such as work, social relations, or looking after oneself. This criterion is critical in determining whether thoughts, emotions, or behaviors represent a mental disorder or are simply unusual.

To fully understand any disorder, psychologists need to investigate it from four perspectives. First, they have to determine **etiology,** that is, the factors that

LEARNING TIP: Limitations of the Criteria for Disordered Emotions, Thoughts, and Behaviors

This table will help you understand the limitations of the four specific criteria for determining when emotions, thoughts, and behaviors are disordered.

CRITERIA	LIMITATION	EXAMPLE
1. Does it deviate from cultural norms for what is acceptable?	People differ in their beliefs of whether something deviates from the cultural norm.	The behavior of the homeless man in Figure 13.3 might be acceptable in some situations, but it is not appropriate in the fashionable area of Notting Hill, London.
2. Is it maladaptive?	Just because it is maladaptive doesn't make it a disorder.	Talking on the cell phone while driving puts us at risk for an accident, but it is not necessarily a psychological disorder.
3. Does it cause the individual personal distress or threaten other people?	It is possible to experience distress without having a mental disorder.	A person might be distressed about how others respond to her sexual orientation, even though that orientation is not a psychological disorder.
	It is also possible to experience a mental disorder without distress.	A person who is a psychopath will take advantage of and hurt others without any concern or remorse.
4. Does it cause discomfort and concern to others?	Something that is not a disorder can cause discomfort to others.	Several people cyberbullied Amanda Todd. This behavior caused Amanda great pain, but it does not mean the bullies had psychological disorders.

contribute to development of the disordered thoughts, emotions, and behaviors. Second, they need to identify and assess the *symptoms* of the disorder to understand what is occurring. Third, they must group symptoms into meaningful *categories* to make a diagnosis. This process of categorization and diagnosis is critical to the fourth perspective, which is identifying possible *treatments*.

For example, the causes of depression may be quite different from the causes of schizophrenia. Likewise, people with depression may show different symptoms than those with schizophrenia. By grouping people into their disorder categories, we can look for commonalities among people within those categories and explore what treatments might help people with similar symptoms. Let's begin by looking at the causes of some common psychological disorders.

There Are Several Causes of Disorders

Psychologists do not completely agree about the causes of most psychological disorders. Still, some factors are generally thought to be important. As we have seen throughout this book, both nature and nurture matter, so we should not try to identify either biology or environment as solely responsible for a given disorder.

DIATHESIS-STRESS MODEL The **diathesis-stress model** (Monroe & Simons, 1991; **Figure 13.4**) explains the mechanism that leads to the onset of psychological illness based on two factors. First, an individual may have an underlying vulnerability or predisposition (known as *diathesis*) to a mental disorder. This vulnerability can be biological, such as a genetic predisposition to a specific disorder, or it can be environmental, such as childhood trauma. The vulnerability may not be enough to trigger a psychological disorder by itself, but a second factor, which is the addition of stressful circumstances, can tip the scales. If the stress level is more than the person can cope with, the symptoms of a psychological disorder may emerge. In this view, a family history of psychological disorder suggests vulnerability rather than destiny. So according to this model, the onset of mental disorders occurs due to both vulnerability for the disorder and the presence of stressful events.

BIOPSYCHOSOCIAL APPROACH Although the diathesis stress model describes a mechanism for the onset of a psychological disorder, today most psychologists approach this model by recognizing that several factors can contribute to psychological disorders. As the name suggests, the *biopsychosocial approach* states that most psychological disorders are influenced by biological, psychological, and sociocultural factors (**Figure 13.5**).

The biological aspect of this approach focuses on how physiological factors, such as brain function, neurotransmitter imbalances, and genetics, all contribute to psychological disorders (Kandel, 1998). Studies comparing the rates of psychological disorders between identical and fraternal twins and individuals who have been adopted have revealed the importance of genetic factors (Kendler, Prescott, Myers, & Neale, 2003; Krueger, 1999; also see Chapter 2).

The psychological aspect of this approach considers that thoughts, emotions, personality, and learned experiences all influence the development of psychological disorders. For example, recall the story in Chapter 6 of how Little Albert learned to fear white rats after experiencing a loud clanging noise that was paired with a rat.

Lastly, sociocultural factors such as family relationships, socioeconomic status, and the cultural context in which a person is born and raised are all related to the development of psychological disorders. Certain disorders, such as schizophrenia,

diathesis-stress model
Proposes that a disorder may develop when an underlying vulnerability is coupled with a precipitating event.

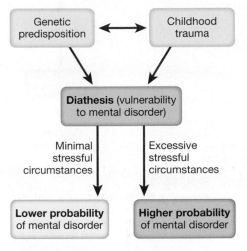

FIGURE 13.4
Diathesis-Stress Model of the Onset of Mental Disorders
This model illustrates how nature and nurture work together in the onset of mental disorders.

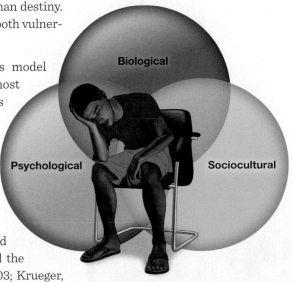

FIGURE 13.5
Biopsychosocial Approach to Psychological Disorders
According to this approach, most psychological disorders are influenced by three factors: biological processes, such as brain function and genetics; psychological processes, including how people think and feel; and sociocultural factors, such as socioeconomic status.

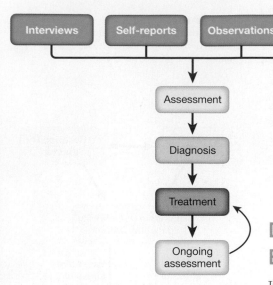

Assessing the Symptoms of a Patient
Clinical psychologists examine a person's mental functions and psychological health to diagnose a mental disorder and determine an appropriate treatment. This flowchart shows the factors that lead to treatment.

appear to be more common among the lower socioeconomic classes. This increased occurrence may be due to differences in lifestyles, in expectations, and in opportunities between the classes. In addition, there may be biases in people's willingness to ascribe disorders to different social classes. As an example, odd behavior by a wealthy person might be tolerated or viewed as amusing. But the same behavior by a person living in poverty might be taken as evidence of a psychological disorder.

The biopsychosocial approach recognizes that each of these factors alone can influence psychological disorders. More important, however, is the idea that the three factors interact with each other in disordered thoughts and behavior.

Disordered Thoughts and Behavior Can Be Assessed and Categorized

If you go to the doctor because you have a discolored patch on your skin, it can be biopsied. If you have an infection, a blood test will reveal the bacteria involved. Determining whether someone has a psychological disorder is not as straightforward. Clinical psychologists often work like detectives, tracking down information from sources, including interviews, self-reports, observations, and psychological testing (**Figure 13.6**). This *assessment* of a person's mental functions and actions allows psychologists to categorize the individual's thoughts, emotions, and behaviors in order to make a *diagnosis* so that appropriate treatment can be provided. The course of the condition and its probable outcome, or *prognosis,* will depend on the particular category of mental disorder that is diagnosed. A correct diagnosis will help the patient, and perhaps the patient's family, understand what the future might bring.

ASSESSMENT OF SYMPTOMS Most psychological problems develop over a fairly long time. Frequently, family members or a physician notice symptoms and encourage the person to seek help. A psychologist's first step in an assessment is often to conduct an *interview,* asking the person about current symptoms and about recent experiences that might be causing distress. For example, if someone is feeling depressed, the psychologist is likely to ask whether he recently experienced some sort of loss. People's *self-reports* can reveal a lot.

A psychological assessor can also gain information through *observations* of the client's behavior. For instance, a client who avoids eye contact during an examination might be experiencing social anxiety disorder (social phobia) or have attention-deficit/hyperactivity disorder. A client whose eyes dart around nervously may feel paranoid. Behavioral assessments often are useful with children. Observing their interactions with other children or seeing whether they can sit still in a classroom, for instance, may tell a psychologist more than the child could herself.

Another source of information regarding psychopathology is *psychological testing.* Personality tests, such as those described in Chapter 12, are one example. Other psychological tests ask the client to perform actions, such as copying a picture or placing blocks into slots on a board while blindfolded, that require abilities such as planning, coordinating, or remembering (**Figure 13.7**). By discovering actions that the client performs poorly, the assessment might indicate problems with a particular brain region. For instance, people who have difficulty categorizing objects may have impairments in the frontal lobes. Subsequent assessment with brain imaging might show brain damage caused by a tumor or by an injury.

Once assessment reveals that someone is experiencing disordered emotions, thoughts, or behavior, the next step is to make a diagnosis in one or more categories of psychological disorder.

Psychological Testing
The assessment depicted here uses a neuropsychological test to examine mental function.

CATEGORIZING DISORDERED THOUGHTS AND BEHAVIOR Throughout most of human history, people showing signs of what we now consider psychological disorders were viewed as suffering from madness. Such a condition was believed to be caused by the gods, witches, or some sort of evil spirits (**Figure 13.8**). But with advances in the medical understanding and treatment of diseases, recognition grew that psychological disorders were not caused by these entities. Eventually, doctors such as Sigmund Freud began to study psychological disorders to find out what caused them. In the late 1800s, the psychiatrist Emil Kraepelin noticed that not all patients experienced the same disorder. Kraepelin identified mental disorders based on the groups of symptoms that occurred together. For instance, he separated disorders of mood, such as depression, from disorders of cognition, such as schizophrenia.

The idea of categorizing mental disorders systematically was not officially adopted until 1952, when the American Psychiatric Association published the first edition of the *Diagnostic and Statistical Manual of Mental Disorders (DSM)*. Since then, the *DSM* has undergone several revisions and remains the standard assessment method in psychology and psychiatry. In the current edition, *DSM-5* (released in 2013), disorders are described in terms of observable symptoms. A patient must meet specific criteria to receive a particular diagnosis. The *DSM-5* consists of three sections: (1) an introduction with instructions for using the manual; (2) diagnostic criteria for all of the disorders, which are grouped so that similar disorders are located near each other; and (3) a guide for future psychopathology research that describes conditions not yet officially recognized as disorders, such as excessive Internet gaming.

However, people seldom fit neatly into the precise categories of psychological disorders. An alternative to categorization by type is the *dimensional approach,* which considers mental disorders along a continuum on which people vary in degree rather than in kind. With categorization, the approach can be compared to a simple switch that turns a light either on or off. By contrast, the dimensional approach is like a dimmer switch, which can provide light in varying amounts. A dimensional approach recognizes that many mental disorders are extreme versions of what we often experience. For example, most of us feel worried on occasion. When we feel worry, we may be slightly anxious (**Figure 13.9**, see line A), somewhat anxious (Figure 13.9, see line B), or very anxious (Figure 13.9, see line C). There is no threshold level in order to meet the formal criteria for anxiety. In the third section of *DSM-5,* researchers are encouraged to examine whether a dimensional approach might be helpful for understanding many psychological disorders, such as personality disorders.

Further, scientific research indicates that many mental disorders occur together even though the *DSM-5* treats them as separate disorders—for example, depression and anxiety, or depression and substance abuse. This state is known as *comorbidity* (**Figure 13.10**). Accordingly, people who are found to be depressed should also be assessed for comorbid conditions. Though they may be diagnosed with two or more disorders, a dual diagnosis offers no advantages in terms of treatment because both conditions usually will respond to the same treatment.

Despite the limitations of *DSM-5* categorization, in the rest of this chapter we consider some of the most common psychological disorders it describes. *DSM-5* describes 19

FIGURE 13.8

Historical View of Psychological Disorders

Throughout history, people believed that the gods, witches, or evil spirits caused psychological disorders.

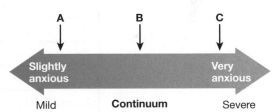

FIGURE 13.9

Dimensional Approach to Psychological Disorders

An alternative to categorizing a psychological disorder as present or absent is to describe the severity of the symptoms along a continuum from mild to severe.

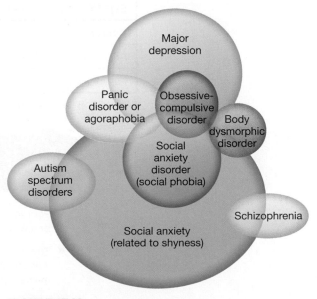

FIGURE 13.10

Comorbidity of Mental Disorders

As this diagram illustrates, psychological disorders commonly overlap. For instance, substance abuse is common across psychological disorders, and people with depression often also have anxiety disorders.

major categories of disorders, each of which has several variations or types (**Table 13.1**). Nearly all psychological disorders involve disturbances in how people feel and how they think, but emotional experiences are more central to some disorders and thought disturbances more central to others. We'll begin in the next section by considering the most common disorders involving emotions.

TABLE 13.1

DSM-5 **Disorders**

CATEGORY	EXAMPLES
Neurodevelopmental disorders	Autism spectrum disorder
Schizophrenia spectrum and other psychotic disorders	Schizophrenia
Bipolar and related disorders	Bipolar I disorder
Depressive disorders	Major depressive disorder
Anxiety disorders	Panic disorder
Obsessive-compulsive and related disorders	Body dysmorphic disorder
Trauma- and stressor-related disorders	Posttraumatic stress disorder
Dissociative disorders	Dissociative amnesia
Somatic symptom and related disorders	Conversion disorder
Feeding and eating disorders	Anorexia nervosa
Elimination disorders	Enuresis (bed wetting)
Sleep-wake disorders	Narcolepsy
Sexual dysfunctions	Erectile disorder
Gender dysphoria	Gender dysphoria
Disruptive, impulse-control, and conduct disorders	Pyromania
Substance-related and addictive disorders	Alcohol use disorder
Neurocognitive disorders	Delirium
Personality disorders	Borderline personality disorder
Paraphilic disorders	Exhibitionist disorder

SOURCE: Based on American Psychiatric Association (2013).

✓ 13.1 CHECKPOINT: What Is a Psychological Disorder?

- People with psychological disorders have emotions, thoughts, and/or behaviors that impair their lives.

- The diathesis-stress model suggests that psychological disorders arise from vulnerability paired with stressful circumstances. Psychological disorders also may arise from biopsychosocial factors.

- Assessment is the process of examining mental functions and actions to classify symptoms into categories.

- The *DSM-5* categorizes symptoms into one or more of 19 major psychological disorders, which allows for diagnosis and treatment.

13.2 How Do People Experience Disorders of Emotion?

LEARNING GOALS	READING ACTIVITIES	LEARN
a. Remember the key terms about disorders of emotion.	List all of the boldface words and write down their definitions.	
b. Apply anxiety disorders to several fictional people.	Describe four imaginary people who show the symptoms of the four anxiety disorders.	
c. Analyze the symptoms of obsessive-compulsive disorder (OCD).	Differentiate between obsessions and compulsions in OCD.	
d. Apply depressive and bipolar disorders.	Describe four imaginary people who show the symptoms of the four depressive and bipolar disorders.	

Almost certainly, you can think of times in your life when you've felt rather emotional, perhaps a bit anxious or down. These feelings are a common experience for most people, and feeling some anxiety can even be useful. It can prepare us for upcoming events and motivate us to learn new ways of coping with life's challenges. Being anxious about tests reminds us to keep up with our homework and study. Being slightly anxious when meeting new people helps us avoid doing bizarre things and making bad impressions. For some people, however, anxiety can become debilitating and interfere with every aspect of life.

Likewise, our moods color every aspect of our lives. When we are happy, the world seems like a wonderful place, and we are filled with boundless energy. When we are sad, we view the world in a decidedly less rosy light, feeling hopeless and isolated. Few of us, however, experience these symptoms day after day. When our emotions, including feeling sad or anxious, go from being a normal part of daily living to being extreme enough to disrupt our ability to work, learn, and play, our emotions are considered to be disordered.

Anxiety Disorders Make People Anxious, Tense, and Apprehensive

We all feel anxious in stressful or threatening situations, but it is abnormal to feel strong chronic anxiety without cause. *Anxiety disorders* are characterized by excessive anxiety in the absence of true danger. Anxious individuals tend to perceive ambiguous situations as threatening, whereas nonanxious individuals assume they are nonthreatening (Eysenck, Mogg, May, Richards, & Matthews, 1991; **Figure 13.11**). Anxious individuals also focus excessive attention on perceived threats (Rinck, Reinecke, Ellwart, Heuer, & Becker, 2005), and they recall threatening events more easily than nonthreatening events. These cognitive biases help to exaggerate the threat and contribute to greater anxiety. More than 1 in 4 Americans will have some type of anxiety disorder during their lifetime (**Figure 13.12**; Kessler & Wang, 2008).

People who experience anxiety disorders feel anxious, tense, and worried about the future. Anxiety disorders are also responsible for many physical ailments, some of which are potentially serious. Constant worry can make falling asleep and staying asleep difficult, and attention span and concentration can be impaired.

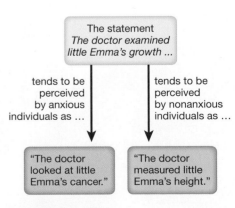

The statement
The doctor examined little Emma's growth ...

tends to be perceived by anxious individuals as ...

tends to be perceived by nonanxious individuals as ...

"The doctor looked at little Emma's cancer."

"The doctor measured little Emma's height."

FIGURE 13.11

Anxiety Disorders Are Characterized by Excessive Worry

As this example illustrates, anxious individuals tend to perceive ambiguous situations as more threatening than do people who are not anxious.

By continually arousing the autonomic nervous system, chronic anxiety also causes bodily symptoms such as sweating, dry mouth, rapid pulse, shallow breathing, and increased muscular tension. Chronic arousal can also result in hypertension, headaches, and intestinal problems and can even cause brain damage. Due to their high levels of autonomic arousal, people who experience anxiety disorders also exhibit restless and useless motor behaviors, such as toe tapping and excessive fidgeting. Problem solving and judgment may be impaired as well. Because chronic stress can damage the body, including the brain, it is important to identify and effectively treat disorders that involve chronic anxiety. Here we discuss four of the main types of anxiety disorders, which are summarized in **Table 13.2.**

SYMPTOMS OF TWO TYPES OF PHOBIAS As we saw in Chapter 6, a **phobia** is a fear of a specific object or situation that is exaggerated and out of proportion to the actual danger. Phobias are classified based on the object of the fear. *DSM-5* describes two types of phobias. *Specific phobias,* which affect about 1 in 8 people, involve particular objects and situations. Common specific phobias include fear of snakes (ophidiophobia), fear of enclosed spaces (claustrophobia), and fear of

FIGURE 13.12

Anxiety Disorders Are Very Common
Like 15 million other Americans, the football player Ricky Williams has been diagnosed with social phobia. Some people thought that Williams was shy or aloof. Instead, he was afraid of interacting with people. Williams could not look people in the eye, dreaded meeting fans on the street, talked to reporters with his helmet on, and could not interact with his daughter. After Williams sought treatment, he began to realize that he wasn't crazy. Soon he was able, he said, "to start acting like the real Ricky Williams."

phobia
Fear of a specific object or situation that is out of proportion with any actual threat.

TABLE 13.2

Four Types of Anxiety Disorders

CATEGORY	DESCRIPTION	EXAMPLE
Phobias	*Specific phobia:* fear of something that is disproportionate to the threat	Rachel is so afraid of snakes that if she sees even a picture of a snake, her heart begins to pound and she feels the need to run away.
	Social anxiety disorder (social phobia): fear of being negatively evaluated by others in a social setting	Linda worries intensely that she will say or do the wrong thing around other people and they will think badly of her. So she prefers to be by herself and avoids being around lots of people.
Generalized anxiety disorder	Nearly constant anxiety not associated with a specific thing	Reginald is feeling very worried and has been for months, but he can't figure out why. It seems as though he is anxious about everything.
Panic disorder	Sudden attacks of overwhelming terror	Jennifer has had several panic attacks and worries she will have another one. This brings on more panic attacks, where she feels extreme fear and her heart pounds in her chest.
Agoraphobia	Fear of being in a situation from which one cannot escape	Rashad works for a company located in a skyscraper, but he is so terrified of not being able to get out of the building that he has begun to have panic attacks at work.

SOURCE: Based on American Psychiatric Association (2013).

heights (acrophobia). Another common specific phobia is fear of flying (aviophobia). Even though the odds of dying in a plane crash, compared with a car crash, are extraordinarily small, some people find flying terrifying. For those who need to travel frequently for their jobs, a fear of flying can cause significant impairment in daily living. **Table 13.3** lists some unusual specific phobias.

Social anxiety disorder, also called *social phobia*, is a fear of being negatively evaluated by others. This specific phobia includes fears of public speaking, speaking up in class, meeting new people, and eating in front of others. About 1 in 8 people will experience social phobia at some point in their lifetimes, and around 1 in 14 are experiencing social phobia at any given time (Ruscio et al., 2008). It is one of the earliest forms of anxiety disorder to develop, often beginning around age 13. The more social fears a person has, the more likely he is to develop other disorders, particularly depression and substance abuse problems. Indeed, assessment must consider the overlap between social phobia and related disorders to make an informed diagnosis (Stein & Stein, 2008).

SYMPTOMS OF GENERALIZED ANXIETY DISORDER Whereas the anxiety in phobic disorders has a specific focus, the anxiety in **generalized anxiety disorder** is diffuse and always present. People with this disorder are constantly anxious and worry incessantly about even minor matters. They even worry about being worried! Because the anxiety is not focused, it can occur in response to almost anything, so the person is constantly on the alert for problems. This high level of alertness results in distractibility, fatigue, irritability, and sleep problems as well as headaches, restlessness, lightheadedness, and muscle pain. Just under 6 percent of the United States population is affected by this disorder at some point in their lives, though women are diagnosed more often than men (Kessler et al., 1994; Kessler & Wang, 2008).

generalized anxiety disorder
A diffuse state of constant anxiety not associated with any specific object or event.

TABLE 13.3

Some Unusual Specific Phobias

• Arachibutyrophobia: fear of peanut butter sticking to the roof of one's mouth
• Automatonophobia: fear of ventriloquists' dummies
• Barophobia: fear of gravity
• Dextrophobia: fear of objects at the right side of the body
• Geliophobia: fear of laughter
• Gnomophobia: fear of garden gnomes
• Hippopotomonstrosesquippedaliophobia: fear of long words
• Ochophobia: fear of being in a moving automobile
• Panophobia: fear of everything
• Pentheraphobia: fear of mothers-in-law
• Triskaidekaphobia: fear of the number 13

panic disorder
An anxiety disorder that consists of sudden, overwhelming attacks of terror.

agoraphobia
An anxiety disorder marked by fear of being in situations from which escape may be difficult or impossible.

SYMPTOMS OF PANIC DISORDER Panic disorder consists of sudden, overwhelming attacks of terror and worry about having additional panic attacks. The attacks seemingly come out of nowhere, though they may be cued by external stimuli or internal thought processes. Panic attacks typically last for several minutes, during which the person may begin to sweat and tremble; feel her heart racing; feel shortness of breath and chest pain; and feel dizzy and lightheaded, with numbness and tingling in the hands and feet. People experiencing panic attacks often feel that they are going crazy, that they are dying, or as if they are about to be hit by a train and cannot escape. Panic disorder affects an estimated 3 percent of the population in a given year, and women are twice as likely to be diagnosed as men (Kessler & Wang, 2008). Those who experience panic attacks attempt suicide much more frequently than those in the general population (Fawcett, 1992; Korn et al., 1992; Noyes, 1991).

SYMPTOMS OF AGORAPHOBIA Loosely translated, *agoraphobia* means "fear of a gathering place." People who have **agoraphobia** fear being in situations from which escape is difficult or impossible—for example, being in a crowded shopping mall or using public transportation. Their fear is so strong that being in such situations causes panic attacks. Indeed, agoraphobia without panic attacks is quite rare (Kessler & Wang, 2008). As a result, people who experience agoraphobia avoid going into open spaces or to places that might have crowds. In extreme cases, these people may feel unable to leave their homes. In addition to fearing the particular situations, many people with agoraphobia fear having a panic attack in public.

DEVELOPMENT OF ANXIETY DISORDERS Although people are anxious about different things, the etiology of various types of anxiety is best explained by the biopsychosocial approach. For example, as we saw in Chapter 12, our temperaments are biologically determined aspects of our personality. Children who have an inhibited temperamental style are usually shy and tend to avoid unfamiliar people and novel objects. These inhibited children are more likely to develop anxiety disorders later in life (Fox, Henderson, Marshall, Nichols, & Ghera, 2005). They are especially at risk for developing social phobia (Biederman et al., 2001). In one study, described in the Scientific Thinking feature, people who had been categorized as inhibited before age 2 showed a threat response to novel faces even as adults many years later (Schwartz, Wright, Shin, Kagan, & Rauch, 2003). This finding suggests that some aspects of childhood temperament are preserved in the adult brain.

We also know that many fears are learned. As we saw in Chapter 6, a person might come to associate something with fear through classical conditioning. For example, someone could develop a fear of flying by observing another person's fearful reaction to the closing of cabin doors. Such a fear might then generalize to other enclosed spaces, resulting in claustrophobia.

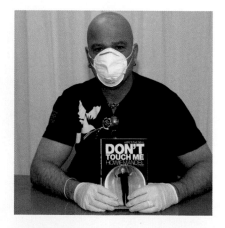

FIGURE 13.13

Howie Mandel's Obsessions and Compulsions
The comedian Howie Mandel has been diagnosed with obsessive-compulsive disorder. Like many people with OCD, Mandel experiences a strong fear of germs. His trademark shaved head helps him with this problem by making him feel cleaner. Mandel even built a second, sterile house, where he can retreat if he feels he might be contaminated by anyone around him. Here Mandel promotes his autobiography, *Here's the Deal: Don't Touch Me* (2009), in which he "comes clean" about his experiences with OCD and other disorders.

Unwanted Thoughts Create Fear in Obsessive-Compulsive Disorder

Game show host Howie Mandel is famous for giving his guests a fist bump rather than shaking hands with them. What viewers didn't know was that Mandel had a serious psychological reason for using his signature greeting: He was obsessed with germs. In 2009, Mandel publicly announced that he had been diagnosed with obsessive-compulsive disorder (OCD), a condition that had been ruling his life for many years (**Figure 13.13**).

Hypothesis: People who had an inhibited temperamental style as children are more likely to show signs of social anxiety later in life.

Research Method:

1 Adults received brain scans while viewing pictures of familiar faces and of novel faces. One group of these adults had been categorized as inhibited before age 2. The other group had been categorized as uninhibited before age 2.

2 Two regions of the brain were more activated by novel faces. These areas were the amygdala (marked "Amy" in the brain scan) and the occipitotemporal cortex (marked "OTC"). The amygdala is normally active when people are threatened. The occipitotemporal cortex is normally active when people see faces, whether the faces are novel or familiar.

Results: Compared with the uninhibited group, the inhibited group showed greater activation of the amygdala while viewing novel faces. Such activation indicated that when seeing novel faces the inhibited group showed greater brain activity associated with threat.

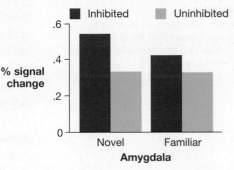

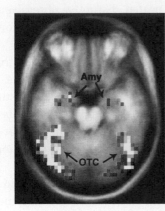

Conclusion: The results suggest that some aspects of childhood temperament are preserved in the adult brain. In particular, biological factors seem to play an important role in social anxiety.

We have seen that many psychological disorders involve both emotional and cognitive impairments. In some cases, the occurrence of unwanted thoughts leads to emotional distress. *DSM-5* categorizes a number of disorders that involve experiencing unwanted thoughts or the desire to engage in maladaptive behaviors. The commonality is the obsession with an idea or thought and the compulsion to repeatedly act in a certain way.

SYMPTOMS OF OBSESSIVE-COMPULSIVE DISORDER **Obsessive-compulsive disorder (OCD)** involves frequent intrusive thoughts and compulsive actions. Affecting 1 percent to 2 percent of the population, OCD is more common in women than men, and it generally begins in early adulthood (Robins & Regier, 1991; Weissman et al., 1994). OCD includes two aspects of disordered thoughts and behaviors. *Obsessions* are recurrent, intrusive, and unwanted thoughts or urges or mental images. They often include intense worry and fears of contamination, of accidents, or of one's own aggression. *Compulsions* are particular acts that the person feels driven to perform over and over again. The most common compulsive behaviors are cleaning, checking, and counting. The key in this disorder is that when the person engages in the compulsive behavior, she experiences a temporary reduction in the anxiety caused by the obsession. For instance, a person who has an obsessive fear of germs might engage in the compulsion of repeatedly washing his hands. People diagnosed with OCD are aware that their obsessions and compulsions are irrational, yet they are unable to stop them.

obsessive-compulsive disorder (OCD)
A disorder characterized by frequent intrusive thoughts that create anxiety and compulsive actions that temporarily reduce the anxiety.

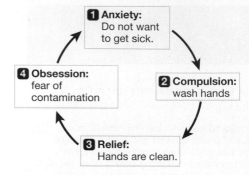

FIGURE 13.14

The Cycle of Obsession and Compulsion

As shown here, the obsession and compulsion aspects of obsessive-compulsive disorder feed into each other in a continuous cycle.

DEVELOPMENT OF OBSESSIVE-COMPULSIVE DISORDER OCD is another example of how the biopsychosocial approach explains the causes of some mental disorders. One explanation is that the disorder results from psychological factors, such as learning by conditioning. Anxiety is somehow paired to a specific event, probably through classical conditioning. The person then engages in behavior that reduces anxiety. The reduction of anxiety is reinforced through operant conditioning, and the chances of engaging in that behavior again are increased. This can happen to anyone. For instance, if you are forced to shake hands with a man who has a bad cold, you will likely feel anxious or uncomfortable because you do not want to get sick (**Figure 13.14,** part 1). As soon as the pleasantries are over, you run to the bathroom and wash your hands (Figure 13.14, part 2). Afterward, you feel relieved (Figure 13.14, part 3). Because you have paired hand-washing with a reduction in anxiety, this increases the chances that you will wash your hands in a similar situation in the future. For someone who develops OCD, however, the compulsive behavior will reduce the anxiety only temporarily, so he will continue to experience repeated, disruptive obsessive thoughts, for example about germs (Figure 13.14, part 4). In turn, he will perform the behavior again and again in attempts to reduce the anxiety.

However, there is also good evidence that the etiology of OCD is in part biological—specifically, genetic—in nature (Crowe, 2000). Indeed, various behavioral genetics methods, such as twin studies, have shown that OCD runs in families. The specific mechanism has not been identified, but the OCD-related genes appear to control the neurotransmitter glutamate (Pauls, 2008). As we saw in Chapter 2, glutamate is the major excitatory transmitter in the brain, causing increased neural firing.

Brain imaging has also provided some evidence regarding which brain systems are involved in OCD. The caudate, a brain structure involved in suppressing impulses, is smaller and has structural abnormalities in people with OCD (Baxter, 2000). It is possible that in people with OCD, the caudate does not function properly to prevent impulses from reaching a person's conscious awareness.

Posttraumatic Stress Disorder Results From Trauma

DSM-5 categorizes a number of disorders together that result from trauma or excessive stress. This category describes *trauma and stressor-related disorders*. For example, a person who cries continually, has difficulty studying, and avoids social settings for 6 months after a romantic breakup may have an *adjustment disorder*. This person is having difficulty adjusting to the stressor.

When people experience severe stress or emotional trauma—such as having a serious accident, being raped, fighting in active combat, or surviving a natural disaster—they often have negative reactions long after the danger has passed. In severe cases, they develop **posttraumatic stress disorder (PTSD),** a disorder that involves frequent and recurring unwanted thoughts related to the trauma, including nightmares, intrusive thoughts, and flashbacks. Around 7 percent of the population will experience PTSD at some point in their lives, and women are more likely to develop the disorder (Kessler et al., 2005).

An opportunity to study susceptibility to PTSD came about because of a tragedy at Northern Illinois University in 2008. On the campus, in front of many observers, a lone gunman killed five people and wounded 21. Among a sample of female students, those with certain genetic markers related to serotonin functioning

posttraumatic stress disorder (PTSD)
A mental disorder that involves frequent nightmares, intrusive thoughts, and flashbacks related to an earlier trauma.

were much more likely to show PTSD symptoms in the weeks after the shooting (Mercer et al., 2011). This finding suggests that some individuals may be more at risk than others for developing PTSD after exposure to a stressful event.

Those with PTSD often have chronic tension, anxiety, and health problems, and they may experience memory and attention problems in their daily lives. PTSD involves an unusual problem in memory—the inability to forget. People with PTSD also pay a lot of attention to stimuli associated with their traumatic events. For instance, soldiers with combat-induced PTSD show increased physiological responsiveness to pictures of troops, sounds of gunfire, and even words associated with combat. It is as if the severe emotional event is "overconsolidated," and incredibly memorable so the person is always on the alert to experience a similar situation (see Chapter 7 for a discussion of consolidation of memory).

Depressive Disorders Are Common

When we feel down, or sad about something happening in our life, we often say we are "depressed." These emotions are relatively common, especially during the winter (see Has It Happened to You?), but only lasting episodes that impair a person's life are diagnosed as depressive disorders. *Depressive disorders* are a type of mood disorder that features persistent and pervasive feelings of sadness. Two types of depressive disorders, and two types of bipolar disorders, are summarized in **Table 13.4.**

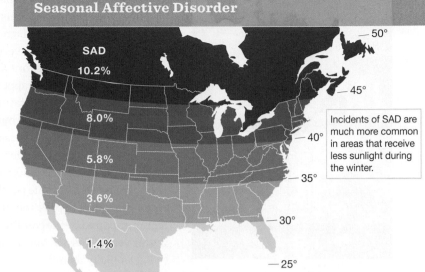

HAS IT HAPPENED TO YOU?
Seasonal Affective Disorder

SAD
10.2%
8.0%
5.8%
3.6%
1.4%

50°
45°
40°
35°
30°
25°

Incidents of SAD are much more common in areas that receive less sunlight during the winter.

Do you tend to feel sad during the winter? If the sadness is severe enough to impair daily functioning, then it is called *seasonal affective disorder (SAD)*. People are more likely to experience this cyclical pattern of depression due to the particularly short days and reduced sunlight in winter. The good news is that people with SAD don't just need to wait for summer to come; easy and effective treatments are available, as described in Chapter 14.

TABLE 13.4
Four Types of Depressive and Bipolar Disorders

DSM-5 CATEGORY	DESCRIPTION	EXAMPLE
Depressive disorders	*Major depressive disorder:* extremely depressed mood or loss of interest in pleasurable activities for two weeks, plus other symptoms, such as changes in weight or sleep	MaryBeth had been deeply depressed for months and had no hope that she would ever feel happy again. She didn't enjoy seeing her friends, she was tired all of the time, and she gained a lot of weight.
	Persistent depressive disorder: mild or moderate depressed mood most days for at least 2 years	Ken used to be a very happy person, but for the past few years he has felt "down" most of the time.
Bipolar and related disorders	*Bipolar I:* extremely elevated moods (manic episodes) lasting at least one week	For 2 weeks, Dory has felt extremely happy and excited, needed very little sleep, and impulsively bought expensive jewelry.
	Bipolar II: alternating between mildly elevated mood for at least 4 days and extremely depressed mood for 2 weeks	Simon would experience weeks of deep sadness. Then his mood would improve and he would be happy and have energy to get things done.

SOURCE: Based on American Psychiatric Association (2013).

SYMPTOMS OF DEPRESSIVE DISORDERS The common feature of all depressive disorders is the presence of sad, empty, or irritable mood, along with bodily symptoms and cognitive problems that interfere with daily life.

The classic disorder in this category is **major depressive disorder.** According to *DSM-5* criteria, to be diagnosed with major depressive disorder a person must have one of two symptoms: very depressed (often irritable) mood, or loss of interest in pleasurable activities for two weeks or more. In addition, the person must have other symptoms, such as appetite and weight changes, sleep disturbances, loss of energy, difficulty concentrating, feelings of self-reproach or guilt, and frequent thoughts of death, perhaps by suicide. Amanda Todd, whose tragic story opened this chapter, had many of these symptoms.

Major depressive disorder affects about 6 percent to 7 percent of Americans in any given year, and approximately 16 percent of Americans will experience major depression at some point in their lives (Kessler & Wang, 2008; **Figure 13.15**). Although major depression varies in severity, those who receive a diagnosis are highly impaired by the condition. It tends to persist over several months, often lasting for years (Kessler, Merikangas, & Wang, 2007; **Figure 13.16**). Women are nearly twice as likely as men to be diagnosed with major depressive disorder (Kessler et al., 2003).

Unlike major depression, **persistent depressive disorder** is of mild to moderate severity. People with persistent depressive disorder—approximately 2 to 3 percent of the population—may have many of the same symptoms as those with major depression, but the symptoms are less intense (see Figure 13.16). To be diagnosed with persistent depressive disorder, someone must have a depressed mood most of the day, more days than not, for at least two years. Periods of persistent depressive disorder last from 2 to 20 or more years, although the typical duration is about 5 to 10 years.

Depression is so prevalent that it is sometimes called the common cold of mental disorders. In its most severe form, depression is the leading cause of disability in the United States and worldwide (Worley, 2006). The stigma associated with this disorder is especially a problem in developing countries, where people do not take advantage of the treatment options because they do not want to admit to being depressed. Depression is the leading risk factor for suicide, which claims approximately a million lives annually around the world and is among the top three causes of death for people between 15 and 35 years of age (Insel & Charney, 2003). One way to combat the stigma of psychological disorders is to focus attention on how common they are and to educate more people about effective treatments (**Figure 13.17**).

FIGURE 13.15

Many People Experience Depressive Disorders

In 1969, the astronaut Buzz Aldrin walked on the moon. But after returning to Earth, he found it substantially difficult to cope with depression combined with alcoholism. In 2009, Aldrin wrote a memoir about his experiences, *Magnificent Desolation*. Now, after three decades of treatment and sobriety, Aldrin says that overcoming his problems has been satisfying because "it has given me a sense of comfort and ease with where I am now."

major depressive disorder
Mood disorder, characterized by extremely depressed moods or a lack of interest in normally pleasurable activities, that persists for two weeks or more.

persistent depressive disorder
Mood disorder, characterized by mildly or moderately depressed moods, that persists for at least two years.

FIGURE 13.16

Depressed Mood in Depressive Disorders

This graphic provides a general way to understand the two main types of depressive disorders in relation to "normal mood." People with major depressive disorder tend to experience extremely depressed moods but for short periods. By contrast, people with persistent depressive disorder experience mildly or moderately depressed moods but for longer periods.

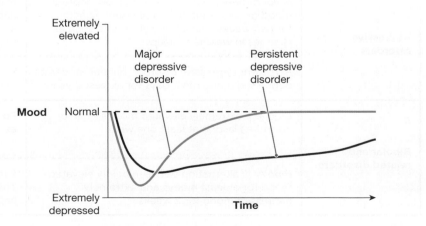

**DEVELOPMENT OF DEPRESSIVE DISORDERS: BIOLOGI-
CAL FACTORS** As with the other psychological disorders we
have discussed, biopsychosocial factors play a role in the etiology
of depression. Studies of twins, of families, and of adoptive children support the notion that depression has a genetic component.
Although there is some variability among studies, it is more likely
that both identical twins will have depression than both fraternal twins (Levinson, 2006). The existence of a genetic component
implies that biological factors are involved in depression. In fact,
there is evidence that major depression involves a deficiency of
neurotransmitters that regulate emotion. As we will see in Chapter
14, medications that increase or decrease the availability of specific
neurotransmitters are used in the treatment of depression.

In addition, studies of brain function have suggested that certain
neural structures may be involved in mood disorders. Damage to
the left prefrontal cortex can lead to depression, but damage to the
right prefrontal cortex does not. Biological rhythms also have been
implicated in depression. Depressed patients enter REM sleep more
quickly and have more of it. In fact, one symptom of depression is
excessive sleeping and tiredness.

**DEVELOPMENT OF DEPRESSIVE DISORDERS: PSYCHOLOGI-
CAL FACTORS** Psychological factors also play a role in the cause
of depression. The bullying of Amanda Todd is only one example. A
number of studies have implicated life stressors, such as the death of a loved one, a
divorce, or multiple negative events, in many cases of depression (Hammen, 2005).

How people react to stress, however, can be influenced by their interpersonal
relationships, and relationships play an extremely important role in depression. A
person who has a close friend or group of friends is less likely to become depressed
when faced with stress. This protective factor is related not to the number of friends,
but to the quality of the friendships: One good friend is more protective than a large
number of casual acquaintances. Nevertheless, regardless of any other factors, relationships contribute to the development of depression and alter people's experiences
when depressed. Ultimately, a relationship may be damaged by the constant needs or
complaints of the person with depression. Over time, people may avoid interactions
with others who are experiencing depression, thus initiating a downward spiral by
making people feel even more depressed.

The psychologist Aaron Beck has hypothesized that a psychological factor associated with depression is how people think of themselves. Specifically, depressed
people think negatively about themselves ("I am worthless"; "I am a failure"; "I am
ugly"), about their situations ("Everybody hates me"; "The world is unfair"), and
about the future ("Things are hopeless"; "I can't change"). Beck refers to these negative thoughts about self, situation, and the future as the *cognitive triad* (Beck, 1967,
1976; **Figure 13.18**).

From Beck's perspective, people likely to develop depression blame misfortunes on personal defects and see positive occurrences as the result of luck. People
who are not prone to depression do the opposite. Beck also notes that people likely
to become depressed make errors in logic. For example, they overgeneralize based
on single events, exaggerate the seriousness of bad events, think in extremes (such
as believing they should either be perfect or not try), and take responsibility for bad
events that actually have little to do with them.

FIGURE 13.17

Informing the Public
Advertisements such as this one, from the
National Institute of Mental Health, are
meant to increase understanding about
psychological disorders. The more we hear
about how common mental illness is, the
more inclined we may be to visit doctors
when problems arise.

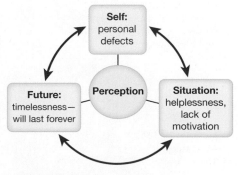

FIGURE 13.18

Cognitive Triad
People who experience depression
perceive themselves, their situations, and
the future negatively. These perceptions
influence each other and contribute to the
disorder.

What to Do if a Person Might Be Thinking of Suicide

Many people consider suicide at some point in their lives. Tragically, as of 2007, suicide was the third leading cause of death among Americans 10 to 24 years old (American Association of Suicidology, 2011). As a result, many college students will be or have been touched by suicide. Perhaps you know someone who died by suicide. Perhaps a friend of yours talks about wanting to die. Or maybe you have thought about taking your own life. Understanding the risk factors associated with suicide is an important step toward preventing suicide. Knowing where and how to find support can save lives.

In his book *Why People Die by Suicide* (2005), the clinical psychologist Thomas Joiner considers two key questions about suicide: Who *wants* to commit suicide? And who *can* commit suicide? In answering the first question, Joiner argues that "people desire death when two fundamental needs are frustrated" (p. 47). The first of these fundamental needs is the need to belong, to feel connected with others. We all want to have positive interactions with others who care about us. Without such interactions, our need to belong is not met. The second fundamental need is the need for competence. If we do not perceive ourselves as able to do the things we think we should be able to do, our need for competence is not met. According to Joiner, when the need to belong and the need for competence are frustrated, we might desire death.

But as Joiner points out, just because a person wants to commit suicide does not mean he will be able to do so. Evolution has hardwired us with a tremendously strong self-preservation instinct. What makes a person able to endure the tremendous physical pain or overwhelming psychological fear many of us would experience if we tried to kill ourselves? Joiner presents a straightforward answer: practice. People who expose themselves to self-injury or get used to dangerous behavior are more likely to go through with suicide. A person who drives recklessly, engages in self-cutting, and/or experiments with drugs may be more likely to have the capacity to carry out lethal self-injury. Joiner's contention is that the individuals who are *most* at risk of dying by suicide both *want* to do so and *are able* to do so.

With such risk factors in mind, what can you do if you think someone you know might be suicidal?

1. **Take all threats of suicide seriously.** You have to assume your friend is actually capable of committing suicide.

2. **Get help.** Someone who is considering suicide should talk with a trained professional as soon as possible. Contact a counselor at your school, ask a religious leader for help, call a local suicide prevention hotline, or speak to someone at the National Suicide Prevention Lifeline: 1-800-273-TALK (8255). These individuals can help you get your friend the support she needs.

3. **Let your friend know you care.** Remember, suicide risk is particularly high when people do not feel a sense of connection with others. You can remind the suicidal person that you value your relationship, that you care about her well-being, and that you would be devastated if she were no longer in your life. These forms of support can challenge the suicidal person's sense that she lacks belongingness. You can also challenge a perceived sense of incompetence by reminding your friend why you admire him, or you can ask him for help on a project or issue you are genuinely struggling with.

Suicide is forever, but the problems that prompt someone to feel suicidal are often temporary. If you ever find yourself or a friend feeling that suicide offers the best way out of an overwhelming or hopeless situation, know that other options exist. You or your friend might not be able to see those options right away. Reach out to someone who can help you or your friend see the ways out of current problems and into the future.

A second cognitive theory of depression is based on *learned helplessness* (Seligman, 1974, 1975). In this case, people come to see themselves as unable to have any effect on events in their lives. The psychologist Martin Seligman based this model on years of animal research. When animals are placed in aversive situations they cannot escape (such as receiving an inescapable shock), the animals eventually become passive and unresponsive. They end up lacking the motivation to try new methods of escape even when given the opportunity. Similarly, people who are experiencing learned helplessness come to expect that bad things will happen to them and believe they are powerless to avoid negative events. Their explanations for negative events refer to personal factors that are unchanging rather than to situational factors that are temporary. This pattern leads them to feel hopeless about making positive changes in their lives (Abramson, Metalsky, & Alloy, 1989; see Using Psychology in Your Life).

DEVELOPMENT OF DEPRESSIVE DISORDERS: CULTURE AND GENDER
Across multiple countries and contexts, twice as many women as men are diagnosed with depression (Ustün, Ayuso-Mateos, Chatterji, Mathers, & Murray, 2004). In fact, suicide is the leading cause of death among young women in India and China (Khan, 2005). The highest rates of depression are found in women in developing countries, and especially high rates are reported for women in rural Pakistan (Mumford, Saeed, Ahmad, Latif, & Mubbashar, 1997). Research in India, Brazil, and Chile shows that low income, lack of education, and difficult family relationships contribute to mental disorders in women (Blue & Harpham, 1996).

Furthermore, gender roles may lead to discrepancies in the experience of depression. One theory is that women respond to stressful events by internalizing their feelings, which leads to depression and anxiety, whereas men externalize with alcohol, drugs, and violence (Holden, 2005).

Bipolar Disorders Involve Mania

Think about how you have been feeling for the past week. Some days you were probably happy, and on others you might have been sad. We all experience variations in mood. Our typical fluctuations from happiness to sadness seem small, however, compared with the extremes experienced by people with *bipolar disorders,* who experience episodes of mania. These changes in mood can vary in degree and are accompanied by major shifts in energy level and physical activity. The two main types of bipolar disorders are summarized in Table 13.4.

SYMPTOMS OF BIPOLAR DISORDERS True *manic episodes* last one week or longer and are characterized by abnormally and persistently elevated mood, increased activity, diminished need for sleep, grandiose ideas, racing thoughts, and extreme distractibility. During episodes of mania, heightened levels of activity and extreme happiness often result in excessive involvement in pleasurable but foolish activities. People may engage in sexual indiscretions, buying sprees, risky business ventures, and similar "out of character" behaviors that they regret once the mania has subsided. They might also have severe thought disturbances and hallucinations. This condition is known as **bipolar I disorder.** Bipolar I disorder is based more on the manic episodes than on depression. Although those with bipolar I disorder often have depressive episodes, such episodes are not necessary for a *DSM-5* diagnosis. The manic episodes in bipolar I disorder cause significant impairment in daily living and often can result in hospitalization (**Figure 13.19**).

Compared to bipolar I disorder, in which people experience true manic episodes, those with **bipolar II disorder** may experience less extreme mood elevations

FIGURE 13.19

Manic Episodes in People With Bipolar Disorder
The actor Carrie Fisher has been diagnosed with bipolar disorder and has managed her symptoms for many years. In 2013, she experienced a bipolar episode during a performance on a cruise ship. She was sleepless, agitated, ranting, and writing manically. After a brief hospitalization and adjustment of her medication, Fisher was able to resume her normal life.

bipolar I disorder
Mood disorder characterized by extremely elevated moods during manic episodes.

bipolar II disorder
Mood disorder characterized by alternating periods of extremely depressed and mildly elevated moods.

FIGURE 13.20
Elevated and Depressed Moods in Bipolar Disorders

This graphic provides a general way to understand two types of bipolar disorders based on what is considered "normal mood." People with bipolar I tend to experience extremely elevated moods. People with bipolar II disorder tend to experience mildly or moderately elevated moods, along with episodes of major depression.

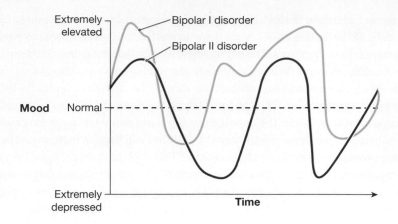

(**Figure 13.20**). These episodes are often characterized by heightened creativity and productivity, and they can be extremely pleasurable and rewarding. The singer Demi Lovato and actor Catherine Zeta-Jones have both revealed that they have been diagnosed with bipolar II disorder. Although these less extreme mood elevations may be somewhat disruptive to a person's life, they do not cause significant impairment in daily living or require hospitalization. However, the bipolar II diagnosis does require at least one episode of major depression. Therefore the depression might cause significant impairments. Thus the impairments to daily living for bipolar I disorder are the manic episodes, whereas the impairments for bipolar II disorder are the major depressive episodes.

A CASE STUDY OF BIPOLAR DISORDER Psychology professor Kay Redfield Jamison acknowledged her own struggles with bipolar disorder in her award-winning memoir *An Unquiet Mind* (1995; **Figure 13.21**). Her work has helped shape the study of the disorder. Her 1990 textbook, coauthored with Frederick Goodwin, is considered the standard for the field (Goodwin & Jamison, 1990).

In *An Unquiet Mind,* Jamison details how as a child she was intensely emotional and occasionally obsessive. When she was 17, she had her first serious bout of what she describes as profoundly suicidal depression. Jamison experienced deepening swings from wild exuberance to paralyzing depression throughout her undergraduate years. In 1975, after obtaining her Ph.D. in clinical psychology, she joined the UCLA Department of Psychiatry, where she directed the Affective Disorders Clinic.

Within months after she began this job, her condition deteriorated dramatically. She began hallucinating and feared that she was losing her mind. This state so terrified her that she sought out a psychiatrist, who quickly diagnosed her as having bipolar disorder and prescribed a drug called lithium. Although lithium has helped Jamison, she also credits the psychological support of her psychiatrist as well as her family and friends.

An unfortunate side effect of lithium is that it blunts positive feelings. People with bipolar disorder experience profoundly enjoyable highs during their manic phases, so they often resent the drug and refuse to take it. Jamison has made the point that lithium can rob people of creative energy. In her 1993 book *Touched with Fire,* Jamison asks whether lithium would have dampened the genius of major artists and writers who may have had bipolar disorders, such as Michelangelo, Vincent van Gogh, Georgia O'Keeffe, Emily Dickinson, and Ernest Hemingway. Jamison demonstrates the strong association between bipolar disorder and artistic genius, and she raises the disturbing question of whether eradicating the

FIGURE 13.21

Kay Redfield Jamison

Jamison was able to overcome bipolar disorder to succeed as a teacher, researcher, and author.

disorder would rob society of much great art. Jamison embodies this irony: Her early career benefited from the energy and creativity of her manic phases even as her personal life was threatened by devastating depression. (For more information about lithium and other treatments for bipolar disorders, see Chapter 14.)

DEVELOPMENT OF BIPOLAR DISORDERS Bipolar disorders are much less common than depression. Around 3–4 percent of the population will experience a bipolar disorder in their lifetimes (Kessler & Wang, 2008). Whereas depression is more common in women, bipolar disorders are equally prevalent in women and men. Bipolar disorders emerge most commonly during late adolescence or early adulthood. Bipolar I disorder is typically diagnosed at an earlier age than bipolar II disorder.

There is a very strong genetic component to bipolar disorders (Belmaker & Agam, 2008). Twin studies reveal that for identical twins, both of them are three times more likely to have the disorder than are both fraternal twins (Nurnberger, Goldin, & Gershon, 1994). In the 1980s, the Amish community—a self-contained religious community centered largely in Pennsylvania—was involved in a genetic research study. The Amish were an ideal population for this sort of research because they keep good family history records, and few outsiders marry into the community. In addition, substance abuse is virtually nonexistent among Amish adults, so psychological disorders are less likely to be confused with it. The research results revealed that bipolar disorders ran in a limited number of families and that all of those afflicted had a similar genetic defect (Egeland et al., 1987).

Genetic research also suggests, however, that the hereditary nature of bipolar disorders is complex and not linked to just one gene. Current research focuses on identifying several genes that may be involved. In addition, it appears that in families with bipolar disorders, the disorders are more severe and appear at younger ages in successive generations (McInnis et al., 1993; Petronis & Kennedy, 1995). Research on this pattern may help reveal the genetics of the disorders, but the specific nature of the heritability of bipolar disorders remains to be discovered.

 13.2 CHECKPOINT: How Do People Experience Disorders of Emotion?

- Anxiety disorders are characterized by excessive anxiety in the absence of danger.

- Obsessive-compulsive disorder (OCD) involves repeated intrusive thoughts and compulsive behaviors that temporarily relieve the anxiety.

- Posttraumatic stress disorder (PTSD) is characterized by unwanted, recurring thoughts about the trauma, nightmares, and flashbacks.

- Depressive disorders include depressed mood that is severe (major depressive disorder) or mild to moderate (persistent depressive disorder).

- Bipolar disorder includes episodes of severe mania (bipolar I) or mild to moderate mania (bipolar II). In bipolar II, people also experience major depression.

13.3 How Do People Experience Disorders of Thought?

✐ LEARNING GOALS	📖 READING ACTIVITIES	LEARN
a. Remember the key terms about disorders of thought.	List all of the boldface words and write down their definitions.	
b. Analyze the five symptoms of schizophrenia.	Distinguish between the five symptoms of schizophrenia.	
c. Apply the types of delusions.	Describe three imaginary people who show symptoms of three types of delusions.	
d. Understand the factors that influence the onset of schizophrenia.	Summarize in your own words how genetic and environmental factors interact in the development of schizophrenia.	

As we have seen, many psychological disorders include impairments in people's emotions that influence how they think. For example, those with depression can have distorted thoughts about themselves or their futures. By contrast, the essence of *psychosis* is a break from reality in which the person has difficulty distinguishing what thoughts or perceptions are real versus what are imagined. The *DSM-5* category of schizophrenia spectrum and other psychotic disorders includes a number of conditions in which thought disturbances are the primary characteristic. People experiencing these disorders have extreme difficulty functioning in everyday life. In this section, we focus on the best-known psychotic disorder, schizophrenia.

Schizophrenia Is a Psychotic Disorder

The term *schizophrenia* literally means "splitting of the mind." The psychological disorder **schizophrenia** is characterized by a split between thought and emotion. According to current estimates, less than 1 percent of the population has schizophrenia (Tandon, Keshavan, & Nasrallah, 2008). The rates for men and women are similar (Saha, Chant, Welham, & McGrath, 2006).

For the person and for the family, schizophrenia may be the most devastating mental disorder. It is characterized by a combination of motor, cognitive, behavioral, and perceptual abnormalities. These abnormalities result in impaired social, personal, or vocational functioning or in some combination of these impairments. According to the *DSM-5*, to be diagnosed with schizophrenia a person has to have shown continuous signs of disturbances for at least 6 months. There are five major *DSM-5* symptoms for schizophrenia: (1) delusions, (2) hallucinations, (3) disorganized speech, (4) disorganized behavior, and (5) negative symptoms. A diagnosis of schizophrenia requires a person to show two or more of these symptoms. At least one of these has to be from among the first three symptoms listed above (i.e., delusions, hallucinations, and disorganized speech). By tradition, researchers tend to group these symptoms into two categories: **Positive symptoms** are excesses. They are positive not in the sense of being good or desirable, but in the sense of adding abnormal behaviors. As you will see, **negative symptoms** are deficits in functioning, such as apathy, lack of emotion, slowed speech, and slowed movement.

schizophrenia
A psychological disorder characterized by a split between thought and emotion where a person has difficulty distinguishing whether altered thoughts, perceptions, and conscious experiences are real versus what are imagined.

positive symptoms
Symptoms of schizophrenia that are marked by excesses in functioning, such as delusions, hallucinations, and disorganized speech or behavior.

negative symptoms
Symptoms of schizophrenia that are marked by deficits in functioning, such as apathy, lack of emotion, and slowed speech and movement.

delusions
False beliefs based on incorrect inferences about reality.

TABLE 13.5

Types of Delusions and Associated Beliefs Associated With Schizophrenia

Persecution	Belief that others are persecuting, spying on, or trying to harm them
Referential	Belief that objects, events, or other people have particular significance to them, such as a belief that a stop sign has a particular personal message for the person
Grandiose	Belief that they have great power, knowledge, or talent
Identity	Belief that they are someone else, such as Jesus Christ or the president of the United States
Guilt	Belief that they have committed a terrible sin
Control	Belief that their thoughts and behaviors are being controlled by external forces

DELUSIONS Delusions are positive symptoms (excess in function) most commonly associated with schizophrenia. Delusions are false beliefs that reflect breaks from reality (**Table 13.5**). Delusional people persist in their beliefs despite clear evidence to the contrary, because their cognitive processes misinform them about what is real and what is not. For example, in his 50s, the early 20th-century artist Louis Wain began to experience delusions of persecution and to have difficulty separating reality from fantasy. Wain was subsequently diagnosed with schizophrenia. Many people believe that changes in his art over time reflect periods where he was experiencing milder or more-severe symptoms (**Figure 13.22**).

Delusions are characteristic of schizophrenia in all cultures, but the type of delusion can be influenced by cultural factors. For instance, Tateyama and colleagues (1993) found that German and Japanese patients with schizophrenia had similar rates of *grandiose delusions,* believing themselves much more powerful and important than they really were. The two groups differed significantly, however, for other types of delusions. The German patients had delusions that involved guilt and sin, particularly as these concepts related to religion. By contrast, the Japanese patients showed beliefs that they were being slandered by others.

HALLUCINATIONS Hallucinations are another positive symptom commonly associated with schizophrenia. **Hallucinations** are perceptual disturbances that are experienced without an external source. Frequently auditory, they can also be visual, olfactory, or bodily. Auditory hallucinations are often accusatory voices that may tell the person he is evil or inept, or they may command him to do dangerous things. Sometimes the person hears a racket of sounds with voices intermingled.

The cause of hallucinations is unclear. Neuroimaging studies suggest that auditory hallucinations are associated with increased activation in brain areas that are activated when people without schizophrenia hear external sounds or are engaged in inner speech (Stein & Richardson, 1999). This finding has led to speculation that auditory hallucinations might be caused by a difficulty in distinguishing the inner speech of talking to oneself (inside their mind) from external sounds. To function in society, people with schizophrenia have to learn to ignore the voices in their heads, but doing so is extremely difficult and sometimes impossible.

FIGURE 13.22

Louis Wain's Paintings May Reveal Symptoms of Schizophrenia
According to some commentators, Wain painted his realistic but fanciful paintings when he was experiencing fewer symptoms of schizophrenia. In this view, the increasingly abstract, frenetic, and hostile feel of his work may reflect his worsening symptoms, including delusions of persecution and visual disturbances.

hallucinations
False sensory perceptions that are experienced without an external source.

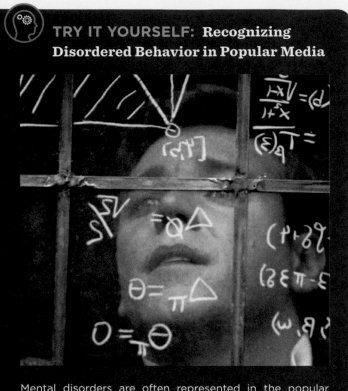

Mental disorders are often represented in the popular media, on television shows, and in the movies, but the characters do not always accurately represent the symptoms of those disorders. An exception to this general rule is the 2001 movie *A Beautiful Mind*, starring Russell Crowe as the real-life Princeton mathematics professor and Nobel laureate John Forbes Nash, who was diagnosed with schizophrenia. If you watch the movie, try to identify the positive and the negative symptoms of the disorder.

disorganized speech
Speaking in an incoherent way that involves frequently changing topics and saying strange or inappropriate things.

disorganized behavior
Acting in strange or unusual ways, including strange movement of limbs and inappropriate self-care, such as failing to dress properly or bathe.

DISORGANIZED SPEECH Another key positive symptom of schizophrenia is **disorganized speech.** The speech is disorganized in the sense that it is incoherent, failing to follow a normal conversational structure. It is very difficult or impossible to follow what people with schizophrenia are talking about because they frequently change topics, which is known as a *loosening of associations*. More-extreme cases involve *clang associations:* the stringing together of words that rhyme but have no other apparent link. People with schizophrenia may also display strange and inappropriate emotions while talking. Such strange speaking patterns make it very difficult for people with schizophrenia to communicate (Docherty, 2005).

DISORGANIZED BEHAVIOR A final common positive symptom of schizophrenia is **disorganized behavior.** In other words, people with schizophrenia often act strangely. They might wear multiple layers of clothing even on hot summer days, walk along muttering to themselves, alternate between anger and laughter, or pace and wring their hands as if extremely worried. They have problems performing many activities, which interferes with daily living.

NEGATIVE SYMPTOMS People with schizophrenia often avoid eye contact and seem apathetic. They do not express emotion even when discussing emotional subjects. Their speech is slowed, they say less than most people, and they use a monotonous tone of voice. Their speech may be characterized by long pauses before answering, failure to respond to a question, or inability to complete saying something after they start it. There is often a similar reduction in their behavior: Patients' movements may be slowed and their overall amount of movement reduced. They may engage in little initiation of behavior and have no interest in social participation. These negative symptoms, though less dramatic than delusions and hallucinations and other positive symptoms, can be equally serious and result in patients' becoming withdrawn and isolated. Negative symptoms are more common in men than in women (Raesaenen, Pakaslahti, Syvaelahti, Jones, & Isohanni, 2000).

DEVELOPMENT OF SCHIZOPHRENIA: BIOLOGICAL FACTORS The etiology of schizophrenia is not well understood. Early theories attributed this disorder to the patient's mother, who had simultaneously accepted and rejected the individual during childhood. Research has revealed, however, that the causes of the disorder are much more complex.

Schizophrenia runs in families, and genetics clearly plays a role in the development of the disorder (**Figure 13.23**). For instance, if one twin develops schizophrenia, the likelihood of the other twin's succumbing is almost 50 percent if the twins are identical but only 14 percent if the twins are fraternal. If one parent has schizophrenia, the risk of a child's developing the disorder is 13 percent. If both parents have schizophrenia, the risk jumps to almost 50 percent (Gottesman, 1991). Nevertheless, the genetic component of schizophrenia represents a predisposition rather than destiny. If schizophrenia were caused solely by genetics, the likelihood of both identical twins having the disorder would approach 100 percent.

Schizophrenia is primarily a brain disorder (Walker, Kestler, Bollini, & Hochman, 2004). As seen in brain imaging, the ventricles are enlarged in people with schizophrenia (**Figure 13.24**). In other words, there is actually less brain tissue, especially in the frontal lobes and medial temporal lobes. Some researchers have speculated, however, that schizophrenia is more likely a problem of connection between brain regions than the result of diminished or changed functions of any particular brain region (Walker et al., 2004).

One possibility is that schizophrenia results from abnormality in neurotransmitters. Since the 1950s, scientists have believed that dopamine may play an important role. Drugs that block dopamine activity decrease symptoms of schizophrenia, whereas drugs that increase the activity of dopamine neurons increase symptoms. Moreover, there is now evidence that a number of other neurotransmitter systems are involved.

If schizophrenia is a brain disorder, when do these brain abnormalities emerge? Schizophrenia is most often diagnosed when people are in their 20s or 30s, but it is hard to assess whether brain impairments actually occur earlier. There is evidence that some neurological signs of schizophrenia can be observed long before the disorder is diagnosed. Elaine Walker and colleagues (2004) have analyzed home movies taken by parents whose children later developed schizophrenia. Compared with their siblings, those who developed the disorder displayed unusual social behaviors, more-severe negative emotions, and motor disturbances. All of these differences often went unnoticed during the children's early years. Such studies suggest that schizophrenia develops over the life course but that obvious symptoms often emerge by late adolescence. Hints of future problems, however, may be evident even in young children.

DEVELOPMENT OF SCHIZOPHRENIA: ENVIRONMENTAL FACTORS

Because genetics do not account fully for the onset and severity of schizophrenia, other factors must also be at work. In those genetically at risk for schizophrenia, environmental stress seems to contribute to its development, a fact that is consistent with the diathesis-stress model described earlier in the chapter (Walker et al., 2004). One study looked at adopted children whose biological mothers were diagnosed with schizophrenia (Tienari et al., 1990, 1994). If the adoptive families were severely disturbed, 11 percent of the children developed schizophrenia and 41 percent had severe psychological disorders. If the adoptive families were psychologically healthy, none of the children developed psychosis. More generally, growing up in a dysfunctional family may increase the risk of developing schizophrenia for those who are genetically at risk (Tienari et al., 2004; **Figure 13.25a**). By contrast, without a genetic risk, a child has a low risk for developing schizophrenia, regardless of whether the family environment is dysfunctional or healthy (**Figure 13.25b**).

Some researchers have also theorized that the increased stress of urban environments can trigger the onset of the disorder, because being born or raised in an

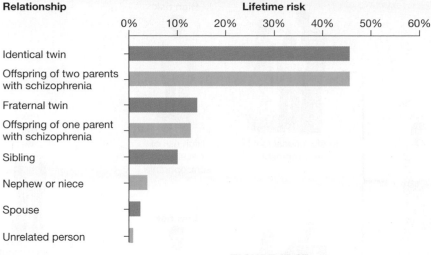

Relationship	Lifetime risk
Identical twin	
Offspring of two parents with schizophrenia	
Fraternal twin	
Offspring of one parent with schizophrenia	
Sibling	
Nephew or niece	
Spouse	
Unrelated person	

FIGURE 13.23

Genetics and Schizophrenia
The more closely related a person is to someone with schizophrenia, the more likely the person is to develop schizophrenia. This finding is evidence of at least a partially genetic basis for schizophrenia.

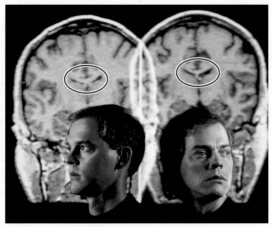

FIGURE 13.24

The Brains of Identical Twins, One of Whom Has Schizophrenia
The MRI scans of these identical twins show the smaller ventricles (these fluid-filled cavities are circled and appear dark in the image) in the brain of the twin without schizophrenia **(left)** versus the larger ventricles in the brain of the twin with schizophrenia **(right)**.

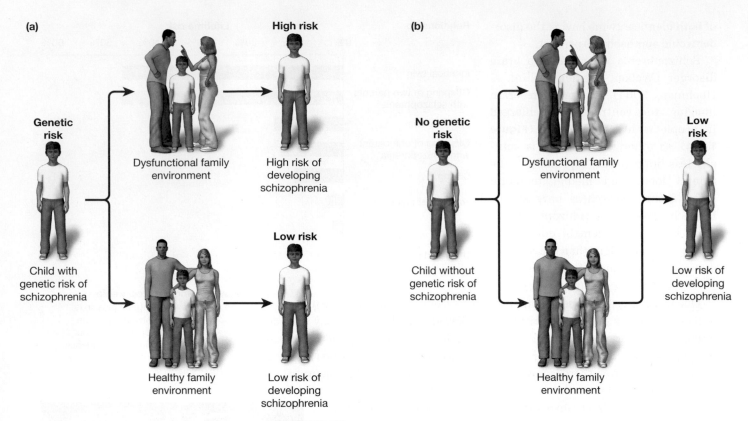

(a)

Genetic risk

Child with genetic risk of schizophrenia

Dysfunctional family environment → **High risk** — High risk of developing schizophrenia

Healthy family environment → **Low risk** — Low risk of developing schizophrenia

(b)

No genetic risk

Child without genetic risk of schizophrenia

Dysfunctional family environment

Healthy family environment

Low risk — Low risk of developing schizophrenia

FIGURE 13.25

Effects of Biology and Environment on Schizophrenia
(a) If a child has a genetic risk for schizophrenia and is raised in a dysfunctional family environment, that child will have a high risk of developing schizophrenia. But if that child is raised in a healthy family environment, that child will have a low risk of developing the disorder. **(b)** By contrast, if a child has no genetic risk of developing schizophrenia, the child will have a low risk of developing the disorder whether the child is raised in a dysfunctional or a healthy family environment.

urban area approximately doubles the risk of developing schizophrenia later in life (Torrey, 1999). Others have speculated that some kind of virus causes schizophrenia. If so, the close quarters of a big city increases the likelihood of the virus spreading. In support of the virus hypothesis, some researchers have reported finding antibodies in the blood of people with schizophrenia but not found in the blood of those without the disorder (Waltrip et al., 1997). According to the evidence, multiple factors may serve as triggers for the development of schizophrenia for those who are genetically susceptible.

 13.3 CHECKPOINT: How Do People Experience Disorders of Thought?

- Schizophrenia is diagnosed according to five criteria: delusions, hallucinations, disorganized speech, disorganized behavior, and negative symptoms.

- Schizophrenia is a genetically related disorder characterized by abnormal brain structures and processes.

- Environmental factors, such as the stress of dysfunctional family dynamics or urban environments, may trigger the onset of schizophrenia.

13.4 How Do People Experience Disorders of Self?

📖 **LEARNING GOALS**	✏️ **READING ACTIVITIES**	LEARN
a. Remember the key terms about personality disorders.	List all of the boldface words and write down their definitions.	
b. Apply the three clusters of personality disorders.	Describe how three imaginary people display the characteristics of three personality disorders, one from each group.	
c. Understand psychopathic tendencies.	Summarize in your own words how psychopathic tendencies could result in someone's being a murderer or a successful businessperson.	
d. Analyze the dissociative disorders.	Compare the similarities and differences in dissociative amnesia, dissociative fugue, and dissociative identity disorder.	

As we saw in Chapter 12, our personality reflects our unique response to our environment; it is part of our identity and our sense of self. Although we change somewhat over time, the ways we interact with the world and cope with events are fairly fixed by the end of adolescence. Some people's identities cause them to interact with the world in maladaptive and inflexible ways. When this style of interaction is long-lasting and causes problems in work and in social situations, it becomes a *personality disorder*. Although people with personality disorders do not hallucinate or experience radical mood swings, their ways of interacting with the world can have serious consequences for the individual, family and friends, and society.

Personality Disorders Are Maladaptive Ways of Relating to the World

The *DSM-5* divides personality disorders into three groups, as listed in **Table 13.6.** Disorders in the first group (Cluster A) are characterized by odd or eccentric behavior. People with *paranoid, schizoid,* and *schizotypal* personality disorders are often reclusive and suspicious. They have difficulty forming personal relationships because of their strange behavior and aloofness. As you might expect, people with personality disorders in this category show some similarities to people with schizophrenia, but their symptoms are far less severe.

Disorders in the second group (Cluster B) are characterized by dramatic, emotional, or erratic behaviors. *Antisocial, borderline, histrionic,* and *narcissistic* personality disorders make up this group. Borderline and antisocial personality disorders have been the focus of much research, so we consider them in more detail in the next section.

Disorders in the third group (Cluster C)—*avoidant, dependent,* and *obsessive-compulsive* personality disorders—are characterized by anxious or fearful behavior. These disorders share some characteristics of anxiety disorders such as social phobia or generalized anxiety disorder. However, personality disorders in this third group refer more to maladaptive ways of interacting with others and of responding to events. People with obsessive-compulsive disorder (OCD) have true obsessions

TABLE 13.6

Personality Disorders and Associated Characteristics

Cluster A: Odd or Eccentric Behavior	
Paranoid	Distrust; suspiciousness
Schizoid	Detachment from social relationships; restricted emotional expression
Schizotypal	Peculiarities of thought, appearance, and behavior that are disconcerting to others; acute discomfort in social relationships
Cluster B: Dramatic, Emotional, or Erratic Behavior	
Antisocial	Disregard for and violation of the rights of others
Borderline	Unstable moods, personal relationships, and self-image; impulsivity
Histrionic	Excessive emotionality; attention seeking
Narcissistic	Pattern of grandiosity; need for admiration; lack of empathy
Cluster C: Anxious or Fearful Behavior	
Avoidant	Social inhibition; feelings of inadequacy; easily hurt and embarrassed
Dependent	Submissive and clinging behavior; excessive need to be taken care of
Obsessive-compulsive	Perfectionistic; preoccupied with orderliness and control

SOURCE: Adapted from American Psychiatric Association (2013).

and compulsions, but people with obsessive-compulsive personality disorder do not. For instance, whereas a person with OCD may be obsessed with germs and have the compulsion to wash her hands, a person with an obsessive-compulsive personality disorder may be excessively neat and orderly. The person might always eat the same food at precisely the same time or perhaps read a newspaper in a particular order each time. People with OCD are often distressed by their rituals. By contrast, people with personality disorders view their behavior as problematic only when it interferes with their lives. For example, people with personality disorders may find it impossible to travel or to maintain relationships.

SYMPTOMS AND DEVELOPMENT OF BORDERLINE PERSONALITY DISORDER Borderline personality disorder is characterized by disturbances in identity, in emotional states, and in impulse control. This complex disorder was officially recognized as a diagnosis in 1980. The term *borderline* was initially used because people with these disorders were considered on the border between normal and psychotic (Knight, 1953). Approximately 1 percent to 2 percent of adults meet the criteria for borderline personality disorder, and the disorder is more than twice as common in women as in men (Lenzenweger et al., 2007).

People with borderline personality disorder seem to lack a strong sense of self. They cannot tolerate being alone and have an intense fear of abandonment. Because they desperately need an exclusive and dependent relationship with another person, they can be very manipulative in their attempts to control relationships. In addition to problems with identity, borderline individuals have affective disturbances. Emotional instability is a key feature. Episodes of depression, anxiety, anger, irritability, or some combination of these states can last from a few hours to a few days. Shifts from one mood to another usually occur for no obvious reason.

borderline personality disorder
A personality disorder characterized by disturbances in identity, in moods, and in impulse control.

antisocial personality disorder (APD)
A personality disorder marked by disregard for and violation of the rights of others and by lack of remorse.

The third key feature of borderline personality disorder is impulsivity, which may explain the much higher rate of the disorder in prisons than in the general population (Conn et al., 2010). Impulsivity can include sexual promiscuity, physical fighting, and binge eating and purging. Self-mutilation, such as cutting and burning of the skin, is commonly associated with this disorder, as is a high risk for suicide.

Borderline personality disorder may have an environmental component because of the strong relationship that exists between the disorder and trauma or abuse (Lieb, Zanarini, Schmahl, Linehan, & Bohus, 2004). Some studies have reported that 70 percent to 80 percent of patients with borderline personality disorder have experienced physical or sexual abuse or observed some kind of extreme violence. Other theories propose that borderline patients may have had caretakers who did not accept them or were unreliable or unavailable. The constant rejection and criticism made it difficult for the patients to learn to regulate their emotions and understand emotional reactions to events (Linehan, 1987). An alternative theory is that caregivers encouraged dependence, preventing the individuals in their charge from adequately developing a sense of self. As a result, the individuals became overly sensitive to others' reactions: If rejected by others, they reject themselves.

SYMPTOMS AND DEVELOPMENT OF ANTISOCIAL PERSONALITY DISORDER During the 1970s, a handsome and charismatic law student named Ted Bundy kidnapped, raped, and murdered 30 or more young women and girls and violated their bodies in appalling ways (**Figure 13.26**). Bundy's behavior is something most people are unable to understand. Even one of Bundy's defense attorneys described him as being heartless and evil. Bundy was eventually executed for his crimes.

According to the *DSM-5*, **antisocial personality disorder (APD)** is the diagnosis for individuals who behave in socially undesirable ways, such as breaking the law and being deceitful and irresponsible. People with APD are willing to take advantage of others and hurt them without showing any concern or remorse for their behavior. Instead, people with this disorder tend to be focused on pleasure, seeking immediate gratification of wants and needs with no thought about others. For example, such individuals could be superficially charming and rational, but they also could be insincere, unsocial, and incapable of love; lack insight; and be shameless. However, not all criminals can be described as having APD.

The term *psychopath* is used to refer to a disorder that is related, but not identical, to APD. People with psychopathic tendencies display more extreme behaviors than those with APD. They also tend to have other personality characteristics not found in those with APD, such as glibness, a grandiose sense of self-worth, shallow affect, and cunning or manipulativeness. They have no remorse, lie and cheat, and lack empathy. Their behavior is particularly dangerous because they can be extremely hard-hearted. For instance, one study of murderers found that those with psychopathic tendencies nearly always kill intentionally. They want to gain something, such as money, sex, or drugs. People without psychopathic tendencies are much more likely to commit murder impulsively, such as when provoked or angry (Woodworth & Porter, 2002). Because of this difference, psychopaths fit the stereotype of cold-blooded killers like Ted Bundy.

Ironically, people with psychopathic traits are often seen as charming and intelligent. For this reason, some psychopaths manage to be successful professionals and conceal the crimes they may commit. Their psychopathic traits may even provide advantages in some occupations, such as business and politics (**Figure 13.27**).

FIGURE 13.26
Ted Bundy
The convicted serial killer Ted Bundy is thought to have had antisocial personality disorder. As a result of this condition, he could be charming when trying to attract women, then lacking remorse for the atrocities he committed upon his victims.

FIGURE 13.27
American Psychopath
In the 2000 movie *American Psycho*, Christian Bale plays Patrick Bateman, who appears to be a suave man-about-town, a successful professional, and also a serial killer.

In the United States, about 1 percent to 4 percent of the population has APD (Compton, Conway, Stinson, Colliver, & Grant, 2005). Less common are people with this condition who also show more-extreme psychopathic traits (Lenzenweger et al., 2007). APD is much more common in men than in women. The disorder is most apparent in late adolescence and early adulthood, and it generally improves on its own around age 40 (Hare, McPherson, & Forth, 1988), at least for those without psychopathic traits.

Various physiological abnormalities may play a role in APD. In 1957, David Lykken reported that psychopaths do not become anxious when they are subjected to aversive stimuli. Lykken and other investigators have continued this line of research, showing that such individuals do not seem to feel fear or anxiety (Lykken, 1995). They do not learn from punishment, because they do not experience punishment as particularly unpleasant. This pattern of reduced psychophysiological response in the face of punishment also occurs in adolescents at risk for developing psychopathy (Fung et al., 2005).

Dissociative Disorders Involve Disruptions in One's Sense of Self

Sometimes we get lost in our thoughts or daydreams, even to the point of losing track of what is going on around us. Many of us have had the experience of forgetting what we are doing while in the middle of an action ("Why was I headed to the kitchen?"). When we wake up in an unfamiliar location, we may be disoriented for a short time and not know where we are. In other words, our thoughts and experiences can become dissociated, or split, from the external world.

Dissociative disorders are extreme versions of this phenomenon. These disorders involve disruptions of identity, memory, or conscious awareness (Kihlstrom, 2005). In all of them, some parts of memory are split off from a person's conscious awareness. Dissociative disorders are believed to result from extreme stress. That is, the person with a dissociative disorder has split off a traumatic event in order to protect his sense of self. Some researchers believe that people prone to dissociative disorders are also prone to PTSD (Cardeña & Carlson, 2011).

SYMPTOMS AND DEVELOPMENT OF DISSOCIATIVE AMNESIA In **dissociative amnesia,** a person forgets that an event happened or loses awareness of a large block of time. For example, the person with this disorder may suddenly lose memory for personal facts, including who she is and where she lives. These memory failures cannot be accounted for by ordinary forgetting (such as briefly forgetting where you parked your car) or by the effects of drugs or alcohol.

Consider the case of Dorothy Joudrie, from Calgary, Canada. In 1995, after suffering years of physical abuse from her husband, Joudrie shot him six times. Her husband survived, and he described her behavior during the shooting as very calm, as if she were detached from what she was doing. When the police arrived, however, Joudrie was extremely distraught. She had no memory of the shooting and told the police that she simply found her husband shot and lying on the garage floor, at which time she called for help. Joudrie was found not criminally responsible for her actions because of her dissociative state (Butcher, Mineka, & Hooley, 2007).

The rarest and most extreme form of dissociative amnesia is *dissociative fugue*. The disorder involves a loss of identity. In addition, it involves traveling to another location (the Latin word *fuga* means "flight") and sometimes assuming a new identity. The fugue state often ends suddenly, leaving the person unsure how he ended

dissociative amnesia
Mental disorder that involves disruptions of memory for personal facts or loss of conscious awareness for a period of time.

up in unfamiliar surroundings. Typically, he does not remember events that took place during the fugue state.

dissociative identity disorder (DID)
The occurrence of two or more distinct identities in the same individual.

SYMPTOMS AND DEVELOPMENT OF DISSOCIATIVE IDENTITY DISORDER An individual with **dissociative identity disorder (DID)** has developed two or more distinct identities. (The condition was formerly called *multiple personality disorder*.) Most people diagnosed with DID are women who report being severely abused as children. According to the most common theory, children who are likely to develop DID cope with abuse by pretending it is happening to someone else. They enter a trancelike state in which they separate their mental states from their physical bodies. Over time, this dissociated state takes on its own identity. Different identities develop to deal with different traumas.

Often the identities have periods of amnesia, and sometimes only one identity is aware of the others. Indeed, diagnosis often occurs only when a person has difficulty accounting for large chunks of his day. The separate identities usually differ substantially in gender, sexual orientation, age, language spoken, interests, physiological profiles, and patterns of brain activation (Reinders et al., 2003). Even their handwriting can differ (**Figure 13.28**).

Despite this evidence, many researchers remain skeptical about whether DID is a genuine mental disorder or even whether it exists at all (Kihlstrom, 2005). Moreover, some people may have hidden motives for claiming DID. A diagnosis of DID often occurs after someone has been accused of committing a crime, raising the possibility that the suspect is pretending to have multiple identities to avoid conviction. Other skeptics point to the sharp rise in reported cases as evidence that the disorder might not be real or that it is diagnosed far too often. Ultimately, how can we know whether a diagnosis of DID is valid? As we have said, most often there is no objective, definitive test for diagnosing a psychological disorder. It can be difficult to tell if a person is faking, has come to believe what a therapist said, or has a genuine mental disorder.

Identity 1

Identity 2

Identity 3

Identity 4

Identity 5

Identity 6

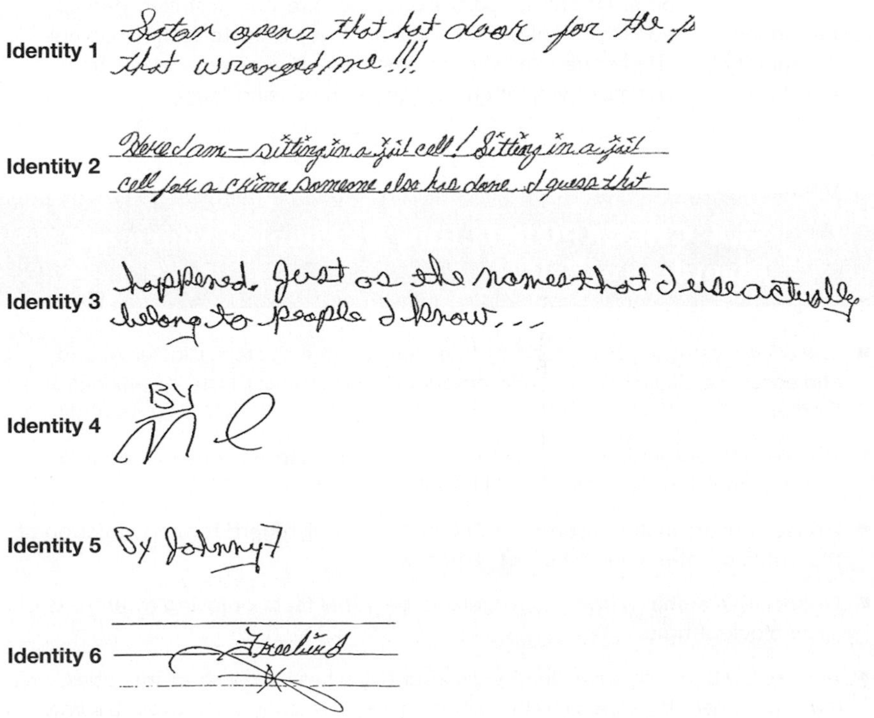

FIGURE 13.28

Handwriting Samples From a Person With Dissociative Identity Disorder When researchers studied 12 murderers diagnosed with DID, writing samples from 10 of the participants revealed markedly different handwriting in each of their identities. Here handwriting samples from one of the participants demonstrate the expression of several different identities.

James had been looking forward to Chapter 13 all semester. Before he started studying psychology, he thought the field was all about mental illness. He had enjoyed learning about the other aspects of thought and behavior that psychologists study, but now he was excited to explore the area that had first interested him.

Recently the news had been filled with stories about mental illness and violent crime. At least, mental illness appeared to be a major factor in so many terrible incidents. Jared Loughner, the man who shot Gabby Giffords and others in Arizona, had been identified as possibly mentally ill. James Holmes, the man who opened fire in a movie theater in Colorado, had been seeing a psychiatrist who had been worried about his behavior. Adam Lanza had shot children and teachers at an elementary school in Connecticut, and before this event his mother had voiced concerns about her son's mental health. *Are these isolated incidents?* James wondered. *Or is there scientific research that links mental illness and violent crime?*

When he did a Google search for "link between mental illness and violent crime," James got 137,000 hits. While many searches yield lots of "unscientific" results, most of what popped up was more legitimate: WebMD, universities, and .org Web sites (the suffix often indicates a not-for-profit or public-interest group). *Each one could provide good information.* James clicked on a link from the University of Washington. Rather than just being a link to a particular study, it was a "fact sheet" about mental illness and violence, presenting facts with research to support each claim. *That's helpful—a site that asks and answers the question with research, and the research references are even included! This looks like a site I should believe.*

The fact sheet explained that most violent crimes are not committed by people with mental illness: "The vast majority of people who are violent do not suffer from mental illness,"

it read. The fact sheet explained the other direction as well: "The contribution of people with mental illnesses to overall rates of violence is small." *So not only do most people who commit violent crimes not have mental illnesses, but most people with mental illness are not committing violent crimes.*

James also read that many people believe, as he had, that mental illness and violent crime go together. In fact, the number of people who believed in the link has been increasing. *Why would opinions about this supposed link be changing? Well, television might be one reason. Lots of shows—the news,* CSI—*hint that there's a link.* The fact sheet backed up this idea.

But to James, the biggest revelation was that a completely different link actually exists. Despite our mistaken perception that mentally ill people are more likely to commit violent crimes, people who are mentally ill are more likely to be *victims* of violent crime, such as rapes and muggings.

13.4 CHECKPOINT: How Do People Experience Disorders of Self?

- The *DSM-5* categorizes personality disorders in three clusters. Cluster A: odd and eccentric; Cluster B: dramatic, emotional, and erratic; Cluster C: anxious and fearful.

- People with borderline personality disorder lack a strong sense of identity and are very emotionally unstable and impulsive.

- Antisocial personality disorder (APD) includes a disregard for and violation of the rights of others and a lack of remorse.

- Dissociative amnesia involves forgetting personal facts or losing awareness of a large block of time.

- A person with dissociative identity disorder (DID) has two or more identities, which may have been developed by the person to help him cope with severe trauma.

13.5 What Disorders Affect Children?

LEARNING GOALS	✏️ READING ACTIVITIES LEARN
a. Remember the key terms about disorders affecting children.	List all of the boldface words and write down their definitions.
b. Apply the characteristics of one of the neurodevelopmental disorders.	Provide a description of a real or imaginary child who shows the symptoms of a specific learning disorder, intellectual disability, or communication or motor disorder.
c. Analyze the severity of autism spectrum disorder.	Differentiate the symptoms of severe autism spectrum disorder and the mild form of the disorder (Asperger's syndrome).
d. Apply the symptoms of attention-deficit/hyperactivity disorder (ADHD).	Provide a description of a real or imaginary child who shows the symptoms of ADHD.

In his classic text on the classification of mental disorders, published in 1883, Emil Kraepelin did not mention childhood disorders. The first edition of the *DSM*, published 70 years later, essentially considered children as small versions of adults and did not consider childhood disorders separately from adulthood disorders. The current version of the *DSM* describes a group of disorders that are most common in children as *neurodevelopmental disorders*. This category includes a wide range of disorders. Some—such as specific learning disorders and communication disorders, such as stuttering—affect only very specific areas of a child's world. Other conditions—such as autism spectrum disorder, attention-deficit/ hyperactivity disorder, and others listed in **Table 13.7**—affect every aspect of a child's life.

All of the neurodevelopmental disorders should be considered within the context of normal childhood development. Some symptoms of childhood psychological disorders are extreme examples of normal behavior or are actually normal behaviors for children at an earlier developmental stage than when they occur. For example, bed-wetting is normal for 2-year-olds but not for 10-year-olds. Other behaviors, however, deviate significantly from normal development. Here we consider autism spectrum disorder and attention-deficit/hyperactivity disorder as illustrations of childhood disorders.

Autism Spectrum Disorder Involves Social Deficits

Autism spectrum disorder is characterized by deficits in social interaction, by impaired communication, and by restricted, repetitive behavior and interests (Volkmar, Chawarska, & Klin, 2005). The disorder was first described in 1943, by the psychiatrist Leo Kanner. Struck by the profound isolation of some children, Kanner coined the term *early infantile autism.*

Approximately 3 to 6 children out of 1,000 show signs of autism spectrum disorder, and males outnumber females 3 to 1 (Muhle, Trentacoste, & Rapin, 2004). From 1991 to 1997, there was a dramatic increase—of 556 percent—in the number of children diagnosed with autism (Stokstad, 2001). This increase

autism spectrum disorder
A developmental disorder characterized by deficits in social interaction, by impaired communication, and by restricted, repetitive behavior and interests.

TABLE 13.7

Neurodevelopmental Disorders That Affect Children

DISORDER	DESCRIPTION	EXAMPLE
Intellectual disabilities	Deficits in intellectual functioning and in adaptive functioning that begin during childhood or adolescence	Emily was 5 years old and showed difficulty learning in a variety of areas. Her problems adapting to the demands of daily living suggested that she would need support both in school and functioning in life.
Communication disorders	Deficits in language, speech, or communications; for example, difficulty learning a language, stuttering, or failure to follow social rules for communication; symptoms begin in childhood	Although Julio was very intelligent, he had a hard time learning to speak as a child. As a teenager he still often made inappropriate responses in conversation, which affected his social life a lot.
Autism spectrum disorder	Persistent impairment in social interaction; unresponsiveness; impaired language, social, cognitive development; restricted, repetitive behavior; symptoms begin in early childhood	Annalise suddenly stopped speaking when she was 2 years old, stopped looking people in the eyes and responding to her name, and began to flap her arms repeatedly when upset.
Attention-deficit/hyperactivity disorder	Hyperactive, inattentive, and impulsive behavior that causes social or academic impairment; begins before age 12	Jacob fidgeted all the time at school, could not pay attention to the teacher or follow instructions to complete tasks, and often disrupted other students.
Specific learning disorder	Difficulty learning and using academic skills; for example, much lower performance in reading, mathematics, or writing than expected for age, education, intelligence; begins during school-age years	Darnell was in third grade, but even though he showed normal intelligence, his reading skills were closer to that of a child in first grade.
Motor disorders	Recurrent motor and/or vocal tics that cause marked distress or impairment or deficits in developing or being able to show coordinated motor skills; symptoms begin in childhood	Cathy is an adolescent who for several years has experienced uncontrollable muscle spasms, called tics, in her face and head.

SOURCE: Based on American Psychiatric Association (2013).

was likely due to a greater awareness of symptoms by parents and physicians and a willingness to apply the diagnosis to a wider array of behaviors (Rutter, 2005).

Autism spectrum disorder varies in severity, from mild social impairments to severe social and intellectual impairments. High-functioning autism is sometimes called *Asperger's syndrome,* named after the pediatrician who first described it. A child with Asperger's has normal intelligence but deficits in social interaction. These deficits reflect an underdeveloped theory of mind. As we discussed in Chapter 4, theory of mind is both the understanding that other people have mental states and the ability to predict their behavior accordingly.

SYMPTOMS OF AUTISM SPECTRUM DISORDER Children with a severe form of autism spectrum disorder are seemingly unaware of others. As babies, they do not smile at their caregivers, do not respond to vocalizations, and may actively reject physical contact with others. These children do not establish eye contact and do not use their gaze to gain or direct the attention of those around them. One group of researchers had participants view video footage of the first birthdays of children with autism to see if characteristics of autism spectrum disorder could be detected before the children were diagnosed (Osterling & Dawson, 1994). By considering only the number of times a child looked at another person's face, the participants were able to classify the children as being either autistic or not autistic with impressive accuracy (**Figure 13.29**).

Deficits in communication are a second characteristic of autism spectrum disorder. Children with autism show severe impairments in verbal and nonverbal communication. Even if they vocalize, it is often not because they are trying to communicate. Such deficits are evident by 14 months of age (Landa, Holman, & Garrett-Mayer, 2007).

A third set of deficits includes restricted, repetitive behaviors and interests. Though children with autism spectrum disorder seem not to notice people around them, they are acutely aware of their surroundings. Most children automatically pay attention to the social aspects of a situation, but those with autism may focus on seemingly trivial details (Klin, Jones, Schultz, & Volkmar, 2003; **Figure 13.30**).

Any changes in daily routine or in the placement of furniture or toys are very upsetting for children with autism spectrum disorder. Once they are upset, the children can become extremely agitated or throw tantrums. The play of children with severe autism spectrum disorder tends to be repetitive and obsessive, and they focus on the sensory aspects of objects. The children may smell and taste objects, or they may spin and flick them for visual stimulation. Other aspects of their behavior also tend to be repetitive and can include strange hand movements, body rocking, and hand flapping. Self-injury is common, and some children must be forcibly restrained to keep them from hurting themselves.

DEVELOPMENT OF AUTISM SPECTRUM DISORDER It is now well established that autism is the result of biological factors. For example, there is evidence for a genetic component to this disorder (Hyman, 2008). Although autism spectrum disorder is heritable, environmental or other factors are also important.

Research into the causes of autism also points to prenatal and/or early childhood events that may result in brain dysfunction. The brains of children with autism spectrum disorder grow unusually large during the first two years of life, and then growth slows until age 5 (Courchesne et al., 2007). The brains of children with autism spectrum disorder also do not develop normally during adolescence

(a)

(b)

FIGURE 13.29

Scenes From Videotapes of Children's Birthday Parties

(a) This child focused more on objects than on people. This child was later diagnosed with autism. **(b)** This child focused appropriately on objects and on people. The child developed normally.

Area focused on by a 2-year-old with autism.

FIGURE 13.30

Toddler With Autism Watching Television

This image from a 1994 study shows the television program being viewed by a 2-year-old with autism and the image of the child's eye as he watches the program **(top left)**. The circled area **(bottom right)** is where the child was looking when watching the television show. This pattern suggested that children with autism will focus on the unimportant details in the scene rather than on the social interaction.

attention-deficit/hyperactivity disorder (ADHD)
A disorder characterized by excessive activity or fidgeting, inattentiveness, and impulsivity.

(Amaral, Schumann, & Nordahl, 2008). Researchers are investigating genetic factors, such as gene mutations, and nongenetic factors that might explain this overgrowth/undergrowth pattern.

In addition, there is evidence that the brains of people with autism have faulty wiring in a large number of areas (Minshew & Williams, 2007). Some of those brain areas are associated with social thinking, and others might support attention to social aspects of the environment.

Attention-Deficit/Hyperactivity Disorder Is Common in Childhood

Consider a child who exhibits hyperactivity. At home, he might have difficulty remembering not to trail his dirty hand along the clean wall as he runs from the front door to the kitchen. While playing games with his peers, he might spontaneously change the rules. At school, he might make warbling noises or other strange sounds that inadvertently disturb anyone nearby. He might seem to have more than his share of accidents: for example, knocking over the tower his classmates are erecting or tripping over the television cord while chasing the family cat (Whalen, 1989).

SYMPTOMS OF ATTENTION-DEFICIT/HYPERACTIVITY DISORDER Symptoms such as these can seem humorous in the retelling, but the reality is a different story. Children with **attention-deficit/hyperactivity disorder (ADHD)** are overly active, inattentive, and impulsive. They need to have directions repeated and rules explained over and over. Although they are often friendly and talkative, these children can have trouble making and keeping friends because they miss subtle social cues and make unintentional social mistakes. Many of these symptoms are exaggerations of typical toddler behavior, and thus the line between normal and abnormal behavior is hard to draw. According to *DSM-5*, children must show symptoms before age 12 to be diagnosed with ADHD. The best available evidence for children in the United States is that 11 percent of boys and 4 percent of girls have ADHD (Bloom & Cohen, 2007).

DEVELOPMENT OF ADHD The causes of ADHD are unknown. One of the difficulties in pinpointing its etiology is that the behavioral profiles of children with ADHD vary, so the causes of the disorder most likely vary as well. Factors such as poor parenting and social disadvantage may contribute to the onset of symptoms, as is true for all psychological disorders. Still, ADHD clearly has a genetic component (Goodman & Stevenson, 1989; Sherman, McGue, & Iacono, 1997).

In an early imaging study, Alan Zametkin and colleagues (1990) found that adults who had been diagnosed with ADHD in childhood had reduced metabolism in brain regions involved in the self-regulation of motor functions and of attentional systems (**Figure 13.31**). These researchers theorized that the connection between the frontal lobes and the limbic system is impaired in ADHD patients. In fact, the symptoms of ADHD are similar to those seen in patients with frontal lobe damage: problems with planning, sustaining concentration, using feedback, and thinking flexibly. In other imaging studies of adolescents with ADHD, difficulty stopping motor responses was associated with abnormal activation of certain frontal regions (Schulz et al., 2004).

HAS IT HAPPENED TO YOU?

ADHD

Do you know a child who seems to "always be on the move"? Maybe he does silly things on impulse and can't seem to control himself. And he seems to not hear directions and reprimands to change his behavior. Many of us can see the characteristics of attention-deficit/hyperactivity disorder (ADHD) in children, or possibly adults, we know. This makes sense because it is one of the most commonly diagnosed disorders of childhood, and the symptoms continue into adulthood. With support, children can learn ways to reduce distractions, follow directions, and stay on task, which can reduce the effects of ADHD in adulthood. On the plus side, both children and adults with ADHD are often friendly and talkative, so they can be fun to be with—as long as they learn social rules and pay attention to subtle social cues.

ADHD ACROSS THE LIFE SPAN Children generally are not diagnosed with ADHD until they enter structured settings where they must conform to rules, get along with peers, and sit in their seats for long periods. In the past, these things happened when children entered school, between ages 5 and 7. Now, with more structured day care settings, the demands on children to conform are occurring much earlier.

According to longitudinal studies, children do not outgrow ADHD by the time they enter adulthood (McGough & Barkley, 2004). The *DSM-5* recognizes that many of the symptoms of ADHD continue well into adulthood. Adults with ADHD symptoms, about 4 percent of the population (Kessler et al., 2006), may struggle academically and vocationally. They generally reach a lower-than-expected socioeconomic level and change jobs more frequently than other adults (Bellak & Black, 1992; Mannuzza et al., 1991). At the same time, many adults with ADHD learn how to adapt to their condition, such as by reducing distractions while they work (**Figure 13.32**).

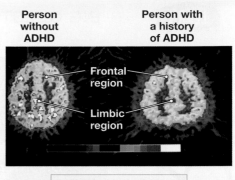

Person without ADHD   Person with a history of ADHD

Frontal region

Limbic region

Red and white indicate the higher levels of activation.

FIGURE 13.31

ADHD and the Brain
The brain image of a person without ADHD **(left)** shows greater activation in the frontal and limbic regions (see red and white areas). By contrast, the brain image of a person with ADHD **(right)** shows less overall activation (less red and white), especially in the frontal and limbic regions.

FIGURE 13.32

Living with ADHD
Paula Luper, of North Carolina, was diagnosed with ADHD in elementary school. Here, as a senior in high school, she is taking a quiz in the teachers' lounge to avoid being distracted.

 13.5 CHECKPOINT: What Disorders Affect Children?

 LEARN

- There are six neurodevelopmental disorders that affect children.

- Autism spectrum disorder is marked by impaired social functioning, poor communication, and restricted, repetitive behavior and interests. Autism has both genetic and environmental causes.

- Asperger's syndrome, a mild form of autism, is characterized by similar impairments but normal intellectual capacities.

- Children with attention-deficit/hyperactivity disorder (ADHD) are overactive, inattentive, and impulsive. Environmental factors, brain function, and genetics all contribute to ADHD.

BIG PICTURE

13.1
What Is a Psychological Disorder?

a. Remember the key terms related to psychological disorders.

b. Apply the idea of disordered thoughts, emotions, and behavior to real life.

c. Apply the diathesis-stress model to the onset of psychological disorders.

d. Understand the classification systems for psychological disorders.

13.2
How Do People Experience Disorders of Emotion?

a. Remember the key terms about disorders of emotion.

b. Apply the anxiety disorders to several fictional people.

c. Analyze the symptoms of obsessive-compulsive disorder (OCD).

d. Apply depressive and bipolar disorders.

13.3
How Do People Experience Disorders of Thought?

a. Remember the key terms about disorders of thought.

b. Analyze the five symptoms of schizophrenia.

c. Apply the types of delusions.

d. Understand the factors that influence the onset of schizophrenia.

13.4
How Do People Experience Disorders of Self?

a. Remember the key terms about personality disorders.

b. Apply the three clusters of personality disorders.

c. Understand psychopathic tendencies.

d. Analyze the dissociative disorders.

13.5
What Disorders Affect Children?

a. Remember the key terms about disorders affecting children.

b. Apply the characteristics of one of the neurodevelopmental disorders.

c. Analyze the severity of autism spectrum disorder.

d. Apply the symptoms of attention-deficit/hyperactivity disorder (ADHD).

KEY TERMS

CHECKPOINT

psychopathology
etiology
diathesis-stress model

- People with psychological disorders have emotions, thoughts, and/or behaviors that impair their lives.

- The diathesis-stress model suggests that psychological disorders arise from vulnerability paired with stressful circumstances. Psychological disorders also may arise from biopsychosocial factors.

- Assessment is the process of examining mental functions and actions to classify symptoms into categories.

- The *DSM-5* categorizes symptoms into one or more of 19 major psychological disorders, which allows for diagnosis and treatment.

phobia
generalized anxiety disorder
panic disorder
agoraphobia
obsessive-compulsive disorder (OCD)
posttraumatic stress disorder (PTSD)
major depressive disorder
persistent depressive disorder
bipolar I disorder
bipolar II disorder

- Anxiety disorders are characterized by excessive anxiety in the absence of danger.

- Obsessive-compulsive disorder (OCD) involves repeated intrusive thoughts and compulsive behaviors that temporarily relieve the anxiety.

- Posttraumatic stress disorder (PTSD) is characterized by unwanted, recurring thoughts about the trauma, nightmares, and flashbacks.

- Depressive disorders include depressed mood that is severe (major depressive disorder) or mild to moderate (persistent depressive disorder).

- Bipolar disorder includes episodes of severe mania (bipolar I) or mild to moderate mania (bipolar II). In bipolar II, people also experience major depression.

schizophrenia
positive symptoms
negative symptoms
delusions
hallucinations
disorganized speech
disorganized behavior

- Schizophrenia is diagnosed according to five criteria: delusions, hallucinations, disorganized speech, disorganized behavior, and negative symptoms.

- Schizophrenia is a genetically related disorder characterized by abnormal brain structures and processes.

- Environmental factors, such as the stress of dysfunctional family dynamics or urban environments, may trigger the onset of schizophrenia.

borderline personality disorder
antisocial personality disorder (APD)
dissociative amnesia
dissociative identity disorder (DID)

- The *DSM-5* categorizes personality disorders in three clusters. Cluster A: odd and eccentric; Cluster B: dramatic, emotional, and erratic; Cluster C: anxious and fearful.

- People with borderline personality disorder lack a strong sense of identity and are very emotionally unstable and impulsive.

- Antisocial personality disorder (APD) includes a disregard for and violation

of the rights of others and a lack of remorse.

- Dissociative amnesia involves forgetting personal facts or losing awareness of a large block of time.

- A person with dissociative identity disorder (DID) has two or more identities, which may have been developed by the person to help him cope with severe trauma.

autism spectrum disorder
attention-deficit/hyperactivity disorder (ADHD)

- There are six neurodevelopmental disorders that affect children.

- Autism spectrum disorder is marked by impaired social functioning, poor communication, and restricted, repetitive behavior and interests. Autism has both genetic and environmental causes.

- Asperger's syndrome, a mild form of autism, is characterized by similar impairments but normal intellectual capacities.

- Children with attention-deficit/ hyperactivity disorder (ADHD) are overactive, inattentive, and impulsive. Environmental factors, brain function, and genetics all contribute to ADHD.

For a self-quiz on this chapter, go to the back of the book and find Appendix B: Quizzes.

14 Psychological Treatments

WHEN DENNIS WAS IN COLLEGE, he often "choked" on exams. When he entered a classroom on exam day, his palms would sweat, his mouth would get dry, and his breathing would become rapid. Some professors were sympathetic, but Dennis's grades suffered. He was placed on academic probation. He ended up leaving college early and taking a job in sales. Dennis's problems with anxiety continued, although their intensity varied. He coped largely by avoiding any situation that made him anxious, such as anywhere that involved crowds.

One day, Dennis was shopping in a mall with his fiancée. He suddenly felt very sick. His hands began to shake, his vision became blurred, and he felt a great deal of pressure in his chest. He started gasping and felt weak all over. Combined with all of this, he had a feeling of overwhelming terror. Without saying what was happening, he ran from the store. He got into the car, where he tried to calm down.

BIG QUESTIONS

FIGURE 14.1

Panic Attacks

For Dennis, the anxiety caused by being in a crowd eventually brought on panic attacks. During these attacks, he felt overwhelming terror along with physical symptoms such as extreme shakiness. Luckily for Dennis and people like him, getting treatment from the right type of provider can help them overcome their anxiety and eliminate panic attacks.

Later, Dennis explained to his fiancée what had happened. He revealed that he had experienced this sort of attack before, so he usually avoided shopping malls and other large, crowded places. At his fiancée's urging, Dennis agreed to see a clinical psychologist.

During his first several treatment sessions, Dennis downplayed his problems. After all, he wasn't "crazy"! But after a few sessions, it became clear that he had a long history of anxiety problems, such as choking on exams. Once Dennis had revealed this history, the therapist explained that Dennis was experiencing panic attacks (**Figure 14.1**).

The therapist believed Dennis's problems were the result of vulnerability to stress combined with thoughts and behaviors that made the anxiety worse. The first step in his therapy was relaxation training. This approach would give Dennis a strategy to use when he became anxious and tense. The next step was to change his maladaptive thought patterns, which interfered with his daily functioning. With his therapist's help, Dennis came to recognize that situations that made him feel anxious might be difficult. Even so, he would be able to manage them.

The final phase of treatment was to address Dennis's avoidance of situations that he associated with panic attacks. First, Dennis and his therapist constructed a list of increasingly stressful situations. Then Dennis exposed himself to them gradually, using relaxation techniques as necessary to control his anxiety.

After six months, Dennis was able to stop his treatment. His anxiety levels were greatly reduced. He was able to get himself to relax when he did become tense. In addition, he had not experienced a panic attack during the time of his treatment and was no longer avoiding situations he had once found stressful (Oltmanns, Martin, Neale, & Davison, 2009). Dennis would always need to make an effort to reduce his anxiety. But with the help he received from psychological treatment, he knew how to handle his anxiety. Now he and his future wife could enjoy their lives together.

Many people have experienced anxiety. But sometimes anxiety interferes with carrying on your life, as it did with Dennis. At that point, it's time to get professional help. This chapter explores the basic principles of therapy. It also describes the various treatment approaches to specific disorders.

14.1 How Are Psychological Disorders Treated?

📖 LEARNING GOALS	✏️ READING ACTIVITIES	**LEARN**
a. Remember the key terms about treatment of psychological disorders.	List all of the boldface words and write down their definitions.	
b. Understand the different forms of psychotherapy.	Describe in your own words the six main approaches to psychotherapy.	
c. Understand the types of psychotropic medications.	Compare the differences between the five main classes of psychotropic medications.	
d. Apply information about mental health practitioners.	Describe two people seeking help for mental illness or life problems and indicate what type of treatment provider might be most appropriate to help each person.	

There are no instant cures for psychological disorders. As in Dennis's situation, disorders need to be managed over time through treatment that helps reduce symptoms so people can function well in their daily lives. This approach includes a continuous cycle of assessment, diagnosis, and treatment, followed by ongoing assessment and continued treatment. Unfortunately, even though psychological disorders are very common, many people who need help do not seek treatment.

When people overcome the barriers to seeking help, many forms of treatment are available. In this section, you will learn about the three main approaches used to treat disorders: psychotherapy, psychotropic medications, and alternative treatments. In the remaining sections of this chapter, you will also learn that most psychological disorders can be treated in more than one way. The choice of treatment depends on the type and severity of symptoms as well as on the specific diagnosis. However, one particular method is often more successful than others for a specific disorder.

Psychotherapy Is Based on Psychological Principles

The name for any formal psychological treatment aimed at changing thoughts and behavior is **psychotherapy.** The particular techniques used may depend on the practitioner's training, but all forms of psychotherapy involve interactions between practitioner and client. These interactions are critical in helping clients understand their symptoms and problems as well as providing solutions for those symptoms and problems. As a result, one especially important factor in the outcome of therapy is the relationship between the therapist and the client. A good relationship can provide hope that help will be received (Miller, 2000; Talley, Strupp, & Morey, 1990).

Therapists generally use psychotherapy to change their clients' patterns of thought or behavior. The methods used to bring about such changes can differ dramatically, however. One researcher estimated that more than 400 approaches to treatment are available (Kazdin, 1994). Many therapists follow an *eclectic* approach. That is, they use a variety of techniques that seem appropriate for a given client. The following discussion highlights the most common approaches to psychotherapy, which are summarized in **Table 14.1.**

PSYCHODYNAMIC THERAPY One of the first people to develop treatments for psychological disorders was Sigmund Freud. Along with Josef Breuer, Freud pioneered the method of *psychoanalysis.* This method was based on the idea that psychological disorders were caused by prior experiences, particularly early traumatic experiences.

Freud's psychoanalytic treatment involved identifying unconscious conflicts in feelings and drives that, he believed, gave rise to maladaptive thoughts and behaviors. Techniques included *free association* and *dream analysis.* In free association, the client would say whatever came to mind and the therapist would look for signs of unconscious conflicts, especially where the client appeared resistant to discussing certain topics. In dream analysis, the therapist would interpret the hidden meaning of the client's dreams. In early forms of psychoanalysis, the client would lie on a couch while the therapist sat out of view (**Figure 14.2**). This method

FIGURE 14.2
Psychodynamic Therapy Aims to Resolve Unconscious Conflicts
As part of the treatment process of psychoanalysis, Freud sat behind his desk (partly visible in the lower left corner). His clients would lie on the couch, facing away from him. Through free association, dream analysis, and other techniques, Freud worked to help the client become aware of unconscious conflicts that were causing distress.

psychotherapy
Treatment for psychological disorders where a therapist works with clients to help them understand their problems and work toward solutions.

TABLE 14.1

Six Approaches to Psychotherapy

APPROACH	THERAPY GOALS	THERAPY METHODS
Psychodynamic therapy	Help clients become aware of unconscious conflicts and defense mechanisms	Psychoanalysis with free association and dream analysis
Humanistic therapy	Help clients fulfill their potential for personal growth	Client-centered therapy with active listening and unconditional positive regard
Behavior therapy	Help clients replace harmful behaviors with beneficial ones	Behavior modification, including rewards and punishments, token economies, social skills training, modeling; may also use cognitive-behavioral therapy
Cognitive therapy	Help clients eliminate harmful thought patterns and replace them with positive ones	Cognitive therapy that includes cognitive restructuring and/or rational-emotive therapy; also can use cognitive-behavioral therapy
Group therapy	Provide support while also improving social skills in a cost-effective manner	Often uses an eclectic mix of therapy approaches
Family therapy	Heal family relationships	Systems approach; often uses an eclectic mix of therapy approaches

psychodynamic therapy
Treatment for psychological disorders where a therapist works with clients to help them become aware of how their unconscious processes may be causing conflict and impairing daily functioning.

humanistic therapy
Treatment for psychological disorders where a therapist works with clients to help them develop their full potential for personal growth through greater self-understanding.

was meant to reduce the client's inhibitions and allow freer access to unconscious thought processes.

The general goal of psychoanalysis is to increase the client's awareness of his own unconscious psychological processes and how these processes affect daily functioning. By gaining this understanding, the client is freed from these unconscious influences. According to psychoanalysis, the client's symptoms diminish as a result of reducing unconscious conflicts.

Psychotherapists later revised some of Freud's ideas and developed a number of adaptations, known collectively as **psychodynamic therapy.** In using the psychodynamic approach, a therapist aims to help a client examine her unconscious needs, motives, and defenses. The resulting insight is meant to help the client understand why she is distressed. Most supporters of the psychodynamic perspective today continue to embrace Freud's "talking therapy." They have replaced the couch with a chair, and the talking tends to be more conversational.

During the past few decades, the use of psychodynamic therapy has become increasingly controversial. Traditional psychodynamic therapy is expensive and time-consuming, sometimes continuing for many years. There is some evidence that this therapy has promise for certain disorders, such as borderline personality disorder (Gibbons, Crits-Chistoph, & Hearon, 2008). There is only weak evidence, however, for its effectiveness in treating most psychological disorders.

HUMANISTIC THERAPY As we saw in Chapter 12, the humanistic approach to personality emphasizes personal experience and the individual's belief systems. The goal of **humanistic therapy** is to treat the person as a whole. In other words, the person is not just a collection of behaviors or a storehouse of repressed thoughts.

One of the best-known humanistic therapies is *client-centered therapy*. This approach was developed by the psychologist Carl Rogers. Client-centered

FIGURE 14.3
Humanistic Therapy Aims to Help People Fulfill Their Potential
Carl Rogers founded the form of humanistic therapy called client-centered therapy. Here, Rogers leads a group therapy session, demonstrating the importance of a safe and comforting environment in the pursuit of greater self-understanding.

therapy encourages people to fulfill their potential for personal growth through greater self-understanding. One key ingredient of client-centered therapy is creation of a safe and comforting setting for clients to access their true feelings. Another key ingredient is *active listening*. The therapist listens attentively to the client, repeats the client's concerns to help her clarify her feelings, and asks for further clarification when necessary (**Figure 14.3**). Therapists strive to be empathic, to take the client's perspective, and to accept the client through *unconditional positive regard*. The therapist does not direct the client's behavior or pass judgment on his actions or thoughts. Instead, the therapist helps the client focus on his subjective experience. Relatively few practitioners follow the principles of humanistic theory strictly. But in establishing a good therapeutic relationship between therapist and client, many practitioners use techniques advocated by Rogers.

BEHAVIOR AND COGNITIVE THERAPIES Many of the most successful therapies involve trying to change a client's cognition and behavior directly. Recall that psychodynamic therapies consider maladaptive behavior the result of an underlying problem. By contrast, behavior and cognitive therapies treat the thoughts and behaviors as the problems. For example, the therapist is not particularly interested in *why* someone has developed a fear of elevators. Instead, the therapist targets the client's thoughts and behaviors as a way of helping her overcome the fear.

FIGURE 14.4
Behavior Therapy Helps People Learn Desired Behaviors
A person can use operant conditioning as a form of behavior therapy. For example, someone who bites his nails can snap a rubber band on his finger or wrist when he performs this behavior. Even this small punishment will decrease the behavior.

The main idea behind **behavior therapy** is that behavior is learned and so it can be unlearned through the use of classical and operant conditioning (**Figure 14.4**). As discussed in Chapter 6, behavior modification is based on operant conditioning. It is a method of helping people to learn desired behaviors and unlearn unwanted behaviors. Desired behaviors are reinforced (reinforcers might include small treats or praise). Unwanted behaviors are ignored or punished (punishments might include groundings, time-outs, or the administration of unpleasant tastes). Many treatment centers use *token economies*. Through these systems, people earn tokens for good behavior and can trade the tokens for rewards or privileges. This technique also increases a person's likelihood of engaging in a desired behavior.

For a desired behavior to be rewarded, however, the client first must exhibit the behavior. A therapist can use *social skills training* to elicit desired behavior. A client who has particular interpersonal difficulties, such as with initiating a conversation, can learn appropriate ways to act in specific social situations. The first step is often *modeling*. Here, the therapist acts out an appropriate behavior. Recall from Chapter 6 that we learn many behaviors by watching others perform them. In modeling, the client is encouraged to imitate the displayed behavior, rehearse it in therapy, and later use the learned behavior in real-world situations. The successful

behavior therapy
Treatment for psychological disorders where a therapist works with clients to help them unlearn learned behaviors that negatively affect their functioning.

cognitive therapy
Treatment for psychological disorders where a therapist works with clients to help them change distorted thought patterns that produce maladaptive behaviors and emotions.

Maladaptive pattern

"My boss yelled at me." → "I'm worthless." → Depression

After cognitive restructuring

"My boss yelled at me." → "My boss was having a bad day." → No depression

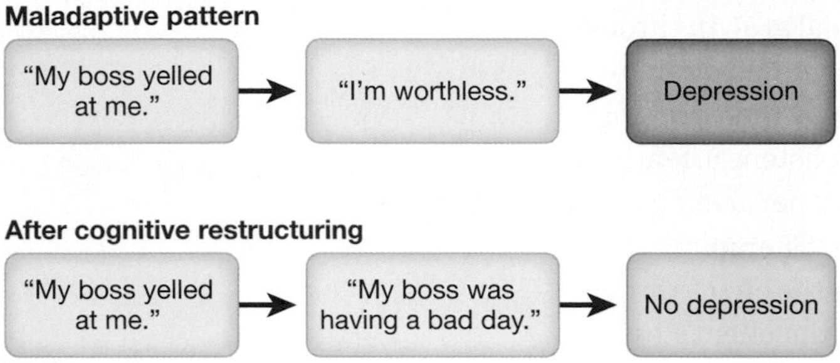

FIGURE 14.5
Cognitive Therapy Helps Change Negative Thought Patterns
A therapist can use cognitive restructuring to help a client learn to replace maladaptive thought patterns with more-realistic, positive ones.

cognitive-behavioral therapy (CBT)
Treatment for psychological disorders where a therapist incorporates techniques from cognitive therapy and behavior therapy to correct faulty thinking and maladaptive behaviors.

use of newly acquired social skills is itself rewarding and encourages the continued use of those skills.

Cognitive therapy is based on the theory that distorted thoughts can produce maladaptive behaviors and emotions. Thus treatment strategies that modify the distorted thought patterns should eliminate the maladaptive behaviors and emotions. Various approaches to cognitive therapy have been proposed. For example, Aaron Beck has advocated *cognitive restructuring*. Through this approach, a clinician seeks to help a client recognize maladaptive thought patterns and replace them with ways of viewing the world that are more in tune with reality (**Figure 14.5**). Albert Ellis, another major thinker in this area, introduced *rational-emotive therapy*. In this approach, the therapist acts as a teacher, explaining the client's errors in thinking and demonstrating more-adaptive ways to think and behave. Although both of these therapies are considered to be cognitive because they primarily target the client's maladaptive thoughts, they also include a behavioral component to help the client change her actions.

Cognitive-behavioral therapy (CBT) incorporates techniques from both cognitive therapy and behavior therapy. CBT tries to correct the client's faulty cognitions and train him to engage in new behaviors. Suppose the client has social anxiety disorder (social phobia)—a fear of being viewed negatively by others. The therapist will encourage the client to examine other people's reactions to him and understand how he might be wrong about how other people view him. At the same time, the therapist will teach the client how to change his behavior. CBT is perhaps the most widely used version of psychotherapy. It is one of the most effective therapies for many types of psychological disorders, especially anxiety disorders and mood disorders (Deacon & Abramowitz, 2004; Hollon, Thase, & Markowitz, 2002).

GROUP THERAPY In the mid-twentieth century, because of the many stresses related to World War II, many people needed therapy. But there were not enough therapists available to treat them. As a result, the idea of treating people in groups became popular. This form of treatment is called *group therapy*. Therapists came to realize that in some instances, group therapy offers advantages over individual therapy. The most obvious benefit is cost. Group therapy is often much less expensive than individual treatment. Because it is less expensive, it is available to more people. In addition, the group setting gives people an opportunity to improve their social skills and learn from each other's experiences.

Group therapies vary widely in the types of clients enrolled in the group, the duration of treatment, the theoretical perspective of the therapist running the group, and the group size (some practitioners believe the ideal number is around eight clients). Many groups are organized around a particular type of problem (e.g., sexual abuse) or a particular type of client (e.g., adolescents). Many groups continue over long periods, during which some members leave the group and others join it at various intervals.

Depending on the therapist's preferred treatment approach, the group may be highly structured. Or, it may be more loosely organized to encourage open discussion. For example, behavior and cognitive-behavioral groups usually are highly structured. They have specific goals and techniques designed to modify the thought and behavior patterns of group members. This type of group has been effective for disorders such as bulimia and obsessive-compulsive disorder. The social support that group members can provide each other is one of the most helpful aspects of this type of therapy. As a result, group therapy is often used in combination with individual psychotherapy.

FAMILY THERAPY When a client is being treated for a psychological disorder, the therapy she receives is of course an important element. But the client's family often plays an almost equally important role, and therefore family therapy attempts to include all family members in the process of therapy (**Figure 14.6**). According to a *systems approach,* an individual is part of a larger context. Any change in individual behavior will affect the whole system. This effect is often easiest to see within families. Each person in a family plays a particular role and interacts with the other members in specific ways. Over the course of therapy, the way the individual thinks, behaves, and interacts with others may change. Such changes can greatly affect the family dynamics. For instance, an alcoholic who gives up drinking may start to criticize other family members when they drink. In turn, the family members might provide less support for the client's continuing to avoid alcohol. After all, if the family members do not have drinking problems, they might resent being criticized. If they do have drinking problems, they might be irritated by the comments because they do not want to give up drinking.

FIGURE 14.6
Family Therapy Heals Relationships
A person with a psychological disorder is part of a larger context. To see the person within at least part of that context, many practitioners take a systems approach to treatment and include family members in therapy.

Biological Therapies Are Effective for Certain Disorders

The psychotherapies we have looked at so far are based on the idea that psychological disorders arise from cognition and behavior. **Biological therapy,** in contrast, is based on the notion that psychological disorders result from abnormalities in bodily processes, so treatment must address these physical problems. Accordingly, biological therapies reflect medical approaches to illness and to disease.

PSYCHOTROPIC MEDICATIONS For some psychological disorders, drugs have proven to offer effective treatment. Their use is based on the assumption that psychological disorders result from imbalances in specific neurotransmitters or from improperly functioning receptors for those neurotransmitters. Drugs that affect mental processes are called **psychotropic medications.** They act by changing brain neurochemistry, for example, either by inhibiting action potentials or by altering how neurotransmitters work in the brain (see Table 2.1) to affect thoughts, emotions, and behavior.

Most psychotropic medications fall into five categories: *anti-anxiety drugs, antidepressants, mood stabilizers, antipsychotics,* and *stimulants*. These medications are generally used to treat specific disorders (see **Table 14.2**). Note, however, that drugs from one category are sometimes used to treat a disorder from another category, such as when antidepressant drugs are used to treat anxiety. One reason for this approach is comorbidity. For example, as discussed in Chapter 13, a substantial number of people experiencing depression also meet diagnostic criteria for an anxiety disorder. Another reason is that in most cases, there is not enough evidence about why a particular drug is effective in reducing symptoms of a psychological disorder. Many questions remain about how brain chemistry is related to psychological disorders, and many drug treatments have been based on trial-and-error clinical trials in which different drugs have been tried to see if they reduce symptoms. In later sections of the chapter, we go into greater detail about how some of these drugs are effective in treating specific disorders.

ALTERNATIVE TREATMENTS FOR EXTREME CASES Unfortunately, not all people experiencing psychological disorders are treated successfully with

biological therapy
Treatment for psychological disorders that is based on medical approaches to illness and to disease.

psychotropic medications
Drugs that affect mental processes and that can be used to treat psychological disorders.

TABLE 14.2

Five Classes of Psychotropic Medications

DRUG CLASSIFICATION	TREATMENT PROVIDED	DRUG TYPE	SIDE EFFECTS	DRUG BRAND NAMES
Anti-anxiety drugs	Temporary sedative, calming effect	Minor tranquilizers	Drowsiness, addiction	• Valium • Xanax • Ativan
Antidepressant drugs	Increase positive mood; reduce emotionality, impulsiveness, and arousal	Selective serotonin reuptake inhibitors (SSRIs)	Sexual dysfunction, nausea, nervousness, weight gain	• Prozac • Paxil • Zoloft
		Tricyclics	Weight gain, dizziness, sexual and digestive problems	• Anafranil • Tofranil • Elavil
Mood stabilizer drugs	Help even out moods, especially manic episodes	Mineral	Blunting of positive affect	• Lithium
Antipsychotic drugs	Reduce positive symptoms (delusions, hallucinations, disorganized speech and behavior)	Conventional antipsychotics (early antipsychotics)	Tardive dyskinesia, seizures, lethargy	• Thorazine • Haldol
	Reduce positive and some negative symptoms (lethargy, lack of emotion)	Atypical antipsychotics (recent antipsychotics)	Potentially fatal loss of white blood cells, seizures, heart rate problems, weight gain, Type 2 diabetes	• Clozaril • Risperdal • Zyprexa
Stimulants	Decrease hyperactivity, distractibility; increase attention, concentration	Methylphenidate	Insomnia, reduced appetite, body twitches, temporary suppression of growth	• Ritalin
		Amphetamine	Insomnia, nausea, weight loss, vomiting, nervousness	• Adderall

electroconvulsive therapy (ECT)
Treatment for psychological disorders that involves administering a strong electrical current to the client's brain to produce a seizure; ECT is effective in some cases of severe depression.

FIGURE 14.7
Electroconvulsive Therapy Can Relieve Depression
A woman being prepared for ECT has a soft object placed between her teeth to prevent her from hurting her tongue. ECT is most commonly used to treat severe depression that has not been responsive to medication or psychotherapy.

psychotherapy, medication, or a combination of both. In extreme treatment-resistant cases, practitioners may suggest alternative biological treatments, such as electrical or magnetic stimulation of the brain, or brain surgery in the most extreme cases. All of these treatments are used to alter brain function. They are often last resorts, because they may have more serious side effects than psychotherapy or medication.

Electroconvulsive therapy (ECT) involves placing electrodes on a client's head and administering an electrical current strong enough to produce a seizure (**Figure 14.7**). This procedure was developed in Europe in the 1930s. It was first tried on a human in 1938. In the 1950s and 1960s, it was commonly and successfully used to treat some psychological disorders, including schizophrenia and depression. However, researchers still do not know precisely how ECT achieves these positive treatment effects.

The general public has a very negative view of ECT. This view comes partly from Ken Kesey's 1962 novel *One Flew over the Cuckoo's Nest,* as well as the award-winning 1975 film version. Kesey graphically depicted ECT and its extreme side effects, as well as the tragic effects of brain surgeries such as lobotomy and abuses in mental health care generally. Although care for the mentally ill is still far from perfect, many reforms have been made. ECT now generally occurs under anesthesia, using powerful muscle relaxants to eliminate muscular convulsions. As you

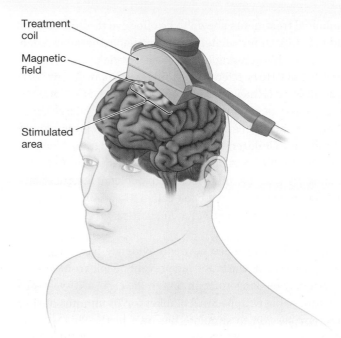

FIGURE 14.8

Transcranial Magnetic Stimulation Treats Depression
In TMS, a wire coil is placed over the scalp where a brain area is to be stimulated. When electrical current passes through the coil, a magnetic field is created. When the coil is turned on and off, this action interrupts brain function in the stimulated region. TMS is used mainly to treat depression.

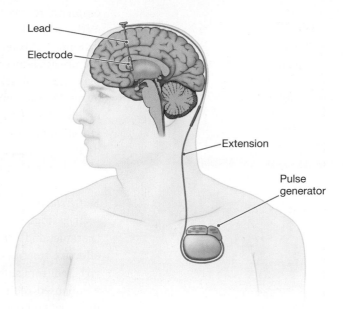

FIGURE 14.9

Deep Brain Stimulation Is Used to Treat Depression and Obsessive-Compulsive Disorder
In DBS, an electrical generator placed just under the skin below the collarbone sends out continuous stimulation to electrodes implanted in the brain. DBS is used to treat OCD and depression.

will learn later in the chapter, ECT is particularly effective for some cases of severe depression, but this treatment still involves some risks.

During **transcranial magnetic stimulation (TMS),** which we discussed in Chapter 2, an electrical current produces a powerful magnetic field. When rapidly switched on and off, this magnetic field creates an electrical current in the brain region directly below the coil, thereby interrupting the activity of neurons in that region (**Figure 14.8**). TMS has been used with some success in cases of depression, as we will see later in this chapter.

One of the most dramatic new techniques for treating severe psychological disorders is **deep brain stimulation (DBS).** This brain surgery technique involves surgically implanting electrodes deep within the brain, at differing sites depending on the disorder. Mild electricity is then used to stimulate the particular region of the brain at an optimal frequency and intensity, much the way a pacemaker stimulates the heart (**Figure 14.9**). DBS is being tested for treating various psychological disorders. As you will learn later in this chapter, DBS might be especially valuable for treating severe obsessive-compulsive disorder (OCD) and depression.

Scientific Evidence Indicates Which Treatments Are Safe and Effective

Reenacting your own birth, screaming, having body parts manipulated—these are a few activities that have been offered as "psychotherapy" (**Figure 14.10**). Do they do any good? Just as we need to use critical thinking to recognize and avoid flawed science, we also need to recognize and avoid therapies that do not have scientific evidence of effectiveness. As we will see in the rest of this chapter,

transcranial magnetic stimulation (TMS)
Treatment for psychological disorders that uses a magnetic field to interrupt function in specific regions of the brain.

deep brain stimulation (DBS)
Treatment for psychological disorders that involves passing electricity through electrodes planted in the client's brain to stimulate the brain at a certain frequency and intensity.

FIGURE 14.10

Rebirthing: A "Therapy" With No Scientific Basis
Some practitioners claim that rebirthing therapy can promote attachment and reduce traumas remaining from birth. However, there is no scientific evidence that rebirthing therapy has any benefit.

most psychologists recommend treatments shown to be effective through careful empirical research (Kazdin, 2008). Unfortunately, many available therapies, such as those listed at the beginning of this paragraph, have no scientific basis.

Some treatments widely believed to be effective not only lack scientific support, but are actually counterproductive (Hines, 2003; Lilienfeld, 2007). For instance, exposing adolescents to prisoners or tough treatments supposedly scares them away from committing crimes, but teens in "scared straight" programs show an increase in conduct problems. Children in drug education programs such as DARE are more likely to drink alcohol and smoke cigarettes than children who do not attend such programs. In addition, many self-help books make questionable claims. Can we trust the information in a book called *Make Anyone Fall in Love with You in 5 Minutes,* or another called *Three Easy Steps for Having High Self-Esteem*?

It is important to recognize the difference between evidence-based psychotherapies and "fringe" therapies because the latter can prevent people from getting effective treatment and even may be dangerous. In one tragic case, a 10-year-old girl died from suffocation after being wrapped in a blanket for 70 minutes during a supposed rebirthing therapy session to simulate her own birth. This was an untested and unscientific method being used to correct the child's unruly behavior (Lowe, 2001). The people conducting the session were unlicensed and had not passed the tests that certify knowledge about psychotherapy.

As with the various psychological theories we have discussed throughout this book, the only way to know whether a treatment is valid is to conduct empirical research. The researchers should compare the treatment with a control condition, such as receiving helpful information or having supportive listeners (Kazdin, 2008). In keeping with good scientific principles, client-participants should be randomly assigned to conditions. The use of *randomized clinical trials* is a hallmark of good research to establish whether a particular treatment is effective. Recall from Chapter 1 that random assignment helps ensure that groups are comparable and also controls for many potential confounds. Psychological disorders should always be treated in ways that scientific research has shown to be effective.

Three features characterize evidence-based psychological treatments (Barlow, 2004). First, treatments vary according to the particular psychological disorder and the client's specific symptoms. Just as treatment for asthma differs from that for psoriasis, treatments for panic disorder are likely to differ from those for bulimia nervosa. Second, the techniques used in these treatments have been developed in the laboratory by psychologists, especially behavioral, cognitive, and social psychologists. Third, no overall grand theory guides treatment. Instead, treatment is based on evidence of its effectiveness.

Various Providers Assist in Treatment for Psychological Disorders

Recall that nearly half of all Americans meet *Diagnostic and Statistical Manual (DSM)* criteria for a psychological disorder at some point in their lives. In any given year, 25 percent of the population meets these criteria (Kessler & Wang, 2008). Who should these people turn to for treatment?

As summarized in **Table 14.3,** the providers of psychological treatment range from those with limited training (e.g., former addicts who provide peer counseling) to those with advanced degrees in psychopathology and its treatment (e.g., clinical psychologists and psychiatrists; **Figure 14.11**). Each type of professional works in

TABLE 14.3
Providers of Psychological Treatment

SPECIALTY	TRAINING	DEGREE	EMPLOYMENT
Psychiatrists	4 years of medical school with 3–5 years of additional specialization in residency programs to treat people with psychological disorders	MD	Client treatment in hospitals or private practice
Clinical psychologists	5–7 years of graduate school conducting research on psychological disorders and treatment, including 1 year of clinical internship	PhD	Primarily research in university settings
	4–6 years of graduate school developing clinical skills to treat people with psychological disorders, followed by 1 year of internship	PsyD	Client treatment in hospitals or other clinical settings
Counseling psychologists	4–6 years of graduate school developing clinical skills to treat clients' adjustment and life stress problems (academic, relationship, work) but not psychological disorders	PhD	Universities, colleges, schools, and private practice
Psychiatric social workers	2–3 years of graduate training on directing clients to appropriate social and community agency resources, plus specialized training in mental health care	MSW	Hospitals, mental health treatment centers, home visits
Psychiatric nurses	2 years for an associate's degree (ASN, RN), 4 years for a bachelor's degree (BSN), or 2–3 additional years of graduate training (MSN), but all focus on nursing plus special training in the care of clients with psychological disorders	ASN; RN; BSN; MSN	Hospitals and residential treatment programs, outpatient clinics
Paraprofessionals	Work under supervision to assist those with mental health problems in the challenges of daily living	Limited advanced training, no advanced degree	Community outreach programs, crisis intervention, pastoral counseling

Note. MD = Doctor of Medicine; PhD = Doctor of Philosophy in Psychology; PsyD = Doctor of Psychology; MSW = Master of Social Work; ASN = Associate of Science in Nursing; RN = Registered Nurse; BSN = Bachelor of Science in Nursing; MSN = Master of Science in Nursing.

(a)

(b)

(c)

FIGURE 14.11
Providers of Psychological Treatment
Many types of professionals provide treatment for psychological disorders. **(a)** Psychiatrists work in hospitals and treatment centers. They can prescribe psychotropic medications. **(b)** Clinical psychologists either work with clients providing therapy or conduct research on the effectiveness of various treatments. **(c)** Paraprofessionals often work in the community and provide outreach services to people with mental illness.

How Do I Find a Provider Who Can Help Me?

Have you ever felt that the stresses or problems of your life were more than you could cope with alone? Perhaps you thought about seeking therapeutic support but were apprehensive. That apprehension is understandable. It's not easy to admit—to yourself or others—that you need extra support. And stepping into a stranger's office and disclosing your personal thoughts and feelings is not easy either. Here are some questions and answers that can help you decide if the time has come, and how to find the right therapist.

How can I know if I need therapy? Many times family members, friends, professors, or physicians encourage college students to seek help for psychological problems. For example, if a student goes to the health center because she feels tired all the time, the doctor might ask if she has been under stress or feeling sad. These conditions might indicate that she is experiencing depression and could be helped by a therapist. Of course, sometimes a student is already aware that he has a psychological problem. For example, a student who struggles night after night to fall asleep because of constant worry about his academic performance might seek help for dealing with anxiety.

You don't have to be 100 percent certain that you need therapy before seeking it out. You can think of the first couple of sessions as a trial period to help you figure out if therapy would be a valuable tool in your situation.

What kinds of issues can therapists help with? According to the psychologist Katherine Nordal, "Psychologists [and other therapists] work with clients who are looking for help in making lifestyle and behavior changes that lead to better physical and mental health. [They] can help people learn to cope with anxiety or depression, deal with stressful situations, overcome addictions, manage chronic illnesses, both physical and psychological, and break past barriers that might prevent them from reaching their goals" (American Psychological Association, 2010). In other words, therapists can help you deal with various issues, ranging from acute stressors (e.g., preparing to move across the country) to chronic concerns (e.g., managing anxiety).

How do I find a therapist who is a good fit for me and my needs? Most college campuses have counselors who can direct students to appropriate treatment providers. In addition, you can ask your friends, teachers, or clergy if they can recommend someone in your area. And organizations such as the American Psychological Association host referral services, many of which are free and Web-based.

But just having a name and phone number does not mean that therapist will be a good fit for you. To figure that out, you will want to do some information gathering up front. First, what are your preferences? Do you think you would be more comfortable working with someone who is the same gender as you? Is it important for the therapist to have a cultural background similar to yours? Second, it is a good idea to ask the therapist about her level of experience in helping people with your particular problem (e.g., depression, procrastination, coming out to your parents). Third, pay attention to your comfort level as you interact with the therapist during the first session or two. It is critical for you to find a therapist who is trustworthy and caring. The initial consultation should make you feel at ease and hopeful that your issue can be resolved.

If you do not feel a connection with one therapist, seek another. It might take more than one try to find someone you want to work with, but the effort will be well spent. Remember, therapy involves a kind of relationship. Just as you would not expect every first date to be a love connection, do not expect every therapist to be a good fit for you. Finding someone you connect with can be difficult, but it is extremely important for ensuring successful treatment.

different settings and provides different services to people who have psychological disorders or who are experiencing life problems. In addition to mental health specialists, regular health care providers (e.g., internists, pediatricians), human-services workers (e.g., school counselors), and volunteers (e.g., self-help groups) provide services related to treatment. No matter who administers the treatment, however, most of the techniques used today have emerged from psychological laboratories.

Choosing the right treatment provider is extremely important for ensuring successful treatment (see Using Psychology in Your Life). That professional must have the appropriate training and experience for the specific psychological disorder or life problem, and the person seeking help must believe the therapist is trustworthy and caring. The initial consultation should make the client feel at ease and hopeful that her psychological problem can be resolved. If not, she should seek another provider.

Medication is normally prescribed only by psychiatrists, because they have a medical degree. However, the ability to prescribe medication should play a minor role in the choice of therapist. Efforts are under way to give more practitioners, such as clinical psychologists, the ability to prescribe medications. In New Mexico and Louisiana, clinical psychologists with specialized training in psychoactive drugs can prescribe medications; similar legislation is being proposed elsewhere in the United States (McGrath, 2010). In addition, almost all practitioners have arrangements with physicians who can prescribe medications if necessary. In searching for a provider who is right for you, the most important thing is to find someone who is both empathic and experienced in the methods known to be effective in treating specific psychological disorders.

It is most important that individuals not feel hopeless in their struggles with mental health problems. They should seek help just as they would for any illness or injury. College students usually have access to low-cost or free therapies at their schools. Most communities have sliding-fee, low-cost, or free facilities to help people who do not have insurance coverage.

14.1 CHECKPOINT: How Are Psychological Disorders Treated?

- Psychotherapies are formal treatments that focus on changing a client's cognition and behavior.

- Biological treatments include psychotropic medications that change neurochemistry.

- When traditional treatments are not successful, therapists may suggest alternative treatments, such as electroconvulsive therapy (ECT), transcranial magnetic stimulation (TMS), and deep brain stimulation (DBS).

- Evidence-based practice provides safe, effective treatment. Therapies not supported by scientific evidence can be dangerous.

- A variety of specialized mental health practitioners have different training that allows them to provide treatment in diverse settings.

14.2 What Are Effective Treatments for Common Disorders?

LEARNING GOALS	READING ACTIVITIES	LEARN
a. Remember the key terms about effective treatments for anxiety disorders, obsessive-compulsive disorder (OCD), depressive disorders, bipolar disorders, and schizophrenia.	List all of the boldface words and write down their definitions.	
b. Apply cognitive-behavioral therapy (CBT) to panic disorder.	Describe how cognitive restructuring and exposure therapy could be used to treat a woman who worries she will die when she has a panic attack.	
c. Analyze the impact of different treatments on OCD.	Differentiate the effects of cognitive-behavioral, drug, and alternative treatments for OCD.	
d. Understand how CBT is used to treat people with depression.	Explain in your own words how people with depression can benefit from treatment of the cognitive triad.	
e. Analyze drug treatments for schizophrenia.	Distinguish the pros and cons in using conventional versus atypical antipsychotics to treat schizophrenia, and explain why atypical antipsychotics are the treatment of choice.	

Think back to the story of Dennis that opened this chapter. Once Dennis found an appropriate therapist, he was able to receive treatment that was effective for his anxiety and could move forward with his life. Not all psychological disorders are so easily treated. Moreover, outcomes are influenced by the interaction of the particular client and therapist, so it is difficult to make comparisons across disorders and therapists. Nevertheless, research over the past three decades has shown that certain types of treatments are particularly effective for specific types of psychological disorders (Barlow, 2004). These best-practice treatments for anxiety, obsessive-compulsive disorder, mood disorders, and schizophrenia are described in this section and are summarized in **Table 14.4.**

Anxiety and Obsessive-Compulsive Disorders Are Best Treated with Cognitive-Behavioral Therapy

Various treatment approaches to anxiety disorders have had mixed success. When Freudian psychoanalytic theory governed the classification of psychological disorders, anxiety disorders were thought to result from repressed sexual and aggressive impulses. The therapist attempted to deal with this underlying cause rather than with specific symptoms. Ultimately, psychoanalytic theory did not prove useful for treating anxiety disorders. There is accumulated evidence that most adult anxiety disorders are best treated with a combination of cognitive and behavior therapies (Hofmann & Smits, 2008; **Figure 14.12**).

Anti-anxiety drugs (see Table 14.2) are also beneficial in some cases because they have a sedative effect that makes people feel calmer. With drugs, however, there are risks of side effects and, after drug treatment is terminated, the risk of relapse. For instance, anti-anxiety drugs work in the short term for generalized

FIGURE 14.12

Anxiety Disorders Can Be Successfully Treated

The actor Kim Basinger is one of the thousands of people who receive treatment each year for anxiety disorders. After extreme social anxiety led to panic attacks, Basinger did not leave her house for six months. While she still feels "shy," psychotherapy has helped Basinger manage her panic disorder and agoraphobia.

TABLE 14.4

Types of Treatment for Common Psychological Disorders

CATEGORY	EXAMPLES OF SPECIFIC DISORDERS	TYPES OF TREATMENT	SAMPLE OF POSSIBLE TECHNIQUES
Anxiety disorders	*Specific phobia:* fear of something out of proportion to the threat	cognitive-behavioral	• changing thoughts about feared stimulus • exposure • systematic desensitization
	Panic disorder: sudden attacks of overwhelming terror	cognitive-behavioral	• cognitive restructuring about panic attacks • exposure
Obsessive-compulsive and related disorders	*Obsessive-compulsive disorder:* frequent intrusive thoughts (obsessions) and actions that are performed repeatedly (compulsions)	cognitive-behavioral	• cognitive restructuring to recognize that all people have intrusive thoughts • exposure and response prevention
		psychotropic medications	• antidepressants
		alternative	• DBS
Depressive disorders	*Major depressive disorder:* depression that is severe, plus other symptoms	psychotropic medications	• antidepressants
		cognitive-behavioral	• alter thinking to address cognitive triad of negative thoughts
		alternative	• phototherapy for SAD • exercise • ECT • TMS • DBS
Bipolar and related disorders	*Bipolar I disorder:* severe mania	psychotropic medications	• lithium • antidepressants may be added with lithium
Schizophrenia spectrum and other psychotic disorders	*Schizophrenia:* psychotic disorder with motor, cognitive, behavioral, and perceptual abnormalities	psychotropic medications	• atypical antipsychotics
		behavior	• social skills training • behavioral training for life skills

Note: DBS = deep brain stimulation; SAD = seasonal affective disorder; ECT = electroconvulsive therapy; TMS = transcranial magnetic stimulation.

anxiety disorder, but they do little to lessen the source of anxiety and are addictive. Therefore, they are not a treatment of choice. By contrast, the effects of cognitive-behavioral therapy (CBT) persist long after treatment, so this remains the best treatment in general for anxiety disorders (Hollon, Stewart, & Strunk, 2006).

SPECIFIC PHOBIAS Learning theory suggests that specific phobias are acquired either by experiencing a trauma or by observing similar fear in others. However, most phobias apparently develop without being brought about by any particular event. Although learning theory cannot completely explain the development of phobias, behavior techniques are the treatment of choice, along with approaches to changing the client's thoughts about the fearful stimulus.

1 The little girl in the white shirt (on the left) has a phobia about dogs.

2 She is encouraged to approach a dog that scares her.

3 From this mild form of exposure she learns that the dog is not dangerous, and she overcomes her fear.

FIGURE 14.13

Using Exposure to Reduce Phobias
Exposure is a common feature of many cognitive-behavioral therapies. In this sequence, exposure is used to help a little girl overcome her fear of dogs. She is not allowed to avoid a dog, and her level of exposure to the dog is gradually increased.

exposure
Therapy technique that involves repeatedly exposing a client to an anxiety-producing stimulus or situation and has the goal of reducing the client's fear.

systematic desensitization
Therapy technique that involves exposing a client to increasingly anxiety-producing stimuli or situations while having the client relax at the same time.

FIGURE 14.14

Using Computer Simulations to Conquer Phobias
Computer-generated images can simulate feared environments or social interactions as part of treatment for phobias. For example, in this "virtual world," the client can stand on the edge of a tall building or fly in an aircraft and practice relaxing to get rid of fear. By using a process of systematic desensitization, the client can conquer the virtual situation before taking on the feared situation in real life.

Many successful behavior therapies for phobias include an **exposure** component. In this technique, which is based on classical conditioning, the client is exposed repeatedly to the anxiety-producing stimulus or situation (**Figure 14.13**). The reasoning behind exposure is that people avoid fearful stimuli or situations to reduce their anxiety, and so they remain afraid of the specific stimuli or situations. Because specific phobias can interfere with daily living, clients need to reduce their fear rather than just avoid what scares them. Repeated exposure to a feared stimulus increases the client's anxiety, but because they cannot avoid it, the link with the escape behavior is broken.

A gradual form of exposure therapy is **systematic desensitization.** In this method, the therapist has the client imagine increasingly anxiety-producing situations and teaches him to relax at the same time. First, the client makes a *fear hierarchy,* a list of situations in which fear develops, in ascending order. An example of a fear hierarchy is shown in Try It Yourself. The next step is relaxation training, in which the client learns to alternate muscular tension with muscular relaxation and to use other relaxation techniques. Exposure therapy is often the next step. While the client is relaxed, he is asked to enact or imagine scenarios from the fear hierarchy that become more and more upsetting.

A recent alternative is to expose clients to fearful situations without putting them in danger by using computers to simulate the environments and the feared objects (**Figure 14.14**). There is substantial evidence that using simulated environments for exposure therapy can reduce fear responses (Rothbaum et al., 1999). Regardless of whether the client enacts the scenario, imagines it, or uses a computer simulation, an important key is that new scenarios are not presented until she is able to maintain relaxation at the previous levels. The theory behind this technique is that the relaxation response competes with and eventually replaces the fear response. However, there is evidence that exposure to the feared object, rather than the relaxation, extinguishes the phobic response. Because of this, many contemporary practitioners leave out the relaxation component.

Psychotropic medication treatments for phobias often include anti-anxiety drugs that are calming (see Table 14.2). These drugs can help people handle immediate fears, but as soon as the drugs wear off, the fears return. Studies have suggested that antidepressants (see Table 14.2) might be useful for social phobia (social anxiety disorder) in a similar way as for specific phobias. Indeed, in one comprehensive study, researchers found that taking an antidepressant or undergoing CBT were equally effective in treating social phobia (Davidson et al., 2004). Those taking the antidepressant, however, had more physical complaints, such as lack of sexual interest. Thus CBTs are the treatments of choice for phobia.

PANIC DISORDER Panic disorder has multiple components, and each symptom may require a different treatment. When people feel anxious, they tend to overestimate the probability of danger, potentially contributing to their rising feelings of panic. This is what happened to Dennis, in the story you read at the start of the chapter. To break the learned association between the physical symptoms of anxiety, such as hyperventilation or heart palpitations, and the feeling of impending doom, CBT can be effective, as it was for Dennis.

Cognitive restructuring is a technique used in cognitive therapy to address ways of reacting to the symptoms of a panic attack. For example, first the client identifies her specific fears, such as having a heart attack or fainting. She then estimates how many panic attacks she has experienced. The therapist helps the client assign percentages to specific fears and then compare these numbers with the actual number of times the fears have been realized. For example, a client might estimate that she fears having a heart attack during 90 percent of her panic attacks and fainting during 85 percent of her attacks. The therapist can then point out that the actual rate of occurrence was zero. In fact, people do not faint during panic attacks. The physical symptoms of a panic attack, such as having a racing heart, are the opposite of fainting.

TRY IT YOURSELF: Using Systematic Desensitization to Reduce Fear

Everyone is afraid of something. But even if our fears are not as extreme as specific phobias, we can use systematic desensitization to help us conquer fears. To try it yourself, first create a fear hierarchy about something you are afraid of. This sample fear hierarchy was created by a person who wanted to conquer a fear of heights so he could go mountain climbing.

Once you have created your own hierarchy, take yourself through it. First put yourself in the least fearful situation, either in real life or in your imagination. Then practice relaxation and breathing until you are calm in that situation. Then proceed to the next fearful situation and repeat the process until you are quite relaxed even in the most fearful situation. This technique may take a while. But by going step by step, you may overcome your fear.

Degree of fear	Situation
10	I'm standing on the balcony of the top floor of an apartment tower.
20	I'm sitting on the slope of a mountain, looking out over the horizon.
30	I'm riding a ski lift 8 feet above the ground.
40	I'm climbing a ladder outside the house to reach a second-story window.
50	I'm scrambling up a rock that is 8 feet high.
60	I'm walking on a wide plateau, 2 feet from the edge of a cliff.
70	I'm walking over a railway trestle.
80	I'm riding a chairlift 15 feet above the ground.
90	I'm walking up (or down) a 15-degree slope on a 3-foot-wide trail. On one side of the trail, the terrain drops down sharply; on the other side is a steep upward slope.
100	I'm walking on a 2-foot-wide ridge. The trail slopes on either side are more than 25 degrees.

exposure and response prevention
Therapy technique that teaches clients to relax as they are gradually exposed to increasingly feared stimuli or situations. The goal of treatment is to reduce the fear.

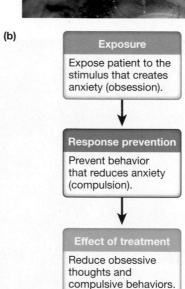

FIGURE 14.15

Using Exposure and Response Prevention to Treat Obsessive-Compulsive Disorder
(a) Someone who obsesses about germs might engage in a compulsive behavior, such as excessive hand washing. **(b)** In exposure and response therapy, the person would be asked to touch something dirty, then would be prevented from hand washing. The effect should be to break the link between the obsession and the compulsion, reducing both.

Even if clients recognize the irrationality of their fears, they may still experience panic attacks. From a cognitive-behavioral perspective, the attacks continue because of a conditioned response to the trigger (e.g., shortness of breath). The goal of therapy is to break the connection between the trigger symptom and the resulting panic. This break can be made by exposure treatment.

In the treatment of panic attacks, CBT appears to be as effective as or more effective than medication (Schmidt & Keough, 2011). For example, David Barlow and colleagues (2000) found that in the short term, the results were the same for CBT alone as for an antidepressant alone. Six months after treatment ended, however, those who had received CBT were less likely to relapse than those who had taken medication. These results support the conclusion that CBT is the treatment of choice for panic disorder.

OBSESSIVE-COMPULSIVE DISORDER As we saw in Chapter 13, obsessive-compulsive disorder (OCD) is a combination of recurrent intrusive thoughts (obsessions) and behaviors that an individual feels compelled to perform over and over (compulsions). CBT is effective for OCD (Franklin & Foa, 2011).

The most important component of the behavior aspect of therapy for OCD is **exposure and response prevention.** This treatment is based on the theory that a particular stimulus triggers anxiety and that performing the compulsive behavior is what reduces the anxiety. For example, a client might obsess about germs and then compulsively wash her hands to reduce anxiety after touching a doorknob, using a public telephone, or shaking hands with someone (**Figure 14.15a**). In this variation of exposure therapy, the client is directly exposed to the anxiety-producing stimuli but is prevented from engaging in the compulsive behavior that reduces the anxiety. So a client who obsesses about germs would be required to touch a dirty doorknob and then be instructed not to engage in the compulsive behavior of washing her hands afterward (**Figure 14.15b**). As with exposure therapy for panic disorder, the goal is to break the conditioned link between a particular stimulus and a compulsive behavior. When this happens, the avoidance response to stimuli that cause obsessive thoughts is eventually extinguished. Anxiety is reduced. The reduced anxiety then reduces the compulsive behavior. This form of therapy is highly effective for treating people with OCD.

Some cognitive therapies are also useful for OCD. For example, cognitive restructuring may help the client recognize that most people occasionally experience unwanted thoughts and compulsions. Indeed, unwanted thoughts and compulsions are a normal part of human experience.

How does drug treatment with an antidepressant compare with CBT for OCD? In one study, the use of exposure and response prevention proved superior to the use of a specific tricyclic antidepressant, although both were better than *placebos,* which are "sugar pills" that contain no active drugs (Foa et al., 2005; **Figure 14.16**). CBT may thus be a more effective way of treating OCD than medication, especially over the long term. There is evidence that, at a minimum, adding CBT to drug treatment with certain antidepressant drugs may improve outcomes (Simpson et al., 2008).

One exciting possibility is that deep brain stimulation (DBS) may be an effective treatment for those with OCD who have not found relief from CBT or medications. Early studies used psychosurgery, such as lobotomy, to remove brain regions thought to contribute to OCD. There were promising outcomes at times, but these techniques could involve destroying large areas of brain tissue, especially in the frontal lobes. And, brain surgery is inherently a risky therapy because it is irreversible. DBS offers new hope.

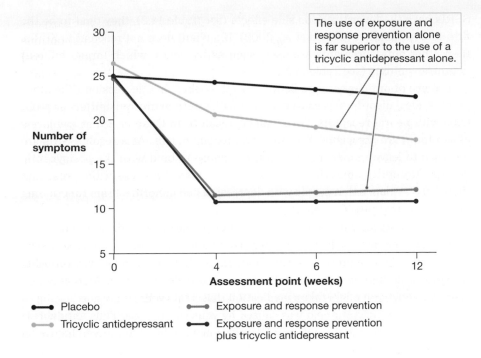

The use of exposure and response prevention alone is far superior to the use of a tricyclic antidepressant alone.

Number of symptoms

Assessment point (weeks)

●─● Placebo
●─● Tricyclic antidepressant
●─● Exposure and response prevention
●─● Exposure and response prevention plus tricyclic antidepressant

FIGURE 14.16

Effectiveness of Treatments for Obsessive-Compulsive Disorder
This graph shows how the numbers of symptoms of OCD changed over a period of 12 weeks based on each type of treatment. The results indicated that treatment with an antidepressant alone did not reduce symptoms as much as did treatment with exposure and response prevention alone.

Many Effective Treatments Are Available for Depressive Disorders

Recall that depressive disorders involve depressed moods that range from mild to extreme, lasting anywhere from two weeks to years. Depression is one of the most widespread psychological disorders among adolescents and adults, and it has become more common over the past few decades (Hollon et al., 2002). Fortunately, scientific research has validated a number of effective treatments. There is no "best" way to treat depression. Many approaches are available (**Figure 14.17**). Ongoing research is determining which type of therapy works best for which types of individuals.

PSYCHOTROPIC DRUG TREATMENT In the 1950s, tuberculosis was a major health problem in the United States, particularly in urban areas. A common drug treatment reduced tuberculosis-related bacteria in patients' saliva. It also stimulated patients' appetites, increased their energy levels, and gave them an overall sense of well-being. In 1957, researchers who had noted the drug's effect on mood reported preliminary success in using it to treat depression. In the following year, nearly half a million people experiencing depression were given the drug. Since then, various drugs have been used to treat depression (see Table 14.2). Each drug has side effects, however, and different antidepressants can affect people in different ways.

Researchers have attempted to determine how particular types of people will respond to antidepressants. Still, physicians often must resort to a trial-and-error approach in treating clients who are experiencing depression to determine what will work for them. Because of this, no single drug stands out as being most effective. Often the decision of which drug to use depends on the client's overall medical health and the possible side effects of each medication. In general, though, because

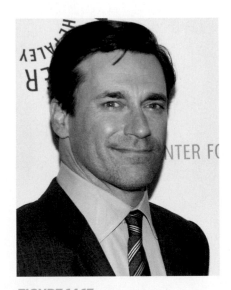

FIGURE 14.17

Depressive Disorders Can Be Successfully Treated
The actor Jon Hamm, from *Mad Men*, has talked publicly about his experiences with chronic depression after the death of his father when Hamm was 20 years old. He credits both psychotherapy and psychotropic medications with helping him overcome the disorder. By using antidepressants, he says, "You can change your brain chemistry enough to think: 'I want to get up in the morning; I don't want to sleep until four in the afternoon. I want to get up and . . . go to work and . . . kick-start the engine!'"

SSRIs have the fewest serious side effects (see Table 14.2), they tend to be the first-line medication (Olfson et al., 2002). If a client does not respond to SSRIs, then other antidepressants are used, such as tricyclics, which target different neurotransmitters (see Table 14.2).

The use of antidepressants is based on the belief that depression (like other psychological disorders) is caused by an imbalance in neurotransmitters or problems with neural receptors. For instance, recall from Chapter 2 that low levels of serotonin are associated with sad and anxious moods. As a result, SSRIs are designed to leave more serotonin in the synapse to bind with the postsynaptic neurons. Recently, some critics have challenged this view. These critics argue that there is no evidence that people with depression had abnormal brain functioning before drug treatment (Angell, 2011).

Indeed, faulty logical reasoning may be at play. The fact that drugs seem to help symptoms of depression has been viewed as evidence that depression is caused by an abnormality in neurotransmitter function. As a critical thinker, you probably recognize that this connection is not necessarily proof of causation. After all, when you have a cold, you might take a medication that treats your runny nose. Doing so does not prove that your cold was caused by your runny nose. Thus antidepressants may help treat the symptoms of depression without having any influence on the underlying cause.

Other critics have questioned whether antidepressants are more effective than placebos in treating depression. According to published studies, approximately 60 percent to 70 percent of clients who take antidepressants experience relief from their symptoms, as compared with about 30 percent who respond to placebos. Such findings indicate that although there are placebo effects in the treatment of depression, antidepressants do seem to lead to greater improvement. Placebos that produce some side effects (such as a dry mouth) are called active placebos, and they are more likely to produce therapeutic gains than placebos that have no side effects (Kirsch, 2011). This result occurs because the placebos' side effects lead clients to think they are receiving real drugs. So when antidepressants are compared with active placebos, the benefits of antidepressants are more modest. Only drug trials that involve individuals with severe depression show clear benefits of drugs over placebos, in part because people with severe depression show less response to placebo treatments (Kirsch et al., 2008).

COGNITIVE-BEHAVIORAL TREATMENT Not all clients benefit from antidepressant medications. In addition, some clients cannot or will not tolerate the side effects. Fortunately, research has shown that cognitive-behavioral therapy (CBT) is just as effective as antidepressants in treating depression (Hollon et al., 2002).

From a cognitive perspective, people become depressed because of automatic, distorted thoughts. According to the cognitive distortion model developed by Aaron Beck, depression is the result of a cognitive triad of negative thoughts about oneself, the situation, and the future (see Figure 13.18). People with depression think about how they have failed in the past, how poorly they are dealing with the present situation, and how terrible the future will be. The goal of CBT for depression is to identify, reevaluate, and change negative thoughts associated with depression. Ultimately, this approach helps the client think more adaptively and eliminate the cognitive triad of negative thoughts. This change is intended to improve mood and behavior. The specific treatment is adapted to the individual client, but some general principles apply. Clients may be asked to recognize and record negative thoughts. Thinking about situations in a negative way can become automatic, and recognizing these thought patterns can be difficult. Once the

As Kim read Chapter 14, she thought about how much she had learned this semester. Many topics in psychology would be helpful once she pursued her career in marketing. For example, research findings about motivation might give her insight into what makes people buy things. Findings about self-esteem might make it easier to sell exercise equipment, makeup, luxury cars....

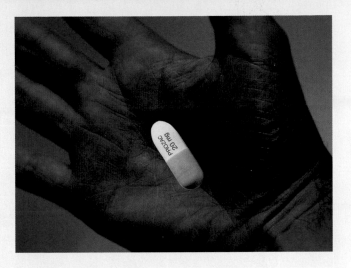

As she learned about treatments for mental illness, Kim pictured some of the television commercials she had seen for antidepressants. How much money did that business take in? She paused in her reading and did a quick Internet search. At the *Consumer Reports* Web site, she discovered that in 2009, $300 million was spent on advertising two antidepressants. *That is a lot of money for just two drugs,* she thought. *The total amount for all antidepressant drugs must have been huge. How much of that buying is inspired by advertising?*

Kim e-mailed her marketing professor, Dr. Haun, to ask if any research had been done on this question. Later the next day, Dr. Haun replied that the topic had been researched by both marketers and psychologists. He attached a paper about the link between familiarity with antidepressant print ads and perceptions of depression (Park & Grow, 2008). Dr. Haun mentioned, however, that neither coauthor was a psychologist. In the study, college students were asked whether they were familiar with ads for five antidepressants. They were then asked to rate their perceived risk of depression ("How likely is it that you will experience depression in your lifetime?") and the prevalence of depression in the general population ("What percentage of the population will experience depression?").

According to the study, being more familiar with drug advertisements was associated with higher ratings of both lifetime personal prevalence of depression and higher ratings of population prevalence. *Interesting! As people's familiarity with these ads increases, they tend to think that their chance of getting depression is higher and that other people's chances of getting depression is higher.* She thought for a minute. *Of course, people's familiarity doesn't necessarily cause their ideas. Isn't it possible that people who have a higher estimate of depression in themselves and in the population will also tend to remember ads for antidepressants?*

The study didn't try to answer that question. However, it took into consideration whether the participants had any interpersonal experience with depression or antidepressants. For example, did they know of any friends or family members who experienced depression, sought treatment for it, or had taken antidepressants? Even when this factor was included, the link existed between ads and ratings of prevalence. *That part of the study is smart. Otherwise, people could criticize the study on the grounds that people who are more familiar with depression would of course be more aware of the ads and would have higher estimates. Although familiarity with depression is associated with awareness of ads and estimates, the study shows that familiarity with ads is related to prevalence estimates even beyond that.*

Kim found this research inspiring in various ways. She wondered whether experimentation had been done on this topic. For example, did any studies look into whether exposure to drug ads leads people to think differently about mental illness and treatment? But above all, Kim was thrilled to find out about research that blended her two favorite subjects: psychology and marketing. *Who knew?*

patterns are identified and monitored, the clinician can help the client recognize other ways of viewing the same situation that are not so dysfunctional (see Try It Yourself on p. 516).

CBT can be effective on its own, but combining it with antidepressant medication can be more effective than either one of these approaches alone (McCullough, 2000). The issue is not drugs versus psychotherapy. The issue is what provides relief for each client. For instance, drug treatment may be the most effective option for clients who are suicidal, in acute distress, or unable to commit to regular attendance with a therapist. For most clients, especially those who have physical problems such as liver impairment or cardiac problems, CBT may be the treatment of

TRY IT YOURSELF: Using a Journal to Reduce Negative Thoughts

We all have negative thoughts at times. These thoughts may be rational or irrational, but they may lead us to feel anxious or sad. In fact, sometimes negative thoughts and the feelings that go with them can appear in patterns. These patterns can be severe enough to be diagnosed as depression.

How can you avoid negative thoughts and negative emotions? Keep a journal to write down your thoughts and emotions. As shown in this sample from a person experiencing depression, you should note the day, the event, your thoughts, and your feelings. Look for patterns in how you think and feel. Use the far column to write down ways to make positive changes in your thoughts and feelings.

Date	Event	Thought	Feeling	Change(s)
April 4	Boss seemed annoyed	*Oh, what have I done now? If I keep making him angry, I am going to get fired.*	Sad, anxious, worried	Explore alternative interpretations. • *Is he annoyed at something other than me?* Don't think of a situation as a catastrophe. • *I am overestimating and probably won't get fired.*
April 5	Husband did not want to make love	*I'm so fat and ugly.*	Sad	Check to see if thinking is distorted by negative views. • *There are positive aspects of my body.*
April 7	Boss yelled at another employee	*I'm next.*	Anxious	Make the best of a bad situation. • *See if I can do anything to help so my boss is less annoyed.*
April 9	Husband said he's taking a long business trip next month	*He's probably got a mistress somewhere. My marriage is falling apart.*	Sad, defeated	Question whether there is evidence to support this idea. • *Is there evidence of an affair?*
April 10	Neighbor brought over some cookies	*She probably thinks that I can't cook. I look like such a mess all the time. And my house was a disaster when she came in.*	A little happy, mostly sad	Stop a cascade of negative thoughts and replace them with positive ones. • *The neighbor just wants to help me.*

choice because it is long-lasting and does not have the side effects associated with medications (Hollon et al., 2006).

ALTERNATIVE TREATMENTS In clients with seasonal affective disorder (SAD), episodes of depression are most likely to occur during winter. Many of these clients respond favorably to **phototherapy.** This treatment involves exposure to a high-intensity light source for part of each day (**Figure 14.18**).

For some clients with depression, regular aerobic exercise can reduce the symptoms and prevent recurrence (Pollock, 2004). Aerobic exercise may reduce depression because it releases endorphins. As discussed in Chapter 2, the release of endorphins can cause an overall feeling of well-being (a feeling runners sometimes experience as "runner's high"). Aerobic exercise may also regularize bodily rhythms, improve self-esteem, and provide social support if people exercise with others. However, clients with depression may have difficulty finding the energy and motivation to begin an exercise regimen.

An alternative treatment that alters the brain's electrical function, such as electroconvulsive therapy (ECT), is very effective for those who are severely depressed and do not respond to conventional treatments (Hollon et al., 2002). ECT might be a preferred treatment for a number of reasons. Antidepressants can take weeks to be effective, whereas ECT works quickly. For a suicidal client, waiting several

phototherapy
Treatment for seasonal affective disorder (SAD) through which the client is exposed to high-intensity light each day.

weeks for relief can literally be deadly. In addition, ECT may be the treatment of choice for pregnant women, because there is no evidence that the seizures harm the developing fetus. Many psychotropic medications, in contrast, can cause birth defects. Most important, ECT has proved effective in clients for whom other treatments have failed.

ECT does, however, have some serious limitations, including a high relapse rate (often necessitating repeated treatments) and memory impairments (Fink, 2001). In most cases, memory loss is limited to the day of ECT treatment, but some clients experience substantial permanent memory loss (Donahue, 2000). Some treatment centers perform ECT only over the brain hemisphere not dominant for language, and this approach seems to reduce memory disruption (Papadimitriou, Zervas, & Papakostas, 2001).

A series of studies have demonstrated that changing brain function by using transcranial magnetic stimulation (TMS) over the left frontal regions of the brain also reduces depression significantly (Chistyakov et al., 2004; George, Lisanby, & Sackheim, 1999; George et al., 1995; Pascual-Leone, Catala, & Pascual-Leone, 1996). Because TMS does not involve anesthesia or have any major side effects other than headache, it can be administered outside hospital settings. Moreover, it is effective even for those who have not responded to treatment with antidepressants (Fitzgerald et al., 2003). In October 2008, the Food and Drug Administration (FDA) approved TMS for the treatment of major depression in clients who are not helped by traditional therapies.

DEEP BRAIN STIMULATION As with obsessive-compulsive disorder, DBS might be valuable for treating severe depression when all other treatments have failed. As described in Scientific Thinking on p. 518, neurosurgeons inserted electrodes into the prefrontal cortex in six clients who had been diagnosed with severe depression (Mayberg et al., 2005; McNeely, Mayberg, Lozano, & Kennedy, 2008). Four of the clients had stunning results. In fact, some of them felt relief as soon as the switch was turned on. For all four, it was as if a horrible noise had stopped and a weight had been lifted. The clients described the result as feeling like they had emerged into a more beautiful world (Dobbs, 2006; Ressler & Mayberg, 2007).

Several studies have been done of using DBS for treatment-resistant depression, and each time at least half the clients benefited from the treatment (Bewernick et al., 2010; Malone et al., 2009). One study followed 20 clients for three to six years and found that about two thirds showed long-lasting benefits from DBS (Kennedy et al., 2011). Before DBS, only 10 percent of the client-participants had been able to work or engage in meaningful activities outside the house, whereas two thirds were able to do so after DBS. Such studies demonstrate that DBS is useful for helping clients lead more productive lives.

Mood Stabilizers Are Most Effective for Bipolar Disorders

In bipolar I disorder, a person exhibits severe mania (see Figure 13.20). The elevated moods in bipolar II disorder cycle between mild or moderate mania and major depressive disorder (also shown in Figure 13.20). Bipolar disorders are one of the few psychological disorders for which there is a clear optimal treatment (**Figure 14.19**). The best practice is to use psychotropic medications, especially the mood stabilizer lithium, which has the effect of regulating mood (see Table 14.2; Geddes, Burgess, Hawton, Jamison, & Goodwin, 2004). In one study, only about 20 percent of bipolar I clients being treated with lithium experienced relapses (Keller & Baker, 1991).

FIGURE 14.18

Phototherapy Is Used to Treat Seasonal Affective Disorder
One treatment for SAD is phototherapy. In this method, the client sits in front of strong lighting for several hours each day to reduce symptoms of depression.

FIGURE 14.19

Bipolar Disorders Can Be Successfully Treated
The actor Catherine Zeta-Jones has been diagnosed with bipolar II disorder. Zeta-Jones manages her symptoms through psychotropic medications and periodic residential treatment.

Hypothesis: Deep brain stimulation of an area of the prefrontal cortex may alleviate depression.

Research Method:

1 A pair of small holes were drilled into the skulls of six participants.

2 A pulse generator was attached under the collarbone, connecting to electrodes that passed through the holes in the skull to a specific area of the prefrontal cortex (see Figure 14.9).

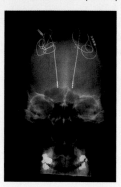

Results: Some participants reported relief as soon as the electrodes were switched on, and two thirds of the participants felt significantly better within months.

Conclusion: DBS may be an especially effective method for clients with depression that is resistant to other treatments.

Just how lithium stabilizes mood is not well understood, but the drug seems to modulate neurotransmitter levels, balancing excitatory and inhibitory activities (Jope, 1999). Because lithium works better on elevated moods than on depressed moods, clients—especially those with bipolar II disorder—often are treated with both lithium and an SSRI antidepressant. SSRIs are preferable to other antidepressants because they are less likely to trigger episodes of mania (Gijsman, Geddes, Rendell, Nolen, & Goodwin, 2004).

As with all psychological disorders, compliance with drug therapy can be a problem for various reasons. Lithium has unpleasant side effects, including thirst, hand tremors, excessive urination, and memory problems. These side effects often diminish after several weeks on the drug. To reduce these effects, some clients may skip doses or stop taking the medication completely. In such situations, cognitive-behavioral therapy can help clients stay on their medication regimen (Miller, Norman, & Keitner, 1989). Clients with bipolar disorder also may stop taking their medications because they miss the "highs" of their manic episodes. Again, psychological therapy can help clients accept their need for medication and understand how much their disorder affects those around them as well as themselves.

Drug Treatments Are Superior for Schizophrenia

In the early 1900s, Freud's psychoanalytic theory and treatments based on it were widely touted as the answer to many psychological disorders. However, even Freud admitted that his techniques were unlikely to benefit people with more-severe psychotic disorders, such as schizophrenia. Psychotic people were difficult to handle and even more difficult to treat, so they generally were institutionalized as patients in large mental hospitals with extremely poor conditions. In such institutions in New York State, for instance, the physician-to-patient ratio in 1934 was less than 1 to 200.

In this undesirable situation, the staff and administration of mental hospitals were willing to try any inexpensive treatment that might help decrease the patient population or that at least might make patients more manageable. Brain surgery, such as lobotomy, was often used for patients with severe psychological disorders. But those with schizophrenia did not seem to improve following the operation, although it did make them easier to handle. Fortunately, the introduction of medications in the 1950s eliminated the use of lobotomy.

PSYCHOTROPIC DRUG TREATMENTS Early antipsychotic drugs, called *conventional antipsychotics* (see Table 14.2), reduced the positive symptoms of schizophrenia, such as delusions, hallucinations, and disorganized speech and behavior. These drugs became the most frequently used treatment for this disorder, and they revolutionized the treatment of schizophrenia. Patients who had been hospitalized for years were able to walk out of mental institutions and live independently. But these medications have little to no effect on the negative symptoms of schizophrenia, which produce deficits in function, such as apathy and lack of emotion. What's more, they have significant side effects. For instance, conventional antipsychotics had significant motor effects that resemble symptoms of Parkinson's disease: immobility of facial muscles, trembling of extremities, muscle spasms, uncontrollable salivation, and a shuffling walk. *Tardive dyskinesia*—involuntary movement of body parts—is another devastating side effect of these medications and is irreversible once it appears (**Figure 14.20**).

The late 1980s saw the introduction of a new group of drugs, called the *atypical antipsychotics* (see Table 14.2). These are significantly different from conventional antipsychotic medications in a number of ways. First, they act on different neurotransmitters. Second, they are beneficial in treating both the positive symptoms of schizophrenia and some of the negative symptoms (**Figure 14.21**). Indeed, many clients who had not responded to the previously available conventional antipsychotics improved after taking a specific atypical antipsychotic. Third, no signs of Parkinson's symptoms or of tardive dyskinesia appeared in any of the clients taking this drug.

While atypical antipsychotics do have fewer side effects than earlier antipsychotic medications, they can have serious side effects. These include seizures, heart rate problems, and substantial weight gain. An even greater concern is that some of these drugs can cause a fatal reduction in white blood cells. Even in spite of the risks, these new drugs are now the first choice in treating schizophrenia (Walker, Kestler, Bollini, & Hochman, 2004).

BEHAVIOR THERAPY Medication is essential in the treatment of schizophrenia. Without it, clients may deteriorate, experiencing more-frequent and more-severe psychotic episodes. When antipsychotic drugs became available, other types of therapies for schizophrenia were virtually dismissed. It became clear over time, however, that although medication can effectively reduce symptoms, clients might still have long-standing social problems. Thus antipsychotic drugs should be combined with other treatments to help people lead productive lives.

Specifically, behavior therapy can include social skills training to elicit desired behavior, such as appropriate ways to act in specific social situations. These clients can also benefit from intensive training in regulating expression of emotion, recognizing social cues, and predicting the effects of their behavior in social situations. With intensive long-term training, clients with schizophrenia can generalize the skills learned in therapy to other social environments. Indeed, the successful use of newly acquired social skills is itself rewarding and encourages the client to continue using those skills. Similarly, when a client's self-care skills are poor, behavioral interventions can focus on areas such as grooming and bathing, managing medications, and financial planning. By contrast, training in specific cognitive skills, such as modifying thinking patterns and coping with auditory hallucinations, has been less effective.

PROGNOSIS IN SCHIZOPHRENIA Most clients diagnosed with schizophrenia experience multiple psychotic episodes over the course of the disorder. In some clients, the disorder apparently gets worse. Each schizophrenic episode lays the groundwork for more and more severe symptoms in the future. Thus it is in the client's best interest to treat the disorder early and aggressively.

A Side Effect of Conventional Antipsychotics Was Tardive Dyskinesia
Conventional antipsychotics were the earliest drugs used to treat schizophrenia. They unfortunately left some clients with a permanent motor disorder called tardive dyskinesia. This disorder caused involuntary movements of the face and neck as well as abnormal posture.

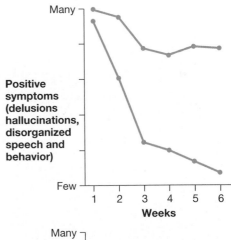

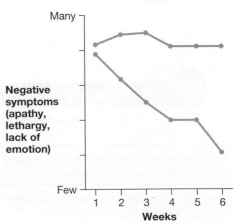

FIGURE 14.21

Effectiveness of Conventional Versus Atypical Antipsychotics
As shown by these graphs, many clients with schizophrenia did not respond to conventional antipsychotics. However, more recently introduced atypical antipsychotics worked well to reduce both positive and negative symptoms.

prognosis
A prediction of the likely course of a psychological (or physical) disorder.

However, most clients with schizophrenia also experience a reduction in symptoms as they get older. One study that followed participants for an average of 32 years showed that between half and two thirds were recovered or had experienced considerable improvement in functioning (Harding, Zubin, & Strauss, 1987). No one knows why most people with schizophrenia apparently improve as they grow older. Perhaps they find a treatment regimen that is most effective for them, or perhaps changes in the brain that occur with aging somehow result in fewer psychotic episodes. Dopamine levels may decrease with age, and this decrease may be related to the improvement in symptoms.

The prospect of recovery, or **prognosis,** for people with schizophrenia depends on factors that include the age of symptom onset, gender, and culture. People with later onset tend to have a more favorable prognosis than people who experience their first symptoms during childhood or adolescence (McGlashan, 1988). Women tend to have better prognoses than men do (Hambrecht, Maurer, Hafner, & Sartorius, 1992), perhaps because schizophrenia in women tends to appear later than in men. Culture also plays a role in prognosis. In developing countries, schizophrenia often is less severe than in developed countries (Jablensky, 1989; Leff, Sartorius, Jablensky, Korten, & Ernberg, 1992). This difference may arise because developing countries have more-extensive family networks that can provide more support for people with schizophrenia.

14.2 CHECKPOINT: **What Are Effective Treatments for Common Disorders?**

- Treatments that focus on behavior and on cognition are superior for anxiety disorders.

- Obsessive-compulsive disorder (OCD) responds to cognitive-behavioral treatment (CBT) and antidepressant medications. Deep brain stimulation (DBS) holds promise for treatment.

- Many antidepressants, CBTs, and alternative therapies are effective for depression.

- Lithium is most effective for stabilizing mood among clients with bipolar disorders. CBT can help support compliance with drug treatment.

- Atypical antipsychotics reduce positive and negative symptoms of schizophrenia. Drug therapy is most effective when combined with behavior therapy.

14.3 Can Personality Disorders Be Treated?

📖 **LEARNING GOALS**	✏️ **READING ACTIVITIES**
a. Remember the key terms about treatment of personality disorders.	List all of the boldface words and write down their definitions.
b. Apply dialectical behavior therapy (DBT) to the treatment of borderline personality disorder.	Describe how a therapist would go through three steps in DBT to treat a woman with borderline personality disorder.
c. Understand the barriers to treatment of antisocial personality disorder (APD).	Explain in your own words why it is so difficult to treat APD.

TABLE 14.5

Types of Treatment for Specific Personality Disorders

CATEGORY	EXAMPLES OF SPECIFIC DISORDERS	TYPES OF TREATMENT	SAMPLE OF POSSIBLE TECHNIQUES
Personality disorder (Cluster B: dramatic, emotional, or erratic behavior)	*Borderline personality disorder:* intense, unstable moods, relationships, and self-image; impulsivity	cognitive-behavioral	• dialectical behavior therapy (DBT)
	Antisocial personality disorder: disregard for and violation of the rights of others; manipulative; lacking guilt	psychotropic medications	• antidepressants
		behavior	• operant procedures

Most therapists agree that personality disorders are very difficult to treat. Clients with these disorders see the environment, not their own behavior, as the cause of their problems. As a result, individuals with personality disorders rarely seek therapy or are very difficult to engage in therapy. Nevertheless, some therapies have proven to be helpful for two of the most disruptive personality disorders, as shown in **Table 14.5.**

Dialectical Behavior Therapy Is Most Successful for Borderline Personality Disorder

The impulsivity, emotional disturbances, and identity disturbances characteristic of borderline personality disorder make it challenging to provide therapy for the people affected. Traditional psychotherapy approaches have been largely unsuccessful, so therapists have attempted to develop approaches specific to borderline personality disorder.

The most successful treatment approach so far was developed by the psychologist Marsha Linehan in the 1980s (**Figure 14.22**). Two decades earlier, as a young woman, Linehan had suffered from extreme social withdrawal, physical self-destructiveness, and recurrent thoughts of suicide (Carey, 2011). Institutionalized and diagnosed as schizophrenic, she was locked in a seclusion room, treated with various medications, given Freudian psychoanalysis, and treated with electroconvulsive therapy (ECT). Eventually, after being released from the hospital with little hope of surviving, Linehan learned to manage her disorder by changing the way she thought; she began to accept herself rather than striving for some impossible ideal.

This idea of "radical acceptance," as she puts it, enabled Linehan to function. She earned her PhD in psychology with the goal of helping people who are chronically self-destructive or even suicidal. Linehan's **dialectical behavior therapy (DBT)** combines elements of behavior, cognitive, and psychodynamic therapies with a mindfulness approach based on Eastern meditative practices (Lieb, Zanarini, Schmahl, Linehan, & Bohus, 2004). All clients are seen in both group and individual sessions, and the responsibilities of the client and the therapist are made explicit.

DBT proceeds in three phases (**Figure 14.23**). In phase 1, the therapist targets the client's most extreme and dysfunctional behaviors. Often these behaviors involve self-cutting and threats of suicide or suicide attempts. The focus is on replacing these behaviors with less destructive ones. The client learns problem-solving techniques and effective ways of coping with her emotions. She is taught to

FIGURE 14.22

Marsha Linehan

The psychologist Marsha Linehan pioneered the therapeutic technique of DBT. Linehan has recently publicly described having experienced the kind of psychological disorder this technique is used to treat.

dialectical behavior therapy (DBT)
Form of therapy used to treat borderline personality disorder.

(a)

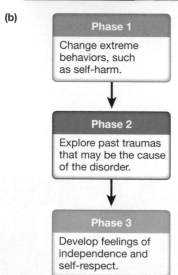

(b)

Phase 1

Change extreme behaviors, such as self-harm.

↓

Phase 2

Explore past traumas that may be the cause of the disorder.

↓

Phase 3

Develop feelings of independence and self-respect.

FIGURE 14.23

Dialectical Behavior Therapy Is Used to Treat Borderline Personality Disorder

(a) Suppose that a client with borderline personality disorder wants to hurt herself. **(b)** In phase 1 of DBT, she will learn to change extreme behaviors through problem solving, coping, and focusing on the present. In phase 2, the therapist helps her explore past traumas underlying her emotional problems. In phase 3, she works to increase her self-esteem and stop depending on others for validation.

control her attention so that she focuses on the present. Strategies for controlling attention are based on mindfulness meditation. In phase 2, the therapist helps the client explore past traumatic experiences that may be at the root of her emotional problems. In phase 3, the therapist helps the client develop self-respect and independent problem solving. This phase is crucial because clients with borderline personality disorder depend heavily on others for support and validation. These clients must be able to develop the appropriate attitudes and necessary skills themselves. Otherwise, they are likely to return to their previous behavior patterns.

Therapeutic approaches targeted at borderline personality disorder—for example, DBT—may improve the prognosis for these clients. Studies have demonstrated that when clients with borderline personality disorder undergo DBT, they are more likely to remain in treatment and less likely to be suicidal than are clients with borderline personality disorder who undergo other types of therapy (Linehan, Armstrong, Suarez, Allmon, & Heard, 1991; Linehan, Heard, & Armstrong, 1993). SSRI antidepressants are often prescribed along with DBT to treat feelings of depression.

Antisocial Personality Disorder Is Extremely Difficult to Treat

Treating clients with borderline personality disorder can be difficult. Treating those with antisocial personality disorder (APD) often seems impossible. These clients lie without thinking twice about it, care little for other people's feelings, and live for the present without considering the future. All these factors decrease the possibility of developing a therapeutic relationship and motivating the client to change. Individuals with this disorder are often more interested in manipulating their therapists than in changing their own behavior. Therapists working with these clients must constantly be on guard.

Numerous treatment approaches have been tried for APD and for the related but more extreme disorder, called *psychopathy*. Individuals with APD apparently have diminished cortical arousal. For this reason, stimulants have been prescribed to normalize arousal levels. There is evidence that these drugs are beneficial in the short term but not the long term. Anti-anxiety drugs may lower hostility levels somewhat, and lithium has shown promise in treating the aggressive, impulsive behavior of violent criminals who are psychopathic. Overall, however, psychotropic medications have not been effective in treating this disorder.

Similarly, most psychotherapies seem of little use in treating APD. Individual therapy sessions, for instance, rarely produce any change in antisocial behavior. Behavior therapy approaches have had some success when they use *operant procedures*. You may recall from Chapter 6 that operant conditioning is a form of learning where people learn to associate certain behaviors with specific outcomes. It can be applied to treatment when a therapist uses reinforcers to increase desirable behaviors (**Figure 14.24**). In this way, treatment using operant procedures can replace maladaptive behavior patterns with behavior patterns that are more socially appropriate. These approaches seem to work best when the therapist controls reinforcement, the client cannot leave treatment, and the client is part of a group. Clearly, this behavior therapy cannot be implemented on an outpatient basis, because the client will receive reinforcement for his antisocial behavior outside of therapy and can leave treatment at any time. For these reasons, therapy for APD is most effective in a residential treatment center or a correctional facility.

However, the prognosis is poor that clients with APD will change their behaviors as a result of any therapy. This conclusion is especially true for clients with psychopathic traits. Some of the more recently developed cognitive techniques show promise, but there is no good evidence that they produce long-lasting or even real changes. Fortunately for society, individuals with APD, but without the more severe disease of psychopathy, typically improve after age 40 with or without treatment.

The reasons for this improvement are unknown, but it may be due to a reduction in biological drives. One alternative theory is that these individuals may gain insight into their self-defeating behaviors. Another possibility is that they may just get worn out and be unable to continue their manipulative ways. The improvement, however, is mainly in the realm of antisocial behavior. The underlying egocentricity, callousness, and manipulativeness can remain unchanged (Harpur & Hare, 1994), especially for those who are psychopathic. Criminal acts and imprisonment decrease among those with APD after age 40 (**Figure 14.25**). Even so, more than half of the individuals with the more severe disorder, psychopathy, continue to be arrested after age 40 (Hare, McPherson, & Forth, 1988). Thus, although some aspects of the behavior of people with APD mellow with age, people with psychopathy remain indifferent to traditional societal norms.

(a)

(b)

Reinforcement

Provide reinforcers for desirable behaviors, such as telling the truth.

Effect of treatment

Increase in desirable behaviors.

FIGURE 14.24

Operant Procedures Are Used to Treat Antisocial Personality Disorder
(a) Someone with APD behaves in socially undesirable ways, such as stealing. (b) No treatment is very successful in treating APD. However, providing reinforcement can increase desired behaviors.

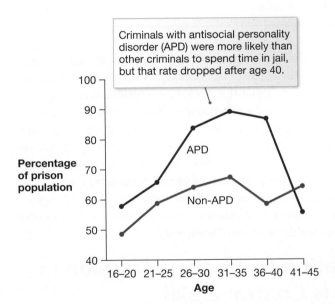

Criminals with antisocial personality disorder (APD) were more likely than other criminals to spend time in jail, but that rate dropped after age 40.

FIGURE 14.25

Rates of Imprisonment for People of Different Ages With Antisocial Personality Disorder
In this five-year longitudinal study, the percentage of prisoners in jail who had APD was greater than prisoners without the disorder. However, after the age of 40, there were relatively fewer prisoners with APD.

 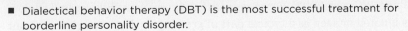

14.3 CHECKPOINT: Can Personality Disorders Be Treated?

LEARN

- Dialectical behavior therapy (DBT) is the most successful treatment for borderline personality disorder.

- DBT combines elements of behavior therapy, psychodynamic therapy, mindfulness meditation, and cognitive therapy.

- DBT therapy has three phases: (1) extreme behaviors are replaced with more-appropriate ones; (2) past traumatic events are explored; and (3) self-respect and independence are developed.

- Antisocial personality disorder (APD) is very difficult to treat. Therapy with operant procedures has had some success, primarily in a controlled residential treatment environment.

14.4 How Can Disorders Be Treated in Children and Adolescents?

FIGURE 14.26

Children and Adolescents Benefit From Treatment for Psychological Disorders

By receiving appropriate treatment early in life, young people can overcome psychological disorders. **(a)** Children often benefit from play therapy. **(b)** Adolescents can benefit from group therapy.

In the United States, an estimated 12 percent to 20 percent of children and adolescents experience psychological disorders (Leckman et al., 1995; Merikangas et al., 2010). As we have seen throughout this book, our experiences and development during early life are critical to our psychological health in adulthood. Problems not addressed during childhood or adolescence may persist into adulthood. Most theories of human development regard children and adolescents as less set in their ways than adults and therefore more open to treatment. Accordingly, there is a benefit to getting treatment early (**Figure 14.26**). In this section, we look at the psychotropic medication, cognitive, and behavior therapy approaches that are most effective for adolescent depression, attention-deficit/hyperactivity disorder (ADHD), and autism spectrum disorder (see **Table 14.6**).

Using Medication to Treat Depression in Adolescents Is Controversial

Adolescent depression is a serious problem. Approximately 8 percent of 12- to 17-year-olds in the United States have reported experiencing a major depressive episode that met *Diagnostic and Statistical Manual (DSM)* criteria (SAMHSA, 2011; **Figure 14.27**). Approximately 5,000 U.S. teenagers kill themselves each year, making suicide the third leading cause of death for that age group (Arias, MacDorman, Strobino, & Guyer, 2003). For many years, depression in children and adolescents was ignored or seen as a typical part of growing up. Even today, only about one third of adolescents with psychological disorders receive any form of treatment (Merikangas et al., 2011). The percentage is even lower for adolescents from racial and ethnic minorities (Cummings & Druss, 2010). Untreated adolescent depression is associated with drug abuse, dropping out of school, and suicide. Understandably, then, many mental health professionals reacted favorably to the initial use of antidepressants to treat adolescent depression.

RISKS OF ANTIDEPRESSANTS FOR ADOLESCENTS Shortly after SSRIs were introduced as treatments for adolescent depression, some mental health researchers raised concerns that the drugs might cause some adolescents to

TABLE 14.6

Types of Treatment for Children and Adolescents Experiencing Psychological Disorders

CATEGORY	EXAMPLES OF SPECIFIC DISORDERS	TYPES OF TREATMENT	SAMPLE OF POSSIBLE TECHNIQUES
Depressive disorders	*Major depressive disorder:* severely depressed mood or loss of interest in pleasurable activities for two weeks, plus other symptoms, such as changes in weight or in sleep	psychotropic medications	• antidepressants
		cognitive-behavioral	• changing negative thoughts associated with depression
Neuro-developmental disorders	*Attention-deficit/hyperactivity disorder:* hyperactivity, inattentiveness, and impulsive behavior with social or academic impairment; begins before age 12	psychotropic medications	• stimulants
		behavior	• operant procedures
	Autism spectrum disorder: persistent unresponsiveness; impaired social interaction, language, and cognitive development; restricted and repetitive behavior; symptoms begin in early childhood	behavior	• applied behavioral analysis

become suicidal (Jureidini et al., 2004). These concerns arose partly from studies with adults that found SSRIs caused some people to feel restless, impulsive, and suicidal. Following a report by one drug company of an increase in suicidal thoughts among adolescents taking its product, the FDA asked all drug companies to analyze their records for similar reports. An analysis of reports on more than 4,400 children and adolescents found that for those taking SSRIs, the number who reported having suicidal thoughts (4 percent) was about twice as high as for those taking a placebo (2 percent).

None of the children or adolescents in the reports actually committed suicide. But evidence of increased thoughts of suicide led the FDA, in 2004, to require warning labels on antidepressant packaging. Physicians also were advised to watch their young clients closely, especially in the first few weeks of treatment. Suddenly, many parents were wondering whether SSRIs were safe for their children.

Many questions about SSRIs and young people need to be answered. First, are SSRIs effective for young people? If so, are they more effective than other treatments? Second, do these drugs cause suicidal feelings, or are young people with depression likely to feel suicidal whether or not they take medication? Finally, how many children and adolescents would be suicidal if their depression were left untreated?

Some of these questions were addressed in the Treatment for Adolescents with Depression Study (TADS, 2004). This ambitious research program was supported by the U.S. National Institutes of Health. TADS provided clear evidence that SSRIs are effective in treating adolescent depression. The study examined 439 adolescents who had experienced depression for an average of 40 weeks before the study began. Participants were assigned randomly to a type of treatment and followed for 12 weeks. Sixty-one percent of participants taking an SSRI showed improvement in symptoms, compared with 43 percent receiving cognitive-behavioral therapy (CBT) and 35 percent taking a placebo. The group that received both an SSRI

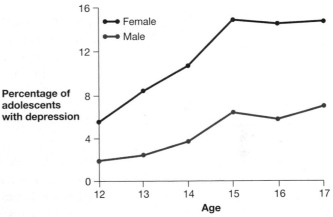

FIGURE 14.27

Rates of Depression in Adolescents
This graph shows results from the National Survey on Drug Use and Health. The survey was undertaken by the Substance Abuse and Mental Health Services Administration (SAMHSA), a branch of the U.S. Department of Health and Human Services. The lines chart the increasing rates of depression among adolescents in 2009.

FIGURE 14.28

Declining Suicide Rates in Adolescents

This graph depicts the declining suicide rates among people from ages 15 to 24 during a 20-year period.

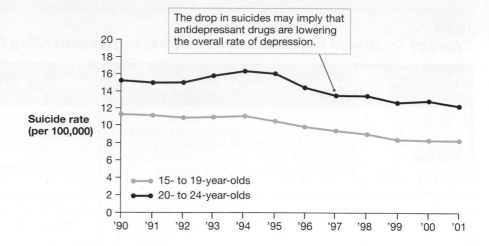

antidepressant and therapy did best (71 percent improved). This latter finding is consistent with studies of adults.

A follow-up study three years after the initial TADS research (March et al., 2007) found that the combined group still had the best outcomes (86 percent improvement). Improvement with CBT alone was similar to that with SSRIs alone (81 percent for both groups). In short, combining drugs and psychotherapy often produces the strongest results for treating depression in adolescents.

FURTHER THOUGHTS ON TREATMENT APPROACHES So can we say that SSRIs are a safe and effective treatment for adolescent depression? Ultimately, the question is whether the millions of children who take antidepressants experience more benefits than risks.

In the TADS report, suicide attempts were quite uncommon (7 of 439 clients). Moreover, only a small number of the 5,000 adolescents who kill themselves each year are taking antidepressants of any kind. Suicide rates have dropped since the use of SSRIs became widespread (**Figure 14.28**). Regions of the United States where SSRIs are most prescribed have seen the greatest reduction in teenage suicides (Olfson, Shaffer, Marcus, & Greenberg, 2003). Thus, not providing SSRIs to adolescents may increase the suicide rate (Brent, 2004).

According to some researchers, however, the relative success of psychotherapy for teenage depression makes it a better treatment choice. Indeed, there is considerable evidence that CBT is effective on its own (Mufson et al., 2004) and that it also enhances drug treatment. But getting adolescents to comply with psychotherapy can be challenging. CBT is also time consuming and expensive, and many health insurance companies provide only minimal support (Rifkin & Rifkin, 2004). It is unrealistic to expect that sufficient resources will be available to provide psychotherapy to all adolescents who need it in the near future.

By contrast, it is relatively easy for pediatricians and family physicians to prescribe drugs. However, general practitioners are not trained in treating psychological disorders. Thus, although prescribing drugs without CBT might be cost-effective (Domino et al., 2008), it may not be in the best interests of adolescents with depression. In short, adolescents with depression should receive CBT if at all possible.

Children With ADHD Can Benefit From Various Approaches

Is attention-deficit/hyperactivity disorder (ADHD) a psychological disorder that should be treated, or is it simply a troublesome behavior pattern that children eventually outgrow? As we discussed in Chapter 13, people have different opinions about this question.

Some individuals diagnosed with ADHD as children do grow out of it. Many more continue to experience the disorder throughout adolescence and adulthood. These people are more likely to drop out of school and to reach a lower socioeconomic level than expected. They show continued patterns of inattention, impulsivity, and hyperactivity, and they are at increased risk for other psychiatric disorders (Wilens, Faraone, & Biederman, 2004). Because of this somewhat bleak long-term prognosis, effective treatment early in life may be crucial.

PSYCHOTROPIC MEDICATION TREATMENT OF ADHD The most common treatment for ADHD is a central nervous system stimulant, such as methylphenidate. This drug is most commonly known by the brand name Ritalin. The drug's actions are not fully understood, but it may affect multiple neurotransmitters, particularly dopamine. Another drug used to treat ADHD is Adderall, which combines stimulants.

At appropriate doses, central nervous system stimulants such as Ritalin and Adderall decrease overactivity and distractibility. They increase attention and the ability to concentrate. Children on these drugs experience a small increase in positive behaviors (**Figure 14.29a**) and a large decrease in negative behaviors (**Figure 14.29b**). The children are able to work more effectively on a task without

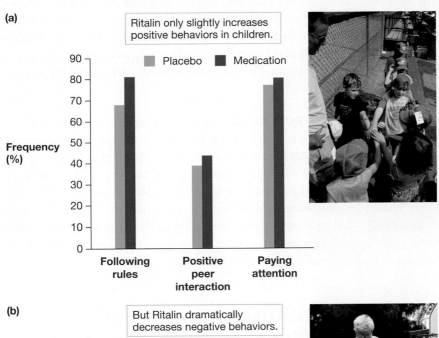

(a)

Ritalin only slightly increases positive behaviors in children.

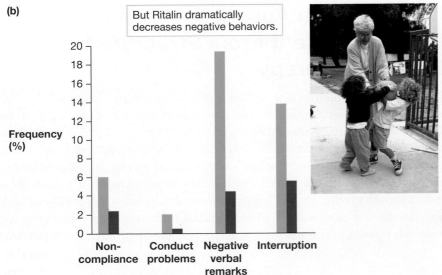

(b)

But Ritalin dramatically decreases negative behaviors.

FIGURE 14.29

The Effects of Ritalin on the Symptoms of ADHD

These graphs compare the effects of Ritalin on the symptoms of ADHD. **(a)** Ritalin only slightly increases positive behaviors in children with ADHD. **(b)** But Ritalin has a large effect on decreasing their negative behaviors.

Perhaps you know a child who was inattentive, hyperactive, and impulsive but who settled down after being treated with stimulants. Maybe even you yourself have been diagnosed with ADHD and have experienced the effects of stimulant drugs, such as Ritalin. It may be surprising that a stimulant would improve these symptoms, because the behavior of children with ADHD seems to suggest that their brains are overactive. However, functional brain imaging shows that children with ADHD have underactive brains. So their hyperactivity may have the effect of raising their arousal levels to a higher, normal level. Stimulant drugs have this same effect. Taking a stimulant means the child no longer needs to behave in ways that increase her arousal level.

interruption and are less impulsive. Studies have shown that children taking Ritalin also are happier, more adept socially, and modestly more successful academically (Chronis, Jones, & Raggi, 2006; Van der Oord et al., 2008).

Such improvements quite likely have contributed to increases in the number of children who take this medication. Parents often feel pressured by school systems to medicate children who have ongoing behavior problems, and parents often pressure physicians to prescribe Ritalin because its effects can make home life much more manageable.

Drugs such as Ritalin have drawbacks, however. Side effects include sleep problems, reduced appetite, body twitches, and temporary slowing of growth (Rapport & Moffitt, 2002; Schachter, Pham, King, Langford, & Moher, 2001). There is evidence that the short-term benefits of stimulants may not be maintained over the long term. In addition, because stimulants affect everyone who takes them, not just those with a diagnosed condition, drug abuse is a very real risk. There are many cases of children and adolescents buying and selling drugs such as Ritalin and Adderall. One study found that nearly 8 percent of college students had taken a nonprescribed stimulant in the past 30 days, and 60 percent reported knowing students who misused stimulants (Weyandt et al., 2009).

Perhaps most important, some children on medication may see their problems as beyond their control. They may not feel responsible for their behaviors and may not learn coping strategies they will need if they stop taking their medication or if it becomes ineffective. Most therapists believe medication should be supplemented by psychological therapies, such as behavior modification. Some therapists even urge that medication be replaced by other treatment approaches when possible.

BEHAVIOR THERAPY FOR ADHD Behavior therapy for ADHD aims to use operant procedures to reinforce positive behaviors and ignore or punish problem behaviors. An analysis of 174 studies consisting of over 2,000 research participants found clear support for the effectiveness of behavior therapy for ADHD (Fabiano et al., 2009). Many therapists advocate combining behavioral approaches with medication. The medication is used to gain control over the behaviors. Once that goal is accomplished, behavior modification techniques can be taught and the medication slowly phased out. Others argue that medication should be used only if behavioral techniques do not reduce inappropriate behaviors.

Children With Autism Spectrum Disorder Benefit From Structured Behavior Therapy

The treatment of children with autism spectrum disorder presents unique challenges to mental health professionals. The core symptoms of autism spectrum disorder are impaired communication, restricted interests, and deficits in social interaction. These symptoms make the children particularly difficult to work with. Their sometimes extreme behaviors—such as hand waving, rocking, humming, and jumping up and down—must be reduced or eliminated before the children can make progress in other areas. Changing these extreme behaviors is difficult to do because effective reinforcers are hard to find. Children without autism respond positively to social praise and small prizes, but children with autism often show no response to these rewards. In some cases, food is the only effective reinforcer in the initial stages of treatment.

Children with autism also tend to be quite selective in what they pay attention to. This tendency to focus on specific details while ignoring others interferes with generalizing learned behavior to other stimuli and situations. For example, a child who learns to set the table with plates may not know what to do when he is asked to use bowls instead. Generalization of skills must be explicitly taught. Thus, for these children, structured therapies are more effective than unstructured interventions such as play therapy (in which the therapist tries to engage the child in conversation while the child plays with toys).

BEHAVIOR THERAPY FOR AUTISM One of the best-known and perhaps most effective treatments was developed in the 1980s by Ivar Lovaas and his colleagues. This program, **applied behavioral analysis,** is based on principles of operant conditioning: Behaviors that are reinforced should increase in frequency, and behaviors that are not reinforced should diminish (**Figure 14.30**). There is evidence that this method can be used successfully to treat autism spectrum disorder (Warren et al., 2011), particularly if treatment is started early in life (Vismara & Rogers, 2010).

This intensive approach requires a minimum of 40 hours of treatment per week. In Lovaas's study (1987), preschool-age children with autism were treated by teachers and by their parents, who received specific training. After more than two years of treatment, the children had gained about 20 IQ points on average. Most of them were able to enter a normal kindergarten program. In contrast, IQ did not change in a control group that received no treatment. Children who received only 10 hours of treatment per week fared no better than those in the control group. Initiating treatment at a younger age yielded better results. Children with better language skills before entering treatment also had better outcomes than those with language impairments.

Lovaas's applied behavioral analysis program has some drawbacks. The most obvious is the time commitment. Parents of children with autism essentially become full-time teachers for years. The financial and emotional drains on the family can be substantial. And other children in the family may feel neglected or jealous due to the amount of time and energy devoted to the child with autism.

BIOLOGICAL TREATMENT FOR AUTISM SPECTRUM DISORDER There is good evidence that autism spectrum disorder is caused by brain dysfunction. Many attempts have been made to use this knowledge to treat the disorder. It is easy to find compelling case studies of children who appear to have benefited from alternative treatment approaches. When the treatments are assessed in controlled studies, however, there is little or no evidence that most of them are effective. Currently, the neurobiology of autism spectrum disorder is not well understood. Attempts to use psychopharmacology to treat the disorder have led to some improvements in behavior, but much remains to be learned.

PROGNOSIS Despite a few reports of remarkable recovery from autism spectrum disorder, the long-term prognosis is poor. One follow-up study revealed that men in their early 20s continued to show the ritualistic, self-stimulating behavior typical of autism spectrum disorder. In addition, nearly three quarters had severe social difficulties and were unable to live and work independently (Howlin, Mawhood, & Rutter, 2000).

FIGURE 14.30

Applied Behavioral Analysis Is Used to Treat Autism Spectrum Disorder
Applied behavioral analysis involves intensive interaction between children with autism and their teachers and parents. In this form of treatment, children perform specific tasks to earn rewards, such as food or stickers. Here, the task is touching blocks with the therapist. Over time, the rewards increase socially desired and appropriate behaviors that help children with autism function in their daily lives.

applied behavioral analysis
An intensive behavior therapy for autism; this treatment is based on operant conditioning.

Several factors affect the chances of recovery. Therapists once believed the prognosis was particularly poor for children whose symptoms were apparent before age 2 (Hoshino et al., 1980). However, it is possible that, before public recognition of the disorder increased, only the most severe cases of autism were diagnosed that early. Early diagnosis clearly allows for more-effective treatments (National Research Council, 2001). Still, severe cases are less likely to improve with treatment. Cases involving notable cognitive deficiencies are particularly resistant to treatment. Early language ability is associated with better outcomes (Howlin et al., 2000). Higher IQ is also associated with better outcomes. Children with autism have difficulty generalizing from the therapeutic setting to the real world, and this limitation severely restricts their social functioning (Handleman, Gill, & Alessandri, 1988). A higher IQ may mean a better ability to generalize learning and therefore a better overall prospect of improvement.

A CASE STUDY OF CHILDHOOD AUTISM SPECTRUM DISORDER Despite the difficulties of dealing with childhood autism spectrum disorder, we can end on a hopeful note. John O'Neil, a deputy editor at the *New York Times,* has described what it is like to be the parent of a child with the disorder (O'Neil, 2004).

O'Neil's son James had been an easy baby. As a toddler, however, he began to show signs of being "different." He seemed to have difficulty looking his parents in the eye and did not display a strong sense of connection. James showed little interest in objects, even toys that were given or shown to him. Instead, he repeated behaviors to the point of harming himself. For example, he pulled his cowboy boots on and off until his feet were raw. He responded to loud noises by crying.

James's behavior really started to deteriorate when he was 2½, following the arrival of a baby brother and a move to a new house. His parents assumed he was overwhelmed, but the director of James's new preschool noticed the telltale signs of autism. On her recommendation, a professional assessed James and determined that he had the disorder. During the first visit to a speech therapist, James's mother learned just how much her son needed treatment: He had forgotten his name.

The discovery of James's autism follows a familiar pattern. Most diagnoses of autism are made by age 3, but the disorder can be detected earlier if parents or pediatricians know what to look for. Luckily for James, the preschool staff recommended a professional evaluation because of his unusual behavior. The earlier treatment begins, the better the prognosis.

The O'Neils were relieved to learn that treatments for autism exist. Then they heard the bad news: Treatment is expensive, difficult, and time consuming. Most versions of treatment are based on applied behavioral analysis. As we described earlier, this type of therapy requires that parents and teachers spend hours working closely with the child. As is the case in many school districts, there were not enough resources for James to receive full treatment in school. Therefore, his mother, a physician, gave up her full-time position to set up a home-based program for James.

James's day might begin with physical activities to strengthen coordination and build body awareness. After this exercise period, he would take a snack break. During the break, appropriate social behaviors were reinforced and language skills were stressed. Each part of the day was designed to work on James's problem areas. He spent up to eight hours every day performing tasks that most children would find extremely boring. For example, he had to repeatedly imitate the therapist's placing two blocks next to each other or touching her nose. Along the way, his progress was charted to guide upcoming sessions. If James was going to be able to attend mainstream school, his language skills had to improve. Encouraged by being given any treat he asked for, James learned to talk.

He started school with the assistance of one of his full-time instructors, who attended class with him. Despite some rocky moments, James made tremendous progress. He still had problems in some areas, such as reading comprehension, math, attention, and social skills. He did not understand why he had a disorder and other kids did not. But James triumphed. Perhaps his biggest accomplishment was making friends with a classmate named Larry (**Figure 14.31**).

Why, O'Neil speculates, was Larry attracted to James as a friend? Perhaps they shared a love of potty humor. Perhaps they were similarly warm and enthusiastic. Whatever the reason, one day, O'Neil overheard the two friends engaged in silly conversation. They were telling stupid jokes and gossiping about their "girlfriends." In that moment, O'Neil realized just how many of his dreams for James had been realized. Psychological research continues to inform the development of effective treatments for disorders such as autism. The goal of this research is to help people like James live happier and healthier lives.

This success story and others like it show that psychological research can help us discover effective treatments for many psychological disorders. These treatments improve the lives of people who have the disorders and their families, and thus the treatments have a positive influence on society.

FIGURE 14.31

James O'Neil
At the time of this photo, James **(center)** was 8 years old. At left is his friend Larry, also 8. At right is James's brother, Miles, who was 6.

 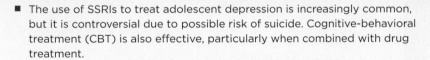

14.4 CHECKPOINT: How Can Disorders Be Treated in Children and Adolescents?

- The use of SSRIs to treat adolescent depression is increasingly common, but it is controversial due to possible risk of suicide. Cognitive-behavioral treatment (CBT) is also effective, particularly when combined with drug treatment.

- Stimulants such as Ritalin are effective in treatment for children with attention-deficit/hyperactivity disorder (ADHD). However, behavior therapy results in better long-term outcomes.

- Children with autism spectrum disorder benefit from applied behavioral analysis, an intensive treatment based on operant conditioning. This treatment diminishes unwanted extreme behaviors and increases socially desirable behaviors.

BIG PICTURE

BIG QUESTION	LEARNING GOALS

14.1
How Are Psychological Disorders Treated?

a. Remember the key terms about treatment of psychological disorders.
b. Understand the different forms of psychotherapy.
c. Understand the types of psychotropic medications.
d. Apply information about mental health practitioners.

14.2
What Are Effective Treatments for Common Disorders?

a. Remember the key terms about effective treatments for anxiety disorders, obsessive-compulsive disorder (OCD), depressive disorders, bipolar disorders, and schizophrenia.
b. Apply cognitive-behavioral therapy (CBT) to panic disorder.
c. Analyze the impact of different treatments on OCD.
d. Understand how CBT is used to treat people with depression.
e. Analyze drug treatments for schizophrenia.

14.3
Can Personality Disorders Be Treated?

a. Remember the key terms about treatment of personality disorders.
b. Apply dialectical behavior therapy (DBT) to the treatment of borderline personality disorder.
c. Understand the barriers to treatment of antisocial personality disorder (APD).

14.4
How Can Disorders Be Treated in Children and Adolescents?

a. Remember the key terms about treatment of psychological disorders experienced by children and adolescents.
b. Evaluate the two treatment options for adolescents with depressive disorders.
c. Apply the treatments for attention-deficit/hyperactivity disorder (ADHD).
d. Understand behavior therapy for autism spectrum disorder.

KEY TERMS

psychotherapy
psychodynamic therapy
humanistic therapy
behavior therapy
cognitive therapy
cognitive-behavioral therapy
   (CBT)
biological therapy
psychotropic medications
electroconvulsive therapy
   (ECT)
transcranial magnetic
   stimulation (TMS)
deep brain stimulation (DBS)

exposure
systematic desensitization
exposure and response
   prevention
phototherapy
prognosis

dialectical behavior therapy
   (DBT)

applied behavioral analysis

CHECKPOINT

- Psychotherapies are formal treatments that focus on changing a client's cognition and behavior.

- Biological treatments include psychotropic medications that change neurochemistry.

- When traditional treatments are not successful, therapists may suggest alternative treatments, such as electroconvulsive therapy (ECT), transcranial magnetic stimulation (TMS), and deep brain stimulation (DBS).

- Evidence-based practice provides safe, effective treatment. Therapies not supported by scientific evidence can be dangerous.

- A variety of specialized mental health practitioners have different training that allows them to provide treatment in diverse settings.

- Treatments that focus on behavior and on cognition are superior for anxiety disorders.

- Obsessive-compulsive disorder (OCD) responds to cognitive-behavioral treatment (CBT) and antidepressant medications. Deep brain stimulation (DBS) holds promise for treatment.

- Many antidepressants, CBTs, and alternative therapies are effective for depression.

- Lithium is most effective for stabilizing mood among clients with bipolar disorders. CBT can help support compliance with drug treatment.

- Atypical antipsychotics reduce positive and negative symptoms of schizophrenia. Drug therapy is most effective when combined with behavior therapy.

- Dialectical behavior therapy (DBT) is the most successful treatment for borderline personality disorder.

- DBT combines elements of behavior therapy, psychodynamic therapy, mindfulness meditation, and cognitive therapy.

- DBT therapy has three phases: (1) extreme behaviors are replaced with more-appropriate ones; (2) past traumatic events are explored; and (3) self-respect and independence are developed.

- Antisocial personality disorder (APD) is very difficult to treat. Therapy with operant procedures has had some success, primarily in a controlled residential treatment environment.

- The use of SSRIs to treat adolescent depression is increasingly common, but it is controversial due to possible risk of suicide. Cognitive-behavioral treatment (CBT) is also effective, particularly when combined with drug treatment.

- Stimulants such as Ritalin are effective in treatment for children with attention-deficit/hyperactivity disorder (ADHD). However, behavior

therapy results in better long-term outcomes.

- Children with autism spectrum disorder benefit from applied behavioral analysis, an intensive treatment based on operant conditioning. This treatment diminishes unwanted extreme behaviors and increases socially desirable behaviors.

For a self-quiz on this chapter, go to the back of the book and find Appendix B: Quizzes.

APPENDIX A: Analyzing Data in Psychological Research

After conducting research, you need to analyze the data to see whether your hypothesis is supported (see Figure 1.24, Step 4). The first step in evaluating data is to inspect the raw values. These data are as close as possible to the form in which they were collected. Recall that in your experiment, the hypothesis was "People who consume more alcohol will tend to display poorer driving skills than people who consume less alcohol." Therefore, the number of accidents that participants had during the driving game would be raw data. In examining raw data, researchers look for errors in data recording. For instance, they remove from the data set any responses that seem especially unlikely (e.g., 50,000 accidents).

Descriptive Statistics Summarize the Data

Once the researchers are satisfied that the raw data make sense, they summarize the basic patterns. Descriptive statistics provide an overall summary of the study's results. For example, descriptive statistics might show how many accidents participants had in the driving game when they had consumed alcohol to obtain a certain BAC level, as compared to the participants who had consumed tonic water.

CENTRAL TENDENCY The simplest descriptive statistics are measures of *central tendency* (**Figure A.1a**). This single value describes a typical response or the behavior of the group as a whole.

The most intuitive measure of central tendency is the mean. The mean is the arithmetic average of a set of numbers. The class average on an exam is an example of a mean score. In your experiment on drinking alcohol and driving performance, you might calculate three means, each based on the number of car accidents during the driving game. You would calculate one mean for those participants who drank alcohol and were at BAC 0.01–0.05 and another for those participants at BAC 0.06–0.10. You would calculate a third mean for those participants who did not drink alcohol. If alcohol affects driving, you would see a difference in the three means for performance of sober and intoxicated driving participants.

A second measure of central tendency is the median. The median is the value in a set of numbers that falls exactly halfway between the lowest and highest values. For instance, if you received the median score on a test, half the people who took the test scored lower than you and half the people scored higher.

Sometimes researchers will summarize data using a median instead of a mean. The median will be more useful than the mean if one or two numbers in the set are dramatically larger or smaller than all the others, because the mean will then give either an inflated or a deflated summary of the average. This effect occurs in studies of average income. Perhaps about 50 percent of Americans make more than $45,000 per year, but a small percentage of people make so much more (multiple millions or billions for the richest) that the mean income is much higher than the median and is not an accurate measure of what most people earn. The median provides a better estimate of how much money the average person makes.

A third measure of central tendency is the mode. The mode is the most frequent score or value in a set of numbers. For instance, the mode of children in an American family is two. This value means that more American families have two children than any other number of children.

VARIABILITY Consider two neighborhoods. One neighborhood is suburban, and most of its residents earn similar salaries. The other neighborhood is urban, and its residents have incomes ranging from low to high. In both neighborhoods, the mean income is $45,000 per year. Despite the differences between these populations, their mean incomes are the same.

What does this example show? Measures of central tendency are not the only important characteristics of data. Also important in a set of numbers is the *variability*, the spread in scores. A simple measure of variability is the range, the distance between the largest and smallest values (**Figure A.1b**).

Say that the top score for an exam is 95 out of a possible 100. The bottom score is 52. The range is 43. This result would be considered large, in that it shows great variability in student performance on the exam. It suggests that the person who scored 52 needs extra help—as do people who earned similar scores.

CORRELATIONS The descriptive statistics we have discussed so far are used for summarizing the central tendency and variability in a set of numbers. Descriptive statistics can also be used to summarize how two variables relate to each other.

Remember that finding the relationship between two variables is the goal of correlational methods. Recall from Chapter 1 that you would have used correlational methods to test the hypothesis "What is the relationship between drinking alcohol and driving skills?" In this case, your first step in examining the

You measure the number of car accidents during the driving game for those participants who drank alcohol to reach BAC 0.06–0.10:

- One has 55 accidents.
- One has 69 accidents.
- One has 56 accidents.
- One has 65 accidents.
- One has 60 accidents.

- Two have 45 accidents.
- One has 48 accidents.
- One has 38 accidents.
- One has 34 accidents.
- One has 25 accidents.

Written in ascending order, the number of accidents per participant looks like this:

25 34 38 45 45 48 55 56 60 65 69

(a) Central tendency

Mean
The arithmetic average of a set of numbers

$$\frac{\text{total \# of accidents}}{\text{total \# of participants}} = \frac{25+34+38+45+45+48+55+56+60+65+69}{11} = \frac{540}{11} = 49$$

Median
The value that falls exactly halfway between the lowest and highest values

25 34 38 45 45   48   55 56 60 65 69 = 48

Mode
The most frequent score or value in a set of numbers

25 34 38 **45 45** 48 55 56 60 65 69 = **45**

(b) Variability

Range
The distance between the largest and smallest values

25 34 38 45 45 48 55 56 60 65 **69** = **69 – 25** = **44**

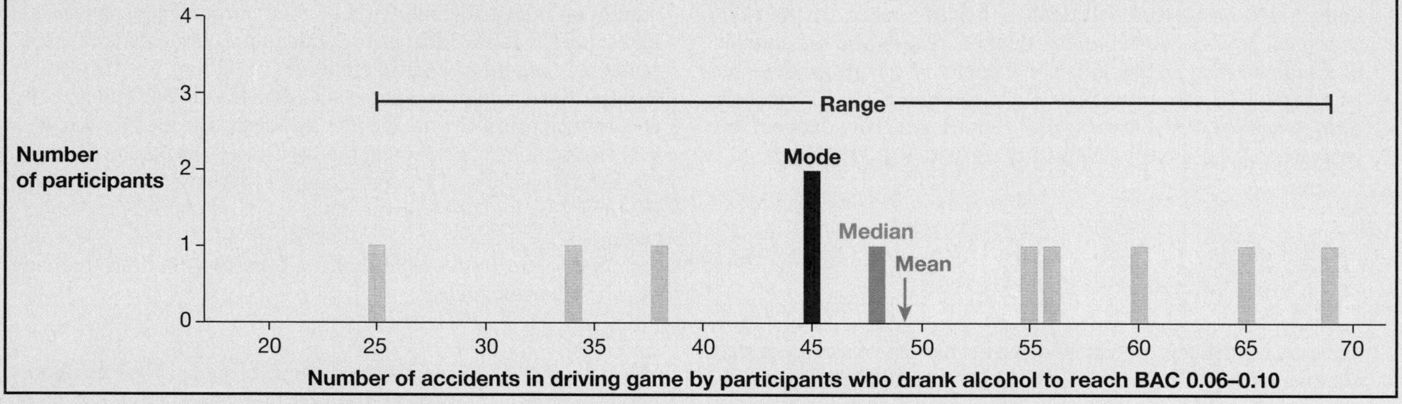

FIGURE A.1

Descriptive Statistics for Experiment on Alcohol Consumption and Driving Skills
Descriptive statistics summarize a data set. Here, the data are for one of three experimental groups in the sample experiment, the group that drank alcohol to reach BAC 0.06–0.10. **(a)** The mean, median, and mode are different measures of central tendency. **(b)** The range is a measure of variability.

relationship between two variables would be to create what is called a scatterplot. This type of graph provides a convenient picture of the data (**Figure A.2**).

In addition to depicting the association in a scatterplot, you would compute a *correlation coefficient*. This descriptive statistic provides a numerical value between −1.0 and +1.0 (see Figure A.2). The correlation coefficient provides two pieces of information that help us understand the relationship between two variables: It describes the direction of the association and the strength of the association.

Both the direction and the strength of associations are shown in the scatterplots in **Figure A.3**. If two variables have a positive correlation, they change in the same direction. That is, they both either increase or decrease together (see graphs 1 and 2). For example, when a person drinks greater amounts of alcohol, that person is more likely to have an accident when driving. If two variables have a negative correlation, they change in opposite directions: As one increases in value, the other decreases in value (see graphs 4 and 5). For example, as a person drinks more alcohol, that person's driving skills decline.

Besides indicating the direction of the association, a correlation coefficient also tells us about the strength of the relationship. Knowing how people measure on one variable enables you to predict how they will measure on the other variable. What signifies a strong relationship? A perfect positive correlation is indicated by a value of +1.0 (see graph 1). A perfect negative correlation is indicated by a value of −1.0 (see graph 5). If two variables show no apparent relationship, the value of the correlation will be a number close to zero (see graph 3).

Inferential Statistics Rule Out Chance Findings

Researchers use descriptive statistics to summarize data sets. They also need to estimate whether differences actually exist in the populations they have drawn their study samples from. For this purpose, researchers use inferential statistics.

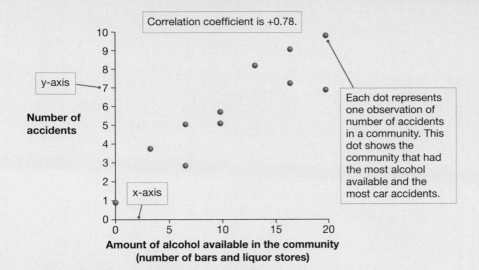

FIGURE A.2

Scatterplot of Correlation Between Alcohol Consumption and Driving Skills
Scatterplots are graphs that illustrate the correlation between two variables. This scatterplot shows data concerning alcohol consumption and car accidents: As alcohol consumption goes up, so do car accidents.

Suppose you find that the mean driving performance for drivers at BAC level 0.06–0.10 in your experiment is lower than the mean driving performance for drivers who did not drink alcohol. How different do these means need to be for you to conclude that your finding is not just an isolated, chance finding?

To answer this question, assume for a moment that intoxication does not influence driving performance. If you measure the driving performances of sober and drunk drivers, just by chance there will be some variability in the mean performance of the two groups. They are not likely to have exactly the same mean, and just by chance you would expect the means to differ a little bit. The key is that if alcohol does not affect driving performance, then a large difference between the two means is relatively unlikely. Researchers use statistical techniques to understand the differences among the sample means. Are these differences (probably) chance variations, or do they reflect meaningful differences in the populations?

When the results obtained from a study would be very unlikely to occur if there really were no differences between the groups of subjects, the researchers conclude that the results are statistically significant. According to generally accepted standards, researchers typically conclude there is a significant effect only if the results would occur by chance less than 5 percent of the time.

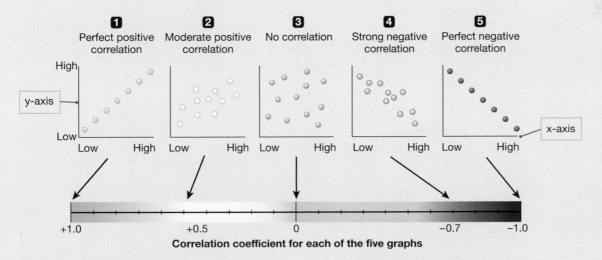

FIGURE A.3

Direction and Strength of Correlations
Correlations are a descriptive statistic of how two variables are associated (or not associated, as in 3). Correlations are characterized by direction. In a positive correlation (1 and 2), two variables change in the same direction. In a negative correlation (4 and 5), the variables change in different directions. Correlations are also characterized by the strength of association between variables. Stronger correlations (1 and 5) are shown by very little scatter or spread, such as when all the values fall on a straight line. Weaker correlations (2 and 4) are shown by more scatter or spread, where the values deviate from a straight line. Other times, there is no correlation between variables (3).

APPENDIX B: Quizzes

CHAPTER 1: INTRODUCING THE WORLD OF PSYCHOLOGY

1. Linda is a psychologist. During her day at work, she is most likely to _____.
   a) investigate export policies
   b) study trends in foreign markets
   c) interpret a European burial site
   d) research thought processes

2. Harry has a different girlfriend every week. William's explanation for Harry's behavior is that Harry has a naturally high level of testosterone. Kate's explanation is that Harry's mother died when he was young. These explanations tell you that William likely believes that _____ influences who we are, whereas Kate believes that _____ influences who we are.
   a) nurture; nature
   b) structuralism; behaviorism
   c) nature; nurture
   d) behaviorism; structuralism

3. Monica believes that the human mind, like a piece of music, must be broken into component parts to be understood. Monica's beliefs best reflect the psychological school of thought called _____.
   a) structuralism
   b) functionalism
   c) psychoanalytic theory
   d) Gestalt theory

4. Frank wants to investigate how mental processes, such as attention, affect the amount of time that a child will work on a difficult task. Frank's research is most similar to the research approach taken by _____.
   a) Lewin, from the school of social psychology
   b) Watson, from the school of behaviorism
   c) Miller, from the school of cognitive psychology
   d) Wertheimer, who helped develop Gestalt theory

5. Victoria and Janelle are studying whether college students have better test performance when taking tests written in their native language or in their second language. This research is focused on investigating psychological phenomena at the _____ level of analysis.
   a) social
   b) individual
   c) biological
   d) cultural

6. Frank is always polite and reserved. Elrico thinks that Frank's behavior can be explained by his shyness. Aidan thinks that Frank's behavior can be explained by his having been raised in rural Kentucky. Elrico's view of Frank's behavior most closely reflects the perspective of _____ psychology, whereas Aidan's view most closely reflects the perspective of _____ psychology.
   a) personality; cultural
   b) personality; developmental
   c) cognitive; cultural
   d) cognitive; developmental

7. Nancy is conducting a study on how couples communicate. However, she doesn't have the money to conduct laboratory tests, so she collects data in the field. To ensure that she does not violate the ethical rule of privacy, Nancy must _____.
   a) observe couples only in public settings
   b) always keep the couples' personal information secret
   c) always obtain informed consent from the couples
   d) observe couples only in their own homes

8. Simon, a psychologist, believes that people who watch a greater amount of TV are more likely to be good at memorizing visual information than those who watch less TV. To investigate this _____, Simon uses the average number of hours of TV watched during one week as the _____ of amount of TV watching.
    a) theory; variable
    b) hypothesis; operational definition
    c) theory; operational definition
    d) hypothesis; variable

9. Jool wants to study whether children in public playgrounds tend to play with children of their own sex. To begin her study, Jool goes to the local playground, watches the kids for about 20 minutes, and takes notes about what she sees. Jool is conducting her research by using the method of a(n) _____.
    a) self-report
    b) case study
    c) experiment
    d) observational study

10. Keyshawn has just learned about variables and correlations, and he is applying these concepts to his own life. He correctly thinks: "One positive correlation in my life is that _____."
    a) my prescription anti-anxiety medicine causes me to be more calm and outgoing
    b) spending more time studying is associated with higher grades
    c) the closer to the front I sit in class, the less likely I am to be called on by the professor
    d) the outfit I choose for the day does NOT influence the way I style my hair

Answers for Chapter 1

1. D
Psychology is the study of human mental activity and behavior.
    For more information, refer to Learning Goal 1.1a.

2. C
The nature/nurture debate considers how thoughts and behaviors are influenced by biological and/or environmental factors.
    For more information, refer to Learning Goal 1.2b.

3. A
Structuralism is the school of psychology that explores conscious experiences by breaking them down into their component parts.
    For more information, refer to Learning Goal 1.2c.

4. C
Cognitive psychology investigates mental activity associated with functions such as intelligence, learning, thinking, and attention.
    For more information, refer to Learning Goal 1.2d.

5. B
The individual level of analysis deals with comparing individual differences in mental processes and how these differences affect perception, understanding, and behavior.
    For more information, refer to Learning Goal 1.3b.

6. A
Personality psychology is the study of enduring characteristics that people display over time (for example, shyness). Cultural psychology examines how people's behavior is influenced by the societal rules, values, and beliefs from their environment.
    For more information, refer to Learning Goal 1.3c.

7. A
According to the ethical guidelines regarding privacy, the couples in a study of this kind must be observed in public settings only, not in private settings.
    For more information, refer to Learning Goal 1.3d.

8. B
Simon has come up with a specific, testable prediction—a hypothesis. He is using a specific criterion—an operational definition—to assess his participants on a particular variable.
    For more information, refer to Learning Goal 1.4b.

9. D
By strictly watching the children and not manipulating any variables, Jool is using the research method of an observational study.
    For more information, refer to Learning Goal 1.4c.

10. B
Keyshawn sees that two variables—studying and getting good grades—are related. When one increases, so does the other, and that effect is a positive correlation.
    For more information, refer to Learning Goal 1.4d.

CHAPTER 2: THE ROLE OF BIOLOGY IN PSYCHOLOGY

1. Marisol knocks over a glass of water and tries to catch it. Neurons firing in her brain enable her quick reaction. Which of the following statements correctly describes the communication of Marisol's neurons in this situation?
   a) The axons of neurons receive neurotransmitters.
   b) The neurons fire stronger action potentials.
   c) The dendrites of neurons receive neurotransmitters.
   d) The neurons are in a resting state.

2. You participate in a medical study testing a drug that temporarily increases the function of the neurotransmitter glutamate. You correctly believe that the increased glutamate will _____.
   a) improve your ability to remember
   b) increase the number of hours you sleep
   c) make you feel more depressed
   d) make you feel less pain from a pin prick

3. Alyssa's grandmother had a stroke. Afterwards, she experienced trouble keeping her balance and stumbled when she walked. Alyssa correctly believes that her grandmother's stroke affected a structure in her _____ called the _____.
   a) hindbrain; cerebellum
   b) forebrain; cerebellum
   c) hindbrain; substantia nigra
   d) forebrain; substantia nigra

4. Ever since he had a motorcycle accident, Cornelius has been unable to form new memories. Cornelius has most likely damaged his _____.
   a) hypothalamus
   b) amygdala
   c) hippocampus
   d) thalamus

5. Dane is looking at a photo that his friend emailed him. During this task, the part of Dane's brain that processes his ability to see the people in the photo is probably most active. This part of the brain is the _____ lobe.
   a) frontal
   b) temporal
   c) parietal
   d) occipital

6. George touches a baby lamb at the local petting zoo. George says the lamb feels "soft." The softness of the fur is a result of how the feel of the lamb was processed in George's _____ system.
   a) autonomic nervous
   b) endocrine
   c) parasympathetic
   d) somatic nervous

7. While walking through the woods one day, Ricardo sees a large bear. His sympathetic nervous system will most likely _____.
   a) cause his heart to beat faster as he prepares to run away
   b) allow him to notice how smooth his can of bear spray feels against his hand
   c) cause a reflexive reaction in his spinal cord that lets him run away
   d) allow his breathing to slow as he relaxes and thinks about what to do next

8. Corbin, a 13-year-old, asks his brother if hormones are responsible for Corbin's sudden growth of facial hair. His brother responds, "Yes, it's because hormones called _____ are being released into your bloodstream, where they affect the organs in your body through the _____ system."
   a) androgens; endocrine
   b) estrogens; central nervous
   c) estrogens; endocrine
   d) androgens; central nervous

9. Dr. Rieker does research in the field of behavioral genetics. He wants to investigate associations between different siblings' grades in school. To study the role of "nature" in siblings' grades, he should conduct _____. By contrast, to study the role of "nurture" in siblings' grades, he should conduct _____.
   a) an experiment on genotypes; an experiment on phenotypes
   b) a twin study; an adoption study
   c) an experiment on phenotypes; an experiment on genotypes
   d) an adoption study; a twin study

10. Louisa had a stroke that damaged the motor cortex in her right hemisphere, making it impossible for her to walk. However, over time and with practice, Louisa started walking again because different, undamaged, parts of her brain took over control of this ability. Louisa was able to walk again most likely because of the influence of _____ on her brain.
    a) genotypes
    b) plasticity
    c) the sympathetic nervous system
    d) the parasympathetic nervous system

Answers for Chapter 2

1. C

If a presynaptic neuron has an action potential, then neurotransmitters are released from the end of the axon, cross the synapse, and bind with the receptors on the dendrites of the postsynaptic neuron. But action potentials are never stronger or weaker—they fire or do not fire, but they always fire at a constant rate.

For more information, refer to Learning Goal 2.1c.

2. A

Glutamate is the primary excitatory neurotransmitter that also assists in learning and memory by reinforcing neural pathways.

For more information, refer to Learning Goal 2.1d.

3. A

The hindbrain is the portion of the brain that contains the cerebellum, which is crucial for motor learning, coordination, and balance.

For more information, refer to Learning Goal 2.2b.

4. C

The hippocampus plays a crucial role in the formation of new memories.

For more information, refer to Learning Goal 2.2c.

5. D

The occipital lobe houses the primary visual cortex and processes visual information.

For more information, refer to Learning Goal 2.2d.

6. D

The somatic nervous system transmits sensory information to the central nervous system, using receptors in the skin, muscles, and joints.

For more information, refer to Learning Goal 2.3b.

7. A

The sympathetic nervous system prepares the body for action and is in charge of the fight-or-flight response. It would most likely be responsible for the increased heart rate that enables Ricardo to run from the bear.

For more information, refer to Learning Goal 2.3c.

8. A

Androgens are hormones, more prevalent in males, that influence the development of secondary sex characteristics, such as the growth of facial hair. As chemical messengers in the endocrine system, hormones act on glands and organs to affect how we think and behave.

For more information, refer to Learning Goal 2.3d.

9. B

A behavioral geneticist examines how genes and environment interact to influence psychology. To focus on how "nature" influences siblings, behavioral geneticists study monozygotic (identical) and dizygotic (fraternal) twins in the same home, because similarities between the twins are thought to be due to genetics. To focus on how "nature" influences siblings, behavioral geneticists use adoption studies, because similarities between biological and adopted siblings are thought to be due to environment.

For more information, refer to Learning Goal 2.4c.

10. B

Plasticity is a property of the brain that enables it to change through experience.

For more information, refer to Learning Goal 2.4d.

CHAPTER 3: CONSCIOUSNESS

1. When Fiona was a child, her grandmother taught her to make lasagna. Now, when Nicholas asks Fiona for her lasagna recipe, she realizes she doesn't know the measurements for the ingredients because she always "just makes it." Fiona's ability to cook lasagna without being aware of measuring the ingredients is best described as an example of _____.
   a) conscious processing
   b) the global workspace model
   c) unconscious processing
   d) subliminal perception

2. Matilda's boyfriend just sent her a beautiful teddy bear as a gift. According to the global workspace model, Matilda's subjective enjoyment of how the teddy bear looks is most likely due to _____.
   a) brain activity in her occipital lobe
   b) the fact that her corpus callosum has been cut
   c) the amount of REM sleep she got last night
   d) her being in an altered state of consciousness

3. Clark's corpus callosum was surgically cut to reduce epilepsy. When a picture of his dog is shown only to Clark's left hemisphere, he will be _____ to name the object as "dog" and will be _____ to use his left hand to pick up a toy dog out of a group of objects.
   a) able; able
   b) able; unable
   c) unable; unable
   d) unable; able

4. Leo is participating in a sleep study. During his sleep, his brain shows delta wave activity. At that point, the researchers wake him up, and he is very disoriented. When the researchers wake Leo up, he is most likely in _____ sleep.
   a) stage 2
   b) REM
   c) stage 1
   d) slow-wave

5. For spring break, you spend ten days with friends, going dancing late every night and not getting enough sleep. According to the consolidation theory of sleep, afterward you will _____.
   a) have trouble remembering things you did during spring break
   b) secrete more growth hormone to restore your body
   c) have fewer dreams for a while because of the REM rebound effect
   d) sleep less during the night for a while because your circadian rhythms have shifted

6. While sleeping, Kevin dreamed about being in a dancing competition. As he dreamed about doing dance moves, he kicked his foot against the wall. The kick was most likely due to _____.
   a) sleep apnea
   b) narcolepsy
   c) somnambulism
   d) REM behavior disorder

7. Remy likes to go home after a hard day at work and relax in a chair, watching the fire roar in his fireplace. In these situations, he often feels "zoned out." His thoughts and the world around him seem less clear. Remy is most likely experiencing _____.
   a) withdrawal
   b) REM sleep
   c) altered consciousness
   d) posthypnotic suggestion

8. Steven goes to a hypnotism show with his friend Missy and is chosen to be brought on stage to be hypnotized. Missy believes in the dissociation theory of hypnosis, so she thinks that when Steven is hypnotized he will _____.
   a) only pretend to act how a hypnotized person should act
   b) NOT be able to experience hypnotic analgesia
   c) actually be in a trancelike state where he can't access his conscious awareness
   d) experience flow

9. Vivian is under the influence of a psychoactive drug. She is experiencing changes in her emotions and perceptions. In particular, she sees in "Technicolor" because everything looks so vivid. Vivian is most likely experiencing the effects of _____ on her consciousness.
   a) stimulants
   b) hallucinogenics
   c) depressants
   d) opiates

10. When Jerry began college, he rarely drank coffee, so it didn't take much coffee to get enough caffeine to make him feel energetic. But now Jerry must drink much more coffee to get enough caffeine to experience the same energy level. However, he experiences no negative side effects from drinking so much coffee. Taken together, this information most likely indicates that Jerry _____.
    a) has developed a tolerance of caffeine
    b) is experiencing flow when he drinks caffeine
    c) has become addicted to caffeine
    d) is experiencing caffeine withdrawal

Answers for Chapter 3

1. C
Unconscious processing occurs when we execute well-learned, routine tasks without devoting much of our attention to the tasks, so we are not fully aware of doing them.
   For more information, refer to Learning Goal 3.1b.

2. A
The global workspace model states that brain activity gives rise to consciousness. Specifically, our conscious experiences are a result of which brain circuits are active at a given time.
   For more information, refer to Learning Goal 3.1d.

3. B
The left hemisphere of the brain is responsible for producing language, so Clark will be able to say "dog". But the left hand is controlled by the right hemisphere. Because his right hemisphere did not receive the image of the dog due to his corpus callosum having been cut, Clark will be unable to pick up the toy with his left hand.
   For more information, refer to Learning Goal 3.1e.

4. D

Slow-wave sleep is characterized by the presence of delta waves. Consciousness is very different in this stage of sleep. People can respond to important information in the environment, such as a baby's cries. But if they wake up from slow-wave sleep, they are often disoriented.

For more information, refer to Learning Goal 3.2b.

5. A

The consolidation theory suggests that the main benefit of sleeping is to help us strengthen and consolidate the neural connections that enable us to learn and remember.

For more information, refer to Learning Goal 3.2c.

6. D

REM behavior disorder occurs when the body's muscles are not paralyzed during REM sleep and people act out their dreams.

For more information, refer to Learning Goal 3.2d.

7. C

During many daily activities, such as watching television or looking at a fire, a person may experience an altered state of consciousness. In an altered state of consciousness, the person has a different quality of awareness. Internal thoughts and external events seem either more or less clear.

For more information, refer to Learning Goal 3.3b.

8. C

According to the dissociative theory of hypnosis, hypnosis is a truly altered state of consciousness in which people's awareness of their conscious experiences are suspended or inaccessible.

For more information, refer to Learning Goal 3.3c.

9. B

Hallucinogenic drugs affect consciousness by altering a person's sensations and perceptions.

For more information, refer to Learning Goal 3.4b.

10. A

The evidence suggests that Jerry has developed a tolerance for caffeine. This form of physical dependence occurs when the body becomes accustomed to certain levels of a substance and needs more of the substance to feel the same effect as when the person first started using it.

For more information, refer to Learning Goal 3.4d.

CHAPTER 4: DEVELOPMENT ACROSS THE LIFE SPAN

1. Latonia is pregnant. Her doctor told her that the baby has developed enough that it can now live outside of the womb. Right now, Latonia is most likely in the _____ period of pregnancy.
   a) fetal
   b) teratogen
   c) embryonic
   d) germinal

2. Reagan is 3 weeks pregnant, but doesn't know it yet. She drinks a few glasses of wine two or three days each week. In this case, alcohol is a _____ that may put her baby at risk for _____.
   a) teratogen; irritability and high-pitched crying
   b) germinal; irritability and high-pitched crying
   c) germinal; malformation of the face and limbs and mental retardation
   d) teratogen; malformation of the face and limbs and mental retardation

3. Dr. Cortez, a pediatrician, focuses on the biological factors that influence physical development. In his view, children learn to walk only after they can stand and crawl. His wife reminds him that their children learned to walk at somewhat different ages, depending on how often each child was willing to practice walking with her. From this information, you might assume that Dr. Cortez believes that physical development is primarily influenced by _____ and his wife believes that it is mainly affected by _____.
   a) maturation; nature
   b) maturation; nurture
   c) dynamic systems theory; nature
   d) dynamic systems theory; nurture

4. Peter is 2 years old, and his mother takes him to see a new dentist. When Peter's mother leaves him alone with the dentist for a few minutes, Peter begins to cry. When his mother returns, she cannot console him. This scenario suggests that Peter has most likely formed a(n) _____ attachment with his mother.
   a) ambivalent
   b) avoidant
   c) secure
   d) anxious

5. Shay's parents pay attention to the new thinking skills that Shay acquires. They realize he has passed out of Piaget's preoperational stage into the next stage of cognitive development when he _____.
   a) plans his next several chess moves in his head when playing chess with his dad.
   b) tells them his "truck is happy" because it got a bath in the washing machine.
   c) found his favorite pacifier hiding under the blanket in his crib.
   d) correctly answered the question "What is 8 minus 2?" with the help of his fingers.

6. Mary and her younger brother Eric are playing in the front yard. Eric has mastered correct syntax in English, but he displays overregularization when he says, _____.
   a) "Ball me pass to play!"
   b) "Water now!"
   c) "Mary! I forgetted to feed my pet worms!"
   d) "We need to play outside and not watch TV!"

7. Juan is a young man from Mexico. He attends college in the United States with the intention of becoming a preschool teacher. However, in his native culture, being a preschool teacher is not generally a job a man would have. Although he is proud to be a Mexican man, Juan is worried enough about people's perceptions that he is also exploring other career options. This scenario indicates that Juan is most likely experiencing _____.
   a) the psychosocial challenge of identity versus role confusion
   b) questions about his gender identity
   c) the psychosocial challenge of industry versus inferiority
   d) questions about his ethnic identity

8. Kurt's friend Friedrich steals an iPad from another student in their dorm. Kurt decides to tell the police what Friedrich did because Kurt thinks that stealing the iPad was against the law. This reasoning reveals that Kurt is most likely in the _____ stage of moral development.
   a) preconventional
   b) postconventional
   c) unconventional
   d) conventional

9. Zach, a 42-year-old, very much wants to have children, but he has never found the right person to have them with. He decides to adopt a child because he wants to make a positive contribution to the future. Zach's decision to adopt and raise a child most likely reflects that he has successfully dealt with the psychosocial challenge of _____.

   a) trust
   b) generativity
   c) integrity
   d) intimacy

10. Tanya is 78 years old and has stayed physically and mentally active, so she is experiencing only the normal cognitive decline of a person her age. As a result, Tanya is least likely to have trouble with _____.
   a) thinking and reacting quickly to road signs when she is driving
   b) trying to remember her grocery list while talking to a friend at the market
   c) remembering what she learned long ago, such as the names of the state capitals
   d) learning the names of several new people that she meets at a party

Answers for Chapter 4

1. A
From 2 months until the birth of the baby, a developing human is a "fetus" and the woman is in the fetal period of prenatal development. Although most pregnancies end with a birth at about 40 weeks of gestation, a fetus can often survive outside the womb after about 28 weeks of gestation.
   For more information, refer to Learning Goal 4.1b.

2. D
Alcohol is an example of a teratogen (that happens to be a legal drug) with severe effects on a developing embryo. Alcohol may lead to birth defects such as facial and limb malformations, heart defects, and mental retardation. For more information, refer to Learning Goal 4.1c.

3. B
The process of maturation occurs when children develop a predictable set of motor skills in the same sequential order within a similar range of time. Maturation was thought to be a purely biological process that reflected the influence of nature on development. But we now know that the influence of nurture—experiences and environment—helps shape an infant's physical development.
   For more information, refer to Learning Goal 4.1d.

4. A
An ambivalent attachment is an insecure attachment. Children with ambivalent attachments cry when their caregiver leaves and are inconsolable upon being reunited with the caregiver.
   For more information, refer to Learning Goal 4.2c.

5. D

If Shay is out of the preoperational stage of cognitive development, he is now in the concrete operational stage. In this stage, he is able to think logically and perform and understand operations on concrete objects. For example, he can do simple math if he uses his fingers or blocks or some other object to help him.

For more information, refer to Learning Goal 4.2d.

6. C

Eric is able to put words together using correct syntax for English. But as a normal part of his language development, he is overapplying certain rules, which is called overregularization. In this case, Eric incorrectly added "-ed" to "forget" to make "forgetted." Instead of using the regular past tense, he should have used the irregular past tense, "forgot."

For more information, refer to Learning Goal 4.2e.

7. A

Juan is struggling with the psychosocial challenge of identity versus role confusion because his first career choice conflicts with his culture's expectations for men. Exploring other career choices suggests he may be experiencing role confusion.

For more information, refer to Learning Goal 4.3c.

8. D

People in the conventional level of moral reasoning are likely to make moral decisions based on laws or social rules. They make decisions in order to avoid breaking laws and going against social norms when doing so would bring about disapproval.

For more information, refer to Learning Goal 4.3d.

9. B

According to Erickson, when most people reach middle age—between about age 40 and 50—they face the challenge of generativity versus stagnation. This challenge reflects the tension between a desire to work hard in one's career and raise children to leave something for future generations versus focusing only on oneself.

For more information, refer to Learning Goal 4.4c.

10. C

As people age, they experience cognitive impairments such as reacting quickly to information, doing two things at one time, and learning new information. But they tend to retain knowledge for facts they learned in the past.

For more information, refer to Learning Goal 4.4d.

CHAPTER 5: SENSATION AND PERCEPTION

1. Mia is taking a hearing test. The technician instructs her to tell him when she hears a sound. The test moves from louder to softer sounds, until Mia can hear a sound of a certain volume only half the time it is given. The technician is determining Mia's _____ for auditory stimuli.
   a) difference threshold
   b) absolute threshold
   c) signal detection
   d) sensory adaptation

2. Pierre, a new father, often thinks he hears his infant daughter crying in the night. Many times, he runs to her bedroom and finds her sleeping quietly. But when she does cry at night, Pierre always hears her and goes to help her right away. According to signal detection theory, in this situation, Pierre shows a high rate of _____ and _____.
   a) misses; correct rejections
   b) false alarms; correct rejections
   c) misses; hits
   d) false alarms; hits

3. Luis stares at Marigold's green dress, then looks at a white wall. On the wall, he sees a red afterimage of the dress. According to _____ theory, this afterimage is due to processing in his _____.
   a) opponent-process; ganglion cells
   b) trichromatic; ganglion cells
   c) opponent-process; cones
   d) trichromatic; cones

4. Benjamin injured one of his eyes and needs to wear an eye patch over it for the next 6 weeks. He finds it difficult to reach out and grab things, such as the buttons on his shirt, because with the use of only one eye he lacks the depth cue of _____.
   a) relative size
   b) occlusion
   c) binocular disparity
   d) linear perspective

5. In a science fiction movie, the villain wants to cause deafness in people by preventing auditory transduction. The villain tries to achieve this goal by _____ in her victims.
   a) removing the thalamus
   b) destroying all the hair cells
   c) fusing the ossicles
   d) damaging the auditory nerve

6. Kai has been attending loud rock concerts for several years. Recently, she has been having problems hearing high-pitched sounds. This loss is most likely due to impaired _____ coding in her _____
   a) temporal; cochlea
   b) temporal; semicircular canals
   c) place; cochlea
   d) place; semicircular canals

7. Roberto has strong taste sensations and is very sensitive to spiciness. Hot spices are almost physically painful to him. To find out if Roberto is a supertaster, you would determine if he has _____.
   a) many papillae, because papillae contain taste receptors
   b) the unusual ability to detect umami
   c) a very responsive olfactory epithelium
   d) a highly active gustatory cortex

8. A rare disease has destroyed Cosette's thalamus. As a result, Cosette can't experience many sensations she used to enjoy. Luckily, _____ is still a pleasure for her, because the sense of _____ is not processed through the thalamus.
   a) listening to music; vision
   b) eating; taste
   c) eating; hearing
   d) listening to music; smell

9. Jase's phone is on vibrate. Jase feels the vibration due to processing by his _____.
   a) kinesthetic sense
   b) fast and slow fibers
   c) pressure receptors
   d) vestibular sense

10. While playing soccer, Viveca was kicked in her thigh. She felt sharp pain due to _____ fibers. The immediacy of this sensation was due to the _____ of myelin on the axons of these fibers.
    a) fast; absence
    b) fast; presence
    c) slow; absence
    d) slow; presence

Answers for Chapter 5

1. B
The technician is attempting to determine when Mia can detect an auditory stimulus half the time. The absolute threshold represents the smallest amount of input needed to detect a stimulus. By contrast, a difference threshold is the ability to distinguish a difference between two or more stimuli.

For more information, refer to Learning Goal 5.1c.

2. D
When Pierre goes to his baby but finds she isn't crying, his response is a false alarm because a signal is not present but he responds anyway. When Pierre goes to his baby and she really is crying, his response is a hit because a signal is present and he responds to it.

For more information, refer to Learning Goal 5.1d.

3. A
The fact that we see some colors as opposites can be explained by opponent-process theory. Activity in some types of ganglion cells makes red and green seem like opposites. Activity in other types of ganglion cells makes yellow and blue seem like opposites.

For more information, refer to Learning Goal 5.2c.

4. C
Binocular disparity is a binocular depth cue, which means that it requires two eyes. It allows you to see depth because the brain calculates how far away objects are based on the slightly different image sent to the retina of each eye. This cue works only for objects that are close to you.

For more information, refer to Learning Goal 5.2e.

5. B
The hair cells are responsible for transduction in the auditory system. That is, the hair cells change sounds waves into signals that the brain ultimately processes as sounds.

For more information, refer to Learning Goal 5.3b.

6. C
Because Kai is having problems hearing high-pitched sounds, she is having difficulty processing high-frequency sound waves. According to place theory, these waves are encoded by receptors at different locations on the basilar membrane in the cochlea.

For more information, refer to Learning Goal 5.3c.

7. A
Papillae are structures on the tongue that contain many taste buds. The taste buds contain the sensory receptors for the gustatory system, called taste receptors. People who have many papillae also have more taste receptors and are more sensitive to certain tastes.

For more information, refer to Learning Goal 5.4b.

8. D

All sensory information is processed through the thalamus in the brain except for the sense of smell, so Cosette can enjoy eating because she can still smell the food.

For more information, refer to Learning Goal 5.4c.

9. C

Pressure receptors, including those that are sensitive to vibration and different types of pressure, are located in the skin and detect tactile stimuli.

For more information, refer to Learning Goal 5.5b.

10. B

Fast fibers carry information that we perceive as sharp pain. These messages are transmitted immediately because the axons of fast fibers are insulated by myelin.

For more information, refer to Learning Goal 5.5c.

CHAPTER 6: LEARNING

1. Rosie wants her cat to meow when the doorbell rings. Each time a visitor rings the bell and the cat meows, Rosie gives him a treat. Soon the cat always meows when the doorbell rings. Rosie's cat is demonstrating _____ learning.
   a) non-associative
   b) observational
   c) vicarious
   d) associative

2. Sanjay got a slight sunburn. At first, he felt very uncomfortable whenever his shirt touched his irritated skin. After a while, he stopped feeling that discomfort. Sanjay's adjustment resulted from a type of learning called _____.
   a) habituation
   b) sensitization
   c) conditioning
   d) modeling

3. Whenever Erin first sees her boyfriend, her heart beats fast. And whenever her boyfriend comes to her dorm room and the door is closed, he knocks five times before entering the room. After a while, Erin's heart jumps with excitement whenever she hears five knocks. The knocking is a(n) _____ for Erin.
   a) unconditioned stimulus
   b) unconditioned response
   c) conditioned stimulus
   d) conditioned response

4. Christopher used to drink water from a drinking fountain just before physics class. One time, he felt nauseated right after drinking the water. After that, to avoid the risk of nausea, he stopped drinking at the fountain. Christopher learned a connection between the water fountain and feeling nauseated because he experienced _____.
   a) acquisition
   b) extinction
   c) spontaneous recovery
   d) counterconditioning

5. Lola's new dog, Hoss, is afraid of loud noises. Every time her cell phone rings, Hoss starts barking out of fear. After a while, Hoss also starts barking when a phone rings on a television show. The fact that Hoss now barks when he hears a telephone ring on TV is most likely due to _____.
   a) stimulus discrimination
   b) stimulus generalization
   c) spontaneous recovery
   d) second-order conditioning

6. Ajeet's younger sister is always bugging him. One day, Ajeet lets her play his video game, and she stops bugging him for several hours. Ajeet now lets her play his video game more and more, because doing so stops her from bugging him. Ajeet's learning in this situation is best explained by _____.
   a) positive reinforcement
   b) negative reinforcement
   c) positive punishment
   d) negative punishment

7. Glen and Lynda are hired to rake leaves. Glen is paid $3 for each bag of leaves he rakes. Lynda is paid $7 for each hour she works. Glen is paid according to a _____ schedule of reinforcement. Lynda is paid according to a _____ schedule.
   a) variable ratio; variable interval
   b) fixed ratio; fixed interval
   c) variable ratio; fixed interval
   d) fixed ratio; variable interval

8. Dante often shopped at the same grocery store. One day, another customer asked Dante if he knew where the plastic storage containers were located in the store. Dante immediately gave directions to the correct aisle, even though he had never bought plastic storage containers from that store. The fact that Dante knew the location of the containers is best explained by _____.
   a) insight learning
   b) vicarious conditioning
   c) latent learning
   d) continuous reinforcement

9. Three-year-old Sam watches as his 5-year-old sister, Mindy, draws on her bedroom wall with crayons. Their mother enters the room, but doesn't yell at Mindy. Instead, as Sam watches, their mother gets cleaning supplies and scrubs the wall clean. The next day, Sam displays modeling when he _____.
    a) stops himself from drawing on the walls to avoid punishment
    b) thinks about where they have a coloring book he can color in
    c) yells at Mindy for drawing on the walls
    d) gets his markers and colors on the laundry room wall

10. During a spelling test, Jung's friend is caught cheating and gets suspended from school for three days. Jung decides not to cheat because she does not want to get suspended for cheating. In this example, Jung is most likely displaying learning that is due to _____.
    a) modeling
    b) observational learning
    c) insight
    d) vicarious conditioning

Answers for Chapter 6

1. D
Rosie is attempting to teach the cat a relationship between two things: the doorbell ringing and the consequences of the cat meowing when the doorbell rings. This relationship represents a form of associative learning—specifically, operant conditioning.

For more information, refer to Learning Goal 6.1b.

2. A
Habituation is a non-associative form of learning. In this case, Sanjay becomes habituated to the discomfort of having his shirt rubbing against his sunburn.

For more information, refer to Learning Goal 6.1c.

3. C
In this scenario, seeing Erin's boyfriend is the unconditioned stimulus. It causes an unconditioned physiological response, a fast heartbeat. For Erin, five knocks have become associated with seeing her boyfriend at her dorm room. So five knocks are now a conditioned stimulus that elicits a conditioned response, a fast heartbeat.

For more information, refer to Learning Goal 6.2b.

4. A
Acquisition is the process of learning an association between two stimuli over a period of time. In this case, the stimuli were the water from that drinking fountain and nausea.

For more information, refer to Learning Goal 6.2c.

5. B
Stimulus generalization occurs when stimuli that are similar (but not identical) to a conditioned stimulus cause the same conditioned response.

For more information, refer to Learning Goal 6.2c.

6. B
Negative reinforcement *increases* the likelihood that a behavior will continue by *removing* a negative stimulus. In this case, Ajeet lets his sister play the game more because doing so reduces the amount of time she bugs him.

For more information, refer to Learning Goal 6.3b.

7. B
With a fixed ratio schedule, a behavior is reinforced after a person does the desired behavior a specific number of times (if Glen is paid $3 per bag and rakes three bags of leaves, he will earn $9). With a fixed interval schedule, a behavior is reinforced after a person does the desired behavior for a specific length of time (if Lynda rakes for an hour, she will earn $7, regardless of how many bags of leaves she rakes).

For more information, refer to Learning Goal 6.3c.

8. C
Latent learning is an example of how learning is influenced by cognition. In particular, latent learning explains how learning can occur even without reinforcement, as it did in Dante's situation.

For more information, refer to Learning Goal 6.3d.

9. D
Modeling is a form of learning that occurs when someone watches the behavior of another person and then imitates that behavior.

For more information, refer to Learning Goal 6.4c.

10. D
Through vicarious conditioning, we can learn to not perform a behavior because we see another person being punished for that behavior, as in the case with Jung. Alternatively, through vicarious conditioning, we can learn to perform a behavior if we see another person being reinforced for it.

For more information, refer to Learning Goal 6.4c.

CHAPTER 7: MEMORY

1. Johanna was asked to remember a string of letters. She heard x during the presentation of the letters. In her brain, this input was changed into the neural code s. Later, when she was asked to recall the letters, Johanna included s, not x, in her list. Johanna most likely made this error on the recall test due to an error in the _____ phase of memory.
   a) encoding
   b) retrieval
   c) acquisition
   d) storage

2. Demetra's husband is watching a football game on television. When Demetra asks if he will pick up their daughter, Zoe, from day care the next day, he doesn't reply. When Demetra asks, "Did you hear me?" her husband replies, "Yes, I heard you. I'll pick up Zoe tomorrow." However, the next day, her husband comes home without Zoe. He claims to have no memory of being asked to pick her up. The fact that he did not have the information about picking up Zoe from day care in _____ storage was most likely due to his _____.
   a) short-term; never having that information in sensory memory
   b) short-term; not paying attention to the request
   c) long-term; never having that information in sensory memory
   d) long-term; not paying attention to the request

3. Lily gets a new debit card and must memorize her password, *vt0806*. To remember this sequence, she thinks of *vt* as representing *Vermont*. She thinks of *0806* as representing *August 6th*, her husband's birthday. With this combination in mind, Lily remembers the password easily. She has used _____.
   a) maintenance rehearsal to encode information into long-term storage
   b) the primacy effect
   c) the working memory strategy of chunking
   d) the recency effect

4. When it comes to solving math problems on tests, Brandon can recall all the formulas perfectly. But as he actively works to solve a problem, he has trouble keeping track of the variables that he manipulates in his mind. This example describes how Brandon most likely has limited _____.
   a) sensory storage
   b) working memory

   c) long-term storage
   d) short-term storage

5. When someone says the word *doctor*, 13-year old Vanessa remembers her most recent medical visit. She also thinks of objects related to the concept of a doctor, such as an examination room, a stethoscope, and an X-ray machine. The fact that a word brings up memories about many related ideas is best explained by _____.
   a) the primacy effect
   b) spreading activation models of memory
   c) the recency effect
   d) level of processing model of memory

6. Nathaniel's friend asks him what he ate for breakfast this morning. When Nathaniel remembers that he ate eggs, toast, and bacon, this recall is an example of _____ memory. When Nathanial tells his friend what he ate, his ability to verbalize that information is an example of _____ memory.
   a) episodic; explicit
   b) episodic; implicit
   c) semantic; explicit
   d) semantic; implicit

7. Professor Linsmeier was recently in a motorcycle accident that left him with brain damage. He has no trouble teaching his economics course, which he has taught for 15 years. However, Professor Linsmeier has lost the ability to remember new information, such as the names of his students. He is most likely experiencing _____.
   a) retrograde amnesia
   b) proactive interference
   c) anterograde amnesia
   d) retroactive interference

8. Louisa recovers from a severe illness. While she used to be a good piano-player, now she cannot remember what finger movements to make to play her favorite pieces. Louisa most likely has damage in her _____.
   a) amygdala
   b) temporal lobe
   c) hippocampus
   d) cerebellum

9. Cadence is currently frustrated with a coworker. She wants to write a recommendation for one of her students, Jamie, who has many talents and is a hard worker. However, as she writes the letter, the only memories that come to mind are times when she was frustrated with Jamie. Cadence's experience of remembering only situations where Jamie frustrated her is best explained by _____.

a) context dependence
b) state dependence
c) retroactive interference
d) proactive interference

10. When Russell was growing up, he thought his Grandma Betty was a hoarder because she had so much junk that you could hardly walk around her house. Now that Russell is an adult, he obsessively buys old board games and action figures that remind him of his youth. He has so many boxes lying around, he can barely make a pathway from his bedroom to his kitchen. Russell claims that he learned to collect from his Grandma Betty, whose house he loved visiting because she "always collected really cool, meaningful stuff." The fact that Russell's memory about his grandmother is currently positive can best be described by _____.
a) forgetting
b) misattribution
c) memory bias
d) suggestibility

Answers for Chapter 7

1. A
When Johanna recalled hearing an *s,* her answer implied that she had stored and retrieved a memory. However, since she recalled the wrong letter, her brain most likely processed the incorrect information during encoding.

For more information, refer to Learning Goal 7.1b.

2. D
In this case, storing information for use the next day is an example of long-term storage. To store memories and retrieve them later on, we must devote attentional resources to the information.

For more information, refer to Learning Goal 7.1c.

3. C
Chunking is the process of using working memory to organize information into meaningful units. This process allows for better transfer into long-term storage.

For more information, refer to Learning Goal 7.2c.

4. B
Knowledge of math formulas is an example of successful long-term storage of relatively permanent information. By contrast, an inability to keep track of a few variables while solving a math problem indicates a deficit in working memory.

For more information, refer to Learning Goal 7.2c.

5. B
According to spreading activation models of memory, activating one idea in semantic long-term storage activates closely linked ideas.

For more information, refer to Learning Goal 7.2e.

6. A
Recalling information about personally experienced events—such as the time, place, and circumstances—is episodic memory. Episodic memory is a type of explicit memory. Explicit memory means memories we are consciously aware of and can describe.

For more information, refer to Learning Goal 7.3b.

7. C
In a case of anterograde amnesia caused by brain injury, someone loses the ability to form new memories. However, the person can remember information learned before the brain injury.

For more information, refer to Learning Goal 7.3c.

8. D
The cerebellum plays a vital role in implicit memory, including procedural memory used to perform many motor behaviors, such as playing the piano. By contrast, the temporal lobe is important for explicit memories, the hippocampus is important for the consolidation of new memories and for spatial memory, and the amygdala is crucial in processing implicit memories about fear learning.

For more information, refer to Learning Goal 7.3d.

9. B
State-dependent memory allows us to retrieve memories that occurred when we were in a physical state that is similar to what we are in now. Because Cadence is currently frustrated, it is easier for her to recall events when she was also frustrated.

For more information, refer to Learning Goal 7.4b.

10. C
Russell's opinion of his grandmother used to be negative because he thought hoarding was unhealthy. Now that he is displaying the same type of behavior, he has changed his memory of his grandmother so that it is consistent with his attitude toward his own behavior. This shift is an example of memory bias, which is one of the ways our memories become distorted.

For more information, refer to Learning Goal 7.4d.

CHAPTER 8: THINKING AND INTELLIGENCE

1. Camden is learning to play pool. He thinks about how his knowledge of physics can help him make different types of shots. Camden is using a(n) _____ to think about how to play pool.
   a) prototype
   b) analogical representation
   c) symbolic representation
   d) heuristic

2. Ayanna doesn't know what a "clunker" is, so her friend Hilary says, "You know that old car Bruce has? That's the best example of a 'clunker.' It has all the characteristics: It's an older car, it looks terrible, it's always breaking down, yet it's still driveable." Hilary's thinking about Bruce's clunker is based on the _____ model of thought.
   a) prototype
   b) exemplar
   c) defining attribute
   d) stereotype

3. Dawson thinks about going to Boston on his vacation. But he remembers the Boston Marathon bombings and decides that Boston is too dangerous. So he books a flight to Orlando instead. Dawson's overestimation of the danger in Boston is a result of _____.
   a) formal reasoning
   b) the availability heuristic
   c) framing
   d) the representativeness heuristic

4. When he works on a Sudoku puzzle, Armando begins by filling in all the number 1's. Then he moves on to all the 2's, then 3's, and so on until he finishes with the number 9's. Armando's problem solving strategy of filling in one number at a time until the entire puzzle is complete is based on _____.
   a) using an analogy
   b) creating subgoals
   c) working backward
   d) experiencing insight

5. Florin wants to go out on Halloween, but he doesn't have a costume. His wife, Ashley, replies, "No problem. Just use this sheet." But Florin doesn't see how the sheet could be a costume. He wife says, "Put this bed sheet over your head, poke out two holes for your eyes, and now you're a ghost!" The fact that Florin didn't see how he could use the sheet as a ghost costume is most likely explained by his experiencing _____.

   a) restructuring
   b) framing
   c) insight
   d) functional fixedness

6. Mrs. Tomaselli knows that her student Eli has an average IQ. She also has observed him having difficulty spelling long words and multiplying double-digit numbers. Because of these facts, Mrs. Tomaselli assumes that Eli will have trouble with other specific abilities, such as solving science problems. Mrs. Tomaselli's assessment of Eli's abilities is best explained by a belief in _____.
   a) general intelligence
   b) multiple intelligences
   c) crystallized intelligence
   d) the triarchic theory of intelligence

7. Fritz is an "A" student who easily learns and remembers facts from school and recalls them for tests. Jason is skilled at analyzing problems with his car and solving them so he can get around. Fritz is most likely considered to be intelligent based on _____, while Jason is most likely considered to be intelligent based on _____.
   a) fluid intelligence; multiple intelligences
   b) fluid intelligence; triarchic theory
   c) crystallized intelligence; triarchic theory
   d) crystallized intelligence; multiple intelligences

8. Carla conducts a study and finds evidence supporting a correlation between "nurture" and intelligence. Which of the following is Carla most likely to have found?
   a) Identical twins receive similar scores on a traditional IQ test.
   b) Adopted siblings vary greatly in their ability to learn new tasks.
   c) Children who are able to teach themselves to read are more likely to go to college.
   d) Children whose parents provide them with many books perform better academically.

9. Dr. Cantor puts several questions about his political views on an American history exam. Students complain that those questions have nothing to do with how well they know American history and should not be used to determine their grades. The students are arguing that the test _____.
   a) lacks reliability
   b) does not have a normal distribution
   c) lacks validity
   d) measures aptitude, not achievement

10. While Felicia has only an average IQ, she is excellent at trivia. Felicia always answers the questions several seconds before anyone else. Felicia's cognitive performance suggests she is intelligent because she _____.
   a) has fast reaction times
   b) has high general intelligence
   c) has good working memory
   d) is a savant

Answers for Chapter 8

1. C
Camden is using a symbolic representation because his thoughts are abstract mental connections consisting of words or ideas about how principles of physics can help him play pool.
   For more information, refer to Learning Goal 8.1b.

2. A
Hilary is describing Bruce's car as a prototype of the category "clunker." A prototype is a "most typical member" of a given category, and it is used to organize concepts.
   For more information, refer to Learning Goal 8.1c.

3. B
The availability heuristic is a "rule of thumb" where our decisions tend to be made based on information that is easily retrieved.
   For more information, refer to Learning Goal 8.2b.

4. B
Armando is using subgoals to solve the puzzle. In this case, he is completing one number at a time—all the 1's, then the 2's, and so on. Each number he gets correct places him one step closer to reaching his ultimate goal of finishing the Sudoku.
   For more information, refer to Learning Goal 8.2c.

5. D
Functional fixedness is an obstacle to problem solving that arises when we rely too heavily on our mental representation of the typical functions for ordinary objects.
   For more information, refer to Learning Goal 8.2d.

6. A
General intelligence is the idea that one general factor underlies intelligence. It is responsible for IQ scores and for a person's performance across a range of tasks that show specific abilities, such as math, writing, drawing, and problem solving.
   For more information, refer to Learning Goal 8.3b.

7. C
Fritz's skills reveal crystallized intelligence, which is long-term memory about facts and knowledge. Jason's skills reflect the triarchic theory of intelligence, which posits that intelligence is comprised of practical intelligence, analytical intelligence, and creative intelligence.
   For more information, refer to Learning Goal 8.3c.

8. D
"Nurture" can play a large role in the development of intelligence through a person's environment, social characteristics, upbringing, and experiences. Thus, out of these options, Carla most likely found that children with lots of books (e.g., an environmental factor) do best academically.
   For more information, refer to Learning Goal 8.3d.

9. C
Validity is an assessment of whether a test measures what it is intended to measure. In this case, the test may be invalid if the questions don't assess knowledge of American history.
   For more information, refer to Learning Goal 8.4a.

10. A
Because Felicia answers the questions quickly, her reaction times are faster. The faster reaction times indicate that her mental processing is more efficient. Indeed, many people argue that fast reaction times indicate increased intelligence.
   For more information, refer to Learning Goal 8.4c.

CHAPTER 9: MOTIVATION AND EMOTION

1. Dwayne enjoys spending calm, quiet evenings at home watching old movies. Debbie likes to do exciting activities, such as skydiving, on her days off. The fact that Dwayne and Debbie choose to spend their free time in these ways is best explained by _____.
   a) satisfaction of needs
   b) incentives
   c) optimal level of arousal
   d) drive reduction

2. Vince and Edith are training for a marathon. When asked why they are running the race, Vince says he wants the medal they give out to everyone who crosses the finish line. Edith responds that she enjoys trying new things. Vince's behavior is most likely explained by _____, whereas Edith's behavior is most likely explained by _____.
   a) extrinsic motivation; intrinsic motivation
   b) intrinsic motivation; extrinsic motivation
   c) self-perception theory; self-determination theory
   d) self-determination theory; self-perception theory

3. When Terry's stomach starts growling, he decides it's time for lunch. After eating a burrito and tortilla chips, he feels full and does not want to eat more. Which of the following does NOT play a role in his short-term feeling of "fullness"?
   a) increased glucose in his bloodstream
   b) decreased ghrelin in his stomach
   c) activation of his hypothalamus
   d) release of leptin in his saliva

4. Thomas sends his daughter Sophia to spend the summer with her grandparents, who eat dinner at 5:00 PM. Upon her return home, Sophia wants to eat dinner at 5:00 PM every night, even though she is not hungry and does not finish all the food on her plate. Sophia's change in desired mealtime has most likely been influenced by _____.
   a) drive reduction
   b) classical conditioning
   c) optimal arousal
   d) low levels of the hormone ghrelin

5. Rick feels lucky that his wife, Rachel, wants to have sex frequently. He thinks Rachel's desire is most likely due to her _____, which influence sexual motivation in women.
   a) low levels of androgens
   b) high levels of androgens
   c) low levels of estrogens
   d) high levels of estrogens

6. Hannah enjoys playing video games because every time she scores a point, processing in her brain simultaneously causes an excited emotion and an increase in her heart rate. The theory that best explains Hannah's experience of emotion is _____.
   a) the Cannon-Bard theory
   b) misattribution of arousal
   c) the James-Lange theory
   d) excitation transfer

7. After Bernadette is in a car accident, she is extra friendly to people she meets. In fact, she does not seem to realize when she might be revealing personal information to untrustworthy strangers. This information suggests that Bernadette may have brain damage in her _____.
   a) right prefrontal cortex
   b) left prefrontal cortex
   c) amygdala
   d) thalamus

8. Bianca is sad and anxious because her sister is moving across the country for a new job. To make herself feel better, Bianca thinks of her sister's new city as a vacation destination—a place Bianca can visit and explore. Bianca is regulating her emotional state by using _____.
   a) rumination
   b) distraction
   c) thought suppression
   d) reappraisal

9. Tori sometimes refrains from arguing with her colleagues in staff meetings because she believes it is not appropriate for women to display anger. Tori's belief about emotional expressiveness in women is best explained by _____.
   a) self-determination theory
   b) thought suppression
   c) display rules
   d) affect-as-information theory

10. Madison frequently checks the cell phone of her husband, Max, to see if he is texting other women. Max catches her and is very hurt by her behavior. Madison loves Max very much and feels bad that she hurt him. In this situation, Madison is most likely to feel the emotion of _____.
    a) guilt
    b) pride
    c) embarrassment
    d) fear

Answers for Chapter 9

1. C
Each person has an optimal level of arousal, which motivates the person to behave in certain ways. Too much arousal overwhelms us, and we need a break; too little arousal leaves us bored.
   For more information, refer to Learning Goal 9.1b.

2. A
Extrinsic motivation is the desire to perform an action to achieve certain external goals. Intrinsic motivation is the desire to perform an action because of the enjoyment it brings.
   For more information, refer to Learning Goal 9.1c.

3. D
Leptin is involved in the biological process of eating. However, this hormone is released by fat cells (not in our saliva) and acts on the hypothalamus. In addition, it affects long-term fat regulation, not short-term motivation for eating.
   For more information, refer to Learning Goal 9.2b.

4. B

Eating meals at a specific time of day is an example of classical conditioning. After spending time with her grandparents, Sophia learned to associate eating dinner with a very specific time of day, so she now prefers to eat at that time.

For more information, refer to Learning Goal 9.2c.

5. B

Androgens—for example, testosterone—are hormones that are more important in influencing sexual behavior than estrogens are. In particular, the more testosterone a woman has, the more likely she is to have sexual thoughts and desires.

For more information, refer to Learning Goal 9.2d.

6. A

The Cannon-Bard theory of emotion says that processing in the brain creates the experience of emotion and physical response in the body at the same time.

For more information, refer to Learning Goal 9.3b.

7. C

The amygdala is associated with various emotional functions. It plays a major role in the perception of social stimuli, such as evaluating the trustworthiness of a stranger or feeling cautious around strangers.

For more information, refer to Learning Goal 9.3c.

8. D

Reappraisal is a method of emotion regulation in which we alter our emotional reactions by thinking of events in more neutral (as opposed to negative) terms.

For more information, refer to Learning Goal 9.3d.

9. C

Tori's belief that women should not show anger suggests she is following display rules, which are rules learned through socialization that dictate how and when people express emotions. These rules are often heavily influenced by factors such as sex and culture.

For more information, refer to Learning Goal 9.4b.

10. A

Guilt can arise from anxiety and remorse in situations when we have harmed another person. Displays of guilt also demonstrate that we care about our relationship partners. By showing that we care, the displays can help strengthen our social bonds.

For more information, refer to Learning Goal 9.4d.

CHAPTER 10: HEALTH AND WELL-BEING

1. Chuck is often stressed because he suffers from severe arthritis and also has to take care of his three young grandchildren. The biopsychosocial model would predict that Chuck is most likely to become ill if he also experiences the psychological factor of _____.
   a) being exposed to a lot of germs
   b) having low self-esteem
   c) missing several important deadlines at work
   d) moving to a new home

2. Emily is of average weight. However, she often hides food in her bedroom and eats late at night when she feels anxious. She compensates for this behavior by chronically abusing laxatives to help her get rid of calories. This information suggests that Emily is most likely to be diagnosed with _____.
   a) bulimia nervosa
   b) binge-eating disorder
   c) anorexia nervosa
   d) obesity

3. Logan works at an investment company and has been embezzling money from his clients. He recently was arrested and sentenced to 10 years in prison. Logan is most likely experiencing stress due to _____.
   a) the alarm phase of the general adaptation syndrome
   b) this daily hassle
   c) the exhaustion phase of the general adaptation syndrome
   d) this major life stressor

4. Kenny has to give an oral presentation in 15 minutes. He is very anxious and experiencing shortness of breath, dilated pupils, and a huge lump in his throat. Kenny is most likely experiencing the _____ stage of Selye's general adaptation syndrome.
   a) immune
   b) resistance
   c) alarm
   d) exhaustion

5. Valerie's home and workplace were destroyed by a tornado. She has been able to find temporary lodging at a cousin's house. She attends support meetings with her neighbors and is trying to get new clothes for her children. Valerie's response to this stressor is best described as a(n) _____ response.
   a) fight-or-flight
   b) general adaptation syndrome
   c) tend-and-befriend
   d) negative stress

6. Although well prepared, John panicked during an exam and failed the test. John's father is confident he will do better next time and suggests John get a tutor. John also plans to solve practice problems with a timer so he is less likely to feel panicked in the future. John's father's support and John's feelings of control over the situation are best described as stress _____ that will _____ the stressful impact of future exams on John.
   a) mediators; increase
   b) mediators; decrease
   c) responses; increase
   d) responses; decrease

7. When faced with stress, Ross reacts with aggressiveness and impatience, whereas Tia is more relaxed and easygoing. In these situations, Ross exhibits a _____ behavior pattern and is _____ likely than Tia to develop heart disease.
   a) type A; less
   b) type B; less
   c) type A; more
   d) type B; more

8. Preston told his supervisor that he is unable to work when he has soccer practice, but she keeps scheduling him for shifts during those times. Preston uses problem-focused coping when he decides to _____.
   a) talk to his friends to reduce his stress
   b) think about whether the situation is stressful enough for him to deal with
   c) take up smoking to relieve some of his stress
   d) remind his supervisor about his schedule conflicts

9. Mark decides to get his employees involved in teambuilding sessions and friendly intra-office competitions, such as a chili cookoff. He also offers to sponsor gym memberships for his employees and their families. Mark's efforts are most likely aimed at increasing the _____ of his employees.
   a) positivity
   b) well-being
   c) happiness
   d) resilience

10. When Lauren is feeling down, she makes an extra effort to feel hopeful about the future and maintain a happy attitude. Lauren is most likely to benefit from her positive attitude by _____.

a) experiencing less hypertension and not developing diabetes
b) having a better-functioning immune system
c) living longer than her peers
d) all of the above

Answers for Chapter 10

1. B
The biopsychosocial model suggests that health (or illness) results from the combined influence of biological, social, and psychological characteristics. In Chuck's case, arthritis, grandchildren, and negative self-evaluations have the potential to make him ill.
   For more information, refer to Learning Goal 10.1b.

2. A
Bulimia nervosa is an eating disorder characterized by alternating between dieting, binge eating, and purging by vomiting or using laxatives.
   For more information, refer to Learning Goal 10.1c.

3. D
A major life stressor—such as a possible prison sentence—is a large disruption that is unpredictable or uncontrollable and that affects the central areas of a person's life.
   For more information, refer to Learning Goal 10.2b.

4. C
The alarm stage of the general adaptation syndrome occurs when the body has an emergency response to a stressor. This response physically prepares us to fight or run away.
   For more information, refer to Learning Goal 10.2c.

5. C
Common in women, the tend-and-befriend response to stress centers around caring for children and forming alliances with others. This response reduces the impact of stressors.
   For more information, refer to Learning Goal 10.2d.

6. B
Stress mediators are factors that influence the amount that a stressor affects your life (or causes a stress response). In this case, John has social support and engages in activities that make him feel more in control of the situation. Both of these factors will make him less likely to respond negatively to the stress of a chemistry exam in the future.
   For more information, refer to Learning Goal 10.3a.

7. C

People with a type A behavior pattern display competitiveness, aggression, impatience, and hostility, whereas people with a type B behavior pattern are more laid-back, easygoing, and accommodating. Research has shown that people with type A behavior patterns are more likely to develop heart disease, among other health problems.

For more information, refer to Learning Goal 10.3b.

8. D

A problem-focused coping method involves taking direct steps to reduce the stressor. In this case, Preston would most likely discuss his scheduling conflicts with his supervisor.

For more information, refer to Learning Goal 10.3c.

9. B

Well-being is a positive state that includes striving for life satisfaction and optimal health. By aiming to improve workplace relationships and supporting healthy behaviors, Mark is trying to promote his employees' well-being.

For more information, refer to Learning Goal 10.4b.

10. D

Positivity—positive emotions, attitudes, and outlooks—helps people to maintain good mental and physical health in all of these ways.

For more information, refer to Learning Goal 10.4c.

CHAPTER 11: SOCIAL PSYCHOLOGY

1. Within a few seconds of meeting her new coworker, Greg, Lucy noticed his nice smile. Because of his smile, Lucy assumed she would enjoy working with Greg. Lucy most likely made a judgment based on _____.
   a) thin slices of behavior
   b) the actor/observer bias
   c) a situational attribution
   d) a self-fulfilling prophecy

2. When Elizabeth's fellow students show up late to class, she thinks they are irresponsible and lazy. But when Elizabeth is late to class, she tells her professor that it is not her fault because her bus was late. Elizabeth's explanations best illustrate the _____.
   a) fundamental attribution error
   b) just world hypothesis
   c) self-fulfilling prophecy
   d) actor/observer bias

3. Troy believes that exercise contributes to positive self-esteem. If Troy formed this attitude through operant conditioning, which of the following situations is most likely?
   a) He drives by a local gym every morning and sees good-looking, happy people.
   b) He exercises on a daily basis, consistently doing the same workout on his treadmill.
   c) He began exercising and is pleased that he can now buy jeans in a smaller size.
   d) His parents routinely exercise and encourage him to do the same.

4. Before a big charity event, Bridget decides to get a haircut at an expensive salon. Afterwards, she doesn't think it looks any different from her normal cut and is worried that she wasted money. A few hours later, she tells her friends that it was the best haircut she has ever gotten. Bridget's change in attitude is best explained by _____.
   a) cognitive dissonance
   b) postdecisional dissonance
   c) the mere exposure effect
   d) attitude accessibility

5. In an advertisement for Activist Group A, a beautiful actor says she is against using animals for testing cosmetics. In an advertisement for Activist Group B, an average-looking research scientist explains how animals are physically harmed in cosmetic testing. According to the elaboration likelihood model, Activist Group A is using the _____ route to influence attitudes, whereas Activist Group B is using the _____ route to influence attitudes.
   a) personal; situational
   b) peripheral; central
   c) situational; personal
   d) central; peripheral

6. Marco will be singing with three other people in his glee club's upcoming performance and has put in many hours of practice. Which of the following statements is the best example of how social facilitation is likely to influence his performance?
   a) Marco will not sing as loudly during the chorus because everyone else is singing very well.
   b) Marco will sing very well because of the presence of other singers.
   c) Marco will forget the words to the song because everyone is watching him.
   d) Marco will pay less attention to his personal standards of singing because all the singers are wearing the same costume.

7. Most of the students in David's introductory psychology class sit in the same seat every day, so David also sits in the same seat every day. On Monday, he has to switch seats because his instructor asks him to move to the front row to help with an in-class demonstration. David's usual choice of seat is influenced by _____, but on Monday he displayed _____.
    a) deindividuation; compliance
    b) conformity; compliance
    c) deindividuation; obedience
    d) conformity; obedience

8. Darren is walking through a busy grocery store when he knocks over a display full of paper towel rolls. Many people see the paper towels fall, but no one helps him pick them up. People's failure to help can most likely be attributed to _____.
    a) altruism
    b) reciprocal helping
    c) frustration-aggression hypothesis
    d) bystander apathy

9. Glenda is 30 and single. Because of the impact of proximity, she is most likely to date which of the following bachelors?
    a) Leon, a friend-of-a-friend she has met twice, who shares her passion for volleyball and vacations in Europe
    b) Dion, a thoughtful and sincere man she met through a dating service
    c) Martin, whom she has sees at the dog park several times a week
    d) Jay, who lives across town and whom she sometimes sees at the grocery store

10. Victoria and Ryne have been married for five years. They still have as much sexual desire for each other as when they first started dating. This information suggests that Victoria and Ryne experience _____.
    a) passionate love
    b) prosocial behavior
    c) companionate love
    d) accommodation

Answers for Chapter 11

1. A
When Lucy determines her feeling about Greg after viewing his facial expression for just a few seconds, she is making a snap judgment based on thin slices of behavior.
    For more information, refer to Learning Goal 11.1b.

2. D
Elizabeth is displaying the actor/observer bias because she is making a personal attribution about her classmates' behavior (they are late because they are lazy) and a situational attribution about her own behavior (she is late because of her bus).
    For more information, refer to Learning Goal 11.1c.

3. C
If Troy has formed an attitude about exercising through operant conditioning, he was most likely reinforced for working out by being able to buy smaller jeans.
    For more information, refer to Learning Goal 11.2b.

4. A
Cognitive dissonance occurs when there is a contradiction between two attitudes or between an attitude and a behavior. Bridget held two conflicting attitudes: An expensive haircut should be better than a cheap haircut, and her expensive haircut did not look any different than her normal one. Taken together, these conflicting ideas led her to be anxious and change her attitude about how her hair looked.
    For more information, refer to Learning Goal 11.2c.

5. B
The peripheral route to persuasion does not elaborate information in a meaningful way or encourage someone to process the information carefully. As a result, persuasion to change attitudes is achieved based on the attractiveness of the messenger. By contrast, the central route for persuasion uses high elaboration and provides the opportunity for someone to carefully process the information presented. In this case, persuasion to change attitudes depends on the quality of the arguments.
    For more information, refer to Learning Goal 11.2d.

6. B
Social facilitation occurs when the mere presence of other people enhances a person's performance.
    For more information, refer to Learning Goal 11.3b.

7. D
When we alter our behavior to match the behavior or expectations of others, we are conforming. Another way we alter our behavior, obedience, occurs when an authority figure such as a parent, teacher, or police officer asks us to behave in a specific way.
    For more information, refer to Learning Goal 11.3c.

8. D
Bystander apathy is when people fail to offer help to someone in need. This effect is particularly strong when many

bystanders are present. In that situation, people will generally expect someone else to offer assistance, relieving them of this responsibility.

For more information, refer to Learning Goal 11.3d.

9. C

Proximity influences our relationships based on how frequently we come into contact with each other. In particular, the more frequently you come into contact with someone, the greater the chance you will like that person. Increased liking may also result from increased familiarity caused when we repeatedly are exposed to someone.

For more information, refer to Learning Goal 11.4b.

10. A

Passionate love describes romantic relationships that include intense physical/sexual desire.

For more information, refer to Learning Goal 11.4c.

CHAPTER 12: SELF AND PERSONALITY

1. Lee is riding an elevator to the top floor of a tall building. During a brief conversation with a stranger in the elevator, Lee mentions that he is afraid of heights, which is not how he normally thinks of himself. After arriving at the top floor, Lee realizes that his fear of heights came to mind because of the elevator ride. This example best illustrates how Lee's thoughts were influenced by _____.
   a) his working self-concept
   b) a sociometer
   c) a self-serving bias
   d) his self-esteem

2. Kelly decides that she is an excellent graduate student because she has several more publications than the other students in her research group. Kelly's high self-esteem in this situation is based on a(n) _____.
   a) upward comparison
   b) sociometer
   c) downward comparison
   d) self-serving bias

3. Holly was raised in a collectivist culture. At school, Holly is most likely to feel high self-esteem when _____.
   a) she works well with a group of students to promote a social event
   b) she expresses her own unique viewpoint during science class
   c) her artwork is displayed in the school's hallway
   d) her teacher praises her work in front of other students

4. When Delaney asks Harvey to give him the cookies from his lunch, Harvey says no. Delaney tells him he is mean. Delaney's negative evaluations have created conditions of worth in Harvey. These conditions of worth may influence the development of Harvey's personality, according to _____.
   a) psychodynamic theory
   b) expectancy theory
   c) the five-factor theory
   d) the person-centered approach

5. Whenever Ella gets an assignment in one of her classes, she immediately writes it down in her planner. At home, Ella keeps a notepad and calendar on her desk so she can stay organized with all her coursework. This information suggests that Ella is likely to score highly on the Big Five personality trait of _____.
   a) extraversion
   b) conscientiousness
   c) agreeableness
   d) neuroticism

6. Justin believes that bad things just happen to him and that he has bad luck. Justin's belief is most consistent with the cognitive approach to personality called _____.
   a) expectancy theory
   b) object relations theory
   c) reciprocal determinism
   d) biological trait theory

7. Julian, a researcher, conducts an adoption study and concludes that "nature" affects shyness. Which of these findings is most consistent with the conclusion of Julian's study?
   a) Children who are biologically related are dissimilar in their degree of shyness.
   b) Children who are biologically related but who are raised in different households are similar in shyness.
   c) A child raised by nonbiological parents is more likely to be shy.
   d) Identical twins are likely to be dissimilar in their levels of shyness.

8. Three-year-old Morris loves being with other children at the park. When his mom tells him it is time to go home, he typically cries and yells at her. This information suggests that Morris is exhibiting two aspects of temperament: _____ and _____.
   a) low sociability; low emotionality
   b) low activity level; low emotionality
   c) high sociability; high emotionality
   d) high activity level; high emotionality

9. Tameka takes a personality test in which she is asked to write lyrics for a piece of music. The personality test that Tameka is most likely taking is a(n) _____.
   a) objective measure
   b) Thematic Apperception Test
   c) projective measure
   d) Rorschach test

10. Jerome, an office worker with a background in psychology, attends a picnic for work. He is surprised to see his usually reserved coworker Ralph singing karaoke and playing games. Jerome believes that the environmental cues at the picnic directly influenced Ralph's personality. This type of environmental influence is called _____. Jerome sees the picnic as a _____.
   a) interactionism; weak situation
   b) situationism; strong situation
   c) interactionism; strong situation
   d) situationism; weak situation

Answers for Chapter 12

1. A
Working self-concept reflects how a person thinks about himself and processes personal information at a given moment.

For more information, refer to Learning Goal 12.1b.

2. C
When a person makes a downward comparison, she is contrasting herself with people worse off than herself in the characteristic she is evaluating. This type of social comparison protects her high self-esteem.

For more information, refer to Learning Goal 12.1c.

3. A
A collectivist culture emphasizes the collective self more than the individual self and teaches its members to value connections to family, social groups, and group cohesiveness. Thus Holly most likely feels good about herself when she is working well with others to promote an event that will bring other people together.

For more information, refer to Learning Goal 12.1d.

4. D
According to Carl Rogers's person-centered approach to personality, an individual's personality is influenced by the person's sense of self and how others evaluate him. Inconsistencies between a person's self-concept and the way others evaluate him may lead to conditions of self-worth. Conditions of self-worth lead to the development of a personality based only on the aspects of the person that are accepted by others.

For more information, refer to Learning Goal 12.2b.

5. B
According to the information presented, Ella appears to be high in conscientiousness. The characteristics of this personality factor include being organized, careful, and self-disciplined.

For more information, refer to Learning Goal 12.2c.

6. A
Justin's explanation that he "has bad luck" is consistent with having an external locus of control, one of two types of personality described by Rotter's expectancy theory. Rotter's work in personality is a cognitive approach because it states that (1) our behaviors are part of our personality and (2) our actions are shaped by our expectations for reinforcement and the values that we ascribe to different reinforcers.

For more information, refer to Learning Goal 12.2d.

7. B
Adoption studies can examine siblings who are biologically related but are raised in different households; similarities between siblings can be attributed to the effect of nature. In this study, the children display similar shyness. This finding suggests that biology (nature) influenced the degree of shyness but that parenting differences (nurture) across the two households did not influence the degrees of shyness.

For more information, refer to Learning Goal 12.3b.

8. C
The description indicates that Morris tends to affiliate with others and to display intense emotional reactions. Morris's temperament is based on high sociability and high emotionality.

For more information, refer to Learning Goal 12.3c.

9. C
A projective personality test presents an ambiguous stimulus or prompt and allows the person to respond freely. The hope is that the person will project her hidden mental processes onto the prompt. This projection may reveal hidden aspects of her personality, such as her unconscious wishes, desires, and so on.

For more information, refer to Learning Goal 12.4b.

10. D
The person/situation debate is about whether personality or situational cues directly influence behavior. Situationism argues that personality is determined more by situational cues, but it recognizes that there are strong situations (those

that mask individual differences in personality due to environment) and weak situations (those that reveal individual differences in personality due to environment).

For more information, refer to Learning Goal 12.4c.

CHAPTER 13: PSYCHOLOGICAL DISORDERS

1. Which of the following college students is most likely at risk of developing psychopathology?
    a) Elijah, who has frequent disagreements with classmates that make them uncomfortable
    b) Jan, who likes to sing and dance at her desk even though her teachers sometimes yell at her for doing it
    c) Jeremy, who has uncontrollable urges to eat nonedible objects, such as chalk, so often that these urges interfere with his life
    d) Emily, who likes to ride the elevator facing backward, even though most people face forward

2. Aya points out that childhood abuse predisposes women for depression when they encounter stress later in life. Alisha argues that depression among women results from a combination of genetic predisposition, oppression in a male-dominated society, and the tendency for women to have negative thoughts. In regard to the etiology of depression, Aya seems to adhere to the _____ approach, whereas Alisha seems to adopt a _____ approach.
    a) assessment; psychopathology
    b) assessment; biopsychosocial
    c) diathesis-stress; psychopathology
    d) diathesis-stress; biopsychosocial

3. Kat constantly worries, even over small things. She is always on high alert and is so easily distracted that she had to quit her job. This information suggests that Kat would most likely be diagnosed with _____.
    a) social anxiety disorder
    b) generalized anxiety disorder
    c) panic disorder
    d) agoraphobia

4. Mary experiences feelings of deep sadness that last for several months at a time and make it hard for her to get out of bed to care for her children. However, she sometimes experiences short periods where she is a bit more creative and energized than normal and is able to succeed at her job as a book illustrator. Mary is most likely experiencing _____ disorder.
    a) bipolar I
    b) major depressive

    c) bipolar II
    d) persistent depressive

5. William hears a voice inside his head that urges him to steal money and lab equipment from a medical research center. William is most likely experiencing _____, which are a _____ symptom of schizophrenia.
    a) hallucinations; positive
    b) delusions; positive
    c) hallucinations; negative
    d) delusions; negative

6. Warren has schizophrenia. He believes that a chip has been implanted in his brain and that it let his boss spy on his thoughts about the company. Warren's belief is best characterized as a _____ delusion.
    a) grandiose
    b) control
    c) referential
    d) persecution

7. During conversations with his therapist, Paul often makes comments that reveal his vast mood swings, unstable relationships, and impulsivity. As a result, Paul's therapist would probably characterize him as having _____ personality disorder.
    a) avoidant
    b) borderline
    c) paranoid
    d) dependent

8. Twin sisters Molly and Holly both have peculiar psychological conditions. Once, Molly woke up on her kitchen floor, not knowing her name or how she came to be in her house. Holly disappeared and turned up a month later in a different state, living as "Nicole" and with no memory of her former life. Molly most likely has dissociative _____, whereas Holly most likely has dissociative _____.
    a) fugue; amnesia
    b) identity disorder; amnesia
    c) amnesia; fugue
    d) identity disorder; fugue

9. Micah is in elementary school and has a very difficult time with reading and writing. In particular, Micah reports that when he reads or writes, the letters get mixed up in his head. Micah may have _____.
    a) a specific learning disorder
    b) an intellectual disability
    c) a motor disorder
    d) autism spectrum disorder

10. Louis, a 7-year-old, has a hard time keeping friends. Although he can be very friendly and outgoing, he is inattentive to classmates. During recess, he acts impulsively, often running from group to group and interrupting their games. Louis's behavior is most consistent with having _____.
    a) autism spectrum disorder
    b) attention-deficit/hyperactivity disorder
    c) Asperger's syndrome
    d) a motor disorder

Answers for Chapter 13

1. C
Psychopathology arises from disordered thoughts, emotions, and/or behaviors that deviate from cultural norms, are maladaptive, cause personal distress, and cause discomfort for others. However, the most important criteria for something to be a psychopathology is that it must interfere with the life of the person being diagnosed.
    For more information, refer to Learning Goal 13.1b.

2. D
Aya adopts the diathesis-stress model: When an individual has a predisposition for a psychopathology, this predisposition may trigger the disorder under stressful circumstances. Alisha adopts the biopsychosocial approach: Psychological disorders are influenced by biological, psychological, and sociocultural factors.
    For more information, refer to Learning Goal 13.1c.

3. B
Generalized anxiety disorder is a diffuse state of constant anxiety not associated with a specific stimulus or event, resulting in distractibility, fatigue, irritability, and sleep problems.
    For more information, refer to Learning Goal 13.2b.

4. C
Mary is most likely to be diagnosed with bipolar II disorder—alternating periods of extreme depression and mildly elevated mood—because her daily functioning is more impaired by her depressive episodes than by her heightened mood.
    For more information, refer to Learning Goal 13.2d.

5. A
William is experiencing hallucinations, which are perceptual disturbances (in this case, auditory) that arise without any actual auditory input. Hallucinations are a positive symptom of schizophrenia, because they represent the addition of an abnormal behavior.
    For more information, refer to Learning Goal 13.3b.

6. D
A person with schizophrenia has a delusion of persecution if he believes that others are persecuting, spying on, or trying to harm him.
    For more information, refer to Learning Goal 13.3c.

7. B
Cluster B personality disorders are characterized by dramatic, emotional, or erratic behaviors. They include antisocial, borderline (as described in the question), histrionic, and narcissistic personality disorders.
    For more information, refer to Learning Goal 13.4b.

8. C
Dissociative amnesia is a disorder that involves disruptions of memory for personal facts, plus loss of conscious awareness for a period of time. Dissociative fugue is a disorder that involves a loss of identity in conjunction with travel to a new location and sometimes assuming a new identity.
    For more information, refer to Learning Goal 13.4d.

9. A
A specific learning disorder occurs when a school-age child has difficulty learning and using academic skills, in particular for math, reading, or writing.
    For more information, refer to Learning Goal 13.5b.

10. B
Attention-deficit/hyperactivity disorder is characterized by excessive activity, inattentiveness, and impulsivity in a child under the age of 12. This disorder often leads to social difficulties.
    For more information, refer to Learning Goal 13.5d.

CHAPTER 14: PSYCHOLOGICAL TREATMENTS

1. Eileen, a psychotherapist, interacts with her clients as an equal as she helps them fulfill their potential for personal growth. She does not give clients advice, but provides the acceptance and support that will allow them to change their own behavior. Eileen most likely uses a _____ therapy approach with clients.
    a) cognitive
    b) psychodynamic
    c) humanistic
    d) behavior

2. The last time Ryan experienced a manic phase, he proposed marriage to four women in one day, maxed out all his credit cards, and quit his job. Ryan's psychiatrist will most likely prescribe a(n) _____ to control his symptoms.
   a) mood stabilizer drug
   b) antipsychotic drug
   c) stimulant
   d) anti-anxiety drug

3. Craig has been successfully treated for severe depression. He has an associate's degree and now volunteers at a suicide crisis center, conducting intake interviews with new patients as a way to help others. Craig is most likely a _____.
   a) clinical psychologist
   b) psychiatric social worker
   c) paraprofessional
   d) counseling psychologist

4. Jonah has panic attacks when he has to give presentations in class. Jonah's therapist helps him change the way he thinks about the symptoms of a panic attack. He also has Jonah practice reading aloud in front of a few people so Jonah will get used to it. Jonah's therapist is using _____ to treat his panic attacks.
   a) exposure and response prevention
   b) cognitive-behavioral therapy
   c) systematic desensitization
   d) group therapy

5. Aidan's therapist believes that cognitive-behavioral therapy will help to relieve the symptoms of his major depressive disorder. As part of this therapy, his therapist will most likely suggest that Aidan _____.
   a) take Zoloft for 8 weeks before coming back for another visit
   b) sit under a high-intensity light source for a short period each day
   c) expose himself to situations that make him feel depressed until his mood improves
   d) keep a journal to track his negative thoughts and then work to change his thoughts

6. Peter, a man with schizophrenia, experiences auditory hallucinations, slow speech, and apathy. His doctor is likely to prescribe a(n) _____ to treat all of these symptoms.
   a) conventional antipsychotic
   b) mood stabilizer
   c) atypical antipsychotic
   d) stimulant

7. Cindy has come to Dr. Lindstrom for assistance with borderline personality disorder. Which of the following treatment approaches is least likely to be part of a successful treatment using dialectical behavior therapy?
   a) discussing childhood abuse
   b) prescribing mood stabilizers
   c) learning problem-solving techniques
   d) working to develop self-respect

8. Hugh, a 35-year-old man, has been diagnosed with antisocial personality disorder. His doctor is concerned that Hugh's prognosis is poor because people with antisocial personality disorder _____.
   a) have a lack of empathy that makes it difficult to develop a therapeutic relationship
   b) have symptoms that get worse after age 40
   c) respond only to extreme measures, such as a type of psychosurgery called lobotomy
   d) are not able to learn positive behaviors through operant procedures

9. Samantha, a 14-year-old, seeks help for depression. Her doctor reviews the literature on treating adolescent depression and concludes that taking Prozac, an SSRI, is usually _____ in treating Samantha's symptoms. He also concludes that cognitive-behavioral therapy may _____ her drug treatment.
   a) effective; improve any impact of
   b) effective; reduce
   c) ineffective; improve
   d) ineffective; reduce

10. Every time her name is spoken, Simone is rewarded with her favorite candy if she makes eye contact with her teacher. Simone most likely has been diagnosed with _____ and is being treated with _____.
    a) ADHD; play therapy
    b) ADHD; applied behavioral analysis
    c) autism spectrum disorder; play therapy
    d) autism spectrum disorder; applied behavioral analysis

Answers for Chapter 14

1. C
The humanistic therapy approach encourages clients to fulfill their potential for personal growth through active listening and unconditional positive regard.
   For more information, refer to Learning Goal 14.1b.

2. A

Mood stabilizers help level out severe shifts in moods and emotions, especially for manic episodes. In particular, lithium is a common mood stabilizer drug for bipolar I disorder.

For more information, refer to Learning Goal 14.1c.

3. C

A paraprofessional has little or no advanced training or education in psychology, but works under supervision in the community to assist people with mental health problems.

For more information, refer to Learning Goal 14.1d.

4. B

Effective therapies for panic attacks, such as cognitive-behavioral therapy, aim to change how people think about their responses to their physical symptoms and may also address the triggers of the attack through exposure techniques.

For more information, refer to Learning Goal 14.2b.

5. D

Cognitive-behavioral therapy can be used to treat the symptoms of depression by identifying, evaluating, and replacing negative thoughts. This treatment will in turn help the patient improve his mood.

For more information, refer to Learning Goal 14.2d.

6. C

Atypical antipsychotics are used for treating both positive and negative symptoms of schizophrenia. Early antipsychotics reduced only positive symptoms and were associated with the negative side effect of tardive dyskinesia.

For more information, refer to Learning Goal 14.2e.

7. B

The most effective treatment for borderline personality disorder is dialectical behavior therapy (DBT). DBT involves three steps: (1) replacing destructive behaviors with less destructive actions and teaching problem-solving skills, (2) exploration of past traumatic experiences, and (3) development of self-respect, independent problem solving, and self-acceptance.

For more information, refer to Learning Goal 14.3b.

8. A

The prognosis for treatment of antisocial personality disorder is poor. In particular, psychotherapy does not work because the manipulative, egotistical characteristics of the patient prevent a positive therapeutic relationship from forming. Moderate gains have been made only in treating antisocial personality disorder with stimulants (in the short term) and operant procedures in residential treatment centers.

For more information, refer to Learning Goal 14.3c.

9. A

Several studies have found that SSRIs are effective at treating depression in adolescents. Cognitive-behavioral therapy is also effective at treating depression on its own, and it enhances the effect of drug treatment with SSRIs.

For more information, refer to Learning Goal 14.4b.

10. D

Autism spectrum disorder, which is marked by difficulties with social and communication skills, can be effectively treated with applied behavioral analysis. In this intensive behavior therapy, desirable behaviors are rewarded in the hope that their frequency will increase.

For more information, refer to Learning Goal 14.4d.

GLOSSARY

absolute threshold The smallest amount of physical stimulation required to detect a sensory input half of the time it is present.

accommodation The process we use to create new frameworks for knowledge or drastically alter existing ones to incorporate new information that otherwise would not fit.

achievement motivation The need, or desire, to attain a certain standard of excellence.

achievement test A psychometric test that is designed to test what knowledge and skills a person has learned.

acquisition The gradual formation of an association between conditioned and unconditioned stimuli.

action potential The neural impulse that travels along the axon and then causes the release of neurotransmitters into the synapse.

activation-synthesis Dreams are the result of the brain's attempts to make sense of random brain activity by synthesizing the activity with stored memories.

actor/observer bias When interpreting our own behavior, we tend to focus on situations. When interpreting other people's behavior, we tend to focus on personal attributes.

addiction Compulsive drug craving and use, despite the negative consequences of using the drug.

affect-as-information theory People use their current moods to make decisions, judgments, and appraisals, even if they do not know the sources of the moods.

aggression Any behavior that involves the intention to harm someone else.

agoraphobia An anxiety disorder marked by fear of being in situations from which escape may be difficult or impossible.

altruism The act of providing help when it is needed, with no apparent reward for doing so.

ambivalent attachment The attachment style for infants who are unwilling to explore an unfamiliar environment but seem to have mixed feelings about the caregiver—they cry when the caregiver leaves the room, but they cannot be consoled by the caregiver upon the caregiver's return.

amygdala A subcortical forebrain structure that serves a vital role in our learning to associate things with emotional responses and in processing emotional information.

analogical representations Mental representations that have some of the physical characteristics of objects.

androgens A class of hormones that are associated with sexual behavior and are more prevalent in males; testosterone is one example.

anorexia nervosa An eating disorder characterized by excessive fear of becoming fat and therefore restricting energy intake to obtain a significantly low body weight.

anterograde amnesia A condition in which people lose the ability to form new memories after experiencing a brain injury.

antisocial personality disorder (APD) A personality disorder marked by disregard for and violation of the rights of others and by lack of remorse.

applied behavioral analysis An intensive behavior therapy for autism; this treatment is based on operant conditioning.

aptitude test A psychometric test that is designed to test a person's ability to learn—that is, the person's future performance.

arousal Physiological activation (such as increased brain activity) or increased autonomic responses (such as increased heart rate, sweating, or muscle tension).

assimilation The process we use to incorporate new information into existing frameworks for knowledge.

attention Focusing mental resources on information; allows further processing for perception, memory, and response.

attention-deficit/hyperactivity disorder (ADHD) A disorder characterized by excessive activity or fidgeting, inattentiveness, and impulsivity.

attitude accessibility Ease of retrieving an attitude from memory.

attitudes People's evaluations of objects, of events, or of ideas.

autism spectrum disorder A developmental disorder characterized by deficits in social interaction, by impaired communication, and by restricted interests.

autonomic nervous system A part of the peripheral nervous system; this part transmits sensory signals and motor signals between the central nervous system and the body's glands and internal organs.

avoidant attachment The attachment style for infants who are somewhat willing to explore an unfamiliar environment, but do not look at the caregiver when the caregiver leaves or returns, as though they have little interest in the caregiver.

axon A long, narrow outgrowth of a neuron that enables the neuron to transmit information to other neurons.

babbling Intentional vocalization, often by an infant, that does not have a specific meaning.

basic tendencies Personality traits that are largely determined by biology and are stable over time.

behaviorism A psychological approach that emphasizes the role of environmental forces in producing behavior.

behavior therapy Treatment for psychological disorders where a therapist works with clients to help them unlearn learned behaviors that negatively affect their functioning.

binge-eating disorder An eating disorder characterized by binge eating that causes significant distress.

binocular depth cues Cues of depth perception that arise because people have two eyes.

biological therapy Treatment for psychological disorders that is based on medical approaches to illness and to disease.

biopsychosocial model A model of health that integrates the effects of biological, behavioral, and social factors on health and illness.

bipolar I disorder Mood disorder characterized by extremely elevated moods during manic episodes.

bipolar II disorder Mood disorder characterized by alternating periods of extremely depressed and mildly elevated moods.

body mass index (BMI) A ratio of body weight to height, used to measure obesity.

borderline personality disorder A personality disorder characterized by disturbances in identity, in moods, and in impulse control.

bottom-up processing The perception of objects is due to analysis of environmental stimulus input by sensory receptors; this analysis then influences the more complex, conceptual processing of that information in the brain.

Broca's area A small portion of the left frontal region of the brain; this area is crucial for producing speech.

bulimia nervosa An eating disorder characterized by dieting, binge eating, and purging.

bystander apathy The failure to offer help to people in need.

Cannon-Bard theory Emotions and bodily responses both occur simultaneously due to how parts of the brain process information.

cell body Part of the neuron where information from thousands of other neurons is collected and integrated.

central nervous system The part of the nervous system that consists of the brain and the spinal cord.

central route A method of persuasion that uses high elaboration—where people pay attention to the arguments and consider all the information in the message. This method usually results in development of stronger attitudes.

cerebellum A hindbrain structure at the back of the brain stem; this structure is essential for coordinated movement and balance.

change blindness An individual's failure to notice large visual changes in the environment.

characteristic adaptations Changes in behavioral expression of basic tendencies based on the demands of specific situations.

chunking Using working memory to organize information into meaningful units to make it easier to remember.

circadian rhythms The regulation of biological cycles into regular, daily patterns.

classical conditioning A type of learned response in which a neutral object comes to elicit a response when it is associated with a stimulus that already produces a response.

cochlea A coiled, bony, fluid-filled tube in the inner ear that houses the sensory receptors.

cognitive approaches Ways of studying personality that recognize the influence of how people think.

cognitive-behavioral therapy (CBT) Treatment for psychological disorders where a therapist incorporates techniques from cognitive therapy and behavior therapy to correct faulty thinking and maladaptive behaviors.

cognitive dissonance An uncomfortable mental state due to a contradiction between two attitudes or between an attitude and a behavior.

cognitive map A visuospatial mental representation of an environment.

cognitive psychology The study of how people think, learn, and remember.

cognitive therapy Treatment for psychological disorders where a therapist works with clients to help them change distorted thought patterns that produce maladaptive behaviors and emotions.

cold receptors Sensory receptors in the skin that detect the temperature of stimuli and transduce it into information processed in the brain as cold.

companionate love A type of romantic relationship that includes strong commitment to supporting and caring for a partner.

compliance The tendency to agree to do things requested by others.

concept A mental representation of objects, events, or relations around common themes.

concrete operational stage The third stage in Piaget's theory of cognitive development; during this stage, children begin to think about and understand logical operations, and they are no longer fooled by appearances.

conditioned response (CR) A response to a conditioned stimulus; a response that has been learned.

conditioned stimulus (CS) A stimulus that elicits a response only after learning has taken place.

cones Sensory receptors in the retina that detect light waves and transduce them into signals that are processed in the brain as vision. Cones respond best to higher levels of illumination, and therefore they are responsible for seeing color and fine detail.

conformity The altering of your own behaviors and opinions to match those of other people or to match other people's expectations.

consciousness The combination of a person's subjective experience of the external world and the person's mental activity; this combination results from brain activity.

consolidation A process by which immediate memories become lasting through long-term storage.

control group In an experiment, a comparison group of participants that receives no intervention or receives an intervention that is unrelated to the independent variable being investigated.

conventional level Middle level of moral development; at this level, strict adherence to societal laws and the approval of others determine what is moral.

correlational methods A research method that examines how variables are naturally related in the real world. The researcher makes no attempt to alter the variables or assign causation between them.

critical thinking Systematically evaluating information to reach reasonable conclusions best supported by evidence.

crystallized intelligence Intelligence that reflects both the knowledge a person acquires through experience and the ability to use that knowledge.

culture The beliefs, values, rules, and customs that exist within a group of people who share a common language and environment and that are transmitted through learning from one generation to the next.

daily hassles Everyday irritations that cause small disruptions, the effects of which can add up to a large impact on health.

decision making Attempting to select the best alternative among several options.

deep brain stimulation (DBS) Treatment for psychological disorders that involves passing electricity through electrodes planted in the client's brain to stimulate the brain at a certain frequency and intensity.

defense mechanisms Unconscious mental strategies that the mind uses to protect itself from distress.

defining attribute model A way of thinking about concepts: A category is characterized by a list of features that determine if an object is a member of the category.

deindividuation A state of reduced individuality, reduced self-awareness, and reduced attention to personal standards; this phenomenon may occur when people are part of a group.

delusions False beliefs based on incorrect inferences about reality.

dementia Severe impairment in intellectual capacity and personality, often due to damage to the brain.

dendrites Branchlike extensions of the neuron with receptors that detect information from other neurons.

dependent variable In an experiment, the variable that is affected by the manipulation of the independent variable.

depressants Psychoactive drugs that decrease both mental processes and physical activity.

descriptive methods A research method that provides a systematic and objective description of what is occurring.

developmental psychology The scientific study of how humans change over the life span, from conception until death.

dialectical behavior therapy (DBT) Form of therapy used to treat borderline personality disorder.

diathesis-stress model Proposes that a disorder may develop when an underlying vulnerability is coupled with a precipitating event.

difference threshold The minimum difference in physical stimulation required to detect a difference between sensory inputs.

discrimination The inappropriate and unjustified treatment of people as a result of prejudice.

disorganized behavior Acting in strange or unusual ways, including strange movement of limbs and inappropriate self-care, such as failing to dress properly or bathe.

disorganized speech Speaking in an incoherent way that involves frequently changing topics and saying strange or inappropriate things.

display rules Rules that are learned through socialization and that dictate what emotions are suitable in certain situations.

dissociation theory of hypnosis Hypnotized people are in an altered state where their awareness is separated from other aspects of consciousness.

dissociative amnesia Mental disorder that involves disruptions of memory for personal facts or loss of conscious awareness for a period of time.

dissociative identity disorder (DID) The occurrence of two or more distinct identities in the same individual.

distortion Human memory is not a perfectly accurate representation of the past, but is flawed.

dizygotic twins Fraternal twins; these siblings result from two separately fertilized eggs, so they are no more similar genetically than non-twin siblings are.

downward comparisons Comparing oneself to another person who is less competent or in a worse situation, which tends to protect a person's high self-esteem.

dreams Products of consciousness during sleep in which a person confuses images and fantasies with reality.

drive A psychological state that, by creating arousal, motivates an organism to engage in a behavior to satisfy a need.

eardrum A thin membrane that marks the beginning of the middle ear; sound waves cause the eardrum to vibrate.

ego In psychodynamic theory, the component of personality that tries to satisfy the wishes of the id while being responsive to the superego.

elaborative rehearsal Using working memory processes to think about how new information relates to ourselves or our prior knowledge (semantic information); provides deeper encoding of information for more successful long-term storage.

electroconvulsive therapy (ECT) Treatment for psychological disorders that involves administering a strong electrical current to the client's brain to produce a seizure; ECT is effective in some cases of severe depression.

embryonic period The period in prenatal development from 2 to 8 weeks after conception, when the brain, spine, major organs, and bodily structures begin to form in the embryo.

emotion Feelings that involve subjective evaluation, physiological processes, and cognitive beliefs.

emotion-focused coping A type of coping in which people try to prevent having an emotional response to a stressor.

encoding The processing of information so that it can be stored.

endocrine system A communication system that uses hormones to influence thoughts and actions.

episodic memory A type of explicit memory that includes a person's personal experiences.

estrogens A class of hormones that are associated with sexual behavior and are more prevalent in females; estradiol is one example.

etiology Factors that contribute to the development of a disorder.

exemplar model A way of thinking about concepts: All concepts in a category are examples (exemplars); together, they form the category.

experimental group In an experiment, one or more treatment groups of participants that receive the intervention of the independent variable being investigated.

experimental methods A research method that tests causal hypotheses by manipulating independent variables and measuring the effects on dependent variables.

explicit attitude An attitude that a person is consciously aware of and can report.

explicit memory The system for long-term storage of conscious memories that can be verbally described.

exposure Therapy technique that involves repeatedly exposing a client to an anxiety-producing stimulus or situation and has the goal of reducing the client's fear.

exposure and response prevention Therapy technique that teaches clients to relax as they are gradually exposed to increasingly feared stimuli or situations. The goal of treatment is to reduce the fear.

extinction A process in which the conditioned response is weakened when the conditioned stimulus is repeated without the unconditioned stimulus.

extrinsic motivation A desire to perform an activity because of the external goals that activity is directed toward.

fast fibers Sensory receptors in skin, muscles, organs, and membranes around both bones and joints; these myelinated fibers quickly convey intense sensory input to the brain, where it is perceived as sharp, immediate pain.

fetal period The period in prenatal development from 8 weeks after conception until birth, when the brain continues developing, bodily structures are refined, and the fetus grows in length and weight and accumulates fat in preparation for birth.

fight-or-flight response The physiological preparedness of animals to deal with danger.

fixed interval schedule (FI) Reinforcing the occurrence of a particular behavior after a pre-determined amount of time since the last reward.

fixed ratio schedule (FR) Reinforcing a particular behavior after that behavior has occurred a predetermined number of times.

flow A highly focused, altered state of consciousness, when awareness of self and time diminishes due to being completely engrossed in an enjoyable activity.

fluid intelligence Intelligence that reflects the ability to process information, particularly in novel or complex circumstances.

forgetting The inability to retrieve a memory from long-term storage, which is often due to interference, blocking, and absentmindedness.

formal operational stage The final stage in Piaget's theory of cognitive development; during this stage, people can think abstractly, and they can formulate and test hypotheses through logic.

framing How information is presented affects how that information is perceived and influences decisions.

frontal lobes Regions of the cerebral cortex at the front of the brain; these regions are important for movement and complex processes (rational thought, attention, social processes, etc.).

frustration-aggression hypothesis The more frustrated we feel, the more likely we are to act aggressively.

functional fixedness A tendency to think of things based on their usual functions, which may make it harder to solve a problem.

functionalism An early school of psychology concerned with the adaptive purpose, or function, of mind and behavior.

fundamental attribution error In explaining other people's behavior, the tendency to overemphasize personality traits and underestimate situational factors.

gender identity Each person's beliefs about being male or female.

gender roles The characteristics associated with being male or being female, because of cultural influence or learning.

general adaptation syndrome (GAS) A consistent pattern of physical responses to stress that consists of three stages: alarm, resistance, and exhaustion.

general intelligence The idea that one general factor underlies intelligence.

generalized anxiety disorder A diffuse state of constant anxiety not associated with any specific object or event.

generativity versus stagnation Seventh stage of Erikson's theory of psychosocial development, where middle-aged adults face the challenge of leaving behind a positive legacy and caring for future generations.

genes The units of heredity, which partially determine an organism's characteristics.

germinal period The period in prenatal development from conception to two weeks after fertilization of the egg, when the zygote divides rapidly and implants in the uterine wall.

Gestalt theory The idea that the whole of personal experience is different from simply the sum of its parts.

ghrelin A hormone that is associated with increasing eating behavior based on short-term signals in the bloodstream.

global workspace model Consciousness is a product of activity in specific brain regions.

grouping The visual system's organization of features and regions to create the perception of a whole, unified object.

guilt A negative emotional state associated with anxiety, tension, and agitation.

habituation A decrease in behavioral response after lengthy or repeated exposure to a stimulus.

hair cells Sensory receptors located in the cochlea that detect sound waves and transduce them into signals that ultimately are processed in the brain as sound.

hallucinations False sensory perceptions that are experienced without an external source.

hallucinogenics Psychoactive drugs that affect perceptual experiences and evoke sensory images even without sensory input.

health psychology A field that integrates research on health and on psychology; it involves the application of psychological principles to promoting health and well-being.

heuristic A shortcut (rule of thumb or informal guideline) used to reduce the amount of thinking that is needed to make decisions.

hippocampus A subcortical forebrain structure that is associated with the formation of memories.

hormones Chemical substances, released from endocrine glands, that travel through the bloodstream to targeted tissues; the tissues are later influenced by the hormones.

humanistic approaches Ways of studying personality that emphasize self-actualization, where people seek to fulfill their potential through greater self-understanding.

humanistic therapy Treatment for psychological disorders where a therapist works with clients to help them develop their full potential for personal growth through greater self-understanding.

hypnosis A social interaction during which a person, responding to suggestions, experiences changes in memory, perception, and/or voluntary action.

hypothalamus A subcortical forebrain structure involved in regulating bodily functions. The hypothalamus also influences our basic motivated behaviors.

hypothesis A specific prediction of what should be observed if a theory is correct.

id In psychodynamic theory, the component of personality that is completely submerged in the unconscious and operates according to the pleasure principle.

identity versus role confusion Fifth stage of Erikson's theory of psychosocial development, where adolescents face the challenge of figuring out who they are.

immune system The body's mechanism for dealing with invading microorganisms, such as allergens, bacteria, and viruses.

implicit attitude An attitude that influences a person's feelings and behavior at an unconscious level.

implicit memory The system for long-term storage of unconscious memories that cannot be verbally described.

incentives External objects or external goals, rather than internal drives, that motivate behaviors.

independent variable In an experiment, the variable that the experimenter manipulates to examine its impact on the dependent variable.

insight learning A sudden understanding of how to solve a problem after a period of either inaction or thinking about the problem.

insomnia A disorder characterized by an inability to sleep.

institutional review boards (IRBs) Groups of people responsible for reviewing proposed research to ensure that it meets the accepted standards of science and provides for the physical and emotional well-being of research participants.

integrity versus despair Eighth stage of Erikson's theory of psychosocial development, where older adults face the challenge of feeling satisfied that they have lived a good life and developed wisdom.

intelligence The ability to use knowledge to reason, make decisions, make sense of events, solve problems, understand complex ideas, learn quickly, and adapt to environmental challenges.

intelligence quotient (IQ) An index of intelligence originally computed by dividing a child's estimated mental age by the child's chronological age, then multiplying this number by 100.

interactionists Theorists who believe that behavior is determined jointly by situations and underlying traits.

intimacy versus isolation Sixth stage of Erikson's theory of psychosocial development, where adolescents face the challenge of forming committed long-term friendships and romances.

intrinsic motivation A desire to perform an activity because of the value or pleasure associated with that activity, rather than for an apparent external goal or purpose.

James-Lange theory Emotions result from the experience of physiological reactions in the body.

latent learning Learning that takes place in the absence of reinforcement.

learning A change in behavior, resulting from experience.

lens The adjustable, transparent structure behind the pupil; this structure focuses light on the retina, resulting in a crisp visual image.

leptin A hormone that is associated with decreasing eating behavior based on long-term body fat regulation.

locus of control The idea that personality is based on a person's perception of whether she controls the rewards and punishments that she experiences (internal locus of control) or does not control them (external locus of control).

long-term storage A memory storage system that allows relatively permanent storage, probably of an unlimited amount of information.

maintenance rehearsal Using working memory processes to repeat information based on how it sounds (acoustic information); provides only shallow encoding of information and less successful long-term storage.

major depressive disorder Mood disorder, characterized by extremely depressed moods or a lack of interest in normally pleasurable activities, that persists for two weeks or more.

major life stressors Large disruptions, especially unpredictable and uncontrollable catastrophic events, that affect central areas of people's lives.

maturation Physical development of the brain and body that prepares an infant for voluntary movement, such as rolling over, sitting, and walking.

meditation A practice in which intense contemplation leads to a deep sense of calmness that has been described as an altered state of consciousness.

melatonin A hormone, released in the brain, that aids regulation of circadian rhythms because bright light reduces production and darkness increases production.

memory The nervous system's capacity to acquire and retain skills and knowledge for later retrieval.

mental age An assessment of a child's intellectual standing compared with that of same-age peers; determined by comparing the child's test score with the average score for children of each chronological age.

mental sets A tendency to approach a problem in the same way that has worked in the past, which may make it harder to solve a problem.

mere exposure effect The increase in liking due to repeated exposure.

modeling The imitation of behavior through observational learning.

monocular depth cues Cues of depth perception that are available to each eye alone.

monozygotic twins Identical twins; these siblings result from one zygote splitting in two, so they share the same genes.

motivation Factors of differing strength that energize, direct, and sustain behavior.

multiple intelligences The idea that people have many different types of intelligence that are independent of one another.

narcolepsy A sleep disorder in which a person experiences excessive sleepiness during normal waking hours, sometimes going limp and collapsing.

natural selection In evolutionary theory, the idea that those who inherit characteristics that help them adapt to their particular environments have a selective advantage over those who do not.

need A state of biological or social deficiency.

need hierarchy An arrangement of needs, in which basic survival needs must be met before people can satisfy higher needs.

need to belong theory The need for interpersonal attachments is a fundamental motive that has evolved for adaptive purposes.

negative punishment The removal of a stimulus to decrease the probability that a behavior will recur.

negative reinforcement The removal of a stimulus to increase the probability that a behavior will be repeated.

negative symptoms Symptoms of schizophrenia that are marked by deficits in functioning, such as apathy, lack of emotion, and slowed speech and movement.

neurons The basic units of the nervous system; cells that receive, integrate, and transmit information in the nervous system. Neurons operate through electrical impulses, communicate with other neurons through chemical signals, and form neural networks.

neurotransmitters Chemical substances that carry signals from one neuron to another.

nervous system A network of billions of cells in the brain and the body, responsible for all aspects of what we feel, think, and do.

obedience Factors that influence people to follow the orders given by an authority.

objective measures Relatively direct assessments of personality, usually based on information gathered through self-report questionnaires or observer ratings.

observational learning The acquisition or modification of a behavior after exposure to at least one performance of that behavior.

obsessive-compulsive disorder (OCD) A disorder characterized by frequent intrusive thoughts that create anxiety and compulsive actions that temporarily reduce the anxiety.

occipital lobes Regions of the cerebral cortex at the back of the brain; these regions are important for vision.

olfactory bulb A brain structure above the olfactory epithelium in the nasal cavity; from this structure, the olfactory nerve carries information about smell to the brain.

olfactory epithelium A thin layer of tissue, deep within the nasal cavity, containing the olfactory receptors; these sensory receptors produce information that is processed in the brain as smell.

operant conditioning A learning process in which the consequences of an action determine the likelihood that the action will be performed in the future.

opponent-process theory The proposal that ganglion cells in the retina receive excitatory input from one type of cone and inhibitory input from another type of cone, creating the perception that some colors are opposites.

overregularization The tendency for young children to incorrectly use a regular syntax rule where they should use an exception to the rule.

panic disorder An anxiety disorder that consists of sudden, overwhelming attacks of terror.

papillae Structures on the tongue that contain groupings of taste buds.

parietal lobes Regions of the cerebral cortex in front of the occipital lobes and behind the frontal lobes; these regions are important for the sense of touch and for picturing the layout of spaces in an environment.

partial-reinforcement extinction effect The greater persistence of behavior under partial reinforcement than under continuous reinforcement.

passionate love A type of romantic relationship that includes intense longing and sexual desire.

perception The processing, organization, and interpretation of sensory signals in the brain; these processes result in an internal neural representation of the physical stimulus.

peripheral nervous system The part of the nervous system that enables nerves to connect the central nervous system with the muscles, organs, and glands.

peripheral route A method of persuasion that uses low elaboration—where people minimally process the message. This method usually results in development of weaker attitudes.

persistence The continual recurrence of unwanted memories from long-term storage.

persistent depressive disorder Mood disorder, characterized by mildly or moderately depressed moods, that persists for at least two years.

personal attributions People's explanations for why events or actions occur that refer to people's internal characteristics, such as abilities, traits, moods, or efforts.

personality The characteristic thoughts, emotional responses, and behaviors that are relatively stable in an individual over time and across circumstances.

persuasion The active and conscious effort to change an attitude through the transmission of a message.

phobia Fear of a specific object or situation that is out of proportion with any actual threat.

phototherapy Treatment for seasonal affective disorder (SAD) through which the client is exposed to high-intensity light each day.

place coding The perception of higher-pitched sounds is a result of the location on the basilar membrane where hair cells are stimulated by sound waves of varying higher frequencies.

plasticity A property of the brain that causes it to change through experience, drugs, or injury.

positive psychology The study of the strengths and virtues that allow people and communities to thrive.

positive punishment The addition of a stimulus to decrease the probability that a behavior will recur.

positive reinforcement The addition of a stimulus to increase the probability that a behavior will be repeated.

positive symptoms Symptoms of schizophrenia that are marked by excesses in functioning, such as delusions, hallucinations, and disorganized speech or behavior.

postconventional level Highest level of moral development; at this level, decisions about morality depend on abstract principles and the value of all life.

posttraumatic stress disorder (PTSD) A mental disorder that involves frequent nightmares, intrusive thoughts, and flashbacks related to an earlier trauma.

preconventional level Earliest level of moral development; at this level, self-interest and event outcomes determine what is moral.

prejudice Negative feelings, opinions, and beliefs associated with a stereotype.

preoperational stage The second stage in Piaget's theory of cognitive development; during this stage, children think symbolically about objects, but they reason based on intuition and superficial appearances rather than logic.

pressure receptors Sensory receptors in the skin that detect tactile stimulation and transduce it into information processed in the brain as different types of pressure on the skin.

primary appraisals Part of coping that involves making decisions about whether a stimulus is stressful or not.

primary emotions Evolutionarily adaptive emotions that are shared across cultures and associated with specific physical states; they include anger, fear, sadness, disgust, happiness, and possibly surprise and contempt.

primary sex characteristics The reproductive organs and genitals that distinguish the sexes and their maturation for reproduction.

proactive interference When access to newer memories is impaired by older memories.

problem-focused coping A type of coping in which people take direct steps to confront or minimize a stressor.

problem solving Finding a way around an obstacle to reach a goal.

procedural memory A type of implicit memory that involves motor skills and behavioral habits.

prognosis A prediction of the likely course of a psychological (or physical) disorder.

projective measures Personality tests that examine unconscious processes by having people interpret ambiguous stimuli.

prosocial Acting in ways that tend to benefit others.

prospective memory Remembering to do something at some future time.

prototype model A way of thinking about concepts: Within each category, there is a best example—a prototype—for that category.

psychodynamic theory Freudian theory that unconscious forces determine behavior.

psychodynamic therapy Treatment for psychological disorders where a therapist works with clients to help them become aware of how their unconscious processes may be causing conflict and impairing daily functioning.

psychology The study of mental activity and behavior, which are based on brain processes.

psychopathology Sickness or disorder of the mind.

psychotherapy Treatment for psychological disorders where a therapist works with clients to help them understand their problems and work toward solutions.

psychotropic medications Drugs that affect mental processes and that can be used to treat psychological disorders.

puberty The physical changes in the body that are a part of sexual development.

random assignment Placing research participants into the conditions of an experiment in such a way that each participant has an equal chance of being assigned to any level of the independent variable.

random sample A sample that fairly represents the population because each member of the population had an equal chance of being included.

reasoning Using information to determine if a conclusion is valid or reasonable.

reliability How consistently a psychometric test produces similar results each time it is used.

REM sleep The stage of sleep when EEGs show beta wave activity associated with an awake, alert mind, and sleepers experience rapid eye movements, dreaming, and paralysis of motor systems.

restructuring Thinking about a problem in a new way in order to solve it.

retina The thin inner surface of the back of the eyeball; this surface contains the sensory receptors.

retrieval The act of recalling or remembering stored information when it is needed.

retrieval cue Anything that helps a person access information in long-term storage.

retroactive interference When access to older memories is impaired by newer memories.

retrograde amnesia A condition in which people lose the ability to access memories they had before a brain injury.

rods Sensory receptors in the retina that detect light waves and transduce them into signals that are processed in the brain as vision. Rods respond best to low levels of illumination, and therefore do not support color vision or seeing fine detail.

schizophrenia A psychological disorder characterized by a split between thought and emotion where a person has difficulty distinguishing whether altered thoughts, perceptions, and conscious experiences are real versus what are imagined.

scientific method A systematic procedure of observing and measuring phenomena (observable things) to answer questions about *what* happens, *when* it happens, *what causes* it, and *why*. This process involves a dynamic interaction between theories, hypotheses, and research methods.

secondary appraisals Part of coping where people decide how to manage and respond to a stressful stimulus.

secondary emotions Blends of primary emotions; they include remorse, guilt, shame, submission, and anticipation.

secondary sex characteristics Sex-differentiating characteristics that are not directly related to reproduction but that develop during the hormonal changes of puberty.

secure attachment The attachment style for most infants, who are confident enough to play in an unfamiliar environment as long as the caregiver is present and are readily comforted by the caregiver during times of distress.

self-esteem The affective aspect of the self.

self-fulfilling prophecy People's tendency to behave in ways that confirm their own expectations or other people's expectations.

self-schema An integrated set of memories, beliefs, and generalizations about the self.

self-serving bias The tendency for people to take personal credit for success but blame failure on external factors.

semantic memory A type of explicit memory that includes a person's knowledge about the world.

sensation The sense organs' detection of external physical stimulus and the transmission of information about this stimulus to the brain.

sensitization An increase in behavioral response after lengthy or repeated exposure to a stimulus.

sensorimotor stage The first stage in Piaget's theory of cognitive development; during this stage, infants acquire information about the world through their senses and motor skills.

sensory adaptation A decrease in sensitivity to a constant level of stimulation.

sensory receptors Sensory organs that detect physical stimulation from the external world and change that stimulation into information that can be processed by the brain.

sensory storage A memory storage system that very briefly holds a vast amount of information from the five senses in close to their original sensory formats.

sexual response cycle A four-stage pattern of physiological and psychological responses during sexual activity.

sexual strategies theory Women and men have evolved distinct mating strategies because they have faced different adaptive problems over the course of human history. The strategies used by each sex maximize the probability of passing along their genes to future generations.

short-term storage A memory storage system that briefly holds a limited amount of information in awareness.

signal detection theory Detection of a faint stimulus requires a judgment—it is not an all-or-none process.

situational attributions People's explanations for why events or actions occur that refer to external events, such as the weather, luck, accidents, or other people's actions.

situationism The theory that behavior is determined more by situations than by personality traits.

sleep apnea A disorder in which a person, while asleep, stops breathing because the throat closes; the condition results in frequent awakenings during the night.

slow fibers Sensory receptors in skin, muscles, organs, and membranes around both bones and joints; these unmyelinated fibers slowly convey intense sensory input to the brain, where it is perceived as chronic, dull, steady pain.

slow-wave sleep Stages 3 and 4 of deep sleep, when EEGs reveal large, regular delta waves and sleepers are hard to awaken.

social facilitation When the mere presence of others enhances performance.

social loafing The tendency for people to work less hard in a group than when working alone.

social norms Expected standards of conduct, which influence behavior.

social psychology The study of how people are influenced by their interactions with others.

sociocognitive theory of hypnosis Hypnotized people are not in an altered state, but they behave in a way that is expected in that situation.

somatic nervous system A part of the peripheral nervous system; this part transmits sensory signals and motor signals between the central nervous system and the skin, muscles, and joints.

split brain A condition in which the corpus callosum is surgically cut, and the two hemispheres of the brain do not receive information directly from each other.

spontaneous recovery A process in which a previously extinguished response reemerges after the conditioned stimulus is presented again.

stereotypes Cognitive schemas that allow for easy, fast processing of information about people, events, or groups, based on their membership in certain groups.

stereotype threat Apprehension about confirming negative stereotypes related to a person's own group.

stimulants Psychoactive drugs that increase both mental processes and physical activity.

stimulus discrimination A differentiation between two similar stimuli when only one of them is consistently associated with the unconditioned stimulus.

stimulus generalization Learning that occurs when stimuli that are similar but not identical to the conditioned stimulus produce the conditioned response.

storage The retention of encoded representations over time.

stress A group of behavioral, psychological, and physiological processess occuring when events match or exceed the organism's ability to respond in a healthy way.

stressor An environmental event or stimulus that threatens an organism.

stress responses Physical, behavioral, and/or psychological responses to stressors.

structuralism An early school of psychology that explored the structures of the mind through introspection.

subliminal perception The processing of information by sensory systems without a person's conscious awareness.

superego In psychodynamic theory, the component of personality that reflects the internalization of societal and parental standards of conduct.

symbolic representations Abstract mental representations that consist of words or ideas.

synapse The site where communication occurs between neurons through neurotransmitters.

systematic desensitization Therapy technique that involves exposing a client to increasingly anxiety-producing stimuli or situations while having the client relax at the same time.

taste buds Structures, located in papillae on the tongue, that contain the sensory receptors called taste receptors.

telegraphic speech The tendency for toddlers to speak using rudimentary sentences that are missing words and grammatical markings but follow a logical syntax and convey a wealth of meaning.

temperament Biologically based tendency to feel or act in certain ways.

temporal coding The perception of lower-pitched sounds is a result of the rate at which hair cells are stimulated by sound waves of lower frequencies.

temporal lobes Regions of the cerebral cortex below the parietal lobes and in front of the occipital lobes; these regions are important for processing auditory information and for perceiving objects and faces.

tend-and-befriend response Females' tendency to respond to stressors by protecting and caring for their offspring and forming social alliances.

teratogens Environmental agents that can harm prenatal development.

thalamus A subcortical forebrain structure; the gateway to the brain for almost all incoming sensory information before that information reaches the cortex.

theory A model of interconnected ideas or concepts that explains what is observed and makes predictions about future events.

thinking The mental manipulation of representations of information we encounter in our environments.

tolerance A physical effect of addiction that occurs when a person needs to take larger doses of a drug to experience its effect.

top-down processing The perception of objects is due to the complex analysis of prior experiences and expectations within the brain; this analysis influences how sensory receptors process stimulus input from the environment.

trait approaches Ways of studying personality that are based on people's characteristics, their tendencies to act in a certain way over time and across circumstances.

transcranial magnetic stimulation (TMS) Treatment for psychological disorders that uses a magnetic field to interrupt function in specific regions of the brain.

transduction A process by which sensory receptors change physical stimuli into signals that are eventually sent to the brain.

triarchic theory The idea that people have three types of intelligence: analytical, creative, and practical.

trichromatic theory There are three types of cone receptor cells in the retina that are responsible for color perception. Each type responds optimally to different, but overlapping, ranges of wavelengths.

two-factor theory How we experience an emotion is influenced by the cognitive label we apply to explain the physiological changes we have experienced.

Type A behavior pattern Personality traits characterized by competitiveness, achievement orientation, aggressiveness, hostility, restlessness, impatience with others, and an inability to relax.

Type B behavior pattern Personality traits characterized by being noncompetitive, relaxed, easygoing, and accommodating.

unconditioned response (UR) A response that does not have to be learned, such as a reflex.

unconditioned stimulus (US) A stimulus that elicits a response that is innate and does not require any prior learning.

upward comparisons Comparing oneself to another person who is more competent or in a better situation, which tends to confirm a person's low self-esteem.

validity How well a psychometric test measures what it is intended to measure.

variable interval schedule (VI) Reinforcing the occurrence of a particular behavior after an unpredictable and varying amount of time since the last reward.

variable ratio schedule (VR) Reinforcing a particular behavior after the behavior has occurred an unpredictable and varying number of times.

vicarious conditioning Learning the consequences of an action by watching others being rewarded or punished for performing the action.

warm receptors Sensory receptors in the skin that detect the temperature of stimuli and transduce it into information processed in the brain as warmth.

well-being A positive state that includes striving for optimal health and life satisfaction.

withdrawal A physical and psychological effect of addiction that occurs when a person experiences anxiety, tension, and cravings after discontinuing use of an addictive drug.

working memory An active processing system that allows manipulation of different types of information to keep it available for current use.

working self-concept Reflects how a person thinks of herself at a certain moment.

REFERENCES

Abel, E. L. (2006). Fetal alcohol syndrome: A cautionary note. *Current Pharmaceutical Design, 12,* 1521–1529.

Abizaid, A. (2009). Ghrelin and dopamine: New insights on the peripheral regulation of appetite. *Journal of Neuroendocrinology, 21,* 787–793.

Abraido-Lanza, A. F., Chao, M. T., & Florez, K. R. (2005). Do healthy behaviors decline with greater acculturation? Implications for the Latino mortality paradox. *Social Science and Medicine, 61,* 1243–1255.

Abramson, L. Y., Metalsky, G., & Alloy, L. (1989). Hopelessness depression: A theory-based subtype of depression. *Psychological Review, 96,* 358–372.

Adolphs, R., Gosselin, F., Buchanan, T. W., Tranel, D., Schyns, P., & Damasio, A. R. (2005). A mechanism for impaired fear recognition after amygdala damage. *Nature, 433,* 68–72.

Adolphs, R., Sears, L., & Piven, J. (2001). Abnormal processing of social information from faces in autism. *Journal of Cognitive Neuroscience, 13,* 232–240.

Agawu, K. (1995). *African rhythm: A northern ewe perspective.* Cambridge, UK: Cambridge University Press.

Ainsworth, M. D. S., Blehar, M. C., Waters, E., & Wall, S. (1978). *Patterns of attachment: A psychological study of the strange situation.* Hillsdale, NJ: Erlbaum.

Albus, C. (2010). Psychological and social factors in coronary heart disease. *Annals of Medicine, 42,* 487–494.

Algoe, S. B., & Fredrickson, B. L. (2011). Emotional fitness and the movement of affective science from lab to field. *American Psychologist, 66,* 35–42.

Alicke, M. D., Klotz, M. L., Breitenbecher, D. L., Yurak, T. J., & Vredenburg, D. S. (1995). Personal contact, individuation, and the better-than-average effect. *Journal of Personality and Social Psychology, 68,* 804–825.

Amaral, D. G., Schumann, C. M., & Nordahl, C. W. (2008). Neuroanatomy of autism. *Trends in Neurosciences, 3,* 137–145.

Amato, P. R., Johnson, D. R., Booth, A., & Rogers, S. J. (2003). Continuity and change in marital quality between 1980 and 2000. *Journal of Marriage and Family, 65,* 1–22.

Ambady, N., & Rosenthal, R. (1993). Half a minute: Predicting teacher evaluations from thin slices of nonverbal behavior and physical attractiveness. *Journal of Personality and Social Psychology, 64,* 431–441.

American Academy of Pediatrics, Committee on Drugs. (1998). Neonatal drug withdrawal. *Pediatrics, 10,* 1079–1088.

American Association of Suicidology. (2011). Youth suicidal behavior [Fact sheet]. Retrieved June 3, 2013, from http://www.suicidology.org/c/document_library/get_file?folderId=232&name=DLFE-335.pdf

American Psychiatric Association. (2000). Practice guidelines for the treatment of patients with eating disorders (revised). *American Journal of Psychiatry, 157* (Suppl.), 1–39.

American Psychiatric Association. (2013). *Diagnostic and statistical manual of mental disorders* (5th ed.). Washington, DC: Author.

American Psychological Association. (2007, February). Guidelines for psychological practice with girls and women. Retrieved June 3, 2013, from http://www.apa.org/practice/guidelines/girls-and-women.pdf

American Psychological Association (2010, May 13). Dr. Katherine C. Nordal on how to find a therapist. Retrieved June 3, 2013, from http://apa.org/news/press/releases/2010/05/locate-a-therapist.aspx

American Psychological Association, Health Psychology Division 38. (n.d.). What is health psychology? Retrieved June 11, 2013, from http://www.health-psych.org/AboutWhatWeDo.cfm

Anderson, A. K., Christoff, K., Stappen, I., Panitz, D., Ghahremani, D. G., Glover, G., et al. (2003). Dissociated neural representations of intensity and valence in human olfaction. *Nature Neuroscience, 6,* 196–202.

Anderson, A. K., & Phelps, E. A. (2000). Expression without recognition: Contributions of the human amygdala to emotional communication. *Psychological Science, 11,* 106–111.

Anderson, C. A., Berkowitz, L., Donnerstein, E., Huesmann, L. R., Johnson, J., Linz, D., et al. (2003). The influence of media violence on youth. *Psychological Science in the Public Interest, 4,* 81–110.

Anderson, N. H. (1968). Likableness ratings of 555 personality-trait words. *Journal of Personality and Social Psychology, 9,* 272–279.

Anderson, R., Lewis, S. Z., Gichello, A. L., Aday, L. A., & Chiu, G. (1981). Access to medical care among the Hispanic population of the Southwestern United States. *Journal of Health and Social Behavior, 22,* 78–89.

Angell, M. (2011, June 23). The Epidemic of Mental Illness: Why? *The New York Review of Books,* p. 14. Retrieved June 11, 2013, http://www.nybooks.com/articles/archives/2011/jun/23/epidemic-mental-illness-why/

Arias, E., MacDorman, M. F., Strobino, D. M., & Guyer, B. (2003). Annual summary of vital statistics: 2002. *Pediatrics, 112*, 1215–1230.

Aronne, L. J., Wadden, T., Isoldi, K. K., & Woodworth, K. A. (2009). When prevention fails: Obesity treatment strategies. *American Journal of Medicine, 122*(4 Suppl. 1), S24–S32.

Aronson, E., & Mills, J. (1959). The effects of severity of initiation on liking for a group. *Journal of Abnormal and Social Psychology, 59*, 177–181.

Asch, S. E. (1955). Opinions and social pressure. *Scientific American, 193*, 31–35.

Asch, S. E. (1956). Studies of independence and conformity: A minority of one against a unanimous majority. *Psychological Monographs, 70*, Whole No. 416.

Austin, E. J., Saklofske, D. H., & Mastoras, S. M. (2010). Emotional intelligence, coping and exam-related stress in Canadian undergraduate students. *Australian Journal of Psychology, 62*, 42–50.

Aviezer, H., Hassin, R. R., Ryan, J., Grady, C., Susskind, J., Anderson, A., et al. (2008). Angry, disgusted, or afraid? Studies on the malleability of emotion perception. *Psychological Science, 19*, 724–732.

Axelsson, J., Sundelin, T., Ingre, M., Van Someren, E. J. W., Olsson, A., & Lekander, M. (2010). Beauty sleep: Experimental study on the perceived health and attractiveness of sleep deprived people. *British Journal of Medicine, 341*. Retrieved June 3, 2013, from http://www.bmj.com/content/341/bmj.c6614.abstract

Baars, B. (1988). *A cognitive theory of consciousness*. Cambridge, UK: Cambridge University Press.

Baddeley, A. D. (2002). Is working memory still working? *European Psychologist, 7*, 85–97.

Baddeley, A. D., & Hitch, G. (1974). Working memory. In G. H. Bower (Ed.), *The psychology of learning and motivation: Advances in research and theory* (Vol. 8, pp. 47–89). New York: Academic Press.

Baillargeon, R. (1987). Object permanence in 3½ and 4½ month old infants. *Developmental Psychology, 23*, 655–664.

Baillargeon, R., Li, J., Ng, W., & Yuan, S. (2009). A new account of infants' physical reasoning. In A. Woodward & A. Needham (Eds.), *Learning and the infant mind* (pp. 66–116). New York: Oxford University Press.

Baker, T. B., Brandon, T. H., & Chassin, L. (2004). Motivational influences on cigarette smoking. *Annual Review of Psychology, 55*, 463–491.

Baldwin, D. A., & Baird, J. A. (2001). Discerning intentions in dynamic human action. *Trends in Cognitive Sciences, 5*, 171–178.

Baler, R. D., & Volkow, N. D. (2006). Drug addiction: The neurobiology of disrupted self-control. *Trends in Molecular Medicine, 12*, 559–566.

Ballantyne, J. C., & LaForge, K. S. (2007). Opioid dependence and addiction during opioid treatment of chronic pain. *Pain, 129*, 235–255.

Balthazard, C. G., & Woody, E. Z. (1992). The spectral analysis of hypnotic performance with respect to "absorption." *International Journal of Clinical and Experimental Hypnosis, 40*, 21–43.

Bandura, A. (1977a). Self-efficacy: Toward a unifying theory of behavioral change. *Psychological Review, 84*, 191–215.

Bandura, A. (1977b). *Social learning theory*. Englewood Cliffs, NJ: Prentice-Hall.

Bandura, A., Ross, D., & Ross, S. (1961). Transmission of aggression through imitation of aggressive models. *Journal of Abnormal and Social Psychology, 66*, 3–11.

Bargh, J. A. (2006). What have we been priming all these years? On the development, mechanisms, and ecology of nonconscious social behavior. *European Journal of Social Psychology, 36*, 168.

Bargh, J. A., & Chartrand, T. L. (1999). The unbearable automaticity of being. *American Psychologist, 54*, 462–479.

Bargh, J. A., & Morsella, E. (2008). The unconscious mind. *Perspectives on Psychological Science, 3*, 73–79.

Barlett, C. P., & Rodeheffer, C. 2009. Effects of realism on extended violent and nonviolent video game play on aggressive thoughts, feelings, and physiological arousal. *Aggressive Behavior, 35*, 213–224.

Barlow, D. H. (2002). *Anxiety and its disorders: The nature and treatment of anxiety and panic* (2nd ed.). New York: Guilford Press.

Barlow, D. H. (2004). Psychological treatments. *American Psychologist, 59*, 869–878.

Baron, A. S., & Banaji, M. R. (2006). The development of implicit attitudes. *Psychological Science, 17*, 53–58.

Bartels, J., Andreasen, D., Ehirim, P., Mao, H., Seibert, S., Wright, E. J., et al. (2008). Neurotrophic electrode: Method of assembly and implantation into human motor speech cortex. *Journal of Neuroscience Methods, 174*, 168–176.

Bartlett, F. C. (1932). *Remembering: A study in experimental and social psychology*. Cambridge, UK: Cambridge University Press.

Bartoshuk, L. M. (2000). Comparing sensory experiences across individuals: Recent psychophysical advances illuminate genetic variation in taste perception. *Chemical Senses, 25*, 447–460.

Basson, M. D., Bartoshuk, L. M., Dichello, S. Z., Panzini, L., Weiffenbach, J. M., & Duffy, V. B. (2005). Association between 6-n-propylthiouracil (PROP) bitterness and colonic neoplasms. *Digestive Diseases and Sciences, 50*, 483–489.

Baumeister, R. F. (1991). *Escaping the self: Alcoholism, spirituality, masochism, and other flights from the burden of selfhood*. New York: Basic Books.

Baumeister, R. F. (2000). Gender differences in erotic plasticity: The female sex drive as socially flexible and responsive. *Psychological Bulletin, 126*, 347–374.

Baumeister, R. F., Campbell, J. D., Krueger, J. I., & Vohs, K. D. (2003). Does high self-esteem cause better performance, interpersonal success, happiness, or healthier lifestyles? *Psychological Science in the Public Interest, 4*, 1–44.

Baumeister, R. F., Campbell, J. D., Krueger, J. I., & Vohs, K. D. (2005, January). Exploding the self-esteem myth. *Scientific American, 292*, 84–91.

Baumeister, R. F., Catanese, K. R., & Vohs, K. D. (2001). Is there a gender difference in strength of sex drive? Theoretical views, conceptual distinctions, and a review of the relevant literature. *Social Psychology Review, 5*, 242–273.

Baumeister, R. F., Dale, K., & Sommers, K. L. (1998). Freudian defense mechanisms and empirical findings in modern social psychology: Reaction formation, projection, displacement, undoing, isolation, sublimation, and denial. *Journal of Personality, 66,* 1081–1124.

Baumeister, R. F., Heatherton, T. F., & Tice, D. (1994). *Losing control: How and why people fail at self-regulation.* San Diego, CA: Academic Press.

Baumeister, R. F., & Leary, M. R. (1995). The need to belong: Desire for interpersonal attachments as a fundamental human motivation. *Psychological Bulletin, 117,* 497–529.

Baumeister, R. F., Smart, L., & Boden, J. M. (1996). Relation of threatened egotism to violence and aggression: The dark side of high self-esteem. *Psychological Review, 103,* 5–33.

Baumgartner, T., Lutz, K., Schmidt, C. F., & Jäncke, L. (2006). The emotional power of music: How music enhances the feeling of affective pictures. *Brain Research, 1075,* 151–164.

Baumrind, D., Larzelere, R. E., & Cowan, P. A. (2002). Ordinary physical punishment: Is it harmful? Comment on Gershoff (2002). *Psychological Bulletin, 128,* 580–589.

Baxter, L. R. (2000). Functional imaging of brain systems mediating obsessive-compulsive disorder. In D. S. Charney, E. J. Nestler, & B. S. Bunney (Eds.), *Neurobiology of mental illness* (pp. 534–547). New York: Oxford University Press.

Baydala, L., Rasmussen, C., Birch, J., Sherman, J., Wikman, E., Charchun, J., et al. (2009). Self-beliefs and behavioural development as related to academic achievement in Canadian Aboriginal children. *Canadian Journal of School Psychology, 24,* 19–33.

Beck, A. T. (1967). *Depression: Clinical, experimental and theoretical aspects.* New York: Harper & Row.

Beck, A. T. (1976). *Cognitive therapy and the emotional disorders.* New York: International Universities Press.

Beck, H. P., Levinson, S., & Irons, G. (2009). Finding Little Albert: A journey to John B. Watson's infant laboratory. *American Psychologist, 64,* 605–614.

Beggs, J. M., Brown, T. H., Byrne, J. H., Crow, T., LeDoux, J. E., LeBar, K., et al. (1999). Learning and memory: Basic mechanisms. In M. J. Zigmond, F. E. Bloom, S. C. Landis, J. L. Roberts, & L. R. Squire (Eds.), *Fundamentals of neuroscience* (pp. 1411–1454). San Diego, CA: Academic Press.

Behne, T., Carpenter, M., Call, J., & Tomasello, M. (2005). Unwilling versus unable: Infants' understanding of intentional action. *Developmental Psychology, 41,* 328–337.

Bellak, L., & Black, R. B. (1992). Attention-deficit hyperactivity disorder in adults. *Clinical Therapeutics, 14,* 138–147.

Belmaker, R. H., & Agam, G. (2008). Major depressive disorder. *New England Journal of Medicine, 358,* 55–68.

Belsky, J. (1990). Children and marriage. In F. D. Fincham & T. N. Bradbury (Eds.), *The psychology of marriage: Basic issues and applications* (pp. 172–200). New York: Guilford Press.

Belsky, J., Houts, R. M., & Fearon, R. M. P. (2010). Infant attachment security and the timing of puberty: Testing an evolutionary hypothesis. *Psychological Science, 21,* 1195–1201.

Bem, D. J. (1967). Self-perception: An alternative explanation of cognitive dissonance phenomena. *Psychological Review, 74,* 183–200.

Bender, H. L., Allen, J. P., McElhaney, K. B., Antonishak, J., Moore, C. M., Kelly, H. O., et al. (2007). Use of harsh physical discipline and developmental outcomes in adolescence. *Development and Psychopathology, 19,* 227–242.

Bentler, P. M., & Newcomb, M. D. (1978). Longitudinal study of marital success and failure. *Journal of Consulting and Clinical Psychology, 46,* 1053–1070.

Berkman, L. F., & Syme, S. L. (1979). Social networks, host resistance, and mortality: A nine-year follow-up study of Alameda County residents. *American Journal of Epidemiology, 109,* 186–204.

Berscheid, E., & Regan, P. (2005). *The psychology of interpersonal relationships.* New York: Prentice-Hall.

Bewernick, B. H., Hurlemann, R., Matusch, A., Kayser, S., Grubert, C., Hadrysiewicz, B., et al. (2010). Nucleus accumbens deep brain stimulation decreases ratings of depression and anxiety in treatment-resistant depression. *Biological Psychiatry, 67,* 110–116.

Bidell, T. R., & Fischer, K. W. (1995). Between nature and nurture: The role of agency in the epigenesis of intelligence. In R. Sternberg & E. Grigorenko (Eds.), *Intelligence: Heredity and environment* (pp. 193–242). New York: Cambridge University Press.

Biederman, J., Hirshfeld-Becker, D. R., Rosenbaum, J. F., Herot, C., Friedman, D., Snidman, N., et al. (2001). Further evidence of association between behavioral inhibition and social anxiety in children. *American Journal of Psychiatry, 158,* 1673–1679.

Biesanz, J., West, S. G., & Millevoi, A. (2007). What do you learn about someone over time? The relationship between length of acquaintance and consensus and self-other agreement in judgments of personality. *Journal of Personality and Social Psychology, 92,* 119–135.

Bjorklund, D. F. (2007). *Why youth is not wasted on the young: Immaturity in human development.* Malden, MA: Blackwell.

Blakemore, S. J., & Choudhury, S. (2006). Development of the adolescent brain: Implications for executive function and social cognition. *Journal of Child Psychology and Psychiatry, 47,* 296–312.

Blass, T. (1991). Understanding behavior in the Milgram obedience experiment: The role of personality, situations, and their interactions. *Journal of Personality and Social Psychology, 60,* 398–413.

Block, J., & Kremen, A. M. (1996). IQ and ego-resiliency: Conceptual and empirical connections and separateness. *Journal of Personality and Social Psychology, 70,* 349–361.

BloodAlcoholContent.Org. (2007–2013). Measuring BAC. Retrieved June 3, 2013, from http://bloodalcoholcontent.org/measuringbac.html

Bloom, B., & Cohen, R. A. (2007). Summary health statistics for U.S. children: National health interview survey, 2006 (Vital and Health Statistics, Series 10, No. 234). Hyattsville, MD: Centers for Disease Control and Prevention.

Blue, I., & Harpham, T. (1996). Urbanization and mental health in developing countries. *Current Issues in Public Health, 2,* 181–185.

Bohlin, G., Hagekull, B., & Rydell, A. M. (2000). Attachment and social functioning: A longitudinal study from infancy to middle childhood. *Social Development, 9,* 24–39.

Bolles, R. C. (1970). Species-specific defense reactions and avoidance learning. *Psychological Review, 77*, 32–48.

Bonanno, G. A. (2004). Loss, trauma, and human resilience: Have we underestimated the human capacity to thrive after extremely aversive events? *American Psychologist, 59*, 20–28.

Bootzin, R. R., & Epstein, D. R. (2011). Understanding and treating insomnia. *Annual Review of Clinical Psychology, 7*, 435–458.

Bornstein, R. F. (1999). Criterion validity of objective and projective dependency tests: A meta-analytic assessment of behavioral prediction. *Psychological Assessment, 11*, 48–57.

Bouchard, C., & Pérusse, L. (1993). Genetics of obesity. *Annual Review of Nutrition, 13*, 337–354.

Bouchard, C., Tremblay, A., Despres, J. P., Nadeau, A., Lupien, J. P., Theriault, G., et al. (1990). The response to long-term overfeeding in identical twins. *New England Journal of Medicine, 322*, 1477–1482.

Bouchard, T. J., Jr., Lykken, D. T., McGue, M., Segal, N. L., & Tellegen, A. (1990). Sources of human psychological differences: The Minnesota study of twins reared apart. *Science, 250*, 223–228.

Bouton, M. E. (1994). Context, ambiguity, and classical conditioning. *Current Directions in Psychological Science, 3*, 49–53.

Bouton, M. E., Westbrook, R. F., Corcoran, K. A., & Maren, S. (2006). Contextual and temporal modulation of extinction: Behavioral and biological mechanisms. *Biological Psychiatry, 60*, 352–360.

Bowlby, J. (1982). Attachment and loss: Retrospect and prospect. *American Journal of Orthopsychiatry, 52*, 664–678.

Bradbury, T. N., & Fincham, F. D. (1990). Attributions in marriage: Review and critique. *Psychological Bulletin, 107*, 3–33.

Bransford, J. D., & Johnson, M. K. (1972). Contextual prerequisites for understanding: Some investigations of comprehension and recall. *Journal of Verbal Learning and Verbal Behavior, 11*, 717–726. (Reprinted and modified in *Human memory*, p. 305, by E. B. Zechmeister & S. E. Nyberg, Eds., Pacific Grove, CA: Brooks Cole, 1982.)

Breland, K., & Breland, M. (1961). The misbehavior of organisms. *American Psychologist, 16*, 681–684.

Brent, D. A. (2004). Antidepressants and pediatric depression: The risk of doing nothing. *New England Journal of Medicine, 351*, 1598–1601.

Brewer, M. B., & Caporael, L. R. (1990). Selfish genes vs. selfish people: Sociobiology as origin myth. *Motivation and Emotion, 14*, 237–243.

Bromley, S. M., & Doty, R. L. (1995). Odor recognition memory is better under bilateral than unilateral test conditions. *Cortex, 31*, 25–40.

Brown, A. S. (1991). A review of the tip-of-the-tongue phenomenon. *Psychological Bulletin, 109*, 204–223.

Brown, B. B., Mounts, N., Lamborn, S. D., & Steinberg, L. (1993). Parenting practices and peer group affiliations in adolescence. *Child Development, 64*, 467–482.

Brown, R. (1973). Development of the first language in the human species. *American Psychologist, 28*, 97–106.

Brown, R., & Kulik, J. (1977). Flashbulb memories. *Cognition, 5*, 73–99.

Brown, R., & McNeill, D. (1966). The "tip-of-the-tongue" phenomenon. *Journal of Verbal Learning and Verbal Behavior, 5*, 325–337.

Brownell, K. D., Greenwood, M. R. C., Stellar, E., & Shrager, E. E. (1986). The effects of repeated cycles of weight loss and regain in rats. *Physiology & Behavior, 38*, 459–464.

Burger, J. M. (2009). Replicating Milgram: Would people still obey today? *American Psychologist, 64*, 1–11.

Bush, E. C., & Allman, J. M. (2004). The scaling of frontal cortex in primates and carnivores. *Proceedings of the National Academy of Sciences, USA, 101*, 3962–3966.

Buss, A. H., & Plomin, R. (1984). *Temperament: Early developing personality traits*. Hillsdale, NJ: Erlbaum.

Buss, D. M. (1989). Sex differences in human mate preferences: Evolutionary hypotheses tested in 37 cultures. *Behavioral and Brain Sciences, 12*, 1–49.

Buss, D. M., & Schmitt, D. P. (1993). Sexual strategies theory: An evolutionary perspective on human mating. *Psychological Review, 100*, 204–232.

Butcher, J. N., Mineka, S., & Hooley, J. M. (2007). *Abnormal psychology* (13th ed.). Boston: Allyn & Bacon.

Byers-Heinlein, K., Burns, T. C., & Werker, J. F. (2010). The roots of bilingualism in newborns. *Psychological Science, 21*, 343–348.

Cacioppo, J. T., Hughes, M. E., Waite, L. J., Hawkley, L. C., & Thisted, R. A. (2006). Loneliness as a specific risk factor for depressive symptoms: Cross sectional and longitudinal analyses. *Psychology and Aging, 21*, 140–151.

Cahill, L., Haier, R. J., White, N. S., Fallon, J., Kilpatrick, L., Lawrence, C., et al. (2001). Sex-related difference in amygdala activity during emotionally influenced memory storage. *Neurobiology of Learning and Memory, 75*, 1–9.

Cahill, L., Prins, B., Weber, M., & McGaugh, J. L. (1994). Beta-adrenergic activation and memory for emotional events. *Nature, 371*, 702–704.

Cahn, B. R., & Polich, J. (2006). Meditation states and traits: EEG, ERP, and neuroimaging studies. *Psychological Bulletin, 132*, 180–211.

Cairns, R. B., & Cairns, B. D. (1994). *Lifelines and risks: Pathways of youth in our times*. Cambridge, UK: Cambridge University Press.

Campbell, W. K., Bush, C. P., Brunell, A. B., & Shelton, J. (2005). Understanding the social costs of narcissism: The case of tragedy of the commons. *Personality and Social Psychology, 31*, 1358–1368.

Campbell, W. K., Foster, C.A., & Finkel, E. J. (2002). Does self-love lead to love for others? A story of narcissistic game playing. *Journal of Personality and Social Psychology, 83*, 340–354.

Campbell, W. K., & Sedikides, C. (1999). Self-threat magnifies the self-serving bias: A meta-analytic integration. *Review of General Psychology, 3*, 23–43.

Canli, T. (2006). *Biology of personality and individual differences*. New York: Guilford Press.

Cannon, W. B. (1927). The James-Lange theory of emotion: A critical examination and an alternative theory. *American Journal of Psychology, 39*, 106–124.

Caramaschi, D., de Boer, S. F., & Koolhaus, J. M. (2007). Differential role of the 5-HT receptor in aggressive and non-aggressive mice: An across-strain comparison. *Physiology & Behavior, 90,* 590–601.

Cardeña, E., & Carlson, E. (2011). Acute stress disorder revisited. *Annual Review of Clinical Psychology, 7,* 245–267.

Carey, B. (2011, June 23). Expert on mental illness reveals her own fight. *The New York Times.* Retrieved June 3, 2013, from http://www.nytimes.com/2011/06/23/health/23lives.html

Carli, L. L., Ganley, R., & Pierce-Otay, A. (1991). Similarity and satisfaction in roommate relationships. *Personality and Social Psychology Bulletin, 17,* 419–426.

Carrère, S., Buehlman, K. T., Gottman, J. M., Coan, J. A., & Ruckstuhl, L. (2000). Predicting marital stability and divorce in newlywed couples. *Journal of Family Psychology, 14,* 42–58.

Carstensen, L. L. (1995). Evidence for a life-span theory of socioemotional selectivity. *Current Directions in Psychological Science, 4,* 151–156.

Case, R. (1992). The role of the frontal lobes in development. *Brain and Cognition, 20,* 51–73.

Casey, B. J., Jones, R. M., & Somerville, L. H. (2011). Braking and accelerating of the adolescent brain. *Journal of Research in Adolescence, 21,* 21–33.

Caspi, A. (2000). The child is father of the man: Personality continuities from childhood to adulthood. *Journal of Personality and Social Psychology, 78,* 158–172.

Caspi, A., & Herbener, E. S. (1990). Continuity and change: Assortative marriage and the consistency of personality in adulthood. *Journal of Personality and Social Psychology, 58,* 250–258.

Caspi, A., McClay, J., Moffitt, T. E., Mill, J., Martin, J., Craig, I. W., et al. (2002). Role of genotype in the cycle of violence in maltreated children. *Science, 29,* 851–854.

Cattell, R. B. (1971). *Abilities: Their structure, growth, and action.* Boston: Houghton Mifflin.

Ceci, S. J. (1999). Schooling and intelligence. In S. J. Ceci & W. M. Williams (Eds.), *The nature-nurture debate: The essential readings* (pp. 168–175). Oxford, UK: Blackwell.

Centers for Disease Control and Prevention, National Center on Birth Defects and Developmental Disabilities. (2004, July). Fetal alcohol syndrome: Guidelines for referral and diagnosis. Retrieved June 11, 2013, from http://www.cdc.gov/ncbddd/fasd/documents/fas_guidelines_accessible.pdf

Centers for Disease Control and Prevention. (2008). Self-reported physically active adults – United States, 2007. *Morbity and Mortality Weekly Report, 57,* 1297-1300. Retrieved June 11, 2013 from http://www.cdc.gov/mmwr/preview/mmwrhtml/mm5748a1.htm

Centers for Disease Control and Prevention. (2010a). How tobacco smoke causes disease: The biology and behavioral basis for smoking-attributable disease: A report of the Surgeon General. Atlanta, GA: Author.

Centers for Disease Control and Prevention, National Center for Health Statistics. (2010b). [Table 22, Life expectancy at birth, at 65 years of age, and at 75 years of age, by race and sex: United States, selected years 1900–2007]. *Health, United States, 2010.* Retrieved June 3, 2013, from http://www.cdc.gov/nchs/data/hus/hus10.pdf#022

Centers for Disease Control and Prevention. (2010c). Tobacco use and United States students. Retrieved June 3, 2013, from http://www.cdc.gov/HealthyYouth/yrbs/pdf/us_tobacco_combo.pdf

Centers for Disease Control and Prevention. (2011). Mental illness surveillance among adults in the United States. *Morbidity and Mortality Weekly Report, 60,* 1–32.

Centers for Disease Control and Prevention. (2013, February). Noise-induced hearing loss. Retrieved June 3, 2013, from http://www.cdc.gov/healthyyouth/noise/

Cepeda, N. J., Pashler, H., Vul, E., Wixted, J. T., & Rohrer, D. (2006). Distributed practice in verbal recall tasks: A review and quantitative synthesis. *Psychological Bulletin, 132,* 354–380.

Certain, L. K., & Kahn, R. S. (2002). Prevalence, correlates, and trajectory of television viewing among infants and toddlers. *Pediatrics, 109,* 634–642.

Chabas, D., Taheri, S., Renier, C., & Mignot, E. (2003). The genetics of narcolepsy. *Annual Review of Genomics & Human Genetics, 4,* 459–483.

Chambers, D. W. (1983). Stereotypic images of the scientist: The draw-a-scientist test. *Science Education, 67,* 255–265.

Chase, W. G., & Simon, H. A. (1973). Perception in chess. *Cognitive Psychology, 4,* 55–81.

Chassin, L., Presson, C. C., & Sherman, S. J. (1990). Social psychological contributions to the understanding and prevention of adolescent cigarette smoking. *Personality and Social Psychology Bulletin, 16,* 133–151.

Cherry, E. C. (1953). Some experiments on the recognition of speech, with one and two ears. *Journal of the Acoustical Society of America, 25,* 975–979.

Chesher, G., & Greeley, J. (1992). Tolerance to the effects of alcohol. *Alcohol, Drugs, and Driving, 8,* 93–106.

Chistyakov, A. V., Kaplan, B., Rubichek, O., Kreinin, I., Koren, D., Feinsod, M., et al. (2004). Antidepressant effects of different schedules of repetitive transcranial magnetic stimulation vs. clomipramine in patients with major depression: Relationship to changes in cortical excitability. *International Journal of Neuropsychopharmacology, 8,* 223–233.

Choi, I., Dalal, R., Kim-Prieto, C., & Park, H. (2003). Culture and judgment of causal relevance. *Journal of Personality and Social Psychology, 84,* 46–59.

Christakis, N. A., & Fowler, J. H. (2007). The spread of obesity in a large social network over 32 years. *New England Journal of Medicine, 357,* 370–379.

Christianson, S. (1992). Emotional stress and eyewitness memory: A critical review. *Psychological Bulletin, 112,* 284–309.

Chronis, A. M., Jones, H. A., & Raggi, V. L. (2006). Evidence-based psychosocial treatments for children and adolescents with attention-deficit/hyperactivity disorder. *Clinical Psychology Review, 26,* 486–502.

Chun, M. M., Golomb, J. D., & Turk-Browne, N. B. (2011). A taxonomy of external and internal attention. *Annual Review of Psychology, 62,* 73–101.

Cialdini, R. B. (2008). *Influence: Science and prejudice* (5th ed.). Boston: Allyn & Bacon.

Clark, R. D., & Hatfield, E. (1989). Gender differences in receptivity to sexual offers. *Journal of Psychology and Human Sexuality, 2*, 39–55.

Clark, S. E., & Wells, G. L. (2008). On the diagnosticity of multiple-witness identifications. *Law and Human Behavior, 32*, 406–422.

Cloninger, C., Adolfsson, R., & Svrakic, N. (1996). Mapping genes for human personality. *Nature and Genetics, 12*, 3–4.

Cohen, D., Nisbett, R. E., Bowdle, B. F., & Schwarz, N. (1996). Insult, aggression, and the southern culture of honor: An "experimental ethnography." *Journal of Personality and Social Psychology, 70*, 945–960.

Cohen, G. L., Garcia, J., Apfel, N., & Master, A. (2006). Reducing the racial achievement gap: A social-psychological intervention. *Science, 313*, 1307–1310.

Cohen, S., Alper, C. M., Doyle, W. J., Treanor, J. J., & Turner, R. B. (2006). Positive emotional style predicts resistance to illness after experimental exposure to rhinovirus or influenza A virus. *Psychomatic Medicine, 68*, 809–815.

Cohen, S., Doyle, W. J., Skoner, D. P., Rabin, B. S., & Gwaltney, J. M. J. (1997). Social ties and susceptibility to the common cold. *Journal of the American Medical Association, 277*, 1940–1944.

Cohen, S., Janicki-Deverts, D., & Miller, G. E. (2007). Psychological stress and disease. *Journal of the American Medical Association, 298*, 1685–1687.

Cohen, S., Tyrrell, D. A. J., & Smith, A. P. (1991). Psychological stress and susceptibility to the common cold. *New England Journal of Medicine, 325*, 606–612.

Colapinto, J. (2000). *As nature made him: The boy who was raised as a girl.* New York: HarperCollins.

Colcombe, S. J., Erickson, K. I., Scalf, P., Kim, J., Prkash, R., McAuley, E., et al. (2006). Aerobic exercise training increases brain volume in aging humans. *Journal of Gerontology: Medical Sciences, 61A*, 1166–1170.

Collins, A. M., & Loftus, E. F. (1975). A spreading activation theory of semantic processing. *Psychologial Review, 82*, 407–428.

Compton, W. M., Conway, K. P., Stinson, F. S., Colliver, J. D., & Grant, B. F. (2005). Prevalence, correlates, and comorbidity of *DSM-IV* antisocial personality syndromes and alcohol and specific drug use disorders in the United States: Results from the national epidemiologic survey on alcohol and related conditions. *Journal of Clinical Psychiatry, 66*, 677–685.

Conn, C., Warden, R., Stuewig, R., Kim, E., Harty, L., Hastings, M., & Tangney, J. P. (2010). Borderline personality disorder among jail inmates: How common and how distinct? *Corrections Compendium, 35*, 6–13.

Conway, A. R. A., Kane, M. J., Bunting, M. F., Hambrick, D. Z., Wilhelm, O., & Engle, R. W. (2005). Working memory span tasks: A methodological review and user's guide. *Psychonomic Bulletin & Review, 12*, 769–786.

Conway, A. R. A., Kane, M. J., & Engle, R. W. (2003). Working memory capacity and its relation to general intelligence. *Trends in Cognitive Sciences, 7*, 547–552.

Cook, G. I., Marsh, R. L., Clark-Foos, A., & Meeks, J. T. (2007, February). Learning is impaired by activated intentions. *Psychonomic Bulletin and Review, 14*, 101–106.

Cook, M., & Mineka, S. (1989). Observational conditioning of fear to fear-relevant versus fear-irrelevant stimuli in rhesus monkeys. *Journal of Abnormal Psychology, 98*, 448–459.

Cooke, S. F., & Bliss, T. V. P. (2006). Plasticity in the human central nervous system. *Brain: A Journal of Neurology, 129*, 1659–1673.

Copeland, W. E., Wolke, D., Angold, A., & Costello, E. J. (2013). Adult psychiatric outcomes of bullying and being bullied by peers in childhood and adolescence. *Journal of the American Medical Association Psychiatry, 70*, 419–426.

Cooper, C. R., Denner, J., & Lopez, E. M. (1999). Cultural brokers: Helping Latino children on pathways toward success. *The Future of Children, 9*, 51–57.

Corder, E. H., Saunders, A. M., Strittmatter, W. J., Schmechel, D. E., Gaskell, P. C., Small, G. W., et al. (1993). Gene dose of apolipoprotein E type 4 allele and the risk of Alzheimer's disease in late onset families. *Science, 261*, 921–923.

Coren, S. (1996). Daylight savings time and traffic accidents. *New England Journal of Medicine, 334*, 924.

Cosmides, L., & Tooby, J. (1997). Evolutionary psychology: A primer. Retrieved June 3, 2013, from http://www.psych.ucsb.edu/research/cep/primer.html

Costa, P. T., Terracciano, A., & McCrae, R. R. (2001). Gender differences in personality traits across cultures: Robust and surprising findings. *Journal of Personality and Social Psychology, 81*, 322–331.

Courchesne, E., Pierce, K., Schumann, C. M., Redcay, E., Buckwalter, J. A., Kennedy, D. P., et al. (2007). Mapping early brain development in autism. *Neuron, 56*, 399–413.

Cowan, C. P., & Cowan, P. A. (1988). Who does what when partners become parents? Implications for men, women, and marriage. In R. Palkovitz & M. B. Sussman (Eds.), *Transitions to parenthood* (pp. 105–132). New York: The Haworth Press.

Cowell, P. E., Turetsky, B. E., Gur, R. C., Grossman, R. I., Shtasel, D. L., & Gur, R. E. (1994). Sex differences in aging of the human frontal and temporal lobes. *Journal of Neuroscience, 14*, 4748–4755.

Craft, L. L., & Perna, F. M. (2004). The benefits of exercise for the clinically depressed. *Journal of Clinical Psychiatry, 6*, 104–111.

Craik, F. I. M., & Lockhart, R. S. (1972). Levels of processing: A framework for memory research. *Journal of Verbal Learning and Verbal Behavior, 11*, 671–684.

Crawford, H. J., Corby, J. C., & Kopell, B. (1996). Auditory event-related potentials while ignoring tone stimuli: Attentional differences reflected in stimulus intensity and latency responses in low and highly hypnotizable persons. *International Journal of Neuroscience, 85*, 57–69.

Crocker, J., & Major, B. (1989). Social stigma and self-esteem: The self-protective properties of stigma. *Psychological Review, 96*, 608–630.

Crocker, J., Niiya, Y., & Mischkowski, D. (2008). Why does writing about important values reduce defensiveness? Self-affirmation and the role of positive other-directed feelings. *Psychological Science, 19*, 740–747.

Crocker, J., Olivier, M., & Nuer, N. (2009). Self-image goals and compassionate goals: Costs and benefits. *Self and Identity, 8*, 251–269.

Crosnoe, R., & Elder, G. H., Jr. (2002). Successful adaptation in the later years: A life-course approach to aging. *Social Psychology Quarterly, 65*, 309–328.

Crothers, T. (2012). *The queen of Katwe: A story of life, chess, and one extraordinary girl's dreams of becoming a grandmaster.* New York: Scribner.

Crowe, R. R. (2000). Molecular genetics of anxiety disorders. In D. S. Charney, E. J. Nestler, & B. S. Bunney (Eds.), *Neurobiology of mental illness* (pp. 451–462). New York: Oxford University Press.

Csikszentmihalyi, M. (1990). *Flow: The psychology of optimal experience.* New York: Harper & Row.

Csikszentmihalyi, M. (1999). If we are so rich, why aren't we happy? *American Psychologist, 54*, 821–827.

Cummings, J. R., & Druss, B. G. (2010). Racial/ethnic differences in mental health service use among adolescents with major depression. *Journal of the American Academy of Child & Adolescent Psychiatry, 50*, 160–170.

Cunningham, M. R., Barbee, A. P., & Druen, P. B. (1996). Social allergens and the reactions they produce: Escalation of annoyance and disgust in love and work. In R. M. Kowalski (Ed.), *Aversive interpersonal behaviors* (pp. 189–214). New York: Plenum Press.

Cunningham, M. R., Roberts, A. R., Barbee, A. P., Druen, P. B., & Wu, C. (1995). Their ideas of beauty are, on the whole, the same as ours: Consistency and variability in the cross-cultural perception of female physical attractiveness. *Journal of Personality and Social Psychology, 68*, 261–279.

Curtiella, C. (2009). *The state of learning disabilities.* New York: National Center for Learning Disabilities.

Curtiss, S. (1977). *Genie: A psycholinguistic study of a modern day "wild child."* New York: Academic Press.

Dalton, M. A., Bernhardt, A. M., Gibson, J. J., Sargent, J. D., Beach, M. L., Adachi-Mejia, et al. (2005). "Honey, have some smokes." Preschoolers use cigarettes and alcohol while role playing as adults. *Archives of Pediatrics & Adolescent Medicine, 159*, 854–859.

Damasio, A. R. (1994). *Descartes' error.* New York: Avon Books.

Damasio, H., Grabowski, T., Frank, R., Galaburda, A. M., & Damasio, A. R. (1994). The return of Phineas Gage: Clues about the brain from the skull of a famous patient. *Science, 264*, 1102–1105.

Darley, J. M., & Batson, C. D. (1973). "From Jerusalem to Jericho": A study of situational and dispositional variables in helping behavior. *Journal of Personality and Social Psychology, 27*, 100–108.

Darwin, C. (1859). *On the origin of species by means of natural selection, or the preservation of favoured races in the struggle for life.* London: John Murray.

Darwin, C. R. (1872). *The expression of the emotions in man and animals.* London: John Murray.

Davidson, J. R., Foa, E. B., Huppert, J. D., Keefe, F. J., Franklin, M. E., Compton, J. S., et al. (2004). Fluoxetine, comprehensive cognitive behavioral therapy, and placebo in generalized social phobia. *Archives of General Psychiatry, 61*, 1005–1013.

Davidson, R. J. (2000). Affective style, psychopathology, and resilience: Brain mechanisms and plasticity. *American Psychologist, 55*, 1196–1214.

Davidson Ward, S. L., Bautisa, D., Chan, L., Derry, M., Lisbin, A., Durfee, M., et al. (1990). Sudden infant death syndrome in infants of substance-abusing mothers. *Journal of Pediatrics, 117*, 876–887.

Deacon, B. J., & Abramowitz, J. S. (2004). Cognitive and behavioral treatments for anxiety disorders: A review of meta-analytic findings. *Journal of Clinical Psychology, 60*, 429–441.

Deary, I. J. (2000). *Looking down on human intelligence.* New York: Oxford University Press.

Deaux, K., & Major, B. (1987). Putting gender into context: An interactive model of gender-related behavior. *Psychological Review, 94*, 369–389. DeCasper, A. J., & Fifer, W. P. (1980, June 6). Of human bonding: Newborns prefer their mothers' voices. *Science, 208*, 1174–1176.

DeCasper, A. J., & Fifer, W. P. (1980). Of human bonding: Newborns prefer their mothers' voices. *Science, 208*, 1174–1176.

DeCasper, A. J., & Spence, M. J. (1986). Prenatal maternal speech influences newborns' perception of speech sounds. *Infant Behavior and Development, 9*, 133–150.

Deci, E. L., & Ryan, R. M. (1987). The support of autonomy and the control of behavior. *Journal of Personality and Social Psychology, 53*, 1024–1037.

Decyk, B. N. (1994). Using examples to teach concepts. In *Changing college classrooms: New teaching and learning strategies for an increasingly complex world* (pp. 39–63). San Francisco: Jossey-Bass.

Dehaene, S., Changeux, J. P., Naccache, L., Sackur, J., & Sergent, C. (2006). Conscious, preconscious, and subliminal processing: A testable taxonomy. *Trends in Cognitive Sciences, 10*, 204–211.

Dejong, W., & Kleck, R. E. (1986). The social psychological effects of overweight. In C. P. Herman, M. P. Zanna, & E. T. Higgins (Eds.), *Physical appearance, stigma and social behavior: The Ontario Symposium* (pp. 65–87). Hillsdale, NJ: Erlbaum.

Demerouti, E. (2006). Job characteristics, flow, and performance: The moderating role of conscientiousness. *Journal of Occupational Health Psychology, 11*, 266–280.

Demos, K.E., Heatherton, T.F., & Kelley, W.M. (2012). Individual differences in nucleus accumben activity to food and sexual images predict weight gain and sexual behavior. *Journal of Neuroscience, 32*, 5549–5552.

de Wijk, R. A., Schab, F. R., & Cain, W. S. (1995). Odor identification. In F. R. Schab (Ed.), *Memory for odors* (pp. 21–37). Mahwah, NJ: Erlbaum.

Diener, E. (2000). Subjective well-being: The science of happiness and a proposal for a national index. *American Psychologist, 55*, 34–43.

Diener, E., Gohm, C. L., Suh, E., & Oishi, S. (2000). Similarity of the relations between marital status and subjective well-being. *Journal of Cross-Cultural Psychology, 31*, 419–436.

Dijksterhuis, A., & Aarts, H. (2010). Goals, attention, and (un)conscious. *Annual Review of Psychology, 61*, 467–490.

Dineley, K. T., Westernman, M., Bui, D., Bell, K., Ashe, K. H., & Sweatt, J. D. (2001). β-amyloid activates the mitogen-activated protein kinase cascade via hippocampal $\alpha 7$ nicotinic acetylcholine receptors: In vitro and in vivo mechanisms related to Alzheimer's disease. *Journal of Neuroscience, 21,* 4125–4133.

Dion, K., Berscheid, E., & Walster, E. (1972). What is beautiful is good. *Journal of Personality and Social Psychology, 24,* 285–290.

Diotallevi, M. (2008). Testimonials versus evidence. *Canadian Medical Association Journal, 179,* 449.

Dobbs, D. (2006, August/September). Turning off depression. *Scientific American Mind,* 26–31.

Dockray, A., & Steptoe, A. (2010). Positive affect and psychobiological process. *Neuroscience and Biobehavioral Reviews, 35,* 69–75.

Domhoff, G. W. (2003). *The scientific study of dreams: Neural networks, cognitive development, and content analysis.* Washington, DC: American Psychological Association.

Domino, M. E., Burns, B. J., Silva, S. G., Kratochvil, C. J., Vitiello, B., Reinecke, M. A., et al. (2008). Cost-effectiveness of treatments for adolescent depression: Results from TADS. *American Journal of Psychiatry, 165,* 588–596.

Domjan, M. (2003). *Principles of learning and behavior* (5th ed.). Belmont, CA: Thomson/Wadsworth.

Donahue, A. B. (2000). Electroconvulsive therapy and memory loss: A personal journey. *Journal of ECT, 16,* 133–143.

Drosopoulos, S., Schulze, C., Fischer, S., & Born, J. (2007). Sleep's function in the spontaneous recovery and consolidation of memories. *Journal of Experimental Psychology: General 136,* 169–183.

Duckworth, A. L., & Seligman, M. E. P. (2005). Self-discipline outdoes IQ in predicting academic performance of adolescents. *Psychological Science, 16,* 939–944.

Dugatkin, L. A. (2004). *Principles of animal behavior.* New York: Norton.

Duncker, K. (1945). On problem solving. *Psychological Monographs, 58*(5, Whole no. 70).

Dutton, D. G., & Aron, A. P. (1974). Some evidence for heightened sexual attraction under conditions of high anxiety. *Journal of Personality and Social Psychology, 30,* 510–517.

Eaker, E. D., Sullivan, L. M., Kelly-Hayes, M., D'Agostino, R. B., Sr., & Benjamin, E. J. (2004). Anger and hostility predict the development of atrial fibrillation in men in the Framingham Offspring Study. *Circulation, 109,* 1267–1271.

Egeland, J. A., Gerhard, D. S., Pauls, D. L., Sussex, J. N., Kidd, K. K., Allen, C. R., et al. (1987). Bipolar affective disorders linked to DNA markers on chromosome 11. *Nature, 325,* 783–787.

Einstein, G. O., & McDaniel, M. A. (2005). Prospective memory. Multiple retrieval processes. *Current Directions in Psychological Science, 14,* 286–290.

Ekelund, J., Lichtermann, D., Jaervelin, M., & Peltonen, L. (1999). Association between novelty seeking and type 4 dopamine receptor gene in a large Finnish cohort sample. *American Journal of Psychiatry, 156,* 1453–1455.

Ekman, P., & Friesen, W. V. (1971). Constants across cultures in the face and emotion. *Journal of Personality and Social Psychology, 17,* 124–129.

Ekman, P., Sorenson, E. R., & Friesen, W. V. (1969). Pancultural elements in facial displays of emotions. *Science, 164,* 86–88.

Engle, R. W., & Kane, M. J. (2004). Executive attention, working memory capacity, and a two-factor theory of cognitive control. In B. Ross (Ed.), *The psychology of learning and motivation* (pp. 145–199). New York: Elsevier.

Engle, R. W., Tuholski, S. W., Laughlin, J. E., & Conway, A. R. A. (1999). Working memory, short-term memory, and general fluid intelligence: A latent variable approach. *Journal of Experimental Psychology: General, 128,* 309–331.

Engwall, M., & Duppils, G. S. (2009). Music as a nursing intervention for postoperative pain: A systematic review. *Journal of Perianesthesia Nursing, 24,* 370–383.

Enns, J. (2005). *The thinking eye, the seeing brain.* New York: Norton.

Epstein, L. H., Robinson, J. L., Roemmich, J. N., Marusewski, A. L., & Roba, L. G. (2010). What constitutes food variety? Stimulus specificity of food. *Appetite, 54,* 23–29.

Era, P., Jokela, J., & Heikkinen, E. (1986). Reaction and movement times in men of different ages: A population study. *Perceptual and Motor Skills, 63,* 111–130.

Erikson, E. H. (1959). *Identity and the life cycle.* New York: International Universities Press.

Erikson, E. H. (1968). *Identity: Youth and crisis.* New York: Norton.

Erikson, E. H. (1980). *Identity and the life cycle.* New York: Norton.

Erk, S., Spitzer, M., Wunderlich, A. P., Galley, L., & Walter, H. (2002). Cultural objects modulate reward circuitry. *Neuroreport, 13,* 2499–2503.

Espelage, D. L., & Holt, M. K. (2012). Understanding and preventing bullying and sexual harassment in school. In K. R. Harris & M. Zeidner (Eds.), *APA educational psychology handbook, Vol. 2: Individual differences and cultural contextual factors* (pp. 391–416). Washington, DC: American Psychologial Association.

Espie, C. A. (2002). Insomnia: Conceptual issues in the development, persistence, and treatment of sleep disorders in adults. *Annual Review of Psychology, 53,* 215–243.

Eysenck, M. W., Mogg, K., May, J., Richards, A., & Matthews, A. (1991). Bias in interpretation of ambiguous sentences related to threat in anxiety. *Journal of Abnormal Psychology, 100,* 144–150.

Fabiano, G. A., Pelham, W. E., Coles, E. K., Gnagy, E. M., Chronis-Tuscano, A., & O'Connor, B. C. (2009). A meta-analysis of behavioral treatments for attention-deficit/hyperactivity disorder. *Clinical Psychology Review, 29,* 129–140.

Fagerström, K. O., & Schneider, N. G. (1989). Measuring nicotine dependence: A review of the Fagerström tolerance questionnaire. *Journal of Behavioral Medicine, 12,* 159–181.

Fallon, A. E., & Rozin, P. (1985). Sex differences in perceptions of desirable body shape. *Journal of Abnormal Psychology, 94,* 102–105.

Fantz, R. L. (1966). Pattern discrimination and selective attention as determinants of perceptual development from birth. In A. H. Kidd & L. J. Rivoire (Eds.), *Perceptual development in children* (pp. 143–173). New York: International Universities Press.

Farooqi, I. S., Bullmore, E., Keogh, J., Gillard, J., O'Rahilly, S., & Fletcher, P. C. (2007). Leptin regulates striatal regions and human eating behavior. *Science, 317*, 1355.

Fawcett, J. (1992). Suicide risk factors in depressive disorders and in panic disorders. *Journal of Clinical Psychiatry, 53*, 9–13.

Fazio, R. H. (1995). Attitudes as object-evaluation associations: Determinants, consequences, and correlates of attitude accessibility. In R. E. Petty & J. A. Krosnick (Eds.), *Attitude strength: Antecedents and consequences* (pp. 247–282). Hillsdale, NJ: Erlbaum.

Fazio, R. H., Eisner, J. R., & Shook, N. J. (2004). Attitude formation through exploration: Valence asymmetries. *Journal of Personality and Social Psychology, 87*, 293–311.

Feingold, A. (1992). Good-looking people are not what we think. *Psychological Bulletin, 111*, 304–341.

Feingold, A. (1994). Gender differences in personality: A meta-analysis. *Psychological Bulletin, 116*, 429–456.

Feldman, S. S., & Rosenthal, D. A. (1991). Age expectations of behavioural autonomy in Hong Kong, Australian and American youth: The influence of family variables and adolescents' values. *International Journal of Psychology, 26*, 1–23.

Feldman Barrett, L., Lane, R. D., Sechrest, L., & Schwartz, G. E. (2000). Sex differences in emotional awareness. *Personality and Social Psychology Bulletin, 26*, 1027–1035.

Fernald, A. (1989). Intonation and communicative intent in mothers' speech to infants: Is the melody the message? *Child Development, 60*, 1497–1510.

Ferrari, P. F., Visalberghi, E., Paukner, A., Fogassi, L., Ruggiero, A., & Suomi, S. (2006). Neonatal imitation in rhesus macaques. *PLoS Biology, 4*, 1501–1508.

Ferry, G. (Writer/Broadcaster). (2002, 12 & 19 November). Hearing colours, eating sounds. *BBC Radio 4, Science.* Retrieved June 3, 2013, from http://www.bbc.co.uk/radio4/science/hearingcolours.shtml

Festinger, L. (1987). A personal memory. In N. E. Grunberg, R. E. Nisbett, J. Rodin, & J. E. Singer (Eds.), *A distinctive approach to psychological research: The influence of Stanley Schachter* (pp. 1–9). New York: Erlbaum.

Festinger, L., & Carlsmith, J. M. (1959). Cognitive consequences of forced compliance. *Journal of Abnormal and Social Psychology, 58*, 203–210.

Fibiger, H. C. (1993). Mesolimbic dopamine: An analysis of its role in motivated behavior. *Seminars in Neuroscience, 5*, 321–327.

Finger, S. (1994). *Origins of neuroscience.* Oxford, UK: Oxford University Press.

Fink, M. (2001). Convulsive therapy: A review of the first 55 years. *Journal of Affective Disorders, 63*, 1–15.

Fischer, C., Hatzidimitriou, G., Wlos, J., Katz, J., & Ricaurte, G. (1995). Reorganization of ascending 5-HT axon projections in animals previously exposed to the recreational drug (+/−)3,4-methylene-dioxymethamphetamine (MDMA, "ecstasy"). *Journal of Neuroscience, 15*, 5476–5485.

Fischer, K. (1980). A theory of cognitive development: The control and construction of hierarchies of skills. *Psychological Review, 87*, 477–531.

Fisher, H. E., Aron, A., & Brown, L. L. (2006). Romantic love: A mammalian brain system for mate choice. *Philosophical Transactions of the Royal Society of London, 361B*, 2173–2186.

Fitzgerald, P. B., Brown, T. L., Marston, N. A., Daskalakis, Z. J., De Castella, A., & Kulkarni, J. (2003). Transcranial magnetic stimulation in the treatment of depression: A double-blind, placebo-controlled trial. *Archives of General Psychiatry, 60*, 1002–1008.

Fixx, J. F. (1978). *Solve it.* New York: Doubleday.

Flegal, K. M., Kit, B. K., Orpana, H., & Graubard, B. I. (2013). Association of all-case mortality with overweight and obesity using standard body mass index categories. *Journal of the American Medical Asssociation, 309*, 71–82.

Flynn, J. R. (2007, October/November). Solving the IQ puzzle. *Scientific American Mind*, 24–31.

Foa, E. B., Liebowitz, M. R., Kozak, M. J., Davies, S., Campeas, R., Franklin, M. E., et al. (2005). Randomized, placebo-controlled trial of exposure and ritual prevention, clomipramine, and their combination in the treatment of obsessive-compulsive disorder. *American Journal of Psychiatry, 162*, 151–161.

Foer, Joshua. (2011, February 20). Secrets of a mind-gamer: How I trained my brain and became a world-class memory athlete. *The New York Times Magazine.* Retrieved June 11, 2013, from http://www.nytimes.com/interactive/2011/02/20/magazine/mind-secrets.html

Foley, K. M. (1993). Opioids. *Neurologic Clinics, 11*, 503–522.

Folkman, S., & Lazarus, R. S. (1988). Coping as a mediator of emotion. *Journal of Personality and Social Psychology, 54*, 466–475.

Folkman, S., & Moskowitz, J. T. (2000). Positive affect and the other side of coping. *American Psychologist, 55*, 647–654.

Forgas, J. P. (1998). Asking nicely: Mood effects on responding to more or less polite requests. *Personality and Social Psychology Bulletin, 24*, 173–185.

Fox, N. A., Henderson, H. A., Marshall, P. J., Nichols, K. E., & Ghera, M. M. (2005). Behavioral inhibition: Linking biology and behavior within a developmental framework. *Annual Review of Psychology, 56*, 235–262.

Franken, R. E. (1998). *Human motivation.* Pacific Grove, CA: Brooks Cole.

Franklin, M. E., & Foa, E. B. (2011). Treatment of obsessive compulsive disorder. *Annual Review of Clinical Psychology, 7*, 229–243.

Fratiglioni, L., Paillard-Borg, S., & Winblad, B. (2004). An active and socially integrated lifestyle in late life might protect against dementia. *Lancet Neurology, 3*, 343–353.

Fredrickson, B. L. (2001). The role of positive emotions in positive psychology: The broaden-and-build theory of positive emotions. *American Psychologist, 56*, 218–226.

Freedman, J. L. (1984). Effects of television violence on aggression. *Psychological Bulletin, 96*, 227–246.

Freedman, J. L., & Fraser, S. C. (1966). Compliance without pressure: The foot-in-the-door technique. *Journal of Personality and Social Psychology, 4*, 196–202.

Freud, A. (1936). *The ego and the mechanisms of defense.* New York: International Universities Press.

Frijda, N. H. (1994). Emotions are functional, most of the time. In P. Ekman & R. J. Davidson (Eds.), *The nature of emotion: Fundamental questions, Vol. 4. Series in affective science* (pp. 112–122). New York: Oxford University Press.

Funder, D. C. (1995). On the accuracy of personality judgment: A realistic approach. *Psychological Review, 102*, 652–670.

Fung, H. H., & Carstensen, L. L. (2004). Motivational changes in response to blocked goals and foreshortened time: Testing alternatives to socioemotional selectivity theory. *Psychology and Aging, 19*, 68–78.

Fung, M. T., Raine, A., Loeber, R., Lynam, D. R., Steinhauer, S. R., Venables, P. D., et al. (2005). Reduced electrodermal activity in psychopathy-prone adolescents. *Journal of Abnormal Psychology, 114*, 187–196.

Galanter, E. (1962). Contemporary psychophysics. In R. Brown (Ed.), *New directions in psychology.* New York: Holt, Rinehart & Winston.

Galef, B. G., Jr., & Whiskin, E. E. (2000). Social influences on the amount eaten by Norway rats. *Appetite, 34*, 327–332.

Gallup. (1995). *Disciplining children in America: A Gallup poll report.* Princeton, NJ: Author.

Gana, K., Bailly, N., Saada, Y., Joulain, M., & Alaphilippe, D. (2013). Does life satisfaction change in old age: Results from an 8-year longitudinal study. *Journals of Gerontology, Series B.*

Garcia, J., & Koelling, R. A. (1966). Relation of cue to consequence in avoidance learning. *Psychonomic Science, 4*, 123–124.

Gardner, H. (1983). *Frames of mind: The theory of multiple intelligences.* New York: Basic Books.

Gardner, W. L., Pickett, C. L., Jefferis, V., & Knowles, M. (2005). On the outside looking in: Loneliness and social monitoring. *Personality and Social Psychology Bulletin, 31*, 1549–1560.

Garon, N., Bryson, S. E., & Smith, I. M. (2008). Executive function in preschoolers: A review using an integrative framework. *Psychological Bulletin, 134*, 31–60.

Gazzaniga, M. S. (2000). Cerebral specialization and interhemispheric communication: Does the corpus callosum enable the human condition? *Brain, 123*, 1293–1326.

Gazzaniga, M. S., & Sperry, R. W. (1967). Language after section of the cerebral commissures. *Brain, 90*, 131–148.

Geddes, J. R., Burgess, S., Hawton, K., Jamison, K., & Goodwin, G. M. (2004). Long-term lithium therapy for bipolar disorder: Systematic review and meta-analysis of randomized controlled trials. *American Journal of Psychiatry, 161*, 217–222.

George, M. S., Lisanby, S. H., & Sackheim, H. A. (1999). Transcranial magnetic stimulation: Applications in neuropsychiatry. *Archives of General Psychiatry, 56*, 300–311.

George, M. S., Wassermann, E. M., Williams, W. A., Callahan, A., Ketter, T. A., Basser, P., et al. (1995). Daily repetitive transcranial magnetic stimulation (rTMS) improves mood in depression. *Neuroreport, 6*, 1853–1856.

Gergely, G., & Csibra, G. (2003). Teleological reasoning in infancy: The naïve theory of rational action. *Trends in Cognitive Sciences, 7*, 287–292.

Gershoff, E. T. (2002). Parental corporal punishment and associated child behaviors and experiences: A meta-analytic and theoretical review. *Psychological Bulletin, 128*, 539–579.

Gibbons, M. B. C., Crits-Christoph, P., & Hearon, B. (2008). The empirical status of psychodynamic therapies. *Annual Review of Clinical Psychology, 4*, 93–108.

Giedd, J. N., Castellanos, F. X., Rajapakse, J. C., Vaituzis, A. C., & Rapoport, J. L. (1997). Sexual dimorphism of the developing human brain. *Progress in Neuro-Psychopharmacology & Biological Psychiatry, 21*, 1185–1201.

Gijsman, H. J., Geddes, J. R., Rendell, J. M., Nolen, W. A., & Goodwin, G. M. (2004). Antidepressants for bipolar depression: A systematic review of randomized, controlled trials. *American Journal of Psychiatry, 161*, 1537–1547.

Gillihan, S. J., & Farah, M. J. (2005). Is self special? A critical review of evidence from experimental psychology and cognitive neuroscience. *Psychological Bulletin, 131*, 76–97.

Gillogley, K. M., Evans, A. T., Hansen, R. L., Samuels, S. J., & Batra, K. K. (1990). The perinatal impact of cocaine, amphetamine, and opiate use detected by universal intrapartum screening. *American Journal of Obstetrics and Gynecology, 163*, 1535–1542.

Gilovich, T. (1991). *How we know what isn't so: The fallibility of human reason in everyday life.* New York: The Free Press.

Gilpin, E. A., Choi, W. S., Berry, C., & Pierce, J. P. (1999). How many adolescents start smoking each day in the United States? *Journal of Adolescent Health, 25*, 248–255.

Gladwell, M. (2005). *Blink: The power of thinking without thinking.* New York: Little, Brown.

Glaser, R. & Kiecolt-Glaser, J. K. (2005). Stress-induced immune dysfunction: Implications for health. *Nature Reviews, 5*, 243–251.

Gonzales, R., Mooney, L., & Rawson, R. A. (2010). The methamphetamine problem in the United States. *Annual Review of Public Health, 31*, 385–398.

Goodall, G. (1984). Learning due to the response-shock contingency in signaled punishment. *Quarterly Journal of Experimental Psychology, 36*, 259–279.

Goodman, R., & Stevenson, J. (1989). A twin study of hyperactivity-II. The aetiological role of genes, family relationships, and perinatal adversity. *Journal of Child Psychology and Psychiatry, 30*, 691–709.

Goodwin, F. K., & Jamison, K. R. (1990). *Manic-depressive illness.* New York: Oxford University Press.

Gosling, S. D. (1998). Personality dimensions in spotted hyenas (*Crocuta crocuta*). *Journal of Comparative Psychology, 112*, 107–118.

Gosling, S. D. (2008). *Snoop: What your stuff says about you.* New York: Basic Books.

Gottesman, I. I. (1991). *Schizophrenia genesis: The origins of madness.* New York: Freeman.

Gottfredson, L. S. (2004a). Intelligence: Is it the epidemiologists' elusive "fundamental cause" of social class inequalities in health? *Journal of Personality and Social Psychology, 86*, 174–199.

Gottfredson, L. S. (2004b, Summer). Schools and the g factor. *Wilson Quarterly, 28*(3), 35–45.

Gottman, J. (1994). *Why marriages succeed or fail . . . and how you can make yours last.* New York: Simon & Schuster.

Graf, P., & Uttl, B. (2001). Prospective memory: A new focus for research. *Consciousness and Cognition, 10,* 437–450.

Granot, D., & Mayseless, O. (2001). Attachment security and adjustment to school in middle childhood. *International Journal of Behavioral Development, 25,* 530–541.

Gray, J. R., & Thompson, P. M. (2004). Neurobiology of intelligence: Science and ethics. *Nature Reviews Neuroscience, 5,* 471–482.

Green, D. M., & Swets, J. A. (1966). *Signal detection theory and psychophysics.* New York: Wiley.

Greenwald, A. G. (1968). Cognitive learning, cognitive response to persuasion, and attitude change. In A. G. Greenwald, T. C. Brock, & T. M. Ostrom (Eds.), *Psychological foundations of attitudes* (pp. 147–170). New York: Academic Press.

Greenwald, A. G. (1992). New look 3: Reclaiming unconscious cognition. *American Psychologist, 47,* 766–779.

Greenwald, A. G., & Banaji, M. R. (1995). Implicit social cognition: Attitudes, self-esteem, and stereotypes. *Psychological Review, 102,* 4–27.

Greenwald, A. G., McGhee, D., & Schwartz, J. (1998). Measuring individual differences in implicit cognition: The implicit association test. *Journal of Personality and Social Psychology, 74,* 1464–1480.

Greitemeyer, T. (2009). Effects of songs with prosocial lyrics on prosocial behavior: Further evidence and a mediating mechanism. *Personality and Social Psychology Bulletin, 35,* 1500–1511.

Gross, J. J. (1999). Emotion and emotion regulation. In L. A. Pervin & O. P. John (Eds.), *Handbook of personality: Theory and research* (2nd ed., pp. 525–552). New York: Guilford Press.

Grossman, L. (2005, January 24). Grow up? Not so fast. *Time, 165,* 42–53.

Grossman, M., & Wood, W. (1993). Sex differences in intensity of emotional experience: A social role interpretation. *Journal of Personality and Social Psychology, 65,* 1010–1022.

Gruber, S. A., Silveri, M. M., & Yurgelun-Todd, D. A. (2007). Neuropsychological consequences of opiate use. *Neuropsychological Review, 17,* 299–315.

Gruenewald, P. J., Millar, A. B., Treno, A. J., Yang, Z., Ponicki, W. R., & Roeper, P. (1996). The geography of availability and driving after drinking. *Addiction, 91,* 967–983.

Gruzelier, J. H. (2000). Redefining hypnosis: Theory, methods, and integration. *Contemporary Hypnosis, 17,* 51–70.

Guenther, F. H., Brumberg, J. S., Wright, E. J., Nieto-Castanon, A., Tourville, J. A., et al. (2009). A wireless brain-machine interface for real-time speech synthesis. *PLoS ONE, 4,* e82128.

Guerin, B. (1994). What do people think about the risks of driving? Implications for traffic safety interventions. *Journal of Applied Social Psychology, 24,* 994–1021.

Guerri, C. (2002). Mechanisms involved in central nervous system dysfunctions induced by prenatal ethanol exposure. *Neurotoxicity Research, 4*(4), 327–335.

Gur, R. C., & Gur, R. E. (2004). Gender differences in the functional organization of the brain. In M. J. Legato (Ed.), *Principles of gender specific medicine* (pp. 63–70). Amsterdam: Elsevier.

Halpern, C. T., Udry, J. R., & Suchindran, C. (1997). Testosterone predicts initiation of coitus in adolescent females. *Psychosomatic Medicine, 59,* 161–171.

Hamann, S. B., Ely, T. D., Grafton, D. T., & Kilts, C. D. (1999). Amygdala activity related to enhanced memory for pleasant and aversive stimuli. *Nature Neuroscience, 2,* 289–293.

Hamann, S., Herman, R. A., Nolan, C. L., & Wallen, K. (2004). Men and women differ in amygdala response to visual sexual stimuli. *Nature Neuroscience, 7,* 411–416.

Hambrecht, M., Maurer, K., Hafner, H., & Sartorius, N. (1992). Transnational stability of gender differences in schizophrenia: Recent findings on social skills training and family psychoeducation. *Clinical Psychology Review, 11,* 23–44.

Hamilton, N. A., Gallagher, M. W., Preacher, K. J., Stevens, N., Nelson, C. A., Karlson, C., et al. (2007). Insomnia and well-being. *Journal of Consulting and Clinical Psychology, 75,* 939–946.

Hammen, C. (2005). Stress and depression. *Annual Review of Clinical Psychology, 1,* 293–319.

Handleman, J. S., Gill, M. J., & Alessandri, M. (1988). Generalization by severely developmentally disabled children: Issues, advances, and future directions. *Behavior Therapist, 11,* 221–223.

Hanewinkel, R., & Sargent, J. D. (2008). Exposure to smoking in internationally distributed American movies and youth smoking in Germany: A cross-cultural cohort study. *Pediatrics, 121,* 108–117.

Haney, C., Banks, C., & Zimbardo, P. (1973). Interpersonal dynamics in a simulated prison. *International Journal of Criminology and Penology, 1,* 69–97.

Hansen, C. J., Stevens, L. C., & Coast, J. R. (2001). Exercise duration and mood state: How much is enough to feel better? *Health Psychology, 20,* 267–275.

Hansen, W. B., Graham, J. W., Sobel, J. L., Shelton, D. R., Flay, B. R., & Johnson, C. A. (1987). The consistency of peer and parental influences on tobacco, alcohol, and marijuana use among young adolescents. *Journal of Behavioral Medicine, 10,* 559–579.

Harburger, L. L., Nzerem, C. K., & Frick, K. M. (2007). Single enrichment variables differentially reduce age-related memory decline in female mice. *Behavioral Neuroscience, 121,* 679–688.

Harding, C. M., Zubin, J., & Strauss, J. S. (1987). Chronicity in schizophrenia: Fact, partial fact, or artifact? *Hospital and Community Psychiatry, 38,* 477–486.

Hare, R. D., McPherson, L. M., & Forth, A. E. (1988). Male psychopaths and their criminal careers. *Journal of Consulting and Clinical Psychology, 56,* 710–714.

Harlow, H. F., & Harlow, M. K (1966). Learning to love. *American Scientist, 54,* 244–272.

Harlow, H. F., Harlow, M. K., & Meyer, D. R. (1950). Learning motivated by a manipulation drive. *Journal of Experimental Psychology, 40,* 228–234.

Harpur, T. J., & Hare, R. D. (1994). Assessment of psychopathy as a function of age. *Journal of Abnormal Psychology, 103,* 604–609.

Hartford, J., Kornstein, S., Liebowitz, M., Pigott, T., Russell, J., Detke, M., et al. (2007). Duloxetine as an SNRI treatment for generalized anxiety disorder: Results from a placebo and active-controlled trial. *International Clinical Psychopharmacology, 22,* 167–174.

Hawkley, L., & Cacioppo, J. T. (2010). Loneliness matters: A theoretical and empirical review of consequences and mechanisms. *Annals of Behavioral Medicine, 40,* 218–227.

Heatherton, T. F. (2011). Neuroscience of self and self-regulation. *Annual Review of Psychology, 62,* 363–390.

Heatherton, T. F., & Baumeister, R. F. (1991). Binge eating as escape from self-awareness. *Psychological Bulletin, 110,* 86–108.

Heine, S. J., & Lehman, D. R. (2004). Move the body, change the self: Acculturative effects on the self-concept. In M. Schaller & C. Crandall (Eds.), *Psychologial Foundations of Culture* (pp. 305–331).Mahwah, NJ: Erlbaum.

Heller, D., Watson, D., & Ilies, R. (2004). The role of person versus situation in life satisfaction: A critical examination. *Psychological Bulletin, 130,* 574–600.

Helmreich, R., Aronson, E., & LeFan, J. (1970). To err is humanizing sometimes: Effects of self-esteem, competence, and a pratfall on interpersonal attraction. *Journal of Personality and Social Psychology, 16,* 259–264.

Henrich, J., Heine, S. J., & Norenzayan, A. (2010). The weirdest people in the world? *Behavioral and Brain Sciences, 33,* 61–83, 111–135.

Herbert, T. B., & Cohen, S. (1993). Stress and immunity in humans: A meta-analytic review. *Psychosomatic Medicine, 55,* 364–379.

Herdener, M., Esposito, F., di Salle, F., Boller, C., Hilti, C. C., et al. (2010). Musical training induces functional plasticity in human hippocampus. *Journal of Neuroscience, 30,* 1377–1384.

Higgins, S. C., Gueorguiev, M., & Korbonits, M. (2007). Ghrelin, the peripheral hunger hormone. *Annals of Medicine, 39,* 116–136.

Hilgard, E. R., & Hilgard, J. R. (1975). *Hypnosis in the relief of pain.* Los Altos, CA: Kaufmann.

Hines, T. (2003). *Pseudoscience and the paranormal.* Amherst, NY: Prometheus.

Hirst, W., Phelps, E. A., Buckner, R. L., Budson, A. E., Cuc, A., Gabrieli, J. D. E., et al. (2009). Long-term memory for the terrorist attack of September 11: Flashbulb memories, event memories, and the factors that influence their retention. *Journal of Experimental Psychology: General, 138,* 161–176.

Hobson, J. A. (1999). Sleep and dreaming. In M. J. Zigmond, F. E. Bloom, S. C. Landis, J. L. Roberts, & L. R. Squire (Eds.), *Fundamental neuroscience* (pp. 1207–1227). San Diego: Academic Press.

Hobson, J. A. (2009). REM sleep and dreaming: Towards a theory of protoconsciousness. *Nature Reviews Neuroscience, 10,* 803–814.

Hobson, J. A., & McCarley, R. (1977.) The brain as a dream state generator: An activation-synthesis hypothesis of the dream process. *American Journal of Psychiatry, 134,* 1335–1348.

Hockley, W. E. (2008). The effect of environmental context on recognition memory and claims of remembering. *Journal of Experimental Psychology: Learning, Memory, and Cognition, 34,* 1412–1429.

Hofmann, S. G., & Smits, J. A. J. (2008). Cognitive-behavioral therapy for adult anxiety disorders: A meta-analysis of randomized placebo-controlled trials. *Journal of Clinical Psychiatry, 69,* 621–632.

Hogan, M. J., Parker, J. D., Wiener, J., Watters, C., Wood, L. M., & Oke, A. (2010). Academic success in adolescence: Relationships among verbal IQ, social support and emotional intelligence. *Australian Journal of Psychology, 62,* 30–41.

Holden, C. (2005). Sex and the suffering brain. *Science, 308,* 1574.

Hollon, S. D., Stewart, M. O., & Strunk, D. (2006). Enduring effects for cognitive behavior therapy in the treatment of depression and anxiety. *Annual Review of Psychology, 57,* 285–315.

Hollon, S. D., Thase, M. E., & Markowitz, J. C. (2002). Treatment and prevention of depression. *Psychological Science in the Public Interest, 3,* 39–77.

Holmbeck, G. N. (1996). A model of family relational transformations during the transition to adolescence: Parent-adolescent conflict and adaptation. In J. A. Graber, J. Brooks-Gunn, & A. C. Petersen (Eds.), *Transitions through Adolescence* (pp. 67–200). Mahwah, NJ: Erlbaum.

Holmes, T. H., & Rahe, R. H. (1967). The social readjustment rating scale. *Journal of Psychosomatic Research, 11,* 213–218.

Holstein, S. B., & Premack, D. (1965). On the different effects of random reinforcement and presolution reversal on human concept-identification. *Journal of Experimental Psychology, 70,* 335–337.

Horn, J. L. (1968). Organization of abilities and the development of intelligence. *Psychological Review, 75,* 242–259.

Horn, J. L., & Hofer, S. M. (1992). Major abilities and development in the adult period. In R. J. Sternberg & C. A. Berg (Eds.), *Intellectual development* (pp. 44–99). New York: Cambridge University Press.

Hoshino, Y., Kumashiro, H., Yashima, Y., Tachibana, R., Watanabe, M., & Furukawa, H. (1980). Early symptoms of autism in children and their diagnostic significance. *Japanese Journal of Child and Adolescent Psychiatry, 21,* 284–299.

Hovland, C. I., Janis, I. L., & Kelley, H. H. (1953). *Communication and persuasion: Psychological studies of opinion change.* New Haven, CT: Yale University Press.

Howard, D. J., Gengler, C., & Jain, A. (1995). What's in a name? A complimentary means of persuasion. *Journal of Consumer Research, 22,* 200–211.

Howard , D. J., Gengler, C., & Jain, A. (1997). The name remembrance effect: A test of alternative explanations. *Journal of Social Behaviour and Personality, 12,* 801–810.

Howlin, P., Mawhood, L., & Rutter, M. (2000). Autism and developmental receptive language disorder—A follow-up comparison in early adult life. II: Social, behavioural, and psychiatric outcomes. *Journal of Child Psychology and Psychiatry and Allied Disciplines, 41,* 561–578.

Hull, C. L. (1943). *Principles of behavior: An introduction to behavior theory.* New York: D. Appleton-Century.

Hulse, G. K., Milne, E., English, D. R., & Holman, C. D. J. (1998). Assessing the relationship between maternal opiate use and ante-partum haemorrhage. *Addiction, 93,* 1553–1558.

Hyde, J. S. (2005). The gender similarities hypothesis. *American Psychologist, 60,* 581–592.

Hyman, S. E. (2008). A glimmer of light for neuropsychiatric disorders. *Nature, 455,* 890–893.

Hymel, S., Rocke-Henderson, N., & Bonanno, R. A. (2005). Moral disengagement: A framework for understanding bullying among adolescents. *Journal of Social Sciences, 8,* 1–11.

Iacoboni, M. (2009). Imitation, empathy, and mirror neurons. *Annual Review of Psychology, 60,* 653–670.

Insel, T. R., & Charney, D. S. (2003). Research on major depression. *Journal of the American Medical Association, 289,* 3167–3168.

Isen, A. M. (1993). Positive affect and decision making. In M. Lewis & J. M. Haviland (Eds.), *Handbook of emotions* (pp. 261–277). New York: Guilford Press.

Iyengar, S. S., & Lepper, M. R. (2000). When choice is demotivating: Can one desire too much of a good thing? *Journal of Personality and Social Psychology, 79,* 995–1006.

Jablensky, A. (1989). Epidemiology and cross-cultural aspects of schizophrenia. *Psychiatric Annals, 19,* 516–524.

Jackson, B., Kubzansky, L. D., Cohen, S., Jacobs, D. R., Jr., & Wright, R. J. (2007). Does harboring hostility hurt? Associations between hostility and pulmonary function in the coronary artery risk development in (young) adults (CARDIA) study. *Health Psychology, 26,* 333–340.

Jackson, S. A., Thomas, P. R., Marsh, H. W., & Smethurst, C. J. (2001). Relationships between flow, self-concept, psychological skills, and performance. *Journal of Applied Sport Psychology, 13,* 129–153.

James, W. (1884). What is an emotion? *Mind, 9,* 188–205.

James, W. (1890). *The principles of psychology.* New York: Henry Holt.

Jamieson, G. A. (2007). *Hypnosis and conscious states: The cognitive neuroscience perspective.* New York: Oxford University Press.

Janata, P. (2009). The neural architecture of music-evoked autobiographical memories. *Cerebral Cortex, 19,* 2579–2594.

Jang, K. L., Livesley, W. J., & Vemon, P. A. (1996). Heritability of the big five personality dimensions and their facets: A twin study. *Journal of Personality, 64,* 577–592.

Jensen, A. R. (1998). *The g factor: The science of mental ability.* Westport, CT: Praeger.

Jiang, Y., Sheikh, K., & Bullock, C. (2006). Is there a sex or race difference in stroke mortality? *Journal of Stroke and Cerebrovascular Disease 15,* 179–186.

John, O. P. (1990). The "Big Five" factor taxonomy: Dimensions of personality in the natural language and in questionnaires. In L. A. Pervin & O. P. John (Eds.), *Handbook of personality: Theory and research* (pp. 66–100). New York: Guilford Press.

Johns, F., Schmader, T., & Martens, A. (2005). Knowing is half the battle—Teaching stereotype threat as a means of improving women's math performance. *Psychological Science, 16,* 175–179.

Johnston, L. D., O'Malley, P. M., Bachman, J. G., & Schulenberg, J. E. (2011). *Monitoring the future national results on adolescent drug use: Overview of key findings, 2010.* Ann Arbor: Institute for Social Research, University of Michigan.

Joiner, T. E. (2005). *Why people die by suicide.* Cambridge, MA: Harvard University Press.

Jones, M. C. (1924). A laboratory study of fear: The case of Peter. *Pedagogical Seminary, 31,* 308–315.

Jope, R. S. (1999). Anti-bipolar therapy: Mechanism of action of lithium. *Molecular Psychiatry, 4,* 117–128.

Jorm, A. F. (2000). Does old age reduce the risk of anxiety and depression? A review of epidemiological studies across the adult life span. *Psychological Medicine, 30,* 3011–3022.

Jureidini, J. N., Doecke, C. J., Mansfield, P. R., Haby, M., Menkes, D. B., & Tonkin, A. L. (2004). Efficacy and safety of antidepressants for children and adolescents. *British Medical Journal, 328,* 879–883.

Kagan, J. (2011). Three lessons learned. *Perspectives in Psychological Science, 6,* 107–113.

Kagan, J., & Snidman, N. (1991). Infant predictors of inhibited and uninhibited profiles. *Psychological Science, 2,* 40–44.

Kalechstein, A. D., De La Garza II, R., Mahoney III, J. J., Fantegrossi, W. E., & Newton, T. F. (2007). MDMA use and neurocognition: A meta-analytic review. *Psychopharmacology, 189,* 531–537.

Kallio, S., & Revonsuo, A. (2003). Hypnotic phenomena and altered states of consciousness: A multi-level framework of description and explanation. *Contemporary Hypnosis, 20,* 111–164.

Kandall, S. R., & Gaines, J. (1991). Maternal substance use and subsequent sudden infant death syndrome (SIDS) in offspring. *Neurotoxicology and Teratology, 13,* 235–240.

Kandel, E. R. (1998). A new intellectual framework for psychiatry. *American Journal of Psychiatry, 155,* 457–469.

Kane, M. J., Hambrick, D. Z., & Conway, A. R. (2005). Working memory capacity and fluid intelligence are strongly related constructs: Comment on Ackerman, Beier, and Boyle (2005). *Psychological Bulletin, 131,* 66–71.

Kaplan, R. M. (2007). Should Medicare reimburse providers for weight loss interventions? *American Psychologist, 62,* 217–219.

Kapur, S. E., Craik, F. I. M., Tulving, E., Wilson, A. A., Houle, S., & Brown, G. R. (1994). Neuroanatomical correlates of encoding in episodic memory: Levels of processing effects. *Proceedings of the National Academy of Sciences, USA, 91,* 2008–2011.

Kawas, C., Gray, S., Brookmeyer, R., Fozard, J., & Zonderman, A. (2000). Age-specific incidence rates of Alzheimer's disease: The Baltimore longitudinal study of aging, *Neurology, 54,* 2072–2077.

Kay, K. N., Naselaris, T., Prenger, R. J., & Gallant, J. L. (2008). Identifying natural images from human brain activity. *Nature, 452,* 352–355.

Kazdin, A. E. (1994). Methodology, design, and evaluation in psychotherapy research. In A. E. Bergin & S. L. Garfield (Eds.), *International handbook of behavior modification and behavior change* (4th ed., pp. 19–71). New York: Wiley.

Kazdin, A. E. (2008). Evidence-based treatment and practice: New opportunities to bridge clinical research and practice, enhance the knowledge base, and improve patient care. *American Psychologist, 63,* 146–159.

Kazdin, A. E., & Benjet, C. (2003). Spanking children: Evidence and issues. *Current Directions in Psychological Science, 12*, 99–103.

Keane, M. (1987). On retrieving analogues when solving problems. *Quarterly Journal of Experimental Psychology, 39A*, 29–41.

Keel, P. K., & Mitchell, J. E. (1997). Outcome in bulimia nervosa. *American Journal of Psychiatry, 154*, 313–321.

Keller, J., & Bless, H. (2008). Flow and regulatory compatibility: An experimental approach to the flow model of intrinsic motivation. *Personality and Social Psychology Bulletin, 34*, 196–209.

Keller, M. B., & Baker, L. A. (1991). Bipolar disorder: Epidemiology, course, diagnosis, and treatment. *Bulletin of the Menninger Clinic, 55*, 172–181.

Kelley, W. T., Macrae, C. N., Wyland, C., Caglar, S., Inati, S., & Heatherton, T. F. (2002). Finding the self? An event-related fMRI study. *Journal of Cognitive Neuroscience, 14*, 785–794.

Keltner, D., & Bonanno, G. A. (1997). A study of laughter and dissociation: Distinct correlates of laughter and smiling during bereavement. *Journal of Personality and Social Psychology, 73*, 687–702.

Keltner, D., Young, R. C., Heerey, E. A., Oemig, C., & Monarch, N. D. (1998). Teasing in hierarchical and intimate relations. *Journal of Personality and Social Psychology, 75*, 1231–1247.

Kendler, K. S., Prescott, C. A., Myers, J., & Neale, M. C. (2003). The structure of genetic and environmental risk factors for common psychiatric and substance use disorders in men and women. *Archives of General Psychiatry, 60*, 929–937.

Kennedy, S. H., Giacobbe, P., Rizvi, S., Placenza, F. M., Nishikawa, Y., Mayberg, H. S., et al. (2011). Deep brain stimulation for treatment-resistant depression: Follow-up after 3 to 6 years. *American Journal of Psychiatry, 168*, 502–510.

Kenrick, D. T., & Funder, D. C. (1991). The person-situation debate: Do personality traits really exist? In V. J. Derlega, B. A. Winstead, & W. H. Jones (Eds.), *Personality: Contemporary theory and research* (pp. 149–174). Chicago: Nelson Hall.

Kessler, R. C., Adler, L., Barkley, R., Biederman, J., Conners, C. K., Demler, O., et al. (2006). The prevalence and correlates of adult ADHD in the United States: Results from the national comorbidity survey replication. *American Journal of Psychiatry, 163*, 716–723.

Kessler, R. C., Berglund, P., Demler, O., Jin, R., Koretz, D., Merikangas, K., et al. (2003). The epidemiology of major depressive disorder: Results from the national comorbidity survey replication (NCS-R). *Journal of the American Medical Association, 289*, 3095–3105.

Kessler, R. C., Chiu, W. T., Demler, O., & Walters, E. E. (2005). Prevalence, severity, and comorbidity of twelve-month *DSM-IV* disorders in the national comorbidity survey replication (NCS-R). *Archives of General Psychiatry, 62*, 617–627.

Kessler, R. C., Demler, O., Frank, R. G., Olfson, M., Pincus, M. A., Walters, E. E., et al. (2005). Prevalence and treatment of mental disorders, 1990 to 2003. *New England Journal of Medicine, 352*, 2515–2523.

Kessler, R. C., McGonagle, K. A., Zhao, S., Nelson, C. B., Hugh, M., Eshleman, S., et al. (1994). Lifetime and 12-month prevalence of *DSM-III-R* psychiatric disorders in the United States: Results from the national comorbidity study. *Archives of General Psychiatry, 51*, 8–19.

Kessler, R. C., Merikangas, K. R., & Wang, P. S. (2007). Prevalence, comorbidity, and service utilization for mood disorders in the United States at the beginning of the twenty-first century. In S. NolenHoeksema, T. Cannon, & T. Widiger (Eds.), *Annual review of clinical psychology: Vol. 3* (pp. 137–158). Palo Alto, CA: Annual Reviews.

Kessler, R. C., Sonnega, A., Bromet, E., Hughes, M., & Nelson, C. B. (1995). Posttraumatic stress disorder in the national comorbidity survey. *Archives of General Psychiatry, 52*, 1048–1060.

Kessler, R. C., & Wang, P. S. (2008). The descriptive epidemiology of commonly occurring mental disorders in the United States. *Annual Review of Public Health, 29*, 115–129.

Keys, A., Brozek, J., Henschel, A. L., Mickelsen, O., & Taylor, H. L. (1950). *The biology of human starvation.* Minneapolis: University of Minnesota Press.

Khan, M. M. (2005). Suicide prevention and developing countries. *Journal of the Royal Society of Medicine, 98*, 459–463.

Kiecolt-Glaser, J. K., & Glaser, R. I. (1988). Immunological competence. In E. A. Blechman & K. D. Brownell (Eds.), *Handbook of behavioral medicine for women* (pp. 195–205). Elmsford, NY: Pergamon Press.

Kihlstrom, J. F. (1985). Hypnosis. *Annual Review of Psychology, 36*, 385–418.

Kihlstrom, J. F. (2005). Dissociative disorder. *Annual Review of Clinical Psychology, 1*, 227–253.

Kihlstrom, J. F., & Eich, E. (1994). Altering states of consciousness. In D. Druckman & R. A. Bjork (Eds.), *Learning, remembering, and believing: Enhancing performance* (pp. 207–248). Washington, DC: National Academy Press.

Kim, S. J., Lyoo, I. K., Hwang, J., Chung, A., Hoon Sung, Y., Kim, J., et al. (2006). Prefrontal grey-matter changes in short-term and long-term abstinent methamphetamine abusers. *International Journal of Neuropsychopharmacology, 9*, 221–228.

Kirsch, I. (2011). The placebo effect has come of age. *Journal of Mind-Body Regulation, 1*, 106–109.

Kirsch, I., Deacon, B. J., Huedo-Medina, T. B., Scoboria, A., Moore, T. J., & Johnson, B. T. (2008). Initial severity and antidepressant benefits: A metaanalysis of data submitted to the Food and Drug Administration. *PLoS Medicine, 5*, e45.

Kirsch, I., & Lynn, S. J. (1995). The altered state of hypnosis: Changes in the theoretical landscape. *American Psychologist, 10*, 846–858.

Klatsky, A. (2009). Alcohol and cardiovascular health. *Physiology and Behavior, 100*, 76–81.

Klin, A., Jones, W., Schultz, R., & Volkmar, F. (2003). The enactive mind, or from actions to cognition: Lessons from autism. *Philosophical Transactions of the Royal Society of London, 358B*, 345–360.

Klump, K. L., & Culbert, K. M. (2007). Molecular genetic studies of eating disorders: Current status and future directions. *Current Directions in Psychological Science, 16*, 37–41.

Knight, R. (1953). Borderline states. *Bulletin of the Menninger Clinic, 17*, 1–12.

Knox, S. S., Weidner, G., Adelman, A., Stoney, C. M., & Ellison, R. C. (2004). Hostility and physiological risk in the national heart, lung, and blood institute family heart study. *Archives of Internal Medicine, 164,* 2442–2447.

Kobasa, S. C. (1979). Personality and resistance to illness. *American Journal of Community Psychology, 7,* 413–423.

Koelsch, S., Offermanns, K., & Franzke, P. (2010). Music in the treatment of affective disorders: A new method for music-therapeutic research. *Music Perception, 27,* 307–316.

Kohlberg, L. (1984). *Essays on moral development: Vol. 2. The psychology of moral development.* San Francisco: Harper & Row.

Köhler, W. (1925). *The mentality of apes.* New York: Harcourt Brace.

Koole, S. L., Dijksterhuis, A., & van Knippenberg, A. (2001). What's in a name: Implicit self-esteem and the automatic self. *Journal of Personality and Social Psychology, 80,* 669–685.

Korn, M. L., Kotler, M., Molcho, A., Botsis, A. J., Grosz, D., Chen, C., et al. (1992). Suicide and violence associated with panic attacks. *Biological Psychiatry, 31,* 607–612.

Kosslyn, S. M., Thompson, W. L., Constantine-Ferrando, M. F., Alpert, N. M., & Spiegel, D. (2000). Hypnotic visual illusion alters color processing in the brain. *American Journal of Psychiatry, 157,* 1279–1284.

Kosslyn, S. M., Thompson, W. L., Kim, I. J., & Alpert, N. M. (1995). Topographical representations of mental images in primary visual cortex. *Nature, 378,* 496–493.

Kowalski, P., & Taylor, A. K. (2004). Ability and critical thinking as predictors of change in students' psychological misconceptions. *Journal of Instructional Psychology, 31,* 297–303.

Krantz, D. S., & McCeney, M. K. (2002). Effects of psychological and social factors on organic disease: A critical assessment of research on coronary heart disease. *Annual Review of Psychology, 53,* 341–369.

Krendl, A. C., Richeson, J. A., Kelley, W. M., & Heatherton, T. F. (2008). The negative consequences of threat: An fMRI investigation of the neural mechanisms underlying women's underperformance in math. *Psychological Science, 19,* 168–175.

Kringelbach, M. L., & Berridge, K. C. (2009). Toward a functional neuroanatomy of pleasure and happiness. *Trends in Cognitive Sciences, 13,* 479–487.

Krueger, R. F. (1999). The structure of common mental disorders. *Archives of General Psychiatry, 56,* 921–926.

Kruesi, M. J., Hibbs, E. D., Zahn, T. P., Keysor, C. S., Hamburger, S. D., Bartko, J. J., et al. (1992). A 2-year prospective follow-up study of children and adolescents with disruptive behavior disorders. Prediction by cerebrospinal fluid 5-hydroxyindoleacetic acid, homovanillic acid, and autonomic measures. *Archives of General Psychiatry, 49,* 429–435.

Krulwich, R. (2007). Sweet, sour, salty, bitter . . . and umami. *NPR: Krulwich on Science.* Retrieved June 3, 2013, from http://www.npr.org/templates/story/story.php?storyId=15819485

Kuhl, P. K. (2006). Is speech learning "gated" by the social brain? *Developmental Science, 10,* 110–120.

Kuhl, P. K., Stevens, E., Hayashi, A., Deguchi, T., Kiritani, S., & Iverson, P. (2006). Infants show a facilitation effect for native language phonetic perception between 6 and 12 months. *Developmental Science, 9,* F13–F21.

Kuhl, P. K., Tsao, F. M., & Liu, H. M. (2003). Foreign-language experience in infancy: Effects of short-term exposure and social interaction on phonetic learning. *Proceedings of the National Academy of Sciences, USA, 100,* 9096–9101.

Kuhn, C., Swartzwelder, S., & Wilson, W. (2003). *Buzzed: The straight facts about the most used and abused drugs from alcohol to ecstasy* (2nd ed.). New York: Norton.

Kuncel, N. R., Hezlett, S. A., & Ones, D. S. (2004). Academic performance, career potential, creativity, and job performance: Can one construct predict them all? *Journal of Personality and Social Psychology, 86,* 148–161.

LaFrance, M. L., & Banaji, M. (1992). Toward a reconsideration of the gender-emotion relationship. In M. Clarke (Ed.), *Review of personality and social psychology* (pp. 178–201). Beverly Hills, CA: Sage.

Laird, J. D. (1974). Self-attribution of emotion: The effects of expressive behavior on the quality of emotional experience. *Journal of Perspectives in Social Psychology, 29,* 475–486.

Landa, R., Holman, K., & Garrett-Mayer, E. (2007). Social and communication development in toddlers with early and later diagnosis of autism spectrum disorders. *Archives of General Psychiatry, 64,* 853–864.

Langlois, J. H., Kalakanis, L., Rubenstein, A. J., Larson, A., Hallam, M., & Smoot, M. (2000). Maxims or myths of beauty? A meta-analytic and theoretical review. *Psychological Bulletin, 126,* 390–423.

Langlois, J. H., Ritter, J. M., Casey, R. J., & Sawin, D. B. (1995). Infant attractiveness predicts maternal behaviors and attitudes. *Developmental Psychology, 31,* 464–472.

Langlois, J. H., & Roggman, L. A. (1990). Attractive faces are only average. *Psychological Science, 1,* 115–121.

Larson, E. B., Wang, L., Bowen, J. D., McCormick, W. C., Teri, L., Crane, P., et al. (2006). Exercise is associated with reduced risk for incident dementia among persons 65 years of age and older. *Annals of Internal Medicine, 144,* 73–81.

Latané, B., & Darley, J. M. (1968). Group inhibition of bystander intervention in emergencies. *Journal of Personality and Social Psychology, 10,* 215–221.

Latané, B., Williams, K., & Harkins, S. G. (1979). Many hands make light the work: The causes and consequences of social loafing. *Journal of Personality and Social Psychology, 37,* 822–832.

Lautenschlager, N. T., Cox, K. L., Flicker, L., Foster, J. K., van Bockxmeer, F. M., Xiao, J., et al. (2008). Effect of physical exercise on cognitive function in older adults at risk for Alzheimer disease. *Journal of the American Medical Association, 300,* 1027–1037.

Lazarus, R. S. (1993). From psychological stress to the emotions: A history of changing outlooks. *Annual Review of Psychology, 44,* 1–21.

Leary, M. R. (2004). The function of self-esteem in terror management theory and sociometer theory: Comment on Pyszczynski et al. *Psychological Bulletin, 130,* 478–482.

Leary, M. R., & MacDonald, G. (2003). Individual differences in self-esteem: A review and theoretical integration. In M. R. Leary & J. P. Tangney (Eds.), *Handbook of self and identity* (pp. 401–418). New York: Guilford Press.

Leary, M. R., Tambor, E. S., Terdal, S. K., & Downs, D. L. (1995). Self-esteem as an interpersonal monitor: The sociometer hypothesis. *Journal of Personality and Social Psychology, 68,* 518–530.

Leckman, J. F., Elliott, G. R., Bromet, E. J., Campbell, M., Cicchetti, D., Cohen, D. J., et al. (1995). Report card on the national plan for research on child and adolescent mental disorders: The midway point. *Archives of General Psychiatry, 34,* 715–723.

LeDoux, J. E. (1996). *The emotional brain: The mysterious underpinnings of emotional life.* New York: Simon & Schuster.

LeDoux, J. E. (2000). Emotion circuits in the brain. *Annual Review of Neuroscience, 23,* 155–184.

LeDoux, J. E. (2002). *Synaptic self.* New York: Viking.

LeDoux, J. E. (2007). The amygdala. *Current Biology, 17,* R868–R874.

Lee, P. A. (1980). Normal ages of pubertal events among American males and females. *Journal of Adolescent Health Care, 1,* 26–29.

Leff, J., Sartorius, N., Jablensky, A., Korten, A., & Ernberg, G. (1992). The international pilot study of schizophrenia: Five-year follow-up findings. *Psychological Medicine, 22,* 131–145.

Lehrner, J. P. (1993). Gender differences in long-term odor recognition memory: Verbal versus sensory influences and the consistency of label use. *Chemical Senses, 18,* 17–26.

Leigh, B. C., & Schafer, J. C. (1993). Heavy drinking occasions and the occurrence of sexual activity. *Psychology of Addictive Behaviors, 7,* 197–200.

Leigh, B. C., & Stacy, A. W. (2004). Alcohol expectancies and drinking in different age groups. *Addiction, 99,* 215–217.

Lenzenweger, M. F., Lane, M. C., Loranger, A. W., & Kessler, R. C. (2007). *DSM-IV* personality disorders in the national comorbidity survey replication. *Biological Psychiatry, 62,* 553–564.

Lepper, M. R., Greene, D., & Nisbett, R. E. (1973). Undermining children's intrinsic interest with extrinsic reward: A test of the "overjustification" hypothesis. *Journal of Personality and Social Psychology, 28,* 129–137.

Lesniak, K. T., & Dubbert, P. M. (2001). Exercise and hypertension. *Current Opinion in Cardiology, 16,* 356–359.

LeVay, S. (1991). A difference in hypothalamic structure between heterosexual and homosexual men. *Science, 253,* 1034–1037.

Leventhal, H., & Cleary, P. D. (1980). The smoking problem: A review of research and theory in behavioral risk modification. *Psychological Bulletin, 88,* 370–405.

Levinson, D. F. (2006). The genetics of depression: A review. *Biological Psychiatry, 60,* 84–92.

Levitin, D. J. (2006). *This is your brain on music: The science of a human obsession.* New York: Dutton/Penguin.

Lieb, K., Zanarini, M. C., Schmahl, C., Linehan, M. M., & Bohus, M. (2004). Borderline personality disorder. *Lancet, 364,* 453–461.

Lieberman, M. D. (2000). Intuition: A social cognitive neuroscience approach. *Psychological Bulletin, 126,* 109–137.

Lieberman, M. D., Ochsner, K. N., Gilbert, D. T., & Schacter, D. L. (2001). Do amnesiacs exhibit cognitive dissonance reduction? The role of explicit memory and attention in attitude change. *Psychological Science, 121,* 135–140.

Lilienfeld, S. O. (2007). Psychological treatments that cause harm. *Perspectives on Psychological Science, 2,* 53–67.

Lindemann, B. (2001). Receptors and transduction in taste. *Nature, 413,* 219–225.

Linehan, M. M. (1987). Dialectical behavior therapy for borderline personality disorder: Theory and method. *Bulletin of the Menninger Clinic, 51,* 261–276.

Linehan, M. M., Armstrong, H. E., Suarez, A., Allmon, D., & Heard, H. (1991). Cognitive behavioral treatment of chronically parasuicidal borderline patients. *Archives of General Psychiatry, 48,* 1060–1064.

Linehan, M. M., Heard, H., & Armstrong, H. E. (1993). Naturalistic follow-up of a behavioral treatment for chronically parasuicidal borderline patients. *Archives of General Psychiatry, 50,* 971–974.

Lledo, P. M., Gheusi, G., & Vincent, J. D. (2005). Information processing in the mammalian olfactory system. *Physiological Review, 85,* 281–317.

Lobue, V. & Deloache, J. S. (2011). Pretty in pink: The early development of gender stereotyped colour preferences. *British Journal of Developmental Psychology, 29,* 656–667.

Locke, E. A., & Latham, G. P. (1990). *A theory of goal setting and task performance.* Englewood Cliffs, NJ: Prentice-Hall.

Loftus, E. F., Miller, D. G., & Burns, H. J. (1978). Semantic integration of verbal information into a visual memory. *Journal of Experimental Psychology: Human Learning and Memory, 4,* 19–31.

Loftus, E. F., & Palmer, J. C. (1974). Reconstruction of automobile destruction: An example of the interaction between language and memory. *Journal of Learning and Verbal Behavior, 13,* 585–589.

Lovaas, O. I. (1987). Behavioral treatment and normal educational and intellectual functioning in young autistic children. *Journal of Consulting and Clinical Psychology, 55,* 3–9.

Lowe, P. (2001, October 12). No prison for Candace's adoptive mom. *Denver Rocky Mountain News,* p. 26A.

Lubinski, D. (2004). Introduction to the special section on cognitive abilities: 100 years after Spearman's (1904) "'General intelligence,' objectively determined and measured." *Journal of Personality and Social Psychology, 86,* 96–111.

Luria, A. R. (1968). *The mind of a mnemonist.* New York: Avon.

Lykken, D. T. (1957). A study of anxiety in the sociopathic personality. *Journal of Abnormal Social Psychology, 55,* 6–10.

Lykken, D. T. (1995). *The antisocial personalities.* Hillsdale, NJ: Erlbaum.

Lykken, D. T. (2000). The causes and costs of crime and a controversial cure. *Journal of Personality, 68,* 560–605.

Lyubomirsky, S., King, L., & Diener, E. (2005). The benefits of frequent positive affect: Does happiness lead to success? *Psychological Bulletin, 131,* 803–855.

Lyubomirsky, S., & Nolen-Hoeksema, S. (1995). Effects of self-focused rumination on negative thinking and interpersonal problem solving. *Journal of Personality and Social Psychology, 69,* 176–190.

Maccoby, E. E., & Jacklin, C. N. (1974). *The psychology of sex differences.* Stanford, CA: Stanford University Press.

MacDonald, G., & Leary, M. R. (2005). Why does social exclusion hurt? The relationship between social and physical pain. *Psychological Bulletin, 131*, 202–223.

Macrae, C. N., Bodenhausen, G. V., & Calvini, G. (1999). Contexts of cryptomnesia: May the source be with you. *Social Cognition, 17*, 273–297.

Macur, J. (2012). A very long journey was very swift. *The New York Times*, p. B11.

Maguire, E. A., Spiers, H. J., Good, C. D., Hartley, T., Frackowiak, R. S. J., & Burgess, N. (2003). Navigation expertise and the human hippocampus: A structural brain imaging analysis. *Hippocampus, 13*, 250–259.

Malone, D. A., Jr., Dougherty, D. D., Rezai, A. R., Carpenter, L. L., Friehs, G. M., Eskandar, E. N., et al. (2009). Deep brain stimulation of the ventral capsule/ventral striatum for treatment-resistant depression. *Biological Psychiatry, 65*, 267–275.

Manhart, K. (2004, December). The limits of multi-tasking. *Scientific American Mind*, 62–67.

Manning, R., Levine, M., & Collins, A. (2007). The Kitty Genovese murder and the social psychology of helping: The parable of the 38 witnesses. *American Psychologist, 62*, 555–562.

Mannuzza, S., Klein, R. G., Bonagura, N., Malloy, P., Giampino, T. L., & Addalli, K. A. (1991). Hyperactive boys almost grown up. Replications of psychiatric status. *Archives of General Psychiatry, 48*, 77–83.

March, J. S., Silva, S., Petrycki, S., Curry, J., Wells, K., Fairbank, J., et al. (2007). The Treatment for Adolescents with Depression Study (TADS): Long-term effectiveness and safety outcomes. *Archives of General Psychiatry, 64*, 1132–1143.

Marcus, G. F. (1996). Why do children say "breaked"? *Current Directions in Psychological Science, 5*, 81–85.

Marcus, G. F., Pinker, S., Ullman, M., Hollander, M., Rosen, T. S., & Xu, F. (1992). Overregularization in language acquisition. *Monographs of the Society for Research in Child Development, 57*(4, serial No. 228), 181.

Markon, J. (2001, October 8). Elderly judges handle 20 percent of U. S. caseload. *The Wall Street Journal*, p. A15.

Markus, H. R. (1977). Self-schemata and processing information about the self. *Journal of Personality and Social Psychology, 35*, 63–78.

Markus, H. R., & Kitayama, S. (1991). Culture and the self: Implications for cognition, emotion, and motivation. *Psychological Review, 98*, 224–253.

Marlatt, G. A. (1999). Alcohol, the magic elixir? In S. Peele & M. Grant (Eds.), *Alcohol and pleasure: A health perspective* (pp. 233–248). Philadelphia: Brunner/Mazel.

Marsland, A. L., Pressman, S., & Cohen, S. (2007). Positive affect and immune function. *Psychoneuroimmunology, 2*, 761–779.

Martin, A., & Chao, L. L. (2001). Semantic memory and the brain: Structure and processes. *Current Opinion in Neurobiology, 11*, 194–201.

Martire, L. M., & Schulz, R. (2007). Involving family in psychosocial interventions for chronic illness. *Current Directions in Psychological Science, 16*, 90–94.

Maruta, T., Colligan, R. C., Malinchoc, M., & Offord, K. P. (2002). Optimism-pessimism assessed in the 1960s and self-reported health status 30 years later. *Mayo Clinic Proceedings, 77*, 748–753.

Maslow, A. (1968). *Toward a psychology of being*. New York: Van Nostrand.

Mayberg, H. S., Lozano, A. M., Voon, V., McNeely, H. E., Seminowicz, D., Hamani, C., et al. (2005). Deep brain stimulation for treatment-resistant depression. *Neuron, 45*, 651–660.

Mayhew, D. R., Brown, S. W., & Simpson, H. M. (2002). *The alcohol-crash problem in Canada: 1999*. Ottawa, Canada: Transport Canada.

McAdams, D. P., & Olson, B. D. (2010). Personality development: Continuity and change over the life course. *Annual Review of Psychology, 61*, 517–542.

McCabe, D. P., Roediger, H. L., McDaniel, M. A., Balota, D. A., & Hambrick, D. Z. (2010). The relationship between working memory capacity and executive functioning: Evidence for a common executive attention construct. *Neuropsychology, 24*, 222–243.

McClelland, D. C. (1987). *Human motivation*. New York: Cambridge University Press.

McClelland, D. C., Koestner, R., & Weinberger, J. (1989). How do self-attributed and implicit motives differ? *Psychological Review, 96*, 690–702.

McCrae, R. R., & Costa, P. T., Jr. (1990). *Personality in adulthood*. New York: Guilford Press.

McCrae, R. R., & Costa, P. T., Jr. (1999). A five-factor theory of personality. In L. A. Pervin & O. P. John (Eds.), *Handbook of personality: Theory and research* (2nd ed., pp. 139–153). New York: Guilford Press.

McCrae, R. R., Costa, P. T., Ostendorf, F., Angleitner, A., Hrebickova, M., Avia, M. D., et al. (2000). Nature over nurture: Temperament, personality, and life span development. *Journal of Personality and Social Psychology, 78*, 173–186.

McCullough, J. P. (2000). *Treatment for chronic depression: Cognitive behavioral analysis system of psychotherapy (CBASP)*. New York: Guilford Press.

McEwen, B. S. (2008). Central effects of stress hormones in health and disease: Understanding the protective and damaging effects of stress and stress mediators. *European Journal of Pharmacology, 583*, 174–185.

McEwen, B. S., & Gianaros, P. J. (2011). Stress- and allostatis-induced brain plasticity. *Annual Review of Medicine, 62*, 431–435.

McGlashan, T. H. (1988). A selective review of recent North American long-term follow-up studies of schizophrenia. *Schizophrenia Bulletin, 14*, 515–542.

McGough, J. J., & Barkley, R. A. (2004). Diagnostic controversies in adult attention deficit hyperactivity disorder. *American Journal of Psychiatry, 161*, 1948–1956.

McGrath, R.W. (2010). Prescriptive authority for psychologists. *Annual Review of Clinical Psychology, 6*, 21–47.

McInnis, M. G., McMahon, F. J., Chase, G. A., Simpson, S. G., Ross, C. A., & DePaulo, J. R. (1993). Anticipation in bipolar affective disorder. *American Journal of Human Genetics, 53,* 385–390.

McKown, C., & Weinstein, R. S. (2008). Teacher expectations, classroom context, and the achievement gap. *Journal of School Psychology, 46,* 235–261.

McNeely, H. E., Mayberg, H. S., Lozano, A. M., & Kennedy, S. H. (2008). Neuropsychological impact of Cg25 deep brain stimulation for treatment-resistant depression: Preliminary results over 12 months. *Journal of Nervous and Mental Disease, 196,* 405–410.

McNeil, D. G., Jr. (2006, November 23). For rare few, taste is in the ear of the beholder. *The New York Times.* Retrieved June 3, 2013, from http://www.nytimes.com/2006/11/23/science/23taste.html

Meddis, R. (1977). *The sleep instinct.* London: Routledge & Kegan Paul.

Mehl, M. R., Gosling, S. D., & Pennebaker, J. W. (2006). Personality in its natural habitat: Manifestations and implicit folk theories of personality in daily life. *Journal of Personality and Social Psychology, 90,* 862–877.

Mehl, M. R., Pennebaker, J. W., Crow, M. D., Dabbs, J., & Price, J. H. (2001). The electronically activated recorder (EAR): A device for sampling naturalistic daily activities and conversations. *Behavior Research Methods, Instruments, and Computers, 33,* 517–523.

Melzack, R., & Wall, P. D. (1982). *The challenge of pain.* New York: Basic Books.

Mennella, J. A., Jagnow, C. P., & Beauchamp, G. K. (2001). Prenatal and postnatal flavor learning by human infants. *Pediatrics, 107,* e88.

Mercer, K. B., Orcutt, H. K., Quinn, J. F., Fitzgerald, C. A., Conneely, K. N., Barfield, R. T., et al. (2012). Acute and posttraumatic stress symptoms in a prospective gene x environment study of a university campus shooting. *Archives of General Psychiatry, 69,* 89–97.

Merikangas, K. R., Burstein, M., Swanson, S. A., Avenevoli, S., Cui, L., Benjet, C., et al. (2010). Lifetime prevalence of mental disorders in U.S. adolescents: Results from the National Comorbidity Survey Replication–Adolescent Supplement (NCS–A). *Journal of the American Academy of Child and Adolescent Psychiatry, 49,* 980–989.

Merikangas, K., He, J., Burstein, M., Swendsen, J., Avenevoli, S., Case, B., et al. (2011). Service utilization for lifetime mental disorders in U.S. adolescents: Results of the National Comorbidity Survey–Adolescent Supplement (NCS–A). *Journal of the American Academy of Child and Adolescent Psychiatry, 50,* 32–45.

Meston, C. M., & Frohlich, P. F. (2000). The neurobiology of sexual function. *Archives of General Psychiatry, 57,* 1012–1030.

Mezulis, A. H., Abramson, L. Y., Hyde, J. S., & Hankin, B. L. (2004). Is there a universal positivity bias in attributions? A meta-analytic review of individual, developmental, and culture differences in the self-serving attributional bias. *Psychological Bulletin, 130,* 711–747.

Milgram, S. (1974). *Obedience to authority: An experimental view.* New York: Harper & Row.

Miller, G. (1956). The magical number seven, plus or minus two: Some limits on our capacity for processing information. *Psychological Review, 63,* 81–97.

Miller, G. (2005). How are memories stored and retrieved? *Science, 309,* 92–93.

Miller, G. E., Freedland, K. E., Carney, R. M., Stetler, C. A., & Banks, W. A. (2003). Cynical hostility, depressive symptoms, and the expression of inflammatory risk markers for coronary heart disease. *Journal of Behavioral Medicine, 26,* 501–515.

Miller, I. W., Norman, W. H., & Keitner, G. I. (1989). Cognitive-behavioral treatment of depressed inpatients: Six- and twelve-month follow-up. *American Journal of Psychiatry, 146,* 1274–1279.

Miller, R. S. (1996). *Embarrassment: Poise and peril in everyday life.* New York: Guilford Press.

Miller, R. S. (1997). We always hurt the ones we love: Aversive interactions in close relationships. In R. M. Kowalski (Ed.), *Aversive interpersonal behaviors* (pp. 11–29). New York: Plenum Press.

Miller, W. T. (2000). Rediscovering fire: Small interventions, large effects. *Psychology of Addictive Behaviors, 14,* 6–18.

Miniño, A. M., & Murphy, S. L. (2012). Deaths in the United States, 2010. NCHS data brief, no 99. Hyattsville, MD: National Center for Health Statistics.

Minshew, N. J., & Williams, D. L. (2007). The new neurobiology of autism: Cortex, connectivity, and neuronal organization. *Archives of Neurology, 64,* 945–950.

Miranda, D., & Claes, M. (2004). Rap music genres and deviant behaviors in French-Canadian adolescents. *Journal of Youth and Adolescence, 33,* 113–122.

Mischel, W., Shoda, Y., & Rodriguez, M. L. (1989). Delay of gratification in children. *Science, 244,* 933–938.

Miyamoto, Y., & Kitayama, S. (2002). Cultural variation in correspondence bias: The critical role of attitude diagnosticity of socially constrained behavior. *Journal of Personality and Social Psychology, 83,* 1239–1248.

Moeller, S. J., & Crocker, J. (2009). Drinking and desired self-images: Path models of self-image goals, coping motives, heavy-episodic drinking, and alcohol problems. *Psychology of Addictive Behaviors, 23,* 334–340.

Moffitt, T. E., Brammer, G. L., Caspi, A., Fawcett, J. P., Raleigh, M., Yuwiler, A., et al. (1998). Whole blood serotonin relates to violence in an epidemiological study. *Biological Psychiatry, 43,* 446–457.

Moll, J., & de Oliveira-Souza, R. (2007). Moral judgments, emotions and the utilitarian brain. *Trends in Cognitive Sciences, 11,* 319–321, ISSN 1364-6613.

Monroe, S. M., & Simons, A. D. (1991). Diathesis-stress theories in the context of life-stress research: Implications for depressive disorders. *Psychological Bulletin, 110,* 406–425.

Montgomery, G. H., DuHamel, K. N., & Redd, W. H. (2000). A meta-analysis of hypnotically induced analgesia: How effective is hypnosis? *International Journal of Clinical and Experimental Hypnosis, 48,* 138–153.

Monti, M. M., Vanhaudenhuyse, A., Coleman, M. R., Boly, M., Pickard, J. D., Tshibanda, L., et al. (2010). Willful modulation of brain activity in disorders of consciousness. *New England Journal of Medicine, 362,* 579–589.

Morin, C. M., Vallières, A., Guay, B., Ivers, H., Savard, J., Mérette, C., et al. (2009). Cognitive behavioral therapy, singly and combined with medication, for persistent insomnia: A randomized controlled trial. *Journal of the American Medical Association, 301,* 2005–2015.

Morris, N. M., Udry, J. R., Khan-Dawood, F., & Dawood, M. Y. (1987). Marital sex frequency and midcycle female testosterone. *Archives of Sexual Behavior, 16,* 27–37.

Mortensen, E. L., Michaelsen, K. F., Sanders, S. A., & Reinisch, J. M. (2002). The association between duration of breastfeeding and adult intelligence. *Journal of the American Medical Association, 287,* 2365–2371.

Morton, J., & Johnson, M. H. (1991). CONSPEC and CONLERN: A two-process theory of infant face recognition. *Psychological Review, 98,* 164–181.

Mowery, P. D., Brick, P. D., & Farrelly, M. (2000). Pathways to established smoking: Results from the 1999 national youth tobacco survey (Legacy First Look Report No. 3). Washington, DC: American Legacy Foundation.

Mroczek, D. K., & Kolarz, C. M. (1998). The effect of age on positive and negative affect: A developmental perspective on happiness. *Journal of Personality and Social Psychology, 75,* 1333–1349.

Mroczek, D. K., & Spiro, A. (2003). Modeling intraindividual change in personality traits: Findings from the Normative Aging Study. *Journal of Gerontology, 58B,* 153–165.

Mufson, L., Dorta, K. P., Wickramaratne, P., Nomura, Y., Olfson, M., & Weissman, M. M. (2004). A randomized effectiveness trial of interpersonal psychotherapy for depressed adolescents. *Archives of General Psychiatry, 61,* 577–584.

Muhle, R., Trentacoste, S. V., & Rapin, I. (2004). The genetics of autism. *Pediatrics, 113,* 472–486.

Mukherjee, R. A. S., Hollins, S., Abou-Saleh, M. T., & Turk, J. (2005). Low levels of alcohol consumption and the fetus. *British Medical Journal, 330*(7488), 375–385.

Mulder, J., Ter Bogt, T.F.M., Raaijmakers, Q.A.W., Nic Gabhainn, S., Monshouwer, K., & Vollebergh, W.A.M. (2009). The soundtrack of substance abuse: Music preference and adolescent smoking and drinking. *Substance Use & Misuse, 44,* 514–531.

Mumford, D. B., Saeed, K., Ahmad, I., Latif, S., & Mubbashar, M. H. (1997). Stress and psychiatric disorder in rural Punjab: A community survey. *British Journal of Psychiatry, 170,* 473–478.

Munson, J. A., McMahon, R. J., & Spieker, S. J. (2001). Structure and variability in the developmental trajectory of children's externalizing problems: Impact of infant attachment, maternal depressive symptomatology, and child sex. *Development and Psychopathology, 13,* 277–296.

Murray, H. A. (1938). *Explorations in personality.* New York: Oxford University Press.

Musella, D. P. (2005). Gallup poll shows that Americans' belief in the paranormal persists. *Skeptical Inquirer, 29,* 5.

Mustanski, B. S., Chivers, M. L., & Bailey, J. M. (2002). A critical review of recent biological research on human sexual orientation. *Annual Review of Sex Research, 13,* 89–140.

Myers, D. G. (2000). The funds, friends, and faith of happy people. *American Psychologist, 55,* 56–67.

Myers, D. G., & Lamm, H. (1976). The group polarization phenomenon. *Psychological Bulletin, 83,* 602–627.

Nadel, L., Hoscheidt, S., & Ryan, L. R. (2013). Spatial cognition and the hippocampus: The anterior–posterior axis. *Journal of Cognitive Neuroscience, 25,* 22–28.

Nader, K., & Einarsson, E. O. (2010). Memory reconsolidation: An update. *Annals of the New York Academy of Sciences, 1191,* 27–41.

Nader, K., Schafe, G. E., & Le Doux, J. E. (2000). Fear memories require protein synthesis in the amygdala for reconsolidation after retrieval. *Nature, 406,* 722–726.

Nakano, K., & Kitamura, T. (2001). The relation of the anger subcomponent of type A behavior to psychological symptoms in Japanese and foreign students. *Japanese Psychological Research, 43,* 50–54.

Nash, M., & Barnier, A. (2008). *The Oxford handbook of hypnosis.* New York: Oxford University Press.

National Institute of Drug Abuse. (2006). NIDA Research report: Methamphetamine abuse and addiction (NIH Publication No. 06–4210). Retrieved June 3, 2013, from http://www.nida.nih.gov/ResearchReports/methamph/methamph.html

National Institute of Drug Abuse. (2010). MDMA (Ecstasy) [Fact sheet]. Retrieved June 3, 2013, from http://teens.drugabuse.gov/facts/facts_xtc1.php

National Research Council. (2006). *When I'm 64.* Washington, DC: National Academy Press.

National Research Council, Committee on Educational Interventions for Children with Autism. (2001). *Educating young children with autism.* Washington, DC: National Academy Press.

Neimeyer, R. A., & Mitchell, K. A. (1988). Similarity and attraction: A longitudinal study. *Journal of Social and Personal Relationships, 5,* 131–148.

Neisser, U. (1967). *Cognitive psychology.* New York: Appleton-Century-Crofts.

Neisser, U., Boodoo, G., Bouchard, T. J., Jr., Boykin, A. W., Brody, N., Ceci, S. J., et al. (1996). Intelligence: Knowns and unknowns. *American Psychologist, 51,* 77–101.

Ng, D. M., & Jeffrey, E. W. (2003). Relationships between perceived stress and health behaviors in a sample of working adults. *Health Psychology, 22,* 638–642.

Nicolini, H., Bakish, D., Duenas, H., Spann, M., Erickson, J., Hallberg, C., et al. (2008). Improvement of psychic and somatic symptoms in adult patients with generalized anxiety disorder: Examination from a duloxetine, venlafaxine extended-release and placebo-controlled trial. *Psychological Medicine, 19,* 1–10.

Nisbett, R. E., & Wilson, T. D. (1977). Telling more than we can know: Verbal reports on mental processes. *Psychological Review, 84,* 231–259.

Nishino, S. (2007). Narcolepsy: Pathophysiology and pharmacology. *Journal of Clinical Psychiatry, 68*(Suppl. 13), 9–15.

Nomura, Y., Halperin, J. M., Newcorn, J. H., Davey, C., Fifer, W. P., Savitz, D. A., et al. (2009). The risk for impaired learning-related abilities in childhood and educational achievement among adults born near-term. *Journal of Pediatric Psychology, 34*, 406–418.

Norcross, J. C., Hedges, M., & Castle, P. H. (2002). Psychologists conducting therapy in 2001. A study of the Division 29 membership. *Psychotherapy: Theory/Research/Practice/ Training, 39*, 97–102.

Nosek, B. A., Hawkins, C. B., & Frazier, R. S. (2011). Implicit social cognition: From measures to mechanisms. *Trends in Cognitive Sciences, 15*, 152–159.

Noyes, R. (1991). Suicide and panic disorder: A review. *Journal of Affective Disorders, 22*, 1–11.

Nurnberger, J. J., Goldin, L. R., & Gershon, E. S. (1994). Genetics of psychiatric disorders. In G. Winokur & P. M. Clayton (Eds.), *The medical basis of psychiatry* (pp. 459–492). Philadelphia: Saunders.

O'Leary, S. G. (1995). Parental discipline mistakes. *Current Directions in Psychological Science, 4*, 11–13.

O'Neil, J. (2004, December 29). Slow-motion miracle: One boy's journey out of autism's grasp. *The New York Times*, p. B8.

O'Neil, S. (1999). Flow theory and the development of musical performance skills. *Bulletin of the Council for Research in Music Education, 141*, 129–134.

O'Toole, A. J., Jiang, F., Abdi, H., & Haxby, J. V. (2005). Partially distributed representations of objects and faces in ventral temporal cortex. *Journal of Cognitive Neuroscience, 17*, 580–590.

Oberauer, K., Schulze, R., Wilhelm, O., & Süß, H. M. (2005). Working memory and intelligence—Their correlation and their relation: Comment on Ackerman, Beier, and Boyle (2005). *Psychological Bulletin, 131*, 61–65.

Obot, I. S., & Room, R. (2005). *Alcohol, gender and drinking problems: Perspectives from low and middle income countries.* Geneva, Switzerland: World Health Organization.

Ochsner, K. N., Bunge, S. A., Gross, J. J., & Gabrieli, J. D. E. (2002). Rethinking feelings: An fMRI study of the cognitive regulation of emotion. *Journal of Cognitive Neuroscience, 14*, 1215–1299.

Ogbu, J. U. (1994). From cultural differences to differences in cultural frames of reference. In P. M. Greenfield & R. R. Cocking (Eds.), *Cross cultural roots of minority child development* (pp. 365–392). Hillsdale, NJ: Erlbaum.

Ogden, C. L., & Carroll, M. (2010). Prevalence of overweight, obesity, and extreme obesity among adults: United States, trends 1976–1980 through 2007–2008. A report of the National Center for Health Statistics. http://www.cdc .gov/NCHS/data/hestat/obesity_adult_07_08/obesity_ adult_07_08.pdf/

Ogden, C. L., Carroll, M. D., Kit, B. K., & Flegal, K. M. (2012). Prevalence of obesity in the United States, 2009–2010. NCHS Data Brief, 82. Washington, DC: U.S. Department of Health and Human Services.

Ogletree, S. M., Turner, G., Vieira, A., & Brunotte, J. (2005). College living: Issues related to housecleaning attitudes. *College Student Journal, 39*, 729–733.

Olfson, M., Marcus, S. C., Druss, B., Elinson, L., Tanielian, T., & Pincus, H. A. (2002). National trends in the outpatient treatment of depression. *Journal of the American Medical Association, 287*, 203–209.

Olfson, M., Shaffer, D., Marcus, S. C., & Greenberg, T. (2003). Relationship between antidepressant medication treatment and suicide in adolescents. *Archives of General Psychiatry, 60*, 978–982.

Olson, R., Hogan, L., & Santos, L. (2006). Illuminating the history of psychology: Tips for teaching students about the Hawthorne studies. *Psychology Learning and Teaching, 5*, 110–118.

Oltmanns, T. F., Martin, M. T., Neale, J. M., & Davison, G. C. (2009). *Case studies in abnormal psychology.* Hoboken, NJ: Wiley.

Onishi, K. H., & Baillargeon, R. (2005). Do 15-month-old infants understand false beliefs? *Science, 308*, 255–258.

Ortigue, S., Bianchi-Demicheli, F., Hamilton, C., & Grafton, S. T. (2007). The neural basis of love as a subliminal prime: An event-related functional magnetic resonance imaging study. *Journal of Cognitive Neuroscience, 19*, 1218–1230.

Osterling, J., & Dawson, G. (1994). Early recognition of children with autism: A study of first birthday home videotapes. *Journal of Autism and Developmental Disorders, 24*, 247–257.

Ottieger, A. E., Tressell, P. A., Inciardi, J. A., & Rosales, T. A. (1992). Cocaine use patterns and overdose. *Journal of Psychoactive Drugs, 24*, 399–410.

Owen, A. M., Coleman, M. R., Boly, M., Davis, M. H., Laureys, S., & Pickard, J. D. (2006). Detecting awareness in the vegetative state. *Science, 313*, 1402.

Pack, A. I., & Pien, G.W. (2011). Update on sleep and its disorders. *Annual Review of Medicine, 62*, 447–460.

Pagnoni, G., & Cekic, M. (2007). Age effects on gray matter volume and attentional performance in Zen meditation. *Neurobiology of Aging, 28*, 1623–1627.

Papadimitriou, G. N., Zervas, I. M., & Papakostas, Y. G. (2001). Unilateral ECT for prophylaxis in affective illness. *Journal of ECT, 17*, 229–231.

Park, J. S., & Grow, J. (2008). The social reality of depression: DTC advertising of antidepressants and perceptions of the prevalence and lifetime risk of depression. *Journal of Business Ethics, 79*, 1–26.

Pascual-Leone, A., Catala, M. D., & Pascual-Leone, P. A. (1996). Lateralized effect of rapid-rate transcranial magnetic stimulation of the prefrontal cortex on mood. *Neurology, 46*, 499–502.

Pasupathi, M., & Carstensen, L. L. (2003). Age and emotional experience during mutual reminiscing. *Psychology and Aging, 18*, 430–442.

Patterson, D., & Jensen, M. (2003). Hypnosis and clinical pain. *Psychological Bulletin, 129*(4), 495–521.

Paul-Labrador, M., Polk, D., Dwyer, J. H., Velasquez, I., Nidich, S., Rainforth, M., et al. (2006). Effects of a randomized controlled trial of transcendental meditation on components of the metabolic syndrome in subjects with coronary heart disease. *Archives of Internal Medicine, 166*, 1218–1224.

Pauls, D. L. (2008). The genetics of obsessive compulsive disorder: A review of the evidence. *American Journal of Medical Genetics, 148C*, 133–139.

Paunonen, S. V., & Ashton, M. C. (2001). Big five factors and facets and the prediction of behavior. *Journal of Personality and Social Psychology, 81*, 524–539.

Pavlov, I. P. (1927). *Conditioned reflexes: An investigation of the physiological activity of the cerebral cortex.* (Translated and edited by G. V. Anrep.) London: Oxford University Press; Humphrey Milford.

Payne, B. K. (2001). Prejudice and perception: The role of automatic and controlled processes in misperceiving a weapon. *Journal of Personality and Social Psychology, 81*, 181–192.

Payne, B. K., Krosnick, J. A., Pasek, J., Lelkes, Y., Akhtar, O., & Tompson, T. (2010). Implicit and explicit prejudice in the 2008 American presidential election. *Journal of Experimental Social Psychology, 46*, 367–374.

Penfield, W., & Jasper, H. (1954). *Epilepsy and the functional anatomy of the human brain.* Boston: Little, Brown.

Peretz, I. (1996). Can we lose memory for music? A case of music agnosia in a nonmusician. *Journal of Cognitive Neuroscience, 8*, 481–496.

Perez-Stable, E. J., Marin, G., & Marin, B. V. (1994). Behavioral risk factors: Comparison of Latinos and non-Latino whites in San Francisco. *American Journal of Public Health, 84*, 971–976.

Perrett, D. I., May, K. A., & Yoshikawa, S. (1994). Facial shape and judgments of female attractiveness. *Nature, 368*, 239–242.

Peterson, L. R., & Peterson, M. J. (1959). Short-term retention of individual verbal items. *Journal of Experimental Psychology, 58*, 193–198.

Petronis, A., & Kennedy, J. L. (1995). Unstable genes—Unstable mind? *American Journal of Psychiatry, 152*, 164–172.

Petty, R. E., & Cacioppo, J. T. (1986). *Communication and persuasion: Central and peripheral routes to attitude change.* New York: Springer-Verlag.

Petty, R. E., & Wegener, D. T. (1998). Attitude change: Multiple roles for persuasion variables. In D. T. Gilbert, S. T. Fiske, & G. Lindzey (Eds.), *The handbook of social psychology* (4th ed., pp. 323–390). Boston: McGraw-Hill.

Phelps, E. A. (2006). Emotion and cognition: Insights from studies of the human amygdala. *Annual Review of Psychology, 57*, 27–53.

Phelps, E. A., Ling, S., & Carrasco, M. (2006). Emotion facilitates perception and potentiates the perceptual benefits of attention. *Psychological Science, 17*, 292–299.

Phinney, J. S. (1990). Ethnic identity in adolescents and adults: Review of research. *Psychological Bulletin, 108*, 499–514.

Pinker, S. (1984). *Language learnability and language development.* Cambridge, MA: Harvard University Press.

Pitman, R., Sanders, K., Zusman, R., Healy, A., Cheema, F., Lasko, N., et al. (2002). Pilot study of secondary prevention of posttraumatic stress disorder with propranolol. *Biological Psychiatry, 51*, 189–192.

Plant, E. A., Hyde, J. S., Keltner, D., & Devine, P. G. (2000). The gender stereotyping of emotions. *Psychology of Women Quarterly, 24*, 81–92.

Plomin, R., & Caspi, A. (1999). Behavioral genetics and personality. In L. A. Pervin & O. P. John (Eds.), *Handbook of personality: Theory and research* (2nd ed., pp. 251–276). New York: Guilford Press.

Plomin, R., & Spinath, F. M. (2004). Intelligence: Genetics, genes, and genomics. *Journal of Personality and Social Psychology, 86*, 112–129.

Polivy, J., & Herman, C. P. (2002). Causes of eating disorders. *Annual Review of Psychology, 53*, 187–213.

Pollock, K. M. (2004). Exercise in treating depression: Broadening the psychotherapist's role. *Journal of Clinical Psychology, 57*, 1289–1300.

Premack, D. (1959). Toward empirical behavior laws: 1. Positive reinforcement. *Psychological Review, 66*, 219–233.

Premack, D. (1970). Mechanisms of self-control. In W. A. Hunt (Ed.), *Learning mechanisms in smoking* (pp. 107–123). Chicago: Aldine.

Prentiss, D., Power, R., Balmas, G., Tzuang, G., & Israelski, D. (2004). Patterns of marijuana use among patients with HIV/AIDS followed in a public health care setting. *Journal of Acquired Immune Deficiency Syndromes, 35*(1), 38–45.

Price, D. D., Harkins, S. W., & Baker, C. (1987). Sensory-affective relationships among different types of clinical and experimental pain. *Pain, 28*, 297–307.

Raesaenen, S., Pakaslahti, A., Syvaelahti, E., Jones, P. B., & Isohanni, M. (2000). Sex differences in schizophrenia: A review. *Nordic Journal of Psychiatry, 54*, 37–45.

Rainville, P., Duncan, G. H., Price, D. D., Carrier, B., & Bushnell, M. C. (1997). Pain affect encoded in human anterior cingulate but not somatosensory cortex. *Science, 277*, 968–971.

Rainville, P., Hofbauer, R. K., Bushnell, M. C., Duncan, G. H., & Price, D. D. (2002). Hypnosis modulates activity in brain structures involved in the regulation of consciousness. *Journal of Cognitive Neuroscience, 14*, 887–901.

Ram, S., Seirawan, H., Kumar, S. K., & Clark, G. T. (2010). Prevalence and impact of sleep disorders and sleep habits in the United States. *Sleep Breath, 14*, 63–70.

Ramachandran, V. S. (2003). Lecture 2: Synapses and the self. BBC Radio 4, *The Reith Lectures 2003: The emerging mind website.* Retrieved June 3, 2013, from http://www.bbc.co.uk/print/radio4/reith2003/lecture2.shtml

Ramachandran, V. S., & Hubbard, E. M. (2001). Psychophysical investigations into the neural basis of synaesthesia. *Proceedings of the Royal Society of London, 268B*, 979–983.

Ramachandran, V. S., & Hubbard, E. M. (2003, May). Hearing colors, tasting shapes: Color-coded world. *Scientific American, 288*, 42–49.

Ramirez, G., & Beilock, S. L. (2011). Writing about testing worries boosts exam performance in the classroom. *Science, 331*, 211–213.

Rapport, M. D., & Moffitt, C. (2002). Attention-deficit/hyperactivity disorder and methylphenidate: A review of the height/weight, cardiovascular, and somatic complaint side effects. *Clinical Psychology Review, 22*, 1107–1131.

Rauscher, F. H., Shaw, G. L., & Ky, K. N. (1993). Music and spatial task performance. *Nature, 365*, 611.

Read, J. P., & Brown, R. A. (2003). The role of exercise in alcoholism treatment and recovery. *Professional Psychology: Research and Practice, 34,* 49–56.

Reddy, L., Tsuchiya, N., & Serre, T. (2010). Reading the mind's eye: Decoding category information during mental information. *Neuroimage, 50,* 818–825.

Reeves, L. M., & Weisberg, R. W. (1994). The role of content and abstract information in analogical transfer. *Psychological Bulletin, 115,* 381–400.

Reinders, A. A., Nijenhuis, E. R., Paans, A. M., Korf, J., Willemsen, A. T., & den Boer, J. A. (2003). One brain, two selves. *Neuroimage, 20,* 2119–2125.

Reis, D. L., Brackett, M. A., Shamosh, N. A., Kiehl, K. A., Salovey, P., & Gray, J. R. (2007). Emotional intelligence predicts individual differences in social exchange reasoning. *Neuroimage, 35,* 1385–1391.

Reis, H. X, Wheeler, L., Spiegel, N., Kernis, M. H., Nezlek, J., & Perri, M. (1982). Physical attractiveness in social interaction: II. Why does appearance affect social experience? *Journal of Personality and Social Psychology, 43,* 979–996.

Rescorla, R. (1966). Predictability and number of pairings in Pavlovian fear conditioning. *Psychonomic Science, 4,* 383–384.

Ressler, K. J., & Mayberg, H. S. (2007). Targeting abnormal neural circuits in mood and anxiety disorders: From the laboratory to the clinic. *Nature Neuroscience, 10,* 1116–1124.

Reyna, C., Brandt, M., & Viki, G. T. (2009). Blame it on hip-hop: Anti-rap attitudes as a proxy for prejudice. *Group Process and Intergroup Relations, 12,* 361–380.

Rhodewalt, F., & Morf, C. C. (1998). On self-aggrandizement and anger: A temporal analysis of narcissism and affective reactions to success and failure. *Journal of Personality and Social Psychology, 74,* 672–685.

Richman, L. S., Kubzansky, L., Maselko, J., Kawachi, I., Choo, P., & Bauer, M. (2005). Positive emotion and health: Going beyond the negative. *Health Psychology, 24,* 422–429.

Rifkin, A., & Rifkin, W. (2004). Adolescents with depression. *Journal of the American Medical Association, 292,* 2577–2578.

Rinck, M., Reinecke, A., Ellwart, T., Heuer, K., & Becker, E. S. (2005). Speeded detection and increased distraction in fear of spiders: Evidence from eye movements. *Journal of Abnormal Psychology, 114,* 235–248.

Roberts, B. W., & Friend-DelVecchio, W. (2000). The rank-order consistency of personality traits from childhood to old age: A quantitative review of longitudinal studies. *Psychological Bulletin, 126,* 3–25.

Robins, L. N., & Regier, D. A. (1991). *Psychiatric disorders in America: The epidemiological catchment areas study.* New York: Free Press.

Robins, R. W., Trzesniewski, K., Tracy, J. L., Gosling, S. D., & Potter, J. (2002). Global self-esteem across the life span. *Psychology and Aging, 17,* 423–434.

Robles, T. F., & Kiecolt-Glaser, J. K. (2003). The physiology of marriage: Pathways to health. *Physiology & Behavior, 79,* 409–416.

Roediger, H. L., III, & Karpicke, J. D. (2006). The power of testing memory: Basic research and implications for educational practice. *Psychological Science, 1,* 181–210.

Roethlisberger, F. J., & Dickson, W. J. (1939). *Management and the worker: An account of a research program conducted by the Western Electric Company, Hawthorne Works, Chicago.* Cambridge, MA: Harvard University Press.

Rogers, T. B., Kuiper, N. A., & Kirker, W. S. (1977). Self-reference and the encoding of personal information. *Journal of Personality and Social Psychology, 35,* 677–688.

Roisman, G. I., Clausell, E., Holland, A., Fortuna, K., & Elieff, C. (2008). Adult romantic relationships as contexts of human development: A multimethod comparison of same-sex couples with opposite-sex dating, engaged, and married dyads. *Developmental Psychology, 44,* 91–101.

Rolls, B. J., Roe, L. S., & Meengs, J. S. (2007). The effect of large portion sizes on energy intake is sustained for 11 days. *Obesity Research, 15,* 1535–1543.

Rolls, E. T. (2007). Sensory processing in the brain related to the control of food intake. *Proceedings of the Nutritional Society, 66,* 96–112.

Rolls, E. T., Burton, M. J., & Mora, F. (1980). Neurophysiological analysis of brain-stimulation reward in the monkey. *Brain Research, 194,* 339–357.

Rosenfeld, M. J. (2010, April). *Meeting online: The rise of the Internet as a social intermediary.* Paper session presented at the Population Association of America Meetings, Dallas, TX.

Rosenman, R. H., Brand, R. J., Jenkins, C. D., Friedman, M., Straus, R., & Wurm, M. (1975). Coronary heart disease in the Western Collaborative Group Study: Final follow-up experience of 8½ years. *Journal of the American Medical Association, 233,* 872–877.

Rosenman, R. H., Friedman, M., Straus, R., Wurm, M., Kositchek, R., Hahn, W., et al. (1964). A predictive study of heart disease. *Journal of the American Medical Association, 189,* 15–22.

Rosenstein, D., & Oster, H. (1988). Differential facial responses to four basic tastes in newborns. *Child Development, 59,* 1555–1568.

Rosenthal, R. (2003). Covert communication in laboratories, classrooms, and the truly real world. *Current Directions in Psychologial Science, 12,* 151–154.

Ross, H. E., & Young, L. J. (2009). Oxytocin and the neural mechanisms regulating social cognition and affiliative behavior. *Frontiers in Neuroendocrinology, 30,* 534–547.

Rothbaum, B. O., Hodges, L., Alarcon, R., Ready, D., Shahar, F., Graap, K., et al. (1999). Virtual reality exposure therapy for PTSD Vietnam veterans: A case study. *Journal of Traumatic Stress, 12,* 263–271.

Rothemund, Y., Preuschhof, C., Bohner, G., Bauknecht, H. C., Klingebiel, R., Flor, H., et al. (2007). Differential activation of the dorsal striatum by high-calorie visual food stimuli in obese individuals. *Neuroimage, 37,* 410–421.

Rotter, J. B. (1954). *Social learning and clinical psychology.* New York: Prentice-Hall.

Rotter, J. (1966). Generalized expectancies for internal versus external control of reinforcements. *Psychological Monographs, 80,* Whole No. 609.

Rubenstein, A. J., Kalakanis, L., & Langlois, J. H. (1999). Infant preferences for attractive faces: A cognitive explanation. *Developmental Psychology, 35,* 848–855.

Rubin, Z. (1970). Measurement of romantic love. *Journal of Personality and Social Psychology, 16*, 265–273.

Rusbult, C. E., & Van Lange, P. A. M. (1996). Interdependence processes. In E. T. Higgins & A. Kruglanski (Eds.), *Social psychology: Handbook of basic principles* (pp. 564–596). New York: Guilford Press.

Ruscio, A. M., Brown, T. A., Chiu, W. T., Sareen, J., Stein, M. B., & Kessler, R. C. (2008). Social fears and social phobia in the USA: Results from the national comorbidity survey replication. *Psychological Medicine, 35*, 15–28.

Russell, M. A. H. (1990). The nicotine trap: A 40-year sentence for four cigarettes. *British Journal of Addiction, 85*, 293–300.

Rutter, M. (2005). Incidence of autism disorders: Changes over time and their meaning. *Acta Paediatrica, 94*, 2–15.

Rymer, R. (1993). *Genie: A scientific tragedy*. New York: HarperCollins.

Sabol, S. Z., Nelson, M. L., Fisher, C., Gunzerath, L., Brody, C. L., Hu, S., et al. (1999). A genetic association for cigarette smoking behavior. *Health Psychology, 18*, 7–13.

Sacks, O. (1995). *An anthropologist on Mars: Seven paradoxical tales*. New York: Knopf.

Saha, S., Chant, D. C., Welham, J. L., & McGrath, J. J. (2006). The incidence and prevalence of schizophrenia varies with latitude. *Acta Psychiatrica Scandinavica, 114*, 36–39.

Salovey, P., & Grewel, D. (2005). The science of emotional intelligence. *Current Directions in Psychological Science, 14*, 281–286.

Salovey, P., & Mayer, J. D. (1990). Emotional intelligence. *Imagination, Cognition, and Personality, 9*, 185–211.

Sanford, A. J., Fay, N., Stewart, A., & Moxey, L. (2002). Perspective in statements of quantity, with implications for consumer psychology. *Psychological Science, 13*, 130–134.

Sargent, J. D., Beach, M. L., Adachi-Mejia, A. M., Gibson, J. J., Titus-Ernstoff, L. T., Carusi, C. P., et al. (2005). Exposure to movie smoking: Its relation to smoking initiation among U.S. adolescents. *Pediatrics, 116*, 1183–1191.

Savitz, D. A., Schwingle, P. J., & Keels, M. A. (1991). Influences of paternal age, smoking, and alcohol consumption on congenital anomalies. *Teratology, 44*, 429–440.

Sayette, M. A. (1993). An appraisal-disruption model of alcohol's effects on stress responses in social drinkers. *Psychological Bulletin, 114*, 459–476.

Schab, F. R. (1991). Odor memory: Taking stock. *Psychological Bulletin, 109*, 242–251.

Schacter, D. L., & Tulving, E. (1994). What are the memory systems of 1994? In D. L. Schacter & E. Tulving (Eds.), *Memory systems 1994* (pp. 1–38). Cambridge, MA: MIT Press.

Schachter, H. M., Pham, B., King, J., Langford, S., & Moher, D. (2001). How efficacious and safe is short-acting methylphenidate for the treatment of attention-deficit hyperactivity disorder in children and adolescents? A meta-analysis. *Canadian Medical Association Journal, 165*, 1475–1488.

Schachter, S. (1951). Deviation, rejection, and communication. *Journal of Abnormal Psychology, 46*, 190–207.

Schachter, S., & Singer, J. (1962). Cognitive, social, and physiological determinants of emotional state. *Psychological Review, 69*, 379–399.

Schaie, K. W. (1990). Intellectual development in adulthood. In J. E. Birren & K. W. Schaie (Eds.), *Handbook of the psychology of aging* (3rd ed., pp. 291–319). New York: Van Nostrand Reinhold.

Scheerer, M. (1963). Problem-solving. *Scientific American, 208*, 118–128.

Schiller, D., Monfils, M., Raio, C., Johnson, D., LeDoux, J. E., & Phelps, E. A. (2010). Preventing the return of fear in humans using reconsolidation update mechanisms. *Nature, 463*, 49–54.

Schmader, T. (2010). Stereotype threat deconstructed. *Current Directions in Psychological Science, 19*, 14–18.

Schmader, T., Johns, M., & Forbes, C. (2008). An integrated process model of stereotype threat effects on performance. *Psychological Review, 115*, 336–356.

Schmidt, N. B., & Keough, M. E. (2011). Treatment of panic. *Annual Review of Clinical Psychology, 6*, 241–256.

Schmitt, D. P., Allik, J., McCrae, R. R., & Benet-Martinez, V. (2007). The geographic distribution of big five personality traits: Patterns and profiles of human self-description across 56 nations. *Journal of Cross-Cultural Psychology, 38*, 173–212.

Schoenemann, P. T., Sheehan, M. J., & Glotzer, L. D. (2005). Prefrontal white matter volume is disproportionately larger in humans than in other primates. *Nature Neuroscience, 8*, 242–252.

Schultz, W. (2010). Dopamine signals for reward value and risk: Basic and recent data. *Behavioral and Brain Functions, 6*, 1–9.

Schulz, K. P., Fan, J., Tang, C. Y., Newcorn, J. H., Buchsbaum, M. S., Cheung, A. M., et al. (2004). Response inhibition in adolescents diagnosed with attention deficit hyperactivity disorder during childhood: An event-related fMRI study. *American Journal of Psychiatry, 161*, 1650–1657.

Schwartz, B. (2004). *The paradox of choice: Why more is less*. New York: Ecco.

Schwartz, C. E., Wright, C. I., Shin, L. M., Kagan, J., & Rauch, S. L. (2003). Inhibited and uninhibited infants "grown up": Adult amygdalar response to novelty. *Science, 300*, 1952–1953.

Schwartz, S., & Maquet, P. (2002). Sleep imaging and the neuropsychological assessment of dreams. *Trends in Cognitive Sciences, 6*, 23–30.

Schwarz, N., & Clore, G. L. (1983). Mood, misattribution, and judgments of well-being: Informative and directive functions of affective states. *Journal of Personality and Social Psychology, 45*, 513–523.

Scislowska, M. (2007, June 4). Man wakes from 19-year coma to "prettier" Poland. Railway worker is shocked at radical changes. *Associated Press*. Retrieved June 3, 2013, from http://www.boston.com/news/world/europe/articles/2007/06/04/man_wakes_from_19_year_coma_to_prettier_poland/

Sclafani, A., & Springer, D. (1976). Dietary obesity in adult rats: Similarities to hypothalamic and human obesity syndromes. *Physiology and Behavior, 17*, 461–471.

Segerstrom, S. C., & Miller, G. E. (2004). Psychological stress and the human immune system: A meta-analytic study of 30 years of inquiry. *Psychological Bulletin, 130*, 601–630.

Seligman, M. E. P. (1970). On the generality of the laws of learning. *Psychological Review, 77*, 406–418.

Seligman, M. E. P. (1974). Depression and learned helplessness. In R. J. Friedman & M. M. Katz (Eds.), *The psychology of depression: Contemporary theory and research* (pp. 83–113). Washington, DC: V. H. Winston.

Seligman, M. E. P. (1975). *Helplessness: On depression, development, and death.* San Francisco: Freeman.

Seligman, M. E. P. (2011). *Flourish.* New York: Simon & Schuster.

Seligman, M. E. P., & Csikszentmihalyi, M. (2000). Positive psychology: An introduction. *American Psychologist, 55*, 5–14.

Seligman, M. E. P., Steen, T. A., Park, N., & Peterson, C. (2005). Positive psychology progress: Empirical validation of interventions. *American Psychologist, 60*, 410–421.

Shapiro, A. F., Gottman, J. M., & Carrère, S. (2000). The baby and the marriage: Identifying factors that buffer against decline in marital satisfaction after the first baby arrives. *Journal of Family Psychology, 14*, 59–70.

Shedler, J., & Block, J. (1990). Adolescent drug use and psychological health: A longitudinal inquiry. *American Psychologist, 45*, 612–630.

Shenkin, S. D., Starr, J. M., & Deary, I. J. (2004). Birth weight and cognitive ability in childhood: A systematic review. *Psychological Bulletin, 130*, 989–1013.

Shephard, R. J. (1997). *Aging, physical activity, and health.* Champaign, IL: Human Kinetics Publishers.

Sher, K. J., Grekin, E. R., & Williams, N. A. (2005). The development of alcohol use disorders. *Annual Review of Clinical Psychology, 1*, 493–523.

Sherif, M., Harvey, O. J., White, B. J., Hood, W. R., & Sherif, C. W. (1961). *Intergroup cooperation and competition: The Robbers Cave experiment.* Norman, OK: University Book Exchange.

Sherman, D. K., McGue, M. K., & Iacono, W. G. (1997). Twin concordance for attention deficit hyperactivity disorder: A comparison of teacher's and mother's reports. *American Journal of Psychiatry, 154*, 532–535.

Sherman, S. J., Presson, C., Chassin, L., Corty, E., & Olshavsky, R. (1983). The false consensus effect in estimates of smoking prevalence: Underlying mechanisms. *Personality and Social Psychology Bulletin, 9*, 197–207.

Sherwin, B. B. (1988). A comparative analysis of the role of androgen in human male and female sexual behavior: Behavioral specificity, critical thresholds, and sensitivity. *Psychobiology, 16*, 416–425.

Sherwin, B. B. (1994). Sex hormones and psychological functioning in postmenopausal women. *Experimental Gerontology, 29*, 423–430.

Sherwin, B. B. (2008). Hormones, the brain, and me. *Canadian Psychology, 49*, 42–48.

Sherwood, R. A., Keating, J., Kavvadia, V., Greenough, A., & Peters, T. J. (1999). Substance misuse in early pregnancy and relationship to fetal outcome. *European Journal of Pediatrics, 158*, 488–492.

Siegler, I. C., Costa, P. T., Brummett, B. H., Helms, M. J., Barefoot, J. C., Williams, R., et al. (2003). Patterns of change in hostility from college to midlife in the UNC alumni heart study predict high-risk status. *Psychosomatic Medicine, 65*, 738–745.

Silber, M., Ancoli-Israel, S., Bonnet, M., Chokroverty, S., Grigg-Damberger, M., Hirshkowitz, M., et al. (2007). The visual scoring of sleep in adults. *Journal of Clinical Sleep Medicine, 3*, 121–131.

Silva, C. E., & Kirsch, I. (1992). Interpretive sets, expectancy, fantasy proneness, and dissociation as predictors of hypnotic response. *Journal of Personality and Social Psychology, 63*, 847–856.

Simner, J., Mulvenna, C., Sagiv, N., Tsakanikos, E., Witherby, S. A., Fraser, C., et al. (2006). Synaesthesia: The prevalence of atypical cross-modal experiences. *Perception, 35*, 1024–1033.

Simon, T. (2003). Photographer's foreword to *The Innocents.* [Electronic version]. Retrieved June 3, 2013, from http://www.pbs.org/wgbh/pages/frontline/shows/burden/innocents/

Simons, D. J., & Levin, D. T. (1998). Failure to detect changes to people during a real-world interaction. *Psychonomic Bulletin and Review, 5*, 644–649.

Sims, H. E. A., Goldman, R. F., Gluck, C. M., Horton, E., Kelleher, P., & Rowe, D. (1968). Experimental obesity in man. *Transactions of the Association of American Physicians, 81*, 153–170.

Sirois, B. C., & Burg, M. M. (2003). Negative emotion and coronary heart disease: A review. *Behavior Modification, 27*, 83–102.

Slovic, P., Finucane, M., Peters, E., & MacGregor, D. (2002). The affect heuristic. In T. Gilovich, D. Griffin, & D. Kahneman (Eds.), *Heuristics and biases: The psychology of intuitive judgment* (pp. 397–420). New York: Cambridge University Press.

Smith, C., & Lapp, L. (1991). Increases in number of REMs and REM density in humans following an intensive learning period. *Sleep, 14*, 325–330.

Smith, L. B., & Thelen, E. (2003, August). Development as a dynamic system. *Trends in Cognitive Sciences, 7*, 343–348.

Smith, T. W., Orleans, C. T., & Jenkins, C. D. (2004). Prevention and health promotion: Decades of progress, new challenges, and an emerging agenda. *Health Psychology, 23*, 126–131.

Solms, M. (2000). Dreaming and REM sleep are controlled by different brain mechanisms. *Behavioral and Brain Sciences, 23*, 793.

Sommerville, J. A., & Woodward, A. L. (2005). Pulling out the intentional structure of action: The relation between action processing and action production in infancy. *Cognition, 95*, 1–30.

Sorensen, T., Holst, C., Stunkard, A. J., & Skovgaard, L. T. (1992). Correlations of body mass index of adult adoptees and their biological and adoptive relatives. *International Journal of Obesity and Related Metabolic Disorders, 16*, 227–236.

Spanos, N. P., & Coe, W. C. (1992). A social-psychological approach to hypnosis. In E. Fromm & M. Nash (Eds.), *Contemporary hypnosis research* (pp. 102–130). New York: Guilford Press.

Spearman, C. (1904). "General intelligence," objectively determined and measured. *American Journal of Psychology, 15*, 201–293.

Spencer, S. J., Steele, C. M., & Quinn, D. M. (1999). Stereotype threat and women's math performance. *Journal of Experimental Social Psychology, 35*, 4–28.

Sperling, G. (1960). The information available in brief visual presentations. *Psychological Monographs, 74*, 1–29.

Spurr, K. F., Graven, M. A., & Gilbert, R. W. (2008). Prevalence of unspecified sleep apnea and the use of continuous positive airway pressure in hospitalized patients, 2004 national hospital discharge survey. *Sleep and Breathing, 12*, 229–234.

Squire, L. R., & Moore, R. Y. (1979). Dorsal thalamic lesion in a noted case of human memory dysfunction. *Annals of Neurology, 6*, 503–506.

Squire, L. R., Stark, C. E. L., & Clark, R. E. (2004). The medial temporal lobe. *Annual Review of Neuroscience, 27*(27), 279–306.

Stark, S. (2000, December 22). "Cast Away" lets Hanks fend for himself. *The Detroit News*. Retrieved from http://www.detnews.com

Steele, C. M., & Aronson, J. (1995). Stereotype threat and the intellectual test performance of African-Americans. *Journal of Personality and Social Psychology, 69*, 797–811.

Stein, J., & Richardson, A. (1999). Cognitive disorders: A question of misattribution. *Current Biology, 9*, R374–R376.

Stein, M. B., & Stein, D. J. (2008). Social anxiety disorder. *Lancet, 371*, 1115–1125.

Steinberg, L., & Sheffield, A. M. (2001). Adolescent development. *Journal of Cognitive Education and Psychology, 2*, 55–87.

Steiner, J. E. (1977). Facial expressions of the neonate infant indicating the hedonics of food-related chemical stimuli. In J. M. Weiffenbach (Ed.), *Taste and development* (pp. 173–189). Bethesda, MD: National Institutes of Health.

Stephenson, M. T., Hoyle, R. H., Palmgreen, P., & Slater. M. D. (2003). Brief measures of sensation seeking for screening and large-scale surveys. *Drug and Alcohol Dependence, 72*, 279–286.

Steriade, M. (1992). Basic mechanisms of sleep generation. *Neurology, 42*(Suppl. 6), 9–18.

Sternberg, R. J. (1986). A triangular theory of love. *Psychological Review, 93*, 119–135.

Sternberg, R. J. (1999). The theory of successful intelligence. *Review of General Psychology, 3*, 292–316.

Stice, E. (2002). Risk and maintenance factors for eating pathology: A meta-analytic review. *Psychological Bulletin, 128*, 825–848.

Stokes, M., Thompson, R., Cusack, R., & Duncan, J. (2009). Top-down activation of shape-specific population codes in visual cortex during mental imagery. *Journal of Neuroscience, 29*, 1565–1572.

Stokstad, E. (2001). New hints into the biological basis of autism. *Science, 294*, 34–37.

Stunkard, A. J. (1996). Current views on obesity. *American Journal of Medicine, 100*, 230–236.

Substance Abuse and Mental Health Services Administration (SAMHSA). (2011). Major depressive episode and treatment among adolescents: 2009. *National Survey on Drug Use and Health*. Retrieved June 3, 2013, from http://www.oas.samhsa.gov/2k11/009/AdolescentDepression.htm

Suchecki, D., Tiba, P., & Machado, R. (2012). REM sleep rebound as an adaptive response to stressful situations. *Frontiers in Neurology, 3*, 41.

Super, C. M. (1976). Environmental effects on motor development: The case of African precocity. *Developmental Medicine and Child Neurology, 18*, 561–567.

Svenson, O. (1981). Are we all less risky and more skillful than our fellow drivers? *Acta Psychologica, 47*, 143–148.

Swaab, D. F. (2004). Sexual differentiation of the human brain: Relevance for gender identity, transsexualism and sexual orientation. *Gynecological Endocrinology, 19*, 301–312.

Talarico, J. M., & Rubin, D. C. (2003). Confidence, not consistency, characterizes flashbulb memories. *Psychological Science, 14*, 455–461.

Talley, P. R., Strupp, H. H., & Morey, L. C. (1990). Matchmaking in psychotherapy: Patient-therapist dimensions and their impact on outcome. *Journal of Consulting and Clinical Psychology, 58*, 182–188.

Tandon, R., Keshavan, M. S., & Nasrallah, H. A. (2008). Schizophrenia, "Just the facts." What we know in 2008. 2. Epidemiology and etiology. *Schizophrenia Research, 102*, 1–18.

Tang, Y. Y., Ma, Y. H., Wang, J. H., Fan, Y. X., Feng, S. G., Lu, Q. L., et al. (2007). Short-term meditation training improves attention and self-regulation. *Proceedings of the National Academy of Sciences, USA, 104*, 17152–17156.

Tateyama, M., Asai, M., Kamisada, M., Hashimoto, M., Bartels, M., & Heimann, H. (1993). Comparison of schizophrenic delusions between Japan and Germany. *Psychopathology, 26*, 151–158.

Taylor, S. E. (2006). Tend and befriend: Biobehavioral bases of affiliation under stress. *Current Directions in Psychological Science, 15*, 273–277.

Taylor, S. E., & Brown, J. D. (1988). Illusion and well-being: A social psychological perspective on mental health. *Psychological Bulletin, 103*, 193–210.

Taylor, S. E., Lewis, B. P., Gruenewald, T. L., Gurung, R. A. R., Updegraff, J. A., & Klein, L. C. (2002). Sex differences in biobehavioral responses to threat: Reply to Geary and Flinn. *Psychological Review, 109*, 751–753.

Teller, D. Y., Morse, R., Borton, R., & Regal, C. (1974). Visual acuity for vertical and diagonal gratings in human infants. *Vision Research, 14*, 1433–1439.

Tesser, A. (1993). The importance of heritability: The case of attitudes. *Psychological Review, 100*, 129–142.

Tessler, L. G. (1997). How college students with learning disabilities can advocate for themselves. Retrieved June 3, 2013, from http://www.ldanatl.org/aboutld/adults/post_secondary/print_college.asp

Thoits, P. A. (2010). Stress and health: Major findings and policy implications. *Journal of Health and Social Behavior, 51*, 41–53.

Thompson, P. M., Hayashi, K. M., Simon, S. L., Geaga, J. A., Hong, M. S., Sui, Y., et al. (2004). Structural abnormalities in the brains of human subjects who use methamphetamine. *Journal of Neuroscience, 24*, 6028–6036.

Tickle, J. J., Sargent, J. D., Dalton, M. A., Beach, M. L., & Heatherton, T. F. (2001). Favorite movie stars, their tobacco use in contemporary movies and its association with adolescent smoking. *Tobacco Control, 10*, 16–22.

Tienari, P., Lahti, I., Sorri, A., Naarala, M., Moring, J., Kaleva, M., et al. (1990). Adopted-away offspring of schizophrenics and controls: The Finnish adoptive family study of schizophrenia. In L. Robins & M. Rutter (Eds.), *Straight and devious pathways from childhood to adulthood* (pp. 365–379). New York: Cambridge University Press.

Tienari, P., Wynne, L. C., Moring, J., Lahti, I., Naarala, M., Sorri, A., et al. (1994). The Finnish adoptive family study of schizophrenia: Implications for family research. *British Journal of Psychiatry, 23*(Suppl.), 20–26.

Tienari, P., Wynne, L. C., Sorri, A., Lahti, I., Laksy, K., Moring, J., et al. (2004). Genotype-environment interaction in schizophrenia spectrum disorder. *British Journal of Psychiatry, 184,* 216–222.

Tollefson, G. D. (1995). Selective serotonin reuptake inhibitors. In A. F. Schatzberg & C. B. Nemeroff (Eds.), *The American Psychiatric Press textbook of psychopharmacology* (1st ed., pp. 161–182). Washington, DC: American Psychiatric Press.

Tolman, E. C., & Honzik, C. H. (1930). Introduction and removal of reward, and maze performance in rats. *University of California Publications in Psychology, 4,* 257–275.

Tombs, S., & Silverman, I. (2004). Pupillometry: A sexual selection approach. *Evolution and Human Behavior, 25,* 221–228.

Tomkins, S. S. (1963). *Affect imagery consciousness: Vol. 2. The negative affects.* New York: Tavistock/Routledge.

Tong, F., Nakayama, K., Vaughan, J. T., & Kanwisher, N. (1998). Binocular rivalry and visual awareness in human extrastriate cortex. *Neuron, 21,* 753–759.

Torrey, E. F. (1999). Epidemiological comparison of schizophrenia and bipolar disorder. *Schizophrenia Research, 39,* 101–106.

Tracy, J. L., & Matsumoto, D. (2008). The spontaneous display of pride and shame: Evidence for biologically innate nonverbal displays. *Proceedings of the National Academy of Sciences, USA, 105,* 11655–11660.

Tracy, J. L., & Robins, R. W. (2008). The nonverbal expression of pride: Evidence for cross-cultural recognition. *Journal of Personality and Social Psychology, 94,* 516–530.

Treatment for Adolescents with Depression Study (TADS) Team. (2004). Fluoxetine, cognitive-behavioral therapy, and their combination for adolescents with depression: Treatment for Adolescents with Depression Study (TADS) randomized controlled trial. *Journal of the American Medical Association, 292,* 807–820.

Treffert, D. A., & Christensen, D. D. (2006, June/July). Inside the mind of a savant. *Scientific American Mind,* 50–55.

Treisman, A., & Gelade, G. (1980). A feature-integration theory of attention. *Cognitive Psychology, 12,* 97–136.

Triandis, H. C. (1989). The self and social behavior in differing cultural contexts. *Psychological Review, 96,* 506–520.

Trivers, R. L. (1971). The evolution of reciprocal altruism. *Quarterly Review of Biology, 46,* 35–57.

Trzesniewski, K. H., Donnellan, M. B., & Roberts, R. W. (2008). Is "generation me" really more narcissistic than previous generations? *Journal of Personality, 76,* 903–918.

Tugade, M. M., & Fredrickson, B. L. (2004). Resilient individuals use positive emotions to bounce back from negative emotional experiences. *Journal of Personality and Social Psychology, 86,* 320–333.

Tulving, E. (1972). Episodic and semantic memory. In E. Tulving & W. Donaldson (Eds.), *Organization of memory* (pp. 381–403). New York: Academic Press.

Twenge, J. M., Konrath, S., Foster, J. D., Campbell, K. W., & Bushman, B. J. (2008). Egos inflating over time: A cross-temporal meta-analysis of the narcissistic personality inventory. *Journal of Personality, 76,* 875–902.

United Nations Office on Drugs and Crime. (2009). World Drug Report 2009. Vienna, Austria: Author. Retrieved June 3, 2013, from http://www.unodc.org/unodc/en/data-and-analysis/WDR-2009.html

United States Bureau of Labor Statistics, U.S. Department of Labor. (2009). *Occupational outlook handbook, 2008–2009 edition: Psychologists.* Retrieved June 3, 2013, from http://www.bls.gov/oco/ocos056.htm

United States Department of Health and Human Services. (2001, January 8). Preventing disease and death from tobacco use [Press release]. Retrieved June 3, 2013, from http://archive.hhs.gov/news/press/2001pres/01fstbco.html

United States Department of Health and Human Services. (2008). Physical activity guidelines for Americans. Retrieved June 3, 2013, from http://www.health.gov/paguidelines

United States Department of Health and Human Services, Office of the Surgeon General (2004, May 27). *The health consequences of smoking: A report of the Surgeon General.* Retrieved June 3, 2013, from http://www.surgeongeneral.gov/library/reports/smokingconsequences

Upton, N. (1994). Mechanisms of action of new antiepileptic drugs: Rational design and serendipitous findings. *Trends in Pharmacological Sciences, 15,* 456–463.

Urberg, K. A., Degirmencioglue, S. M., Tolson, J. M., & Halliday-Scher, K. (1995). The structure of adolescent peer networks. *Developmental Psychology, 31,* 540–547.

Ustün, T. B., Ayuso-Mateos, J. L., Chatterji, S., Mathers, C., & Murray, C. J. (2004). Global burden of depressive disorders in the year 2000. *British Journal of Psychiatry, 184,* 386–392.

Vallabha, G. K., McClelland, J. L., Pons, F., Werker, J. F., & Amano, S. (2007). Unsupervised learning of vowel categories from infant-directed speech. *Proceedings of the National Academy of Sciences, USA, 104,* 13273–13278.

Van der Oord, S., Prins, P. J. M., Oosterlaan, J., & Emmelkamp, P. M. G. (2008). Efficacy of methylphenidate, psychosocial treatments and their combination in school-aged children with ADHD: A meta-analysis. *Clinical Psychology Review, 28,* 783–800.

van IJzendoom, M. H. (1995). Adult attachment representations, parental responsiveness, and infant attachment: A meta-analysis on the predictive validity of the Adult Attachment Interview. *Psychologial Bulletin, 117,* 387–403.

Vargas-Reighley, R. V. (2005). *Bicultural competence and academic resilience among immigrants.* El Paso, TX: LFB Scholarly Publishing.

Vargha-Khadem, F., Gadian, D. G., Watkins, K. E., Connelly, A., Van Paesschen, W., & Mishkin, M. (1997). Differential effects of early hippocampal pathology on episodic and semantic memory. *Science, 277,* 376–380.

Vazire, S. (2010). Who knows what about a person? The self-other knowledge asymmetry (SOKA) model. *Journal of Personality and Social Psychology, 98*, 281–300.

Vazire, S., & Carlson, E. N. (2011). Others sometimes know us better than we know ourselves. *Current Directions in Psychological Science, 20*, 104–108.

Vismera, L., & Rogers, S. (2010). Behavioral treatments in autism spectrum disorders: What do we know? *Annual Review of Clinical Psychology, 6*, 447–468.

Volkmar, F., Chawarska, K., & Klin, A. (2005). Autism in infancy and early childhood. *Annual Review of Psychology, 56*, 1–21.

Volkow, N. D. (2007, September). This is your brain on food. Interview by Kristin Leutwyler-Ozelli. *Scientific American, 297*, 84–85.

Volkow, N. D., Wang, G. J., & Baler, R. D. (2011). Reward, dopamine, and the control of food intake: Implications for obesity. *Trends in Cognitive Science, 15*, 37–46.

Waite, L. J. (1995). Does marriage matter? *Demography, 32*, 483–507.

Walker, E., Kestler, L., Bollini, A., & Hochman, K. M. (2004). Schizophrenia: Etiology and course. *Annual Review of Psychology, 55*, 401–430.

Walker, M. P., & Stickgold, R. (2006). Sleep, memory, and plasticity. *Annual Review of Psychology, 57*, 139–166.

Walton, G. M., & Spencer, S. J. (2009). Latent ability: Grades and test scores systematically underestimate the intellectual ability of negatively stereotyped students. *Psychological Science, 20*, 1132–1139.

Waltrip, R. W., Buchanan, R. W., Carpenter, W. T., Kirkpatrick, B., Summerfelt, A., Breier, A., et al. (1997). Borna disease virus antibodies and the deficit syndrome of schizophrenia. *Schizophrenia Research, 23*, 253–257.

Wamsley, E. J., Tucker, M., Payne, J. D., Benavides, J. A., & Stickgold, R. (2010). Dreaming of a learning task is associated with enhanced sleep-dependent memory consolidation. *Current Biology, 20*, 850–855.

Wardle, J., Carnell, S., Haworth, C. M., & Plomin, R. (2008). Evidence for a strong genetic influence on childhood adiposity despite the force of the obesogenic environment. *American Journal of Clinical Nutrition, 87*, 398–404.

Warren, Z., McPheeters, M., Sathe, N., Foss-Feig, J. H., Glasser, A., et al. (2011). A systematic review of early intensive intervention for autism spectrum disorders. *Pediatrics, 127*, e1303–1311.

Waters, E., Matas, L., & Sroufe, L. A. (1975). Infants' reactions to an approaching stranger: Description, validation, and functional significance of wariness. *Child Development, 46*, 348–356.

Watson, D., & Clark, L. A. (1997). Extraversion and its positive emotional core. In R. Hogan, J. Johnson, & S. Briggs (Eds.), *Handbook of personality psychology* (pp. 767–793). San Diego, CA: Academic Press.

Watson, D., Wiese, D., Vaidya, J., & Tellegen, A. (1999). The two general activation systems of affect: Structural findings, evolutionary considerations, and psychobiological evidence. *Journal of Personality and Social Psychology, 76*, 820–838.

Watson, J. B. (1924). *Behaviorism.* New York: Norton.

Wegner, D., Shortt, J., Blake, A., & Page, M. (1990). The suppression of exciting thoughts. *Journal of Personality and Social Psychology, 58*, 409–418.

Weiner, B. (1974). *Achievement motivation and attribution theory.* Morristown, NJ: General Learning Press.

Weiss, A., Bates, T. C., & Luciano, M. (2008). Happiness is a personal(ity) thing: The genetics of personality and well-being in a representative sample. *Psychological Science, 19*, 205–210.

Weissman, M. M., Bland, R. C., Canino, G. J., Greenwald, S., Hwu, H. G., Lee, C. K., et al. (1994). The cross national epidemiology of obsessive compulsive disorder. The cross national collaborative group. *Journal of Clinical Psychiatry, 55*, 5–10.

Wells, G. L. (2008). Field experiments on eyewitness identification: Towards a better understanding of pitfalls and prospects. *Law and Human Behavior, 32*, 6–10.

Wells, G. L., Small, M., Penrod, S., Malpass, R. S., Fulero, S. M., & Brimacombe, C. A. E. (1998). Eyewitness identification procedures: Recommendations for lineups and photospreads. *Law and Human Behavior, 22*, 603–647.

West, G., Anderson, A., & Pratt, J. (2009). Motivationally significant stimuli show visual prior entry: Direct evidence for attentional capture. *Journal of Experimental Psychology: Human Perception and Performance, 35*, 1032–1042.

Westen, D. (1998). The scientific legacy of Sigmund Freud: Toward a psychodynamically informed psychological science. *Psychological Bulletin, 124*, 333–371.

Weyandt, L. L., Janusis, G., Wilson, K., Verdi, G., Paquin, G., Lopes, J., et al. (2009). Nonmedical prescription stimulant use among a sample of college students: Relationships with psychological variables. *Journal of Attention Disorders, 13*, 284–296.

Whalen, C. K. (1989). Attention deficit and hyperactivity disorders. In T. H. Ollendick & M. Herson (Eds.), *Handbook of child psychopathology* (2nd ed., pp. 131–169). New York: Plenum Press.

Whalen, P. J., Rauch, S. L., Etcoff, N. L., McInerney, N. L., Lee, M. B., & Jenike, M. A. (1998). Masked presentations of emotional facial expressions modulate amygdala activity without explicit knowledge. *Journal of Neuroscience, 18*, 411–418.

Wheatley, T., & Haidt, J. (2005). Hypnotic disgust makes moral judgments more severe. *Psychological Science, 16*, 780–784.

Wierson, M., Long, P. J., & Forehand, R. L. (1993). Toward a new understanding of early menarche: The role of environmental stress in pubertal timing. *Adolescence, 28*, 913–924.

Wilens, T. E., Faraone, S. V., & Biederman, J. (2004). Attention-deficit/hyperactivity disorder in adults. *Journal of the American Medical Association, 292*, 619–623.

Wilfley, D. E., Bishop, M., Wilson, G. T., & Agras, W. S. (2007). Classification of eating disorders: Toward *DSM-V. International Journal of Eating Disorders, 40*(Suppl.), S123–S129.

Williams, K., Harkins, S. G., & Latané, B. (1981). Identifiability as a deterrent to social loafing: Two cheering experiments. *Journal of Personality and Social Psychology, 40*, 303–311.

Williams, L. E., & Bargh, J. A. (2008). Experiences of physical warmth influence interpersonal warmth. *Science, 322*, 606–607.

Williams, R. B., Jr. (1987). Refining the type A hypothesis: Emergence of the hostility complex. *American Journal of Cardiology, 60,* 27J–32J.

Wills, T. A., DuHamel, K., & Vaccaro, D. (1995). Activity and mood temperament as predictors of adolescent substance use: Test of a self-regulation mediational model. *Journal of Personality and Social Psychology, 68,* 901–916.

Wilsnack, R. W., Wilsnack, S. C., & Obot, I. S. (2005). Why study gender, alcohol and culture? In I. S. Obot & R. Room (Eds.), *Alcohol, gender and drinking problems: Perspectives from low and middle income countries* (pp. 1–23). Geneva, Switzerland: World Health Organization.

Wilson, A. E., & Ross, M. (2001). From chump to champ: People's appraisals of their earlier and present selves. *Journal of Personality and Social Psychology, 80,* 572–584.

Wilson, M. A., & McNaughton, B. L. (1994). Reactivation of hippocampal ensemble memories during sleep. *Science, 265,* 676–679.

Wise, R. A., & Rompre, P. P. (1989). Brain dopamine and reward. *Annual Review of Psychology, 40,* 191–225.

Wolpe, J. (1997). Thirty years of behavior therapy. *Behavior Therapy, 28,* 633–635.

Wood, J. M., Garb, H. N., Lilienfeld, S. O., & Nezworski, M. T. (2002). Clinical assessment. *Annual Review of Psychology, 53,* 519–543.

Woodworth, M., & Porter, S. (2002). In cold blood: Characteristics of criminal homicides as a function of psychopathy. *Journal of Abnormal Psychology, 111,* 436–445.

World Health Organization. (2008). WHO Report on the global tobacco epidemic. Retrieved June 3, 2013, from http://www.who.int/tobacco/mpower/en/

World Health Organization. (2011). The top ten causes of death [Fact sheet]. Retrieved June 3, 2013, from http://www.who.int/mediacentre/factsheets/fs310/en/index.html

Worley, H. (2006, June). Depression: A leading contributor to global burden of disease: Myriad obstacles—particularly stigma—block better treatment in developing countries. Retrieved June 3, 2013, from http://www.prb.org/Articles/2006/DepressionaLeadingContributortoGlobalBurdenofDisease.aspx

Yerkes, R. M., & Dodson, J. D. (1908). The relation of strength of stimulus to rapidity of habit formation. *Journal of Comparative Neurology & Psychology, 18,* 459–482.

Yeshurun, Y., & Sobel, N. (2010). An odor is not worth a thousand words: From multidimensional odors to unidimensional odor objects. *Annual Review of Psychology, 61,* 219–241.

Yoo, S. S., Hu, P. T., Gujar, N., Jolesz, F. A., & Walker, M. P. (2007). A deficit in the ability to form new human memories without sleep. *Nature Neuroscience, 10,* 385–392.

Zahn-Waxler, C., & Robinson, J. (1995). Empathy and guilt: Early origins of feelings of responsibility. In J. P. Tangney & K. W. Fischer (Eds.), *Self-conscious emotions: The psychology of shame, guilt, embarrassment, and pride* (pp. 143–173). New York: Guilford Press.

Zajonc, R. B. (1968). Attitudinal effects of mere exposure. *Journal of Personality and Social Psychology Monographs, 9,* 1–27.

Zajonc, R. B. (1980). Feeling and thinking: Preferences need no inferences. *American Psychologist, 35,* 151–175.

Zajonc, R. B. (2001). Mere exposure: A gateway to the subliminal. *Current Directions in Psychological Science, 10,* 224–228.

Zametkin, A. J., Nordahl, T. E., Gross, M., King, A. C., Stemple, W. E., Rumsey, J., et al. (1990). Cerebral glucose metabolism in adults with hyperactivity of childhood onset. *New England Journal of Medicine, 323,* 1361–1366.

Ziv, N., & Goshen, M. (2006). The effect of "sad" and "happy" background music on the interpretation of a story in 5- to 6-year-old children. *British Journal of Music Education, 23,* 303–314.

Zorrilla, E. P., Iwasaki, S., Moss, J. A., Chang, J., Otsuji, J., Inoue, K., et al. (2006). Vaccination against weight gain. *Proceedings of the National Academy of Sciences, USA, 103,* 13226–13231.

PERMISSIONS ACKNOWLEDGMENTS

Title spread: (photo) Shutterstock

CHAPTER 1

Opener: (photo) Getty Images/Cultura RF

Fig. 1.1: provided by the Raffaele family

Fig. 1.2: FS2 WENN Photos/Newscom

Fig. UN1.1, p. 6: (left to right) Will Steacy/Getty Images; Paper Boat Creative/Getty Images; Blue Jean Images/SuperStock; Prisma/SuperStock; iStockphoto

Fig. 1.3: (photo) Blue Jean Images/Alamy

Fig. 1.4: (a) UpperCut Images/Alamy; (b) Juice Images/Alamy; (c) Jim West/Photo Edit

Fig. UN1.2, p. 9: Geomphotography/Alamy

Fig. 1.6: Center for the History of Psychology/The University of Akron

Fig. 1.8: (photo) YAY Media AS/Alamy

Fig. 1.12: BSIP SA/Alamy

Fig. UN1.3: from *American Journal of Psychology* © 1974 by the Board of Trustees of the University of Ilinois. Used with permission of the University of Illinois Press

Fig. 1.15: Exactostock/SuperStock

Fig. 1.17: Jeff Greenberg/Getty Images

Fig. 1.19: Lisa Peardon/Getty Images

Fig. UN1.4, p. 19: (top to bottom) SIU/Peter Arnold Images; Stockbyte/Alamy; Somos Images LLC/Alamy; Bruno De Hogues/Getty

Fig. 1.20: Levitin, D. J., and Menon, V. (2003)

Fig. 1.21a: (a) Augusta Chronicle/ZUMAPRESS/Alamy; (b) Han Myung-Gu/WireImage/Getty Images

Fig. 1.24: (photos, top to bottom) Ocean/Corbis; Steve Skjold/Photo Edit; Ace Stock Limited/Alamy; Christy Varonfakis Johnson/Alamy

Fig. 1.26: (left) Lawrence S. Sugiyama/University of Oregon/(right) Karl Ammann/Corbis

Fig. UN1.5, p. 27: Roethlisberger, F. J., & Dickson, W. J. (1939). Management and the worker: An account of a research program conducted by the Western Electric Company, Hawthorne Works, Chicago. Cambridge, MA: Harvard University Press

Fig. 1.27: (left) Janine Wiedel Photolibrary/(right) Alamy; John Birdsall/The Image Works

Fig. 1.28: (left) AP Photo/Jason DeCrow; (right) Kateleen Foy/Getty Images

Fig. 1.29: Peter Arnold, Inc./Alamy

Fig. UN1.4, p. 31: Annie Engel/Corbis

Fig. 1.32: Marmaduke St. John/Alamy

CHAPTER 2

Opener: (photo) Joe McBride/Getty Images

Fig. 2.1: David Aguilera/BuzzFoto/FilmMagic/Getty Images

Fig. UN2.1, p. 41: Alamy

Fig. 2.3: James Cavallini/Photo Researchers

Fig. 2.7: Newscom

Fig. 2.8: SuperStock

Fig. UN2.2, p. 48: Getty Images/Cultura RF

Fig. 2.9: (a) Alamy; (b) Bettmann/CORBIS

Fig. 2.10: (a) *Nature Reviews Neuroscience 5*, 812–819 (October 2004)

Fig. 2.11: (a) AJPhoto/Photo Researchers; James Cavallini/Photo Researchers; (b) Mark Harmel/Alamy; Courtesy of Psych Central; (c) Marcello Massimini/University of Wisconsin-Madison; Dr K Singh, Liverpool University/Dr S Hamdy & Dr Q Aziz, Manchester University

Fig. 2.18: from Penfield, Wilder (1958), The excitable cortex in conscious man. Liverpool University Press

Fig. 2.20: (a) Collection of Jack and Beverly Wilgus; (b) www.hbs.deakin.edu.au/gagepage/pgage.htm; (c) Hanna Damasio, © 2004 Massachusetts Medical Society

Fig. 2.21: Bettmann/Corbis

Fig. UN2.5, p. 62: Alamy

Fig. 2.24: AP Photo/Courtesy of Harpo Studios, Inc., George Burns

Fig. 2.25: Conor Caffrey/Science Source

Fig. UN2.6, p. 67: Harry B. Clay, Jr.

Fig. 2.26: (a) Tony Freeman/PhotoEdit/(b) Bob Sacha

Fig. 2.27: provided by the Mack family

Fig. UN2.7, p. 71: AP Photo

Fig. UN2.8, p. 72: incamerastock/Alamy

Fig. 2.28: Indiana University School of Medicine

CHAPTER 3

Opener: (photo) Sverre Haugland/Image Source/Corbis

Fig. 3.1: (a) Courtesy Michael Schiavo/(b) Bogdan Hrywniak/AFP/Getty Images

Fig. 3.2: Blend Images/SuperStock

Fig. UN3.1, p. 80: JGI/Daniel Grill/Getty Images

Fig. UN3.2, p. 81: The Photo Works

Fig. 3.9: (photo) James King-Holmes/Photo Researchers

Fig. 3.12: Blickwinkel/Alamy

Fig. 3.13: Chris Rout/Alamy

Fig. 3.14: PHOTOTAKE Inc./Alamy

Fig. UN3.5, p. 96: (a) Greg Ceo/Getty Images; (b) Heidi Coppock-Beard/Getty Images

Fig. UN3.6, p. 97: Radius Images/Alamy

Fig. 3.15: *Science 8*, September 2006, Vol. 313, no. 5792, p. 1402DOI, Fig. 1: 10

Fig. 3.16: Newscom

Fig. 3.17: David Young-Wolff/Getty Images

Fig. 3.18: Ed Kashi/Corbis

Fig. 3.19: Eckehard Schulz/AP

Fig. 3.21: Kim, S. J., Lyoo, I. K., Hwang, J., Chung, A., Hoon Sung, Y., Kim, J., Kwon, D. H., Chang, K. H., & Renshaw, P. F. (2006)

Fig. 3.22: Multnomah County Sheriff's Office

Fig. 3.23: fifth edition of the textbook *Biological Psychology: An Introduction to Behavioral, Cognitive, and Clinical Neuroscience,* by Breedlove, Rosenzweig, and Watson (Sinauer Associates)

Fig. 3.25: (a) Janine Wiedel Photolibrary/Alamy; (b) Blend Images/SuperStock

CHAPTER 4

Opener: (photo) Rhea Anna/Gallery Stock

Fig. 4.1: Sebastien Micke/Paris Match via Getty Images

Fig. 4.2: (photos, clockwise from upper left) Getty Images; Ellen Senisi/The Image Works; Gale Zucker/Getty Images

Fig. 4.3: (a) Dr. Yorgos Nikas/Phototake; (b) Petit Format/Photo Researchers; (c) Biophoto Associates/Photo Researchers, Inc.

Fig. 4.5: Gallo Images/Alamy

Fig. 4.6: AP Photo/Baptist Hospital

Fig. 4.7: courtesy of Sterling K. Clarren, MD, Clinical Professor of Pediatrics, University of British Columbia Faculty of Medicine

Fig. 4.8: (a) Peter Turnley/CORBIS; (b) From studies conducted by researchers from the ChildTrauma Academy (www.ChildTrauma.org) led by Bruce D. Perry, M.D., Ph.D.; (c) Yagi Studio/Getty Images

Fig. 4.9: (a & b) Bubbles Photolibrary/Alamy; (c) Petit Format/Photo Researchers

Fig. 4.11: (clockwise from upper left) Sergio Pitamitz/Marka/AgeFotostock I; Panos Pictures; Larry Mayer/Billings Gazette/AP; Monica Almeida/The New York Times/Redux

Fig. 4.12: Stock Boston, LLC/Spencer Grant

Fig. 4.14: Ashley Gill/Getty Images

Fig. UN4.1, p. 125: Nina Leen/Time Life Pictures/Getty Images

Fig. 4.15: (photo) James R. Clarke/Alamy

Fig. UN4.3, p. 128: Angela Georges/Getty Images

Fig. 4.17: Bill Anderson/Photo Researchers

Fig. 4.19: (top to bottom) Sally and Richard Greenhill/Alamy; Tom Mareschal/Alamy; Alamy; Jon Feingersh/Getty Images

Figure 4.20: Marmaduke St. John/Alamy

Fig. 4.21: Sarah Grison

Fig. 4.24: (photo) Ellen Senisi/The Image Works

Fig. 4.26: (a) ClassicStock.com/SuperStock; (b) Exactostock/SuperStock

Fig. 4.27: courtesy David Reimer; from Colapinto, John, As nature made him: The boy who was raised as a girl (2000), HarperCollins Publishers Inc.

Fig. 4.28: Reuters Newsmedia Inc./Corbis

Fig. 4.29: (a) Gale Zucker/Getty Images ; (b) Peter Turnley/Corbis

Fig. UN4.6, p. 142: Alamy

Fig. 4.30: Chris McGrath/Getty Images

Fig. 4.31: (a) Alamy; (b) R. Matina/Agefotostock; (c) Alamy

Fig. 4.32: Stephanie Maze/Corbis

Fig. 4.33: Getty Images

CHAPTER 5

Opener: (photo) Shutterstock

Fig. UN5.1, p. 156: Road & Track Magazine/Richard Ba/Transtock/Corbis

Fig. 5.4: (photo) Blend Images/SuperStock

Fig. UN5.3, p. 159: PhotoAlto/Alamy

Fig. 5.5: (photo) Karolina Webb/Alamy

Fig. 5.6: (photo) GlowImages/Alamy

Fig. 5.14: (a) Rick Price/Getty Images; (b) A Hawthorne/Arctic Photo

Fig. 5.16: (photo) Kumar Sriskandan/Alamy

Fig. 5.17: From *The Art Pack* by Christopher Frayling, Helen Frayling, and Ron Van der Meer, copyright 1992 by Singram Company Ltd. *The Art Pack* copyright 1992 by Van der Meer Paper Design Ltd. Text copyright 1992 by Christopher & Helen Frayling. Copyright 1992 by The Art Pack. Used by permission of Alfred A. Knopf, a division of Random House, Inc.

Fig. UN5.5, p. 174: Marcos Welsh/AgeFotostock

Fig. 5.18: (photo) Image Source/Getty Images

Fig. 5.20: (photo) Stephen Dalton/NHPA

Fig. UN5.6, p. 180: Linus Gelber/Alert the Medium/Getty Images

Fig. 5.21: Marcy Maloy/Getty Images

Fig. UN5.7, p. 181: (left) Steven Errico/Digital Vision/Getty Images; (right) Jose Luis Pelaez Inc./Blend Images/Getty Images

Fig. 5.22: (photo) Anna Zielinska/Getty Images

Fig. UN5.8, p. 184: Blend Images/SuperStock

Fig. 5.23: (photo) John Bazemore/AP

Fig. UN5.9, p. 187: Westend61 GmbH/Alamy

Fig. 5.24: Art Directors & TRIP/Alamy

Fig. 5.25: (a) Jose Luis Pelaez Inc/Getty Images; (b) Andre Bernardo/Getty Images

CHAPTER 6

Opener: (man and dog) Bela Szandelszky/AP/Corbis; (tree background) Shutterstock

Fig. 6.1: Angelo Gandolfi/Nature Picture Library

Fig. 6.2a: (a) Mark Peterson/Corbis; (b) Dave & Les Jacobs/Blend Images/Corbis

Fig. UN6.3, p. 198: iStockphoto

Fig. 6.3: (photo) Bettmann/Corbis

Fig. 6.4: courtesy Everett Collection

Fig. 6.6: (a) Scott Camazine/Alamy; (b) Alamy; (c) Journal-Courier/Steve Warmowski/The Image Works

Fig. 6.7: Archives of the History of American Psychology, The Center for the History of Psychology, The University of Akron

Fig. 6.8: Alamy

Fig. 6:10: (photo) Yerkes, Robert M. Manuscripts & Archives, Yale University

Fig. 6.13: Sozaijiten/Datacraft/Getty Images

Fig. 6.16: Getty Images/Comstock Images

Fig. 6.17: Mary Kate Denny/Photo Edit

Fig. UN6.4, p. 217: Hero Images/Corbis

Fig. 6.18: Javier M. Gonzalez

Fig. UN6.5, p. 221: Albert Bandura, Dept. of Psychology, Stanford University

Fig. 6.20: Ronnie Kaufman/Larry Hirshowitz/Getty Images

Fig. 6.21: Geri Engberg/The Image Works

Fig. 6.22: Francois Duhamel/© Columbia Pictures/courtesy Everett Collection

Fig. 6.23: Penny Tweedie/Getty Images

Fig. UN6.7, p. 224: David J. Green—Lifestyle/Alamy

Fig. 6.24: F. B. M. deWaal

CHAPTER 7

Opener: (photo) Gallery Stock

Fig. 7.1: AP Photo/Alex Brandon

Fig. 7.2: (photo) Image Source/Getty Images

Fig. 7.3: Alamy

Fig. UN7.2, p. 234: courtesy Daniel J. Simons

Fig. 7.6: Keith R. Allen/Getty Images/Flickr RF

Fig. UN7.3, p. 237: Erik Reis/agefotostock

Fig. 7.12: Suzanne Corkin, used with permission of The Wylie Agency LLC

Fig. 7.15: (a) David Turnley/Getty Images; (b) Newscom

Fig. 7.17: (a) Tips Images/Tips Italia Srl a socio unico/Alamy; (b) Michael Blann/Getty Images

Fig. 7.18: (a) Flirt/SuperStock; (b) Stephen Morris/Getty Images

Fig. 7.20: from Wheeler, M. E., Petersen, S. E., & Buckner, R. L. (2000). Memory's echo: vivid remembering reactivates sensory specific cortex. *Proceedings of the National Academy of Sciences, 97,* 11125–11129

Fig. UN7.5, p. 253: iStockphoto

Fig. 7.21: Focus Features/courtesy Everett Collection

Fig. 7.22: (photo) Chris A. Crumley/Alamy

Fig. 7.25: Robert E. Klein/AP

Fig. 7.26: (a) AP Photo/Charles Krupa; (b) Spencer Platt/Getty Images

Fig. 7.27: Joe Raedle/Getty Images

Fig. 7.28: AP/Wide World Photos

Fig. 7.29: Tony Gutierrez/AP

CHAPTER 8

Opener: (photo) Muro/F1 Online/Corbis

Fig. 8.1a: (a) Rex Features via AP Images; (b) Michele Sibiloni/AFP/Getty Images

Fig. 8.4: (a) Richard A. Cooke/Corbis; (b) Renee Jones Schneider/Minneapolis Star Tribune/ZUMAPRESS.com/Alamy

Fig. 8.7: Wong Pun Keung/Xinhua Press/Corbis

Fig. UN8.1, p. 274: (right side up, left to right) imagebroker/Alamy; Steven Vidler/Eurasia Press/Corbis; Warner Bros./Courtesy Everett Collection; Artisan Entertainment/Courtesy Everett Collection

Fig. 8.9: Peter Arnold, Inc./Alamy

Fig. 8.10: (a) Ryan Mcvay/Getty Images; (b) Gregor Schlaeger/VISUM/The Image Works

Fig. UN8.2, p. 276: Dalton, M. A., Bernhardt, A. M., Gibson, J. J., Sargent, J. D., Beach, M. L., Adachi-Mejia, A. M., Titus-Ernstoff, L. T., & Heatherton, T. F. (2005). "Honey, have some smokes." Preschoolers use cigarettes and alcohol while role playing as adults. *Archives of Pediatrics & Adolescent Medicine, 159,* 854–859

Fig. 8.11: (a) STR/Rene Werse/AFP/Getty Images; (b) JSP Studios/Alamy

Fig. 8.12: Mario Tama/Getty Images

Fig. 8.13: Larry Downing/Reuters/Landov

Fig. 8.14a–b: courtesy Sheena Iyengar. Iyengar, S. S., & Lepper, M. R. (2000). *Journal of Personality and Social Psychology, 79,* 995–1006

Fig. UN8.3, p. 281: Laura Dwight/Photo Edit

Fig. 8.17: American Philosophical Society

Fig. 8.20: (a) Interfoto/Alamy; (b) Meghann Myers/Medill News Service/MCT via Getty Images; (c) Jeff Kravitz/FilmMagic/Getty Images: (d) AP Photo/Red Bull Stratos; (e) Jason LaVeris/FilmMagic/Getty Images

Fig. UN8.4, p. 291: vario images GmbH & Co. KG/Alamy

Fig. 8.27: (a) Image Source/Alamy; (b) Alamy

Fig. 8.29: Syracuse Newspapers/Caroline Chen/The Image Works

Fig. 8.34: Jim Ross for *The New York Times*

Fig. 8.35: Dan Kitwood/Getty Images

Fig. 8.36: (a) Image Source/Alamy; (b) Mandel Ngan/AFP/Getty Images

CHAPTER 9

Opener: (photo) Getty Images/Blend Images

Fig. 9.1: (a) Martin Schoeller; (b) Emmanuel Dunand/AFP/GettyImages

Fig. 9.2: (a) Cultura Creative/Alamy; (b) Tetra Images/Alamy; (c) Chad Ehlers/Alamy; (d) Jose Luis Pelaez Inc./Getty Images

Fig. UN9.1: (left) Tim Gainey/Alamy; (right) Bill Aron/Photo Edit

Fig. 9.7: (a) Radius Images/Alamy; (b) 2happy/Alamy

Fig. 9.8: (a) Bruce Forster/Getty Images; (b) MBI/Alamy

Fig. UN9.2, p. 317: Heather Bragman/Syracuse Newspapers/The Image Works

Fig. 9.10: Alberto Pomares/Getty Images

Fig. 9.11: (a) Anyka/Alamy; (b) Susanna Blavarg/Getty Images

Fig. 9.12: Reuters/Corbis

Fig. UN9.3, p. 326: www.beautycheck.de

Fig. 9.16: Fred R. Conrad/The New York Times/Redux

Fig. 9.17: (a) Peter Casolino/Alamy; (b) Marmaduke St. John/Alamy

Fig. 9.19: courtesy of W. W. Norton & Co., Inc.

Fig. 9.22: Chris Lisle/Corbis

Fig. UN9.4, p. 334: Andrew Burton/Reuters/Newscom

Fig. 9.25: Aviezer, H., Hassin, R. R., Ryan, J., Grady, C., Susskind, J., Anderson, A., Moscovitch, M., & Bentin, S.

Fig. UN9.6, p. 339: Ekman (1972-2004)

Fig. UN9.4: Facial and emotional reactions to Duchenne and non-Duchenne smiles. *International Journal of Psychophysiology 29*, 1, 1 June 1998, 23-33. Photo courtesy of Veikko Surakka

Fig. 9.26: Tracy & Matsumoto (2008)/courtesy of Jessica Tracy

Fig. 9.27: Brian H. Thomas/Alamy

Fig. 9.28: courtesy of Dacher Keltner

CHAPTER 10

Opener: (photo) Shutterstock

Fig. 10.1: Jim Mahoney/Dallas Morning News

Fig. 10.2: Ana Nance/Redux

Fig. 10.5: (photo) Tim Hill/Food and Drink/SuperStock

Fig. 10.6: (a) Sam Edwards/Getty Images; (b) nobleIMAGES/Alamy

Fig. 10.7: (a) Douglas Peebles/Photolibrary; (b) Francois Guillot/AFP/Getty Images

Fig. 10.8: (a) Teh Eng Koon/AFP/Getty; (b) Travel Ink/Getty Images

Fig. 10.10: Lisa Peardon/Getty Images

Fig. 10.11: (a) Bon Appetit/Alamy; (b) yellowdog/Getty Images

Fig. 10.12: (a) Stan Honda/AFP/Getty Images; (b) Jeff Greenberg/Alamy

Fig. UN10.3, p. 363: Marc Romanelli/Alamy

Fig. 10.14: Bertram Henry/Getty Images

Fig. UN10.4, p. 364: Purestock/Getty Images

Fig. 10.15: Mel Yates/Getty Images

Fig. 10.17: (a) Dex Image/Alamy; (b) Jetta Productions/Getty Images; (c) Digital Vision/Getty Images

Fig. 10.18: (a) Peter Dazeley/Getty Images; (b) SuperStock

Fig. UN10.5, p. 369: Corbis

Fig. 10.19: (a) AP Photo/Ross D. Franklin; (b) AP Photo/Altaf Qadri

Fig. UN10.5, p. 371: Digital Vision/Getty Images

Fig. 10.21: AFP/Getty Images

Fig. 10.23: Alamy

Fig. 10.24: David J. Green—lifestyle themes/Alamy

CHAPTER 11

Opener: (photo) Getty Images

Fig. 11.1: AP Photo/Julio Cortez

Fig. 11.2: (photo) Blend Images/Alamy

Fig. 11.3: Mike Kittrell/The Press-Register/Landov

Fig. 11.4: (a) Ryan Remorz/The Canadian Press; (b) Chelsea Lauren/WireImage/Getty Images

Fig. 11.5: Ronald Zak/AP

Fig. 11.6: (photos) courtesy Keith Pyne, Washington University

Fig. 11.7a: (a) Glyn Kirk/AFP/Getty Images; (b) Clive Brunskill/Getty Images

Fig. 11.8: (photo) David S. Holloway/Getty Images

Fig. UN11.1, p. 390: The Star-Ledger/Aristide Economopoulos/The Image Works

Fig. 11.9: Jeff Kravitz/FilmMagic/Getty Images

Fig. 11.10: Paul Robbins/Alamy

Fig. 11.12: courtesy of Terp Weekly Edition

Fig. UN11.12, p. 394: Drazen Vukelic/Getty Images

Fig. 11.14: (a) Gabriel Bouys/AFP/GettyImages; (b) David J. Green—work themes/Alamy

Fig. 11.15: (a) AP; (b) Philip G. Zimbardo, PhD

Fig. 11.16: (a) Joe Robbins/Getty Images; (b) SMI/Newscom

Fig. UN11.3, p. 398: Kablonk/SuperStock

Fig. 11.17: (a) Hybrid Images/Getty images; (b) Mohamed Omar/EPA/Landov

Fig. 11.20: Belinda Images/SuperStock

Fig. 11.23: Andrew Burton/Reuters/Newscom

Fig. 11.24: New York Times Pictures

Fig. 11.26: AP Photo/Ramon Espinosa

Fig. UN11.06, p. 410: from Perrett, D. I., May, K. A., & Yoshikawa, S. (1994). Facial shape and judgments of female attractiveness. Reprinted by permission from *Nature*, 1994, vol. 386, 238-242. Copyright 2002 Macmillan Publishers Ltd. Images courtesy D. I. Perrett, University of St. Andrews

Fig. 11.27: from Langlois, J. H., & Ruggerman, L. A. (1990). Attractive faces are only average. *Psychological Science 1*, 115-121. Photographs courtesy Judith Hall Langlois, UT Austin

Fig. 11.28: (a) VStock/Alamy; (b) Asia Images Group Pte Ltd/Alamy

Fig. 11.29: Catchlight Visual Services/Alamy

Fig. UN11.7, p. 413: Gabe Palmer/Alamy

CHAPTER 12

Opener: (photo) Dave & Les Jacobs/Blend Images/Corbis

Fig. 12.2: Josef Lindau/Corbis

Fig. 12.9: (a) Kyodo via AP Images; (b) David R. Frazier Photolibrary, Inc./Alamy

Fig. UN12.1, p. 425: GoGo Images Corporation/Alamy

Fig. 12.11: (a) JB Lacroix/WireImage/Getty Images; (b) NBCU Photo Bank via Getty Images; (c) George Napolitano/FilmMagic/Getty Images

Fig. 12.13: iStockphoto

Fig. 12.14: Jessica Peterson/Tetra Images/Corbis

Fig. 12.15: Imaginechina/Corbis

Fig. 12.16: (photo) Masterfile

Fig. UN12.04, p. 438: courtesy Dr. Christine Drea

Fig. 12.19: (a) Big Cheese Photo/Corbis; (b) Tony Freeman/PhotoEdit

Fig. 12.20: (a) Photodisc/Getty Images; (b) Agnieszka Kirinicjanow/Getty Images; (c) Randy Faris/Corbis

Fig. 12.25: (a) Westend61 GmbH/Alamy; (b) SuperStock

Fig. 12.26: (photo) Bill Aron/Photo Edit

Fig. 12.27: Tek Image/Photo Researchers

Fig. UN12.4, p. 449: John Birdsall/The Image Works

Fig. 12.29: (a) Alamy; (b) Martin Thomas Photography/Alamy

CHAPTER 13

Opener: (photo) Vetta/Getty Images

Fig. 13.1: courtesy of Carol Todd

Fig. 13.3: David Hoffman/Photo Library/Alamy

Fig. 13.7: courtesy of Richard F. Kaplan

Fig. 13.8: Francisco Jose de Goya y Lucientes (1746-1828), *The Witches' Sabbath* (oil on canvas)/Museo Lazaro Galdiano, Madrid, Spain/Giraudon/The Bridgeman Art Library

Fig. 13.12: Ronald C. Modra/Sports Imagery/Getty Images

Fig. 13.13: Charles Eshelman/FilmMagic/Getty Images

Fig. UN13.1: (left) PhotoStock-Israel/Photo Edit; (middle) Carl E. Schwartz et al., *Science 300*, 1952 (2003); DOI: 10.1126/science.1083703

Fig. 13.15: Paul Zimmerman/Getty Images

Fig. 13.17: NIMH National Institute of Mental Health

Fig. UN13.3, p. 472: YouTube

Fig. 13.19: Jason LaVeris/Getty Images

Fig. 13.21: Thomas Traill

Fig. 13.22: (top to bottom) *Cat and Her Kittens,* Louis Wain (1860-1939)/private collection/photo © Bonhams, London, UK/The Bridgeman Art Library; Eileen Tweedy/The Art Archive at Art Resource, NY; © Lebrecht Music and Arts Photo Library/Alamy

Fig. UN13.02, p. 478: Mary Evans/Universal Pictures/Dreamworks/Imagine Entertainment/Ronald Grant/Everett Collection

Fig. 13.24: Joe McNally

Fig. 13.26: AP Photo

Fig. 13.27: courtesy of Everett Collection

Fig. 13.28: *Abnormal Psychology,* 4th ed., by Seligman, Walker, and Rosenhan. Copyright W. W. Norton & Company, Inc. Used by permission of W. W. Norton & Co., Inc.

Fig. UN13.4: Diverse Images/Universal Images Group/Getty Images

Fig. 13.29: from Osterlin, J., & Dawson, G. (1994). Early recognition of children with autism. A study of first birthday home videotapes. *Journal of Autism and Developmental Disorders, 24,* 247-257. Photographs courtesy of Geraldine Dawson

Fig. 13.30: courtesy of Dr. Ami Klin. (2003). The enactive mind from actions to cognition: Lessons from autism. *Philosophical Transactions of the Royal Society*

Fig. UN13.5, p. 490: Carey Kirkella/Getty Images

Fig. 13.31: from Zametkin, A. J., Nordhal, T. E., Gross, M., et al. (1990). Cerebral glucose metabolism in adults with hyperactivity of childhood onset. *New England Journal of Medicine, 323*(0), 1361-1366. Images courtesy of Alan Zametkin, NIH

Fig. 13.32: Juli/Leonard/MCT/Landov

CHAPTER 14

Opener: (photo) Walter Zerla/Getty Images

Fig. 14.1: Israel Images/Alamy

Fig. 14.2: Bettmann/Corbis

Fig. 14.3: Michael Rougier/Time Life Pictures/Getty Images

Fig. 14.4: iStockphoto

Fig. 14.6: David Grossman/Alamy

Fig. 14.7: Will McIntyre/Photo Researchers, Inc.

Fig. 14.10: Horacio Sormani/Science Source

Fig. 14.11: (a) BSIP/UIG Via Getty Images; (b) Alina Solovyova-Vincent/Getty Images; (c) Jeff Greenberg/Photo Edit

Fig. UN14.1, p. 506: Alamy

Fig. 14.12: Gregg DeGuire/FilmMagic/Getty Images

Fig. 14.14: AP Photo/Bebeto Matthews

Fig. 14.15a: (photo) Photofusion/UIG via Getty Images

Fig. 14.17: Eugene Gologursky/WireImage/Getty Images

Fig. UN14.2, p. 515: Terry Why/Newscom

Fig. 14.18: Pascal Goetheluck/Science Photo Library/Photo Researchers, Inc.

Fig. 14.19: Paul Drinkwater/NBC/NBCU Photo Bank via Getty Images

Fig. UN14.3, p. 518: *Scientific American Mind*, p. 31, courtesy of Helen Mayberg, M.D., Professor, Psychiatry and Behavioral Sciences

Fig. 14.20: Art Directors & TRIP/Alamy

Fig. 14.22: Peter Yates/The New York Times/REDUX

Fig. 14.23: (photo) Zave Smith/Corbis

Fig. 14.24: (photo) ableimages/Alamy

Fig. 14.26: (a) Stockbyte/Getty Images; (b) Steve Debenport/Getty Images

Fig. 14.29: (photo a) DMAC/Alamy; (photo b) Mary Kate Denny/PhotoEdit

Fig. 14.30: iStockphoto

Fig. 14.31: Richard Perry/The New York Times

NAME INDEX

Page numbers in *italics* refer to illustrations.

SUBJECT INDEX

Page numbers in *italics* refer to illustrations.

modeling and, *222*
observational learning and, 276
circadian rhythms, 88, 93
classical conditioning, 196, 198–207, *199,*
201, 204, 247
advertising and, 391
client-centered therapy, 498–99, *499*
cliques, 141
closure, *168,* 169
Coca-Cola, 105, *105*
cocaine, 104, *105,* 118
cochlea, 173, *174, 175*
codeine, 106
cognition, 205–7, *207*
cognitive approach to personality, *428,*
434–35
cognitive-behavioral therapy (CBT), 500,
514–16
cognitive development, 128–33, *129, 133*
cognitive dissonance, 392
cognitive map, 219
cognitive psychology, *12,* 16–17, *17*
cognitive restructuring, 500, 511–12
cognitive therapy, *498,* 500, *500*
cognitive triad, 71, 471, *471*
Colapinto, John, 139
cold receptors, 185
collectivist cultures, 425–27, *425, 427*
College Entrance Examination Board, 423
color mixing, 166, *166*
color opposites, 167, *167*
color perception, 154, 164–67, *165, 166*
coma, 76, 78, 99
communication disorders, 488
comorbidity, 461–62
companionate love, 411
competition, cooperation and, 387–88
compliance strategies, 399–401, *401*
compulsions, 108, 467, *468,* 512
concentrative mediation, 102
concepts, 271, *271*
concrete operational stage of cognitive
development, *129,* 132
conditioned response (CR), 199–201
conditioned stimulus (CS), 199–201
conditioned taste aversion, 192, 194, 206
condom use, 376
cones, 162, *162, 166*
conformity, 398–99, *399*
confound, 33
consciousness, 76–111
altered states of, 98–109
brain activity and, 81–86
learning and, *80*
sleep and, 87–98
conservation, law of, 131, *131, 133*
consolidation of memories, 93, 251–52
constraint, 437
context-dependent memory, 255–56, *255*
continuity, *168,* 169
continuous reinforcement, 213

control delusions, 477
control group, 33
conventional antipsychotics, 518–19, *519*
conventional level, 143
conversion therapy, 328
Cooke, Edward, 230
cooperation, competition and, 387–88
coping behavior, 521
differences in, 370–71, *370*
types of, 368–70, *368*
cornea, 161, *162*
corpus callosum, 57, *57,* 83
correctional facility, 522
correct rejection, 159, *159*
correlational methods, *26,* 29–31, *29,* 72,
224, 291
counterconditioning, 205
Cowell, Simon, *428*
CR (conditioned response), 199–201
cranial nerves, 186, *187*
creative intelligence, 290, *290*
creativity, 314
critical thinking, 4, 6–8, 132
Crowe, Russell, 478
crying, in infants, 124
cryptomnesia, 262, *262*
crystallized intelligence, 288–89, *288, 289*
CS (conditioned stimulus), 199–201
CSI (TV show), 486
cues, 4, 88, 170–71, 177, 250, 255–56, 383
cultural bias, psychometric testing and,
297–98, *298*
cultural level of analysis, *19,* 20
culture, 20, *20*
depression and, 473
discrimination and, 301, *301*
diversity and, *21,* 73, 107, 223, 326
self-concept and, 425–27
cutting, 456, 472, 521
cyberbullying, 142, 456

daily hassles, 360, *360*
DARE, 504
Darwin, Charles, *12,* 14, *14,* 338
data analysis, 25
DBS (deep brain stimulation), 503, *503,*
517–18
DBT (dialectical behavior therapy), 521–22,
521, 522
decision making, 277–81, *278,* 397–98
deep brain stimulation (DBS), 503, *503,*
517–18
defense mechanisms, 430, *430*
defining attribute model of concepts,
272–73, *272, 273*
deindividuation, 396–97, *396, 397*
delayed gratification, 316
delta waves, 89–90, *89*
delusions, 476–77, *476*
dementia, 148
denial, 430

dendrites, 42
dependent personality disorders, 481, *482*
dependent variable, 32
depressants, 104, 106–8
depression, depressive disorders, 454, 456,
463, *470*
development of, 471–73
symptoms of, 469–70
treatment of, 501–3, *509,* 513–17, *517, 525*
types of, *469*
depth perception, 170
Descartes, Rene, *11,* 79
descriptive methods, descriptive statistics,
24–29
despair, integrity vs., *138,* 146, 147
development, developmental psychology,
112–49
of adolescents, 136–34
of adults, 144–49
Erikson's theory of, 137–38, *138,* 145
of infants and children, 119–35
Piaget's theory of, 128–33, *129*
prenatal, 114–18
Diagnostic and Statistical Manual of Mental
Disorders (DSM), 354, 461, 504, 524
dialectical behavior therapy (DBT), 521–22,
521, 522
diathesis-stress model, 459
Dickinson, Emily, 474
DID (dissociative identity disorder), 485,
485
dieting, 353
difference threshold, 158–59
dimensional approach, 461
directionality problem, 29
discrimination, 301, 386
disorders:
in children, 487–91, *488, 489, 491,* 524–31
of emotion, 463–75
of personality, 481–86, *482*
of thought, 476–80
disorganized behavior and speech, 476, 478
displacement, 430
display rules, 340
dissociation theory of hypnosis, 101
dissociative amnesia, 484–85
dissociative disorders, 484–85
dissociative fugue, 484
dissociative identity disorder (DID), 485,
485
dissonance, 392–93
distortion of memory, *255,* 260–63
distracted driving law, *4*
distraction, 337
Dizygotic (fraternal) twins, 68
DNA evidence, *263*
door-in-the-face compliance strategy, 401,
401
dopamine, *46,* 47, 106, 108, 218
reinforcement and, 218
Dorr, Richard, *327*

intelligence, 266–68, 286–303
  birth weight and, *293*
  definition of, 286–87
  differences in, 301–3
  environment and, 292–93
  genetics and, 291–92, *292*
  measurement of, 294–99
  tests of, 287, 295–96
  theories of, 287–90, *288*
intelligence quotient (IQ), 266, *268*, 287, 291, 296
intelligence tests, 295–96
interactionists, 450
interference, 255, 258
internal clock, 321
internal locus of control, 434
Internet, 224, 252, 456
  dating on, 416, 423
  gaming on, 461
interpersonal intelligence, 289, *289*
interpreter, 85–86, *86*
intimacy, isolation vs., *138*, 145
intrapersonal intelligence, 289, *289*
intrinsic motivation, 314
introspection, 13, *13*
introverts, introversion, 437, 442–43
intuition, 334, 457
iPod, 174
IQ (intelligence quotient), 266, *268*, 287, 291, 301
IQ scores, distribution of, 296, *296*
IRBs (institutional review boards), 13
iris, 161
isolation, intimacy vs., *138*, 145

Jackson, Randy, 298
Jackson, William, *262*
James, William, *12*, *13*, 209
James-Lange theory of emotion, 330–31, *330*
  facial feedback hypothesis and, 331, *331*
Jamison, Kay Redfield, 474–75, *474*
Jaws (film), *201*
Jay Z, *409*
Jell-O, 248, 322
Jennings, Ken, *248*
Jeopardy! (TV show), *248*
jigsaw classroom, 388
"Jim twins," 68
Johnson, Virginia, 322
Joiner, Thomas, 472
Joudrie, Dorothy, 484
journaling, 516
justification of effort, 393, *393*
just world hypothesis, 384

Kahneman, Daniel, 278, 280
K-complex, *89*
Keillor, Garrison, 424
Keltner, Dacher, *343*
Kennedy, John F., assassination of, 260

Kim Jae-beom, 103
Kim Yun-jeong, 103
kinesthetic sense, 189, *189*
Kinsey, Alfred, 322
Kipsigi, infant development among, 122–23
knee-jerk reflex, 62
Kohlberg, Lawrence, 141, 142
Köhler, Wolfgang, *12*, 15, 283, *283*
Kohwet village, Kenya, 122
Korsakoff's syndrome, 107
Kushner, Harold, 375

Lady Gaga, *5*
language, development of, 133–34, *134*
Lanza, Adam, *28*, 486
latency stage, 431
latent content, 92
latent learning, 219, *219*
laughing club, *373*
law of effect, 209
L cones, *166*
L-DOPA, 47
learned helplessness, 473
learning, 80, 192–225
  by classical conditioning, 196, 198–208, *199*, *200*, *202*, *204*
  consciousness and, 80
  definition of, 195
  healthy coping and, 376–77
  by operant conditioning, 196–97, 208–220, *210*
  to speak, 134
  types of, 194–97, *196*
  by watching others, 196–97, 220–25
learning disabilities, 71, 488
left brain hemisphere, 56–57, 83–86, *84*, *85*
left-handedness, 32
lens, 162
Leonardo da Vinci, 170
levels of processing model, 240
Levitin, Daniel, 176
Lewin, Kurt, *12*, 17, *17*
libido, 429
lie detection, 333–35, *335*
Lie to Me (TV show), 334
life expectancy, U.S., 144
life satisfaction, 147, 149
life support, 78
light cues, 88
light waves, *162*
Lima, Adriana, 230
limbic system, 54, 108
linear perspective, 170, *171*
Linehan, Marsha, *521*
linguistic intelligence, 289, *289*
listening time, 175
lithium, 474–75, 518, 522
"Little Albert" case study, 204–5, *204*
lobotomy, 61, *61*, 502, 518
localization of sound, 177–78, *177*
Locke, John, 195

locus of control, 434
logic, 7, 471
logical thinking, 132
London, England, *300*
longevity, *349*
long-term potentiation (LTP), 197
long-term storage, *236*, 240–53, *247*, *289*
loudness, 175, 176, *176*, *177*
Loughner, Jared, 486
Lovato, Demi, 474
love, companionate vs. passionate, 411
lowballing, 401
LTP (long-term potentiation), 197
Luper, Paula, *491*

Ma, Yo-Yo, *259*
Mace, John, *327*
Mack, Michelle, 70, *70*
Mad Men (TV show), *513*
Madonna, 145
magnetic resonance imaging (MRI), 252, *479*
Magnificent Desolation (Aldrin), *470*
maintenance rehearsal, 240
major depressive disorder, 470, *470*
major life stressors, 360, *360*
Mandel, Howie, *466*
mania, manic episodes, 473–74, *473*
manifest content, 92
mantra, 102
marijuana, 105–6, *118*
  medical use of, 106
marriage, 146–47, *146*, 374
  health and, 374–75, *374*
Maryland, University of, *393*
Maslow, Abraham, 309, 433
Masters, William, 322
materialism, 79
math ability, *287*
mathematical/logical intelligence, 289, *289*
maturation, 121–22, *121*, *136*
maximizers, 281
M cones, *166*
MDMA (ecstasy), 105–6, *106*
media reports, *7*, 30
medications for psychological disorders, *see* psychotropic medications
meditation, 101–2, *101*, 521
melatonin, 88
membrane, 43
memes, 223, *224*
memory, memories, 228–63
  accessing of, 254–63, *254*
  acquiring of, 230–35
  autism spectrum disorder and, 300
  brain regions and, 251–53, *251*, *252*
  intelligence and, 148, 184
  long-term storage of, 236, *236*, 240–53, *241*, *244*
  loss of, 107, 149, 246, *246*
  research on, 245–46

retrieval of, *231, 232,* 254–63

    sensory storage of, 236, *236,* 237–38, *237*

    short-term storage of, 236, *236,* 238–39, *239*

    smell and, 184

Memory Championship, USA, 228, *230,* 254

memory encoding, 230–35, *231,* 240–41, *241*

memory jogs, 260

    smartphone as, 217, 250

    sticky notes as, 250

memory span, 239

memory tests, 299, *299*

memory traces, 9

meningitis, 205

Mensa, 266, *268,* 287, 296, 301

mental activity, 5–6

    neurotransmitters and, 45–48

mental age, 296

mental health care, abuses of, 502, 518

mental health professionals, finding, 506

mental illness, *see* psychological disorders

mental maps, 270, *270*

mental states, 285

"mental walk," 230

mercury, *118*

mere exposure effect, 390–91, *391*

methamphetamine (meth), 105–6, *105, 106*

method of loci, 256

metronome, 199

Michelangelo, 474

"micro-emotions," 334

midbrain, 52–54, *52, 53*

middle ear, 173, *174*

Miller, George, *12,* 16–17, *16,* 239

Miller Analogy Test, 296–97

Milner, Brenda, 247

mind, 5

mind/body problem, 11

mindfulness, 102, 521–22

minimally conscious state, 78, *78,* 99

Minnesota Twin Project, 68

mirror image, 391

mirror neurons, 224

misattribution, 260, 261–62

    of arousal, 332, *332*

miscarriage, 116

miss, 159, *159*

mistrust, trust vs., *138*

mnemonics, 256, 257

modeling, 196–97, 222–23, *222,* 499

    cigarette smoking and, *222*

Molaison, Henry (H.M.), 245–46, *245, 246, 249, 249*

monocular depth cues, 170, *171*

monozygotic (identical) twins, 68

mood stabilizers, 501, *502,* 517–18, *518*

moral development, 141–43

moral disengagement, 142

moral reasoning, 143

morphemes, 133, *134*

morphine, 106

Motherjones.com, 291

motion aftereffects, 171

motion perception, 170–72

motivation, 306–8

    behavior and, 309–19, *309*

    eating behavior and, 319–22

    emotion and, *308,* 337–43

    sexual behavior and, 322–28

motor cortex, *56, 58, 59, 84, 91*

motor disorders, 488

motor skills, 120–23

Mount Erebus, *169*

Mozart effect, 7

MRI (magnetic resonance imaging), *252, 479*

MS (multiple sclerosis), 38, 40, *40,* 57, 66

multiple intelligence theory, *288,* 289–90, *289, 290*

multiple personality disorder, 485

multiple sclerosis (MS), 38, 40, *40,* 44, 57, 66

musical intelligence, 289, *289*

music perception, 174, 175, 176

music therapy, 20, 189

Mutesi, Phiona, 268, *268,* 285

myelin sheath, 44

MySpace, 422

NAAFA (National Association to Advance Fat Acceptance), 348

Nadeau, Maxime, 99

narcissism, 422, 481, *482*

narcolepsy, *see* sleep, disorders of

nasal passage, *182*

Nash, John Forbes, 478

National Association to Advance Fat Acceptance (NAAFA), 348

National Center for Learning Disabilities, 71

National Highway Traffic Safety Administration, 4

National Institute of Drug Abuse, 105

National Institute of Mental Health, *471*

National Institutes of Health, 71, 525

National Research Council, 145, 530

National Sleep Foundation, 96

National Suicide Prevention Lifeline, 472

National Survey on Drug Use and Health, *525*

natural selection, 14, *14*

nature/nurture debate, 11, 40, 66–73, 428, 439, 442

need, 309

need hierarchy, 309–10

need to belong, 109, 141, 316, 318, 472

negative punishment, 212–13, *212*

negative reinforcement, 212, *212*

negative symptoms, 476

negative thinking, 496

neglect, impact of, *120,* 127

Neisser, Ulrich, *12,* 16

NEO Personality Inventory, 447

nerve cells, 42–45, *42*

nerve fiber, *180*

nervous system, 40–48, *41,* 62

    disorders of, 38, 40, 47, 48

networks of association, 243–44, *244*

neural communication, 43–44, *43,* 154

neural signals, *156*

neurodevelopmental disorders, 487, *488*

    see also childhood disorders

neurons, 42–45, *42,* 79, 157

neurotic personality, 437

neurotransmitters, 45–48, *45, 46*

    behavior and, 45–48

    mental activity and, 45–48

neutral stimulus, 199

Newman, Levey, *69*

Newman, Mark, *69*

Newtown, Conn., shooting, *28,* 224, 486

New York State, Same-Sex Marriage Act in, 327, *327*

New York Times, 263, 308, 530

Ng, Konrad, *301*

nicotine, 104, *118*

night driving, 148

night vision, 163

NIHL (noise-induced hearing loss), 174

9/11 terrorist attacks, 261

No Child Left Behind Act, 294

nocturnal birds, 177

noise-induced hearing loss (NIHL), 174

noisy environment, 175, 195

non-associative learning, 195–96

Nordal, Katherine, 506

norepinephrine, *46,* 47

normal distribution, 296

normative influence, 398, *398*

Northern Illinois University shooting, 468–69

Obama, Barack, *301,* 392

obedience, 401–3, *402*

obesity, *348,* 350–55, *351, 352*

objective measures of personality, 446–47, *447*

objectivity, 79

object perception, 167–69, *167*

object permanence, 131

object relations theory, 432

observational learning, 196–97, 220–25, *221,* 276

observational studies, 26–27, *26*

observer bias, 26

obsessions, 467, *468,* 512

obsessive-compulsive disorder (OCD), 466–68, *466, 468,* 481, *482*

    treatment of, 508, *509,* 512–13, *512, 513*

obstacles, overcoming, 283–85, 308

occipital lobe, 52, 56–57, *56, 83, 157*

occlusion, 170, *171*

OCD, *see* obsessive-compulsive disorder

odorants, 182, *182*

psychological analysis, 19–20, *19*
psychological dependence, 108, *108*
psychological disorders, 454–91
    assessment of, 460–61
    causes of, 459–60
    classification of, *462*
    criteria for, 457–58
    treatment of, 494–533, *509, 525*
    see also specific disorders and therapies
psychologists, *21, 505*
psychology:
    contemporary research in, 4, 18–35, *26,*
      224
    critical thinking skills and, 6–8
    definition of, 5–6
    philosophical origins of, 11
    real-life applications of, 5, 8–10, 142, 194,
      217, 257, 281, 413, 472
    schools of thought in, 12–17, *12*
    as scientific field of study, 11
    subfields of, 21–22, *22*
psychometric testing, 294–99, *294*
psychopathy, 457, 460, 483, *483,* 522–23
psychosexual development, 431–32
psychosis, 476
psychosocial development, 137–38, *138*
psychotherapy, 497–501, *498, 499, 500, 501,*
    524
psychotic disorders, 476
psychoticism, 437
psychotropic medications, 501, *502,* 513–14,
    513, 517–19, 522
    anti-anxiety drugs, 501, *502,* 508, 522
    antidepressants, 501, *502,* 512, 513–14,
      513, 524–26
    antipsychotics, 501, *502,* 518–19
    mood stabilizers, 501, *502,* 517–18, *518*
    stimulants, 104–5, 501, *502,* 522
PTSD (posttraumatic stress disorder),
    259–60, 468–69, 522
puberty, 136–37, *136*
punishment, 212–16, *215*
pupil, 161, *162*

radiation (X-rays), *118*
radical acceptance, 521
Raffaele, Bonnie, *4*
Raffaele, Kelsey, 4, *4*
Rain Man (film), 300
random assignment, 34, *34,* 224
randomized clinical trials, 504
random sample, random sampling, *34,* 35
rapid eye movement (REM) sleep, 90–91,
    471
RAS (reticular activating system), 442
rational-emotive therapy, 500
rationalization, 430
reaction formation, 430
reaction time, 12, 299
reactivity, 27
reality principle, 430

reasoning, 7, 277–78
rebirthing, 503–4, *503*
recency effect, 242, *242*
reception phase of neural communication,
    43
receptors, 44
reciprocal determinism, 435–36, *436*
reciprocal helping, 406
reconsolidation, 252–53
recticular activating system (RAS), 442
referential delusions, 477
reflected appraisal, 421
reflexes, 11, 62
Reimer, Brian, 139, *139*
Reimer, David, 139–40, *140*
reinforcers, reinforcement, 108, 210–12,
    210, 212, 217, 528
    biological predisposition and, 218
    dopamine and, 218
    schedules of, 213–14, *213,* 217
relationships, 408–13
relative size, 170, *171*
relaxation response, 510
relaxation techniques, 496, 510
reliability of testing, 294, 296–97, *297,* 298
religious ecstasy, *102*
REM behavior disorder, 97
REM (rapid eye movement) sleep, 90–91,
    471
representativeness heuristic, 279–80
repression, 430
research, psychological, 4, 18–25, 224
    methods of, 25–35, *26*
residential treatment center, 522
resilience, 370, *370*
response, 159
response cycles, sexual behavior and,
    322–23
resting state, 43
restorative theory, 93
restructuring, 284–85, *284*
reticular activating system (RAS), 442
retina, 162, *162*
retirement, 146
retrieval cues, *255*
retroactive interference, 258, *258*
retrograde amnesia, 246, *246*
reward, 212
right brain hemisphere, 56–57, 83–86, *84, 85*
ringing ears, 175
risk/benefit ratio, 23, 407
risky-shift effect, 397
Ritalin, 527–28, *527*
rods, 162, *162*
Rogers, Carl, 433, 498, *499*
Rolling Stones, 145, *145*
romantic relationships, 411–13, *411*
roommate relationships, 449
rooting reflex, 120–22, *121*
Rorschach inkblot test, 446, *446*
Ross Ice Shelf, 169, *169*

rumination, 336–37
runner's high, 48, 102, 135, 516

SAD (seasonal affective disorder), 469,
    516
safe sex, 376
sales techniques, *see* compliance strategies
salty taste, 179
Same-Sex Marriage Act, New York, 327
SAMHSA (Substance Abuse and Mental
    Health Services Administration), 525
sample, 35
Sandy, Hurricane, *279, 360, 382, 405*
Sandy Hook Elementary School, *28*
SAT (standardized aptitude test), 294
satisfaction of needs, 309–10
satisficers, 281
saturation, 164, *165*
savants, 300
scalloping, 214
Schacter-Singer, *see* two-factor theory of
    emotion
schemas, 128–30, 243, 271, *271, 275, 276*
Schiavo, Terri, 78, *78, 99*
schizoid personality, 481, *482*
schizophrenia, 476–80, *509*
    treatment of, *509,* 518–20
schizotypal personality disorder, 481, *482*
scientific method, 24–25, *25*
S cones, *166*
score distribution, 296
Scripps National Spelling Bee, *286*
seasonal affective disorder (SAD), 469,
    516
Seattle Longitudinal Study, 148
secondary appraisals, 368
secondary reinforcers, 211
secondary sex characteristics, *136,* 137
second-order conditioning, 204
secure attachment, 127
selective attention, 233–34
selective listening, 232, 233
self-actualization, 310, 433
self-concept, 419–27, *419*
    cultures and, 425–27
self-determination theory, 314–15
self-efficacy, 315–16
self-esteem, 421, *423,* 522
    life outcomes and, 422–23
self-fulfilling prophecy, 385–86
self-help books, 504
self-hypnosis, 101
self-perception theory, 314–15
self-reports, 27–28, *28, 301,* 449
self-schema, 429, *429*
self-serving bias, 424–25
Selye, Hans, 64
semantic memory, *247,* 248, *248*
semicircular canals, *174*
senior moments, 148
sensation, 155, *156, 162, 174, 180, 182, 186*